Moral Controversies

Moral Controversies

Race, Class, and Gender

in Applied Ethics

Edited by
Steven Jay Gold
Southern Connecticut State University

Wadsworth Publishing Company
Belmont, California
A Division of Wadsworth, Inc.

Philosophy Editor: Kenneth King
Editorial Assistant: Gay Meixel
Production: Cecile Joyner, The Cooper Company
Print Buyer: Diana Spence
Permissions Editor: Robert Kauser
Designer: Vargas/Williams/Design
Copy Editor: Micky Lawler
Cover Designer: Image House
Cover Painting: Gene Davis, *Moondog*. Rose Art Museum,
Brandeis University (Anonymous Gift)
Signing Representative: Maria Tarantino
Compositor: Kachina Typesetting
Printer: Malloy Lithographing, Inc.

*This book is printed on
acid-free recycled paper.*

1 2 3 4 5 6 7 8 9 10—97 96 95 94 93

Library of Congress Cataloging-in-Publication Data

Moral controversies : race, class, and gender in applied ethics /
  Steven Jay Gold, editor.
      p.   cm.
    Includes bibliographical references.
    ISBN 0-534-19662-4
    1. Social ethics.   2. Social problems.   3. Sociological
jurisprudence.   4. United States—Moral conditions.   I. Gold,
Steven Jay.
HM216.M652   1992
303.3'72—dc20   92-19977

For Susan, David, and Lauryn Rose,
who provide the love and laughter in my life

Contents

3   Gay Rights   101

Introduction   102

4   Euthanasia   141

Introduction   142

5 Testing 189

Introduction 190

6 The Death Penalty 235

Introduction 236

10   Affirmative Action, Comparable Worth, and Sexual Harassment 471

Introduction 472

Preface

Universities across the country are beginning to recognize the need to make courses sensitive to diversity. *Moral Controversies* allows instructors to integrate race and gender concerns into their moral issues courses while still preserving traditional perspectives; the book offers a balance of new material and traditional pieces, conventional orientations and radical perspectives.

As part of this book's orientation toward diversity, articles and cases are included that address issues crucial to women, people of color, gays and lesbians, and so on. An original article offers a Native-American perspective on property rights and economic justice. Other topics covered include "environmental racism," race and the death penalty, race and abortion, racism and rape, justice for farm workers, and more.

Feminism and gender issues are infused throughout the text. Beyond simply illustrating feminist positions on abortion and pornography, I have included feminist perspectives on the environment, euthanasia, welfare, surrogacy, sexual harassment, and lesbian issues, as well as an entire chapter on acquaintance rape.

A successful moral problems course must largely be discussion. Cases have to be selected that will challenge students to think. The cases in this text were chosen to reflect the tough social problems students read about every day, an approach that enables the students to identify with the problems and get excited. This text includes discussion material on such topics as:

- Abortion: parental consent; sex selection; fathers' rights
- Surrogate motherhood
- Gay partners and the family; gays in the military
- Euthanasia: Baby Doe cases; Dr. Kevorkian and assisted suicide
- Polygraph testing; drug testing; HIV testing
- The death penalty: psychiatrists' role; victims' role; rehabilitation
- Acquaintance rape case studies
- Pornography: censorship in the arts; Mapplethorpe v. rap music
- Welfare rights cases
- Affirmative action: minority set-asides; comparable worth
- Sexual harassment: the Hill-Thomas hearings; the Lisa Olson case
- Acid rain; environmental racism; Native American grave sites at risk
- Animal experimentation

This text also provides some new twists on very traditional issues. On euthanasia and abortion, for example, an article is included that covers both by arguing that, from a *feminist* perspective, the corpse of a *brain-dead pregnant woman* should not be kept ventilated for the sake of the fetus. The chapter on gay rights features the long battle by Sharon Kowalski's lover for custody after a crippling accident, an issue that challenges our conception of the traditional "family." On surrogacy, a case is included on gestational, as well as traditional, surrogacy arrangements. The chapter on acquaintance rape discusses rape on campus and questions the role fraternities may play in contributing to violence against women.

I would like to thank the Connecticut State University for research funding, as well as Project IMPACT Director Penelope Lisi and the Project IMPACT participants. Further debts are owed to Bat-Ami Bar On of SUNY Binghamton, to Ward Churchill and Evelyn Hu DeHart of the University of Colorado–Boulder, to Ken Gatzke of Southern Connecticut State University, to the many people on the electronic mail networks who responded to my perpetual questions about the text, and to Susan Adler-Gold for her constant critical assessments of the project and her un-failing moral support. I would like to thank the reviewers for their comments: Susan J. Brison, Dartmouth College; Andrew Mc-Laughlin, City University of New York, Herbert H. Lehman College; Sheila Ruth, Southern Illinois University at Edwardsville; Kathy Squadrito, Indiana University–Purdue University at Fort Wayne; and William F. Waber, Ohio Wesleyan University. I would also like to thank Ken King at Wadsworth for his endless energy, encouragement, and motivation (through seemingly impossible deadlines).

Steven Jay Gold

Abortion

Abortion, or the termination of pregnancy, has become as divisive an issue as any in the history of the United States. The rights of individual women to privacy and to control over their own reproductive systems have been challenged by those who feel that the right to life of the fetus outweighs the rights of the woman. Almost everyone agrees that, when a woman's life is directly in danger, an abortion is acceptable. The question then becomes "Under what *other* conditions, if any, can abortions be allowed?"

Women have abortions for many reasons. Death or severe physical/emotional harm to the mother, rape, incest, deformity or other damage to the fetus, financial well-being, or other difficult personal life situations are common conditions people use to justify abortions. Abortion has even been used as a means of sex selection. Some proponents suggest that a woman should be allowed to have an abortion any time she desires—what is called "abortion on demand."

Currently a woman's legal right to an abortion stems from the constitutional protection of individual privacy. Although privacy is never explicitly mentioned in the Bill of Rights, it was said, in the precedent decision *Griswold* v. *Connecticut* (1965), to be one of the rights reserved to the people in the Ninth Amendment. In *Griswold* a Connecticut law limiting information about birth control to married couples was struck down as an unconstitutional violation of the right to sexual privacy within marriage. Later, in *Eisenstadt* v. *Baird,* the right to privacy was extended to individuals. And, in 1973, *Roe* v. *Wade* guaranteed abortion as fundamental to an individual woman's right to privacy.

It is typically asked "At what point in development does the fetus become a person?" Sperm and egg combine into a zygote, which, after gradual implantation in the uterus, becomes an embryo and, later, a fetus. Somewhere around the fourth month movement, or what was traditionally called "quickening," can be detected. Between the sixth and seventh months the fetus becomes viable—that is, able to live outside the womb with only normal assistance.

The conservative position, at its most extreme, typically holds that a fetus becomes a person in the morally relevant sense at the moment of conception. Defenders of this position often refer to the difficulty in drawing a particular line, to the religious argument that the fetus gets a "soul" at the moment of conception, or to some sufficient condition for personhood—e.g., the full genetic code (of course, every cell in the body has this)—or simply to the argument that, if we do not know if it is a person, we must err on the side of caution.

Those who favor abortion often argue that, although the fetus is a *human* fetus, it is not a person in any morally significant sense. The claim centers on the idea that a fetus shares few characteristics with postpartum humans. This position leads those at this extreme to conclude that abortion on demand is morally acceptable. Of course, at some point in pregnancy the fetus is practically indistinguishable from a newborn baby.

Many in the debate take on a more moderate perspective. Jane English, whose article is included here, attempts to moderate the conservative position by showing that some forms of abortion constitute self-defense. In these cases, the purpose of the abortion outweighs any claim to life the fetus might have. Others have attempted to moderate the liberal perspective by showing that the fetus, in the later stages, is *sentient,* possessing the basic cognitive equipment necessary for acting as a full person.

On the legal status of the fetus, the U.S. Constitution is fairly clear. The 14th Amendment grants citizenship, due process, and equal protection of the laws to "all persons born or naturalized" in the United States. Since abortion was a common practice even in revolutionary times (let alone in 1868), it was never intended that the unborn had the rights of citizens. It is for this reason that pro-life advocates push hard for a "human life amendment" to the Constitution.

The relevant precedent decision, *Roe* v. *Wade* (1973), never suggests that the fetus is a person. Justice Harry Blackmun ruled in *Roe* that any restrictions on abortion in the first trimester unconstitutionally violated a woman's right to privacy. In the second trimester, abortion may be regulated for important medical reasons only. In the last trimester, however, after the fetus is viable, states may proscribe abortion to protect interests in the *potentiality* of life, as well as for medical reasons.

As for the facts concerning abortion, first-trimester abortions are usually performed by uterine aspiration, whereby the contents of the uterus are simply vacuumed out. This is a safe and simple procedure that entails less risk to the woman than carrying the child to term. Later abortions are done by injecting a saline solution into the amniotic cavity and inducing labor. This is a considerably more intrusive and dangerous procedure, although, if done with proper care, it is no more dangerous than many other routine surgical procedures. Recently an "abortion pill," otherwise known as RU486, has been developed in France. Although not yet available in the United States, RU486 has been shown to be a success-ful, nonintrusive option for many women.

Statistically, every year in the United States 3 out of 100 women aged 15–44 have an abortion. Women under 30, especially 18–19-year-olds, have the most abortions; Hispanic women are 60% more likely to have abortions than non-Hispanic women but somewhat less likely than African-American women. Poor women are three times more likely to have abortions, and Catholic women are more likely to have abortions than Jewish or Protestant women (30% higher than Protestant women in fact). Most women who have abortions after 15 weeks experienced problems detecting the pregnancy and delayed the decision for lack of funding. [Data from The Alan Guttmacher Institute, October 6, 1988, as seen in *From Abortion to Reproductive Freedom: Transforming the Movement,* by Marlene Gerber-Fried (Boston: South End Press, 1990, pp. 129–130).]

1. Abortion and the Concept of a Person

Jane English

English argues that, even if a fetus is a person, abortion may often be permissible; and abortion may often be impermissible even if the fetus is not a person. Using a self-defense model, English concludes that abortion as terminating a person can be morally defensible. She further maintains that, even if the fetus is not a person, it so closely resembles one at the later stages that abortion may not be morally acceptable.

The abortion debate rages on. Yet the two most popular positions seem to be clearly mistaken. Conservatives maintain that a human life begins at conception and that therefore abortion must be wrong because it is murder. But not all killings of humans are murders. Most notably, self defense may justify even the killing of an innocent person.

Liberals, on the other hand, are just as mistaken in their argument that since a fetus does not become a person until birth, a woman may do whatever she pleases in and to her own

This article is reprinted from the *Canadian Journal of Philosophy,* 5, no. 2 (October 1975) by permission of the Canadian Association for Publishing in Philosophy.

body. First, you cannot do as you please with your own body if it affects other people adversely.[1] Second, if a fetus is not a person, that does not imply that you can do to it anything you wish. Animals, for example, are not persons, yet to kill or torture them for no reason at all is wrong.

At the center of the storm has been the issue of just when it is between ovulation and adulthood that a person appears on the scene. Conservatives draw the line at conception, liberals at birth. In this paper I first examine our concept of a person and conclude that no single criterion can capture the concept of a person and no sharp line can be drawn. Next I argue that if a fetus is a person, abortion is still justifiable in many cases; and if a fetus is not a person, killing it is still wrong in many cases. To a large extent, these two solutions are in agreement. I conclude that our concept of a person cannot and need not bear the weight that the abortion controversy has thrust upon it.

I

The several factions in the abortion argument have drawn battle lines around various proposed criteria for determining what is and what is not a person. For example, Mary Anne Warren[2] lists five features (capacities for reasoning, self-awareness, complex communication, etc.) as her criteria for personhood and argues for the permissibility of abortion because a fetus falls outside this concept. Baruch Brody[3] uses brain waves. Michael Tooley[4] picks having-a-concept-of-self as his criterion and concludes that infanticide and abortion are justifiable, while the killing of adult animals is not. On the other side, Paul Ramsey[5] claims a certain gene structure is the defining characteristic. John Noonan[6] prefers conceived-of-humans and presents counterexamples to various other candidate criteria. For instance, he argues against viability as the criterion because the newborn and infirm would then be non-persons, since they cannot live without the aid of others. He rejects any criterion that calls upon the sorts of sentiments a being can evoke in adults on the grounds that this would allow us to exclude other races as non-persons if we could just view them sufficiently unsentimentally.

These approaches are typical: foes of abortion propose sufficient conditions for personhood which fetuses satisfy, while friends of abortion counter with necessary conditions for personhood which fetuses lack. But these both presuppose that the concept of a person can be captured in a straightjacket of necessary and/or sufficient conditions.[7] Rather, "person" is a cluster of features, of which rationality, having a self-concept and being conceived of humans are only part.

What is typical of persons? Within our concept of a person we include, first, certain biological factors: descended from humans, having a certain genetic make-up, having a head, hands, arms, eyes, capable of locomotion, breathing, eating, sleeping. There are psychological factors: sentience, perception, having a concept of self and of one's own interests and desires, the ability to use tools, the ability to use language or symbol systems, the ability to joke, to be angry, to doubt. There are rationality factors: the ability to reason and draw conclusions, the ability to generalize and to learn from past experience, the ability to sacrifice present interests for greater gains in the future. There are social factors: the ability to work in groups and respond to peer pressures, the ability to recognize and consider as valuable the interests of others, seeing oneself as one among "other minds," the ability to sympathize, encourage, love, the ability to evoke from others the responses of sympathy, encouragement, love, the ability to work with others for mutual advantage. Then there are legal factors: being subject to the law and protected by it, having the ability to sue and enter contracts, being counted in the census, having a name and citizenship, the ability to own property, inherit, and so forth.

Now the point is not that this list is incomplete, or that you can find counterinstances to each of its points. People typically exhibit rationality, for instance, but someone who was irrational would not thereby fail to qualify as a person. On the other hand, something could exhibit the majority of these features and still fail to be a person, as an advanced robot might. There is no single core of necessary and sufficient features which we can draw upon with the assurance that they constitute what really makes a person; there are only features that are more or less typical.

This is not to say that no necessary or sufficient conditions can be given. Being alive is a necessary condition for being a person, and being a U.S. Senator is sufficient. But rather than falling inside a sufficient condition or outside a necessary one, a fetus lies in the penumbra region where our concept of a person is not so simple. For this reason I think a conclusive answer to the question whether a fetus is a person is unattainable.

Here we might note a family of simple fallacies that proceed by stating a necessary condition for personhood and showing that a fetus has that characteristic. This is a form of the fallacy of affirming the consequent. For example, some have mistakenly reasoned from the premise that a fetus is human (after all, it is a human fetus rather than, say, a canine fetus), to the conclusion that it is a human. Adding an equivocation of "being," we get the fallacious argument that since a fetus is something both living and human, it is a human being.

Nonetheless, it does seem clear that a fetus has very few of the above family of characteristics, whereas a newborn baby exhibits a much larger proportion of them—and a two-year-old has even more. Note that one traditional anti-abortion argument has centered on pointing out the many ways in which a fetus resembles a baby. They emphasize its development ("It already has ten fingers . . .") without mentioning its dissimilarities to adults (it still has gills and a tail). They also try to evoke the sort of sympathy on our part that we only feel toward other persons ("Never to laugh . . . or feel the sunshine?"). This all seems to be a relevant way to argue, since its purpose is to persuade us that a fetus satisfies so many of the important features on the list that it ought to be treated as a person. Also note that a fetus near the time of birth satisfies many more of these factors than a fetus in the early months of development. This could provide reason for making distinctions among the different stages of pregnancy, as the U.S. Supreme Court has done.[8]

Historically, the time at which a person has been said to come into existence has varied widely. Muslims date personhood from fourteen days after conception. Some medievals followed Aristotle in placing ensoulment at forty days after conception for a male fetus and eighty days for a female fetus.[9] In European common law since the Seventeeth Century, abortion was considered the killing of a person only after quickening, the time when a pregnant woman first feels the fetus move on its own. Nor is this variety of opinions surpris-

ing. Biologically, a human being develops gradually. We shouldn't expect there to be any specific time or sharp dividing point when a person appears on the scene.

For these reasons I believe our concept of a person is not sharp or decisive enough to bear the weight of a solution to the abortion controversy. To use it to solve that problem is to clarify *obscurum per obscurius*.

II

Next let us consider what follows if a fetus is a person after all. Judith Jarvis Thomson's landmark article, "A Defense of Abortion,"[10] correctly points out that some additional argumentation is needed at this point in the conservative argument to bridge the gap between the premise that a fetus is an innocent person and the conclusion that killing it is always wrong. To arrive at this conclusion, we would need the additional premise that killing an innocent person is always wrong. But killing an innocent person is sometimes permissible, most notably in self defense. Some examples may help draw out our intuitions or ordinary judgments about self defense.

Suppose a mad scientist, for instance, hypnotized innocent people to jump out of the bushes and attack innocent passers-by with knives. If you are so attacked, we agree you have a right to kill the attacker in self defense, if killing him is the only way to protect your life or to save yourself from serious injury. It does not seem to matter here that the attacker is not malicious but himself an innocent pawn, for your killing of him is not done in a spirit of retribution but only in self defense.

How severe an injury may you inflict in self defense? In part this depends upon the severity of the injury to be avoided: you may not shoot someone merely to avoid having your clothes torn. This might lead one to the mistaken conclusion that the defense may only equal the threatened injury in severity; that to avoid death you may kill, but to avoid a black eye you may only inflict a black eye or the equivalent. Rather, our laws and customs seem to say that you may create an injury somewhat, but not enormously, greater than the injury to be avoided. To fend off an attack whose outcome would be as serious as rape, a severe beating or the loss of a finger, you may shoot; to avoid having your clothes torn, you may blacken an eye.

Aside from this, the injury you may inflict should only be the minimum necessary to deter or incapacitate the attacker. Even if you know he intends to kill you, you are not justified in shooting him if you could equally well save yourself by the simple expedient of running away. Self defense is for the purpose of avoiding harms rather than equalizing harms.

Some cases of pregnancy present a parallel situation. Though the fetus is itself innocent, it may pose a threat to the pregnant woman's well-being, life prospects or health, mental or physical. If the pregnancy presents a slight threat to her interests, it seems self defense cannot justify abortion. But if the threat is on a par with a serious beating or the loss of a finger, she may kill the fetus that poses such a threat, even if it is an innocent person. If a lesser harm to the fetus could have the same defensive effect, killing it would not be justified. It is unfortunate that the only way to free the woman from the pregnancy entails the death of the fetus (except in very late stages of pregnancy). Thus a self defense model supports Thomson's point that the woman has a right only to be freed from the fetus, not a right to demand its death.[11]

The self defense model is most helpful when we take the pregnant woman's point of view. In the pre-Thomson literature, abortion is often framed as a question for a third party: do you, a doctor, have a right to choose between the life of the woman and that of the fetus? Some have claimed that if you were a passer-by who witnessed a struggle between the innocent hypnotized attacker and his equally innocent victim, you would have no reason to kill either in defense of the other. They have concluded that the self defense model implies that a woman may attempt to abort herself, but that a doctor should not assist her. I think the position of the third party is somewhat more complex. We do feel some inclination to intervene on behalf of the victim rather than the attacker, other things equal. But if both parties are innocent, other

factors come into consideration. You would rush to the aid of your husband whether he was attacker or attackee. If a hypnotized famous violinist were attacking a skid row bum, we would try to save the individual who is of more value to society. These considerations would tend to support abortion in some cases.

But suppose you are a frail senior citizen who wishes to avoid being knifed by one of these innocent hypnotics, so you have hired a body-guard to accompany you. If you are attacked, it is clear we believe that the body-guard, acting as your agent, has a right to kill the attacker to save you from a serious beating. Your rights of self defense are transferred to your agent. I suggest that we should similarly view the doctor as the pregnant woman's agent in carrying out a defense she is physically incapable of accomplishing herself.

Thanks to modern technology, the cases are rare in which a pregnancy poses as clear a threat to a woman's bodily health as an attacker brandishing a switchblade. How does self defense fare when more subtle, complex and long-range harms are involved?

To consider a somewhat fanciful example, suppose you are a highly trained surgeon when you are kidnapped by the hypnotic attacker. He says he does not intend to harm you but to take you back to the mad scientist who, it turns out, plans to hypnotize you to have a permanent mental block against all your knowledge of medicine. This would automatically destroy your career which would in turn have a serious adverse impact on your family, your personal relationships and your happiness. It seems to me that if the only way you can avoid this outcome is to shoot the innocent attacker, you are justified in so doing. You are defending yourself from a drastic injury to your life prospects. I think it is no exaggeration to claim that unwanted pregnancies (most obviously among teenagers) often have such adverse life-long consequences as the surgeon's loss of livelihood.

Several parallels arise between various views on abortion and the self defense model. Let's suppose further that these hypnotized attackers only operate at night, so that it is well known that they can be avoided completely by the considerable inconvenience of never leaving your house after dark. One view is that since you could stay home at night, therefore if you go out and are selected by one of these hypnotized people, you have no right to defend yourself. This parallels the view that abstinence is the only acceptable way to avoid pregnancy. Others might hold that you ought to take along some defense such as Mace which will deter the hypnotized person without killing him, but that if this defense fails, you are obliged to submit to the resulting injury, no matter how severe it is. This parallels the view that contraception is all right but abortion is always wrong, even in cases of contraceptive failure.

A third view is that you may kill the hypnotized person only if he will actually kill you, but not if he will only injure you. This is like the position that abortion is permissible only if it is required to save a woman's life. Finally we have the view that it is all right to kill the attacker, even if only to avoid a very slight inconvenience to yourself and even if you knowingly walked down the very street where all these incidents have been taking place without taking along any Mace or protective escort. If we assume that a fetus is a person, this is the analogue of the view that abortion is always justifiable, "on demand."

The self defense model allows us to see an important difference that exists between abortion and infanticide, even if a fetus is a person from conception. Many have argued that the only way to justify abortion without justifying infanticide would be to find some characteristic of personhood that is acquired at birth. Michael Tooley, for one, claims infanticide is justifiable because the really significant characteristics of person are acquired some time after birth. But all such approaches look to characteristics of the developing human and ignore the relation between the fetus and the woman. What if, after birth, the presence of an infant or the need to support it posed a grave threat to the woman's sanity or life prospects? She could escape this threat by the simple expedient of running away. So a solution that does not entail the death of the infant is available. Before birth, such solutions are not available because of the biological dependence of the fetus on the woman. Birth is the crucial point not because of any characteristics

the fetus gains, but because after birth the woman can defend herself by a means less drastic than killing the infant. Hence self defense can be used to justify abortion without necessarily thereby justifying infanticide.

III

On the other hand, supposing a fetus is not after all a person, would abortion always be morally permissible? Some opponents of abortion seem worried that if a fetus is not a full-fledged person, then we are justified in treating it in any way at all. However, this does not follow. Non-persons do get some consideration in our moral code, though of course they do not have the same rights as persons have (and in general they do not have moral responsibilities), and though their interests may be overridden by the interests of persons. Still, we cannot just treat them in any way at all.

Treatment of animals is a case in point. It is wrong to torture dogs for fun or to kill wild birds for no reason at all. It is wrong Period, even though dogs and birds do not have the same rights persons do. However, few people think it is wrong to use dogs as experimental animals, causing them considerable suffering in some cases, provided that the resulting research will probably bring discoveries of great benefit to people. And most of us think it all right to kill birds for food or to protect our crops. People's rights are different from the consideration we give to animals, then, for it is wrong to experiment on people, even if others might later benefit a great deal as a result of their suffering. You might volunteer to be a subject, but this would be supererogatory; you certainly have a right to refuse to be a medical guinea pig.

But how do we decide what you may or may not do to non-persons? This is a difficult problem, one for which I believe no adequate account exists. You do not want to say, for instance, that torturing dogs is all right whenever the sum of its effects on people is good—when it doesn't warp the sensibilities of the torturer so much that he mistreats people. If that were the case, it would be all right to torture dogs if you did it in private, or if the torturer lived on a desert island or died soon afterward, so that his actions had no effect on people. This is an inadequate account, because whatever moral consideration animals get, it has to be indefeasible, too. It will have to be a general proscription of certain actions, not merely a weighing of the impact on people on a case-by-case basis.

Rather, we need to distinguish two levels on which consequences of actions can be taken into account in moral reasoning. The traditional objections to Utilitarianism focus on the fact that it operates solely on the first level, taking all the consequences into account in particular cases only. Thus Utilitarianism is open to "desert island" and "lifeboat" counterexamples because these cases are rigged to make the consequences of actions severely limited.

Rawls's theory could be described as a teleological sort of theory, but with teleology operating on a higher level.[12] In choosing the principles to regulate society from the original position, his hypothetical choosers make their decision on the basis of the total consequences of various systems. Furthermore, they are constrained to choose a general set of rules which people can readily learn and apply. An ethical theory must operate by generating a set of sympathies and attitudes toward others which reinforces the functioning of that set of moral principles. Our prohibition against killing people operates by means of certain moral sentiments including sympathy, compassion and guilt. But if these attitudes are to form a coherent set, they carry us further: we tend to perform supererogatory actions, and we tend to feel similar compassion toward person-like non-persons.

It is crucial that psychological facts play a role here. Our psychological constitution makes it the case that for our ethical theory to work, it must prohibit certain treatment of non-persons which are significantly person-like. If our moral rules allowed people to treat some person-like non-persons in ways we do not want people to be treated, this would undermine the system of sympathies and attitudes that makes the ethical system work. For this reason, we would choose in the original

position to make mistreatment of some sorts of animals wrong in general (not just wrong in the cases with public impact), even though animals are not themselves parties in the original position. Thus it makes sense that it is those animals whose appearance and behavior are most like those of people that get the most consideration in our moral scheme.

It is because of "coherence of attitudes," I think, that the similarity of a fetus to a baby is very significant. A fetus one week before birth is so much like a newborn baby in our psychological space that we cannot allow any cavalier treatment of the former while expecting full sympathy and nurturative support for the latter. Thus, I think that anti-abortion forces are indeed giving their strongest arguments when they point to the similarities between a fetus and a baby, and when they try to evoke our emotional attachment to and sympathy for the fetus. An early horror story from New York about nurses who were expected to alternate between caring for six-week premature infants and disposing of viable 24-week aborted fetuses is just that—a horror story. These beings are so much alike that no one can be asked to draw a distinction and treat them so very differently.

Remember, however, that in the early weeks after conception, a fetus is very much unlike a person. It is hard to develop these feelings for a set of genes which doesn't yet have a head, hands, beating heart, response to touch or the ability to move by itself. Thus it seems to me that the alleged "slippery slope" between conception and birth is not so very slippery. In the early stages of pregnancy, abortion can hardly be compared to murder for psychological reasons, but in the latest stages it is psychologically akin to murder.

Another source of similarity is the bodily continuity between fetus and adult. Bodies play a surprisingly central role in our attitudes toward persons. One has only to think of the philosophical literature on how far physical identity suffices for personal identity or Wittgenstein's remark that the best picture of the human soul is the human body. Even after death, when all agree the body is no longer a person, we still observe elaborate customs of respect for the human body; like people who torture dogs, necrophiliacs are not to be trusted with people.[13] So it is appropriate that we show respect to a fetus as the body continuous with the body of a person. This is a degree of resemblance to persons that animals cannot rival.

Michael Tooley also utilizes a parallel with animals. He claims that it is always permissible to drown newborn kittens and draws conclusions about infanticide.[14] But it is only permissible to drown kittens when their survival would cause some hardship. Perhaps it would be a burden to feed and house six more cats or to find other homes for them. The alternative of letting them starve produces even more suffering than the drowning. Since the kittens get their rights secondhand, so to speak, *via* the need for coherence in our attitudes, their interests are often overriden by the interests of full-fledged persons. But if their survival would be no inconvenience to people at all, then it is wrong to drown them, *contra* Tooley.

Tooley's conclusions about abortion are wrong for the same reason. Even if a fetus is not a person, abortion is not always permissible, because of the resemblance of a fetus to a person. I agree with Thomson that it would be wrong for a woman who is seven months pregnant to have an abortion just to avoid having to postpone a trip to Europe. In the early months of pregnancy when the fetus hardly resembles a baby at all, then, abortion is permissible whenever it is in the interests of the pregnant woman or her family. The reasons would only need to outweigh the pain and inconvenience of the abortion itself. In the middle months, when the fetus comes to resemble a person, abortion would be justifiable only when the continuation of the pregnancy or the birth of the child would cause harms—physical, psychological, economic or social—to the woman. In the last months of pregnancy, even on our current assumption that a fetus is not a person, abortion seems to be wrong except to save a woman from significant injury or death.

The Supreme Court has recognized similar gradations in the alleged slippery slope stretching between conception and birth. To this point, the present paper has been a discussion of the moral status of abortion only, not its legal status. In view of the great physical, financial and sometimes psychological costs of abortion, perhaps the legal arrangement most compatible with the proposed moral solution would be the absence of restrictions, that is, so-called abortion "on demand."

So I conclude, first, that application of our concept of a person will not suffice to settle the abortion issue. After all, the biological development of a human being is gradual. Second, whether a fetus is a person or not, abortion is justifiable early in a pregnancy to avoid modest harms and seldom justifiable late in pregnancy except to avoid significant injury or death.

Notes

1. We also have paternalistic laws which keep us from harming our own bodies even when no one else is affected. Ironically, anti-abortion laws were originally designed to protect pregnant women from a dangerous but tempting procedure.

2. Mary Anne Warren, "On the Moral and Legal Status of Abortion," *Monist* 5 (1973), p. 55.

3. Baruch Brody, "Fetal Humanity and the Theory of Essentialism," in Robert Baker and Frederick Elliston (eds.), *Philosophy and Sex* (Buffalo, N.Y., 1975).

4. Michael Tooley, "Abortion and Infanticide," *Philosophy and Public Affairs* 1 (1971).

5. Paul Ramsey, "The Morality of Abortion," in James Rachels (ed.), *Moral Problems* (New York, 1971).

6. John Noonan, "Abortion and the Catholic Church: A Summary History," *Natural Law Forum* 12 (1967), pp. 125–131.

7. Wittgenstein has argued against the possibility of so capturing the concept of a game, *Philosophical Investigations* (New York, 1958), §66–71.

8. Not because the fetus is partly a person and so has some of the rights of persons but rather because of the rights of person-like non-persons. This I discuss in part III.

9. Aristotle himself was concerned, however, with the different question of when the soul takes

form. For historical data, see Jimmye Kimmey, "How the Abortion Laws Happened," *Ms.* 1 (April, 1973), pp. 48ff and John Noonan, *loc. cit.*

10. J. J. Thomson, "A Defense of Abortion," *Philosophy and Public Affairs* 1 (1971).

11. *Ibid.,* p. 52.

12. John Rawls, *A Theory of Justice* (Cambridge, Mass., 1971), §§3–4.

13. On the other hand, if they can be trusted with people, then our moral customs are mistaken. It all depends on the facts of psychology.

14. *Op. cit.,* pp. 40, 60–61.

2. Ethics, Feminism, and Abortion

Milton Fisk

Milton Fisk assesses the abortion issue and liberal political theory within the larger political context of problems facing the women's movement. He analyzes the right to organize against sexual oppression within a liberal state. Looking at individual actions as parts of group actions, Fisk examines abortion and reproductive control in terms of patriarchal domination.

Introduction

A great source of confusion and mystification in moral philosophy in the United States today is the implicit and explicit use of the liberal theory of human nature as bedrock. This theory is associated with a view of individual rights which lies in the background of many concrete moral discussions. The course of events sometimes ignores the liberal theory, as is evident from the great movements of our time. People see their grievances as shared grievances, thus prompting them to act in solidarity with those whose roles are similar to their own.

Little motivation comes from within philosophy for philosophers to abandon points of view that can no longer serve a practical purpose. Such motivation can come only from identification with a movement outside philosophy. Philosophy can then perhaps provide a model that adds coherence to the moral patterns developing in such a movement.[1]

From *Applied Ethics and Ethical Theory,* by David M. Rosenthal and Fadlov Shehad. © 1988 by University of Utah Press. Reprinted by permission.

And with that added coherence, partisans of the movement can have lifted from them the suspicion that somewhere the intellectuals of the day have justified a higher morality than that of their movement.

To illustrate this conception of the relation of philosophy to morality, I choose the example of the feminist movement. If we are to deal coherently with the ethical questions arising within feminism and about feminism, a social conception of human nature needs to replace the liberal theory of the individual. Liberal theory attempts to deal with these questions as though there were no such thing as a feminist movement. This leads to treating formulations such as, "Do women have rights to their own bodies as property?" and "Does the fetus have the full range of rights of a person?" as starting places, rather than as problems arising where the points of struggle of a group have first been identified.

Arguing that a change in the model of the individual is needed here is, I think, a philosophical project. It is rarely the role of the philosopher to tell a movement what it wants or what is right for it. But, when enemies of the movement tell it that what it wants is forbidden fruit, it is important that the movement have a response. A movement is, after all, about the business of winning partisans, and silence in the face of criticism will not pull people off the fence. The opposition would like to monopolize all the models with which legitimate discourse can operate. The availability of alternative models is the task of the philosophy of any movement.

Organizing against Oppression

Liberal theory has little tolerance toward organizing for special interests. This can be seen by examining how it views conflict and conflict resolution.

Given a multitude of independently defined centers of action whose actual social roles are accidental in relation to what they are—the conflicts that occur will be rooted in squabbles among individuals. Lust, greed, ambition, and pride will set individuals on collision courses with one another. The mechanism needed to prevent such collisions can be a third party who, without prior allegiance to either side, has good enough sense to intervene before maximum damage is done.[2] Since such collisions are widespread and since reasonable third parties cannot be expected simply to volunteer their services, the state is formed as an overarching third party.

The state in liberal theory is, then, a neutral force protecting rights wherever they might be threatened. The sheer variety of the invasions of rights rules out the usefulness of a partisan force. After all, no organization could rightfully be dedicated to protecting the rights of women alone, for there are plenty of cases in which men's rights are invaded by women. If women set up a partisan force to protect their rights, men would form a counter organization. We would end with something more than individual squabbles between men and women; there would now be group warfare between organizations of men and organizations of women.[3] If men do seem on the whole to be more in the wrong than women, this is no reason for bypassing the state with special-interest organizations. The state was designed to limit wrongdoing without taking the side of

the most frequently wronged. After all, it is not a question of who is most often wrong but of how to stop the individual squabbles. Philosophers can, it is supposed, be of help in listing the rights that individuals have. In this way the state is informed about when it should intervene to protect rights. Those rights are antecedent to the squabbles in which they are infringed.

Moreover, by taking individuals to be independently defined centers of action, liberal theory makes the whole enterprise of independent organization against oppression suspect. In the first place, the very idea of social oppression is suspect. To the ears of the liberal theorist it suggests the implausible idea of a relatively permanent and systematic conspiracy of the members of one group against those of another. This implausibility follows from treating the individual as an independently defined center of action. In contrast, if individuals are social in nature, oppression need not be said to involve a conspiracy. It becomes thoroughly plausible within the framework of group opposition.

In the second place, the very idea of threatening to redress grievances through independent group action is seen as an unwarranted attack on the social bond.[4] It short-circuits the process of petitioning the state to redress grievances. The social bond depends on the recognition of the sovereignty of the state in the handling of disputes. If there is no satisfaction from the state, then civil disobedience is allowable. But, generally, civil disobedience implies an acceptance of the state as sovereign even when it is fallible, slow, and insensitive in providing redress.

Independent organization against oppression is a challenge to this sovereignty. Independent organizations not only do not subordinate their decisions to oppressing groups but do not subordinate them to state organizations. They need not project the overthrow of the state, but at least they posit a dual center of political initiative and of social and economic power.

A neutral state enveloping atomized individuals and their squabbles is too simple a model for a society where people are organizing themselves both against oppression and for oppression. Adding to the model the liberal right to form factions fails to provide the needed complexity. The liberal right to form political factions amounts to no more than the right to contest control of the state from within the established mechanisms of change of office and representation. The Republican challenge to the Democrats in the U.S. or the Communist challenge to the Christian Democrats in Italy is legitimated by this right to factions. But a black movement and a feminist movement are not legitimated by this liberal right. Still, many influential members of these movements, as well as many influential people with no sympathy for these movements, have done all in their power to bring these movements within the established mechanisms, where they would be legitimated by the liberal right to factionalize.

The Right to Organize against Sexual Oppression

The right to organize for any purpose is to be considered in light of the interests of a group. It is not derivative from the rights of individuals in a state of nature. But it is not a right that conflicts with what people in the group are. They are what they are as members of this group, and its interests are among the interests its members have. There are lots of problems about how wide and how narrow groups of the sort relevant to morality can be. Instead of dealing with those problems, it is best here to concentrate on the main lines of the difference with liberal theory.

Suppose the grievances that women have with individual men are treated as local squabbles, instead of as part of a pattern of grievances. A man's beating his wife would then be merely an instance of the schema "Person x beats person y." His beating her is treated as just another beating. The wife might, from this perspective, just as well have beaten the man, had she been as angry and had she thought to grab the poker in order to stun him first. And so it seems that one should not take the side of one gender in these squabbles, but only attempt to prevent them or prevent them from going to dangerous extremes.

We think we know why such interpretations are inadequate. For it seems clear that many men believe that society gives them control over their wives. They exercise this control in many matters without any sanction from society. And, if they cannot control their wives to their satisfaction, who is to tell them that they cannot subdue them by violence? The society may interfere at this point, but the ambivalence of the interference reflects the wide recognition that a man has control over his wife. Thus the wife did not grab the poker to stun him and then beat him senseless. Since she did not have control over him, her anger expressed itself rather in hysterical shouting or sobbing.

Shelters for abused women exist not because women are merely an identifiable segment of all those in the population who get beaten, but because abused women are victims of efforts to enforce male control. The organization of those shelters is an organization against aspects of male control, insofar as shelters allow women and their children to escape male control when it is enforced with violence.

This will serve as an illustration of the kind of thing I am driving at when I say that liberal theory has trouble seeing beyond local squabbles. To say that wife beating reflects social oppression is to cease to view the man and his wife as independently defined centers of action. One must see them both as actors within a system of male control. Many men become members of the dominant group in that system, and many women become members of the dominated group in that system. Actors so defined can do more than engage in local squabbles; their conflicts need to be understood as part of a pattern of conflicts. These actors are only acting out who they are in the system of male control when they attempt to organize either as oppressors or as the oppressed. In so doing, they join with those like them to struggle against the counterforce of the other group. The asocial individuals of liberal theory are not distinguished by such conflicting roles, and thus they would be organizing against their own kind if they did more than organize a neutral state as a power outside themselves.

The idea that the state is neutral seems plausible when it is counterposed to individuals and their isolated squabbles. But once we have said that the society includes a system of domination within which one group is decidedly dominant, the neutral state looks less plausible. Relative to the power of the neutral state, individuals are supposed to be equal. Yet the forces supporting male control are not in general equal before the state to those against it. The state itself acts in a patriarchal fashion. The welfare state relates to its recipients as fathers do to their children and dependents. And, without continuing pressure from women, the state does little to shake entrenched standards of male control. The lack of neutrality is to be found counterfactually in what would remain in the absence of a determined struggle.[5] So, with the abandonment of the liberal model of individual and conflict, the liberal model of the state crumbles.

This analysis clears the obstacles placed by liberal theory in the way of a right to organize independently against male control. Since the state leans toward perpetuating social oppression, independent organization to overcome oppression—through a challenge to the state's role as resolver of conflicts—is thoroughly warranted. Not relying on the state breaks no social bond that was not already broken.

The acid test for any kind of organizing, such as the setting up of shelters, is whether it contributes to the interests of the oppressed group. The characteristic thing about *an oppressed group* is that its members get what is required to satisfy their basic needs only by accepting conditions which are imposed by another group and which impede the realization of other aspects of what those in the oppressed group are. Workers get their livelihood only if they accept the necessity of producing a surplus for the owners. Women can get companionship in the family, a livelihood in the workplace, and benefits from the state only if they accept the decisions of men and the secondary social and economic status that results from this. To make claim to what they get without accepting the imposed conditions is rebellion and an assertion of the right to liberation.

Once people only half perceive the possibility of obtaining what they need without paying the price of conditions imposed by another group, they will begin, however tentatively, to organize against their oppression. This may be self-destructive in the absence of a clear vision of the path. But, once rage has been combined with a conception of where it is possible to take the struggle without disastrous defeats, an internal morality begins to take shape within the movement of the oppressed itself. And one of the first clear precepts of such a morality is that there is a right to organize independently against oppression.

Who is obliged to recognize this right? How is it frequently denied? On what does the right rest? If, as I contend, the right rests on the interests of the group or, equivalently, on what those in the group are, then its validity does not depend on its confirmation by other groups, unless of course their interests are tied up with the interests of the given oppressed group. It is, for example, necessary for the men in the working class to recognize the right of women to organize against male control. Without this recognition the solidarity needed for overcoming exploitation will be impossible.[6] The struggle to overcome sexism is, then, part of the class struggle. It is not a problem at the edge of the class struggle, to be dealt with at some later time when male workers find it convenient.

The right-wing movement of the 1980s in the United States wishes to deny women the right to organize against their oppression. It sees its interests as tied to continuing male domination. It then violates no right and hence misses no obligation in rejecting independent organization by women. Attributing such an obligation to the right wing would have no practical effect anyway. This movement senses that social control is effective only under conditions of stability, yet to allow liberation in one area would lead to its spilling over in another. It wants a stable system of "growth"—growth through reproduction in the family, exploitation in the workplace, and rolling back communism in the world. Domination over workers, women, minorities, and other states is, then, a seamless system. To say that the right wing is wrong in failing to grant a right to independent organization by the oppressed is merely to say that *from the point of view of the oppressed* there should not be any oppressors.[7]

The anti-feminist "right to life" movement is not an instance of independent organization against oppression. It is neither against women's oppression nor independent. It is clearly subordinate to male-dominated groups of the right-wing movement.[8] The American feminist movement is itself divided between currents favoring independent organization and others tending to fold the movement into mainstream politics. Among basically independent movements—the Polish Solidarity movement, the Palestine liberation movement, the Salvadorean liberation movement—it is usually possible to find both currents.

The Right to Choose

The issue of abortion becomes public through struggle. The rise of the women's movement in the 1960s brought it to the fore, and now the right-wing backlash keeps it there. Even liberal theorists have taken to writing about the problem in these periods, though they write about it as an eternal question. The connection between feminism and abortion is, though, not accidental; for a woman's right to choose is counterposed to the male's right to make choices for her.

If our model switches from persons as independently defined centers of action to persons as in important ways group-defined centers of action, then what had been thought of as rights based on the universal feature of being a person become rights based on being a person in a certain group. The effect of making this switch is frequently canceled by harmonistic assumptions about groups. On the one hand, it is admitted that the model of a person in liberal theory is an abstraction, but, on the other hand, it is claimed to be a useful abstraction, since individuals of the major groups of a society have complementary rather than conflicting interests.

These harmonistic assumptions are of a piece with the liberal theory of the neutral state. They limit inevitable conflicts to local affairs, whereas social conflicts are to be resolved by conversation between groups. It is not claimed that at any given time there is harmony, but it is proposed, for example, by Jürgen Habermas[9] and Richard Rorty,[10] that conversation can be pursued between the parties till it is evident that the further we go in dialogue the more the motives for a fight are alleviated. This is traditionally the tactic of the party that holds all the cards. But occasionally it is the expression of the naiveté of the weaker party, as when in 1979 the National Organization of Women sought to reason with the right-to-lifers over the issue of attacking abortion clinics.

Is there a way of choosing between the practice of the harmonizers and that of those who fight against oppression? Presumably some moral principle will enable us to make this choice if the choice is not arbitrary. It is indeed not arbitrary, but there is no moral principle for the job that stands above groups. Those in an oppressed group will have a morality, more or less articulate, that condemns deals with the oppressor which compromise the goal of liberation. Movements against the oppressor will come and go against the background of an implicit understanding that some way out of the system of oppression must be used.[11] The existence of such a morality is a factional threat, but it is not a bit less legitimate for that. A philosophical model merely puts this legitimacy on a footing that makes sense to the practitioner of the morality of the oppressed.

The morality of the harmonizers also has a historical basis, however much it would like to claim a timeless pedigree. It is the morality of the cultural, political, religious, economic, and educational institutions dedicated to ensuring that the dominant social order is not destabilized. The existence of such a morality is a threat to factional movements. Through its institutional dissemination it exists, alongside the morality of the oppressed, in the oppressed themselves. Ultimately it is a morality that serves the interests of oppressing groups, since its universalistic form serves to limit protest from oppressed groups to issues affecting a "common good."

A moral philosophy linked with the cause of the oppressed has, then, a relativist thrust. When a universalist culture puts itself forward as a higher culture, a philosophy of the oppressed needs to point out that the place of harmonizing universalist ideas is itself a historical place. It needs to reiterate that this place is found alongside other historical places and has a validity that is local despite its universalist form. This relativist thrust gains some plausibility if we look at the way in which institutions supposedly representing universalist interests treat abortion.

According to *Genesis* women are deservedly an oppressed group. The weakness of Eve was the source of patriarchy, since God gave husbands the right to rule over their wives because of Eve's eating of the forbidden fruit. Henceforth the lot of woman would be to have her childbirths multiplied and made sorrowful. The rights of God's children were then decided by Him in typical patriarchal fashion.

The U.S. Supreme Court has consistently seen the protection of potential life as a legitimate concern of the various states. Its interpretation of what this concern implies has changed. In *Roe v. Wade* in 1973, the Court ruled that abortion was a constitutional right, but it gave the states the right to regulate or prescribe third-trimester abortions, in view of their interest in potential life. A woman's medical need was, though, allowed precedence over the state's interest in potential life in the second trimester. And no restrictions were placed on abortions in the first trimester. But, in 1977, the Court ruled that individual states could refuse to fund nontherapeutic abortions. And, in 1980, in *Harris v. McRae*, the Court upheld the Hyde Amendment, passed in Congress in 1976; federal funds could be used for abortions only in cases of rape, incest, and danger to the mother's life. This left it open to the states to withdraw matching funds in all but these cases. The argument was that the states' interests in protecting potential life was more important than equal protection of the right to choose as between rich and poor women. The rights of women are decided here by a male-controlled court to be limited by male-controlled states.

But, if women's oppression is not the price of original sin, if women are not children of the courts, if, in short, women's rights are not to be defined by male-dominated institutions, and if universalism cannot function except as a vehicle for men so long as men are the oppressors, then there is no obstacle in the way of seeing women as having a right to fight in a manner consistent with their liberation. The right to choose on reproductive matters is central in this fight. So long as the interests of states, the dictates of the Church, certification by doctors, or obedience to a husband is allowed to override the interests of women in the choices of reproduction, there is cooperation with the structures of male dominance.

In the United States in the nineteenth century, it was the efforts of doctors to expand their control to reproductive matters that was behind the antiabortion movement.[12] Midwives had regularly performed abortions; medical practice had to be snatched away from them. With 73 percent of American Catholics thinking that abortion should be legal in all or at least some circumstances in 1977, the National Conference of Catholic Bishops thought it necessary to involve the Church in lobbying for a "Human Life Amendment" to the U.S. Constitution and to make the Church the major institutional and financial force behind local and national right-to-life committees. The amendment was introduced into both houses of Congress in January 1981, but so far has gone nowhere.

The right to choose on reproductive matters is incorrectly represented by its critics as a matter of selfish individualism. With this it has little to do. It is a matter of women who identify themselves as members of an oppressed gender saying that, whether they choose in individual cases to have an abortion or not, unless they are allowed to make this choice they will be denied other choices that are crucial to their liberation. To let Justice Potter Stewart, who wrote the Court's position in *Harris v. McRae,* or Pope John Paul II, who spoke against abortion during his American trip, decide about abortion is to let men determine the outcome of efforts for child care and for women's gaining equal status in the church.

It is not just that these things are linked. Reproductive choices are where it all starts: they determine the capitalist's next-generation labor force, the bishop's next-generation flock, the husband's heir and pride, and the state's new taxpayers. Naturally, the thinking male supremacist is not going to agree to the idea that mere women should be handed this key to the future of the ever-so-painstakingly constructed man's world. It is difficult to see, then, how a feminist movement could consistently neglect the fight for the right to choose in all reproductive matters.

In sum, women have the right to choose an abortion. This right is based on several things. At the concrete level, it is based on the key role the right to choose has among other rights women are struggling for. At a more general level, it is based on the way the morality of an oppressed group is formed by the goal of liberation for that group. That group takes precedence as regards morality over others—the church, the state, the medical profession, the nation. Such a precedence looks like a step backward from the standpoint of a universalist culture. For it accords privileges to particular interests over the universal interests of some qualified elite or of humanity itself. Here is precisely where the battle over philosophical models occurs.

The liberal version of universalist culture holds out for a uniformity in human nature which makes any kind of particularism in morality rest on what is contingent and accidental in people. This model of human nature leads to a call for a mechanism for adjusting conflict that treats all parties to the conflict as equals. One such mechanism is the neutral state; another is dialogue.

In contrast, the group model of human nature presented here considers some failures of universality to be based on what people truly are rather than on what is accidental to them. From the perspective of this model, the morality of a group fighting oppression can be valid, not because it might be universal, but because it properly interprets the interests of that group in winning liberation. This model is useful for purposes of understanding the liberal theory in its various forms. It sees liberal theory as useful to those who have some stake in making oppression only an accidental fact about those who are oppressed. The needs of the oppressed can then wait until the neutral state or dialogue becomes effective in satisfying them.

The Right to Life

One approach to the problem of abortion is to treat the matter, as we have just done, from a group perspective. From the perspective of women as a group seeking liberation, the fetus may have no right to life. But let us return for the moment to treating the problem of abortion in the absence of any consideration of groups. Appeal will be made directly to the rights of persons. All persons will then have rights which women in their struggle must respect. In particular, if the fetus is a person, he or she has rights that cannot be subordinated to the liberation of women. We shall find that, upon application of this nongroup view, difficulties emerge which lead us back to the group model.

A right in one person is usually thought to imply support from other persons. Otherwise a right is no more than a permission to do something. With a right to life the fetus has a call upon others to support his or her life. In particular, the fetus has a call upon the mother to the use of her body until he or she becomes independently viable. One of the fuzzy facts about a right is, though, that, even with widespread recognition of the right, there is unclarity about *how much* others must sacrifice in order to provide the called-for support.

Judith Jarvis Thomson has dramatized the issue of the degree of sacrifice with her hypothetical plugged-in violinist whose life depends on his blood being run through someone else's kidneys. How much support does the violinist's right to life demand? Must someone spend the rest of his/her life plugged in to the violinist to support his life? Thomson and both her critics and supporters have intuitions to offer in profusion, but they have no systematic way of answering the question about the degree of sacrifice.[13] It won't do here to counterpose a presumptive right of the mother to the use of her own body. This only adds another right to the list, and adding it doesn't tell us how it is to be weighed against the fetus's right to life.

If we limit considerations to individuals taken by themselves, there seems to be no basis for saying what the degree of support for a right should be. Should the degree of support I give be such that it does not inconvenience me? Should it be such that it is compatible with my life plan? My convenience seems a lame excuse for avoiding the sacrifices required to protect the rights of others. And an individual whose life plan could be defined without relation to any group would, at least from a naturalist view of ethics, fail to fall within the domain of the moral. A duty to support the rights of others would not apply to such a being.

On the group model for human nature and morality, the way sacrifices to protect rights would affect groups becomes relevant.[14] A right exists when to deny it would be incompatible with the interests characteristic of the group relative to which there is the right. And it must be supported when not doing so would go against those interests. But there are limits to the degree of support, limits to be defined in terms of these group interests. When giving support calls for sacrifices that would be a greater setback to the group than would result from giving no support, we have reached those limits.

Of course, there must be some way to identify interests characteristic of a group. This will be no easy job for any group, owing in large part to group overlappings and to the ideology promoted by official institutions. Women will be divided by class, by religion, by race, and by politics. There will be no consensus on feminist issues among women, just as there is no consensus within the working class on class issues. Despite the overlapping, women from all groups have participated in movements that have recognized the oppression of women. Those movements—the women's rights and suffrage movement of the late nineteenth and the early twentieth centuries and the liberation movement beginning in the 1960s—overcame some of the divisions through struggle around concrete issues. In those struggles a wide sense of the need to eliminate sexual oppression caught hold and

for a time did not lose its grip, even after the struggles subsided and backlash eroded commitment.

It is in the context of struggles focusing on sources of oppression that consciousness of interests develops. Struggles that do not focus on sources of oppression but pit women allied with their oppressors against other women will not have the same potential for revealing group interests. The interests characteristic of a group are to be decided not abstractly but in conjunction with struggle against oppression. The moral philosopher must look to these struggles, rather than to moral intuitions acquired in isolation from those struggles, in attempting to decide what sacrifices have to be made to protect rights.

There are limits to the degree of sacrifice that must be made for the fetus's right to life. What those limits are will depend on the group relative to which those limits are to be determined. When that group is the female gender, those limits are determined on the basis of the goal of overthrowing male control. If what is sacrificed by a general policy of supporting the fetus's right to life is the ability of women to carry on an effective struggle against male control, then they have gone beyond what is required. Going beyond what is required to support the fetus will lead many women to accept the responsibilities of motherhood in a society in which men still refuse an equal share in child rearing, will lead many women to accept the financial responsibility for child rearing when they cannot afford adequate medical care, housing, and child care, and will lead many women to accept the traditional family simply because the single mother finds it difficult to survive on the low-paying jobs open to her.

Childbearing in the circumstances many women find themselves in today thus puts women in a position that strengthens the power of men over them. If this is the case for a large number of women, as it surely is, then it will tend to strengthen male control as an overall institution. Thus it is in the interests of women generally, insofar as they are opposed to male control, to support the right of women to choose whether they will carry a fetus to term or not. This does not mean that the right choice will be made in every case, but that women have the right to decide how far to go in supporting the life of the fetus on the basis of their interests as women.

This argument still holds in the case of the viable fetus. Medical technology has pushed the point of viability to earlier and earlier stages of pregnancy. So the right to abortion becomes more and more restricted if only the nonviable fetus may be aborted. Yet the argument above disallows such a restriction. Whether the fetus could survive a premature delivery or not leaves unchanged the fact that, under circumstances faced by many women today, childbearing strengthens the power of men over them. Putting up the neonate for adoption does not solve this problem. For male control is maintained by women's being forced to deliver a viable fetus and to undergo the wrenching experience of giving it away. Is this compulsion still illegitimate if the viable fetus has a right to life? This question takes us back to the issue of the limits on sacrifices for protecting rights. Those sacrifices need not be made if they set back the struggle against male control.[15]

I turn now to another issue about sacrifices for rights. Some liberal philosophers have claimed that the sacrifices to be made for the life of the fetus are to be greater when the mother is responsible for the pregnancy. The sorts of matters thought to reduce this responsibility are the condom's breaking or intercourse while under the influence of alcohol. Joel Feinberg helpfully lists a spectrum of responsibility, beginning with rape and ending with a joint decision to have a child.[16] But, like other moral concepts, the concept of responsibility cannot be treated apart from groups.[17]

Those forces in society which want to reinforce the male-dominated family, which want women to constitute a cheap labor force, and which do not want to take responsibility for making child rearing less a burden for women find it convenient to say that, except in cases of physical coercion, the woman is responsible for her pregnancy and thus should go through with it. Their sense of the meaning of responsibility derives from the realization that they would be threatened with the realization of many of the ideals of women's liberation if the woman did not take responsibility for her pregnancy. They do not hold consistently to this sense of responsibility on all occasions. Individual men will urge abortions on their girl friends when they want to avoid financial responsibility for the offspring of short-term relationships. But some of the same men would be outraged if their wives unilaterally decided to abort their potential heirs.

From the perspective of the struggle against male control, responsibility looks quite different. From this perspective there is a variety of ways in which the woman's responsibility for the dependent unborn person in reduced. It must be recognized that the mother alone cannot always meet the needs of the fetus and the neonate. The surrounding society must provide some support. When the mother herself is needy, the society can provide pregnancy care, decent conditions for childbirth, and a promise of adequate conditions for child rearing. In addition, the surrounding society must avoid restricting the woman's freedom. Wanting the child before the pregnancy should not result from an ideology that makes motherhood the chief role of the woman. Equally, the pregnancy should not be the result of social circumstances that make companionship with children born out of wedlock preferable to the domination of male partners. All these things affect the degree of responsibility of the mother for the dependent fetus. When the society fails to take its share of the responsibility and when it constrains the woman to seek motherhood, she can rightly refuse to take full responsibility for the fetus's life.

Saying that the woman is responsible for the life of the fetus she has got through voluntary sex is, then, a form of guilt-tripping. If the society can exist only through being reproduced and if it promotes its existence with the cult of motherhood, then it shares responsibility with the mother for the life of the fetus. A male-dominated society will still tell the woman she has full responsibility for seeing that the fetus is carried to term. For the woman, the only way to avoid taking most of the responsibility is, in many cases, to have an abortion. Representative Hyde, whose amendment cutting off federal funds for most abortions was supported by the Supreme Court, has supported bills to cut the Food Stamp Program and to cut back decent public housing.[18] His view would have to be that pregnancies resulting from voluntary sex impose no responsibility on society, but considerable responsibility on the woman. The interesting thing is that liberal philosophers fall right in with this atomized view of responsibility because they do not take the point of view of women as a group in determining responsibility to the fetus. Liberal theory was not designed to support factional causes, and it is no wonder that it has such limited success when used on women's issues.

Conclusion

Philosophy as I have spoken of it here is not speculative in the sense that nothing is ever done with it. Yet it is not practical in the sense that it would be merely the application of good sense to thinking about knotty problems. It stands in the middle as interpretive. It involves the proposal of a model about human nature that might itself be put to speculative uses, but is in fact used to interpret writing and action that has come from the women's movement. Using the model to interpret that writing and action involves showing how their parts fall into place when looked at in terms of the model.

Women are asking for something that pertains to them as women; specifically they are asking for the ability to determine their lives as producers of new life. A model of human nature as determined by groups and, derivatively, a model of morality as relative to groups would seem to be helpful in this context. It provides a unity that the liberal theory of human nature cannot provide for the women's movement. That movement is not about civil rights, at which the liberal theory is moderately good. It is not just about human rights because part of it is about the right to organize against the sectors of humanity defending male-supremacist institutions and part of it is about women as the reproducers of life.

What the relations between men and women might be as male control sinks to ex-

tinction is a matter of speculation until the struggle develops further. But as far as the present stage of the struggle is concerned, it is being suggested here that it would be fruitful for the women's movement to recognize the limitations of interpreting itself in terms of liberal theory and the advantages of interpreting itself in terms of the group model of human nature. The continuity of the movement and the development of its perspective depends on the presence of some unifying model at this general level. Otherwise the movement is condemned after lulls to bring itself to life again by piecing together random new bits from the history of oppression in the absence of any foundation. The critique of old models like the liberal one will have to be redone, and momentum will build up without a clear direction.

Notes

1. Antonio Gramsci, "The Study of Philosophy," in *The Modern Prince and Other Writings*, L. Marks, trans. (New York: International Publishers, 1957), p. 63. Such interpretive models do not always come from within the movements that make use of them. After rightly criticizing Engels' subordination of the women's movement to the class movement, feminists have been able to employ Engels' idea that capitalism opens up the possibility of women's liberation by eliminating the patriarchal family as the unit of production, even though in other ways it is a major obstacle to women's liberation. And, after rightly criticizing Freud's sexism, feminists have been able to employ his conceptions of the Oedipus and Electra complexes to forward their understanding of male control today. On both points, see Juliet Mitchell, *Psychoanalysis and Feminism* (New York: Pantheon, 1974).

2. John Rawls, *A Theory of Justice* (Cambridge, Mass.: Harvard University Press, 1971), pp. 240, 268, 336.

3. Pluralism did, to be sure, get grafted onto liberal theory; see John Dewey, *Reconstruction in Philosophy* (Boston: Beacon Press, 1957), pp. 203–204. But there is no inherent reason for the groups recognized by pluralist theory to do battle

with one another. When they do have squabbles, they submit to the adjudication of the state, the neutral power set above them. By contrast, movements against oppression do not characteristically submit to such a discipline. There will, though, be wings of most movements that push in the direction of putting pressure on the state rather than on developing a more independent form of organization.

4. John Locke, *The Second Treatise of Government,* ch. III, "Of the State of War," #21: "Had there been any such court, and superior jurisdiction on earth, to determine the right between Jephthah and the Ammonites, they had never come to a state of war; but we see he was forced to appeal to heaven . . . and then prosecuting and relying on his appeal, he leads out his army to battle."

5. Nicos Poulantzas, *Classes in Contemporary Capitalism,* D. Fernbach, trans. (London: Verso, 1978), p. 161.

6. Compare the analogous thesis about the right of oppressed nations to organize in V. I. Lenin, "The Right of Nations to Self-determination," *Collected Works* (Moscow: Progress Publishers, 1964), vol. 20, pp. 395–454.

7. What is of practical significance is the reluctance of much of the left really to believe that women have the right to organize independently of men and of the institutions men have dominated. It is of practical significance since there are ways of demonstrating that this reluctance is plainly counter to the best interests of the groups the left takes itself to be representing. See my "Feminism, Socialism, and Historical Materialism," *Praxis International,* II (1982): 117–40.

8. Deirdre English, "The War against Choice," *Mother Jones* (February/March, 1981): 16–32.

9. "On Systematically Distorted Communication," *Inquiry,* XIII (1970): 205–218; "Toward a Theory of Communicative Competence." *ibid.,* 360–75.

10. "Pragmatism, Relativism, and Irrationalism," Presidential Address, Eastern Division American Philosophical Association, December 1979, part III; reprinted in Rorty's *The Consequences of Pragmatism* (Minneapolis: University of Minnesota Press, 1983).

11. Simone de Beauvoir, *The Second Sex,* H. M. Parshley, trans. (New York: Vintage, 1974), p. 546.

12. *Women under Attack: Abortion, Sterilization Abuse, and Reproductive Freedom,* Committee for Abortion Rights and against Sterilization Abuse, PO Box 124, Cathedral Station, New York, N.Y., 10025, 1979, Chapter III. Incredibly, the right-to-life ideologue John T. Noonan, Jr., in *A Private Choice* (New York: Free Press, 1979), p. 52, takes Dr. Horatio R. Stoner's 1859 AMA statement against "snuffing out life in the making" at face value.

13. "A Defense of Abortion," *Philosophy and Public Affairs,* I (1971): 47–66.

14. See my *Ethics and Society* (New York: N.Y.U. Press, 1980), p. 203.

15. Mary Anne Warren, "On the Moral and Legal Status of Abortion" and "Postscript on Infanticide," in J. P. Sterba, ed., *Morality in Practice* (Belmont, Calif.: Wadsworth, 1984), p. 153.

16. "Abortion," in T. Regan, ed., *Matters of Life and Death* (New York: Random House, 1980), pp. 212–13.

17. See my *Ethics and Society,* pp. 194–96.

18. *Women under Attack,* chapter V. In response to this type of argument, Noonan contrives the following sophism: "The liberty [to abort] is oppressive to the poor. Its existence has led to depriving the pregnant poor of assistance for their independent unborn children" (*A Private Choice,* p. 190).

3. Why Abortion Is Immoral

Don Marquis

Don Marquis argues that abortion is, in most circumstances, morally unaccept-able. His argument is based on the claim that killing an innocent human being is almost always wrong. Abortion takes away the fetus's ability to pursue a future life, with all the enjoyments available to any human.

The view that abortion is, with rare exceptions, seriously immoral has received little support in the recent philosophical literature. No doubt most philosophers affiliated with secular institutions of higher education believe that the anti-abortion position is either a symptom of irrational religious dogma or a conclusion generated by seriously confused philosophical argument. The purpose of this essay is to undermine this general belief. This essay sets out an argument that purports to show, as well as any argument in ethics can show, that abortion is, except possibly in rare cases, seriously immoral, that it is in the same moral category as killing an innocent adult human being.

The argument is based on a major assumption. Many of the most insightful and careful writers on the ethics of abortion—such as Joel Feinberg, Michael Tooley, Mary Anne Warren, H. Tristram Engelhardt, Jr., L. W. Sumner, John T. Noonan, Jr., and Philip Devine[1]—believe that whether or not abortion is morally permissible stands or falls on whether or not a fetus is the sort of being whose life it is seriously wrong to end. The argument of this essay will assume, but not argue, that they are correct.

Also, this essay will neglect issues of great importance to a complete ethics of abortion. Some anti-abortionists will allow that certain abortions, such as abortion before implantation or abortion when the life of a woman is threatened by a pregnancy or abortion after rape, may be morally permissible. This essay will not explore the casuistry of these hard cases. The purpose of this essay is to develop a general argument for the claim that the overwhelming majority of deliberate abortions are seriously immoral.

From *The Journal of Philosophy*, LXXXVI, 4 (April 1989), pp. 183–202. Reprinted by permission.

I

A sketch of standard anti-abortion and pro-choice arguments exhibits how those arguments possess certain symmetries that explain why partisans of those positions are so convinced of the correctness of their own positions, why they are not successful in convincing their opponents, and why, to others, this issue seems to be unresolvable. An analysis of the nature of this standoff suggests a strategy for surmounting it.

Consider the way a typical anti-abortionist argues. She will argue or assert that life is present from the moment of conception or that fetuses look like babies or that fetuses possess a characteristic such as a genetic code that is both necessary and sufficient for being human. Anti-abortionists seem to believe that (1) the truth of all of these claims is quite obvious, and (2) establishing any of these claims is sufficient to show that abortion is morally akin to murder.

A standard pro-choice strategy exhibits similarities. The pro-choicer will argue or assert that fetuses are not persons or that fetuses are not rational agents or that fetuses are not social beings. Pro-choicers seem to believe that (1) the truth of any of these claims is quite obvious, and (2) establishing any of these claims is sufficient to show that an abortion is not a wrongful killing.

In fact, both the pro-choice and the anti-abortion claims do seem to be true, although the "it looks like a baby" claim is more difficult to establish the earlier the pregnancy. We seem to have a standoff. How can it be resolved?

As everyone who has taken a bit of logic knows, if any of these arguments concerning abortion is a good argument, it requires not only some claim characterizing fetuses, but also some general moral principle that ties a characteristic of fetuses to having or not having the right to life or to some other moral characteristic that will generate the obligation or the lack of obligation not to end the life of a fetus. Accordingly, the arguments of the anti-abortionist and the pro-choicer need a bit of filling in to be regarded as adequate.

Note what each partisan will say. The anti-abortionist will claim that her position is supported by such generally accepted moral principles as "It is always prima facie seriously wrong to take a human life" or "It is always prima facie seriously wrong to end the life of a baby." Since these are generally accepted moral principles, her position is certainly not obviously wrong. The pro-choicer will claim that her position is supported by such plausible moral principles as "Being a person is what gives an individual intrinsic moral worth" or "It is only seriously prima facie wrong to take the life of a member of the human community." Since these are generally accepted moral principles, the pro-choice position is certainly not obviously wrong. Unfortunately, we have again arrived at a standoff.

Now, how might one deal with this standoff? The standard approach is to try to show how the moral principles of one's opponent lose their plausibility under analysis. It is easy to see how this is possible. On the one hand, the anti-abortionist will defend a moral principle concerning the wrongness of killing which tends to be broad in scope in order that even fetuses at an early stage of pregnancy will fall under it. The problem with broad principles is that they often embrace too much. In this particular instance, the principle "It is always prima facie wrong to take a human life" seems to entail that it is wrong to end the existence of a living human cancer-cell culture, on the grounds that the culture is both living and human. Therefore, it seems that the anti-abortionist's favored principle is too broad.

On the other hand, the pro-choicer wants to find a moral principle concerning the wrongness of killing which tends to be narrow in scope in order that fetuses will *not* fall under it. The problem with narrow principles is that they often do not embrace enough. Hence, the needed principles such as "It is prima facie seriously wrong to kill only persons" or "It is prima facie wrong to kill only rational agents" do not explain why it is wrong to kill infants or young children or the severely retarded or even perhaps the severely mentally ill. Therefore, we seem again to have a standoff. The anti-abortionist charges, not unreasonably, that pro-choice principles concerning killing are too narrow to be acceptable; the pro-choicer charges, not unreasonably, that anti-abortionist principles concerning killing are too broad to be acceptable.

Attempts by both sides to patch up the difficulties in their positions run into further difficulties. The anti-abortionist will try to remove the problem in her position by reformulating her principle concerning killing in terms of human beings. Now we end up with: "It is always prima facie seriously wrong to end the life of a human being." This principle has the advantage of avoiding the problem of the human cancer-cell culture counterexample. But this advantage is purchased at a high price. For although it is clear that a fetus is both human and alive, it is not at all clear that a fetus is a human *being*. There is at least something to be said for the view that something becomes a human being only after a process of development, and that therefore first trimester fetuses and perhaps all fetuses are not yet human beings. Hence, the anti-abortionist, by this move, has merely exchanged one problem for another.[2]

The pro-choicer fares no better. She may attempt to find reasons why killing infants, young children, and the severely retarded is wrong which are independent of her major principle that is supposed to explain the wrongness of taking human life, but which will not also make abortion immoral. This is no easy task. Appeals to social utility will seem satisfactory only to those who resolve not to think of the enormous difficulties with a utilitarian account of the wrongness of killing and the significant social costs of preserving the lives of the unproductive.[3] A pro-choice strategy that extends the definition of "person" to infants or even to young children seems just as arbitrary as an anti-abortion strategy that extends the definition of "human being" to fetuses. Again, we find symmetries in the two positions and we arrive at a standoff.

There are even further problems that reflect symmetries in the two positions. In addition to counterexample problems, or the arbitrary application problems that can be exchanged for them, the standard anti-abortionist principle "It is prima facie seriously wrong to kill a human being," or one of its variants, can be objected to on the grounds of ambiguity. If "human being" is taken to be a *biological* category, then the anti-abortionist is left with the problem of explaining why a merely biological category should make a moral difference. Why, it is asked, is it any more reasonable to base a moral conclusion on the number of chromosomes in one's cells than on the color of one's skin?[4] If "human being," on the other hand, is taken to be a *moral* category, then the claim that a fetus is a human being cannot be taken to be a premise in the anti-abortion argument, for it is precisely what needs to be established. Hence, either the anti-abortionist's main category is a morally irrelevant, merely biological category, or it is of no use to the anti-abortionist in establishing (noncircularly, of course) that abortion is wrong.

Although this problem with the anti-abortionist position is often noticed, it is less often noticed that the pro-choice position suffers from an analogous problem. The principle "Only persons have the right to life" also suffers from an ambiguity. The term "person" is typically defined in terms of psychological characteristics, although there will certainly be disagreement concerning which characteristics are most important. Supposing that this matter can be settled, the pro-choicer is left with the problem of explaining why *psychological* characteristics should make a *moral* difference. If the pro-choicer should attempt to deal with this problem by claiming that an explanation is not necessary, that in fact we do treat such a cluster of psychological properties as having moral significance, the sharp-witted anti-abortionist should have a ready response. We do treat being both living and human as hav-

ing moral significance. If it is legitimate for the pro-choicer to demand that the anti-abortionist provide an explanation of the connection between the biological character of being a human being and the wrongness of being killed (even though people accept this connection), then it is legitimate for the anti-abortionist to demand that the pro-choicer provide an explanation of the connection between psychological criteria for being a person and the wrongness of being killed (even though that connection is accepted).[5]

Feinberg has attempted to meet this objection (he calls psychological personhood "commonsense personhood"):

The characteristics that confer commonsense personhood are not arbitrary bases for rights and duties, such as race, sex or species membership; rather they are traits that make sense out of rights and duties and without which those moral attributes would have no point or function. It is because people are conscious; have a sense of their personal identities; have plans, goals, and projects; experience emotions; are liable to pains, anxieties, and frustrations; can reason and bargain, and so on—it is because of these attributes that people have values and interests, desires and expectations of their own, including a stake in their own futures, and a personal well-being of a sort we cannot ascribe to unconscious or nonrational beings. Because of their developed capacities they can assume duties and responsibilities and can have and make claims on one another. Only because of their sense of self, their life plans, their value hierarchies, and their stakes in their own futures can they be ascribed fundamental rights. There is nothing arbitrary about these linkages (*op. cit.*, p. 270).

The plausible aspects of this attempt should not be taken to obscure its implausible features. There is a great deal to be said for the view that being a psychological person under some description is a necessary condition for having duties. One cannot have a duty unless one is capable of behaving morally, and a being's capability of behaving morally will require having a certain psychology. It is far from obvious, however, that having rights entails consciousness or rationality, as Feinberg suggests. We speak of the rights of the severely retarded or the severely mentally ill, yet some of these persons are not rational. We speak of the rights of the temporarily unconscious. The New Jersey Supreme Court based their decision in the Quinlan case on Karen Ann Quinlan's right to privacy, and she was known to be permanently unconscious at that time. Hence, Feinberg's claim that having rights entails being conscious is, on its face, obviously false.

Of course, it might not make sense to attribute rights to a being that would never in its natural history have certain psychological traits. This modest connection between psychological personhood and moral personhood will create a place for Karen Ann Quinlan and the temporarily unconscious. But then it makes a place for fetuses also. Hence, it does not serve Feinberg's pro-choice purposes. Accordingly, it seems that the pro-choicer will have as much difficulty bridging the gap between psychological personhood and personhood in the moral sense as the anti-abortionist has bridging the gap between being a biological human being and being a human being in the moral sense.

Furthermore, the pro-choicer cannot more escape her problem by making 'person' a purely moral category than the anti-abortionist could escape by the analogous move. For if person is a moral category, then the pro-choicer is left without any means for establishing (noncircularly, of course) the claim that a fetus is not a person. This is an essential premise in her argument. Thus, we have both a symmetry and a supportive... pro-choice and anti-abortion...

Passions in the abortion... There are both plausible... with the standard positions... hardly surprising that partisans... embrace with fervor the moral generalizations that support the conclusions... they analytically favor, and reject with disdain the moral generalizations of their opponents as being subject to inescapable difficulties. It is easy to believe that the counterexamples to one's own moral principles are merely tempo-

rary difficulties that will dissolve in the wake of further philosophical research, and that the counterexamples to the principles of one's opponents are as straightforward as the contradiction between *A* and *O* propositions in traditional logic. This might suggest to an impartial observer (if there are any) that the abortion issue is unresolvable.

There is a way out of this apparent dialectical quandary. The moral generalizations of both sides are not quite correct. The generalizations hold for the most part, for the usual cases. This suggests that they are all *accidental* generalizations, that the moral claims made by those on both sides of the dispute do not touch on the *essence* of the matter.

This use of the distinction between essence and accident is not meant to invoke obscure metaphysical categories. Rather, it is intended to reflect the rather atheoretical nature of the abortion discussion. If the generalization a partisan in the abortion dispute adopts were derived from the reason why ending the life of a human being is wrong, then there could not be exceptions to that generalization unless some special case obtains in which there are even more powerful countervailing reasons. Such generalizations would not be merely accidental generalizations; they would point to, or be based upon, the essence of the wrong... what it is that makes killing... suggests that a necessary condition... abortion controversy is a... the wrongness of... believe, but do...

[handwritten annotations overlaid:]
→ Language difference b/w fetus vs. adult human being
→ Both arguments are rooted in too broad of statements
→ person defined by psychological characteristics – no resources for establishing a fetus is not a person
→ loss of experiences, projects etc. is what makes killing wrong

...an account, we can... [f]ollowing unproblematic... our own case: it is... hy is it wrong? Some answer... eliminated. It might be said that... killing us wrong is that a killing brutalizes the one who kills. But the brutalization consists of being inured to the performance of an act that is hideously immoral; hence, the brutalization does not explain the immorality. It might be said that what makes killing us wrong is the great loss others would experience due to our absence. Although such hubris is understandable, such an explanation does not account for the wrongness of killing hermits, or those whose lives are relatively independent and whose friends find it easy to make new friends.

A more obvious answer is better. What primarily makes killing wrong is neither its effect on the murderer nor its effect on the victim's friends and relatives, but its effect on the victim. The loss of one's life is one of the greatest losses one can suffer. The loss of one's life deprives one of all the experiences, activities, projects, and enjoyments that would otherwise have constituted one's future. Therefore, killing someone is wrong, primarily because the killing inflicts (one of) the greatest possible losses on the victim. To describe this as the loss of life can be misleading, however. The change in my biological state does not by itself make killing me wrong. The effect of the loss of my biological life is the loss to me of all those activities, projects, experiences, and enjoyments which would otherwise have constituted my future personal life. These activities, projects, experiences. and enjoyments are either valuable for their own sakes or are means to something else that is valuable for its own sake. Some parts of my future are not valued by me now, but will come to be valued by me as I grow older and as my values and capacities change. When I am killed, I am deprived both of what I now value which would have been part of my future personal life, but also what I would come to value. Therefore, when I die, I am deprived of all of the value of my future. Inflicting this loss on me is ultimately what makes killing me wrong. This being the case, it would seem that what makes killing *any* adult human being prima facie seriously wrong is the loss of his or her future.[6]

How should this rudimentary theory of the wrongness of killing be evaluated? It cannot be faulted for deriving an "ought" from an "is," for it does not. The analysis assumes that killing me (or you, reader) is prima facie seriously wrong. The point of the analysis is to establish which natural property ultimately explains the wrongness of the killing, given that it is wrong. A natural property will ultimately explain the wrongness of killing, only if (1) the explanation fits with our intuitions about the matter and (2) there is no other natural property that provides the basis for a better explanation of the wrongness of killing. This analysis rests on the intuition that what makes killing a particular human or animal wrong is what it does to that particular human or animal. What makes killing wrong is some natural effect or other of the killing. Some would deny this. For instance, a divine-command theorist in ethics would deny it. Surely this denial is, however, one of those features of divine-command theory which renders it so implausible.

The claim that what makes killing wrong is the loss of the victim's future is directly supported by two considerations. In the first place, this theory explains why we regard killing as one of the worst of crimes. Killing is especially wrong, because it deprives the victim of more than perhaps any other crime. In the second place, people with AIDS or cancer who know they are dying believe, of course, that dying is a very bad thing for them. They believe that the loss of a future to them that they would otherwise have experienced is what makes their premature death a very bad thing for them. A better theory of the wrongness of killing would require a different natural property associated with killing which better fits with the attitudes of the dying. What could it be?

The view that what makes killing wrong is the loss to the victim of the value of the victim's future gains additional support when some of its implications are examined. In the first place, it is incompatible with the view that it is wrong to kill only beings who are biologically human. It is possible that there exists a different species from another planet whose members have a future like ours. Since having a future like that is what makes killing someone wrong, this theory entails that it would be wrong to kill members of such a species. Hence, this theory is opposed to the claim that only life that is biologically human has great moral worth, a claim which many antiabortionists have seemed to adopt. This opposition, which this theory has in common with personhood theories, seems to be a merit of the theory.

In the second place, the claim that the loss of one's future is the wrong-making feature of one's being killed entails the possibility that the futures of some actual nonhuman mammals on our own planet are sufficiently like ours that it is seriously wrong to kill them also. Whether some animals do have the same right to life as human beings depends on adding to the account of the wrongness of killing some additional account of just what it is about my future or the futures of other adult human beings which makes it wrong to kill us. No such additional account will be offered in this essay. Undoubtedly, the provision of such an account would be a very difficult matter. Undoubtedly, any such account would be quite controversial. Hence, it surely should not reflect badly on this sketch of an elementary theory of the wrongness of killing that it is indeterminate with respect to some very difficult issues regarding animal rights.

In the third place, the claim that the loss of one's future is the wrong-making feature of one's being killed does not entail, as sanctity-of-human-life theories do, that active euthanasia is wrong. Persons who are severely and incurably ill, who face a future of pain and despair, and who wish to die will not have suffered a loss if they are killed. It is, strictly speaking, the value of a human's future which makes killing wrong in this theory. This being so, killing does not necessarily wrong some persons who are sick and dying. Of course, there may be other reasons for a prohibition of active euthanasia, but that is another matter. Sanctity-of-human-life theories seem to hold that active euthanasia is seriously wrong even in an individual case where there seems to be good reason for it independently of public policy considerations. This consequence is most implausible, and it is a plus for the claim that the loss of a future of value is what makes killing wrong that it does not share this consequence.

In the fourth place, the account of the wrongness of killing defended in this essay does straightforwardly entail that it is prima facie seriously wrong to kill children and infants, for we do presume that they have futures of value. Since we do believe that it is wrong to kill defenseless little babies, it is im-

portant that a theory of the wrongness of killing easily account for this. Personhood theories of the wrongness of killing, on the other hand, cannot straightforwardly account for the wrongness of killing infants and young children.[7] Hence, such theories must add special ad hoc accounts of the wrongness of killing the young. The plausibility of such ad hoc theories seems to be a function of how desperately one wants such theories to work. The claim that the primary wrong-making feature of a killing is the loss to the victim of the value of its future accounts for the wrongness of killing young children and infants directly; it makes the wrongness of such acts as obvious as we actually think it is. This is a further merit of this theory. Accordingly, it seems that this value of a future-like-ours theory of the wrongness of killing shares strengths of both sanctity-of-life and personhood accounts while avoiding weaknesses of both. In addition, it meshes with a central intuition concerning what makes killing wrong.

The claim that the primary wrong-making feature of a killing is the loss to the victim of the value of its future has obvious consequences for the ethics of abortion. The future of a standard fetus includes a set of experiences, projects, activities, and such which are identical with the futures of adult human beings and are identical with the futures of young children. Since the reason that is sufficient to explain why it is wrong to kill human beings after the time of birth is a reason that also applies to fetuses, it follows that abortion is prima facie seriously morally wrong.

This argument does not rely on the invalid inference that, since it is wrong to kill persons, it is wrong to kill potential persons also. The category that is morally central to this analysis is the category of having a valuable future like ours; it is not the category of personhood. The argument to the conclusion that abortion is prima facie seriously morally wrong proceeded independently of the notion of person or potential person or any equivalent. Someone may wish to start with this analysis in terms of the value of a human future, conclude that abortion is, except perhaps in rare circumstances, seriously morally wrong, infer that fetuses have the right to life, and then call fetuses "persons" as a result of their having the right to life. Clearly, in this case, the category of person is being used to state the *conclusion* of the analysis rather than to generate the *argument* of the analysis.

The structure of this anti-abortion argument can be both illuminated and defended by comparing it to what appears to be the best argument for the wrongness of the wanton infliction of pain on animals. This latter argument is based on the assumption that it is prima facie wrong to inflict pain on me (or you, reader). What is the natural property associated with the infliction of pain which makes such infliction wrong? The obvious answer seems to be that the infliction of pain causes suffering and that suffering is a misfortune. The suffering caused by the infliction of pain is what makes the wanton infliction of pain on me wrong. The wanton infliction of pain on other adult humans causes suffering. The wanton infliction of pain on animals causes suffering. Since causing suffering is what makes the wanton infliction of pain wrong and since the wanton infliction of pain on animals causes suffering, it follows that the wanton infliction of pain on animals is wrong.

This argument for the wrongness of the wanton infliction of pain on animals shares a number of structural features with the argument for the serious prima facie wrongness of abortion. Both arguments start with an obvious assumption concerning what it is wrong to do to me (or you, reader). Both then look for the characteristic or the consequence of the wrong action which makes the action wrong. Both recognize that the wrong-making feature of these immoral actions is a property of actions sometimes directed at individuals other than postnatal human beings. If the structure of the argument for the wrongness of the wanton infliction of pain on animals is sound, then the structure of the argument for the prima facie serious wrongness of abortion is also sound, for the structure of the two arguments is the same. The structure common to both is the key to the explanation of how the wrongness of abortion can be demonstrated without recourse to the category of person. In neither argument is that category crucial.

This defense of an argument for the wrongness of abortion in terms of a structurally similar argument for the wrongness of the wanton infliction of pain on animals succeeds only if the account regarding animals is the correct account. Is it? In the first place, it seems plausible. In the second place, its major competition is Kant's account. Kant believed that we do not have direct duties to animals at all, because they are not persons. Hence, Kant had to explain and justify the wrongness of inflicting pain on animals on the grounds that "he who is hard in his dealings with animals becomes hard also in his dealing with men."[8] The problem with Kant's account is that there seems to be no reason for accepting this latter claim unless Kant's account is rejected. If the alternative to Kant's account is accepted, then it is easy to understand why someone who is indifferent to inflicting pain on animals is also indifferent to inflicting pain on humans, for one is indifferent to what makes inflicting pain wrong in both cases. But, if Kant's account is accepted, there is no intelligible reason why one who is hard in his dealings with animals (or crabgrass or stones) should also be hard in his dealings with men. After all, men are persons: animals are no more persons than crabgrass or stones. Persons are Kant's crucial moral category. Why, in short, should a Kantian accept the basic claim in Kant's argument?

Hence, Kant's argument for the wrongness of inflicting pain on animals rests on a claim that, in a world of Kantian moral agents, is demonstrably false. Therefore, the alternative analysis, being more plausible anyway, should be accepted. Since this alternative analysis has the same structure as the anti-abortion argument being defended here, we have further support for the argument for the immorality of abortion being defended in this essay.

Of course, this value of a future-like-ours argument, if sound, shows only that abortion is prima facie wrong, not that it is wrong in any and all circumstances. Since the loss of the future to a standard fetus, if killed, is, however, at least as great a loss as the loss of the future to a standard adult human being who is killed, abortion, like ordinary killing, could be justified only by the most compelling reasons. The loss of one's life is almost the greatest misfortune that can happen to one. Presumably abortion could be justified in some circumstances, only if the loss consequent on failing to abort would be at least as great. Accordingly, morally permissible abortions will be rare indeed unless, perhaps, they occur so early in pregnancy that a fetus is not yet definitely an individual. Hence, this argument should be taken as showing that abortion is presumptively very seriously wrong, where the presumption is very strong—as strong as the presumption that killing another adult human being is wrong.

III

How complete an account of the wrongness of killing does the value of a future-like-ours account have to be in order that the wrongness of abortion is a consequence? This account does not have to be an account of the necessary conditions for the wrongness of killing. Some persons in nursing homes may lack valuable human futures, yet it may be wrong to kill them for other reasons. Furthermore, this account does not obviously have to be the sole reason killing is wrong where the victim did have a valuable future. This analysis claims only that, for any killing where the victim did have a valuable future like ours, having that future by itself is sufficient to create the strong presumption that the killing is seriously wrong.

One way to overturn the value of a future-like-ours argument would be to find some account of the wrongness of killing which is at least as intelligible and which has different implications for the ethics of abortion. Two rival accounts possess at least some degree of plausibility. One account is based on the obvious fact that people value the experience of living and wish for that valuable experience to continue. Therefore, it might be said, what makes killing wrong is the discontinuation of that experience for the victim. Let us call this the *discontinuation account*.[9] Another rival account is based upon the obvious fact that people strongly desire to continue to live. This suggests that what makes killing us so wrong is that it interferes with the fulfillment of a strong and fundamental desire, the fulfillment of which is necessary for the fulfillment of any other desires we might have. Let us call this the *desire account*.[10]

Consider first the desire account as a rival account of the ethics of killing which would provide the basis for rejecting the anti-abortion position. Such an account will have to be stronger than the value of a future-like-ours account of the wrongness of abortion if it is to do the job expected of it. To entail the wrongness of abortion, the value of a future-like-ours account has only to provide a sufficient, but not a necessary, condition for the wrongness of killing. The desire account, on the other hand, must provide us also with a necessary condition for the wrongness of killing in order to generate a pro-choice conclusion on abortion. The reason for this is that presumably the argument from the desire account moves from the claim that what makes killing wrong is interference with a very strong desire to the claim that abortion is not wrong because the fetus lacks a strong desire to live. Obviously, this inference fails if someone's having the desire to live is not a necessary condition of its being wrong to kill that individual.

One problem with the desire account is that we do regard it as seriously wrong to kill persons who have little desire to live or who have no desire to live or, indeed, have a desire not to live. We believe it is seriously wrong to kill the unconscious, the sleeping, those who are tired of life, and those who are suicidal. The value-of-a-human-future account renders standard morality intelligible in these cases: these cases appear to be incompatible with the desire account.

The desire account is subject to a deeper difficulty. We desire life, because we value the goods of this life. The goodness of life is not secondary to our desire for it. It this were not so, the pain of one's own premature death could be done away with merely by an appropriate alteration in the configuration of one's desires. This is absurd. Hence, it would seem that it is the loss of the goods of one's future, not the interference with the fulfillment of a strong desire to live, which accounts ultimately for the wrongness of killing.

It is worth noting that, if the desire account is modified so that it does not provide a necessary, but only a sufficient, condition for the wrongness of killing, the desire account is compatible with the value of a future-like-ours account. The combined accounts will yield an anti-abortion ethic. This suggests that one can retain what is intuitively plausible about the desire account without a challenge to the basic argument of this paper.

It is also worth noting that, if future desires have moral force in a modified desire account of the wrongness of killing, one can find support for an anti-abortion ethic even in the absence of a value of a future-like-ours account. If one decides that a morally relevant property, the possession of which is sufficient to make it wrong to kill some individual, is the desire at some future time to live—one might decide to justify one's refusal to kill suicidal teenagers on these grounds, for example— then, since typical fetuses will have the desire in the future to live, it is wrong to kill typical fetuses. Accordingly, it does not seem that a desire account of the wrongness of killing can provide a justification of a pro-choice ethic of abortion which is nearly as adequate as the value of a human-future justification of an anti-abortion ethic.

The discontinuation account looks more promising as an account of the wrongness of killing. It seems just as intelligible as the value of a future-like-ours account, but it does not justify an anti-abortion position. Obviously, if it is the continuation of one's activities, experiences, and projects, the loss of which makes killing wrong, then it is not wrong to kill fetuses for that reason, for fetuses do not have experiences, activities, and projects to be continued or discontinued. Accordingly, the discontinuation account does not have the anti-abortion consequences that the value of a future-like-ours account has. Yet, it seems as intelligible as the value of a future-like-ours account, for when we think of what would be wrong with our being killed, it does seem as if it is the discontinuation of what makes our lives worthwhile which makes killing us wrong.

Is the discontinuation account just as good an account as the value of a future-like-ours account? The discontinuation account will not be adequate at all, if it does not refer to the *value* of the experience that may be discontinued. One does not want the discontinuation account to make it wrong to kill a patient who begs for death and who is in severe pain that cannot be relieved short of killing. (I leave open the question of whether it is wrong for other reasons.) Accordingly, the discontinua-

tion account must be more than a bare discontinuation account. It must make some reference to the positive value of the patient's experiences. But, by the same token, the value of a future-like-ours account cannot be a bare future account either. Just having a future surely does not itself rule out killing the above patient. This account must make some reference to the value of the patient's future experiences and projects also. Hence, both accounts involve the value of experiences, projects, and activities. So far we still have symmetry between the accounts.

The symmetry fades, however, when we focus on the time period of the value of the experiences, etc., which has moral consequences. Although both accounts leave open the possibility that the patient in our example may be killed, this possibility is left open only in virtue of the utterly bleak future for the patient. It makes no difference whether the patient's immediate past contains intolerable pain, or consists in being in a coma (which we can imagine is a situation of indifference), or consists in a life of value. If the patient's future is a future of value, we want our account to make it wrong to kill the patient. If the patient's future is intolerable, whatever his or her immediate past, we want our account to allow killing the patient. Obviously, then, it is the value of that patient's future which is doing the work in rendering the morality of killing the patient intelligible.

This being the case, it seems clear that whether one has immediate past experiences or not does no work in the explanation of what makes killing wrong. The addition the discontinuation account makes to the value of a human future account is otiose. Its addition to the value-of-a-future account plays no role at all in rendering intelligible the wrongness of killing. Therefore, it can be discarded with the discontinuation account of which it is a part.

IV

The analysis of the previous section suggests that alternative general accounts of the wrongness of killing are either inadequate or unsuccessful in getting around the anti-abortion consequences of the value of a future-like-ours argument. A different strategy for avoiding these anti-abortion consequences involves limiting the scope of the value-of-a-future argument. More precisely, the strategy involves arguing that fetuses lack a property that is essential for the value-of-a-future argument (or for any anti-abortion argument) to apply to them.

One move of this sort is based upon the claim that a necessary condition of one's future being valuable is that one values it. Value implies a valuer. Given this one might argue that, since fetuses cannot value their futures, their futures are not valuable to them. Hence, it does not seriously wrong them deliberately to end their lives.

This move fails, however, because of some ambiguities. Let us assume that something cannot be of value unless it is valued by someone. This does not entail that my life is of no value unless it is valued by me. I may think, in a period of despair, that my future is of no worth whatsoever, but I may be wrong because others rightly see value—even great value—in it. Furthermore, my future can be valuable to me even if I do not value it. This is the case when a young person attempts suicide, but is rescued and goes on to significant human achievements. Such young people's futures are ultimately valuable to them, even though such futures do not seem to be valuable to them at the moment of attempted suicide. A fetus's future can be valuable to it in the same way. Accordingly, this attempt to limit the anti-abortion argument fails.

Another similar attempt to reject the anti-abortion position is based on Tooley's claim that an entity cannot possess the right to life unless it has the capacity to desire its continued existence. It follows that, since fetuses lack the conceptual capacity to desire to continue to live, they lack the right to life. Accordingly, Tooley concludes that abortion cannot be seriously prima facie wrong (*op. cit.*, pp. 46/7).

What could be the evidence for Tooley's basic claim? Tooley once argued that individuals have a prima facie right to what they desire and that the lack of the capacity to desire something undercuts the basis of one's right to it (*op. cit.*, pp. 44/5). This argument plainly will not succeed in the context of the analysis of this essay, however, since the point here is to establish the fetus's right to life on other grounds. Tooley's argument assumes that the right to life cannot be established in general on some basis other than the desire for life. This position was considered and rejected in the preceding section of this paper.

One might attempt to defend Tooley's basic claim on the grounds that, because a fetus cannot apprehend continued life as a benefit, its continued life cannot be a benefit or cannot be something it has a right to or cannot be something that is in its interest. This might be defended in terms of the general proposition that, if an individual is literally incapable of caring about or taking an interest in some X, then one does not have a right to X or X is not a benefit or X is not something that is in one's interest.[11]

Each member of this family of claims seems to be open to objections. As John C. Stevens[12] has pointed out, one may have a right to be treated with a certain medical procedure (because of a health insurance policy one has purchased), even though one cannot conceive of the nature of the procedure. And, as Tooley himself has pointed out, persons who have been indoctrinated, or drugged, or rendered temporarily unconscious may be literally incapable of caring about or taking an interest in something that is in their interest or is something to which they have a right, or is something that benefits them. Hence, the Tooley claim that would restrict the scope of the value of a future-like-ours argument is undermined by counterexamples.[13]

Finally, Paul Bassen[14] has argued that, even though the prospects of an embryo might seem to be a basis for the wrongness of abortion, an embryo cannot be a victim and therefore cannot be wronged. An embryo cannot be a victim, he says, because it lacks sentience. His central argument for this seems to be that, even though plants and the permanently unconscious are alive, they clearly cannot be victims. What is the explanation of this? Bassen claims that the explanation is that their lives consist of mere metabolism and mere metabolism is not enough to ground victimizability. Mentation is required.

The problem with this attempt to establish

the absence of victimizability is that both plants and the permanently unconscious clearly lack what Bassen calls "prospects" or what I have called "a future life like ours." Hence, it is surely open to one to argue that the real reason we believe plants and the permanently unconscious cannot be victims is that killing them cannot deprive them of a future life like ours; the real reason is not their absence of present mentation.

Bassen recognizes that his view is subject to this difficulty, and he recognizes that the case of children seems to support this difficulty, for "much of what we do for children is based on prospects." He argues, however, that, in the case of children and in other such cases, "potentiality comes into play only where victimizability has been secured on other grounds" (*ibid.*, p. 333).

Bassen's defense of his view is patently question-begging, since what is adequate to secure victimizability is exactly what is at issue. His examples do not support his own view against the thesis of this essay. Of course, embryos can be victims: when their lives are deliberately terminated, they are deprived of their futures of value, their prospects. This makes them victims, for it directly wrongs them.

The seeming plausibility of Bassen's view stems from the fact that paradigmatic cases of imagining someone as a victim involve empathy, and empathy requires mentation of the victim. The victims of flood, famine, rape, or child abuse are all persons with whom we can empathize. That empathy seems to be part of seeing them as victims.[15]

In spite of the strength of these examples, the attractive intuition that a situation in which there is victimization requires the possibility of empathy is subject to counterexamples. Consider a case that Bassen himself offers: "Posthumous obliteration of an author's work constitutes a misfortune for him only if he had wished his work to endure" (*op. cit.*, p. 318). The conditions Bassen wishes to impose upon the possibility of being victimized here seem far too strong. Perhaps this author, due to his unrealistic standards of excellence and his low self-esteem, regarded his work as unworthy of survival, even though it possessed genuine literary merit. Destruction of such work would

surely victimize its author. In such a case, empathy with the victim concerning the loss is clearly impossible.

Of course, Bassen does not make the possibility of empathy a necessary condition of victimizability; he requires only mentation. Hence, on Bassen's actual view, this author, as I have described him, can be a victim. The problem is that the basic intuition that renders Bassen's view plausible is missing in the author's case. In order to attempt to avoid counterexamples, Bassen has made his thesis too weak to be supported by the intuitions that suggested it.

Even so, the mentation requirement on victimizability is still subject to counterexamples. Suppose a severe accident renders me totally unconscious for a month, after which I recover. Surely killing me while I am unconscious victimizes me, even though I am incapable of mentation during that time. It follows that Bassen's thesis fails. Apparently, attempts to restrict the value of a future-like-ours argument so that fetuses do not fall within its scope do not succeed.

V

In this essay, it has been argued that the correct ethic of the wrongness of killing can be extended to fetal life and used to show that there is a strong presumption that any abortion is morally impermissible. If the ethic of killing adopted here entails, however, that contraception is also seriously immoral, then there would appear to be a difficulty with the analysis of this essay.

But this analysis does not entail that contraception is wrong. Of course, contraception prevents the actualization of a possible future of value. Hence, it follows from the claim that futures of value should be maximized that contraception is prima facie immoral. This obligation to maximize does not exist, however; furthermore, nothing in the ethics of killing in this paper entails that it does. The ethics of killing in this essay would entail that contraception is wrong only if something were denied a human future of value by contraception. Nothing at all is denied such a future by contraception, however.

Candidates for a subject of harm by contraception fall into four categories: (1) some sperm or other, (2) some ovum or other, (3) a sperm and an ovum separately, and (4) a sperm and an ovum together. Assigning the harm to some sperm is utterly arbitrary, for no reason can be given for making a sperm the subject of harm rather than an ovum. Assigning the harm to some ovum is utterly arbitrary, for no reason can be given for making an ovum the subject of harm rather than a sperm. One might attempt to avoid these problems by insisting that contraception deprives both the sperm and the ovum separately of a valuable future like ours. On this alternative, too many futures are lost. Contraception was supposed to be wrong, because it deprived us of one future of value, not two. One might attempt to avoid this problem by holding that contraception deprives the combination of sperm and ovum of a valuable future like ours. But here the definite article misleads. At the time of contraception, there are hundreds of millions of sperm, one (released) ovum and millions of possible combinations of all of these. There is no actual combination at all. Is the subject of the loss to be a merely possible combination? Which one? This alternative does not yield an actual subject of harm either. Accordingly, the immorality of contraception is not entailed by the loss of a future-like-ours argument simply because there is no nonarbitrarily identifiable subject of the loss in the case of contraception.

VI

The purpose of this essay has been to set out an argument for the serious presumptive wrongness of abortion subject to the assumption that the moral permissibility of abortion stands or falls on the moral status of the fetus. Since a fetus possesses a property, the possession of which in adult human beings is sufficient to make killing an adult human being wrong, abortion is wrong. This way of dealing

with the problem of abortion seems superior to other approaches to the ethics of abortion, because it rests on an ethics of killing which is close to self-evident, because the crucial morally relevant property clearly applies to fetuses, and because the argument avoids the usual equivocations on "human life," "human being," or "person." The argument rests neither on religious claims nor on Papal dogma. It is not subject to the objection of "speciesism." Its soundness is compatible with the moral permissibility of euthanasia and contraception. It deals with our intuitions concerning young children.

Finally, this analysis can be viewed as resolving a standard problem—indeed, *the* standard problem—concerning the ethics of abortion. Clearly, it is wrong to kill adult human beings. Clearly, it is not wrong to end the life of some arbitrarily chosen single human cell. Fetuses seem to be like arbitrarily chosen human cells in some respects and like adult humans in other respects. The problem of the ethics of abortion is the problem of determining the fetal property that settles this moral controversy. The thesis of this essay is that the problem of the ethics of abortion, so understood, is solvable.

Notes

1. Feinberg, "Abortion," in *Matters of Life and Death: New Introductory Essays in Moral Philosophy*, Tom Regan, ed. (New York: Random House, 1986), pp. 256–293; Tooley, "Abortion and Infanticide," *Philosophy and Public Affairs*, II, 1 (1972):37–65, Tooley, *Abortion and Infanticide* (New York: Oxford, 1984); Warren, "On the Moral and Legal Status of Abortion," *The Monist*, LVII, 1 (1973):43–61; Engelhardt, "The Ontology of Abortion," *Ethics*, LXXXIV, 3 (1974):217–234; Sumner, *Abortion and Moral Theory* (Princeton: University Press, 1981); Noonan, "An Almost Absolute Value in History," in *The Morality of Abortion: Legal and Historical Perspectives*, Noonan, ed. (Cambridge: Harvard, 1970); and Devine, *The Ethics of Homicide* (Ithaca: Cornell, 1978).

2. For interesting discussions of this issue, see

Warren Quinn, "Abortion: Identity and Loss," *Philosophy and Public Affairs*, XIII, 1 (1984):24–54; and Lawrence C. Becker, "Human Being: The Boundaries of the Concept," *Philosophy and Public Affairs*, IV, 4 (1975):334–359.

3. For example, see my "Ethics and The Elderly: Some Problems," in Stuart Spicker, Kathleen Woodward, and David Van Tassel, eds., *Aging and the Elderly: Humanistic Perspectives in Gerontology* (Atlantic Highlands, NJ: Humanities. 1978), pp. 341–355.

4. See Warren, *op. cit.*, and Tooley, "Abortion and Infanticide."

5. This seems to be the fatal flaw in Warren's treatment of this issue.

6. I have been most influenced on this matter by Jonathan Glover, *Causing Death and Saving Lives* (New York: Penguin, 1977), ch. 3; and Robert Young, "What Is So Wrong with Killing People?" *Philosophy*, LIV, 210 (1979):515–528.

7. Feinberg, Tooley, Warren, and Engelhardt have all dealt with this problem.

8. "Duties to Animals and Spirits," in *Lectures on Ethics*, Louis Infeld, trans. (New York: Harper, 1963), p. 239.

9. I am indebted to Jack Bricke for raising this objection.

10. Presumably a preference utilitarian would press such an objection. Tooley once suggested that his account has such a theoretical underpinning. See his "Abortion and Infanticide," pp. 44/5.

11. Donald VanDeVeer seems to think this is self-evident. See his "Whither Baby Doe?" in *Matters of Life and Death*, p. 233.

12. "Must the Bearer of a Right Have the Concept of That to Which He Has a Right?" *Ethics*, XCV, 1 (1984):68–74.

13. See Tooley again in "Abortion and Infanticide," pp. 47–49.

14. "Present Sakes and Future Prospects: The Status of Early Abortion," *Philosophy and Public Affairs*, XI, 4 (1982):322–326.

15. Note carefully the reasons he gives on the bottom of p. 316.

4. Racism, Birth Control, and Reproductive Rights

Angela Davis

Noted scholar and activist Angela Davis gives us a perspective on abortion, birth control, and the movement for reproductive freedom that focuses on race. Placing the abortion-rights movement within the context of racial domination allows us to understand the social functions of the movement.

When nineteenth-century feminists raised the demand for "voluntary motherhood," the campaign for birth control was born. Its proponents were called radicals and they were subjected to the same mockery as had befallen the initial advocates of woman suffrage. "Voluntary motherhood" was considered audacious, outrageous, and outlandish by those who insisted that wives had no right to refuse their husbands' sexual urges. Eventually, of course, the right to birth control, like women's right to vote, would be more or less taken for granted by U.S. public opinion. Yet in 1970, a full century later, the call for legal and easily accessible abortions was no less controversial than the issue of "voluntary motherhood" which had originally launched the birth control movement of the United States.

Birth control—individual choice, safe contraceptive methods, as well as abortions when necessary—is a fundamental prerequisite for the emancipation of women. Since the right of

This article is excerpted from Angela Y. Davis, *Women, Race, & Class*, Chapter 12 (New York: Random House, 1981). © 1981 by Angela Davis. Reprinted by permission of Random House, Inc.

birth control is obviously advantageous to women of all classes and races, it would appear that even vastly dissimilar women's groups would have attempted to unite around this issue. In reality, however, the birth control movement has seldom succeeded in uniting women of different social backgrounds, and rarely have the movement's leaders popularized the genuine concerns of working-class women. Moreover, arguments advanced by birth control advocates have sometimes been based on blatantly racist premises. The progressive potential of birth control remains indisputable. But in actuality, the historical record of this movement leaves much to be desired in the realm of challenges to racism and class exploitation.

The most important victory of the contemporary birth control movement was won during the early 1970s when abortions were at last declared legal. Having emerged during the infancy of the new women's liberation movement, the struggle to legalize abortions incorporated all the enthusiasm and the militancy of the young movement. By January 1973, the abortion rights campaign had reached a triumphant culmination. In *Roe v. Wade* (410 U.S.) and *Doe v. Bolton* (410 U.S.), the U.S. Supreme Court ruled that a woman's right to personal privacy implied her right to decide whether or not to have an abortion.

The ranks of the abortion rights campaign did not include substantial numbers of women of color. Given the racial composition of the larger women's liberation movement, this was not at all surprising. When questions were raised about the absence of racially oppressed women in both the larger movement and in the abortion rights campaign, two explanations were commonly proposed in the discussions and literature of the period: women of color were overburdened by their people's fight against racism, and/or they had not yet become conscious of the centrality of sexism. But the real meaning of the almost lily-white complexion of the abortion rights campaign was not to be found in ostensibly myopic or underdeveloped consciousness among women of color. The truth lay buried in the ideological underpinnings of the birth control movement itself.

The failure of the abortion rights campaign to conduct a historical self-evaluation led to a dangerously superficial appraisal of Black people's suspicious attitudes toward birth control in general. Granted, when some Black people unhesitatingly equated birth control with genocide, it did appear to be an exaggerated—even paranoiac—reaction. Yet white abortion rights activists missed a profound message, for underlying these cries of genocide were important clues about the history of the birth control movement. This movement, for example, had been known to advocate involuntary sterilization—a racist form of mass "birth control." If ever women would enjoy the right to plan their pregnancies, legal and easily accessible birth control measures and abortions would have to be complemented by an end to sterilization abuse.

As for the abortion rights campaign itself, how could women of color fail to grasp its urgency? They were far more familiar than their white sisters with the murderously clumsy scalpels of inept abortionists seeking profit in illegality. In New York, for instance, during the several years preceding the decriminalization of abortions in that state, some 80 percent of the deaths caused by illegal abortions involved Black and Puerto Rican women.[1] Immediately afterward, women of color received close to half of all the legal abortions. If the abortion rights campaign of the early 1970s needed to be reminded that women of color wanted desperately to escape the back-room quack abortionists, they should also have realized that these same women were not about to express pro-abortion sentiments. They were in favor of *abortion rights,* which did not mean that they were proponents of abortion. When Black and Latina women resort to abortions in such large numbers, the stories they tell are not so much about the desire to be free of their pregnancy, but rather about the miserable social conditions which dissuade them from bringing new lives into the world.

Black women have been aborting themselves since the earliest days of slavery. Many slave women refused to bring children into a world of interminable forced labor, where chains and floggings and sexual abuse for women were the everyday conditions of life. A doctor practicing in Georgia around the middle of the last century noticed that abortions and miscarriages were far more common among his slave patients than among the white women he treated.

*   *   *

Why were self-imposed abortions and reluctant acts of infanticide such common occurrences during slavery? Not because Black women had discovered solutions to their predicament, but rather because they were desperate. Abortions and infanticides were acts of desperation, motivated not by the biological birth process but by the oppressive conditions of slavery. Most of these women, no doubt, would have expressed their deepest resentment had someone hailed their abortions as a stepping stone toward freedom.

During the early abortion rights campaign, it was too frequently assumed that legal abortions provided a viable alternative to the myriad problems posed by poverty. As if having fewer children could create more jobs, higher wages, better schools, etc. This assumption reflected the tendency to blur the distinction between *abortion rights* and the general advocacy of *abortions*. The campaign often failed to provide a voice for women who wanted the *right* to legal abortions while deploring the social conditions that prohibited them from bearing more children.

The renewed offensive against abortion rights that erupted during the latter half of the 1970s has made it absolutely necessary to focus more sharply on the needs of poor and racially oppressed women. By 1977, the passage of the Hyde Amendment in Congress had mandated the withdrawal of federal funding for abortions, causing many state legislatures to follow suit. Black, Puerto Rican, Chicana, and Native American Indian women, together with their impoverished white sisters, were thus effectively divested of the right to legal abortions. Since surgical sterilizations, funded by the Department of Health, Education and Welfare [now the Department of Health and Human Services], remained free on demand, more and more poor women have been forced to opt for permanent infertility. What is urgently required is a broad campaign to defend the reproductive rights of all women—and especially those women whose economic circumstances often compel them to relinquish the right to reproduction itself.

*   *   *

While women have probably always dreamed of infallible methods of birth control, it was not until the issue of women's rights in general became the focus of an organized movement that reproductive rights could emerge as a legitimate demand. In an essay entitled "Marriage," written during the 1850s, Sarah Grimke argued for a ". . . right on the part of woman to decide *when* she shall become a mother, how often and under what circumstances."[2]

*   *   *

Sarah Grimke advocated women's right to sexual abstinence.

*   *   *

The notion that women could refuse to submit to their husbands' sexual demands eventually became the central idea of the call for "voluntary motherhood." By the 1870s, when the woman suffrage movement had reached its peak, feminists were publicly advocating voluntary motherhood.

*   *   *

It was not a coincidence that women's consciousness of their reproductive rights was born within the organized movement for women's political equality. Indeed, if women remained forever burdened by incessant childbirths and frequent miscarriages, they would hardly be able to exercise the political rights they might win. Moreover, women's new dreams of pursuing careers and other paths of self-development outside marriage and motherhood could only be realized if they could limit and plan their pregnancies. In this sense, the slogan "voluntary motherhood" contained a new and genuinely progressive vision of womanhood. At the same time, however, this vision was rigidly bound to the lifestyle enjoyed by the middle classes and the bourgeoisie. The aspirations underlying the demand for "voluntary motherhood" did not reflect the conditions of working-class women, engaged as they were in a far more fundamental fight for economic survival. Since this first call for birth control was associated with goals which could only be achieved by women possessing material wealth, vast numbers of poor and working-class women would find it rather difficult to identify with the embryonic birth control movement.

Toward the end of the 19th century the white birth rate in the United States suffered a significant decline. Since no contraceptive innovations had been publicly introduced, the drop in the birth rate implied that women were substantially curtailing their sexual activity. By 1890, the typical native-born white woman was bearing no more than four children.[3] Since U.S. society was becoming increasingly urban, this new birth pattern should not have been a surprise. While farm life demanded large families, they became dysfunctional within the context of city life. Yet this phenomenon was publicly interpreted in a racist and anti-working-class fashion by the ideologues of rising monopoly capitalism. Since native-born white women were bearing fewer children, the specter of "race suicide" was raised in official circles.

In 1905, President Theodore Roosevelt concluded his Lincoln Day Dinner speech with the proclamation that "race purity must be maintained."[4] By 1906, he blatantly equated the falling birth rate among native-born whites with the impending threat of "race suicide." In his State of the Union message that year, Roosevelt admonished the well-born white women who engaged in "willful sterility—the one sin for which the penalty is national death, race suicide."[5] These comments were made during a period of accelerating racist ideology and of great waves of race riots and lynchings on the domestic scene.

* * *

How did the birth control movement respond to Roosevelt's accusation that their cause was promoting race suicide? The President's propagandistic ploy was a failure, according to a leading historian of the birth control movement, for, ironically, it led to greater support for its advocates. Yet, as Linda Gordon maintains, this controversy ". . . also brought to the forefront those issues that most separated feminists from the working class and the poor."[6]

This happened in two ways. First, the feminists were increasingly emphasizing birth control as a route to careers and higher education—goals out of reach of the poor with or without birth control. In the context of the whole feminist movement, the race-suicide episode was an additional factor identifying feminism almost exclusively with the aspirations of the more privileged women of the society. Second, the pro-birth control feminists began to popularize the idea that poor people had a moral obligation to restrict the size of their families, because large families create a drain on the taxes and charity expenditures of the wealthy and because poor children were less likely to be "superior."[7]

The acceptance of the race-suicide thesis, to a greater or lesser extent, by women such as Julia Ward Howe and Ida Husted Harper reflected the suffrage movement's capitulation to the racist posture of Southern women. If the suffragists acquiesced to arguments invoking the extension of the ballot to women as the saving grace of white supremacy, then birth control advocates either acquiesced to or supported the new arguments invoking birth control as a means of preventing the proliferation of the "lower classes" and as an antidote to race suicide. Race suicide could be prevented by the introduction of birth control among Black people, immigrants, and the poor in general. In this way, the prosperous whites of solid Yankee stock could maintain their superior numbers within the population. Thus class bias and racism crept into the birth control movement when it was still in its infancy. More and more, it was assumed within birth control circles that poor women, Black and immigrant alike, had a "moral obligation to restrict the size of their families."[8] What was demanded as a "right" for the privileged came to be interpreted as a "duty" for the poor.

* * *

During the first decades of the 20th century, the rising popularity of the eugenics movement was hardly a fortuitous development. Eugenic ideas were perfectly suited to the ideological needs of the young monopoly capitalists. Imperialist incursions in Latin America and in the Pacific needed to be justified, as did the intensified exploitation of Black workers in the South and immigrant workers in the North and West. The pseudo-scientific racial theories associated with the eugenics campaign furnished dramatic apologies for the conduct of the young monopolies. As a result, this movement won the unhesitating support of such leading capitalists as the Carnegies, the Harrimans, and the Kelloggs.[9]

By 1919, the eugenic influence on the birth control movement was unmistakably clear. In an article published by Margaret Sanger in the American Birth Control League's journal, she defined "the chief issue of birth control" as "more children from the fit, less from the unfit."[10] Around this time the American Birth Control League (ABCL) heartily welcomed the author of *The Rising Tide of Color Against White World Supremacy* into its inner sanctum.[11] Lothrop Stoddard, Harvard professor and theoretician of the eugenics movement, was offered a seat on the ABCL board of directors. In the pages of the ABCL's journal, articles by Guy Irving Birch, director of the American Eugenics Society, began to appear. Birch advocated birth control as a weapon to

> . . . prevent the American people from being replaced by alien or Negro stock, whether it be by immigration or by overly high birth rates among others in this country.[12]

By 1932, the Eugenics Society could boast that at least 26 states had passed compulsory sterilization laws and that thousands of "unfit" persons had already been surgically prevented from reproducing.[13] Margaret Sanger offered her public approval of this development. "Morons, mental defectives, epileptics, illiterates, paupers, unemployables, criminals, prostitutes and dope fiends" ought to be surgically sterilized, she argued in a radio talk.[14] She did not wish to be so intransigent as to leave them with no choice in the matter; if they wished, she said, they should be able to choose a life-long segregated existence in labor camps.

Within the ABCL, the call for birth control among Black people acquired the same racist edge as the call for compulsory sterilization. In 1939, its successor, the Birth Control Federation of America, planned a "Negro Project." In the Federation's words,

> [t]he mass of Negroes, particularly in the South, still breed carelessly and disastrously, with the result that the increase among Negroes, even more than among whites, is from that portion of the population least fit, and least able to rear children properly.[15]

Calling for the recruitment of Black ministers to lead local birth control committees, the Federation's proposal suggested that Black people should be rendered as vulnerable as possible to their birth control propaganda. "We do not want word to get out," wrote Margaret Sanger in a letter to a colleague,

> that we want to exterminate the Negro population and the minister is the man who can straighten out that idea if it ever occurs to any of their more rebellious members.[16]

This episode in the birth control movement confirmed the ideological victory of the racism associated with eugenic ideas. It had been robbed of its progressive potential, advocating for people of color not the individual right to *birth control*, but rather the racist strategy of *population control*. The birth control campaign would be called upon to serve in an essential capacity in the execution of the U.S. government's imperialist and racist population policy.

The abortion rights activists of the early 1970s should have examined the history of their movement. Had they done so, they might have understood why so many of their Black sisters adopted a posture of suspicion toward their cause. They might have understood how important it was to undo the racist deeds of their predecessors, who had advocated birth control as well as compulsory sterilization as a means of eliminating the "unfit" sectors of the population. Consequently, the young white feminists might have been more receptive to the suggestion that their campaign for abortion rights include a vigorous condemnation of sterilization abuse, which had become more widespread than ever.

It was not until the media decided that the casual sterilization of two Black girls in Montgomery, Alabama, was a scandal worth reporting that the Pandora's box of sterilization abuse was finally flung open. But by the time the case of the Relf sisters broke, it was practically too late to influence the politics of the abortion rights movement. It was the summer of 1973 and the Supreme Court decision legalizing abortions had already been announced in January. Nevertheless, the urgent need for mass opposition to sterilization abuse became tragically clear. The facts surrounding the Relf sisters' story were horrifyingly simple. Minnie Lee, who was 12 years old, and Mary Alice, who was 14, had been unsuspectingly carted into an operating room, where surgeons irrevocably robbed them of their capacity to bear children.[17] The surgery had been ordered by the HEW-funded Montgomery Community Action Committee after it was discovered that Depo-Provera, a drug previously administered to the girls as a birth prevention measure, caused cancer in test animals.[18]

After the Southern Poverty Law Center filed suit on behalf of the Relf sisters, the girls' mother revealed that she had unknowingly "consented" to the operation, having been deceived by the social workers who handled her daughters' case. They had asked Mrs. Relf, who was unable to read, to put her "X" on a document, the contents of which were not described to her. She assumed, she said, that it authorized the continued Depo-Provera injections. As she subsequently learned, she had authorized the surgical sterilization of her daughters.[19]

In the aftermath of publicity exposing the Relf sisters' case, similar episodes were brought to light. In Montgomery alone, 11 girls, also in their teens, had been similarly sterilized. HEW-funded birth control clinics in other states, as it turned out, had also subjected young girls to sterilization abuse. Moreover, individual women came forth with equally outrageous stories. Nial Ruth Cox, for example, filed suit against the state of North Carolina. At the age of 18—eight years before her suit—officials had threatened to discontinue her family's welfare payments if she refused to submit to surgical sterilization.[20] Before she assented to the operation, she was assured that her infertility would be temporary.[21]

Nial Ruth Cox's lawsuit was aimed at a state which had diligently practiced the theory of eugenics. Under the auspices of the Eugenics Commission of North Carolina, so it was learned, 7,686 sterilizations had been carried out since 1933. Although the operations were justified as measures to prevent the reproduction of "mentally deficient persons," about 5,000 of the sterilized persons had been Black.[22] According to Brenda Feigen Fasteau, the ACLU attorney representing Nial Ruth Cox, North Carolina's recent record was not much better.

> As far as I can determine, the statistics reveal that since 1964, approximately 65 percent of the women sterilized in North Carolina were Black and approximately 35 percent were white.[23]

As the flurry of publicity exposing sterilization abuse revealed, the neighboring state of South Carolina had been the site of further atrocities. Eighteen women from Aiken, South Carolina, charged that they had been sterilized by a Dr. Clovis Pierce during the early 1970s. The sole obstetrician in that small town, Pierce had consistently sterilized Medicaid recipients with two or more children. According to a nurse in his office, Dr. Pierce insisted that pregnant welfare women "will have to submit [sic] to voluntary sterilization" if they wanted him to deliver their babies.[24] While he was ". . . tired of people running around and having babies and paying for them with my taxes,"[25] Dr. Pierce received some $60,000 in taxpayers' money for the sterilizations he performed. During his trial he was supported by the South Carolina Medical Association, whose members declared that doctors ". . . have a moral and legal right to insist on sterilization permission before accepting a patient, if it is done on the initial visit."[26]

Revelations of sterilization abuse during that time exposed the complicity of the federal government. At first the Department of Health, Education and Welfare claimed that approximately 16,000 women and 8,000 men had been sterilized in 1972 under the auspices of federal programs.[27] Later, however, these figures underwent a drastic revision. Carl Shultz, director of HEW's Population Affairs Office, estimated that between 100,000 and 200,000 sterilizations had actually been funded that year by the federal government.[28] During Hitler's Germany, incidentally, 250,000 sterilizations were carried out under the Nazis' Hereditary Health Law.[29] Is it possible that the record of the Nazis, through the years of their reign, may have been almost equaled by U.S. government-funded sterilizations in the space of a single year?

Given the historical genocide inflicted on the native population of the United States, one would assume that Native American Indians would be exempted from the government's sterilization campaign. But according to Dr. Connie Uri's testimony in a Senate committee hearing, by 1976 some 24 percent of all Indian women of childbearing age had been sterilized.[30] "Our blood lines are being stopped," the Choctaw physician told the Senate committee, "Our unborn will not be born ... This is genocidal to our people."[31] According to Dr. Uri, the Indian Health Services Hospital in Claremore, Oklahoma, had been sterilizing one out of every four women giving birth in that federal facility.[32]

*   *   *

The domestic population policy of the U.S. government has an undeniably racist edge. Native American, Chicana, Puerto Rican and Black women continue to be sterilized in disproportionate numbers. According to a national fertility study conducted in 1970 by Princeton University's Office of Population Control, 20 percent of all married Black women have been permanently sterilized.[33] Approximately the same percentage of Chicanas have been rendered surgically infertile.[34] Moreover, 43 percent of the women sterilized through federally subsidized programs were Black.[35]

The astonishing number of Puerto Rican women who have been sterilized reflects a special government policy that can be traced back to 1939. In that year President Roosevelt's Interdepartmental Committee on Puerto Rico issued a statement attributing the island's economic problems to the phenomenon of overpopulation.[36] This committee proposed that efforts be undertaken to reduce the birth rate to no more than the level of the death rate.[37] Soon afterward, an experimental sterilization campaign was undertaken in Puerto Rico. Although the Catholic Church initially opposed this experiment and forced the cessation of the program in 1946, it was converted during the early 1950s to the teachings and practice of population control.[38] In this period, over 150 birth control clinics were opened, resulting in a 20 percent decline in population growth by the mid-1960s.[39] By the 1970s, over 35 percent of all Puerto Rican women of childbearing age had been surgically sterilized.[40]

*   *   *

The prevalence of sterilization abuse during the latter 1970s may be greater than ever before. Although the Department of Health, Education and Welfare issued guidelines in 1974, which were ostensibly designed to prevent involuntary sterilizations, the situation has nonetheless deteriorated. When the American Civil Liberties Union's Reproductive Freedom Project conducted a survey of teaching hospitals in 1975, it discovered that 40 percent of those institutions were not even aware of the regulations issued by HEW.[41] Only 30 percent of the hospitals examined by the ACLU were even attempting to comply with the guidelines.[42]

The 1977 Hyde Amendment added yet another dimension to coercive sterilization practices. As a result of this law passed by Congress, federal funds for abortions were eliminated in all cases but those involving rape and the risk of death or severe illness. According to Sandra Salazar of the California Department of Public Health, the first victim of the Hyde Amendment was a 27-year-old Chicana woman from Texas. She died as a result of an illegal abortion in Mexico shortly after Texas discontinued government-funded abortions. There have been many more victims—women for whom sterilization has become the only alternative to the abortions, which are currently beyond their reach. Sterilizations continue to be federally funded and free, to poor women, on demand.

Over the last decade the struggle against sterilization abuse has been waged primarily by Puerto Rican, Black, Chicana and Native American women. Their cause has not yet been embraced by the women's movement as a whole. Within organizations representing the interests of middle-class white women, there has been a certain reluctance to support the demands of the campaign against sterilization abuse, for these women are often denied their individual rights to be sterilized when they desire to take this step. While women of color are urged, at every turn, to become permanently infertile, white women enjoying prosperous economic conditions are urged, by the same forces, to reproduce themselves. They therefore sometimes consider the "waiting period" and other details of the demand for "informed consent" to sterilization as further inconveniences for women like themselves. Yet whatever the inconveniences for white middle-class women, a fundamental reproductive right of racially oppressed and poor women is at stake. Sterilization abuse must be ended.

Notes

1. Edwin M. Gold *et al.,* "Therapeutic Abortions in New York City: A Twenty-Year Review," *American Journal of Public Health,* Vol. LV (July, 1965), pp. 964–972. Quoted in Lucinda Cisler, "Unfinished Business: Birth Control and Women's Liberation," in Robin Morgan, ed., *Sisterhood Is Powerful: An Anthology of Writings From the Women's Liberation Movement* (New York: Vintage Books, 1970), p. 261. Also quoted in Robert Staples, *The Black Woman in America* (Chicago: Nelson Hall, 1974), p. 146.

2. Gerda Lerner, *The Female Experience: An American Documentary* (Indianapolis: Bobbs-Merrill, 1977), p. 91.

3. Mary P. Ryan, *Womanhood in America from Colonial Times to the Present* (New York: Franklin Watts, Inc., 1975), p. 162.

4. Melvin Steinfeld, *Our Racist Presidents* (San Ramon, California: Consensus Publishers, 1972), p. 212.

5. Bonnie Mass, *Population Target: The Political Economy of Population Control in Latin America* (Toronto, Canada: Women's Educational Press, 1977), p. 20.

6. Linda Gordon, *Woman's Body, Woman's Right: A Social History of Birth Control in America* (New York: Penguin Books, 1976), p. 157.

7. *Ibid.,* p. 158.

8. *Ibid.*

9. Mass, *op. cit.,* p. 20.

10. Gordon, *op. cit.,* p. 281.

11. Mass, *op. cit.,* p. 20.

12. Gordon, *op. cit.,* p. 283.

13. Herbert Aptheker, "Sterilization, Experimentation and Imperialism," *Political Affairs,* Vol. LIII, No. 1 (January, 1974), p. 44.

14. Gena Corea, *The Hidden Malpractice* (New York: A Jove/HBJ Book, 1977), p. 149.

15. Gordon, *op. cit.,* p. 332.

16. *Ibid.,* pp. 332–333.

17. Aptheker, "Sterilization," p. 38. See also Anne Braden, "Forced Sterilization: Now Women Can Fight Back," *Southern Patriot,* September, 1973.

18. *Ibid.*

19. Jack Slater, "Sterilization, Newest Threat to the Poor," *Ebony,* Vol. XXVIII, No. 12 (October, 1973), p. 150.

20. Braden, *op. cit.*

21. Les Payne, "Forced Sterilization for the Poor?" *San Francisco Chronicle,* February 26, 1974.

22. Harold X., "Forced Sterilization Pervades South," *Muhammed Speaks,* October 10, 1975.

23. Slater, *op. cit.*

24. Payne, *op. cit.*

25. *Ibid.*

26. *Ibid.*

27. Aptheker, "Sterilization," p. 40.

28. Payne, *op. cit.*

29. Aptheker, "Sterilization," p. 48.

30. Arlene Eisen, "They're Trying to Take Our Future—Native American Women and Sterilization," *The Guardian,* March 23, 1972.

31. *Ibid.*

32. *Ibid.*

33. Quoted in a pamphlet issued by the Committee to End Sterilization Abuse, Box A244, Cooper Station, New York 10003.

34. *Ibid.*

35. *Ibid.*

36. Gordon, *op. cit.,* p. 338.

37. *Ibid.*

38. Mass, *op. cit.,* p. 92.

39. *Ibid.,* p. 91.

40. Gordon, *op. cit.,* p. 401. See also pamphlet issued by the Committee to End Sterilization Abuse.

41. Rahemah Aman, "Forced Sterilization," *Union Wage,* March 4, 1978.

42. *Ibid.*

5. *Webster* v. *Reproductive Health Services*

U.S. Supreme Court

Chief Justice Rehnquist, writing for the majority, argues that the Missouri law prohibiting the use of public facilities or employees for performing abortions, and requiring physicians to conduct viability tests prior to performing abortions, does not violate the First, Fourth, Ninth, or 14th Amendments to the Constitution. Rehnquist argues that the state is not required to provide abortions, only not to proscribe them. Furthermore, Rehnquist cites the *Row* v. *Wade* decision's concern for protecting potential life as the reason for forcing doctors to conduct viability tests. Justices Blackmun, Brennan, and Marshall dissent by arguing that such decisions must be left to the woman and that the trimester format in *Roe* is adequate for determining viability.

Chief Justice *Rehnquist* announced the judgment of the Court.

In June 1986, the Governor of Missouri signed into law Missouri Senate Committee Substitute for House Bill No. 1596 (hereinafter Act or statute), which amended existing state law concerning unborn children and abortions. The Act consisted of 20 provisions, 5 of which are now before the Court. The first provision, or preamble, contains "findings" by the state legislature that "[t]he life of each human being begins at conception," and that "unborn children have protectable interests in life, health, and well-being." . . . The Act further requires that all Missouri laws be interpreted to provide unborn children with the same rights enjoyed by other persons, subject to the Federal Constitution and this Court's precedents. Among its other provisions, the Act requires that, prior to performing an abortion on any woman whom a physician has reason to believe is 20 or more weeks pregnant, the physician ascertain whether the fetus is viable by performing "such medical examinations and tests as are necessary to make a finding of the gestational age, weight, and lung maturity of the unborn child." The Act also prohibits the use of public employees and facilities to perform or assist abortions not necessary to save the mother's life, and it prohibits the use of public funds, employees, or facilities for the purpose of "encouraging or counseling" a woman to have an abortion not necessary to save her life. . . .

In July 1986, five health professionals employed by the State and two nonprofit corporations brought this class action in the United States District Court for the Western District of Missouri to challenge the constitutionality of the Missouri statute. Plaintiffs, appellees in this Court, sought declaratory and injunctive relief on the ground that certain statutory provisions violated the First, Fourth, Ninth, and Fourteenth Amendments to the Federal Constitution. . . . They asserted violations of various rights, including the "privacy rights of pregnant women seeking abortions"; the "woman's right to an abortion"; the "righ[t] to privacy in the physician-patient relationship"; the physician's "righ[t] to practice medicine"; the pregnant woman's "right to life due to inherent risks involved in childbirth"; and the woman's right to "receive . . . adequate medical advice and treatment" concerning abortions. . . .

Several weeks after the complaint was filed, the District Court temporarily restrained enforcement of several provisions of the Act. Following a 3-day trial in December 1986, the District Court declared seven provisions of the Act unconstitutional and enjoined their enforcement. . . . These provisions included the preamble, . . . the "informed consent" provision, which required physicians to inform the pregnant woman of certain facts before performing an abortion, . . . the requirement that post-16-week abortions be performed only in hospitals, . . . the mandated tests to determine viability, and the prohibition on the use of public funds, employees, and facilities to perform or assist nontherapeutic abortions, and the restrictions on the use of public funds, employees, and facilities to encourage or counsel women to have such abortions, . . .

. . . The Court of Appeals determined that Missouri's declaration that life begins at conception was "simply an impermissible state adoption of a theory of when life begins to justify its abortion regulations." . . . It further held that the requirement that physicians perform viability tests was as unconstitutional legislative intrusion on a matter of medical skill and judgment. . . . The Court of Appeals invalidated Missouri's prohibition on the use of public facilities and employees to perform or assist abortions not necessary to save the mother's life. . . . It distinguished our decisions in *Harris v. McRae*, . . . and *Maher v. Roe*, on the ground that " '[t]here is a fundamental difference between providing direct funding to effect the abortion decision and allowing staff physicians to perform abortions at an existing publicly owned hospital.' " . . . The Court of

Appeals struck down the provision prohibiting the use of public funds for "encouraging or counseling" women to have nontherapeutic abortions, for the reason that this provision was both overly vague and inconsistent with the right to an abortion enunciated in *Roe v. Wade*. . . .

[The Act] provides that "[i]t shall be unlawful for any public employee within the scope of his employment to perform or assist an abortion, not necessary to save the life of the mother," . . . [and] makes it "unlawful for any public facility to be used for the purpose of performing or assisting an abortion not necessary to save the life of the mother." The Court of Appeals held that these provisions contravened this Court's abortion decisions. . . . We take the contrary view.

As we said earlier this Term in *DeShaney v. Winnebago County Dept. of Social Services*, . . . "our cases have recognized that the Due Process Clauses generally confer no affirmative right to governmental aid, even where such aid may be necessary to secure life, liberty, or property interests of which the government itself may not deprive the individual." In *Maher v. Roe*, . . . the Court upheld a Connecticut welfare regulation under which Medicaid recipients received payments for medical services related to childbirth, but not for nontherapeutic abortions. The Court rejected the claim that this unequal subsidization of childbirth and abortion was impermissible under *Roe v. Wade*. As the Court put it:

> The Connecticut regulation before us is different in kind from the laws invalidated in our previous abortion decisions. The Connecticut regulation places no obstacles—absolute or otherwise—in the pregnant woman's path to an abortion. An indigent woman who desires an abortion suffers no disadvantage as a consequence of Connecticut's decision to fund childbirth; she continues as before to be dependent on private sources for the service she desires. The State may have made childbirth a more attractive alternative, thereby influencing the woman's decision, but it has imposed no restriction on access to abortions that was not already there. The indigency that

may make it difficult—and in some cases, perhaps, impossible—for some women to have abortions is neither created nor in any way affected by the Connecticut regulation. . . .

The Court of Appeals distinguished these cases on the ground that "[t]o prevent access to a public facility does more than demonstrate a political choice in favor of childbirth; it clearly narrows and in some cases forecloses the availability of abortion to women." . . . The court reasoned that the ban on the use of public facilities "could prevent a woman's chosen doctor from performing an abortion because of his unprivileged status at other hospitals or because a private hospital adopted a similar anti-abortion stance." *Ibid.* It also thought that "[s]uch a rule could increase the cost of obtaining an abortion and delay the timing of it as well." . . .

We think that this analysis is much like that which we rejected in *Maher, Poelker,* and *McRae.* As in those cases, the State's decision here to use public facilities and staff to encourage childbirth over abortion "places no governmental obstacle in the path of a woman who chooses to terminate her pregnancy." . . . Just as Congress' refusal to fund abortions in *McRae* left "an indigent woman with at least the same range of choice in deciding whether to obtain a medically necessary abortion as she would have had if Congress had chosen to subsidize no health care costs at all," . . . Missouri's refusal to allow public employees to perform abortions in public hospitals leaves a pregnant woman with the same choices as if the State had chosen not to operate any public hospitals at all. The challenged provisions only restrict a woman's ability to obtain an abortion to the extent that she chooses to use a physician affiliated with a public hospital. This circumstance is more easily remedied, and thus considerably less burdensome, than indigency, which "may make it difficult—and in some cases, perhaps, impossible—for some women to have abortions" without public funding. . . . Having held that the State's refusal to fund abortions does not violate *Roe v. Wade,* it strains logic to reach a contrary result for the use of public facilities and employees. If the State may "make a value judgment favoring

childbirth over abortion and . . . implement that judgment by the allocation of public funds," . . . surely it may do so through the allocation of other public resources, such as hospitals and medical staff. . . .

The Missouri Act provides:

> Before a physician performs an abortion on a woman he has reason to believe is carrying an unborn child of twenty or more weeks gestational age, the physician shall first determine if the unborn child is viable by using and exercising that degree of care, skill, and proficiency commonly exercised by the ordinarily skillful, careful, and prudent physician engaged in similar practice under the same or similar conditions. In making this determination of viability, the physician shall perform or cause to be performed such medical examinations and tests as are necessary to make a finding of the gestational age, weight, and lung maturity of the unborn child and shall enter such findings and determination of viability in the medical record of the mother.

As with the preamble, the parties disagree over the meaning of this statutory provision. The State emphasizes the language of the first sentence, which speaks in terms of the physician's determination of viability being made by the standards of ordinary skill in the medical profession. . . . Appellees stress the language of the second sentence, which prescribes such "tests as are necessary" to make a finding of gestational age, fetal weight, and lung maturity. . . .

The Court of Appeals read [the Act] as requiring that after 20 weeks "doctors *must* perform tests to find gestational age, fetal weight and lung maturity." . . . The court indicated that the tests needed to determine fetal weight at 20 weeks are "unreliable and inaccurate" and would add $125 to $250 to the cost of an abortion. . . . It also stated that "amniocentesis, the only method available to determine lung maturity, is contrary to accepted medical practice until 28–30 weeks of gestation, expensive, and imposes significant health risks for both the pregnant woman and the fetus." . . .

We must first determine the meaning of [the Act] under Missouri law. Our usual practice is to defer to the lower court's construction of a state statute, but we believe the Court of Appeals has "fallen into plain error" in this case. . . .

We think the viability-testing provision makes sense only if the second sentence is read to require only those tests that are useful to making subsidiary findings as to viability. If we construe this provision to require a physician to perform those tests needed to make the three specified findings *in all circumstances,* including when the physician's reasonable professional judgment indicates that the tests would be irrelevant to determining viability or even dangerous to the mother and the fetus, the second sentence . . . would conflict with the first sentence's *requirement* that a physician apply his reasonable professional skill and judgment. It would also be incongruous to read this provision, especially the word "necessary," to require the performance of tests irrelevant to the expressed statutory purpose of determining viability. It thus seems clear to us that the Court of Appeals' construction of [the Act] violates well-accepted canons of statutory interpretation used in the Missouri courts. . . .

The viability-testing provision of the Missouri Act is concerned with promoting the State's interest in potential human life rather than in maternal health. [The Act] creates what is essentially a presumption of viability at 20 weeks, which the physician must rebut with tests indicating that the fetus is not viable prior to performing an abortion. It also directs the physician's determination as to viability by specifying consideration, if feasible, of gestational age, fetal weight, and lung capacity. The District Court found that "the medical evidence is uncontradicted that a 20-week fetus is *not* viable," and that "23½ to 24 weeks gestation is the earliest point in pregnancy where a reasonable possibility of viability exists." . . . But it also found that there may be a 4-week error in estimating gestational age, . . . which supports testing at 20 weeks.

In *Roe v. Wade,* the Court recognized that the State has "important and legitimate" interests in protecting maternal health and in the potentiality of human life. . . . During the second trimester, the State "may, if it chooses, regulate the abortion procedure in ways that are reasonably related to maternal health." . . . After viability, when the State's interest in potential human life was held to become compelling, the State "may, if it chooses, regulate, and even proscribe, abortion except where it is necessary, in appropriate medical judgment, for the preservation of the life or health of the mother." . . .

In *Colautti v. Franklin,* . . . upon which appellees rely, the Court held that a Pennsylvania statute regulating the standard of care to be used by a physician performing an abortion of a possibly viable fetus was void for vagueness. . . . But in the course of reaching that conclusion, the Court reaffirmed its earlier statement in *Planned Parenthood of Central Missouri v. Danforth,* . . . that " 'the determination of whether a particular fetus is viable is, and must be, a matter for the judgment of the responsible attending physician.' " . . . The dissent, . . . 6, ignores the statement in *Colautti* that "neither the legislature nor the courts may proclaim one of the elements entering into the ascertainment of viability—be it weeks of gestation or fetal weight or any other single factor—as the determinant of when the State has a compelling interest in the life or health of the fetus." . . . To the extent that [the Act] regulates the method for determining viability, it undoubtedly does superimpose state regulation on the medical determination of whether a particular fetus is viable. The Court of Appeals and the District Court thought it unconstitutional for this reason. . . . To the extent that the viability tests increase the cost of what are in fact second-trimester abortions, their validity may also be questioned under *Akron,* . . . where the Court held that a requirement that second-trimester abortions must be performed in hospitals was invalid because it substantially increased the expense of those procedures.

We think that the doubt cast upon the Missouri statute by these cases is not so much a flaw in the statute as it is a reflection of the fact that the rigid trimester analysis of the course of a pregnancy enunciated in *Roe* has resulted in subsequent cases like *Colautti* and *Akron* making constitutional law in this area a virtual Procrustean bed. . . .

Stare decisis is a cornerstone of our legal system, but it has less power in constitutional cases, where, save for constitutional amendments, this Court is the only body able to make needed changes. . . . We have not refrained from reconsideration of a prior construction of the Constitution that has proved "unsound in principle and unworkable in practice." . . . We think the *Roe* trimester framework falls into that category.

In the first place, the rigid *Roe* framework is hardly consistent with the notion of a Constitution cast in general terms, as ours is, and usually speaking in general principles, as ours does. The key elements of the *Roe* framework—trimesters and viability—are not found in the text of the Constitution or in any place else one would expect to find a constitutional principle. Since the bounds of the inquiry are essentially indeterminate, the result has been a web of legal rules that have become increasingly intricate, resembling a code of regulations rather than a body of constitutional doctrine. As Justice *White* has put it, the trimester framework has left this Court to serve as the country's "*ex officio* medical board with powers to approve or disapprove medical and operative practices and standards throughout the United States." . . .

In the second place, we do not see why the State's interest in protecting potential human life should come into existence only at the point of viability, and that there should therefore be a rigid line allowing state regulation after viability but prohibiting it before viability. The dissenters in *Thornburgh,* writing in the context of the *Roe* trimester analysis, would have recognized this fact by positing against the "fundamental right" recognized in *Roe* the State's "compelling interest" in protecting potential human life throughout pregnancy. . . .

The tests that [the Act] requires the physician to perform are designed to determine viability. The State here has chosen viability as the point at which its interest in potential human life must be safeguarded. . . . It is true that the tests in question increase the expense of abortion, and regulate the discretion of the physician in determining the viability of the fetus. Since the tests will undoubtedly show in many cases that the fetus is not viable, the tests

will have been performed for what were in fact second-trimester abortions. But we are satisfied that the requirement of these tests permissibly furthers the State's interest in protecting potential human life, and we therefore believe [the Act] to be constitutional.

The dissent takes us to task for our failure to join in a "great issues" debate as to whether the Constitution includes an "unenumerated" general right to privacy as recognized in cases such as *Griswold v. Connecticut,* . . . and *Roe.* But *Griswold v. Connecticut,* unlike *Roe,* did not purport to adopt a whole framework, complete with detailed rules and distinctions, to govern the cases in which the asserted liberty interest would apply. As such, it was far different from the opinion, if not the holding, of *Roe v. Wade,* which sought to establish a constitutional framework for judging state regulation of abortion during the entire term of pregnancy. That framework sought to deal with areas of medical practice traditionally subject to state regulation, and it sought to balance once and for all by reference only to the calendar the claims of the State to protect the fetus as a form of human life against the claims of a woman to decide for herself whether or not to abort a fetus she was carrying. The experience of the Court in applying *Roe v. Wade* in later cases, . . . suggests to us that there is wisdom in not unnecessarily attempting to elaborate the abstract differences between a "fundamental right" to abortion, as the Court described it in *Akron,* . . . a "limited fundamental constitutional right," which Justice Blackmun's dissent today treats *Roe* as having established, . . . or a liberty interest protected by the Due Process Clause, which we believe it to be. The Missouri testing requirement here is reasonably designed to ensure that abortions are not performed where the fetus is viable—an end which all concede is legitimate—and that is sufficient to sustain its constitutionality.

The dissent also accuses us, . . . of cowardice and illegitimacy in dealing with "the most politically divisive domestic legal issue of our time." . . . There is no doubt that our holding today will allow some governmental regulation of abortion that would have been prohibited under the language of cases such as *Colautti v. Franklin,* . . . and *Akron v. Akron Center for Reproductive Health.* . . . But the goal of constitutional adjudication is surely not to remove inexorably "politically divisive" issues from the ambit of the legislative process, whereby the people through their elected representatives deal with matters of concern to them. The goal of constitutional adjudication is to hold true the balance between that which the Constitution puts beyond the reach of the democratic process and that which it does not. We think we have done that today. The dissent's suggestion, . . . that legislative bodies, in a Nation where more than half of our population is women, will treat our decision today as an invitation to enact abortion regulation reminiscent of the dark ages not only misreads our views but does scant justice to those who serve in such bodies and the people who elect them. . . .

Justice *Blackmun,* with whom Justice *Brennan* and Justice *Marshall* join, concurring in part and dissenting in part.

Today, *Roe v. Wade,* . . . and the fundamental constitutional right of women to decide whether to terminate a pregnancy, survive but are not secure. Although the Court extricates itself from this case without making a single, even incremental, change in the law of abortion, the plurality and Justice Scalia would overrule *Roe* (the first silently, the other explicitly) and would return to the States virtually unfettered authority to control the quintessentially intimate, personal, and life-directing decision whether to carry a fetus to term. Although today, no less than yesterday, the Constitution and the decisions of this Court prohibit a State from enacting laws that inhibit women from the meaningful exercise of that right, a plurality of this Court implicitly invites every state legislature to enact more and more restrictive abortion regulations in order to provoke more and more test cases, in the hope that sometime down the line the Court will return the law of procreative freedom to the severe limitations that generally prevailed in this country before January 22, 1973. Never in my memory has a plurality announced a judgment of this Court that so foments disregard for the law and for our standing decisions.

Nor in my memory has a plurality gone about its business in such a deceptive fashion.

At every level of its review, from its effort to read the real meaning out of the Missouri statute, to its intended evisceration of precedents and its deafening silence about the constitutional protections that it would jettison, the plurality obscures the portent of its analysis. With feigned restraint, the plurality announces that its analysis leaves *Roe* "undisturbed," albeit "modif[ied] and narrow[ed]." . . . But this disclaimer is totally meaningless. The plurality opinion is filled with winks, and nods, and knowing glances to those who would do away with *Roe* explicitly, but turns a stone face to anyone in search of what the plurality conceives as the scope of a woman's right under the Due Process Clause to terminate a pregnancy free from the coercive and brooding influence of the State. The simple truth is that *Roe* would not survive the plurality's analysis, and that the plurality provides no substitute for *Roe's* protective umbrella.

I fear for the future. I fear for the liberty and equality of the millions of women who have lived and come of age in the 16 years since *Roe* was decided. I fear for the integrity of, and public esteem for, this Court. . . .

In the plurality's view, the viability-testing provision imposes a burden on second-trimester abortions as a way of furthering the State's interest in protecting the potential life of the fetus. Since under the *Roe* framework, the State may not fully regulate abortion in the interest of potential life (as opposed to maternal health) until the third trimester, the plurality finds it necessary, in order to save the Missouri testing provision, to throw out *Roe's* trimester framework. . . . In flat contradiction to *Roe,* . . . the plurality concludes that the State's interest in potential life is compelling before viability, and upholds the testing provision because it "permissibly furthers" that state interest. . . .

At the outset, I note that in its haste to limit abortion rights, the plurality compounds the errors of its analysis by needlessly reaching out to address constitutional questions that are not actually presented. The conflict between [the Act] and *Roe's* trimester framework, which purportedly drives the plurality to reconsider our past decisions, is a contrived conflict: the product of an aggressive misreading of the viability-testing requirement and a needlessly wooden application of the *Roe* framework. . . .

Abruptly setting aside the construction of [the Act] adopted by both the District Court and Court of Appeals as "plain error," the plurality reads the viability-testing provision as requiring only that before a physician may perform an abortion on a woman whom he believes to be carrying a fetus of 20 or more weeks gestational age, the doctor must determine whether the fetus is viable and, as part of that exercise, must, to the extent feasible and consistent with sound medical practice, conduct tests necessary to make findings of gestational age, weight, and lung maturity. . . . But the plurality's reading of the provision, according to which the statute requires the physician to perform tests only in order to determine *viability,* ignores the statutory language explicitly directing that "the physician *shall* perform or cause to be performed such medical examinations and tests as are *necessary to make a finding of the gestational age, weight, and lung maturity* of the unborn child and *shall* enter such findings" in the mother's medical record. . . . The statute's plain language requires the physician to undertake whatever tests are necessary to determine gestational age, weight, and lung maturity, regardless of whether these tests are necessary to a finding of viability, and regardless of whether the tests subject the pregnant woman or the fetus to additional health risks or add substantially to the cost of an abortion.

Had the plurality read the statute as written, it would have had no cause to reconsider the *Roe* framework. As properly construed, the viability-testing provision does not pass constitutional muster under even a rational-basis standard, the least restrictive level of review applied by this Court. . . . By mandating tests to determine fetal weight and lung maturity for every fetus thought to be more than 20 weeks gestational age, the statute requires physicians to undertake procedures, such as amniocentesis, that, in the situation presented, have no medical justification, impose significant additional health risks on both the pregnant woman and the fetus, and bear no rational relation to the State's interest in protecting fetal life. As written, [the Act] is an arbitrary imposition of discomfort, risk, and expense, furthering no discernible interest except to make the procurement of an abortion as arduous and difficult as possible. Thus, were it not for the plurality's tortured effort to avoid the plain import of . . . [the Act], it could have struck down the testing provision as patently irrational irrespective of the *Roe* framework.

The plurality eschews this straightforward resolution, in the hope of precipitating a constitutional crisis. Far from avoiding constitutional difficulty, the plurality attempts to engineer a dramatic retrenchment in our jurisprudence by exaggerating the conflict between its untenable construction of [the Act] and the *Roe* trimester framework.

No one contests that under the *Roe* framework the State, in order to promote its interest in potential human life, may regulate and even proscribe non-therapeutic abortions once the fetus becomes viable. . . . If, as the plurality appears to hold, the testing provision simply requires a physician to use appropriate and medically sound tests to determine whether the fetus is actually viable when the estimated gestational age is greater than 20 weeks . . . then I see little or no conflict with *Roe.* Nothing in *Roe,* or any of its progeny, holds that a State may not effectuate its compelling interest in the potential life of a viable fetus by seeking to ensure that no viable fetus is mistakenly aborted because of the inherent lack of precision in estimates of gestational age. A requirement that a physician make a finding of viability, one way or the other, for every fetus that falls within the range of possible viability does no more than preserve the State's recognized authority. Although, as the plurality correctly points out, such a testing requirement would have the effect of imposing additional costs on second-trimester abortions where the tests indicated that the fetus was not viable, these costs would be merely incidental to, and a necessary accommodation of, the State's unquestioned right to prohibit nontherapeutic abortions after the point of viability. In short, the testing provision, as construed by the plurality is consistent with the *Roe* framework and could be upheld effortlessly under current doctrine.

How ironic it is, then, and disingenuous, that the plurality scolds the Court of Appeals for adopting a construction of the statute that fails to avoid constitutional difficulties. . . . By distorting the statute, the plurality manages to avoid invalidating the testing provision on what should have been noncontroversial constitutional grounds; having done so, however, the plurality rushes headlong into a much deeper constitutional thicket, brushing past an obvious basis for upholding [the Act] in search of a pretext for scuttling the trimester framework. Evidently, from the plurality's perspective, the real problem with the Court of Appeals' construction of [the Act] is not that it raised a constitutional difficulty, but that it raised the wrong constitutional difficulty—one not implicating *Roe*. The plurality has remedied that, traditional canons of construction and judicial forbearance notwithstanding.

Having set up the conflict between [the Act] and the *Roe* trimester framework, the plurality summarily discards *Roe's* analytic core as " 'unsound in principle and unworkable in practice.' " . . . This is so, the plurality claims, because the key elements of the framework do not appear in the text of the Constitution, because the framework more closely resembles a regulatory code than a body of constitutional doctrine, and because under the framework the State's interest in potential human life is considered compelling only after viability, when, in fact, that interest is equally compelling throughout pregnancy. . . . The plurality does not bother to explain these alleged flaws in *Roe*. Bald assertion masquerades as reasoning. The object, quite clearly, is not to persuade, but to prevail.

The plurality opinion is far more remarkable for the arguments that it does not advance than for those that it does. The plurality does not even mention, much less join, the true jurisprudential debate underlying this case: whether the Constitution includes an "unenumerated" general right to privacy as recognized in many of our decisions, most notably *Griswold v. Connecticut*, . . . and *Roe*, and, more specifically, whether and to what extent such a right to privacy extends to matters of childbearing and family life, including abortion. . . . These are questions of unsurpassed significance in this Court's interpretation of the Constitution, and mark the battleground upon which this case was fought, by the par-

ties, by the Solicitor General as *amicus* on behalf of petitioners, and by an unprecedented number of *amici*. On these grounds, abandoned by the plurality, the Court should decide this case.

But rather than arguing that the text of the Constitution makes no mention of the right to privacy, the plurality complains that the critical elements of the *Roe* framework—trimesters and viability—do not appear in the Constitution and are, therefore, somehow inconsistent with a Constitution cast in general terms. . . . Were this a true concern, we would have to abandon most of our constitutional jurisprudence. As the plurality well knows, or should know, the "critical elements" of countless constitutional doctrines nowhere appear in the Constitution's text. The Constitution makes no mention, for example, of the First Amendment's "actual malice" standard for proving certain libels, . . . or of the standard for determining when speech is obscene. . . . Similarly, the Constitution makes no mention of the rational-basis test, or the specific verbal formulations of intermediate and strict scrutiny by which this Court evaluates claims under the Equal Protection Clause. The reason is simple. Like the *Roe* framework, these tests or standards are not, and do not purport to be, rights protected by the Constitution. Rather, they are judge-made methods for evaluating and measuring the strength and scope of constitutional rights or for balancing the constitutional rights of individuals against the competing interests of government.

With respect to the *Roe* framework, the general constitutional principle, indeed the fundamental constitutional right, for which it was developed is the right to privacy, . . . a species of "liberty" protected by the Due Process Clause, which under our past decisions safeguards the right of women to exercise some control over their own role in procreation. As we recently reaffirmed in *Thornburgh v. American College of Obstetricians and Gynecologists*, . . . few decisions are "more basic to individual dignity and autonomy" or more appropriate to that "certain private sphere of individual liberty" that the Constitution reserves from the intrusive reach of government than the right to make the uniquely personal, intimate, and self-defining decision whether to end a pregnancy. . . . It is this general principle, the " 'moral fact that a person belongs to himself and not others nor to society as a whole,' " . . . that is found in the Constitution. . . . The trimester framework simply defines and limits that right to privacy in the abortion context to accommodate, not destroy, a State's legitimate interest in protecting the health of pregnant women and in preserving potential human life. . . . Fashioning such accommodations between individual rights and the legitimate interests of government, establishing benchmarks and standards with which to evaluate the competing claims of individuals and government, lies at the very heart of constitutional adjudication. To the extent that the trimester framework is useful in this enterprise, it is not only consistent with constitutional interpretation, but necessary to the wise and just exercise of this Court's paramount authority to define the scope of constitutional rights.

The plurality next alleges that the result of the trimester framework has "been a web of legal rules that have become increasingly intricate, resembling a code of regulations rather than a body of constitutional doctrine." . . . Again, if this were a true and genuine concern, we would have to abandon vast areas of our constitutional jurisprudence. The plurality complains that under the trimester framework the Court has distinguished between a city ordinance requiring that second-trimester abortions be performed in clinics and a state law requiring that these abortions be performed in hospitals, or between laws requiring that certain information be furnished to a woman by a physician or his assistant and those requiring that such information be furnished by the physician exclusively. . . . Are these distinctions any finer, or more "regulatory," than the distinctions we have often drawn in our First Amendment jurisprudence, where, for example, we have held that a "release time" program permitting public-school students to leave school grounds during school hours to receive religious instruction does not violate the Establishment Clause, even though a release-time program permitting religious instruction on school grounds does violate the Clause? . . . Our Fourth Amendment jurisprudence recognizes

factual distinctions no less intricate. Just this Term, for example, we held that while an aerial observation from a helicopter hovering at 400 feet does not violate any reasonable expectation of privacy, such an expectation of privacy would be violated by a helicopter observation from an unusually low altitude. . . . Similarly, in a Sixth Amendment case, the Court held that although an overnight ban on attorney-client communication violated the constitutionally guaranteed right to counsel, . . . that right was not violated when a trial judge separated a defendant from his lawyer during a 15-minute recess after the defendant's direct testimony. . . .

Finally, the plurality asserts that the trimester framework cannot stand because the State's interest in potential life is compelling throughout pregnancy, not merely after viability. The opinion contains not one word of rationale for its view of the State's interest. This "it-is-so-because-we-say-so" jurisprudence constitutes nothing other than an attempted exercise of brute force; reason, much less persuasion, has no place.

In answering the plurality's claim that the State's interest in the fetus is uniform and compelling throughout pregnancy, I cannot improve upon what Justice *Stevens* has written:

> I should think it obvious that the State's interest in the protection of an embryo—even if that interest is defined as 'protecting those who will be citizens' . . . —increases progressively and dramatically as the organism's capacity to feel pain, to experience pleasure, to survive, and to react to its surroundings increases day by day. The development of a fetus—and pregnancy itself—are not static conditions, and the assertion that the government's interest is static simply ignores this reality. . . . [U]nless the religious view that a fetus is a 'person' is adopted . . . there is a fundamental and well-recognized difference between a fetus and a human being; indeed, if there is not such a difference, the permissibility of terminating the life of a fetus could scarcely be left to the will of the state legislatures. And if distinctions may be drawn between a fetus and a human be-

ing in terms of the state interest in their protection—even though the fetus represents one of 'those who will be citizens'—it seems to me quite odd to argue that distinctions may not also be drawn between the state interest in protecting the freshly fertilized egg and the state interest in protecting the 9-month-gestated, fully sentient fetus on the eve of birth. Recognition of this distinction is supported not only by logic, but also by history and by our shared experiences. . . .

For my own part, I remain convinced, as six other Members of this Court 16 years ago were convinced, that the *Roe* framework, and the viability standard in particular, fairly, sensibly, and effectively functions to safeguard the constitutional liberties of pregnant women while recognizing and accommodating the State's interest in potential human life. The viability line reflects the biological facts and truths of fetal development; it marks that threshold moment prior to which a fetus cannot survive separate from the woman and cannot reasonably and objectively be regarded as a subject of rights or interests distinct from, or paramount to, those of the pregnant woman. At the same time, the viability standard takes account of the undeniable fact that as the fetus evolves into its postnatal form, and as it loses its dependence on the uterine environment, the State's interest in the fetus' potential human life, and in fostering a regard for human life in general, becomes compelling. As a practical matter, because viability follows "quickening"—the point at which a woman feels movement in her womb—and because viability occurs no earlier than 23 weeks gestational age, it establishes an easily applicable standard for regulating abortion while providing a pregnant woman ample time to exercise her fundamental right with her responsible physician to terminate her pregnancy. Although I have stated previously for a majority of this Court that "[c]onstitutional rights do not always have easily ascertainable boundaries," to seek and establish those boundaries remains the special responsibility of this Court. . . . In *Roe,* we discharged that responsibility as logic

and science compelled. The plurality today advances not one reasonable argument as to why our judgment in that case was wrong and should be abandoned.

Having contrived an opportunity to reconsider the *Roe* framework, and then having discarded that framework, the plurality finds the testing provision unobjectionable because it "permissibly furthers the State's interest in protecting potential human life." . . . This newly minted standard is circular and totally meaningless. Whether a challenged abortion regulation "permissibly furthers" a legitimate state interest is the *question* that courts must answer in abortion cases, not the standard for courts to apply. In keeping with the rest of its opinion, the plurality makes no attempt to explain or to justify its new standard, either in the abstract or as applied in this case. Nor could it. The "permissibly furthers" standard has no independent meaning, and consists of nothing other than what a majority of this Court may believe at any given moment in any given case. The plurality's novel test appears to be nothing more than a dressed-up version of rational-basis review, this Court's most lenient level of scrutiny. One thing is clear, however: were the plurality's "permissibly furthers" standard adopted by the Court, for all practical purposes, *Roe* would be overruled.

The "permissibly furthers" standard completely disregards the irreducible minimum of *Roe:* the Court's recognition that a woman has a limited fundamental constitutional right to decide whether to terminate a pregnancy. That right receives no meaningful recognition in the plurality's written opinion. Since, in the plurality's view, the State's interest in potential life is compelling as of the moment of conception, and is therefore served only if abortion is abolished, every hindrance to a woman's ability to obtain an abortion must be "permissible." Indeed, the more severe the hindrance, the more effectively (and permissibly) the State's interest would be furthered. A tax on abortions or a criminal prohibition would both satisfy the plurality's standard. So, for that matter, would a requirement that a pregnant woman memorize and recite today's plurality opinion before seeking an abortion.

The plurality pretends that *Roe* survives,

explaining that the facts of this case differ from those in *Roe:* here, Missouri has chosen to assert its interest in potential life only at the point of viability, whereas, in *Roe,* Texas had asserted that interest from the point of conception, criminalizing all abortions, except where the life of the mother was at stake. . . . This, of course, is a distinction without a difference. The plurality repudiates every principle for which *Roe* stands; in good conscience, it cannot possibly believe that *Roe* lies "undisturbed" merely because this case does not call upon the Court to reconsider the Texas statute, or one like it. If the Constitution permits a State to enact any statute that reasonably furthers its interest in potential life, and if that interest arises as of conception, why would the Texas statute fail to pass muster? One suspects that the plurality agrees. It is impossible to read the plurality opinion and especially its final paragraph, without recognizing its implicit invitation to every State to enact more and more restrictive abortion laws, and to assert their interest in potential life as of the moment of conception. All these laws will satisfy the plurality's non-scrutiny, until sometime, a new regime of old dissenters and new appointees will declare what the plurality intends: that *Roe* is no longer good law.

Thus, "not with a bang, but a whimper," the plurality discards a landmark case of the last generation, and casts into darkness the hopes and visions of every woman in this country who had come to believe that the Constitution guaranteed her the right to exercise some control over her unique ability to bear children. The plurality does so either oblivious or insensitive to the fact that millions of women, and their families, have ordered their lives around the right to reproductive choice, and that this right has become vital to the full participation of women in the economic and political walks of American life. The plurality would clear the way once again for government to force upon women the physical labor and specific and direct medical and psychological harms that may accompany carrying a fetus to term. The plurality would clear the way again for the State to conscript a woman's body and to force upon her a "distressful life and future." . . .

The result, as we know from experience, . . . would be that every year hundreds of thousands of women, in desperation, would defy the law, and place their health and safety in the unclean and unsympathetic hands of back-alley abortionists, or they would attempt to perform abortions upon themselves, with disastrous results. Every year, many women, especially poor and minority women, would die or suffer debilitating physical trauma, all in the name of enforced morality or religious dictates or lack of compassion, as it may be.

Of the aspirations and settled understandings of American women, of the inevitable and brutal consequences of what it is doing, the tough-approach plurality utters not a word. This silence is callous. It is also profoundly destructive of this Court as an institution. To overturn a constitutional decision is a rare and grave undertaking. To overturn a constitutional decision that secured a fundamental personal liberty to millions of persons would be unprecedented in our 200 years of constitutional history. Although the doctrine of *stare decisis* applies with somewhat diminished force in constitutional cases generally, . . . even in ordinary constitutional cases "any departure from *stare decisis* demands special justification." . . . This requirement of justification applies with unique force where, as here, the Court's abrogation of precedent would destroy people's firm belief, based on past decisions of this Court, that they possess an unabridgeable right to undertake certain conduct.

As discussed at perhaps too great length above, the plurality makes no serious attempt to carry "the heavy burden of persuading . . . that changes in society or in the law dictate" the abandonment of *Roe* and its numerous progeny, . . . much less the greater burden of explaining the abrogation of a fundamental personal freedom. Instead, the plurality pretends that it leaves *Roe* standing, and refuses even to discuss the real issue underlying this case: whether the Constitution includes an unenumerated right to privacy that encompasses a woman's right to decide whether to terminate a pregnancy. . . .

This comes at a cost. The doctrine of *stare decisis* "permits society to presume that bedrock principles are founded in the law rather than in the proclivities of individuals, and thereby contributes to the integrity of our constitutional system of government, both in appearance and in fact." . . . Today's decision involves the most politically divisive domestic legal issue of our time. By refusing to explain or to justify its proposed revolutionary revision in the law of abortion, and by refusing to abide not only by our precedents, but also by

our canons for reconsidering those precedents, the plurality invites charges of cowardice and illegitimacy to our door. I cannot say that these would be undeserved.

For today, at least, the law of abortion stands undisturbed. For today, the women of this Nation still retain the liberty to control their destinies. But the signs are evident and very ominous, and a chill wind blows.

I dissent.

Case 1.a *Foe* v. *Vanderhoof:*
Parental Consent for Abortion

U.S. District Court, Disctrict of Colorado

The Colorado District Court in 1975 struck down a Colorado statute requiring an unmarried woman under 18 to obtain the consent of parents or a guardian before obtaining an abortion. The plaintiff was a 16-year-old unmarried, second-trimester pregnant woman with a 5-month-old child and was living in a foster home with the support of public assistance. The woman intended to enroll in school and was described by the court as "an alert, mature and reasonably intelligent young person."

FINESILVER, Judge.

In our view, the right to privacy as expounded in *Roe* and *Doe* to include a decision to terminate a pregnancy extends to minors. The right is a personal one guaranteeing to the individual the right to make basic decisions concerning his or her life without interference from the goverment. . . . Minors are entitled to this personal right as well as adults. The Court in *Eisenstadt*, . . . explained the right to privacy as:

> . . . the right of the *individual,* married or single, to be free from unwarranted governmental intrusion into matters so fundamentally affecting a person as the decision whether to bear or beget a child. *Id.* 405 U.S. at 453,92 S.Ct. at 1038. [emphasis supplied]

The state has demonstrated no reason why this personal and fundamental right should not be guaranteed to pregnant women under eighteen as well as those over eighteen. The detriments discussed in *Roe* . . . which would be suffered by a woman should the state totally deny her the choice to have an abortion are equally applicable to a minor as to an adult.

The right to privacy in regard to an abortion decision extends to minors, particularly, where as here, the minor is living away from home and has made a voluntary and informed decision regarding abortion. . . .

However, the right to privacy, as is true of other constitutional rights, is not absolute. . . . The Court's decisions recognizing the right of privacy have concluded that some state regulation in the area may be appropriate. . . .

Thus the state may infringe on the constitutional right to privacy; however, before it may do so, it must demonstrate interests so compelling as to justify the instrusion on the fundamental right involved. The legislation must be narrowly drawn and confined or restricted to the compelling state interests. . . .

In considering the interests of the state in regard to C.R.S. § 18-6-101(1) (1973), the central issue is whether the state has a compelling interest in requiring that before any woman under the age of eighteen may obtain an abortion, she must acquire the consent of her parents or guardian.

The Court in *Roe* and *Doe* recognized that at some point during pregnancy, the state's interests in maternal health and the life of the fetus become compelling. Thus, after the first trimester, the state's interest in maternal health becomes sufficiently compelling to permit the state to legitimately intervene in order to protect that health by regulating the abortion procedure. This regulation includes requirements relating to the qualifications and licensing of persons who may perform abortions and the regulation of facilities where they may be performed. After the fetus becomes viable, the state may intervene and regulate, or even proscribe, abortions in furtherance of its interest in protecting fetal life.

However, the Court in *Roe* and *Doe,* concluded that there were no compelling state interests which would justify the interference of the state in the abortion decision during the first trimester of a woman's pregnancy. The decision to abort in the first three months is to be made by the woman and her physician alone. . . .

The Colorado statute requiring parental consent for an abortion performed on a woman under eighteen does not serve to further these legitimate state interests recognized in *Roe* as it makes no differentiation according to length of pregnancy nor does it specify reasons for which consent may be withheld. The statute contains an unconditional requirement of adult consent regardless of any danger to maternal health or viability of the fetus. We have been shown no distinction in regard to either of these interests between the pregnancy of a minor and that of an adult which would justify the difference in treatment contained in the statute. . . .

In the instant case, plaintiff was in her second trimester of pregnancy. The only legitimate interest recognized by *Roe* which a state may assert during this trimester is an interest in regulating the procedure for obtaining an abortion in order to protect the mother's health. The Colorado statute under challenge goes far beyond furthering that interest. The operation of the statute unequivocally denies plaintiff her choice of obtaining an abortion.

However, a state may have additional interests in regulating a minor's abortion not present in the case of an adult. The major interests asserted by the state in requiring parental consent for a minor's abortion and interests which have been recognized in other contexts in regard to minors are the protection of the minor and providing for her welfare, and fostering parental control. Analysis of these interests demonstrates that they do not justify the blanket requirement of parental or guardian consent contained in C.R.S. § 18-6-101(1) (1973).

The state certainly has some interest in protecting minors from improvident, hasty, and uninformed decisions. The state also has an interest in providing for the well-being of its youth. However, the statute in question does not achieve those objectives.

The Colorado abortion statute makes no exceptions for minors who are supporting themselves, who are mature, emancipated, or those who receive counseling and guidance from physicians or others in regard to the consequences of their decision to have an abortion.

In the present situation, plaintiff is a mature, emancipated woman who made a serious decision to seek an abortion after consultation with a physician, her social worker, and others. The Court conducted its own investigation to determine if plaintiff had made an informed and intelligent decision and concluded that she had. Thus the statute did not operate to protect her from an improvident decision or to protect her welfare, but gave to another absolute authority to decide for her the question of an abortion.

We have considered and reject defendants' argument that the state as *parens patriae* may act to safeguard the well-being of its youth through the statute in question. . . . We do not believe that this is a situation where the state is acting as *parens patriae* to protect minors, but rather is affording third parties exclusive control over the activities of minors in this area. That doctrine is inapplicable.

We also note that Colorado has passed several statutes which allow minors to consent to medical care without the necessity of parental consent in various situations: C.R.S. § 13-22-103(1) (1973) (minor over 14 who is living apart from parents and managing his or her own financial affairs or is married may consent to any medical and surgical treatment except abortion); C.R.S. § 13-22-103(3) (1973) (any minor parent may consent to medical care for his or her child); C.R.S. § 13-22-105 (1973) (minor may receive birth control information and devices without knowledge of parents); C.R.S. § 13-22-102 (1973) (minor may consent to treatment for drug addiction or use); C.R.S. § 25-4-402(4) (1973) (minor may consent to examination and treatment for venereal disease); C.R.S. § 25-6-102 (1973) (policy statement—all contraceptive devices shall be available to all persons regardless of age).

The state has demonstrated no compelling reason why abortions should be singled out for different treatment than other surgical procedures. The statutory exception contained in the challenged statute seems inconsistent with the philosophy of the state to allow minors, particularly emancipated ones, to consent to virtually any other medical treatment. The state has not demonstrated that its interest in protecting minors and providing for their well-being is different in the case of abortions than in regard to other medical procedures.

The interest of the state in fostering parental control or parental interests and responsibility in raising their children is perhaps the strongest interest asserted by the state in regard to the statute. . . .

However, those cases which have considered parental control of children have involved conflicts between parents and the state wherein the courts have considered intrusions by the state into the area of parental values—particularly religious values. Cases which have upheld parental control have not involved a situation where the parent and child differ and the state is imposing the parents' views on the minor.

These cases are thus inapplicable to the instant question. We do not believe that the state has demonstrated that its interest in fostering parental control is sufficiently compelling to justify the broad and unrestricted intrusion into a minor's own constitutional rights which is the result of the application of the statute in question.

We conclude that the state has not shown that its interests in protecting minors or fostering parental control are sufficiently compelling to justify a blanket requirement of parental or guardian consent in all cases of minors seeking abortions. Nor is the statute narrowly drawn to legitimately further those interests. . . .

The state has not demonstrated any compelling interests in regard to C.R.S. § 18-6-101(1) (1973) which will overcome the fundamental right of plaintiff to privacy and equal protection of the laws. None of the interests urged by the state are sufficiently compelling to justify the statute's broad requirement that parental or guardian consent must be obtained in every case of a minor seeking an abortion. In effect, this statute denies a minor the individual ability to decide to terminate her pregnancy solely because of her age. The state may well have some legitimate interests in the regulation of a minor's abortion which differ from its interests in regard to an adult's abortion; however, this statute is not drawn so as to further only those interests.

Accordingly, it is hereby ordered that C.R.S. § 18-6-101(1) (1973) insofar as it requires the consent of a parent or guardian before a minor may obtain an abortion is declared unconstitutional, and consequently invalid.

Judgment shall enter for the plaintiff.

Case 1.b   Fatal Knowledge?
Prenatal Diagnosis and Sex Selection

Dorothy C. Wertz and John C. Fletcher

Recent advances in prenatal screening allow parents to know the sex of their child prior to birth. Some parents have opted for abortion as a means of selecting the sex of the child—i.e., waiting for a pregnancy with a child of the preferred sex. This article assesses the arguments vis à vis sexism, genetic engineering, and cultural biases and attempts to provide some solutions.

Examining the ethical arguments on sex selection through prenatal diagnosis and their implications for social policy is now an urgent task for three reasons: (1) Recent data suggest that physicians in the U.S. and some other nations may comply with prenatal requests for sex selection, (2) advances in genetic knowledge, such as international projects to map the human genome, beg a question whether sex selection is a precedent for direct genetic "tinkering" with human characteristics having little or nothing to do with disease, and (3) preconceptual sex determination may become scientifically reliable in the future. Unfortunately, no studies exist on how often patients actually ask for sex selection by prenatal diagnosis or what physicians actually do in practice. Such studies may be impossible to carry out because patients may mask their real intent. Those who do make direct requests for sex selection tend to be in extreme or unusual situations. Some examples:

Case 1. A couple with four healthy daughters desire a son. They request prenatal diagnosis solely to learn the fetus's sex, in the absence of any medical indications. They tell the doctor that if the fetus is a female they will abort it. Further, they say that if the doctor will not grant their request for prenatal diagnosis they will have an abortion rather than risk having a fifth girl.

Case 2. A couple with three sons in their late teens think their family is completed, but the woman finds herself unexpectedly pregnant at

From The Hastings Center Report, May/June 1989. Reprinted by permission.

age forty-two. She has always wanted a daughter. Still, the couple is ambivalent; though they are not eager for a fourth child, they are tempted by the possibility of continuing the pregnancy long enough to have prenatal diagnosis, which is medically indicated at the woman's age, finding out the fetus's sex, and then making their decision about abortion.

Case 3. An immigrant woman from an Asian nation where sons are strongly preferred requests prenatal diagnosis for fetal sexing. She already has three daughters and says her husband will divorce her, send her home, and "throw her on the dung heap" if she has another.

By revealing fetal sex, prenatal diagnosis presents prospective parents with a new and troubling possibility: choosing their children's sex through selective abortion. In contrast to past practice, today doctors are much more willing to comply with such requests. When presented with Case 1, 62 percent in a 1985 survey of 295 United States geneticists said that they would either perform prenatal diagnosis for this couple (34%) or would refer them to someone who would perform it (28%).[1] When asked why, most phrased their answers in terms of respect for patients' autonomy and rights of choice. Many regarded sex choice as a logical extension of parents' rights to control the number, timing, spacing, and quality of their offspring. Others said that as long as abortion is available on demand, it should not be denied for specific purposes. Some clearly regarded themselves as technicians who provided services nonjudgmentally; what patients subsequently did with the information was not their business. Few were

55

swayed by the couple's stated intention to abort if they could not discover the fetus's sex. Most considered this a bluff, or at least not a matter of moral concern for the physician.

Geneticists in some other Western nations are not far behind the United States in willingness to permit prenatal sex selection. Sizeable percents in Hungary (60%), Canada (47%), Sweden (38%), Israel (33%), Brazil (30%), Greece (29%), and the United Kingdom (24%) would either perform prenatal diagnosis for this couple or refer. Hungarian geneticists took the threat of abortion seriously; all who would perform prenatal diagnosis said that they were doing so solely to give the fetus at least a 50 percent chance of survival. Elsewhere patterns of moral reasoning were similar to those in the United States. Few (less than 4%) in any Western nation mentioned social issues such as the place of women in society, maintaining a balanced sex ratio, or limiting the population.

Our international study in the medical genetics community asked respondents about a specific case. Three other studies, with very different populations and purposes, have asked questions about sex choice and prenatal diagnosis. In 1972–73, only 1 percent of 448 MD/PhDs in genetics polled by Sorenson, most of whom were researchers, said they would "approve the use of amniocentesis to determine the sex of the fetus to satisfy parental curiosity."[2] At the time, clinical genetics, where patients are seen in counseling, was a small enterprise, amniocentesis was unproven and considered risky, and Sorenson's question itself suggested frivolity. In 1975, Fraser and Pressor learned that among 149 clinically oriented genetic counselors, 15 percent would recommend amniocentesis for sex selection or refer in general, while 28 percent indicated they would do so in response to a case where a well-informed couple with one girl wanted to be sure that their final child was a son.[3] In 1988, Evans surveyed members of the Society for Perinatal Obstetricians about selective termination of multiple fetuses, and included a question on their views of abortion for sex choice.[4] Evans found that of the 308 respondents, 10.3 percent agreed that this was morally acceptable in the first trimester of pregnancy and 5.3 percent in the second trimester.

Due to differences in method, direct comparison of our study with the Sorenson and Evans surveys is not advisable. Our findings are, however, comparable to those of Fraser and Pressor. Their sample was also clinical, and their study also called for response to a hypothetical case. Apparently, attitudes of clinical geneticists about sex selection are even more tolerant today than in 1975.

What explains this changing moral appraisal of sex selection? In the background is a popular desire for the perfect, tailor-made child, a desire to which medicine has contributed by offering the possibility of control over more and more aspects of pregnancy and birth. For some, control over the child's sex seems a logical extension of other kinds of control and respect for reproductive freedom. Further, the consumer movement in the United States has forced doctors to be more open with patients. Many doctors now regard injecting their moral beliefs into the doctor-patient relationship as paternalistic.

Geneticists are in a peculiarly sensitive position, because giving advice or withholding services leaves them open to accusations of practicing eugenics or acting as the gatekeepers to life. The new fields of medical genetics and genetic counseling that developed after World War II stressed "nondirectiveness," support for patients' decisions, whatever these decisions were, and refusal to "tell patients what to do."[5] Today the stance of nondirectiveness (ethical neutrality) in genetic counseling is ubiquitous.[6] A stated practice of nondirectiveness makes it difficult for some practitioners to refuse a service without appearing judgmental. Nevertheless, few desire to remove all moral values from the doctor-patient relationship. There is something distinctly unnerving in the idea of a doctor as pure technician.

The Ethics of Sex Selection

Sex selection through prenatal diagnosis asks us to decide upon the limits to reproductive choice. Mary Anne Warren and other feminist authors have considered some central moral arguments on sex selection.[7]

Warren observes that even in a nonsexist society there would remain a natural desire for a child of one's own sex. This desire is not sexism, but a desire for companionship with which most of us sympathize. Meeting this desire is perhaps the strongest argument for sex selection (except to make a prenatal diagnosis of a sex-linked genetic disease, for example, before there was an exact way to diagnose hemophilia or Duchenne's muscular dystrophy by using DNA techniques). We discuss the companionship motive below.

Warren also examines three claims: first, that sex choice would enhance quality of life more for a child of the "wanted" sex than a child of the "unwanted" sex, second, would provide better quality of life for the family that has the "balance" it desires, and third, a better quality of life for the mother, because she will undergo fewer births to have the desired number of children of each sex. Each of these arguments, however, is premised upon the existence of a sexist society. The perception of "better quality of life" would not be comprehensible except against the background of preferential treatment of one sex (usually the male). To practice sex selection for these reasons, Warren maintains, serves not only to perpetuate a sexist society but further would not, in the context of a sexist society, lead to the desired results.

Warren claims, moreover, that there is no evidence that sex selection would result in a better quality of family life; in fact, there are several ways in which it could worsen it. Sex selection could encourage favored treatment of a child whose sex was deliberately selected by parents and result in neglect of existing children whose sex was determined by nature. Sex selection also may occasion marital conflict about family composition, and, in societies where women possess little power, foreclose their only chance to have a girl.

In addition, improved quality of life for women by sex choice is an illusion. Warren argues on consequentialist grounds that (assuming persons would act on their preferences, if they could) in most societies, sex selection would tend to be used against women. Even in the U.S., where most couples desire to have one child of each sex, there are preferences for boys.[8] Even if the selection

were in favor of girls, however, the fact remains that sex selection is inherently sexist because it is premised upon a belief in sexual inequality. We agree with Warren's conclusion that there appear to be no valid arguments for sex selection on the basis of "quality of life."

Another argument to justify sex selection is that it would help to limit the population. Families would not have six girls to have their desired son, for example. But there is no evidence that population trends result from a desire to have sons. Rather, most families try to have the number of children that seems most economically advantageous. If they could select sex, and if one sex presented an economic advantage over the other, some families might actually have more children than they would have had in the absence of sex selection.

The most convincing moral arguments against sex choice, however, would refute the "desire for companionship" argument described above, and show that sex choice would be wrong (except perhaps in one very limited case), based on violations of equality, even were preconceptual methods available. Additional arguments are that sex selection may be held to undermine the most important moral reason that justifies prenatal diagnosis—the prevention of serious and untreatable genetic disease, increase morally unjustifiable abortions and thereby threaten reproductive freedom, and pose a precedent for the abuse of genetic knowledge and preconceptual sex determination in the future.

Equality and Justice

The President's Commission recommended that geneticists reject sex selection because it violates the principle of equality between females and males.[9] However, the Commission did not provide moral arguments to support its position.

Can reasons be offered for sex preferences that are defensible in terms of serious tests of rationality? Michael Bayles has examined the concerns one might advance for sex preference, including replacing oneself biologically; carrying on the family name; rights of inheritance; pleasures associated with one or the other sex (the "desire for companionship"); or jobs that require either males or females.[10]

Bayles rejects each reason, although he is not responsible for all of the reasoning we present here. The sex of one child does not make her or him anymore "my" child than one of the other sex; genetically, parents contribute equally to each child. Women can carry on the family name. They do so increasingly in the United States by retaining their maiden names, hyphenating their last names, or using the husband's family name only in society's private sector. In almost all nations, males and females are now more equal in the capacity to inherit the estates of parents or others. Any normal pleasure that can be enjoyed with a child of one sex such as sports, vacations, hobbies, games, art, and literature can be enjoyed with a child of the other sex. Few jobs exist that women cannot perform as well as or better than men when performance is the criterion for evaluation. Our analysis does not diminish the power of biologically or culturally based sex preferences, but the desire itself cannot directly be acted upon, especially in deliberate choices about sex selection, without a prior admission that it is irrational to do so.

There may be one real exception to the moral case against sex selection when parents want to reduce the harms of sexism and also desire to balance their family in gender. Suppose a future in which a proven, safe, and inexpensive method of preconceptual sex determination exists. Further, suppose that like most Americans you would use natural sex determination with your first child. Whatever the gender of your first child, by prior agreement with your spouse, for subsequent births you want to use sex determination to balance your family.

We find no moral reasons to condemn the desire to balance gender in families, especially if used by parents who want their children to respect sex-based differences and to learn fairness to the opposite sex by practicing it at home. No intrinsic link exists between sexism and the desire for a balanced family. However, there may be serious considerations against sex determination based on potentially harmful consequences. In a society that condemns abortion for sex choice, wide use of preconceptual sex determination could increase the need to ascertain in pregnancy that the "right gender" was indeed selected, with abortion as an option. Parents with a very strong motive to determine the sex of a second or third child would probably not always accept physicians' claims that methods for sex determination are effective. Secondly, preconceptual sex selection could contribute to gender stereotyping before birth and perpetuate sexism in society. Finally, sex determination could harm the parents themselves. If, after sex determination, a child is born with serious health problems, parents could all too readily blame themselves for contributing to *this* child's suffering by having determined his or her origin in a special way.

Thus, though the desire for balance might be beneficially used by parents in this one instance, we believe that most parents would prefer to limit reproductive freedom to avoid possibly harmful consequences of sex predetermination, even under the best of motives.

Misuse of Prenatal Diagnosis

Societal arguments against using prenatal diagnosis for sex selection include the possibility of unbalancing the sex ratio, diminishing the status of women (assuming that sex preference would be for males), and unbalancing the birth order if, for example, most families acted upon their preference for first-born boys. There is, of course, no real proof that any of these things would happen in Western societies. Although families in Western nations may state sex or birth order preferences when answering a survey, these preferences are slight. It is doubtful that many would go to the length of having trial pregnancies and abortions for the purpose of tailoring their families to fit their survey responses. Unbalancing sex ratios through prenatal diagnosis alone seems a very remote possibility. Preconceptual sex selection—at present not a reliable option—may be a greater danger.

Use of prenatal diagnosis may also contravene the principle of distributive justice, however. The provision of this service for sex selection is a misuse of costly medical resources. In rural and remote sections of the U.S., prenatal diagnosis is still a scarce resource; and the majority of women for whom prenatal diagnosis is medically indicated on the basis of age (over 35) do not receive it.[11] The use of costly, limited medical resources for nonmedical purposes as long as there are women with medical/genetic indications who need this service, and who cannot afford it, is contrary to our beliefs in fairness.

But suppose there were an abundance of prenatal diagnostic services, and public funds or insurance reimbursement to provide unlimited procedures to all who request them. What then? Already some communities in the United States are rapidly approaching the situation where prenatal diagnosis is no longer a "scarce" resource. Under these conditions, some doctors would hesitate to withhold it from almost anyone who asks. Risks to the fetus are now considered so minimal, at least for amniocentesis and chorionic villus sampling, that for many doctors they are not an argument for withholding the service, provided that the parents are informed.

A stronger reason to oppose sex selection by prenatal diagnosis is that, whenever it is done, it undermines the major moral reason that justifies prenatal diagnosis and selective abortion—the prevention of serious and untreatable genetic disease. Gender is not a disease. Prenatal diagnosis for a nonmedical reason makes a mockery of medical ethics.

Physicians are not supposed to give tests or treatments except for indications that meet a "standard of care." Fetal sexing, unrelated to genetic disease, has never appeared on any list of medical indications for prenatal diagnosis. In fact, an NIH consensus development conference, a Hastings Center interdisciplinary group, an international meeting of geneticists, and the President's Commission advise against use of prenatal diagnosis for sex choice.[12] Physicians who do provide it are flaunting these well-considered recommendations.

The U.S. public's view of the indications for genetic testing rely on the principle of relief or prevention of suffering. The best study of this question, among a national probability sample of 1,273 American adults by the Harris organization, shows overwhelming support (89%) for making genetic testing available for *serious and fatal genetic diseases.* Eighty-three percent would take such a test themselves for that reason, including 81 percent who describe themselves as very religious.[13]

Prenatal Diagnosis and Selective Abortion

Parents who request prenatal diagnosis for sex choice act outside the limits of a moral consensus about the medical uses of genetic knowledge. Furthermore, those who try to "bluff" physicians or fabricate reasons for prenatal diagnosis violate the ethical norms of the patient role. And threatening abortion to obtain prenatal diagnosis is a form of moral blackmail unacceptable in any circle. It betrays the intuition that abortion of a normal fetus for sex selection, absent any higher moral claims such as the mother's health or a serious, untreatable genetic disease, is morally unjustifiable. Encouraging or increasing abortions for this reason, however few in number they may be, may indirectly contribute to the erosion of women's freedom to choose abortion when there are strong moral reasons to do so. Feminists have long opposed sex choice abortions because these acts "trivialize" the moral seriousness of abortion decisions. Reproductive choices are not unlimited, especially when they threaten fairness to others.

Perfect Children?

Another argument against sex selection—one that anticipates completion of the human genome map—is that by selecting for sex we set precedents for attempts to select other characteristics that have nothing to do with disease, for instance, height, eye and hair color, thinness, skin color, and straight teeth. Many parents already include some of these characteristics in visualizing their perfect children. If sex selection is permitted, will it not be a precedent for other requests from anxious parents in the next century? Why stop at gender selection? What else will geneticists be asked to do if and when they can understand and determine the expression of several genes? Parents could argue that having a child with "undesirable" characteristics—shortness, nearsightedness, color-blindness, or just an average IQ would make them miserable, make the child miserable, and lower the quality of their family life (especially if they already had several such children)—many of the same arguments given for sex selection. For some minority groups, this precedent could lead in another direction: the temptation to select lighter-skinned fetuses, knowing that skin color is historically related to upward mobility in the United States. These choices are still in the realm of science fiction, but gender selection is not. Within the next twenty years, or sooner, however, some of the more exotic choices may be technically possible, especially those related to body size and height. At the extreme, such prenatal tinkering with desired characteristics could lead to positive eugenics. Further, unless there are radical changes in the U.S. system of medical care, the capacity to use genetic knowledge will reside with those who can pay for eugenic interventions.

What happens now, with sex selection, sets precedents for moral acceptance or rejection of future choices. If the medical profession provides prenatal diagnosis for sex choice, nonjudgmentally, why withhold it for other purposes? If, on the other hand, geneticists and allied professionals were to adopt a code of ethics that opposed sex selection through prenatal diagnosis, this could help to prevent misguided "cosmetic" uses of genetic knowledge in the future.[14]

It is important for a final reason to take a stand on sex selection now. Preconceptual sex selection, though at present not scientifically reliable, may someday become feasible. Unlike sex selection through abortion, preconceptual selection could gain widespread popular acceptance and could more easily affect sex ratios or birth order, with unknown social repercussions. This is more likely to happen if there has been previous cultural acceptance of or neutrality toward sex selection through prenatal diagnosis. If responsible medical professionals were to oppose tinkering with the natural lottery for sex selection, this might help to prepare the public for very limited, medically indicated uses of preconceptual methods, such as to avoid sex-linked genetic disorder.

Knowledge as Temptation

The moral and social arguments seem to weigh heavily against performing prenatal diagnosis solely for sex selection. Direct requests for this information, however, are likely to be few in Western nations. Instead, more moral problems will evolve from the knowledge about sex that is incidental to prenatal diagnosis performed for other purposes. Our second case is likely to be most representative of couples in the United States. This couple is clearly eligible for prenatal diagnosis because of the increased risk of chromosomal abnormalities after age thirty-five. Before prenatal diagnosis was widely available, they could have simply had an abortion. Now they face the tempting possibility of waiting, having prenatal diagnosis for chromosome abnormalities (as early as the eighth week if they use chorionic villus sampling), finding out the fetus's sex, and then making their decision. Three instances known to one of us followed this scenario. In all three, the desired sex was female. In one case, the couple had three boys and the husband wanted no more children. When the wife unexpectedly became pregnant, he threatened to leave her. She wanted the child, whatever the sex, but also wanted to preserve the family. Finally they struck a bargain: if the fetus were female, she would carry it to term, otherwise she would abort. It was a girl, and she continued the pregnancy. In a second case, the family had four sons and severe financial hardships. They did not want a fifth child, but said that they would "try harder" if it were a girl. This couple did not take abortion lightly. When prenatal diagnosis revealed a boy and they had the abortion, they spent a long time holding the fetus afterward and grieving. In the third case, the couple had two teen-aged sons and the wife was tempted to continue her unexpected pregnancy long enough to find out if the fetus was female. Her husband convinced her that sex choice was immoral, and she subsequently had an abortion without learning the fetus's sex. Several years later she believes that this decision, though morally correct, was "wrong" for her, and regrets her lost opportunity of perhaps having a girl.

Some parents may welcome the possibility of making such decisions, but for many it is an unwanted, agonizing choice. They are faced with a decision that may cause moral agony, not so much because they make the "wrong" choice, but because the choice exists. In William Styron's novel, *Sophie's Choice*, Sophie is forced to decide which of her two children to send to the gas chamber. Her subsequent nightmare is not that she chose the wrong child, but that *she* had to make the *choice*. The possibility of sex selection presents parents with a similar moral nightmare. Most would not seek to have prenatal diagnosis solely for sex selection, but their eligibility for the procedure on other grounds presents a temptation.[15]

Maternal Anxiety

The problem will be exacerbated if prenatal diagnosis is used in borderline situations like "maternal anxiety." By providing the procedure to any woman who says she is anxious about the fetus's health, doctors also open the gate to the possibility of sex selection. "Anxiety" is already a medical indication in Denmark, Sweden, and Switzerland, and accounts for roughly 10 percent of prenatal diagnoses in these nations.[16] According to our survey, the majority of geneticists around the world (73%, including 89% in the United States) would perform prenatal diagnosis for a twenty-five-year-old anxious woman with no family history of genetic disorder or toxic exposure, or would refer her to someone who would perform it.

When asked to justify their actions, some doctors point to the special anxieties of women who work in institutions for the mentally retarded or whose friends have given birth to children with Down syndrome. Others believe that every pregnant woman should have the opportunity to have her anxieties relieved. They see prenatal diagnosis as a beneficient procedure that promotes the mother's mental health and that may thereby lead to a healthier pregnancy.

There is a clear link between willingness to do prenatal diagnosis for anxiety—which amounts to prenatal diagnosis on request—and the possibility of sex selection. Swedish doctors performed prenatal diagnosis for the Asian woman described in Case 3 on the basis of the anxiety engendered by her husband's threat. If doctors continue to do prenatal diagnosis for maternal anxiety, prenatal diagnosis could soon become routine in most pregnancies.

Although the more invasive and riskier methods, such as amniocentesis and CVS, may in the future be restricted to those at genuinely high risk, they will likely be replaced in mass pregnancy screening by noninvasive methods such as ultrasound and recovery of fetal cells from maternal blood. It is already possible to determine fetal sex from ultrasound, sometimes as early as nine to eleven weeks, and techniques are improving. Fetal chromosome analysis may one day be possible through a maternal blood test that poses no risk to mother or fetus. Such tests could become routine, and the sex of the fetus determined in the first trimester as part of routine prenatal care. Before this day arrives, we must have some preventive solutions for the attendant moral and social problems.

Some Possible Solutions

Laws against using prenatal diagnosis for sex selection would probably be disadvantageous in most Western nations. Women have only recently won control over their reproductive lives, and legal measures prohibiting prenatal diagnosis or abortion for a specific purpose would be a step backward toward other restrictive controls. Furthermore, laws against sex selection would be impossible to enforce, for few people in Western nations would make direct requests. In the U.S. it would be possible, within the framework of *Roe v. Wade* to prohibit abortions done for a specific reason, such as sex selection, using the analogy of laws that prohibit the sale of guns to those who say they will use them to murder people. This is not a particularly helpful analogy, for few would-be murderers tell gunshop owners that they intend to shoot people, and few prospective parents tell doctors that their real reason for having prenatal diagnosis is to discover fetal sex.

Judicious use of hospital and laboratory policy seems a more effective alternative, especially in countries with a national health service. In nations such as the United States, professional codes of medical ethics, including those of national specialty boards and state medical societies, could be used to discourage private doctors from using prenatal diagnosis for sex selection. The codes of state medical societies are particularly important, because these societies ordinarily control licensure and can discipline or suspend physicians who flagrantly violate the code. Such moral guidance by the profession would not prevent all sex selection, for codes would vary from state to state and it is likely that only the most obvious violators would be disciplined. Nevertheless, a professional stand on the question could go a long way toward preventing widespread abuse.

Most prospective parents would probably agree with this approach, which helps to remove a temptation. A few doctors would continue to practice sex selection, but it is better to permit this freedom to the few than to start hedging reproduction with restrictive laws. Discouraging the use of prenatal diagnosis for sex selection will not necessarily result in fewer abortions; it may actually result in more, because those who are undecided about continuing a pregnancy may be more willing to abort if they are unable to find out the fetus's sex.

Why not simply withhold information about sex, rather than withholding prenatal diagnosis? This would seem a logical solution to the problem. Sex is not a disease, and it would probably be legal for doctors to withhold the information about gender as clinically irrelevant. This alternative has not yet been put to a legal test. Withholding information of

any kind, however, is a very sensitive moral issue. Patients in the United States have become used to asking for full disclosure, and ethicists have tried to educate professionals to convey the "whole truth" to competent patients. Withholding information puts control into the hands of doctors, not patients, and sets a precedent for a resurgence of medical paternalism.

Yet doctors do withhold some types of nonmedical information routinely. In our survey, 96 percent of geneticists said they would not tell a woman's husband that he is not the biological father of her child. Instead, most (83%) would tell the woman alone, so that she could use the information to plan the rest of her reproductive life, and let her decide whether to tell her husband. The decision to withhold information from the husband in the interests of protecting family unity is analogous to withholding other types of "incidental" information learned from genetic testing.

The disanalogous aspect of the false paternity example is that few husbands ask "Am I the father?" and more parents ask if they can know the gender. However, a similar practice of not revealing incidental information, unless asked, could be applied to fetal sex. Parents would thereby be spared the temptation to abort on the basis of sex. They would also avoid gender stereotyping their children before birth.[17] Such a policy of not revealing fetal sex was recently instituted in prenatal diagnostic laboratories in the Birmingham Region of England, not because parents were requesting sex selection, but because some parents complained that they wished they had not known the fetus's sex.[18] In 1987–1988, when the information was no longer made available as a matter of course, of 3,883 amniotic fluid analyses there were only 95 (2.4%) parental requests to know fetal sex. This policy takes a "middle ground": the information is available if patients request it, but is not routinely provided in the laboratory report to the patient's doctor. Therefore the doctor does not know something that the patient does not know—thus avoiding a circumstance that irks some patients and leads them to request information. Instead, the information resides at further remove in the laboratory files. While this will not prevent sex selection if someone is determined to do it, it does minimize opportunities for abuse.

Professional Responsibility

We hold that a very strong normative case exists against sex selection that transcends cultural boundaries, especially based on claims of equal worth of both sexes and justice in social life. Because of studies that trace the evolution of more openness in physicians' attitudes about sex choice, we believe that it is important that the medical profession take a stand now against sex selection. A posture of ethical neutrality on this issue could lead to unfortunate precedents in moral thinking about future uses of genetic knowledge and preconceptual sex determination. Such neutrality undermines the morality that supports prenatal diagnosis and may encourage legal attacks on morally justified reproductive choices, such as genetic services themselves or abortions to prevent a serious and untreatable genetic disorder. To protect more important reproductive choices, the profession will have to abandon its nonjudgmental stance and offer moral guidance. To fail to do so may encourage third parties, courts, or governments to intervene.

Notes

1. Dorothy C. Wertz and John C. Fletcher, *Ethics and Human Genetics: A Cross-Cultural Perspective* (Heidelberg: Springer-Verlag, 1989); "Ethics and Medical Genetics in the United States: A National Survey," *American Journal of Medical Genetics* 29 (1988), 815–27; "Ethical Problems in Prenatal Diagnosis: A Cross-Cultural Survey of Medical Geneticists in 18 Nations," *Prenatal Diagnosis* 8 (1989), 1–13; "Ethical Aspects of Prenatal Diagnosis: Views of U.S. Medical Geneticists," *Clinics in Perinatology* 14:2 (1987), 293–312.

2. James R. Sorenson, "From Social Movement to Clinical Medicine: The Role of Law and the Medical Profession in Regulating Applied Human Genetics," in *Genetics and the Law*, Aubrey Milunsky and George J. Annas, eds. (New York: Plenum, 1976), 467–85.

3. F. Clarke Fraser and C. Pressor, "Attitudes of Counselors in Relation to Prenatal Sex Determination for Choice of Sex," in *Genetic Counseling*, Herbert A. Lubs and Felix de la Cruz, eds. (New York: Raven, 1977), 109–112.

4. Mark I. Evans, Hutzel Hospital, Wayne State University, Detroit, MI, personal communication.

5. F. Clarke Fraser, "Genetic Counseling," *American Journal of Human Genetics* 26 (1974), 636–59; James R. Sorenson, Judith P. Swazey, and Norman A. Scotch, *Reproductive Pasts, Reproductive Futures: Genetic Counseling and its Effectiveness* (New York: Alan R. Liss, 1981).

6. Dorothy C. Wertz and John C. Fletcher, "Attitudes of Genetic Counselors: A Multinational Survey," *American Journal of Human Genetics* 42:4 (1988), 592–600.

7. Mary Anne Warren, *Gendercide: The Implications of Sex Selection* (Totowa, NJ: Rowman & Allanheld, 1985); Christine Overall, *Ethics and Human Reproduction: A Feminist Analysis* (Boston: Allen & Unwin, 1987), 17–39; Helen Bequaert Holmes, "Review of *Gendercide*," *Bioethics* 1:1 (1987), 100–110.

8. Anne R. Pebley and Charles F. Westhoff, "Women's Sex Preferences in the United States: 1970 to 1975," *Demography* 19:2 (1982), 177–89; Charles F. Westhoff and Ronald R. Rindfuss, "Sex Preselection in the United States," *Science* 184 (1974), 633–36; Roberta Steinbacher and Helen B. Holmes, "Sex Choice: Survival and Sisterhood," in *Man-Made Women: How New Reproductive Technologies Affect Woman*, Gena Corea et al., eds. (Bloomington: Indiana University Press, 1987), 52–63; Mary E. Pharis and Martin Manosevitz, "Sexual Stereotyping of Infants: Implications for Social Work Practice," *Social Work Research and Abstracts* 20 (1984), 7–12.

9. President's Commission for the Study of Ethical Problems in Medicine and Biomedical and Behavioral Research, *Screening and Counseling for Genetic Conditions* (Washington, DC: US Government Printing Office, 1983), 58–59.

10. Michael D. Bayles, *Reproductive Ethics* (Englewood Cliffs, NJ: Prentice-Hall, Inc., 1984), 33–37.

11. John J. Mulvihill, Leroy Walters, and

Dorothy C. Wertz, "Ethics and Medical Genetics in the United States of America," in *Ethics and Human Genetics,* 419–56.

12. U.S. Department of Health, Education, and Welfare, National Institutes of Health, *Antenatal Diagnosis,* (Bethesda, MD: U.S. Government Printing Office/NIH, 1979), 1–77; Tabitha M. Powledge and John C. Fletcher, "Guidelines for the Ethical, Social, and Legal Issues in Prenatal Diagnosis," *New England Journal of Medicine* 300:4 (1979), 168–72; John L. Hamerton, *et al.,* "Chromosome Disease," in *Prenatal Diagnosis: Past, Present, and Future,* Report of an International Workshop, *Prenatal Diagnosis* (Special Issue, 1980), 11.

13. U.S. Congress Office of Technology Assessment, *New Developments in Biotechnology* (Washington, DC: U.S. Government Printing Office, May 1987), 74–75.

14. John C. Fletcher, Kare Berg, and Knut Erik Tranøy, "Ethical Aspects of Medical Genetics: A Proposal for Guidelines in Genetic Counseling, Prenatal Diagnosis and Screening," *Clinical Genetics* 27 (1985), 199–205; Dorothy C. Wertz, John C. Fletcher, and John J. Mulvihill, "Ethics and Medical Genetics in 18 Nations: A Proposal for a Professional Code of Ethics for Medical Geneticists," *American Journal of Human Genetics* (submitted in revision).

15. In a Swedish study, 16 percent of women having prenatal diagnosis on the basis of advanced age said that the fetus's sex would affect their decisions about abortion. Berit Sjogren, "Parental Attitudes to Prenatal Information About the Sex of the Fetus," *Acta Obstetrica Gynecologia Scandinavia* 67 (1988), 43–46.

16. Sjogren, "Parental Attitudes."

17. Barbara Katz Rothman, *The Tentative Pregnancy: Prenatal Diagnosis and the Future of Motherhood* (New York: Viking, 1986), 116–54.

18. Maj Hulten, East Birmingham Hospital, Birmingham, U.K., personal communication.

Case 1.c   *Doe* v. *Doe:* Fathers' Rights?

Massachusetts State Supreme Court

The Does (a pseudonym) were married in April 1974, and, after suffering a miscarriage in August, the wife again became pregnant. Although the pregnancy was welcomed, the marriage deteriorated and the couple separated. At first Mr. Doe wanted nothing to do with the child, expressly stating his wish to have his name withheld from the birth certificate. When Mrs. Doe decided that she would have an abortion (she was 18 weeks pregnant), Mr. Doe brought suit to stop termination of the pregnancy.

Before TAURO, C. J., and REARDON, QUIRICO, BRAUCHER, HENNESSEY, KAPLAN and WILKINS, JJ.

BRAUCHER, Justice.

. . . The husband contends that he has a fundamental right, guaranteed by the Constitution of the United States, to determine that his child shall not be aborted, citing the concurring opinion of Mr. Justice Goldberg in Griswold v. Connecticut, 381 U.S. 479, 493, 85 S.Ct. 1678 (1965). It is true that in various contexts the Supreme Court has declared that certain interests associated with the marital relationship give rise to rights guaranteed by the Federal Constitution. . . . But all those cases involved a shield for the private citizen against government action, not a sword of government assistance to enable him to overturn the private decisions of his fellow citizens. . . . We find no basis for the husband's assertion that the Constitution enables him to summon the Commonwealth to help him in a dispute with his wife.

. . . The husband does not claim support for his position from any statute of the Commonwealth. Nor could he. Our statute on abortion, like the traditional statutes of most States, is a criminal statute, forbidding an abortion unless performed "in good faith and in an honest belief that it is necessary for the preservation of the life *or health* of the woman" (emphasis supplied). . . . The statute was rendered inoperative for the purposes of the present case by the decision in Roe v. Wade, 410 U.S. 113, 166, 93 S.Ct. 705 (1973). . . .

In other States, recent statutes have dealt in various ways with the issue now before us. The Am. Law Inst., Model Penal Code, § 230.3 (Proposed Official Draft, 1962), the Uniform Abortion Act (1971), and the statutes of many States make no mention of the husband's consent. . . . Statutes in some States provide for the consent of the husband. In several of those States the husband's consent is given effect only where the wife is a minor or incompetent. In several his consent is required only if the parties are living together or is dispensed with in cases of separation or abandonment.

In neither Roe v. Wade nor Doe v. Bolton [410 U.S. 179, 93 S.Ct. 739 (1973)] did the Supreme Court "discuss the father's rights, if any exist in the constitutional context, in the abortion decision." No paternal rights had been asserted in either of the cases, and the governing "statutes on their face take no cognizance of the father." The court found it unnecessary to "decide whether provisions" recognizing the father in certain circumstances "are constitutional." . . . In lower courts statutes requiring the husband's consent have not withstood constitutional attack. Gerstein v. Coe, 376 F.Supp. 695 (S.D.Fla.1973), app. dism. and cert. den., 417 U.S. 279, 94 S.Ct. 2246, 41 L.Ed.2d 68 (1974). Doe v. Rampton, 366 F.Supp. 189, 192 (D.Utah 1973). . . .

After the 1973 decisions, recognition of an enforceable right in the husband to prevent the abortion would raise serious constitutional questions. Although the court did not pass on the husband's right, it used language inconsistent with such a right. It recognized "a right of personal privacy, or a guarantee of certain areas or zones of privacy . . . broad enough to encompass a woman's decision whether or not to terminate her pregnancy." . . . During the first trimester "the attending physician, in consultation with his patient, is free to determine, without regulation by the State, that, in his medical judgment the patient's pregnancy should be terminated." . . . Thereafter, until the fetus is viable, "the State, in promoting its interest in the health of the mother, may, if it chooses, regulate the abortion procedure in ways that are reasonably related to maternal health." . . .

The cases since Roe v. Wade give little support to the husband's claim. In a case involving an unmarried woman during the first trimester of pregnancy, a Florida court ruled that the putative father's claim was not covered by the Florida statute and denied relief apart from statute. Jones v. Smith, 278 So.2d 339, 344 (Fla.App.1973), cert. den., 415 U.S. 958, 94 S.Ct. 1486 (1974). . . . A lower court in Illinois has apparently denied relief to a husband in a similar case. Pound v. Pound, (January 31, 1974) 42 U.S.L.Week 2456 (Ill.Cir.Ct.). If the State cannot interfere with the abortion decision, before the fetus is viable, except in ways reasonably related to maternal health, it seems highly doubtful that it can come to the husband's assistance with authority it does not itself possess. . . .

If it is within our power, free of constitutional prohibition, to fashion a rule of decision recognizing an enforceable right in the husband, we decline to do so, at least where the fetus is not viable. . . . Injunctions and other threats against licensed physicians may drive determined women into the waiting offices of persons not licensed. . . . Except in cases involving divorce or separation, our law has not in general undertaken to resolve the many delicate questions inherent in the marriage relationship. We would not order either a husband or a wife to do what is necessary to conceive a child or to prevent conception, any more than we would order either party to do what is necessary to make the other happy. We think the same considerations prevent us from forbidding the wife to do what is necessary to bring about or to prevent birth, at least before the fetus is viable and in the absence of any danger to maternal life or health. Some things must be left to private agreement.

Nothing we say here is intended to affirm or deny a right in the husband to divorce, separation, child custody, or the like by reason of an abortion procured by his wife without his consent. We are deeply conscious of the husband's interest in the abortion decision, at least while the parties are living together in harmony. Surely that interest is legitimate. Surely, if the family life is to prosper, he should participate with his wife in the decision. But it does not follow that he must have an absolute veto, or that his veto, reasoned or unreasoned, can be enforced by the Commonwealth.

HENNESSEY, Justice (dissenting in part).

. . . I concur with the court's decision not to enjoin the wife from procuring the abortion. . . .

At the same time, I dissent from the court's determination that the husband has no legal rights. I would have, while denying injunctive relief, simultaneously declared that the husband has fundamental rights here and that in the circumstances of this case the wife has a duty to forbear the abortion. Justice required such a declaration even though injunctive relief was denied.

. . . I cannot join the majority of my colleagues of the Supreme Judicial Court in a voluntary extension of the rules of the cases of Roe v. Wade and Doe v. Bolton. For it is clear that the *Wade* and *Bolton* cases are not directly controlling here. Indeed the *Wade* case expressly reserves . . . the question now before us of the father's rights. Further, in the *Bolton* case . . . the court said that a woman's constitutional right to an abortion is not absolute.

Nor, in my view, are the father's claims disposed of by any acceptable extension of the basic premises of the *Wade* and *Bolton* cases. The Supreme Court has stated in essence that the woman has a fundamental right of private decision to terminate the pregnancy. No right of the fetus is recognized by that court, at least during the first two trimesters.

But the father has rights. They are familial. They antedate the Constitution; they are about as old as civilization itself. They center in a main potentiality of his marriage: the birth and raising of children. Few human experiences have meaning comparable to parenthood. The father's rights asserted here are surely among the fundamental rights protected by the Constitution.

In the circumstances of the case before us, the father's rights were dominant. The woman's health was not a factor. She had separated from her husband and did not want the child because she doubted her ability to care for the child and because she said her husband had indicated to her that he would not support it. The husband wanted the pregnancy to continue to full term and a normal birth. He stated that he would be willing to assume custody, and care for the child, in the event that the wife would not. The wife's assertions were not supportable by contrast with those of her husband. Thus, justice to her husband, at the very least, required forbearance by the wife.

REARDON, Justice (dissenting).

This is a case where a court order has taken from a potential father the right to have his child born, a child which he and his wife both wanted at the time of conception. . . .

We have here a situation in which the loss suffered by the husband is dramatically and utterly irreversible and where the severity of the deprivation can be gauged only by the most sensitive and profound human faculties. . . . I am persuaded that a legitimate and judicially cognizable interest of the husband was at stake in this case and that it was appropriate to grant relief to preserve it.

[Justice REARDON pointed to a number of cases which turned on the right of privacy as a bar to governmental interference with the fundamental right to procreate and to rear children. He went on to say:]

. . . In each case the right of privacy was but the correlative of the duty of the State to refrain from activity to which, by virtue of the limited nature of our constitutional government, it was obliged to remain a stranger. But who will assert that the husband here is, or could ever be, a stranger to the destruction of the fetus which he begot or to the possible future birth of his child? At base it was respect for the intimacy of certain sectors of human life which compelled the decisions of the Supreme Court insisting that government refrain from interfering in these private determinations. It is that same respect which informs us that a potential father's rights in the birth of a child cannot be dissolved by unreasoned reference to the Fourteenth Amendment.

I believe that the interests of fathers in the birth of offspring en ventre sa mère may be discerned in the constitutional and common law of the Commonwealth. To find its roots we need look no further than the Preamble to our Constitution which declares among the purposes of the Commonwealth the provision to its citizens of "the power of enjoying in safety and tranquility their natural rights." Article 1 of our Declaration of Rights proclaims the existence of "natural, essential, and unalienable" rights. The broad and elusive character of such "natural rights" makes their invocation a serious and even dangerous business, one never to be lightly undertaken. But when a citizen comes before this court asking for the protection of an interest which is plainly grounded in the most universal of human emotions, and which has in related forms been recognized and nurtured for centuries by the common law, he raises a cogent claim to judicial recognition of his natural right.

. . . The "right of privacy" cases discussed above have as an implicit assumption that as matter of practical universal agreement and natural right there exists a critical interest in individual control of certain aspects of human lives. The explicitly defined prohibition of State interference with these rights evinces an implicit recognition that to some degree these interests are protectible against private persons as well. Thus there is a cognizable private interest in begetting and raising children and, indeed, in the termination of a pregnancy. It is, I submit, equally true that such an interest exists in the father with respect to the completion in birth of an existing pregnancy.

The existence of this interest is further evidenced by long lived and undisputed rights which the common law has recognized. The presumptive common law rule, in the absence of statute or court decree, is that custody of children is in the father. . . . While more enlightened times have raised the position of the mother to equality in matters of custody, this

has not been at the expense of the father-child relationship. The rights of the father may not be extinguished when the mother and a second husband seek adoption without the father's consent. . . . The law thus clearly recognizes what nature has made inevitable: the universal bond of affection and devotion between father and child.

Furthermore, it would be absurd to posit that this interest springs into existence full grown on the day of birth. As in the case of the mother, the period of gestation is for the father one of anxiety, anticipation, and growth in feeling for the unborn child. . . . The modern trend is for fathers to take a more active role in the pregnancy and, indeed, to participate during the mother's labor and delivery of the child. . . . The law has not been insensitive to the undeniable interest of parents in their children even prior to their birth. Thus over a period of years the law has recognized remedies for injuries to unborn children in tort and under the wrongful death statute. . . . Perhaps the most obvious legal recognition of the fact that the parental interest in children precedes birth is in the area of the distribution of estates. Thus a class gift to children by a testator is ordinarily construed to include posthumously born children since this is quite rightly deemed to be within the scope of the intended gift. . . . Moreover, under the theory of the pretermitted child statute, the law again quite properly deems a testator not to have omitted a bequest to any child including one yet unborn unless an intention to do so is clearly indicated. . . . In these areas and others the idea that a parent's interest in children preceded the birth is not a novelty to our law. Thus, not only as a matter of common sense and feeling but also as a natural extension of familiar legal principles, it would be only expected that, were no other rights involved, a court of equity would protect a father's interest by prohibiting the destruction of a fetus in utero.

. . . Neither the interest of the father in bringing the pregnancy to term nor that of the mother in terminating the pregnancy has been declared to be absolute and to cancel the other. The balance of these two rights, each of such a sensitive and personal nature, is, as I see it, the real task confronting the court. The factors which might bear on this decision and the weight to which they should be accorded are matters which would be peculiarly suited for legislative determination as indicated by the statutes from other States cited in the majority opinion. In the absence of such guidelines, however, I believe it is the duty of the court to deal with the question on the facts before it as best it can. The interests of the mother in this case were certainly significant but they were in large measure temporary. The husband stood ready to assume at birth the responsibility for the care and raising of his child. He furthermore was willing to defray all the medical expenses of the pregnancy and the delivery. The wife's association with and responsibility for the child could have ended at birth. There was medical testimony that no unusual medical risks or complications were to be anticipated. I do not for a moment wish to minimize the very serious burden which would be imposed on the wife. The physical discomfort and inevitable risks to health in carrying the pregnancy to term are significant. There is also the distinct possibility of psychological damage lingering even after the birth. But a major part of the interest of the pregnant wife must be the continuing responsibility for the welfare of the child. . . . That part of the interest, at least, is not present in this case. On the other hand the injury to the husband in terminating the pregnancy is unmistakably palpably permanent. There is no speculation, no question, that the husband will never experience the satisfaction, the comfort, the affection, or the sense of fulfilment which might have been provided him by the birth and growing up of the child whose life he petitioned this court to assure. On this record I believe the balance of perceptible interests falls in favor of the potential father. I would have granted the injunction prayed for.

Surrogate Motherhood

Advances in reproductive technology have generated a vast array of means to have children beyond natural sexual intercourse. Doctors have been using, for some time, artificial means to impregnate women. Among the more contentious practices involving artificial insemination is surrogate motherhood. When a woman is incapable of having children, the couple can turn to a "surrogate" who will be inseminated with the husband's sperm and bear the child for them. In some cases, referred to as "gestational surrogacy," the wife's egg is fertilized with her husband's sperm and then implanted in a surrogate's uterus. Here the child is the biological offspring of the father and his spouse, but not of the woman who carries and gives birth to the child.

Often, but not always, there is a commercial surrogate contract entered into. The surrogate is paid a fee, typically around $10,000, for carrying the baby to term. Problems arise when one or both parties seek to void the contract. In some cases the surrogate mother "bonds" with the baby and wishes to keep the child. In others the couple paying the surrogate refuse to accept the child; prob-

lems such as these arise when the child is in some way deformed or when the couple break up or simply decide they do not wish to have the child. There has even been a case in which twins were conceived, and the contracting couple wished to accept only one of the children. Questions arise here as to who deserves custody of the child and who is responsible for the child's welfare.

Surrogacy raises serious moral concerns even without a desire to void the contract. Feminists argue that surrogacy exploits poor women and women of color, who through indigency lease their bodies to wealthy couples. It is often pointed out, however, that feminists advocate the woman's total control over her reproductive system in abortion areas and hence are committed to allowing the choice here.

Another area of concern involves prenatal care and abortion. Does a woman in this situation surrender all of her privacy rights in this contract? The extent of control that the biological parent has over the surrogate raises serious questions about the woman's physical privacy.

6. Selling Babies and Selling Bodies

Sara Ann Ketchum

Sara Ann Ketchum argues that a free market in the production of babies, or in the use of women's bodies for that purpose, violates Kantian principles of personhood. Furthermore, Ketchum contends that surrogacy is contrary to the feminist principle that men do not have the right to the reproductive use of women's bodies.

The "Baby M" case has turned into something approaching a national soap opera, played out in newspapers and magazines. The drama surrounding the case tends to obscure the fact that the case raises some very abstract philosophical and moral issues. It forces us to examine questions about the nature and meaning of

From *Hypatia*, Vol. 4, no. 3 (Fall 1989). © by Sara Ann Ketchum.

parenthood, of the limits of reproductive autonomy, of how the facts of pregnancy should affect our analysis of sexual equality,[1] and of what counts as selling people and of what forms (if any) of selling people we should honor in law and what forms we should restrict. It is this last set of questions whose relevance I will be discussing here. One objection to what is usually called "surrogate motherhood" and which I will call "contracted motherhood" (CM) or "baby contracts"[2] is that it commercializes reproduction and turns human beings (the mother and/or the baby) into objects of sale. If this is a compelling objection, there is a good argument for prohibiting (and/or not enforcing contracts for) commercial CM. Such a prohibition would be similar to laws on black market adoptions and would have two parts, at least: 1) a prohibition of commercial companies who make the arrangements and/or 2) a prohibition on the transfer of money to the birth mother for the transfer of custody (beyond expenses incurred) (Warnock 1985, 46–7). I will also argue that CM law should follow adoption law in making clear that pre-birth agreements to relinquish parental rights are not binding and will not be enforced by the courts (the birth mother should not be forced to give up her child for adoption).[3]

CM and AID: The Real Difference Problem

CM is usually presented as a new reproductive technology and, moreover, as the female equivalent of AID (artificial insemination by donor) and, therefore, as an extension of the right to privacy or the right to make medical decisions about one's own life. There are two problems with this description: 1) CM uses the same technology as AID—the biological arrangements are exactly the same—but intends an opposite assignment of custody. 2) No technology is necessary for CM as is evidenced by the biblical story of Abraham and Sarah who used a "handmaid" as a birth mother. Since artificial insemination is virtually uncontroversial[4] it seems clear that what makes CM controversial is not the technology, but the social arrangements—that is, the custody assignment. CM has been defended on the ground that such arrangements enable fertile men who are married to infertile women to reproduce and, thus, are parallel to AID which enables fertile women whose husbands are infertile to have children. It is difficult not to regard these arguments as some-

what disingenuous. The role of the sperm donor and the role of the egg donor/mother are distinguished by pregnancy, and pregnancy is, if anything is, a "real difference" which would justify us in treating women and men differently. To treat donating sperm as equivalent to biological motherhood would be as unfair as treating the unwed father who has not contributed to his children's welfare the same as the father who has devoted his time to taking care of them. At most, donating sperm is comparable to donating ova; however, even that comparison fails because donating ova is a medically risky procedure, donating sperm is not.

Therefore, the essential morally controversial features of CM have to do with its nature as a social and economic institution and its assignment of family relationships rather than with any technological features. Moreover, the institution of CM requires of contracting birth mothers much more time commitment, medical risk, and social disruption than AID does of sperm donors. It also requires substantial male control over women's bodies and time, while AID neither requires nor provides any female control over men's bodies. Christine Overall (1987, 181–185) notes that when a woman seeks AID, she not only does not usually have a choice of donor, but she also may be required to get her husband's consent if she is married. The position of the man seeking CM is the opposite; he chooses a birth mother and his wife does not have to consent to the procedure (although the mother's husband does).[5] The contract entered into by Mary Beth Whitehead and William Stern contains a number of provisions regulating her behavior, including: extensive medical examinations, an agreement about when she may or may not abort, an agreement to follow doctors' orders, and agreements not to take even prescription drugs without the doctor's permission. Some of these social and contractual provisions are eliminable. But the fact that CM requires a contract and AID does not reflects the differences between pregnancy and ejaculation. If the sperm donor wants a healthy child (a good product), he needs to control the woman's behavior. In contrast, any damage the sperm-donor's behavior will have on the child will be present in the sperm and could, in principle, be tested for before the woman enters the AID procedure. There is no serious moral problem with discarding defective sperm; discarding defective children is a quite different matter.

Commodification

There are three general categories of moral concern with commercializing either adoption (baby selling) or reproductive activities. The three kinds of argument are not always separated and they are not entirely separable:

(1) There is the Kantian argument, based on a version of the Second Formulation of the Categorical Imperative. On this argument, selling people is objectionable because it is treating them as means rather than as ends, as objects rather than as persons. People who can be bought and sold are being treated as being of less moral significance than are those who buy and sell. Allowing babies to be bought and sold adds an extra legal wedge between the status of children and that of adults, and allowing women's bodies to be bought and sold (or "rented" if you prefer) adds to the inequality between men and women. Moreover, making babies and women's bodies available for sale raises specters of the rich "harvesting" the babies of the poor. (2) Consequentialist objections are fueled by concern for what may happen to the children and women who are bought and sold, to their families, and to the society as a whole if we allow an area of this magnitude and traditional intimacy to become commercialized. (3) Connected to both 1 and 2, are concerns about protecting the birth mother and the mother-child relationship from the potential coerciveness of commercial transactions. These arguments apply slightly differently depending on whether we analyze the contracts as baby contracts (selling babies) or as mother contracts (as a sale of women's bodies), although many of the arguments will be very similar for both.

Selling Babies

The most straightforward argument for prohibiting baby-selling is that it is selling a hu-

man being and that any selling of a human being should be prohibited because it devalues human life and human individuals. This argument gains moral force from its analogy with slavery. Defenders of baby contracts argue that baby-selling is unlike selling slaves in that it is a transfer of parental rights rather than of ownership of the child—the adoptive parents cannot turn around and sell the baby to another couple for a profit (Landes and Posner 1978, 344). What the defenders of CM fail to do is provide an account of the wrongness of slavery such that baby-selling (or baby contracts) do not fall under the argument. Landes and Posner, in particular, would, I think, have difficulty establishing an argument against slavery because they are relying on utilitarian arguments. Since one of the classic difficulties with utilitarianism is that it cannot yield an argument that slavery is wrong in principle, it is hardly surprising that utilitarians will find it difficult to discover within that theory an argument against selling babies. Moreover, their economic argument is not even utilitarian because it only counts people's interest to the extent that they can pay for them.

Those who, unlike Landes and Posner, defend CM while supporting laws against baby-selling, distinguish CM from paid adoptions in that in CM the person to whom custody is being transferred is the biological (genetic) father. This suggests a parallel to custody disputes, which are not obviously any more appropriately ruled by money than is adoption. We could argue against the commercialization of either on the grounds that child-regarding concerns should decide child custody and that using market criteria or contract considerations would violate that principle by substituting another, unrelated, and possibly conflicting, one. In particular, both market and contract are about relations between the adults involved rather than about the children or about the relationship between the child and the adult.

Another disanalogy cited between preadoption contracts and CM is that, in preadoption contracts the baby is already there (that is, the preadoption contract is offered to a woman who is already pregnant, and, presumably, planning to have the child), while the mother contract is a contract to create a child who does not yet exist, even as an embryo. If our concern is the commodification of children, this strikes me as an odd point for the *defenders* of CM to emphasize. Producing a child to order for money is a paradigm case of commodifying children. The fact that the child is not being put up for sale to the highest bidder, but is only for sale to the genetic father, may reduce some of the harmful effects of an open market in babies but does not quiet concerns about personhood.

Arguments for allowing CM are remarkably similar to the arguments for legalizing black-market adoptions in the way they both define the problem. CM, like a market for babies, is seen as increasing the satisfaction and freedom of infertile individuals or couples by increasing the quantity of the desired product (there will be more babies available for adoption) and the quality of the product (not only more white healthy babies, but white healthy babies who are genetically related to one of the purchasers). These arguments tend to be based on the interests of infertile couples and obscure the relevance of the interests of the birth mothers (who will be giving the children up for adoption) and their families, the children who are produced by the demands of the market, and (the most invisible and most troubling group) needy children who are without homes because they are not "high-quality" products and because we are not, as a society, investing the time and money needed to place the hard to adopt children. If we bring these hidden interests to the fore, they raise a host of issues about consequences—both utilitarian issues and issues about the distribution of harms and benefits.

Perhaps the strongest deontological argument against baby-selling is an objection to the characterization of the mother-child relationship (and, more generally, of the adult-child relationship) that it presupposes. Not only does the baby become an object of commerce, but the custody relationship of the parent becomes a property relationship. If we see parental custody rights as correlates of parental responsibility or as a right to maintain a relationship, it will be less tempting to think of them as something one can sell. We have good reasons for allowing birth mothers to relinquish their children because otherwise we

would be forcing children into the care of people who either do not want them or feel themselves unable to care for them. However, the fact that custody may be waived in this way does not entail that it may be sold or transferred. If children are not property, they cannot be gifts either. If a mother's right is a right to maintain a relationship (see Ketchum 1987), it is implausible to treat it as transferrable; having the option of terminating a relationship with A does not entail having the option of deciding who A will relate to next—the right to a divorce does not entail the right to transfer one's connection to one's spouse to someone else. Indeed, normally, the termination of a relationship with A ends any right I have to make moral claims on A's relationships. Although in giving up responsibilities I may have a responsibility to see to it that someone will shoulder them when I go, I do not have a right to choose that person.

Selling Women's Bodies

Suppose we do regard mother contracts as contracts for the sale or rental of reproductive capacities. Is there good reason for including reproductive capacities among those things or activities that ought not to be bought and sold? We might distinguish between selling reproductive capacities and selling work on a number of grounds. A conservative might argue against commercializing reproduction on the grounds that it disturbs family relationships,[6] or on the grounds that there are some categories of human activities that should not be for sale. A Kantian might argue that there are some activities that are close to our personhood[7] and that a commercial traffic in these activities constitutes treating the person as less than an end (or less than a person).

One interpretation of the laws prohibiting baby-selling is that they are an attempt to reduce or eliminate coercion in the adoption process, and are thus based on a concern for the birth mother rather than (or as well as) the child. All commercial transactions are at least potentially coercive in that the parties to them are likely to come from unequal bargaining positions and in that, whatever we have a market in, there will be some people who will be in a position such that they have to sell it in order to survive. Such concerns are important to arguments against an open market in human organs or in the sexual use of people's bodies as well as arguments against baby contracts of either kind.

As Margaret Radin suggests (1987, 1915–1921), the weakness of arguments of this sort—that relationships or contracts are exploitative on the grounds that people are forced into them by poverty—is that the real problem is not in the possibility of commercial transactions, but in the situation that makes these arrangements attractive by comparison. We do not end the feminization of poverty by forbidding prostitution or CM. Indeed, if we are successful in eliminating these practices, we may be reducing the income of some women (by removing ways of making money) and, if we are unsuccessful, we are removing these people from state protection by making their activities illegal. Labor legislation which is comparably motivated by concern for unequal bargaining position (such as, for example, minimum wage and maximum hours laws, and health and safety regulations) regulates rather than prevents that activity and is thus less vulnerable to this charge. Radin's criticism shows that the argument from the coerciveness of poverty is insufficient as a support for laws rejecting commercial transactions in personal services. This does not show that the concern is irrelevant. The argument from coercion is still an appropriate response to simple voluntarist arguments—those that assume that these activities are purely and freely chosen by all those who participate in them. Given the coerciveness of the situation, we cannot assume that the presumed or formal voluntariness of the contract makes it nonexploitative.

If the relationship of CM is, by its nature, disrespectful of personhood, it can be exploitative despite short-term financial benefits to some women. The disrepect for women as persons that is fundamental to the relationship lies in the concept of the woman's body (and of the child and mother-child relationship) implicit in the contract. I have argued elsewhere (1984), that claiming a welfare right to another person's body is to treat that person as an object:

An identity or intimate relation between persons and their bodies may or may not be essential to our metaphysical understanding of a person, but it is essential to a minimal moral conceptual scheme. Without a concession to persons' legitimate interests and concerns for their physical selves, most of our standard and paradigm moral rules would not make sense; murder might become the mere destruction of the body; assault, a mere interference with the body . . . and so on. We cannot make sense out of the concept of assault unless an assault on S's body is ipso facto an assault on S. By the same token, treating another person's body as part of my domain—as among the things that I have a rightful claim to—is, if anything is, a denial that there is a person there. (1984, 34–35)

This argument is, in turn, built on the analysis of the wrongness of rape developed by Marilyn Frye and Carolyn Shafer in "Rape and Respect" (1977):

The use of a person in the advancement of interests contrary to its own is a limiting case of disrespect. It reveals the perception of the person simply as an object which can serve some purpose, a tool or a bit of material, and one which furthermore is dispensable or replaceable and thus of little value even as an object with a function. (341)

We can extend this argument to the sale of persons. To make a person or a person's body an object of commerce is to treat the person as part of another person's domain, particularly if the sale of A to B gives rights to A or to A's body. What is objectionable is a claim—whether based on welfare or on contract—to a right to another person such that that person is part of my domain. The assertion of such a right is morally objectionable even without the use of force. For example, a man who claims to have a *right* to sexual intercourse with his wife, on the grounds of the marriage relationship, betrays a conception of her body, and thus her person, as being properly within his domain, and thus a conception of her as an object rather than a person.

Susan Brownmiller, in *Against Our Will* (1975) suggests that prostitution is connected to rape in that prostitution makes women's bodies into consumer goods that might—if not justifiably, at least understandably—be forcibly taken by those men who see themselves as unjustly deprived.

> When young men learn that females may be bought for a price, and that acts of sex command set prices, then how should they not also conclude that that which may be bought may also be taken without the civility of a monetary exchange? . . . legalized prostitution institutionalizes the concept that it is a man's monetary right, if not his divine right, to gain access to the female body, and that sex is a female service that should not be denied the civilized male. (391, 392)

The same can be said for legalized sale of women's reproductive services. The more hegemonic this commodification of women's bodies is, the more the woman's lack of consent to sex or to having children can present itself as unfair to the man because it is arbitrary.

A market in women's bodies—whether sexual prostitution or reproductive prostitution—reveals a social ontology in which women are among the things in the world that can be appropriately commodified—bought and sold and, by extension, stolen. The purported freedom that such institutions would give women to enter into the market by selling their bodies is paradoxical. Sexual or reproductive prostitutes enter the market not so much as *agents* or subjects, but as commodities or objects. This is evidenced by the fact that the pimps and their counterparts, the arrangers of baby contracts, make the bulk of the profits. Moreover, once there is a market for women's bodies, all women's bodies will have a price, and the woman who does not sell her body becomes a hoarder of something that is useful to other people and is financially available. The market is a hegemonic institution; it determines the meanings of actions of people who choose not to participate as well as of those who choose to participate.

Contract

The immediate objection to treating the Baby M case as a contract dispute is that the practical problem facing the court is a child custody problem and to treat it as a contract case is to deal with it on grounds other than the best interests of the child. That the best interests of the child count need not entail that contract does not count, although it helps explain one of the reasons we should be suspicious of this particular contract. There is still the question of whether the best interests of the child will trump contract considerations (making the contract nonbinding) or merely enter into a balancing argument in which contract is one of the issues to be balanced. However, allowing contract to count at all raises some of the same Kantian objections as the commodification problem. As a legal issue, the contract problem is more acute because the state action (enforcing the contract) is more explicit.

Any binding mother contract will put the state in the position of enforcing the rights of a man to a woman's body or to his genetic offspring. But this is to treat the child or the mother's body as objects of the sperm donor's rights, which, I argued above, is inconsistent with treating them as persons. This will be clearest if the courts enforce specific performance[8] and require the mother to go through with the pregnancy (or to abort) if she chooses not to or requires the transfer of custody to the contracting sperm donor on grounds other than the best interests of the child. In those cases, I find it hard to avoid the description that what is being awarded is a person and what is being affirmed is a right to a person. I think the Kantian argument still applies if the court refuses specific performance but awards damages. Damages compensate for the loss of something to which one has a right. A judge who awards damages to the contracting sperm donor for having been deprived of use of the contracting woman's reproductive capacities or for being deprived of custody of the child gives legal weight to the idea that the contracting sperm donor had a legally enforceable *right* to them (or, to put it more bluntly, to those commodities or goods).

The free contract argument assumes that Mary Beth Whitehead's claim to her daughter are rights (rather than, for example, obligations or a more complex relationship), and, moreover, that they are alienable, as are property rights. If the baby is not something she has an alienable right to, then custody of the baby is not something she can transfer by contract. In cases where the state is taking children away from their biological parents and in custody disputes, we do want to appeal to some rights of the parents. However, I think it would be unfortunate to regard these rights as rights to the child, because that would be to treat the child as the object of the parents' rights and violate the principles that persons and persons' bodies cannot be the objects of other people's rights. The parents' rights in these cases should be to consideration, to nonarbitrariness and to respect for the relationship between the parent and the child.

Concluding Remarks

The Kantian, person-respecting arguments I have been offering do not provide an account of all of the moral issues surrounding CM. However, I think that they can serve as a counter-balance to arguments (also Kantian) for CM as an expression of personal autonomy.[9] They might also add some weight to the empirical arguments against CM that are accumulating. There is increasing concern that women cannot predict in advance whether or not they and their family[10] will form an attachment to the child they will bear nor can they promise not to develop such feelings (as some of the contracts ask them to do). There is also increasing concern for the birth-family and for the children produced by the arrangement (particularly where there is a custody dispute). A utilitarian might respond that the problems are outweighed by the joys of the adopting/sperm-donor families, but, if so, we must ask: are we simply shifting the

misery from wealthy (or wealthier) infertile couples to poorer fertile families and to the "imperfect" children waiting for adoption?

These considerations provide good reason for prohibiting commercialization of CM. In order to do that we could adopt new laws prohibiting the transfer of money in such arrangements or simply extend existing adoption laws, making the contracts non-binding as are pre-birth adoption contracts (Cohen 1984, 280–284) and limiting the money that can be transferred. There are some conceptual problems remaining about what would count as prohibiting commodification. I find the English approach very attractive. This approach has the following elements: 1) it strictly prohibits third parties from arranging mother contracts; 2) if people arrange them privately, they are allowed; 3) the contracts are not binding. If the birth-mother decides to keep the baby, her decision is final[11] (*and* the father may be required to pay child-support; that may be too much for Americans). 4) Although, in theory, CM is covered by limitations on money for adoption, courts have approved payments for contracted motherhood, and there is never criminal penalty on the parents for money payments.[12]

Notes

1. In "Is There a Right to Procreate?" (1987a), I argue that there is an asymmetry between the right not to reproduce (as in the right to access to abortion and contraception) and the right to reproduce in that a decision to reproduce (unlike a decision not to reproduce) involves two other persons—the person who is to be produced and the person who is the other biological parent. Thus, the claim of a privacy right to reproduce is a claim to a right to make decisions about other people's lives, and those people's rights and interests must be weighed in the balance. Furthermore, I will argue (and this paper is part of that argument) that issues of reproductive privacy cannot be entirely separated from issues of sexual equality.

2. Terms such as "surrogate mother" and "rent-

ing a womb" are distortions—the surrogate mother *is* the mother, and she is giving up her child for adoption just as is the birth mother who gives up her child for adoption by an unrelated person. This language allows the defenders of paternal rights to argue for the importance of biological (genetic) connection when it comes to the *father's* rights, but bury the greater physical connection between the mother and the child in talk that suggests that mothers are mere receptacles (shades of Aristotle's biology) or that the mother has a more artificial relationship to the child than does the father or the potential adoptive mother. But, at the time of birth, the natural relationship is between the mother and child. [I discuss this issue further in "New Reproductive Technologies and the Definition of Parenthood: A Feminist Perspective" (1987).] A relationship created by contract is the paradigm of artificiality, of socially created relationship, and the most plausible candidate for a natural social relationship is the mother-child bond. I will be using "contracted motherhood" and "baby contracts" (a term offered by Elizabeth Bartholet) rather than "surrogate motherhood" and "surrogacy." I will use "baby contracts" as the more general term, covering paid adoption contracts as well as so called "surrogate mother" arrangements. I have not yet found a term that is either neutral between or inclusive of the motherhood aspects and the baby-regarding aspects.

3. She may still lose a custody fight, since the male of the adopting couple is the genetic father of the child, but in that case, she would still be the legal mother of the child and have a right to maintain a relationship.

4. I do not mean to suggest that there are no moral problems with AID. See Krimmel (1983) for an approach that presents arguments against both.

5. Indeed, there is a technical reason for her not to sign the contract. The wife of the sperm donor in CM intends to adopt the resulting child. If she is a party to the contract, it would be more difficult to avoid the conclusion that the arrangement exchanges money for adoption and is thus contrary to baby-selling laws.

6. Robert C. Black (1981) argues, in response to an argument of this sort, that: "In any realistic view of the situation, the only true 'family' whose future is at stake is the one the child is pre-destined to enter—that of the childless married couple—not the *nominal, intentionally temporary 'family'* represented by the surrogate mother" (382, emphasis added). Surely, this is a disingenuous response. Mary Beth Whitehead's family is just as much a family as the Sterns' (and it is larger); even if we are to ignore her, we must consider the interests of her children (what effect does it have on them that their half-sister is being sold to another family?) and her husband and the integrity of the family unit. Some surrogates report problems their children have with the arrangement in, "Baby M: Surrogate Mothers Vent Feelings," by Iver Peterson (1987).

7. This is the position that Margaret Radin (1987) develops and relies on in "Market-Inalienability." "Market-inalienability ultimately rests on our best conception of human flourishing . . ." (1937). Radin's article provides a very thorough discussion of and argument for prohibiting commodification of personal services.

8. M. Louise Graham (1982) argues that traditional contract doctrine and precedent would prohibit requiring specific performance against the birth mother: "The rule that a contract for distinctly personal, nondelegable services will not be enforced by specific performance is nearly universal. The reasons given for the refusal to enforce are the difficulty of gauging the quality of any performance rendered, prejudice against a species of involuntary servitude, and a reluctance to force a continued relationship between antagonistic parties." (301)

9. See, for example, Joan Hollinger (1985, 865–932) for a well developed analysis of new reproductive technology issues as pure (or almost pure) autonomy issues.

10. One former surrogate reports that her daughter (11 at the time of the birth and now 17) is still having problems: "Nobody told me that a child could bond with a baby while you're still pregnant. I didn't realize then that all the times she listened to his heartbeat and felt his legs kick that she was becoming attached to him." Another quotes her son as having asked, "You're not going to give them me, are you?" (Peterson 1987, B1).

11. This presupposes a presumption in favor of the birth mother as custodial or deciding parent. I have argued for that position on the grounds that, at the time of birth, the gestational mother

has a concrete relationship to the child that the genetic father (and the genetic mother, if she is not the gestational mother) does not have. Without that presumption and without a presumption of sale or contract, each case would be subject to long custody disputes.

12. This, I think, helps us get around Radin's double-bind problem (1987, 1915–1921).

References

Black, Robert. 1981. Legal problems of surrogate motherhood. *New England Law Review* 16 (3): 380–392.

Brownmiller, Susan. 1975. *Against our will: Men, women, and rape.* New York: Simon and Schuster.

Cohen, Barbara. 1984. Surrogate mothers: Whose baby is it? *American Journal of Law and Medicine* 10: 243–285.

Frye, Marilyn and Carolyn Shafer. 1977. Rape and respect. In *Feminism and philosophy.* Mary Vetterling-Braggin, Frederick A. Elliston and Jane English, eds. Totowa, N.J.: Littlefield, Adams and Co.

Graham, M. Louise. 1982. Surrogate gestation and the protection of choice. *Santa Clara Law Review* 22: 291–323.

Hollinger, Joan Heifetz. 1985. From coitus to commerce: Legal and social consequences of noncoital reproduction. *Michigan Journal of Law Reform* 18: 865–932.

Ketchum, Sara Ann. 1987. New reproductive technologies and the definition of parenthood: A feminist perspective. Presented at Feminism and legal theory: Women and intimacy, a conference sponsored by the Institute for Legal Studies at the University of Wisconsin-Madison.

Ketchum, Sara Ann. 1987a. Is there a right to procreate? Presented at the Pacific Division Meetings of the American Philosophical Association.

Ketchum, Sara Ann. 1984. The moral status of the bodies of persons. *Social Theory and Practice* 10: 25–38.

Krimmel, Herbert. 1983. The case against surrogate parenting. *Hastings Center Report* 13 (5): 35–39.

Landes, Elizabeth A. and Richard M. Posner. 1978. The economics of the baby shortage. *Journal of Legal Studies* 7.

Overall, Christine. 1987. *Ethics and human reproduction.* Boston: Allen & Unwin.

Peterson, Iver. 1987. Baby M: Surrogate mothers vent feelings. *New York Times,* March 2, 1987: B1 and B4.

Radin, Margaret. 1987. Market-Inalienability. *Harvard Law Review* 100: 1849–1937.

Warnock, Mary. 1985. *A question of life: The Warnock report on human fertilization and embryology.* Oxford: Basil Blackwell.

7.   Commodification or Compensation: A Reply to Ketchum

H. M. Malm

Professor Malm, responding to Sara Ann Ketchum's claim that paid surrogacy is unacceptable because it treats persons as objects, points out that these arrangements provide compensation for the woman's services. Malm also rejects the ideas that paid surrogacy involves exploitation or violates custodial rights.

The practice of surrogate motherhood raises at least three sorts of moral questions.[1] First, there are questions about the nature of sur-

From *Hypatia,* Vol. 4, no. 3 (Fall 1989). © by H. M. Malm.

rogate motherhood itself. Is there something inherently wrong, for example, with intentionally becoming pregnant when one does not intend to raise the child? Second, there are questions about the status of the arrangements when they involve a transfer of money. Is it morally wrong for one person to offer, and another person to accept, payment for being a surrogate mother? What is being purchased? Third, there are questions about the legal status of the arrangements. Should they be regarded as binding contracts?

Sara Ketchum (1988) addresses questions of the second sort in "Selling Babies and Selling Bodies." She argues for a ban on paid surrogacy arrangements by arguing that persons are not the sort of thing that may be bought, sold, or rented. In one sense Ketchum's arguments are successful. She has shown us, or perhaps reminded us of *why* it is wrong to treat persons as objects of sale. In another sense they are unsuccessful. For while she intends her arguments to provide grounds for prohibiting paid surrogacy arrangements, she has not argued that these arrangements *do in fact* treat persons as objects of sale. That is, while she has defended premise 1 in the following argument, she has not defended premise 2.

1. It is morally wrong to treat persons, including babies, as objects of sale.
2. Paid surrogate motherhood arrangements treat persons as objects of sale.
3. Therefore, paid surrogacy arrangements are morally objectionable.

The failure to defend premise 2 is not simply a failure to defend the obvious. Though it is possible that the payments made in paid surrogacy arrangements are payments for the baby, or for the use of the woman's body, it is also possible that they are not. They may be payments for the woman's services—compensation, that is, for the efforts and risks of bearing a child, e.g., not drinking coffee or alcohol for nine months, not engaging in enjoyable but potentially dangerous activities, for the risks involved in giving birth, and for the effort it may take to return her body to the condition it was in prior to pregnancy.

In this essay I develop the distinction between compensating a woman for her services, and paying a woman for the use of her body, and then evaluate some of Ketchum's arguments in its light. I argue that since this dis-

tinction allows us to reject premise 2, we cannot prohibit paid surrogacy arrangements on the grounds that they treat persons as objects of sale. I then discuss some of Ketchum's arguments that can be offered against the compensation-view of the payments. I argue that they too provide inadequate grounds for prohibiting the arrangements.[2]

I

Ketchum's acceptance of premise 2 can be seen in the structure of her paper and in some of its particular passages. After introducing the topic of paid surrogacy arrangements, she distinguishes three sorts of arguments that may be raised against the commodification of persons.

> 1) There is the Kantian argument . . . [that] selling people is objectionable because it is treating them as means rather than ends, as objects rather than persons. . . . 2) Consequentialist objections are fueled by concern for what may happen to the *children and women who are bought and sold*. . . . 3) Connected to both 1 and 2, there are concerns about protecting the birth mother and the mother-child relationship from the potential coerciveness of commercial transactions. These arguments apply slightly differently *depending on whether we analyze the contracts as baby contracts (selling babies) or as mother contracts (as the sale of women's bodies)* although many of the arguments will apply to both. (emphasis added) (Ketchum 1989, 118)

She then offers a number of particular arguments explaining why it is wrong to treat persons as objects of sale, and concludes by claiming "these considerations provide good reason for prohibiting commercialization of [surrogate] motherhood" (Ketchum 1989, 124). But absent from Ketchum's discussion is an argument that *connects* paid surrogacy arrangements *with* the commodification of persons. Without this argument, even the most forceful arguments about the wrongness of selling people cannot do the work she wants them to do.

The question before us may be stated as follows: Are we committed to viewing the payments made in paid surrogacy arrangements as payments for either the baby itself or for the use of the woman's body? To see that we are not, it will be helpful if we first grant, as Ketchum does, that the payments made are not necessarily for the baby itself, and then examine what Ketchum finds wrong with paying a woman for the use of her body. In the section titled "Selling Bodies," Ketchum writes:

> The disrespect for women as persons that is fundamental to the [surrogacy] relationship lies in the concept of the woman's body implicit in the contract. I have argued elsewhere, in the context of abortion laws, that claiming a welfare right to another person's body is to treat that person as an object. . . .[T]reating another person's body as a part of my domain—as among the things that I have a rightful claim to—is, if anything is, a denial that there is a person there. . . .
> We can extend this argument to the sale of persons. To make a person or a person's body an object of commerce is to treat the person as part of another person's domain, particularly if the sale of A to B gives B rights to A or to A's body. . . .(Ketchum 1989, 121–122)

Ketchum seems to be assuming that if I pay you to bear a child for me, then I acquire a right to your body, treat you as an object of my domain, and (or) deny that you are a person. But this assumption is flawed. It fails to take into account the difference between (a) my paying you for *me* to use your body in a way that benefits me, and (b) my paying you for *you* to use your body in a way that benefits me. The difference between these two is important because it determines whether my payments to you give me a right to your body, and thus whether they treat your body as an object of commerce and you as less than a person. To illustrate it, suppose that you own a lawnmower. (I do not mean to suggest that women's bodies are on a par with machines.) If I need to have my lawn mowed then I may (a) pay you for *me* to use your lawnmower to mow my lawn, in which case I *rent* your lawnmower from you, or (b) pay you for *you* to use your lawnmower to mow my lawn, in which case I pay you for your *services*. In the former case I acquire a right to your lawnmower—the right to use it for a limited period of time. In the latter case I do not. Any right I have here is at most a right to insist that you do with your lawnmower what you said you would. But that is not a right to your lawnmower.

When we apply this distinction to the issue of surrogate motherhood we see that there is no need to view the payments to the woman as payments for the use (i.e., rental) of her body—the customer does not acquire a space over which he (or she)[3] then has control. He may not paint it blue, keep a coin in it, or do whatever else he wishes provided that he does not cause permanent damage. Instead, the woman is being paid for *her* to use her body in a way that benefits him—she is being compensated for her services.[4] But this does not treat her body as an object of commerce, or her as less than a person, any more than does my paying a surgeon to perform an operation, a cabby to drive a car, or a model to pose for a statue. My payments to the surgeon do not give me a right to her arm, make her an object of my domain, nor deny that she is a person. Indeed, recognizing that persons can enter into agreements to use their own bodies in ways that benefit others *reaffirms* their status as persons—as agents—rather than denies it. Given this, we cannot prohibit paid surrogacy arrangements on the grounds that they involve the buying and selling or renting of babies and women's bodies.

II

Though Ketchum does not address the compensation-view of the payments, some of her arguments against paid surrogacy arrangements may seem to stand even given that view. In the section titled "Selling Babies" she writes:

Perhaps the strongest argument against baby selling is an objection to the characterization of the mother-child relationship that it presupposes. Not only does the baby become an object of commerce, but the custodial relationship of the parent becomes a property relationship. If we see parental custodial rights as correlates of parental responsibility or as a right to maintain a relationship, it will be less tempting to think of them as something one can sell. We have good reasons for allowing birth-mothers to relinquish their children because otherwise we would be forcing children into the care of people who either do not want them or feel themselves unable to care for them. However, that custody is waivable in this way does not entail that it is saleable or even transferrable. If children are not property they cannot be gifts either. (Ketchum 1989, 119–120)

As this passage suggests, one may object to paid surrogacy arrangements on the grounds that (a) since they require that custody of the child be *transferred* (by sale or gift) from one person to another, then (b) they require that we view the parent-child relationship as a property relationship. And that is morally objectionable.

Let us grant that the parent-child relationship is not a property relationship, as well as adopt Ketchum's suggestion that parental custodial rights be viewed as rights to maintain a relationship. The problem with the above argument is that there is nothing in the nature of surrogate motherhood arrangements that requires that custody be transferred rather than waived. In order for one parent to gain sole custody of a child, he or she need not acquire the other parent's parental custodial right, such that he or she would then have two parental custodial rights—two rights to maintain a relationship—when before he or she had only one. Instead, one parent may obtain sole custody of a child merely by the other parent's *waiving* his or her custodial right. The one would then have sole custody because he or she is then the only one *with* custody. But his or her right to maintain a relationship has not, somehow, doubled in size. (This is supported by the fact that a judge is not required

to find a parent with sole custody *twice* as unfit as a parent who shares custody, before she would be justified in removing a child from that parent's care. Indeed, we may think it should be just the reverse.)

Another way to object to paid surrogacy arrangements, given the compensation-view of the payments, is to argue that there is an important moral difference between compensating a woman for the efforts and risks of bearing a child, and compensating a woman for the efforts and risks of, say, mowing a lawn, posing for a drawing, or performing an operation. But making this argument requires that we can explain what that difference is, and the differences suggested by Ketchum seem to me to be inadequate. She writes:

> We might distinguish between selling reproductive capacities and selling work on a number of grounds. A conservative might argue against commercializing reproduction on the grounds that it disturbs family relationships, or on the grounds that there are some categories of human activities that should not be for sale. A Kantian might argue that there are some activities that are close to our personhood and that a commercial traffic in these activities constitutes treating the person as less than an end (or as less than a person). (Ketchum 1989, 120)

Ketchum's first suggestion, that paid surrogacy arrangements disturb family relationships (while typical forms of work do not?), won't draw an appropriate line because many forms of work run that risk. Laura Purdy (1989) points out that women risk their lives and health by building bridges, working on farms, and even for the postal service. Yet few of us would regard the disruption of the family that would be occasioned by the woman's death or serious illness, as legitimate grounds for prohibiting women (or mothers) from these jobs. Further, divorce, remarriage, and adoption all risk disruption of the family, yet we would not want to deny a woman these options simply because she is a mother.

The second suggestion, that "some categories of human activities should not be for sale," is also inadequate. In order to make use of it, we would have to know what these categories are or at least how to distinguish them from others. But Ketchum does not tell us. Her comment that "some activities are close to our personhood . . ." is likewise of little help. (It is not clear whether this is offered as a third suggestion or as way to clarify the second.) If, on the one hand, it refers to those activities that distinguish persons from other beings, then reproduction is certainly not one of them. On the other hand, if it refers to those activities that we *identify* with—those by which we conceive of ourselves—then it is a mistake to think that all women (or all women in their child-bearing years) conceive of themselves as essentially child-bearers. What we do with some parts of our lives need not define who we are; a woman who is paid to bear a child for another need not conceive of herself as essentially a child-bearer any more than a woman who is paid to teach a college course need conceive of herself as essentially a teacher.

Perhaps there are ways to mark an important moral difference between compensating a woman for the efforts and risks of bearing a child, and compensating her for the efforts and risks of typical (and unobjectionable) ways that she uses her body to benefit others. But Ketchum has not told us what they are. And without that information we cannot use the difference in a case against surrogate motherhood.

The last objection I will address focuses on coercion and exploitation. Ketchum writes:

All commercial transactions are at least potentially coercive in that the parties to them are likely to come from unequal bargaining positions and in that, whatever we have a market in, there will be some people who will be in a position such that they have to sell that in order to survive. Such concerns are important to arguments . . . against baby selling and surrogate contracts. (Ketchum 1989, 120)

It is true that offers to enter into paid surrogacy arrangements are *potentially* coercive. It is also true that by permitting these offers we increase the risk that poor women will be exploited. The question, however, is whether these risks provide adequate grounds for pro-

hibiting paid surrogacy arrangements. The following four points should help to show that they do not.[5]

First, as John Robertson (1983, 28) discusses, offers to be paid to bear a child for another are not "unjustly" coercive. They do not leave the recipient worse off than before the offer was made. (For contrast, consider the gunman's "Your money or your life" offer which does leave the recipient worse off.) Second, there is evidence that the opportunity to be paid for one's services in bearing a child has not been widely exploitive of poor women. Statistics indicate that the "average surrogate mother is white, attended two years of college, married young, and has all the children she and her husband want."[6] These are not the characteristics of the group we envision when we express concerns about protecting the poor from exploitation.

Third, though it is possible that the opportunity to be paid for one's services in bearing a child *will become* widely exploitive of poor women (as the arrangements increase in popularity), the same may be true of any opportunity to be paid for one's services. Yet we would not serve the interests of poor women in general if, in the efforts to protect them from exploitation, we prohibited them the means of escaping poverty. (Ketchum recognizes this point and cites Radin (1988, 1915) in its defense.)

Finally, the concern about exploitation and coercion seems to presuppose that the act of bearing a child for another is so detestable, so degrading, that few women would enter into the arrangements were they not forced to do so out of economic necessity. But the statistics mentioned above suggest that this is not the case. Further, some women enjoy being pregnant and may view their act as altruistic.[7] They are doing for another what that other cannot do for him or herself, and thereby allowing that other to know the joys (and pains) of raising an offspring. And if our aim is to protect those women who *do* view bearing a child for another as degrading, but nonetheless feel forced to do so out of economic necessity, then we can protect those women by putting restrictions on who can *enter into* paid surrogacy arrangements—we do not need to prohibit the arrangements entirely. One may object that such restrictions would be *unfair* because they would prohibit poor women from doing something that other women were allowed to do. But that seems to presuppose that the restrictions would be denying poor women a good, rather than protecting them from a harm, which, if true, would suggest that our initial concerns about coercion and exploitation were misguided.

Notes

1. Though I will continue to use the lay term "surrogate motherhood," it is a misleading name for the practice it identifies. In typical cases (i.e., those not involving embryo transfer) the woman bearing the child is both the genetic mother of the child and the birth mother. The only "mother" role she does not (intend to) fulfill is the social one. Were this enough to render her a surrogate mother then we should have to refer to women who relinquish their children for adoption, and to men who donate sperm to sperm banks, as "surrogate mothers" and "surrogate fathers." The term seems to be rooted in the oppressive notion that a woman's proper role in life is to be a child-bearer for a mate. Were that the case, then the woman being paid to bear a child could be viewed as a surrogate for another woman.

2. Some of the arguments I discuss are also discussed (and some in more detail) in my "Paid surrogacy: Arguments and responses" (1989). Also, it is worth noting that my arguments defend only the permissibility of the arrangements. Their legal enforcement is a separate issue.

3. Though I use the masculine pronoun when referring to a customer of surrogate motherhood arrangements, the customer need not be male. A woman with ova but no uterus may wish to have one of her ova fertilized, in vitro, with sperm from a sperm bank and then pay another woman to carry the conceptus to term. The possibility that a woman may be a customer of surrogate mother arrangements counsels against our objecting to these arrangements on the grounds that they treat women as "fungible baby-makers for men whose seed must be carried on" (Radin 1988, 1935). (Radin makes this objection within the context of our current gender ideologies.)

4. Laura Purdy (1989) raises the possibility that "lurking behind objections to surrogacy is some feeling that it is wrong to earn money by letting your body work, without active effort on your part. But this would rule out sperm selling as well as using women's beauty to sell products and services." Notice that on the compensation-view of the payments the woman is not being paid for something her body does. She is being compensated for the efforts she must make, and the risks she incurs, in the nine month process of bearing a child.

5. Purdy (1989) offers some different, and in many ways more detailed, responses to the argument from exploitation.

6. The statistics are from "Surrogate motherhood: A practice that's still undergoing birth pangs," *Los Angeles Times,* March 22, 1987. Radin (1988) cites them as well.

7. Radin rejects this point on the grounds that "even if surrogate mothering is subjectively experienced as altruism, the surrogate's self-conception as nurturer, caretaker, and service-giver might be viewed as a kind of gender-role oppression" (Radin 1988, 1930). I respond to this claim in "Paid surrogacy: Arguments and responses."

References

Ketchum, Sara. 1984. The moral status of the bodies of persons. *Social Theory and Practice* 10: 25–38.

Ketchum, Sara. 1989. Selling babies and selling bodies: Surrogate motherhood and the problem of commodification. *Hypatia* 4 (3): 116–127.

Malm, H. M. forthcoming. Paid surrogacy: Arguments and responses. *Public Affairs Quarterly* 3 (2): 57–66.

Purdy, Laura. 1989. Surrogate mothering: Exploitation or empowerment? *Bioethics* 3 (1): 18–34.

Radin, Margaret. Market inalienability. *Harvard Law Review* 100 (8): 1849–1937.

Robertson, John. 1983. Surrogate mothers: Not so novel after all. *Hastings Center Report* 13: 28–34.

8.   Surrogate Motherhood:
The Challenge for Feminists

Lori B. Andrews

After presenting an explanation of the legacy of feminism, Lori B. Andrews addresses the various arguments against surrogacy. Andrews looks at the arguments about symbolic harm to society, the harm to women, and the potential harm to potential children and suggests that feminists would be better off opposing all forms of governmental control.

Surrogate motherhood presents an enormous challenge for feminists. During the course of the *Baby M* trial, the New Jersey chapter of the National Organization of Women met and could not reach consensus on the issue. "The feelings ranged the gamut," the head of the chapter, Linda Bowker, told the *New York Times*. "We did feel that it should not be made illegal, because we don't want to turn women into criminals. But other than that, what you may feel about the Baby M case may not be what you feel about another.

"We do believe that women ought to control their own bodies, and we don't want to play big brother or big sister and tell them what to do," Ms. Bowker continued. "But on the other hand, we don't want to see the day when women are turned into breeding machines."[1]

Other feminist groups have likewise been split on the issue, but a vocal group of feminists came to the support of Mary Beth Whitehead with demonstrations[2] and an amicus brief[3]; they are now seeking laws that would ban surrogate motherhood altogether. However, the rationales that they and others are using to justify this governmental intrusion into reproductive choice may come back to haunt feminists in other areas of procreative policy and family law.

As science fiction has taught us, the types of technologies available shape the nature of a society. Equally important as the technologies—and having much farther-reaching

implications—are the policies that a society devises and implements to deal with technology. In Margaret Atwood's *A Handmaid's Tale*, a book often cited as showing the dangers of the technology of surrogacy, it was actually policy changes—the criminalization of abortion and the banning of women from the paid labor force—that created the preconditions for a dehumanizing and harmful version of surrogacy.

The Feminist Legacy

In the past two decades, feminist policy arguments have refashioned legal policies on reproduction and the family. A cornerstone of this development has been the idea that women have a right to reproductive choice—to be able to contracept, abort, or get pregnant. They have the right to control their bodies during pregnancy, such as by refusing Cesarean sections. They have a right to create non-traditional family structures such as lesbian households or single-parent families facilitated by artificial insemination by donor. According to feminist arguments, these rights should not be overridden by possible symbolic harms or speculative risks to potential children.

Another hallmark of feminism has been that biology should not be destiny. The equal treatment of the sexes requires that decisions about men and women be made on other than biological grounds. Women police officers can

From *Surrogate Motherhood: Politics and Privacy*, ed. Larry Gostin. Bloomington: Indiana University Press, 1990, pp. 167–182. Reprinted by permission.

be as good as men, despite their lesser strength on average. Women's larger role in bearing children does not mean they should have the larger responsibility in rearing children. And biological fathers, as well as nonbiological mothers or fathers, can be as good parents as biological mothers.

The legal doctrine upon which feminists have pinned much of their policy has been the constitutional protection of autonomy in decisions to bear and rear one's biological children.[4] Once this protection of the biologically related family was acknowledged, feminists and others could argue for the protection of non-traditional, non-biological families on the grounds that they provide many of the same emotional, physical, and financial benefits that biological families do.[5]

In many ways, the very existence of surrogacy is a predictable outgrowth of the feminist movement. Feminist gains allowed women to pursue educational and career opportunities once reserved for men, such as Betsy Stern's position as a doctor and medical school professor. But this also meant that more women were postponing childbearing, and suffering the natural decline in fertility that occurs with age. Women who exercised their right to contraception, such as by using the Dalkon Shield, sometimes found that their fertility was permanently compromised. Some women found that the chance for a child had slipped by them entirely and decided to turn to a surrogate mother.

Feminism also made it more likely for other women to feel comfortable being surrogates. Feminism taught that not all women relate to all pregnancies in the same way. A woman could choose not to be a rearing mother at all. She could choose to lead a child-free life by not getting pregnant. If she got pregnant, she could choose to abort. Reproduction was a condition of her body over which she, and no one else, should have control. For some women, those developments added up to the freedom to be a surrogate.

In the surrogacy context, feminist principles have provided the basis for a broadly held position that contracts and legislation should not restrict the surrogate's control over her body during pregnancy (such as by a requirement that the surrogate undergo amniocentesis or abort a fetus with a genetic defect). The argument against enforcing such contractual provisions resounds with the notion of gender equality, since it is in keeping with common law principles that protect the bodily integrity of both men and women, as well as with basic contract principles rejecting specific performance of personal-services provisions.[6] It is also in keeping with constitutional principles giving the pregant woman, rather than the male progenitor, the right to make abortion decisions. In this area, feminist lobbying tactics have met with considerable success. Although early bills on surrogacy contained provisions that would have constrained surrogates' behavior during pregnancy, most bills regulating surrogacy that have been proposed in recent years specifically state that the surrogate shall have control over medical decisions during the pregnancy.[7] Even the trial court decision in the Baby M case, which enforced the surrogacy contract's termination of parental rights, voided the section that took from the surrogate the right to abort.[8]

Now a growing feminist contingent is moving beyond the issue of bodily control during pregnancy and is seeking to ban surrogacy altogether. But the rationales for such a ban are often the very rationales that feminists have fought against in the contexts of abortion, contraception, non-traditional families, and employment. The adoption of these rationales as the reasons to regulate surrogacy could severely undercut the gains previously made in these other areas. These rationales fall into three general categories: the symbolic harm to society of allowing paid surrogacy, the potential risks to the women of allowing paid surrogacy, and the potential risks to the potential child of allowing paid surrogacy.

The Symbolic Harm to Society

For some feminists, the argument against surrogacy is a simple one: it demeans us all as a society to sell babies. And put that way, the argument is persuasive, at least on its face. But as a justification for policy, the argument is reminiscent of the argument that feminists roundly reject in the abortion context: that it demeans us as a society to kill babies.

Both arguments, equally heartfelt, need closer scrutiny if they are to serve as a basis for policy. In the abortion context, pro-choice people criticize the terms, saying we are not talking about "babies" when the abortion is done on an embryo or fetus still within the woman's womb. In the surrogacy context, a similar assault can be made on the term "sale." The baby is not being transferred for money to a stranger who can then treat the child like a commodity, doing anything he or she wants with the child. The money is being paid to enable a man to procreate his biological child; this hardly seems to fit the characterization of a sale. Am I buying a child when I pay a physician to be my surrogate fallopian tubes through in vitro fertilization (when, without her aid, I would remain childless)? Am I buying a child when I pay a physician to perform a needed Cesarean section, without which my child would never be born alive?

At most, in the surrogacy context, I am buying not a child but the preconception termination of the mother's parental rights. For decades, the pre-conception sale of a father's parental rights has been allowed with artificial insemination by donor. This practice, currently facilitated by statutes in at least thirty states, has received strong feminist support. In fact, when, on occasion, such sperm donors have later felt a bond to the child and wanted to be considered legal fathers, feminist groups have litigated to hold them to their pre-conception contract.[9]

Rather than focusing on the symbolic aspects of a sale, the policy discussion should instead analyze the advisability of pre-conception terminations for both women and men. For example, biological parenting may be so important to both the parent and the child that either parent should be able to assert these rights after birth (or even later in the child's life). This would provide sperm donors in artificial insemination with a chance to have a relationship with the child.

Symbolic arguments and pejorative language seem to make up the bulk of the policy arguments and media commentary against surrogacy. Surrogate motherhood has been described by its opponents not only as the buying and selling of children but as reproductive prostitution,[10] reproductive slavery,[11] the renting of a womb,[12] incubatory servitude,[13] the factory method of childbearing,[14] and cutting up women into genitalia.[15] The women who are surrogates are labeled paid breeders,[16] biological entrepreneurs,[17] breeder women,[18] reproductive meat,[19] interchangeable parts in the birth machinery,[20] manufacturing plants,[21] human incubators,[22] incubators for men's sperm,[23] a commodity in the reproductive marketplace,[24] and prostitutes.[25] Their husbands are seen, alternatively, as pimps[26] or cuckolds.[27] The children conceived pursuant to a surrogacy agreement have been called chattel[28] or merchandise to be expected in perfect condition.[29]

Feminists opposing surrogacy have also relied heavily on a visual element in the debate over Baby M. They have been understandably upset at the vision of a baby being wrenched from its nursing mother or being slipped out a back window in a flight from governmental authorities. But relying on the visceral and visual, a long-standing tactic of the right-to-life groups, is not the way to make policy. Conceding the value of symbolic arguments for the procreative choice of surrogacy makes it hard to reject them for other procreative choices.

One of the greatest feminist contributions to policy debates on reproduction and the family has been the rejection of arguments relying on tradition and symbolism and an insistence on an understanding of the nature and effects of an actual practice in determining how it should be regulated. For example, the idea that it is necessary for children to grow up in two-parent, heterosexual families has been contested by empirical evidence that such traditional structures are not necessary for children to flourish.[30] This type of analysis should not be overlooked in favor of symbolism in discussions of surrogacy.

The Potential Harm to Women

A second line of argument opposes surrogacy because of the potential psychological and physical risks that it presents for women. Many aspects of this argument, however, seem ill founded and potentially demeaning to women. They focus on protecting women against their own decisions because those decisions might later cause them regret, be unduly influenced by others, or be forced by financial motivations.

Reproductive choices are tough choices, and any decision about reproduction—such as abortion, sterilization, sperm donation, or surrogacy—might later be regretted. The potential for later regrets, however, is usually not thought to be a valid reason to ban the right to choose the procedure in the first place.

With surrogacy, the potential for regret is thought by some to be enormously high. This is because it is argued (in biology-is-destiny terms) that it is unnatural for a mother to give up a child. It is assumed that because birth mothers in traditional adoption situations often regret relinquishing their children, surrogate mothers will feel the same way. But surrogate mothers are making their decisions about relinquishment under much different circumstances. The biological mother in the traditional adoption situation is already pregnant as part of a personal relationship of her own. In many, many instances, she would like to keep the child but cannot because the relationship is not supportive or she cannot afford to raise the child. She generally feels that the relinquishment was forced upon her (for example, by her parents, a counselor, or her lover).[31]

The biological mother in the surrogacy situation seeks out the opportunity to carry a child that would not exist were it not for the couple's desire to create a child as a part of their relationship. She makes her decision in advance of pregnancy for internal, not externally enforced reasons. While 75 percent of the biological mothers who give a child up for adoption later change their minds,[32] only around 1 percent of the surrogates have similar changes of heart.

Entering into a surrogacy arrangement does present potential psychological risks to women. But arguing for a ban on surrogacy seems to concede that the *government,* rather than the individual woman, should determine what risks a woman should be allowed to face. This conflicts with the general legal policy allowing competent individuals to engage in potentially risky behavior so long

as they have given their voluntary, informed consent.

Perhaps recognizing the dangers of giving the government widespread powers to "protect" women, some feminists do acknowledge the validity of a general consent to assume risks. They argue, however, that the consent model is not appropriate to surrogacy since the surrogate's consent is neither informed nor voluntary.

It strikes me as odd to assume that the surrogate's consent is not informed. The surrogacy contracts contain lengthy riders detailing the myriad risks of pregnancy, so potential surrogates are much better informed on that topic than are most women who get pregnant in a more traditional fashion. In addition, with volumes of publicity given to the plight of Mary Beth Whitehead, all potential surrogates are now aware of the possibility that they may later regret their decisions. So, at that level, the decision is informed.

Yet a strong element of the feminist argument against surrogacy is that women cannot give an informed consent until they have had the experience of giving birth. Robert Arenstein, an attorney for Mary Beth Whitehead, argued in congressional testimony that a "pre-birth or at-birth termination, is a termination without informed consent. I use the words informed consent to mean full understanding of the personal psychological consequences at the time of surrender of the child."[33] The feminist amicus brief in *Baby M* made a similar argument.[34]

The New Jersey Supreme Court picked up this characterization of informed consent, writing that "quite clearly any decision prior to the baby's birth is, in the most important sense, uninformed."[35] But such an approach is at odds with the legal doctrine of informed consent. Nowhere is it expected that one must have the experience first before one can make an informed judgment about whether to agree to the experience. Such a requirement would preclude people from ever giving informed consent to sterilizations, abortions, sex change operations, heart surgery, and so forth. The legal doctrine of informed consent presupposes that people will predict in advance of the experience whether a particular course will be beneficial to them.

A variation of the informed consent argument is that while most competent adults can make such predictions, hormonal changes during pregnancy may cause a woman to change her mind. Virtually a whole amicus brief in the *Baby M* appeal was devoted to arguing that a woman's hormonal changes during pregnancy make it impossible for her to predict in advance the consequences of her relinquishment.[36] Along those lines, adoption worker Elaine Rosenfeld argues that

> [t]he consent that the birth mother gives prior to conception is not the consent of . . . a woman who has gone through the chemical, biological, endocrinological changes that have taken place during pregnancy and birth, and no matter how well prepared or well intentioned she is in her decision prior to conception, it is impossible for her to predict how she will feel after she gives birth.[37]

In contrast, psychologist Joan Einwohner, who works with a surrogate mother program, points out that

> women are fully capable of entering into agreements in this area and of fulfilling the obligations of a contract. Women's hormonal changes have been utilized too frequently over the centuries to enable male dominated society to make decisions for them. The Victorian era allowed women no legal rights to enter into contracts. The Victorian era relegated them to the status of dependent children. Victorian ideas are being given renewed life in the conviction of some people that women are so overwhelmed by their feelings at the time of birth that they must be protected from themselves.[38]

Surrogate Carol Pavek is similarly uncomfortable with hormonal arguments. She posits that if she is allowed the excuse of hormones to change her mind (thus harming the expectant couple and subjecting the child to the trauma of litigation), what's to stop men from using their hormones as an excuse for rape or other harms? In any case, feminists should be wary of a hormone-based argument, just as they have been wary of the hormone-

related criminal defense of premenstrual syndrome.

The consent given by surrogates is also challenged as not being voluntary. Feminist Gena Corea, for example, in writing about another reproduction arrangement, in vitro fertilization, asks, "What is the real meaning of a woman's 'consent' . . . in a society in which men as a social group control not just the choices open to women but also women's *motivation* to choose?"[39]

Such an argument is a dangerous one for feminists to make. It would seem to be a step backward for women to argue that they are incapable of making decisions. That, after all, was the rationale for so many legal principles oppressing women for so long, such as the rationale behind the laws not allowing women to hold property. Clearly, any person's choices are motivated by a range of influences—economic, social, religious.

At a recent conference of law professors, it was suggested that surrogacy was wrong because women's boyfriends might talk them into being surrogates and because women might be surrogates for financial reasons. But women's boyfriends might talk them into having abortions or women might have abortions for financial reasons; nevertheless, feminists do not consider those to be adequate reasons to ban abortions. The fact that a woman's decision could be influenced by the individual men in her life or by male-dominated society does not by itself provide an adequate reason to ban surrogacy.

Various feminists have made the argument that the financial inducement to a surrogate vitiates the voluntariness of her consent. Many feminists have said that women are exploited by surrogacy.[40] They point out that in our society's social and economic conditions, some women—such as those on welfare or in dire financial need—will turn to surrogacy out of necessity, rather than true choice. In my view, this is a harsh reality that must be guarded against by vigilant efforts to assure that women have equal access to the labor market and that there are sufficient social services so that poor women with children do not feel they must enter into a surrogacy arrangement in order to obtain money to provide care for their existing children.

However, the vast majority of women who have been surrogates do not allege that they have been tricked into surrogacy, nor have they done it because they needed to obtain a basic of life such as food or health care. Mary Beth Whitehead wanted to pay for her children's education. Kim Cotton wanted money to redecorate her house.[41] Another surrogate wanted money to buy a car. These do not seem to be cases of economic exploitation; there is no consensus, for example, that private education, interior decoration, and an automobile are basic needs, nor that society has an obligation to provide those items. Moreover, some surrogate mother programs specifically reject women who are below a certain income level to avoid the possibility of exploitation.

There is a sexist undertone to an argument that Mary Beth Whitehead was exploited by the paid surrogacy agreement into which she entered to get money for her children's education. If Mary Beth's husband, Rick, had taken a second job to pay for the children's education (or even to pay for their mortgage), he would not have been viewed as exploited. He would have been lauded as a responsible parent.

It undercuts the legitimacy of women's role in the workforce to assume that they are being exploited if they plan to use their money for serious purchases. It seems to harken back to a notion that women work (and should work) only for pin money (a stereotype that is the basis for justifying the firing of women in times of economic crisis). It is also disturbing that in most instances, when society suggests that a certain activity should be done for altruism, rather than money, it is generally a woman's activity.

Some people suggest that since there is a ban on payment for organs, there should be a ban on payment to a surrogate.[42] But the payment for organs is different from the payment to a surrogate, when viewed from either the side of the couple or the side of the surrogate. As the New Jersey Supreme Court has stated, surrogacy (unlike organ donation) implicates a fundamental constitutional right—the right to privacy in making procreative decisions.[43] The court erroneously assumed that the constitutional right did not extend to commercial applications. This is in conflict with the hold-ings of other right-to-privacy cases regarding reproductive decisions. In *Carey v. Population Services*, for example, it was acknowledged that constitutional protection of the use of contraceptives extended to their commercial availability.[44] The Court noted that "in practice, a prohibition against all sales, since more easily and less offensively enforced, might have an even more devastating effect on the freedom to choose contraception" than a ban on their use.[45]

Certainly, feminists would feel their right to an abortion was vitiated if a law were passed prohibiting payment to doctors performing abortions; such a law would erect a major barrier to access to the procedure. Similarly, a ban on payment to surrogates would inhibit the exercise of the right to produce a child with a surrogate. For such reasons, it could easily be argued that the couple's right to pay a surrogate is constitutionally protected (unlike the right to pay a kidney donor).

From the surrogate's standpoint, the situation is different as well. An organ is not meant to be removed from the body; it endangers the life of the donor to live without the organ. In contrast, babies are conceived to leave the body and the life of the surrogate is not endangered by living without the child.[46]

At various legislative hearings, women's groups have virtually begged that women be protected against themselves, against their own decisions. Adria Hillman testified against a New York surrogacy bill on behalf of the New York State Coalition on Women's Legislative Issues. One would think that a women's group would criticize the bill as unduly intruding into women's decisions—it requires a double-check by a court on a contract made by a woman (the surrogate mother) to assure that she gave voluntary, informed consent and does not require oversight of contracts made by men. But the testimony was just the opposite. The bill was criticized as empowering the court to assess whether a surrogacy agreement protects the health and welfare of the potential child, without specifying that the judge should look into the agreement's potential effect on the natural mother.[47] What next? Will women have to go before a court when they are considering having an affair—to have a judge discern whether they will be psychologically harmed by, or later regret, the relationship?

Washington Post writer Jane Leavy has written:

> I have read volumes in defense of Mary Beth, her courage in taking on a lonely battle against the upper classes, the exploited wife of a sanitation man versus the wife of a biochemist, a woman with a 9th grade education versus a pediatrician. It all strikes me as a bit patronizing.
> Since when do we assume that a 29-year-old mother is incapable of making an adult decision and accepting the consequences of it?[48]

Surrogate mother Donna Regan similarly testified in New York that her will was not overborne in the surrogacy context: "No one came to ask me to be a surrogate mother. I went to them and asked them to allow me to be a surrogate mother.[49]

"I find it extremely insulting that there are people saying that, as a woman, I cannot make an informed choice about a pregnancy that I carry," she continued, pointing out that she, like everyone, "makes other difficult choices in her life."[50]

Potential Harm to Potential Children

The third line of argument opposes surrogacy because of the potential harm it represents to potential children. Feminists have had a long-standing concern for the welfare of children. But much feminist policy in the area has been based on the idea that mothers (and family) are more appropriate decision-makers about the best interests of children than the government. Feminists have also fought against using traditions, stereotypes, and societal tolerance or intolerance as a driving force for determining what is in a child's best interest. In that respect, it is understandable that feminists rallied to the aid of Mary Beth Whitehead in order to expose and oppose the faulty grounds on which custody was being determined.[51]

However, the opposition to stereotypes being used to determine custody in a best-interests analysis is not a valid argument against surrogacy itself (which is premised not on stereotypes about the child's best interest being used to determine custody, but on a preconception agreement being used to determine custody). And when the larger issue of the advisability of surrogacy itself comes up, feminists risk falling into the trap of using arguments about potential harm to the child that have as faulty a basis as those they oppose in other areas of family law.

For example, one line of argument against surrogacy is that it is like adoption and adoption harms children. However, such an argument is not sufficiently borne out in fact. There is evidence that adopted children do as well as non-adopted children in terms of adjustment and achievement.[52] A family of two biological parents is not necessary to assure the child's well-being.

Surrogacy has also been analogized to baby-selling. Baby-selling is prohibited in our society, in part because children need a secure family life and should not have to worry that they will be sold and wrenched from their existing family. Surrogacy is distinguishable from baby-selling since the resulting child is never in a state of insecurity. From the moment of birth, he or she is under the care of the biological father and his wife, who cannot sell the child. There is thus no psychological stress to that child or to *any other existing child* that he or she may someday be sold. Moreover, no matter how much money is paid through the surrogacy arrangement, the child, upon birth, cannot be treated like a commodity—a car or a television set. Laws against child abuse and neglect come into play.

Paying a biological mother to give her child up for traditional adoption is criticized since the child may go to an "undeserving" stranger, whose mere ability to pay does not signify sufficient merit for rearing a child. In paid surrogacy, by contrast, the child is turned over to the biological father. This biological bond has traditionally been considered to be a sufficient indicator of parental merit.

Another argument about potential harm to the resulting children is that parents will expect more of a surrogate child because of the $10,000 they have spent on her creation. But many couples spend more than that on infertility treatments without evidence that they expect more of the child. A Cesarean section costs twice as much as natural childbirth, yet the parents don't expect twice as much of the children. Certainly, the $10,000 is a modest amount compared to what parents will spend on their child over her lifespan.

Surrogacy has also been opposed because of its potential effect on the surrogate's other children. Traditionally, except in cases of clear abuse, parents have been held to be the best decision-makers about their children's best interests. Applying this to surrogacy, the surrogate (and not society) would be the best judge of whether or not her participation in a surrogacy program will harm her children. Not only are parents thought best able to judge their child's needs, but parents can profoundly influence the effects of surrogacy on the child. Children take their cues about things from the people around them. There is no reason to believe that the other children of the surrogate will necessarily feel threatened by their mother's contractual pregnancy. If the children are told from the beginning that this is the contracting couple's child—not a part of their own family—they will realize that they themselves are not in danger of being relinquished.

Surrogate Donna Regan told her child that "the reason we did this was because they [the contracting couple] wanted a child to love as much as we love him." Regan contrasted her case to the Whitehead case: "In the Mary Beth Whitehead case, the child did not see this as something her mother was doing for someone else, so, of course, the attitude that she got from that was that something was being taken away rather than something being given."[53]

It seems ironic for feminists to embrace the argument that certain activities might inherently lead their children to fear abandonment, and that consequently such activities should be banned. Feminists have fought hard to gain access for women to amniocentesis and late-stage abortions of fetuses with a genetic defect[54]—even in light of similarly anecdotal evidence that when the woman aborts, her *other* children will feel that they, too, might be "sent to heaven" by their mother.[55] Indeed, it could be argued that therapeutic abortion is

more devastating to the remaining children than is surrogacy. After all, the brother or sister who is aborted was intended to be part of the family; moreover, he or she is dead, not just living with other people. I personally do not feel that the potential effect of either therapeutic abortion or surrogacy on the pregnant woman's other children is a sufficient reason to ban the procedures, particularly in light of the fact that parents can mediate how their children perceive and handle the experiences.

The reactions of outsiders to surrogacy may, however, be beyond the control of parents and may upset the children. But is this a sufficient reason to ban surrogacy? William Pierce seems to think so. He says that the children of surrogates "are being made fun of. Their lives are going to be ruined."[56] It would seem odd to let societal intolerance guide what relationships are permissible. Along those lines, a judge in a lesbian custody case replied to the argument that children could be harmed by stigma by stating:

> It is just as reasonable to expect that they will emerge better equipped to search out their own standards of right and wrong, better able to perceive that the majority is not always correct in its moral judgments, and better able to understand the importance of conforming their beliefs to the requirements of reasons and tested knowledge, not the constraints of currently popular sentiment or prejudice.[57]

Feminism Revisited

Feminists are taking great pride that they have mobilized public debate against surrogacy. But the precedent they are setting in their alliance with politicians like Henry Hyde and groups like the Catholic church is one whose policy is "protect women, even against their own decisions" and "protect children at all costs" (presumably, in latter applications, even against the needs and desires of women). This is certainly the thrust of the New Jersey Supreme Court decision against surrogacy, which cites as support for its holding the notorious *In re A. C.* case. In that case a woman's decision to refuse a Cesarean section was overridden based on an unsubstantiated possibility of benefit to her future child.[58]

In fact, the tenor of the New Jersey Supreme Court decision is reminiscent of earlier decisions "protecting" women that have been roundly criticized by feminists. The U.S. Supreme Court in 1872 felt it was necessary to prevent Myra Bradwell and all other women from practicing law—in order to protect women and their children. And when courts upheld sexist employment laws that kept women out of employment that men were allowed to take, they used language that might have come right out of the New Jersey Supreme Court's decision in the Baby M case. A woman's

> physical structure and a proper discharge of her maternal functions—having in view not merely her health, but the well-being of the race—justify legislation to protect her from the greed as well as the passion of man. The limitations which this statute place upon her contractual powers, upon her right to agree with her employer as to the time she shall labor, are not imposed solely for her benefit, but also largely for the benefit of all.[59]

The New Jersey Supreme Court rightly pointed out that not everything should be for sale in our society. But the examples given by the court, such as occupational safety and health laws prohibiting workers from voluntarily accepting money to work in an unsafe job, apply to both men and women. In addition, an unsafe job presents risks that we would not want people to undertake, whether or not they received pay. In contrast, a policy against paid surrogacy prevents women from taking risks (pregnancy and relinquishment) that they are allowed to take for free. It applies disparately—men are still allowed to relinquish their parental rights in advance of conception and to receive money for their role in providing the missing male factor for procreation.

Some feminists are comfortable with advocating disparate treatment on the grounds that gestation is such a unique experience that it has no male counterpart at law and so deserves a unique legal status.[60] The special nature of gestation, according to this argument, gives rise to special rights—such as the right for the surrogate to change her mind and assert her legal parenthood after the child is born.

The other side of the gestational coin, which has not been sufficiently addressed by these feminists, is that with special rights come special responsibilities. If gestation can be viewed as unique in surrogacy, then it can be viewed as unique in other areas. Pregnant women could be held to have responsibilities that other members of society do not have—such as the responsibility to have a Cesarean section against their wishes in order to protect the health of a child (since only pregnant women are in the unique position of being able to influence the health of the child).

Some feminists have criticized surrogacy as turning participating women, albeit with their consent, into reproductive vessels. I see the danger of the anti-surrogacy arguments as potentially turning *all* women into reproductive vessels, without their consent, by providing government oversight for women's decisions and creating a disparate legal category for gestation. Moreover, by breathing life into arguments that feminists have put to rest in other contexts, the current rationales opposing surrogacy could undermine a larger feminist agenda.

Notes

1. Iver Peterson, "Baby M Custody Trial Splits Ranks of Feminists over Issue of Exploitation," *New York Times,* Feb. 24, 1987 (quoting Linda Bowker).

2. Bob Port, "Feminists Come to the Aid of Whitehead's Case," *St. Petersburg Times,* Feb. 23, 1987, 1A.

3. Brief filed on behalf of Amici Curiae, the Foundation on Economic Trends et al., In the matter of Baby M, New Jersey Supreme Court, Docket No. FM-25314–86E (hereafter cited as "Brief"). (The feminists joining in the brief in-

cluded Betty Friedan, Gloria Steinem, Gena Corea, Barbara Katz Rothman, Lois Gould, Michelle Harrison, Kathleen Lahey, Phyllis Chesler, and Letty Cottin Pogrebin.)

4. See, e.g., Roe v. Wade, 410 U.S. 113 (1973); Griswold v. Connecticut, 381 U.S. 479 (1965); Meyer v. Nebraska, 262 U.S. 390 (1923); Pierce v. Society of Sisters, 268 U.S. 510 (1928).

5. See, e.g., Karst, "The Freedom of Intimate Association," *Yale Law Journal,* 89 (1980): 624.

6. Prior to conception and during pregnancy, the surrogate mother contract is a personal service contract. However, after the child's birth, no further services on the part of the surrogate are needed. Thus, enforcing a provision providing for the father's custody of the child is not the enforcement of a personal services contract. It is like the enforcement of a court order on custody or the application of a paternity statute.

7. Lori Andrews, "The Aftermath of Baby M: Proposed State Laws on Surrogate Motherhood," *Hastings Center Report,* 17 (Oct./Nov. 1987): 31–40, at 37.

8. In re Baby M, 217 N.J. Super. 313, 525 A.2d 1128, 1159 (1987).

9. Jhordan C. v. Mary K., 179 Cal. App. 3d 386, 224 Cal. Rptr. 530 (1986).

10. *Surrogate Parenthood and New Reproductive Technologies, A Joint Public Hearing, before the N.Y. State Assembly, N.Y. State Senate, Judiciary Committees* (Oct. 16, 1986) (statement of Bob Arenstein at 103–4, 125); *In The Matter of a Hearing on Surrogate Parenting before the N.Y. Standing Committee on Child Care* (May 8, 1987) (statement of Adria Hillman at 174, statement of Mary Ann Dibari at 212 ["the prostitution of motherhood"]).

11. *Surrogacy Arrangements Act of 1987: Hearing on H. R. 2433, before the Subcomm. on Transportation, Tourism, and Hazardous Materials,* 100th Cong., 1st Sess. (Oct. 15, 1987) (statement of Gena Corea at 3, 5); Robert Gould, N.Y. Testimony (May 8, 1987), supra note 10, at 233 (slavery).

12. Arthur Morrell, U.S. Testimony (Oct. 15, 1987), supra note 11, at 1.

13. William Pierce, U.S. Testimony (Oct. 15, 1987), supra note 11, at 2, citing Harvard Law Professor Lawrence Tribe.

14. Brief, supra note 3, at 19.

15. Port, supra note 2, at 7A, quoting Phyllis Chesler.

16. Gena Corea, U.S. Testimony (Oct. 15, 1987), supra note 11, at 3; Hillman, N.Y. Testimony (May 8, 1987), supra note 10, at 174.

17. Ellen Goodman, "Checking the Baby M Contract," *Boston Globe,* March 24, 1987, 15.

18. Gena Corea, U.S. Testimony (Oct. 15, 1987), supra note 11, at 5; Hillman, N.Y. Testimony (May 8, 1987) supra note 10, at 174.

19. Gena Corea, U.S. Testimony (Oct. 15, 1987), supra note 11, at 5.

20. Id.

21. Id.: 2.

22. Elizabeth Kane, U.S. Testimony (Oct. 15, 1987), supra note 11, at 1.

23. Kay Longcope, "Standing up for Mary Beth," *Boston Globe,* March 5, 1987, 81, 83 (quoting Janice Raymond).

24. Brief, supra note 3, at 14.

25. Robert Gould, N.Y. Testimony (May 8, 1987), supra note 10, at 232.

26. Judianne Densen-Gerber, N.Y. Testimony (May 8, 1987), supra note 10, at 253; Robert Gould, N.Y. Testimony (May 8, 1987), supra note 10, at 232.

27. Robert Gould, N.Y. Testimony (May 8, 1987), supra note 10, at 232.

28. Henry Hyde, U.S. Testimony (Oct. 15, 1987), supra note 11, at 1 ("Commercial surrogacy arrangements, by rendering children into chattel, are in my opinion, immoral."); DiBari, N.Y. Testimony (May 8, 1987), supra note 10, at 212.

29. John Ray, U.S. Testimony (Oct. 15, 1987), supra note 11, at 7.

30. See, e.g., Maureen McGuire and Nancy J. Alexander, "Artificial Insemination of Single Women," *Fertility and Sterility,* 43 (Feb. 1985): 182–84; Raschke and Raschke, "Family Conflict and Children's Self-Concept: A Comparison of Intact and Single Parent Families," *Journal of Marriage and the Family,* 41 (1979): 367; Weiss, "Growing up a Little Faster," *Journal of Social Issues,* 35 (1979): 97.

31. See, e.g., Rynearson, "Relinquishment and Its Maternal Complications: A Preliminary Study," *American Journal of Psychiatry,* 139 (1982): 338; Deykin, Campbell, Patti, "The Postadoption

Experience of Surrendering Parents," *American Journal of Orthopsychiatry,* 54 (1984): 271.

32. Betsy Aigen, N.Y. Testimony (May 8, 1987), supra note 10, at 18.

33. Robert Arenstein, U.S. Testimony (Oct. 15, 1987), supra note 11, at 9.

34. Brief, supra note 3, at 30–31.

35. In re Baby M, 109 N.J. 396; 537 A.2d 1227, 1248 (1988).

36. See Brief filed on behalf of Amicus Curiae the Gruter Institute, In the Matter of Baby M, New Jersey Supreme Court, Docket No. FM-25314-86E.

37. *Hearing in re Surrogate Parenting: Hearing on S. B. 1429, before Senators Goodhue, Dunne, Misters Balboni, Abramson, and Amgott* (April 10, 1987) (statement of Elaine Rosenfeld at 187). A similar argument made by Adria Hillman, N.Y. Testimony (May 8, 1987), supra note 10, at 175.

38. Joan Einwohner, N.Y. Testimony (April 10, 1987), supra note 37, at 110–11.

39. Gena Corea, *The Mother Machine* (New York: Harper & Row, 1985), 3.

40. Brief, supra note 3, at 10, 13; Judy Briedbart, N.Y. Testimony (May 8, 1987), supra note 10, at 168.

41. K. Cotton and D. Winn, *Baby Cotton: For Love and Money* (1985).

42. Karen Peters, N.Y. Testimony (May 8, 1987), supra note 10, at 121.

43. In re Baby M, 109 N.J. 396; 537 A.2d 1227, 1253 (1988).

44. Carey v. Population Services Int'l., 431 U.S. 678 (1977).

45. Carey v. Population Services Int'l., 431 U.S. 678, 688 (1976) (citation omitted).

46. Betsy Aigen, N.Y. Testimony (May 8, 1987), supra note 10, at 11–12.

47. Adria Hillman, N.Y. Testimony (May 8, 1987), supra note 10, at 177–78.

48. Jane Leavy, "It Doesn't Take Labor Pains to Make a Real Mom," *Washington Post,* April 4, 1987.

49. Donna Regan, N.Y. Testimony (May 8, 1987), supra note 10, at 157.

50. Id.

51. Michelle Harrison, "Social Construction of Mary Beth Whitehead," *Gender and Society,* 1 (Sept. 1987): 300–311.

52. Teasdale and Owens, "Influence of Paternal Social Class on Intelligence Level in Male Adoptees and Non-Adoptees," *British Journal of Educational Psychology,* 56 (1986): 3.

53. Donna Regan, N.Y. Testimony (May 8, 1987), supra note 10, at 156.

54. See, e.g., the briefs filed by feminist organizations in Thornburgh v. American College of Obstetricians, 476 U.S. 747 (1986).

55. See, e.g., J. Fletcher, *Coping with Genetic Disorders: A Guide for Counseling* (San Francisco: Harper & Row, 1982).

56. William Pierce, N.Y. Testimony (May 8, 1987), supra note 10, at 86. It should be pointed out that kids hassle other kids for a wide range of reasons. A child might equally be made fun of for being the recipient of a kidney transplant or being the child of a garbage man.

57. M. P. v. S. P., 169 N.J. Super. 425, 438, 404 A.2d 1256, 1263 (Super. Ct. App. Div. 1979).

58. In re Baby M, 109 N.J. 396; 537 A.2d 1227, 1254 n. 13 (1988), citing In re A. C., 533 A.2d 611 (D.C. App. 1987).

59. Muller v. Oregon, 208 U.S. 412, 422 (1907).

60. See Brief, supra note 3, at 11.

Case 2.a   Baby M

In 1986 Mary Beth Whitehead contracted with Elizabeth and William Stern to be inseminated with Mr. Stern's sperm and act as surrogate for the birth of a child for $10,000. After the birth, however, Mrs. Whitehead decided she could not give up the child. Although the court eventually awarded custody to the Sterns, the surrogacy issue has yet to be fully settled.

On March 30, 1986, Dr. Elizabeth Stern, a professor of pediatrics, and her husband, William, accepted from Mary Beth Whitehead a baby who had been born four days earlier. The child's biological mother was Mrs. Whitehead, but she had been engaged by the Sterns as a surrogate mother. Even so, it was not until almost exactly a year later that the Sterns were able to claim legal custody of the child.

The Sterns, working through the Infertility Center of New York, had first met with Mrs. Whitehead and her husband, Richard, in January of 1985. Mrs. Whitehead, who already had a son and a daughter, had indicated her willingness to become a surrogate mother by signing up at the Infertility Center. "What brought her there was empathy with childless couples who were infertile," her attorney later stated. Her own sister had been unable to conceive.

According to court testimony, the Sterns considered Mrs. Whitehead a "perfect person" to bear a child for them. Mr. Stern said that it was "compelling" for him to have children, for he had no relatives "anywhere in the world." He and his wife planned to have children, but they put off attempts to conceive until his wife completed her medical residency in 1981. However, in 1979 she was diagnosed as having an eye condition indicating that she probably had multiple sclerosis. When she learned that the symptoms of the disease might be worsened by pregnancy and that she might become temporarily or even permanently paralyzed, the Sterns "decided the risk wasn't worth it." It was this decision that led them to the Infertility Center and to Mary Beth Whitehead.

The Sterns agreed to pay Mrs. Whitehead $10,000 to be artifically inseminated with Mr. Stern's sperm and to bear a child. Mrs. Whitehead would then turn the child over to the Sterns, and Dr. Stern would be allowed to adopt the child legally. The agreement was drawn up by a lawyer specializing in surrogacy arrangements. Mr. Stern later testified that Mrs. Whitehead seemed perfectly pleased with the agreement and expressed no interest in

keeping the baby she was to bear. "She said she would not come to our doorstep," he said. "All she wanted from us was a photograph each year and a little letter on what transpired that year."

The baby was born on March 27, 1986. According to Dr. Stern, the first indication that Mrs. Whitehead might not keep the agreement was her statement to the Sterns in the hospital two days after the baby's birth. "She said she didn't know if 'I can go through with it,'" Dr. Stern testified. Although Mrs. Whitehead did turn the baby over to the Sterns on March 30, she called a few hours later. "She said she didn't know if she could live any more," Dr. Stern said. She called again the next morning and asked to see the baby, and she and her sister arrived at the Sterns' house before noon.

According to Dr. Stern, Mrs. Whitehead told her that she "woke up screaming in the middle of the night" because the baby was gone, that her husband was threatening to leave her, and that she had "considered taking a bottle of Valium." Dr. Stern quoted Mrs. Whitehead as saying, "I just want her for a week, and I'll be out of your lives forever." The Sterns allowed Mrs. Whitehead to take the baby home with her.

Mrs. Whitehead then refused to return the baby voluntarily and took the infant with her to the home of her parents in Florida. The Sterns obtained a court order, and on July 31 the child was seized from Mrs. Whitehead. The Sterns were granted temporary custody. Then Mr. Stern, as the father of the child, and Mrs. Whitehead, as the mother, each sought permanent custody from the Superior Court of the State of New Jersey.

The seven-week trial attracted considerable attention, for the legal issues were virtually without precedent. Mrs. Whitehead was the first to challenge the legal legitimacy of a surrogate agreement in a U.S. court. She argued that the agreement was "against public policy" and violated New Jersey prohibitions against selling babies. In contrast, Mr. Stern was the first to seek a legal decision to uphold the "specific performance" of the terms of a surrogate contract. In particular, he argued that Mrs. Whitehead should be ordered to uphold her agreement and to surrender her parental rights and permit his wife to become the baby's legal mother. In addition to the contractual issues, the judge had to deal with the "best interest" of the child as required by New Jersey child-custody law. In addition to being a vague concept, the "best interest" standard had never been applied in a surrogacy case.

On March 31, 1987, Judge Harvey R. Sorkow announced his decision. He upheld the legality of the surrogate-mother agreement between the Sterns and Mrs. Whitehead and dismissed all arguments that the contract violated public policy or prohibitions against selling babies. Immediately after he read his decision, Judge Sorkow summoned Elizabeth Stern into his chambers and allowed her to sign documents permitting her to adopt the baby she and her husband called Melissa. The court decision effectively stripped Mary Beth Whitehead of all parental rights concerning this same baby, the one she called Sara.

The Baby M story did not stop with Judge Sorkow's decision. Mrs. Whitehead's attorney appealed the ruling to the New Jersey Supreme Court, and on February 3, 1988, the seven members of the court, in a unanimous decision, reversed Judge Sorkow's ruling on the surrogacy agreement. The court held that the agreement violated the state's adoption laws, because it involved a payment for a child. "This is the sale of a child, or at the very least, the sale of a mother's right to her child," Chief Justice Wilentz wrote. The agreement "guarantees the separation of a child from its mother . . .; it takes the child from the mother regardless of her wishes and her maternal fitness . . .; and it accomplishes all of its goals through the use of money." The court held that surrogacy agreements might be acceptable if they involved no payment and if a surrogate mother voluntarily surrendered her parental rights. In the present case, though, the court regarded paying for surrogacy "illegal, perhaps criminal, and potentially degrading to women."

The court let stand the award of custody to the Sterns, because "Their household and their personalities promise a much more likely foundation for Melissa to grow and thrive." Mary Beth Whitehead, having divorced her husband three months earlier, was romantically involved with a man named Dean Gould and was pregnant at the time of the court decision.

Despite awarding custody to the Sterns, the court set aside the adoption agreement signed by Elizabeth Stern. Mary Beth Whitehead remained a legal parent of Baby M, and the court ordered a lower court hearing to consider visitation rights for the mother.

The immediate future of the child known to the court and to the public as Baby M was settled. Neither the Sterns nor Mary Beth Whitehead had won exactly what they had sought, but neither had they lost all.

Case 2.b   Carrying for Your Daughter: The Case of Arlette Schweitzer

Arlette Schweitzer, age 42, decided to carry a child for her daughter Christa, who was born without a uterus. At the University of Minnesota hospital, eggs from Christa's ovaries were removed, fertilized with sperm from her husband, and implanted in her mother. Shortly thereafter, Mrs. Schweitzer was found to be carrying her daughter's twins.

Eyes twinkling, hands folded across her swelling belly, Arlette Schweitzer imagines the headlines a tabloid might concoct to

From "All in the Family," *Time*, August 19, 1991. Copyright 1991 The Time Inc. Magazine Company. Reprinted by permission.

sensationalize her admittedly unusual condition. The exercise amuses her no end—probably because there is nothing the least bit bizarre about this cheerful 42-year-old librarian who lives with her husband Dan, a fluffy white cat named Boom Boom and a cocker spaniel named Special on a tree-lined street in Aberdeen, S. Dak. What a visitor notices above all in their cozy, split-level house is the photographs of smiling kids: grandchildren, nieces and nephews and, over the living-room sofa, two large color portraits of the Schweitzers' son Curtis, 26, and daughter Christa, 22.

Now that Christa has, well, got her mother in a family way, newspaper writers and TV crews are camped outside. Since the New York *Times* put her on Page One, producers for talk shows have kept calling, photographers have continually rung her doorbell, and somehow, through it all, Arlette Schweitzer has continued to radiate a sense of calm. "Christa has no . . ." a reporter hesitantly ventures. "That's right," replied Arlette, her voice as clear and as strong as a church bell. "Christa has no uterus."

When this misfortune was discovered eight years ago, her mother patiently explains, Christa was only 14, and even then she was absolutely devastated by the news. "When Christa was just a little girl," recalls Arlette, "all she could talk about was becoming a mother." Two years later, during a visit to the Mayo Clinic, Arlette observed to a physician who examined her daughter, "I wish you could transplant my uterus because I certainly have no use for it anymore." The doctor looked at her curiously. "He asked me how old I was. I said I was 36, which I was at the time. Suddenly it was like a light bulb switched on for all three of us. She was born without a uterus. I was young enough to lend her mine."

In February of this year, at the University of Minnesota Hospital and Clinic in Minneapolis, eggs taken from Christa's ovaries were fertilized with her husband Kevin Uchytil's sperm, then implanted in Arlette's uterus. Ten days later, Arlette telephoned her daughter and son-in-law, who live in Sioux City, Iowa. "Congratulations!" she triumphantly exclaimed. "*You're* pregnant." Not long thereafter, Christa, viewing an ultrasound picture of her mother's tummy, saw two heartbeats and realized that her mother would give birth to twins. "How lucky could I be!" Christa said. "This just takes my breath away."

Becoming a surrogate mother, stresses Arlette, is sort of like running a triathlon: the experience may be exhilarating, but it is not entirely painless. For 89 days, she had to inject herself with hormones. "I still have scars on both my hips," she says with a grin. "But as long as you know there's an end to it, I think you can bear almost anything. For 89 days, I think you could even walk on burning coals if you had to. I feel so responsible. This really is a one-shot chance, and so I'm trying to do everything right."

Arlette grew up in Lemmon, S. Dak., where her father was a jeweler. At 15, she surprised her parents by dropping out of school to marry Dan, now a sales representative for the Keebler Co. She had her children early and was for years a stay-at-home mom. "I played house, and I loved every minute of it," she says. Then when Christa was in third grade, Arlette went back to school. For the past two years, she has taken charge of the library at Aberdeen's Simmons Junior High. "My whole life," she says impishly, "I've done in reverse. I feel like Frank Sinatra. I've done it my way."

The idea of surrogate parenting has kept professional ethicists and jurists wringing their hands ever since the first case surfaced in 1978. Is it proper to "rent" a womb by paying a stranger to bear a child? What if the surrogate mother changes her mind? But now a heartwarming situation has come along in which the moral quandaries pale before that most basic of human instincts: the desire of a parent to take on and take away the pain of a child.

With refreshing, down-to-earth pragmatism, Arlette, a devout Roman Catholic, says she had no doubts about her decision. "If you can give the gift of life," she asks, "why not? If medical science affords that opportunity, why not take it?" Far more problematic, in her view, is the more typical situation—such as that involving Mary Beth Whitehead in 1987—in which a surrogate mother is also the biological mother. "These are Christa's eggs and Kevin's sperm," Arlette says. "There's no doubt about whose children these are!"

Asked by her seven-year-old grandson whether Grandma was going to have a baby, Arlette replied, "Christa and Kevin's babies are going to use Grandma's uterus until they're old enough to be born." That made perfect sense to him. "Children are very accepting," observes Arlette. "It's adults who cloud the matter. Maybe it's not quite the same old birds and bees. Maybe now there are birds and bees and butterflies too."

So why not go ahead and congratulate the medical butterflies responsible for this unorthodox biological event? That's what Arlette and Dan and Christa and Kevin plan to do when they welcome their miracle babies into the world this October. "Dan will be up there coaching me," imagines Arlette fondly, "while Kevin and Christa will be getting ready to grab the babies and run." Then Arlette and Dan will settle back to their normal role—that of happy grandparents.

Case 2.c   The Gestational Surrogate: The Case of Anna Johnson

After a hysterectomy, Crispina Calvert decided she still wanted children. She and her husband, Mark, then contracted with Anna Johnson to bear their child for $10,000. The child genetically would be theirs, since the sperm and egg would come from Mr. and Mrs. Calvert, although Ms. Johnson would carry the child in her uterus. Around the seventh month, however, Anna Johnson changed her mind and, arguing that she was not simply a "baby carrier," insisted on keeping the child. In 1990 the California Superior Court gave custody to the Calverts.

Disease forced Crispina Calvert of Orange County, California, to have a hysterectomy, but only her uterus was removed by surgery, not her ovaries. She and her husband, Mark, wanted a child of their own, but without a uterus Crispina would not be able to bear it. For a fee of $10,000 they arranged with Anna Johnson to act as a surrogate.

Unlike the more common form of surrogate pregnancy, Johnson would have no genetic investment in the child. The ovum that would be fertilized would not be hers. Mary Beth Whitehead, the surrogate in the controversial Baby M case, had received artificial insemination. Thus, she made as much genetic contribution to the child as did the biological father.

Johnson, however, would be the gestational surrogate. In a standard in vitro fertilization process, ova were extracted from Crispina Calvert and mixed with sperm from Mark. A fertilized ovum was implanted in Anna Johnson's uterus, and a fetus began to develop.

Johnson's pregnancy proceeded along a

normal course, but in her seventh month she announced that she had changed her mind about giving up the child. She filed suit against the Calverts to seek custody of the unborn child. "Just because you donate a sperm and an egg doesn't make you a parent," said Johnson's attorney. "Anna is not a machine, an incubator."

"That child is biologically Chris and Mark's," said the Calverts' lawyer. "That contract is valid."

Johnson was not the first woman to serve as a gestational surrogate. No official records are kept, but the Center for Surrogate Parenting in Beverly Hills estimates that about 80 such births have occurred since 1987. This compares to some 2,000 surrogate pregnancies during the same period. According to the Center's figures, probably around 4,000 surrogate births have occurred since the late 1970s.

Critics of genetic surrogate pregnancy are equally critical of gestational surrogate pregnancy. Both methods, some claim, exploit women, particularly poor women. Further, in gestational pregnancy the surrogate is the one who must run the risks and suffer the discomforts and dangers of pregnancy. She has a certain biological claim to be the mother, because it was her body that produced the child according to the genetic information.

Defenders of surrogate pregnancy respond to the first criticism by denying that surrogates are exploited. They enter freely into a contract to serve as a surrogate for pay, just as anyone might agree to perform any other form of service for pay. Pregnancy has hazards and leaves its marks on the body, but so do many other paid occupations. As far as gestational surrogacy is concerned, defenders say, since the surrogate makes no genetic contribution to the developing child, in no reasonable way can she be regarded as the child's parent.

The Ethics Committee of the American Fertility Society has endorsed a policy opposing surrogate pregnancy "for non-medical reasons." The apparent aim of the policy is to permit the use of gestational surrogate pregnancy in cases like that of Mrs. Calvert, while condemning it when its motivation is mere convenience or an unwillingness to be pregnant. When a woman is fertile but, because of diabetes, uncontrollable hypertension, or some other life-threatening disorder, is unable to bear the burden of pregnancy, then gestational surrogacy would be a legitimate medical option.

The child carried by Anna Johnson, a boy, was born on September 19, and for a while, under a court order, Johnson and the Calverts shared visitation rights. Then, in October, 1990, a California Superior Court denied to Anna Johnson the parental rights she had sought. Justice R. N. Parslow awarded complete custody of the child to the Calverts and terminated Johnson's visitation rights.

"I decline to split the child emotionally between two mothers," the judge said. He said Johnson had nurtured and fed the fetus in the way a foster parent might take care of a child, but she was still a "genetic stranger" to the boy and could not claim parenthood because of surrogacy.

Justice Parslow found the contract between the Calverts and Johnson to be valid, and he expressed doubt about Johnson's contention that she had "bonded" with the fetus she was carrying. "There is substantial evidence in the record that Anna Johnson never bonded with the child till she filed her lawsuit, if then," he said. While the trial was in progress, Johnson had been accused of planning to sue the Calverts from the beginning to attempt to make the case famous so she could make money from book and movie rights.

Justice Parslow also urged the California Legislature to establish legal guidelines to deal with surrogacy cases. He suggested a process in which all parties undergo psychological evaluation and agree at the beginning that the surrogate mother will have no custody rights. He also suggested that a surrogate be required to have had previous successful experience with childbirth and that surrogacy be used only in cases in which the genetic mother is unable to give birth.

"I see no problem with someone getting paid for her pain and suffering," he said. "There is nothing wrong with getting paid for nine months of what I understand is a lot of misery and a lot of bad days. They are not selling a baby; they are selling pain and suffering."

The Calverts were overjoyed by the decision.

Gay Rights

Issues related to the rights of lesbians and gay men, people who prefer same-sex relationships, do not relate simply to sexuality or to privacy. This chapter, however, attempts to address the most fundamental aspect of gay life: the right to be a homosexual and join with a partner. Whereas the right to sexual privacy within heterosexual marriage was established in *Griswold* v. *Connecticut* (1965), and later extended to single heterosexuals in *Eisenstadt* v. *Baird* (1972), this fundamental right has been denied to homosexuals in *Bowers* v. *Hardwick* (1988). The decriminalization of same-sex relationships and of sexual practices performed in the privacy of their own home has yet to happen for homosexuals. Sodomy laws make anal sex, oral sex, and bestiality (sex with animals) illegal. Whereas anal and oral sex can be performed by heterosexuals, as well as by gay men and lesbians, sodomy laws are almost exclusively applied against gay men. In the recent *Bowers* decision, such an application of the law was held to be constitutional.

Opposition to homosexuality derives principally from traditional Western religious values. This tradition sees same-sex relationships as "unnatural." The position stems from the claim that the "natural purpose" of sexual organs is for the reproduction of the species. This "teleological," or function-oriented, view of sexuality leads to the conclusion that homosexuality is unnatural, as are all acts of sodomy (many instances of oral or anal sex even among heterosexuals are called "crimes against nature").

Myths and distortions related to homosexuality remain in our culture today. First, it is often suggested that all gays are promiscuous and molest children. No evidence exists to show that homosexuals molest children any more than heterosexuals do. Furthermore, lesbians and gay men have no more tendency to be promiscuous than heterosexual people. Society often reduces gay people to their sexuality, as if it were more central to who they are than it is to heterosexual people.

In general, lesbians and gay men face serious obstacles in their attempts to live life as they wish. Job discrimination, the inability to have their partner acknowledged legally as such, harassment, overt violence, and simply the lack of any fundamental right to sexual privacy all make being gay in today's society a difficult challenge.

Traditionally most people have strongly rejected the idea that lesbians and gay men should be allowed to marry and to adopt or have custody of children. However, several cities in the United States have enacted "domestic partner" laws, which allow live-in and gay couples to be legally recognized. These laws allow same-sex partners to have the same benefits, health insurance, life insurance, etc., as legally acknowledged heterosexual couples.

9. Is Homosexuality Bad Sexuality?

Michael Ruse

Michael Ruse responds to claims that homosexuality is unnatural and abnormal. He examines homosexuality in ancient Greece, in the Judeo-Christian tradition, and in terms of modern ethical theory. Ruse concludes that homosexuality does not constitute sexual perversion.

Is homosexuality, inclination and behaviour, an acceptable way for a human being to feel and act, or is it pernicious? Undoubtedly,

From *Homosexuality* by Michael Ruse. Oxford: Basil Blackwell Publishers, 1988, pp. 177–202, 270. Reprinted by permission.

although there will be less unanimity on this matter today than there would have been (say) a hundred years ago, for a good many people the answer will seem obvious—that homosexuality is aesthetically revolting and morally gross; that in all its aspects it is wrong, and that this is a conclusion not merely confirmed by modern thought but underlined by the whole western religious/philosophical tradition.

Whether or not this is really the case is the topic of this chapter.

Greek Homosexuality

The major formative influences on western civilization, particularly in the areas of morality and behaviour, were those of the Ancient Greeks and of the Jews. Very roughly speaking, from the Greeks we inherit the attempt to see and live in the world guided by our physical senses and our reason, and from the Jews we inherit the attempt to see and live in the world guided by our faith and our religious sense. I suspect that if most people were questioned, they would be inclined to argue that over the matter of homosexuality, Greek and Jewish thought come into conflict, and that it is the Jewish tradition which triumphs. The Greeks, so the story would go, accepted and even promoted homosexual relations. Furthermore, this attitude is to be found in the greatest of their philosophers, most especially Plato. The Jews, however, both those of the Old and New Testaments, uniformly and unambiguously condemned all forms of homosexuality. It merited the punishment of man and of God. And it is this latter position which has prevailed ever since, thanks to the rise of Christianity, a religion which has such deep roots in Judaism.

But is this story true? Let us turn to the sources, beginning first with the Greeks. As is so often the case, popular opinion has a very inadequate grasp of the whole (Dover 1973, 1978; Verstraete 1977; Ungaretti 1982). It is indeed true that by the time of 'classical Greece' (from 480 BC, the date of the rejection of Persian colonial aspirations, to the coming of the Romans, 146 BC)—a time which firmly includes the life span of the philosopher Plato (428–347 BC)—overt homosexuality was a well-established tradition and acceptable part of the Greek life style. But the sexuality of classical Greece was apparently not simply an unrestrained free-for-all, with any two or more people doing whatsoever they

liked, to whomsoever they liked. Specifically, the homosexuality one hears about was very much an upper-class phenomenon, strongly associated with the enforced segregation of the sexes, and highly stylized, with emotions rather than actions playing a major role. The central focus was a bond which would be formed between a somewhat older and a somewhat younger man (ideally, a 25-year-old paired with a 15-year-old). It seems to have been rare indeed (and certainly not proper) for two men of exactly the same age to have fallen in love and to have had any kind of physical relationship. Moreover, after marriage the need for (and acceptability of) homosexual relations fell away rapidly. (It is assumed that an analogous story can be told about women, although we know far less about lesbianism. It seems, for some unknown reason, to have been a taboo subject for the male writers. . . .)

The constraint about ages was accompanied also by a constraint about emotions. The older man (the *erastes* or lover) was expected to feel strong sexual emotion for the younger man or boy (the *eromenos* or loved one), admiring his beauty, wanting to get physically close to him, and being prepared to court him with gifts and favours. The boy, however, was not expected to feel the same kind of sexual attraction in response, but rather to admire his older lover, looking upon him as an ideal or model, and wanting to make him happy. This convention about love and ages helped dictate the nature of the physical sexual relations. Officially at least, sodomy was definitely taboo, not to mention things like fellatio. Being sodomized was considered far too degrading—indeed, someone who indulged too freely in this in his youth, certainly someone who rented his body for such favours, stood in grave danger of losing various powers as a citizen. Hence, the usual method of intercourse between upper-class lovers was somewhat limited, in a stylized manner. The erastes, the older, would push his penis between the thighs of the eromenos, the younger, and bring himself to ejaculation this way, "intercrurally." The boy was not supposed to ejaculate in return—indeed, he was supposed to find the whole business rather asexual, and to remain unaroused throughout. No doubt there was frequently a gap between the ideal and the actual.

Against this background we can understand Plato's position of homosexuality. As is well known, Plato was the student and follower of Socrates, who was put to death on a charge of corrupting the youth, because he filled the heads of young aristocrats with all sorts of radical ideas. Reputedly, Socrates had a strong heterosexual appetite (all of his appetites were strong) and he was married, although supposedly his wife was somewhat of a shrew. Plato, tradition has it, was unmarried and fairly exclusively homosexual in orientation. Be this as it may, Socrates and his (exclusively male) companions lived, thought, and behaved very much in the homosexual milieu described above as being the norm for upper-class Athenians. In Plato's early writings (which report, fairly authentically, on actual Socratic discussions or dialogues), we get repeated, unselfconscious references to the sexual pangs that an older man would feel for a boy or younger man, and the liaisons that would spring up between them. The following translation of a passage from the *Charmides* (an early dialogue) needs no further comment:

> Then I just didn't know what to do, and all the confidence that I'd previously felt, in the belief that I'd find it easy to talk to him, was knocked out of me. When Kritias told him that I was the man who knew the cure [for headache], and he looked me in the eye—oh, what a look! and made as if to ask me, and everyone in the wrestling-school crowded close all round us, that was the moment when I saw inside his cloak, and I was on fire, absolutely beside myself . . . All the same, when he asked me if I knew the cure for his head, I did somehow manage to answer that I knew it. (Dover 1978: 155)

However, with this much said, matters start to get a little more complicated. Although there is much talk of sexual desire, which seems even to be cherished, both Socrates and Plato unambiguously reject and condemn all taking of homosexual attraction to the point of intercourse and orgasm. According to Xenophon, Kritias and Socrates fell out over this very point, because Kritias wanted to copulate with his lover Euthydemos and Socrates thought he ought not. And in the greatest of all of Plato's works, the *Republic* (which, although it uses the historical Socrates as a mouthpiece, probably more truly represents Plato's own ideas), Socrates, in describing the nature of the ideal state, endorses homosexual attractions and liaisons and yet strictly prohibits the taking of them to the physical climax.

Why were Socrates and Plato so strongly against physical homosexual relations? There is an obvious reason, which had nothing to do with homosexuality per se. Both Socrates and Plato were reflecting an important attitude of their society and class, namely a great respect for self-constraint and control. Emotions were seen as things which took control of one, and the man who could withstand them gained stature in his and his colleagues' eyes. This applies to any kind of emotion, including homosexual impulses. Yet given that there was this condemnation of the fulfilment of homosexual feelings, were not Socrates and Plato somewhat inconsistent in apparently accepting the feelings themselves? Making the distinction between homosexual orientation (even if only partial) and homosexual behaviour, for consistency should not Socrates and Plato at least have regretted homosexual inclinations rather than accepting them? The answer to this question probably lies in the fact that Plato (and Socrates also) saw them as inevitable, rather like the feelings of hunger and thirst. They are thrust upon you, so no moral opprobrium can be attached to them. Morality enters in only at the point of action.

Indeed, for Plato, so obvious and inevitable were homosexual urges, and so crucial was their control, he gave both parts a central place in his metaphysics. As is well known, Plato argued that there is a world of ultimate reality, the unchanging eternal world of the Forms, which are (among other things) the universals, like the Form of Bed, or Horse, or Happiness. The highest Form is that of the Good, which in some sense both illuminates the other Forms and is the source of their being. The ultimate in human philosophical achievement is to gaze upon the Form of the

Good, which we are to do in some way through our rational or intuitive faculty. (See the *Republic* and Cross and Woozley 1964.) But we cannot just do this as soon as we feel so inclined. It requires long years of rigorous training; and a key part of this route of achievement involves homosexual attraction. We start by gazing upon and being overwhelmed by beautiful boys. From this we can go on to contemplate beautiful souls and pursuits (like the fascination of the quest for knowledge). As we do so, we start to realize that it is not the particular beautiful thing which attracts us, but the element in which they all participate, the Form of Beauty or the Good. So, finally, having restrained ourselves in the physical (genital) realm, we come to be rewarded by what is almost literally a philosophical orgasm. As in the physical world, at the moment of climax we get a real sense of oneness with everything. (See the *Symposium* 211 c–e.)

For the mature Plato, therefore, control is essential. To read Plato's early and middle writings as providing a licence for homosexual inclination and behaviour is not to read them properly. Homosexual attraction is accepted and even venerated, but consummation is condemned. The man who lets his passions thus govern his reason is an object of pity. This, however, is not quite all that there is to Plato's treatment of homosexuality. Towards the end of his life he developed his ideas yet further, and indeed he arrived at a position by a line of argument that was profoundly to influence subsequent thinking on the matter of homosexuality. Simply and categorically Plato condemned homosexual behaviour because it is 'unnatural'. It is not done by the animals. No more should it be done by us.

> Anyone who, in conformity with nature, proposes to re-establish the law as it was before Laios, declaring that it was right not to join with men and boys in sexual intercourse as with females, adducing as evidence the nature of animals and pointing out that [among them] male does not touch male for sexual purposes, since that is not natural, he could, I think, make a very strong case. (Plato, *Laws*, 836c–e, trans. Dover 1978: 166)

The opposition to homosexual acts becomes absolute. And, although the third of the great Greek philosophers, Aristotle, said little on the topic of homosexuality, what little he did say could be taken as underlining this point. Under the classification of pleasures which do not come about naturally, and under the sub-classification of things which are found pleasurable by those with bad natures ('disease-like or as a result of habituation'), Aristotle includes pulling out one's hair, eating earth, and "the disposition of sexual intercourse for males" (Aristotle, *Nichomachean Ethics*, 1148b 15–19a 20, trans. Dover 1978: 168). Probably, given all we know of his society, Aristotle here was more concerned with (condemning) the passive role in sodomy. But, be this as it may, there was no challenge to the finality of Plato.

The Judaeo/Christian Tradition

Let us turn now to Judaism and its breakaway offspring, Christianity. Here, on the surface at least, popular opinion does seem closer to the truth. The primary source of information about the positions of the Jews and the early Christians is obviously the Bible, Old and New Testaments. In the Old Testament, there are two main sources of information about the position taken by God and his chosen people on the subject of homosexuality: the story of Sodom and Gomorrah, and various scattered dictates about homosexual practices. Both sources apparently tell the same tale: homosexual behaviour is abhorrent in the eyes of the Lord and therefore morally barred to humankind. As it happens, the Sodom and Gomorrah story about the citizens of Sodom, who wanted to have homosexual intercourse with two of God's angels, has been the subject of much Biblical reinterpretation. Most pertinently, it has been argued that the homosexual theme of the Sodom and Gomorrah story is a later interpolation (Bailey 1955). But the 'holiness Code' of Leviticus is unambiguous.

Thou shalt not lie with mankind, as with

womankind: it is abomination. (Leviticus xviii.22)

If a man also lie with mankind, as he lieth with a woman, both of them have committed an abomination: they shall surely be put to death; their blood shall be upon them. (Leviticus xx.13)

In the New Testament, one likewise finds passages which categorically prohibit homosexual behaviour. As is usual on matters of sex, it was not the founder himself who pronounced on these matters, but his chief proselytizer, Paul.

the men, leaving the natural use of the woman, burned in their lust one toward another, men with men working unseemliness, and receiving in themselves that recompense of their error which was due. (Romans i.27)

Be not deceived: neither fornicators, nor idolators, nor adulterers, nor effeminate, nor abusers of themselves with men, nor thieves, nor covetous, nor drunkards, nor revilers, nor extortioners, shall inherit the kingdom of God. (I Corinthians vi.9–10)

law is not made for a righteous man, but for the lawless and unruly . . . for abusers of themselves with men . . . (I Timothy i.9–10)

Nor is lesbian behaviour neglected.

God gave them up unto vile passions: for their women changed the natural use into that which is against nature . . . (Romans i.26)

Of course, as you might imagine, there has been no shortage of voices prepared to argue that these passages do not really mean what they say. We are told that the condemnations are really against homosexual prostitution, and the like (Horner 1978). If so, one can only wish that God had chosen a less ambiguous scribe than Paul. What is clear, however, is that (much like the Greeks) both the Old and the New Testament authors are really concerned with *behaviour*. Attitudes and orientation go unmentioned and uncondemned.

Turning now to the great Christian philosophers, not unexpectedly we find that they too take a negative view of homosexual activity. Fairly typical was St Augustine (354–430), whose philosophical thought was a subtle blend of Neo-Platonism and Christianity. He saw homosexual acts as a failure to love either God or one's neighbour, writing that:

. . . those shameful acts against nature, such as were committed in Sodom, ought everywhere and always to be detested and punished. If all nations were to do such things, they would be held guilty of the same crime by the law of God, which has not so made men that they should use one another in this way. (Augustine, *Confessions*. III, viii (15), trans. Bailey 1955: 83)

Indeed, Augustine went so far as to say that in order to avoid homosexual advances one is permitted to commit acts which in other circumstances would be considered sins, like lying.

But the most detailed philosophical discussion of homosexuality by a Christian thinker is to be found in the writings of the thirteenth-century theologian St Thomas Aquinas (1968). Aquinas's treatment of homosexuality, as of most moral issues, depends crucially on the notion of "natural law." Essentially, he saw the whole world as created and regulated according to divine reason, which gives rise to eternal law ("This rational guidance of created things on the part of God . . . we can call the Eternal law"). Then, in turn, Aquinas thought that humans, inasmuch as we ourselves can control our destinies, have an obligation to fit with this eternal law. "This participation in the Eternal law by rational creatures is called the Natural law" (Aquinas, *Summa Theologiae*, 1a 2ae, quae. 91, art. 1). Coming to sexuality, Aquinas (who was much influenced by Aristotle) did not ask the straightforward causal question. "How do things work?" but rather the teleological question. "What are things for? What end do they serve?" And the answer he gave is that sex exists for the procreation and raising of children. This is why God made us sexual beings, and this therefore is the end towards which we must strive if we are not to violate natural law, that area of the eternal law where we ourselves must make a contribution.

The consequence of Aquinas's position, as he thought, is that all sex outside marriage is wrong because it is a violation of natural law. Thus, quite apart from homosexuality's prohibition on Biblical grounds, for Aquinas it is necessarily barred as being against natural law: as being in conflict with "right reason" (Aquinas 1968, p. 245). Homosexual encounters do not lead to children, therefore they must be wrong. But there is rather more than this. All lust is immoral, but some acts are doubly to be condemned, because "they are in conflict with the natural pattern of sexuality for the benefit of the species" (p. 245). These are termed "unnatural vices" *("vitiae contra naturum")*. There are four kinds of such vices: masturbation, bestiality, homosexuality, and sex acts where "the natural style of intercourse is not observed, as regards the proper organ or according to other rather beastly and monstrous techniques" (p. 245). Unnatural vices are the worst kinds of sins of lust (worse even than incest), and they are ordered according to the object being abused. Hence in the depths of depravity comes bestiality, then homosexuality, then "lechery which does not observe the due mode of intercourse," and at the top of a sorry lot comes masturbation.

And in quite unchanged form, this is the official Catholic position unto this day: "To choose someone of the same sex for one's sexual activity is to annul the rich symbolism and meaning, not to mention the goals of the creator's sexual design" (letter from Cardinal Ratzinger of the Sacred Congregation for the Doctrine of the Faith, to Catholic bishops: reported in *The Times*, 31 October 1986).[1]

Modern Ethical Philosophies

Let us turn now to the modern era, the time after the scientific revolution. There are two major, secular moral philosophies, those of the German thinker, Immanuel Kant (1949, 1959), and the (primarily) British utilitarians. Both groups thought their views threw light on the status of homosexual behaviour (again,

feelings get short shrift). Let us take them in turn.

Kant thought humans are subject to an overriding and necessary moral law, a supreme directive, the "categorical imperative." It is this law which tells us what we ought to do; wherein lies our duty. There are various ways in which Kant formulated his maxim (Körner 1955 gives a readable introduction). At one point he suggested that the key lies in the need to be able to *universalize* our actions: never do anything which you would not want to say that anybody and everybody should be able to do in a similar situation. Wanton cruelty is therefore wrong because one would not want to give people licence to do it to oneself. Another formulation of the categorical imperative is that one should always treat people as ends and not as means. In other words, one ought not simply use people for one's own benefit or for the benefit of others. People must be treated as subjective worthy beings in their own right.

As Kant (1963) himself recognized, at a quite general level sex and the categorical imperative have a rather uneasy relationship. The starting point to sex is the sheer desire of a person for the body of another. One wants to feel the skin, to smell the hair, to see the eyes— one wants to bring one's own genitals into contact with those of the other, and to reach orgasm. This gets dangerously close to treating the other as a means to the fulfilment of one's own sexual desire—as an object, rather than as an end. And this, according to the categorical imperative, is immoral. To escape from this dilemma, and one surely must if the end of the human race is not to be advocated on moral grounds, one must go on to treat the object of one's sexual advances as an end. One does this by broadening one's feelings, so that the personhood of the object of one's desire is brought within one's attraction, and by giving oneself reciprocally—by yielding oneself, body and soul, one shows respect for the other as an end, and not just as a means.

But what about a sincere commitment between two people of the same sex, the sort of homosexual equivalent of heterosexual marriage? At this point Kant invokes the notion of a *crimina carnis*, an abuse of one's sexuality. There are two kinds. First, there are acts which are contrary to sound reason, *crimina carnis secundum naturam*. These are immoral acts which go against the moral code imposed upon us as humans, and include such things as adultery. Second, there are acts contrary to our animal nature, *crimina carnis contra naturam*. These include masturbation, sex with animals, and homosexuality. They are the lowest and most disgusting sort of vice, worse in a sense even than suicide, and they are practices that we hesitate to mention. In fact, Kant found himself in something of a dilemma: mention the vices and you draw people's attention to them; fail to mention them and you do not warn people of them.

On balance, though, because they involve so great a violation of the categorical imperative, something must be said:

> A second *crimen carnis contra naturam* is intercourse between *sexus homogenii*, in which the object of sexual impulse is a human being but there is homogeneity instead of heterogeneity of sex, as when a woman satisfies her desire on a woman, or a man on a man. This practice too is contrary to the ends of humanity; for the end of humanity in respect of sexuality is to preserve the species without debasing the person; but in this instance the species is not being preserved (as it can be by a *crimen carnis secundum naturam*), but the person is set aside, the self is degraded below the level of the animals, and humanity is dishonoured. (Kant 1963: 170)

Contrasting with Kantian ethics is that of the utilitarians, the most prominent of whom were Jeremy Bentham and the two Mills, James (father) and John Stuart (son). For them, the key to ethical theory is happiness: "The creed which accepts as the foundation of morals utility or the greatest happiness principle holds that actions are right in proportion as they tend to promote happiness; wrong as they tend to produce the reverse of happiness" (Mill 1910: 6). Of course, there is a lot more to the theory than this, particularly revolving around what one might mean by "happiness" and "pleasure". To the more intellectually robust Bentham, "quantity of pleasure being

equal, pushpin is as good as poetry" (Bentham 1834). To the more sensitive (and greater) John Stuart Mill, "better to be Socrates dissatisfied than a fool satisfied" (Mill 1910: 9). But the important point is that to evaluate a moral action, one simply judges its consequences in terms of happiness (or pleasure) and unhappiness. And one action is better than another, and consequently that which one ought to do or approve, if it leads to greater happiness and to less unhappiness than the other.

Like Kant, Bentham applied his ethical theory to homosexual behaviour. Yet although they were writing at the same time, and although Bentham's language is frequently uncomplimentary, they might as well have been in different worlds. Bentham thinks homosexual interactions as acceptable morally as Kant finds them pernicious. Such interactions give pleasure to the people engaged in them, and so by the greatest happiness principle they ought to be valued. "As to any primary mischief, it is evident that [a homosexual interaction] produces no pain in anyone. On the contrary it produces pleasure . . ." (Bentham 1978: 390). Bentham is not advocating homosexual behaviour for everyone, only for those who want to so indulge. Then, there will be no harm. Nor is there any real problem stemming from the possibility that homosexual practices might incline or influence others into similar behaviour. People who indulge homosexual appetites seem to enjoy themselves; so at most one is inclining others to enjoyable practices.

What of the claim that homosexual behaviour runs one down physically, thus as it were reducing one's long-term pleasure in life? Bentham's conclusion is that there is no evidence to this effect. In any case, being in line with medical opinion of the time, and accepting that masturbation is physically debilitating, Bentham pointed out the injustice of trying to eliminate homosexuality through the law, when one did (and obviously could) do nothing about self-abuse. What of the claim that homosexuality is a threat to the keeping of population numbers up to an acceptable level? (Bentham had no doubts that a sizeable population is a good thing.) Again Bentham saw no danger on this score. Men's sexual appetites and capabilities far exceed those of females, particularly in the sense that a man can fertilize many more times than a fertilized female can give birth. Hence, for homosexuality to be a threat to population numbers "the nature of the human composition must receive a total change" (Bentham 1978: 396). Indeed, suggested Bentham rather tongue in cheek, with more homosexuality we should need fewer (heterosexual) prostitutes. These women, who rarely give birth, would therefore be freed for child-bearing purposes.

What about the idea that homosexuality amongst men deprives women of sex and marriage? Here, Bentham shows that what he is concerned to defend is the right of anyone to have homosexual relations, including those people chiefly of a heterosexual bent.

> Were the prevalence of this taste to rise to ever so great a height the most considerable part of the motives to marriage would remain entire. In the first place, the desire of having children, in the next place the desire of forming alliances between families, thirdly the convenience of having a domestic companion whose company will continue to be agreeable throughout life, fourthly the convenience of gratifying the appetite in question at any time when the want occurs and without the expense and trouble of concealing it or the danger of a discovery. (p. 400)

I take it that Bentham's concern with the right of heterosexuals to indulge homosexuality was (in part) a function of the fact that he was dealing with a society much like the Ancient Greeks', where upper-class young men were segregated from members of the opposite sex.

Bentham does incidentally make brief acknowledgement of the fact of lesbianism, but although noting that "where women contrive to procure themselves the sensation by means of women, the ordinary course of nature is as much departed from as when the like abomination is practised by men with men" (p. 100), he says nothing at all about its moral status. Presumably, he considered lesbian behaviour as no more immoral than male homosexual behaviour. It should be noted

that Bentham's failure to discuss lesbianism in detail was not sexist bias. In writing on male homosexuality he was trying to show that it did not merit the very severe legal penalties to which it was then subject. There were no such laws against lesbianism in England at the time that he was writing.

Bentham never published his ideas—perhaps out of prudence. We never therefore got public debate and opposition between the great ethical philosophers. But, with respect to homosexual activity, the difference is about as great as one could get. And this being so, we have reached a good point to stop and take stock.[2]

Is Homosexual Behaviour Biologically Unnatural?

I take it that the switch we have now encountered, from the focus (in previous chapters) on sexual orientation to the present concern with homosexual activity, is understandable and relatively uncontroversial. Homosexual orientation is something thrust upon you. You have no choice or freedom in the matter. Consequently, in this respect you are not a moral agent. Homosexual behaviour, however, is a question of choice. Here you do have the power to make decisions, to act rationally. Here, therefore, it is appropriate to make value judgements.

Turning now to discussion, as a philosopher I shall not presume to judge the purely religious input to the question of the moral status of homosexual behaviour. I shall use my exposition primarily to ferret out religious themes which sneak into ostensibly philosophical theses, and conversely. Indeed, with respect to homosexual activity it seems to me as an outsider that the religious position is thoroughly ambiguous. On the one hand, however much reinterpretation you may do, the Biblical prohibitions really are explicit. On the other hand, does the Christian truly have to take as literal everything in Leviticus or in the epistles of St Paul? You simply cannot make a reasonable decision about the moral status of homosexual activity, without some philosophical input—a conclusion which is supported by the fact that there are as many different stands on the homosexual question as there are religious denominations. [Batchelor 1980 carries an excellent survey of the various (American) church positions on homosexuality.]

We turn to philosophy, and as always we turn back to Plato, for it was he who introduced the argument which has had the greatest influence on western thought about the worth of homosexuality. Plato stated categorically that homosexuality (the behaviour at least) is wrong because it is unnatural—it is not something done by the animals. "Our citizens should not be inferior to birds and many species of animals . . ." (Plato, *Laws,* 840de, tr. Dover 1978: 166). And this is an argument which repeats itself through history. There are some things which ought not to be done because they go against nature in some way, and homosexual acts must be included. Our bodies are "designed" for proper functioning, and the genitalia specifically are designed for heterosexual relations, which are themselves the beginning step on the way to reproduction and thence to the creation of new humans. A penis in a vagina is doing what it was intended to do; a penis in an anus is not; and this is all there is to the matter. We learn this fact directly from the non-human world where, uncorrupted by perverted lusts, animals behave in their proper fashion, that is to say where they behave heterosexually. Homosexuality is unnatural, because it goes against our biology. Therefore it is immoral. Christian philosophers like Aquinas (1968) sing the theme; Kant (1963) finds homosexuality worse than suicide because of this; and there are loud echoes of it today. Undoubtedly the average (heterosexual!) woman or man would condemn homosexuality because it "goes against nature."

At least, now, we can see fully why so many radical thinkers were so hostile to biology, especially to a biology being applied to the understanding of homosexuality. It is biology which is the strongest plank in the barrier against the permissibility of same-gender sex. But should *we* condemn homosexual behaviour as immoral because it is unnatural, in the sense of being against biology? Should we

say that animals do not behave homosexually; therefore humans should not behave homosexually? Is it true that genitals were "designed" for heterosexual ends and that all other uses are a wicked corruption? We must try to answer these questions for ourselves, and to this end a number of points must be raised.

First, it is simply not true, if by "unnatural" one means "not performed by animals" or even "not commonly performed by animals," that homosexuality is unnatural. We know that in species after species, right through the animal kingdom, students of animal behaviour report unambiguous evidence of homosexual attachments and behaviour—in insects, fish, birds, and lower and higher mammals (reviewed in Weinrich 1982). Of course, you can always maintain that animal homosexual behaviour is not really homosexual behaviour. But granting that talk of animal homosexuality is not a conceptual confusion—and I have said all I have to say on that topic in the context of Dörner's rats—there are the kinds of behaviour and bonds occurring in nature that fully fit the description. There is evidence of anal penetration of one male by another and emission of semen (Denniston 1980), and one cannot go further than that. Whatever the moral implications of homosexuality and naturalness may be, it is false that homosexuality is immoral because it does not exist amongst animals. It has taken people a long time to realize how universal animal homosexual behaviour really is, or perhaps we should say that it has taken a long time for those knowledgeable about animal homosexuality (such as farmers and naturalists) to pass on their knowledge to those interested in the possibility of animal homosexuality (such as philosophers and theologians). But it does exist nevertheless, and we cannot pretend otherwise.

A second point is that, if by "unnatural" we mean "going against our biology"—and this is the sense of "unnatural" we are considering in this section—then if there is any truth at all in the sociobiological hypotheses, much human homosexuality (no doubt like much animal homosexuality) has a solid biological basis. It is something maintained by natural selection. To say, for example, that vaginas were designed for penises and that anuses were not so designed is simply not relevant. If, as a consequence of putting his penis in another man's anus, or allowing his own anus to be so used, a man better replicates his genes than if he were to devote his attention to seeking out vaginas, then biologically speaking this is perfectly proper or natural. Admittedly, anuses are also for defecating; but then, penises are also for urinating. There is a popular joke amongst gay men: "If God had meant us to be homosexuals, then he would have given us all anuses."

A third point against the thesis that homosexuality is biologically unnatural is that humans are not mere animals. This remains true even after Darwin. Humans have a social and cultural realm to a degree virtually inconceivable, by comparison with animals (Boyd and Richerson 1985). I see, therefore, no reason why things as important to our social and general life as our sexual emotions and attachments should be judged by animal standards. I do not condemn the male walrus for being polygamous; but neither do I suggest that therefore humans have the universal right to be polygamous (Barash 1977). Why should the male walrus be a standard for me? Or why should the (supposedly) heterosexual birds be a standard?

I think, in fact, that one can take this argument a little further. One sociobiological claim which does seem reasonably uncontentious is that humans, because they need so much parental care, have evolved sexual habits somewhat different from the rest of the animal world. In particular, unlike most mammals the male human must get involved in child rearing (Hrdy 1981). One way in which the female keeps the male in attendance is by being continuously sexually receptive. This means that much human sexual intercourse—the heterosexual variety—does not have the direct biological end of reproduction, in the sense of insemination. Hence, the whole set of arguments that any kind of sex that could not potentially lead to conception is unnatural is simply based on bad biology. Even if humans were physiologically like monkeys or rats in their reproductive mechanisms (and we have seen that in some respects they certainly are not), still at the non-cultural biological level

humans differ essentially from monkeys and rats (Meyer-Bahlburg 1984b). What is natural for others is not necessarily natural for us, nor do all human organs have simple, obvious uses.

A fourth and perhaps related point is that, even if it turns out that some kinds of sexual behaviour have nothing to do with straight biology, even if it turns out that the homosexual is doing him/herself a biological disservice and perhaps even his/her race or species a similar disservice, this does not as such imply that anything sexual, including homosexual, is immoral. What moral obligation has the individual got to reproduce (Ruse 1984b)? What moral obligation has the individual got to help his/her species reproduce?[3] It might be argued that any behaviour which is so disruptive of society that society itself fails to reproduce is immoral; but this is a contingent claim and one must justify it (Gray 1978). One has to show first that any such behaviour is in fact so disruptive of society, and secondly either that society's reproduction is a morally good thing, or that the disruption in itself causes so much trouble as to be a bad thing.

But, in reply, first of all it is obvious that homosexual activity today is not so disruptive of society as to prevent overall reproduction. Second, the moral importance of society's reproduction is not that obvious. We may have an obligation to future generations not so to pollute our planet that life for them becomes depressingly difficult, but do we have an obligation to produce future generations? I confess that I see no straightforward reasons to suggest that we do. Of course, if people want society to continue, then that is reason enough, and I think most people do want the human race to continue. But if enough of us felt otherwise, then why should their wish be wrong? (I am not saying that it would be moral to destroy all living people.) Third, even if homosexual activity were reducing population numbers, it would hardly be that disruptive of heterosexuals. No one is arguing that heterosexuals must be castrated, merely that those who do not want to reproduce need not.

The morality of homosexuality, therefore, must be judged on grounds other than those of biological naturalness. If what is natural is judged by what occurs in the animal world, then homosexuality is not unnatural. If what is natural is what it is biologically advantageous to do, then homosexuality is not obviously unnatural. And even if one agreed that naturalness for humans could be defined in terms of biological advantage, and even if one also agreed (which I do not) that homosexuality is unnatural, then it still would not necessarily be immoral. Its wrongness would have to be judged on other grounds. I am not denying that there is any concept of naturalness which is appropriate for humans; nor am I denying that violations of this concept might be, or be considered, bad things. When you have an argument with the ongoing appeal that the one we are now considering obviously has, it would be rash to pretend that there is nothing to it. Indeed, I shall be suggesting shortly that there may well be something to a notion of naturalness which is connected to value—although where this will leave homosexual behaviour is another matter. What I am saying is that one cannot tease out the moral status of human homosexual behaviour on grounds of *biological* naturalness. (This whole argument about biological unnaturalness strikes me as being a conceptual sibling of many of the arguments for evolutionary ethics; and with about as much validity. See Flew 1967; Ruse 1986.)

Obviously, one might try to resurrect the argument by appealing to additional premises. One possible way in which one could keep defending the thesis that homosexuality is immoral because it is biologically unnatural is along the lines suggested by Aquinas, where that which is biologically natural is seen as the rationale of boundaries that God wants us to respect. But apart from the fact that we still have the problem of explicating what is biologically natural for humans, we have also got to prove that it is God's will that we stay within bounds. Of course, Aquinas thinks he can do this and sets about the task with much subtlety and brilliance. But here, clearly, we move again from the philosophical to the theological. I can respect the Catholic doctrine of natural law, but it is not my job to believe it, defend it, or attack it. The fact remains that, on its own, the argument that homosexuality is biologically unnatural and hence immoral, fails. And with it goes much of the mainstay of the traditional critique of homosexual activity.

Homosexuality and the Modern Philosophers

We come to the present. Some radical thinkers would have us jettison all established moral principles, relying merely on intuitions and feelings. Thus, Jeffrey Weeks writes:

> If we endorse the radical approach that no erotic act has any intrinsic meaning this suggests that, though they may not be the conclusive factors, subjective feelings, intentions and meanings are vital elements in deciding on the merits of an activity. The decisive factor is an awareness of context, of the situation in which choices are made. (Weeks 1985: 219)

But this leaves you quite powerless, Both Adolf Hitler and Mother Teresa were aware in their different ways; yet we must evaluate their actions differently. Throwing out moral principles sacrifices integrity on the altar of subjectivity.

We would do better to stay with the great ethical theories of the modern era, Kantianism and utilitarianism. We have seen how Kant and the major utilitarian thinker Jeremy Bentham reached almost diametrically opposed positions on the morality of homosexual behaviour. Given that both thinkers explicitly and (I think) genuinely referred to their ethical foundations to justify their conclusions, one may conclude that this is all there is to the matter. I am not sure, however, that this is quite so. I suspect that the Kantian position is, if anything, somewhat more conservative than the utilitarian position, or at least some versions of the position, but I remain unconvinced that (as moral philosophies) they lead to totally different conclusions on the question of homosexual behaviour. On neither scheme will the Greek admiration for personal restraint be entirely lost.

Speaking of sexuality generally, Kant (1963) argued that the danger in any erotic encounter lies in the using of one's partner simply as an end to one's own (orgasmic) ends. Only through marriage can one achieve sex without violation of the categorical imperative.

Here, one enters into an agreement to let another have complete rights over oneself, in return for equal rights over that person.

> if I yield myself completely to another and obtain the person of the other in return, I win myself back; I have given myself up as the property of another, but in turn I take that other as my property, and so win myself back again in winning the person whose property I have become. (p. 167)

I get myself back as an end and treat my partner as an end in some way, because I have given myself absolutely to another who has given him/herself absolutely to me.

Now, putting matters this way, legal questions about marriage aside, I simply cannot see that a homosexual relationship is any less a potentially full, moral encounter than is a heterosexual relationship. There is no reason why homosexuals should reach out in a loving and giving relationship any less than do heterosexuals. At this level, whatever Kant himself says to the contrary, homosexuality is quite compatible with the categorical imperative—it is a good, even. Kant himself, as we saw, speaks of the self being "degraded" and of humanity being "dishonoured," and I am sure that he thought that in homosexual acts people—including oneself—were being used as means rather than ends. Again, he spoke of "the species not being preserved" and, considering the categorical imperative as a demand that actions be universalizable, no doubt, he thought that if we were all homosexual then humankind would come to a rapid halt. But if you remove the biology-as-unnatural-therefore-immoral element, then nothing remains to Kant's objections. We are no longer degraded by being lower than the animals, and even if we were different—breaking from the "naturalness" of animals—then so what? Humans uniquely cook their meat. Does this debase us? And, in any case, preservation of the species is not an ultimate, either in biology or morality. Of course, I would like the human species to continue. Kant would like the species to continue. But these desires do not stem from the categorical imperative.

I expect there will be those Kantians who try a different tack, arguing on empirical grounds that full, loving homosexual relationships are impossible. The empirical information of the first chapter, and the causal discussions of the succeeding chapters (especially the critique of the phobic theorists) is my backing against this, and if more is needed, it will be found in the discussion of health and disease in the next chapter.[4] I am not, of course, arguing that homosexuality is a good above heterosexuality, and ought therefore to be practised by heterosexuals. For the sake of argument, at this point, I am prepared even to accept a conservative claim that, perhaps if there are no children, a homosexual relationship will be less fulfilled than a heterosexual relationship. My point simply is that for those whose inclinations tend to homosexuality, and who can and would enter into full relationships that way, it is a good on Kantian grounds. It is certainly morally superior to the alternatives, which are either that homosexuals enter into heterosexual relationships or that they suffer an imposed celibacy. (I shall leave until the final chapter all of the somewhat convoluted arguments about "setting an example." Here, I shall assume that two homosexuals, living in a loving relationship, do not cause a collapse in the wellbeing of all of the heterosexuals around them.)

Nevertheless, all of this talk of intense, one-to-one relationships, does rather raise the question of casual sexual encounters. These, heterosexual as well as homosexual, are far more difficult to justify within a Kantian framework (despite what some modern interpreters have implied to the contrary: Elliston 1975). It is true that, however casual an encounter, one can give one's body reciprocally to one's partner; but one is caught in a situation where people are treating each other as objects to such an extent that I doubt that this giving fully compensates. Obviously, this is a matter of degress: not all casual sex is as impersonal as fellatio with a stranger through a hole in the wall in a public lavatory. But generally speaking, in a transient sexual encounter one seems not to be involved with the other person as a person. If nothing else, the case can surely be made that in casual sex one is sexually desensitizing oneself, so the full-blown sexual relationship—precious precisely because it is unique—is made that much more difficult. Hence, I suspect that the promiscuous lifestyles of so many male homosexuals transgress the categorical imperative. (I will take as given all of the qualifications one must now make in this era of AIDS. Even if "safe sex" is, or becomes, possible, the Kantian has trouble with promiscuity—although, I confess that the thought of several hundred men, in an abandoned warehouse, clad in nothing but gym-shoes, engaging in group masturbation, strikes me as more ludicrous than positively evil. I assume that if one is knowingly engaging in any sex that might infect others, this is wrong to the Kantian—or to any other moral theorist, for that matter. Whether running a risk for oneself is immoral is a nice point. Kant would have thought it is. Since none of us is Robinson Crusoe, I would myself probably argue likewise, if not for the same reasons.)

Turning to the utilitarian position, Bentham (1978) is surely right in concluding that, judged by the criterion of pleasure, there is nothing immoral in homosexuality per se. If people who indulge in such activities get pleasure from the activities, then so be it. It may be objected that homosexuals on average are less happy than heterosexuals. However, even if this objection were true (and we shall be turning to this matter in the next chapter), it would hardly be all that relevant. The point is whether people of homosexual inclination get more pleasure from homosexual activities than they would from enforced heterosexual activities, and there is no question about the answer to this. They are happier in freely chosen homosexual activity than they would be in compulsory heterosexuality. Nor is it plausible that the discomfort caused to heterosexuals by homosexuals' practices alters the overall calculus of pleasure. Letting homosexuals behave after their inclinations increases the total pleasure. Therefore homosexual activity is not a moral evil. It is a positively good thing, in fact. (As noted above, in the final chapters I shall discuss in detail the whole question of the homosexual and society at large.)

I suspect that the Benthamite version of the greatest happiness principle most probably extends to an endorsement of fairly casual sexual affairs as well as long-term, deep, loving relationships. If people get pleasure from casual sex acts at whatever level, then they are accept-able. "Push-pin is as good as poetry." The only qualifications would come from the above mentioned dangers of disease. However, in this context of casual sex one really ought to mention the views of John Stuart Mill (1910) and his distinction between qualities of pleasures. Mill certainly does not want to rule out sex entirely. He himself was for years deeply in love with Harriet Taylor, finally marrying her. But his position, borne out by his own relationship with Mrs Taylor, is that a sexual relationship must be part of an overall relationship: a union demanding intellect and emotions, if it is to achieve true happiness and be morally worthwhile. I see nothing in any of this which would bar a homosexual relationship from reaching just such a desirable state as a heterosexual relationship. However, I really cannot imagine that Mill would rate casual encounters very high on the happiness scale. Quite apart from the pleasure-destroying risks that such encounters carry, he would surely think that the efforts expounded on them could be better employed elsewhere. For Mill, physical pleasures are far outweighed by pleasures which involve the intellect or meaningful interaction between people: "Human beings have faculties more elevated than the animal appetites, and when once made conscious of them, do not regard anything as happiness which does not include their gratification" (1910: 7). Undoubtedly, this eliminates casual encounters as objects of moral desirability—certainly casual encounters which do not go beyond the level of physical animal sex.

My conclusions, therefore, are that once you strike out fallacious arguments about biological naturalness, and bring forward modern realizations of the possibilities for homosexuals of meaningful relationships, the Kantian and utilitarian positions come very much closer together. Certainly, at a minimum, there is moral worth in the close-coupled relationships of the Second Kinsey study, and probably more. Yet, Benthamite utilitarianism excepted, there simply has to be concern at total sexual promiscuity. To radicals, this may sound like retreat. But moral philosophies, if they are to have any bite, have to draw the line somewhere—and I believe they draw the line here.

I have no wish, myself, to hide behind the great names of the past. I have elsewhere argued for the central worth of both Kantian and (Millian) utilitarian moral philosophies (Ruse 1986). I see no reason now to back off from what I take to be their consequences qua homosexual behaviour. Homosexuality within a loving relationship is a morally good thing. Casual promiscuity threatens us all, heterosexual and homosexual. One qualification must be added, however. It is a great deal easier to avoid wrongdoing, if you are not tempted. Thinking now especially of the average heterosexual male, to sleep with 1003 women would truly demand the charm and dedication of Don Giovanni, not to mention the assistance of Leporello. For the average homosexual male, the opportunities are readily available and the numbers easily passed (qualifications about AIDS, and so forth, taken as read). Also—whether the reasons be biological or cultural—the actual harm done in 1003 homosexual encounters might be much, much less than the harm done in 1003 heterosexual encounters (Symons 1979). I defy anyone to have 1003 heterosexual encounters without an extraordinary amount of cheating and lying—even if you do not end by killing a Commandatore. For these and like reasons, I think the moral philosopher—Kantian or utilitarian—should be very wary of rushing in and, although allowing the ideal of a homosexual relationship, denying the reality as it affects many (if not most) homosexual males. (Since lesbians apparently are far less promiscuous than male homosexuals, these qualifying words hardly apply to them.)

Sexual Perversion

In theory, this should conclude our discussion at this point. Once you have strained out religious elements, once you have dropped outmoded scientific claims, once you have sorted through the proper relationship between "is" and "ought," once you have discovered a little bit about what homosexuals are really like rather than what you think they might be like, moral conclusions start to fall

fairly readily into place. Yet there is something about homosexual activity—and, indeed, the whole overt homosexual life style—that other people find disturbing and threatening; something which drives people to conclude that, for all of the fancy arguments of the philosophers, homosexual activity is a wrong: a moral evil. (The feeling is particularly strong of males, by males—an asymmetry to which I shall return.)

What is it about homosexuality—what is it about male homosexuality in particular—that brings forth such negative judgements? One thing, above all else, comes across. Listen to the eminent theologian Karl Barth (1980): "[Homosexuality] is the physical, psychological and social sickness, the phenomenon of perversion, decadence and decay, which can emerge when man refuses to admit the validity of the divine command in the sense in which we are now considering it" (p. 49). Forget about the sickness part of the complaint. God does not condemn the diabetic. What troubles Barth and his God—what troubles virtually all of those who hate homosexuality—is that they see it as a *perversion*. It is the epitome of wrongdoing, and therefore must be censored in the strongest possible way.

Obviously, from our perspective, we have seen a paradox. Homosexual behaviour seems not so very morally pernicious; yet, through the notion of perversion, this is precisely how it appears to many people—in our society, at least. How can we resolve it? Fortunately, some help is at hand, for the notion of perversion has been much discussed by analytic philosophers in recent years.[5] Typical in many respects, certainly in that which ties in best with our previous discussion, is an analysis by Sara Ruddick (1975). Trying to capture the concept, she turns to traditional arguments, claiming that what people have been arguing about down through the ages is less a moral question and more one of perversity. She suggests that the natural end of sex is reproduction: that all and only acts which tend to lead to reproduction are natural, and that all unnatural acts are perverted.

The ground for classifying sexual acts as either natural or unnatural is that the former type serve or could serve the evolutionary and biological function of sexuality—namely, reproduction. "Natural" sexual desire has as its "object" living persons of the opposite sex, and in particular their postpubertal genitals. The "aim" of natural sexual desire—that is, the act that "naturally" completes it—is genital intercourse. Perverse sex acts are deviations . . . (p. 91)

Clearly, on her criterion, Ruddick finds homosexual acts perverse. However, unlike many, Ruddick sees nothing morally inferior about perverted sex acts. Indeed she goes so far as to say that, all other things being equal, "perverted sex acts are preferable to natural ones if the latter are less pleasurable or less complete" (p. 96).

As Ruddick's proposal stands, it obviously will not do. Apart from the difficulties with the notion of "biological naturalness," how do you deal with non-obviously sexual perversions? I should say that a man who spreads his sheets with faeces before he hops into bed is perverse. Yet Ruddick's analysis tells us nothing of it. Conversely, are we supposed to believe that such non-reproductive sex as using a condom is perverse? And, in any case, although I agree that homosexuality per se is not immoral, Ruddick—in what one critic has called the "over-intellectualized-approach" typical of philosophers (Goldman 1977)—surely misses what is most central to the notion of perversion: the very strong emotional reaction that perverse acts raise in us. To most people, to say "perverted sex acts are preferable to natural ones" is virtually a contradiction in terms. Perversion *is* a value concept. (Weeks 1985 is quite right in connecting judgements of perversion with political commitments—the latter are value notions also.)

So, how does one do better? Naturalness keeps coming up. Perhaps the time has come to make it work for us, rather than against us. And indeed, this is a reasonable move, for people like Ruddick are surely right in thinking naturalness important. The pervert who spreads faeces all over his bedsheets is unnatural. And, because he is unnatural, he is a pervert. Yet a biological definition will not do. Perhaps the time has come to make a break. We are human beings: that means we live in a

cultural realm, unlike animals who are fundamentally trapped down at the level of pure biology. What I argue, therefore, is that naturalness ought to be defined in terms of culture and not simple biology. What is unnatural, and what is consequently in some important sense perverse, is what goes against or breaks with our culture. It is what violates the ends or aims that human beings think are important or worth striving for. This may include reproduction, but extends to all the things we hold dear, the things that make us happy and make life worth living generally. And this is why perversity is indeed a value laden term, because a perversion puts itself against human norms and values. (In invoking culture to define perversion. I am with Gray 1978, and Margolis 1975, although I doubt they would agree with all that I would claim.)

We have to go a little bit further than just referring to culture to define perversion, however. Stealing or murder go against western culture's rules, but one would not want to say that the thief qua thief or the murderer qua murderer was a pervert. It is true indeed that some who break society's moral rules are perverts, but I suspect that the breaking of the rules and the perversity are not quite logically identical, even though they may coincide. Reginald Halliday Christie used to get a sexual thrill from murdering women while having intercourse with them (Kennedy 1960). He was a pervert. But his perversity lay not in the murder per se but in his sexual propensities. Conversely, not all perversities violate moral rules, at least not in a straightforward way. A person who eats 10 kg of chocolates per day, and then vomits them up, is close to perversion—even though there may not be much immoral about the action. Had Christie confined his activities to copulating with (suitably hollowed) cabbages, tearing them to shreds at the point of orgasm, he would still have been a pervert, although his actions would not have been immoral.

This is the key to perversions: what I like to call the "Ugh! factor." A perversion involves a breaking not of a moral rule, but more of an aesthetic rule. We find perversions disgusting, revolting. But why is this? I would suggest the following reason. A perversion involves going against one of culture's values or ends or things considered desirable, and other members of society cannot understand why one would want to go against the value. People cannot empathize with the pervert or understand why he/she has done what he/she has (Stoller 1975). One may not approve of what the murderer has done, but at least one can understand the action. We have all felt hate for others, even wishing that people were dead. Very few of us have felt the urge to strangle our partner during copulation, or think we or anyone else could enjoy it.

Put matters this way: in the *Republic* (11. 359–60), Plato tells the story of Gyges who found a magic ring which would make him invisible at will. Hence, he had full power to do and get whatever he wanted. Gyges in fact killed the king, and seduced the queen, and set himself up in power. We may not approve: we can understand. Were Gyges to have stolen 10 kg of chocolates per day, or copulated with cabbages, we simply would not have understood. Nor would we have understood had he wanted to strangle the queen during intercourse. (By understand here, I do not mean "understand causally": I mean "feel an empathy with a fellow human being." Of course, causal understanding may lead to empathy.) My point, therefore, is that a perversion is something which goes against the very things we hold worthwhile: that we could not imagine wanting to do, even if we could.

Note that a perversion does not necessarily involve doing something that one does not want to do. I may not want to become a celibate monk, but such a monk is not therefore a pervert. I can understand a monk's feelings well enough to empathize. I simply cannot so empathize with a child molester. Note also that although a perversion is not immoral because it is a perversion, often its perversity lies in that which makes it immoral. We find it so alien to use a person as Christie used his victims that we think his actions perverse. This explains why many perversions are not merely aesthetically revolting but also morally pernicious.

We have come back to the original Platonic position—but with crucial shifts. Unnaturalness is connected to culture, not biology. (As a

Darwinian, though, I would never deny that the former comes from and is moulded by the latter. That is why many perversions do involve biologically unsavoury acts—like eating faeces.) And the values involved are not so much moral as aesthetic. So what about homosexuality? Are homosexual acts perverse acts, and is the inclination to such acts a perverse inclination? Acknowledging that I am trying to offer a descriptive rather than prescriptive analysis, I do not think there is any straightforward answer to these questions. But I look upon this as a strength of my analysis, not a weakness! I think the question of the perversity of homosexuality is to a great extent an empirical matter. How do people feel about homosexual behaviour? Can they in some sense relate to it, whether or nor they want to do it themselves and whether or not they have homosexual inclinations? The answer surely is that some people can—homosexuals themselves and some heterosexuals. Many others, like Karl Barth, cannot—they find it totally alien and disgusting. Hence, I suggest that for some people in our society homosexuality is not a perversion and for some it is. Some other societies have seen homosexuality totally as a perversion. Some other societies have not seen it as a perversion at all (Churchill 1967; Bullough 1976; Blackwood 1985).

What I am arguing, therefore, is that, faced with divided opinion in our society about the perverted nature of homosexuality (inclination and behaviour), neither side is absolutely right and neither side is absolutely wrong. There is a crucial element of subjectivity at work here, as with liking or disliking spinach. Perversion, especially as it applies to homosexuality, is a relative concept. But this does not mean that people's minds on the subject cannot be changed, or that one has no obligation to change people's minds. If one agrees that homosexuality is not immoral, then surely one ought to persuade people not to regard homosexuals and their habits with loathing. Certainly, one ought to persuade people not to confuse their disgust at a perversion with moral indignation. This does not mean that one should try to turn everyone or anyone into a homosexual; but, given that feelings of loathing are hurtful to people in a society, if there is good reason for the feelings (that is, if they do not reinforce moral norms), then they are simply divisive, and one should try to end them. And not simply for the sake of those despised. Homophobics are not paradigmatically happy people (De Cecco 1984).

Conclusion

This brings this part of the discussion to an end. If you need further argument to convince you of the truth of what I have been saying, let me remind you of the curious phenomenon of lesbianism and the law. Morally, I defy you to find any difference between a male homosexual act and a lesbian act. Yet western law, as enforcer of morals, has always been more strict against the former than against the latter. It has not been from the reluctance of the (almost invariably) male legislators to judge female morality—the laws against adultery usually fall more heavily on women than on men. The answer lies in the fact that the average male heterosexual can regard lesbianism without strong counter-emotions. He finds it erotic, even. Thus, he does not stand in danger of confusing disgust at perversion with moral outrage. . . .

For men, it is otherwise. Many people have strongly negative feelings about male homosexuality. What I suggest is that they mistake the nature of their emotions. In their disgust, they make moral judgements whereas (at most) they should admit to aesthetic judgements. This is not to say that people cannot back up their feelings with moral arguments. But if these latter can be dismissed—and I have given my opinion on this—then we should work on our feelings. Not to do so is morally wrong. Indeed, it is important that this chapter end with this point resonating in your mind. Heterosexuals are only too ready to make moral judgements about homosexuals. Unrestrained homophobia is a far worse sin than two or twenty homosexuals grappling together.

Notes

1. Boswell (1980), in what is recognized as the authoritative source on the history of the attitude of the Catholic church towards homosexuality in the first twelve centuries of its existence, shows that—despite the arguments of the philosophers—in thought and behaviour authorities were often tolerant of homosexuality in its various forms. I do think Boswell underestimates the subtlety and integrity of Aquinas's arguments—but, of course, as a fellow philosopher I am defending one of my own.

2. Since the eighteenth century, there has been comparatively little written on the topic of homosexuality by professional philosophers. One who does touch on the subject is the French existentialist, Jean-Paul Sartre; but he is mainly interested in using the refusal to accept homosexual identity as an example of bad faith ("*mauvais fois*"). See Sartre 1965; also 1947, 1962.

3. Already, here, with the emphasis on the group we are going beyond biology, but let it pass. Today's evolutionists emphasize that natural selection works for, and only for, the species. Anyone who says that the homosexual is letting down the side, biologically speaking, is twenty years out of date, biologically speaking.

4. An interesting Kantian-like suggestion from Scruton (1986) is that perhaps homosexual relationships fail to measure with heterosexual relationships because, being narcissus-like, they do not involve the same level of mystery (and consequent need to risk oneself) as is required when dealing with a person of the other gender. Perhaps paradoxically, given that I am more sympathetic to the significance of human biology than is Scruton, I would claim that any relationship with another requires such a self-transcending commitment.

5. The classic article in this field is by Thomas Nagel (1969). But I agree with his critics that he speaks less of the sexually perverse and more of the sexually complete or incomplete. I take it that the Freudian notion of "perversion". . . is a technical term, with no immediate connection to the general sense being discussed here.

10. Why Homosexuality Is Abnormal

Michael Levin

Michael Levin argues that homosexuality is inherently abnormal and immoral. He contends that homosexuality constitutes a misuse of important body parts and that such misuse can be connected to human unhappiness.

Introduction

This paper defends the view that homosexuality is abnormal and hence undesirable—not because it is immoral or sinful, or because it weakens society or hampers evolutionary development, but for a purely mechanical reason. It is a misuse of bodily parts. Clear empirical sense attaches to the idea of *the use* of such bodily parts as genitals, the idea that they are *for* something, and consequently to the idea of their misuse. I argue on grounds involving natural selection that misuse of bodily parts can with high probability be connected to unhappiness. I regard these matters as prolegomena to such policy issues as the rights of homosexuals, the rights of those desiring not to associate with homosexuals, and legislation concerning homosexuality, issues which I shall not discuss systematically here. However, I do in the last section draw a seemingly evident corollary from my view that homosexuality is abnormal and likely to lead to unhappiness.

I have confined myself to male homosexuality for brevity's sake, but I believe that much of what I say applies *mutatis mutandis* to lesbianism. There may well be significant differences between the two: the data of [2], for example, support the popular idea that sex *per se* is less important to women and in particular lesbians than it is to men. On the other hand, lesbians are generally denied motherhood, which seems more important to women than is fatherhood—normally denied homosexual males—to men. On this matter, [2] offers no

data. Overall, it is reasonable to expect general innate gender differences to explain the major differences between male homosexuals and lesbians.

Despite the publicity currently enjoyed by the claim that one's "sexual preference" is nobody's business but one's own, the intuition that there is something unnatural about homosexuality remains vital. The erect penis fits the vagina, and fits it better than any other natural orifice; penis and vagina seem made for each other. This intuition ultimately derives from, or is another way of capturing, the idea that the penis is not *for* inserting into the anus of another man—that so using the penis is not the way it is *supposed*, even *intended*, to be used. Such intuitions may appear to rest on an outmoded teleological view of nature, but recent work in the logic of functional ascription shows how they may be explicated, and justified, in suitably naturalistic terms. Such is the burden of Section 2, the particular application to homosexuality coming in Section 3. Furthermore, when we understand the sense in which homosexual acts involve a misuse of genitalia, we will see why such misuse is bad and not to be encouraged. (The case for this constitutes the balances of Section 3.) . . .

But before turning to these issues, I want to make four preliminary remarks. The first concerns the explicitness of my language in the foregoing paragraph and the rest of this paper. Explicit mention of bodily parts and the frank description of sexual acts are necessary to keep the phenomenon under discussion in clear focus. Euphemistic vagary about "sexual orientation" or "the gay lifestyle" encourage one to slide over homosexuality without having to face or even acknowledge what it really is. Such talk encourages one to treat "sexual preference" as if it were akin to preference among flavors of ice-cream. Since unusual taste in ice-cream is neither right nor wrong, this usage suggests, why should unusual taste in sex be regarded as objectionable? Opposed to this usage is the unblinkable fact that the sexual preferences in question are such acts as mutual fellation. Is one man's taste for pistachio ice-cream really just like another man's taste for fellation? Unwillingness to call this particular spade a spade allows delicacy to award the field by default to the view that homosexuality is normal. Anyway, such delicacy is misplaced in a day when "the love that dare not speak its name" is shouting its name from the rooftops.*

My second, related, point concerns the length of the present paper. . . . [We have shortened Levin's paper considerably.—Eds.]

The third point is this. The chain of intuitions I discussed earlier has other links, links connected to the conclusion that homosexuality is bad. They go something like this: Homosexual acts involve the use of the genitals for what they aren't for, and it is a *bad* or at least *unwise* thing to use a part of your body for what it isn't for. Calling homosexual acts "unnatural" is intended to sum up this entire line of reasoning. "Unnatural" carries disapprobative connotations, and any explication of it should capture this. . . . To have anything to do with our intuitions—even if designed to demonstrate them groundless—an explication of "abnormal" must capture the analytic truth that the abnormality of a practice is a reason for avoiding it. If our ordinary concept of normality turns out to be ill-formed, so that various acts are at worst

"abnormal" in some nonevaluative sense, this will simply mean that, as we ordinarily use the expression, *nothing is abnormal*. (Not that anyone really believes this—people who deny that cacophagia or necrophilia are abnormal do so only to maintain the appearance of consistency.)

Fourth, I should mention Steven Goldberg's defense of a position similar to mine ([3]). . . .

On "Function" and Its Cognates

To bring into relief the point of the idea that homosexuality involves a misuse of bodily parts, I will begin with an uncontroversial case of misuse, a case in which the clarity of our intuitions is not obscured by the conviction that they are untrustworthy. Mr. Jones pulls all his teeth and strings them around his neck because he thinks his teeth look nice as a necklace. He takes puréed liquids supplemented by intravenous solutions for nourishment. It is surely natural to say that Jones is misusing his teeth, that he is not using them for what they are for, that indeed the way he is using them is incompatible with what they are for. Pedants might argue that Jones's teeth are no longer part of him and hence that he is not misusing any bodily parts. To them I offer Mr. Smith, who likes to play "Old MacDonald" on his teeth. So devoted is he to this amusement, in fact, that he never uses his teeth for chewing—like Jones, he takes nourishment intravenously. Now, not only do we find it perfectly plain that Smith and Jones are misusing their teeth, we predict a dim future for them on purely physiological grounds; we expect the muscles of Jones's jaw that are used for—that *are* for—chewing to lose their tone, and we expect this to affect Jones's gums. Those parts of Jones's digestive tract that are for processing solids will also suffer from disuse. The net result will be deteriorating health and perhaps a shortened life. Nor is this all. Human beings enjoy chewing. Not only has natural selection selected in muscles for chewing and favored creatures with such muscles, it has

---

*"Sexual preference" typifies the obfuscatory language in which the homosexuality debate is often couched. "Preference" suggests that sexual tastes are voluntarily chosen, whereas it is a commonplace that one cannot decide what to find sexually stimulating. True, we talk of "preferences" among flavors of ice-cream even though one cannot choose what flavor of ice-cream to like; such talk is probably a carryover from the voluntariness of *ordering* ice-cream. "Sexual preference" does not even sustain this analogy, however, since sex is a forced choice for everyone except avowed celibates, and especially for the relatively large number of homosexuals who cruise regularly (see Appendix [deleted from this abridged version of Levin's essay—Eds.]).

selected a tendency to find the use of those muscles reinforcing. Creatures who do not enjoy using such parts of their bodies as deteriorate with disuse, will tend to be selected out. Jones, product of natural selection that he is, descended from creatures who at least tended to enjoy the use of such parts. Competitors who didn't simply had fewer descendants. So we expect Jones sooner or later to experience vague yearnings to chew something, just as we find people who take no exercise to experience a general listlessness. Even waiving for now my apparent reification of the evolutionary process, let me emphasize how little anyone is tempted to say "each to his own" about Jones or to regard Jones's disposition of his teeth as simply a deviation from a statistical norm. This sort of case is my paradigm when discussing homosexuality.

The main obstacle to talk of what a process or organic structure is for is that, literally understood, such talk presupposes an agent who intends that structure or process to be used in a certain way. Talk of function derives its primitive meaning from the human use of artifacts, artifacts being for what purposive agents intend them for. Indeed, there is in this primitive context a natural reason for using something for what it is for: to use it otherwise would frustrate the intention of some purposeful agent. Since it now seems clear that our bodily parts were not emplaced by purposeful agency, it is easy to dismiss talk of what they are for as "theologically" based on a faulty theory of how we came to be built as we are:

> The idea that sex was designed for propagation is a theological argument, but not a scientific one. . . . To speak of the "fit" of penis and vagina as proof of nature's intention for their exclusive union is pure theological reasoning—imposing a meaning or purpose upon a simple, natural phenomenon ([4], 63).

Barash—who elsewhere uses its cognates freely—dismisses "unnatural" as a mere term of abuse: "people with a social or political axe to grind will call what they don't like 'unnatural' and what they do, 'natural' " ([1], 237). Hume long ago put the philosopher's case against the term 'natural' with characteristic succinctness: " 'Tis founded on final Causes; which is a consideration, that appears to me pretty uncertain & unphilosophical. For pray, what is the End of Man? Is he created for Happiness or for Virtue? For this Life or the next? For himself or for his Maker?" ([5], 134). . . .

An organ is for a given activity if the organ's performing that activity helps its host or organisms suitably related to its host, *and* if this contribution is how the organ got and stays where it is. . . . This definition . . . distinguishes what something is for from what it may be *used* for on some occasion. Teeth are for chewing—we have teeth because their use in chewing favored the survival of organisms with teeth—whereas Jones is using his teeth for ornamentation.

[This account of what it is for an organ to be *for* a certain activity] explains our intuition that, since their efficacy in chewing got them selected in, teeth are for masticating and Jones is preventing his teeth from doing their proper job. . . . Nature is interested in making its creatures like what is (inclusively) good for them. A creature that does not enjoy using its teeth for chewing uses them less than does a toothed competitor who enjoys chewing. Since the use of teeth for chewing favors the survival of an individual with teeth, and, other things being equal, traits favorable to the survival of individuals favor survival of the relevant cohort, toothed creatures who do not enjoy chewing tend to get selected out. We today are the filtrate of this process, descendants of creatures who liked to chew. . . .

Jones's behavior is ill-advised not only because of the avertible objective consequences of his defanging himself, but because he will feel that something is missing. Similarly, this is why you should exercise. It is not just that muscles are for running. We have already heard the sceptic's reply to that: "So what? Suppose I don't mind being flabby? Suppose I don't give a hang about what will propagate my genetic cohort?" Rather, running is good because nature made sure people like to run. This is, of course, the prudential "good," not the moral "good"—but I disavowed at the outset the doctrine that misuse of bodily parts is *morally* bad, at least in any narrow sense. You ought to run because running was once necessary for catching food: creatures who did not enjoy running, if there ever were any, caught less food and reproduced less frequently than competitors who enjoyed running. These competitors passed on their appetites along with their muscles *to you.* This is not to say that those who suffer the affective consequences of laziness must recognize them as such, or even be able to identify them against their general background feeling-tone. They may not realize they would feel better if they exercised. They may even doubt it. They may have allowed their muscles to deteriorate beyond the point at which satisfying exercise is possible. For all that, evolution has decreed that a life involving regular exercise is on the whole more enjoyable than a life without. The same holds for every activity that is the purpose of an organ.

Applications to Homosexuality

The application of this general picture to homosexuality should be obvious. There can be no reasonable doubt that one of the functions of the penis is to introduce semen into the vagina. It does this, and it has been selected in because it does this. . . . Nature has consequently made this use of the penis rewarding. It is clear enough that any proto-human males who found unrewarding the insertion of penis into vagina have left no descendants. In particular, proto-human males who enjoyed inserting their penises into each other's anuses have left no descendants. This is why homosexuality is abnormal, and why its abnormality counts prudentially against it. Homosexuality is likely to cause unhappiness because it leaves unfulfilled an innate and innately rewarding desire. And should the reader's environmentalism threaten to get the upper hand, let me remind him again of an unproblematic case. Lack of exercise is bad and even abnormal not only because it is unhealthy but also because one feels poorly without regular exercise. Nature made exercise rewarding because, until recently, we had to

exercise to survive. Creatures who found running after game unrewarding were eliminated. Laziness leaves unreaped the rewards nature has planted in exercise, even if the lazy man cannot tell this introspectively. If this is a correct description of the place of exercise in human life, it is by the same token a correct description of the place of heterosexuality.

It hardly needs saying, but perhaps I should say it anyway, that this argument concerns tendencies and probabilities. Generalizations about human affairs being notoriously "true by and large and for the most part" only, saying that homosexuals are bound to be less happy than heterosexuals must be understood as short for "Not coincidentally, a larger proportion of homosexuals will be unhappy than a corresponding selection of the heterosexual population." There are, after all, genuinely jolly fat men. To say that laziness leads to adverse affective consequences means that, because of our evolutionary history, the odds are relatively good that a man who takes no exercise will suffer adverse affective consequences. Obviously, some people will get away with misusing their bodily parts. Thus, when evaluating the empirical evidence that bears on this account, it will be pointless to cite cases of well-adjusted homosexuals. I do not say they are nonexistent; my claim is that, of biological necessity, they are rare. . . .

Talk of what is "in the genes" inevitably provokes the observation that we should not blame homosexuals for their homosexuality if it is "in their genes." True enough. Indeed, since nobody decides what he is going to find sexually arousing, the moral appraisal of sexual object "choice" is entirely absurd. However, so saying is quite consistent with regarding homosexuality as a misfortune, and taking steps—this being within the realm of the will—to minimize its incidence, especially among children. Calling homosexuality involuntary does not place it outside the scope of evaluation. Victims of sickle-cell anemia are not blameworthy, but it is absurd to pretend that there is nothing wrong with them. Homosexual activists are partial to genetic explanations and hostile to Freudian environmentalism in part because they see a genetic cause as exempting homosexuals from blame. But surely people are equally blameless for indelible traits acquired in early childhood. And anyway, a blameless condition may still be worth trying to prevent. . . .

Utilitarians must take the present evolutionary scenario seriously. The utilitarian attitude toward homosexuality usually runs something like this: even if homosexuality is in some sense unnatural, as a matter of brute fact homosexuals take pleasure in sexual contact with members of the same sex. As long as they don't hurt anyone else, homosexuality is as great a good as heterosexuality. But the matter cannot end here. Not even a utilitarian doctor would have words of praise for a degenerative disease that happened to foster a certain kind of pleasure (as sore muscles uniquely conduce to the pleasure of stretching them). A utilitarian doctor would presumably try just as zealously to cure diseases that feel good as less pleasant degenerative diseases. A pleasure causally connected with great distress cannot be treated as just another pleasure to be toted up on the felicific scoreboard. Utilitarians have to reckon with the inevitable consequences of pain-causing pleasure. . . .

On Policy Issues

Homosexuality is intrinsically bad only in a prudential sense. It makes for unhappiness. However, this does not exempt homosexuality from the larger categories of ethics—rights, duties, liability. Deontic categories apply to acts which increase or decrease happiness or expose the helpless to the risk of unhappiness.

If homosexuality is unnatural, legislation which raises the odds that a given child will become homosexual raises the odds that he will be unhappy. The only gap in the syllogism is whether legislation which legitimates, endorses or protects homosexuality does increase the chances that a child will become homosexual. If so, such legislation is *prima facie* objectionable. The question is not whether homosexual elementary school teachers will molest their charges. Prohomosexual legislation might increase the incidence of homosexuality in subtler ways. If it does, and if the protection of children is a fundamental obligation of society, legislation which legitimates homosexuality is a dereliction of duty. I am reluctant to deploy the language of "children's rights," which usually serves as one more excuse to interfere with the prerogatives of parents. But we do have obligations to our children, and one of them is to protect them from harm. If, as some have suggested, children have a right to protection from a religious education, they surely have a right to protection from homosexuality. So protecting them limits somebody else's freedom, but we are often willing to protect quite obscure children's rights at the expense of the freedom of others. There is a movement to ban TV commercials for sugar-coated cereals, to protect children from the relatively trivial harm of tooth decay. Such a ban would restrict the freedom of advertisers, and restrict it even though the last clear chance of avoiding the harm, and thus the responsibility, lies with the parents who control the TV set. I cannot see how one can consistently support such legislation and also urge homosexual rights, which risk much graver danger to children in exchange for increased freedom for homosexuals. (If homosexual behavior is largely compulsive, it is falsifying the issue to present it as balancing risks to children against the freedom of homosexuals.) The right of a homosexual to work for the Fire Department is not a negligible good. Neither is fostering a legal atmosphere in which as many people as possible grow up heterosexual.

It is commonly asserted that legislation granting homosexuals the privilege or right to be firemen endorses not homosexuality, but an expanded conception of human liberation. It is conjectural how sincerely this can be said in a legal order that forbids employers to hire whom they please and demands hours of paperwork for an interstate shipment of hamburger. But in any case legislation "legalizing homosexuality" cannot be neutral because passing it would have an inexpunge-able speech-act dimension. Society cannot grant unaccustomed rights and privileges to homosexuals while remaining neutral about the value of homosexuality. Working from the assumption that society rests on the family and its consequences, the Judaeo-Christian tradition has deemed homosexuality a sin and withheld many privileges from homosexuals. Whether or not such denial was right, for our society to grant these privileges to homosexuals *now* would amount to declaring that it has rethought the matter and decided that homosexuality is not as bad as it had previously supposed. . . .

Up to now, society has deemed homosexuality so harmful that restricting it outweighs putative homosexual rights. If society reverses itself, it will in effect be deciding that homosexuality is not as bad as it once thought.

Notes

1. Barash, D. *The Whispering Within.* New York: Harper & Row, 1979.

2. Bell, A. and M. Weinberg. *Homosexualities.* New York: Simon and Schuster, 1978.

3. Goldberg, S. "What is 'Normal'? Logical Aspects of the Question of Homosexual Behavior." *Psychiatry* (1975).

4. Gould, R, "What We Don't Know about Homosexuality." *New York Times Magazine,* Feb. 24, 1974.

5. Gary, R. "Sex and Sexual Perversion." *Journal of Philosophy* 74 (1978): 189–99.

6. Mossner, E. *The Life of David Hume,* 1st. ed. New York: Nelson & Sons, 1954.

---

11. *Bowers* v. *Hardwick*

U.S. Supreme Court

Justice White argues for the majority that the Georgia sodomy law is constitutional. He concludes that, unlike the rights of married people to sexual privacy, or the rights of individual heterosexuals, the Constitution does not protect such rights for gay people. In dissent, Justices Blackmun et al. argue that prior decisions naturally extend the right to sexual privacy to homosexuals.

Justice *White* delivered the opinion of the Court.

In August 1982, respondent Hardwick (hereafter respondent) was charged with violating the Georgia statute criminalizing sodomy[1] by committing that act with another adult male in the bedroom of respondent's home. After a preliminary hearing, the District Attorney decided not to present the matter to the grand jury unless further evidence developed.

Respondent then brought suit in the Federal District Court, challenging the constitutionality of the statute insofar as it criminalized consensual sodomy. He asserted that he was a practicing homosexual, that the Georgia sodomy statute, as administered by the defendants, placed him in imminent danger of arrest, and that the statute for several reasons violates the Federal Constitution. The District Court granted the defendants' motion to dismiss for failure to state a claim. . . .

A divided panel of the Court of Appeals for the Eleventh Circuit reversed. . . . The court went on to hold that the Georgia statute violated respondent's fundamental rights because his homosexual activity is a private and intimate association that is beyond the reach of state regulation by reason of the Ninth

Amendment and the Due Process Clause of the Fourteenth Amendment. The case was remanded for trial, at which, to prevail, the State would have to prove that the statute is supported by a compelling interest and is the most narrowly drawn means of achieving that end.

. . . We agree with petitioner that the Court of Appeals erred, and hence reverse its judgment.

This case does not require a judgment on whether laws against sodomy between consenting adults in general, or between homosexuals in particular, are wise or desirable. It raises no question about the right or propriety of state legislative decisions to repeal their laws that criminalize homosexual sodomy, or of state-court decisions invalidating those laws on state constitutional grounds. The issue presented is whether the Federal Constitution confers a fundamental right upon homosexuals to engage in sodomy and hence invalidates the laws of the many States that still make such conduct illegal and have done so for a very long time. The case also calls for some judgment about the limits of the Court's role in carrying out its constitutional mandate.

We first register our disagreement with the Court of Appeals and with respondent that the Court's prior cases have construed the Constitution to confer a right of privacy that extends to homosexual sodomy and for all intents and purposes have decided this case. . . . [These cases have been] described as dealing with child rearing and education; with family relationships; with procreation; with marriage; with contraception; and with abortion. [The cases dealing with contraception and abortion] were interpreted as construing the Due Process Clause of the Fourteenth Amendment to confer a fundamental individual right to decide whether or not to beget or bear a child.

Accepting the decisions in these cases and the above description of them, we think it evident that none of the rights announced in those cases bears any resemblance to the claimed constitutional right of homosexuals to engage in acts of sodomy that is asserted in this case. No connection between family, marriage, or procreation on the one hand and homosexual activity on the other has been demonstrated, either by the Court of Appeals or by respondent. Moreover, any claim that these cases nevertheless stand for the proposition that any kind of private sexual conduct between consenting adults is constitutionally insulated from state proscription is unsupportable. . . .

Precedent aside, however, respondent would have us announce, as the Court of Appeals did, a fundamental right to engage in homosexual sodomy. This we are quite unwilling to do. It is true that despite the language of the Due Process Clauses of the Fifth and Fourteenth Amendments, which appears to focus only on the processes by which life, liberty, or property is taken, the cases are legion in which those Clauses have been interpreted to have substantive content, subsuming rights that to a great extent are immune from federal or state regulation or proscription. Among such cases are those recognizing rights that have little or no textual support in the constitutional language. . . .

Striving to assure itself and the public that announcing rights not readily identifiable in the Constitution's text involves much more than the imposition of the Justices' own choice of values on the States and the Federal Government, the Court has sought to identify the nature of the rights qualifying for heightened judicial protection. In *Palko* v. *Connecticut* (1937), it was said that this category includes those fundamental liberties that are "implicit in the concept of ordered liberty," such that "neither liberty nor justice would exist if [they] were sacrificed." A different description of fundamental liberties appeared in *Moore* v. *East Cleveland* (1977), where they are characterized as those liberties that are "deeply rooted in this Nation's history and tradition."

It is obvious to us that neither of these formulations would extend a fundamental right to homosexuals to engage in acts of consensual sodomy. Proscriptions against that conduct have ancient roots. Sodomy was a criminal offense at common law and was forbidden by the laws of the original 13 States when they ratified the Bill of Rights. In 1868, when the Fourteenth Amendment was ratified, all but 5 of the 37 States in the Union had criminal sodomy laws. In fact, until 1961, all 50 States outlawed sodomy, and today, 24 States and the

District of Columbia continue to provide criminal penalties for sodomy performed in private and between consenting adults. Against this background, to claim that a right to engage in such conduct is "deeply rooted in this Nation's history and tradition" or "implicit in the concept of ordered liberty" is, at best, facetious.

Nor are we inclined to take a more expansive view of our authority to discover new fundamental rights imbedded in the Due Process Clause. The Court is most vulnerable and comes nearest to illegitimacy when it deals with judge-made constitutional law having little or no cognizable roots in the language or design of the Constitution. . . .

Respondent, however, asserts that the result should be different where the homosexual conduct occurs in the privacy of the home. He relies on *Stanley* v. *Georgia* (1969), where the Court held that the First Amendment prevents conviction for possessing and reading obscene material in the privacy of one's home: "If the First Amendment means anything, it means that a State has no business telling a man, sitting alone in his house, what books he may read or what films he may watch."

Stanley did protect conduct that would not have been protected outside the home, and it partially prevented the enforcement of state obscenity laws; but the decision was firmly grounded in the First Amendment. The right pressed upon us here has no similar support in the text of the Constitution, and it does not qualify for recognition under the prevailing principles for construing the Fourteenth Amendment. Its limits are also difficult to discern. Plainly enough, otherwise illegal conduct is not always immunized whenever it occurs in the home. Victimless crimes, such as the possession and use of illegal drugs, do not escape the law where they are committed at home. *Stanley* itself recognized that its holding offered no protection for the possession in the home of drugs, firearms, or stolen goods. And if respondent's submission is limited to the voluntary sexual conduct between consenting adults, it would be difficult, except by fiat, to limit the claimed right to homosexual conduct while leaving exposed to prosecution adultery, incest, and other sexual crimes even though they are committed in the home. We are unwilling to start down that road.

Even if the conduct at issue here is not a fundamental right, respondent asserts that there must be a rational basis for the law and that there is none in this case other than the presumed belief of a majority of the electorate in Georgia that homosexual sodomy is immoral and unacceptable. This is said to be an inadequate rationale to support the law. The law, however, is constantly based on notions of morality, and if all laws representing essentially moral choices are to be invalidated under the Due Process Clause, the courts will be very busy indeed. Even respondent makes no such claim, but insists that majority sentiments about the morality of homosexuality should be declared inadequate. We do not agree, and are unpersuaded that the sodomy laws of some 25 States should be invalidated on this basis.

Accordingly, the judgment of the Court of Appeals is *Reversed.*

Justice *Blackmun*, dissenting.

This case is no more about "a fundamental right to engage in homosexual sodomy," as the Court purports to declare, than *Stanley* v. *Georgia* (1969) was about a fundamental right to watch obscene movies, or *Katz* v. *United States* (1967) was about a fundamental right to place interstate bets from a telephone booth. Rather, this case is about "the most comprehensive of rights and the right most valued by civilized men," namely, "the right to be let alone."

The statute at issue, Ga. Code Ann. § 16-6-2 (1984), denies individuals the right to decide for themselves whether to engage in particular forms of private, consensual sexual activity. The Court concludes that § 16-6-2 is valid essentially because "the laws of . . . many States . . . still make such conduct illegal and have done so for a very long time." But the fact that the moral judgments expressed by statutes like § 16-6-2 may be " 'natural and familiar . . . ought not to conclude our judgment upon the question whether statutes embodying them conflict with the Constitution of the United States.' " Like Justice Holmes, I believe that "[i]t is revolting to have no better reason for a rule of law than that so it was laid down in the time of Henry IV. It is still more revolting if the grounds upon which it was laid down have vanished long since, and the rule simply persists from blind imitation of the past." I believe we must analyze respondent Hardwick's claim in the light of the values that underlie the constitutional right to privacy. If that right means anything, it means that, before Georgia can prosecute its citizens for making choices about the most intimate aspects of their lives, it must do more than assert that the choice they have made is an " 'abominable crime not fit to be named among Christians.' "

I

. . . A fair reading of the statute and of the complaint clearly reveals that the majority has distorted the question this case presents.

. . . The Court's almost obsessive focus on homosexual activity is particularly hard to justify in light of the broad language Georgia has used. . . . Georgia has provided that "[a] person commits the offense of sodomy when he performs or submits to any sexual act involving the sex organs of one person and the mouth or anus of another." The sex or status of the persons who engage in the act is irrelevant as a matter of state law. . . . Michael Hardwick's standing may rest in significant part on Georgia's apparent willingness to enforce against homosexuals a law it seems not to have any desire to enforce against heterosexuals. But his claim that § 16-6-2 involves an unconstitutional intrusion into his privacy and his right of intimate association does not depend in any way on his sexual orientation. . . .

. . . I believe that Hardwick has stated a cognizable claim that § 16-6-2 interferes with constitutionally protected interests in privacy and freedom of intimate association. . . . The Court's cramped reading of the issue before it makes for a short opinion, but it does little to make for a persuasive one.

II

"Our cases long have recognized that the Constitution embodies a promise that a certain private sphere of individual liberty will be kept largely beyond the reach of government." In construing the right to privacy, the Court has proceeded along two somewhat distinct, albeit complementary, lines. First, it has recognized a privacy interest with reference to certain *decisions* that are properly for the individual to make. Second, it has recognized a privacy interest with reference to certain *places* without regard for the particular activities in which the individuals who occupy them are engaged. The case before us implicates both the decisional and the spatial aspects of the right to privacy.

A

The Court concludes today that none of our prior cases dealing with various decisions that individuals are entitled to make free of governmental interference "bears any resemblance to the claimed constitutional right of homosexuals to engage in acts of sodomy that is asserted in this case." While it is true that these cases may be characterized by their connection to protection of the family, the Court's conclusion that they extend no further than this boundary ignores the warning . . . against "clos[ing] our eyes to the basic reasons why certain rights associated with the family have been accorded shelter under the Fourteenth Amendment's Due Process Clause." We protect those rights not because they contribute, in some direct and material way, to the general public welfare, but because they form so central a part of an individual's life. "[T]he concept of privacy embodies the 'moral fact that a person belongs to himself and not others nor to society as a whole.' " And so we protect the decision whether to marry precisely because marriage "is an association that promotes a way of life, not causes; a harmony in living, not political faiths; a bilateral loyalty, not commercial or social projects." We protect the decision whether to have a child because parenthood alters so dramatically an individual's self-definition, not because of demographic considerations or the Bible's command to be fruitful and multiply. And we protect the family because it contributes so powerfully to the happiness of individuals, not because of a preference for stereotypical households. The Court [has] recognized . . . that the "ability independently to define one's identity that is central to any concept of liberty" cannot truly be exercised in a vacuum; we all depend on the "emotional enrichment from close ties with others."

Only the most willful blindness could obscure the fact that sexual intimacy is "a sensitive, key relationship of human existence, central to family life, community welfare, and the development of human personality." The fact that individuals define themselves in a significant way through their intimate sexual relationships with others suggests, in a Nation as diverse as ours, that there may be many "right" ways of conducting those relationships, and that much of the richness of a relationship will come from the freedom an individual has to *choose* the form and nature of these intensely personal bonds.

In a variety of circumstances we have recognized that a necessary corollary of giving individuals freedom to choose how to conduct their lives is acceptance of the fact that different individuals will make different choices. For example, in holding that the clearly important state interest in public education should give way to a competing claim by the Amish to the effect that extended formal schooling threatened their way of life, the Court declared: "There can be no assumption that today's majority is 'right' and the Amish and others like them are 'wrong.' A way of life that is odd or even erratic but interferes with no rights or interests of others is not to be condemned because it is different." The Court claims that its decision today merely refuses to recognize a fundamental right to engage in homosexual sodomy; what the Court really has refused to recognize is the fundamental interest all individuals have in controlling the nature of their intimate associations with others.

B

The behavior for which Hardwick faces prosecution occurred in his own home, a place to which the Fourth Amendment attaches special significance. The Court's treatment of this aspect of the case is symptomatic of its overall refusal to consider the broad principles that have informed our treatment of privacy in specific cases. Just as the right to privacy is more than the mere aggregation of a number of entitlements to engage in specific behavior, so too, protecting the physical integrity of the home is more than merely a means of protecting specific activities that often take place there. Even when our understanding of the contours of the right to privacy depends on "reference to a 'place,' the essence of a Fourth Amendment violation is 'not the breaking of [a person's] doors, and the rummaging of his drawers,' but rather is 'the invasion of his indefeasible right of personal security, personal liberty and private property.' "

The Court's interpretation of the pivotal case of *Stanley* v. *Georgia* (1969) is entirely unconvincing. *Stanley* held that Georgia's undoubted power to punish the public distribution of constitutionally unprotected, obscene material did not permit the State to punish the private possession of such material. According to the majority here, *Stanley* relied entirely on the First Amendment, and thus, it is claimed, sheds no light on cases not involving printed materials. But that is not what *Stanley* said. Rather, the *Stanley* Court anchored its holding in the Fourth Amendment's special protection for the individual in his home. . . .

. . . *Stanley* rested as much on the Court's understanding of the Fourth Amendment as it did on the First. . . . "The right of the people to be secure in their . . . houses," expressly guaranteed by the Fourth Amendment, is perhaps the most "textual" of the various constitutional provisions that inform our understanding of the right to privacy, and thus I cannot agree with the Court's statement that "[t]he right pressed upon us here has no . . . support in the text of the Constitution." Indeed, the right of an individual to conduct intimate relationships in the intimacy of his or her own home seems to me to be the heart of the Constitution's protection of privacy.

III

The Court's failure to comprehend the magnitude of the liberty interests at stake in this case leads it to slight the question whether petitioner, on behalf of the State, has justified Georgia's infringement on these interests. I believe that neither of the two general justifications for § 16-6-2 that petitioner has advanced warrants dismissing respondent's challenge for failure to state a claim.

First, petitioner asserts that the acts made criminal by the statute may have serious adverse consequences for "the general public health and welfare," such as spreading communicable diseases or fostering other criminal activity. Inasmuch as this case was dismissed by the District Court on the pleadings, it is not surprising that the record before us is barren of any evidence to support petitioner's claim. In light of the state of the record, I see no justification for the Court's attempt to equate the private, consensual sexual activity at issue here with the "possession in the home of drugs, firearms, or stolen goods," to which *Stanley* refused to extend its protection. None of the behavior so mentioned in *Stanley* can properly be viewed as "[v]ictimless": drugs and weapons are inherently dangerous, and for property to be "stolen," someone must have been wrongfully deprived of it. Nothing in the record before the Court provides any justification for finding the activity forbidden by § 16-6-2 to be physically dangerous, either to the persons engaged in it or to others.

The core of petitioner's defense of § 16-6-2, however, is that respondent and others who engage in the conduct prohibited by § 16-6-2 interfere with Georgia's exercise of the " 'right of the Nation and of the States to maintain a decent society.' " Essentially, petitioner argues, and the Court agrees, that the fact that the acts described in § 16-6-2 "for hundreds of years, if not thousands, have been uniformly condemned as immoral" is a sufficient reason to permit a State to ban them today.

I cannot agree that either the length of time a majority has held its convictions or the passions with which it defends them can withdraw legislation from this Court's scrutiny. As Justice Jackson wrote so eloquently, . . . "we apply the limitations of the Constitution with no fear that freedom to be intellectually and spiritually diverse or even contrary will distintegrate the social organization. . . .[F]reedom to differ is not limited to things that do not matter much. That would be a mere shadow of free-

dom. The test of its substance is the right to differ as to things that touch the heart of the existing order." It is precisely because the issue raised by this case touches the heart of what makes individuals what they are that we should be especially sensitive to the rights of those whose choices upset the majority.

The assertion that "traditional Judeo-Christian values proscribe" the conduct involved cannot provide an adequate justification for § 16-6-2. That certain, but by no means all, religious groups condemn the behavior at issue gives the State no license to impose their judgments on the entire citizenry. The legitimacy of secular legislation depends instead on whether the State can advance some justification for its law beyond its conformity to religious doctrine. Thus, far from buttressing his case, petitioner's invocation of Leviticus, Romans, St. Thomas Aquinas, and sodomy's heretical status during the Middle Ages undermines his suggestion that § 16-6-2 represents a legitimate use of secular coercive power. A State can no more punish private behavior because of religious intolerance than it can punish such behavior because of racial animus. "The Constitution cannot control such prejudices, but neither can it tolerate them. Private biases may be outside the reach of the law, but the law cannot, directly or indirectly, give them effect." No matter how uncomfortable a certain group may make the majority of this Court, we have held that "[m]ere public intolerance or animosity cannot constitutionally justify the deprivation of a person's physical liberty."

Nor can § 16-6-2 be justified as a "morally neutral" exercise of Georgia's power to "protect the public environment." Certainly, some private behavior can affect the fabric of society as a whole. Reasonable people may differ about whether particular sexual acts are moral or immoral, but "we have ample evidence for believing that people will not abandon morality, will not think any better of murder, cruelty and dishonesty, merely because some private sexual practice which they abominate is not punished by the law." Petitioner and the Court fail to see the difference between laws that protect public sensibilities and those that enforce private morality. Statutes banning public sexual activity are entirely consistent with protecting the individual's liberty interest in decisions concerning sexual relations: the same recognition that those decisions are intensely private which justifies protecting them from governmental interference can justify protecting individuals from unwilling exposure to the sexual activities of others. But the mere fact that intimate behavior may be punished when it takes place in public cannot dictate how States can regulate intimate behavior that occurs in intimate places.

This case involves no real interference with the rights of others, for the mere knowledge that other individuals do not adhere to one's value system cannot be a legally cognizable interest, let alone an interest that can justify invading the houses, hearts, and minds of citizens who choose to live their lives differently.

IV

It took but three years for the Court to see the error in its analysis in *Minersville School District* v. *Gobitis* (1940) and to recognize that the threat to national cohesion posed by a refusal to salute the flag was vastly outweighed by the threat to those same values posed by compelling such a salute. I can only hope that here, too, the Court soon will reconsider its analysis and conclude that depriving individuals of the right to choose for themselves how to conduct their intimate relationships poses a far greater threat to the values most deeply rooted in our Nation's history than tolerance of nonconformity could ever do. Because I think the Court today betrays those values, I dissent.

Case 3.a   The Sharon Kowalski Case: Sexual Dissent and the Family

Nan D. Hunter

Sharon Kowalski and Karen Thompson had exchanged rings in a ceremony, pledging to love each other for life. After Sharon suffered serious brain damage in a car accident, her parents became her guardians and refused to allow Karen to visit. After years of legal battles, Karen Thompson was finally awarded custody of Sharon Kowalski. In this discussion of the case, Nan D. Hunter focuses on the impact these issues have on our concept of the family.

No connection between family, marriage, or procreation on the one hand and homosexual activity on the other has been demonstrated.—Supreme Court, *Bowers* v. *Hardwick*, 1986

Sharon Kowalski is the child of a divorce between her consanguineous family and her family of affinity, the petitioner Karen Thompson. . . . That Sharon's

From *The Nation*, October 7, 1991. © 1991 by The Nation Co., Inc. Reprinted by permission.

family of affinity has not enjoyed societal recognition in the past is unfortunate.
—Minnesota State District Court In re: Guardianship of Sharon Kowalski, Ward, 1991

In the effort to end second-class citizenship for lesbian and gay Americans, no obstacle has proved tougher to surmount than the cluster of issues surrounding "the family." For the past twenty years, the concept of family has functioned as a giant cultural screen. Projected onto it, contests over race, gender, sexuality and a range of other "domestic" issues from crime to taxes constantly create and recreate a newly identified zone of social combat, the politics of the family. Activists of all persuasions eagerly seek to enter the discursive field, ever-ready to debate and discuss: Who counts as a family? Which "family values" are the authentic ones? Is there a place in the family for queers? As battles are won and lost in this cultural war, progressives and conservatives agree on at least one thing—the family is highly politicized terrain.

For lesbians and gays, these debates have dramatic real-life consequences, probably more so than with any other legal issue. Relationship questions touch almost every person's life at some point, in a way that military issues, for example, do not. Further, the unequal treatment is blatant, de jure and universal, as compared with the employment arena, where discrimination may be more subtle and variable. No state allows a lesbian or gay couple to marry. No state recognizes (although sixteen counties and cities do) domestic partnership systems under which unmarried couples (gay or straight) can become eligible for certain benefits usually available only to spouses. The fundamental inequity is that, barring mental incompetence or consanguinity, virtually any straight couple has the option to marry and thus establish a next-of-kin relationship that the state will enforce. No lesbian or gay couple can. Under the law, two women or two men are forever strangers, regardless of their relationship.

One result is that every lesbian or gay man's nightmare is to be cut off from one's primary other, physically incapacitated, stranded, unable to make contact, without legal recourse. It is a nightmare that could not happen to a married couple. But it did happen to two Minnesota women, Sharon Kowalski and Karen Thompson, in a remarkable case that has been threading its way through the courts for six years.

Sharon Kowalski, notwithstanding the Minnesota State District Court's characterization of her as a "child of divorce," is an adult with both a committed life partner and parents who bitterly refuse to acknowledge either her lesbianism or her lover. Kowalski is a former physical education teacher and amateur athlete, whose Minnesota women's high school shot-put record still stands. In 1983, she was living with her lover, Thompson, in the home they had jointly purchased in St. Cloud. Both women were deeply closeted; they exchanged rings with each other but told virtually no one of their relationship. That November, Kowalski suffered devastating injuries in a car accident, which left her unable to speak or walk, with arms deformed and with major brain damage, including seriously impaired short-term memory.

After the accident, both Thompson and Kowalski's father petitioned to be appointed Sharon's guardian; initially, an agreement was entered that the father would become guardian on the condition that Thompson retain equal rights to visit and consult with doctors. By the summer of 1985, after growing hostilities, the father refused to continue the arrangement and persuaded a local court that Thompson's visits caused Kowalski to feel depressed. One doctor hired by the father wrote a letter stating that Kowalski was in danger of sexual abuse. Within twenty-four hours after being named sole guardian, the father cut off all contact between Thompson and Kowalski, including mail. By this time, Kowalski had been moved to a nursing home near the small town where she grew up in the Iron Range, a rural mining area in northern Minnesota.

Surely one reason the Kowalski case is so compelling is that for millions of parents, learning that one's son is gay or daughter is lesbian would be *their* worst nightmare. That is all the more true in small-town America, among people who are religiously observant and whose expectations for a daughter are primarily marriage and motherhood. "The good Lord put us here for reproduction, not that kind of way," Donald Kowalski told the *Los Angeles Times* in 1988. "It's just not a normal life style. The Bible will tell you that." Karen Thompson, he told other reporters, was "an animal" and was lying about his daughter's life. "I've never seen anything that would make me believe" that she is lesbian, he said to *The New York Times* in 1989. How much less painful it must be to explain a lesbian daughter's life as seduction, rather than to experience it as betrayal.

Since 1985, Kowalski's parents and her lover have been locked in litigation, seeking review as far as the Supreme Court (which declined to hear the case). Thompson's stubborn struggle to "bring Sharon home" has now entered a new stage. In late 1988 a different judge, sitting in Duluth, ordered Kowalski moved to a new facility for medical evaluation. Soon thereafter, based on staff recommendations from the second nursing facility, the court ordered that Thompson be allowed to visit. The two women saw each other again in the spring of 1989, after three and a half years of forced separation. For the past two years, Thompson has visited Kowalski frequently. Kowalski, who can communicate by typing on a special keyboard, has said that she wants to live in "St. Cloud with Karen."

Since their daughter was moved to the new facility near Minneapolis, Donald and Della Kowalski have made only a handful of trips to see her. In May 1990, citing a heart condition for which he had been hospitalized, Donald Kowalski resigned as his daughter's guardian. This resignation set the stage for Thompson to file a renewed petition for appointment as guardian, which she did. But in an April 1991 ruling, Minnesota State District Court Judge Robert Campbell selected as guardian Karen Tomberlin—a friend of both Kowalski and her parents, who supported Tomberlin's request. On the surface, the court sought balance. The judge characterized the Kowalski parents and Karen Thompson as the "two wings" of Sharon Kowalski's family. He repeatedly asserted that both must have ample access to visitation with Kowalski. He described Tomberlin as a neutral third party who would not exclude either side. But the biggest single reason behind the decision, the one that he characterized as "instrumental," seemed to be the judge's anger at Thompson for ever telling Kowalski's parents (in a private letter), and then the world at large, that she and Kowalski were lovers.

The court condemned Thompson's revelation of her own relationship as the "outing" of Sharon Kowalski. Thompson did write the letter to Kowalski's parents without telling Kowalski (who was at the time just emerging from a three-month coma after the accident) and did build on her own an active political organization around the case, composed chiefly of disability and lesbian and gay rights groups. Of course, for most of that period, she could not have consulted Kowalski because the two were cut off from each other.

In truth, though, the judge's concern seemed to be more for the outing of Kowalski's parents. He describes the Kowalskis as "outraged and hurt by the public invasion of Sharon's privacy and their privacy," and he blames this outing for the bitterness between Thompson and the parents. Had Thompson simply kept this to herself, the court implies, none of these nasty facts would ever have had to be discussed. But then Thompson would never had been able to maintain her relationship with her lover.

An openly stated preference for ignorance over knowledge is remarkable in a judicial opinion. Ultimately, that is what this latest decision in the Kowalski-Thompson litigation saga is about. One imagines the judge silently cursing Thompson for her arrogance in claiming the role of spouse, and for her insistence on shattering the polite fiction of two gym teachers living and buying a house together as just good friends. Women, especially, aren't supposed to be so stubborn or uppity. One can sense the court's empathetic response of shared embarrassment with the parents, of the desire not to be told and thus not to be forced to speak on this subject.

The conflict in the Kowalski case illustrates one of the prime contradictions underlying all the cases seeking legal protection for lesbian and gay couples. This culture is deeply invested with a notion of the ideal family as not only a zone of privacy and a structure of authority (preferably male in the conservative view) but also as a barrier against unlicensed sexuality. Even many leftists and progressives, who actively contest male authority and at least some of the assumptions behind privacy, are queasy about constructing a family politics with queer sex on the inside rather than the outside.

When such sexuality is culturally recognized *within* family bounds, "the family" ceases to function as an enforcer of sexual norms. That's why the moms and dads in groups like P-FLAG, an organization primarily of parents supportive of their lesbian and gay children, make such emotionally powerful spokespersons for the cause of civil rights. Parents who welcome sexual dissenters within the family undermine the notion that such dissent is intrinsically antithetical to deep human connection.

The theme of cultural anxiety about forms of sexuality not bounded and controlled by the family runs through a series of recent judicial decisions. In each case, the threat to norms came not from an assault on the prerogatives of family by libertarian outsiders, a prospect often cited by the right wing to trigger social anxieties. Instead, each court faced the dilemma of how to repress, at least in the law, the anomaly of unsanctioned sexuality within the family.

In a stunning decision two years ago, the Supreme Court ruled in *Michael H. v Gerald D.* that a biological father had no constitutionally protected right to a relationship with his daughter, despite both paternity (which was not disputed) and a psychological bond that the two had formed. Instead, the Court upheld the rule that because the child's mother—who had had an affair with the child's biological father—was married to another man, the girl would be presumed to be the husband's child. It was more important, the Court declared, to protect the "unitary family," i.e., the marriage, than to subject anyone to "embarrassment" by letting the child and her father continue to see each other. The Court ruled that a state could properly force the termination of that bond rather than "disrupt an otherwise harmonious and apparently exclusive marital relationship." We are not bound, the Court said, to protect what it repeatedly described as "adulterous fathers."

In *Hodgson v. Minnesota* last year, the Supreme Court upheld a Minnesota requirement that a pregnant teenager had to notify both her parents—even if they were divorced or if there was a threat of violence from her family—prior to obtaining an abortion, so long as she had the alternative option to petition a court. The decision was read primarily as an abortion decision and a ruling on the extent of privacy protection that will be accorded a minor who decides to have an abortion. But the case was also, at its core, about sex in the family and specifically about whether parents could rely on the state for assistance in learning whether a daughter is sexually active.

In two very similar cases this past spring, appellate courts in New York and California ruled that a lesbian partner who had co-parented a child with the biological mother for some years had no standing to seek visitation after the couple split up. Both courts acknowledged that the best interests of the child would be served by allowing a parental relationship to continue, but both also ruled that the law would not recognize what the New York court called "a biological stranger." Such a person could be a parent only if there had been a marriage or an adoption.

Indeed, perhaps the most important point in either decision was the footnote in the California ruling that invited lesbian and gay couples to adopt children jointly: "We see nothing in these [statutory] provisions that would preclude a child from being jointly adopted by someone of the same sex as the natural parent." This opens the door for many more such adoptions, at least in California, which is one of six states where lesbian or gay-couple adoption has occurred, although rarely. The New York court made no such overture.

The effort to legalize gay marriage will almost certainly emerge as a major issue in the next decade. In the past year, lawsuits seeking a right to marry have been filed in the District of Columbia and Hawaii, and activists in other states are contemplating litigation. In 1989 the Conference of Delegates of the State Bar of California endorsed an amendment of that state's law to permit lesbian and gay couples to marry.

A debate continues within the lesbian and gay community about whether such an effort is assimilationist and conservatizing and whether same-sex marriage would simply constitute the newest form of boundary. Much of that debate, however, simply assumes that the social meaning of marriage is unchanging and timeless. If same-sex couples could marry, the profoundly gendered structure at the heart of marriage would be radically disrupted. Who *would* be the "husband" in a marriage of two men, or the "wife" in a marriage of two women? And either way—if there can be no such thing as a female husband or a male wife, as the right wing argues with contempt; or if indeed in some sense there *can* be, as lesbian and gay couples reconfigure these roles on their own terms—the absolute conflation of gender with role is shattered. What would be the impact on heterosexual marriage?

The law's changes to protect sexual dissent within the family will occur at different speeds in different places, which might not be so bad. Family law has always been a province primarily of state rather than federal regulation and often has varied from state to state; grounds for divorce, for example, used to differ dramatically depending on geography. What seems likely to occur in the next wave of family cases is the same kind of variability in the legal definition of the family itself. Those very discrepancies may help to denaturalize concepts like "marriage" and "parent" and expose the utter contingency of the sex-

ual conventions that, in part, construct the family.

[EDITOR'S NOTE: On December 17, 1991, a three-judge panel unanimously awarded Karen Thompson full guardianship of Sharon Kowalski. Minnesota Court of Appeals Judge Jack Davis found that State District Court Judge Robert Campbell disregarded medical evidence and abused his discretion by denying Thompson's petition for guardianship. In a stunning precedent for the domestic-partners rights movement, the court said that Thompson and Kowalski are "a family of affinity and ought to be accorded respect." The decision coincided with the 12th anniversary of the commitment ceremony in which the two women had exchanged rings and vowed to love each other for the rest of their lives.]

Case 3.b   *Watkins* v. *U.S. Army*

U.S. Ninth Circuit Court of Appeals

In 1982 the Army attempted to discharge Perry Watkins, an admitted homosexual, based on regulations concerning "sexual perversion or homosexuality." Watkins was reinstated by the court, which found that the Army's policy discriminates against homosexuals on the basis of sexual orientation. Since the right to equal protection was violated, the court contended, homosexuals represented a constitutionally "suspect class." Hence the state must show that the rule is a necessary means to a compelling state interest, rather than employing the weaker "rational means" test used when no constitutional right is violated.

Norris, Circuit Judge:

In August 1967, at the age of 19, Perry Watkins enlisted in the United States Army. In filling out the Army's pre-induction medical form, he candidly marked "yes" in response to a question whether he had homosexual tendencies. The Army nonetheless considered Watkins "qualified for admission" and inducted him into its ranks. Watkins served fourteen years in the Army, and became, in the words of his commanding officer, "one of our most respected and trusted soldiers." . . .

Even though Watkins'[s] homosexuality was always common knowledge, . . . the Army has never claimed that his sexual orientation or behavior interfered in any way with military functions. To the contrary, an Army review board found "there is no evidence suggesting that his behavior has had either a degrading effect upon unit performance, morale or discipline, or upon his own job performance." . . .[1]

In 1981 the Army promulgated new regulations which mandated the disqualification of all homosexuals from the Army without regard to the length or quality of their military service. Pursuant to these new regulations, the Army notified Watkins that he would be discharged and denied reenlistment because of his homosexuality. In this federal court action, Watkins challenges the Army's actions and new regulations on various statutory and constitutional grounds. . . .

We now turn to the threshold question raised by Watkins'[s] equal protection claim: Do the Army's regulations discriminate based on sexual orientation? . . .

We conclude that these regulations, on their face, discriminate against homosexuals on the basis of their sexual orientation. Under the regulations any homosexual act or statement of homosexuality gives rise to a presumption of homosexual orientation, and anyone who fails to rebut that presumption is conclusively barred from Army service. In other words, the regulations target homosexual orientation itself. The homosexual acts and statements are merely relevant, and rebuttable, indicators of that orientation.

. . . The Army . . . argues that the Supreme Court's decision in *Bowers v. Hardwick,* 478 U.S. 186 . . . (1986), forecloses Watkins'[s] equal protection challenge to its regulations. In *Hardwick,* the Court rejected a claim by a homosexual that a Georgia statute criminalizing sodomy deprived him of his liberty without due process of law in violation of the Fourteenth Amendment. More specifically, the Court held that the constitutionally protected right to privacy—recognized in cases such as *Griswold v. Connecticut,* 381 U.S. 479 . . . (1965), and *Eisenstadt v. Baird,* 405 U.S. 438 . . . (1972)—does not extend to acts of consensual homosexual sodomy. . . . The Court's holding was limited to this due process question. The parties did not argue and the Court explicitly did not decide the question whether the Georgia sodomy statute might violate the equal protection clause. . . .

The Army nonetheless argues that it would be "incongruous" to hold that its regulations deprive gays of equal protection of the laws when *Hardwick* holds that there is no constitutionally protected privacy right to engage in homosexual sodomy. . . . We disagree. First, while *Hardwick* does indeed hold that the due process clause provides no substantive privacy protection for acts of private homosexual sodomy, nothing in *Hardwick* suggests that the state may penalize gays for their sexual orientation. . . .

. . . Second, although *Hardwick* held that the due process clause does not prevent states from criminalizing acts of homosexual sodomy, . . . nothing in *Hardwick* actually holds that the state may make invidious distinctions when regulating sexual conduct. . . .

. . . We cannot read *Hardwick* as standing for the proposition that government may outlaw sodomy only when committed by a disfavored class of persons. Surely, for example, *Hardwick* cannot be read as a license for the government to outlaw sodomy only when committed by blacks. If government insists on regulating private sexual conduct between consenting adults, it must, at a minimum, do so evenhandedly—prohibiting all persons from engaging in the proscribed sexual acts rather than placing the burden of sexual restraint solely on a disfavored minority.[2] . . .

We now address the merits of Watkins'[s] claim that we must subject the Army's regulations to strict scrutiny because homosexuals constitute a suspect class under equal protection jurisprudence. The Supreme Court has identified several factors that guide our suspect class inquiry.

The first factor the Supreme Court generally considers is whether the group at issue has suffered a history of purposeful discrimination. . . .

. . . As the Army concedes, it is indisputable that "homosexuals have historically been the object of pernicious and sustained hostility." . . .

. . . Homosexuals have been the frequent victims of violence and have been excluded from jobs, schools, housing, churches, and even families. . . .

The second factor that the Supreme Court considers in suspect class analysis is difficult to capsulize and may in fact represent a cluster of factors grouped around a central idea—whether the discrimination embodies a gross unfairness that is sufficiently inconsistent with the ideals of equal protection to term it invidious. Considering this additional factor makes sense. After all, discrimination exists against some groups because the animus is warranted—no one could seriously argue that burglars form a suspect class.

... In giving content to this concept of gross unfairness, the Court has considered (1) whether the disadvantaged class is defined by a trait that "frequently bears no relation to ability to perform or contribute to society," *Frontiero,* 411 U.S. at 686 . . . (plurality); (2) whether the class has been saddled with unique disabilities because of prejudice or inaccurate stereotypes; and (3) whether the trait defining the class is immutable. . . .

Sexual orientation plainly has no relevance to a person's "ability to perform or contribute to society." Indeed, the Army makes no claim that homosexuality impairs a person's ability to perform military duties. Sergeant Watkins'[s] exemplary record of military service stands as a testament to quite the opposite. . . . Moreover, as the Army itself concluded, there is not a scintilla of evidence that Watkins'[s] avowed homosexuality "had either a degrading effect upon unit performance, morale or discipline, or upon his own job performance." . . .

This irrelevance of sexual orientation to the quality of a person's contribution to society also suggests that classifications based on sexual orientation reflect prejudice and inaccurate stereotypes—the second indicia of a classification's gross unfairness.

[The] Army suggests that the public opprobrium directed towards gays does not constitute prejudice in the pejorative sense of the word, but rather represents appropriate public disapproval of persons who engage in immoral behavior. The Army equates homosexuals with sodomists and justifies its regulations as simply reflecting a rational bias against a class of persons who engage in criminal acts of sodomy. In essence, the Army argues that homosexuals, like burglars, cannot form a suspect class because they are criminals.

The Army's argument, essentially adopted by the dissent, rests on two false premises. First, the class burdened by the regulations is defined by the sexual *orientation* of its members, not by their sexual conduct. . . . To our knowledge, homosexual orientation itself has never been criminalized in this country. Moreover, any attempt to criminalize the status of an individual's sexual orientation would present grave constitutional problems. . . .

Second, little of the homosexual *conduct* covered by the regulations is criminal. The regulations reach many forms of homosexual conduct other than sodomy such as kissing, handholding, caressing, and hand-genital contact. Yet, sodomy is the only consensual adult sexual conduct that Congress has criminalized. . . .

Finally, we turn to immutability as an indicator of gross unfairness. . . .

... Although the Supreme Court considers immutability relevant, it is clear that by "immutability" the Court has never meant strict immutability in the sense that members of the class must be physically unable to change or mask the trait defining their class. People can have operations to change their sex. Aliens can ordinarily become naturalized citizens. The status of illegitimate children can be changed. People can frequently hide their national origin by changing their customs, their names, or their associations. Lighter skinned blacks can sometimes "pass" for white, as can Latinos for Anglos, and some people can even change their racial appearance with pigment injections. . . . At a minimum, then, the Supreme Court is willing to treat a trait as effectively immutable if changing it would involve great difficulty, such as requiring a major physical change or a traumatic change of identity. Reading the case law in a more capacious manner, "immutability" may describe those traits that are so central to a person's identity that it would be abhorrent for government to penalize a person for refusing to change them, regardless of how easy that change might be physically. Racial discrimination, for example, would not suddenly become constitutional if medical science developed an easy, cheap, and painless method of changing one's skin pigment. . . .

Under either formulation, we have no trouble concluding that sexual orientation is immutable for the purposes of equal protection doctrine. Although the causes of homosexuality are not fully understood, scientific research indicates that we have little control over our sexual orientation and that, once acquired, our sexual orientation is largely impervious to change. . . . Scientific proof aside, it seems appropriate to ask whether heterosexuals feel capable of changing *their* sexual orientation. Would heterosexuals living in a city that passed an ordinance banning those who engaged in or desired to engage in sex with persons of the *opposite* sex find it easy not only to abstain from heterosexual activity but also to shift the object of their sexual desires to persons of the same sex? It may be that some heterosexuals and homosexuals can change their sexual orientation through extensive therapy, neurosurgery or shock treatment. . . .

. . . But the possibility of such a difficult and traumatic change does not make sexual orientation "mutable" for equal protection purposes. To express the same idea under the alternative formulation, we conclude that allowing the government to penalize the failure to change such a central aspect of individual and group identity would be abhorrent to the values animating the constitutional ideal of equal protection of the laws. . . .

Having concluded that homosexuals constitute a suspect class, we must subject the Army's regulations facially discriminating against homosexuals to strict scrutiny. Consequently, we may uphold the regulations only if " '*necessary* to promote a *compelling* governmental interest.' " . . .

[Even] granting special deference to the policy choices of the military, we must reject many of the Army's asserted justifications because they illegitimately cater to private biases. . . .

The Army's defense of its regulations, however, goes beyond its professed fear of prejudice in the ranks. Apparently, the Army believes that its regulations rooting out persons with certain sexual tendencies are not merely a response to prejudice, but are also grounded in legitimate moral norms. In other words, the Army believes that its ban against homosexuals simply codifies society's moral consensus that homosexuality is evil. Yet, even accepting *arguendo* this proposition that antihomosexual animus is grounded in morality (as opposed to prejudice masking as morality), equal protection doctrine does not permit notions of majoritarian morality to serve as compelling justification for laws that discriminate against suspect classes. . . .

. . . Although courts may sometimes have to accept society's moral condemnation as a jus-

tification even when the morally condemned activity causes no harm to interests outside notions of morality, . . . our deference to majoritarian notions of morality must be tempered by equal protection principles which require that those notions be applied evenhandedly. Laws that limit the acceptable focus of one's sexual desires to members of the opposite sex, like laws that limit one's choice of spouse (or sexual partner) to members of the same race, cannot withstand constitutional scrutiny absent a compelling governmental justification. . . .

Reversed and remanded.

Reinhardt, Circuit Judge, dissenting.

With great reluctance, I have concluded that I am unable to concur in the majority opinion. Like the majority, I believe that homosexuals have been unfairly treated both historically and in the United States today. Were I free to apply my own view of the meaning of the Constitution and in that light to pass upon the validity of the Army's regulations, I too would conclude that the Army may not refuse to enlist homosexuals. I am bound, however, as a circuit judge to apply the Constitution as it has been interpreted by the Supreme Court and our own circuit, whether or not I agree with those interpretations. Because of this requirement, I am sometimes compelled to reach a result I believe to be contrary to the proper interpretation of constitutional principles. This is, regrettably, one of those times.

In this case we consider the constitutionality of a regulation which bars homosexuals from enlisting in the Army. Sergeant Perry Watkins challenges that regulation under the Equal Protection Clause. The majority holds that homosexuals are a suspect class, and that the regulation cannot survive strict scrutiny. Because I am compelled by recent Supreme Court and Ninth Circuit precedent to conclude first, that homosexuals are not a suspect class and second, that the regulation survives both rational and intermediate level scrutiny, I must dissent. . . .

Bowers v. Hardwick . . . is the landmark case involving homosexual conduct. In *Hardwick*, the Supreme Court decided that homosexual sodomy is not protected by the right to privacy, and thus that the states are free to criminalize that conduct. Because Hardwick did not challenge the Georgia sodomy statute under the Equal Protection Clause, and neither party presented that issue in its briefs or at oral argument, the Court limited its holding to due process and properly refrained from reaching any direct conclusion regarding an equal protection challenge to the statute. . . . However, the fact that *Hardwick* does not address the equal protection question directly does not mean that the case is not of substantial significance to such an inquiry. . . .

In my opinion, *Hardwick must* be read as standing precisely for the proposition the majority rejects. To put it simply, I believe that after *Hardwick* the government may outlaw homosexual sodomy even though it fails to regulate the private sexual conduct of heterosexuals. In *Hardwick* the Court took great care to make clear that it was saying only that *homosexual* sodomy is not constitutionally protected, and not that all sexual acts—both heterosexual and homosexual—that fall within the definition of sodomy can be prohibited. . . .

The majority opinion concludes that under the criteria established by equal protection case law, homosexuals must be treated as a suspect class. . . . Were it not for *Hardwick* (and other cases discussed *infra*), I would agree, for in my opinion the group meets all the applicable criteria. . . . However, after *Hardwick*, we are no longer free to reach that conclusion.

The majority opinion treats as a suspect class a group of persons whose defining characteristic is their desire, predisposition, or propensity to engage in conduct that the Supreme Court has held to be constitutionally unprotected, an act that the states can—and approximately half the states have—criminalized. Homosexuals are different from groups previously afforded protection under the equal protection clause in that homosexuals are defined by their conduct—or, at the least, by their desire to engage in certain conduct. With other groups, such as blacks or women, there is no connection between particular conduct and the definition of the group. When conduct that plays a central role in defining a group may be prohibited by the state, it

cannot be asserted with any legitimacy that the group is specially protected by the Constitution.[3]

. . . Laws against sodomy do not affect homosexuals and heterosexuals equally. Homosexuals are more heavily burdened by such legislation, even if we ignore the governmental tendency to prosecute general sodomy statutes selectively against them. . . . Oral sex, a form of sodomy, is the primary form of sexual activity among homosexuals; however, sexual intercourse is the primary form of sexual activity among heterosexuals. If homosexuals were in fact a suspect class, a statute criminalizing sodomy would still not survive equal protection analysis. For the prohibition to be equal, the government would have to prohibit sexual intercourse—conduct as basic to heterosexuals as sodomy is to homosexuals. This, obviously, the government would not and could not do. Therefore, if equal protection rules apply (i.e., if homosexuals are a suspect class), a ban on homosexual sodomy could not stand no matter how the statute was drawn. *Hardwick* makes it plain that the contrary is true. . . .

Before concluding my discussion of *Hardwick*, I wish to record my own view of the opinion. I have delayed doing so until I have applied the case as I believe we have a duty to apply it. Now, I must add that as I understand our Constitution, a state simply has no business treating any group of persons as the State of Georgia and other states with sodomy statutes treat homosexuals. In my opinion, invidious discrimination against a group of persons with immutable characteristics can never be justified on the grounds of society's moral disapproval. No lesson regarding the meaning of our Constitution could be more important for us as a nation to learn. I believe that the Supreme Court egregiously misinterpreted the Constitution in *Hardwick*. In my view, *Hardwick* improperly condones official bias and prejudice against homosexuals, and authorizes the criminalization of conduct that is an essential part of the intimate sexual life of our many homosexual citizens, a group that has historically been the victim of unfair and irrational treatment. I believe that history will view *Hardwick* much as it views *Plessy v. Fergu-*

son, 163 U.S. 537 . . . (1896). And I am confident that, in the long run, *Hardwick,* like *Plessy,* will be overruled by a wiser and more enlightened Court.

Notes

1. In this opinion we use the term "sexual orientation" to refer to the orientation of an individual's sexual preference, not to his actual sexual conduct. Individuals whose sexual orientation creates in them a desire for sexual relationships with persons of the opposite sex have a heterosexual orientation. Individuals whose sexual orientation creates in them a desire for sexual relationships with persons of the same sex have a homosexual orientation.

In contrast, we use the terms "homosexual conduct" and "homosexual acts" to refer to sexual activity between two members of the same sex whether their orientations are homosexual, heterosexual, or bisexual, and we use the terms "heterosexual conduct" and "heterosexual acts" to refer to sexual activity between two members of the opposite sex whether their orientations are homosexual, heterosexual, or bisexual.

Throughout this opinion, the terms "gay" and "homosexual" will be used synonymously to denote persons of homosexual orientation.

2. The dissent's interpretation of *Hardwick*—that it authorizes the state to single out homosexual conduct for criminal sanction *because* that conduct is committed by homosexuals—is wide of the mark. *Hardwick* explicitly focused on the question whether the right to privacy extends constitutional protection to the commission of homosexual sodomy. . . . In essence, the dissent shifts *Hardwick's* focus away from substantive due process and the right to privacy towards the right of homosexuals to enjoy equal treatment under the laws. Such an expansively anti-homosexual reading of *Hardwick* is unsupported and unfair both to homosexuals and the Supreme Court.

We also cannot agree with the dissent's assertion that the equal protection clause is entirely "procedural in nature" and that, therefore, our equal protection analysis is coherent "[o]nly if heterosexual sodomy is *not* protected by the right to privacy." . . . However the Supreme Court defines the right to privacy—whether that definition includes a right to engage in heterosexual sodomy, homosexual sodomy, neither, or both— the equal protection clause imposes an independent obligation on government not to draw invidious distinctions among its citizens. . . . We do not read *Hardwick* as in any way eroding that principle.

3. Thus, it is not even necessary to decide whether the majority's view of *Hardwick*—that it is based on a condemnation of sodomy rather than of homosexuality—is correct. Whatever the explanation for the Court's willingness to allow sodomy to be criminalized—whether its decision is based on its views as to the morality of homosexuality or on its disapproval of sodomy, including the heterosexual variety—that willingness is inconsistent with affording special constitutional protection to homosexuals—a group whose primary form of sexual activity, the Court tells us, may be declared criminal.

Euthanasia

Advances in technology now allow us to prolong human life beyond the point (some suggest) where it has any value. Indeed, people who are technically already dead (i.e., have no detectable brain activity) can be kept alive almost indefinitely. These advances raise questions as to when technology should be withheld or withdrawn, when we should fail to treat, and when, if ever, we should actually assist in the death of a terminally ill patient. Conditions range from complete coma, a vegetative state with no hope of recovery, to cases in which pain and/or deterioration caused by a disease radically compromises the person's capacity to enjoy life, so that death seems like the only fair option. The basic dilemma lies in balancing the patient's right to a dignified and peaceful death with concerns over the devaluation of life, and in allowing doctors to make these life-and-death decisions.

Such cases are by no means limited to adults. Babies born *anencephalic* (that is, with partial or near-total absence of a brain) or those with other birth defects, such as *Tay-Sachs disease,* may live only a short time and often in great pain. Should these babies be treated, left to die, or perhaps even terminated? Here we must question whether we are harming or helping by prolonging life. Are we preserving dignity by allowing people to die, or even by actively killing them, or should we preserve life at all costs?

Passive euthanasia, whereby a patient is allowed to die, is legal in the United States. *Active euthanasia,* whereby a doctor actually takes steps to cause or assist in the death of a patient, has been rejected by the American Medical Association and is illegal in all 50 states. James Rachels, in his article included in this section, suggests that there is no morally relevant difference between the two.

In euthanasia cases we must always be concerned first with the wishes of the patient. Euthanasia can be *voluntary,* in which case the patient's wishes are known either directly or indirectly. It is becoming a common practice for people to write a *living will.* In these legal documents, individuals make clear their desires with reference to extraordinary medical treatment. Problems arise, of course, when the doctor and/or family is unsure of the decisions of the patient; euthanasia in these cases is referred to as *involuntary.*

Questions are often raised about the differences between *extraordinary* and *ordinary* care. Extraordinary means, such as heart/lung machines and transplants, can be withheld or even withdrawn, and the measures can still be considered passive euthanasia. Controversy typically stems from withdrawing or withholding ordinary care. We typically think of basic medicines, antibiotics, saline IVs, nasal feeding tubes, and the like as ordinary care. Withholding these treatments from a patient, thereby causing the patient's death, is largely illegal.

Recently the euthanasia debate has been taken one step further. People have begun to argue for the right to a dignified death for those who are terribly afflicted with a disease but are not diagnosed as terminal. Many persons are in horrible pain and discomfort and yet are not able to take their own lives. If they wish to die, can a doctor aid in their suicide? Is suicide like euthanasia? A case study is included in this section discussing the work of Dr. Jack Kevorkian.

12. Active and Passive Euthanasia

James Rachels

In this article, James Rachels argues that there is no necessary moral difference between active euthanasia (killing) and passive euthanasia (letting die) and that active euthanasia can often be more humane. Since the moral status of killing depends on intentions and circumstances, Rachels concludes that, depending on these conditions, active euthanasia can be morally preferable.

The distinction between active and passive euthanasia is thought to be crucial for medical ethics. The idea is that it is permissible, at least in some cases, to withhold treatment and allow a patient to die, but it is never permissible to take any direct action designed to kill the patient. This doctrine seems to be accepted by most doctors, and it is endorsed in a statement adopted by the House of Delegates of the American Medical Association on December 4, 1973:

> The intentional termination of the life of one human being by another—mercy killing—is contrary to that for which the medical profession stands and is contrary to the policy of the American Medical Association.
>
> The cessation of the employment of extraordinary means to prolong the life of the body when there is irrefutable evidence that biological death is imminent is the decision of the patient and/or his immediate family. The advice and judgment of the physician should be freely available to the patient and/or his immediate family.

However, a strong case can be made against this doctrine. In what follows I will set out some of the relevant arguments, and urge doctors to reconsider their views on this matter.

To begin with a familiar type of situation, a patient who is dying of incurable cancer of the throat is in terrible pain, which can no longer be satisfactorily alleviated. He is certain to die within a few days, even if present treatment is continued, but he does not want to go on living for those days since the pain is unbearable. So he asks the doctor for an end to it, and his family joins in the request.

Suppose the doctor agrees to withhold treatment, as the conventional doctrine says he may. The justification for his doing so is that the patient is in terrible agony, and since he is going to die anyway, it would be wrong to prolong his suffering needlessly. But now notice this. If one simply withholds treatment, it may take the patient longer to die, and so he may suffer more than he would if more direct action were taken and a lethal injection given. This fact provides strong reason for thinking that, once the initial decision not to prolong his agony has been made, active euthanasia is actually preferable to passive euthanasia, rather than the reverse. To say otherwise is to endorse the option that leads to more suffering rather than less, and is contrary to the humanitarian impulse that prompts the decision not to prolong his life in the first place.

Part of my point is that the process of being "allowed to die" can be relatively slow and painful, whereas being given a lethal injection is relatively quick and painless. Let me give a different sort of example. In the United States about one in 600 babies is born with Down's syndrome. Most of these babies are otherwise healthy—that is, with only the usual pediatric care, they will proceed to an otherwise normal infancy. Some, however, are born with congenital defects such as intestinal obstructions that require operations if they are to live. Sometimes, the parents and the doctor will decide not to operate, and let the infant die. Anthony Shaw describes what happens then:

Reprinted by permission from the *New England Journal of Medicine* 292, no. 2 (January 9, 1975): 78–80.

. . . When surgery is denied [the doctor] must try to keep the infant from suffering while natural forces sap the baby's life away. As a surgeon whose natural inclination is to use the scalpel to fight off death, standing by and watching a salvageable baby die is the most emotionally exhausting experience I know. It is easy at a conference, in a theoretical discussion, to decide that such infants should be allowed to die. It is altogether different to stand by in the nursery and watch as dehydration and infection wither a tiny being over hours and days. This is a terrible ordeal for me and the hospital staff—much more so than for the parents who never set foot in the nursery.[1]

I can understand why some people are opposed to all euthanasia, and insist that such infants must be allowed to live. I think I can also understand why other people favor destroying these babies quickly and painlessly. But why should anyone favor letting "dehydration and infection wither a tiny being over hours and days"? The doctrine that says that a baby may be allowed to dehydrate and wither, but may not be given an injection that would end its life without suffering, seems so patently cruel as to require no further refutation. The strong language is not intended to offend, but only to put the point in the clearest possible way.

My second argument is that the conventional doctrine leads to decisions concerning life and death made on irrelevant grounds.

Consider again the case of the infants with Down's syndrome who need operations for congenital defects unrelated to the syndrome to live. Sometimes, there is no operation, and the baby dies, but when there is no such defect, the baby lives on. Now, an operation such as that to remove an intestinal obstruction is not prohibitively difficult. The reason why such operations are not performed in these cases is, clearly, that the child has Down's syndrome and the parents and doctor judge that because of that fact it is better for the child to die.

But notice that this situation is absurd, no matter what view one takes of the lives and potentials of such babies. If the life of such an infant is worth preserving, what does it matter

if it needs a simple operation? Or, if one thinks it better that such a baby should not live on, what difference does it make that it happens to have an unobstructed intestinal tract? In either case, the matter of life and death is being decided on irrelevant grounds. It is the Down's syndrome, and not the intestines, that is the issue. The matter should be decided, if at all, on that basis, and not be allowed to depend on the essentially irrelevant question of whether the intestinal tract is blocked.

What makes this situation possible, of course, is the idea that when there is an intestinal blockage, one can "let the baby die," but when there is no such defect there is nothing that can be done, for one must not "kill" it. The fact that this idea leads to such results as deciding life or death on irrelevant grounds is another good reason why the doctrine should be rejected.

One reason why so many people think that there is an important moral difference between active and passive euthanasia is that they think killing someone is morally worse than letting someone die. But is it? Is killing, in itself, worse than letting die? To investigate this issue, two cases may be considered that are exactly alike except that one involves killing whereas the other involves letting someone die. Then, it can be asked whether this difference makes any difference to the moral assessments. It is important that the cases be exactly alike, except for this one difference, since otherwise one cannot be confident that it is this difference and not some other that accounts for any variation in the assessments of the two cases. So, let us consider this pair of cases:

In the first, Smith stands to gain a large inheritance if anything should happen to his six-year-old cousin. One evening while the child is taking his bath, Smith sneaks into the bathroom and drowns the child, and then arranges things so that it will look like an accident.

In the second, Jones also stands to gain if anything should happen to his six-year-old cousin. Like Smith, Jones sneaks in planning to drown the child in his bath. However, just as he enters the bathroom Jones sees the child slip and hit his head, and fall face down in the water. Jones is delighted; he stands by, ready to push the child's head back under if it is necessary, but it is not necessary. With only a little thrashing about, the child drowns all by himself, "accidentally," as Jones watches and does nothing.

Now Smith killed the child, whereas Jones "merely" let the child die. That is the only difference between them. Did either man behave better, from a moral point of view? If the difference between killing and letting die were in itself a morally important matter, one should say that Jones's behavior was less reprehensible than Smith's. But does one really want to say that? I think not. In the first place, both men acted from the same motive, personal gain, and both had exactly the same end in view when they acted. It may be inferred from Smith's conduct that he is a bad man, although that judgment may be withdrawn or modified if certain further facts are learned about him—for example, that he is mentally deranged. But would not the very same thing be inferred about Jones from his conduct? And would not the same further considerations also be relevant to any modification of this judgment? Moreover, suppose Jones pleaded, in his own defense, "After all, I didn't do anything except stand there and watch the child drown. I didn't kill him; I only let him die." Again, if letting die were in itself less bad than killing, this defense should have at least some weight. But it does not. Such a "defense" can only be regarded as a grotesque perversion of moral reasoning. Morally speaking, it is no defense at all.

Now, it may be pointed out, quite properly, that the cases of euthanasia with which doctors are concerned are not like this at all. They do not involve personal gain or the destruction of normal healthy children. Doctors are concerned only with cases in which the patient's life is of no further use to him, or in which the patient's life has become or will soon become a terrible burden. However, the point is the same in these cases: the bare difference between killing and letting die does not, in itself, make a moral difference. If a doctor lets a patient die, for humane reasons, he is in the same moral position as if he had given the patient a lethal injection for humane reasons. If his decision was wrong—if, for example, the patient's illness was in fact curable—the decision would be equally regrettable no matter which method was used to carry it out. And if the doctor's decision was the right one, the method used is not in itself important.

The AMA policy statement isolates the crucial issue very well; the crucial issue is "the intentional termination of the life of one human being by another." But after identifying this issue, and forbidding "mercy killing," the statement goes on to deny that the cessation of treatment is the intentional termination of a life. This is where the mistake comes in, for what is the cessation of treatment, in these circumstances, if it is not "the intentional termination of the life of one human being by another"? Of course it is exactly that, and if it were not, there would be no point to it.

Many people will find this judgment hard to accept. One reason, I think, is that it is very easy to conflate the question of whether killing is, in itself, worse than letting die, with the very different question of whether most actual cases of killing are more reprehensible than most actual cases of letting die. Most actual cases of killing are clearly terrible (think, for example, of all the murders reported in the newspapers), and one hears of such cases every day. On the other hand, one hardly ever hears of a case of letting die, except for the actions of doctors who are motivated by humanitarian reasons. So one learns to think of killing in a much worse light than of letting die. But this does not mean that there is something about killing that makes it in itself worse than letting die, for it is not the bare difference between killing and letting die that makes the difference in these cases. Rather, the other factors—the murderer's motive of personal gain, for example, contrasted with the doctor's humanitarian motivation—account for different reactions to the different cases.

I have argued that killing is not in itself any worse than letting die; if my contention is right, it follows that active euthanasia is not any worse than passive euthanasia. What arguments can be given on the other side? The most common, I believe, is the following:

"The important difference between active and passive euthanasia is that, in passive euthanasia, the doctor does not do anything to bring about the patient's death. The doctor does nothing, and the patient dies of whatever ills already afflict him. In active euthanasia, however, the doctor does something to bring about the patient's death: he kills him. The doctor who gives the patient with cancer a lethal injection has himself caused his patient's death; whereas if he merely ceases treatment, the cancer is the cause of the death."

A number of points need to be made here. The first is that it is not exactly correct to say that in passive euthanasia the doctor does nothing, for he does do one thing that is very important: he lets the patient die. "Letting someone die" is certainly different, in some respects, from other types of action—mainly in that it is a kind of action that one may perform by way of not performing certain other actions. For example, one may let a patient die by way of not giving medication, just as one may insult someone by way of not shaking his hand. But for any purpose of moral assessment, it is a type of action nonetheless. The decision to let a patient die is subject to moral appraisal in the same way that a decision to kill him would be subject to moral appraisal: it may be assessed as wise or unwise, compassionate or sadistic, right or wrong. If a doctor deliberately let a patient die who was suffering from a routinely curable illness, the doctor would certainly be to blame for what he had done, just as he would be to blame if he had needlessly killed the patient. Charges against him would then be appropriate. If so, it would be no defense at all for him to insist that he didn't "do anything." He would have done something very serious indeed, for he let his patient die.

Fixing the cause of death may be very important from a legal point of view, for it may determine whether criminal charges are brought against the doctor. But I do not think that this notion can be used to show a moral difference between active and passive euthanasia. The reason why it is considered bad to be the cause of someone's death is that death is regarded as a great evil—and so it is. However, if it has been decided that euthanasia—even passive euthanasia—is desirable in a given case, it has also been decided that in this instance death is no greater an evil than the patient's continued existence. And if this is true, the usual reason for not wanting to be the cause of someone's death simply does not apply.

Finally, doctors may think that all of this is only of academic interest—the sort of thing that philosophers may worry about but that has no practical bearing on their own work. After all, doctors must be concerned about the legal consequences of what they do, and active euthanasia is clearly forbidden by the law. But even so, doctors should also be concerned with the fact that the law is forcing upon them a moral doctrine that may well be indefensible, and has a considerable effect on their practices. Of course, most doctors are not now in the position of being coerced in this matter, for they do not regard themselves as merely going along with what the law requires. Rather, in statements such as the AMA policy statement that I have quoted, they are endorsing this doctrine as a central point of medical ethics. In that statement, active euthanasia is condemned not merely as illegal but as "contrary to that for which the medical profession stands," whereas passive euthanasia is approved. However, the preceding considerations suggest that there is really no moral difference between the two, considered in themselves (there may be important moral differences in some cases in their *consequences,* but, as I pointed out, these differences may make active euthanasia, and not passive euthanasia, the morally preferable option). So, whereas doctors may have to discriminate between active and passive euthanasia to satisfy the law, they should not do any more than that. In particular, they should not give the distinction any added authority and weight by writing it into official statements of medical ethics.

Note

1. A. Shaw, "Doctor, Do We Have a Choice?" *The New York Times Magazine,* January 30, 1972, p. 54.

13. Must Patients Always Be Given Food and Water?

Joanne Lynn and James F. Childress

Joanne Lynn and James F. Childress argue that in some instances it is acceptable to withhold food and water from terminal patients. According to Lynn and Childress, feeding tubes are no different from any other medical procedure and can be withheld or withdrawn if the case is futile, if there would be no benefit to the patient, or if any benefit would be outweighed by the costs to the patient.

Many people die from the lack of food or water. For some, this lack is the result of poverty or famine, but for others it is the result of disease or deliberate decision. In the past, malnutrition and dehydration must have accompanied nearly every death that followed an illness of more than a few days. Most dying patients do not eat much on their own, and nothing could be done for them until the first flexible tubing for instilling food or other liquid into the stomach was developed about a hundred years ago. Even then, the procedure was so scarce, so costly in physician and nursing time, and so poorly tolerated that it was used only for patients who clearly could benefit. With the advent of more reliable and efficient procedures in the past few decades, these conditions can be corrected or ameliorated in nearly every patient who would otherwise be malnourished or dehydrated. In fact, intravenous lines and nasogastric tubes have become common images of hospital care.

Providing adequate nutrition and fluids is a high priority for most patients, both because they suffer directly from inadequacies and because these deficiencies hinder their ability to overcome other diseases. But are there some patients who need not receive these treatments? This question has become a prominent public policy issue in a number of recent cases. In May 1981, in Danville, Illinois, the parents and the physician of newborn conjoined twins with shared abdominal organs decided not to

feed these children. Feeding and other treatments were given after court intervention, though a grand jury refused to indict the parents.[1] Later that year, two physicians in Los Angeles discontinued intravenous nutrition to a patient who had severe brain damage after an episode involving loss of oxygen following routine surgery. Murder charges were brought, but the hearing judge dismissed the charges at a preliminary hearing. On appeal, the charges were reinstated and remanded for trial.[2]

In April 1982, a Bloomington, Indiana, infant who had tracheoesophageal fistula and Down Syndrome was not treated or fed, and he died after two courts ruled that the decision was proper but before all appeals could be heard.[3] When the federal government then moved to ensure that such infants would be fed in the future,[4] the Surgeon General, Dr. C. Everett Koop, initially stated that there is never adequate reason to deny nutrition and fluids to a newborn infant.

While these cases were before the public, the nephew of Claire Conroy, an elderly incompetent woman with several serious medical problems, petitioned a New Jersey court for authority to discontinue her nasogastric tube feedings. Although the intermediate appeals court has reversed the ruling,[5] the trial court held that he had this authority since the evidence indicated that the patient would not have wanted such treatment and that its value to her was doubtful.

In all these dramatic cases and in many more that go unnoticed, the decision is made to deliberately withhold food or fluid known

Reprinted by permission of the authors and The Hastings Center from *Hastings Center Report 13* (October 1983), pp. 17–21.

to be necessary for the life of the patient. Such decisions are unsettling. There is now widespread consensus that sometimes a patient is best served by not undertaking or continuing certain treatments that would sustain life, especially if these entail substantial suffering.[6] But food and water are so central to an array of human emotions that it is almost impossible to consider them with the same emotional detachment that one might feel toward a respirator or a dialysis machine.

Nevertheless, the question remains: Should it ever be permissible to withhold or withdraw food and nutrition? The answer in any real case should acknowledge the psychological contiguity between feeding and loving and between nutritional satisfaction and emotional satisfaction. Yet this acknowledgment does not resolve the core question.

Some have held that it is intrinsically wrong not to feed another. The philosopher G. E. M. Anscombe contends: "For wilful starvation there can be no excuse. The same can't be said quite without qualification about failing to operate or to adopt some courses of treatment."[7] But the moral issues are more complex than Anscombe's comment suggests. Does correcting nutritional deficiencies always improve patients' well-being? What should be our reflective moral response to withholding or withdrawing nutrition? What moral principles are relevant to our reflections? What medical facts about ways of providing nutrition are relevant? And what policies should be adopted by the society, hospitals, and medical and other health care professionals?

In our effort to find answers to these questions, we will concentrate upon the care of patients who are incompetent to make choices for themselves. Patients who are competent to determine the course of their therapy may refuse any and all interventions proposed by others, as long as their refusals do not seriously harm or impose unfair burdens upon others.[8] A competent patient's decision regarding whether or not to accept the provision of food and water by medical means such as tube feeding or intravenous alimentation is unlikely to raise questions of harm or burden to others.

What then should guide those who must decide about nutrition for a patient who cannot decide? As a start, consider the standard by which other medical decisions are made: one should decide as the incompetent person would have if he or she were competent, when that is possible to determine, and advance that person's interests in a more generalized sense when individual preferences cannot be known.

The Medical Procedures

There is no reason to apply a different standard to feeding and hydration. Surely, when one inserts a feeding tube, or creates a gastrostomy opening, or inserts a needle into a vein, one intends to benefit the patient. Ideally, one should provide what the patient believes to be of benefit, but at least the effect should be beneficial in the opinions of surrogates and caregivers.

Thus, the question becomes, is it ever in the patient's interest to become malnourished and dehydrated, rather than to receive treatment? Posing the question so starkly points to our need to know what is entailed in treating these conditions and what benefits the treatments offer.

The medical interventions that provide food and fluids are of two basic types. First, liquids can be delivered by a tube that is inserted into a functioning gastrointestinal tract, most commonly through the nose and esophagus into the stomach or through a surgical incision in the abdominal wall and directly into the stomach. The liquids used can be specially prepared solutions of nutrients or a blenderized version of an ordinary diet. The nasogastric tube is cheap; it may lead to pneumonia and often annoys the patient and family, sometimes even requiring that the patient be restrained to prevent its removal.

Creating a gastrostomy is usually a simple surgical procedure, and, once the wound is healed, care is very simple. Since it is out of sight, it is aesthetically more acceptable and restraints are needed less often. Also, the gastrostomy creates no additional risk of pneumonia. However, while elimination of a nasogastric tube requires only removing the tube, a gastrostomy is fairly permanent, and can be closed only by surgery.

The second type of medical intervention is intravenous feeding and hydration, which also has two major forms. The ordinary hospital or peripheral IV, in which fluid is delivered directly to the bloodstream through a small needle, is useful only for temporary efforts to improve hydration and electrolyte concentrations. One cannot provide a balanced diet through the veins in the limbs: to do that requires a central line, or a special catheter placed into one of the major veins in the chest. The latter procedure is much more risky and vulnerable to infections and technical errors, and it is much more costly than any of the other procedures. Both forms of intravenous nutrition and hydration commonly require restraining the patient, cause minor infections and other ill effects, and are costly, especially since they ordinarily require the patient to be in a hospital.

None of these procedures, then, is ideal; each entails some distress, some medical limitations, and some costs. When may a procedure be forgone that might improve nutrition and hydration for a given patient? Only when the procedure and the resulting improvement in nutrition and hydration do not offer the patient a net benefit over what he or she would otherwise have faced.

Are there such circumstances? We believe that there are; but they are few and limited to the following three kinds of situations: (1) the procedures that would be required are so unlikely to achieve improved nutritional and fluid levels that they could be correctly considered futile; (2) the improvement in nutritional and fluid balance, though achievable, could be of no benefit to the patient; (3) the burdens of receiving the treatment may outweigh the benefit.

When Food and Water May Be Withheld

Futile Treatment

Sometimes even providing "food and water" to a patient becomes a monumental task. Con-

sider a patient with a severe clotting deficiency and a nearly total body burn. Gaining access to the central veins is likely to cause hemorrhage or infection, nasogastric tube placement may be quite painful, and there may be no skin to which to suture the stomach for a gastrostomy tube. Or consider a patient with severe congestive heart failure who develops cancer of the stomach with a fistula that delivers food from the stomach to the colon without passing through the intestine and being absorbed. Feeding the patient may be possible, but little is absorbed. Intravenous feeding cannot be tolerated because the fluid would be too much for the weakened heart. Or consider the infant with infarction of all but a short segment of bowel. Again, the infant can be fed, but little if anything is absorbed. Intravenous methods can be used, but only for a short time (weeks or months) until their complications, including thrombosis, hemorrhage, infections, and malnutrition, cause death.

In these circumstances, the patient is going to die soon, no matter what is done. The ineffective efforts to provide nutrition and hydration may directly cause suffering that offers no counterbalancing benefit for the patient. Although the procedures might be tried, especially if the competent patient wanted them or the incompetent patient's surrogate had reason to believe that this incompetent patient would have wanted them, they cannot be considered obligatory. To hold that a patient must be subjected to this predictably futile sort of intervention just because protein balance is negative or the blood serum is concentrated is to lose sight of the moral warrant for medical care and to reduce the patient to an array of measurable variables.

No Possibility of Benefit

Some patients can be reliably diagnosed to have permanently lost consciousness. This unusual group of patients includes those with anencephaly, persistent vegetative state, and some preterminal comas. In these cases, it is very difficult to discern how any medical intervention can benefit or harm the patient. These patients cannot and never will be able to experience any of the events occurring in the world or in their bodies. When the diagnosis is exceedingly clear, we sustain their lives vigorously mainly for their loved ones and the community at large.

While these considerations probably indicate that continued artificial feeding is best in most cases, there may be some cases in which the family and the caregivers are convinced that artificial feeding is offensive and unreasonable. In such cases, there seems to be more adequate reason to claim that withholding food and water violates any obligations that these parties or the general society have with regard to permanently unconscious patients. Thus, if the parents of an anencephalic infant or of a patient like Karen Quinlan in a persistent vegetative state feel strongly that no medical procedures should be applied to provide nutrition and hydration, and the caregivers are willing to comply, there should be no barrier in law or public policy to thwart the plan.[9]

Disproportionate Burden

The most difficult cases are those in which normal nutritional status or fluid balance could be restored, but only with a severe burden for the patient. In these cases, the treatment is futile in a broader sense—the patient will not actually benefit from the improved nutrition and hydration. A patient who is competent can decide the relative merits of the treatment being provided, knowing the probable consequences, and weighing the merits of life under various sets of constrained circumstances. But a surrogate decision maker for a patient who is incompetent to decide will have a difficult task. When the situation is irremediably ambiguous, erring on the side of continued life and improved nutrition and hydration seems the less grievous error. But are there situations that would warrant a determination that this patient, whose nutrition and hydration could surely be improved, is not thereby well served?

Though they are rare, we believe there are such cases. The treatments entailed are not benign. Their effects are far short of ideal. Furthermore, many of the patients most likely to have inadequate food and fluid intake are also likely to suffer the most serious side effects of these therapies.

Patients who are allowed to die without artificial hydration and nutrition may well die more comfortably than patients who receive conventional amounts of intravenous hydration.[10] Terminal pulmonary edema, nausea, and mental confusion are more likely when patients have been treated to maintain fluid and nutrition until close to the time of death.

Thus, those patients whose "need" for artificial nutrition and hydration arises only near the time of death may be harmed by its provision. It is not at all clear that they receive any benefit in having a slightly prolonged life, and it does seem reasonable to allow a surrogate to decide that, for this patient at this time, slight prolongation of life is not warranted if it involves measures that will probably increase the patient's suffering as he or she dies.

Even patients who might live much longer might not be well served by artificial means to provide fluid and food. Such patients might include those with fairly severe dementia for whom the restraints required could be a constant source of fear, discomfort, and struggle. For such a patient, sedation to tolerate the feeding mechanisms might preclude any of the pleasant experiences that might otherwise have been available. Thus, a decision not to intervene, except perhaps briefly to ascertain that there are no treatable causes, might allow such a patient to live out a shorter life with fair freedom of movement and freedom from fear, while a decision to maintain artificial nutrition and hydration might consign the patient to end his or her life in unremitting anguish. If this were the case a surrogate decision-maker would seem to be well justified in refusing the treatment.

Inappropriate Moral Constraints

Four considerations are frequently proposed as moral constraints on forgoing medical feeding and hydration. We find none of these to dictate that artificial nutrition and hydration must always be provided.

The Obligation to Provide "Ordinary" Care

Debates about appropriate medical treatment are often couched in terms of "ordinary" and "extraordinary" means of treatment. Historically, this distinction emerged in the Roman Catholic tradition to differentiate optional treatment from treatment that was obligatory for medical professionals to offer and for patients to accept.[11] These terms also appear in many secular contexts, such as court decisions and medical codes. The recent debates about ordinary and extraordinary means of treatment have been interminable and often unfruitful, in part because of a lack of clarity about what the terms mean. Do they represent the premises of an argument or the conclusion, and what features of a situation are relevant to the categorization as "ordinary" or "extraordinary"?[12]

Several criteria have been implicit in debates about ordinary and extraordinary means of treatment; some of them may be relevant to determining whether and which treatments are obligatory and which are optional. Treatments have been distinguished according to their simplicity (simple/complex), their naturalness (natural/artificial), their customariness (usual/unusual), their invasiveness (noninvasive/invasive), their chance of success (reasonable chance/futile), their balance of benefits and burdens (proportionate/disproportionate), and their expense (inexpensive/costly). Each set of paired terms or phrases in the parentheses suggests a continuum: as the treatment moves from the first of the paired terms to the second, it is said to become less obligatory and more optional.

However, when these various criteria, widely used in discussions about medical treatment, are carefully examined, most of them are not morally relevant in distinguishing optional from obligatory medical treatments. For example, if a rare, complex, artificial, and invasive treatment offers a patient a reasonable chance of nearly painless cure, then one would have to offer a substantial justification not to provide that treatment to an incompetent patient.

What matters, then, in determining whether to provide a treatment to an incompe- tent patient is not a prior determination that this treatment is "ordinary" per se, but rather a determination that this treatment is likely to provide this patient benefits that are sufficient to make it worthwhile to endure the burdens that accompany the treatment. To this end, some of the considerations listed above are relevant: whether a treatment is likely to succeed is an obvious example. But such considerations taken in isolation are not conclusive. Rather, the surrogate decision-maker is obliged to assess the desirability to this patient of each of the options presented, including nontreatment. For most people at most times, this assessment would lead to a clear obligation to provide food and fluids.

But sometimes, as we have indicated, providing food and fluids through medical interventions may fail to benefit and may even harm some patients. Then the treatment cannot be said to be obligatory, no matter how usual and simple its provision may be. If "ordinary" and "extraordinary" are used to convey the conclusion about the obligation to treat, providing nutrition and fluids would have become, in these cases, "extraordinary." Since this phrasing is misleading, it is probably better to use "proportionate" and "disproportionate," as the Vatican now suggests,[13] or "obligatory" and "optional."

Obviously, providing nutrition and hydration may sometimes be necessary to keep patients comfortable while they are dying even though it may temporarily prolong their dying. In such cases, food and fluids constitute warranted palliative care. But in other cases, such as a patient in a deep and irreversible coma, nutrition and hydration do not appear to be needed or helpful, except perhaps to comfort the staff and family.[14] And sometimes the interventions needed for nutrition and hydration are so burdensome that they are harmful and best not utilized.

The Obligation to Continue Treatments Once Started

Once having started a mode of treatment, many caregivers find it very difficult to discontinue it. While this strongly felt difference between the ease of withholding a treatment and the difficulty of withdrawing it provides a psychological explanation of certain actions, it does not justify them. It sometimes even leads to a thoroughly irrational decision process. For example, in caring for a dying, comatose patient, many physicians apparently find it harder to stop a functioning peripheral IV than not to restart one that has infiltrated (that is, has broken through the blood vessel and is leaking fluid into surrounding tissue), especially if the only way to reestablish an IV would be to insert a central line into the heart or to do a cutdown (make an incision to gain access to the deep large blood vessels).[15]

What factors might make withdrawing medical treatment morally worse than withholding it? Withdrawing a treatment seems to be an action, which, when it is likely to end in death, initially seems more serious than an omission that ends in death. However, this view is fraught with errors. Withdrawing is not always an act: failing to put the next infusion into a tube could be correctly described as an omission, for example. Even when withdrawing is an act, it may well be morally correct and even morally obligatory. Discontinuing intravenous lines in a patient now permanently unconscious in accord with that patient's well-informed advance directive would certainly be such a case. Furthermore, the caregiver's obligation to serve the patient's interests through both acts and omissions rules out the exculpation that accompanies omissions in the usual course of social life. An omission that is not warranted by the patient's interests is culpable.

Sometimes initiating a treatment creates expectations in the minds of caregivers, patients, and family that the treatment will be continued indefinitely or until the patient is cured. Such expectations may provide a reason to continue the treatment as a way to keep a promise. However, as with all promises, caregivers could be very careful when initiating a treatment to explain the indications for its discontinuation, and they could modify preconceptions with continuing reevaluation and education during treatment. Though all patients are entitled to expect the continuation of care in the patient's best interests, they are not and should not be entitled to the continuation of a particular mode of care.

Accepting the distinction between withholding and withdrawing medical treatment as morally significant also has a very unfortunate implication: caregivers may become unduly reluctant to begin some treatments precisely because they fear that they will be locked into continuing treatments that are no longer of value to the patient. For example, the physician who had been unwilling to stop the respirator while the infant Andrew Stinson died over several months is reportedly "less eager to attach babies to respirators now."[16] But if it were easier to ignore malnutrition and dehydration and to withhold treatments for these problems than to discontinue the same treatments when they have become especially burdensome and insufficiently beneficial for the patient, then the incentives would be perverse. Once a treatment has been tried, it is often much clearer whether it is of value to the patient, and the decision to stop it can be made more reliably.

The same considerations should apply to starting as to stopping a treatment, and whatever assessment warrants withholding should also warrant withdrawing.

The Obligation to Avoid Being the Unambiguous Cause of Death

Many physicians will agree with all that we have said and still refuse to allow a choice to forgo food and fluid because such a course seems to be a "death sentence." In this view death seems to be more certain from malnutrition and dehydration than from forgoing other forms of medical therapy. This implies that it is acceptable to act in ways that are likely to cause death, as in not operating on a gangrenous leg, only if there remains a chance that the patient will survive. This is a comforting formulation for caregivers, to be sure, since they can thereby avoid feeling the full weight of the responsibility for the time and manner of a patient's death. However, it is not a persuasive moral argument.

First, in appropriate cases discontinuing certain medical treatments is generally accepted despite the fact that death is as certain as with nonfeeding. Dialysis in a patient without kidney function or transfusions in a patient with severe aplastic anemia are obvious examples. The dying that awaits such patients often is not greatly different from dying of dehydration and malnutrition.

Second, the certainty of a generally undesirable outcome such as death is always relevant to a decision, but it does not foreclose the possibility that this course is better than others available to this patient.[17] Ambiguity and uncertainty are so common in medical decision-making that caregivers are tempted to use them in distancing themselves from direct responsibility. However, caregivers are in fact responsible for the time and manner of death for many patients. Their distaste for this fact should not constrain otherwise morally justified decisions.

The Obligation to Provide Symbolically Significant Treatment

One of the most common arguments for always providing nutrition and hydration is that it symbolizes, expresses, or conveys the essence of care and compassion. Some actions not only aim at goals, they also express values. Such expressive actions should not simply be viewed as means to ends; they should also be viewed in light of what they communicate. From this perspective food and water are not only goods that preserve life and provide comfort; they are also symbols of care and compassion. To withhold or withdraw them—to "starve" a patient—can never express or convey care.

Why is providing food and water a central symbol of care and compassion? Feeding is the first response of the community to the needs of newborns and remains a central mode of nurture and comfort. Eating is associated with social interchange and community, and providing food for someone else is a way to create and maintain bonds of sharing and expressing concern. Furthermore, even the relatively low levels of hunger and thirst that most people have experienced are decidedly uncomfortable, and the common image of severe malnutrition or dehydration is one of unremitting agony. Thus, people are rightly eager to provide food and water. Such provision is essential to minimally tolerable existence and a powerful symbol of our concern for each other.

However, *medical* nutrition and hydration,

we have argued, may not always provide net benefits to patients. Medical procedures to provide nutrition and hydration are more similar to other medical procedures than to typical human ways of providing nutrition and hydration, for example, a sip of water. It should be possible to evaluate their benefits and burdens, as we evaluate any other medical procedure. Of course, if family, friends, and caregivers feel that such procedures affirm important values even when they do not benefit the patient, their feelings should not be ignored. We do not contend that there is an obligation to withhold or to withdraw such procedures (unless consideration of the patient's advance directives or current best interest unambiguously dictates that conclusion); we only contend that nutrition and hydration may be forgone in some cases.

The symbolic connection between care and nutrition or hydration adds useful caution to decision making. If decision makers worry over withholding or withdrawing medical nutrition and hydration, they may inquire more seriously into the circumstances that putatively justify their decisions. This is generally salutary for health care decision making. The critical inquiry may well yield the sad but justified conclusion that the patient will be served best by not using medical procedures to provide food and fluids.

A Limited Conclusion

Our conclusion—that patients or their surrogates, in close collaboration with their physicians and other caregivers and with careful assessment of the relevant information, can correctly decide to forgo the provision of medical treatments intended to correct malnutrition and dehydration in some circumstances—is quite limited. Concentrating on incompetent patients, we have argued that in most cases such patients will be best served by providing nutrition and fluids. Thus, there should be a presumption in favor of providing nutrition and fluids as part of the broader presumption to provide means that prolong life. But this presumption may be rebutted in particular cases.

We do not have enough information to be able to determine with clarity and conviction whether withholding or withdrawing nutrition and hydration was justified in the cases that have occasioned public concern, though it seems likely that the Danville and Bloomington babies should have been fed and that Claire Conroy should not.

It is never sufficient to rule out "starvation" categorically. The question is whether the obligation to act in the patient's best interests was discharged by withholding or withdrawing particular medical treatments. All we have claimed is that nutrition and hydration by medical means need not always be provided. Sometimes they may not be in accord with the patient's wishes or interests. Medical nutrition and hydration do not appear to be distinguishable in any morally relevant way from other life-sustaining medical treatments that may on occasion be withheld or withdrawn.

Notes

1. John A. Robertson, "Dilemma in Danville," *Hastings Cent. Rep.* 11: 5–8 (October 1981).

2. T. Rohrlich, "2 Doctors Face Murder Charges in Patient's Death." *L.A. Times,* August 19, 1982, A-1; Jonathan Kirsch, "A Death at Kaiser Hospital." *Calif. Mag.* (1982), 79ff; Magistrate's findings. California v. Barber and Nejdl, No. A 925586, Los Angeles Man. Ct. Cal. (March 9, 1983); Superior Court of California, County of Los Angeles, California v. Barber and Nejdl, No. A0 25586k tentative decision May 5, 1983.

3. *In re* Infant Doe, No. GU 8204-00 (Cir. Ct. Monroe County, Ind., April 12, 1982), *writ of mandamus dismissed sub nom.* State ex rel. Infant Doe v. Baker, No. 482 S140 (Indiana Supreme Ct., May 27, 1982).

4. Office of the Secretary, Department of Health and Human Services, "Nondiscrimination on the Basis of Handicap," *Federal Register* 48 (1983), 9630-32. (Interim final rule modifying 45 C.F.R. #84.61.) See Judge Gerhard Gesell's decision, American Academy of Pediatrics v. Heckler, No. 83-0774, U.S. District Court, D.C., April 24,

1983; and also George J. Annas, "Disconnecting the Baby Doe Hotline," *Hastings Cent. Rep.* 13: 14–16 (June 1983).

5. *In re* Conroy, 190 N.J. Super. 453, 464 A.2d 303 (App. Div. 1983).

6. President's Commission for the Study of Ethical Problems in Medicine and Biomedical and Behavioral Research. *Deciding to Forego Life-Sustaining Treatment.* Washington, D.C.: U.S. Government Printing Office (1982).

7. G. E. M. Anscombe, "Ethical Problems in the Management of Some Severely Handicapped Children: Commentary 2," *J. Med. Ethics* 7: 117–124 (1981).

8. See, e.g., President's Commission for the Study of Ethical Problems in Medicine and Biomedical and Behavioral Research, *Making Health Care Decisions,* Washington, D.C.: U.S. Government Printing Office (1982).

9. President's Commission, *Deciding to Forego,* at 171–196.

10. Joyce V. Zerwekh, "The Dehydration Question," *Nursing 83,* 47–51 (1983) with comments by Judith R. Brown and Marion B. Dolan. See also chapter 3.

11. James J. McCartney, "The Development of the Doctrine of Ordinary and Extraordinary Means of Preserving Life in Catholic Moral Theology before the Karen Quinlan Case," *Linacre Q.* 47: 215 (1980).

12. President's Commission. *Deciding to Forego,* at 82–90. For an argument that fluids and electrolytes can be "extraordinary," see Carson Strong, "Can Fluids and Electrolytes be 'Extraordinary' Treatment?" *J. Med. Ethics* 7: 83–85 (1981).

13. The Sacred Congregation for the Doctrine of the Faith, Declaration on Euthanasia, Vatican City, May 5, 1980.

14. Paul Ramsey, *The Patient as Person,* New Haven: Yale University Press (1970), 128–129; Paul Ramsey, *Ethics at the Edges of Life: Medical and Legal Intersections,* New Haven: Yale University Press (1978), 275; Bernard Towers, "Irreversible Coma and Withdrawal of Life Support: Is It Murder If the IV Line Is Disconnected?" *J. Med. Ethics* 8: 205 (1982).

15. See Kenneth C. Micetich, Patricia H. Steinecker, and David C. Thomasma, "Are Intravenous Fluids Morally Required for a Dying

Patient?" *Arch. Intern. Med.* 143: 975–978 (1983), also chapter 4.

16. Robert and Peggy Stinson, *The Long Dying of*

Baby Andrew, Boston: Little, Brown and Co. (1983), 355.

17. See chapter 4 [in original volume].

14. Objections to the Institutionalisation of Euthanasia

Stephen G. Potts

Physician Stephen G. Potts argues that any attempt to institutionalize active voluntary euthanasia entails risks to the development of new treatments, decreases patient hope, increases fear, and brings pressures on patients. Potts is also concerned with the difficulties in implementation and with social costs. He concludes by arguing that patients do not have the right to be provided with a means of death.

[I am opposed] to any attempt to institutionalise euthanasia . . . because the risks of such institutionalisation are so grave as to outweigh the very real suffering of those who might benefit from it.

Risks of Institutionalisation

Among the potential effects of a legalised practice of euthanasia are the following:

1. Reduced Pressure to Improve Curative or Symptomatic Treatment If euthanasia had been legal forty years ago, it is quite possible that there would be no hospice movement today. The improvement in terminal care is a direct result of attempts made to minimise suffering. If that suffering had been extinguished by extinguishing the patients who bore it, then we may never have known the advances in the control of pain, nausea, breathlessness and other terminal symptoms that the last twenty years have seen.

Some diseases that were terminal a few dec-

From Stephen G. Potts, "Looking for the Exit Door: Killing and Caring in Modern Medicine," *Houston Law Review,* vol. 25 (1988), pp. 504–509, 510–511. Reprinted by permission of the *Houston Law Review.*

ades ago are now routinely cured by newly developed treatments. Earlier acceptance of euthanasia might well have undercut the urgency of the research efforts which led to the discovery of those treatments. If we accept euthanasia now, we may well delay by decades the discovery of effective treatments for those diseases that are now terminal.

2. Abandonment of Hope Every doctor can tell stories of patients expected to die within days who surprise everyone with their extraordinary recoveries. Every doctor has experienced the wonderful embarrassment of being proven wrong in their pessimistic prognosis. To make euthanasia a legitimate option as soon as the prognosis is pessimistic enough is to reduce the probability of such extraordinary recoveries from low to zero.

3. Increased Fear of Hospitals and Doctors Despite all the efforts at health education, it seems there will always be a transference of the patient's fear of illness from the illness to the doctors and hospitals who treat it. This fear is still very real and leads to large numbers of late presentations of illnesses that might have been cured if only the patients had sought help earlier. To institutionalise euthanasia, however carefully, would undoubtedly magnify all the latent fear of doctors and hospitals harbored by the public. The inevitable result would be a rise in late presentations and, therefore, preventable deaths.

4. Difficulties of Oversight and Regulation Both the Dutch and the Californian proposals list sets of precautions designed to prevent abuses. They acknowledge that such abuses are a possibility. I am far from convinced that the precautions are sufficient to prevent either those abuses that have been foreseen or those that may arise after passage of the law. The history of legal "loopholes" is not a cheering one: Abuses might arise when the patient is wealthy and an inheritance is at stake, when the doctor has made mistakes in diagnosis and treatment and hopes to avoid detection, when insurance coverage for treatment costs is about to expire, and in a host of other circumstances.

5. Pressure on the Patient Both sets of proposals seek to limit the influence of the patient's family on the decision, again acknowledging the risks posed by such influence. Families have all kinds of subtle ways, conscious and unconscious, of putting pressure on a patient to request euthanasia and relieve them of the financial and social burden of care. Many patients already feel guilty for imposing burdens on those who care for them, even when the families are happy to bear that burden. To provide an avenue for the discharge of that guilt in a request for euthanasia is to risk putting to death a great many patients who do not wish to die.

6. Conflict with Aims of Medicine The pro-euthanasia movement cheerfully hands the dirty work of the actual killing to the doctors who, by and large, neither seek nor welcome the responsibility. There is little examination of the psychological stresses imposed on those whose training and professional outlook are geared to the saving of lives by asking them to start taking lives on a regular basis. Euthanasia advocates seem very confident that doctors can be relied on to make the enormous efforts sometimes necessary to save some lives, while at the same time assenting to requests to take

other lives. Such confidence reflects, perhaps, a high opinion of doctors' psychic robustness, but it is a confidence seriously undermined by the shocking rates of depression, suicide, alcoholism, drug addiction, and marital discord consistently recorded among this group.

7. Dangers of Societal Acceptance It must never be forgotten that doctors, nurses, and hospital administrators have personal lives, homes, and families, or that they are something more than just doctors, nurses or hospital administrators. They are *citizens* and a significant part of the society around them. I am very worried about what the institutionalisation of euthanasia will do to society, in general, and, particularly how much it will further erode our attachment to the sixth commandment. ["Thou shalt not kill."] How will we regard murderers? What will we say to the terrorist who justifies killing as a means to his political end when we ourselves justify killing as a means to a humanitarian end? I do not know and I daresay the euthanasia advocates do not either, but I worry about it and they appear not to. They need to justify their complacency.

8. The Slippery Slope How long after acceptance of voluntary euthanasia will we hear the calls for nonvoluntary euthanasia? There are thousands of comatose or demented patients sustained by little more than good nursing care. They are an enormous financial and social burden. How soon will the advocates of euthanasia be arguing that we should "assist them in dying"—for, after all, they won't mind, will they?

How soon after *that* will we hear the calls for involuntary euthanasia, the disposal of the burdensome, the unproductive, the polluters of the gene pool? We must never forget the way the Nazi euthanasia programme made this progression in a few short years. "Oh, but they were barbarians," you say, and so they were, but not at the outset.

If developments in terminal care can be represented by a progression from the CURE mode of medical care to the CARE mode, enacting voluntary euthanasia legislation would permit a further progression to the KILL mode. The slippery slope argument represents the fear that, if this step is taken, then it will be difficult to avoid a further progression to the CULL mode, as illustrated:

CURE   The central aim of medicine

CARE   The central aim of terminal care once patients are beyond cure

KILL   The aim of the proponents of euthanasia for those patients beyond cure and not helped by care

CULL   The feared result of weakening the prohibition on euthanasia

I do not know how easy these moves will be to resist once voluntary euthanasia is accepted, but I have seen little evidence that the modern euthanasia advocates care about resisting them or even worry that they might be possible.

9. *Costs and Benefits*   Perhaps the most disturbing risk of all is posed by the growing concern over medical costs. Euthanasia is, after all, a very cheap service. The cost of a dose of barbiturates and curare and the few hours in a hospital bed that it takes them to act is minute compared to the massive bills incurred by many patients in the last weeks and months of their lives. Already in Britain, there is a serious under-provision of expensive therapies like renal dialysis and intensive care, with the result that many otherwise preventable deaths occur. Legalising euthanasia would save substantial financial resources which could be diverted to more "useful" treatments. These economic concerns already exert pressure to accept euthanasia, and, if accepted, they will inevitably tend to enlarge the category of patients for whom euthanasia is permitted.

Each of these objections could, and should, be expanded and pressed harder. I do not propose to do so now, for it is sufficient for my purposes to list them as *risks*, not inevitabilities. Several elements go into our judgment of the severity of a risk: the *probability* that the harm in question will arise (the odds), the *severity* of the harm in question (the stakes), and the ease with which the harm in question can be corrected (the *reversibility*). The institutionalisation of euthanasia is such a radical departure from anything that has gone before in West-

ern society that we simply cannot judge the probability of any or all of the listed consequences. Nor can we rule any of them out. There must, however, be agreement that the severity of each of the harms listed is enough to give serious cause for concern, and the severity of all the harms together is enough to horrify. Furthermore, many of the potential harms seem likely to prove very difficult, if not impossible, to reverse by reinstituting a ban on euthanasia.

Weighing the Risks

For all these reasons, the burden of proof *must* lie with those who would have us gamble by legalising euthanasia. They should demonstrate beyond reasonable doubt that the dangers listed will not arise, just as chemical companies proposing to introduce a new drug are required to demonstrate that it is safe as well as beneficial. Thus far, the proponents of euthanasia have relied exclusively on the compassion they arouse with tales of torment mercifully cut short by death, and have made little or no attempt to shoulder the burden of proving that legalising euthanasia is safe. Until they make such an attempt and carry it off successfully, their proposed legislation must be rejected outright.

The Right to Die and the Duty to Kill

The nature of my arguments should have made it clear by now that I object, not so much to individual acts of euthanasia, but to institutionalising it as a practice. All the pro-euthanasia arguments turn on the individual case of the patient in pain, suffering at the center of an intolerable existence. They exert powerful calls on our compassion, and appeal to our pity, therefore, we assent too readily when it is claimed that such patients have a *"right to die"* as an escape from torment. So long as the right to die means no more than the right to refuse life-prolonging treatment and the right to rational suicide, I agree. The advocates of euthanasia want to go much further than this though. They want to extend the right to die to encompass the right to receive assistance in suicide and, beyond that, the right to be killed. Here, the focus shifts from the patient to the agent, and from the killed to the killer; but, the argument begins to break down because our compassion does not extend this far.

If it is true that there is a right to be assisted in suicide or a right to be killed, then it follows that someone, somewhere, has a *duty* to provide the assistance or to do the killing. When we look at the proposed legislation, it is very clear upon whom the advocates of euthanasia would place this duty: the doctor. It would be the doctor's job to provide the pills and the doctor's job to give the lethal injection. The regulation of euthanasia is meant to prevent anyone, other than the doctor, from doing it. Such regulation would ensure that the doctor does it with the proper precautions and consultations, and would give the doctor security from legal sanctions for doing it. The emotive appeal of euthanasia is undeniably powerful, but it lasts only so long as we can avoid thinking about who has to do the killing, and where, and when, and how. Proposals to institutionalise euthanasia force us to think hard about these things, and the chill that their contemplation generates is deep enough to freeze any proponent's ardor. . . .

[One final objection to the institutionalisation of euthanasia] relates to another set out above (#5. Pressure on the patient). The objection turns on the concern that many requests for euthanasia will not be truly voluntary because of pressure on the patient or the patient's fear of becoming a burden. There is a significant risk that legalising voluntary euthanasia out of respect for the *right* to die will generate many requests for euthanasia out of a perceived *duty* to die. . . .

15. Should Pregnancies Be Sustained in Brain-Dead Women? A Philosophical Discussion of Postmortem Pregnancy

Julien S. Murphy

Professor Julien S. Murphy argues against keeping the bodies of brain-dead women functioning for the purpose of preserving a fetus. She bases her claim on the feminist definition of pregnancy, which requires human consciousness and the woman's choice to be pregnant. Since the brain-dead woman is no longer alive, and no longer has "choice" in the matter of pregnancy, Murphy argues that no state of pregnancy exists and the woman's cadaver should not be ventilated.

Life keeps me alive; all its tubes
and wires are connected to me and give
support

From *Healing Technology: Feminist Perspectives,* edited by Kathryn Strother Ratcliff. Copyright 1989 by The University of Michigan. Published by the University of Michigan Press. Used by permission.

in ways that life determines for my
needs.
On a bed of earth, in house, its calendars
and clocks are programmed to me: the
various airs
of mornings, evenings, noontimes, in and
out.

—William Bronk, "Life Supports"

As the current abortion debates indicate, the relationship between a woman and her fetus in pregnancy has become far more than a biological matter. It is one of the most complex social, legal, and ethical controversies of the twentieth century.[1] Opinions vary widely on the rights and responsibilities of women in pregnancy, as the frequent criticisms of *Roe v. Wade* show. Moreover, the continual innovations in reproductive technology present, almost daily, new possibilities that may alter the very meaning of *pregnancy*. One irony of our century may be that, although we are biologically dependent on pregnancy for the survival of our species, we could end the century lacking agreement on such formerly basic matters as what pregnancy is, what one is pregnant with, and who or what is pregnant. Amid the flurry of high-tech possibilities (embryo transfer, donor eggs, frozen embryos), a little-mentioned low-tech procedure, seldom applicable, may tilt the meaning of pregnancy in the most unfamiliar and perhaps dangerous direction: the use of *postmortem maternal ventilation* (PMV) to sustain pregnancy in brain-dead women.[2] PMV marks a shift in the use of respiratory systems away from use on patients who might otherwise recover to those whose lives will thereafter be terminated. Like much of low technology, PMV is cost-effective. It requires standard hospital life-support equipment and decreases the need for high-cost prenatal technology.

Postmortem maternal ventilation is the term I have selected to refer to the practice of applying ventilation (i.e., life-support machine) to a brain-dead pregnant patient to sustain the maternal vital functions necessary for continued fetal development. If PMV is successful, the subsequent postmortem caesarean section results in a live birth. I will refer to the brain-dead pregnant patient as a *pregnant cadaver* and when PMV is in progress, as a *ventilated pregnant cadaver*. Both terms stress the fact that the body to which PMV is being applied is a dead body since it has been judged brain-dead, fulfilling the medical and legal criteria for determining the person dead. The Uniform Determination of Death Act approved in 1980 and adopted in twenty-three states includes brain death in its definition of death:

An individual who has sustained either (1) irreversible cessation of circulatory and respiratory functions, or (2) irreversible cessation of all functions of the entire brain, including the brain stem, is dead. A determination of death must be made in accordance with accepted medical standards. (*Uniform Laws Annotated* 1988, 293)

A ventilated cadaver may simulate the state of being "alive" by retaining a fleshy skin color, by being warm to the touch, and by lacking the coloration and stiffness of a dead body. Since its vital circulatory and respiratory processes have irreversibly failed, however, it is not a live body. Whereas other brain-dead bodies are usually removed from live support systems and interred, or are used for organ transplants or medical research before interment, the pregnant cadaver presents a unique case, for a healthy pregnancy can continue to thrive in a ventilated pregnant cadaver.

The philosophical significance of PMV is the challenge it poses to these assumptions, which I will argue, are basic to pregnancy: *that a woman must be alive to be pregnant* and *that the mother in pregnancy must be a person*. The use of PMV depends on a refusal to think that the pregnancy must end with the death of the mother and an assumption that a mother, when alive, adds nothing essential to her pregnancy. The challenge to both of these formerly taken-for-granted beliefs is unsettling. Common-sense attitudes conceal the deeply rooted philosophical issues inherent in PMV: either people are quickly pleased at the unexpected prospect of fetal survival and favor PMV or they find PMV grotesquely necrophilic and undesirable. Proponents are fascinated with the possibility of continuing pregnancy in a body after death or are concerned with maintaining fetal life, either because they may believe that a fetus always has a right to life or because the fetus is favored out of love for the mother, as a way in which some part of her can live on beyond her death.

While sociologists might look for a correlation between views on PMV and views on either abortion or euthanasia, the philosopher's task is to evaluate the implications of the practice of PMV for the social community and to ask how PMV might affect the discourse about pregnancy, especially assumptions about pregnancy and social policy. Despite the appeal that PMV may have to medical practitioners and interested parties, serious ethical objections can be raised about its underlying implications. Feminists and those concerned with the value priorities of medical technology can find strong grounds from which to argue against PMV even though the choice not to use PMV may result in the death of an otherwise healthy fetus.

This discussion will oppose PMV on the moral grounds that there is a feminist definition of pregnancy and that this definition precludes even the deliberate choice of PMV. The feminist view of pregnancy advanced here asserts two fundamental requirements: first, that *human consciousness is necessary to pregnancy*. Pregnancy ought to include the conscious state of being pregnant. A woman need not be conscious all the time (i.e., in sleep, blackouts, light comas) but she must at least have the capacity for consciousness in order for her activity of "being pregnant" to be properly a human activity. Second, *pregnancy ought to result from a choice a woman makes to be pregnant*. The choice to be pregnant is essentially a woman's choice, as it is her body that sustains the pregnancy. One who is pregnant ought to be one who is choosing pregnancy as an existential project. A woman may not have deliberately chosen to become pregnant (i.e., conception could result from a contraceptive failure), but if she remains pregnant it should be the result of her conscious choice of pregnancy as an activity.

While other medical practices that seek to separate pregnancy from maternal consciousness outside of women's bodies (i.e., experimentation on pregnancy in vitro) may be objectionable on other grounds, in this paper I will argue that in vivo pregnancies, those occurring in women's bodies, require the possibility of maternal consciousness if the pregnancy is to uphold respect for women as persons. In fact, the practice of PMV undermines women as persons precisely because the female role in reproduction occurs in a nonperson form of a woman. I argue that a careful examination of the practice of PMV along with the medical, philosophical, and legal problems inherent in this new obstetric practice will reveal an eliminative view of pregnancy. Any mandatory PMV policy can be seen as directly violating women's reproductive freedoms and brain-dead patients' right to privacy. Any voluntary PMV policy must assume that PMV is similar to organ donation, that the allocation of medical resources for PMV is justifiable by community health needs, and that the practice of PMV is not detrimental to persons. All three of these assumptions can be shown to be problematic. I will conclude that the practice of PMV should not continue unless such issues are resolved.

The Practice of Postmortem Maternal Ventilation

Difficult ethical issues arise in considering whether or not pregnancy should be sustained in nonconscious female bodies, where the woman may either be reversibly comatose or even brain dead. While pregnancy has been sustained in comatose women for as long as twenty-eight weeks (See table 1, case 2), life support was not required for these patients and they were by no means dead.[3] In fact, in case two, the child was born by a vaginal delivery even though the mother remained comatose. Whether or not pregnancy should be sustained in comatose women is a difficult issue as all but those in an irreversible comatose state are technically alive and no "extraordinary means" are needed to sustain bodily life. Admittedly, the stage of pregnancy as well as the stage of coma may be difficult to discern in comatose women. Whatever decision is made about sustaining pregnancy in comatose cases, it must be remembered that as long as the woman can survive without life support she is medically defined as alive.

The practice of PMV, however, continues pregnancy in patients classified as dead. PMV practices apply life support to brain-dead comatose patients whose bodies have not been otherwise severely damaged. The definition of brain death is a recent development in medicine. It developed as a result of the need to distinguish other comatose patients from those irreversibly comatose patients on life

Table 1. U.S. cases of sustaining pregnancies in comatose women

Place and Date	Age of Woman (years)	Cause of Maternal Coma	Onset of Coma[a]	Length of Coma at Birth (in weeks)	Maternal Death[b]	Live Birth	Birth Weight (oz.)	Court Battle for Abortion	Court Ruling
S. Dakota, 1977	30	Brain injury from car accident	6	27	Yes	Yes vaginal delivery	58	None	
Florida, Feb.–Aug. 1984	16	Brain injury from car accident	12	24	c	Yes c-sect.	c	None	
New York, March 1985	21	Anticancer drug mistakenly injected into spinal column	25	1	c	Yes c-sect.	34	None	
Connecticut, January 1986	24	Oxygen loss in attempted hanging	9	15	Yes	No		Yes	Sustain pregnancy

[a]gestational age in weeks

[b]maternal death following the birth

[c]information unknown

support who have no central nervous system activity. This distinction aids physicians in determining when life support is futile and should be ended. It is particularly suitable for determining the point at which organs can be removed from a brain-dead donor. A team of researchers at the Harvard Medical School in 1965 established a set of criteria for determining the state of irreversible coma, establishing it as a definitive way to determine brain death in a patient and judge the patient as "dead." The team claimed "that responsible medical opinion is ready to adopt new criteria for pronouncing death to have occurred in an individual sustaining irreversible coma as a result of permanent brain damage" (Harvard Ad Hoc Committee 1968).

The Harvard Brain-Death Criteria which are used in PMV as well as organ transplant cases consist of four components: (1) unreceptivity and unresponsivity, (2) lack of movements or breathing, (3) absence of reflexes, and (4) flat electroencephalogram (Harvard Ad Hoc Committee 1968). In PMV cases, the Harvard Criteria are slightly altered. Normally, the respirator is turned off for three-minute intervals to see if the patient can breathe spontaneously. This usual test is not performed to prevent possible fetal damage. According to the Harvard team, the patient should be declared dead *before* the respirator is turned off, to provide legal protection for physicians. Hence if life support is continued after the test confirms brain death, then life support is being applied to a dead body. It is also recommended that, in order to avoid a conflict of interests, the physician making the diagnosis of brain death should not also be involved in subsequent transplant efforts using organs from the same patient. It is unclear whether this restriction is included in the application of the Harvard Criteria to PMV cases.

The instances of brain death during pregnancy in the United States are quite rare. Even more unusual are pregnancies in brain-dead women in which neither the mother's internal organs nor the fetus is damaged. Yet at least seven cases suitable for PMV practices have been reported in the United States since 1976 (table 2), and the known instances may increase with the apparent tendency to bring such cases into court in recent years.[4]

Only one of the seven publicized PMV cases (Buffalo, 1981) has been written up in the medical journals by the medical team (Dillon et al. 1982). Writing about the Buffalo case, they describe a young epileptic woman, who shortly after hospital admission, suffered irreversible neurological deterioration— slurred speech, ataxic gait, respiratory collapse. Despite ventilation and intubation, the woman, while twenty-five weeks pregnant, began to die: "her pupils were fixed and dilated," and two days later "her reflexes were absent; and all sedation and anti-seizure medications were withdrawn" (Dillon et al. 1982, 1090). But as long as the mother's body was artificially aerified and fed, it remained capable of sustaining the fetus. The mother herself "had no spontaneous respirations; all limbs were flaccid; deep-tendon reflexes were absent throughout. The eyes were fixed in the midline. . . ." and "she was unresponsive to deep pain." The fetus, however, continued to thrive: "the fetal heart rate was audible and ranged between 140 and 160 beats per minute after the mother was diagnosed as brain-dead" (1089–91). PMV enabled the pregnancy to continue until the twenty-sixth week when the onset of fetal distress indicated cessation of PMV and a birth by caesarean section. Not only was the Buffalo case successful, but it was offered as grounds to recommend life-support measures in appropriate brain-dead pregnancies (Dillon et al. 1982, 1090). The authors' recommendation states:

> Having established a diagnosis of brain-death in a patient with a potentially viable fetus (24–27 weeks' gestation), we recommend that vigorous maternal support and fetal monitoring be instituted. . . . Our experience indicates that after 24 weeks' gestation, each extra week in utero increases the chances for fetal survival. (1090)

The goal of PMV is to sustain the fetus in its mother's ventilated cadaver until the fetus can survive on its own. Whereas abortion discussions emphasize fetal viability (the earliest

Table 2. U.S. cases of PMV pregnancies

Place and Date	Age of Woman (years)	Cause of Maternal Brain Death	Onset of PMV[a]	End of PMV	Reason for Ending PMV	Live Birth	Birth Weight (oz.)	Court Battle over PMV	Court Ruling
Colorado, Dec. 1976	b	b	b	b	Futile	No	b	No	None
Brooklyn, N.Y., Dec. 1977	27	Coma	16	17	Maternal heart attack	No	b	No	None
Buffalo, N.Y., Jan. 1981	24	Encephalitis	25	26	Maternal instability	Yes	32	No	None
San Francisco, Calif., March 1983	b	Seizure	22	31	Fetal maturity	Yes	48	No	None
Roanoke, Vir., July 1983	b	b	c	c	b	Yes	59	No	None
Santa Clara, Calif., July 1986	34	Brain tumor	24	31	Fetal maturity	Yes	69	Yes	Sustain pregnancy
Augusta, Geo., Aug. 1986	25	Drug overdose	17	24	b	No	17	Yes	Sustain pregnancy

[a] gestational age in weeks

[b] information unknown

[c] 84 days of PMV

point in fetal development in which the fetus would be likely to survive birth), PMV aims to sustain the fetus in utero until fetal pulmonary maturity, the point somewhat beyond viability at which it is likely that the fetal respiratory system is fully developed. The odds of a live birth increase dramatically as fetal development approaches fetal pulmonary maturity. The onset of PMV has begun as early as the sixteenth week of gestation (case 2) and as late as the twenty-fifth week (case 3). In the Buffalo case, life support was applied latest in pregnancy of all seven cases. Nevertheless, its eight days of ventilation did not set the record for the longest use of PMV. Since then, three cases have exceeded that duration: (case 4) with sixty-three days of ventilation, (case 6) with fifty-three days of ventilation, and (case 5) with eighty-four days of ventilation. The trend to maintain ventilation in pregnant cadavers for a matter of weeks or even months makes Dillon's suggested management of PMV pregnancies conservative. The two limiting factors for determining the duration of PMV are indications of maternal instability and indications of fetal distress. Barring these, the fetus can be sustained in utero after maternal brain death for long periods.

Sustaining pregnancy in a ventilated cadaver is no easy matter. The Buffalo team recognized that "the medical problems encountered in attempting this are profound and time-consuming but not insurmountable" (Dillon et al. 1982, 1091). For instance, the fetus must receive nourishment through the cadaver, so the cadaver must be given intravenous infusions of nutrients as well as antibiotics to prevent infection; the respirator must be continually adjusted; and the body temperature of the cadaver must be regulated by applying warm or cooled blankets. And PMV is not merely a matter of applying machines to a pregnant cadaver, but involves medical staff in daily services to the cadaver. In case 4, environmental stimulation for the fetus was supplied by nurses who "stroked the mother's abdomen and murmured soothing words," and played music on a tape recorder near the bed (*Newsweek* 1983). The vital role that nurses play in the care of ventilated pregnant cadavers calls forth a complex range of attitudes. Some nurses believe the mother is actually a live person and value their role in the pregnancy, while other nurses see the mother as dead and find it difficult to provide the necessary services. A wide range of attitudes from approval to disgust also mark the legal controversy surrounding PMV.

The Legal Controversy over PMV

Along with medical difficulties that arise in ventilating a pregnant cadaver, conceptual difficulties are inherent in the very nature of the practice. To begin with, confusion exists about how the ventilated cadaver is to be regarded, what rights if any it has, and whether any possible rights of the cadaver could outweigh claims of fetal rights. The confusion is found in Dillon et al., who diagnosed their patient as brain dead and yet referred to it not as a cadaver but as "a fatally ill pregnant woman whose vital functions have been preserved" (1089). They speak of their attempts "to prolong maternal life in the face of brain death" (1089). But as Siegler and Wikler note in their preface to the Dillon et al. report "one cannot prolong life in a dead body" (1982, 1101). Dillon et al. refer to the maintenance of "somatic life" in their patient (1982, 1089). However, if one grants somatic life in a ventilated cadaver, it is artificially sustained somatic life and not spontaneous somatic life as in a patient in a vegetative state. And if somatic life essentially means the ability of an organism to sustain itself spontaneously, then it is inappropriate to grant somatic life to ventilated cadavers. Even with a general acceptance of brain-death criteria among physicians, evidence suggests that many doctors would not turn off the respirators of patients who satisfied the Harvard Criteria for Brain Death (Pinkus 1984). Siegler and Wikler claim that "clinicians who find it congenial to speak of brain-dead patients as 'terminally ill' (and the like) do not, on our interpretation, really view the bodies of these patients as dead" (1982, 1101).

Amidst the conceptual disagreement about the status of brain-dead patients in general, little clear-cut legal ground exists to guide physicians through the perplexing ethical issues of PMV. Since PMV is a new practice and since brain death occurred quite unexpectedly in the cited cases, there was no opportunity to obtain consent from the women prior to death. In the Buffalo case not even paternal consent was obtained for PMV. Also there was no clear legal authority for researchers to keep a pregnant cadaver on life support for the sake of the fetus. The authors acknowledged that they chose "to sin bravely," by proceeding with PMV (Dillon et al. 1982, 1091). Apparently their intent was to provide the best care possible for the fetus. Their decision presupposes that PMV for the sake of fetal survival outweighed all other possible considerations. The nature of this controversial decision is indicated by court battles over the use and continuation of PMV in two of the seven cases. In fact, without patient consent the legal grounds are not clear for postmortem caesarean sections in unventilated cases even when they would be routine in late trimester pregnancies. As one physician advised his colleagues in a medical journal:

. . . (failing consent) perform the procedure [postmortem caesarean section] even without consent because (a) even if you are sued, the likelihood of being found liable is slim (no one has so far), and (b) the courts may well hold next that you MAY be sued, if you FAIL to perform the section, by the legal representatives of the child (and that case may be yours). (Arthur 1978, 179)

In PMV cases, it can be claimed either that the mother has no interests because she is dead, and hence the protection of fetal life warrants PMV, or that the mother's death should be respected and not artificially postponed, so PMV should be prohibited. On both sides, there may be benevolent wishes—those of well-meaning relatives who want the fetus to survive, and those of well-meaning relatives who want no further treatment applied to a mother who is clinically dead. The claim that the mother's interests die with her is commonly held. Siegler and Wikler, for instance, argue that as the mother in the Buffalo case

gave no prior request prohibiting PMV and as the physicians were unable to restore the mother to health or consciousness, "the mother's interests, apart from earlier desires to bear a healthy child, were not at issue. Further treatment could be considered neither beneficial nor harmful" (1982, 1101).

In both legal battles over PMV (cases 6 and 7), the court ruled for the continuation of life support. In case 6 the brain-dead patient's parents protested life support while the father of the fetus, supported by the court, demanded it. The intentions of the father in supporting PMV appeared to be based on his love for his brain-dead fiancée and his desire for their child, for after the successful PMV birth, the father told the press, "I'm very happy about the outcome for Michele (the baby), but I'm still grieving a little bit. Michele's birth today makes things a little easier. When I looked into her eyes, I could see the extension from Odette into her" (Associated Press 1986b, 1).

In the second legal battle over PMV (case 7), the brain-dead patient's husband was not the father of the fetus and the two men disagreed about PMV. Her husband protested life support while, once again, it was the father of the fetus who demanded it. This case presented an interesting legal conflict of rights, for the patient's husband presumably had the right to consent concerning medical treatment for his spouse, but would have no paternity rights over the fetus. The biological father might have paternity rights over the fetus but no right to consent for the brain-dead patient. The lawyer for the biological father, along with lawyers representing the fetus and the hospital argued for continuation of PMV as a right-to-life issue. It was claimed that discontinuing maternal life support was tantamount to feticide under Georgia law, which prohibits killing a fetus that is capable of movement (quickening), and that the mother's right to privacy, upheld by *Roe*, ended with her brain death, and hence "the state may intervene. . . . The state has an interest in the protection of human life" (Associated Press 1986a, Georgia Superior Court 1986). While the state attorney asked for a dismissal of the case, finding it outside of the court's jurisdiction because the fetus could not survive outside the womb, the court did not dismiss the case, but ordered in favor of PMV. Despite the court ruling, the life support was prematurely ended due to maternal instability. The fetus died.

The court rulings in PMV cases have been consistently in favor of continuing ventilation on pregnant cadavers. Such rulings assume either that the brain-dead mother no longer has rights or that her rights are not sufficient to outweigh those of the fetus. What is most alarming in the legal controversy over PMV is the failure to recognize the mother's right to a speedy death. In particular, it is important to examine the parameters of reproductive freedom to show that they include women's right to die.

PMV: An Eliminative View of Pregnancy

At one level, PMV seems to show that no matter how valuable higher brain functions might be within our society, they are not required in the third trimester of pregnancy. In fact, at the very stage in fetal development when the fetus is becoming neurologically advanced, it appears that it can be sustained in a body lacking all neurological activity. This point is not astounding from a medical standpoint, for it has been known that brain-dead patients on life support could maintain respiratory, circulatory, and digestive functions, and even generate new tissue. But, from an ethical point of view, the practice of PMV suggests that its proponents do not believe that maternal brain activity *ought* to be a requirement for pregnancy. Such a belief suggests an eliminative view of pregnancy. Eliminative views subtract or leave out one or more otherwise essential requirements of a definition. An eliminative view of pregnancy eliminates consciousness from the essential requirements for pregnancy, reducing women from "pregnant persons" to "pregnant bodies." The use of PMV suggests that pregnancy is a mindless act, and that what women themselves, as conscious beings, contribute to their pregnancies in the third trimester is not essential to the moral community. To imagine a dead woman's body as "artificially" pregnant is to claim that a woman's connection to her pregnancy is neither vital nor necessary, since PMV finishes a woman's pregnancy in her aerated and intubated remains. Once again, the point is not that the pregnancy is "artificial" or "unnatural" but that the cadaver is used to extort in death the female work of reproduction unfinished in life. Would we think nothing of mechanically ventilating and automating the bodies of brain-dead workers for the purpose of extracting additional labor from them? Both acts would eliminate consciousness as a necessary requirement for extracting work from human bodies and diminish the status of persons in the moral community by using human bodies for labor after their human life had ceased. The danger of eliminative views of human activities, such as pregnancy, is that they further diminish the human community by granting no special status to dead bodies as opposed to living ones. One difficulty in combating an eliminative view of pregnancy, such as that found in PMV, is that the right to privacy, which has been the framework for respecting human beings in matters of reproduction and health, is itself under attack, and not an obvious right as critics of *Roe* point out.

PMV, *Roe*, and Reproductive Freedom

The initiation of PMV is an instance of how the relationship between a woman and her fetus is interpreted from a sexist point of view. It poses a serious challenge to the right to abortion by obscuring even further the relationship between a pregnant woman and her fetus. The obscuring of the relationship between a pregnant woman and her fetus begins with conservative interpretations of the Supreme Court decision, *Roe v. Wade* (1973). The Supreme Court, when deciding in favor of Roe, granted women the right to abortion in early trimester pregnancies while leaving to each state the possibility of refusing abortion to women in third trimester pregnancies, the trimester most suitable for PMV, provided a state could show a "compelling interest" in fetal life. Conservatives interpret *Roe* as validating fetal life from the point of fetal viability. *Roe* defines fetal viability as the capacity for meaningful life outside the mother's womb even if it requires technological assistance for an ex utero fetus. One could argue that there is only a slight difference between life support for a twenty-seven week infant and life support for a maternal cadaver twenty-seven weeks' pregnant. Yet to blur the distinction is to undermine the assumption behind abortion rights, namely, that reproductive freedom must include the right not to be pregnant against one's will. For women, PMV raises the dangerous possibility that it could be claimed that every brain-dead pregnant woman with a healthy fetus *ought* to be ventilated. PMV could become mandatory for all suitable cases, particularly those in the third trimester, requiring of women that they finish their pregnancies even beyond the point of their own deaths. Just as women resorted to back-street abortions before *Roe,* relatives and friends of brain-dead pregnant women might need to resort to "back-street burials" or seek out physicians who might agree to claim that PMV would be "unfeasible" in particular cases.

If the practice of PMV were to become not only a medical option for physicians but a legal requirement in all appropriate cases, women would be forced into pregnancy beyond the point of their deaths, and it would be much harder to convince people that women should not be pregnant against their will in life. Clearly there are moral grounds to argue against mandatory PMV. *Roe* does not imply that (live) women are "natural" life support machines for the fetus, nor does *Roe* always require women to remain pregnant even in the third trimester. Hence, *Roe* is a decision that supports women's reproductive freedom, specifically the freedom to terminate pregnancy.

PMV, on the other hand, plays havoc with women's freedom in pregnancy by allowing for the condition of pregnancy without a woman's capacity for choice. A woman's will, her desire, is nonexistent in her ventilated pregnant cadaver. Even more oppressive than the most restrictive state abortion regulations, PMV practices are using women's bodies without their prior consent solely for the maintenance of pregnancies. Women's bodies, in the practice of PMV, are exclusively means to ends.

In PMV practices, the body of a brain-dead pregnant woman continues to labor under the functions of an artificially sustained pregnancy despite the fact that the woman, qua woman, no longer exists.

Roe reaffirmed the necessary connection between a right to one's body and a right to terminate pregnancy through its appeal to the right of privacy. The right to privacy had successfully been used prior to *Roe* to guarantee the right for adult bedroom pornography and contraception. But the Court's understanding of privacy has not granted women full protection in pregnancy. By granting the possibility of states claiming a compelling interest in viable fetuses, *Roe* has implied that women's bodies in pregnancy both are and are not their own, declaring the right to privacy a contingent right for pregnant women:

> The right to privacy, whether it be founded in the 14th Amendment's concept of personal liberty and restrictions upon state action, as we feel it is, or as the District Court determined, in the 9th Amendment's reservation of rights to the people, is broad enough to encompass a woman's decision whether or not to terminate her pregnancy. (*Roe v. Wade* 1973)

And yet, *Roe* also says:

> The pregnant woman cannot be isolated in her privacy. She carries an embryo, and later, a fetus. . . . The woman's privacy is no longer sole and any right of privacy she possesses must be measured accordingly. (*Roe v. Wade* 1973)

Hence, it is suggested by the Court that the right to privacy, which guarantees persons the "right to be let alone," is a right for the pregnant woman in early trimester pregnancies, but a right that can become increasingly contingent as her pregnancy develops, if a state chooses to claim a compelling interest. The longer a woman remains pregnant, the less right to her body she may be seen to have. Limitations on the right to privacy for pregnant women undermine the basis for reproductive freedoms including the freedom to not be pregnant when dead.

Reproductive freedom means the freedom to engage in or refrain from acts of reproduction. Human reproduction ought to be based upon free acts of consenting adults. An act of "consent" is one in which the agent of the act does not feel motivated primarily by coercion, but rather enters the act willingly and of her own accord. Coercion can happen to an individual as well as on a social level. A person could feel coerced into an action if another individual through threat of physical or psychological force demands performance of the action. In such a case, the act will have been done at the expense of her liberty. Coercion at the social level happens when a person finds a particular action appealing only in virtue of a complex social context of major incentives and penalties linked with a particular scheme of choices. Of course, it can be argued that no choice is totally free of cultural values. But the crucial issue is whether or not reproductive freedom ought to be a basic freedom in human societies, deeply rooted in the very foundation of rights that makes individual liberties possible. I would argue that reproductive freedom is basic to a system of rights in human communities, as evidenced by public outrage at instances of reproductive coercion, such as forced sterilization of workers. If the right to reproduce is judged to be integral to one's freedom and basic sense of dignity as a human being, then similarly, the right not to reproduce must be equally vital. Nothing should take precedence over a woman's right to engage in or terminate her pregnancy freely. Acts of either the legal system or individuals that threaten women with restrictions on their liberties in reproduction are tantamount to acts of coercion. Any mandatory PMV policy would similarly be coercive for women in pregnancy, for it would take away a woman's liberty not to be pregnant after she had ceased to exist.

PMV and Cadaver Rights

PMV raises the issue of the rights of persons after the clinical diagnosis of death. Do dead bodies have rights? Specifically, can a cadaver be harmed and if so, does the act of ventilation bring about harm to that cadaver? Or do dead bodies have a right to privacy that would exclude the possibility of PMV?

Clearly, brain-dead bodies do have some rights: the right not to be exploited, invaded, mutilated, mishandled. It is illegal to willfully, recklessly, or negligently mutilate a body after death. But are laws prohibiting cadaver abuse meant to protect the cadaver itself, the deceased person, the friends and family of the deceased, or the moral community as such? It seems that the capacity to be harmed requires the capacity to suffer, either physically by feeling pain, or emotionally by realizing the wrong that has been committed. Hence, since a cadaver has no central nervous system activity and is incapable of consciousness, it cannot be harmed. Only the living can be harmed. Cadaver abuse is an act of harm inflicted on the living. This view is consistent with legal assumptions inherent in Abuse of Corpse Laws. There is liability for cadaver abuse to relatives who are entitled to damages because they have the obligation to bury the cadaver and are seen to suffer "mental anguish," which means "grievous injury to their feelings" from cadaver abuse. The fact that it is the relatives who are able to collect damages for abuse to a cadaver evidences the assumption that harm to a cadaver is harm to those who hold the memory of the deceased in high regard. But what if relatives do not claim to suffer mental anguish from a case of cadaver abuse? Has harm occurred? Nonrelatives, even strangers, might be capable of being harmed by cadaver abuse in the sense that abusive treatment of any human cadaver has implications for the regard for persons in general within the community. How we treat our dead can be seen as a reflection of our regard for the living. If PMV harms, it harms the moral community as well as those directly associated with the deceased.

Does a right to privacy preclude the possibility of PMV? If we assume, along with the Harvard team, that brain death and an irreversibly comatose state are equivalent and result in the diagnosis of death, then, along with the Supreme Court of New Jersey in the Karen Quinlan case, we can grant brain-dead bodies a right to privacy. It was assumed that Karen Quinlan was an irreversibly comatose patient, completely dependent on life support. In the Quinlan case, the Supreme Court of New Jersey granted Quinlan's legal guardian the right to stop life support on privacy grounds, finding that ventilation, intubation, drugs, and constant medical care, which Quinlan required, constituted extreme bodily invasion, particularly since Quinlan could never recover consciousness:

> We think that the State's interest *contra* weakens and the individual's right to privacy grows as the degree of bodily invasion increases and the prognosis dims. Ultimately there comes a point at which the individual's rights overcome the State interest. (*Atlantic Reporter* 1976)

The Quinlan case showed that the right to privacy included the right not to have one's body unduly maintained by life-support machines. The privacy that was protected could be seen as belonging to a body capable of being judged dead. After the court ruling, the respirator was turned off and Quinlan, surprisingly, was able to breathe spontaneously and lived for several years after the court ruling. Yet, the importance of the Quinlan case was that when the court assumed she was irreversibly comatose (brain dead), she was granted a right to privacy. In cases of ventilated brain-dead cadavers, the same invasive treatment is required as was required for Quinlan. Do the philosophical differences between a brain-dead patient and a pregnant brain-dead patient warrant that the same treatment not be regarded as invasive in the latter? Does pregnancy in death, as well as possibly in life, diminish women's right to privacy?

The potential conflict between a pregnant woman's right to privacy and a state's right to protect an interest in fetal life occurs in PMV cases as well as abortion cases. At least one court battle over PMV (case 7) illustrates the confusion of attributing a privacy right to a ventilated cadaver. In the hearing for continuation of PMV, the hospital lawyer claimed that "Mrs. Piazzi is dead. . . . She has no more right of privacy," while hospital officials who were advocates of PMV appealed to Mrs. Piaz-

zi's right to privacy as grounds for the refusal of details about the time and manner of childbirth (Associated Press 1986a). Does PMV violate a dead woman's right to privacy? In the case of ventilated bodies diagnosed as brain dead, it seems that a right to privacy can be understood to include the right to a bodily death. Every body that cannot be returned to a state of consciousness or at least spontaneous respiration would therefore have a right to be allowed to die, which includes the right not to have the process of dying interrupted. Ventilated brain-dead cases have a right to privacy, for though they are classified as "dead patients" they have not been granted the right to a full bodily death. Ventilated bodies have the processes of death postponed. Although it makes sense for the right to privacy to end with death, full bodily death has not occurred in PMV cases.

The major difference between PMV and the Quinlan case is that PMV offers a benefit: the possibility that the fetus might survive. A feminist view opposing PMV must show that the harm of PMV to women and the moral community in general outweighs the benefits of a possible live birth. I have already argued that PMV can be seen as harming the moral community and violating the brain-dead patient's right to privacy. I further contend that it is inappropriate to require the bodies of women to remain pregnant in death but not in life, unless a dead body has some reproductive obligation that a live body does not have. Do cadavers have reproductive obligations? Clearly not, since an obligation requires an agent capable of fulfilling the obligation by performing an act. As a cadaver is incapable of being the agent of an act, a cadaver cannot be seen to have any obligations. Others may have obligations vis à vis the cadaver, for instance the obligation to bury it, but the cadaver itself is incapable of being obligated or responsible for anything. Someone might claim that the woman herself is obligated from life, to have her pregnancy continued beyond the point of her brain death. Such a view might point to other obligations in life that are interrupted by one's death, for instance a parent's death interrupts the parent's abilities to fulfill obligations toward her children. Death always interrupts one's financial obligations. But it has been argued that PMV cannot help meet a woman's obligation to continue her pregnancy because she ought not be obligated to be pregnant. And if a cadaver has no reproductive obligations, then it cannot have reproductive rights. In fact, cadavers are excluded from reproductive rights precisely because they are cadavers. Reproductive freedom is properly attributed to people, not cadavers. PMV violates the reproductive freedom of women. The stronger opponents of this view would argue that PMV would create no harm to the moral community if it were based on consent and seen as an instance of organ donation, but this results from conceptual confusion about the nature of consent, organ donations, and pregnancy.

PMV and Individual Consent

Would PMV be riddled with problems if it were not mandatory, but based on consent? Like much reproductive technology, PMV is expensive, has a high failure rate, and undermines women by emphasizing pregnancy as a woman's highest fulfillment. Nevertheless, some women might want the chance to participate in PMV for individual reasons—to have an heir, to leave their spouses with a last child, to have their deaths afford something positive, to have their own processes of death delayed. It is feasible that some women might choose PMV, prior to brain death, as the possibility of PMV becomes more widely known. Physicians might even decide to discuss PMV routinely with every pregnant woman in order to be informed of her wishes in the unusual event of sudden brain death.

If consent were the essential moral requirement for PMV, whose consent is necessary? The woman's own? In which case there ought to be PMV consent forms available in every obstetric practice. Should the biological father have a right to consent to PMV? If so, how would a conflict between the mother's and the father's wishes be resolved? Should the mother's wishes take precedence because it is her body? Or should the father's wishes take precedence because he has paternal responsibilities if the fetus were to be born alive? A woman's interest in terminating the pregnancy

ought to outweigh the interests of her sexual partner with respect to PMV, for I believe that it would be inconsistent with the abortion right to assume that a father has rights to an in utero fetus if the mother is dead, but not if she is alive.

If PMV were based on consent, there would always be cases in which consent was unclear, as well as current cases in which consent was not given because no one envisioned that a particular pregnant case might be appropiate for ventilation. Is it plausible for physicians to assume that because, in all seven PMV cases cited, the women had not terminated their pregnancies before the onset of brain death, they would have wanted their pregnancies continued beyond their brain deaths? Clearly, one cannot infer that any intention in life applies as well to intentions in death. For instance, if my neighbor donates blood regularly in blood-drives, I cannot automatically infer that it would be his intention to make a large donation of his blood upon his death. There might be reasons for donating blood in life that would not be valid in death. For instance, suppose my neighbor was an active blood donor primarily because he liked chatting with the nurses at the bloodmobile. This motive would not be served by donating blood after his death. Similarly, if a woman has not terminated her pregnancy before suffering brain death it cannot be inferred that she would desire her pregnancy to continue beyond the point of her brain death. For instance, lacking a partner, she may not want to bring a child into the world with no one designated to care for it, or she may not want her body to be seen by others and artificially sustained after her brain death.

As one cannot infer consent to be pregnant in death from consent to be pregnant in life, a physician cannot properly infer that a woman would have wanted PMV simply from the fact that she had not aborted earlier in pregnancy. Such an inference would confuse the intent to sustain one's pregnancy in life with the intent to have one's pregnancy artificially sustained in one's ventilated corpse. The two intentions are quite distinct, as are a conscious body and a brain-dead body. Moreover, the fact that a woman is pregnant now does not mean it is her intent to remain pregnant in the future.

Hence, physicians must consider the possibility that a pregnant brain-dead woman is not necessarily a woman who desires her pregnancy to continue. Of course, it could be argued that it would violate a woman's wishes to infer that she doesn't want the pregnancy continued. However, as PMV requires the active maintenance of life in a cadaver, and as we do not routinely apply active measures when no consent is given, it would be inappropriate to apply active "extraordinary" measures automatically in pregnant cases. Though a physician's duty is to save lives, this is not a duty without limitations. A physician is not expected, for instance, to use cadavers as incubators for the nurturing of previable life, anymore than the physician is expected to find tissue mediums where aborted fetuses might possibly be sustained. After all, the physician's patient is the woman, not the fetus, and the physician owes her patient a speedy and dignified death. She is obligated to treat the fetus as a vital part of her patient's body, providing sound medical advice and obstetric care, but it would be exploitive of the pregnant woman for a physician to elevate fetal interests over the welfare of the mother herself.

The right to consent to PMV ought to include the right to refuse PMV. Living wills, typically used to indicate a patient's wishes in cases of terminal illness, might contain requests regarding PMV. Currently, there are living will acts in thirty-five states. But living wills tend to favor the fetus and not the pregnant woman. Twenty-seven acts include a pregnancy clause that forbids implementation if the patient is pregnant (MacAvoy-Snitzer 1987). In order for women to be able to prohibit PMV in a living will, pregnancy clauses would need to be invalidated.

It has been assumed that consent might make PMV morally permissible, but consent alone does not make an act morally permissible. PMV would not be morally permissible if the violations of rights outweigh the benefits of possible live birth. PMV violates women's reproductive freedoms by failing to treat the bodies of brain-dead women as ends in themselves. There is a need for maternal brain death to be a clear and steady marker beyond which a woman and her body should no longer be pregnant. Otherwise, the distinction between the dead and the living disintegrates. For if pregnant cadavers ought to be used for reproductive work, then *any* cadaver might be seen as obligated to partake of service in sustaining human life. Not only could we find ourselves in intensive care wards full of plugged-in cadavers functioning as uteri, kidney machines, transplant banks, and tissue suppliers, but the implications of attributing obligations to cadavers would include a deterioration in the status of the right to one's body and the regard we might have for each person as an end in herself.

One could imagine a woman's request for PMV as a way in which she regarded herself as an end. She might desire PMV in order to actualize her life and plead with her physician before the onset of brain death, "Keep my baby alive. Do all you can to save this pregnancy. The birth of my child matters to me more than anything I have ever done in my whole life." Even though this wish might reflect the patriarchal socialization of women for motherhood, nonetheless, it demonstrates that pregnancy has become a very meaningful choice for the woman herself within her unique life situation. Still, the harm to fundamental personal freedoms can be judged more significant than the harm of denying an individual's wish for PMV. For neither moral decisions nor technological practices can be isolated from the context of social and political meanings that structure reality.

PMV as Organ Donation

It might be argued that PMV ought to be seen as an instance of a woman donating her cadaver to be used for sustaining the fetus, and hence analogous to the practice of donating organs for human transplants or donating one's entire body to medical research. Exploring PMV as an instance of organ donation reveals a significant aspect of the ontological relationship between a woman and her fetus in pregnancy. Whether one donates a ventilated cadaver for research, or a ventilated pregnant cadaver for fetal support, a positive end results. Since cadaver donations for both research and transplants are legal in all fifty states under the Uniform Donor Act, it might be claimed that PMV also ought to be legal, for it is simply another case of donating one's cadaver for use by the living (Schwartz 1985).

But differences in intent and end result indicate an ontological difference between cadaver donations and PMV. Only PMV uses a cadaver for maintaining another (living) body, the fetus, which would not otherwise qualify as a transplant recipient. The pregnant cadaver is not transplanted into the fetus, like an organ donation, nor does it require the surgical connection between the donor and the recipient, for the fetus has been in utero since conception. Most importantly, PMV greatly alters the ontological relationship between a woman and her fetus in pregnancy. In pregnancies in living women, the fetus is biologically contingent on the woman's body. In PMV the woman's body is contingent on the fetus—somatic life will be sustained in the woman's body only as long as the fetus is present and thriving. Once the fetus is born, life support on the woman's body is ended, natural bodily death is allowed to occur, and the woman's remains are interred. If PMV is to be seen as merely another case covered by the Uniform Donor Act, it must be argued that the PMV cadaver is analogous to donated cadaver organs, yet the analogy breaks down because the ontological relationship between the donated organ and the human recipient undergoes no reversal. Further, the organ recipient is not using the donated organ while it is still a part of the donor. Nor does the transplant recipient use the donor's body to grow its own new organs. The fact is, the pregnant body has never been disconnected from the fetus after conception, unlike other donations. Live pregnancies similarly are not donor/recipient relationships. A pregnant woman is not "donating" her body temporarily for the maintenance of the fetus. Rather, pregnant women are autonomous beings engaged in a variety of projects, not the least of which is the project of growing a fetus. Hence, neither in life nor in death can pregnancy be seen as an instance of organ donation. Organ donation is a false analogy for PMV, for pregnancy, as always, is a special case. A pregnant body affords no suitable analogies. What is needed is clarification of what pregnancy is and discussion about the parameters of pregnancy that make it a human endeavor. Were PMV to become standard obstetric practice, it would suggest that the moral community values fetal survival more than the privacy rights of pregnant persons.

Pregnancy Rights

Ours is a century in which reproductive technology is increasingly expanding alternatives to traditional reproductive practices. Yet the technology is too often placed in the control of medical professionals, which supercedes women's control over their pregnancies. PMV is another procedure that threatens to separate pregnancy from women's control while altering the social meaning of pregnancy (Lenow 1983, Johnsen 1986). Neither *Roe*, the right to privacy, nor the Uniform Donor Act is able to subsume the issues of PMV. Even an appeal to cadaver rights provides no basis for the prohibition of PMV as long as it can be claimed that the pregnant cadaver is a "special case." Clearly, without a definition of pregnancy, human rights can be seen as inapplicable to women in pregnancy, leading to such preposterous claims as the belief that pregnant women are entitled to less control over their bodies, less protection from bodily mutilation in noncognitive states, less of a right to immediate bodily death, less of a right to privacy, less of a right to have their cadavers protected from exploitative medical uses. Rather than sorting out women's rights in pregnancy by direct application of basic human rights to the "special case" of pregnancy, a definition of pregnancy should be established at the outset and women's rights in pregnancy derived from this definition. Needless to say, feminists must take an active role in establishing any definition of pregnancy to be used to determine women's legal rights.

If we understand the mother/fetus relationship in pregnancy as determined solely by the mother, who is the only autonomous party in the relationship, and who sustains the relationship only insofar as she regards it as a meaningful project resulting from her own free choice, then the practice of PMV would be impermissible. PMV fundamentally alters the mother/fetus relationship in pregnancy by making the mother contingent on the fetus and severing pregnancy from human consciousness. PMV poses a serious threat to abortion rights by sustaining pregnancy in a female cadaver without prior consent.

Serious objections have been raised about PMV within a patriarchal society. However, at least two kinds of objections to PMV could be raised even in an egalitarian society. First, PMV might still have serious implications for reproductive freedom. One would need to consider whether or not PMV necessarily presupposes an eliminative view of pregnancy. If so, then PMV would be undesirable. Of course if the egalitarian society had a high infertility rate and if brain death in pregnancy became quite common, then the society might be in dire need of live births and a limited use of PMV might be justifiable. Assuming that this extreme situation does not exist, an egalitarian society would need to consider whether or not PMV would be a fair use of medical technology. In the United States, PMV perpetuates the unequal allocation of scarce medical resources. PMV requires that technology, staff, and medical resources be used not for the treatment of human beings but for the sake of saving previable fetuses. Moreover, PMV is an arbitrary use of medicine. It is used to maintain a few previable pregnancies in cadavers (some of whom were from working class and black families) while thousands of pregnant women, often in the same city in which the practice of PMV occurred, lack a minimal level of prenatal care. Isn't it alarming that the country with the greatest number of publicized PMV cases is also the country that ranks seventeenth in low infant mortality rates in the West? The individual benefits of PMV cannot outweigh such an allocation of medical resources. There are better ways to use and distribute our technological resources that would effectively serve the common good. A poet writes

> We study the wrong subject in the maze
> of inquiry, we took a false corner. The
> ways we came to there are known and
> plotted but we end, still, at a blind wall.
> —William Bronk, "The False Corner"

Like other new possibilities for pregnancy, PMV perpetuates the desire to control life and deny death. PMV, like modern medicine in general, is based on an assumption of meta-physical dualism: that the body can be perceived and managed by seeing it as separate from human consciousness. Higher human activities such as consciousness, cognition, and imagination are devalued. We cannot diminish the value of human pregnancy without diminishing the value of being human. PMV is but one instance of such an attempt, an instance of one of the limitless uses for cadavers and technology. Yet the measure of our social community lies not in the number of its technological exploits, but in the ends we strive for. The most fundamental human end is the valuation of human consciousness. Postmortem maternal ventilation, by requiring pregnancy of women after their brain deaths, fails to envision what the capacity for maternal consciousness in pregnancy should mean to a human community.

Notes

1. This discussion applies to U.S. pregnancies. For European discussion of PMV see Metter and Estel (1972) and Pietchowiak (1984). The legal ambiguities of *Roe v.Wade* are further explored in Rhoden (1986), Rice (1983), and Martyn (1981–82).

2. For analysis of the exploitation of women in embryo transfer research see my article (1984). For discussion of the legal issues in reproductive technology see Smith (1985). For analysis of the effects of reproductive technology on abortion rights, see my article (1986).

3. The table is by no means a complete registry of cases. (1) Sampson (1979), (2) Associated Press (1984), (3) Sampson (1979), (4) Associated Press (1987a,b).

4. The table is by no means a complete registry of cases. (1) and (2) Meyer (1977), (3) Associated Press (1982), (4) Associated Press (1983a,b), (5) Associated Press (1983c), (6) Associated Press (1986b), (7) Associated Press (1986a,c,d).

References

Ad Hoc Committee of the Harvard Medical School to Examine the Definition of Brain-

Death. 1968. A definition of irreversible coma. *Journal of the American Medical Association* 205, no. 6: 337–40.

Arthur, Robert K. 1978. Postmortem caesarean section. *American Journal of Obstetrics and Gynecology* 132, no. 2: 175–79.

Associated Press. 1982. Doctors report birth of baby in 1981 to brain-dead woman. *New York Times*, September 5, 1982.

———. 1983a. Life from death. *New York Times*, October 16, 1983.

———. 1983b. Woman legally dead gives birth to a boy. *New York Times*, March 31, 1983.

———. 1983c. Brain-dead mother dies. *New York Times*, July 7, 1983.

———. 1984. Healthy baby delivered from mother in coma. *New York Times*, August 21, 1984.

———. 1986a. Ruling by a court keeps fetus alive: Man who claims fatherhood wins fight for life support for brain-dead woman. *New York Times*, July 26, 1986.

———. 1986b. Baby born to dead woman. *Portland Press Herald* (Portland, Maine), July 31, 1986.

———. 1986c. Baby is weak after birth to brain-dead woman. *New York Times*, August 16, 1986.

———. 1986d. Baby in court battle dies after one day. *New York Times*, August 17, 1986.

———. 1987a. Mother chooses for comatose daughter, fetus. *Hartford Courant*. March 19, 1987.

———. 1987b. Comatose woman's fetus is focus of dispute. *New York Times*, March 8, 1987.

Atlantic Reporter. 1976. "In the matter of Karen Quinlan, an alleged incompetent," Supreme Court of New Jersey, 2D, 355:647, March 31, 1976.

Bronk, Willliam. 1982. Life supports and the false corner. In *Life Supports*. San Francisco: North Point Press.

Dillon, William P., Richard V. Lee, Sharon Buckwald, Michael Tronolone, and Ronald J. Foote. 1982. Life support and maternal brain death during pregnancy. *Journal of the American Medical Association* 248, no. 9: 1089–91.

Johnsen, Dawn E. 1986. The creation of fetal rights: Conflicts with women's constitutional rights to liberty, privacy, and equal protection. *Yale Law Journal* 95, no. 599: 21–47.

Lenow, Jeffrey L. 1983. The fetus as patient: Emerging rights as a person? *American Journal of Law and Medicine* 9, no. 1: 1–29.

MacAvoy-Snitzer, Janice. 1987. Pregnancy clauses in living will statutes. *Columbia Law Review* 87: 1,280–1,300.

Martyn, Ken. 1981–82. Technological advances and Roe v. Wade: The need to rethink abortion law. *UCLA Law Review* 29, nos. 5,6: 1.194–1.215.

Metter, D., and C. Estel. 1972. Arztliche und rechtliche probleme der sectio in mortua et in moribunda (Medical and legal problems of death and dying). *Zeitschrift fur arztliche Fortbildung* 66, No. 6: 351–53.

Meyer, Lawrence, 1977. Two lives involved: "Brain-dead" mother kept alive in effort to save four month fetus. *Washington Post*, December 2, 1977.

Murphy, Julien S. 1984. Egg-farming and women's future. In *Test-Tube Women*, eds. R. Arditti, R. Klein, and S. Minden, 66–75. New York: Routledge and Kegan Paul.

———. 1986. Abortion rights and fetal termination. *Journal of Social Philosophy* 17, no. 1: 11–16.

Newsweek, 1983. Out of death, a new life comes. April 11, 1983.

Piechowiak, J. 1984. Der mutterliche hirntod am ende des zweiten trimenons. *Rundschau Med. Praxis* 73, no. 12: 361–62.

Pinkus, Rosa Lynn. 1984. Families, brain death, and traditional medical excellence. *Journal of Neurosurgery* 60: 1.192–94.

Rhoden, Nancy K. 1986. Trimesters and technology: Revamping Roe v. Wade. *Yale Law Journal*, 95, no. 4: 739–97.

Rice, Julie E. 1983. Fetal rights: Defining "persons" under 42 U.S.C. 1983. *University of Illinois Law Review*, no. 1: 347–66.

Roe v. Wade, 410 US 113 (1973).

Sampson, Milo B., and Loren P. Petersen. 1979. Post-traumatic coma during pregnancy. *Obstetrics and Gynecology* 53, no. 3: 2–3.

Schwartz, Howard S. 1985. Bioethical and legal considerations in increasing the supply of transplantable organs: from UAGA to "Baby Fae." *American Journal of Law and Medicine* 10, no. 4: 397–437.

Siegler, Mark, and Daniel Wikler. 1982. Brain death and live birth. *Journal of the American Medical Association* 248, no. 9: 1101.

Smith, George P., II. 1985. Australia's frozen "orphan" embryos: A medical, legal and ethi-

cal dilemma. *Journal of Family Law* 24, no. 1: 27–58.

Uniform Laws Annotated. 1988. Uniform determination of death act. Supplement. 12: 293–96. St. Paul: West Publishing.

University Health Services v. Piazzi. 1986. Document no. CV86-RCCV-464. Georgia Superior Court, August 4, 1986.

Case 4.a *Cruzan v. Director, Missouri Department of Health*

U.S. Supreme Court

The parents of Nancy Beth Cruzan requested that the Missouri trial court authorize the withdrawal of feeding tubes and IV hydration when she was in an irreversible coma brought about by an automobile accident. The trial court accepted their arguments, but the Supreme Court of Missouri disagreed. Justice Rehnquist upheld the Supreme Court of Missouri's decision, arguing that an *incompetent* person cannot give consent to refuse life-saving treatment. Since conclusive evidence about her wishes was not submitted, Rehnquist asserted that she could not be allowed to die. (Further evidence about her wishes was later submitted to the Missouri court, and withdrawal of treatment was authorized. Nancy Cruzan died in December 1990.)

Justice *Rehnquist* delivered the majority opinion:

Petitioner Nancy Beth Cruzan was rendered incompetent as a result of severe injuries sustained during an automobile accident. Co-petitioners Lester and Joyce Cruzan, Nancy's parents and co-guardians, sought a court order directing the withdrawal of their daughter's artificial feeding and hydration equipment after it became apparent that she had virtually no chance of recovering her cognitive faculties. The Supreme Court of Missouri held that because there was no clear and convincing evidence of Nancy's desire to have life-sustaining treatment withdrawn under such circumstances, her parents lacked authority to effectuate such a request. We . . . now affirm.

On the night of January 11, 1983, Nancy Cruzan lost control of her car as she traveled down Elm Road in Jasper County, Missouri. The vehicle overturned, and Cruzan was discovered lying face down in a ditch without detectable respiratory or cardiac function. Paramedics were able to restore her breathing and heartbeat at the accident site, and she was transported to a hospital in an unconscious state. An attending neurosurgeon diagnosed her as having sustained probable cerebral contusions compounded by significant anoxia (lack of oxygen). The Missouri trial court in this case found that permanent brain damage generally results after 6 minutes in an anoxic state; it was estimated that Cruzan was deprived of oxygen from 12 to 14 minutes. She remained in a coma for approximately three weeks and then progressed to an unconscious state in which she was able to orally ingest some nutrition. In order to ease feeding and further the recovery, surgeons implanted a gastrostomy feeding and hydration tube in

Cruzan with the consent of her then husband. Subsequent rehabilitative efforts proved unavailing. She now lies in a Missouri state hospital in what is commonly referred to as a persistent vegetative state: generally, a condition in which a person exhibits motor reflexes but evinces no indications of significant cognitive function.[1] The State of Missouri is bearing the cost of her care.

After it had become apparent that Nancy Cruzan had virtually no chance of regaining her mental faculties her parents asked hospital employees to terminate the artificial nutrition and hydration procedures. All agree that such a removal would cause her death. The employees refused to honor the request without court approval. The parents then sought and received authorization from the state trial court for termination. The court found that a person in Nancy's condition had a fundamental right under the State and Federal Constitutions to refuse or direct the withdrawal of "death prolonging procedures." The court also found that Nancy's "expressed thoughts at age twenty-five in somewhat serious conversation with a housemate friend that if sick or injured she would not wish to continue her life unless she could live at least halfway normally suggests that given her present condition she would not wish to continue on with her nutrition and hydration."

The Supreme Court of Missouri reversed by a divided vote. The court recognized a right to refuse treatment embodied in the common-law doctrine of informed consent, but expressed skepticism about the application of that doctrine in the circumstances of this case. The court also declined to read a broad right of privacy into the State Constitution which would "support the right of a person to refuse medical treatment in every circumstance," and expressed doubt as to whether such a right existed under the United States Constitution. It then decided that the Missouri Living Will statute (1986) embodied a state policy strongly favoring the preservation of life. The court found that Cruzan's statements to her roommate regarding her desire to live or die under certain conditions were "unreliable for the purpose of determining her intent," "and thus insufficient to support the co-guardians claim to exercise substituted judgment on Nancy's

behalf." It rejected the argument that Cruzan's parents were entitled to order the termination of her medical treatment, concluding that "no person can assume that choice for an incompetent in the absence of the formalities required under Missouri's Living Will statutes or the clear and convincing, inherently reliable evidence absent here." . . .

We granted certiorari to consider the question of whether Cruzan has a right under the United States Constitution which would require the hospital to withdraw life-sustaining treatment from her under these circumstances.

At common law, even the touching of one person by another without consent and without legal justification was a battery. Before the turn of the century, this Court observed that "[n]o right is held more sacred, or is more carefully guarded, by the common law, than the right of every individual to the possession and control of his own person, free from all restraint or interference of others, unless by clear and unquestionable authority of law." This notion of bodily integrity has been embodied in the requirement that informed consent is generally required for medical treatment. Justice Cardozo, while on the Court of Appeals of New York, aptly described this doctrine: "Every human being of adult years and sound mind has a right to determine what shall be done with his own body; and a surgeon who performs an operation without his patient's consent commits an assault, for which he is liable in damage." The informed consent doctrine has become firmly entrenched in American tort law.

The logical corollary of the doctrine of informed consent is that the patient generally possesses the right not to consent, that is, to refuse treatment. Until about 15 years ago and the seminal decision [of the New Jersey Supreme Court] in *In re Quinlan* (1976), the number of right-to-refuse-treatment decisions were relatively few. Most of the earlier cases involved patients who refused medical treatment forbidden by their religious beliefs, thus implicating First Amendment rights as well as common law rights of self-determination. More recently, however, with the advance of medical technology capable of sustaining life well past the point where natural forces would have brought certain death in earlier times, cases involving the right to refuse life-sustaining treatment have burgeoned.

In the *Quinlan* case, young Karen Quinlan suffered severe brain damage as the result of anoxia, and entered a persistent vegetative state. Karen's father sought judicial approval to disconnect his daughter's respirator. The New Jersey Supreme Court granted the relief, holding that Karen had a right of privacy grounded in the Federal Constitution to terminate treatment. Recognizing that this right was not absolute, however, the court balanced it against asserted state interests. Noting that the State's interest "weakens and the individual's right to privacy grows as the degree of bodily invasion increases and the prognosis dims," the court concluded that the state interests had to give way in that case. The court also concluded that the "only practical way" to prevent the loss of Karen's privacy right due to her incompetence was to allow her guardian and family to decide "whether she would exercise it in these circumstances."

After *Quinlan,* however, most courts have based a right to refuse treatment either solely on the common law right to informed consent or on both the common law right and a constitutional privacy right. . . .

. . . State courts have available to them for decision a number of sources—state constitutions, statutes, and common law—which are not available to us. In this Court, the question is simply and starkly whether the United States Constitution prohibits Missouri from choosing the rule of decision which it did. This is the first case in which we have been squarely presented with the issue of whether the United States Constitution grants what is in common parlance referred to as a "right to die." We follow the judicious counsel . . . that in deciding "a question of such magnitude and importance . . . it is the [better] part of wisdom not to attempt, by any general statement, to cover every possible phase of the subject."

The Fourteenth Amendment provides that no State shall "deprive any person of life, liberty, or property, without due process of law." The principle that a competent person has a constitutionally protected liberty interest in refusing unwanted medical treatment may be inferred from our prior decisions. In *Jacob-*

son v. *Massachusetts* (1905), for instance, the Court balanced an individual's liberty interest in declining an unwanted smallpox vaccine against the State's interest in preventing disease. . . .

Just this Term, in the course of holding that a State's procedures for administering antipsychotic medication to prisoners were sufficient to satisfy due process concerns, we recognized that prisoners possess "a significant liberty interest in avoiding the unwanted administration of antipsychotic drugs under the Due Process Clause of the Fourteenth Amendment." Still other cases support the recognition of a general liberty interest in refusing medical treatment.

But determining that a person has a "liberty interest" under the Due Process Clause does not end the inquiry;[2] "whether respondent's constitutional rights have been violated must be determined by balancing his liberty interests against the relevant state interests."

Petitioners insist that under the general holdings of our cases, the forced administration of life-sustaining medical treatment, and even of artificially-delivered food and water essential to life, would implicate a competent person's liberty interest. Although we think the logic of the cases [referred to] above would embrace such a liberty interest, the dramatic consequences involved in refusal of such treatment would inform the inquiry as to whether the deprivation of that interest is constitutionally permissible. But for purposes of this case, we assume that the United States Constitution would grant a competent person a constitutionally protected right to refuse life-saving hydration and nutrition.

Petitioners go on to assert that an incompetent person should possess the same right in this respect as is possessed by a competent person. . . .

The difficulty with petitioners' claim is that in a sense it begs the question: an incompetent person is not able to make an informed and voluntary choice to exercise a hypothetical right to refuse treatment or any other right. Such a "right" must be exercised for her, if at all, by some sort of surrogate. Here, Missouri has in effect recognized that under certain circumstances a surrogate may act for the patient in electing to have hydration and nutrition withdrawn in such a way as to cause death, but it has established a procedural safeguard to assure that the action of the surrogate conforms as best it may to the wishes expressed by the patient while competent. Missouri requires that evidence of the incompetent's wishes as to the withdrawal of treatment be proved by clear and convincing evidence. The question, then, is whether the United States Constitution forbids the establishment of this procedural requirement by the State. We hold that it does not.

Whether or not Missouri's clear and convincing evidence requirement comports with the United States Constitution depends in part on what interests the State may properly seek to protect in this situation. Missouri relies on its interest in the protection and preservation of human life, and there can be no gainsaying this interest. As a general matter, the States—indeed, all civilized nations—demonstrate their commitment to life by treating homicide as serious crime. Moreover, the majority of States in this country have laws imposing criminal penalties on one who assists another to commit suicide. We do not think a State is required to remain neutral in the face of an informed and voluntary decision by a physically-able adult to starve to death.

But in the context presented here, a State has more particular interests at stake. The choice between life and death is a deeply personal decision of obvious and overwhelming finality. We believe Missouri may legitimately seek to safeguard the personal element of this choice through the imposition of heightened evidentiary requirements. It cannot be disputed that the Due Process Clause protects an interest in life as well as an interest in refusing life-sustaining medical treatment. Not all incompetent patients will have loved ones available to serve as surrogate decisionmakers. And even where family members are present, "[t]here will, of course, be some unfortunate situations in which family members will not act to protect a patient." A State is entitled to guard against potential abuses in such situations. Similarly, a State is entitled to consider that a judicial proceeding to make a determination regarding an incompetent's wishes may very well not be an adversarial one, with the added guarantee of accurate factfind-

ing that the adversary process brings with it. Finally, we think a State may properly decline to make judgments about the "quality" of life that a particular individual may enjoy, and simply assert an unqualified interest in the preservation of human life to be weighed against the constitutionally protected interests of the individual.

In our view, Missouri has permissibly sought to advance these interests through the adoption of a "clear and convincing" standard of proof to govern such proceedings. "The function of a standard of proof, as that concept is embodied in the Due Process Clause and in the realm of factfinding, is to 'instruct the factfinder concerning the degree of confidence our society thinks he should have in the correctness of factual conclusions for a particular type of adjudication.' " . . .

We think it self-evident that the interests at stake in the instant proceedings are more substantial, both on an individual and societal level, than those involved in a run-of-the-mine civil dispute. But not only does the standard of proof reflect the importance of a particular adjudication, it also serves as "a societal judgment about how the risk of error should be distributed between the litigants." The more stringent the burden of proof a party must bear, the more that party bears the risk of an erroneous decision. We believe that Missouri may permissibly place an increased risk of an erroneous decision on those seeking to terminate an incompetent individual's life-sustaining treatment. An erroneous decision not to terminate results in a maintenance of the status quo; the possibility of subsequent developments such as advancements in medical science, the discovery of new evidence regarding the patient's intent, changes in the law, or simply the unexpected death of the patient despite the administration of life-sustaining treatment, at least create the potential that a wrong decision will eventually be corrected or its impact mitigated. An erroneous decision to withdraw life-sustaining treatment, however, is not susceptible of correction. . . .

In sum, we conclude that a State may apply a clear and convincing evidence standard in proceedings where a guardian seeks to discontinue nutrition and hydration of a person diagnosed to be in a persistent vegetative state. . . .

The Supreme Court of Missouri held that in this case the testimony adduced at trial did not amount to clear and convincing proof of the patient's desire to have hydration and nutrition withdrawn. In so doing, it reversed a decision of the Missouri trial court which had found that the evidence "suggest[ed]" Nancy Cruzan would not have desired to continue such measures, but which had not adopted the standard of "clear and convincing evidence" enunciated by the Supreme Court. The testimony adduced at trial consisted primarily of Nancy Cruzan's statements made to a housemate about a year before her accident that she would not want to live should she face life as a "vegetable," and other observations to the same effect. The observations did not deal in terms with withdrawal of medical treatment or of hydration and nutrition. We cannot say that the Supreme Court of Missouri committed constitutional error in reaching the conclusion that it did.[3]

Petitioners alternatively contend that Missouri must accept the "substituted judgment" of close family members even in the absence of substantial proof that their views reflect the views of the patient. . . .

No doubt is engendered by anything in this record but that Nancy Cruzan's mother and father are loving and caring parents. If the State were required by the United States Constitution to repose a right of "substituted judgment" with anyone, the Cruzans would surely qualify. But we do not think the Due Process Clause requires the State to repose judgment on these matters with anyone but the patient herself. Close family members may have a strong feeling—a feeling not at all ignoble or unworthy, but not entirely disinterested, either—that they do not wish to witness the continuation of the life of a loved one which they regard as hopeless, meaningless, and even degrading. But there is no automatic assurance that the view of close family members will necessarily be the same as the patient's would have been had she been confronted with the prospect of her situation while competent. All of the reasons previously discussed for allowing Missouri to require clear and convincing evidence of the patient's wishes lead us to conclude that the State may choose to defer only to those wishes, rather than confide the decision to close family members.

The judgment of the Supreme Court of Missouri is *Affirmed.*

Notes

1. The State Supreme Court, adopting much of the trial court's findings, described Nancy Cruzan's medical condition as follows: ". . . In sum, Nancy is diagnosed as in a persistent vegetative state. She is not dead. She is not terminally ill. Medical experts testified that she could live another thirty years." . . .

2. Although many state courts have held that a right to refuse treatment is encompassed by a generalized constitutional right of privacy, we have never so held. We believe this issue is more properly analyzed in terms of a Fourteenth Amendment liberty interest. See *Bowers* v. *Hardwick* (1986).

3. The clear and convincing standard of proof has been variously defined in this context as "proof sufficient to persuade the trier of fact that the patient held a firm and settled commitment to the termination of life supports under the circumstances like those presented," and as evidence which "produces in the mind of the trier of fact a firm belief or conviction as to the truth of the allegations sought to be established, evidence so clear, direct and weighty and convincing as to enable [the factfinder] to come to a clear conviction, without hesitancy, of the truth of the precise facts in issue." . . .

Case 4.b   The Baby Doe Rule: Still a Threat

John C. Moskop and Rita L. Saldanha

Moskop and Saldanha respond to the 1985 Department of Health and Human Services rule on terminating severely defective newborns, or what has been called a "Baby Doe rule." Concerned with unjustified prolongation of suffering, the physician's duty not to harm, and the effects on distribution of health care, Moskop and Saldanha argue that this Baby Doe rule is inadequate.

On April 15, 1985, the Department of Health and Human Services published a final rule entitled "Child Abuse and Neglect Prevention and Treatment Program," its fifth attempt in two years to formulate regulations regarding medical treatment of severely handicapped newborns. Like its predecessors, all of which were either struck down in the courts or revised in response to public comments . . . this latest "Baby Doe" rule has serious weaknesses.

The final regulations may indeed represent the best compromise achievable in the current political atmosphere. There remains, however, a major question: Should physicians feel confident that the new regulations will allow them to provide appropriate care for handicapped infants in all circumstances? We will argue that they should not.

The intent of the current policy can be summarized in a single phrase from the rule: to prevent "the withholding of medically indicated treatment from a disabled infant with a life-threatening condition" by making such withholding an instance of medical neglect. The key term "withholding of medically indicated treatment" is further defined as ". . . the failure to respond to the infant's life-threatening conditions by providing treatment . . . which, in the treating physician's . . . reasonable medical judgment, will be most likely to be effective in ameliorating or correcting all such conditions." According to this policy, if there is a treatment that can ameliorate

or correct an infant's life-threatening condition, that treatment must be provided.

The regulations go on to recognize three specific exceptions to this policy, that is, three circumstances in which treatment is not required. These exceptions are: (1) when "the infant is chronically and irreversibly comatose"; (2) when "treatment would merely prolong dying, not be effective in ameliorating or correcting all of the infant's life-threatening conditions, or otherwise be futile in terms of the survival of the infant"; and (3) when "treatment would be virtually futile in terms of the survival of the infant and the treatment itself under such circumstances would be inhumane."

How Will Doctors React?

Several discussions of the April 15 final Baby Doe rule have offered a benign interpretation. One striking example of this view was expressed by Thomas Murray, . . . who argues that the rule is mainly symbolic and will have minimal impact on medical practice.[1]

This appraisal strikes us as extremely optimistic for several reasons. First of all, Murray takes certain liberties with the language of the rule. Nowhere does the rule say that inhumane treatments in and of themselves are not mandatory, as Murray claims; rather it makes an exception for treatments whose provision "would be virtually futile in terms of the survival of the infant *and . . .* would be in-

Reprinted by permission of the authors and The Hastings Center from *Hastings Center Report*, Vol. 16, No. 2 (April 1986), pp. 8–14.

humane." Thus, a treatment judged "inhumane" may be withheld only if it is also "virtually futile" in terms of survival.

Second, the rule does not state that any "reasonable medical opinion" is to be respected, as Murray suggests; rather it requires physicians to use "reasonable medical judgment" in deciding which (if any) treatment will be most likely to be effective in ameliorating or correcting an infant's life-threatening condition(s) and in deciding whether one of the three exceptions applies. In other words, physicians are expected to use reasonable medical judgment in applying the rule, but they may not appeal to medical judgment to justify a decision to ignore or violate this rule.

Finally, Murray claims that the maximum sanction for violating the rule would be the withholding of federal child abuse funding from states. He acknowledges, however, that there is a "faint possibility" that physicians or parents might be charged under state child abuse and neglect statutes. But is this possibility so faint, when the regulation explicitly defines withholding treatment from handicapped infants (except in three specific circumstances) as an instance of medical neglect and requires state child protection agencies to have procedures for identifying and investigating such instances?

In today's malpractice-wary climate, will physicians choose to ignore the rule or to interpret its exceptions very broadly so as to include almost all infants for whom withholding treatment is contemplated? In our opinion, physicians (and perhaps infant care review committees as well) are far more likely to react by treating aggressively in all but the most clearly hopeless cases so as to avoid the real possibility of criminal and civil liability for medical neglect. Such a reaction would surely be understandable, if not exactly praiseworthy, in the already high-risk fields of obstetrics and neonatology. We believe that the final Baby Doe rule, like its predecessors, will continue to have a significant chilling effect on decisions not to treat handicapped infants.

This is particularly true, as Murray acknowledges, with respect to withholding nutrition and fluids. The rule explicitly states that "appropriate nutrition, hydration, and medication" must be provided to all infants without exception, thus leaving almost no room for medical judgment about their advisability.

Because the final rule still requires treatment in all but a very few extreme circumstances, we maintain that basic federal policy has not changed significantly from the first "Baby Doe" regulations proposed in March 1983, although it is more carefully and extensively explicated. The procedures for reviewing treatment decisions and protecting endangered infants have been significantly modified, however, and the new review mechanisms included in the regulations can be very useful. Infant care review committees, for example, may help physicians make decisions in difficult cases, support physicians in those decisions, and obviate the need for external review or investigation. Likewise, state child protective services may well be the most appropriate oversight agencies in these cases. Nevertheless, both infant care review committees and child protective service agencies must abide by the substantive federal policy regarding treatment of disabled infants stated in the DHHS final rule. This is the policy we find most problematic.

The goal of this policy, namely, to protect handicapped infants from medical neglect, is surely important, and the policy may result in long-term benefits for some infants who would otherwise have died for lack of treatment. Despite the highly publicized Bloomington "Baby Doe" case, however, it is not clear that very many infants in recent years have been harmed by withholding or withdrawing medical care. In fact, largely *because* of widespread scholarly criticism of an earlier decision to withhold treatment from an infant with Down syndrome and duodenal atresia, the 1971 Johns Hopkins case,[2] and a widely distributed film dramatization of this case called "Who Should Survive?" which was produced by the Joseph P. Kennedy, Jr. Foundation, such neglect probably occurred infrequently. In contrast to its 1983 warnings of widespread physician neglect of handicapped infants, DHHS now argues that its most recent regulations will affect the care of so few infants that no regulatory impact analysis is required.

Thus, there may not have been a compelling need for new federal regulation in this area, especially since the current policy has at least three significant drawbacks. First, though it may prevent harm to some infants, the current policy threatens the significant harm of unjustified prolongation of life to other seriously handicapped infants. Second, because of the harm it would cause, the policy would force physicians to violate their traditional and fundamental obligation to do no harm without compensating benefit. Third, the policy may exacerbate existing problems or create new problems in the distribution of health care. These three problems will be examined in turn.

Unjustified Prolongation of Life

Current federal policy threatens to create significant harms of unjustified prolongation of life to some seriously handicapped infants. In requiring that any infant whose life can be more than temporarily prolonged must be treated (provided that the infant is not irreversibly comatose), the policy comes close to supporting the principle of "vitalism": namely, as Father John Paris describes it, that "life is the ultimate value, and something that is to be preserved regardless of prognosis, regardless of cost, and regardless of social considerations."[3] The policy's only departures from this principle are its statements that infants who are permanently comatose, who are in the process of dying, or who are highly unlikely to survive need not be treated.

The policy assumes, in other words, that noncomatose, nonterminal life is always preferable to nonexistence; it expressly prohibits consideration of the future quality of life of the infant. This, however, is not a plausible assumption; there are conditions other than irreversible coma or death in the near future in which people would overwhelmingly choose a shorter span of life over a longer life of very poor quality. Treatment policies for adult patients recognize this possibility by requiring that physicians ordinarily obtain the informed consent of the patient even for life-saving or life-prolonging treatment.[4]

An obvious difficulty in determining the value of life-prolonging care for infants is that infants cannot express preferences regarding the continuation of their lives: indeed, they do not have any such preferences. But this incapacity does not require that we doom some infants to longer lives of significant suffering. Where treatment has a high probability of causing significant pain and suffering and a low probability of preserving a life valuable to the patient, should we not permit a decision to withhold it?

In requiring that seriously handicapped infants be treated in almost all circumstances, the policy departs from a growing trend to allow legal guardians or next of kin in many circumstances to authorize the withholding or withdrawal of life-prolonging treatment that is not in the best interests of incompetent patients. The use of family contracts in extended care facilities and durable power of attorney designations for health care are examples of this trend.[5]

Infants whose conditions are severe enough to raise questions about the wisdom of aggressive treatment are fairly common in neonatal intensive care units (NICUs). Among such conditions are extreme prematurity, severe intracranial hemorrhage, severe asphyxia, trisomy 13 and 18, and multiple severe congenital anomalies (such as high-lesion meningomyelocele with hydrocephalus, quadriplegia, scoliosis, and incontinence). Sophisticated life-support systems make it possible to sustain the lives of infants with these conditions, at least for a time, but technology frequently cannot ameliorate the severe underlying handicaps. Neither do life support systems prevent life-threatening complications associated with prematurity, such as bronchopulmonary dysplasia (chronic lung disease), necrotizing enterocolitis (gangrene of the intestines), and severe intracranial hemorrhage.

Do No Harm

In view of the suffering and uncertain prognosis of many of these infants, parents and health care professionals have found it extremely difficult to make decisions about withholding or withdrawing aggressive treatment.

We recognize this difficulty and do not believe that a set of moral or technical criteria can be developed that would provide simple and clear solutions in all cases. We are concerned, however, that current federal policy significantly restricts the circumstances in which physicians and parents can act on their own considered judgments about what would be in the infant's best interests; instead it substitutes a hard and fast rule—whenever current technology can prolong life (that is, can prolong noncomatose life beyond the "near future"), it must be employed.

Admittedly, this policy greatly simplifies treatment decisions; parents and professionals need not, indeed may not, consider the "salvageable" infant's life prospects, no matter how harmful they may appear. A graphic illustration of the potential for harm in the treatment of a handicapped infant is provided by Robert and Peggy Stinson's account of their son Andrew, who was born on December 17, 1976 at a gestational age of 24 ½ weeks and a weight of 800 grams. He was placed on a respirator against his parents' wishes and without their consent on January 13, and remained dependent on the respirator until June 14, when he was finally permitted to die.

> The sad list of Andrew's afflictions, almost all of which were iatrogenic, reveals how disastrous this hospitalization was. Andrew had a months-long, unresolved case of bronchopulmonary dysplasia, sometimes referred to as "respirator lung syndrome." He was "saved" by the respirator to endure countless episodes of bradycardia and cyanosis, countless suctionings and tube insertions and blood samplings and blood transfusions, "saved" to develop retrolental fibroplasia, numerous infections, demineralized and fractured bones, an iatrogenic cleft palate, and, finally, as his lungs became irreparably diseased, pulmonary artery hypertension and seizures of the brain. He was, in effect "saved" by the respirator to die five long, painful, and expensive months later of the respirator's side effects.[6]

We grant that this case may represent one of the worst treatment outcomes neonatolo-gists could expect and that some of the elder Stinsons' problems may have been due to a poor relationship with their son's physicians. Nevertheless, as we understand the current policy, aggressive treatment of Andrew would be required until a judgment could be made that continued treatment was highly unlikely to prevent his death in the near future or that he was irreversibly comatose, that is, probably not before the last few weeks (or months) of his life.

How common is Andrew Stinson's plight? This is difficult to estimate. The medical literature is not rife with similar case reports; physicians are understandably reluctant to dwell on the details of their failures. There are, however, statistical data on mortality and morbidity for very small infants like Andrew. Infants who fall into the lowest birth weight category of 500 to 1000 grams (between 1.1 and 2.2 pounds) are only a small percentage of total births (3.4 to 4 per 1000 live births in one study[7]), but a significant percentage of the patient population of neonatal intensive care units. Over the last twenty years, neonatal intensive care has significantly improved their prospects for survival. Nevertheless, mortality rates for infants in this category remain very high; using somewhat different inclusion criteria, three recently published studies report mortality rates of 48 to 66 percent.[8] Some of these infants will exhibit uncorrectable lethal conditions or irreversible coma at birth or shortly thereafter. Many very low birthweight infants, however, will not, or at least not immediately, satisfy the Baby Doe exception criteria, despite poor longer term survival prospects and the expectation of significant morbidity associated with painful aggressive treatment and with severe mental and physical handicaps. Because the Baby Doe rule does not allow physicians and parents even to take the latter criteria into account in making treatment decisions, it threatens harmful overtreatment for at least some of these infants.

If Mr. and Mrs. Stinson are correct in their judgment that aggressive treatment significantly harmed their son without the prospect of greater compensating benefits, then the physicians who treated him violated an ancient and honored Hippocratic principle of professional ethics, *"Primum non nocere,"* "First, do no harm." In an era in which powerful treatments often produce significant harms as well as benefits, this principle requires interpretation. One obvious interpretation is that, absent special circumstances such as a patient's specific request, treatments that promise greater overall harm than benefit to the patient ought not be provided. As already noted, determining when prolonging treatment constitutes a harm to the patient is not a simple matter, but neither is it impossible or purely arbitrary. At some point, the harms of painful and disabling treatment must surely outweigh the benefit of some chance at survival with a much diminished quality of life. At that point, providing further treatment violates the physician's commitment to do no harm.

A Shortage of Beds?

What about the impact of this federal policy regarding treatment of handicapped infants on the distribution of health care? As a high-technology, labor-intensive area of medical care, neonatal intensive care is very expensive. One 1980 study put the total annual cost of neonatal intensive care at $1.5 billion for 150,000 patients, for an average of $10,000 per patient.[9] Another study cited by DHHS reports an average cost per patient at over $20,000.[10] Charges vary widely depending on the severity of the case; Andrew Stinson's bill for six months of hospitalization in 1977 amounted to $104,403. A Canadian study calculated the cost in 1978 dollars of neonatal intensive care at $52,182 per survivor for newborns weighing 1000 to 1499 grams and $89,892 per survivor for newborns weighing 500 to 999 grams.[11]

Infants of poor families are disproportionately represented in NICUs, probably due to their mothers' poorer overall health status, younger age, and limited use of prenatal care. Because many poor families lack health insurance and are unable to pay for their infants' care, hospitals are naturally reluctant to expand NICUs and assume a greater risk of financial losses. Dr. Arthur Kopelman, director of the NICU at East Caro-

lina University School of Medicine, described the situation *before* the publication of the current federal policy in these terms:

> To be blunt, there are inadequate resources available to provide optimal care for every sick infant. The resources available reflect federal and state funding decisions. Intensive care nurseries often run out of space to admit more infants, but somehow we have always found a place for each infant at some center within our State. Our situation is neither unique nor the worst; sick neonates have on occasion been transferred to us who were born in hospitals several states distant because bed space was unavailable any closer. This is the best we can do under the circumstances, but it is not optimal. Because time is critical for these sick neonates, it would be better and much safer if they could be admitted to an intensive care unit close to where they are born.[12]

Current federal policy requiring treatment under almost all circumstances can only intensify this problem. NICUs will likely have to devote a larger and larger proportion of their beds to the most severely and chronically disabled infants, infants like Andrew Stinson who will have very lengthy stays in intensive care, some with limited prospects of ever leaving the unit. As this occurs it will become more and more difficult to provide intensive care promptly for all those infants with acute but completely reversible life-threatening conditions. Such infants may need to be transported long distances to secure care; occasionally their condition may deteriorate or they may die while they are waiting for a bed to become available.

This shortage of neonatal intensive care beds could be ameliorated by special programs to support NICUs or by increasing reimbursement through programs like Medicaid and Crippled Children's Services, for which a significant number of such infants may qualify. Instead, however, current budget proposals seek to make further deep cuts in health care programs, along with most other domestic programs.

Fear of potential legal liability and financial losses may also prompt smaller hospitals to engage in "dumping." Hospitals that formerly accepted some handicapped infants may now invariably transfer such infants to tertiary care centers, further worsening the NICU bed shortage and creating severe and perhaps unnecessary financial and emotional stresses on families. Paradoxically, then, a policy designed to protect infants from medical neglect may, by prolonging the lives of a small but increasing number of the most compromised infants, result in higher overall morbidity and mortality for all those infants needing intensive care.

Recent and proposed cuts in federal health care and social welfare programs also jeopardize continuing care for those infants who finally leave intensive care units with severe disabilities. Does current policy "save" these infants from medical neglect in the neonatal period only to neglect their continuing substantial needs? Whether life will be of value for a handicapped infant obviously depends to some extent on what resources are available to help the infant develop his or her potentialities and meet future crises. A strong network of services providing custodial, medical, habilitative, and educational support for handicapped infants bolsters claims that such infants will benefit from neonatal intensive care. Current federal policies, however, mandate such care while seeking to dismantle many of the services on which handicapped individuals will later depend.[13]

Why Single Out Infants?

Finally, if this federal policy is justified in order to prevent the medical neglect of handicapped infants, then presumably we could justify a similar policy to protect all incompetent patients who cannot protect their own interests. As a final test of the soundness of this policy, then, consider whether aggressive treatment should be required for all incompetent patients unless death will occur in the near future or the patient is irreversibly comatose.

Is it always in the best interest of the elderly senile patient with advanced cancer to receive chemotherapy or radiation therapy until he is highly unlikely to survive beyond the near future? Should the severely debilitated (but not comatose) stroke victim be resuscitated an indefinite number of times until respiration cannot be restored by any means? Providing treatment in such circumstances seems to us clearly not always in the best interests of such patients. There comes a point at which further prolongation of one's life simply does not make up for the burden of continued aggressive treatment, especially if the quality of life prolonged is diminished by suffering and incapacity. If it would be cruel to prolong the life of adult patients under these circumstances, then it must also be cruel to prolong the life of handicapped infants under comparable circumstances.

Potential cruelty to patients would not be the only problem of such a policy; finding the resources to support a greatly increased reliance on sophisticated medical care would also be extremely difficult. Recent studies have suggested that a very large percentage of health care costs are incurred by patients in the last two years of life.[14] Requiring that all potentially life-prolonging treatments be provided would increase this percentage significantly. Because such last-ditch efforts for seriously ill patients often fail, our policy would then likely place us in the curious position of requiring those treatments which will have the least favorable cost-benefit ratio. We would then be forced either to pay much more for health care than we do today or to cut back on effective treatments for conditions that are not life-threatening.

Neither alternative seems wise. The former, providing unlimited funds for life-prolonging care, would represent a capitulation to the technological imperative. Do we, for example, want to try to provide an artificial heart for all of the 140,000 potential candidates for this procedure, at a cost of $3 to $5 billion annually?[15] Since this treatment does appear to have the potential to prolong life, there would be tremendous pressure to make it widely available under a policy that required the provision of all life-prolonging treatments. The latter alternative, cutting back on treatment for nonlife-threatening conditions, would sacrifice quality of life and long-term life expectancy to short-term prolongation of life. It thus seems highly undesirable to apply the current policy regarding treatment of handicapped infants to all incompetent patients. Why then single out infants and require that they alone receive aggressive treatment?

For all the above reasons, the threat of unjustified prolongation of life, the violation of the physician's duty to do no harm, and undesirable effects on the distribution of health care, the continuing attempt to enforce treatment by federal regulation is an ill-advised response to the problem of caring sensitively for severely compromised infants. We should be proud that our health care system is able to care for very sick newborns, but also recognize that there are limits to our powers. In medicine as elsewhere, advanced technology cannot cure all the ills to which we are heir. And, as the power of any technology increases, so does its potential for harm.

Notes

1. Thomas H. Murray, "The Final, Anticlimactic Rule on Baby Doe." *Hastings Center Report* 15:3 (1985), 5–9.

2. See, e.g., James M. Gustafson, "Mongolism, Parental Desires and the Right to Life," *Perspectives in Biology and Medicine* 16 (1973), 529–57.

3. John J. Paris, "Terminating Treatment for Newborns: A Theological Perspective," *Law, Medicine, and Health Care* 10 (1983), 120–24.

4. Virginia Abernethy and Keith Lundin, "Competency and the Right to Refuse Medical Treatment," in *Frontiers in Medical Ethics*, edited by Virginia Abernethy (Cambridge: Ballinger, 1980), pp. 79–98.

5. For a discussion of durable powers of attorney, see President's Commission for the Study of Ethical Problems in Medicine and Biomedical and Behavioral Research, *Deciding to Forego Life-Sustaining Treatment* (Washington, 1983), pp. 145–53.

6. Robert Stinson and Peggy Stinson, "On the Death of a Baby," *Atlantic Monthly* (July 1979), pp. 64–65.

7. Sargent P. Horwood et al., "Mortality and Morbidity of 500- to 1499-Gram Birth Weight Infants Live-born to Residents of a Defined Geographic Region Before and After Neonatal Intensive Care." *Pediatrics* 69 (1982), 616.

8. Sharon Buckwald et al., "Mortality and Follow-Up Data for Neonates Weighing 500 to 800 g at Birth," *American Journal of Diseases of Children* 138 (1984), 779–82; William Kitchen and Laurence J. Murton, "Survival Rates of Infants with Birth Weight Between 501 and 1000 g," *AJDC*, 139 (1985), 470–71; Ernest Kraybill et al., "Infants with Birth Weights Less Than 1001 g," *AJDC*, 138 (1984), 837–42.

9. Peter P. Budetti et al., *The Cost Effectiveness of Neonatal Intensive Care* (Washington: Office of Technology Assessment, 1980), cited in Andrew T. Griffin and David C. Thomasma, "Triage and Critical Care of Children," *Theoretical Medicine* 4 (1983), 157.

10. Department of Health and Human Services, "Child Abuse and Neglect Prevention and Treatment Program," *Federal Register* 50 (1985), 14873–92.

11. Michael H. Boyle et al., "Economic Evaluation of Neonatal Intensive Care of Very-Low-Birthweight Infants," *New England Journal of Medicine* 308 (1983), 1330–37.

12. Arthur E. Kopelman, "Dilemmas in the Neonatal Intensive Care Unit," in *Ethics and Mental Retardation,* edited by Loretta Kopelman and John C. Moskop (Dordrecht: D. Reidel, 1984), p. 243.

13. See, for example, Peter P. Budetti et al., "Federal Health Program Reforms: Implications for Child Health Care," *Milbank Memorial Fund Quarterly* 60 (1982), 155–181, and Mary O. Mundinger, "Health Service Funding Cuts and the Declining Health of the Poor," *New England Journal of Medicine* 313 (1985), 44–47.

14. See, for example, Steven A. Schroeder et al., "Survival of Adult High-Cost Patients," *Journal of the American Medical Association* 245 (1981), 1446–1449, and Christopher J. Zook and Francis D. Moore, "High-Cost Users of Medical Care," *New England Journal of Medicine* 302 (1980), 996–1002.

15. Penelope Rowlands, "Bionic Bill's Heart: Critics Say Deficient," *Medical News and International Report* 9:3 (Feb. 4, 1985), 9.

Case 4.c   Assisted Suicide:
The Case of Dr. Kevorkian

In a campaign to allow physician-assisted suicide, Dr. Jack Kevorkian has helped a number of nonterminally ill but seriously impaired people to take their own lives. In recent cases, Kevorkian assisted in the deaths of two Michigan women, one with multiple sclerosis and the other with a painful pelvic disease. Currently, Dr. Kevorkian is facing murder charges.

If you are dying, you may view Dr. Jack Kevorkian as a courageous crusader for your rights. If you are a doctor, he may seem more like a cheap purveyor of easy death. Either way, he has become the lightning rod of the right-to-die movement and a gifted promoter of a cause he desperately believes in—and shockingly abets. Last week the doctor who has made his name by hastening death rather than forestalling it helped two more women kill themselves in Michigan. Lawmakers and doctors may debate the ethics of euthanasia endlessly; but while that argument unfolds, the activists have again decided to take life-and-death matters into their own hands.

In the vanguard is Kevorkian, a retired Michigan pathologist who appeared on every television talk show and news program in the country last year in the 24 hours after he helped Alzheimer's patient Janet Adkins commit suicide. He hooked her up to a homemade contraption that allowed her to push a button and send lethal potassium chloride into her veins. A Michigan judge chose not to prosecute Kevorkian for murder, since the state has no laws against assisted suicide, but forbade him to use the machine again. By last week, Dr. Death had found a way around that injunction.

The two most recent recipients of his care were likewise from Michigan: Sherry Miller, 43, had multiple sclerosis, and Marjorie Wantz, 58, suffered from a painful pelvic disease. While her husband watched, Wantz received a lethal injection from a device similar to the one Adkins used. Miller, attended by

her best friend, suffocated on carbon monoxide breathed through a mask. Neither one was a patient of Kevorkian's, and neither was terminally ill. The doctor was present throughout, said his lawyer, Geoffrey Fieger. "He provided the expertise. He provided the equipment."

Public parks remain Kevorkian's preferred treatment centers. Adkins' suicide occurred in a rusting van parked in a campground; this time the two women were found dead in a cabin in the Bald Mountain recreation area, about 40 miles north of Detroit. Kevorkian himself called the police to report the fatalities. "The people were still hooked up to the machines when the sheriffs got there," said county sheriff sergeant Dale Romeo.

In the months since Kevorkian last detonated the euthanasia debate, the public's craving for information has grown. The strangest best seller in memory still hovers at the top of the charts: *Final Exit*, by Derek Humphry, founder of the Hemlock Society, instructs people on how to die, or to kill. Last summer, Wantz said, she tried to follow the directions in the book. When she failed, she turned to Kevorkian.

Humphry, like Kevorkian, has urged physicians to assist in patient suicides. But much of the medical community remains deeply divided over this issue. Doctors see firsthand the agony that confronts the terminally ill and the resources spent prolonging some lives that might be diverted to improving the lives of others. Many thus favor laws that make it easier for patients to reject aggressive medical care, and urge the stricken to make out living wills so that their wishes are met.

Some jurisdictions are prepared to go even

187

further. Next month Washington state will vote on an initiative that would legalize physician-assisted suicide for patients with six months or less to live. If the proposal passes, Washington would become the first state to legalize active euthanasia. No Western country has yet done so. Earlier this year, Dr. Timothy Quill of Rochester, N.Y., wrote in the *New England Journal of Medicine* about helping a patient with acute leukemia kill herself with barbiturates. A state panel of physicians found his actions medically and legally appropriate, and a local grand jury cleared him of any criminal charges. Yet Quill, like many doctors, rejects Kevorkian's macabre approach. "He certainly doesn't stand for the mainstream," Quill says. "This will again muddy the water."

Defenders of the right to die point to the need for careful safeguards around the process: Kevorkian ignored them all. There were no second opinions, no consent forms, no examinations to make sure that Kevorkian's "patients" were of sound mind as they made their decision. As a pathologist more accustomed to dealing with people after they have died, Kevorkian was in no position to confirm the diagnosis of any of the women he helped kill themselves. And his defiant pursuit of publicity suggests a man more obsessed with the justice of his cause than with the interests of his patients.

Death in a rusting van or a remote cabin is hardly a death with dignity. But, as the numbers of people who came to Kevorkian's defense yet again last week indicate, many among the general public have a profound fear that one day they too might lose control of their life and be left at technology's mercy. Until the medical profession and state legislatures address the issue systematically, a retired doctor with a bagful of poisons and an obsession will be viewed as a savior by frightened people in search of final peace.

Testing

Across the country there has been a disturbing trend toward subjecting workers to tests of all different types. Many kinds of tests are necessary for reasons of health and safety, but concern is mounting over issues of privacy, confidentiality, tampering, selective enforcement, and errors in test results. Testing for truth telling, drugs, and the HIV virus are three of the most common forms of testing.

Polygraph Testing

More and more businesses today are requiring applicants and employees to submit to polygraphs, or so-called lie-detector tests. During a polygraph, a person has electrodes attached to various parts of his or her body that record physiological changes. It is assumed that, if a person gives a response to a question, and then the polygraph operator notices a change in blood pressure, pulse, respiration, etc., the person is not responding truthfully.

Corporations use polygraph tests for a variety of reasons. Certainly among the most important reasons given for these tests is the enormous amount of employee theft occurring today. More "stock shrinkage" is attributed to employee theft than to spoilage, breakage, or shoplifting. Hence, by asking personal questions about past behavior, companies believe that they will screen out applicants who are likely to steal. Companies are also worried about drug and alcohol abuse as well as about other dangerous behavior in the workplace. Thus they also screen for previous substance abuse, police records, and so on. Moreover, companies often use polygraphs as an inexpensive alternative to background checks— that is, as a way of determining if people have lied on their employment applications (about such things as education, past employment and salary, and so forth).

People object to polygraph tests for a variety of reasons. First, the tests are a violation of privacy. A person's *physical* privacy is violated in that his or her body is hooked up to machines while vital signs are monitored. From the perspective of *informational* privacy, polygraphs often probe very personal information. On many tests employers ask about sexual preference, sexual fantasies, previous drug problems, and other personal issues.

Polygraphs are also thought to be a violation of the Fifth-Amendment right against self-incrimination. People subjected to polygraphs are often forced to reveal incriminating information about prior drug, alcohol, or criminal activity. Furthermore, opponents argue that the Fourth-Amendment injunction against warrantless search and seizure is violated by random screening of employees. In the absence of some individualized suspicion, it is wrong to subject employees to a search.

The use of polygraphs, like all tests, involves serious due-process problems. If the results are leaked, or otherwise not kept confidential, the information could be extremely damaging. One rarely, with these tests, is able to appeal a condemning judgment. Furthermore, tampering with the results and selectively enforcing the testing for the purpose of discrimination based on race, gender, union affiliation, etc., are quite possible.

Probably the most important reason for opposing polygraphs is the reliability issue. Polygraph tests are not admissible in a court of law, and their accuracy is highly debatable. *False negative* results mean that the people this test is supposed to screen out get through anyway. Polygraphs can be beaten. Similarly, *false positive* results mean that some people will be incriminated unjustly.

Drug Testing

Businesses, schools, and government agencies all seem to be racing to see who can test the most people for drug use. In many cases these tests may be extremely important. In others, however, such testing can be disastrous.

Institutions test for drugs for many reasons. Companies concerned about productivity, employee absences, safety issues, and theft routinely test employees. Probably the most valid justification for drug testing, of course, involves public safety. Employers of airline pilots, bus drivers, railroad engineers, etc., face serious problems if these workers use drugs on the job. Drug users pose a danger to other employees as well as to customers.

Athletic organizations, concerned about health and unfair competition, test for steroids. In order to succeed in viciously competitive sports industries, athletes often turn to dangerous growth hormones to build strength and speed. Sports teams and associations feel that testing may deter steroid use and save lives.

Of course, many institutions are also legitimately concerned about property interests. People on drugs may steal to support their habits or may seriously damage company equipment. And, of course, many institutions drug-test for reasons of image and public relations.

Again, the main concern about drug testing is privacy, both physical and informational. Testees may be required to provide samples of blood, urine, and hair for analysis. To prevent cheating on these tests, supervisors often watch employees urinate in order to ensure that the urine is not switched. This, from the perspective of physical privacy, can be extremely humiliating. With respect to informational privacy, drug tests can reveal crucial personal information. Pregnancy is detectable, and it is hardly contentious to suggest that pregnant women are discriminated against in the workplace. HIV and other physical problems can also be detected and used against an employee.

With random drug tests there is a concern that the Fourth-Amendment injunction against search and seizure without probable cause is violated. Similarly, drug tests are incriminating. And, again, due-process issues are important. Confidentiality, appeal processes, selective enforcement, and, especially, tampering are at issue. Accusations have been made that companies routinely hold the results of drug tests, or tamper with them, in order to use the results against individuals involved in union activities.

Finally, there is a serious concern about the accuracy of drug tests. The larger the number of people being tested, the greater the chance that mistakes will be made. Some laboratories are unlicensed, and some of the types of tests used are significantly prone to error. Again,

false-negative results mean that people who use drugs will not be caught. And false-positive results will incriminate those who never used drugs to begin with.

HIV Testing

HIV, the virus that is responsible for the disease known as AIDS (Acquired Immune Deficiency Syndrome), has been a cause for alarm for over a decade. Now that a test is available, widespread calls for testing of employees, health professionals, teachers, food-service professionals, and others have been heard. Some people even advocate mandatory mass testing and compiling of lists of known HIV carriers. The issues related to HIV testing are somewhat different from those related to polygraph and drug testing, yet there are also striking similarities.

Again, a major concern is safety. People who work in areas in which the transmission of bodily fluids is possible are being subjected to HIV tests. A recent disclosure that a single Florida dentist may have infected several of his patients with the HIV virus touched off a major push to test health professionals. Congress responded by proposing mandatory testing for health-care workers and a jail sentence of up to ten years for failing to inform patients of possible exposure.

Some say that the risks associated with health-care workers are overblown. Tens of thousands of health-care workers are infected, and yet the only known case of transmission involved one dentist who clearly did not follow safety rules. Patients are at a much greater risk of being killed by an impaired, negligent, or incompetent doctor than they are of contracting AIDS from an infected physician.

Insurance companies have used HIV testing as an underwriting tool to screen applicants for health insurance. Needless to say, treatment for AIDS is incredibly expensive and often involves untried and experimental procedures. Unfortunately, many are concerned that HIV testing by the insurance industry will promote discrimination against gays and others who are at risk.

As with all tests, there is a serious concern for privacy, due process, confidentiality, and discrimination. Fatal diseases like AIDS have a tendency to engender substantial hysteria. Concern has been raised for the livelihoods of people with HIV and for the terrible costs to their families when their disease is made public. It is argued that mandatory testing will only drive people underground. Knowing that they will have their name on a list that can be leaked will lead many persons to refuse testing that they might have done voluntarily. The expense of mandatory HIV testing, along with the inevitable "witch hunts" against targeted groups, makes such testing unacceptable to many people.

16.   Privacy, Polygraphs, and Work

George G. Brenkert

In this article, George G. Brenkert attempts to clarify the philosophical and moral issues surrounding polygraph testing in employment. Brenkert's essential thinking revolves around the polygraph's effect on personal privacy. He is concerned with the nature of the information involved, the use of the test itself, and the putatively overriding concerns of property and theft.

The rights of prospective employees have been the subject of considerable dispute, both past and present. In recent years, this dispute has focused on the use of polygraphs to verify the claims which prospective employees make on employment application forms. With employee theft supposedly amounting to approximately ten billion dollars a year, with numerous businesses suffering sizeable losses and even being forced into bankruptcy by employee theft, significant and increasing numbers of employers have turned to the use of polygraphs.[1] Their right to protect their property is in danger, they insist, and the use of the polygraph to detect and weed out the untrustworthy prospective employee is a painless, quick, economical, and legitimate way to defend this right. Critics, however, have questioned both the reliability and validity of polygraphs, as well as objected to the use of polygraphs as demeaning, affronts to human dignity, violations of self-incrimination prohi-

bitions, expressions of employers' mistrust, and violations of privacy.[2] Though there has been a great deal of discussion of the reliability and validity of polygraphs, there has been precious little discussion of the central moral issues at stake. Usually terms such as "dignity," "privacy," and "property rights" are simply bandied about with the hope that some favorable response will be evoked. The present paper seeks to redress this situation by discussing one important aspect of the above dispute—the supposed violation of personal privacy. Indeed, the violation of "a right to privacy" often appears to be the central moral objection to the use of polygraphs. However, the nature and basis of this claim have not yet been clearly established.[3] If they could be, there would be a serious reason to oppose the use of polygraphs on prospective employees.

There are three questions which must be faced in the determination of this issue. First, is the nature of the information which polygraphing seeks to verify, information which can be said to violate, or involve the violation of, a person's privacy? Second, does the use of the polygraph itself as the means to corroborate the responses of the job applicant violate the applicant's privacy? Third, even if—for either of the two preceding reasons—the polygraph does violate a person's privacy, might this violation still be justified by the appeal to more weighty reasons, e.g., the defense of property rights?

I

In order to determine what information might be legitimately private to an individual who seeks employment we must consider the nature of the employer/(prospective) employee relationship. The nature of this relationship depends upon the customs, conventions and rules of the society. These, of course, are in flux at any time—and particularly so in the present case. They may also need revision. Further, the nature of this relationship will depend upon its particular instances—e.g., that of the employer of five workers or of five thousand workers, the kind of work involved, etc. In essence, however, we have a complex relationship in which an employer theoretically contracts with a person(s) to perform certain services from which the employer expects to derive a certain gain for himself. In the course of the employee's performance of these services, the employer entrusts him with certain goods, money, etc.; in return for such services he delivers to the employee a certain remuneration and (perhaps) benefits. The goals of the employer and the employee are not at all, on this account, necessarily the same. The employee expects his remuneration (and benefits) even if the services, though adequately performed, do not result in the end the employer expected. Analogously, the employer expects to derive a certain gain for the services the employee has performed even if the employee is not (fully) satisfied with his work or remuneration. On the other hand, if the employer is significantly unable to achieve the ends sought through the contract with the employee, the latter may not receive his full remuneration (should the employer go bankrupt) and may even lose his job. There is, in short, a complicated mixture of trust and antagonism, connectedness and disparity of ends in the relation between employer and employee.

Given this (brief) characterization of the relationship between employer and employee, the information to which the employer qua employer is entitled about the (prospective) employee is that information which regards his possible acceptable performance of the services for which he might be hired. Without such information the employer could not fulfill the role which present society sanctions. There are two aspects of the information to which the employer is entitled given the employer/employee relationship. On the one hand, this information will relate to and vary in accordance with the services for which the person is to be hired. But in any case, it will be limited by those services and what they require. In short, one aspect of the information to which the employer is entitled is "job relevant" information. Admittedly the criterion of job relevancy is rather vague. Certainly there are few aspects of a person which might not affect his job performance—aspects including his sex life, etc. How then does the "job relevancy" criterion limit the questions asked or the information sought? It does so by limiting the information sought to that which is directly connected with the job description. If a typist is sought, it is job relevant to know whether or not a person can type—typing tests are legitimate. If a store manager is sought, it is relevant to know about his abilities to manage employees, stock, etc. That is, the description of the job is what determines the relevancy of the information to be sought. It is what gives the employer a right to know certain things about the person seeking employment. Accordingly, if a piece of information is not "job relevant" then the employer is not entitled qua employer to know it. Consequently, since sexual practices, political beliefs, associational activities, etc. are not part of the description of most jobs, that is, since they do not directly affect one's job performance, they are not legitimate information for an employer to know in the determination of the hiring of a job applicant.[4]

However, there is a second aspect to this matter. A person must be able not simply to perform a certain activity, or provide a service, but he must also be able to do it in an acceptable manner—i.e., in a manner which is approximately as efficient as others, in an honest manner, and in a manner compatible with others who seek to provide the services for which they were hired. Thus, not simply one's abilities to do a certain job are relevant, but also aspects of one's social and moral character are pertinent. A number of qualifications are needed for the purport of this claim to be clear. First, that a person must be able to work in an acceptable manner is not intended to legitimize the consideration of the prejudices of other employees. It is not legitimate to give weight in moral deliberations to the immoral and/or morally irrelevant beliefs which people hold concerning the characteristics of others. That one's present employees can work at a certain (perhaps exceptional) rate is a legitimate consideration in hiring other workers. That one's present employees have prejudices against certain religions, sexes, races, political views, etc. is not a morally legitimate consideration. Second, it is not, or should not be, the motives, beliefs, or attitudes underlying the job relevant character traits, e.g., honest, efficient, which are pertinent, but rather the fact that a person does or does not perform according to these desirable character traits. This is not to say, it should be noted, that a person's beliefs and attitudes about the job itself, e.g., how it is best to be done, what one knows or believes about the job, etc., are irrelevant. Rather it is those beliefs, attitudes and motives underlying one's desired character traits which are not relevant. The contract of the employer with the employee is for the latter to perform acceptably certain services—it is not for the employee to have certain underlying beliefs, motives, or attitudes. If I want to buy something from someone, this commercial relation does not entitle me to probe the attitudes, motives, and beliefs of the person beyond his own statements, record of past actions, and the observations of others. Even the used car salesman would correctly object that his right to privacy was being violated if he was required to submit to Rorschach tests, an attitude survey test, truth serums, and/or the polygraph in order to determine his real beliefs about selling cars. Accordingly, why the person acts the way in which he acts ought not to be the concern of the employer. Whether a person is a good working colleague simply be-

cause he is congenial, because his ego needs the approval of others, or because he has an oppressive superego is, in this instance, morally irrelevant. What is relevant is whether this person has, by his past actions, given some indication that he may work in a manner compatible with others.

Consequently, a great deal of the information which has been sought in preemployment screening through the use of polygraph tests has violated the privacy of individuals. Instances in which the sex lives, for example, of applicants have been probed are not difficult to find. However, privacy violations have occurred not simply in such generally atypical instances but also in standard situations. To illustrate the range of questions asked prospective employees and the violations of privacy which have occurred we need merely consider a list of some questions which one of the more prominent polygraph firms includes in its current tests:

Have you ever taken any of the following without the advice of a doctor? If Yes, please check: Barbiturates, Speed, LSD, Tranquilizers, Amphetamines, Marijuana, Others.

In the past five years about how many times, if any, have you bet on horse races at the race track?

Do you think that policemen are honest?

Did you ever think about committing a robbery?

Have you been refused credit or a loan in the past five years?

Have you ever consulted a doctor about a mental condition?

Do you think that it is okay to get around the law if you don't actually break it?

Do you enjoy stories of successful crimes and swindles?[5]

Such questions, it follows from the above argument, are for any standard employment violations of one's right to privacy. An employer might ask if a person regularly takes certain narcotic drugs, if he is considering him for a job which requires handling narcotics. An employer might ask if a person has been convicted of a larceny, etc. But whether the person enjoys stories about successful larcenists, whether a person has ever taken any prescription drugs without the advice of a doctor, or whether a person bets on the horses should be considered violations of one's rightful privacy.

The upshot of the argument in the first two sections is, then, that some information can be considered rightfully private to an individual. Such information is rightfully private or not depending on the relationship in which a person stands to another person or institution. In the case of the employer/employee relationship, I have argued that that information is rightfully private which does not relate to the acceptable performance of the activities as characterized in the job description. This excludes a good many questions which are presently asked in polygraph tests, but does not, by any means, exclude all such questions. There still remain many questions which an employer might conceivably wish to have verified by the use of the polygraph. Accordingly, I turn in the next section to the question whether the verification of the answers to legitimate questions by the use of the polygraph may be considered a violation of a person's right to privacy. If it is, then the violation obviously does not stem from the questions themselves but from the procedure, the polygraph test, whereby the answers to those questions are verified.

II

A first reason to believe that use of the polygraph occasions a violation of one's right to privacy is that, even though the questions to be answered are job relevant, some of them will occasion positive, lying reactions which are not necessarily related to any past misdeeds. Rather, the lying reaction indicated by the polygraph may be triggered because of unconscious conflicts, fears and hostilities a person has. It may be occasioned by conscious anxieties over other past activities and observations. Thus, the lying reaction indicated by the polygraph need not positively identify actual lying or the commission of illegal activities. The point, however, is not to question the validity of the polygraph. Rather, the point is that the validity of the polygraph can only be

maintained by seeking to clarify whether or not such reactions really indicate lying and the commission of past misdeeds. But this can be done only by the polygraphist further probing into the person's background and inner thoughts. However, inasmuch as the questions can no longer be restrained in this situation by job relevancy considerations, but must explore other areas to which an employer is not necessarily entitled knowledge, to do this will violate a person's right to privacy.

A second reason why the polygraph must be said to violate a job applicant's right to privacy relates to the monitoring of a person's physiological responses to the questions posed to him. By measuring these responses, the polygraph can supposedly reveal one's mental processes. Now even though the questions posed are legitimate questions, surely a violation of one's right to privacy occurs. Just because I have something which you are entitled to see or know, it does not follow that you can use any means to fulfill that entitlement and not violate my privacy. Consider the instance of two good friends, one of whom has had some dental work done which puts him in a situation such that he can tune in the thoughts and feelings of his friend. Certain facts about, and emotional responses of, his friend—aspects which his friend (we will assume) would usually want to share with him—simply now stream into his head. Even though the friendship relation generally entitles its members to know personal information about the other person, the friend with the dental work is not entitled to such information in this direct and immediate way. This manner of gaining this information simply eliminates any private reserves of the person; it wholly opens his consciousness to the consciousness of another. Surely this would be a violation of his friend's right to privacy, and his friend would rightfully ask that such dental work be modified. Even friends do not have a right to learn in this manner of each other's inner thoughts and feelings.

Such fancy dental work may, correctly, be said to be rather different from polygraphs. Still the point is that though one is entitled to some information about another, one is not entitled to use any means to get it. But why should the monitoring by an employer or his agent of one's physiological responses to legitimate questions be an invasion of privacy—especially if one has agreed to take the test? There are several reasons.

First, the claim that one freely agrees or consents to take the test is surely, in many cases, disingenuous.[6] Certainly a job applicant who takes the polygraph test is not physically forced or coerced into taking the exam. However, it is quite apparent that if he did not take the test and cooperate during the test, his application for employment would either not be considered at all or would be considered to have a significant negative aspect to it. This is surely but a more subtle form of coercion. And if this be the case, then one cannot say that the person has willingly allowed his reactions to the questions to be monitored. He has consented to do so, but he has consented under coercion. Had he a truly free choice, he would not have done so.

Now the whole point of the polygraph test is, of course, not simply to monitor physiological reactions but to use these responses as clues, indications, or revelations of one's mental processes and acts. The polygraph seeks to make manifest to others one's thoughts and ideas. However, unless we freely consent, we are entitled to the privacy of our thoughts, that is, we have a prima facie right not to have our thoughts exposed by others, even when the information sought is legitimate. Consider such analogous cases as a husband reading his wife's diary, a person going through a friend's desk drawers, a stranger reading personal papers on one's desk, an F.B.I. agent going through one's files. In each of these cases, a person attempts to determine the nature of someone else's thoughts by the use of clues and indications which those thoughts left behind. And, in each of these cases, though we may suppose that the person seeks to confirm answers to legitimate questions, we may also say that, if the affected person's uncoerced consent is not forthcoming, his or her right to privacy is violated. Morally, however, there is no difference between ascertaining the nature of one's thoughts by the use of a polygraph, or reading notes left in a drawer, going through one's diary, etc. Hence, unless there are overriding considerations to consent to such revelations of one's thoughts, the use of the polygraph is a violation of one's right to privacy.[7]

Second, if we value privacy not simply as a barrier to the intrusion of others but also as the way by which we define ourselves as separate, autonomous persons, individuals with an integrity which lies at least in part in the ability to make decisions, to give or withhold information and access, then the polygraph strikes at this fundamental value.[8] The polygraph operates by turning part of us over which we have little or no control against the rest of us. If a person were an accomplished yogi, the polygraph would supposedly be useless—since that person's physiological reactions would be fully under his control. The polygraph works because most of us do not have that control. Thus, the polygraph is used to probe people's reactions which they would otherwise protect, not expose to others. It uses part of us to reveal the rest of us. It takes the "shadows" consciousness throws off within us and reproduces them for other people. As such, the use of the polygraph undercuts the decision-making aspect of a person. It circumvents the person. The person says such and such, but his uncontrolled reactions may say something different. He does not know—even when honest—what his reactions might say. Thus it undercuts and demeans that way by which we define ourselves as autonomous persons—in short, it violates our privacy. Suppose one said something to another—but his Siamese and undetached twin, who was given to absolute truth and who correctly knew every thought, past action, and feeling of the person said: "No, he does not really believe that." I think the person would rightfully complain that his twin had better remain silent. Just so, I have a right to complain when my own feelings are turned on me. This subtle form of self-incrimination is a form of invading one's privacy. An employer is entitled to know certain facts about one's background, but this relationship does not entitle him—or his agents—to probe one's emotional responses, feelings, and thoughts.

Thus, it follows that even if the only questions asked in a polygraph test are legitimate ones, the use of the polygraph for the screening of job applicants still violates one's privacy. In this case, the violation of privacy stems from the procedure itself, and not the questions. Accordingly, one can see the lameness of the defense of polygraphing which maintains that if a person has nothing to hide, he should not object to the polygraph tests. Such a defense is mistaken at least on two counts. First, just because someone believes something to be private does not mean that he believes that what is private is wrong, something to be ashamed about or to be hidden. Second, the polygraph test has been shown to violate a person's privacy, whether one person has really something to hide or not—whether he is dishonest or not. Consequently, if the question is simply whether polygraphing of prospective employees violates their privacy the answer must be affirmative.

III

There remains one possible defense of the use of polygraphs for screening prospective employees. This is to admit that such tests violate the applicant's privacy but to maintain that other considerations outweigh this fact. Specifically, in light of the great amount of merchandise and money stolen, the right of the employers to defend their property outweighs the privacy of the applicant. This defense is specious, I believe, and the following arguments seek to show why.

First, surely it would be better if people who steal or are dishonest were not placed in positions of trust. And if the polygraphs were used in only these cases, one might well maintain that the use of the polygraph, though it violates one's privacy, is legitimate and justified. However, the polygraph cannot be so used, obviously, only in these cases—it must be used more broadly on both honest and dishonest applicants. Further, if a polygraph has a 90% validity then out of 1,000 interviewees, a full 100 will be misidentified.[9] Now if 10% of the interviewees are thieves, then 10 out of the 100 will steal, but 90 would not; in addition 90 out of the 900 would be thieves, and supposedly correctly identified. This means that 90 thieves would be correctly identified, 10 thieves would be missed, and 90 honest people would be said not to have cleared the test. Thus, for every thief "caught," one honest person would also be "caught"—the former would be correctly identified as one who would steal, while the latter could not be cleared of the suspicion that he too would steal. The point, then, is that this means of defending property rights is one that excludes not simply thieves but honest people as well—and potentially in equal numbers. Such a procedure certainly appears to constitute not simply a violation of privacy rights, but also, and more gravely, an injustice to those honest people stigmatized as not beyond suspicion and hobbled in their competition with others to get employment. If then using polygraph tests to defend property rights is not simply like preventing a thief from breaking into the safe, but more like keeping a thief from the safe plus binding the leg of an innocent bystander in his competition with others to gain employment, then one may legitimately doubt that this procedure to protect property rights is indeed defensible.[10]

Second, it has been claimed that just as the use of blood tests on suspected drunken drivers and the use of baggage searches at the airport are legitimate, so too is the polygraphing of prospective employees. Both of the former kinds of searches may also be said to violate a person's privacy; still they are taken to be justified whether the appeal is to the general good they produce or to the protection of the rights of other drivers or passengers and airline employees. However, neither the blood test nor the baggage search is really analogous to the use of the polygraph on job applicants. Blood tests are only administered to those drivers who have given police officers reason to believe that they (the drivers) are driving while under the influence of alcohol. The polygraph, however, is not applied only to those suspected of past thefts; it is applied to others as well. Further, the connection between driving while drunk and car accidents is quite direct; it immediately endangers both the safety and lives of others. The connection between polygraph tests of a diverse group of applicants (some honest and some dishonest) and future theft is not nearly so direct nor do the thefts endanger the lives of others. Baggage searches are a different matter. They are similar to polygraphing in that they are required of everyone. They are dissimilar in that they are made because of fears concerning the safety of other people. Further, surely there is a dissimilarity between officials searching one's baggage for lethal objects which one is presently trying to sneak on board, and employers searching one's mind for the true nature of one's past behavior which may or may not lead to future criminal intentions. Finally, there are signs at airports warning people, before they are searched, against carrying weapons on airplanes; such weapons could at that time be declared and sent, without prejudice, with the regular baggage. There is no similar aspect to polygraph tests. Thus, the analogies suggested do not hold. Indeed, they suggest that we allow for a violation of privacy only in very different circumstances than those surrounding the polygraphing of job applicants.

Third, the corporate defense of polygraphs seems one-sided in the sense that employers would not really desire the universalization of their demands. Suppose that the businesses in a certain industry are trying to get a new government contract. The government, however, has had difficulties with other corporations breaking the rules of other contracts. As a result it has lost large sums of money. In order to prevent this in the present case it says that it is going to set up devices to monitor the reactions of board members and top managers when a questionnaire is sent to them which they must answer. Any business, of course, need not agree to this procedure but if it does then it will be noted in their file regarding this and future government contracts. The questionnaire will include questions about the corporations' past fulfillment of contracts, competency to fulfill the present contract, loopholes used in past contracts, collusion with other companies, etc. The reactions of the managers and board members, as they respond to these questions, will be monitored and a decision on the worthiness of that corporation to receive the contract will be made in part on this basis.

There can be little doubt, I think, that the management and directors of the affected corporations would object to the proposal even though the right of the government to defend itself from the violation of its contracts and

serious finanical losses is at stake. It would be said to be an unjustified violation of the privacy of the decision-making process in a business; an illegitimate encroachment of the government on free enterprise. But surely if this is the legitimate response for the corporate job applicant, the same kind of response would be legitimate in the case of the individual job applicant.

Finally, it is simply false that there are not other measures which could be taken which could not help resolve the problem of theft. The fact that eighty percent of industry does not use the polygraph is itself suggestive that business does not find itself absolutely forced into the use of polygraphs. It might be objected that that does not indicate that certain industries might need polygraphs more than others—e.g., banks and drug companies more than auto plants and shipyards. But even granting this point there are other measures which businesses can use to avoid the problem of theft. Stricter inventory controls, different kinds of cash registers, educational programs, hot lines, incentives, etc. could all be used. The question is whether the employer, management, can be imaginative and innovative enough to move in these directions.

Notes

1. Cf. Harlow Unger, "Lie Detectors: Business Needs Them to Avoid Costly Employee Rip-Offs," *Canadian Business,* Vol. 51 (April, 1978), p. 30. Other estimates may be found in "Outlaw Lie-Detector Tests?", *U.S. News & World Report,* Vol. 84, No. 4 (January 1978), p. 45, and Victor Lipman, "New Hiring Tool: Truth Tests," *Parade* (October 7, 1979), p. 19.

2. Both the AFL-CIO and the ACLU have raised these objections to the use of the polygraph for screening job applicants: cf. *AFL-CIO Executive Council Statements and Reports: 1956–1975* (Westport, Conn.: Greenwood Press, 1977), p. 1422. See also ACLU Policy #248.

3. See, for example, Alan F. Westin. *Privacy and Freedom* (New York: Atheneum, 1967), p. 238.

4. This would have to be qualified for security jobs and the like.

5. John E. Reid and Associates, *Reid Report* (Chicago: By the author, 1978), passim.

6. The reasons why people do not submit to the polygraph are many and various. Some might have something to hide; others may be scared of the questions, supposing that some of them will not be legitimate; some may feel that they are being treated like criminals; others may fear the jaundiced response of the employer to the applicant's honest answers to legitimate questions: finally some may even object to the polygraph on moral grounds, e.g., it violates one's right to privacy.

7. See Section III below.

8. Cf. Jeffrey H. Reiman, "Privacy, Intimacy, and Personhood," *Philosophy and Public Affairs*, Vol. VI (Fall, 1976).

9. Estimates of the validity of the polygraph range widely. Professor David Lykken has been reported as maintaining that the most prevalent polygraph test is correct only two-thirds of the time (cf. Bennett H. Beach, "Blood, Sweat and Fears," *Time*, September 8, 1980, p. 44). A similar figure of seventy percent is reported by Richard A. Sternbach et al., "Don't Trust the Lie Detector," *Harvard Business Review*, Vol. XL (Nov.-Dec., 1962), p. 130. Operators of polygraphs, however, report figures as high as 95% accuracy; cf. Sternbach, p. 129.

10. This argument is suggested by a similar argument in David T. Lykken, "Guilty-Knowledge Test: The Right Way to Use a Lie Detector," *Psychology Today* (March, 1975), p. 60.

---

17. The Coors Polygraph Test

Because of concern with safety and employee theft, the Coors Corporation instituted a polygraph test that was extremely invasive. In response to the subsequent workers' protest strike, Coors changed the questions on the test to make them somewhat less invasive and more job related. The question remains: does the change make the test morally acceptable?

On April 5, 1977, the members of Brewery Workers Local No. 366 walked off the job at the Adolf Coors Brewery Plant in Golden, Colorado.[1] The wildcat strike was motivated in part by Coors's use of lie detector tests in a preemployment examination required of prospective employees. Said an officer of the union: "When you get through being grilled on that lie detector, you feel dirty."[2]

To support their case the union collected several notarized affidavits in which striking employees alleged that the company had asked them improper questions during the lie

"The Coors Polygraph Test," from Manuel G. Velasquez, *Business Ethics: Concepts and Cases,* 3rd ed., pp. 430–431. © 1992 Prentice Hall, Inc. Reprinted by permission of Prentice Hall, Englewood Cliffs, New Jersey.

detector test. Two of the notarized affidavits read in part as follows:[3]

> In April of 1973, I, John A. K. _____, had to submit to a polygraph test for employment at the Adolph Coors Company in Golden, Colorado. Of the many personal questions asked, the two listed below were particularly aggravating.
> 1.   Are you a homosexual?
> 2.   Do you know of any reason that you could be blackmailed?

> I, Oliver A. D. __, was hired by the Adolph Coors Company on October 23, 1972. Below are listed some of the questions I was asked on the lie detector while going through my screening for a job.

Do you get along with your wife?
What is your sex preference?
Are you a communist?
Do you have money in the bank?
Have you ever stolen anything and
    was [sic] not caught at it?

I feel that these questions were degrading and an invasion of my privacy. I also feel these questions are unnecessary for the Coors Company to ask of anyone seeking a job with them.

Coors executives responded to these allegations by saying that they did not know these alleged questions were being asked of their prospective employees. The polygraph questionnaires, they said, were administered by an outside agency which Coors had hired before 1975.[4]

However, Coors was unwilling to give up using polygraph tests altogether. In 1960, a member of the Coors family had been kidnapped and killed. In August 1977, a bomb was planted in a Coors recycling plant. Chairman William Coors and his brother, Joseph Coors, both said they wanted to ensure that they did not hire someone who might again endanger their families or their employees. In addition, the Coors brothers felt that the polygraph tests would reveal some information that the company should have:

[The tests reveal] whether the applicant may be hiding some health problem . . . [and ensure that] the applicant does not want the job for some subversive reason such as sabotaging our operation. [Statement of William Coors]

Coors therefore continued to use the polygraph test but formulated a standard questionnaire that the polygraph agency was to use in the preemployment examination. The new questionnaire consisted of seven question areas. Before a job applicant even made an appointment with the polygraph agency, the applicant was given a copy of the questions and was asked to review the questions carefully. If he had any hesitations about answering the questions on a lie detector, he was invited

to discuss his problems with the employment staff. The seven questions were as follows:

1. Did you tell the complete truth on the employment application?
2. Have you ever used any form of illegal drug or narcotic on the job?
3. Has the use of alcohol frequently impaired your ability to perform on the job?
4. Are you concealing any information about subversive, revolutionary, or communistic activity?
5. Are you applying for a job with this company so you can do it or any of its employees harm?
6. Are you presently wanted by the authorities for a felony?
7. Have you ever stolen any kind of merchandise, material, or money from an employer?[5]

Coors assured each applicant that these were the only questions that he or she had to answer. The polygraph agency was to adhere to the questionnaire.

1. Would Coors have been justified in using a polygraph and in asking the questions alleged in the notarized affidavits? Explain your answer fully in terms of the ethical principles involved.
2. Was Coors justified in using a polygraph to gather responses to any or all of the seven questions in its revised questionnaire? Explain your answer fully.
3. Could Coors have protected its interests by using any other methods? Explain your answer fully.

Notes

1. "Bitter Beercott," *Time*, 26 December 1977, p. 15.
2. *Ibid.*
3. Copies of these affidavits were obtained from Brewery Bottling, Can and Allied Industrial Un-

ion-Local No. 366; 4510 Indiana Street, Golden, Colorado.

4. "Bitter Beercott."

5. A copy of the questionnaire was also obtained from Brewery Bottling, Can, and Allied Industrial Union-Local No. 366.

18.   Drug Testing in Employment

Joseph R. DesJardins and Ronald Duska

Joseph R. DesJardins and Ronald Duska examine the basic arguments in favor of drug testing. They reject the claim that drug testing is job relevant with respect to job performance; however, they agree with the issues concerning safety in certain circumstances, provided that procedural guarantees are strictly adhered to. They conclude by examining the issue of voluntary compliance.

We take privacy to be an "employee right," by which we mean a presumptive moral entitlement to receive certain goods or be protected from certain harms in the workplace.[1] Such a right creates a prima facie obligation on the part of the employer to provide the relevant goods or, as in this case, refrain from the relevant harmful treatment. These rights prevent employees from being placed in the fundamentally coercive position where they must choose between their jobs and other basic human goods.

Further, we view the employer–employee relationship as essentially contractual. The employer–employee relationship is an economic one and, unlike relationships such as those between a government and its citizens or a parent and a child, exists primarily as a means for satisfying the economic interests of the contracting parties. The obligations that each party incurs are only those that it voluntarily takes on. Given such a contractual relationship, certain areas of the employee's life remain his or her own private concern, and no employer has a right to invade them. On these presumptions we maintain that certain information about an employee is rightfully private, in other words, that the employee has a right to privacy.

Reprinted by permission from Joseph R. DesJardins and John J. McCall, eds., *Contemporary Issues in Business Ethics,* 2nd ed. (Belmont, Calif.: Wadsworth, 1990).

The Right to Privacy

George Brenkert has described the right to privacy as involving a three-place relation between a person A, some information X, and another person B. The right to privacy is violated only when B deliberately comes to possess information X about A and no relationship between A and B exists that would justify B's coming to know X about A.[2] Thus, for example, the relationship one has with a mortgage company would justify that company's coming to know about one's salary, but the relationship one has with a neighbor does not justify the neighbor's coming to know that information.

Hence, an employee's right to privacy is violated whenever personal information is requested, collected, or used by an employer in a way or for any purpose that is *irrelevant to* or *in violation of* the contractual relationship that exists between employer and employee.

Since drug testing is a means for obtaining information, the information sought must be relevant to the contract if the drug testing is not to violate privacy. Hence, we must first decide whether knowledge of drug use obtained by drug testing is job relevant. In cases in which the knowledge of drug use is *not* relevant, there appears to be no justification for subjecting employees to drug tests. In cases in which information of drug use is job relevant, we need to consider if, when, and under what conditions using a means such as drug testing to obtain that knowledge is justified.

Is Knowledge of Drug Use Job-Relevant Information?

Two arguments are used to establish that knowledge of drug use is job-relevant information. The first argument claims that drug use adversely affects job performance, thereby leading to lower productivity, higher costs, and consequently lower profits. Drug testing is seen as a way of avoiding these adverse effects. According to some estimates $25 billion are lost each year in the United States through loss in productivity, theft, higher rates in health and liability insurance, and similar costs incurred because of drug use.[3] Since employers are contracting with an employee for the performance of specific tasks, employers seem to have a legitimate claim upon whatever personal information is relevant to an employee's ability to do the job.

The second argument claims that drug use has been and can be responsible for considerable harm to individual employees, to their fellow employees, and to the employer, and third parties, including consumers. In this case drug testing is defended because it is seen as a way of preventing possible harm. Further, since employers can be held liable for harms done to employees and customers, knowledge of employee drug use is needed so that employers can protect themselves from risks related to such liability. But how good are these arguments?

The First Argument: Job Performance and Knowledge of Drug Use

The first argument holds that drug use lowers productivity and that consequently, an aware-ness of drug use obtained through drug testing will allow an employer to maintain or increase productivity. It is generally assumed that the performance of people using certain drugs is detrimentally affected by such use, and any use of drugs that reduces productivity is consequently job relevant. If knowledge of such drug use allows the employer to eliminate production losses, such knowledge is job relevant.

On the surface this argument seems reasonable. Obviously some drug use, in lowering the level of performance, can decrease productivity. Since the employer is entitled to a certain level of performance and drug use adversely affects performance, knowledge of that use seems job-relevant.

But this formulation of the argument leaves an important question unanswered. To what level of performance are employers entitled? Optimal performance, or some lower level? If some lower level, what? Employers have a valid claim upon some *certain level* of performance, such that a failure to perform at this level would give the employer a justification for disciplining, firing, or at least finding fault with the employee. But that does not necessarily mean that the employer has a right to a maximum or optimal level of performance, a level above and beyond a certain level of acceptability. It might be nice if the employee gives an employer a maximum effort or optimal performance, but that is above and beyond the call of the employee's duty and the employer can hardly claim a right at all times to the highest level of performance of which an employee is capable. . . .

If the person is producing what is expected, knowledge of drug use on the grounds of production is irrelevant since, by this hypothesis, the production is satisfactory. If, on the other hand, the performance suffers, then to the extent that it slips below the level justifiably expected, the employer has preliminary grounds for warning, disciplining, or releasing the employee. But the justification for this action is the person's unsatisfactory performance, not the person's use of drugs. Accordingly, drug use information is either unnecessary or irrelevant and consequently there are not sufficient grounds to override the right of privacy. Thus, unless we can argue that an employer is entitled to optimal performance, the argument fails.

The counterargument should make it clear that the information that is job relevant, and consequently is not rightfully private, is information about an employee's level of performance and not information about the underlying causes of that level. The fallacy of the argument that promotes drug testing in the name of increased productivity is the assumption that each employee is obliged to perform at an optimal or at least quite high level. But this is required under few if any contracts. What is required contractually is meeting the normally expected levels of production or performing the tasks in the job description adequately (not optimally). If one can do that under the influence of drugs, then on the grounds of job-performance at least, drug use is rightfully private. An employee who cannot perform the task adequately is not fulfilling the contract, and knowledge of the cause of the failure to perform is irrelevant on the contractual model.

Of course, if the employer suspects drug use or abuse as the cause of the unsatisfactory performance, then she might choose to help the person with counseling or rehabilitation. However, this does not seem to be something morally required of the employer. Rather, in the case of unsatisfactory performance, the employer has a prima facie justification for dismissing or disciplining the employee. . . .

The Second Argument: Harm and the Knowledge of Drug Use to Prevent Harm

---

The performance argument is inadequate, but there is an argument that seems somewhat stronger. This is an argument that takes into account the fact that drug use often leads to harm. Using a variant of the Millian argument, which allows interference with a person's rights in order to prevent harm, we could argue that drug testing might be justified if such testing led to knowledge that would enable an employer to prevent harm.

Drug use certainly can lead to harming others. Consequently, if knowledge of such drug use can prevent harm, then knowing whether or not an employee uses drugs might be a legitimate concern of an employer in certain circumstances. This second argument claims that knowledge of the employee's drug use is job relevant because employees who are under the influence of drugs can pose a threat to the health and safety of themselves and others, and an employer who knows of that drug use and the harm it can cause has a responsibility to prevent it.

Employers have both a general duty to prevent harm and the specific responsibility for harms done by their employees. Such responsibilities are sufficient reason for any employer to claim that information about an employee's drug use is relevant if that knowledge can prevent harm by giving the employer grounds for dismissing the employee or not allowing him or her to perform potentially harmful tasks. Employers might even claim a right to reduce unreasonable risks, in this case the risks involving legal and economic liability for harms caused by employees under the influence of drugs, as further justification for knowing about employee drug use.

This second argument differs from the first, in which only a lowered job performance was relevant information. In this case, even to allow the performance is problematic, for the performance itself, more than being inadequate, can hurt people. We cannot be as sanguine about the prevention of harm as we can about inadequate production. Where drug use may cause serious harms, knowledge of that use becomes relevant if the knowledge of such use can lead to the prevention of harm and drug testing becomes justified as a means for obtaining that knowledge.

Jobs with Potential to Cause Harm

In the first place, it is not clear that every job has a potential to cause harm—at least, not a potential to cause harm sufficient to override a prima facie right to privacy. To say that employers can use drug testing where that can prevent harm is not to say that every employer has the right to know about the drug use of every employee. Not every job poses a threat serious enough to justify an employer coming to know this information.

In deciding which jobs pose serious-enough threats, certain guidelines should be followed. First the potential for harm should be *clear* and *present*. Perhaps all jobs in some extended way pose potential threats to human well-being. We suppose an accountant's error could pose a threat of harm to someone somewhere. But some jobs—like those of airline pilots, school bus drivers, public transit drivers, and surgeons—are jobs in which unsatisfactory performance poses a clear and present danger to others. It would be much harder to make an argument that job performances by auditors, secretaries, executive vice-presidents for public relations, college teachers, professional athletes, and the like could cause harm if those performances were carried on under the influence of drugs. They would cause harm only in exceptional cases.[4]

Not Every Person Is to Be Tested

But, even if we can make a case that a particular job involves a clear and present danger for causing harm if performed under the influence of drugs, it is not appropriate to treat everyone holding such a job the same. Not every jobholder is equally threatening. There is less reason to investigate an airline pilot for drug use if that pilot has a twenty-year record of exceptional service than there is to investigate a pilot whose behavior has become erratic and unreliable recently, or one who reports to work smelling of alcohol and slurring his words. Presuming that every airline pilot is equally threatening is to deny individuals the respect that they deserve as autonomous, rational agents. It is to ignore their history and the significant differences between them. It is also probably inefficient and leads to the lowering of morale. It is the likelihood of causing harm, and not the fact of being an airline pilot per se, that is relevant in deciding which employees in critical jobs to test.

So, even if knowledge of drug use is justifiable to prevent harm, we must be careful to limit this justification to a range of jobs and people where the potential for harm is clear and present. The jobs must be jobs that clearly can cause harm, and the specific employee should not be someone who has a history of reliability. Finally, the drugs being tested should be those drugs that have genuine potential for harm if used in the jobs in question.

Limitations on Drug-Testing Policies

Even when we identify those situations in which knowledge of drug use would be job relevant, we still need to examine whether some procedural limitations should not be placed upon the employer's testing for drugs. We have said when a real threat of harm exists and when evidence exists suggesting that a particular employee poses such a threat, an employer could be justified in knowing about drug use in order to prevent the potential harm. But we need to recognize that so long as the employer has the discretion for deciding when the potential for harm is clear and present, and for deciding which employees pose the threat of harm, the possibility of abuse is great. Thus, some policy limiting the employer's power is called for.

Just as criminal law imposes numerous restrictions protecting individual dignity and liberty on the state's pursuit of its goals, so we should expect that some restrictions be placed on employers to protect innocent employees from harm (including loss of job and damage to one's personal and professional reputation). Thus, some system of checks upon an employer's discretion in these matters seems advisable.

A drug-testing policy that requires all employees to submit to a drug test or to jeopardize their jobs would seem coercive and therefore unacceptable. Being placed in such a fundamentally coercive position of having to choose between one's job and one's privacy does not provide the conditions for a truly free consent. Policies that are unilaterally established by employers would likewise be unacceptable. Working with employees to develop company policy seems the only way to ensure that the policy will be fair to both parties.

Prior notice of testing would also be required in order to give employees the option of freely refraining from drug use. Preventing drug use is morally preferable to punishing users after the fact, because this approach treats employees as capable of making rational and informed decisions.

Further procedural limitations seem advisable as well. Employees should be notified of the results of the test, they should be entitled to appeal the results (perhaps through further tests by an independent laboratory), and the information obtained through tests ought to be kept confidential. In summary, limitations upon employer discretion for administering drug tests can be derived from the nature of the employment contract and from the recognition that drug testing is justified by the desire to prevent harm, not the desire to punish wrongdoing.

The Illegality Contention

At this point critics might note that the behavior which testing would try to deter is, after all, illegal. Surely this excuses any responsible employer from being overprotective of an employee's rights. The fact that an employee is doing something illegal should give the employer a right to that information about his or her private life. Thus it is not simply that drug use might pose a threat of harm to others, but that it is an *illegal* activity that threatens others. But again, we would argue that illegal activity itself is irrelevant to job performance. At best, *conviction* records might be relevant, but since drug tests are administered by private employers we are not only ignoring the question of conviction, we are also ignoring the fact that the employee has not even been arrested for the alleged illegal activity.

Further, even if the due process protections and the establishment of guilt are acknowledged, it still does not follow that employers have a claim to know about all illegal activity on the part of their employees.

Consider the following example: Suppose you were hiring an auditor whose job required certifying the integrity of your firm's tax and financial records. Certainly, the personal integrity of this employee is vital to adequate job performance. Would we allow the employer to conduct, with or without the employee's consent, an audit of the employee's own personal tax return? Certainly if we discover that this person has cheated on a personal tax return we will have evidence of illegal activity that is relevant to this person's ability to do the job. Given one's own legal liability for filing falsified statements, the employee's illegal activity also poses a threat to others. But surely, allowing private individuals to audit an employee's tax returns is too intrusive a means for discovering information about that employee's integrity. The government certainly would never allow this violation of an employee's privacy. It ought not to allow drug testing on the same grounds. Why tax returns should be protected in ways that urine, for example, is not, raises interesting questions of fairness. Unfortunately, this question would take us beyond the scope of this paper.

Voluntariness

A final problem that we also leave undeveloped concerns the voluntariness of employee consent. For most employees, being given the choice between submitting to a drug test and risking one's job by refusing an employer's request is not much of a decision at all. We believe that such decisions are less than voluntary and thereby hold that employers cannot escape our criticisms simply by including within the employment contract a drug-testing clause.[5] Furthermore, there is reason to believe that those most in need of job security will be those most likely to be subjected to drug testing. Highly skilled, professional employees with high job mobility and security will be in a stronger position to resist such intrusions than will less skilled, easily replaced workers. This is why we should not anticipate surgeons and airline pilots being tested and should not be surprised when public transit and factory workers are. A serious question of fairness arises here as well.

Drug use and drug testing seem to be our

most recent social "crisis." Politicians, the media, and employers expend a great deal of time and effort addressing this crisis. Yet, unquestionably, more lives, health, and money are lost each year to alcohol abuse than to marijuana, cocaine, and other controlled substances. We are well advised to be careful in considering issues that arise from such selective social concern. We will let other social commentators speculate on the reasons why drug use has received scrutiny while other white-collar crimes and alcohol abuse are ignored. Our only concern at this point is that such selective prosecution suggests an arbitrariness that should alert us to questions of fairness and justice.

In summary, then, we have seen that drug use is not always job relevant, and if drug use is not job relevant, information about it is certainly not job relevant. In the case of performance it may be a cause of some decreased performance, but it is the performance itself that is relevant to an employee's position, not what prohibits or enables that employee to do the job. In the case of potential harm being done by an employee under the influence of drugs, the drug use seems job relevant, and in this case drug testing to prevent harm might be legitimate. But how this is practicable is another question. It would seem that standard motor dexterity or mental dexterity tests given immediately prior to job performance are more effective in preventing harm, unless one concludes that drug use invariably and necessarily leads to harm. One must trust the individuals in any system for that system to work. One cannot police everything. Random testing might enable an employer to find drug users and to weed out the few to forestall possible future harm, but are the harms prevented sufficient to override the rights of privacy of the people who are innocent and to overcome the possible abuses we have mentioned? It seems not.

Clearly, a better method is to develop safety checks immediately prior to the performance of a job. Have a surgeon or a pilot or a bus driver pass a few reasoning and motor-skill tests before work. The cause of the lack of a skill, which lack might lead to harm, is really a secondary issue.

Notes

1. "A Defense of Employee Rights," Joseph DesJardins and John McCall, *Journal of Business Ethics* 4 (1985). We should emphasize that our concern is with the *moral* rights of privacy for employees and not with any specific or prospective *legal* rights. Readers interested in pursuing the legal aspects of employee drug testing should consult "Workplace Privacy Issues and Employer Screening Policies" by Richard Lehr and David Middlebrooks in *Employee Relations Law Journal*, vol. 11, no. 3, 407–421; and "Screening Workers for Drugs: A Legal and Ethical Framework," Mark Rothstein, in *Employee Relations Law Journal*, vol. 11, no. 3, 422–436.

2. "Privacy, Polygraphs, and Work," George Brenkert, *Journal of Business and Professional Ethics*, vol. 1, no. 1 (Fall 1981). For a more general discussion of privacy in the workplace see "Privacy in Employment" by Joesph DesJardins, in *Moral Rights in the Workplace*, edited by Gertrude Ezorsky (SUNY Press, 1987). A good resource for philosophical work on privacy can be found in "Recent Work on the Concept of Privacy" by W. A. Parent, in *American Philosophical Quarterly*, vol. 20 (Oct. 1983) 341–358.

3. *U.S. News and World Report*, 22 Aug. 1983; *Newsweek*, 6 May 1983.

4. Obviously we are speaking here of harms that go beyond the simple economic harm that results from unsatisfactory job performance. These economic harms are discussed in the first argument above. Further, we ignore such "harms" as providing bad role models for adolescents, harms often used to justify drug tests for professional athletes. We think it unreasonable to hold an individual responsible for the image he or she provides to others.

5. It might be argued that since we base our critique upon the contractual relationship between employers and employees, our entire position can be undermined by a clever employer who places within the contract a privacy waiver for drug tests. A full answer to this would require an account of the free and rational subject that

the contract model presupposes. While acknowledging that we need such an account to prevent just any contract from being morally legitimate, we will have to leave this debate to another time. Interested readers might consult "The Moral Contract between Employers and Employees" by Norman Bowie in *The Work Ethic in Business,* edited by W. M. Hoffman and T. J. Wyly (Cambridge, MA: Oelgeschlager and Gunn, 1981) 195–202.

19. The Federal Railroad Association Drug Test

The Federal Railroad Association decided to implement a policy to test employees for alcohol and drug use after a train accident. Although the U.S. Court of Appeals felt that this was a violation of the Fourth Amendment's injunction against warrantless search and seizure, the Supreme Court disagreed.

On August 2, 1985, the Federal Railroad Administration (FRA) issued regulations requiring mandatory blood and urine tests of railroad employees after certain accidents, incidents, and rule violations. After initial legal challenges by the Railroad Labor Executives' Association (RLEA), an association representing all crafts of railroad workers, these regulations went into effect on February 10, 1986. The RLEA sued the Department of Transportation and on February 11, 1988, the United States Court of Appeals ruled in favor of the RLEA and invalidated these regulations.

The regulations required alcohol and drug testing for all employees involved in accidents that resulted in fatalities, release of hazardous materials, injuries, or damage to railroad property exceeding $50,000. Further, the regulations required that employees submit to breath or urine tests when a supervisor has a reasonable suspicion that an employee is under the influence or impaired by alcohol or drugs. To require a urine test, two supervisors must have a reasonable suspicion, and if drug use is suspected, one of them must have been trained in spotting drug use. The railroads may also require testing when an employee

Reprinted by permission from Joseph R. DesJardins and John C. McCall, eds., *Contemporary Issues in Business Ethics,* 2nd ed. (Belmont, CA: Wadsworth, 1990).

violates certain rules of train operation. Refusal to provide a sample would result in a nine-month suspension.

The appeals court reasoned that these regulations constituted a violation of the Fourth Amendment's prohibition of "unreasonable searches." The railroad industry argued that since the regulations authorized testing by *private* companies and did not involve government action, the Fourth Amendment should not apply. The court rejected this argument, reasoning that "the government participates in a significant way" in the railroad industry and in the formulation of these regulations. Thus these regulations were held to involve a "search" in the relevant sense.

But are these regulations "reasonable"? Ordinarily, a warrant is needed to make a search "reasonable," but the Supreme Court has ruled that certain warrantless searches are constitutional. The appeals court ruled that the railroad case failed to meet the necessary standards for warrantless searches on two grounds. First, the standard of reasonableness requires that the search be based upon "individualized" or "particularized" suspicion. The court decided that accidents, incidents, and rule violations were not themselves sufficiently reasonable grounds for testing any one railroad employee, much less an entire train crew. Further, these tests were found not to be reasonable on grounds relating to the very goals that justified interfering with employees in the first place. Specifically, the court ruled that the goal of the testing is to measure *present* intoxication or impairment, but the tests themselves can detect only metabolites of drugs, which may remain in the body's system for days or weeks after the intoxication or impairment. The court left some room for testing, but only when individualized suspicion and observable symptoms of present impairment exist. The drug test could then provide confirming evidence and a sound basis for disciplinary action.

The Department of Transportation appealed this decision to the Supreme Court.

On March 21, 1989, in a 7 to 2 decision, the Supreme Court overturned the appeals court judgment and ruled that drug testing was constitutionally valid. The majority opinion stated that employees' expectation of privacy can be overriden by the safety concerns of the railroads. The Court also ruled that in this case "individualized suspicion" was not necessary, thus allowing drug tests for the entire crew of a train involved in an accident.

In November 1988 the Department of Transportation announced plans to require drug tests for over 4 million workers in the trucking, airline, and mass transit industries. This Supreme Court decision would seem to remove the last obstacle to this program.

---

20.   The Case against Compulsory Casefinding in Controlling AIDS

Lawrence O. Gostin, William J. Curran, and Mary E. Clark

Gostin, Curran, and Clark argue against HIV testing and general screening on the grounds that such programs will be of little value in protecting public health but will entail substantial human and economic costs. In the absence of any significant treatment for AIDS, forced testing does little to help the infected person and, in fact, may be worse than voluntary testing. They go on to discuss proposed criteria for mandatory testing, high-risk groups, transmission risks, use and consequences of the tests, and the possibility of less intrusive means of testing. The authors examine proposals for mandatory HIV testing in schools and in premarital screening.

. . . Mandatory screening programs for selected populations are unlikely to achieve any clear public health benefit. Knowledge of seropositivity cannot be used to alleviate a person's infectious condition since there is currently no vaccine for prevention or treatment which cures HIV infection. HIV is unlike venereal disease, where the chain of infection can be broken by simple antibiotic treatment.

From "The Case against Compulsory Casefinding in Controlling AIDS—Testing, Screening, and Reporting," *American Journal of Law and Medicine* 12 (1987): 7–53. Footnotes have been omitted. Reprinted by permission.

Thus, even with early information of a person's serological status, medicine cannot alter the cycle of infection. Although knowledge of seropositivity enables a person to seek early treatment with such developing therapies as azidothymidine (AZT), AZT presently is not clinically indicated for asymptomatic HIV carriers. Accordingly, early knowledge of seropositivity does not produce any advantage in enabling the person to seek early treatment. Members of high risk groups who clinically present with signs of immunodeficiency can be tested for HIV antibodies for diagnostic purposes with their informed consent. It is difficult to sustain an argument for compulsory screening of large populations in the hope that some might have access to an experimental treatment sooner than they would otherwise by visiting their physician at the first sign of a clinical problem.

In the absence of an effective vaccine or treatment, public health arguments for compulsory screening of large populations must be based upon the premise that widespread serological testing will lead to behavior modification among persons who test positive. The critical unanswered question, however, is whether knowledge of seropositivity influences behavior and in what direction. The appropriate precautions in personal conduct to reduce the spread of HIV are already well-known to most members of high risk groups. The spread of HIV can be reduced only through the willingness of individuals to avoid unsafe intimate sexual and needle sharing behavior. The introduction of compulsory screening may have the reverse effect of causing persons vulnerable to HIV to avoid coming forward for testing, counselling, and treatment.

Given the absence of an established prevention or treatment, and the lack of any evidence that compulsory screening would lead to voluntary changes in behavior, the public health benefit of such a program is likely to be marginal or even counterproductive. Balanced against this marginal public health benefit is the potential for substantial harm to those screened. Each person screened, whether seropositive or not, must submit involuntarily to the taking of a blood sample and the collection of sensitive health care information. Moreover, collection of information creates a demand for its use. Unauthorized disclosure of that information could result in opprobrium among family and friends and discrimination in employment, housing, and insurance. The adverse consequences of screening are serious enough for true positives, even though the great majority are likely to be asymptomatic. In addition, there will be a number of individuals who test positive in the ELISA and supplementary tests, but who do not harbor the virus. The price of screening includes the potential for stigma and discrimination to the false positive population.

Widespread screening has public resource,

as well as personal, implications. Screening requires the administration and interpretation of the ELISA together with supplementary procedures. This entails significant expense for the administration of laboratories, test equipment, and personnel. The costs of investing in a screening program must be measured against similar levels of expenditures needed for research, education, and counselling.

The personal and economic costs engendered by a program of compulsory screening are likely to be disproportionate to the marginal public health benefit. The objective of screening is to obtain shifts in behavior and early treatment among groups most vulnerable to HIV infection. This objective can be achieved in a more effective and less restrictive way by a comprehensive voluntary program of public health education and professional testing and counselling services. Those inclined to seek treatment and behavior control are likely to respond to cost free, readily available education and services. Such a voluntary program would achieve the same public health advantages as a mandatory program, but without the significant detriments of the widespread use of compulsion.

Next, a series of criteria are proposed for assessing the merits of compulsory screening. Then, these criteria are applied, together with the general arguments just made, to specific legislative screening proposals.

Proposed Criteria for Assessing Mandatory Population Screening

. . . In this section, we will develop general standards for use in cases where compulsory screening is proposed. No single formula can always determine whether screening of particular populations is appropriate public policy. Yet, attempts to evaluate each proposal without a systematic theory of analysis could reach inconsistent results. Accordingly, general criteria should be applied in each case where screening is proposed. In most cases, a reasoned positive response to each of the following criteria is desirable before concluding that compulsory screening is warranted.

High Reservoir of Infection

Screening necessarily entails a restriction on individuals' rights to privacy; it involves blood sampling and the collection of sensitive information. Screening expends scarce health care resources, including the cost of using professionals to administer the test and laboratory equipment and personnel to analyze results. Moreover, properly conducted screening programs should provide health care information and professional counselling, adding to the cost of the program. Wherever possible, therefore, screening programs should be narrowly targeted to select populations with a potentially high reservoir of infection, such as a program administered in a treatment center for sexually transmitted diseases or for IV drug abuse.

Screening programs in large populations with a predictably low frequency of infection, such as pre-marital screening, have a number of disadvantages: a large number of people will have their privacy unnecessarily invaded; procedures will have to be adopted to keep a large amount of health care data confidential; and a significant amount of scarce resources will be expended. Finally, even the ELISA test loses a great deal of its accuracy when it is applied to a population with a low reservoir of infection. Accordingly, the application of the ELISA test to a general population will create a high ratio of false to true positives.

Significant Risk of Transmission

To establish the effectiveness of a screening program, it is necessary to demonstrate not only a high reservoir of infection, but also a high risk of transmission. Effective screening programs require a setting where transmission of infection is reasonably likely to occur. Screening decisions should be grounded upon the best scientific and epidemiologic evidence relating to transmission of the infection. To date, four primary means of transmission have been clearly established: sexual contact involving the exchange of bodily fluids, intravenous

drug administration with contaminated needles, use of contaminated blood or blood products, and in utero or intrapartum transmission or transmission postnatally possibly from ingestion of breast milk. There has been considerable research into the possibility of transmission by other routes such as by casual association or intimate caring and nursing functions undertaken within families and health care settings. There is increasingly strong evidence indicating that the virus is not transmitted through casual contact. Thus, there is no public health justification for screening where the only expected association among the population is casual, such as in school settings. However, where the population (e.g., prostitutes or IV drug users) or the environment in which the population operates (e.g., bathhouses) involves the possible exchange of bodily fluids, the public health justification for screening is stronger.

Effective Use of Test Results

If all persons within a selected population are to be screened, the resulting information must be used effectively to reduce the spread of infection. If the precautions that might be taken cannot reduce transmission, there is no purpose to a screening program. Further, if the proposed action or precautions should be taken whether or not the test is given, the action raises the question whether systematic population screening is needed. For example, if hospitals have adopted or should adopt general safety precautions in handling all specimens whether or not they are infected, the rationale for screening specimens is undermined.

Critical Consequences of Screening Should Not Outweigh Benefits

Screening may have many critical consequences for the individual. Screening programs require the collection of personal information. This information may be disclosed to family, employers, landlords, insurers, and others, possibly resulting in opprobrium and discriminatory action against the infected person. Where public health officials screen populations, the information may be used as a condition precedent to other more intrusive public health actions such as sexual contact tracing or isolation. Screening programs and ensuing intrusive actions may have some effect in reducing HIV transmission. Yet, the personal or social costs of these actions may be disproportionate to their expected benefits. The "critical consequences" criterion involves a judgment as to whether the health benefit of screening outweighs the personal, social, and economic costs for those who test positive.

No Less Restrictive or Intrusive Means

Public health law should protect the health of the community with as few restrictions on the rights of individuals as possible. From an individual perspective, this criterion is important because those subjected to public health actions should be allowed as much freedom as possible without imposing significant costs on the public health. The principle of the least restrictive alternative can also further public health interests. A major strategy in combatting the spread of AIDS is to foster voluntary cooperation, such as through notification of contacts and reduction of high risk behavior. The use of involuntary, highly restrictive measures may deter members of high risk groups from cooperating with public health officials or from attending public health programs, such as clinics for the treatment of sexually transmitted diseases or the treatment of drug or alcohol abuse.

Health care professionals may have difficulty with the principle of the least restrictive alternative because public health measures traditionally have been predicated on the notion that it is best to err on the side of caution. Under this philosophy, public health takes precedence over individual rights, and if a control measure might promote the public health, it should be implemented. But, the principle of the least restrictive alternative is not necessarily inconsistent with this view. It does not require a less effective measure merely because it is less intrusive. It requires a less intrusive measure only if it is equally, or more efficacious.

It would be an error to implement a compulsory screening program until the proposed criteria have been applied to the program. . . .

Screening of Selected Populations: Illustrative Cases

Screening in Schools

United States Public Health Service guidelines on "Education and Foster Care of Children Infected with HTLV-III/LAV" advise against mandatory screening as a condition of school entry. The guidelines recommend that infected school-age children be allowed to attend school and after-school day care programs. This is particularly so where they exhibit no higher risk behavior patterns or conditions such as abnormal biting, drooling, open sores, or bleeding. Despite these recommendations, a number of jurisdictions have sought to automatically exclude HIV-infected children from school. A concurrent resolution has been proposed in Congress stating that public schools should not permit students with AIDS to attend regular classes and that schools should make alternative arrangements for education. Although the resolution is cast as a way of "respecting the education" of children with AIDS, its impact would be to isolate these children from their peers. Exclusion of children who test positive for HIV antibody is a critical consequence of testing; the merits of such exclusion are examined below.

1. Risk of Transmission in Schools. None of the identified high risk behaviors are an inherent part of school activities, and they can be virtually ruled out as means of transmission among younger children. The great majority of children with HIV infection contract the virus from their infected mothers. If evidence emerged that some schools had a high reservoir of infection and that transmission was occurring through shared needles or sexual activities, measures to control these activities could be legally justified. It should be noted that these activities are prohibited already on school grounds.

The Public Health Service conclusion that there is no risk of communication of the virus in a normal school environment is based upon a number of studies of families with an infected member. Studies demonstrate that casual contact within the secretion-rich environment of the family does not cause transmission of HIV. There is also evidence demonstrating the difficulty of transmitting HIV in health care settings. While rare cases of parenteral transmission have occurred, no case of transmission from such causes as open wounds or attending to sanitary needs of patients has been documented.

The potential for viral transmission in schools through child-to-child contact is purely theoretical, supported by not a single documented case. Parental fears have been increased by reports of live virus isolated in tears and saliva. Yet, attempts to isolate HIV in saliva are generally quite unsuccessful. All available evidence points to school children having the most remote possibility of contracting the virus on school grounds.

School children are perceived to be a vulnerable population, and it is understandable that parents would adopt a highly conservative formula for risk management; and lethal risk is unacceptable if it can be prevented by exclusion of the infected child. Yet, negligible risks are part of life and society accepts them. Any social activity entails some small risk such as going to school in a motor vehicle or crossing the street. As long as the risks of an activity are outweighed by the benefits of that activity, society condones the activity.

2. The Critical Consequences of Exclusion from School. Balanced against the remote risk entailed in allowing infected children to attend school is the critical consequence of excluding them. Compelling a child to forego the enriching experience of social integration at school is a harsh consequence. Education is a constitutionally protected right. Even if basic education could be provided elsewhere, exclusion denies the child the right to association with his or her peers. In *New York State Association for Retarded Children, Inc.* v. *Carey* (612 F.2d 644, 1979), the Second Circuit Court of Appeals held that exclusion or isolation of students, merely because they have a medical condition (hepatitis B) that may pose a remote risk of transmission, violates section 504 of the Federal Rehabilitation Act of 1983. The court found that such students were "handicapped" within the meaning of the statute and were unlawfully excluded from participation in a federally assisted activity on the basis of that handicap. The *Carey* court stated that even separate educational facilities would discriminate against infected children as such a separation would "limit the extent to which they can participate in school-wide activities such as meals, recesses, and assemblies, and will reinforce the stigma to which these children have already been subjected."

The decision in *Carey* that there was no justification in excluding hepatitis B carriers from school should similarly apply to children with HIV. Since the risk of transmission of hepatitis B is greater than HIV, the rationale for exclusion of children with AIDS is even less apparent. . . .

The exclusion of children with AIDS or HIV infection from school represents a restriction of freedom of association and educational benefit. This deprivation is a high price to exact in exchange for a negligible benefit to public health, and thus violates one of the proposed criteria for screening programs. Therefore, whether viewed from a constitutional or statutory perspective, policies which automatically exclude such children from school are unjustified. . . .

Pre-Marital Screening

Pre-marital screening is one of the most frequently proposed measures in state legislatures. Under such proposals an HIV antibody test would be required prior to the issuance of a marriage license. This is similar to current requirements in many states for a recognized serological test for syphilis; if the test is positive, proof that the infection is not communicable is necessary before the certificate is issued. No state, however, has yet adopted a pre-marital screening program for HIV infection.

Despite the current popularity of pre-marital screening proposals, application of the five criteria indicate that such screening would not be effective in controlling the spread of

HIV. Under state legislative proposals, pre-marital screening would be required of all applicants for a marriage license. If implemented in every state, this would require serological testing for approximately 1.7 million couples. In a normal healthy population, approximately four out of every 10,000 people are infected with HIV. Thus, the reservoir of infection among marriage license applicants is likely to be exceedingly low, particularly in states with a low incidence of HIV. Use of the ELISA test on a large population with a low frequency of infection would cause potentially insurmountable problems. The ELISA test is highly accurate when applied within a high risk population, but it would produce a significant number of false positive results when applied to a normal healthy population. Under optimal circumstances, a single ELISA test would be expected to produce at least one or two false positives for every true positive within a healthy population. A confirmatory Western Blot test would sharply reverse the ratio of true to false positives to approximately seventy to one. Yet, when such ratios are applied to a large population, the total number of false positives would be significant.

Pre-marital testing programs present other problems. The state must fully plan the program and incur the expense of providing the laboratories, test equipment, and personnel necessary for administering and interpreting the ELISA test, administering a second ELISA and Western Blot test for all positive testing applicants, and providing the professional psychological and social work services needed to counsel and support confirmed positive applicants. A testing program, without competent laboratory services to ensure accuracy and a full range of counselling and support services, would fail to meet any valid public health objective.

More important than the economic cost of implementing a system of pre-marital screening is the personal cost to individual privacy. A pre-marital screening requirement tests a large population, the majority of which has not been exposed to HIV. Information concerning those who test positive, including false positives, will be conveyed to prospective spouses and kept by public health officials.

The substantial economic and privacy costs

incurred in a widespread program of pre-marital screening may be justified by a strong public health benefit. The objectives of a pre-marital screening program are to identify positive-testing individuals and to prevent transmission of the virus to spouses and offspring. Prevention of transmission may be achieved either by prohibiting marriage to a positive testing applicant, or by educating the couple about the dangers of unprotected sex and childbirth. Before enacting such a proposal, a legislature must determine whether a pre-marital screening program would achieve this objective or whether less intrusive measures would be as effective.

Since marriage is not necessary for intercourse or impregnation, pre-marital screening will not prevent all cases of transmission to the partners and offspring. Many applicants for marriage will already have had sexual relations. Further, a pre-marital screening requirement does not assure any change in future sexual or child-rearing behavior.

Some pre-marital screening proposals would withhold a marriage license where one party is HIV positive. In the venereal disease context, the existence of antibiotics to cure the syphilis infection makes pre-marital screening feasible. Since there is no prevention of or cure for the HIV infection, however, the legislature could not require a therapeutic intervention as a condition of approval for the marriage certificate. It would be contrary to public policy to bar marriage to sero-positive individuals. Such a proposal would face serious constitutional challenge because the Supreme Court in *Zablocki* v. *Redhail* (434 U.S. 374, 1978) reaffirmed that marriage is a fundamental right. The Court stated that if "a statutory classification significantly interferes with the exercise of a fundamental right, it cannot be upheld unless it is supported by sufficiently important state interests and is closely tailored to effectuate only those interests." Courts may not find a tight fit between HIV antibody screening and a compelling public purpose due to the screening's unproven impact on impeding the spread of infection to spouses or offspring.

Two other alternatives could achieve the public health objective in a less intrusive manner. Screening could be offered on a voluntary basis, and the results used solely to inform both partners of their serologic status and to determine the need for counselling. Test results would be kept confidential. Thus, partners could choose to enter the marriage prepared to engage in safe methods of sex and birth control. The other alternative has been passed by the California legislature. California imposes a duty on public health officials to provide full information concerning the risk groups for HIV, the importance of testing, and the need for safer behavior to all marriage license applicants. Legislatures considering this approach should provide free and confidential testing and counselling services as an adjunct to this informational requirement. Members of high risk groups intending to marry could thus be provided with a needed incentive to undergo testing voluntarily. . . .

Individual Confidentiality and Public Health

The screening of selective populations involves the systematic collection of information about the health status of a class of individuals. Screening creates a conflict between the individual's interest in controlling access to personal information and society's right to know and use this information for public health purposes. The conflict between public health and confidentiality is apparent on two levels. First, knowledge that a person is infectious may create a duty to breach confidentiality in order to protect third parties. Second, reporting statutes require states to collect confidential personal information which they use for epidemiologic purposes to control the spread of infection. Balancing individual and collective rights is the most difficult task of legislators and judges when considering the use of information obtained from screening programs.

Confidentiality

Individuals infected with HIV are concerned with maintaining the confidentiality of their health status. HIV infection is associated with sexual practice and drug use, universally regarded as personal and sensitive activities. Consequently, the process of case identification *per se* triggers a concern of confidentiality. Also, the majority of people infected with HIV in the United States are members of groups subject to persistent prejudice and discrimination. Unauthorized disclosure of a person's serological status can lead to social opprobrium among family and friends, and to loss of employment, housing, and insurance. There is also a wide, constitutionally-protected zone of privacy which extends to intimate personal relationships. There are public health pressures to obtain detailed, sensitive information through medical surveillance and contact tracing, such as intrusive observation and forced disclosure of sexual partners.

Persons at risk of HIV infection, therefore, have strong grounds for desiring personal privacy and confidentiality of medical information. Their cooperation with public health authorities and treatment centers is dependent upon expectations of confidentiality. Efforts to control the spread of AIDS currently rely upon voluntary restraint of behaviors likely to spread HIV. Therefore, the public health objective should be to influence the behavior of those infected with HIV. Trust in and compliance with public health programs depend upon the maintenance of confidentiality.

Most state public health statutes contain provisions protecting confidentiality. Typically, these provisions apply to venereal or sexually transmitted diseases (STDs) because of the deeply rooted personal values implicated by sexual behavior. Currently, one out of the twelve major jurisdictions studied by the federal government reports AIDS as a sexually transmitted disease; the remaining eleven classify it either as a communicable disease or simply as a reportable disease. This presents a major obstacle since communicable diseases are not generally covered by strong confidentiality statutes. While classifying AIDS as a sexually transmitted disease strengthens the confidentiality protections, it also makes individuals potentially subject to compulsory measures such as quarantine, which are often specifically targeted at such diseases.

Several states have enacted legislation or

regulations to protect the confidentiality of HIV antibody test results. There is considerable variation in the confidentiality protection offered within these states. For example, California protects test results from subpoena, while Massachusetts simply requires laboratories to develop unspecified procedures for confidentiality.

A public health confidentiality statute should contain the following elements: a specific requirement that informed consent be given before the release of any information or records relating to known or suspected cases of infection, an exemption protecting the information from subpoena, and a testimonial privilege protecting state and local health officials, private health care professionals, and other holders of information. . . .

Conclusion

Every individual who becomes infected with HIV has approximately a 35 percent chance of developing clinical AIDS and ultimately dying of the disease. The protection of uninfected persons is critical. Infected individuals must be identified on a voluntary basis, and a comprehensive program of focused education and counselling is essential. To accomplish this, there must be a fully planned distribution of test sites in areas with high infection rates, and accessible, high quality public education and individual counselling services should be provided. This requires a political commitment of major resources toward prevention and infection control strategies. Yet, the Office of Technological Assessment in February, 1985 noted that "relatively few funds were allocated to public education" (Herdman, Behney, and Milkey, *Review of the Public Health Service's Response to AIDS: A Technical Memorandum*, 1985).

States must also enact statutes to protect the confidentiality of sensitive information obtained during testing, counselling, and contact tracing. Only by establishing a basis of trust in the privacy of public health programs can cooperation from vulnerable groups be fostered.

High quality testing and counselling services can help promote behavior change. Experience with hepatitis B virus, which is transmitted in much the same way as HIV, has demonstrated that voluntary compliance can reduce the spread of the disease. Emerging evidence on AIDS shows significant voluntary alteration of behavior is necessary to reduce the spread of the disease within vulnerable groups. In the absence of evidence that compulsory testing, screening, and reporting alters behavior more effectively than voluntary education and counselling programs, federal and state public health authorities should design their strategies and devote their resources toward voluntary services for groups vulnerable to HIV.

21. HIV Testing: Voluntary, Mandatory, or Routine?

Theresa L. Crenshaw

A member of the President's Commission on the HIV epidemic, Dr. Theresa L. Crenshaw argues that mandatory HIV testing will be beneficial and that the concerns about it are unwarranted. She asserts that AIDS victims are already underground, that testing is reliable, that testing will have tremendous social utility, and that problems of confidentiality and privacy are, as in other testing situations, entirely manageable.

The AIDS virus is formidable. For a preventable disease, it continues to spread at an alarming rate. As long as 90 percent of those who are infected—1.5 million people or more in the United States—don't know it and continue to spread it to others, we have little hope of controlling this epidemic.

Yet, there are many dilemmas and questions that face us as individuals and as a society. Isn't it better for a person who is infected not to know? How can one expect an infected person to stop having sex when he or she is already suffering more than a human being can bear? Are condoms sufficient protection? Is testing dependable? How can we protect the civil rights of the ill and the civil rights of the healthy?

There is no simple solution. Testing alone is not enough. We need all of our resources: common sense, sexual integrity, compassion, love, exclusivity, education, discipline, testing, condoms, and spermicides—to name just a few. We also need an emphatic, positive message that promotes *quality* sex rather than *quantity* sex. Multiple partners and casual sex are not in the best interest of health, but within an exclusive relationship quality sex can thrive.

In this context, perhaps we could take an in-depth look at the controversial issue of HIV-testing. Widespread voluntary testing, if encouraged by health officials and physicians, will most probably be successful, making widespread mandatory testing unnecessary. The

From *The Humanist*, January/February 1988, pp. 29–34. Reprinted by permission.

general population will cooperate. However, under certain circumstances, required or routine testing might be considered and could be implemented whenever common sense dictates without the feared repercussions of quarantine and discrimination. Regardless of whether testing is voluntary, required, or routine, maintaining confidentiality is critical. It is vitally important to understand that public health officials are trained to maintain confidentiality in all cases; they do not put advertisements in the newspaper or call a person's employer.

Confidentiality is nonetheless a genuine concern. Lists of infected persons have been stolen. There is probably no way humanly possible to ensure against any and all breaches of confidentiality throughout the United States and the world. It would be unrealistic to falsely assure individuals that confidentiality would be 100 percent secure. On the other hand, we must do everything within our power to come as close as possible to 100 percent confidentiality and to assure those who are concerned that these efforts are being made. There are many things we can do to improve our recording and to improve confidentiality systems. These aspects are being investigated and will hopefully be implemented by federal, state, and local authorities.

An encouraging point is that in Colorado, where HIV-positive status is reportable and contact tracing is routine, *there has not been one episode of breach of confidentiality*, demonstrating that when extra care is taken there can be great success. Often forgotten is the fact that confidentiality is equally important for voluntary, required, and routine testing. It must be applied to *all* forms of testing, and it must not be used to distinguish between them.

Mandatory testing brings to mind visions of concentration camps and human beings subjected to arbitrary and insensitive public health tactics. In practice, however, nothing could be further from the truth. Urine tests and blood counts are routinely required upon hospital admission. If a patient refuses, he or she will generally not be accepted by the hospital and certainly won't be allowed to undergo surgery. That's mandatory testing, but we take it in stride. And it has no hint of repressiveness; it is simply a reasonable measure for the protection and well-being of both the patient and the hospital.

Likewise, tests for syphilis are mandatory in many states. In many countries, certain tests and inoculations are required before one can travel. In the not-so-distant past, health cards had to be carried by travelers along with their passports, proving that they had had certain immunizations. There is also required testing of school children for childhood diseases, which includes the tuberculin skin test, and various inoculations, without which they are not permitted to enter school. These are just a few examples of mandatory testing or treatments that are routine in our everyday lives—and that do not compromise our civil rights. However, since the term *mandatory* is emotionally charged, substituting the term *required* might more accurately reflect the intent.

Our society takes in stride sensible, necessary tests and treatments which in many circumstances are required in order to travel abroad or to perform certain jobs. However, strenuous arguments against any form of required testing for AIDS persist. The following are some of the issues most commonly raised by opponents of mandatory testing. I have attempted to analyze each argument.

Mandatory testing will drive infected individuals underground. They will hide out and refuse to be tested.

Since 90 percent of the 1.5 million or more individuals who are infected within the United States don't even know it, *they are already underground.* While certain numbers of people may use creative methods to avoid testing procedures, we would be able to reduce that percentage of people who do not know their HIV status to 10 percent instead of 90 percent, because most people would cooperate voluntarily.

Testing would cause more problems than it solves because huge numbers of people would receive false positive test results. Their lives would be destroyed by such test results.

The enzyme linked immunosorbent assay, or ELISA test, does have a high percentage of false positives, just as the tuberculin skin test has a high percentage of false positives. *That does not mean it is without value.* Whenever a test such as this is performed, a physician never stops at screening tests. Follow-up studies are required to confirm a positive test result. For example, with tuberculosis, chest X-rays and sputum cultures are performed until a positive diagnosis of tuberculosis can be made. The tuberculin skin test is used to determine whether there are indications for further studies. The AIDS antibody test is used in the same fashion. If the ELISA is positive, it should be repeated again and the Western Blot test performed. If these are all positive, the likelihood of the result being a false positive approaches zero (per 400,000, according to Dr. James Curran of the Centers for Disease Control). Immune system studies can then be done and, although it is expensive and somewhat logistically difficult, a patient who wants additional proof of infection can request actual viral cultures. Since recent research demonstrates that there can be a year or more during which the virus is present but antibodies have not yet developed—the so-called window in time—the far greater problem with testing is the high number of false negatives that still will be missed. Another study by A. Ranki et al., in the September 12, 1987, issue of *Lancet*, indicates that up to 36 percent of ELISAs are false negatives in those individuals who have had sex with an infected person. As you see, the screening test is not perfect. There will be false negatives that escape detection, so the test should be repeated periodically. All false positives would be followed up with additional tests until a confirmed positive result can be established. In the near future, we will have a test for the virus itself, solving some of the problems we now face, especially the "window in time" between infection and antibody development.

There is no point in having yourself tested because there is no cure.

Although there is no cure, and indeed *because* there is no cure, it is even more essential to be tested and to know what your antibody status is, because, if you test positive, you must take every precaution not to infect another person. If this disease were curable, perhaps we could be more cavalier. But since we must protect individuals in society from it, we must motivate those who are already infected not to infect anyone else. To assume that everyone should and will behave as though they were infected is optimistic and unreasonable, although I think many can achieve this end. It is unlikely, however, for an individual to take complete responsibility for his or her actions without definitive knowledge of infection. Even then it is a challenge.

There are other reasons for being tested. Someone who tests positive will live longer if counseled not to become exposed unnecessarily to other infections by visiting sick friends at home or in the hospital or by traveling extensively to countries where foreign organisms can cause unusual infections. Additional health counseling can lead to a healthier lifestyle, the avoidance of other opportunistic infections or cofactors, improved nutrition, and planning for the future—which includes estate planning, a will, and making other practical arrangements as indicated.

Perhaps the most important reason for being tested early is that many of the treatments becoming available are more effective the earlier they are instituted. If you know you are HIV-positive, you can apply for research projects for experimental protocols or arrange to take AZT (which is now available) or other similar drugs when they become approved for clinical use. In short, the reasons for being tested far outweigh the reasons for not being tested.

Testing is undesirable for many individuals who are unable to cope with the knowledge that they are infected. These people are better off not being tested.

Anyone who is asked whether or not they think they will be able to cope with the news of an HIV-positive test result would ordinarily say no. It is normal not to be able to cope well with a deadly, incurable disease. Most people who are tested receive pretest counseling. Often pretest counseling, advertently or inadvertently, dissuades individuals from being tested. At a recent conference in New York cosponsored by the American Medical Association and the Centers for Disease Control, one physician said that, with just three minutes on the telephone with someone inquiring about being tested, he succeeds in talking 57 percent of potential patients out of being tested. In the anonymous testing centers, we need only look at the numbers of people who show up for testing compared to those who leave without being tested to assess the effectiveness of some counseling in discouraging testing.

Yet, imagine an analogous situation for a woman needing a breast biopsy. If the physician asked, "Are you sure you want this biopsy? Do you realize that the results could show that you have cancer? Are you prepared to live with that? If the biopsy is positive, you'll need to have your breast removed. Do you think you can cope? How do you think your husband will feel about you sexually? What if the cancer is incurable and you're given a short time to live? Do you think you can handle that?" Of course, the answer to most of these questions would be "no," and many women needing breast biopsies would not pursue them. Instead, doctors help a woman confront the need for the biopsy. They support her in helping her to deal with the natural reluctance and fear involved and help her to find the courage and determination to proceed.

We must do the same with AIDS testing. Instead of asking, "Are you sure you want this test?" and "Do you think you can cope?" the physician, psychologist, or therapist must take the same kind of approach they do with other necessary or valuable medical procedures. Assume it is a good idea to be tested. Compliment the person for his or her courage and self-responsibility in pursuing the test. Let each person know that you intend to help him or her get through some of the difficulties and will be there to talk in detail about the issues should that person's test turn out to be positive. Let patients know that you appreciate the courage it takes for them to proceed with the test. Emphasize that the test will be of value to them whether it turns out to be negative or positive. By taking the approach that it is valuable and worthwhile to be tested, counselors can help patients deal with their fear and discomfort rather than contribute to it. Many counseling centers are beginning to change to this approach, but too many still follow the one that effectively discourages testing.

Testing isn't cost effective except in high-risk populations. Required testing will simply waste a lot of money getting nothing but negative results.

A negative result is exceedingly valuable and can be utilized to maintain health. Any individual who tests negative should be given written, taped, or individual information on how to remain uninfected so that they are motivated to protect that fortunate status. Some studies have found that an HIV-negative result alone is sometimes not sufficient to motivate a change in sexual behavior. It is exceedingly worthwhile to test negative, especially if it can be combined with some information or counseling so that the individual can be given an opportunity to remain HIV-negative for life.

The cost of testing the entire population and counseling those who are HIV-positive on how not to spread the disease is a fraction of the cost that would be required to care for those who would otherwise become infected.

Testing is no good. The day after someone has the test they could become infected. That's why safe sex cards don't work.

It is true that moments after blood has been drawn for an AIDS test the person could have sex and become infected. There is no question that the test is only as good as the behavior that follows it. On the other hand, if a person gets tested fairly regularly (every six months or once a year) and you meet that person five years after their first test and learn that that person has had the discipline and the concern about his or her health to remain negative for that period of time, it tells you something about that person's judgment and health sta-

tus. One test may not carry a great deal of meaning, except to the individual who knows whether or not his or her behavior has been risky since the last test. On the other hand, a series of tests that are negative makes a statement of great importance.

It is also important to emphasize that testing is not enough. I do not support safe sex cards if they are used in singles clubs with the recommendation that anyone who tests negative and carries a card can have sex with anyone else holding a similar card. Multiple partners multiplies the possible error. On the other hand, I think that one or more tests are very valuable if used as a prerequisite to a monogamous relationship and if condoms and spermicide are also used until at least a year has passed to protect against the window in time mentioned earlier.

If you institute mandatory testing, what are you going to do with the individuals who test positive? Isolate them? Quarantine them?

Society will do the same thing with individuals who test HIV-positive on mandatory testing that they will do with any individuals who test HIV-positive on widespread voluntary testing. Most people who are fighting mandatory testing are actually fighting quarantine, afraid that one will lead to the other. I would much prefer that they support the valuable and meaningful step of testing and fight the issue of quarantine, rather than fight step two to avoid step three.

You should not test because some people will panic when they are told of a positive result and commit suicide.

This is one of the most worrisome consequences of testing. It is understandable that someone who tests positive would fleetingly consider taking his or her own life, and some individuals might progress to actually doing so. This is one of the reasons a positive test result should never be given by phone. A patient should be called to see his or her physician or counselor or to the anonymous testing center so that he or she can be counseled extensively at that moment.

There are no guarantees that will ensure that someone would not commit suicide, but we must do everything humanly possible to prevent it—short of not testing. The reason for this is simple: if that person were not tested and did not know that he or she were HIV-positive, the odds are good that that person would take someone else's life unknowingly through continued sexual activity. So, even in this case, informing and counseling the individual are preferable to allowing that person to remain ignorant and perhaps infect not one but many others, thereby sentencing them to death.

Contact tracing is of no value, requires too much manpower, and violates privacy.

Contact tracing is *always* voluntary. A patient must be willing to identify sexual partners for it to be successful. When the public health department performs contact tracing, it contacts the sexual partner without giving him or her the name of the person involved. Instead, health officials say, "It has come to our attention that you have been exposed to the AIDS virus and it is important that you be tested in order to determine whether you have become infected." It is true that if the individual has had only one sexual partner in his or her entire life he or she will be able to deduce who the person was. Since this is the exception rather than the general rule, and since the incubation period of this disease might go back a decade or more, in most cases it would be very difficult to identify the other individual involved.

Under what circumstances could required testing be instituted, and what rationale would justify implementing this system?

Hospital admission is an important opportunity for mandatory or required testing. In order to give the best care to a patient who is HIV-positive, a physician must know the patient's antibody status. A physician would treat a post-operative infection or any other infection far more aggressively with antibiotics in a patient that the physician knew to be HIV-positive than in one who did not have the potential for immune system compromise. Anyone admitted with an infection would be watched more closely if HIV-positive and would probably be treated earlier than someone whose immune system was more dependable.

Many argue that the doctor should use his or her discretion on whom to test. I argue that that feeds into a discriminatory bias suggesting that one can prejudge who might be suspiciously gay. There are no indicators in the healthy HIV-positive person to cause a physician to suspect which person needs testing.

One case history was particularly convincing that physicians need the test to help make a proper diagnosis. A woman called a television program in San Francisco. She said that she had AIDS. Several months before, she had flown to San Diego to donate blood for her mother's elective surgery. Subsequently, she returned to San Francisco, had several additional sexual partners, and eventually was admitted to San Francisco General Hospital for acute respiratory distress. She was treated for allergies and asthma but almost died. During the time that she was in the hospital, she received a letter from the blood bank informing her that her blood had tested HIV-positive. She asked her roommate to open the letter. The doctors then made the diagnosis of Pneumocystis pneumonia, treated her, and she was discharged from the hospital a few days later.

San Francisco General is one of the hospitals that has the most experience in diagnosing and dealing with the AIDS virus. They missed this diagnosis and might not have made it without the aid of the mandatory AIDS test performed by the blood bank. The patient would have died without a change in treatment approach. It seems to me that if such a sophisticated treatment center can miss the diagnosis it would be common in less experienced hospitals. Physicians need the assistance of this kind of testing to guide them.

This also pertains to mental hospital admissions. AIDS dementia and central nervous system infection are proving to be more common than uncommon. Some researchers believe that over 90 percent of those infected manifest some degree of central nervous system involvement. Most psychologists and psychiatrists would still not suspect organic disease due to AIDS when a patient manifests acute or chronic depression, psychoses, schizophrenia, sociopathy, or aggressive or violent behavior. The virus can infect any part of the brain and, depending upon the location of infection, the resultant behavioral changes can be quite varied.

Should HIV testing be required for any special jobs?

Another challenging aspect of HIV infection not yet confronted by our society is the otherwise asymptomatic individual who has extensive central nervous system or brain infection causing impaired judgment and interference with fine motor coordination. Pilots, air traffic controllers, and those in similar professions could be affected Testing for the AIDS virus under these circumstances is common sense, not discrimination.

Mandatory or routine testing has been suggested for many other situations and occupations. Testing is already common in the military, prisons, and during immigration. Other situations becoming more common opportunities for testing are during prenatal examinations and in substance abuse programs. Other situations being heatedly debated are premarital testing and testing for food handlers, teachers, health care workers, and business travelers. . . .

Having reviewed the common arguments against mandatory or required testing, we have only to devise methods that will alleviate the concerns of those who oppose mandatory testing. The two greatest obstacles are concerns about confidentiality and fear of quarantine. Everything possible must be done to improve the security of our record-keeping systems. Simultaneously, society must be taught that everyone who is ill deserves our compassion, care, and respect, regardless of the source of infection.

The issue of testing must be separated from the issue of quarantine. We have tested and reported people with AIDS to the public health department for many years, and there has been no hint of quarantining unless violent or aggressive behavior put others in danger. The issue of quarantining is independent, but related, and should be fought on a different front.

Mandatory, or preferably "required," testing under certain circumstances incorporates all the virtues of voluntary testing without the drawbacks. We do not now have widespread compliance with voluntary testing. Many individuals still prefer not to know. If only one person's health were at stake, this privilege could persist. However, the ostrich approach has never demonstrated itself to be of much value. In order to deal with reality, one must face it. Self-responsibility and responsibility to others require it.

There would be widespread voluntary compliance with required testing just as there is for blood counts and tuberculin tests once it becomes widely recognized as a matter of common sense for health—for the benefit of every individual—and not an issue of coercion.

Voluntary testing is ideal but unrealistic in many situations. Required testing under certain circumstances is best for all concerned if handled with confidentiality and consideration. Routine testing in other circumstances will naturally evolve out of the preceding two. Should these trends materialize, being tested for AIDS will become a way of life. The challenge then becomes how to preserve the quality of life for everyone—the healthy and the ill.

22. HIV-Infected Physicians and the Practice of Seriously Invasive Procedures

Lawrence O. Gostin

Physician Lawrence O. Gostin argues that, even in the absence of instances in which a physician infects a patient (this article was written before the first recorded case of transmission between a Florida dentist and several patients), a case can be made for testing physicians and informing patients. Gostin feels that the risks inherent in seriously invasive procedures are great enough to make HIV testing and information crucial.

AIDS is increasingly being viewed as an occupational disease for physicians despite the evidence that human immunodeficiency virus (HIV) is exceedingly hard to transmit in health care settings.[1] Physicians who carry out seriously invasive procedures claim the "right to know" whether their patients are infected with HIV, including the right to screen patients for the virus.[2] Some hospitals, irrespective of what the law may allow, already screen their patients without specific informed consent.[3]

Conversely, patients undergoing seriously invasive procedures claim the right to know if their physician is infected with HIV. Eighty-six percent of a Gallup Poll sample taken in 1987 said patients should be told if their physician has AIDS.[4] Most patients would choose not to receive treatment from an infected physician. Their case has been buttressed by a policy statement from the American Medical Association that "a physician who knows that he or she is seropositive should not engage in any activity that creates a risk of transmission of the disease to others."[5] Presumably this advice would extend to other health care workers involved in performing seriously invasive procedures. If it is wrong for infected physicians to treat patients invasively, does this create a correlative duty on the part of hospitals to screen physicians before they carry out such treatment? The prospect of a "right to know" the health status of both doctor and

From *The Hastings Center Report*, January/February 1989, pp. 32–39. Reprinted by permission.

patient, with calls for screening on both sides, together with the potential of litigation for avoidable transmission of HIV, undermine trust within the health care system.

The concept of a "right to know" the serologic status of physician or patient is misplaced. Information that a patient is HIV positive is of very limited use to the physician. Physicians have a professional,[6] if not a legal,[7] responsibility to treat infected patients. It is usually not possible to utilize *different* methods for treating HIV-positive patients to reduce the risk of contracting the infection; and in some cases different methods could result in prolongation of operative time, potentially having an adverse effect on the patient. Further, the Centers for Disease Control recommends,[8] and the Occupational Health and Safety Administration requires,[9] the universal application of barrier protection in all cases of exposure to blood. Information that a patient is HIV-positive should not significantly affect the precautions taken in most cases.[10]

Patients, on the other hand, clearly would act upon the knowledge that their physicians were infected with HIV, and when they could choose many would not opt for a physician who is infected with HIV. However, it is not always reasonable for the patient to expect this information. The certain consequence of informing patients that their physician is HIV-positive would be the abandonment of the physician's practice.

This article, therefore, does not make a case for a patient's "right to know." Rather, it argues that the risks inherent in seriously in-

222

vasive procedures are sufficient for the profession to take patient safety seriously, even before the first case of HIV-transmission to a patient occurs. Professional guidance is required to identify the circumstances where a physician should withdraw from performing certain seriously invasive procedures. This conclusion is based upon the doctrine of informed consent and evolving standards of professional care. Failure to take appropriate preventive action now may result in policies that are overly restrictive. For example, Cook County Hospital already has a policy of allowing patients to refuse to be treated by HIV-positive physicians who "routinely provide direct patient care."[11] The policy would appear to put the careers of infected physicians at risk even if they do not perform seriously invasive procedures. This article also makes the case for protecting the privacy of infected physicians and safeguarding against discrimination by their employers and others.

Risks of HIV Transmission in Health Care Settings

There has been no scrutiny of transmission of HIV from physicians to patients, and there is no recorded case where it has occurred.[12] This is not surprising since there has been no systematic attempt to discover which physicians are HIV positive. But there has been careful examination of transmission from patient to health care worker,[13] and some indication of the level of risk in both directions can be ascertained. The possibility of transmission in health care settings has been demonstrated by approximately sixteen cases where health care workers seroconverted from occupational exposure to HIV.[14]

The sixteen reported cases of occupational exposure to HIV appear insignificant given the frequency of contacts between health care workers and HIV-infected patients. Several prospective studies show there is a risk in the range of 0.03 to 0.9 percent that a health care worker will contract HIV following a documented case of percutaneous or mucous membrane exposure to HIV-infected blood.[15] This is relatively low compared to the risk of 12 to 17 percent seroconversion after accidental percutaneous injection from patients with hepatitis B, even after passive immunization of recipients by immune serum globulin.[16]

Physicians performing seriously invasive procedures, such as surgeons, have a potential to cut or puncture their skin with sharp surgical instruments, needles, or bone fragments. Studies indicate that a surgeon will cut a glove in approximately one out of every four cases,[17] and probably sustain a significant skin cut in one out of every forty cases.[18] Given these data, it has been calculated that the risk of contracting HIV in a single surgical operation on an HIV-infected patient is remote—in the range of 1/130,000 to 1/4,500.[19]

It is impossible accurately to calculate the level of risk of HIV transmission from surgeon to patient. Surgeons who cut or puncture themselves do not necessarily expose the patient to their blood, and even if they do the volume is extremely small. A small inoculum of contaminated blood is unlikely to transmit the virus.[20] This suggests that the risk of infection from surgeon to patient is much lower than in the opposite direction. Nonetheless, the fact that the surgeon is in significant contact with the patient's blood and organs, together with the high rate of torn gloves, makes it reasonable to assume that the risk runs in both directions, as is the case with the hepatitis B virus. The cumulative risk to surgical patients, arguably, is higher. While an HIV-infected patient is likely to have relatively few seriously invasive procedures, the infected surgeon, even if the virus drastically shortens his surgical career, can be expected to perform numerous operations. Assuming that the surgical patient's risk is exceedingly low (1/130,000), the risk that one of his patients will contract HIV becomes more realistic the more operations he performs—1/1,300 (assuming 100 operations) or 1/126 (assuming 500 operations). Patients, of course, cannot expect a wholly risk-free environment in a hospital. But there does come a point where the risk of a detrimental outcome becomes sufficiently real that it is prudent for the profession to establish guidelines.

Patient Treatment Decisions

The doctrine of informed consent can help clarify the physician's duties toward his patient. In many jurisdictions, the law of informed consent lays down a patient-oriented standard for the information that must be disclosed by the physician.[21] It is for the patient to assess the risk and to determine where his or her interests lie. If the risk would be intolerable for the reasonably prudent patient he or she is entitled to make that judgment, however unwise the assessment of relative risk is in the eyes of the medical profession.[22] Courts, therefore, require the physician to provide all information that a reasonable patient would find relevant to make an informed decision on whether to undergo a medical procedure.[23] Risks that are relevant or "material" depend upon their severity, the probability that they would occur, and the circumstances under which they would be endured.[24] As the severity of a potential harm becomes greater the need to disclose improbable risks grows, though courts have yet to assign a threshold for the probability of a grave harm beyond which it must be disclosed.[25]

A reasonably prudent patient would find information that his physician is infected with HIV material to his decision to consent to a seriously invasive procedure because the potential harm is severe and the risk, while low, is not negligible. Moreover, he can avoid the risk entirely without any adverse consequences for his health: By choosing another equally competent physician (where available) he can obtain all the therapeutic benefit without the risk of contracting HIV from his physician. The patient, then, can demonstrate not only that the information is material to his decision, but that he would have made a *different* decision had he been given the facts.

Courts have usually been concerned with risks inherent in the treatment, rather than risks associated with a physician's physical condition or skill. Although courts have required disclosure of risks as low as 1 percent or less,[26] they have not required disclosure of risks that are simply unforeseeable—because no case has

ever occurred, or the risk is minute (on the order of 1 in 100,000).[27] The risk of transmission of HIV in the ordinary physician/patient relationship where exposure to large amounts of blood is unlikely is too remote to be foreseeable. Nonetheless, the risks inherent in seriously invasive treatments may well reach the threshold where they become relevant to a rational assessment by the patient.

Courts have been highly consistent in elucidating valid reasons for nondisclosure, all ostensibly for the patient's therapeutic benefit.[28] Relevant information may be withheld when the treatment is necessary in an emergency[29] or is nonelective; the patient is incompetent;[30] or disclosure would be harmful to his psychological state.[31] Nondisclosure of a physician's seropositive status is not founded upon the patient's interests, however, but expressly on the physician's, particularly with respect to rights to privacy and confidentiality.

In *Piper v. Menifee* the court held that a physician was liable to the patient and his family when he failed to inform them that he was attending another patient infected with smallpox. The court held that "if a physician, knowing he has an infectious disease, continues to visit his patients without apprising them of the fact . . . [he] is guilty of a breach of duty."[32]

While few cases affirm the holding in *Piper*, there is ample judicial authority that a physician has a duty to notify third parties who might be exposed to his patient's contagious disease.[33] If a physician has a duty to inform and protect third parties, he owes at least as great a duty toward his own patients.

Yet the right to be informed of a physician's seropositive status requires a finely balanced assessment. There are limits to what society reasonably can expect of a physician in disclosing remote risks. The *Piper* case and more recent duty-to-inform cases involved more substantial risks of contracting disease. There are, moreover, many risks posed by the physician himself, such as inexperience in performing highly technical operations, that are not traditionally disclosed in modern medicine. Nevertheless, the increasing focus of modern law on the patient's rights should require a seropositive physician to withdraw from performing seriously invasive procedures if there is a significant risk to the surgeon's patients.

The Evolving Standard of Professional Care

A physician is expected in law to exercise the care ordinarily used by members of the medical profession in his specialty. Failure to exercise that standard of care is negligence, and a physician will be liable to his patient if harm results.[34] Most cases of medical negligence involve lack of due professional care in providing treatment, but in addition to *Piper* a few demonstrate that a physician may be negligent for continuing to practice when he knows, or reasonably should know, that his physical condition may pose a risk to the patient.

An oral surgeon paid a substantial settlement for transmission of hepatitis B to his patient, and through her to her husband and her child in utero.[35] The employing hospital of a potentially dangerous physician can also be held liable for allowing an infectious or incompetent physician to treat patients.[36]

Both the physician and hospital, therefore, may be negligent for treating a patient in circumstances where the professional standard of care is to refrain from practicing. There is little doubt that a malpractice case would succeed if adequate infection control guidelines had not been followed and, as a result, HIV was transmitted to the patient.[37]

What if HIV is transmitted even though all reasonable infection control procedures are followed? The outcome of a malpractice case would be uncertain. A court might well take cognizance of the fact that there has been no documented case of transmission of HIV from health care worker to patient,[38] and that Boards of Registration in medicine and individual physicians have made conflicting statements of principle.[39]

Nevertheless, the evolving standard of professional care is for an HIV-infected physician to refrain from performing seriously invasive procedures. Physicians have a special responsibility in practicing their profession because of the guardianship of their patients' health. The American Medical Association states that a

> physician who knows that he or she has an infectious disease should not engage in any activity that creates a risk of transmission of the disease to others . . . [P]atients are entitled to expect that their physicians will not increase their exposure to the risk of contracting an infectious disease, even minimally.[40]

The U.S. Public Health Service also recommends an individual assessment to determine whether an HIV-infected health care worker "can adequately and safely be allowed to perform patient care duties or whether their work assignments should be changed . . ."[41]

The American Hospital Association, state hospital associations and state public health departments have likewise acknowledged the risk of transmission of HIV from health care worker to patient in performing invasive procedures.[42] Each group has recognized the legitimacy of an individual determination limiting the practice of invasive procedures by HIV-infected physicians.

While the Public Health Service and professional medical associations have indicated that HIV-infected physicians may pose unacceptable risks for patients when they perform medical procedures, they have not identified those procedures. In each case HIV-infected physicians are told to seek advice and counseling from their personal physician, employing hospital, and colleagues to determine any restrictions on their practice of medicine. The AMA Board, for example, has said that "the decision must be determined on an individual basis founded on the opinions of the worker's personal physician and those of the medical directors and personnel health service staff of the employing institution."[43]

There is a need for national guidance on which procedures should be avoided by infected physicians. Clear guidance would help set a uniform standard of practice across the country; reduce the burden on individual physicians and hospitals to make difficult assessments of risk; prevent inconsistent practice in different hospitals and geographic regions leading to loss of patient confidence;

and reduce the possibility of legal liability for infected physicians and hospitals that countenance allowing an infected physician to continue performing seriously invasive treatment. The absence of prospective guidelines issued by the medical profession could well result in undesirable retrospective standards laid down by the courts.

Physician Screening

If legal and public health policy require the HIV-infected physician to refrain from performing certain seriously invasive procedures, does the hospital have an obligation to screen physicians? The law holds physicians and hospitals accountable, not only for what they know, but for what they reasonably should know. If a physician has engaged in high risk behavior such as homosexual activity or sharing of needles, and failed to be tested or to make any disclosure to the hospital, the courts probably would put him in the same position as if he knew he were seropositive. Any other rule of law would provide an incentive for physicians to avoid being tested and counseled. The prudent course, then, is for physicians who are at increased risk for HIV to obtain confidential testing and counseling, and to inform the health care facility of a positive test result, before performing seriously invasive medical procedures.[44]

Physicians who are not at increased risk for HIV or those who do not perform seriously invasive procedures have no legal or ethical obligation to be tested; and there should be no duty on health care facilities to screen them routinely. In such cases, the social, personal, and financial costs of a comprehensive screening program outweigh the public health benefit. The disadvantages of mandatory physician screening are similar to those in other low risk populations, and have been explicated elsewhere.[45]

A positive test result in a health care professional who is not in fact infected could have devastating personal consequences. A negative test result, moreover, does not guarantee that a physician is free from infection. There is a period of up to twelve weeks or longer before antibodies are produced and detectable after infection; or the physician could contract the virus at some future time, necessitating periodic retesting at considerable expense to the health care facility.

Systematic collection of highly sensitive health care data would place considerable burdens on hospitals. They would be required to keep the information confidential and could be liable for intentional or negligent disclosure.[46] Hospitals would also have to decide whether to disclose the information to patients or third parties under a duty to warn theory.[47]

The legal and ethical quandaries, therefore, posed for the hospital by systematic collection of the HIV status of all physicians would be disproportionate to any public health benefit. The medical literature is replete with documented cases of transmission of hepatitis B in health care settings,[48] and there are some one hundred health care worker deaths each year attributable to HBV. The risk of transmission and cumulative morbidity and mortality associated with HBV are greater than for HIV. Yet there is no systematic screening for HBV, and restrictions on the practice of invasive procedures often occur only after a physician has transmitted HBV (sometimes repeatedly).[49] If the case for screening for hepatitis B has never been sustained, what new facts or data mandate screening for the AIDS virus?

Finally, a systematic program of screening for HIV among physicians might well violate constitutional protection of a person's right to be free from "unreasonable search and seizures." A blood test for HIV with important personal consequences, like a test for drugs or alcohol,[50] may infringe upon a person's "expectation of privacy."[51] In *Glover v. Eastern Nebraska Community Office of Mental Retardation*, a federal district court held that screening for HIV among certain employees in a mental retardation facility constituted unreasonable search and seizure because the risk to clients "is extremely low and approaches zero."[52] It is possible that the courts may find a greater public health interest in a screening program more narrowly focused on health care workers involved in seriously invasive procedures; yet any widespread screening policy is likely to be found unconstitutional.

An effective argument could be made that, once it is determined that HIV-positive physicians should refrain from seriously invasive treatment, it necessarily follows that they should be screened before performing such procedures. I do not accept, however, that screening is a logically necessary result. There are many well-accepted situations in modern medicine where legally and ethically it is advisable for physicians to restrict their medical practice but which do not require systematic screening. A surgeon with HBV, TB or who is drug or alcohol impaired should not continue to practice without the hospital's knowledge and review. It does not necessarily follow (nor might it even be constitutionally permitted) systematically to screen all surgeons for HBV, TB, drugs, and alcohol. Rather, I argue that a physician who knows, or ought to know, that he or she is HIV-positive, should voluntarily refrain from practicing seriously invasive procedures. The cost of such a professional rule is not prohibitive and can be ameliorated by transfer to other duties and by equitable compensation programs. However, the sheer social and personal burdens of systematic screening on physicians, hospitals, and the entire health care system substantially outweigh its public health benefit.

Consequences for the Physician

The standards developed thus far for HIV-infected physicians are strict and based upon prevention of even a minimal risk of transmission. If the physician is expected voluntarily to disclose his serological status to the patient and/or to refrain from performing certain seriously invasive procedures, he is entitled to protection from the consequences of his good faith actions. The right to practice medicine is "sufficiently precious to surround it with a panoply of legal protections."[53] Any public health policy on HIV-infected physicians, therefore, must ensure confidentiality and nondiscriminatory treatment including reasonable accommodation.

Confidentiality. HIV-infected physicians, like other seropositive individuals, are concerned with maintaining confidentiality. Because the majority of physicians infected with HIV are members of risk groups subject to persistent prejudice and discrimination, unauthorized disclosure of their serological status can lead to social opprobrium among family and friends, and to loss of employment, housing and insurance. Consequently, physicians have strong grounds for desiring personal privacy and confidentiality of medical information. Their cooperation with the hospital in protecting against the spread of infections relies upon their trust that their serological status will be kept confidential.

Physicians have a right to confidentiality of intimate health care information based upon a number of legal grounds. First, physicians with HIV are treated by a personal physician and are entitled to the protection of confidentiality inherent in the physician/patient relationship. Second, employees have the right to expect that sensitive health care information will not be disclosed by their employers without their permission.[54] While health care employers may have a legitimate interest in knowing if a physician is HIV positive, they have no legitimate interest in disclosing this information to patients, other employees, or individuals or organizations outside of the hospital. Third, statutes in several states and municipalities specifically protect the confidentiality of HIV-positive test results. These statutes generally provide civil liability for disclosing the result of a serological test without the individual's written informed consent.[55]

Two cases establish the importance of confidentiality for the physician, at least against media disclosure to the general public. In *X. v. Y.* the British High Court issued a permanent injunction against a national newspaper publishing confidential information about a physician with AIDS. The court held that "the public interest in the freedom of the press and informed debate on AIDS was outweighed by the public interest in maintaining the confidentiality of actual or potential AIDS sufferers."[56]

In a similar case the *Miami Herald* filed suit against the Dade County Health Department and the hospital to gain access to the medical records and death certificate of a urologist.

The newspaper's intention was to confirm that the urologist had practiced medicine for several years while he had AIDS. The court did not allow release of this confidential information,[57] basing its decision upon the state Public Records Act, which regards such information as confidential unless the person claiming the information has a "direct and tangible" interest in it.

Confidentiality for the HIV-infected physician not only safeguards his personal rights, but also is in the public interest.[58] The right to confidentiality will encourage physicians to disclose their serological status to their employers, and to seek counseling, treatment, and peer review of the safety of their continued medical practice.

Antidiscrimination. Discrimination against a physician because of his HIV status is just as repugnant as discrimination on other morally irrelevant grounds such as race or gender. The United States Supreme Court in *School Board of Nassau County v. Arline* condemned irrational prejudice based upon a person's infectious condition noting that:

> Society's accumulated myths and fears about disease are as handicapping as are the physical limitations that flow from actual impairment. Few aspects give rise to the same level of public fear and misapprehension as contagiousness.[59]

AIDS has been held to be a handicap within the meaning of section 504 of the Federal Rehabilitation Act of 1973 and similar state statutes.[60] The Civil Rights Restoration Act 1988 states that section 504 is applicable to a person with a contagious disease if he does not pose "a direct threat to the health or safety of other individuals or . . . who is unable to perform the duties of the job." The congressional history of the 1988 Act shows that the language "direct threat" embodies the standard of "significant risk of transmission" articulated by the Supreme Court in *Arline*.[61]

Physicians, then, have a right under federal and state handicap laws not to be denied the right to practice medicine or to be reassigned to an administrative position unless there is a significant risk of HIV transmission. Any limitation on the right of a physician to practice must be reasonably related to the achievement of greater patient safety. Narrow limitations on the practice of seriously invasive procedures may thus be found not to be discriminatory.

In *Doe v. Cook County Hospital* U.S. District Court Judge John A. Nordberg required the signing of a consent decree to protect an HIV-infected neurologist from unreasonable limitations placed on his right to practice.[62] The physician agreed to special surveillance; to double glove before performing invasive procedures; and not to perform three procedures—muscle biopsy, sural nerve biopsy and cerebral arteriography—formally a part of his credentialing, but which he had not performed in recent years. The judge, in language mirroring the *Arline* decision, held that future alterations in clinical practice could be permitted only if the physician posed "a significant health or safety risk to himself or others"; and, except in an emergency, the neurologist received seven days' notice of any alteration.

The Cook County Hospital case establishes the need for balance between a physician's rights and a patient's safety. Yet the concept of "significant risk" needs further clarification. "Significant risk" should be based upon epidemiologic evidence of the gravity of the harm and the probability of it occurring. A risk is significant if: the mode of transmission is well established, even if the risk is small; the potential harm is serious; and the public health intervention is efficacious and does not pose disproportionate burdens on individual rights. Withdrawal of an HIV-infected physician from performing seriously invasive procedures, provided the information can be kept confidential, does not pose an unbearable burden on the physician or the health care system. Reassignment to noninvasive procedures virtually eliminates any risk of harm.

The Cook County case also shows the futility of a case-by-case determination by courts of which medical procedures are sufficiently safe for an HIV-infected physician to perform. It is not the proper function of the courts to list a detailed set of allowed and prohibited medical procedures. The court's decision simply underlines the need for forward-looking professional guidelines to assess which medical procedures pose a risk to the health of patients.

The federal Rehabilitation Act requires employers to make reasonable accommodation for handicapped workers. Health care facilities should ensure that HIV-infected physicians have the opportunity for a wide-ranging clinical practice that is both professionally rewarding and remunerative. The professional guidance called for in this essay should reflect the rich variety of clinical practice infected physicians could safely engage in, ranging from internal medicine and psychiatry to pediatrics and neurology.

The right to confidentiality and antidiscrimination including reasonable accommodation for physicians should be viewed as a *quid pro quo* for the physician's good faith fulfillment of his or her special professional and ethical obligations. The physician has made a substantial human and financial investment in medical education. He is expected to provide treatment for HIV-infected patients despite the occupational risks. Given these special societal burdens on the physician, it is reasonable to protect his personal rights and professional livelihood.

Notes

1. See for example, Centers for Disease Control, "Recommendations for Prevention of HIV Transmission in Health-care Settings," *Morbidity & Mortality Weekly Report* 36:2S (1987), 3S–18S.

2. The Surgeon General, for example, has advocated HIV screening of all preoperative patients. Dennis L. Breo, "Dr. Koop Calls for AIDS Tests Before Surgery," *American Medical News,* 26 June 1987, 1, 21–25.

3. Keith Henry, Karen Willenbring and Kent Crossley, "Human Immunodeficiency Virus Antibody Testing: A Description of Practices and Policies at U.S. Infectious Disease Teaching Hospitals and Minnesota Hospitals," *Journal of the American Medical Association* 259:12 (1988), 1819–22.

4. *Medical Staff News* (August 1987), 2.

5. Council on Ethical and Judicial Affairs, Amer-

ican Medical Association, "Ethical Issues Involved in the Growing AIDS Crisis," *Journal of the American Medical Association* 259:9 (1988), 1360–61.

6. Council on Ethical and Judicial Affairs, "Ethical Issues."

7. George J. Annas, "Not Saints, But Healers: The Legal Duties of Health Care Professionals in the AIDS Epidemic," *American Journal of Public Health* 78:17 (1988), 844–49.

8. Centers for Disease Control, "Recommendations."

9. Department of Labor and Department of Health and Human Services, "Joint Advisory Notice: Protection against Occupational Exposures to Hepatitis B Virus (HBV) and Human Immunodeficiency Virus (HIV)," *Federal Register* 52:10 (1987), 41818–23.

10. J. Louise Gerberding and the University of California, San Francisco Task Force on AIDS, "Recommended Infection Control Policies for Patients With Human Immunodeficiency Virus Infection: An Update," *New England Journal of Medicine* 315:24 (1986), 1562–64.

11. "Chicago Patients Gain Curb on AIDS Carriers," *New York Times,* 22 September 1988, A34.

12. Centers for Disease Control, "Recommendations," 65–75.

13. James R. Allen, "Health Care Workers and the Risk of HIV Transmission," *Hastings Center Reprot* 18:2 (1988), Special Supplement, 2–5.

14. Deborah M. Barnes, "Health Care Workers and AIDS: Questions Persist," *Science* 241 (1988), 161–62.

15. Centers for Disease Control, "Recommendations"; Gerald H. Friedland and Robert S. Klein, "Transmission of the Human Immunodeficiency Virus," *New England Journal of Medicine* 317:18 (1987), 1125–35.

16. Barbara G. Werner and George F. Grady, "Accidental Hepatitis B-Surface-Antigen-Positive Inoculations: Use of e Antigen to Estimate Infectivity," *Annals of Internal Medicine* 97:3 (1982), 367–9.

17. Peter J. E. Cruse and Rosemary Foord, "The Epidemiology of Wound Infection," *Surgical Clinics of North America* 60:1 (1980), 27–40.

18. Michael D. Hagen, Klemens B. Meyer and

Stephen G. Parker, "Routine Pre-Operative Screening for HIV: Does the Risk to the Surgeon Outweigh the Risk to the Patient?" *Journal of the American Medical Association* 259:9 (1988), 1357–59.

19. Hagen *et al.*, "Routine Pre-Operative Screening."

20. Friedland and Klein, "Transmission of the Human Immunodeficiency Virus."

21. See for example, *Harnish v. Children's Hospital Medical Center*, 387 Mass. 152, 439 N.E.2d 240 (1982).

22. *Wikinson v. Vesey*, 110 R.I. 606, 624 (1972).

23. *Canterbury v. Spence. Cobbs v. Grant*, 8 Cal. 3d 229 (1972).

24. *Precourt v. Frederick*, 395 Mass. 689, 694–95 (1985).

25.See *Precourt v. Frederick*, 395 Mass. 689, 697 (1985). The development of law as to which risks are too remote to require disclosure must await future cases.

26. *Salis v. United States*, 522 F. Supplement 989 (Md. and Pa. 1981).

27. See for example, *Precourt v. Frederick. Henderson v. Milobsky*, 595 F.2d 654 (D.C. Cir 1978). It is difficult to predict how the courts would respond in a case of an HIV-infected surgeon, since the risk to any *single* patient is highly remote.

28. See *Mroczkowski v. Staub Clinic and Hospital*, 732 P.2d 1255 (Hawaii App. 1987).

29. *Keegan v. Holy Family Hospital*, 95 Wn.2d 306, 622 P.2d 1246 (1980).

30. See A. Meisel, "The 'Exceptions' to the Informed Consent Doctrine: Striking a Balance Between Competing Values in Decisionmaking," *Wisconsin Law Review* (1979), 413.

31. *Harnish v. Children's Hospital Medical Center*.

32. *Ben Monroe's Reports*, Winter Term 465 (Winter Term 1851).

33. See generally, Lawrence Gostin, William Curran, and Mary Clark, "The Case Against Compulsory Casefinding in Controlling AIDS: Testing, Screening and Reporting," *American Journal of Law and Medicine* 12:1 (1986), 7–53; Lawrence Gostin and William Curran, "AIDS Screening, Confidentiality and the Duty to Warn," *American Journal of Public Health* 77:3 (1987), 361–65.

34. See for example, *Cross v. Huttenlocher*, 440 A.2d 952 (Conn. 1981).

35. *Ruffin v. Harris,* No 80-00627835, New London, Conn., August 1983.

36. See *Opithorne v. Framingham Union Hospital,* 401 Mass. 860 (1988); *Penn Tanker Company v. United States,* 310 F. Supplement 613 (1970).

37. See for example, *LaRoche v. United States* 730 F. 2d, 538 (8th Cir. 1984).

38. Jeffrey J. Sacks, "AIDS in a Surgeon," *New England Journal of Medicine* 313:16 (1985), 1017–18.

39. J. H. Morton, "One More Article About AIDS," *Federation Bulletin* 75:2 (1988), 62–64; Cf. R. J. Feinstein, "When Should the Sick Doctor Stop Caring for Patients, And Who Will Make That Decision?" *Journal of the Florida Medical Association* 73:1 (1986), 43–45.

40. Council on Ethical and Judicial Affairs, "Ethical Issues."

41. Centers for Disease Control, "Recommendations," 16S.

42. American Hospital Association, AIDS Task Force, *AIDS and the Law: Responding to the Special Concerns of Hospitals* (Chicago: AHA, 1987), 52–54; Massachusetts Hospital Association, *AIDS: Administrative Reference Manual* (1987), 64; Massachusetts Department of Public Health, *Governor's Task Force on AIDS Policies and Recommendations* (1987), 4–9.

43. Mary M. Devlin, "Ethical Issues in the AIDS Crisis: The HIV-Positive Practitioner," *Journal of the American Medical Association* 260:6 (1988), 790.

44. A related issue is presented by the case of a physician who is stuck with a needle from an HIV-infected patient. Should he refrain from doing invasive procedures for the time it takes to learn whether he seroconverted? In such a case the risk might fall below a reasonable range for concern (a small probability that the surgeon became positive multiplied by a small probability that he could transfer the infection).

45. Paul Cleary, *et al.,* "Compulsory Premarital Screening for the Human Immunodeficiency Virus: Technical and Public Health Considerations," *Journal of the American Medical Association* 258:13 (1987), 1757–62; Lawrence Gostin, "Screening for AIDS: Efficacy, Cost, and Consequences," *AIDS & Public Policy Journal* 2:4 (1987), 14–24; Ronald Bayer, Carol Levine, Susan M. Wolf, "HIV Antibody Screening: An Ethical Framework for Evaluating Proposed Pro-

grams," *Journal of the American Medical Association* 256:13 (1986), 1768–74.

46. Many state supreme courts have held that disclosure of confidential health care information can result in liability; see for example, *Alberts v. Devine*, 395 Mass. 59 (1985). Moreover, several jurisdictions have now enacted statutes prohibiting unauthorized disclosure of an HIV test. See Larry Gostin and Andrew Ziegler, "A Review of AIDS-Related Legislative and Regulatory Policy in the United States," *Law, Medicine and Health Care* 15:1–2 (1987), 5–16.

47. Gostin and Curran, "AIDS Screening."

48. Frederic E. Shaw, Charles L. Barrett and Robert Hamm, "Lethal Outbreak of Hepatitis B in a Dental Practice," *Journal of the American Medical Association* 255:23 (1986), 3260–64; Robert J. Gerety, "Hepatitis B Transmission Between Dental or Medical Workers and Patients," *Annals of Internal Medicine* 95:2 (1981), 229.

49. W. W. Williams, "Guidelines for Infection Control in Hospital Personnel," *Infection Control* 4:4 (1983), 326–49; Ludwig A. Lettau *et al.*, "Transmission of Hepatitis B with Resultant Restriction of Surgical Practice," *Journal of the American Medical Association* 255:7 (1986), 934–37.

50. See *Schmerber v. California*, 384 U.S. 757 (1966).

51. *O'Connor v. Ortega*, 107 S. Ct. 1492, 1497 (1987) (quoting *United States v. Jacobsen*, 466 U.S. 109, 113 (1984)).

52. *Glover v Eastern Nebraska Community Office of Mental Retardation*, 686 F. Supp. 243 (D. Neb. 1988).

53. *Grannis v. Board of Medical Examiners*, 96 Cal. Rptr. 863, 870, 19 Cal. App. 3d 551, 561 (1971).

54. See *Bratt v. International Business Machine Corporation*, 785 F. 2d 352 (1st Cir. 1986).

55. See Gostin and Ziegler, "A Review of AIDS-Related Legislative and Regulatory Policy."

56. Diana Brahams, "Confidentiality for Doctors Who are HIV Positive," *The Lancet*, 21 November 1987, 1221–22.

57. *Yeste v. Miami Herald Publishing Company*, 451 So.2d 491 (Fla. App. 3 Dist. 1984). See Feinstein, "When Should the Sick Doctor Stop Caring for Patients?"

58. Gostin and Curran, "AIDS Screening."

59. 107 S. Ct. 1123 (1987).

60. *Chalk v. Orange County Department of Education*, 832 F.2d 1158 (9th Cir. 1987); *Shuttleworth v. Broward County*, 639 F. Supplement 654 (S.D. Fla. 1986).

61. 134 *Congressional Record* S1738-1740, (daily ed. March 2, 1988) (statement of Sen. Harkin).

62. No. 87 C 6888, Consent Decree filed 21 February 1988, N.D. Illinois.

23. Compulsory HIV Tests for Hospitalized Patients

Joel D. Howell and Carl Cohen

Joel D. Howell and Carl Cohen comment on a case in which a doctor wishes to test an incoming patient for the HIV virus without her consent. Professor Howell argues that the risk to the patient is too great, and the promise of benefits too small, to force the test without consent. Professor Cohen argues that the doctors have a duty to treat the patient and need full information to do so.

G.L. was a sixty-seven-year-old woman transferred to a university medical center for evaluation of pancytopenia of two

From *The Hastings Center Report*, August/September 1988, pp. 18–20. Reprinted by permission.

years' duration and the recent onset of jaundice. Her clinical presentation was characterized by generalized weakness, a strong history of tuberculosis exposure, transfusion of two units of blood five years ago, splenomegaly, hemolytic anemia, and an abnormal chest X-ray. After several days of intense investigation, her underlying disease remained confusing to both her primary care physician and to several consulting physicians.

While reviewing her hospital course, the attending physician noted that an HIV antibody test had been requested; results pending. The test had been ordered in light of G.L.'s blood transfusion five years earlier, when blood supplies were not being screened routinely for the presence of antibodies to the AIDS virus. Further discussion with the house staff participating in the patient's care revealed that no one had discussed ordering the HIV antibody test with her or told her that such a test was being performed, despite the fact that her mental status was completely normal. When queried about their behavior, the house staff responded that the HIV serology was medically indicated, and that blood samples are routinely drawn from hospitalized patients without obtaining specific consent for each test.

Should hospitalized patients know, and give consent, before their HIV antibody status is determined?

Commentary by
Joel D. Howell

Yes, hospitalized patients, like any other persons, should be asked to consent before having blood drawn to determine their HIV antibody status. One could argue, of course, that however theoretically ideal it might be to obtain consent for every test, it is neither practical nor common procedure to do so in a hospital setting. Hospitalized patients have their blood drawn regularly. Physicians do not ask their consent to check a blood count, to monitor antibiotic levels, to assess thyroid status, or to do other "routine" tests. In the interest of efficiency, we do not ask specific consent for each laboratory examination. Despite this,

we generally acknowledge that competent adult patients—and certainly G.L. would be included in this group—have the right to know what tests are being drawn, to refuse them, indeed, to refuse hospitalization.

Unlike the situation for routine blood tests, physicians do ask consent before inserting tubes into patients' hearts, seeking consent because such invasive procedures involve an element of significant risk to the patient. Thus, physicians ask permission for procedures that could harm the patient.

Into what category does drawing blood for an HIV antibody test fall? It is a procedure for which physicians should obtain consent from the patient, because it places the patient at greater risk for adverse consequences than other blood tests. First, there is the risk of a false-positive test result, the magnitude of which depends on the pretest probability that a patient has been infected with the HIV virus. In G.L.'s case this probability is quite low. A false-positive test should be detected by additional testing, but in the interim the patient would suffer. Graver risks would come from true-positive test results: risks to G.L.'s relationships (both sexual and social if test results were inappropriately disclosed), to her treatment by medical personnel, to her insurability, to schooling, to housing, and were she employed, to job security.

On the other hand, there are potential benefits to drawing an HIV antibody test. The results could give G.L. information about her prognosis and possibly save her the indignities or hazards of further diagnostic evaluation. Knowledge of a positive test result might prompt her to alter her behavior to decrease the probability of transmitting the HIV virus to sexual partners and, were she in her childbearing years, to her potential children. Society, too, could benefit if she refrained from donating blood. Society could also benefit from an increased knowledge about the clinical presentation of AIDS and from a small increment in knowledge about its epidemiology.

Unfortunately, because we have little hope for palliation or cure, the clinical benefits to G.L. of a positive HIV test would be small. The benefits of testing would more likely accrue to physicians. Probably the most powerful motivation behind testing in this case is physicians' natural desire to make a diagnosis, thus fulfilling both role expectations to which they are socialized and the intellectual curiosity that underlies much of medical practice. Those directly involved in caring for G.L. might also perceive some personal benefit from knowing the results. Were the results negative, they might have less sense of personal risk while caring for her. Were they positive, caregivers might take additional precautions, though studies have failed to demonstrate an increased risk of infection among clinicians working with AIDS or HIV-positive patients. Universal secretion precautions are more effective than screening patients thought to be at risk.

Thus, the risks and benefits involved in performing the HIV antibody test must be balanced. In assessing the complex and competing priorities involved, the patient should actively participate in the decision-making process. And here, as always, informed consent means just that; it implies more than a technical exposition and platitudes about confidentiality. It requires an honest effort by the patient's physician to make her aware of the full range of potential risks and benefits, and to counsel her both prior to and following testing. Aware of the potential results of their actions, patients—such as G.L.—can then choose what they wish to do.

Unfortunately, G.L. was not given the opportunity to make this choice. What should the attending physician do now? If the test has not yet been performed, he or she must decide if any HIV test may be indicated. If the answer is no, the attending physician should countermand the resident and cancel the test. If the answer is yes, he or she should, together with the resident, explain to G.L. what has occurred, and after properly informing her of the risks and benefits, request permission to perform an HIV antibody test. The physicians should then abide by her wishes.

If, however, results are obtained before the attending physician can intervene, G.L. should be told of the results even though she did not know that an HIV antibody test was being drawn. For her caregivers to know G.L.'s HIV status while she does not would only compound the initial error made in her care.

Finally, this incident should (and did) prompt discussion with house staff about the need to obtain consent before drawing an HIV test.

AIDS has forced us to reassess traditional hospital practice. This new disease should make physicians think about their patients within a larger social context, rather than an exclusively scientific context, the latter a goal toward which American medicine has strived during much of the twentieth century. The purely technical risk to having a blood test drawn may be minimal, be it a CBC or an HIV, but the social risk for having an HIV drawn is considerable. Hence, the correct response is to obtain hospitalized patients' consent before drawing an HIV antibody test.

Commentary by Carl Cohen

This case presents two distinct issues. First, may the test for antibodies to HIV be performed without the specific consent of the patient? Second, must the patient be informed of her HIV antibody status once that is determined?

The latter question is the easier. The patient has entered the hospital to determine the cause(s) of a long-continued illness; investigation has been "intense"; many lab tests will have been run, and the patient will very likely be anxious about their results. Whatever her state of mind, G.L. surely has a right to full and truthful disclosure of what is known, or has been concluded with high probability, that may help to explain her jaundice, weakness, and other symptoms.

Should G.L. test positive for antibodies to HIV, this may prove difficult for her to accept. The task of informing her of such test results should be approached with care and compassion, in the most constructive and supportive way possible. That it is unpleasant is no reason for keeping the truth from her.

The more difficult question concerns the permissibility of such testing without specific consent of the patient. Its fatal outcome and social stigmatization give grounds for treating routine AIDS testing among healthy persons (even supposing all risk of false positives could be eliminated) with the greatest caution.

But G.L. is not healthy; she suffers from anemia and has received an unscreened blood transfusion. Under such circumstances, it is the duty of the health professionals to whom G.L. has committed her care to undertake the laboratory tests that may help to identify the problem. Failing to determine her antibody status might leave a critical gap in the medical understanding of her condition.

Must the doctors ask her first, however, before testing for antibodies to HIV? No, unless the tests for this disease are different from tests for other conditions routinely tested, in ways that make specific consent a necessary condition of the inquiry.

The patient's consent—to have blood drawn and tested and to have various laboratory tests performed upon tissue taken from her—must certainly be obtained before invasive procedures are initiated. But G.L. gave *that* consent, in general form, when she voluntarily entered the hospital for diagnosis.

Normally, we do not think it essential to receive the patient's specific consent for inquiry into each possible condition from which she may be suffering. The complexities of indirect causation, of complicated probability calculations, and of various possible responses to the test outcomes encountered, make explaining to the patient why each test is being run a practical impossibility in the normal hospital setting. The practice of not seeking specific consent for testing each possible condition is a recognition of the different levels of medical understanding normally possessed by

doctors and their patients, and should not be viewed as a form of condescending paternalism. It also protects the patient from unwarranted fears and anxieties arising from the physician's need to eliminate certain improbable but nonetheless possible causes.

Why might one think that specific consent for HIV antibody testing is nonetheless required? Is it because of the *gravity* of AIDS? The possibility that it may prove necessary to convey very bad news to a patient surely provides no reason for failing to determine her condition. Is specific consent deemed necessary because of the special *stigma* associated with AIDS? G.L., a sixty-seven-year-old who has received an unscreened transfusion, is not likely to suffer the aversion and revulsion experienced by some patients with AIDS or HIV infection even in the unlikely event that she does test positive.

The chief point, however, is that the proper task of those who care for G.L. is to diagnose her disease, and that it is their duty to perform those tests and make those inquiries that are reasonably called for to achieve that end. Had G.L. stipulated on her admission to the hospital that she not be tested for antibodies to HIV, her specific consent before performing such a test would of course be required. Since her admission presumably conformed to standard procedures, it is no infringement upon her interests or her rights to proceed with the laboratory tests that might normally be undertaken—thus doing for her what she came to have her doctors do.

The Death Penalty

Of all the industrialized societies in the world, the United States is among the last still inflicting capital punishment. Is the death penalty a just punishment for heinous crimes, or is it an inhumane and unnecessarily barbaric practice? Is it cruel and unusual punishment, prohibited by the Eighth Amendment, or is it a fitting retribution for certain reprehensible offenses?

Those in favor of the death penalty, typically called *retentionists,* argue that the death penalty fits certain crimes—that it is just retribution. The concept of retributive justice, or *lex taliones* (the law of retribution), goes back to biblical days. The criminal, it is suggested, deserves a punishment proportional to the crime; and for many crimes—especially particularly heinous murders—death amounts to a fair punishment.

As for social utility, retentionists will argue that the death penalty deters and incapacitates. The latter is most certainly true: people who have been executed do not go on to commit further crimes. And this is no small matter. The irreformable maniacal killer may represent a danger to others no matter how well he or she is imprisoned. As for deterrence, this is an open question. Retentionists like to suggest that a strongly enforced death penalty will reduce the number of murders. There is widespread disagreement on this empirical issue.

Retentionists are not in complete agreement over the types of crimes that warrant the death penalty. Murder with special circumstances (such as rape, multiple homicide, or particularly cruel circumstances), murder during a drug deal, murder of a peace officer, murder for hire, and treason or espionage are often considered to be conditions where the death penalty "fits." Of course, the debate also centers on exceptions to the death penalty, such as for being under-age at the time of the crime or having diminished capacity from either drug use or mental retardation.

Abolitionists, or those who oppose the death penalty, often argue against the death penalty on the grounds of the sanctity of life. Each human being is a unique member of society with an *inalienable* right to life. It is also argued that the death penalty is cruel and unusual. Capital punishment, abolitionists assert, involves wanton pain and violence, violates all decent community standards, and, despite the best efforts of lawmakers, is still administered in an arbitrary and capricious manner. The death penalty often discriminates against indigent people of color, since poor legal representation and a biased legal system make it difficult for poor people, especially people of color, to get a fair trial.

Furthermore, the death penalty is wide open to mistakes. Death is irreversible. As for deterrence, life in prison does just as well, the abolitionists argue, and does just as good a job at incapacitation. Hence, it is suggested that the death penalty is excessive.

In the case of *Furman* v. *Georgia* (1972), the Supreme Court ruled that the death penalty was not inherently cruel and unusual but was administered in an arbitrary and capricious manner. The majority of the Court asserted that, once the purportedly appropriate procedures were developed to check the prejudice and unbridled discretion of jury decisions, the death penalty was perfectly acceptable. Hence, in *Gregg* v. *Georgia* (1976), it was decided that currently adopted criteria were adequate to make the application of the death penalty constitutional. In dissent, Justice Marshall argued that most Americans would find the death penalty cruel and unusual if they knew what it involved.

24.   Capital Punishment, Retributive Justice, and Social Defense

Hugo Adam Bedau

Bedau argues against the death penalty, on the grounds of social utility, by first distinguishing between prevention and deterrence. The death penalty prevents crime by incapacitation and deters it by intimidating those who would otherwise commit a capital offense. Since neither, Bedau argues, works any better than a long prison sentence, the death penalty cannot be defended on grounds of social utility. He concludes that the severe costs associated with capital punishment far outweigh what few plausible benefits it might have. From the perspective of retributive justice, Bedau argues against the death penalty on the grounds of proportionality. He suggests that the simple "a life for a life" conception plays little role in our criminal justice system. Furthermore, he asserts that the death penalty, which is administered in an arbitrary and capricious manner, cheapens and degrades our respect for human life.

Capital Punishment and Social Defense

The Analogy with Self-Defense

Capital punishment, it is sometimes said, is to the body politic what self-defense is to the individual. If the latter is not morally wrong, how can the former be morally wrong? In order to assess the strength of this analogy, we need first to inspect the morality of self-defense.

Except for absolute pacifists, who believe it is morally wrong to use violence even to defend themselves or others from unprovoked and undeserved aggression, most of us believe that it is not morally wrong and may even be our moral duty to use violence to prevent aggression directed either against ourselves or against innocent third parties. The law has long granted persons the right to defend themselves against the unjust aggressions of others, even to the extent of using lethal force to kill a would-be assailant. It is very difficult

From T. Regan, ed., *Matters of Life and Death*, 2nd ed. Copyright 1986 by McGraw-Hill, Inc. Reprinted by permission. Footnotes omitted.

to think of any convincing argument that would show it is never rational to risk the death of another in order to prevent death or grave injury to oneself. Certainly self-interest dictates the legitimacy of self-defense. So does concern for the well-being of others. So also does justice. If it is unfair for one person to inflict violence on another, then it is hard to see how morality could require the victim to acquiesce in the attempt by another to hurt him or her, rather than to resist it, even if that resistance involves or risks injury to the assailant.

The foregoing account assumes that the person acting in self-defense is innocent of any provocation of the assailant. It also assumes that there is no alternative to victimization except resistance. In actual life, both assumptions—especially the second—are often false, because there may be a third alternative: escape, or removing oneself from the scene of danger and imminent aggression. Hence, the law imposes on us the "duty to retreat." Before we use violence to resist aggression, we must try to get out of the way, lest unnecessary violence be used to resist aggression. Now suppose that unjust aggression is imminent, and there is no path open for escape. How much violence may justifiably be used to ward off aggression? The answer is: No more violence

237

than is necessary to prevent the aggressive assault. Violence beyond that is unnecessary and therefore unjustified. We may restate the principle governing the use of violence in self-defense in terms of the use of "deadly force" by the police in the discharge of their duties. The rule is this: Use of deadly force is justified only to prevent loss of life in immediate jeopardy where a lesser use of force cannot reasonably be expected to save the life that is threatened.

In real life, violence in self-defense in excess of the minimum necessary to prevent aggression, even though it is not justifiable, is often excusable. One cannot always tell what will suffice to deter or prevent becoming a victim, and so the law looks with a certain tolerance upon the frightened and innocent would-be victim who in self-protection turns upon a vicious assailant and inflicts a fatal injury even though a lesser injury would have been sufficient. What is not justified is deliberately using far more violence than is necessary to prevent becoming a victim. It is the deliberate, not the impulsive or the unintentional use of violence that is relevant to the death-penalty controversy, since the death penalty is enacted into law and carried out in each case only after ample time to weigh alternatives. Notice that we are assuming that the act of self-defense is to protect one's person or that of a third party. The reasoning outlined here does not extend to the defense of one's property. Shooting a thief to prevent one's automobile from being stolen cannot be excused or justified in the way that shooting an assailant charging with a knife pointed at one's face can be. In terms of the concept of "deadly force," our criterion is that deadly force is never justified to prevent crimes against property or other violent crimes not immediately threatening the life of an innocent person.

The rationale for self-defense as set out above illustrates two moral principles of great importance to our discussion. . . . One is that if a life is to be risked, then it is better that it be the life of someone who is guilty (in our context, the initial assailant) rather than the life of someone who is not (the innocent potential victim). It is not fair to expect the innocent prospective victim to run the added risk of severe injury or death in order to avoid using violence in self-defense to the extent of possibly killing his assailant. It is only fair that the guilty aggressor run the risk.

The other principle is that taking life deliberately is not justified so long as there is any feasible alternative. One does not expect miracles, of course, but in theory, if shooting a burglar through the foot will stop the burglary and enable one to call the police for help, then there is no reason to shoot to kill. Likewise, if the burglar is unarmed, there is no reason to shoot at all. In actual life, of course, burglars are likely to be shot at by aroused householders because one does not know whether they are armed, and prudence may dictate the assumption that they are. Even so, although the burglar has no right to commit a felony against a person or a person's property, the attempt to do so does not give the chosen victim the right to respond in whatever way one pleases, and then to excuse or justify such conduct on the ground that one was "only acting in self-defense." In these ways the law shows a tacit regard for the life of even a felon and discourages the use of unnecessary violence even by the innocent; morality can hardly do less.

Preventing versus Deterring Crime

The analogy between capital punishment and self-defense requires us to face squarely the empirical questions surrounding the preventive and deterrent effects of the death penalty. Executing a murderer in the name of punishment can be seen as a crime-*preventive* measure just to the extent it is reasonable to believe that if the murderer had not been executed he or she would have committed other crimes (including, but not necessarily confined to, murder). Executing a murderer can be seen as a crime *deterrent* just to the extent it is reasonable to believe that by the example of the execution other persons would be frightened off from committing murder. Any punishment can be a crime preventive without being a crime deterrent, just as it can be a deterrent without being a preventive. It can also be both or neither. Prevention and deterrence are theoretically independent because they operate by different methods. Crimes can be prevented by taking guns out of the hands of criminals, by putting criminals behind bars, by alerting the public to be less careless and less prone to victimization, and so forth. Crimes can be deterred only by making would-be criminals frightened of being arrested, convicted, and punished for crimes—that is, making persons overcome their desire to commit crimes by a stronger desire to avoid the risk of being caught and punished.

The Death Penalty as a Crime Preventive

Capital punishment is unusual among penalties because its preventive effects limit its deterrent effects. The death penalty can never deter the executed person from further crimes. At most, it can prevent a person from committing them. Popular discussions of the death penalty are frequently confused because they so often assume that the death penalty is a perfect and infallible deterrent so far as the executed criminal is concerned, whereas nothing of the sort is true. What is even more important, it is also wrong to think that in every execution the death penalty has proved to be an infallible crime preventive. What is obviously true is that once an offender has been executed, it is physically impossible for that person to commit any further crimes, since the punishment is totally incapacitative. But incapacitation is not identical with prevention. Prevention by means of incapacitation occurs only if the executed criminal would have committed other crimes if he or she had not been executed and had been punished only in some less incapacitative way (e.g., by imprisonment).

What evidence is there that the incapacitative effects of the death penalty are an effective crime preventive? From the study of imprisonment, parole, release records, this much is clear: If the murderers and other criminals who have been executed are like the murderers who were convicted but not executed, then (1) executing all convicted murderers would have prevented many crimes, but not many murders (less than one convicted murderer in five hundred commits another murder); and (2) convicted murder-

ers, whether inside prison or outside after release, have at least as good a record of no further criminal activity as any other class of convicted felon.

These facts show that the general public tends to overrate the danger and threat to public safety constituted by the failure to execute every murderer who is caught and convicted. While it would be quite wrong to say that there is no risk such criminals will repeat their crimes—or similar ones—if they are not executed, it would be equally erroneous to say that by executing every convicted murderer many horrible crimes will be prevented. All we know is that a few such crimes will never be committed; we do not know how many or by whom they would have been committed. (Obviously, if we did know we would have tried to prevent them!) This is the nub of the problem. There is no way to know in advance which if any of the incarcerated or released murderers will kill again. It is useful in this connection to remember that the only way to guarantee that no horrible crimes ever occur is to execute *everyone* who might conceivably commit such a crime. Similarly, the only way to guarantee that no convicted murderer ever commits another murder is to execute them all. No modern society has ever done this, and for two hundred years ours has been moving steadily in the opposite direction.

These considerations show that our society has implicitly adopted an attitude toward the risk of murder rather like the attitude it has adopted toward the risk of fatality from other sources, such as automobile accidents, lung cancer, or drowning. Since no one knows when or where or upon whom any of these lethal events will fall, it would be too great an invasion of freedom to undertake the severe restrictions that alone would suffice to prevent any such deaths from occurring. It is better to take the risks and keep our freedom than to try to eliminate the risks altogether and lose our freedom in the process. Hence, we have lifeguards at the beach, but swimming is not totally prohibited; smokers are warned, but cigarettes are still legally sold; pedestrians may be given the right of way in a crosswalk, but marginally competent drivers are still allowed to operate motor vehicles. Some risk is therefore imposed on the innocent; in the name of our right to freedom, our other rights are not protected by society at all costs.

The Death Penalty as a Crime Deterrent

Determining whether the death penalty is an effective deterrent is even more difficult than determining its effectiveness as a crime preventive. In general, our knowledge about how penalties deter crimes and whether in fact they do—whom they deter, from which crimes, and under what conditions—is distressingly inexact. Most people nevertheless are convinced that punishments do deter, and that the more severe a punishment is the better it will deter. For half a century, social scientists have studied the questions whether the death penalty is a deterrent and whether it is a better deterrent than the alternative of imprisonment. Their verdict, while not unanimous, is nearly so. Whatever may be true about the deterrence of lesser crimes by other penalties, the deterrence achieved by the death penalty for murder is not measurably any greater than the deterrence achieved by long-term imprisonment. In the nature of the case, the evidence is quite indirect. No one can identify for certain any crimes that did not occur because the would-be offender was deterred by the threat of the death penalty and could not have been deterred by a less severe threat. Likewise, no one can identify any crimes that did occur because the offender was not deterred by the threat of prison even though he would have been deterred by the threat of death. Nevertheless, such evidence as we have fails to show that the more severe penalty (death) is really a better deterrent than the less severe penalty (imprisonment) for such crimes as murder.

If the conclusion stated above is correct, and the death penalty and long-term imprisonment are equally effective (or ineffective) as deterrents to murder, then the argument for the death penalty on grounds of deterrence is seriously weakened. One of the moral principles identified earlier now comes into play. It is the principle that unless there is a good reason for choosing a more rather than a less severe punishment for a crime, the less severe penalty is to be preferred. This principle obviously commends itself to anyone who values human life and who concedes that, all other things being equal, less pain and suffering is always better than more. Human life is valued in part to the degree that it is free of pain, suffering, misery, and frustration, and in particular to the extent that it is free of such experiences when they serve no purpose. If the death penalty is not a more effective deterrent than imprisonment, then its greater severity is gratuitous, purposeless suffering and deprivation. Accordingly, we must reject it in favor of some less severe alternative, unless we can identify some more weighty moral principle that the death penalty protects better than any less severe mode of punishment does. Whether there is any such principle is unclear.

A Cost/Benefit Analysis of the Death Penalty

A full study of the costs and benefits involved in the practice of capital punishment would not be confined solely to the question of whether it is a better deterrent or preventive of murder than imprisonment. Any thoroughgoing utilitarian approach to the death-penalty controversy would need to examine carefully other costs and benefits as well, because maximizing the balance of all the social benefits over all the social costs is the sole criterion of right and wrong according to utilitarianism. . . . Let us consider, therefore, some of the other costs and benefits to be calculated. Clinical psychologists have presented evidence to suggest that the death penalty actually incites some persons of unstable mind to murder others, either because they are afraid to take their own lives and hope that society will punish them for murder by putting them to death, or because they fancy that they, too, are killing with justification analogously to the lawful and presumably justified killing involved in capital punishment. If such evidence is sound, capital punishment can serve as a counterpreventive or even an incitement to murder; such incited murders become part of its social cost. Imprisonment, however, has not been known to incite any murders or other crimes of violence in a comparable fashion. (A possible exception might be found in the imprisonment of terrorists, which has inspired other terrorists to take hostages as part of a scheme to force the authorities to release their imprisoned comrades.) The risks of executing the innocent are also part of the social cost. The historical record is replete with innocent persons arrested, indicted, convicted, sentenced, and occasionally legally executed for crimes they did not commit. This is quite apart from the guilty persons unfairly convicted, sentenced to death, and executed on the strength of perjured testimony, fraudulent evidence, subornation of jurors, and other violations of the civil rights and liberties of the accused. Nor is this all. The high costs of a capital trial and of the inevitable appeals, the costly methods of custody most prisons adopt for convicts on "death row," are among the straightforward economic costs that the death penalty incurs. Conducting a valid cost/benefit analysis of capital punishment is extremely difficult, and it is impossible to predict exactly what such a study would show. Nevertheless, based on such evidence as we do have, it is quite possible that a study of this sort would favor abolition of all death penalties rather than their retention.

What If Executions Did Deter?

From the moral point of view, it is quite important to determine what one should think about capital punishment if the evidence were clearly to show that the death penalty is a distinctly superior method of social defense by comparison with less severe alternatives. Kantian moralists . . . would have no use for such knowledge, because their entire case for the morality of the death penalty rests on the way it is thought to provide just retribution, not on the way it is thought to provide social defense. For a utilitarian, however, such knowledge would be conclusive. Those who follow Locke's reasoning would also be gratified, because they defend the morality of the death penalty both on the ground that it is retributively just and on the ground that it provides needed social defense.

What about the opponents of the death penalty, however? To oppose the death penalty in the face of incontestable evidence that it is an effective method of social defense violates the moral principle that where grave risks are to be run, it is better that they be run by the guilty than by the innocent. Consider in this connection an imaginary world in which by executing the murderer his victim is invariably restored to life, whole and intact, as though the murder had never occurred. In such a miraculous world, it is hard to see how anyone could oppose the death penalty on moral grounds. Why shouldn't a murderer die if that will infallibly bring the victim back to life? What could possibly be morally wrong with taking the murderer's life under such conditions? The death penalty would now be an instrument of perfect restitution, and it would give a new and better meaning to *lex talionis*, "a life for a life." The whole idea is fanciful, of course, but it shows as nothing else can how opposition to the death penalty cannot be both moral and wholly unconditional. If opposition to the death penalty is to be morally responsible, then it must be conceded that there are conditions (however unlikely) under which that opposition should cease.

But even if the death penalty were known to be a uniquely effective social defense, we could still imagine conditions under which it would be reasonable to oppose it. Suppose that in addition to being a slightly better preventive and deterrent than imprisonment, executions also have a slight incitive effect (so that for every ten murders an execution prevents or deters, it also incites another murder). Suppose also that the administration of criminal justice in capital cases is inefficient, unequal, and tends to secure convictions and death sentences only for murderers who least "deserve" to be sentenced to death (including some death sentences and a few executions of the innocent). Under such conditions, it would still be reasonable to oppose the death penalty, because on the facts supposed more (or not fewer) innocent lives are being threatened and lost by using the death penalty than would be risked by abolishing it. It is important to remember throughout our evaluation of the deterrence controversy that we cannot ever apply the principle . . . that advises us to risk the lives of the guilty in order to save the lives of the innocent. Instead, the most we can do is weigh the risk for the general public against the execution of those who are *found* guilty by an imperfect system of criminal justice. These hypothetical factual assumptions illustrate the contingencies upon which the morality of opposition to the death penalty rests. And not only the morality of opposition; the morality of any defense of the death penalty rests on the same contingencies. This should help us understand why, in resolving the morality of capital punishment one way or the other, it is so important to know, as well as we can, whether the death penalty really does deter, prevent, or incite crime, whether the innocent really are ever executed, and how likely is the occurrence of these things in the future.

How Many Guilty Lives Is One Innocent Life Worth?

The great unanswered question that utilitarians must face concerns the level of social defense that executions should be expected to achieve before it is justifiable to carry them out. Consider three possible situations: (1) At the level of a hundred executions per year, each additional execution of a convicted murderer reduces the number of murder victims by ten. (2) Executing every convicted murderer reduces the number of murders to 5,000 victims annually, whereas executing only one out of ten reduces the number to 5,001. (3) Executing every convicted murderer reduces the murder rate no more than does executing one in a hundred and no more than does a random pattern of executions.

Many people contemplating situation (1) would regard this as a reasonable trade-off: The execution of each further guilty person saves the lives of ten innocent ones. (In fact, situation (1) or something like it may be taken as a description of what most of those who defend the death penalty on grounds of social defense believe is true.) But suppose that, instead of saving 10 lives, the number dropped to 0.5, i.e., one victim avoided for each two additional executions. Would that be a reasonable price to pay? We are on the road toward the situation described in situation (2), where a drastic 90 percent reduction in the number of persons executed causes the level of social defense to drop by only 0.0002 percent. Would it be worth it to execute so many more murderers at the cost of such a slight decrease in social

defense? How many guilty lives is one innocent life worth? (Only those who think that guilty lives are *worthless* can avoid facing this problem.) In situation (3), of course, there is no basis for executing all convicted murderers, since there is no gain in social defense to show for each additional execution after the first out of each hundred has been executed. How, then, should we determine which out of each hundred convicted murderers is the unlucky one to be put to death?

It may be possible, under a complete and thoroughgoing cost/benefit analysis of the death penalty, to answer such questions. But an appeal merely to the moral principle that if lives are to be risked then let it be the lives of the guilty rather than of the innocent will not suffice. (We have already noticed . . . that this abstract principle is of little use in the actual administration of criminal justice, because the police and the courts do not deal with the guilty as such but only with those *judged* guilty.) Nor will it suffice to agree that society deserves all the crime prevention and deterrence it can get as a result of inflicting severe punishments. These principles are consistent with too many different policies. They are too vague by themselves to resolve the choice on grounds of social defense when confronted with hypothetical situations like those proposed above.

Since no adequate cost/benefit analysis of the death penalty exists, there is no way to resolve these questions from that standpoint at this time. Moreover, it can be argued that we cannot have such an analysis without already establishing in some way or other the relative value of innocent lives versus guilty lives. Far from being a product of cost/benefit analysis, a comparative evaluation of lives would have to be available to us before we undertook any such analysis. Without it, no cost/benefit analysis can get off the ground. Finally, it must be noted that our knowledge at present does not approximate to anything like the situation described above in (1). On the contrary, from the evidence we do have it seems we achieve about the same deterrent and preventive effects whether we punish murder by death or by imprisonment. . . . Therefore, something like the situation in (2) or in (3) may be correct. If so, this shows that the choice between the two policies of capital punishment and life imprisonment for murder will probably have to be made on some basis other than social defense; on that basis alone, the two policies are equivalent and therefore equally acceptable.

Capital Punishment and Retributive Justice

As we have noticed earlier in several contexts, there are two leading principles of retributive justice relevant to the capital punishment controversy. One is the principle that crimes should be punished. The other is the principle that the severity of a punishment should be proportional to the gravity of the offense. They are moral principles of recognized weight. No discussion of the morality of punishment would be complete without taking them into account. Leaving aside all questions of social defense, how strong a case for capital punishment can be made on their basis? How reliable and persuasive are these principles themselves?

Crime Must Be Punished

Given the general rationale for punishment sketched earlier . . ., there cannot be any dispute over this principle. In embracing it, of course, we are not automatically making a fetish of "law and order," in the sense that we would be if we thought that the most important single thing to do with social resources is to punish crimes. In addition, this principle need not be in dispute between proponents and opponents of the death penalty. Only those who completely oppose punishment for murder and other erstwhile capital crimes would appear to disregard this principle. Even defenders of the death penalty must admit that putting a convicted murderer in prison for years is a punishment of that criminal. The principle that crime must be punished is neutral to our controversy, because both sides acknowledge it.

It is the other principle of retributive justice that seems to be a decisive one. Under the principle of retaliation, *lex talionis,* it must al-

ways have seemed that murderers ought to be put to death. Proponents of the death penalty, with rare exceptions, have insisted on this point, and it seems that even opponents of the death penalty must give it grudging assent. The strategy of opponents of the death penalty is to argue either that (1) this principle is not really a principle of justice after all, or that (2) to the extent it is, it does not require death for murderers, or that (3) in any case it is not the only principle of punitive justice. As we shall see, all these objections have merit.

Is Murder Alone to Be Punished by Death?

Let us recall, first, that not even the Biblical world limited the death penalty to the punishment of murder. Many other nonhomicidal crimes also carried this penalty (e.g., kidnapping, witchcraft, cursing one's parents). In our own nation's recent history, persons have been executed for aggravated assault, rape, kidnapping, armed robbery, sabotage, and espionage. It is not possible to defend *any* of these executions (not to mention some of the more bizarre capital statutes, like the one in Georgia that used to provide an optional death penalty for desecration of a grave) on grounds of just retribution. This entails that either such executions are not justified or that they are justified on some ground other than retribution. In actual practice, few if any defenders of the death penalty have ever been willing to rest their case entirely on the moral principle of just retribution as formulated in terms of "a life for a life." (Kant seems to have been a conspicuous exception.) Most defenders of the death penalty have implied by their willingness to use executions to defend not only life but limb and property as well, that they did not place much value on the lives of criminals when compared to the value of both lives and things belonging to innocent citizens.

Are All Murders to Be Punished by Death?

European civilization for several centuries has tended to limit the variety of criminal homicides punishable by death. Even Kant took a casual attitude toward a mother's killing of her illegitimate child. ("A child born into the world outside marriage is outside the law . . ., and consequently it is also outside the protection of the law.") In our society, the development nearly two hundred years ago of the distinction between first- and second-degree murder was an attempt to narrow the class of criminal homicides deserving the death penalty. Yet those dead owing to manslaughter, or to any kind of unintentional, accidental, unpremeditated, unavoidable, unmalicious killing are just as dead as the victims of the most ghastly murder. Both the law in practice and moral reflection show how difficult it is to identify all and only the criminal homicides that are appropriately punished by death (assuming that any are). Individual judges and juries differ in the conclusions they reach. The history of capital punishment for homicides reveals continual efforts, uniformly unsuccessful, to identify before the fact those homicides for which the slayer should die. Sixty years ago, Benjamin Cardozo, then a justice of the United States Supreme Court, said of the distinction between degrees of murder that it was

. . . so obscure that no jury hearing it for the first time can fairly be expected to assimilate and understand it. I am not at all sure that I understand it myself after trying to apply it for many years and after diligent study of what has been written in the books. Upon the basis of this fine distinction with its obscure and mystifying psychology, scores of men have gone to their death.

Similar skepticism has been expressed on the reliability and rationality of death-penalty statutes that give the trial court the discretion ot sentence to prison or to death. As Justice John Marshall Harlan of the Supreme Court observed more than a decade ago,

Those who have come to grips with the hard task of actually attempting to draft means of channeling capital sentencing discretion have confirmed the lesson taught by history. . . . To identify before

the fact those characteristics of criminal homicide and their perpetrators which call for the death penalty, and to express these characteristics in language which can be fairly understood and applied by the sentencing authority, appear to be tasks which are beyond present human ability.

The abstract principle that the punishment of death best fits the crime of murder turns out to be extremely difficult to interpret and apply.

If we look at the matter from the standpoint of the actual practice of criminal justice, we can only conclude that "a life for a life" plays little or no role whatever. Plea bargaining (in which a person charged with a crime pleads guilty in exchange for a less severe sentence than he might have received if his case went to trial and he was found guilty), even where murder is concerned, is widespread. Studies of criminal justice reveal that what the courts (trial or appellate) in a given jurisdiction decide on a given day is first-degree murder suitably punished by death could just as well be decided in a neighboring jurisdiction on another day either as second-degree murder or as first-degree murder but without the death penalty. The factors that influence prosecutors in determining the charge under which they will prosecute go far beyond the simple principle of "a life for a life." Cynics, of course, will say that these facts show that our society does not care about justice. To put it succinctly, either justice in punishment does not consist of retribution, because there are other principles of justice; or there are other moral considerations besides justice that must be honored; or retributive justice is not adequately expressed in the idea of "a life for a life"; or justice in the criminal justice system is beyond our reach.

Is Death Sufficiently Retributive?

Those who advocate capital punishment for murder on retributive grounds must face the objection that, on their own principles, the death penalty in some cases is morally inadequate. How could death in the electric chair or the gas chamber or before a firing squad or on a gallows suffice as just retribution, given the savage, brutal, wanton character of so many murders? How can retributive justice be served by anything less than equally savage methods of execution? From a retributive point of view, the oft-heard exclamation, "Death is too good for him!" has a certain truth. Are defenders of the death penalty willing to embrace this consequence of their own doctrine?

If they were, they would be stooping to the methods and thus to the squalor of the murderer. Where the quality of the crime sets the limits of just methods of punishment, as it will if we attempt to give exact and literal implementation to *lex talionis*, society will find itself descending to the cruelties and savagery that criminals employ. What is worse, society would be deliberately authorizing such acts, in the cool light of reason, and not (as is often true of vicious criminals) impulsively or in hatred and anger or with an insane or unbalanced mind. Moral restraints, in short, prohibit us from trying to make executions perfectly retributive. Once we grant that such restraints are proper, it is unreasonable to insist that the principle of "a life for a life" nevertheless by itself justifies the execution of murderers.

Other considerations take us in a different direction. Few murders, outside television and movie scripts, involve anything like an execution. An execution, after all, begins with a solemn pronouncement of the death sentence from a judge; this is followed by long detention in maximum security awaiting the date of execution, during which various complex and protracted appeals will be pursued; after this there is a clemency hearing before the governor, and then "the last mile" to the execution chamber itself. As the French writer Albert Camus once remarked,

For there to be an equivalence, the death penalty would have to punish a criminal who had warned his victim of the date at which he would inflict a horrible death on him and who, from that moment onward, had confined him at his mercy for

months. Such a monster is not encountered in private life.

Differential Severity Does Not Require Executions

What, then, emerges from our examination of retributive justice and the death penalty? If retributive justice is thought to consist in *lex talionis,* all one can say is that this principle has never exercised more than a crude and indirect effect on the actual punishments meted out by society. Other principles interfere with a literal and single-minded application of this one. Some homicides seem improperly punished by death at all; others would require methods of execution too horrible to inflict; in still other cases any possible execution is too deliberate and monstrous given the nature of the motivation culminating in the murder. In any case, proponents of the death penalty rarely confine themselves to reliance on nothing but this principle of just retribution, since they rarely confine themselves to supporting the death penalty only for all murders.

But retributive justice need not be thought of as consisting in *lex talionis.* One may reject that principle as too crude and still embrace the retributive principle that the severity of punishments should be graded according to the gravity of the offense. Even though one need not claim that life imprisonment (or any kind of punishment other than death) "fits" the crime of murder, one can claim that this punishment is the proper one for murder. To do this, the schedule of punishments accepted by society must be arranged so that this mode of imprisonment is the most severe penalty used. Opponents of the death penalty need not reject this principle of retributive justice, even though they must reject a literal *lex talionis.*

Equal Justice and Capital Punishment

During the past generation, the strongest practical objection to the death penalty has been the inequities with which it has been applied. As the late Supreme Court Justice William O. Douglas once observed, "One searches our chronicles in vain for the execution of any member of the affluent strata of this society." One does not search our chronicles in vain for the crime of murder committed by the affluent. All the sociological evidence points to the conclusion that the death penalty is the poor man's justice; hence the slogan, "Those without the capital get the punishment." The death penalty is also racially sensitive. Every study of the death penalty for rape (unconstitutional only since 1977) has confirmed that black male rapists (especially where the victim is a white female) are far more likely to be sentenced to death and executed than white male rapists. Convicted black murderers are more likely to end up on "death row" than are others, and the killers of whites (whether white or nonwhite) are more likely to be sentenced to death than are the killers of nonwhites.

Let us suppose that the factual basis for such a criticism is sound. What follows for the morality of capital punishment? Many defenders of the death penalty have been quick to point out that since there is nothing intrinsic about the crime of murder or rape dictating that only the poor or only racial-minority males will commit it, and since there is nothing overtly racist about the statutes that authorize the death penalty for murder or rape, capital punishment itself is hardly at fault if in practice it falls with unfair impact on the poor and the black. There is, in short, nothing in the death penalty that requires it to be applied unfairly and with arbitrary or discriminatory results. It is at worst a fault in the system of administering criminal justice. (Some, who dispute the facts cited above, would deny even this.) There is an adequate remedy—execute more whites, women, and affluent murderers.

Presumably, both proponents and opponents of capital punishment would concede that it is a fundamental dictate of justice that a punishment should not be unfairly—inequitably or unevenly—enforced and applied. They should also be able to agree that when the punishment in question is the extremely severe one of death, then the requirement to be fair in using such a punishment becomes even more stringent. There should be no dispute in the death penalty controversy over these principles of justice. The dispute begins as soon as one attempts to connect the principles with the actual use of this punishment.

In this country, many critics of the death penalty have argued, we would long ago have got rid of it entirely if it had been a condition of its use that it be applied equally and fairly. In the words of the attorneys who argued against the death penalty in the Supreme Court during 1972, "It is a freakish aberration, a random extreme act of violence, visibly arbitrary and discriminatory—a penalty reserved for unusual application because, if it were usually used, it would affront universally shared standards of public decency." It is difficult to dispute this judgment, when one considers that there have been in the United States during the past fifty years about half a million criminal homicides but only about 3,900 executions (all but 33 of which were of men).

We can look at these statistics in another way to illustrate the same point. If we could be assured that the nearly 4,000 persons executed were the worst of the bad, repeated offenders incapable of safe incarceration, much less of rehabilitation, the most dangerous murderers in captivity—the ones who had killed more than once and were likely to kill again, and the least likely to be confined in prision without chronic danger to other inmates and the staff—then one might accept half a million murders and a few thousand executions with a sense that rough justice had been done. But the truth is otherwise. Persons are sentenced to death and executed not because they have been found to be uncontrollably violent or hopelessly poor confinement and release risks. Instead, they are executed because they have a poor defense (inexperienced or overworked counsel) at trial; they have no funds to bring sympathetic witnesses to court; they are transients or strangers in the community where they are tried; the prosecuting attorney wants the publicity that goes with "sending a killer to the chair"; there are no funds for an appeal or for a transcript of the trial record; they are members of a despised racial or political minority. In short, the actual study of why particular persons have been sentenced to death and executed does not show any careful winnowing of the worst from the bad. It shows that the executed were usually the unlucky victims of prejudice and discrimination, the losers in an arbitrary lottery that could just as well have spared them, the victims of the disadvantages that almost always go with poverty. A system like this does not enhance human life; it cheapens and degrades it. However heinous murder and other crimes are, the system of capital punishment does not compensate for or erase those crimes. It only tends to add new injuries of its own to the catalogue of human brutality.

Conclusion

Our discussion of the death penalty from the moral point of view shows that there is no one moral principle the validity of which is paramount and that decisively favors one side of the controversy. Rather, we have seen how it is possible to argue either for or against the death penalty, and in each case to be appealing to moral principles that derive from the worth, value, or dignity of human life. We have also seen how it is impossible to connect any of these abstract principles with the actual practice of capital punishment witout a close study of sociological, psychological, and economic factors. By themselves, the moral principles that are relevant are too abstract and uncertain in application to be of much help. Without the guidance of such principles, of course, the facts (who gets executed, and why) are of little use, either.

My own view of the controversy is that, given the moral principles we have identified in the course of our discussion (including the overriding value of human life), and given all the facts about capital punishment, the balance of reasons favors abolition of the death penalty. The alternative to capital punishment that I favor, as things currently stand, is long-term imprisonment. Such a punishment is retributive and can be made appropriately severe to reflect the gravity of the crime. It gives adequate (though hardly perfect) protection to the public. It is free of the worst defect to which the death penalty is liable: execution of the innocent. It tacitly acknowledges that there is no way for a criminal, alive or dead, to make complete amends for murder or other grave crimes against the person. Last but not least, it has symbolic significance. The death penalty, more than any other kind of killing, is done by officials in the name of society and on its behalf. Yet each of us has a hand in such killings. Unless they are absolutely necessary they cannot be justified. Thus, abolishing the death penalty represents extending the hand of life even to those who by their crimes have "forfeited" any right to live. It is a tacit admission that we must abandon the folly and pretense of attempting to secure perfect justice in an imperfect world.

Searching for an epigram suitable for our times, in which governments have waged war and suppressed internal dissent by using methods that can only be described as savage and criminal, Camus was prompted to admonish: "Let us be neither victims nor executioners." Perhaps better than any other, this exhortation points the way between forbidden extremes if we are to respect the humanity in each of us.

25. On Deterrence and the Death Penalty

Ernest Van Den Haag

Ernest Van Den Haag argues that the death penalty must be retained as a deterrent. He gives us an elaborate psychological explanation for deterrence as a response to danger. Although it cannot be proven that the death penalty deters, he suggests that retention will provide benefits in crime reduction.

I

If rehabilitation and the protection of society from unrehabilitated offenders were the only purposes of legal punishment, the death penalty could be abolished: It cannot attain the first end, and is not needed for the second. No case for the death penalty can be made unless "doing justice" or "deterring others" is among our penal aims.[1] Each of these purposes can justify capital punishment by itself; opponents, therefore, must show that neither actually does, while proponents can rest their case on either.

Although the argument from justice is intellectually more interesting, and, in my view, decisive enough, utilitarian arguments have more appeal: The claim that capital punishment is useless because it does not deter others is most persuasive. I shall, therefore, focus on this claim. Lest the argument be thought to be unduly narrow, I shall show, nonetheless, that some claims of injustice rest on premises which the claimants reject when arguments for capital punishment are derived therefrom; while other claims of injustice have no independent standing: Their weight depends on the weight given to deterrence.

II

Capital punishment is regarded as unjust because it may lead to the execution of inno-

Reprinted by special permission of the *Journal of Criminal Law, Criminology, and Police Science*, © 1969 by Northwestern University School of Law, Vol. 60, No. 2, pp. 141–147.

cents, or because the guilty poor (or disadvantaged) are more likely to be executed than the guilty rich.

Regardless of merit, these claims are relevant only if "doing justice" is one purpose of punishment. Unless one regards it as good, or, at least, better, that the guilty be punished rather than the innocent, and that the equally guilty be punished equally,[2] unless, that is, one wants penalties to be just, one cannot object to them because they are not. However, if one does include justice among the purposes of punishment, it becomes possible to justify any one punishment—even death—on grounds of justice. Yet, those who object to the death penalty because of its alleged injustice usually deny not only the merits, or the sufficiency, of specific arguments based on justice, but the propriety of justice as an argument: They exclude "doing justice" as a purpose of legal punishment. If justice is not a purpose of penalties, injustice cannot be an objection to the death penalty, or to any other; if it is, justice cannot be ruled out as an argument for any penalty.

Consider the claim of injustice on its merits now. A convicted man may be found to have been innocent; if he was executed, the penalty cannot be reversed. Except for fines, penalties never can be reversed. Time spent in prison cannot be returned. However, a prison sentence may be remitted once the prisoner serving it is found innocent; and he can be compensated for the time served (although compensation ordinarily cannot repair the harm). Thus, though (nearly) all penalties are irreversible, the death penalty, unlike others, is irrevocable as well.

Despite all precautions, errors will occur in judicial proceedings: The innocent may be found guilty,[3] or the guilty rich may more easily escape conviction, or receive lesser penalties than the guilty poor. However, these injustices do not reside in the penalties inflicted but in their maldistribution. It is not the penalty—whether death or prison—which is unjust when inflicted on the innocent, but its imposition on the innocent. Inequity between poor and rich also involves distribution, not the penalty distributed.[4] Thus injustice is not an objection to the death penalty but to the distributive process—the trial. Trials are more likely to be fair when life is at stake—the death penalty is probably less often unjustly inflicted than others. It requires special consideration not because it is more, or more often, unjust than other penalties, but because it is always irrevocable.

Can any amount of deterrence justify the possibility of irrevocable injustice? Surely injustice is unjustifiable in each actual individual case; it must be objected to whenever it occurs. But we are concerned here with the process that may produce injustice, and with the penalty that would make it irrevocable—not with the actual individual cases produced, but with the general rules which may produce them. To consider objections to a general rule (the provision of any penalties by law) we must compare the likely net result of alternative rules and select the rule (or penalty) likely to produce the least injustice. For however one defines justice, to support it cannot mean less than to favor the least injustice. If the death of innocents because of judicial error is unjust, so is the death of innocents by murder. If some murders could be avoided by a penalty conceivably more deterrent than others—such as the death penalty—then the question becomes: Which penalty will minimize the number of innocents killed (by crime and by punishment)? It follows that the irrevocable injustice sometimes inflicted by the death penalty would not significantly militate against it, if capital punishment deters enough murders to reduce the total number of innocents killed so that fewer are lost than would be lost without it.

In general, the possibility of injustice argues against penalization of any kind only if the expected usefulness of penalization is less important than the probable harm (particularly to innocents) and the probable inequities. The possibility of injustice argues against the death penalty only inasmuch as the added usefulness (deterrence) expected from irrevocability is thought less important than the added harm. (Were my argument specifically concerned with justice, I could compare the injustice inflicted by the courts with the injustice—outside the courts—avoided by the judicial process. *I.e.*, "important" here may be used to include everything to which importance is attached.)

We must briefly examine now the general use and effectiveness of deterrence to decide whether the death penalty could add enough deterrence to be warranted.

III

Does any punishment "deter others" at all? Doubts have been thrown on this effect because it is thought to depend on the incorrect rationalistic psychology of some of its 18th- and 19th-century proponents. Actually deterrence does not depend on rational calculation, on rationality or even on capacity for it; nor do arguments for it depend on rationalistic psychology. Deterrence depends on the likelihood and on the regularity—not on the rationality—of human responses to danger; and further on the possibility of reinforcing internal controls by vicarious external experiences.

Responsiveness to danger is generally found in human behavior; the danger can, but need not, come from the law or from society; nor need it be explicitly verbalized. Unless intent on suicide, people do not jump from high mountain cliffs, however tempted to fly through the air; and they take precautions against falling. The mere risk of injury often restrains us from doing what is otherwise attractive; we refrain even when we have no direct experience, and usually without explicit computation of probabilities, let alone conscious weighing of expected pleasure against possible pain. One abstains from dangerous acts because of vague, inchoate, habitual and, above all, preconscious fears. Risks and rewards are more often felt than calculated; one abstains without accounting to oneself, because "it isn't done," or because one literally does not conceive of the action one refrains from. Animals as well refrain from painful or injurious experiences presumably without calculation; and the threat of punishment can be used to regulate their conduct.

Unlike natural dangers, legal threats are constructed deliberately by legislators to restrain actions which may impair the social order. Thus legislation transforms social into individual dangers. Most people further transform external into internal danger: They acquire a sense of moral obligation, a conscience, which threatens them, should they do what is wrong. Arising originally from the external authority of rulers and rules, conscience is internalized and becomes independent of external forces. However, conscience is constantly reinforced in those whom it controls by the coercive imposition of external authority on recalcitrants and on those who have not acquired it. Most people refrain from offenses because they feel an obligation to behave lawfully. But this obligation would scarcely be felt if those who do not feel or follow it were not to suffer punishment.

Although the legislators may calculate their threats and the responses to be produced, the effectiveness of the threats neither requires nor depends on calculations by those responding. The predictor (or producer) of effects must calculate; those whose responses are predicted (or produced) need not. Hence, although legislation (and legislators) should be rational, subjects, to be deterred as intended, need not be: They need only be responsive.

Punishments deter those who have not violated the law for the same reasons—and in the same degrees (apart from internalization: moral obligation) as do natural dangers. Often natural dangers—all dangers not deliberately created by legislation (e.g., injury of the criminal inflicted by the crime victim) are insufficient. Thus, the fear of injury (natural danger) does not suffice to control city traffic; it must be reinforced by the legal punishment meted out to those who violate the rules. These punishments keep most people observing the regulations. However, where (in the absence of natural danger) the threatened punishment is so light that the advantage of violating rules tends to exceed the disad-

vantage of being punished (divided by the risk), the rule is violated (i.e., parking fines are too light). In this case the feeling of obligation tends to vanish as well. Elsewhere punishment deters.

To be sure, not everybody responds to threatened punishment. Non-responsive persons may be (a) self-destructive or (b) incapable of responding to threats, or even of grasping them. Increases in the size, or certainty, of penalties would not affect these two groups. A third group (c) might respond to more certain or more severe penalties.[5] If the punishment threatened for burglary, robbery, or rape were a $5 fine in North Carolina, and 5 years in prison in South Carolina, I have no doubt that the North Carolina treasury would become quite opulent until vigilante justice would provide the deterrence not provided by law. Whether to increase penalties (or improve enforcement) depends on the importance of the rule to society, the size and likely reaction of the group that did not respond before, and the acceptance of the added punishment and enforcement required to deter it. Observation would have to locate the points—likely to differ in different times and places—at which diminishing, zero, and negative returns set in. There is no reason to believe that all present and future offenders belong to the a priori non-responsive groups, or that all penalties have reached the point of diminishing, let alone zero returns.

IV

Even though its effectiveness seems obvious, punishment as a deterrent has fallen into disrepute. Some ideas which help explain this progressive heedlessness were uttered by Lester Pearson, then Prime Minister of Canada, when, in opposing the death penalty, he proposed that instead "the state seek to eradicate the causes of crime—slums, ghettos and personality disorders."[6]

"Slums, ghettos, and personality disorders" have not been shown, singly or collectively, to be "the causes" of crime.

(1) The crime rate in the slums is indeed

higher than elsewhere; but so is the death rate in hospitals. Slums are no more "causes" of crime than hospitals are of death; they are locations of crime, as hospitals are of death. Slums and hospitals attract people selectively; neither is the "cause" of the condition (disease in hospitals, poverty in slums) that leads to the selective attraction.

As for poverty which draws people into slums, and, sometimes, into crime, any relative disadvantage may lead to ambition, frustration, resentment and, if insufficiently restrained, to crime. Not all relative disadvantages can be eliminated; indeed very few can be, and their elimination increases the resentment generated by the remaining ones; not even relative poverty can be removed altogether. (Absolute poverty—whatever that may be—hardly affects crime.) However, though contributory, relative disadvantages are not a necessary or sufficient cause of crime: Most poor people do not commit crimes, and some rich people do. Hence, "eradication of poverty" would, at most, remove one (doubtful) cause of crime.

In the United States, the decline of poverty has not been associated with a reduction of crime. Poverty measured in dollars of constant purchasing power, according to present government standards and statistics, was the condition of ½ of all our families in 1920; of ⅕ in 1962; and of less than ⅙ in 1966. In 1967, 5.3 million families out of 49.8 million were poor—⅑ of all families in the United States. If crime has been reduced in a similar manner, it is a well-kept secret.

Those who regard poverty as a cause of crime often draw a wrong inference from a true proposition: The rich will not commit certain crimes—Rockefeller never riots; nor does he steal. (He mugs, but only on T.V.) Yet while wealth may be the cause of not committing (certain) crimes, it does not follow that poverty (absence of wealth) is the cause of committing them. Water extinguishes or prevents fire; but its absence is not the cause of fire. Thus, if poverty could be abolished, if everybody had all "necessities" (I don't pretend to know what this would mean), crime would remain, for, in the words of Aristotle, "the greatest crimes are committed not for the sake of basic necessities but for the sake of

superfluities." Superfluities cannot be provided by the government; they would be what the government does not provide.

(2) Negro ghettos have a high, Chinese ghettos have a low crime rate. Ethnic separation, voluntary or forced, obviously has little to do with crime; I can think of no reason why it should.[7]

(3) I cannot see how the state could "eradicate" personality disorders even if all causes and cures were known and available. (They are not.) Further, the known incidence of personality disorders within the prison population does not exceed the known incidence outside—though our knowledge of both is tenuous. Nor are personality disorders necessary or sufficient causes for criminal offenses, unless these be identified by means of (moral, not clinical) definition with personality disorders. In this case, Mr. Pearson would have proposed to "eradicate" crime by eradicating crime—certainly a sound, but not a helpful idea.

Mr. Pearson's views are part as well of the mental furniture of the former U.S. Attorney General Ramsey Clark, who told a congressional committee that ". . . only the elimination of the causes of crime can make a significant and lasting difference in the incidence of crime." Uncharitably interpreted, Mr. Clark revealed that only the elimination of causes eliminates effects—a sleazy cliché and wrong to boot. Given the benefit of the doubt, Mr. Clark probably meant that the causes of crime are social; and that therefore crime can be reduced "only" by non-penal (social) measures.

This view suggests a fireman who declines fire-fighting apparatus by pointing out that "in the long run only the elimination of the causes" of fire "can make a significant and lasting difference in the incidence" of fire, and that fire-fighting equipment does not eliminate "the causes"—except that such a fireman would probably not rise to fire chief. Actually, whether fires are checked depends on equipment and on the efforts of the firemen using it no less than on the presence of "the causes": inflammable materials. So with crimes. Laws, courts and police actions are no less important in restraining them than "the causes" are in impelling them. If firemen (or attorneys general) pass the buck and refuse to use the means available, we may all be burned while waiting for "the long run" and "the elimination of the causes."

Whether any activity—be it lawful or unlawful—takes place depends on whether the desire for it, or for whatever is to be secured by it, is stronger than the desire to avoid the costs involved. Accordingly people work, attend college, commit crimes, go to the movies—or refrain from any of these activities. Attendance at a theatre may be high because the show is entertaining and because the price of admission is low. Obviously the attendance depends on both—on the combination of expected gratification and cost. The wish, motive or impulse for doing anything—the experienced, or expected, gratification—is the cause of doing it; the wish to avoid the cost is the cause of not doing it. One is no more and no less "cause" than the other. (Common speech supports this use of "cause" no less than logic: "Why did you go to Jamaica?" "*Because* it is such a beautiful place." "Why didn't you go to Jamaica?" "*Because* it is too expensive."—"Why do you buy this?" "*Because* it is so cheap." "Why don't you buy that?" "*Because* it is too expensive.") Penalties (costs) are causes of lawfulness, or (if too low or uncertain) of unlawfulness, of crime. People do commit crimes because, given their conditions, the desire for the satisfaction sought prevails. They refrain if the desire to avoid the cost prevails. Given the desire, low cost (penalty) causes the action, and high cost restraint. Given the cost, desire becomes the causal variable. Neither is intrinsically more causal than the other. The crime rate increases if the cost is reduced or the desire raised. It can be decreased by raising the cost or by reducing the desire.

The cost of crime is more easily and swiftly changed than the conditions producing the inclination to it. Further, the costs are very largely within the power of the government to change, whereas the conditions producing propensity to crime are often only indirectly affected by government action, and some are altogether beyond the control of the government. Our unilateral emphasis on these conditions and our undue neglect of costs may contribute to an unnecessarily high crime rate.

V

The foregoing suggests the question posed by the death penalty: Is the deterrence added (return) sufficiently above zero to warrant irrevocability (or other, less clear, disadvantages)? The question is not only whether the penalty deters, but whether it deters more than alternatives and whether the difference exceeds the cost of irrevocability. (I shall assume that the alternative is actual life imprisonment so as to exclude the complication produced by the release of the unrehabilitated.)

In some fairly infrequent but important circumstances the death penalty is the only possible deterrent. Thus, in case of acute *coups d'état*, or of acute substantial attempts to overthrow the government, prospective rebels would altogether discount the threat of any prison sentence. They would not be deterred because they believe the swift victory of the revolution will invalidate a prison sentence and turn it into an advantage. Execution would be the only deterrent because, unlike prison sentences, it cannot be revoked by victorious rebels. The same reasoning applies to deterring spies or traitors in wartime. Finally, men who, by virtue of past acts, are already serving, or are threatened, by a life sentence could be deterred from further offenses only by the threat of the death penalty.[8]

What about criminals who do not fall into any of these (often ignored) classes? Prof. Thorsten Sellin has made a careful study of the available statistics: He concluded that they do not yield evidence for the deterring effect of the death penalty.[9] Somewhat surprisingly, Prof. Sellin seems to think that this lack of evidence for deterrence is evidence for the lack of deterrence. It is not. It means that deterrence has not been demonstrated statistically—not that non-deterrence has been.

It is entirely possible, indeed likely (as Prof. Sellin appears willing to concede), that the statistics used, though the best available, are nonetheless too slender a reed to rest conclusions on. They indicate that the homicide rate does not vary greatly between similar areas with or without the death penalty, and in the same area before and after abolition.

However, the similar areas are not similar enough; the periods are not long enough; many social differences and changes, other than the abolition of the death penalty, may account for the variation (or lack of it) in homicide rates with and without, before and after abolition; some of these social differences and changes are likely to have affected homicide rates. I am unaware of any statistical analysis which adjusts for such changes and differences. And logically, it is quite consistent with the postulated deterrent effect of capital punishment that there be less homicide after abolition: With retention there might have been still less.

Homicide rates do not depend exclusively on penalties any more than do other crime rates. A number of conditions which influence the propensity to crime, demographic, economic or generally social changes or differences—even such matters as changes of the divorce laws or of the cotton price—may influence the homicide rate. Therefore variation or constancy cannot be attributed to variations or constancy of the penalties, unless we know that no other factor influencing the homicide rate has changed. Usually we don't. To believe the death penalty deterrent does not require one to believe that the death penalty, or any other, is the only or the decisive causal variable; this would be as absurd as the converse mistake that "social causes" are the only or always the decisive factor. To favor capital punishment, the efficacy of neither variable need be denied. It is enough to affirm that the severity of the penalty may influence some potential criminals, and that the added severity of the death penalty adds to deterrence, or may do so. It is quite possible that such a deterrent effect may be offset (or intensified) by non-penal factors which affect propensity; its presence or absence therefore may be hard, and perhaps impossible to demonstrate.

Contrary to what Prof. Sellin *et al.* seem to presume, I doubt that offenders are aware of the absence or presence of the death penalty state by state or period by period. Such unawareness argues against the assumption of a calculating murderer. However, unawareness does not argue against the death penalty if by deterrence we mean a preconscious, general response to a severe, but not neccessarily spe-

cifically and explicitly apprehended, or calculated threat. A constant homicide rate, despite abolition, may occur because of unawareness and not because of lack of deterrence: People remain deterred for a lengthy interval by the severity of the penalty in the past, or by the severity of penalties used in similar circumstances nearby.

I do not argue for a version of deterrence which would require me to believe that an individual shuns murder while in North Dakota, because of the death penalty, and merrily goes to it in South Dakota since it has been abolished there; or that he will start the murderous career from which he had hitherto refrained, after abolition. I hold that the generalized threat of the death penalty may be a deterrent, and the more so, the more generally applied. Deterrence will not cease in the particular areas of abolition or at the particular times of abolition. Rather, general deterrence will be somewhat weakened, through local (partial) abolition. Even such weakening will be hard to detect owing to changes in many offsetting, or reinforcing, factors.

For all of these reasons, I doubt that the presence or absence of a deterrent effect of the death penalty is likely to be demonstrable by statistical means. The statistics presented by Prof. Sellin *et al.* show only that there is no statistical proof for the deterrent effect of the death penalty. But they do not show that there is no deterrent effect. Not to demonstrate presence of the effect is not the same as to demonstrate its absence; certainly not when there are plausible explanations for the nondemonstrability of the effect.

It is on our uncertainty that the case for deterrence must rest.[10]

VI

If we do not know whether the death penalty will deter others, we are confronted with two uncertainties. If we impose the death penalty, and achieve no deterrent effect thereby, the life of a convicted murderer has been expended in vain (from a deterrent viewpoint).

There is a net loss. If we impose the death sentence and thereby deter some future murderers, we spared the lives of some future victims (the prospective murderers gain too; they are spared punishment because they were deterred). In this case, the death penalty has led to a net gain, unless the life of a convicted murderer is valued more highly than that of the unknown victim, or victims (and the non-imprisonment of the deterred non-murderer).

The calculation can be turned around, of course. The absence of the death penalty may harm no one and therefore produce a gain—the life of the convicted murderer. Or it may kill future victims of murderers who could have been deterred, and thus produce a loss—their life.

To be sure, we must risk something certain—the death (or life) of the convicted man, for something uncertain—the death (or life) of the victims of murderers who may be deterred. This is in the nature of uncertainty—when we invest, or gamble, we risk the money we have for an uncertain gain. Many human actions, most commitments—including marriage and crime—share this characteristic with the deterrent purpose of any penalization, and with its rehabilitative purpose (and even with the protective).

More proof is demanded for the deterrent effect of the death penalty than is demanded for the deterrent effect of other penalties. This is not justified by the absence of other utilitarian purposes such as protection and rehabilitation; they involve no less uncertainty than deterrence.[11]

Irrevocability may support a demand for some reason to expect more deterrence than revocable penalties might produce, but not a demand for more proof of deterrence, as has been pointed out above. The reason for expecting more deterrence lies in the greater severity, the terrifying effect inherent in finality. Since it seems more important to spare victims than to spare murderers, the burden of proving that the greater severity inherent in irrevocability adds nothing to deterrence lies on those who oppose capital punishment. Proponents of the death penalty need show only that there is no more uncertainty about it than about greater severity in general.

The demand that the death penalty be proved more deterrent than alternatives can not be satisfied any more than the demand that six years in prison be proved to be more deterrent than three. But the uncertainty which confronts us favors the death penalty as long as by imposing it we might save future victims of murder. This effect is as plausible as the general idea that penalties have deterrent effects which increase with their severity. Though we have no proof of the positive deterrence of the penalty, we also have no proof of zero or negative effectiveness. I believe we have no right to risk additional future victims of murder for the sake of sparing convicted murderers; on the contrary, our moral obligation is to risk the possible ineffectiveness of executions. However rationalized, the opposite view appears to be motivated by the simple fact that executions are more subjected to social control than murder. However, this applies to all penalties and does not argue for the abolition of any.

Notes

1. Social solidarity of "community feeling" (here to be ignored) might be dealt with as a form of deterrence.

2. Certainly a major meaning of *suum cuique tribue*.

3. I am not concerned here with the converse injustice, *which I regard as no less grave*.

4. Such inequity, though likely, has not been demonstrated. Note that, since there are more poor than rich, there are likely to be more guilty poor; and, if poverty contributes to crime, the proportion of the poor who are criminals also should be higher than of the rich.

5. I neglect those motivated by civil disobedience or, generally, moral or political passion. Deterring them depends less on penalties than on the moral support they receive, though penalties play a role. I also neglect those who may belong to all three groups listed, some successively, some even simultaneously, such as drug addicts. Finally, I must altogether omit the far-from-negligible role that problems of apprehension and conviction play in deterrence—beyond saying that, by reducing the government's ability to apprehend

and convict, courts are able to reduce the risks of offenders.

6. I quote from the *New York Times* (November 24, 1967, p. 22). The actual psychological and other factors which bear on the disrepute—as distinguished from the rationalizations—cannot be examined here.

7. Mixed areas, incidentally, have higher crime rates than segregated ones (see, e.g., R. Ross and E. van den Haag, *The Fabric of Society* (New York: Harcourt, Brace & Co., 1957), pp. 102–4. Because slums are bad (morally) and crime is, many people seem to reason that "slums spawn crime"—which confuses some sort of moral with a causal relation.

8. Cautious revolutionaries, uncertain of final victory, might be impressed by prison sentences—but not in the acute stage, when faith in victory is high. And one can increase even the severity of a life sentence in prison. Finally, harsh punishment of rebels can intensify rebellious impulses. These points, though they qualify it, hardly impair the force of the argument.

9. Sellin considered mainly homicide statistics. His work may be found in his *Capital Punishment* (New York: Harper & Row, 1967); or, most conveniently, in H. A. Bedau, *The Death Penalty in America* (Garden City, N.Y.: Doubleday & Co., 1964), which also offers other material, mainly against the death penalty.

10. In view of the strong emotions aroused (itself an indication of effectiveness to me: Might not murderers be as upset over the death penalty as those who wish to spare them?) and because I believe penalties must reflect community feeling to be effective, I oppose mandatory death sentences and favor optional, and perhaps binding, recommendations by juries after their finding of guilt. The opposite course risks the non-conviction of guilty defendants by juries who do not want to see them executed.

11. Rehabilitation or protection are of minor importance in our actual penal system (though not in our theory). We confine many people who do not need rehabilitation and against whom we do not need protection (e.g., the exasperated husband who killed his wife); we release many unrehabilitated offenders against whom protection is needed. Certainly rehabilitation and protection are not, and deterrence is, the main actual function of legal punishment if we disregard nonutilitarian ones.

---

26. *Furman* v. *Georgia*

U.S. Supreme Court

In their 1972 decision on *Furman* v. *Georgia*, the United States Supreme Court invalidated the death penalty on procedural grounds. Concurring with the Court's findings, Justice William Brennan set out what is among the most succinct statements by the Court defining cruel and unusual punishment. For a penalty not to be cruel and unusual, it must not by its severity be degrading to human dignity, there must not be a strong possibility that it is administered in a wholly arbitrary fashion, it must not be substantially rejected by society, and it should serve no greater purpose than that done by a lesser penalty.

Mr. Justice *Brennan*, concurring.

. . . There are, then, four principles by which we may determine whether a particular punishment is "cruel and unusual." The primary principle, which I believe supplies the essential predicate for the application of the others, is that a punishment must not by its severity be degrading to human dignity. The paradigm violation of this principle would be the infliction of a torturous punishment of the type that the Clause has always prohibited.

Yet "[i]t is unlikely that any State at this moment in history," *Robinson* v. *California*, 370 U.S., at 666, would pass a law providing for the infliction of such a punishment. Indeed, no such punishment has ever been before this Court. The same may be said of the other principles. It is unlikely that this Court will confront a severe punishment that is obviously inflicted in wholly arbitrary fashion; no State would engage in a reign of blind terror. Nor is it likely that this Court will be called upon to review a severe punishment that is clearly and totally rejected throughout society; no legislature would be able even to authorize the infliction of such a punishment. Nor, finally, is it likely that this Court will have to consider a severe punishment that is patently unnecessary; no State today would inflict a severe punishment knowing that there was no reason whatever for doing so. In short, we are unlikely to have occasion to determine that a punishment is fatally offensive under any one principle.

Since the Bill of Rights was adopted, this Court has adjudged only three punishments to be within the prohibition of the Clause. See *Weems* v. *United States*, 217 U.S. 349 (1910) (12 years in chains at hard and painful labor); *Trop* v. *Dulles*, 356 U.S. 86 (1958) (expatriation); *Robinson* v. *California*, 370 U.S. 660 (1962) (imprisonment for narcotics addiction). Each punishment, of course, was degrading to human dignity, but of none could it be said conclusively that it was fatally offensive under one or the other of the principles. Rather, these "cruel and unusual punishments" seriously implicated several of the principles, and it was the application of the principles in combination that supported the judgment. That, indeed, is not surprising. The function of these principles, after all, is simply to provide means by which a court can determine whether a challenged punishment comports with human dignity. They are, therefore, interrelated, and in most cases it will be their convergence that will justify the conclusion that a punishment is "cruel and unusual." The test, then, will ordinarily be a cumulative one: If a punishment is unusually severe, if there is a strong probability that it is inflicted arbitrarily, if it is substantially rejected by contemporary society, and if there is no reason to believe that it serves any penal purpose more effectively than some less severe punishment, then the continued infliction of that punishment violates the command of the Clause that the State may not inflict inhuman and uncivilized punishments upon those convicted of crimes.

. . . The question, then, is whether the deliberate infliction of death is today consistent with the command of the Clause that the State may not inflict punishments that do not comport with human dignity. I will analyze the punishment of death in terms of the principles set out above and the cumulative test to which they lead: It is a denial of human dignity for the State arbitrarily to subject a person to an unusually severe punishment that society has indicated it does not regard as acceptable, and that cannot be shown to serve any penal purpose more effectively than a significantly less drastic punishment. Under these principles and this test, death is today a "cruel and unusual" punishment.

Death is a unique punishment in the United States. In a society that so strongly affirms the sanctity of life, not surprisingly the common view is that death is the ultimate sanction. This natural human feeling appears all about us. There has been no national debate about punishment, in general or by imprisonment, comparable to the debate about the punishment of death. No other punishment has been so continuously restricted, see *infra,* at 296–298, nor has any State yet abolished prisons, as some have abolished this punishment. And those States that still inflict death reserve it for the most heinous crimes. Juries, of course, have always treated death cases differently, as have governors exercising their communication powers. Criminal defendants are of the same view. "As all practicing lawyers know, who have defended persons charged with capital offenses, often the only goal possible is to avoid the death penalty." *Griffin* v. *Illinois*, 351 U.S. 12, 28 (1956) (Burton and Minton, JJ., dissenting). Some legislatures have required particular procedures, such as two-stage trials and automatic appeals, applicable only in death cases. "It is the universal experience in the administration of criminal justice that those charged with capital offenses are granted special considerations." *Ibid.* See *Williams* v. *Florida*, 399 U.S. 78, 103 (1970) (all

States require juries of 12 in death cases). This Court, too, almost always treats death cases as a class apart. And the unfortunate effect of this punishment upon the functioning of the judicial process is well known; no other punishment has a similar effect.

The only explanation for the uniqueness of death is its extreme severity. Death is today an unusually severe punishment, unusual in its pain, in its finality, and in its enormity. No other existing punishment is comparable to death in terms of physical and mental suffering. Although our information is not conclusive, it appears that there is no method available that guarantees an immediate and painless death. Since the discontinuance of flogging as a constitutionally permissible punishment, *Jackson* v. *Bishop,* 404 F. 2d 571 (CA8 1968), death remains as the only punishment that may involve the conscious infliction of physical pain. In addition, we know that mental pain is an inseparable part of our practice of punishing criminals by death for the prospect of pending execution exacts a frightful toll during the inevitable long wait between the imposition of sentence and the actual infliction of death. Cf *Ex parte Medley,* 134 U.S. 160, 172 (1890). As the California Supreme Court pointed out, "the process of carrying out a verdict of death is often so degrading and brutalizing to the human spirit as to constitute psychological torture." *People* v. *Anderson,* 6 Cal. 3d 628, 649, 493 P. 2d 880, 894 (1972). Indeed, as Mr. Justice Frankfurter noted, "the onset of insanity while awaiting execution of a death sentence is not a rare phenomenon." *Solesbee* v. *Balkcom,* 339 U.S. 9, 14 (1950) (dissenting opinion). The "fate of ever-increasing fear and distress" to which the expatriate is subjected, *Trop* v. *Dulles,* 356 U.S., at 102, can only exist to a greater degree for a person confined in prison awaiting death.

The unusual severity of death is manifested most clearly in its finality and enormity. Death, in these respects, is in a class by itself. Expatriation, for example, is a punishment that "destroys for the individual the political existence that was centuries in the development," that "strips the citizen of his status in the national and international political community," and that puts "[h]is very existence" in

jeopardy. Expatriation thus inherently entails "the total destruction of the individual's status in organized society." *Id.,* at 101. "In short, the expatriate has lost the right to have rights." *Id.,* at 102. Yet, demonstrably, expatriation is not "a fate worse than death." *Id.,* at 125 (Frankfurter, J., dissenting). Although death, like expatriation, destroys the individual's "political existence" and his "status in organized society," it does more, for, unlike expatriation, death also destroys "[h]is very existence." There is, too at least the possibility that the expatriate will in the future regain "the right to have rights." Death forecloses even that possibility.

Death is truly an awesome punishment. The calculated killing of a human being by the State involves, by its very nature, a denial of the executed person's humanity. The contrast with the plight of a person punished by imprisonment is evident. An individual in prison does not lose "the right to have rights." A prisoner retains, for example, the constitutional rights to the free exercise of religion, to be free of cruel and unusual punishments, and to treatment as a "person" for purposes of due process of law and the equal protection of the laws. A prisoner remains a member of the human family. Moreover, he retains the right of access to the courts. His punishment is not irrevocable. Apart from the common charge, grounded upon the recognition of human fallibility, that the punishment of death must inevitably be inflicted upon innocent men, we know that death has been the lot of men whose convictions were unconstitutionally secured in view of later, retroactively applied, holdings of this Court. The punishment itself may have been unconstitutionally inflicted, see *Witherspoon* v. *Illinois,* 391 U.S. 510 (1968), yet the finality of death precludes relief. An executed person has indeed "lost the right to have rights." As one 19th century proponent of punishing criminals by death declared, "When a man is hung, there is an end of our relations with him. His execution is a way of saying, 'You are not fit for this world, take your chance elsewhere.'"

In comparison to all other punishments today, then, the deliberate extinguishment of human life by the State is uniquely degrading to human dignity. I would not hesitate to hold, on that ground alone, that death is today a "cruel and unusual" punishment, were it not that death is a punishment of longstanding usage and acceptance in this country. I therefore turn to the second principle—that the State may not arbitrarily inflict an unusually severe punishment.

. . . When the punishment of death is inflicted in a trivial number of the cases in which it is legally available, the conclusion is virtually inescapable that it is being inflicted arbitrarily. Indeed, it smacks of little more than a lottery system. The States claim, however, that this rarity is evidence not of arbitrariness, but of informed selectivity: Death is inflicted, they say, only in "extreme" cases.

Informed selectivity, of course, is a value not to be denigrated. Yet presumably the States could make precisely the same claim if there were 10 executions per year, or five, or even if there were but one. That there may be as many as 50 per year does not strengthen the claim. When the rate of infliction is at this low level, it is highly implausible that only the worst criminals or the criminals who commit the worst crimes are selected for this punishment. No one has yet suggested a rational basis that could differentiate in those terms the few who die from the many who go to prison. Crimes and criminals simply do not admit of a distinction that can be drawn so finely as to explain, on that ground, the execution of such a tiny sample of those eligible. Certainly the laws that provide for this punishment do not attempt to draw that distinction; all cases to which the laws apply are necessarily "extreme." Nor is the distinction credible in fact. If, for example, petitioner Furman or his crime illustrates the "extreme," then nearly all murderers and their murders are also "extreme." Furthermore, our procedures in death cases, rather than resulting in the selection of "extreme" cases for this punishment, actually sanction an arbitrary selection. For this Court has held that juries may, as they do, make the decision whether to impose a death sentence wholly unguided by standards governing that decision. *McGautha* v. *California*, 402 U.S. 183, 196–208 (1971). In other words, our procedures are not constructed to guard against the totally capricious selection of criminals for the punishment of death.

Although it is difficult to imagine what further facts would be necessary in order to prove that death is, as my Brother Stewart puts it, "wantonly and . . . freakishly" inflicted, I need not conclude that arbitrary infliction is patently obvious. I am not considering this punishment by the isolated light of one principle. The probability of arbitrariness is sufficiently substantial that it can be relied upon, in combination with the other principles, in reaching a judgment on the constitutionality of this punishment.

When there is a strong probability that an unusually severe and degrading punishment is being inflicted arbitrarily, we may well expect that society will disapprove of its infliction. I turn, therefore, to the third principle. An examination of the history and present operation of the American practice of punishing criminals by death reveals that this punishment has been almost totally rejected by contemporary society.

. . . The progressive decline in, and the current rarity of, the infliction of death demonstrate that our society seriously questions the appropriateness of this punishment today. The States point out that many legislatures authorize death as the punishment for certain crimes and that substantial segments of the public, as reflected in opinion polls and referendum votes, continue to support it. Yet the availability of this punishment through statutory authorization, as well as the polls and referenda, which amount simply to approval of that authorization, simply underscores the extent to which our society has in fact rejected this punishment. When an unusually severe punishment is authorized for wide-scale application but not, because of society's refusal, inflicted save in a few instances, the inference is compelling that there is a deep-seated reluctance to inflict it. Indeed, the likelihood is great that the punishment is tolerated only because of its disuse. The objective indicator of society's view of an unusually severe punishment is what society does with it, and today society will inflict death upon only a small sample of the eligible criminals. Rejection could hardly be more complete without becoming absolute. At the very least, I must conclude that contemporary society views this punishment with substantial doubt.

The final principle to be considered is that an unusually severe and degrading punishment may not be excessive in view of the purposes for which it is inflicted. This principle, too, is related to the others. When there is a strong probability that the State is arbitrarily inflicting an unusually severe punishment that is subject to grave societal doubts, it is likely also that the punishment cannot be shown to be serving any penal purpose that could not be served equally well by some less severe punishment.

The States' primary claim is that death is a necessary punishment because it prevents the commission of capital crimes more effectively than any less severe punishment. The first part of this claim is that the infliction of death is necessary to stop the individuals executed from committing further crimes. The sufficient answer to this is that if a criminal convicted of a capital crime poses a danger to society, effective administration of the States' pardon and parole laws can delay or deny his release from prison, and techniques of isolation can eliminate or minimize the danger while he remains confined.

The more significant argument is that the threat of death prevents the commission of capital crimes because it deters potential criminals who would not be deterred by the threat of imprisonment. The argument is not based upon evidence that the threat of death is a superior deterrent. Indeed, as my Brother Marshall establishes, the available evidence uniformly indicates, although it does not conclusively prove, that the threat of death has no greater deterrent effect than the threat of imprisonment. The States argue, however, that they are entitled to rely upon common human experience, and that experience, they say, supports the conclusion that death must be a more effective deterrent than any less severe punishment. Because people fear death the most, the argument runs, the threat of death must be the greatest deterrent.

It is important to focus upon the precise import of this argument. It is not denied that many, and probably most, capital crimes cannot be deterred by the threat of punishment. Thus the argument can apply only to those who think rationally about the commission of capital crimes. Particularly is that true when

the potential criminal, under this argument, must not only consider the risk of punishment, but also distinguish between two possible punishments. The concern, then, is with a particular type of potential criminal, the rational person who will commit a capital crime knowing that the punishment is long-term imprisonment, which may well be for the rest of his life, but will not commit the crime knowing that the punishment is death. On the face of it, the assumption that such persons exist is implausible.

In any event, this argument cannot be appraised in the abstract. We are not presented with the theoretical question whether under any imaginable circumstances the threat of death might be a greater deterrent to the commission of capital crimes than the threat of imprisonment. We are concerned with the practice of punishing criminals by death as it exists in the United States today. Proponents of this argument necessarily admit that its validity depends upon the existence of a system in which the punishment of death is invariably and swiftly imposed. Our system, of course, satisfies neither condition. A rational person contemplating a murder or rape is confronted, not with the certainty of a speedy death, but with the slightest possibility that he will be executed in the distant future. The risk of death is remote and improbable; in contrast, the risk of long-term imprisonment is near and great. In short, whatever the speculative validity of the assumption that the threat of death is a superior deterrent, there is no reason to believe that as currently administered the punishment of death is necessary to deter the commission of capital crimes. Whatever might be the case were all or substantially all eligible criminals quickly put to death, unverifiable possibilities are an insufficient basis upon which to conclude that the threat of death today has any greater deterrent efficacy than the threat of imprisonment.

There is, however, another aspect to the argument that the punishment of death is necessary for the protection of society. The infliction of death, the States urge, serves to manifest the community's outrage at the commission of the crime. It is, they say, a concrete public expression of moral indignation that inculcates respect for the law and helps assure a more peaceful community. Moreover, we are told, not only does the punishment of death exert this widespread moralizing influence upon community values, it also satisfies the popular demand for grievous condemnation of abhorrent crimes and thus prevents disorder, lynching, and attempts by private citizens to take the law into their own hands.

The question, however, is not whether death serves these supposed purposes of punishment, but whether death serves them more effectively than imprisonment. There is no evidence whatever that utilization of imprisonment rather than death encourages private blood feuds and other disorders. Surely if there were such a danger, the execution of a handful of criminals each year would not prevent it. The assertion that death alone is a sufficiently emphatic denunciation for capital crimes suffers from the same defect. If capital crimes require the punishment of death in order to provide moral reinforcement for the basic values of the community, those values can only be undermined when death is so rarely inflicted upon the criminals who commit the crimes. Furthermore, it is certainly doubtful that the infliction of death by the State does in fact strengthen the community's moral code; if the deliberate extinguishment of human life has any effect at all, it more likely tends to lower our respect for life and brutalize our values. That, after all, is why we no longer carry out public executions. In any event, this claim simply means that one purpose of punishment is to indicate social disapproval of crime. To serve that purpose our laws distribute punishments according to the gravity of crimes and punish more severely the crimes society regards as more serious. That purpose cannot justify any particular punishment as the upper limit of severity.

27. *Gregg* v. *Georgia*

U.S. Supreme Court

In this 1976 precedent death penalty case, Justice Potter Stewart, arguing for the majority, reaffirms the decision in *Furman* that the death penalty does not violate the Eighth Amendment. Having satisfied the procedural concerns expressed in the *Furman* decision, Stewart then proceeds to argue that, substantively, the death penalty does not amount to cruel and unusual punishment. Since it accords with "evolving standards of decency" and does not entail wanton pain and violence or gross disproportionality, and since it may be necessary for deterrence and retribution, the death penalty stands.

Judgment of the Court, and opinion of Mr. Justice Stewart, Mr. Justice Powell, and Mr. Justice Stevens, announced by Mr. Justice Stewart.

The issue in this case is whether the imposition of the sentence of death for the crime of murder under the law of Georgia violates the Eighth and Fourteenth Amendments.

I

The petitioner, Troy Gregg, was charged with committing armed robbery and murder. In accordance with Georgia procedure in capital cases, the trial was in two stages, a guilt stage and a sentencing stage. The evidence at the guilt trial established that on November 21, 1973, the petitioner and a traveling companion, Floyd Allen, while hitchhiking north in Florida were picked up by Fred Simmons and Bob Moore. Their car broke down, but they continued north after Simmons purchased another vehicle with some of the cash he was carrying. While still in Florida, they picked up another hitchhiker, Dennis Weaver, who rode with them to Atlanta where he was let out about 11 P.M. A short time later the four men interrupted their journey for a rest stop along the highway. The next morning the bodies of Simmons and Moore were discovered in a ditch nearby.

On November 23, after reading about the shootings in an Atlanta newspaper, Weaver communicated with the Gwinnet County police and related information concerning the journey with the victims, including a description of the car. The next afternoon, the petitioner and Allen, while in Simmons' car, were arrested in Asheville, N.C. In the search incident to the arrest a .25 caliber pistol, later shown to be that used to kill Simmons and Moore, was found in the petitioner's pocket. After receiving the warnings required by *Miranda* v. *Arizona,* 384 U.S. 436 (1966), and signing a written waiver of his rights, the petitioner signed a statement in which he admitted shooting, then robbing Simmons and Moore. He justified the slayings on grounds of self-defense. The next day, while being transferred to Lawrenceville, Ga., the petitioner and Allen were taken to the scene of the shootings. Upon arriving there, Allen recounted the events leading to the slayings. His version of these events was as follows: After Simmons and Moore left the car, the petitioner stated that he intended to rob them. The petitioner then took his pistol in hand and positioned himself on the car to improve his aim. As Simmons and Moore came up an embankment toward the car, the petitioner fired three shots and the two men fell near a ditch. The petitioner, at close range, then fired a shot into the head of each. He robbed them of valuables and drove away with Allen.

A medical examiner testified that Simmons died from a bullet wound in the eye and that Moore died from bullet wounds in the cheek and in the back of the head. He further testi-

fied that both men had several bruises and abrasions about the face and head which probably were sustained either from the fall into the ditch or from being dragged or pushed along the embankment. Although Allen did not testify, a police detective recounted the substance of Allen's statements about the slayings and indicated that directly after Allen had made these statements the petitioner had admitted that Allen's account was accurate. The petitioner testified in his own defense. He confirmed that Allen had made the statements described by the detective, but denied their truth or ever having admitted to their accuracy. He indicated that he had shot Simmons and Moore because of fear and in self-defense, testifying they had attacked Allen and him, one wielding a pipe and the other a knife.

The trial judge submitted the murder charges to the jury on both felony-murder and nonfelony-murder theories. He also instructed on the issue of self-defense but declined to instruct on manslaughter. He submitted the robbery case to the jury on both an armed-robbery theory and on the lesser included offense of robbery by intimidation. The jury found the petitioner guilty of two counts of armed robbery and two counts of murder.

At the penalty stage, which took place before the same jury, neither the prosecutor nor the petitioner's lawyer offered any additional evidence. Both counsel, however, made lengthy arguments dealing generally with the propriety of capital punishment under the circumstances and with the weight of the evidence of guilt. The trial judge instructed the jury that it could recommend either a death sentence or a life prison sentence on each count. The judge further charged the jury that in determining what sentence was appropriate the jury was free to consider the facts and circumstances, if any, presented by the parties in mitigation or aggravation.

Finally, the judge instructed the jury that it "would not be authorized to consider [imposing] the penalty of death" unless it first found beyond a reasonable doubt one of these aggravating circumstances:

"One—That the offense of murder was committed while the offender was engaged in the commission of two other capital felonies, to-wit the armed robbery of [Simmons and Moore].

"Two—That the offender committed the offense of murder for the purpose of receiving money and the automobile described in the indictment.

"Three—The offense of murder was outrageously and wantonly vile, horrible and inhuman, in that they [*sic*] involved the depravity of [the] mind of the defendant." Tr. 476–477.

Finding the first and second of these circumstances, the jury returned verdicts of death on each count.

The Supreme Court of Georgia affirmed the convictions and the imposition of the death sentences for murder. 233 Ga. 177, 210 S. E. 2d 659 (1974). After reviewing the trial transcript and the record, including the evidence, and comparing the evidence and sentence in similar cases in accordance with the requirements of Georgia law, the court concluded that, considering the nature of the crime and the defendant, the sentences of death had not resulted from prejudice or any other arbitrary factor and were not excessive or disproportionate to the penalty applied in similar cases. The death sentences imposed for armed robbery, however, were vacated on the grounds that the death penalty had rarely been imposed in Georgia for that offense and that the jury improperly considered the murders as aggravating circumstances for the robberies after having considered the armed robberies as aggravating circumstances for the murders. *Id.,* at 127, 210 S. E. 2d, at 667.

We granted the petitioner's application for a writ of certiorari limited to his challenge to the imposition of the death sentences in this case as "cruel and unusual" punishment in violation of the Eighth and the Fourteenth Amendments . . .

Four years ago, the petitioners in *Furman* and its companion cases predicated their argument primarily upon the asserted proposition that standards of decency had evolved to the point where capital punishment no longer could be tolerated. The petitioners in those cases said, in effect, that the evolutionary pro-

cess had come to an end, and that standards of decency required that the Eighth Amendment be construed finally as prohibiting capital punishment for any crime regardless of its depravity and impact on society. This view was accepted by two Justices. Three other Justices were unwilling to go so far; focusing on the procedures by which convicted defendants were selected for the death penalty rather than on the actual punishment inflicted, they joined in the conclusion that the statutes before the Court were constitutionally invalid.

The petitioners in the capital cases before the Court today renew the "standards of decency" argument, but developments during the four years since *Furman* have undercut substantially the assumptions upon which their argument rested. Despite the continuing debate, dating back to the 19th century, over the morality and utility of capital punishment, it is now evident that a large proportion of American society continues to regard it as an appropriate and necessary criminal sanction.

The most marked indication of society's endorsement of the death penalty for murder is the legislative response to *Furman*. The legislatures of at least 35 States have enacted new statutes that provide for the death penalty for at least some crimes that result in the death of another person. And the Congress of the United States, in 1974, enacted a statute providing the death penalty for aircraft piracy that results in death. These recently adopted statutes have attempted to address the concerns expressed by the Court in *Furman* primarily (i) by specifying the factors to be weighed and the procedures to be followed in deciding when to impose a capital sentence, or (ii) by making the death penalty mandatory for specified crimes. But all of the post-*Furman* statutes make clear that capital punishment itself has not been rejected by the elected representatives of the people.

In the only statewide referendum occurring since *Furman* and brought to our attention, the people of California adopted a constitutional amendment that authorized capital punishment, in effect negating a prior ruling by the Supreme Court of California in *People* v. *Anderson*, 6 Cal. 3d 628, 493 P. 2d 880, cert. denied, 406 U.S. 958 (1972), that the death penalty violated the California Constitution.

The jury also is a significant and reliable objective index of contemporary values because it is so directly involved. See *Furman* v. *Georgia*, 408 U.S., at 439–440 (POWELL, J., dissenting). See generally Powell, Jury Trial of Crimes, 23 Wash. & Lee L. Rev. 1(1966). The Court has said that "one of the most important functions any jury can perform in making . . . a selection [between life imprisonment and death for a defendant convicted in a capital case] is to maintain a link between contemporary community values and the penal system." *Witherspoon* v. *Illinois*, 391 U.S. 510, 519 n. 15 (1968). It may be true that evolving standards have influenced juries in recent decades to be more discriminating in imposing the sentence of death. But the relative infrequency of jury verdicts imposing the death sentence does not indicate rejection of capital punishment *per se.* Rather, the reluctance of juries in many cases to impose the sentence may well reflect the humane feeling that this most irrevocable of sanctions should be reserved for a small number of extreme cases. See *Furman* v. *Georgia*, *supra*, at 388 (BURGER, C. J., dissenting). Indeed, the actions of juries in many States since *Furman* are fully compatible with the legislative judgments, reflected in the new statutes, as to the continued utility and necessity of capital punishment in appropriate cases. At the close of 1974 at least 254 persons had been sentenced to death since *Furman,* and by the end of March 1976, more than 460 persons were subject to death sentences.

As we have seen, however, the Eighth Amendment demands more than that a challenged punishment be acceptable to contemporary society. The Court also must ask whether it comports with the basic concept of human dignity at the core of the Amendment. *Trop* v. *Dulles*, 356 U.S., at 100 (plurality opinion). Although we cannot "invalidate a category of penalties because we deem less severe penalties adequate to serve the ends of penology," *Furman* v. *Georgia*, *supra*, at 451 (POWELL, J., dissenting), the sanction imposed cannot be so totally without penological justification that it results in the gratuitous infliction of suffering. *Cf. Wilkerson* v. *Utah*, 99 U.S., at 135–136; *In re Kemmler*, 136 U.S., at 447.

The death penalty is said to serve two principal social purposes: retribution and deterrence of capital crimes by prospective offenders.

In part, capital punishment is an expression of society's moral outrage at particularly offensive conduct. This function may be unappealing to many, but it is essential in an ordered society that asks its citizens to rely on legal processes rather than self-help to vindicate their wrongs.

"The instinct for retribution is part of the nature of man, and channeling that instinct in the administration of criminal justice serves an important purpose in promoting the stability of a society governed by law. When people begin to believe that organized society is unwilling or unable to impose upon criminal offenders the punishment they 'deserve' then there are sown the seeds of anarchy—of self-help, vigilante justice, and lynch law." *Furman* v. *Georgia*, *supra*, at 308 (STEWART, J., concurring).

"Retribution is no longer the dominant objective of the criminal law," *Williams* v. *New York*, 337 U.S. 241, 248 (1949), but neither is it a forbidden objective nor one inconsistent with our respect for the dignity of men. *Furman* v. *Georgia*, 408 U.S., at 394–395 (Burger, C. J., dissenting); id., at 452–454 (Powell, J., dissenting); *Powell* v. *Texas*, 392 U.S., at 531 535–536 (plurality opinion). Indeed, the decision that capital punishment may be the appropriate sanction in extreme cases is an expression of the community's belief that certain crimes are themselves so grievous an affront to humanity that the only adequate response may be the penalty of death: . . .

We now turn to consideration of the constitutionality of Georgia's capital-sentencing procedures. In the wake of *Furman*, Georgia amended its capital punishment statute, but chose not to narrow the scope of its murder provisions. See Part II, *supra*. Thus, now as before *Furman*, in Georgia "[a] person commits murder when he unlawfully and with malice aforethought, either express or implied, causes the death of another human being." Ga. Code Ann., § 26-1101 (a) (1972). All persons convicted of murder "shall be punished by death or by imprisonment for life." § 26-1101 (c) (1972).

Georgia did act, however, to narrow the class of murderers subject to capital punishment by specifying 10 statutory aggravating circumstances, one of which must be found by the jury to exist beyond a reasonable doubt before a death sentence can ever be imposed. In addition, the jury is authorized to consider any other appropriate aggravating or mitigating circumstances. § 27-2534.1 (b) (Supp. 1975). The jury is not required to find any mitigating circumstance in order to make a recommendation of mercy that is binding on the trial court, see §27-2302 (Supp. 1975), but it must find a *statutory* aggravating circumstance before recommending a sentence of death.

These procedures require the jury to consider the circumstances of the crime and the criminal before it recommends sentence. No longer can a Georgia jury do as Furman's jury did: reach a finding of the defendant's guilt and then, without guidance or direction, decide whether he should live or die. Instead, the jury's attention is directed to the specific circumstances of the crime: Was it committed in the course of another capital felony? Was it committed for money? Was it committed upon a peace officer or judicial officer? Was it committed in a particularly heinous way or in a manner that endangered the lives of many persons? In addition, the jury's attention is focused on the characteristics of the person who committed the crime: Does he have a record of prior convictions for capital offenses? Are there any special facts about this defendant that mitigate against imposing capital punishment (*e.g.,* his youth, the extent of his cooperation with the police, his emotional state at the time of the crime)? As a result, while some jury discretion still exists, "the discretion to be exercised is controlled by clear and objective standards so as to produce nondiscriminatory application." *Coley* v. *State,* 231 Ga. 829, 834, 204 S. E. 2d 612, 615 (1974).

As an important additional safeguard against arbitrariness and caprice, the Georgia statutory scheme provides for automatic appeal of all death sentences to the State's Supreme Court. That court is required by statute to review each sentence of death and determine whether it was imposed under the influence of passion or prejudice, whether the evidence supports the jury's finding of a statutory aggravating circumstance, and whether the sentence is disproportionate compared to those sentences imposed in similar cases. § 27-2537 (c) (Supp. 1975).

In short, Georgia's new sentencing procedures require as a prerequisite to the imposition of the death penalty, specific jury findings as to the circumstances of the crime or the character of the defendant. Moreover, to guard further against a situation comparable to that presented in *Furman,* the Supreme Court of Georgia compares each death sentence with the sentences imposed on similarly situated defendants to ensure that the sentence of death in a particular case is not disproportionate. On their face these procedures seem to satisfy the concerns of *Furman.* No longer should there be "no meaningful basis for distinguishing the few cases in which [the death penalty] is imposed from the many cases in which it is not." 408 U.S., at 313 (White, J., concurring).

The petitioner contends, however, that the changes in the Georgia sentencing procedures are only cosmetic, that the arbitrariness and capriciousness condemned by *Furman* continue to exist in Georgia—both in traditional practices that still remain and in the new sentencing procedures adopted in response to *Furman.*

1

First, the petitioner focuses on the opportunities for discretionary action that are inherent in the processing of any murder case under Georgia law. He notes that the state prosecutor has unfettered authority to select those persons whom he wishes to prosecute for a capital offense and to plea bargain with them. Further, at the trial the jury may choose to convict a defendant of a lesser included offense rather than find him guilty of a crime punishable by death, even if the evidence would support a capital verdict. And finally, a defendant who is convicted and sentenced to die may have his sentence commuted by the Governor of the State and the Georgia Board of Pardons and Paroles.

The existence of these discretionary stages is not determinative of the issues before us. At each of these stages an actor in the criminal justice system makes a decision which may remove a defendant from consideration as a candidate for the death penalty. *Furman*, in contrast, dealt with the decision to impose the death sentence on a specific individual who had been convicted of a capital offense. Nothing in any of our cases suggests that the decision to afford an individual defendant mercy violates the Constitution. *Furman* held only that, in order to minimize the risk that the death penalty would be imposed on a capriciously selected group of offenders, the decision to impose it had to be guided by standards so that the sentencing authority would focus on the particularized circumstances of the crime and the defendant.

2

The petitioner further contends that the capital-sentencing procedures adopted by Georgia in response to *Furman* do not eliminate the dangers of arbitrariness and caprice in jury sentencing that were held in *Furman* to be violative of the Eighth and Fourteenth Amendments. He claims that the statute is so broad and vague as to leave juries free to act as arbitrarily and capriciously as they wish in deciding whether to impose the death penalty. While there is no claim that the jury in this case relied upon a vague or overbroad provision to establish the existence of a statutory aggravating circumstance, the petitioner looks to the sentencing system as a whole (as the Court did in *Furman* and we do today) and argues that it fails to reduce sufficiently the risk of arbitrary infliction of death sentences. Specifically, Gregg urges that the statutory aggravating circumstances are too broad and too vague, that the sentencing procedure allows for arbitrary grants of mercy, and that the scope of the evidence and argument that can be considered at the presentence hearing is too wide.

The petitioner attacks the seventh statutory aggravating circumstance, which authorizes

imposition of the death penalty if the murder was "outrageously or wantonly vile, horrible or inhuman in that it involved torture, depravity of mind, or an aggravated battery to the victim," contending that it is so broad that capital punishment could be imposed in any murder case. It is, of course, arguable that any murder involves depravity of mind or an aggravated battery. But this language need not be construed in this way, and there is no reason to assume that the Supreme Court of Georgia will adopt such an open-ended construction. In only one case has it upheld a jury's decision to sentence a defendant to death when the only statutory aggravating circumstance found was that of the seventh, see *McCorquodale* v. *State*, 233 Ga. 369, 211 S. E. 2d 577 (1974), and that homicide was a horrifying torture-murder.

The petitioner also argues that two of the statutory aggravating circumstances are vague and therefore susceptible of widely differing interpretations, thus creating a substantial risk that the death penalty will be arbitrarily inflicted by Georgia juries. In light of the decisions of the Supreme Court of Georgia we must disagree. First, the petitioner attacks that part of § 27-2534.1 (b)(1) that authorizes a jury to consider whether a defendant has a "substantial history of serious assaultive criminal convictions." The Supreme Court of Georgia, however, has demonstrated a concern that the new sentencing procedures provide guidance to juries. It held this provision to be impermissibly vague in *Arnold* v. *State*, 236 Ga. 534, 540, 224 S. E. 2d 386, 391 (1976), because it did not provide the jury with "sufficiently 'clear and objective standards.'" Second, the petitioner points to §27-2534.1 (b)(3) which speaks of creating a "great risk of death to more than one person." While such a phrase might be susceptible of an overly broad interpretation, the Supreme Court of Georgia has not so construed it. The only case in which the court upheld a conviction in reliance on this aggravating circumstance involved a man who stood up in a church and fired a gun indiscriminately into the audience. See *Chenault* v. *State*, 234 Ga. 216, 215 S. E. 2d 223 (1975). On the other hand, the court expressly reversed a finding of great risk when the victim was simply kidnapped in a parking lot. See

Jarrell v. *State,* 234 Ga. 410, 424, 216 S. E. 2d 258, 269 (1975).

The petitioner next argues that the requirements of *Furman* are not met here because the jury has the power to decline to impose the death penalty even if it finds that one or more statutory aggravating circumstances are present in the case. This contention misinterprets *Furman.* See *supra,* at 198–199. Moreover, it ignores the role of the Supreme Court of Georgia which reviews each death sentence to determine whether it is proportional to other sentences imposed for similar crimes. Since the proportionality requirement on review is intended to prevent caprice in the decision to inflict the penalty, the isolated decision of a jury to afford mercy does not render unconstitutional death sentences imposed on defendants who were sentenced under a system that does not create a substantial risk of arbitrariness or caprice.

The petitioner objects, finally, to the wide scope of evidence and argument allowed at presentence hearings. We think that the Georgia court wisely has chosen not to impose unnecessary restrictions on the evidence that can be offered at such a hearing and to approve open and far-ranging argument. See, *e.g., Brown* v. *State,* 235 Ga. 644, 220 S. E. 2d 922 (1975). So long as the evidence introduced and the arguments made at the presentence hearing do not prejudice a defendant, it is preferable not to impose restrictions. We think it desirable for the jury to have as much information before it as possible when it makes the sentencing decision. See *supra, at* 189–190.

3

Finally, the Georgia statute has an additional provision designed to assure that the death penalty will not be imposed on a capriciously selected group of convicted defendants. The new sentencing procedures require that the State Supreme Court review every death sentence to determine whether it was imposed under the influence of passion, prejudice, or any other arbitrary factor, whether the evidence supports the findings of a statutory aggravating circumstance, and "[w]hether the sentence of death is excessive or disproportionate to the penalty imposed in sim-

ilar cases, considering both the crime and the defendant." § 27-2537 (c)(3) (Supp. 1975). In performing its sentence-review function, the Georgia court has held that "if the death penalty is only rarely imposed for an act or it is substantially out of line with sentences imposed for other acts it will be set aside as excessive." *Coley* v. *State,* 231 Ga., at 834, 204 S. E. 2d, at 616. The court on another occasion stated that "we view it to be our duty under the similarity standard to assure that no death sentence is affirmed unless in similar cases throughout the state the death penalty has been imposed generally. . . ." *Moore* v. *State,* 233 Ga. 861, 864, 213 S. E. 2d 829, 832 (1975). See also *Jarrell* v. *State, supra,* at 425, 216 S. E. 2d, at 270 (standard is whether "juries generally throughout the state have imposed the death penalty"); *Smith* v. *State,* 236 Ga. 12, 24, 222 S. E. 2d 308, 318 (1976) (found "a clear pattern" of jury behavior).

It is apparent that the Supreme Court of Georgia has taken its review responsibilities seriously. In *Coley,* it held that "[t]he prior cases indicate that the past practice among juries faced with similar factual situations and like aggravating circumstances has been to impose only the sentence of life imprisonment for the offense of rape, rather than death." 231 Ga., at 835, 204 S. E. 2d, at 617. It thereupon reduced Coley's sentence from death to life imprisonment. Similarly, although armed robbery is a capital offense under Georgia law, § 26-1902 (1972), the Georgia court concluded that the death sentences imposed in this case for that crime were "unusual in that they are rarely imposed for [armed robbery]. Thus, under the test provided by statute, . . . they must be considered to be excessive or disproportionate to the penalties imposed in similar cases." 233 Ga., at 127, 210 S. E. 2d, at 667. The court therefore vacated Gregg's death sentences for armed robbery and has followed a similar course in every other armed robbery death penalty case to come before it. See *Floyd* v. *State,* 233 Ga. 280, 285, 210 S. E. 2d 810, 814 (1974); *Jarrell* v. *State,* 234 Ga., at 424–425, 216 S. E. 2d, at 270. See *Dorsey* v. *State,* 236 Ga. 591, 225 S. E. 2d 418 (1976).

The provision for appellate review in the Georgia capital-sentencing system serves as a check against the random or arbitary imposition of the death penalty. In particular, the proportionality review substantially eliminates the possibility that a person will be sentenced to die by the action of an aberrant jury. If a time comes when juries generally do not impose the death sentence in a certain kind of murder case, the appellate review procedures assure that no defendant convicted under such circumstances will suffer a sentence of death.

II

The basic concern of *Furman* centered on those defendants who were being condemned to death capriciously and arbitrarily. Under the procedures before the Court in that case, sentencing authorities were not directed to give attention to the nature or circumstances of the crime committed or to the character or record of the defendant. Left unguided, juries imposed the death sentence in a way that could only be called freakish. The new Georgia sentencing procedures, by contrast, focus the jury's attention on the particularized nature of the crime and the particularized characteristics of the individual defendant. While the jury is permitted to consider any aggravating or mitigating circumstances, it must find and identify at least one statutory aggravating factor before it may impose a penalty of death. In this way the jury's discretion is channeled. No longer can a jury wantonly and freakishly impose the death sentence; it is always circumscribed by the legislative guidelines. In addition, the review function of the Supreme Court of Georgia affords additional assurance that the concerns that prompted our decision in *Furman* are not present to any significant degree in the Georgia procedure applied here.

For the reasons expressed in this opinion, we hold that the statutory system under which Gregg was sentenced to death does not violate the Constitution. Accordingly, the judgment of the Georgia Supreme Court is affirmed.

28.   Race and the Death Penalty

Anthony G. Amsterdam

Anthony G. Amsterdam argues against the Supreme Court's ruling in the *McCleskey* case, in which an African American was sentenced to death in spite of overwhelming statistical evidence that the Georgia courts were imposing the death penalty in a pattern that reflected the race of the defendant. Amsterdam maintains that allowing such discriminatory sentencing patterns amounts to a license to discriminate against people of color.

There are times when even truths we hold self-evident require affirmation. For those who have invested our careers and our hopes in the criminal justice system, this is one of those times. Insofar as the basic principles that give value to our lives are in the keeping of the

From *Criminal Justice Ethics*, Vol. 7, No. 1 (Winter/Spring 1988), pp. 2, 84–86. Reprinted by permission of The Institute for Criminal Justice Ethics, 899 Tenth Ave., New York, NY 10019.

law and can be vindicated or betrayed by the decisions of any court, they have been sold down the river by a decision of the Supreme Court of the United States less than a year old.

I do not choose by accident a metaphor of slavery. For the decision I am referring to is the criminal justice system's *Dred Scott* case. It is the case of Warren McCleskey, a black man sentenced to die for the murder of a white man in Georgia. The Supreme Court held that McCleskey can be constitutionally put to death despite overwhelming unrebutted and un-explained statistical evidence that the death penalty is being imposed by Georgia juries in a pattern which reflects the race of convicted murderers and their victims and cannot be accounted for by any factor other than race.

This is not just a case about capital punishment. The Supreme Court's decision, which amounts to an open license to discriminate against people of color in capital sentencing, was placed upon grounds that implicate the entire criminal justice system. Worse still, the Court's reasoning makes us all accomplices in its toleration of a racially discriminatory administration of criminal justice.

Let us look at the *McCleskey* case. His crime was an ugly one. He robbed a furniture store at gunpoint, and he or one of his accomplices killed a police officer who responded to the scene. McCleskey may have been the trigger-man. Whether or not he was, he was guilty of murder under Georgia law.

But his case in the Supreme Court was not concerned with guilt. It was concerned with why McCleskey had been sentenced to death instead of life imprisonment for his crime. It was concerned with why, out of seventeen defendants charged with the killings of police officers in Fulton County, Georgia, between 1973 and 1980, only Warren McCleskey—a black defendant charged with killing a white officer—had been chosen for a death sentence. In the only other one of these seventeen cases in which the predominantly white prosecutor's office in Atlanta had pushed for the death penalty, a black defendant convicted of killing a black police officer had been sentenced to life instead.

It was facts of that sort that led the NAACP Legal Defense Fund to become involved in McCleskey's case. They were not unfamiliar facts to any of the lawyers who, like myself, had worked for the Legal Defense Fund for many years, defending Blacks charged with serious crimes throughout the South. We knew that in the United States black defendants convicted of murder or rape in cases involving white victims have always been sentenced to death and executed far out of proportion to their numbers, and under factual circumstances that would have produced a sentence of imprisonment—often a relatively

light sentence of imprisonment—in identical cases with black victims or white defendants or both.

Back in the mid-sixties the Legal Defense Fund had presented to courts evidence of extensive statistical studies conducted by Dr. Marvin Wolfgang, one of the deans of American criminology, showing that the grossly disproportionate number of death sentences which were then being handed out to black defendants convicted of the rape of white victims could not be explained by any factor other than race. Prosecutors took the position then that these studies were insufficiently detailed to rule out the influence of every possible non-racial factor, and it was largely for that reason that the courts rejected our claims that our black death-sentenced clients had been denied the Equal Protection of the Laws. Fortunately, in 1972 we had won a Supreme Court decision that saved the lives of all those clients and outlawed virtually every death penalty statute in the United States on procedural grounds; and when the States enacted new death-penalty laws between 1973 and 1976, only three of them reinstated capital punishment for rape. Now that it no longer mattered much, the prosecutors could afford to take another tack. When we argued against the new capital murder statutes on the ground that the Wolfgang studies had shown the susceptibility of capital sentencing laws to racially discriminatory application, the Government of the United States came into the Supreme Court against us saying, Oh, yes, Wolfgang was "a careful and comprehensive study, and we do not question its conclusion that during the twenty years between [1945 and 1965] . . ., in southern states, there was discrimination in rape cases." However, said the Government, this "research does not provide support for a conclusion that racial discrimination continues, . . . or that it applies to murder cases."

So we were well prepared for this sort of selective agnosticism when we went to court in the *McCleskey* case. The evidence that we presented in support of McCleskey's claim of racial discrimination left nothing out. Our centerpiece was a pair of studies conducted by Professor David Baldus, of the University of Iowa, and his colleagues, which examined 2,484 cases of murder and non-negligent manslaughter that occurred in Georgia between 1973, the date when its present capital murder statute was enacted, and 1979, the year after McCleskey's own death sentence was imposed. The Baldus team got its data on these cases principally from official state records, supplied by the Georgia Supreme Court and the Georgia Board of Pardons and Paroles.

Through a highly refined protocol, the team collected information regarding more than five hundred factors in each case—information relating to the demographic and individual characteristics of the defendant and the victim, the circumstances of the crime and the strength of the evidence of guilt, and the aggravating and mitigating features of each case: both the features specified by Georgia law to be considered in capital sentencing and every factor recognized in the legal and criminological literature as theoretically or actually likely to affect the choice of life or death. Using the most reliable and advanced techniques of social-science research, Baldus processed the data through a wide array of sophisticated statistical procedures, including multiple-regression analyses based upon alternative models that considered and controlled for as few as 10 or as many as 230 sentencing factors in each analysis. When our evidentiary case was presented in court, Baldus reanalyzed the data several more times to take account of every additional factor, combination of factors, or model for analysis of factors suggested by the State of Georgia's expert witnesses, its lawyers, and the federal trial judge. The Baldus study has since been uniformly praised by social scientists as the best study of any aspect of criminal sentencing ever conducted.

What did it show? That death sentences were being imposed in Georgia murder cases in a clear, consistent pattern that reflected the race of the victim and the race of the defendant and could not be explained by any non-racial factor. For example:

(1) Although less than 40 percent of Georgia homicide cases involve white victims, in 87 percent of the cases in which a death sentence is imposed, the victim is white. White-victim cases are almost eleven times more likely to produce a death sentence than are black-victim cases.

(2) When the race of the defendant is con-

sidered too, the following figures emerge: 22 percent of black defendants who kill white victims are sentenced to death; 8 percent of white defendants who kill white victims are sentenced to death; 1 percent of black defendants who kill black victims are sentenced to death; 3 percent of white defendants who kill black victims are sentenced to death. It should be noted that out of the roughly 2,500 Georgia homicide cases found, only 64 involved killings of black victims by white defendants, so the 3 percent death-sentencing rate in this category represents a total of two death sentences over a six-year period. Plainly, the reason why racial discrimination against black defendants does not appear even more glaringly evident is that most black murderers kill black victims; almost no identified white murderers kill black victims; and virtually nobody is sentenced to death for killing a mere black victim.

(3) No non-racial factor explains these racial patterns. Under multiple regression analysis, the model with the maximum explanatory power shows that after controlling for legitimate non-racial factors, murderers of white victims are still being sentenced to death 4.3 times more often than murderers of black victims. Multiple regression analysis also shows that the race of the victim is as good a basis for predicting whether or not a murderer will be sentenced to death as are the aggravating circumstances which the Georgia statute explicitly says should be considered in favor of a death sentence, such as whether the defendant has a prior murder conviction, or whether he is the primary actor in the present murder.

(4) Across the whole universe of cases, approximately 5 percent of Georgia killings result in a death sentence. Yet when more than 230 non-racial variables are controlled for, the death-sentencing rate is 6 percentage points higher in white-victim cases than in black-victim cases. What this means is that in predicting whether any particular person will get the death penalty in Georgia, it is less important to know whether or not he committed a homicide in the first place than to know whether, if he did, he killed a white victim or a black one.

(5) However, the effects of race are not uniform across the entire range of homicide cases. As might be expected, in the least aggra-

vated sorts of cases, almost no one gets a death sentence; in the really gruesome cases, a high percentage of both black and white murderers get death sentences; so it is in the mid-range of cases—cases like McCleskey's—that race has its greatest impact. The Baldus study found that in these mid-range cases the death-sentencing rate for killers of white victims is 34 percent as compared to 14 percent for killers of black victims. In other words, out of every thirty-four murderers sentenced to death for killing a white victim, twenty of them would not have gotten death sentences if their victims had been black.

The bottom line is this: Georgia has executed eleven murderers since it passed its present statute in 1973. Nine of the eleven were black. Ten of the eleven had white victims. Can there be the slightest doubt that this revolting record is the product of some sort of racial bias rather than a pure fluke?

A narrow majority of the Supreme Court pretended to have such doubts and rejected McCleskey's Equal-Protection challenge to his death sentence. It did not question the quality or the validity of the Baldus study, or any of the findings that have been described here. It admitted that the manifest racial discrepancies in death sentencing were unexplained by any non-racial variable, and that Baldus's data pointed to a "likelihood" or a "risk" that race was at work in the capital sentencing process. It essentially conceded that if a similar statistical showing of racial bias had been made in an employment-discrimination case or in a jury-selection case, the courts would have been required to find a violation of the Equal Protection Clause of the Fourteenth Amendment. But, the Court said, racial discrimination in capital sentencing cannot be proved by a pattern of sentencing results: a death-sentenced defendant like McCleskey must present proof that the particular jury or the individual prosecutor, or some other decision-maker in his own case, was personally motivated by racial considerations to bring about his death. Since such proof is never possible to obtain, racial discrimination in capital sentencing is never possible to prove.

The Court gave four basic reasons for this result. First, since capital sentencing decisions are made by a host of different juries and prosecutors, and are supposed to be based upon "innumerable factors that vary according to the characteristics of the individual defendant and the facts of the particular capital offense," even sentencing patterns that are explicable by race and inexplicable except by race do not necessarily show that any single decision-maker in the system is acting out of a subjective purpose to discriminate. Second, capital punishment laws are important for the protection of society; the "[i]mplementation of these laws necessarily requires discretionary judgments"; and, "[b]ecause discretion is essential to the criminal justice process, we [sh]ould demand exceptionally clear proof before we . . . infer that the discretion has been abused." Third, this same respect for discretionary judgments makes it imprudent to require juries and prosecutors to explain their decisions, so it is better to ignore the inference of racial discrimination that flows logically from their behavior than to call upon them to justify such behavior upon non-racial grounds.

Fourth, more is involved than capital punishment. "McCleskey's claim . . . throws into serious question the principles that underlie our entire criminal justice system." This is so because "the Baldus study indicates a discrepancy that appears to correlate with race," and "[a]pparent disparities in sentencing are an inevitable part of our criminal justice system." "Thus," says the Court, "if we accepted McCleskey's claim that racial bias has impermissibly tainted the capital sentencing decision, we could soon be faced with similar claims as to other types of penalty. Moreover, the claim that . . . sentence rests on the irrelevant factor of race easily could be extended to apply to claims based on unexplained discrepancies that correlate to membership in other minority groups, and even to gender"— and even to claims based upon "the defendant's facial characteristics, or the physical attractiveness of the . . . victim." In other words, if we forbid racial discrimination in meting out sentences of life or death, we may have to face claims of discrimination against Blacks, or against women, or perhaps against ugly people, wherever the facts warrant such claims, in the length of prison sentences, in the length of jail sentences, in the giving of suspended sentences, in the making of pretrial release decisions, in the invocation of recidivist sentencing enhancements, in the prosecutor's decisions whether to file charges, and how heavily to load up the charges, against black defendants as compared with white defendants or against ugly defendants as compared with ravishingly beautiful defendants; and of course the whole criminal justice system will then fall down flat and leave us in a state of anarchy. In thirty years of reading purportedly serious judicial opinions, I have never seen one that came so close to Thomas De Quincy's famous justification for punishing the crime of murder: "If once a man indulges himself in murder, very soon he comes to think little of robbing; and from robbing he next comes to drinking and Sabbath-breaking, and from that to incivility and procrastination."

Notice that the Court's version of this slippery-slope argument merely makes explicit what is implied throughout its opinion in the *McCleskey* case. Its decision is not limited to capital sentencing but purports to rest on principles which apply to the whole criminal justice system. Every part of that system from arrest to sentencing and parole, in relation to every crime from murder to Sabbath-breaking, involves a multitude of separate decision-makers making individualized decisions based upon "innumerable [case-specific] factors." All of these decisions are important for the protection of society from crime. All are conceived as "necessarily requir[ing] discretionary judgments." In making these discretionary judgments, prosecutors and judges as well as jurors have traditionally been immunized from inquiry into their motives. If this kind of discretion implies the power to treat black people differently from white people and to escape the responsibility for explaining why one is making life-and-death decisions in an apparently discriminatory manner, it implies a tolerance for racial discrimination throughout the length and breadth of the administration of criminal justice. What the Supreme Court has held, plainly, is that the very nature of the criminal justice system requires that its workings be excluded from the ordinary rules of law and even logic that guarantee equal protection to racial minorities in our society.

And it is here, I suggest, that any self-respecting criminal justice professional is obliged to speak out against this Supreme Court's conception of the criminal justice system. We must reaffirm that there can be no justice in a system which treats people of color differently from white people, or treats crimes against people of color differently from crimes against white people.

We must reaffirm that racism is itself a crime, and that the toleration of racism cannot be justified by the supposed interest of society in fighting crime. We must pledge that when anyone—even a majority of the Supreme Court—tells us that a power to discriminate on grounds of race is necessary to protect society from crime, we will recognize that we are probably being sold another shipment of propaganda to justify repression. Let us therefore never fail to ask the question whether righteous rhetoric about protecting society from crime really refers to protecting only white people. And when the answer, as in the McCleskey case, is that protecting only white people is being described as "protecting society from crime," let us say that we are not so stupid as to buy this version of the Big Lie, nor so uncaring as to let it go unchallenged.

Let us reaffirm that neither the toleration of racism by the Supreme Court nor the pervasiveness of racism in the criminal justice system can make it right, and that these things only make it worse. Let us reaffirm that racism exists, and is against the fundamental law of this Nation, whenever people of different races are treated differently by any public agency or institution as a consequence of their race and with no legitimate non-racial reason for the different treatment. Let us dedicate ourselves to eradicating racism, and declaring it unlawful, not simply in the superficial, short-lived situation where we can point to one or another specific decision-maker and show that his decisions were the product of conscious bigotry, but also in the far more basic, more intractable, and more destructive situation where hundreds upon hundreds of different public decision-makers, acting like Georgia's prosecutors and judges and juries—without collusion and in many cases without consciousness of their own racial biases—combine to produce a pattern that bespeaks the profound prejudice of an entire population.

Also, let us vow that we will never claim—or stand by unprotestingly while others claim for us—that, because our work is righteous and important, it should be above the law. Of course, controlling crime is vital work; that is why we give the agencies of criminal justice drastic and unique coercive powers, including the powers of imprisonment and death. And of course discretion in the execution of such powers is essential. But it is precisely because the powers that the system regulates are so awesome, and because the discretion of its actors is so broad, that it cannot be relieved of accountability for the exercise of that discretion. Nor can it be exempted from the scrutiny that courts of law are bound to give to documented charges of discrimination on the ground of race by any agency of government. Let us declare flatly that we neither seek nor will accept any such exemption, and that we find it demeaning to be told by the Supreme Court that the system of justice to which we

have devoted our professional lives cannot do its job without a special dispensation from the safeguards that assure to people of every race the equal protection of the law.

This is a stigma criminal justice practitioners do not deserve. Service in the criminal justice system should be a cause not for shame but for pride. Nowhere is it possible to dedicate one's labors to the welfare of one's fellow human beings with a greater sense that one is needed and that the quality of what one does can make a difference. But to feel this pride, and to deserve it, we must consecrate ourselves to the protection of all people, not a privileged few. We must be servants of humanity, not of caste. Whether or not the Supreme Court demands this of us, we must demand it of ourselves and of our coworkers in the system. For this is the faith to which we are sworn by our common calling: that doing justice is never simply someone else's job; correcting injustice is never simply someone else's responsibility.

---

29. This Man Has Expired: Witness to an Execution

Robert Johnson

Robert Johnson provides us with an inside look into an execution. He explains the role of the executioners and their assistants, the death watch team, and the death watch itself (which involves keeping the prisoner alive and "on schedule"). Johnson also describes witnessing the execution itself, as well as events of the morning after. This unique insight into how the death penalty is carried out raises serious questions about the nature of "breaking a person's spirit" prior to the execution as cruel and unusual punishment. It also sheds light on the issue of retributive justice.

The death penalty has made a comeback in recent years. In the late sixties and through most of the seventies, such a thing seemed impossible. There was a moratorium on executions in the U.S., backed by the authority of

From *Commonweal*, January 13, 1989, pp. 9–15. Copyright © 1989 Commonweal Foundation. Reprinted by permission.

the Supreme Court. The hiatus lasted roughly a decade. Coming on the heels of a gradual but persistent decline in the use of the death penalty in the Western world, it appeared to some that executions would pass from the American scene [cf. *Commonweal*, January 15, 1988]. Nothing could have been further from the truth.

Beginning with the execution of Gary Gilmore in 1977, over 100 people have been put to death, most of them in the last few years. Some 2,200 prisoners are presently confined on death rows across the nation. The majority of these prisoners have lived under sentence of death for years, in some cases a decade or more, and are running out of legal appeals. It is fair to say that the death penalty is alive and well in America, and that executions will be with us for the foreseeable future.

Gilmore's execution marked the resurrection of the modern death penalty and was big news. It was commemorated in a best-selling tome by Norman Mailer, *The Executioner's Song*. The title was deceptive. Like others who have examined the death penalty, Mailer told us a great deal about the condemned but very little about the executioners. Indeed, if we dwell on Mailer's account, the executioner's story is not only unsung; it is distorted.

Gilmore's execution was quite atypical. His was an instance of state-assisted suicide accompanied by an element of romance and played out against a backdrop of media fanfare. Unrepentant and unafraid, Gilmore refused to appeal his conviction. He dared the state of Utah to take his life, and the media repeated the challenge until it became a taunt that may well have goaded officials to action. A failed suicide pact with his lover staged only days before the execution, using drugs she delivered to him in a visit marked by unusual intimacy, added a hint of melodrama to the proceedings. Gilmore's final words, "Let's do it," seemed to invite the lethal hail of bullets from the firing squad. The nonchalant phrase, at once fatalistic and brazenly rebellious, became Gilmore's epitaph. It clinched his outlaw-hero image, and found its way onto tee shirts that confirmed his celebrity status.

Befitting a celebrity, Gilmore was treated with unusual leniency by prison officials during his confinement on death row. He was, for example, allowed to hold a party the night before his execution, during which he was free to eat, drink, and make merry with his guests until the early morning hours. This is not entirely unprecedented. Notorious English convicts of centuries past would throw farewell balls in prison on the eve of their executions. News accounts of such affairs sometimes in-

cluded a commentary on the richness of the table and the quality of the dancing. For the record, Gilmore served Tang, Kool-Aid, cookies, and coffee, later supplemented by contraband pizza and an unidentified liquor. Periodically, he gobbled drugs obligingly provided by the prison pharmacy. He played a modest arrangement of rock music albums but refrained from dancing.

Gilmore's execution generally, like his parting fete, was decidedly out of step with the tenor of the modern death penalty. Most condemned prisoners fight to save their lives, not to have them taken. They do not see their fate in romantic terms; there are no farewell parties. Nor are they given medication to ease their anxiety or win their compliance. The subjects of typical executions remain anonymous to the public and even to their keepers. They are very much alone at the end.

In contrast to Mailer's account, the focus of the research I have conducted is on the executioners themselves as they carry out typical executions. In my experience executioners—not unlike Mailer himself—can be quite voluble, and sometimes quite moving, in expressing themselves. I shall draw upon their words to describe the death work they carry out in our name.

Death Work and Death Workers

Executioners are not a popular subject of social research, let alone conversation at the dinner table or cocktail party. We simply don't give the subject much thought. When we think of executioners at all, the imagery runs to individual men of disreputable, or at least questionable, character who work stealthily behind the scenes to carry out their grim labors. We picture hooded men hiding in the shadow of the gallows, or anonymous figures lurking out of sight behind electric chairs, gas chambers, firing blinds, or, more recently, hospital gurneys. We wonder who would do such grisly work and how they sleep at night.

This image of the executioner as a sinister

and often solitary character is today misleading. To be sure, a few states hire free-lance executioners and traffic in macabre theatrics. Executioners may be picked up under cover of darkness and some may still wear black hoods. But today, executions are generally the work of a highly disciplined and efficient team of correctional officers.

Broadly speaking, the execution process as it is now practiced starts with the prisoner's confinement on death row, an oppressive prison-within-a-prison where the condemned are housed, sometimes for years, awaiting execution. Death work gains momentum when an execution date draws near and the prisoner is moved to the death house, a short walk from the death chamber. Finally, the process culminates in the death watch, a twenty-four-hour period that ends when the prisoner has been executed.

This final period, the death watch, is generally undertaken by correctional officers who work as a team and report directly to the prison warden. The warden or his representative, in turn, must by law preside over the execution. In many states, it is a member of the death watch or execution team, acting under the warden's authority, who in fact plays the formal role of executioner. Though this officer may technically work alone, his teammates view the execution as a shared responsibility. As one officer on the death watch told me in no uncertain terms: "We all take part in it; we all play 100 percent in it, too. That takes the load off this one individual [who pulls the switch]." The formal executioner concurred. "Everyone on the team can do it, and nobody will tell you I did it. I know my team." I found nothing in my research to dispute these claims.

The officers of these death watch teams are our modern executioners. As part of a larger study of the death work process, I studied one such group. This team, comprised of nine seasoned officers of varying ranks, had carried out five electrocutions at the time I began my research. I interviewed each officer on the team after the fifth execution, then served as an official witness at a sixth electrocution. Later, I served as a behind-the-scenes observer during their seventh execution. The results of this phase of my research form the substance of this essay.

The Death Watch Team

The death watch or execution team members refer to themselves, with evident pride, as simply "the team." This pride is shared by other correctional officials. The warden at the institution I was observing praised members of the team as solid citizens—in his words, country boys. These country boys, he assured me, could be counted on to do the job and do it well. As a fellow administrator put it, "an execution is something [that] needs to be done and good people, dedicated people who believe in the American system, should do it. And there's a certain amount of feeling, probably one to another, that they're part of that—that when they have to hang tough, they can do it, and they can do it right. And that it's just the right thing to do."

The official view is that an execution is a job that has to be done, and done right. The death penalty is, after all, the law of the land. In this context, the phrase "done right" means that an execution should be a proper, professional, dignified undertaking. In the words of a prison administrator, "We had to be sure that we did it properly, professionally, and [that] we gave as much dignity to the person as we possibly could in the process. . . . If you've gotta do it, it might just as well be done the way it's supposed to be done—without any sensation."

In the language of the prison officials, "proper" refers to the procedures that go off smoothly; "professional" means without personal feelings that intrude on the procedures in any way. The desire for executions that take place "without any sensation" no doubt refers to the absence of media sensationalism, particularly if there should be an embarrassing and undignified hitch in the procedures, for example, a prisoner who breaks down or becomes violent and must be forcibly placed in the electric chair as witnesses, some from the media, look on in horror. Still, I can't help but note that this may be a revealing slip of the tongue. For executions are indeed meant to go off without any human feeling, without any sensation. A profound absence of feeling would seem to capture the bureaucratic ideal embodied in the modern execution.

The view of executions held by the execution team members parallels that of correctional administrators but is somewhat more restrained. The officers of the team are closer to the killing and dying, and are less apt to wax abstract or eloquent in describing the process. Listen to one man's observations:

It's a job. I don't take it personally. You know, I don't take it like I'm having a grudge against this person and this person has done something to me. I'm just carrying out a job, doing what I was asked to do. . . . This man has been sentenced to death in the courts. This is the law and he broke this law, and he has to suffer the consequences. And one of the consequences is to put him to death.

I found that few members of the execution team support the death penalty outright or without reservation. Having seen executions close up, many of them have lingering doubts about the justice or wisdom of this sanction. As one officer put it:

I'm not sure the death penalty is the right way. I don't know if there is a right answer. So I look at it like this: if it's gotta be done, at least it can be done in a humane way, if there is such a word for it. . . . The only way it should be done, I feel, is the way we do it. It's done professionally; it's not no horseplaying. Everything is done by documentation. On time. By the book.

Arranging executions that occur "without any sensation" and that go "by the book" is no mean task, but it is a task that is undertaken in earnest by the execution team. The tone of the enterprise is set by the team leader, a man who takes a hard-boiled, no-nonsense approach to correctional work in general and death work in particular. "My style," he says, "is this: if it's a job to do, get it done. Do it and that's it." He seeks out kindred spirits, men who see killing condemned prisoners as a job—a dirty job one does reluctantly, perhaps, but above all a job one carries out dispassionately and in the line of duty.

To make sure that line of duty is a straight and accurate one, the death watch team has been carefully drilled by the team leader in the mechanics of execution. The process has been broken down into simple, discrete tasks and practiced repeatedly. The team leader describes the division of labor in the following exchange:

The execution team is a nine-officer team and each one has certain things to do. When I would train you, maybe you'd buckle a belt, that might be all you'd have to do. . . . And you'd be expected to do one thing and that's all you'd be expected to do. And if everybody does what they were taught, or what they were trained to do, at the end the man would be put in the chair and everything would be complete. It's all come together now.

So it's broken down into very small steps. . . .

Very small, yes. Each person has *one* thing to do.

I see. What's the purpose of breaking it down into such small steps?

So people won't get confused. I've learned it's kind of a tense time. When you're executin' a person, killing a person—you call it killin', executin', whatever you want—the man dies anyway. I find the less you got on your mind, why, the better you'll carry it out. So it's just very simple things. And so far, you know, it's all come together, we haven't had any problems.

This division of labor allows each man on the execution team to become a specialist, a technician with a sense of pride in his work. Said one man,

My assignment is the leg piece. Right leg. I roll his pants leg up, place a piece [electrode] on his leg, strap his leg in. . . . I've got all the moves down pat. We train from different posts: I can do any of them. But that's my main post.

The implication is not that the officers are incapable of performing multiple or complex tasks, but simply that it is more efficient to focus each officer's efforts on one easy task.

An essential part of the training is practice. Practice is meant to produce a confident group, capable of fast and accurate performance under pressure. The rewards of practice are reaped in improved performance. Executions take place with increasing efficiency, and eventually occur with precision. "The first one was grisly," a team member confided to me. He explained that there was a certain amount of fumbling, which made the execution seem interminable. There were technical problems as well: The generator was set too high so the body was badly burned. But that is the past, the officer assured me. "The ones now, we know what we're doing. It's just like clockwork."

The Death Watch

The death-watch team is deployed during the last twenty-four hours before an execution. In the state under study, the death watch starts at 11 o'clock the night before the execution and ends at 11 o'clock the next night when the execution takes place. At least two officers would be with the prisoner at any given time during that period. Their objective is to keep the prisoner alive and "on schedule." That is, to move him through a series of critical and cumulatively demoralizing junctures that begin with his last meal and end with his last walk. When the time comes, they must deliver the prisoner up for execution as quickly and unobtrusively as possible.

Broadly speaking, the job of the death watch officer, as one man put it, "is to sit and keep the inmate calm for the last twenty-four hours—and get the man ready to go." Keeping a condemned prisoner calm means, in part, serving his immediate needs. It seems paradoxical to think of the death watch officers as providing services to the condemned, but the logistics of the job make service a central obligation of the officers. Here's how one officer made this point:

Well, you can't help but be involved with many of the things that he's involved with. Because if he wants to make a call to his family, well, you'll have to dial the number. And you keep records of whatever calls he makes. If he wants a cigarette, well he's not allowed to keep matches so you light it for him. You've got to pour his coffee, too. So you're aware what he's doing. It's not like you can just ignore him. You've gotta just be with him whether he wants it or not, and cater to his needs.

Officers cater to the condemned because contented inmates are easier to keep under control. To a man, the officers say this is so. But one can never trust even a contented, condemned prisoner.

The death-watch officers see condemned prisoners as men with explosive personalities. "You don't know what, what a man's gonna do," noted one officer. "He's liable to snap, he's liable to pass out. We watch him all the time to prevent him from committing suicide. You've got to be ready—he's liable to do anything." The prisoner is never out of at least one officer's sight. Thus surveillance is constant, and control, for all intents and purposes, is total.

Relations between the officers and their charges during the death watch can be quite intense. Watching and being watched are central to this enterprise, and these are always engaging activities, particularly when the stakes are life and death. These relations are, nevertheless, utterly impersonal; there are no grudges but neither is there compassion or fellow-feeling. Officers are civil but cool; they keep an emotional distance from the men they are about to kill. To do otherwise, they maintain, would make it harder to execute condemned prisoners. The attitude of the officers is that the prisoners arrive as strangers and are easier to kill if they stay that way.

During the last five or six hours, two specific team officers are assigned to guard the prisoner. Unlike their more taciturn and aloof colleagues on earlier shifts, these officers make a conscious effort to talk with the prisoner. In one officer's words, "We keep them right there and keep talking to them—about anything except the chair." The point of these conversations is not merely to pass time; it is to keep tabs on the prisoner's state of mind, and to steer him away from subjects that might depress, anger, or otherwise upset him. Sociability, in other words, quite explicitly serves as a source of social control. Relationships, such as they are, serve purely manipulative ends. This is impersonality at its worst, masquerading as concern for the strangers one hopes to execute with as little trouble as possible.

Generally speaking, as the execution moves closer, the mood becomes more somber and subdued. There is a last meal. Prisoners can order pretty much what they want, but most eat little or nothing at all. At this point, the prisoners may steadfastly maintain that their executions will be stayed. Such bravado is belied by their loss of appetite. "You can see them going down," said one officer. "Food is the last thing they got on their minds."

Next the prisoners must box their meager worldly goods. These are inventoried by the staff, recorded on a one-page checklist form, and marked for disposition to family or friends. Prisoners are visibly saddened, even moved to tears, by this procedure, which at once summarizes their lives and highlights the imminence of death. At this point, said one of the officers, "I really get into him; I watch him real close." The execution schedule, the officer pointed out, is "picking up momentum, and we don't want to lose control of the situation."

This momentum is not lost on the condemned prisoner. Critical milestones have been passed. The prisoner moves in a limbo existence devoid of food or possessions; he has seen the last of such things, unless he receives a stay of execution and rejoins the living. His identity is expropriated as well. The critical juncture in this regard is the shaving of the man's head (including facial hair) and right leg. Hair is shaved to facilitate the electrocution; it reduces physical resistance to electricity and minimizes singeing and burning. But the process has obvious psychological significance as well, adding greatly to the momentum of the execution.

The shaving procedure is quite public and intimidating. The condemned man is taken from his cell and seated in the middle of the tier. His hands and feet are cuffed, and he is dressed only in undershorts. The entire death watch team is assembled around him. They stay at a discrete distance, but it is obvious that they are there to maintain control should he resist in any way or make any untoward move. As a rule, the man is overwhelmed. As one officer told me in blunt terms, "Come eight o'clock, we've got a dead man. Eight o'clock is when we shave the man. We take his identity; it goes with the hair." This taking of identity is indeed a collective process—the team makes a forceful "we," the prisoner their helpless object. The staff is confident that the prisoner's capacity to resist is now compromised. What is left of the man erodes gradually and, according to the officers, perceptibly over the remaining three hours before the execution.

After the prisoner has been shaved, he is then made to shower and don a fresh set of clothes for the execution. The clothes are unremarkable in appearance, except that velcro replaces buttons and zippers, to reduce the chance of burning the body. The main significance of the clothes is symbolic: they mark the prisoner as a man who is ready for execution. Now physically "prepped," to quote one team member, the prisoner is placed in an empty tomblike cell, the death cell. All that is left is the wait. During this fateful period, the prisoner is more like an object "without any sensation" than like a flesh-and-blood person on the threshold of death.

For condemned prisoners, like Gilmore, who come to accept and even to relish their impending deaths, a genuine calm seems to prevail. It is as if they can transcend the dehumanizing forces at work around them and go to their deaths in peace. For most condemned prisoners, however, numb resignation rather than peaceful acceptance is the norm. By the account of the death-watch officers, these more typical prisoners are beaten men. Listen to the officers' accounts:

A lot of 'em die in their minds before they go to that chair. I've never known of one or heard of one putting up a fight. . . . By the time they walk to the chair, they've completely faced it. Such a reality most people can't understand. Cause they don't fight it. They don't seem to have anything to say. It's just something like "Get it over with." They may be numb, sort of in a trance.

They go through stages. And, at this stage, they're real humble. Humblest bunch of people I ever seen. Most all of 'em is real, real weak. Most of the time you'd only need one or two people to carry out an execution, as weak and as humble as they are.

These men seem barely human and alive to their keepers. They wait meekly to be escorted to their deaths. The people who come for them are the warden and the remainder of the death watch team, flanked by high-ranking correctional officials. The warden reads the court order, known popularly as a death warrant. This is, as one officer said, "the real deal," and nobody misses its significance. The condemned prisoners then go to their deaths compliantly, captives of the inexorable, irresistible momentum of the situation. As one officer put it. "There's no struggle. . . . They just walk right on in there." So too, do the staff "just walk right on in there," following a routine they have come to know well. Both the condemned and the executioners, it would seem, find a relief of sorts in mindless mechanical conformity to the modern execution drill.

Witness to an Execution

As the team and administrators prepare to commence the good fight, as they might say, another group, the official witnesses, are also preparing themselves for their role in the execution. Numbering between six and twelve for any given execution, the official witnesses are disinterested citizens in good standing drawn from a cross-section of the state's population. If you will, they are every good or decent person, called upon to represent the community and use their good offices to testify to the propriety of the execution. I served as an official witness at the execution of an inmate.

At eight in the evening, about the time the prisoner is shaved in preparation for the execution, the witnesses are assembled. Eleven in all, we included three newspaper and two television reporters, a state trooper, two police officers, a magistrate, a businessman, and myself. We were picked up in the parking lot behind the main office of the corrections department. There was nothing unusual or even memorable about any of this. Gothic touches were notable by their absence. It wasn't a dark and stormy night; no one emerged from the shadows to lead us to the prison gates.

Mundane considerations prevailed. The van sent for us was missing a few rows of seats so there wasn't enough room for all of us. Obliging prison officials volunteered their cars. Our rather ordinary cavalcade reached the prison but only after getting lost. Once within the prison's walls, we were sequestered for some two hours in a bare and almost shabby administrative conference room. A public information officer was assigned to accompany us and answer our questions. We grilled this official about the prisoner and the execution procedure he would undergo shortly, but little information was to be had. The man confessed ignorance on the most basic points. Disgruntled at this and increasingly anxious, we made small talk and drank coffee.

At 10:40 P.M., roughly two-and-a-half hours after we were assembled and only twenty minutes before the execution was scheduled to occur, the witnesses were taken to the basement of the prison's administrative building, frisked, then led down an alleyway that ran along the exterior of the building. We entered a neighboring cell block and were admitted to a vestibule adjoining the death chamber. Each of us signed a log, and was then led off to the witness area. To our left, around a corner some thirty feet away, the prisoner sat in the condemned cell. He couldn't see us, but I'm quite certain he could hear us. It occurred to me that our arrival was a fateful reminder for the prisoner. The next group would be led by the warden, and it would be coming for him.

We entered the witness area, a room within the death chamber, and took our seats. A picture window covering the front wall of the witness room offered a clear view of the electric chair, which was about twelve feet away from us and well illuminated. The chair, a large, high-back solid oak structure with imposing black straps, dominated the death chamber. Behind it, on the back wall, was an open panel full of coils and lights. Peeling paint hung from the ceiling and walls; water stains from persistent leaks were everywhere in evidence.

Two officers, one a hulking figure weighing some 400 pounds, stood alongside the electric chair. Each had his hands crossed at the lap and wore a forbidding, blank expression on his face. The witnesses gazed at them and the chair, most of us scribbling notes furiously. We did this, I suppose, as much to record the experience as to have a distraction from the growing tension. A correctional officer entered the witness room and announced that a trial run of the machinery would be undertaken. Seconds later, lights flashed on the control panel behind the chair indicating that the chair was in working order. A white curtain, opened for the test, separated the chair and the witness area. After the test, the curtain was drawn. More tests were performed behind the curtain. Afterwards, the curtain was reopened, and would be left open until the execution was over. Then it would be closed to allow the officers to remove the body.

A handful of high-level correctional officials were present in the death chamber, standing just outside the witness area. There were two regional administrators, the director of the Department of Corrections, and the prison warden. The prisoner's chaplain and lawyer were also present. Other than the chaplain's black religious garb, subdued grey pinstripes and bland correctional uniforms prevailed. All parties were quite solemn.

At 10:58 the prisoner entered the death chamber. He was, I knew from my research, a man with a checkered, tragic past. He had been grossly abused as a child, and went on to become grossly abusive of others. I was told he could not describe his life, from childhood on, without talking about confrontations in defense of a precarious sense of self—at home, in school, on the streets, in the prison yard. Belittled by life and choking with rage, he was hungry to be noticed. Paradoxically, he had found his moment in the spotlight, but it was a dim and unflattering light cast before a small and unappreciative audience. "He'd pose for cameras in the chair—for the attention," his counselor had told me earlier in the day. But the truth was that the prisoner wasn't smiling, and there were no cameras.

The prisoner walked quickly and silently toward the chair, an escort of officers in tow. His eyes were turned downward, his expression a bit glazed. Like many before him, the prisoner had threatened to stage a last stand. But that was lifetimes ago, on death row. In the death house, he joined the humble bunch and kept to the executioner's schedule. He appeared to have given up on life before he died in the chair.

En route to the chair, the prisoner stumbled slightly, as if the momentum of the event had overtaken him. Were he not held securely by two officers, one at each elbow, he might have fallen. Were the routine to be broken in this or indeed any other way, the officers believe, the prisoner might faint or panic or become violent, and have to be forcibly placed in the chair. Perhaps as a precaution, when the prisoner reached the chair he did not turn on his own but rather was turned, firmly but without malice, by the officers in his escort. These included the two men at his elbows, and four others who followed behind him. Once the prisoner was seated, again with help, the officers strapped him into the chair.

The execution team worked with machine precision. Like a disciplined swarm, they enveloped him. Arms, legs, stomach, chest, and head were secured in a matter of seconds. Electrodes were attached to the cap holding his head and to the strap holding his exposed right leg. A leather mask was placed over his face. The last officer mopped the prisoner's brow, then touched his hand in a gesture of farewell.

During the brief procession to the electric chair, the prisoner was attended by a chaplain. As the execution team worked feverishly to secure the condemned man's body, the chaplain, who appeared to be upset, leaned over him and placed his forehead in contact with the prisoner's, whispering urgently. The priest might have been praying, but I had the impression he was consoling the man, perhaps assuring him that a forgiving God awaited him in the next life. If he heard the chaplain, I doubt the man comprehended his message. He didn't seem comforted. Rather, he looked stricken and appeared to be in shock. Perhaps the priest's urgent ministrations betrayed his doubts that the prisoner could hold himself together. The chaplain then withdrew at the warden's request, allowing the officers to affix the death mask.

The strapped and masked figure sat before us, utterly alone, waiting to be killed. The cap and mask dominated his face. The cap was nothing more than a sponge encased in a leather shell with a metal piece at the top to accept an electrode. It looked decrepit and resembled a cheap, ill-fitting toupee. The mask, made entirely of leather, appeared soiled and worn. It had two parts. The bottom part covered the chin and mouth, the top the eyes and lower forehead. Only the nose was exposed. The effect of a rigidly restrained body, together with the bizarre cap and the protruding nose, was nothing short of grotesque. A faceless man breathed before us in a tragicomic trance, waiting for a blast of electricity that would extinguish his life. Endless seconds passed. His last act was to swallow, nervously, pathetically, with his Adam's apple bobbing. I was struck by that simple movement then, and can't forget it even now. It told me, as nothing else did, that in the prisoner's restrained body, behind that mask, lurked a fellow human being who, at some level, however primitive, knew or sensed himself to be moments from death.

The condemned man sat perfectly still for what seemed an eternity but was in fact no more than thirty seconds. Finally the electricity hit him. His body stiffened spasmodically, though only briefly. A thin swirl of smoke trailed away from his head and then dissipated quickly. The body remained taut, with the right foot raised slightly at the heel, seemingly frozen there. A brief pause, then another minute of shock. When it was over, the body was flaccid and inert.

Three minutes passed while the officials let the body cool. (Immediately after the execution, I'm told, the body would be too hot to touch and would blister anyone who did.) All eyes were riveted to the chair; I felt trapped in my witness seat, at once transfixed and yet eager for release. I can't recall any clear

thoughts from that moment. One of the death watch officers later volunteered that he shared this experience of staring blankly at the execution scene. Had the prisoner's mind been mercifully blank before the end? I hoped so.

An officer walked up to the body, opened the shirt at chest level, then continued on to get the physician from an adjoining room. The physician listened for a heartbeat. Hearing none, he turned to the warden and said, "This man has expired." The warden, speaking to the director, solemnly intoned: "Mr. Director, the court order has been fulfilled." The curtain was then drawn and the witnesses filed out.

The Morning After

As the team prepared the body for the morgue, the witnesses were led to the front door of the prison. On the way, we passed a number of cell blocks. We could hear the normal sounds of prison life, including the occasional catcall and lewd comment hurled at uninvited guests like ourselves. But no trouble came in the wake of the execution. Small protests were going on outside the walls, we were told, but we could not hear them. Soon the media would be gone; the protestors would disperse and head for their homes. The prisoners, already home, had been indifferent to the proceedings, as they always are unless the condemned prisoner had been a figure of some consequence in the convict community. Then there might be tension and maybe even a modest disturbance on a prison tier or two. But few convict luminaries are executed, and the dead man had not been one of them. Our escort officer offered a sad tribute to the prisoner: "The inmates, they didn't care about this guy."

I couldn't help but think they weren't alone in this. The executioners went home and set about their lives. Having taken life, they would savor a bit of life themselves. They showered, ate, made love, slept, then took a day or two off. For some, the prisoner's image would linger for that night. The men who strapped him in remembered what it was like to touch him; they showered as soon as they got home to wash off the feel and smell of death. One official sat up picturing how the prisoner looked at the end. (I had a few drinks myself that night with the same image for company.) There was some talk about delayed reactions to the stress of carrying out executions. Though such concerns seemed remote that evening, I learned later that problems would surface for some of the officers. But no one on the team, then or later, was haunted by the executed man's memory, nor would anyone grieve for him. "When I go home after one of these things," said one man, "I sleep like a rock." His may or may not be the sleep of the just, but one can only marvel at such a thing, and perhaps envy such a man.

Case 6.a   Treating the Condemned to Death

Douglas A. Sargent

> Douglas A. Sargent argues that psychiatrists ought to refrain from treating mentally disturbed death-row inmates for the purpose of returning them to mental health and, hence, to execution. Such conduct is forbidden by the American Medical Association Code, goes against the basic oaths of a physician, and is reminiscent of the behavior of Nazi doctors.

The debate over capital punishment continues to polarize society. Physicians often side with those who oppose execution since killing people is inconsistent with the healer's role. But, while other physicians can easily sidestep professional involvement in executions, psychiatrists practicing in states that permit capital punishment cannot, since they may be pressed into evaluating or treating the condemned. Recently the U.S. Supreme Court upped the ante for psychiatry when it held, in a divided opinion in *Ford v. Wainwright*,[1] that executing an incompetent person offends the Eighth Amendment bar against cruel and unusual punishment.

Alvin Ford was condemned to death for murder, but over the eleven years he spent on death row during exhaustive appeals he had become psychotic. This was not only the opinion of his legal counsel but also of several psychiatrists, including two of the three appointed by the governor of Florida to appraise his competence. (The third found him to be "malingering.") Despite his psychosis, after a half-hour group evaluation the

governor's panel of psychiatrists found Ford "competent to be executed." Ford appealed this finding to the U.S. Supreme Court, and the American Psychiatric Association (APA) filed an *amicus* brief criticizing, among other things, the adequacy of the evaluation process.

The Court's decision not only accepted the APA's position, but went well beyond it. While the *amicus* brief merely hoped to persuade the Court that the procedures used to establish Ford's mental competency to be executed were seriously flawed, the court established a constitutional right for mentally incompetent persons not to be executed.

The decision benefits Ford temporarily, but the APA's "victory" may prove a mixed blessing for psychiatrists. The decision sharpens the conflict many psychiatrists face when dealing with condemned persons, a conflict between the professional's wish to evaluate "the competency to be executed" and treat those found incompetent because of mental disease, and the uneasy feeling that psychiatrists should not be involved in the process at all. While *Ford* was still undecided, psychiatry could content itself with criticizing the clinical shortcomings of the psychiatric evaluations done on Ford and others similarly situated.

From *The Hastings Center Report,* December 1986, pp. 5–6. Reprinted by permission.

Now psychiatrists must face the general and more difficult question: Does evaluating and treating condemned persons in order to restore their competence to be executed constitute "participation in an execution"? Such participation is explicitly forbidden by the AMA Principles of Medical Ethics.[2]

Psychiatrists usually get drawn into the act when a warden learns that a prisoner on death row is behaving strangely. The warden notifies the governor that the prisoner may be mentally ill. In most of the thirty-seven states with capital punishment the governor must determine if the prisoner is "competent to be executed." The usual test is that the condemned person must understand the effect of the death penalty and why it is being applied to him. Psychiatrists usually evaluate the prisoner and if, because of mental disease or defect, he fails either part of the test, execution is postponed until competence is restored. When, as is often the case, the disease or defect is unremitting, hospitalization is extended and the stay of execution becomes a *de facto* commutation.

Ralph Slovenko of Wayne State University Law School believes the procedure allows society to achieve the catharsis of a death sentence without the inconvenience of actually carrying it out. It thus preserves lives that, with more rigorous application of due process, might be lost. To question its fairness or logic may be to cast the searchlight of publicity into a corner that the condemned might prefer to leave dark.

Nevertheless, the psychiatrist working in this area faces daunting logical and ethical problems. First, a psychiatrist is being asked to remove a condition that is the only thing standing between the patient and his demise. Second, to fail to warn the patient that the therapist is colluding with the state in removing the last barrier to execution is dishonest.

Any therapy not grounded in the patient's welfare is inherently dishonest. Behind the acknowledged realities of death row therapy prisoners harbor unarticulated, trustful expectations that the encounter with the physician will prove beneficial. Such expectations flow from encounters with physicians in childhood and from the benevolent medical image

that the profession has taken great pains to foster. It is this implicit trust that our ethical guidelines buttress. We betray that trust when we treat patients so that they may be executed. To many physicians this may seem like "treating the patient to death." Such patients ought to be reminded at every stage that execution will follow recovery. But how many therapists can bring to death row this macabre degree of frankness?

Since informed consent to treatment is not possible under these circumstances, the therapist who complies with an order to treat cannot escape acting as a double agent in the service of the patient and the state. Yet the right to refuse treatment seems more critical on death row than in most settings. Many psychiatrists believe that the patient's explicit or implicit consent to treatment ought to be an absolute precondition for psychiatric treatment. Obviously the patient on death row is compelled and cannot refuse treatment. A landmark Michigan case, *Kaimowitz v. the Michigan Department of Mental Health*,[3] held that prisons are inherently coercive places and thus inmates are incapable of giving voluntary consent to treatment. Although the condemned prisoner's consent to treatment is not a *legal* requirement (there may not be a *legal* right to refuse treatment in this context), it should be of concern to the psychiatrist, who is free to refuse to participate in such coercion.

Further, to label as "treatment" a medical act that can only lead to the patient's death is Newspeak, especially in view of medicine's first rule: *primum non nocere* (First, do no harm). After Texas and Oklahoma introduced execution by lethal injection, the AMA ruled that participation of physicians in executions is unethical. They did so by adopting the recommendation of the Council of Ethical and Judicial Affairs, which stated: "A physician, as a member of a profession dedicated to preserving life when there is hope of doing so, should not be a participant in a legally authorized execution."

Since treatment and a subsequent psychiatric opinion restoring the prisoner's lost competence are the necessary preconditions to execution, it strains logic to think that these acts are anything less than the proscribed "participation." Moving beyond the semantics of "participation," the ethical proscription is grounded in the principle that a physician should not engage voluntarily in behavior that will bring about the death of a patient who does not want to die and who, but for the physician's intervention, would not.

Recently a committee of the APA wrestled with these issues.[4] In attempting to salve the anguish of the psychiatrist who is asked to declare that this patient is now fit for execution, the committee thought it had found a secure foothold on what it called a "slippery ethical slope." It recommended insulating the therapist from the necessity of reporting the patient's recovery to the authorities or reevaluating his competency to be executed.

But concern for the anguish of therapists seems misplaced, as does the desire to spare them from acknowledging that treatment has brought the patient to the foot of the gallows. Besides, unlike the patient, the clinician can always avoid that position. Dividing the grim task of reporting the readiness for execution between the diagnostic and treatment "teams," so that the latter can garner comfort from ignorance about the patient's progress, has little to recommend it except as a "least-restrictive self-deception."

But what about making a *diagnosis* of competency to be executed? If such a determination results in an execution that would not have taken place otherwise, is diagnosis not also a proscribed medical act? Perhaps this is best asked another way: is it ethical to do evaluations if one may occasionally save condemned prisoners' lives by a psychiatric determination that mental illness renders them incompetent for execution? The short answer to this question is "no" if we consider the case of Josef Mengele.

Mengele was a Nazi physician who earned the sobriquet, The Angel of Death. He used his diagnostic skills to determine which prisoners at Auschwitz should live because they had enough vitality to do useful work, and which should die because they did not. (Occasionally he selected special prisoners for "medical experiments," but they were spared only as long as his "experiments" lasted, an exception from which we can draw no comfort: we spare *our*

patients on death row only so long as *our* treatments last.) The general rule of the state was that all prisoners were condemned, but those whose lives could in some other way serve the state were spared for a time. Mengele's medical triage function implemented this "legal" determination, which was a logical outcome of the Nuremberg racial laws promulgated by the Nazis in the late 1930s that deprived certain citizens of their rights.

In his review of Robert Lifton's *The Nazi Doctors: Medical Killing and the Psychology of Genocide*, Bruno Bettelheim asks: "How could physicians become killers?" His answer: "They could do it by taking pride in their professional skills, irrespective of what purposes they served." Bettelheim finds it particularly distressing that "doctors, whom we are accustomed to respect as healers, were the systematic killers of millions, not just passively letting the killing happen, but actually selecting the prisoners to be killed."[5] Some may see in the story of the Nazi physicians an unpleasant parallel to psychiatry's diagnostic role in executions; others may not.

Refined objections to diagnosing and treating the condemned are superfluous if the whole process lies outside the scope of ethical activity. To attempt to prescribe the details of acts that are forbidden is like the executioner concerning himself with the niceties of sterile technique. As the Reagan administration steps up its efforts to widen the number of crimes that can result in capital punishment, *Ford* will be used as a device to lengthen the lives of prisoners. When the medical minuet steps to the tempo of a dirge, however, revising the choreography isn't enough. Physicians might better stay off the dance floor.

Notes

---

1. *Ford v. Wainwright*, No. 85-5542, 54 U.S.L.W. 4799 (U.S. Sup. Ct. June 26, 1986), 2nd, 526 (1985).

2. AMA Principles of Medical Ethics. Adopted

from Recommendations of the Council of Ethical and Judicial Affairs, June 20, 1980.

3. *Kaimowitz v. Mich. Dept. of Mental Health* Summary, 42 U.S.L.W. 2063 (July 31, 1973).

4. Competency to be Executed. APA Council

on Psychiatry and the Law, Revised June 19, 1985.

5. Bruno Bettelheim, "Their Specialty Was Murder," *New York Times Book Review*, October 5, 1986, pp. 1, 61–62.

Case 6.b   What Say Should Victims Have?

Walter Shapiro

Walter Shapiro discusses the question raised in the U.S. Supreme Court case *Payne* v. *Tennessee*, where it is asked if the nature of the victim's life should be at issue in determining if the defendant will be subject to capital punishment. The problems associated with "victim impact statements" and their use in 47 different states, as well as fundamental issues of fairness, are raised by Shapiro.

If, as the Declaration of Independence so eloquently declares, "all men are created equal," then can society place an unequal weight on the tragically lost lives of murder victims?

This is not an exam question in a college philosophy course but a moral conundrum at the core of perhaps the most intriguing case facing the U.S. Supreme Court, *Payne* v. *Tennessee*. Justice David Souter, the court's swing vote, asked during oral argument last month whether "it really is legitimate to value victims differently depending upon the circumstances of the lives that they have chosen to lead." Tennessee Attorney General Charles Burson's response was unequivocal: "There can be no doubt that the taking of the life of the President creates much more societal harm than the taking of the life of the homeless person."

Just 25 years ago, such stark legal reasoning was virtually unknown in modern American jurisprudence. Punishment was meted out because of the nature of the crime, devoid of any reference to the social identity of the victim. But since then, compassion and political calculation have combined to transform crime victims and their advocates into a potent lobbying force.

From *Time*, May 27, 1991. Copyright 1991 The Time Inc. Magazine Company. Reprinted by permission.

Beginning with California in 1978, 47 states now allow some form of so-called victim-impact statements to be included among the evidence weighed during the sentencing phase of criminal trials. Congress endorsed the principle in 1982 by approving victim-impact statements in federal cases. But the Supreme Court, by a 5-to-4 vote in 1987, carved out a crucial exception: neither the life of the victim nor the suffering of his survivors could be a factor in any state or federal case punishable by death. Now the court appears about to reverse itself in its forthcoming decision in *Payne*.

The details of the case are grisly: in 1987 a three-year-old boy, Nicholas Christopher, watched as his mother and baby sister were stabbed to death in Millington, Tenn., a Memphis suburb. The murders were committed by Pervis Tyrone Payne, a 20-year-old retarded man, who also badly wounded the boy. Payne's guilt is not in question; in 1988 he was convicted by a Tennessee court.

Instead, what is at issue before the Supreme Court is the legal validity of evidence the prosecution presented to the jury before it decreed death rather than life imprisonment for Payne. The most controversial testimony was provided by the boy's grandmother, Mary Zvolanek, who recounted in heartrending fashion how Nicholas cries out almost daily for his dead sister. The prosecutor ended his final argument to the jury with this emotive passage: "Somewhere down the road, Nicholas . . . is going to know what happened to his baby sister and his mother. He is going to know what type of justice was done. With your verdict, you will provide the answer."

But should young Nicholas' anguish have a direct bearing on Payne's punishment? Will a Supreme Court decision upholding Payne's sentence create a climate where the wails of a murder victim's relatives will ordain vengeance in the form of capital punishment? During the oral argument, Chief Justice William Rehnquist probably reflected his own views when he asked Payne's attorney, "Are you suggesting that the jury's feeling of sympathy or perhaps outrage at the crime and what it's left the victim with is not a permissible factor at all?"

Like the debate over capital punishment itself, the *Payne* case is rife with emblematic importance, yet it is only tangentially connected with the nation's alarming murder rate. Currently, the death penalty is decreed in only 3% of all murder convictions, and only a small percentage of these lead to actual executions. "The significance of *Payne* is more societal in terms of what it says about the proper role of the crime victim in the criminal-justice system," argues Richard Samp, a lawyer with the conservative Washington Legal Foundation, which is representing the Zvolanek family. This political symbolism has not been lost on the Bush Administration: Attorney General Dick Thornburgh made a rare appearance before the Supreme Court to argue that a jury should be given "the full picture of the nature and extent of the harm that's been caused to the family."

Critics of the government's position raise provocative philosophical and practical objections to an additional legal enshrinement of victims' rights. "It will take a giant step away from presumptions of equality in the worth of lives," broods Tufts University philosophy professor Hugo Bedau. "The criminal-justice system has traditionally been held to the myth of equal treatment of all who come before it."

With serious questions of racial and class bias already swirling around capital punishment, there are concerns that a decision upholding Payne's death sentence will produce further inequities. Hypothetically, the grieving family of a murdered bank president would be persuasive witnesses for the death penalty, while no one would speak for a slain prostitute. Diann Rust-Tierney of the A.C.L.U. is worried that the Supreme Court will "sanction different punishment based on the worth of the victim and aggravate an already pronounced discrimination in the way that the death penalty is applied."

There is, sad to say, no way society can ever provide more than token recompense to the relatives of murder victims. That is why it is an illusion—born of compassion, it is true—that justice can be found by adding their pain to the calculus of retribution in the courtroom.

Case 6.c   Saving Lives in Prison:
The Case of Wilbert Lee Evans

Justice Thurgood Marshall's Dissent

In 1984 Wilbert Lee Evans was sentenced to death for murder on the grounds that he represented a "future danger to society." The district court in Richmond, Virginia, granted a stay of execution after Mr. Evans played a pivotal role in stopping a prison riot. The Fourth Circuit Court of Appeals lifted the stay. The Supreme Court shortly thereafter upheld the Court of Appeals ruling, and Evans was executed in the electric chair. The following is from the dissent of Justice Thurgood Marshall.

The Court's approval of the death penalty has turned on the premise that given sufficient procedural safeguards, the death penalty may be administered fairly and reliably. Wilbert Evans's plea to be spared from execution demonstrates the fallacy of this assumption. Notwithstanding the panoply of procedural protections afforded Evans by this Court's capital jurisprudence, Evans today faces an imminent execution that even the State of Virginia (now) appears to concede is indefensible. Because an execution under these circumstances highlights the inherently cruel and unusual character of capital punishment, I dissent.

Evans was convicted of capital murder and sentenced to death. At the sentencing phase, the jury's verdict was predicated on a single aggravating circumstance: that if allowed to live Evans would pose a serious threat of future danger to society. Without this finding Evans could not have been sentenced to death.

While Evans was on death row at the Mecklenburg Correctional Facility, an event occurred that casts grave doubt on the jury's prediction of Evans's future dangerousness. On May 31, 1984, six death row inmates at Mecklenburg attempted to engineer an escape. (Prison officials attest that Evans played no role in instigating the riot.) Armed with makeshift knives, these inmates took hostage twelve prison guards and two female nurses. The guards were stripped of their clothes and weapons, bound, and blindfolded. The nurses were stripped of their clothes, and one was bound to an inmate's bed.

According to uncontested affidavits presented by guards taken hostage during the uprising, Evans took decisive steps to calm the riot, saving the lives of several hostages and preventing the rape of one of the nurses. For instance, Officer Ricardo Holmes, who was bound by escaping inmates and forced into a closet with other hostages, states that he heard Evans imploring the escaping inmates, "Don't hurt anybody and everything will be all right." Officer Holmes continues:

> It was very clear to me that [Evans] was trying to keep [the escaping inmates] calm and prevent them from getting out of control. It is my belief that had it not been for Evans, I might not be here today.

Other guards taken hostage during the uprising verify Officer Holmes's judgment that Evans protected them and the other hostages from danger. According to Officer Prince Thomas, Evans interceded to prevent the rape of Nurse Ethel Barksdale. Officers Holmes, Thomas, and Crutchfield and five other prison officials all attest that Evans's conduct during the May 31, 1984, uprising was consistent with his exemplary behavior during his close to ten years on death row.

Remarkably, the State of Virginia's opposition to Evans's application to stay the execution barely contests Evans's depiction of the relevant events or Evans's conclusion that these events reveal the clear error of the jury's prediction of Evans's future dangerousness. In other words, the State concedes that the sole basis for Evans's death sentence—future dangerousness—in fact *does not exist*.

The only ground asserted by the State for permitting Evans's execution to go forward is its interest in procedural finality. According to the State, permitting a death row inmate to challenge a finding of future dangerousness by reference to facts occurring after the sentence will unleash an endless stream of litigation. Each instance of inmate's post-sentencing nonviolent conduct, the State argues, will form the basis of a new attack upon a jury's finding of future dangerousness, and with each new claim will come appeals and collateral attacks. By denying Evans's application for a stay, the Court implicitly endorses the State's conclusion that it is entitled to look the other way when late-arriving evidence upsets its determination that a particular defendant can lawfully be executed.

In my view, the Court's decision to let Wilbert Evans be put to death is a compelling statement of the failure of this Court's capital jurisprudence. This Court's approach since *Gregg* v. *Georgia* has blithely assumed that strict procedures will satisfy the dictates of the Eighth Amendment's ban on cruel and unusual punishment. As Wilbert Evans's claim makes crystal clear, even the most exacting procedures are fallible. Just as the jury occasionally "gets it wrong" about whether a defendant charged with murder is innocent or guilty, so too can the jury "get it wrong" about

whether a defendant convicted of murder is deserving of death, notwithstanding the exacting procedures imposed by the Eighth Amendment. The only difference between Wilbert Evans's case and that of many other capital defendants is that the defect in Evans's sentence has been made unmistakably clear for us even before his execution is to be carried out.

The State's interest in "finality" is no answer to this flaw in the capital-sentencing system. It may indeed be the case that a state cannot realistically accommodate post-sentencing evidence casting doubt on a jury's finding of future dangerousness, but it hardly follows from this that it is *Wilbert Evans* who should bear the burden of this procedural limitation. In other words, if it is impossible to construct a system capable of accommodating *all* evidence relevant to a man's entitlement to be spared death—no matter when the evidence is disclosed—then it is the *system,* not the life of the man sentenced to death, that should be dispatched.

The indifferent shrug of the shoulders with which the Court answers the failure of its procedures in this case reveals the utter bankruptcy of its notion that a system of capital punishment can coexist with the Eighth Amendment. A death sentence that is *dead wrong* is no less so simply because its deficiency is not uncovered until the eleventh hour. A system of capital punishment that would permit Wilbert Evans's execution, notwithstanding as-to-now unrefuted evidence showing that death is an improper sentence, is a system that cannot stand.

I would stay Wilbert Evans's execution.

Acquaintance Rape

Violence against women is a pervasive, shocking, and serious problem in our society that gets very little attention. This chapter focuses on what has been called "acquaintance rape," whereby a woman is forced to have sex with a man she knows. Most women are raped by men they know—men they work with, go to school with, or even have as close friends. Less than a third of all rapes fit the stereotype of the unknown man in the park who assaults the unsuspecting woman. The term "acquaintance rape," unfortunately, is too awkward, and perhaps not flashy enough, for the general media. Hence, many call it "date rape." However, only a portion of acquaintance rapes happen on or after a date. All too often this crime occurs on college campuses. And it is the need to begin a discussion among college students that motivates the inclusion of this issue in this volume.

Probably the most problematic element of acquaintance rape is the difficulty of proof. Generally these crimes occur in private, go unreported, and are largely not taken seriously by institutional authorities. Those who dominate institutional power structures are usually men, who dismiss instances of acquaintance rape as mere complaints by women who fail to take responsibility for their own actions. Furthermore, when women actually can face the horror of reporting a rape, their past sex life, personal character, and actions immediately before and after the rape are probed mercilessly. Rape is perhaps the only crime for which the victim is treated worse at a trial than the defendant.

In many ways the question of "consent" is central. When a woman says no to sex, and a man forces her to submit, that, by definition, is rape. And yet many people are concerned by certain seemingly "consensual" elements. In the recent William Kennedy Smith acquaintance rape case, Smith was accused of raping a woman after meeting her at a bar, drinking with her, and taking a walk with her on a deserted beach at 3:00 A.M. Many people felt that this was not morally the same as the case of a woman being raped while jogging through Central Park. For many, the woman's conduct prior to the rape is important.

Feminists, on the other hand, argue that any conduct on the part of the woman, other than explicit consent, is morally irrelevant. In another recent celebrated case, boxer Mike Tyson was convicted, and sentenced to six years in prison, for raping a woman who came to his room early in the morning after an evening of drinking. Although her behavior may have been imprudent, feminists argue that this says nothing about the culpability of Tyson's conduct. When a woman protests, there is no consent; it is rape, pure and simple.

Many men still respond that, with changing social norms and behaviors, it is hard to see where the lines are to be drawn. When women are expected to feel perfectly comfortable going to a man's room and drinking late at night, ambiguities are perceived. On the other hand, some find a response in the simple T-shirt slogan "Exactly what part of 'no' don't you understand?" Changing social behaviors simply do not give men the right to rape women.

In 1975 Susan Brownmiller's book *Against Our Will: Men, Women, and Rape* provided a new way of thinking about rape. Brownmiller argued that rape is not a sex act but essentially a crime of violence used to intimidate women, keep them in a state of fear, and maintain patriarchal domination. Men, Brownmiller argues, are socialized to see women as less important and as existing for their pleasure. Many feminists wish to expand the term "rape" to any form of gender oppression, even nonsexual forms.

Rape, of course, goes beyond the issue of acquaintance rape. Racial issues can be very important. When an African-American male rapes a white woman, the criminal justice system responds quite differently than when the rapist is white. Moreover, one can explore the issue of marital rape. In England quite recently, for the first time, a man was convicted of raping his estranged wife. Because of the general issues surrounding rape, this chapter also provides several articles on the social functions of rape, the media, racism, and more.

30. Fallen Angels: The Representation of Violence against Women in Legal Culture

Kristin Bumiller

Kristin Bumiller analyzes the importance of the media and symbolic trials in perpetuating rape as a means for the social control of women. According to Bumiller, trials that deal with sexual violence, despite the pretense at justice, in fact reinforce dominant perceptions about violence against women. Bumiller pays special attention to the 1984 gang-rape trial in New Bedford, Massachusetts.

Introduction

One of the most frequent sources of the public's contact with legal ideas is through the reporting of trials about notorious crimes and persons. For the casual observer, these trials are worthy of attention because they capture the imagination or generate uncertainty about the law's ability to deal with human tragedy and depravity. Yet avid interest in media reports spawned by notable criminal cases is more than a spectator sport, these reports are the means by which symbolic representations of victims and criminals are produced for consumption in popular culture. The messages that are disseminated in democratic societies by the media about the causes and consequences of crime and the behavior of the principal actors in courtroom dramas are a prolific source of powerful legal symbols. This essay examines the ways in which symbolic trials concerning sexual violence, despite ostensibly promoting justice in individual cases, may actually reinforce dominant preconceptions about women, men, and crimes of sexual violence.

From the perspective of the mass audience, all criminal trials are symbolic, since defendants and victims come to represent social roles. Each trial has within it a message about the way to reconcile the social vision of a good society with justice in the individual case

From *International Journal of the Sociology of Law*, Vol. 18, pp. 125–142. Reprinted by permission.

(Kirchheimer, 1961). Yet these public morality plays, often about disturbing and incomprehensible acts of brutality against isolated victims, evoke in the mass consciousness conflicted emotions: genuine soul-searching for a more humane society mixed with superficial evaluations of dangerous stereotypes and misconceptions about criminals and victims (see Enzensberger, 1974; Lazere, 1987). Even though the stories are controversial, they serve to portray the event as a tragedy and thus relieve anxieties about the sources of violence and the legal system's ability to control them (Edelman, 1977).

The subject of this inquiry is a major symbolic trial that focused attention in its community and the wider world on the American justice system's treatment of sexual violence and ethnic prejudice. My mode of analysis is influenced by linguistics, feminism, and post-structuralist political philosophy. The symbolic trial is viewed as a signifier within the dominant legal culture: it is a forum that projects authoritative messages through language and legal form about identity and social relationships in a struggle between the antagonistic world views of the defense and the prosecution (Bordieu, 1987). The symbolic power of the law is projected through linguistic attributions concerning the character and motives of defendants, victims, and legal professionals (see Santos, 1982). Because dominant modes of constituting the self (as a woman, criminal, or victim, for example) are maintained through the conventions of legal language, symbolic trials are moments when the rejection of those categories may come about through resistance to legal discourse (Bordieu, 1987; see also Foucault, 1977).

Drawing on political and feminist theory (see Spivak, 1987; Moi, 1985), the following passages interpret messages about sexual violence that originate from sources outside and within a controversial rape trial. Interpretations are presented from three vantage points. First, one form of communication that mediates legal issues for the mass public, the newspaper stories that report the initial incident and the legal proceedings, generates accounts that structure perceptions of the crime. Second, accounts are provided from the principal lawyers that reflect their professional identity and their assumptions about the scope and purpose of criminal law. A third dimension is presented through the interpretation of the trial proceedings, and in particular the victim's testimony. This discourse reveals how her speech in a courtroom both conforms to legal ways of understanding violence and yet embodies resistance to accepted modes of expression. The analysis will show how multiple levels of discourse in a symbolic trial, in particular the public and professional language, frame public perceptions and constitute barriers to the articulation of the victim's perspective.

This essay presents a story about women and violence that is rarely written about or discussed in the context of a legal case. Generally, the story line that captures the public interest involves the curious circumstances of the individuals brought into the drama as well as evaluations of their moral character. The public audience plays the role of a jury of one's peers; each person evaluates the credibility of the charges based upon incomplete and fallible renditions of the facts. The themes developed here, however, do not turn on the factual premises of the case. The symbolic import of the trial depends less on the witnesses' adherence to or betrayal of the truth, and more on the way the stories told resonate with images of victims and thus form the context for interpretation.

This rape trial displays the multiple meanings implied in a woman's image of innocence. Simply stated, when the claim that a woman has been sexually assaulted is made, it is often based upon her blamelessness in contributing to her own harm. Thus, the claim to innocence is not easily made, for the shadow of guilt lingers (as with the defendants). More significantly, the multifaceted meanings of innocence widen the scope of judgment about a woman's worth. The "innocence" of a female accuser is lost with her initial charge that she has been touched by sexual violence, and is further eroded as her moral purity becomes an issue in court.

The trial turns on her "innocence of experience" or "freedom from guilt"; this has powerful symbolic consequences, for it reinforces the presumption that punishing violent men is justified to the extent that women are worthy of trust and protection. This presumption is symbolically as threatening as the actual violence of rape, for it exposes a woman's intimate life in the courtroom. The accuser is forced into the role of an "angel" who must defend her heavenly qualities after her fall from grace. The symbolic message is, in some degree, an expression of the legal system's high tolerance for violence against women and its low threshold for the measure of her unworthiness. The various meanings attached to the concept of a woman's innocence in the following interpretations of a major rape trial illustrate the vulnerability of the woman as an accuser in contemporary legal culture.

The Public Trial

The 1984 rape trial of six Portuguese immigrant men in New Bedford, Massachusetts, was a celebrated moment of media attention to issues of sex and violence.[1] The political language of the media reporting of the New Bedford incident encouraged the public audience to vicariously imagine and draw judgments about the sequence of events in the bar called Big Dan's. The media constructed the story in a way that intensified and polarized issues for purposes of the alternative agendas of the feminist and Portuguese communities (e.g., Edelman, 1977, 1988; see also Smart and Smart, 1978, pp. 91, 101–2). Rather than inscribing these acts of violence with meaning, the newspapers reported a lurid "spectacle" in which a "gang" of Portuguese men engaged in "senseless brutality" against a lone woman pinned down on a pool table. Although violent sexual assaults occur frequently in New Bedford and other communities across the country, this case was the subject of immense publicity because it was depicted as an inconceivably brutal gang rape cheered on by pitiless bystanders.

Six Portuguese immigrants were tried for aggravated sexual assault and sexual assault in a Falls River, Massachusetts courtroom about one year after the incident in Big Dan's. Because it received massive local and international newspaper coverage, the rape became an important symbol in popular culture and a focal point for the mobilization of feminist groups. The extensive publicity surrounding the Big Dan's incident's disputability may have arisen from the uniqueness of the circumstances, yet by subjecting the issue of gang rape to public scrutiny, the media constructed powerful images of the case through selective reporting of information and structuring of perceptions for the popular audience. While the power of the media to set agendas and to mobilize interest groups is often regarded with suspicion, the media's role in the creation of dominant images is ignored by skeptics unaware of the more subtle role of news accounts in constructing the conceptual framework within which conflictual events are interpreted and understood.[2]

In the *New Bedford Standard-Time's* characterization of the incident, the implied motives and intentions of the victim and defendants moved in and out of focus within a larger picture which included legal authorities and community organizations. Although a considerable amount of reporting space was allotted to the defendants (their arrest, court hearings, personal information, and statements by their attorneys), the language employed by the press, at least superficially, placed the spotlight on the victim. One news story, for example, described the rape as the "victim's ordeal," in which "ordeal" broadly referred to the acts of violent sexual aggression, the trial, and the publicity surrounding the trial. For the most part, references to the victim ignored her as an individual who had

her own specific responses to rape. Either the victim was named by her formal legal status and demographic qualities (e.g., the "complainant," "young woman," "21-year-old city woman"), or more elaborate discussion of the victim was carried out through references to "generic" victims of rape (e.g., anti-rape activists' statements of solidarity with the victim and special reporting features about rape crisis centers' efforts to respond to the psychological trauma of victims).

The majority of stories were unqualified in their description of the brutality of the crime and full of general sympathy for the victim and hostility toward the perpetrators. The newspapers told of a mob scene: "[according to police and witness reports] the bar was whipped into a lurid, cheering frenzy, as they watched the sexual assault." A rape reform activist is reported to have said: "The rapists knew exactly what they were doing. It went on so long, they obviously had a chance to consider what they were undertaking. The bail is ridiculously low." Her words are one example of the panoply of law-and-order demands that gain their intensity from the symbolic invocation of enemies. Thus, the Portuguese defendants metaphorically took on the instinctive qualities and look of uncivilized people, for example, one news report quoted a Portuguese man in the neighborhood referring to the accused as "barbarians."

Although the references to the victim tended to be sympathetic, there were ambivalent undercurrents in her portrayal. A New Bedford reporter attributed a heavenly innocence to the victim through the rhetorical questioning of an investigating police officer: "Where will she go from here? She'll probably have to leave New Bedford. . . . She won't be able to handle the memories. Look at her angelic face. It's *almost* full of innocence. She'll never be innocent again." She is not attributed earthly innocence, but the innocence of an angel fallen from grace.

The most conspicuous aspect of the event in terms of its symbolic representation in popular legal culture is not the portrayal of either the victim or the defendants, but the emphasis on the setting of the crime. The tone was set by the first major local newspaper story about the rape, which included a large photograph of

Big Dan's Tavern. Thus, attention was drawn to the incompatibility of the setting with expected norms of human behavior. The fact that the incident occurred in a *public* place, in a barroom and on a pool table, is discordant with the social conception of consensual sex as a private and intimate act. The public nature of the crime has significance beyond its location; the image of a gang, yelling, mocking, and humiliating the woman, jars common sensibilities about personal dignity in social interactions. The early coverage employed the shock of these circumstances as a rhetorical device to establish that illegitimate sex occurred. The effect was to inhibit further speculation about the woman's responsibility for the violence. Reporting about the scene of the crime implied that "no woman" would want "that" to happen. In such cases, the woman's private intentions regarding her intimate behavior are considered irrelevant as long as the news reporting focuses on a bar portrayed as a "sore spot" where only the "riff-raff go."

The language describing the setting of the crime creates a picture of the personalities of the actors and sets the framework for popular interpretations. The structuring of public perceptions about this particular incident intensified hostilities over the description of the social setting of the rape, which in this case involved immigrant defendants from a primarily ethnic community. Because popular cultural interpretations emphasized setting, the terms of political discourse were polarized between the response of the Portuguese community that New Bedford is a decent place to live and the demand of advocates of women's rights that women must have the freedom to associate safely in public places. For the "Take Back the Night" protesters, the setting of the crime clarified the underlying moral issue, that regardless of this woman's character and circumstances, *any* woman should have the freedom of movement to enter a public bar without the fear of being gang-raped. Supporters of the Portuguese defendants objected to newspaper reporting that, in their view, employed inappropriate references to the ethnic origins of the defendants. Moreover, concerns were raised that characterizations of Big Dan's as a bad establishment in a marginal neighborhood in the city were responsible for creating the impression that New Bedford was the Portuguese "rape capital" of the country.

At the level of the public trial, the news media both linguistically and visually created a story about brutal and public sexual violence and narrowed the interpretative framework for understanding the crime. In the actual trial, the setting of the rape was also recreated, but often by testimony that recast the scene in terms of precise movements indicated by pointing to a scaled down replica of Big Dan's in front of the witness stand. For the defense attorneys, once the case was brought to trial, their stated objective was to reconstruct the image of the bar so that a plausible story about human behavior would account for and justify the men's actions.

The Courtroom Trial

My ethnographic observations, obtained from interviews three years after the trial, offer an interpretation of the events that differs from the symbolically constructed accounts by the media.[3] From the perspective of the principal legal actors in the trial, the professional discourse of the law protects defendants from unbridled public hostility. The attorneys chose to analyze events by employing a language of equilibrium that employed commonsense personifications of good and evil, as well as of commendable and unworthy character.

From the defense attorneys' standpoint, the case was notable for its mundane nature rather than its notoriety; the case was nothing other than "a routine sexual assault case," "a dull, dull case," or "a classic case based on the mistrust of government witnesses." For these professional participants, the trial was similar to other rape trials and operated according to a predictable set of norms and procedures. The most perceptive of the defense attorneys recognized (similar to the social scientist) that social reality is reconstructed for the purposes of any trial. Several of the attorneys involved readily admitted that the reality of what happened in Big Dan's was unclear and were willing to entertain three possibilities: (1) that a brutal rape occurred; (2) that "something consensual" happened in the bar that night; or (3) that "something consensual" crossed the line into a criminal act. As a group, they openly discussed which image of the bar fit their reading of the facts and would best serve the interests of the defendants. As good criminal defense lawyers, their objective became to turn this incredible scenario into a story that made sense to a jury.

These lawyers confronted the ambiguity of the case but not without acknowledging the life-and-death consequences for a "lone defendant fighting for freedom" or experiencing the sheer scariness of one's heart pounding in making one's way through the mob on the courthouse steps. The defense attorneys identified with what they saw as the human side of the case. For one lawyer, the defendant was "gentle" Joseph Viera and the victim was a survivor: "she is no weeping willow or shrinking violet. She is a tough woman defending something. She has a big interest in the trial—her most important relationships are at stake. That is her public position, not what the people in L.A. think about her, but what the people around her and closest to her think of her." For the advocate, intuition about the victim is necessary to convince the jury that she was both consciously and unconsciously self-protective; that is, not to create the pretense that there was no rape, but to convince the jury that since the first experience of the victim after the attack was a confrontation with an accusatory grandmother, then she should no longer be seen as capable of expressing unadulterated truth. As the lawyer explains, "Why should I subordinate my perceptions about what the battle is about in the courtroom to [feminists'] demands that society devalues the victim because her boyfriend is a schmuck, because she is not married, or had a child out of wedlock—when the fellow next to me has his life on the line?" The bottom line for this defense attorney is that society cannot put its faith in the victim because she "has no commitment to justice."

The moral passion of the defense attorneys both recognizes and buries one truth. As actors in these roles they live with the dilemma that no language is able to express all aspects

of the truth—yet all language carries the force and power of the word—and these words that may be employed to condone violence against women carry the force of the law.

The Victim's Trial

The victim's testimony in the courtroom, reviewed from the videotaped record of the proceedings,[4] provides another kind of symbolic interpretation that connects the presentation of events inside the courtroom with the social construction of sexual relationships. The victim's accounts give authority to the perspectives of women and other excluded voices that are revealed neither by controversies generated by legal analysis nor by public speculation about personalities and circumstances. Yet, these accounts confront barriers to a full understanding of the person, or self, as an actor in the social world (Cassirer, 1985; Merleau-Ponty, 1964; Taylor, 1985a). The move to ground understanding in discourse, in particular the discourse of women and other victimized groups, can be seen as a straightforward strategy to give authority to their speech. But their perceptions of social reality, and our ability to reflect upon and understand their reality, are bounded by their capacities to express themselves in language. The political implication of this epistemological problem is that the discourse of excluded groups provides us with socially constructed "ways of knowing" that are partial and as a result can be employed to undermine their interests (Belenky et al., 1986). As my reading of the trial will show, however, these interpretations give utterance to the strengths as well as the vulnerability and duplicity of victims. These expressions, therefore, must be reconciled within a political context and ultimately evaluated in the larger scheme of institutional life.

The predominant theme of the trial was the inquiry into the "innocence" of the victim, who I call Diana. Both the prosecution and the defense produced theories to account for her motivations in going to the bar and the appropriateness of her behavior. As defense attorney Lindahl questioned: "At first your only intention was to buy cigarettes . . .; at some point you decided to stay . . . *That's the decision* you regret most about that night?" Defense attorney Edward Harrington posed the question: "If you're living with a man, what are you doing running around the streets getting raped?" (see MacKinnon, 1987, p. 80). This frame of reference inevitably flows from the definition of rape that forces the prosecution to show nonconsent in order to prove that a sexual assault has been committed. The state of mind of the victim is the window to the *mens rea* that establishes the culpability of the defendant. Since the social construction of rape in the courtroom or in society ignores the victim's perception of the attack, she becomes the object of a theory about nonconsent that uses information not only about her behavior on the day of the rape but also about the moral choices she has made throughout her lifetime.

The best defense in a rape trial, therefore, is often the indictment of the victim. That is why the defense attorneys attempted to incriminate Diana by posing a series of questions intended to raise doubts about the sincerity of her charge of rape: Was she desperate to have sex that night? So desperate that she would agree to sex in a public place? Was her behavior irresponsible or inviting? Was she too drunk to know what was happening?

The testimony of witnesses who actually heard and saw Diana that night, along with her own testimony, provides us with an account of her motives, words, and actions. Each element of evidence, however, derives its authority from the source and form of communication. For example, Diana's own accounts were different immediately after the rape from what she said at the trial and were given in the form of recollections, written police reports, and reports of witnessed confrontations in the bar or police station. Even as stories unfold in the courtroom, the value of the "facts" the court will call evidence has been predetermined by the social mechanisms that privilege certain forms of communication. In this case, it means that the simple and direct recollection of the facts she gave in court would stand against the enormous collection of documents already recording the events of the crime and her life.

As she testified in a calm monotone, she tried to present herself in society's image of an innocent victim rather than revealing weakness and anger. Adopting the pose of the innocent victim required her to show that her actions conformed to what is expected of a person of good character: consistency, sobriety, and responsibility. While the defense attorney's questions constrained her ability to explain her actions, her responses were also limited by the prosecution which was concerned that her testimony would contradict the police officers' official version and the testimony of witnesses who were in the tavern during the rape (see McBarnett, 1984). The defense attempted to question her credibility by pointing out inconsistencies in the accounts she gave to the police; even her private conferences with a rape counselor were introduced into evidence. Faced with such constraints, her strategy was not to reveal the "whole" story, but to construct a narrative that she felt would best establish her innocence. In a firm voice she recounted what she believed to be the truth about her victimization.

Given the focus on her innocence, the task was to convince the court of her capability to be cognizant of and explain all that had happened to her. This meant she had to draw a line in her description of her own emotional distress that preserved the credibility of her statements. When subjected to an extensive cross-examination that disputed the version of the facts she gave immediately after the rape, she defended her ability to perceive and report events in a state of mind that was (in her words) *near* hysterical and *slightly* confused.

The major challenge to her credibility rested on the record of her "exaggerations" in the police report written the night of the attack. In subsequent police reports she retracted the claim that there were fifteen men involved, including six who had sexual intercourse with her, and said she "lost count." She also modified the statement that "the men had knives" to "one man held a knife in front of her face" (then again, she "admits" he did not *say* anything threatening to her). She was continually questioned by the defense attorneys about these inconsistencies, to which her response was frequently that she "doesn't know" how to account for them.

Ultimately, none of her explanations captured the shock or trauma she had experienced. Instead, she offered admissions that she was tired and slightly confused. She said, "the events are clearer now than then"; and about the first police report, "I don't remember anything I said"; "I was tired, I didn't want to talk to anybody and I wanted to be left alone." Defense attorney Lindahl's effort to get her to justify her statement to the police produced this moment in the trial:

Lindahl: Did you tell [officer Sacramento] 12 or 15 men were involved?

Diana: Every man there was involved.

Lindahl: Did you say six men had sexual intercourse with you; when in fact two men had intercourse?

Diana: Yes.

Lindahl: Is this your testimony to the jury today? If you said twelve or fifteen; if you said sixteen or more; if you said—

Diana: *I believe everybody that was there was guilty!*

Lindahl: Objection!

[At this point the jury was asked to disregard the witness's statement.]

At the same time she spontaneously blurted out that everyone was guilty, she was able to characterize her "exaggerations" as a product of the horror she experienced in the bar that night. Yet Lindahl's next question was, "Maybe you were so upset you exaggerated." Diana's response was, "no." Her denial indicated both that she felt uncomfortable about the manner in which the prosecutors were using the law to try to place blame on her and that she was willing to defend her own view of moral responsibility that accounted for her rage against all of the men in the tavern.

Incriminating statements about Diana were not only used to undermine her credibility,

they were also developed into theories about consent by comparing the victim's character with the moral position of other women who were principal actors in the retelling of the story. These comparisons are poignantly brought forth in the testimony of the women who were with Diana during the day she was raped. The first witness called by the defense was Rosetta, who testified about their activities during the afternoon before Diana went to Big Dan's. Rosetta was asked a series of questions about their consumption of drinks at the Knotty Pine, an Italian restaurant and bar, where they stopped to get soup for their boyfriends. Defense attorney Harrington appeared disappointed with her testimony, as if he expected her to provide a more definitive answer to whether or not Diana had any alcoholic drinks that afternoon. However, the defense was able to establish that Diana had asked Rosetta if she would like to go out with her for a drink. The defense attorney initiated the following exchange on cross-examination:

Waxler: [Diana] wanted more to drink?

Rosetta: Yes.

Waxler: What did you say?

Rosetta: I told her she should *just* go home.

Waxler: Did she respond?

Rosetta: No.

Waxler: Did she say anything further?

Rosetta: No.

The purpose of this exchange was to attempt to establish that Diana intended to go out drinking when she left the house at dusk, but Rosetta insinuated that she disapproved of Diana's desire to get out of the house and, and in so doing, implied that Diana's own restlessness was responsible for her being raped at Big Dan's. Her testimony also enabled the defense to draw a contrast between Rosetta, who had recently married her boyfriend and made the wise decision of staying home, and Diana, who lived with the father of her two children and made the fateful decision to go out that night.

Another incriminating voice came from the other woman who had been in Big Dan's. Marie was introduced to the court as a reliable person with professional credentials: she is employed as a nurse and is much older than Diana (probably in her forties). (She was referred to as the "fat lady" in the testimony by the men in the bar who did not know her name.) She went out that night to get something to eat, but when she discovered the restaurant across the street was closed, she decided to see if she could get a sandwich at Big Dan's. Marie was a regular in the bar, and in fact, knew several of the men quite well. Previously, she had helped the defendant Victor Rapozo get a job. Marie gave the following description of Diana's actions in the tavern:

Harrington:	What did you see her do?
Marie:	She went to the bar to get a drink.
Harrington:	Were you seated at the table?
Marie:	Yes.
Harrington:	Did she come to the table?
Marie:	Next thing she did is, [she] came over and asked if [she] could sit down.
Harrington:	Then?
Marie:	I said you can sit down, but I am leaving shortly.
Harrington:	What observations did you make about the young lady?
Marie:	She was bubbly; she was bouncing 'round the chair; she never stood still, her pupils were very large and her eyes were glassy.

A few moments later, Marie added that during their ten minute conversation Diana had told her that "she didn't have sex for several months, I think nine months," and that her "boyfriend or ex-husband [suggested that she]

should get out and meet people because she is a lonely person."

A third confrontation with the morality of other women came from her closest relative and substitute parent, her grandmother. This confrontation was also recorded for the official record because it was overheard by the police officer accompanying her to the hospital and by the nurse. Her grandmother, when she first saw Diana in the hospital, called her a drunk, accused her of shaming the family, and asked her why she was not at home with her children. Diana was reluctant to talk about her grandmother's denouncements, and at one point insisted that they were irrelevant:

Lindahl:	Do you remember the conversation with your grandmother?
Diana:	I don't want my grandmother brought into this.
Lindahl:	The reason you didn't remember is because you didn't want to talk about your grandmother?
Diana:	Yes, it is.
Lindahl:	It was true you didn't remember?
Diana:	It wasn't a lie. I don't think it should have been brought up.
Lindahl:	Isn't it true, whenever you don't want anything brought up, you say I don't remember?

Diana obviously cared deeply about her grandmother's opinion of her, yet she explained her grandmother's reaction by asserting that she must have been so upset that she did not realize her words were harmful. Diana tried to present the story as if there had been no direct conversation, as if her grandmother had been screaming and as if most of the actual conversation had been directed at her grandfather. The re-enactment in the trial of her grandmother's assault on her character not only revealed the powerful forces of condemnation at work in her private life but brought these painful experiences into the realm of public judgment.

Using the morality of other women to incriminate Diana exemplifies how the social conception of rape finds authority in the woman's duty to protect herself. The defendants, however, relied on more overt challenges based on their ordinary treatment of women. As defendant John Cordeiro told the court, in his testimony on his own behalf, he was surprised to hear the next morning that the police were looking for him because there had been a rape in Big Dan's Tavern. He said, "A rape? Nobody raped anybody." When asked in the trial if he knew what rape was. Cordeiro responded. "It is when you tear off their clothes . . ." In Cordeiro's account of that night, he left Big Dan's for a short while, and when he came back he saw Diana on the pool table with defendant Joe Viera on top of her. He watched defendant Rapozo put his penis in her mouth and then did the same thing, while Diana was "smiling and laughing at them." Cordeiro was relatively unconcerned about talking to the police the next morning, because all he believed he had to do was to "tell the truth . . . *the truth never hurts.*" His confidence turned out to be misplaced, but his lack of concern reflects the unproblematic state of mind of the rapist. There was initially no reason for him to doubt his own opinion about what the woman wanted to have happen to her that night.

Defendant Daniel Silva's story was less frank and based upon more complicated assumptions about how Diana had communicated her desire to be raped. Silva claimed that he had met Diana a few months before and had had a short conversation with her in a cafe named Pals Four. By his account, Diana approached him and asked if he had any drugs. After a few more words, she asked, "Do you want to play, fool around?" He reportedly responded "yes" and claimed she "looked very happy." He explained to her that he could not take her home, however, because he lived with his mother. As they continued to fool around with each other, the only thing that concerned Silva was that he "thought she was holding me too tight; like a hysterical woman; like she wanted something." Daniel

Silva portrayed the situation in Big Dan's as an ordinary "pick-up" in a bar, at least until the other men started making fun of him and then participated in the attack.

The challenges from the women and the defendants were based upon assumptions about how men and women communicate sexual aggression and desire. The proceedings became a search for facts that would explain a cause and effect sequence in which the defendant makes "reasonable" judgments about her desires and the victim either rebukes him or acquiesces in his actions. In this construction of the social interaction, there are "spaces" open for speculation about typical behavior that allows the defense to draw upon images in society that hold women responsible for their own victimization.

Implications for Feminist Strategies

In this essay, the New Bedford trial was analyzed as a spectacle that projected symbolic messages about sexual violence: it presented a story, reconstructed in different media, about a woman's life and her responses to a violent sexual assault. The trial was a moment at which the violation of women's sexuality was reproduced for mass public consumption in a manner to satisfy the internal logic of the legal system.

Although the ultimate conviction of four of the defendants might be seen as symbolic vindication of the victim's innocence, my reading of the trial suggests that even in a situation of multiple acts of violence (in the presence of witnesses) the victim was subject to the vulnerabilities of a woman as an accusor. From the initial media presentation of the case, it appeared that the "public" nature of the violent act served to affirm the assumption of the victim's "innocence" while vilifying the Portuguese defendants and their conduct in the community. As the "facts" became public knowledge, however, the unnamed complaining witness was portrayed as a confused young woman of unreliable character. The public persona of the victim was transformed by a reconstructed account that scrutinized her behavior in the tavern by comparing it to "reasonable" standards of women's propriety. Within the legal forum, her fearful assertion of violation was obscured by questioning that implied personal irresponsibility in protecting herself from male aggression while raising suspicion about her sexual motivations as a woman: she was forced to defend the propriety of her actions while being held suspect for female capriciousness.

Feminist reformers have tried to use the trial forum to raise public awareness about the prevalence of rape and other violent crimes affecting women. The rhetorical stance of these reformers, however, has accepted the presumption of legal realists that trials have an educative function. As a result, the publicity generated by organized courtwatchers and statements of outrage about particular cases are intended to educate an insensitive audience that violence against women had become commonplace both on the streets and in the courtroom (see Pitch, 1985; Fineman, 1983). This analysis, however, demonstrates that publicity encouraged by rape reform advocates may have failed to focus discontent, while generating ambiguous messages about the motivations of victims and the nature of feminine "innocence."

The legal realist's vision of the symbolic trial is adhered to by the professionals in the courtroom, despite realism's arguable inability to capture the social meaning of controversial events. Both the physical setting of the courtroom scene and the procedures and language of the trial create the image of law as separating out the truth from the hysteria of the victim. The prosecutors and defense attorneys act as guardians of this order and are resistent to any form of dialogue that attempts to make sense of the violence in a way that does not fit the legal models of guilt or innocence. For example, in the New Bedford rape trial a motion for mistrial arose from District Attorney Kane's reference to police officer Carol Sacramento's statement. "How did this happen?" Kane repeated it several times during his opening statement, as if this was the question he wanted to leave foremost in the jury's mind. Defense attorney Coffin argued that this inappropriate statement was inadmissible as evidence and therefore should not have been included in his opening statement. Moreover, he claimed that "How did it happen?" is an ambiguous question because it could have meant either "How could this rape have happened?" or "How could these consensual acts have happened?"

Kane's response to the motion for mistrial was that the court should recognize that Sacramento's amazement was part of the proof that the rape occurred: since the rape was an extraordinary event, it was important to point out that those who first heard the complaint that night would have responded to it in an extraordinary manner. Yet the prosecution's willingness to stimulate our bewilderment was limited. As participants in professional legal discourse, the prosecutors tried to discourage speculation about how society's approval of violence against women created the conditions for the rape at Big Dan's. From the prosecution's perspective, the case was simply about a tragedy that involved a confused young woman. In fact, the District Attorney attempted to explain the inconsistencies in his case by arguing, in his closing statement, that this was a story without "heroes." Diana was portrayed as a character in a human tragedy who must confront, like all tragic figures, her own faults and vulnerabilities.

But to call this trial a tragedy is to individualize Diana's misfortune and ignore the way that the ordinary has been given larger than life significance. It is a tragedy only if one believes that the event is otherwise inexplicable and that the cause of the attack did not grow out of the group dynamic in the tavern but arose instead from an evil that lurked within the victim. The District Attorney's analogy to a tragedy was meant to reassure the jury that the trial is the best method to bring forth the truth, and that these truths must self-evidently account for the rape.

Yet, the legal system is itself implicated in the tragedy unless one is willing to agree with defendant John Cordeiro that the "truth never hurts." As the trial is interpreted in its symbolic context, one sees how truths that are partial may become powerful instruments that can assign blame and absolve guilt. From the perspective of legal professionals, partial truths are defensible as part of a larger battle in the pursuit of justice. Defense attorney Lindahl, for example, defended the trial to the press because, "in our attempts to protect those who are truly victims, we better take care that we don't victimize not only the men accused, but all of us if we give up the confrontation inherent in a trial."[5] But the symbolism of this trial involved more than rituals of confrontation; the trial produced messages which served to disempower women both inside and outside of the courtroom. Lindahl's concerns focused on the search for justice in the individual case, and were warranted if the only threat to justice is the excessive power of the state and the unbridled vengeance that stems from victimization. Otherwise, she has ignored the way that law has unleashed metaphors that attack basic notions of human decency. The celebrated trial has an impact far greater, and a message more complicated, than the realists envisioned. Their claim that these contests affirm a legalistic society's reliance on procedure can be made only at the risk of ignoring these trials' cultural significance and meaning.

The narrative constructed in this essay suggests that those who purposely desire to use the trial forum to send a message condemning sexual violence confront a dilemma-ridden strategy. The more vehemently reformers maintain that "objective" evidence can be provided to prove the abuse of victims, the more necessary it becomes to establish the victim's innocence according to commonly held notions of verifiability (Griffin, 1986). The reliance on objective evidence, therefore, forces the defenders of victims' rights to resort to tactics that narrow or limit the telling of the woman's story. The claim of objectivity may also have the effect of making it more difficult to establish the woman's "innocence" in more ambiguous situations where rape differs from

the overt violence of "real rape" (Estrich, 1987), which is marked by a relationship of strangers, the use of a weapon, and a public scene. The forms of communication that are appropriate in a courtroom and that are disseminated by the media conform to conventions of the "public" discourse of news reporting and the "professional" discourse of criminal procedure. If reformers strive toward transforming the social construction of rape, even abandoning the model of consent, then changes in the public understanding of the crime may only come about with challenges to the dominance of legal discourse.

Notes

1. Four of the six defendants were convicted, see *Commonwealth* v. *Rapozo, Cordeiro, Silva, and Viera* (Mass. Super. Ct., Mar. 17, 1984).

2. The following analysis is based upon content analysis of national and local newspaper reports on the incident and the trial, including the *New York Times*, the *Boston Globe*, and the *New Bedford Standard-Times*. All quotations in this paper are from the *New Bedford Standard-Times*, March 1983–April 1984, unless otherwise indicated.

3. Interviews were conducted with five defense attorneys, one prosecutor, and the presiding judge.

4. The entire trial was videotaped and televised by a local New Bedford public television station. The videotapes were obtained from the archives at the Harvard Law Library. All excerpts from the trial are my own transcriptions from the videotaped record.

5. Quoted in a signed article in the *New York Times*, "The Rape Trial," written by Sidney H. Schamberg, March 27, 1984.

31. "The Mind That Burns in Each Body": Women, Rape, and Racial Violence

Jacquelyn Dowd Hall

Building on the feminist claim that rape is a form of male domination, Jacquelyn Dowd Hall expands the understanding to include racial considerations. She argues that, in the post-Reconstruction South, the act of rape was functionally inseparable from the act of lynching as a means of dominating African Americans. Rape, she says, was not simply an act of violence but a story that legitimized violence per se—a story that must be challenged for feminists to succeed in opposing male violence.

I. Hostility Focused on Human Flesh

FLORIDA TO BURN NEGRO AT STAKE: SEX CRIMINAL SEIZED FROM JAIL, WILL BE MUTILATED, SET AFIRE IN EXTRA-LEGAL VENGEANCE FOR DEED
> —Dothan (Alabama)
> *Eagle*, October 26, 1934

After taking the nigger to the woods . . . they cut off his penis. He was made to eat it. Then they cut off his testicles and made him eat them and say he liked it.
> —Member of a lynch mob, 1934[1]

Lynching, like rape, has not yet been given its history. Perhaps it has been too easily relegated to the shadows where "poor white" stereotypes dwell. Perhaps the image of absolute victimization it evokes has been too difficult to reconcile with what we know about black resilience and resistance. Yet the impact of lynching, both as practice and as symbol, can hardly be underestimated. Between 1882 and 1946 almost 5,000 people died by lynching. The lynching of Emmett Till in 1955 for whistling at a white woman, the killing of three civil rights workers in Mississippi in the 1960s,

and the hanging of a black youth in Alabama in 1981 all illustrate the persistence of this tradition of ritual violence in the service of racial control, a tradition intimately bound up with the politics of sexuality.

Vigilantism originated on the eighteenth-century frontier where it filled a vacuum in law enforcement. Rather than passing with the frontier, however, lynching was incorporated into the distinctive legal system of southern slave society.[2] In the nineteenth century, the industrializing North moved toward a modern criminal justice system in which police, courts, and prisons administered an impersonal, bureaucratic rule of law designed to uphold property rights and discipline unruly workers. The South, in contrast, maintained order through a system of deference and customary authority in which all whites had informal police power over all blacks, slave owners meted out plantation justice undisturbed by any generalized rule of law, and the state encouraged vigilantism as part of its overall reluctance to maintain a strong system of formal authority that would have undermined the planter's prerogatives. The purpose of one system was class control, of the other, control over a slave population. And each tradition continued into the period after the Civil War. In the North, factory-like penitentiaries warehoused displaced members of the industrial proletariat. The South maintained higher rates of personal violence than any other region in the country and lynching crossed over the line from informal law enforcement into outright political terrorism.

White supremacy, of course, did not rest on force alone. Routine institutional arrangements denied to the freedmen and women the opportunity to own land, the right to vote, access to education, and participation in the administration of the law. Lynching reached its height during the battles of Reconstruction and the Populist revolt; once a new system of disfranchisement, debt peonage, and segregation was firmly in place, mob violence gradually declined. Yet until World War I, the average number of lynchings never fell below two or three a week. Through the twenties and thirties, mob violence reinforced white dominance by providing planters with a quasi-official way of enforcing labor contracts and crop lien laws and local officials with a means of extracting deference, regardless of the letter of the law. Individuals may have lynched for their own twisted reasons, but the practice continued only with tacit official consent.[3]

Most importantly, lynching served as a tool of psychological intimidation aimed at blacks as a group. Unlike official authority, the lynch mob was unlimited in its capriciousness. With care and vigilance, an individual might avoid situations that landed him in the hands of the law. But a lynch mob could strike anywhere, any time. Once the brush fire of rumor began, a manhunt was organized, and the local paper began putting out special editions announcing a lynching in progress, there could be few effective reprieves. If the intended victim could not be found, an innocent bystander might serve as well.

It was not simply the threat of death that gave lynching its repressive power. Even as outbreaks of mob violence declined in frequency, they were increasingly accompanied by torture and sexual mutilation. Descriptions of the first phase of Hitler's death sweep are chillingly applicable to lynching: "Killing was ad hoc, inventive, and in its dependence on imagination, peculiarly expressive . . . this was murder uncanny in its anonymous intimacy, a hostility so personally focused on human flesh that the abstract fact of death was not enough."[4]

At the same time, the expansion of communications and the development of photography in the late nineteenth and early twentieth centuries gave reporting a vividness it had never had before. The lurid evocation of human suffering implicated white readers in each act of aggression and drove home to blacks the consequences of powerlessness. Like whipping under slavery, lynching was an instrument of coercion intended to impress not only the immediate victim but all who saw or heard about the event. And the mass media spread the imagery of rope and faggot far beyond the community in which each lynching took place. Writing about his youth in the rural South in the 1920s, Richard Wright describes the terrible climate of fear:

> The things that influenced my conduct as a Negro did not have to happen to me directly; I needed but to hear of them to feel their full effects in the deepest layers of my consciousness. Indeed, the white brutality that I had not seen was a more effective control of my behavior than that which I knew. The actual experience would have let me see the realistic outlines of what was really happening, but as long as it remained something terrible and yet remote, something whose horror and blood might descend upon me at any moment, I was compelled to give my entire imagination over to it.[5]

A penis cut off and stuffed in a victim's mouth. A crowd of thousands watching a black man scream in pain. Such incidents did not have to occur very often, or be witnessed directly, to be burned indelibly into the mind.

II. Never against Her Will

> White men have said over and over—and we have believed it because it was repeated so often—that not only was there no such thing as a chaste Negro woman—but that a Negro woman could not be assaulted, that it was never against her will.
>
> —Jessie Daniel Ames (1936)

Schooled in the struggle against sexual rather than racial violence, contemporary feminists may nevertheless find familiar this account of lynching's political function, for analogies between rape and lynching have often surfaced in the literature of the anti-rape movement. To carry such analogies too far would be to fall into the error of radical feminist writing that misconstrues the realities of racism in the effort to illuminate sexual subordination.[6] It is the suggestion of this essay, however, that there is a significant resonance between these two forms of violence. We are only beginning to understand the web of connections among racism, attitudes toward women, and sexual ideologies. The purpose of looking more closely at the dynamics of repressive violence is not to reduce sexual assault and mob murder to static equivalents but to illuminate some of the strands of that tangled web.

The association between lynching and rape emerges most clearly in their parallel use in racial subordination. As Diane K. Lewis has pointed out, in a patriarchal society, black men, as men, constituted a potential challenge to the established order.[7] Laws were formulated primarily to exclude black men from adult male prerogatives in the public sphere, and lynching meshed with these legal mechanisms of exclusion. Black women represented a more ambiguous threat. They too were denied access to the politico-jural domain, but since they shared this exclusion with women in general, its maintenance engendered less anxiety and required less force. Lynching served primarily to dramatize hierarchies among men. In contrast, the violence directed at black women illustrates the double jeopardy of race and sex. The records of the Freedmen's Bureau and the oral histories collected by the Federal Writers' Project testify to the sexual atrocities endured by black women as whites sought to reassert their command over the newly freed slaves. Black women were sometimes executed by lynch mobs, but more routinely they served as targets of sexual assault.

Like vigilantism, the sexual exploitation of black women had been institutionalized under slavery. Whether seized through outright force or voluntarily granted within the master-slave relation, the sexual access of white men to black women was a cornerstone of patriarchal power in the South. It was used as a

punishment or demanded in exchange for leniency. Like other forms of deference and conspicuous consumption, it buttressed planter hegemony. And it served the practical economic purpose of replenishing the slave labor supply.

After the Civil War, the informal sexual arrangements of slavery shaded into the use of rape as a political weapon, and the special vulnerability of black women helped shape the ex-slaves' struggle for the prerequisites of freedom. Strong family bonds had survived the adversities of slavery; after freedom, the black family served as a bulwark against a racist society. Indeed, the sharecropping system that replaced slavery as the South's chief mode of production grew in part from the desire of blacks to withdraw from gang labor and gain control over their own work, family lives, and bodily integrity. The sharecropping family enabled women to escape white male supervision, devote their productive and reproductive powers to their own families, and protect themselves from sexual assault.[8]

Most studies of racial violence have paid little attention to the particular suffering of women.[9] Even rape has been seen less as an aspect of sexual oppression than as a transaction between white and black men. Certainly Claude Lévi-Strauss's insight that men use women as verbs with which to communicate with one another (rape being a means of communicating defeat to the men of a conquered tribe) helps explain the extreme viciousness of sexual violence in the post-emancipation era.[10] Rape *was* in part a reaction to the effort of the freedmen to assume the role of patriarch, able to provide for and protect his family. Nevertheless, as writers like Susan Griffin and Susan Brownmiller and others have made clear, rape is first and foremost a crime against women.[11] Rape sent a message to black men, but more centrally, it expressed male sexual attitudes in a culture both racist and patriarchal.

Recent historians of Victorian sexuality have traced the process by which a belief in female "passionlessness" replaced an older notion of women's dangerous sexual power.[12] Even at the height of the "cult of true womanhood" in the nineteenth century, however, views of women's sexuality remained ambivalent and double-edged. The association between women and nature, the dread of women's treacherous carnality, persisted, rooted, as Dorothy Dinnerstein persuasively argues, in the earliest experiences of infancy.

In the United States, the fear and fascination of female sexuality was projected onto black women; the passionless lady arose in symbiosis with the primitively sexual slave. House slaves often served as substitute mothers; at a black woman's breast white men experienced absolute dependence on a being who was both a source of wish-fulfilling joy and of grief-producing disappointment. In adulthood, such men could find in this black woman a ready object for the mixture of rage and desire that so often underlies male heterosexuality. The black woman, already in chains, was sexually available, unable to make claims for support or concern; by dominating her, men could replay the infant's dream of unlimited access to the mother.[13] The economic and political challenge posed by the black patriarch might be met with death by lynching, but when the black woman seized the opportunity to turn her maternal and sexual resources to the benefit of her own family, sexual violence met her assertion of will. Thus rape reasserted white dominance and control in the private arena as lynching reasserted hierarchical arrangements in the public transactions of men.

III. Lynching's Double Message

The crowds from here that went over to see [Lola Cannidy, the alleged rape victim in the Claude Neal lynching of 1934] said he was so large he could not assault her until he took his knife and cut her, and also had either cut or bit one of her breast [sic] off.

—Letter to Mrs. W. P. Cornell, October 29, 1934, Association of Southern Women for the Prevention of Lynching Papers

. . . more than rape itself, the fear of rape permeates our lives. . . . and the

best defense against this is not to be, to deny being in the body, as a self, to . . . avert your gaze, make yourself, as a presence in the world, less felt.

—Susan Griffin
Rape: The Power of Consciousness (1979)

In the 1920s and 1930s, the industrial revolution spread through the South, bringing a demand for more orderly forms of law enforcement. Men in authority, anxious to create a favorable business climate, began to withdraw their tacit approval of extralegal violence. Yet lynching continued, particularly in rural areas, and even as white moderates criticized lynching in the abstract, they continued to justify outbreaks of mob violence for the one special crime of sexual assault. For most white Americans, the association between lynching and rape called to mind not twin forms of white violence against black men and women, but a very different image: the black rapist, "a monstrous beast, crazed with lust";[14] the white victim—young, blond, virginal; her manly Anglo-Saxon avengers. Despite the pull of modernity, the emotional logic of lynching remained: only swift, sure violence, unhampered by legalities, could protect white women from sexual assault.

The "protection of white womanhood" was a pervasive fixture of racist ideology. In 1839, for example, a well-known historian offered this commonly accepted rationale for lynching: black men find "something strangely alluring and seductive . . . in the appearance of the white woman; they are aroused and stimulated by its foreignness to their experience of sexual pleasures, and it moves them to gratify their lust at any cost and in spite of every obstacle." In 1937, echoing an attitude that characterized most local newspapers, the Jackson, Mississippi, *Daily News* published what it felt was the *coup de grace* to antilynching critics: "What would you do if your wife, daughter, or one of your loved ones was ravished? You'd probably be right there with the mob." Two years later, 65 percent of the white respondents in an anthropological survey believed that lynching was justified in cases of sexual assault.[15] Despite its tenacity, however, the myth of the black rapist was never founded on objective reality. Less than a quarter of lynch victims were even accused of rape or attempted rape. Down to the present, almost every study has underlined the fact that rape is overwhelmingly an intraracial crime, and the victims are more often black than white.[16]

A major strategy of anti-lynching reformers, beginning with Ida B. Wells in the 1880s and continuing with Walter White of the NAACP and Jessie Daniel Ames of the Association of Southern Women for the Prevention of Lynching, was to use such facts to undermine the rationalizations for mob violence. But the emotional circuit between interracial rape and lynching lay beyond the reach of factual refutation. A black man did not literally have to attempt sexual assault for whites to perceive some transgression of caste mores as a sexual threat. White women were the forbidden fruit, the untouchable property, the ultimate symbol of white male power. To break the racial rules was to conjure up an image of black over white, of a world turned upside down.

Again, women were a means of communication and, on one level, the rhetoric of protection, like the rape of black women, reflected a power struggle among men. But impulses toward women as well as toward blacks were played out in the drama of racial violence. The fear of rape was more than a hypocritical excuse for lynching; rather, the two phenomena were intimately intertwined. The "southern rape complex" functioned as a means of both sexual and racial suppression.[17]

For whites, the archetypal lynching for rape can be seen as a dramatization of cultural themes, a story they told themselves about the social arrangements and psychological strivings that lay beneath the surface of everyday life. The story such rituals told about the place of white women in southern society was subtle, contradictory, and demeaning. The frail victim, leaning on the arms of her male relatives, might be brought to the scene of the crime, there to identify her assailant and witness his execution. This was a moment of humiliation. A woman who had just been raped, or who had been apprehended in a clandestine interracial affair, or whose male relatives were pretending that she had been raped, stood on display before the whole community. Here was the quintessential Woman as Victim: pol-luted, "ruined for life," the object of fantasy and secret contempt. Humiliation, however, mingled with heightened worth as she played for a moment the role of the Fair Maiden violated and avenged. For this privilege—if the alleged assault had in fact taken place—she might pay with suffering in the extreme. In any case, she would pay with a lifetime of subjugation to the men gathered in her behalf.

Only a small percentage of lynchings, then, revolved around charges of sexual assault; but those that did received by far the most attention and publicity—indeed, they gripped the white imagination far out of proportion to their statistical significance. Rape and rumors of rape became the folk pornography of the Bible Belt. As stories spread the rapist became not just a black man but a ravenous brute, the victim a beautiful young virgin. The experience of the woman was described in minute and progressively embellished detail, a public fantasy that implied a group participation in the rape as cathartic as the subsequent lynching. White men might see in "lynch law" their ideal selves: patriarchs, avengers, righteous protectors. But, being men themselves, and sometimes even rapists, they must also have seen themselves in the lynch mob's prey.

The lynch mob in pursuit of the black rapist represented the trade-off implicit in the code of chivalry: for the right of the southern lady to protection presupposed her obligation to obey. The connotations of wealth and family background attached to the position of the lady in the antebellum South faded in the twentieth century, but the power of "ladyhood" as a value construct remained. The term denoted chastity, frailty, graciousness. "A lady," noted one social-psychologist, "is always in a state of becoming: one acts like a lady, one attempts to be a lady, but one never *is* a lady." Internalized by the individual, this ideal regulated behavior and restricted interaction with the world.[18] If a woman passed the tests of ladyhood, she could tap into the reservoir of protectiveness and shelter known as southern chivalry. Women who abandoned secure, if circumscribed, social roles forfeited the claim to personal security. Together the practice of ladyhood and the etiquette of chivalry controlled white women's behavior even as they guarded caste lines.

Proslavery theorist Thomas R. Dew spelled out this dialectic. The "essence of manhood," he wrote, is "predation." The essence of womanhood is "allure." Only the rise of gallantry and the patriarchal family offered a haven from male aggression. Stripped to its bare essentials, then, the difference between the sexes was the opposition between the potential rapist and the potential victim of sexual assault, and the family metaphor that justified slavery offered the exchange of dependence for protection to the mistress as well as to the slaves. Dew's notion of female sexuality, however, did not deny her passions of her own. On the contrary, because her role was not to seek, "but to be sought . . . not to woo, but to be wooed," she was forced to suppress her "most violent feelings . . . her most ardent desires."[19] In general, the law of rape expressed profound distrust of women, demanding evidence of "utmost resistance," corroboration by other witnesses in addition to the victim's word, and proof of the victim's chastity—all contrary to the rules of evidence in other forms of violent crime. In sharp contrast, however, when a black man and a white woman were concerned intercourse was prima facie evidence of rape. The presiding judge in the 1931 Scottsboro trial, in which nine black youths were accused of rape, had this to say:

> Where the woman charged to have been raped, as in this case is a white woman, there is a very strong presumption under the law that she would not and did not yield voluntarily to intercourse with the defendant, a Negro; and this is true, whatever the station in life the prosecutrix may occupy, whether she be the most despised, ignorant and abandoned woman of the community, or the spotless virgin and daughter of a prominent home of luxury and learning.[20]

Lynching, then, like laws against intermarriage, masked uneasiness over the nature of white women's desires. It aimed not only to engender fear of sexual assault but also to prevent voluntary unions. It upheld the comforting fiction that at least in relation to black men, white women were always objects and never agents of sexual desire.

Although the nineteenth-century women's movement for the most part advocated higher moral standards for men, not sexual liberation for women, opponents insisted that it threatened the family and painted feminists as spinsters or libertines, sexual deviants in either case. It may be no accident, then, that the vision of the black man as a threatening beast flourished during the first phase of the southern women's rights movement, a fantasy of aggression against boundary-transgressing women as well as a weapon of terror against blacks. Certainly the rebelliousness of that feminist generation was circumscribed by the feeling that women were hedged about by a "nameless horror." The South, wrote one turn-of-the-century woman, had become "a smoldering volcano, the dark of its quivering night . . . pierced through by the cry of some outraged woman."[21]

When women in the 1920s and 1930s did begin to assert their right to sexual expression and to challenge the double standard Thomas Dew's injunctions implied, inheritors of the plantation legend responded with explicit attacks that revealed the sanctions at the heart of the chivalric ideal. William Faulkner's *The Sanctuary*, published in 1931, typified a common literary reaction to the fall of the lady. The corncob rape of Temple Drake—a "new woman" of the 1920s—was the ultimate revenge against the abdicating white virgin. Her fate represented the "desecration of a cult object," the implicit counterpoint to the idealization of women in a patriarchal society.[22]

IV. Lady Insurrectionists

The lady insurrectionists gathered together in one of our southern cities. . . . They said calmly that they were not afraid of being raped; as for their sacredness, they would take care of it themselves; they did not need the chivalry of lynching to protect them and did not want it.

—Lillian Smith, *Killers of the Dream* (1949)

On November 1, 1930, twenty-six white women from six southern states met in Atlanta to form the Association of Southern Women for the Prevention of Lynching. Organized by Texas suffragist Jessie Daniel Ames, the association had a central, ideological goal: to break the circuit between the tradition of chivalry and the practice of mob murder. The association was part of a broader interracial movement; its contribution to the decline of lynching must be put in the perspective of the leadership role played by blacks in the national anti-lynching campaign. But it would be a mistake to view the association simply as a white women's auxiliary to black-led struggles. Rather, it represented an acceptance of accountability for a racist mythology that white women had not created but that they nevertheless served, a point hammered home by black women's admonitions that "when Southern white women get ready to stop lynching, it will be stopped and not before."[23]

Jessie Ames, the association's leader, stood on the brink between two worlds. Born in 1883 in a small town in East Texas, a regional hotbed of mob violence, she directed the anti-lynching campaign from Atlanta, capital of the New South. She drew eclectically on the nineteenth-century female reform tradition and advocated an implicitly feminist antiracism that looked backward to the abolitionist movement as well as forward to feminists of our own times.

Ames had come to maturity in a transitional phase of the women's movement, when female reformers used the group consciousness and Victorian sense of themselves as especially moral beings to justify a great wave of female institution building. When Jessie Ames turned from suffrage to the reform of race relations, she looked naturally to this heritage for her constituency and tactics. The association drew its members from among small-town church women, schooled for decades in running their own affairs within YWCAs, women's clubs, and missionary societies and sensitized by the temperance and suffrage movements to a politics that simultaneously stressed domestic order and women's rights.[24] Ames's strategy for change called for enfranchised women to exercise moral influence over the would-be lynchers in their own homes, political influence over the public officials who collaborated with them, and cultural influence over the editors and politicians who created an atmosphere where mob violence flourished. Like Frances Willard and the temperance campaign, she sought to extend women's moral guardianship into the most quintessentially masculine affairs.

Ames's tenacity and the emotional energy of her campaign derived from her perception that lynching was a women's issue: not only an obstacle to regional development and an injustice to blacks, but also an insult to white women. Along with black women leaders before her, who had perceived that the same sexual stereotyping that allowed black women to be exploited caused black men to be feared, she challenged both racist and patriarchal ideas.[25] Disputing the notion that blacks provoked mob action by raping white women, association members traced lynching to its roots in white supremacy.[26] More central to their campaign was an effort to dissociate the image of the lady from its connotations of sexual vulnerability and retaliatory violence. If lynching held a covert message for white women as well as an overt one for blacks, then the anti-lynching association represented a woman-centered reply. Lynching, it proclaimed, far from offering a shield against sexual assault, served as a weapon of both racial and sexual terror, planting fear in women's minds and dependency in their hearts. It thrust them in the role of personal property or sexual objects, ever threatened by black men's lust, ever in need of white men's protection. Asserting their identity as autonomous citizens, requiring not the paternalism of chivalry but the equal protection of the law, association members resisted the part assigned to them.

If, as Susan Brownmiller claims, the larger anti-lynching movement paid little attention to lynching's counterpart, the rape of black women, the women's association could not ignore the issue. For one thing, black women in the interracial movement continually brought it to their attention, prodding them to take responsibility for stopping both lynching and sexual exploitation. For another, from slavery on, interracial sex had been a chronic source of white women's discontent.[27] In

1920, for example, a white interracialist and women's rights leader, who had come to her understanding of racial issues through pioneering meetings with black women, warned a white male audience:

> The race problem can never be solved as long as the white man goes unpunished [for interracial sex], while the Negro is burned at the stake. I shall say no more, for I am sure you need not have anything more said. When the white men of the South have come to that position, a single standard for both men and women, then you will accomplish something in this great problem.[28]

In the winter of 1931, Jessie Daniel Ames called a meeting of black and white women for an explicit discussion of the split female image and the sexual double standard. The women, she thought, should gather in closed session with no men present "because there are some vices of Southern life which contribute subtly to [lynching] that we want to face by ourselves." The black leader Nannie Burroughs agreed: "All meetings with white and colored women on this question should be held behind closed doors and men should not be admitted." White male attitudes, the group concluded, originated in a slave system where black women "did not belong to themselves but were in effect the property of white men." They went on to explore the myths of black women's promiscuity and white women's purity, and noted how this split image created a society that "considers an assault by a white man as a moral lapse upon his part, better ignored and forgotten, while an assault by a Negro against a white woman is a hideous crime punishable with death by law or lynching." Relationships among women interracialists were far from egalitarian, nor could they always overcome the impediments to what Ames called "free and frank" discussion.[29] Yet on occasions like this one the shared experience of gender opened the way for consciousness-raising communication across the color line.

If such discussions of male behavior had to be held behind closed doors, even more treacherous was the question of sex between black men and white women. In 1892, Memphis anti-lynching reformer and black women's club leader Ida B. Wells was threatened with death and run out of town for proclaiming that behind many lynchings lay consensual interracial affairs. Over sixty years later, in the wake of the famous Scottsboro case, Jessie Daniel Ames began delving beneath the surface of lynchings in which white women were involved. Like Barnett, she found that black men were sometimes executed not for rape but for interracial sex. And she used that information to disabuse association members of one of the white South's central fictions: that, as a Mississippi editor put it, there had never been a southern white woman so depraved as to "bestow her favors on a black man."[30]

But what of lynching cases in which rape actually had occurred? Here association leaders could only fall back on a call for law and order, for they knew from their own experience that the fear engendered in their constituency by what some could bring themselves to call only "the unspeakable crime" was all too real. "Whether their own minds perceive danger where none exists, or whether the fears have been put in their minds by men's fears," Ames commented, women could not but see themselves as potential victims of black assault.[31] It would be left to a future generation to point out that the chief danger to white women came from white men and to see rape in general as a feminist concern. Association leaders could only exorcise their own fears of male aggression by transferring the means of violence from mobs to the state and debunking the myth of the black rapist.

In the civil rights movement of the 1960s, white women would confront the sexual dimensions of racism and racial violence by asserting their right to sleep with black men. Anti-lynching reformers of the 1930s obviously took a very different approach. They abhorred male violence and lynching's eroticism of death, and asserted against them a feminine standard of personal and public morality. They portrayed themselves as moral beings and independent citizens rather than vulnerable sexual objects. And the core of their message lay more in what they were than in what they said: southern ladies who needed only their own rectitude to protect them from interracial sex and the law to guard them from sexual assault. When Jessie Ames referred to "the crown of chivalry that has been pressed like a crown of thorns on our heads," she issued a cry of protest that belongs to the struggle for both racial and sexual emancipation.[32]

V. The Decline of Chivalry

As male supremacy becomes ideologically untenable, incapable of justifying itself as protection, men assert their domination more directly, in fantasies and occasionally in acts of raw violence.

—Christopher Lasch,
Marxist Perspectives (1978)

In the 1970s, for the second time in the nation's history, rape again attracted widespread public attention. The obsession with interracial rape, which peaked at the turn of the nineteenth century but lingered from the close of the Civil War into the 1930s, became a magnet for racial and sexual oppression. Today the issue of rape has crystallized important feminist concerns.

Rape emerged as a feminist issue as women developed an independent politics that made sexuality and personal life a central arena of struggle. First in consciousness-raising groups, where autobiography became a politicizing technique, then in public "speakouts," women broke what in retrospect seems a remarkable silence about a pervasive aspect of female experience. From that beginning flowed both an analysis that held rape to be a political act by which men affirm their power over women and strategies for change that ranged from the feminist self-help methods of rape crisis centers to institutional reform of the criminal justice and medical care systems. After 1976, the movement broadened to include wife-battering, sexual harassment, and, following

the lead of Robin Morgan's claim that "pornography is the theory, rape the practice," media images of women.[33]

By the time Susan Brownmiller's *Against Our Will: Men, Women and Rape* gained national attention in 1975, she could speak to and for a feminist constituency already sensitized to the issue by years of practical, action-oriented work. Her book can be faulted for supporting a notion of universal patriarchy and timeless sexual victimization; it leaves no room for understanding the reasons for women's collaboration, their own sources of power (both self-generated and derived), the class and racial differences in their experience of discrimination and sexual danger. But it was an important milestone, pointing the way for research into a subject that has consistently been trivialized and ignored. Many grassroots activists would demur from Brownmiller's assertion that all men are potential rapists, but they share her understanding of the continuum between sexism and sexual assault.[34]

The demand for control over one's own body—control over whether, when, and with whom one has children, control over how one's sexuality is expressed—is central to the feminist project because, as Rosalind Petchesky persuasively argues, it is essential to "a sense of being a person, with personal and bodily integrity," able to engage in conscious activity and to participate in social life.[35] It is this right to bodily integrity and self-determination that rape, and the fear of rape, so thoroughly undermines. Rape's devastating effect on individuals derives not so much from the sexual nature of the crime (and anti-rape activists have been concerned to revise the idea that rape is a "fate worse than death" whose victims, if no longer "ruined for life," are at least so traumatized that they must rely for recovery on therapeutic help rather than on their own resources) as from the experience of helplessness and loss of control, the sense of one's self as an object of rage. And women who may never be raped share, by chronic attrition, in the same helplessness, "otherness," lack of control. The struggle against rape, like the anti-lynching movement, addresses not only external dangers but also internal consequences: the bodily muting, the self-censorship that limits one's capacity to "walk freely in the world."[36]

The focus on rape, then, emerged from the internal dynamics of feminist thought and practice. But it was also a response to an objective increase in the crime. From 1969 to 1974, the number of rapes rose 49 percent, a greater increase than for any other violent crime. Undoubtedly rape statistics reflect general demographic and criminal trends, as well as a greater willingness of victims to report sexual attacks (although observers agree that rape is still the most underreported of crimes).[37] But there can be no doubt that rape is a serious threat and that it plays a prominent role in women's subordination. Using recent high-quality survey data, Allan Griswold Johnson has estimated that, at a minimum, 20 to 30 percent of girls now twelve years old will suffer a violent attack sometime in their lives. A woman is as likely to be raped as she is to experience a divorce or to be diagnosed as having cancer.[38]

In a recent anthology on women and pornography, Tracey A. Gardner has drawn a parallel between the wave of lynching that followed Reconstruction and the increase in rapes in an era of anti-feminist backlash.[39] Certainly, as women enter the workforce, postpone marriage, live alone or as single heads of households, they become easier targets for sexual assault. But observations like Gardner's go further, linking the intensification of sexual violence directly to the feminist challenge. Such arguments come dangerously close to blaming the victim for the crime. But they may also contain a core of truth. Sociological research on rape has only recently begun, and we do not have studies explaining the function and frequency of the crime under various historical conditions; until that work is done we cannot with certainty assess the current situation. Yet it seems clear that just as lynching ebbed and flowed with new modes of racial control, rape—both as act and idea—cannot be divorced from changes in the sexual terrain.

In 1940, Jessie Ames released to the press a statement that, for the first time in her career, the South could claim a "lynchless year," and in 1942, convinced that lynching was no longer widely condoned in the name of white womanhood, she allowed the Association of Southern Women for the Prevention of Lynching to pass quietly from the scene. The women's efforts, the larger, black-led anti-lynching campaign, black migration from the rural South, the spread of industry—these and other developments contributed to the decline of vigilante justice. Blacks continued to be victimized by covert violence and routinized court procedures that amounted to "legal lynchings." But after World War II, public lynchings, announced in the papers, openly accomplished, and tacitly condoned, no longer haunted the land, and the black rapist ceased to be a fixture of political campaigns and newspaper prose.

This change in the rhetoric and form of racial violence reflected new attitudes toward women as well as toward blacks. By the 1940s few southern leaders were willing, as Jessie Ames put it, to "lay themselves open to ridicule" by defending lynching on the grounds of gallantry, in part because gallantry itself had lost conviction.[40] The same process of economic development and national integration that encouraged the South to adopt northern norms of authority and control undermined the chivalric ideal. Industrial capitalism on the one hand and women's assertion of independence on the other weakened paternalism and with it the conventions of protective deference.[41] This is not to say that the link between racism and sexism was broken; relations between white women and black men continued to be severely sanctioned, and black men, to the present, have drawn disproportionate punishment for sexual assault. The figures speak for themselves: of the 455 men executed for rape since 1930, 405 were black, and almost all the complainants were white.[42] Nevertheless, "the protection of white womanhood" rang more hollow in the postwar New South and the fear of interracial rape became a subdued theme in the nation at large rather than an openly articulated regional obsession.

The social feminist mainstream, of which Jessie Ames and the anti-lynching association were a part, thus chipped away at a politics of gallantry that locked white ladies in the home under the guise of protecting them from the world. But because such reformers held to the genteel trappings of their role even as they asserted their autonomous citizenship, they offered reassurance that women's influence could be expanded without mortal danger to male prerogatives and power. Contemporary feminists have eschewed some of the comforting assumptions of their nineteenth-century predecessors: women's passionlessness, their limitation to social housekeeping, their exclusive responsibility for childrearing and housekeeping. They have couched their revolt in explicit ideology and unladylike behavior. Meanwhile, as Barbara Ehrenreich has argued, Madison Avenue has perverted the feminist message into the threatening image of the sexually and economically liberated woman. The result is a shift toward the rapaciousness that has always mixed unstably with sentimental exaltation and concern. Rape has emerged more clearly into the sexual domain, a crime against women most often committed by men of their own race rather than a right of the powerful over women of a subordinate group or a blow by black men against white women's possessors.[43]

It should be emphasized, however, that the connection between feminism and the upsurge of rape lies not so much in women's gains but in their assertion of rights within a context of economic vulnerability and relative powerlessness. In a perceptive article published in 1901, Jane Addams traced lynching in part to "the feeling of the former slave owner to his former slave, whom he is now bidden to regard as his fellow citizen."[44] Blacks in the post-Reconstruction era were able to express will and individuality, to wrest from their former masters certain concessions and build for themselves supporting institutions. Yet they lacked the resources to protect themselves from economic exploitation and mob violence. Similarly, contemporary feminist efforts have not yet succeeded in overcoming women's isolation, their economic and emotional dependence on men, their cultural training toward submission. There are few restraints against sexual aggression, since up to 90 percent of rapes go unreported, 50 percent of assailants who are reported are never caught, and seven out of ten prosecutions end in acquittal.[45] Provoked by the commercialization of sex, cut loose from traditional commu-

nity restraints, and "bidden to regard as his fellow citizen" a female being whose subordination has deep roots in the psyches of both sexes, men turn with impunity to the use of sexuality as a means of asserting dominance and control. Such fear and rage are condoned when channeled into right-wing attacks on women's claim to a share in public power and control over their bodies. Inevitably they also find expression in less acceptable behavior. Rape, like lynching, flourishes in an atmosphere in which official policies toward members of a subordinate group give individuals tacit permission to hurt and maim.

In 1972 Anne Braden, a southern white woman and long-time activist in civil rights struggles, expressed her fear that the new anti-rape movement might find itself "objectively on the side of the most reactionary social forces" unless it heeded a lesson from history. In a pamphlet entitled *Open Letter to Southern White Women*—much circulated in regional women's liberation circles at the time—she urged anti-rape activists to remember the long pattern of racist manipulation of rape fears. She called on white women, "for their own liberation, to refuse any longer to be used, to act in the tradition of Jessie Daniel Ames and the white women who fought in an earlier period to end lynching," and she went on to discuss her own politicization through left-led protests against the prosecution of black men on false rape charges. Four years later, she joined the chorus of black feminist criticism of *Against Our Will*, seeing Brownmiller's book as a realization of her worst fears.[46]

Since this confrontation between the Old Left and the New, between a white woman who placed herself in a southern tradition of feminist anti-racism and a radical feminist from the North, a black women's movement has emerged, bringing its own perspectives to bear. White activists at the earliest "speakouts" had acknowledged "the racist image of black men as rapists," pointed out the large number of black women among assault victims, and debated the contradictions involved in looking for solutions to a race and class-biased court system. But not until black women had developed their own autonomous organizations and strategies were true alliances possible across racial lines.

A striking example of this development is the Washington, D.C., Rape Crisis Center. One of the first and largest such groups in the country, the center has evolved from a primarily white self-help project to an aggressive interracial organization with a multifaceted program of support services, advocacy, and community education. In a city with an 80 percent black population and more than four times as many women as men, the center has recruited black leadership by channeling its resources into staff salaries and steering clear of the pitfalls of middle-class voluntarism on the one hand and professionalism on the other. It has challenged the perception of the anti-rape movement as a "white woman's thing" by stressing not only rape's devastating effect on women but also its impact on social relations in the black community. Just as racism undermined working-class unity and lynching sometimes pitted poor white against blacks, sexual aggression now divides the black community against itself. In a society that defines manhood in terms of power and possessions, black men are denied the resources to fulfill their expected roles. Inevitably, they turn to domination of women, the one means of manhood within their control. From consciousness-raising groups for convicted rapists to an intensive educational campaign funded by the city's public school system and aimed at both boys and girls from elementary through high school, the center has tried to alter the cultural plan for both sexes that makes men potential rapists and women potential victims.[47]

As the anti-rape movement broadens to include Third World women, analogies between lynching and rape and the models of women like Ida B. Wells and Jessie Daniel Ames may become increasingly useful. Neither lynching nor rape is the "aberrant behavior of a lunatic fringe."[48] Rather, both grow out of everyday modes of interaction. The view of women as objects to be possessed, conquered, or defiled fueled racial hostility; conversely, racism has continued to distort and confuse the struggle against sexual violence. Black men receive harsher punishment for raping white women, black rape victims are especially demeaned

and ignored, and, until recently, the different historical experience of black and white women has hindered them from making common cause. Taking a cue from the women's anti-lynching campaign of the 1930s as well as from the innovative tactics of black feminists, the anti-rape movement must not limit itself to training women to avoid rape or depending on imprisonment as a deterrent, but must aim its attention at changing the behavior and attitudes of men. Mindful of the historical connection between rape and lynching, it must make clear its stand against *all* uses of violence in oppression.

Notes

1. Quoted in Howard Kester, *The Lynching of Claude Neal* (New York: National Association for the Advancement of Colored People, 1934).

2. Michael Stephen Hindus, *Prison and Plantation: Crime, Justice, and Authority in Massachusetts and South Carolina, 1767–1878* (Chapel Hill: University of North Carolina Press, 1980), pp. xix, 31, 124, 253.

3. For recent overviews of lynching, see Robert L. Zangrando, *The NAACP Crusade Against Lynching, 1909–1950* (Philadelphia: Temple University Press, 1980); McGovern, *Anatomy of a Lynching;* and Hall, *Revolt Against Chivalry.*

4. Terrence Des Pres. "The Struggle of Memory," *The Nation,* 10 April 1982, p. 433.

5. Quoted in William H. Chafe, *Women and Equality: Changing Patterns in American Culture* (New York: Oxford University Press, 1977), p. 60.

6. Margaret A. Simons, "Racism and Feminism: A Schism in the Sisterhood," *Feminist Studies* 5 (Summer 1979): 384–401.

7. Diane K. Lewis, "A Response to Inequality: Black Women, Racism, and Sexism," *Signs* 3 (Winter 1977): 341–42.

8. Jacqueline Jones, *Freed Women?: Black Women, Work, and the Family During the Civil War and Reconstruction,* Working Paper No. 61, Wellesley College, 1980; Roger L. Ransom and Richard Sutch, *One Kind of Freedom: The Economic Consequences of Emancipation* (New York: Cambridge University Press, 1977), pp. 87–103.

9. Gerda Lerner, *Black Women in White America: A Documentary History* (New York: Random House, 1972), is an early and important exception.

10. Robin Morgan, "Theory and Practice: Pornography and Rape," *Take Back the Night: Women on Pornography*, ed. Laura Lederer (New York: William Morrow, 1980), p. 140.

11. Susan Griffin, "Rape: The All-American Crime," *Ramparts* (September 1971): 26–35; Susan Brownmiller, *Against Our Will: Men, Women, and Rape* (New York: Simon and Schuster, 1975). See also Kate Millet, *Sexual Politics* (Garden City, N.Y.: Doubleday & Co., 1970).

12. Nancy F. Cott, "Passionlessness: An Interpretation of Victorian Sexual Ideology, 1790–1850," *Signs* 4 (Winter 1978): 219–36.

13. Dorothy Dinnerstein, *The Mermaid and the Minotaur: Sexual Arrangements and Human Malaise* (New York: Harper and Row, 1977). See also Phyllis Marynick Palmer, "White Women/Black Women: The Dualism of Female Identity and Experience," unpublished paper presented at the American Studies Association, September 1979, pp. 15–17. Similarly, British Victorian eroticism was structured by class relations in which upper-class men were nursed by lower-class country women. See Ellen Ross and Rayna Rapp in this volume.

14. A statement made in 1901 by George T. Winston, president of the University of North Carolina, typifies these persistent images: "The southern woman with her helpless little children in a solitary farm house no longer sleeps secure. . . . The black brute is lurking in the dark, a monstrous beast, crazed with lust. His ferocity is almost demoniacal. A mad bull or a tiger could scarcely be more brutal" (quoted in Charles Herbert Stember, *Sexual Racism: The Emotional Barrier to an Integrated Society* [New York: Elsevier, 1976], p. 23).

15. Philip Alexander Bruce, *The Plantation Negro as a Freeman* (New York: Putnam's, 1889), pp. 83–84; Jackson *Daily News*, 27 May 1937; Hortense Powdermaker, *After Freedom: A Cultural Study in the Deep South* (1939; New York: Atheneum, 1969), pp. 54–55, 389.

16. For a contradictory view, see, for example, S. Nelson and M. Amir, "The Hitchhike Victim of Rape: A Research Report," in *Victimology: A New Focus. Vol. 5: Exploiters and Exploited*, ed. M. Agopian, D. Chappell, and G. Geis, and I. Drapkin

and E. Viano (1975), p. 47; and "Black Offender and White Victim: A Study of Forcible Rape in Oakland, California," in *Forcible Rape: The Crime, The Victim, and the Offender* (New York: Columbia University Press, 1977).

17. Winthrop Jordan, *White over Black: American Attitudes Toward the Negro, 1550–1812* (Baltimore: Penguin Books, 1969); W. J. Cash, *The Mind of the South* (New York: Knopf, 1941), p. 117.

18. This reading of lynching as a "cultural test" is modeled on Clifford Geertz, "Deep Play: Notes on the Balinese Cockfight," in *The Interpretation of Cultures: Selected Essays by Clifford Geertz* (New York: Basic Books, 1973), pp. 412–53. For "ladyhood," see Greer Litton Fox, " 'Nice Girl': Social Control of Women Through a Value Construct," *Signs* 2 (Summer 1977): 805–17.

19. Quoted in William R. Taylor, *Cavalier and Yankee: The Old South and American National Character* (Garden City, N.Y.: Doubleday/Anchor, 1963), pp. 148–51.

20. Dan T. Carter, *Scottsboro: An American Tragedy* (Baton Rouge: Louisiana State University Press, 1969), p. 36.

21. Belle Kearney, *A Slaveholder's Daughter* (New York: Abbey Press, 1900), p. 96; Myrta Lockett Avary, *Dixie after the War* (1906; New York: Negro Universities Press, 1969), pp. 377–90. See also John E. Talmadge, *Rebecca Latimer Felton: Nine Stormy Decades* (Athens: University of Georgia Press, 1960), pp. 98–124.

22. Leslie Fiedler, *Love and Death in the American Novel* (New York: Delta, 1966), pp. 320–24.

23. Rich, "Disloyal to Civilization"; Jessie Daniel Ames to Mary McLeod Bethune. 9 March 1938, Association of Southern Women for the Prevention of Lynching (ASWPL) Papers, Atlanta University, Atlanta, Georgia. (henceforth cited as ASWPL Papers). For black women's prior activities, see Ida B. Wells, *Crusade for Justice: The Autobiography of Ida B. Wells* (Chicago: University of Chicago Press, 1970); Lerner, *Black Women*, pp. 194–215; Bettina Aptheker, *Lynching and Rape: An Exchange of Views*, Occasional Paper No. 25, American Institute of Marxist Studies (1977); and Angela Y. Davis, *Women, Race, and Class* (New York: Random House, 1982), pp. 169–98.

24. For this reform tradition, see Estelle Freedman, "Separatism as Strategy: Female Institution Building and American Feminism, 1870–1930," *Feminist Studies* 5 (Fall 1979): 512–29; Mari Jo

Buhle, *Women and American Socialism, 1780–1920* (Urbana: University of Illinois Press, 1981); and Barbara Leslie Epstein, *The Politics of Domesticity: Women, Evangelism, and Temperance in Nineteenth-Century America* (Middletown, Conn.: Wesleyan University Press, 1981).

25. Deb Friedman, "Rape, Racism—and Reality," *Aegis* (July/August, 1978): 17–26.

26. Jessie Daniel Ames to Miss Doris Loraine, 5 March 1935, ASWPL Papers.

27. Anne Firor Scott, "Women's Perspective on the Patriarchy in the 1850's," *Journal of American History* 6 (June 1974): 52–64.

28. Carrie Parks Johnson Address, Commission on Interracial Cooperation (CIC), CIC Papers, Atlanta University, Atlanta, Georgia.

29. Jessie Daniel Ames to Nannie Burroughs, 24 October 1931; Burroughs to Ames, 30 October 1931, ASWPL Papers; "Appendix F, Digest of Discussion," n.d. [November 20, 1931], Jessie Daniel Ames Papers, University of North Carolina at Chapel Hill.

30. Jackson (Mississippi) *Daily News*, February 1931, ASWPL Papers.

31. Jesse Daniel Ames, "Lynchers' View on Lynching," ASWPL Papers.

32. Quoted in Wilma Dykeman and James Stokely, *Seeds of Southern Change: The Life of Will Alexander* (Chicago: University of Chicago Press, 1962), p. 143.

33. Noreen Connell and Cassandra Wilsen, eds., *Rape: The First Sourcebook for Women* (New York: New American Library, 1974); Morgan, "Theory and Practice."

34. Interview with Janet Colm, director of the Chapel Hill-Carrboro (North Carolina) Rape Crisis Center, April 1981. Two of the best recent analyses of rape are Ann Wolbert Burgess and Lynda Lytle Holmstrom, *Rape: Crisis and Recovery* (Bowie, Md.: Robert J. Brady Co., 1979) and Lorenne M. G. Clark and Debra J. Lewis, *Rape: The Price of Coercive Sexuality* (Toronto: Canadian Women's Educational Press, 1977).

35. Rosalind Pollack Petchesky, "Reproductive Freedom: Beyond 'A Woman's Right to Choose,'" *Signs* 5 (Summer 1980): 661–85.

36. Adrienne Rich, "Taking Women Students Seriously," in *Lies, Secrets and Silences*, p. 242.

37. Vivian Berger, "Man's Trial, Woman's Tribulation: Rape Cases in the Courtroom," *Columbia Law Review* 1 (1977): 3–12. Thanks to Walter Dellinger for this reference.

38. Allan Griswold Johnson, "On the Prevalence of Rape in the United States," *Signs* 6 (Fall 1980): 136–46.

39. Tracey A. Gardner, "Racism in Pornography and the Women's Movement," in *Take Back the Night*, p. 111.

40. Jessie Daniel Ames, "Editorial Treatment of Lynching," *Public Opinion Quarterly* 2 (January 1938): 77–84.

41. For a statement of this theme, see Christopher Lasch, "The Flight from Feeling: Sociopsychology of Sexual Conflict," *Marxist Perspectives* 1 (Spring 1978): 74–95.

42. Berger, "Man's Trial, Woman's Tribulation," p. 4. For a recent study indicating that the harsher treatment accorded black men convicted of raping white women is not limited to the South and has persisted to the present, see Gary D. LaFree, "The Effect of Sexual Stratification by Race on Official Reactions to Rape," *American Sociological Review* 45 (October 1980): 842–54. Thanks to Darnell Hawkins for this reference.

43. Barbara Ehrenrich, "The Women's Movement: Feminist and Antifeminist," *Radical America* 15 (Spring 1981): 93–101; Lasch, "Flight from Feeling." Because violence against women is so inadequately documented, it is impossible to make accurate racial comparisons in the incidence of the crime. Studies conducted by Menachen Amir in the late 1950s indicated that rape was primarily intraracial, with 77 percent of rapes involving black victims and black defendants and 18 percent involving whites. More recent investigations claim a somewhat higher percentage of interracial assaults. Statistics on reported rapes show that black women are more vulnerable to assault than white women. However, since black women are more likely than white women to report assaults, and since acquaintance rape, most likely to involve higher status white men, is the most underreported of crimes, the vulnerability of white women is undoubtedly much greater than statistics indicate (Berger, "Man's Trial, Woman's Tribulation," p. 3, n. 16; LaFree, "Effect of Sexual Stratification," p. 845, n. 3; Johnson, "On the Prevalence of Rape," p. 145).

44. Quoted in Aptheker, *Lynching and Rape*, pp. 10–11.

45. Berger, "Man's Trial, Woman's Tribulation," p. 6; Johnson, "On the Prevalence of Rape," p. 138.

46. Anne Braden, "A Second Open Letter to Southern White Women," *Generations: Women in the South,* a special issue of *Southern Exposure* 4 (Winter 1977), edited by Susan

Angell, Jacquelyn Dowd Hall, and Candace Waid.

47. Interview with Loretta Ross and Nkenge Toure, Washington, D.C., May 12, 1981. See also Rape Crisis Center of Washington, D.C., *How to Start a Rape Crisis Center* (1972, 1977).

48. Johnson, "On the Prevalence of Rape," p. 137.

---

32.   Date Rape: A Feminist Analysis

Lois Pineau

> Lois Pineau begins her analysis of date rape by discussing the philosophical and legal considerations surrounding the concept of *mens rea,* or "guilty mind." In criminal law, a defendant must display the appropriate mental state (knowledge or intent) as well as the *actus reus* (in this case, the physical action of engaging in nonconsensual sex). Pineau then attempts to dispel many of the myths surrounding date rape—principally the "she asked for it" justification, holding that women in some way generate a contractual obligation for sex based on seductive behavior.

Date rape is nonaggravated sexual assault, nonconsensual sex that does not involve physical injury, or the explicit threat of physical injury. But because it does not involve physical injury, and because physical injury is often the only criterion that is accepted as evidence that *actus reas* is nonconsensual, what is really sexual assault is often mistaken for seduction. The replacement of the old rape laws with the new laws on sexual assault have done nothing to resolve this problem.

Rape, defined as nonconsensual sex, usually involving penetration by a man of a woman who is not his wife, has been replaced in some criminal codes with the charge of sexual assault. This has the advantage both of extending the range of possible victims of sexual assault, the manner in which people can be assaulted, and replacing a crime which is exclusive of consent, with one for which consent is a defence. But while the consent of a woman

From *Law and Philosophy* No. 8, 1989, pp. 217–243. Reprinted by permission of Kluwer Academic Publishers.

is now consistent with the conviction of her assailant in cases of aggravated assault, nonaggravated sexual assault is still distinguished from normal sex solely by the fact that it is not consented to. Thus the question of whether someone has consented to a sexual encounter is still important, and the criteria for consent continues to be the central concern of discourse on sexual assault.

However, if a man is to be convicted, it does not suffice to establish that the *actus reas* was nonconsensual. In order to be guilty of sexual assault a man must have the requisite *mens rea,* i.e., he must either have believed that his victim did not consent or that she was probably not consenting. In many common law jurisdictions a man who sincerely believes that a woman consented to a sexual encounter is deemed to lack the required *mens rea,* even though the woman did not consent, and even though his belief is not reasonable. Recently, strong dissenting voices have been raised against the sincerity condition, and the argument made that *mens rea* be defeated only if the defendant has a reasonable belief that the plaintiff consented. The introduction of legislation which excludes "honest belief" (unreasonable sincere belief) as a defence, will certainly help to provide women with greater protection against violence. But while this will be an important step forward, the question of what constitutes a reasonable belief, the problem of evidence when rapists lie, and the problem of the entrenched attitudes of the predominantly male police, judges, lawyers, and jurists who handle sexual assault cases, remains.

The criteria for *mens rea*, for the reasonableness of belief, and for consent are closely related. For although a man's sincere belief in the consent of his victim may be sufficient to defeat *mens rea*, the court is less likely to believe his belief is sincere if his belief is unreasonable. If his belief is reasonable, they are more likely to believe in the sincerity of his belief. But evidence of the reasonableness of his belief is also evidence that consent really did take place. For the very things that make it reasonable for *him* to believe that the defendant consented are often the very things that incline the court to believe that she consented. What is often missing is the voice of the woman herself, an account of what it would be reasonable for *her* to agree to, that is to say, an account of what is reasonable from *her* standpoint.

Thus, what is presented as reasonable has repercussions for four separate but related concerns: (1) the question of whether a man's belief in a woman's consent was reasonable; (2) the problem of whether it is reasonable to attribute *mens rea* to him; (3) the question of what could count as reasonable from the woman's point of view; (4) the question of what is reasonable from the court's point of view. These repercussions are of the utmost practical concern. In a culture which contains an incidence of sexual assault verging on epidemic, a criterion of reasonableness which regards mere submission as consent fails to offer persons vulnerable to those assaults adequate protection.

The following statements by self-confessed date rapists reveal how our lack of a solution for dealing with date rape protects rapists by failing to provide their victims with legal recourse:

All of my rapes have been involved in a dating situation where I've been out with a woman I know. . . . I wouldn't take no for an answer. I think it had something to do with my acceptance of rejection. I had low self-esteem and not much self-confidence and when I was rejected for something which I considered to be rightly mine, I became angry and I went ahead anyway. And this was the same in any situation, whether it was rape or it was something else.

When I did date, when I was younger, I would pick up a girl and if she didn't come across I would threaten her or slap her face then tell her she was going to fuck—that was it. But that's because I didn't want to waste time with any come-ons. It took too much time. I wasn't interested because I didn't like them as people anyway, and I just went with them just to get laid. Just to say that I laid them.

There is, at this time, nothing to protect women from this kind of unscrupulous victimization. A woman on a casual date with a virtual stranger has almost no chance of bringing a complaint of sexual assault before the courts. One reason for this is the prevailing criterion for consent. According to this criterion, consent is implied unless some emphatic episodic sign of resistance occurred, and its occurrence can be established. But if no episodic act occurred, or if it did occur, and the defendant claims that it didn't, or if the defendant threatened the plaintiff but won't admit it in court, it is almost impossible to find any evidence that would support the plaintiff's word against the defendant. This difficulty is exacerbated by suspicion on the part of the courts, police, and legal educators that even where an act of resistance occurs, this act should not be interpreted as a withholding of consent, and this suspicion is especially upheld where the accused is a man who is known to the female plaintiff.

In Glanville William's classic textbook on criminal law we are warned that where a man is unknown to a woman, she does not consent if she expresses her rejection in the form of an episodic and vigorous act at the "vital moment." But if the man is known to the woman she must, according to Williams, make use of "all means available to her to repel the man." Williams warns that women often welcome a "mastery advance" and present a token resistance. He quotes Byron's couplet,

A little still she strove, and much repented

And whispering "I will ne'er consent"—consented

by way of alerting law students to the difficulty of distinguishing real protest from pretence. Thus, while in principle, a firm unambiguous stand, or a healthy show of temper ought to be sufficient, if established, to show nonconsent, in practice the forceful overriding of such a stance is apt to be taken as an indication that the resistance was not seriously intended, and that the seduction had succeeded. The consequence of this is that it is almost impossible to establish the defendant's guilt beyond a reasonable doubt.

Thus, on the one hand, we have a situation in which women are vulnerable to the most exploitive tactics at the hands of men who are known to them. On the other hand, almost nothing will count as evidence of their being assaulted, including their having taken an emphatic stance in withholding their consent. The new laws have done almost nothing to change this situation. Yet clearly, some solution must be sought. Moreover, the road to that solution presents itself clearly enough as a need for a reformulation of the criterion of consent. It is patent that a criterion that collapses whenever the crime itself succeeds will not suffice. . . .

The reasoning that underlies the present criterion of consent is entangled in a number of mutually supportive mythologies which see sexual assault as masterful seduction, and silent submission as sexual enjoyment. Because the prevailing ideology has so much informed our conceptualization of sexual interaction, it is extraordinarily difficult for us to distinguish between assault and seduction, submission and enjoyment, or so we imagine. At the same time, this failure to distinguish has given rise

to a network of rationalizations that support the conflation of assault with seduction, submission and enjoyment. . . .

Rape Myths

The belief that the natural aggression of men and the natural reluctance of women somehow makes date rape understandable underlies a number of prevalent myths about rape and human sexuality. These beliefs maintain their force partly on account of a logical compulsion exercised by them at an unconscious level. The only way of refuting them effectively, is to excavate the logical propositions involved, and to expose their misapplication to the situations to which they have been applied. In what follows, I propose to excavate the logical support for popular attitudes that are tolerant of date rape. These myths are not just popular, however, but often emerge in the arguments of judges who acquit date rapists, and policemen who refuse to lay charges.

The claim that the victim provoked a sexual incident, that "she asked for it," is by far the most common defence given by men who are accused of sexual assault. Feminists, rightly incensed by this response, often treat it as beneath contempt, singling out the defence as an argument against it. On other fronts, sociologists have identified the response as part of an overall tendency of people to see the world as just, a tendency which disposes them to conclude that people for the most part deserve what they get. However, an inclination to see the world as just requires us to construct an account which yields this outcome, and it is just such an account that I wish to examine with regard to date rape.

The least sophisticated of the "she asked for it" rationales, and in a sense, the easiest to deal with, appeals to an injunction against sexually provocative behaviour on the part of women. If women should not be sexually provocative, then, from this standpoint, a woman who is sexually provocative deserves to suffer the consequences. Now it will not do to respond that women get raped even when they are not sexually provocative, or that it is men who get to interpret (unfairly) what counts as sexually provocative. The question should be: Why shouldn't a woman be sexually provocative? Why should this behaviour warrant any kind of aggressive response whatsoever?

Attempts to explain that women have a right to behave in sexually provocative ways without suffering dire consequences still meet with surprisingly tough resistance. Even people who find nothing wrong or sinful with sex itself, in any of its forms, tend to suppose that women must not behave sexually unless they are prepared to carry through on some fuller course of sexual interaction. The logic of this response seems to be that at some point a woman's behaviour commits her to following through on the full course of a sexual encounter as it is defined by her assailant. At some point she has made an agreement, or formed a contract, and once that is done, her contractor is entitled to demand that she satisfy the terms of that contract. Thus, this view about sexual responsibility and desert is supported by other assumptions about contracts and agreement. But we do not normally suppose that casual nonverbal behaviour generates agreements. Nor do we normally grant private persons the right to enforce contracts. What rationale would support our conclusion in this case?

The rationale, I believe, comes in the form of a belief in the especially insistent nature of male sexuality, an insistence which lies at the foot of natural male aggression, and which is extremely difficult, perhaps impossible to contain. At a certain point in the arousal process, it is thought, a man's rational will gives way to the prerogatives of nature. His sexual need can and does reach a point where it is uncontrollable, and his natural masculine aggression kicks in to assure that this need is met. Women, however, are naturally more contained, and so it is their responsibility not to provoke the irrational in the male. If they do go so far as that, they have both failed in their responsibilities, and subjected themselves to the inevitable. One does not go into the lion's cage and expect not to be eaten. Natural feminine reluctance, it is thought, is no protection against a sexually aroused male.

This belief about the normal aggressiveness of male sexuality is complemented by common knowledge about female gender development. Once, women were taught to deny their sexuality and to aspire to ideals of chastity. Things have not changed so much. Women still tend to eschew conquest mentalities in favour of a combination of sex and affection. Insofar as this is thought to be merely a cultural requirement, however, there is an expectation that women will be coy about their sexual desire. The assumption that women both want to indulge sexually, and are inclined to sacrifice this desire for higher ends, gives rise to the myth that they want to be raped. After all, doesn't rape give them the sexual enjoyment they *really* want, at the same time that it relieves them of the responsibility for admitting to and acting upon what they want? And how then can we blame men, who have been socialized to be aggressively seductive precisely for the purpose of overriding female reserve? If we find fault at all, we are inclined to cast our suspicions on the motives of the woman. For it is on her that the contradictory roles of sexual desirer and sexual denier has been placed. Our awareness of the contradiction expected of her makes us suspect her honesty. In the past, she was expected to deny her complicity because of the shame and guilt she felt at having submitted. This expectation persists in many quarters today, and is carried over into a general suspicion about her character, and the fear that she might make a false accusation out of revenge, or some other low motive.

But if women really want sexual pleasure, what inclines us to think that they will get it through rape? This conclusion logically requires a theory about the dynamics of sexual pleasure that sees that pleasure as an emergent property of overwhelming male insistence. For the assumption that a raped female experiences sexual pleasure implies that the person who rapes her knows how to cause that pleasure independently of any information she might convey on that point. Since her ongoing protest is inconsistent with requests to be touched in particular ways in particular places, to have more of this and less of that, then we must believe that the person who touches her knows these particular ways and places instinctively, without any directives from her.

Thus, we find, underlying and reinforcing this belief in incommunicative male prowess, a conception of sexual pleasure that springs from wordless interchanges, and of sexual success that occurs in a place of meaningful silence. The language of seduction is accepted as a tacit language: eye contact, smiles, blushes, and faintly discernible gestures. It is, accordingly, imprecise and ambiguous. It would be easy for a man to make mistakes about the message conveyed, understandable that he should mistakenly think that a sexual invitation has been made, and a bargain struck. But honest mistakes, we think, must be excused.

In sum, the belief that women should not be sexually provocative is logically linked to several other beliefs, some normative, some empirical. The normative beliefs are that (1) people should keep the agreements they make, (2) that sexually provocative behaviour, taken beyond a certain point, generates agreements, (3) that the peculiar nature of male and female sexuality places such agreements in a special category, one in which the possibility of retracting an agreement is ruled out, or at least made highly unlikely, (4) that women are not to be trusted, in sexual matters at least. The empirical belief, which turns out to be false, is that male sexuality is not subject to rational and moral control.

Dispelling the Myths

The "she asked for it" justification of sexual assault incorporates a conception of a contract that would be difficult to defend in any other context and the presumptions about human sexuality which function to reinforce sympathies rooted in the contractual notion of just deserts are not supported by empirical research.

The belief that a woman generates some sort of contractual obligation whenever her behaviour is interpreted as seductive is the most indefensible part of the mythology of rape. In law, contracts are not legitimate just because a promise has been made. In particular, the use of pressure tactics to extract agreement is frowned upon. Normally, an agreement is upheld only if the contractors were

clear on what they were getting into, and had sufficient time to reflect on the wisdom of their doing so. Either there must be a clear tradition in which the expectations involved in the contract are fairly well known (marriage), or there must be an explicit written agreement concerning the exact terms of the contract and the expectations of the persons involved. But whatever the terms of a contract, there is no private right to enforce it. So that if I make a contract with you on which I renege, the only permissible recourse for you is through due legal process.

Now it is not clear whether sexual contracts can be made to begin with, or if so, what sort of sexual contracts would be legitimate. But assuming that they could be made, the terms of those contracts would not be enforceable. To allow public enforcement would be to grant the State the overt right to force people to have sex, and this would clearly be unacceptable. Granting that sexual contracts are legitimate, state enforcement of such contracts would have to be limited to ordering non-sexual compensation for breaches of contract. So it makes no difference whether a sexual contract is tacit or explicit. There are no grounds whatsoever that would justify enforcement of its terms.

Thus, even if we assume that a woman has initially agreed to an encounter, her agreement does not automatically make all subsequent sexual activity to which she submits legitimate. If during coitus a woman should experience pain, be suddenly overcome with guilt or fear of pregnancy, or simply lose her initial desire, those are good reasons for her to change her mind. Having changed her mind, neither her partner nor the state has any right to force her to continue. But then if she is forced to continue she is assaulted. Thus, establishing that consent occurred at a particular point during a sexual encounter should not exclusively establish the legitimacy of the encounter. What is needed is a reading of whether she agreed throughout the encounter.

If the "she asked for it" contractual view of sexual interchange has any validity, it is because there is a point at which there is no stopping a sexual encounter, a point at which that encounter becomes the inexorable outcome of the unfolding of natural events. If a sexual encounter is like a slide on which I cannot stop halfway down, it will be relevant whether I enter the slide of my own free will, or am pushed.

But there is no evidence that the entire sexual act is like a slide. While there may be a few seconds in the "plateau" period just prior to orgasm in which people are "swept" away by sexual feelings to the point where we could justifiably understand their lack of heed for the comfort of their partner, the greater part of a sexual encounter comes well within the bounds of morally responsible control of our own actions. Indeed, the available evidence shows that most of the activity involved in sex has to do with building the requisite level of desire, a task that involves the proper use of foreplay, the possibility of which implies control over the form that foreplay will take. Modern sexual therapy assumes that such control is universally accessible, and so far there has been no reason to question that assumption. Sexologists are unanimous, moreover, in holding that mutual sexual enjoyment requires an atmosphere of comfort and communication, a minimum of pressure, and an ongoing check-up on one's partner's state. They maintain that different people have different predilections, and that what is pleasurable for one person is very often anathema to another. These findings show that the way to achieve sexual pleasure, at any time at all, let alone with a casual acquaintance, decidedly does not involve overriding the other person's express reservations and providing them with just any kind of sexual stimulus. And while we do not want to allow science and technology a voice in which the voices of particular women are drowned, in this case science seems to concur with women's perception that aggressive in-communicative sex is not what they want. But if science and the voice of women concur, if aggressive seduction does not lead to good sex, if women do not like it, or want it, then it is not rational to think that they would agree to it. Where such sex takes place, it is therefore rational to presume that the sex was not consensual.

The myth that women like to be raped, is closely connected, as we have seen, to doubt about their honesty in sexual matters, and this

suspicion is exploited by defence lawyers when sexual assault cases make it to the courtroom. It is an unfortunate consequence of the presumption of innocence that rape victims who end up in court frequently find that it is they who are on trial. For if the defendant is innocent, then either he did not intend to do what he was accused of, or the plaintiff is mistaken about his identity, or she is lying. Often the last alternative is the only plausible defence, and as a result, the plaintiff's word seldom goes unquestioned. Women are frequently accused of having made a false accusation, either as a defensive mechanism for dealing with guilt and shame, or out of a desire for revenge.

Now there is no point in denying the possibility of false accusation, though there are probably better ways of seeking revenge on a man than accusing him of rape. However, we can now establish a logical connection between the evidence that a woman was subjected to high-pressure aggressive "seduction" tactics, and her claim that she did not consent to that encounter. Where the kind of encounter is not the sort to which it would be reasonable to consent, there is a logical presumption that a woman who claims that she did not consent is telling the truth. Where the kind of sex involved is not the sort of sex we would expect a woman to like, the burden of proof should not be on the woman to show that she did not consent, but on the defendant to show that contrary to every reasonable expectation she did consent. The defendant should be required to convince the court that the plaintiff persuaded him to have sex with her even though there are no visible reasons why she should.

In conclusion, there are no grounds for the "she asked for it" defence. Sexually provocative behaviour does not generate sexual contracts. Even where there are sexual agreements, they cannot be legitimately enforced either by the State, or by private right, or by natural prerogative. Secondly, all the evidence suggests that neither women nor men find sexual enjoyment in rape or in any form of noncommunicative sexuality. Thirdly, male sexual desire is containable, and can be subjected to moral and rational control. Fourthly, since there is no reason why women should not be sexually provocative, they do not "deserve" any sex they do not want. This last is a welcome discovery. The taboo on sexual provocativeness in women is a taboo both on sensuality and on teasing. But sensuality is a source of delight, and teasing is playful and inspires wit. What a relief to learn that it is not sexual provocativeness, but its enemies, that constitutes a danger to the world. . . .

In thinking about sex we must keep in mind its sensual ends, and the facts show that aggressive high-pressure sex contradicts those ends. Consensual sex in dating situations is presumed to aim at mutual enjoyment. It may not always do this, and when it does, it might not always succeed. There is no logical incompatibility between wanting to continue a sexual encounter, and failing to derive sexual pleasure from it.

But it seems to me that there is a presumption in favour of the connection between sex and sexual enjoyment, and that if a man wants to be sure that he is not forcing himself on a woman, he has an obligation either to ensure that the encounter really is mutually enjoyable, or to know the reasons why she would want to continue the encounter in spite of her lack of enjoyment. A closer investigation of the nature of this obligation will enable us to construct a more rational and more plausible norm of sexual conduct.

Onara O'Neill has argued that in intimate situations we have an obligation to take the ends of others as our own, and to promote those ends in a non-manipulative and non-paternalistic manner. Now it seems that in honest sexual encounters just this is required. Assuming that each person enters the encounter in order to seek sexual satisfaction, each person engaging in the encounter has an obligation to help the other seek his or her ends. To do otherwise is to risk acting in opposition to what the other desires, and hence to risk acting without the other's consent.

But the obligation to promote the sexual ends of one's partner implies that obligation to know what those ends are, and also the obligation to know how those ends are attained. Thus, the problem comes down to a problem of epistemic responsibility, the responsibility to know. The solution, in my view, lies in the practice of a communicative sexuality, one which combines the appropriate knowledge of

the other with respect for the dialectics of desire. . . .

Cultural Presumptions

Now it may well be that we have no obligation to care for strangers, and I do not wish to claim that we do. Nonetheless, it seems that O'Neill's point about the special moral duties we have in certain intimate situations is supported by a conceptual relation between certain kinds of personal relationships and the expectation that it should be a communicative relation. Friendship is a case in point. It is a relation that is greatly underdetermined by what we usually include in our sets of rights and obligations. For the most part, rights and obligations disappear as terms by which friendship is guided. They are still there, to be called upon, in case the relationship breaks down, but insofar as the friendship is a friendship, it is concerned with fostering the quality of the interaction and not with standing on rights. Thus, because we are friends, we share our property, and property rights between us are not invoked. Because we are friends, privacy is not an issue. Because we are friends we may see to each other's needs as often as we see to our own. The same can be said for relations between lovers, parents and dependent children, and even between spouses, at least when interaction is functioning at an optimal level. When such relations break down to the point that people must stand on their rights, we can often say that the actors ought to make more of an effort, and in many instances fault them for their lack of charity, tolerance, or benevolence. Thus, although we have a right to end friendships, it may be a reflection on our lack of virtue that we do so, and while we cannot be criticized for violating other people's rights, we can be rightfully deprecated for lacking the virtue to sustain a friendship.

But is there a similar conceptual relation between the kind of activity that a date is, and the sort of moral practice that it requires? My claim is that there is, and that this connection is easily established once we recognize the cultural presumption that dating is a gesture of friendship and regard. Traditionally, the decision to date indicates that two people have an initial attraction to each other, that they are disposed to like each other, and look forward to enjoying each other's company. Dating derives its implicit meaning from this tradition. It retains this meaning unless other aims are explicitly stated, and even then it may not be possible to alienate this meaning. It is a rare woman who will not spurn a man who states explicitly, right at the onset, that he wants to go out with her solely on the condition that he have sexual intercourse with her at the end of the evening, and that he has no interest in her company apart from gaining that end, and no concern for mutual satisfaction.

Explicit protest to the contrary aside, the conventions of dating confer on it its social meaning, and this social meaning implies a relationship which is more like friendship than the cutthroat competition of opposing teams. As such, it requires that we do more than stand on our rights with regard to each other. As long as we are operating under the auspices of a dating relationship, it requires that we behave in the mode of friendship and trust. But if a date is more like a friendship than a business contract, then clearly respect for the dialectics of desire is incompatible with the sort of sexual pressure that is inclined to end in date rape. And clearly, also, a conquest mentality which exploits a situation of trust and respect for purely selfish ends is morally pernicious. Failure to respect the dialectics of desire when operating under the auspices of friendship and trust is to act in flagrant disregard of the moral requirement to avoid manipulative, coercive, and exploitive behaviour. Respect for the dialectics of desire is *prima facie* inconsistent with the satisfaction of one person at the expense of the other. The proper end of friendship relations is mutual satisfaction. But the requirement of mutuality means that we must take a communicative approach to discovering the ends of the other, and this entails that we respect the dialectics of desire.

But now that we know what communicative sexuality is, and that it is morally required, and that it is the only feasible means to mutual sexual enjoyment, why not take this model as the norm of what is reasonable in sexual interaction. The evidence of sexologists strongly indicates that women whose partners are aggressively uncommunicative have little chance of experiencing sexual pleasure. But it is not reasonable for women to consent to what they have little chance of enjoying. Hence it is not reasonable for women to consent to aggressive noncommunicative sex. Nor can we reasonably suppose that women have consented to sexual encounters which we know and they know they do not find enjoyable. With the communicative model as the norm, the aggressive contractual model should strike us as a model of deviant sexuality, and sexual encounters patterned on that model should strike us as encounters to which *prima facie* no one would reasonably agree. But if acquiescence to an encounter counts as consent only if the acquiescence is reasonable, something to which a reasonable person, in full possession of knowledge relevant to the encounter, would agree, then acquiescence to aggressive noncommunicative sex is not reasonable. Hence, acquiescence under such conditions should not count as consent.

Thus, where communicative sexuality does not occur, we lack the main ground for believing that the sex involved was consensual. Moreover, where a man does not engage in communicative sexuality, he acts either out of reckless disregard, or out of willful ignorance. For he cannot know, except through the practice of communicative sexuality, whether his partner has any sexual reason for continuing the encounter. And where she does not, he runs the risk of imposing on her what she is not willing to have. All that is needed then, in order to provide women with legal protection from "date rape" is to make both reckless indifference and willful ignorance a sufficient condition of *mens rea* and to make communicative sexuality the accepted norm of sex to which a reasonable woman would agree. Thus, the appeal to communicative sexuality as a norm for sexual encounters accomplishes two things. It brings the aggressive sex involved in "date rape" well within the realm of sexual assault, and it locates the guilt of date rapists in the failure to approach sexual relations on a communicative basis.

33. Fraternities and Rape on Campus

Patricia Yancey Martin and Robert A. Hummer

Martin and Hummer focus on the all-too-common rape scenario on college campuses: the fraternity house. The physical and sociocultural contexts of fraternities, and the lack of university supervision, encourage the sexual coercion of women in these environments.

Rapes are perpetrated on dates, at parties, in chance encounters, and in specially planned circumstances. That group structure and processes, rather than individual values or characteristics, are the impetus for many rape episodes was documented by Blanchard (1959) 30 years ago (also see Geis 1971), yet sociologists have failed to pursue this theme (for an exception, see Chancer 1987). A recent review of research (Muehlenhard and Linton 1987) on sexual violence, or rape, devotes only a few pages to the situational context of rape events, and these are conceptualized as potential risk factors for individuals rather than qualities of rape-prone social contexts.

Many rapes, far more than come to the public's attention, occur in fraternity houses on college and university campuses, yet little research has analyzed fraternities at American colleges and universities as rape-prone contexts (cf. Ehrhart and Sandler 1985). Most of the research on fraternities reports on samples of individual fraternity men. One group of studies compares the values, attitudes, perceptions, family socioeconomic status, psychological traits (aggressiveness, dependence), and so on, of fraternity and nonfraternity men (Bohrnstedt 1969; Fox, Hodge, and Ward 1987; Kanin 1967; Lemire 1979; Miller 1973). A second group attempts to identify the effects of fraternity membership over time on the values, attitudes, beliefs, or moral precepts of members (Hughes and Winston 1987; Marlowe and Auvenshine 1982; Miller 1973; Wilder, Hoyt, Doren, Hauck, and Zettle 1978; Wilder, Hoyt, Surbeck, Wilder, and Carney

From: *Gender & Society* 3 (December 1989): 457–473. Reprinted by permission of Sage Publications, Inc.

1986). With minor exceptions, little research addresses the group and organizational context of fraternities or the social construction of fraternity life (for exceptions, see Letchworth 1969; Longino and Kart 1973; Smith 1964).

Gary Tash, writing as an alumnus and trial attorney in his fraternity's magazine, claims that over 90 percent of all gang rapes on college campuses involve fraternity men (1988, p. 2). Tash provides no evidence to substantiate this claim, but students of violence against women have been concerned with fraternity men's frequently reported involvement in rape episodes (Adams and Abarbanel 1988). Ehrhart and Sandler (1985) identify over 50 cases of gang rapes on campus perpetrated by fraternity men, and their analysis points to many of the conditions that we discuss here. Their analysis is unique in focusing on conditions in fraternities that make gang rapes of women by fraternity men both feasible and probable. They identify excessive alcohol use, isolation from external monitoring, treatment of women as prey, use of pornography, approval of violence, and excessive concern with competition as precipitating conditions to gang rape (also see Merton 1985; Roark 1987).

The study reported here confirmed and complemented these findings by focusing on both conditions and processes. We examined dynamics associated with the social construction of fraternity life, with a focus on processes that foster the use of coercion, including rape, in fraternity men's relations with women. Our examination of men's social fraternities on college and university campuses as groups and organizations led us to conclude that fraternities are a physical and sociocultural context that encourages the sexual coercion of women. We make no claims that all fraternities are "bad" or that all fraternity men are rapists. Our observations indicated, however, that rape is especially probable in fraternities because of the kinds of organizations they are, the kinds of members they have, the practices their members engage in, and a virtual absence of university or community oversight. Analyses that lay blame for rapes by fraternity men on "peer pressure" are, we feel, overly simplistic (cf. Burkhart 1989; Walsh 1989). We suggest, rather, that fraternities create a sociocultural context in which the use of coercion in sexual relations with women is normative and in which the mechanisms to keep this pattern of behavior in check are minimal at best and absent at worst. We conclude that unless fraternities change in fundamental ways, little improvement can be expected.

Methodology

Our goal was to analyze the group and organizational practices and conditions that create in fraternities an abusive social context for women. We developed a conceptual framework from an initial case study of an alleged gang rape at Florida State University that involved four fraternity men and an 18-year-old coed. The group rape took place on the third floor of a fraternity house and ended with the "dumping" of the woman in the hallway of a neighboring fraternity house. According to newspaper accounts, the victim's blood-alcohol concentration, when she was discovered, was .349 percent, more than three times the legal limit for automobile driving and an almost lethal amount. One law enforcement officer reported that sexual intercourse occurred during the time the victim was unconscious: "She was in a life-threatening situation" (*Tallahassee Democrat*, 1988b). When the victim was found, she was comatose and had suffered multiple scratches and abrasions. Crude words and a fraternity symbol had been written on her thighs (*Tampa Tribune*, 1988). When law enforcement officials tried to investigate the case, fraternity members refused to cooperate.

This led, eventually, to a five-year ban of the fraternity from campus by the university and by the fraternity's national organization.

In trying to understand how such an event could have occurred, and how a group of over 150 members (exact figures are unknown because the fraternity refused to provide a membership roster) could hold rank, deny knowledge of the event, and allegedly lie to a grand jury, we analyzed newspaper articles about the case and conducted open-ended interviews with a variety of respondents about the case and about fraternities, rapes, alcohol use, gender relations, and sexual activities on campus. Our data included over 100 newspaper articles on the initial gang rape case; open-ended interviews with Greek (social fraternity and sorority) and non-Greek (independent) students (N = 20); university administrators (N = 8, five men, three women); and alumni advisers to Greek organizations (N = 6). Open-ended interviews were held also with judges, public and private defense attorneys, victim advocates, and state prosecutors regarding the processing of sexual assault cases. Data were analyzed using the grounded theory method (Glaser 1978; Martin and Turner 1986). In the following analysis, concepts generated from the data analysis are integrated with the literature on men's social fraternities, sexual coercion, and related issues.

Fraternities and the Social Construction of Men and Masculinity

Our research indicated that fraternities are vitally concerned—more than with anything else—with masculinity (cf. Kanin 1967). They work hard to create a macho image and context and try to avoid any suggestion of "wimpishness," effeminacy, and homosexuality. Valued members display, or are willing to go along with, a narrow conception of masculinity that stresses competition, athleticism, dominance, winning, conflict, wealth, material posessions, willingness to drink alcohol, and sexual prowess vis-à-vis women.

Valued Qualities of Members

When fraternity members talked about the kind of pledges they prefer, a litany of stereotypical and narrowly masculine attributes and behaviors was recited and feminine or woman-associated qualities and behaviors were expressly denounced (cf. Merton 1985). Fraternities seek men who are "athletic," "big guys," good in intramural competition, "who can talk college sports." Males "who are willing to drink alcohol," "who drink socially," or "who can hold their liquor" are sought. Alcohol and activities associated with the recreational use of alcohol are cornerstones of fraternity social life. Nondrinkers are viewed with skepticism and rarely selected for membership.

Fraternities try to avoid "geeks," nerds, and men said to give the fraternity a "wimpy" or "gay" reputation. Art, music, and humanities majors, majors in traditional women's fields (nursing, home economics, social work, education), men with long hair, and those whose appearance or dress violate current norms are rejected. Clean-cut, handsome men who dress well (are clean, neat, conforming, fashionable) are preferred. One sorority woman commented that "the top ranking fraternities have the best looking guys."

One fraternity man, a senior, said his fraternity recruited "some big guys, very athletic" over a two-year period to help overcome its image of wimpiness. His fraternity had won the interfraternity competition for highest grade-point average several years running but was looked down on as "wimpy, dancy, even gay." With their bigger, more athletic recruits, "our reputation improved; we're a much more recognized fraternity now." Thus a fraternity's reputation and status depends on members' possession of stereotypically masculine qualities. Good grades, campus leadership, and community service are "nice" but masculinity dominance—for example, in athletic events, physical size of members, athleticism of members—counts most.

Certain social skills are valued. Men are sought who "have good personalities," are friendly, and "have the ability to relate to girls" (cf. Longino and Kart 1973). One fraternity man, a junior, said: "We watch a guy [a potential pledge] talk to women . . . we want guys who can relate to girls." Assessing a pledge's ability to talk to women is, in part, a preoccupation with homosexuality and a conscious avoidance of men who seem to have effeminate manners or qualities. If a member is suspected of being gay, he is ostracized and informally drummed out of the fraternity. A fraternity with a reputation as wimpy or tolerant of gays is ridiculed and shunned by other fraternities. Militant heterosexuality is frequently used by men as a strategy to keep each other in line (Kimmel 1987).

Financial affluence or wealth, a male-associated value in American culture, is highly valued by fraternities. In accounting for why the fraternity involved in the gang rape that precipitated our research project had been recognized recently as "the best fraternity chapter in the United States," a university official said: "They were good-looking, a big fraternity, had lots of BMWs [expensive, German-made automobiles]." After the rape, newspaper stories described the fraternity members' affluence, noting the high number of members who owned expensive cars (*St. Petersburg Times*, 1988).

The Status and Norms of Pledgeship

A pledge (sometimes called an associate member) is a new recruit who occupies a trial membership status for a specific period of time. The pledge period (typically ranging from 10 to 15 weeks) gives fraternity brothers an opportunity to assess and socialize new recruits. Pledges evaluate the fraternity also and decide if they want to become brothers. The socialization experience is structured partly through assignment of a Big Brother to each pledge. Big Brothers are expected to teach pledges how to become a brother and to support them as they progress through the trial membership period. Some pledges are repelled by the pledging experience, which can entail physical abuse; harsh discipline; and demands to be subordinate, follow orders, and engage in demeaning routines and activities, similar to those used by the military to "make men out of boys" during boot camp.

Characteristics of the pledge experience are

rationalized by fraternity members as necessary to help pledges unite into a group, rely on each other, and join together against outsiders. The process is highly masculinist in execution as well as conception. A willingness to submit to authority, follow orders, and do as one is told is viewed as a sign of loyalty, togetherness, and unity. Fraternity pledges who find the pledge process offensive often drop out. Some do this by openly quitting, which can subject them to ridicule by brothers and other pledges, or they may deliberately fail to make the grades necessary for initiation or transfer schools and decline to reaffiliate with the fraternity on the new campus. One fraternity pledge who quit the fraternity he had pledged described an experience during pledgeship as follows:

> This one guy was always picking on me. No matter what I did, I was wrong. One night after dinner, he and two other guys called me and two other pledges into the chapter room. He said, "Here, X, hold this 25 pound bag of ice at arms' length 'til I tell you to stop." I did it even though my arms and hands were killing me. When I asked if I could stop, he grabbed me around the throat and lifted me off the floor. I thought he would choke me to death. He cussed me and called me all kinds of names. He took one of my fingers and twisted it until it nearly broke. . . . I stayed in the fraternity for a few more days, but then I decided to quit. I hated it. Those guys are sick. They like seeing you suffer.

Fraternities' emphasis on toughness, withstanding pain and humiliation, obedience to superiors, and using physical force to obtain compliance contributes to an interpersonal style that de-emphasizes caring and sensitivity but fosters intragroup trust and loyalty. If the least macho or most critical pledges drop out, those who remain may be more receptive to, and influenced by, masculinist values and practices that encourage the use of force in sexual relations with women and the covering up of such behavior (cf. Kanin 1967).

Norms and Dynamics of Brotherhood

Brother is the status occupied by fraternity men to indicate their relations to each other and their membership in a particular fraternity organization or group. Brother is a male-specific status; only males can become brothers, although women can become "Little Sisters," a form of pseudomembership. "Becoming a brother" is a rite of passage that follows the consistent and often lengthy display by pledges of appropriately masculine qualities and behaviors. Brothers have a quasi-familial relationship with each other, are normatively said to share bonds of closeness and support, and are sharply set off from nonmembers. Brotherhood is a loosely defined term used to represent the bonds that develop among fraternity members and the obligations and expectations incumbent upon them (cf. Marlowe and Auvenshine [1982] on fraternities' failure to encourage "moral development" in freshman pledges).

Some of our respondents talked about brotherhood in almost reverential terms, viewing it as the most valuable benefit of fraternity membership. One senior, a business-school major who had been affiliated with a fairly high-status fraternity throughout four years on campus, said:

> Brotherhood spurs friendship for life, which I consider its best aspect, although I didn't see it that way when I joined. Brotherhood bonds and unites. It instills values of caring about one another, caring about community, caring about ourselves. The values and bonds [of brotherhood] continually develop over the four years [in college] while normal friendships come and go.

Despite this idealization, most aspects of fraternity practice and conception are more mundane. Brotherhood often plays itself out as an overriding concern with masculinity and, by extension, femininity. As a consequence, fraternities comprise collectivities of highly masculinized men with attitudinal qualities and behavioral norms that predispose them to sexual coercion of women (cf. Kanin 1967; Merton 1985; Rapaport and Burkhart 1984). The norms of masculinity are complemented by conceptions of women and femininity that are equally distorted and stereotyped and that may enhance the probability of women's exploitation (cf. Ehrhart and Sandler 1985; Sanday 1981, 1986).

Practices of Brotherhood

Practices associated with fraternity brotherhood that contribute to the sexual coercion of women include a preoccupation with loyalty, group protection and secrecy, use of alcohol as a weapon, involvement in violence and physical force, and an emphasis on competition and superiority.

Loyalty, Group Protection, and Secrecy   Loyalty is a fraternity preoccupation. Members are reminded constantly to be loyal to the fraternity and to their brothers. Among other ways, loyalty is played out in the practices of group protection and secrecy. The fraternity must be shielded from criticism. Members are admonished to avoid getting the fraternity in trouble and to bring all problems "to the chapter" (local branch of a national social fraternity) rather than to outsiders. Fraternities try to protect themselves from close scrutiny and criticism by the Interfraternity Council (a quasi-governing body composed of representatives from all social fraternities on campus), their fraternity's national office, university officials, law enforcement, the media, and the public. Protection of the fraternity often takes precedence over what is procedurally, ethically, or legally correct. Numerous examples were related to us of fraternity brothers' lying to outsiders to "protect the fraternity."

Group protection was observed in the alleged gang rape case with which we began our study. Except for one brother, a rapist who turned state's evidence, the entire remaining fraternity membership was accused by the university and criminal justice officials of lying to protect the fraternity. Members

consistently failed to cooperate even though the alleged crimes were felonies, involved only four men (two of whom were not even members of the local chapter), and the victim of the crime nearly died. According to a grand jury's findings, fraternity officers repeatedly broke appointments with law enforcement officials, refused to provide police with a list of members, and refused to cooperate with police and prosecutors investigating the case (*Florida Flambeau*, 1988).

Secrecy is a priority value and practice in fraternities, partly because full-fledged membership is premised on it (for confirmation, see Ehrhart and Sandler 1985; Longino and Kart 1973; Roark 1987). Secrecy is also a boundary-maintaining mechanism, demarcating in-group from out-group, us from them. Secret rituals, handshakes, and mottoes are revealed to pledge brothers as they are initiated into full brotherhood. Since only brothers are supposed to know a fraternity's secrets, such knowledge affirms membership in the fraternity and separates a brother from others. Extending secrecy tactics from protection of private knowledge to protection of the fraternity from criticism is a predictable development. Our interviews indicated that individual members knew the difference between right and wrong, but fraternity norms that emphasize loyalty, group protection, and secrecy often overrode standards of ethical correctness.

Alcohol as Weapon   Alcohol use by fraternity men is normative. They use it on weekdays to relax after class and on weekends to "get drunk," "get crazy," and "get laid." The use of alcohol to obtain sex from women is pervasive—in other words, it is used as a weapon against sexual reluctance. According to several fraternity men whom we interviewed, alcohol is the major tool used to gain sexual mastery over women (cf. Adams and Abarbanel 1988; Ehrhart and Sandler 1985). One fraternity man, a 21-year-old senior, described alcohol use to gain sex as follows: "There are girls that you know will fuck, then some you have to put some effort into it. . . . You have to buy them drinks or find out if she's drunk enough. . . ."

A similar strategy is used collectively. A

fraternity man said that at parties with Little Sisters: "We provide them with 'hunch punch' and things get wild. We get them drunk and most of the guys end up with one." " 'Hunch punch,' " he said, "is a girls' drink made up of overproof alcohol and powdered Kool-Aid, no water or anything, just ice. It's very strong. Two cups will do a number on a female." He had plans in the next academic term to surreptitiously give hunch punch to women in a "prim and proper" sorority because "having sex with prim and proper sorority girls is definitely a goal." These women are a challenge because they "won't openly consume alcohol and won't get openly drunk as hell." Their sororities have "standards committees" that forbid heavy drinking and easy sex.

In the gang rape case, our sources said that many fraternity men on campus believed the victim had a drinking problem and was thus an "easy make." According to newspaper accounts, she had been drinking alcohol on the evening she was raped; the lead assailant is alleged to have given her a bottle of wine after she arrived at his fraternity house. Portions of the rape occurred in a shower, and the victim was reportedly so drunk that her assailants had difficulty holding her in a standing position (*Tallahassee Democrat*, 1988a). While raping her, her assailants repeatedly told her they were members of another fraternity under the apparent belief that she was too drunk to know the difference. Of course, if she was too drunk to know who they were, she was too drunk to consent to sex (cf. Allgeier 1986; Tash 1988).

One respondent told us that gang rapes are wrong and can get one expelled, but he seemed to see nothing wrong in sexual coercion one-on-one. He seemed unaware that the use of alcohol to obtain sex from a woman is grounds for a claim that a rape occurred (cf. Tash 1988). Few women on campus (who also may not know these grounds) report date rapes, however; so the odds of detection and punishment are slim for fraternity men who use alcohol for "seduction" purposes (cf. Byington and Keeter 1988; Merton 1985).

Violence and Physical Force Fraternity men have a history of violence (Ehrhart and Sandler 1985; Roark 1987). Their record of hazing,

fighting, property destruction, and rape has caused them problems with insurance companies (Bradford 1986; Pressley 1987). Two university officials told us that fraternities "are the third riskiest property to insure behind toxic waste dumps and amusement parks." Fraternities are increasingly defendants in legal actions brought by pledges subjected to hazing (Meyer 1986; Pressley 1987) and by women who were raped by one or more members. In a recent alleged gang rape incident at another Florida university, prosecutors failed to file charges but the victim filed a civil suit against the fraternity nevertheless (*Tallahassee Democrat*, 1989).

Competition and Superiority Interfraternity rivalry fosters in-group identification and out-group hostility. Fraternities stress pride of membership and superiority over other fraternities as major goals. Interfraternity rivalries take many forms, including competition for desirable pledges, size of pledge class, size of membership, size and appearance of fraternity house, superiority in intramural sports, highest grade-point averages, giving the best parties, gaining the best or most campus leadership roles, and, of great importance, attracting and displaying "good looking women." Rivalry is particularly intense over members, intramural sports, and women (cf. Messner 1989).

Fraternities' Commodification of Women

In claiming that women are treated by fraternities as commodities, we mean that fraternities knowingly, and intentionally, *use* women for their benefit. Fraternities use women as bait for new members, as servers of brothers' needs, and as sexual prey.

Women as Bait Fashionably attractive women help a fraternity attract new members. As one fraternity man, a junior, said, "They are good bait." Beautiful, sociable women are believed to impress the right kind of pledges and give the impression that the fraternity can deliver this type of woman to its members. Photographs of shapely, attractive coeds are printed in fraternity brochures and videotapes that are distributed and shown to potential pledges. The women pictured are often dressed in bikinis, at the beach, and are pictured hugging the brothers of the fraternity. One university official says such recruitment materials give the message: "Hey, they're here for you, you can have whatever you want," and, "we have the best looking women. Join us and you can have them too." Another commented: "Something's wrong when males join an all-male organization as the best place to meet women. It's so illogical."

Fraternities compete in promising access to beautiful women. One fraternity man, a senior, commented that "the attraction of girls [i.e., a fraternity's success in attracting women] is a big status symbol for fraternities." One university official commented that the use of women as a recruiting tool is so well entrenched that fraternities that might be willing to forgo it say they cannot afford to unless other fraternities do so as well. One fraternity man said, "Look, if we don't have Little Sisters, the fraternities that do will get all the good pledges." Another said, "We won't have as good a rush [the period during which new members are assessed and selected] if we don't have these women around."

In displaying good-looking, attractive, skimpily dressed, nubile women to potential members, fraternities implicitly, and sometimes explicitly, promise sexual access to women. One fraternity man commented that "part of what being in a fraternity is all about is the sex" and explained how his fraternity uses Little Sisters to recruit new members:

> We'll tell the sweetheart [the fraternity's term for Little Sister], "You're gorgeous; you can get him." We'll tell her to fake a scam and she'll go hang all over him during a rush party, kiss him, and he thinks he's done wonderful and wants to join. The girls think it's great too. It's flattering for them.

Women as Servers   The use of women as servers is exemplified in the Little Sister program. Little Sisters are undergraduate women who are rushed and selected in a manner parallel to the recruitment of fraternity men. They are affiliated with the fraternity in a formal but unofficial way and are able, indeed required, to wear the fraternity's Greek letters. Little Sisters are not full-fledged fraternity members, however; and fraternity national offices and most universities do not register or regulate them. Each fraternity has an officer called Little Sister Chairman who oversees their organization and activities. The Little Sisters elect officers among themselves, pay monthly dues to the fraternity, and have well-defined roles. Their dues are used to pay for the fraternity's social events, and Little Sisters are expected to attend and hostess fraternity parties and hang around the house to make it a "nice place to be." One fraternity man, a senior, described Little Sisters this way: "They are very social girls, willing to join in, be affiliated with the group, devoted to the fraternity." Another member, a sophomore, said: "Their sole purpose is social—attend parties, attract new members, and 'take care' of the guys."

Our observations and interviews suggested that women selected by fraternities as Little Sisters are physically attractive, possess good social skills, and are willing to devote time and energy to the fraternity and its members. One undergraduate woman gave the following job description for Little Sisters to a campus newspaper:

> It's not just making appearances at all the parties but entails many more responsibilities. You're going to be expected to go to all the intramural games to cheer the brothers on, support and encourage the pledges, and just be around to bring some extra life to the house. [As a Little Sister] you have to agree to take on a new responsibility other than studying to maintain your grades and managing to keep your checkbook from bouncing. You have to make time to be a part of the fraternity and support the brothers in all they do. (*The Tomahawk*, 1988)

The title of Little Sister reflects women's subordinate status; fraternity men in a parallel role are called Big Brothers. Big Brothers assist a sorority primarily with the physical work of sorority rushes, which, compared to fraternity rushes, are more formal, structured, and intensive. Sorority rushes take place in the daytime and fraternity rushes at night so fraternity men are free to help. According to one fraternity member, Little Sister status is a benefit to women because it gives them a social outlet and "the protection of the brothers." The gender-stereotypic conceptions and obligations of these Little Sister and Big Brother statuses indicate that fraternities and sororities promote a gender hierarchy on campus that fosters subordination and dependence in women, thus encouraging sexual exploitation and the belief that it is acceptable.

Women as Sexual Prey Little Sisters are a sexual utility. Many Little Sisters do not belong to sororities and lack peer support for refraining from unwanted sexual relations. One fraternity man (whose fraternity has 65 members and 85 Little Sisters) told us they had recruited "wholesale" in the prior year to "get lots of new women." The structural access to women that the Little Sister program provides and the absence of normative supports for refusing fraternity members' sexual advances may make women in this program particularly susceptible to coerced sexual encounters with fraternity men.

Access to women for sexual gratification is a presumed benefit of fraternity membership, promised in recruitment materials and strategies and through brothers' conversations with new recruits. One fraternity man said: "We always tell the guys that you get sex all the time, there's always new girls. . . . After I became a Greek, I found out I could be with females at will." A university official told us that, based on his observations, "no one [i.e., fraternity men] on this campus wants to have 'relationships.' They just want to have fun [i.e., sex]." Fraternity men plan and execute strategies aimed at obtaining sexual gratification, and this occurs at both individual and collective levels.

Individual strategies include getting a woman drunk and spending a great deal of money on her. As for collective strategies, most of our undergraduate interviewees agreed that fraternity parties often culminate

in sex and that this outcome is planned. One fraternity man said fraternity parties often involve sex and nudity and can "turn into orgies." Orgies may be planned in advance, such as the Bowery Ball party held by one fraternity. A former fraternity member said of this party:

> The entire idea behind this is sex. Both men and women come to the party wearing little or nothing. There are pornographic pinups on the walls and usually porno movies playing on the TV. The music carries sexual overtones. . . . They just get schnockered [drunk] and, in most cases, they also get laid.

When asked about the women who come to such a party, he said: "Some Little Sisters just won't go. . . . The girls who do are looking for a good time, girls who don't know what it is, things like that."

Other respondents denied that fraternity parties are orgies but said that sex is always talked about among the brothers and they all know "who each other is doing it with." One member said that most of the time, guys have sex with their girlfriends "but with socials, girlfriends aren't allowed to come and it's their [members'] big chance [to have sex with other women]." The use of alcohol to help them get women into bed is a routine strategy at fraternity parties.

Conclusions

In general, our research indicated that the organization and membership of fraternities contribute heavily to coercive and often violent sex. Fraternity houses are occupied by same-sex (all men) and same-age (late teens, early twenties) peers whose maturity and judgment is often less than ideal. Yet fraternity houses are private dwellings that are mostly off-limits to, and away from scrutiny of, university and community representatives, with the result that fraternity house events seldom come to the attention of outsiders. Practices associated with the social construction of fraternity brotherhood emphasize a macho conception of men and masculinity, a narrow, stereotyped conception of women and femininity, and the treatment of women as commodities. Other practices contributing to coercive sexual relations and the cover-up of rapes include excessive alcohol use, competitiveness, and normative support for deviance and secrecy (cf. Bogal-Allbritten and Allbritten 1985; Kanin 1967).

Some fraternity practices exacerbate others. Brotherhood norms require "sticking together" regardless of right or wrong; thus rape episodes are unlikely to be stopped or reported to outsiders, even when witnesses disapprove. The ability to use alcohol without scrutiny by authorities and alcohol's frequent association with violence, including sexual coercion, facilitates rape in fraternity houses. Fraternity norms that emphasize the value of maleness and masculinity over femaleness and femininity and that elevate the status of men and lower the status of women in members' eyes undermine perceptions and treatment of women as persons who deserve consideration and care (cf. Ehrhart and Sandler 1985; Merton 1985).

Androgynous men and men with a broad range of interests and attributes are lost to fraternities through their recruitment practices. Masculinity of a narrow and stereotypical type helps create attitudes, norms, and practices that predispose fraternity men to coerce women sexually, both individually and collectively (Allgeier 1986; Hood 1989; Sanday 1981, 1986). Male athletes on campus may be similarly disposed for the same reasons (Kirshenbaum 1989; Telander and Sullivan 1989).

Research into the social contexts in which rape crimes occur and the social constructions associated with these contexts illuminate rape dynamics on campus. Blanchard (1959) found that group rapes almost always have a leader who pushes others into the crime. He also found that the leader's latent homosexuality, desire to show off to his peers, or fear of failing to prove himself a man are frequently an impetus. Fraternity norms and practices contribute to the approval and use of sexual coercion as an accepted tactic in relations with women. Alcohol-induced compliance is normative, whereas, presumably, use of a knife, gun, or threat of bodily harm would not

be because the woman who "drinks too much" is viewed as "causing her own rape" (cf. Ehrhart and Sandler 1985).

Our research led us to conclude that fraternity norms and practices influence members to view the sexual coercion of women, which is a felony crime, as sport, a contest, or a game (cf. Sato 1988). This sport is played not between men and women but between men and men. Women are the pawns or prey in the interfraternity rivalry game; they prove that a fraternity is successful or prestigious. The use of women in this way encourages fraternity men to see women as objects and sexual coercion as sport. Today's societal norms support young women's right to engage in sex at their discretion, and coercion is unnecessary in a mutually desired encounter. However, nubile young women say they prefer to be "in a relationship" to have sex while young men say they prefer to "get laid" without a commitment (Muehlenhard and Linton 1987). These differences may reflect, in part, American puritanism and men's fears of sexual intimacy or perhaps intimacy of any kind. In a fraternity context, getting sex without giving emotionally demonstrates "cool" masculinity. More important, it poses no threat to the bonding and loyalty of the fraternity brotherhood (cf. Farr 1988). Drinking large quantities of alcohol before having sex suggests that "scoring" rather than intrinsic sexual pleasure is a primary concern of fraternity men.

Unless fraternities' composition, goals, structures, and practices change in fundamental ways, women on campus will continue to be sexual prey for fraternity men. As all-male enclaves dedicated to opposing faculty and administration and to cementing ingroup ties, fraternity members eschew any hint of homosexuality. Their version of masculinity transforms women, and men with womanly characteristics, into the out-group. "Womanly men" are ostracized; feminine women are used to demonstrate members' masculinity. Encouraging renewed emphasis on their founding values (Longino and Kart 1073), service orientation and activities (Lemire 1979), or members' moral development (Marlowe and Auvenshine 1982) will have little effect on fraternities' treatment of women.

A case for or against fraternities cannot be made by studying individual members. The fraternity qua group and organization is at issue. Located on campus along with many vulnerable women, embedded in a sexist society, and caught up in masculinist goals, practices, and values, fraternities' violation of women—including forcible rape—should come as no surprise.

Note

1. Recent bans by some universities on open-keg parties at fraternity houses have resulted in heavy drinking before coming to a party and an increase in drunkenness among those who attend. This may aggravate, rather than improve, the treatment of women by fraternity men at parties.

References

Adams, Aileen and Gail Abarbanel. 1988. *Sexual Assault on Campus: What Colleges Can Do.* Santa Monica, CA: Rape Treatment Center.

Allgeier, Elizabeth. 1986. "Coercive Versus Consensual Sexual Interactions." G. Stanley Hall Lecture to American Psychological Association Annual Meeting, Washington, DC, August.

Blanchard, W. H. 1959. "The Group Process in Gang Rape." *Journal of Social Psychology* 49:259–66.

Bogal-Allbritten, Rosemarie B. and William L. Allbritten. 1985. "The Hidden Victims: Courtship Violence Among College Students." *Journal of College Student Personnel* 43:201–4.

Bohrnstedt, George W. 1969. "Conservatism, Authoritarianism and Religiosity of Fraternity Pledges." *Journal of College Student Personnel* 27:36–43.

Bradford, Michael. 1986. "Tight Market Dries Up Nightlife at University," *Business Insurance* (March 2): 2, 6.

Burkhart, Barry. 1989. Comments in Seminar on Acquaintance/Date Rape Prevention: A National Video Teleconference, February 2.

Burkhart, Barry R. and Annette L. Stanton. 1985. "Sexual Aggression in Acquaintance Relationships." Pp. 43–65 in *Violence in Intimate Relationships,* edited by G. Russell. Englewood Cliffs, NJ: Spectrum.

Byington, Diane B. and Karen W. Keeter. 1988. "Assessing Needs of Sexual Assault Victims on a University Campus." Pp. 23–31 in *Student Services: Responding to Issues and Challenges.* Chapel Hill: University of North Carolina Press.

Chancer, Lynn S. 1987. "New Bedford, Massachusetts, March 6, 1983–March 22, 1984: The 'Before and After' of a Group Rape." *Gender & Society* 1:239–60.

Ehrhart, Julie K. and Bernice R. Sandler. 1985. *Campus Gang Rape: Party Games?* Washington, DC: Association of American Colleges.

Farr, K. A. 1988. "Dominance Bonding Through the Good Old Boys Sociability Network." *Sex Roles* 18:259–77.

Florida Flambeau. 1988. "Pike Members Indicted in Rape" (May 19):1, 5.

Fox, Elaine, Charles Hodge, and Walter Ward. 1987. "A Comparison of Attitudes Held by Black and White Fraternity Members." *Journal of Negro Education* 56:521–34.

Geis, Gilbert. 1971. "Group Sexual Assaults." *Medical Aspects of Human Sexuality* 5:101–13.

Glaser, Barney G. 1978. *Theoretical Sensitivity: Advances in the Methodology of Grounded Theory.* Mill Valley, CA: Sociology Press.

Hood, Jane. 1989. "Why Our Society Is Rape-Prone." *New York Times,* May 16.

Hughes, Michael J. and Roger B. Winston, Jr. 1987. "Effects of Fraternity Membership on Interpersonal Values." *Journal of College Student Personnel* 45:405–11.

Kanin, Eugene J. 1967. "Reference Groups and Sex Conduct Norm Violations." *The Sociological Quarterly* 8:495–504.

Kimmel, Michael, ed. 1987. *Changing Men: New Directions in Research on Men and Masculinity.* Newbury Park, CA: Sage.

Kirshenbaum, Jerry. 1989. "Special Report, An American Disgrace: A Violent and Unprecedented Lawlessness Has Arisen Among College Athletes in all Parts of the Country." *Sports Illustrated* (February 27): 16–19.

Lemire, David. 1979. "One Investigation of the Stereotypes Associated with Fraternities and Sororities." *Journal of College Student Personnel* 37:54–57.

Letchworth, G. E. 1969. "Fraternities Now and in the Future." *Journal of College Student Personnel* 10:118–22.

Longino, Charles F., Jr., and Cary S. Kart. 1973. "The College Fraternity: An Assessment of Theory and Research." *Journal of College Student Personnel* 31:118–25.

Marlowe, Anne F. and Dwight C. Auvenshine. 1982. "Greek Membership: Its Impact on the Moral Development of College Freshmen." *Journal of College Student Personnel* 40:53–57.

Martin, Patricia Yancey and Barry A. Turner. 1986. "Grounded Theory and Organizational Research." *Journal of Applied Behavioral Science* 22:141–57.

Merton, Andrew. 1985. "On Competition and Class: Return to Brotherhood." *Ms.* (September): 60–65, 121–22.

Messner, Michael. 1989. "Masculinities and Athletic Careers." *Gender & Society* 3:71–88.

Meyer, T. J. 1986. "Fight Against Hazing Rituals Rages on Campuses." *Chronicle of Higher Education* (March 12):34–36.

Miller, Leonard D. 1973. "Distinctive Characteristics of Fraternity Members." *Journal of College Student Personnel* 31:126–28.

Muehlenhard, Charlene L. and Melaney A. Linton. 1987. "Date Rape and Sexual Aggression in Dating Situations: Incidence and Risk Factors." *Journal of Counseling Psychology* 34:186–96.

Pressley, Sue Anne. 1987. "Fraternity Hell Night Still Endures." *Washington Post* (August 11):B1.

Rapaport, Karen and Barry R. Burkhart. 1984. "Personality and Attitudinal Characteristics of Sexually Coercive College Males." *Journal of Abnormal Psychology* 93:216–21.

Roark, Mary L. 1987. "Preventing Violence on College Campuses." *Journal of Counseling and Development* 65:367–70.

St. Petersburg Times. 1988. "A Greek Tragedy." (May 29):1F, 6F.

Sanday, Peggy Reeves. 1981. "The Socio-Cultural Context of Rape: A Cross-Cultural Study." *Journal of Social Issues* 37:5–27.

———. 1986. "Rape and the Silencing of the Feminine." Pp. 84–101 in *Rape*, edited by S. Tomaselli and R. Porter. Oxford: Basil Blackwell.

Sato, Ikuya. 1988. "Play Theory of Delinquency: Toward a General Theory of 'Action.'" *Symbolic Interaction* 11:191–212.

Smith, T. 1964. "Emergence and Maintenance of Fraternal Solidarity." *Pacific Sociological Review* 7:29–37.

Tallahassee Democrat. 1988a. "FSU Fraternity Brothers Charged" (April 27):1A, 12A.

———. 1988b. "FSU Interviewing Students About Alleged Rape" (April 24):1D.

———. 1989. "Woman Sues Stetson in Alleged Rape" (March 19):3B.

Tampa Tribune. 1988. "Fraternity Brothers Charged in Sexual Assault of FSU Coed" (April 27):6B.

Tash, Gary B. 1988. "Date Rape." *The Emerald of Sigma Pi Fraternity* 75(4):1–2.

Telander, Rick and Robert Sullivan. 1989. "Special Report, You Reap What You Sow." *Sports Illustrated* (February 27):20–34.

The Tomahawk. 1988. "A Look Back at Rush, A Mixture of Hard Work and Fun" (April/May):3D.

Walsh, Claire. 1989. Comments in Seminar on Acquaintance/Date Rape Prevention: A National Video Teleconference. February 2.

Wilder, David H., Arlyne E. Hoyt, Dennis M. Doren, William E. Hauck, and Robert D. Zettle. 1978. "The Impact of Fraternity and Sorority Membership on Values and Attitudes." *Journal of College Student Personnel* 36:445–49.

Wilder, David H., Arlyne E. Hoyt, Beth Shuster Surbeck, Janet C. Wilder, and Patricia Imperatrice Carney. 1986. "Greek Affiliation and Attitude Change in College Students." *Journal of College Student Personnel* 44:510–19.

Case 7.a Date Rape Case Studies

Robin Warshaw

The following cases, taken from Robin Warshaw's book *I Never Called It Rape*, tell a frightening story of the different acquaintance rape situations women are subject to. A young woman set up by a friend for a double date, a teenager, a college student, a single working woman, and an older woman, all devastated from being raped by men they knew, make it clear that acquaintance rape can happen to any woman.

Lori's Story

How can a date be a rape?

The pairing of the word "date," which conjures up an image of fun shared by two companions, with the word "rape," which evokes the total loss of control by one person to the will of another, results in the creation of a new phrase that is nearly impossible for most people to comprehend. To understand how date rape happens, let's look at a classic case.

The Setup It was natural. Normal. Lori's friend Amy wanted to go out with Paul, but felt awkward and shy about going out with him alone. So when Paul's roommate, Eric, suggested that he and Lori join Amy and Paul for a double date, it made sense. "I didn't feel anything for Eric except as a friend," Lori says of her reaction to the plan. "I said, 'Okay, maybe it will make Amy feel better.'"

Agreeing to go out with Eric was no great act of charity on Lori's part. He *was* attractive—tall, good-looking, in his mid-20s and from a wealthy family. Lori, who was 19 at the time, knew Eric and Paul as frequent customers at the popular Tampa Bay restaurant where she worked as a waitress when she was between college semesters.

On the day of the date, Eric called several times to change their plans. Finally, he phoned to say that they would be having a barbecue with several of his friends at the house he and Paul shared. Lori agreed.

We went to his house and I mentioned something about Paul and Amy and he kind of threw it off, like "Yeah, yeah." I didn't think anything of it. There we are, fixing steaks, and he was saying, "Well, this is obviously something to help Amy."

He kept making drinks all night long. He kept saying, "Here, have a drink," "Here, drink this." I didn't because I didn't want it. He was just downing them right and left.

The Attack Unknown to Lori, Amy had canceled her plans to see Paul the day before. Paul told Eric, but Eric never told Lori. As the barbecue party progressed and her friend failed to show up, Lori questioned Eric again. He then lied, telling her that Paul had just called to say he and Amy weren't coming.

I was thinking to myself, "Well, okay." Not in my wildest dreams would I have thought he was plotting something. Then all of his friends started leaving. I began to think, "Something is wrong, something is going on," but I've been known to overreact to things, so I ignored it.

After his friends left, we're sitting on the couch and he leans over and he kisses me and I'm thinking, "It's a date, it's no big deal." So then we started kissing a little bit more and I'm thinking, "I'm starting to enjoy this, maybe this isn't so bad." Then the phone rang and when he came back I was standing up. He grabbed me from behind and picked me up. He had his hands over my eyes and we were walking through his house. It was really dark and I didn't know where on earth he was taking me. I had never actually walked through his house.

He laid me down [on a bed] and kissed me. . . . He starts taking off my clothes and I said, "Wait—time out! This is not what I want, you know," and he said to me something like this is what I owed him because he made me dinner.

I said, "This is wrong, don't do this. I didn't go out with you with this intent."

He said, "What do you call that on the couch?"

I said, "I call it a kiss, period."

And he said, "Well, I don't."

The two struggled until Eric rolled off her momentarily. Lori jumped up and went into the bathroom. Her plan was to come out in a few minutes and tell him it was time to take her home.

The whole time I'm thinking, "I don't believe this is happening to me." I didn't even have time to walk fully out of the bathroom door when he grabbed me and threw me on the bed and started taking my clothes off. I'm yelling and hitting and pushing on him and he just liked that. He says, "I know you must like this because a lot of women like this kind of thing." Then he says, "This is the adult world. Maybe you ought to grow up some."

I finally got to the point where there was nothing I could do.

Eric pushed his penis into her and, after a few minutes, ejaculated. Lori had had only one other experience with sexual intercourse, about a year before with a longtime boyfriend.

Then Eric just rolled over and I started to get my clothes together. He said, "Don't tell me you didn't like that." I looked at him and said, "No," and by this time I'm crying because I don't know what else to do. I never heard of anybody having that happen to them.

The Aftermath   Finally, Eric took her home.

In the car he said, "Can I call you tomorrow? Can I see you next weekend?" I just looked at him and he just looked at me and started laughing.

My mom had gone out and I just laid on my bed with the covers up. Everything I could possibly put on I think I put on that night—leg warmers, thermal underwear—everything imaginable in the middle of summer I put on my body. That night I dreamed it was all happening again. I dreamed I was standing there watching him do it.

For two weeks I couldn't talk. People would talk to me and I felt nothing. I felt like a zombie. I couldn't cry, I couldn't smile, I couldn't eat. My mom said, "What's wrong with you? Is something going on?" I said, "Nothing's wrong."

I thought it was my fault. What did I do to make him think he could do something like that? Was I wrong in kissing him? Was I wrong to go out with him, to go over to his house?

After two weeks, she told her mother what happened and they talked about what to do. Lori decided not to report it to the police for fear Eric would blame her. Eric continued to frequent the restaurant where she worked. Several weeks after their date, he cornered her in a hallway near the kitchen.

He touched me and I said, "Get your hands off me." At first, he thought it was funny. He said, "What's wrong?" then he started pulling me, trying to hug me. I pushed him and said, "Leave me alone," and I was starting to get a little loud. As I was walking away, he said, "Oh, I guess you didn't get enough."

I walked in the kitchen and I picked up this tray full of food. I don't know how it happened, I just dropped the whole tray and it went everywhere. My friend, another waitress, went to the manager and said, "She's not going to be much good to you tonight," so they sent me home.

Lori decided to move to a town about 150 miles away to avoid continued encounters with Eric. There she found work as an office assistant and cashier and enrolled for a few classes at a new college.

Sitting in a darkened restaurant on her lunch break one year after the rape, Lori is still looking for answers.

When I moved here, nobody knew about it. I just figured, this only happened to me. Then my roommate told me it happened to her in Ohio. We talked about it once and that was it. It just upset me too much to talk about it anymore. I mean, she understood, it upset her a lot, too, so we just don't bring it up.

How do other women handle it? I work two jobs and I go to school because I don't want to have to deal with the situation of having somebody ask me on a date. If I go out with a guy, I'm wondering, is he thinking dinner means "I'll get you into bed"?

I'm not going to be stupid enough to put myself in that situation again. I grew out of being naive just like that. This experience grew me up in about two weeks.

Jill: A Teenager

Jill lives in a cottage in the fog-shrouded foothills of Washington state near where

she grew up. Now 25, she works hard all day at her secretarial job and then comes home to help her 8-year-old son Donny with his homework. Jill loves her son, but she tries to block the memory of why she became a mother at such a young age: Donny is the result of a date rape that happened when Jill was 16, during the summer between her junior and senior year in high school.

She was on an outing with several male and female friends to a lake when she met the man who would later rape her.

We asked him to come over and sit with us. Later on, I gave him my phone number and he called me up to take me out. He was really cute, but he was older.

His seeming maturity (he was in his early 20s) made him attractive, as did his sandy-colored beard and hair and the fact that he was a carpenter, not a high schooler. But Jill worried about what her parents would think. She still didn't date much, although, unknown to her mother and father, she had had one experience of sexual intercourse with a steady boyfriend her own age several months before.

The day of the date arrived and the sandy-haired man rode up to Jill's house on a motorcycle. She climbed aboard and they drove further into the countryside, to a secluded spot near a river.

We were talking, it was just like a date, you know, when he pulled a gun out of the bag on the back of his motorcycle and started playing with it. I don't like guns. My parents don't have guns. I said, "Oh, gee, that's not loaded, is it?" and he said, "Oh, yeah."

I was very scared.

Jill's date laid the gun down on the blanket they were sharing. He then put his arm around her and started kissing her, but just briefly. He almost immediately proceeded to have intercourse with her.

I remember at the time I thought, "Just go along, it doesn't matter." I didn't want to take any chances. I just wanted to get home and get out of that situation.

Like date rapists then and now, the handsome carpenter never thought about birth control or the possibility of sexually transmitting disease to his victim. He drove her home and Jill was grounded for being late; she went to her room vowing to tell no one.

She made good on that vow for several months, until her pregnancy forced her to confide in a friend. Jill wanted to have an abortion until the medical procedure that would be used was explained to her. That, coupled with her parents' feelings against abortion, led her to decide to remain pregnant and keep the child. Always a good student, Jill went through her senior year pregnant and maintained an A average. She went to graduation with her son in her arms and her dreams of going to art school set aside; instead, she faced the reality of supporting a child.

Rachel: A College Student

Rachel blends in easily with the attractive young crowd filling a downtown Boston street on a mild spring afternoon. Her spiky short brown hair is the arty fashion of the season; her big hoop earrings mimic the large roundness of her eyes. She comes from an intelligent and loving family. Her father is a lawyer; her mother teaches.

Rachel was raped during her freshman year in college. She has never told her parents.

I was at a big university. We had coed dorms, with two hallways on each floor being girls and two hallways were guys. This guy was a football player, about six foot five and 265 pounds. I knew he lived down the hall from me, but I didn't really know him. I thought he was an attractive guy. He was a junior.

There was a party on our floor with all the guys and girls from our floor. There were kegs and stuff. The drinking age was 18, but even though I wasn't

quite 18 they let me into the party. We had already been drinking a lot and we got to the party and this guy [the football player] was talking to me.

Rachel was flattered by the attention.

He wasn't drinking, but he was feeding me alcohol. He asked me to come back to his room—it was right down the hall from where all of us were. I was just so out of it, I said, "Sure." I had no idea. I didn't think he'd hurt me.

I thought there would be other people there. I thought it was just like, "Let's get out of this party." When we got to his room and I saw there was nobody there, I didn't think I could do anything about it.

We started kissing and then he started taking off my clothes. I kept telling him to stop and I was crying. I was scared of him and thought he was going to hurt me. . . . He had a hand over my face. I was five foot two and weighed 110 pounds. I didn't have any choice.

The assault lasted about half an hour. When it was over, Rachel went to her own room, just down the hall. She went to sleep praying that she wasn't pregnant.

I just wanted to block it out. I felt ashamed because it happened. I just felt dirty, violated. I thought it was my fault. It wasn't like he did something to me, it was like I let him do something to me, so I felt very bad about myself.

He came to my room the next day and wanted to go out with me. He felt that was the normal thing to do, I guess.

Rachel turned him down, but offered no explanation. She also did not report the rape.

Who would believe me? He was a really good football player. No one would have believed me if I said anything. I wouldn't have dreamed of saying anything.

Rachel's perception about not being believed would prove prescient. Later that year, her residence hall adviser (an older student) was raped by another athlete who came into her room as she lay in bed in a drunken stupor after a party. A university disciplinary board decided that since the woman was unconscious, the action could only be considered sexual misconduct, not rape. The male student received a light reprimand.

Four years later, Rachel finally began to tell people about the rape. Her friends, men and women, have been sympathetic and supportive. One friend even related her own date-rape experience. Talking about it has helped in Rachel's recovery, helped her believe in herself again. "I made some stupid choices, but him hurting me is not my fault," she says.

You know, you're away from home for the first time and you want to go wild. You don't know what you're getting into. You just don't think people are going to hurt you.

I just had no concept that anyone would do something like that to me.

Paula: A Young Single Working Woman

Paula is a social service professional who lives in the South with her young daughter. When she was 22, she worked as a hospital ward clerk at a Virginia medical facility. For several weeks, one of the young doctors, a resident specializing in the care of cancer patients, had been pressuring her to go out with him. "He had kind of a reputation (for dating a lot of women) around the hospital," she says. "I was aware of that, which is probably why I resisted seeing him for so long." But he was tall, good-looking, and successful, traits which probably had much to do with his popularity. "He had been bugging me for maybe two months, saying, 'I just want you to come over for dinner. Nothing's going to happen.' I mean, he made a really big production out of assuring me of that," she says.

Paula had recently broken up with her boyfriend. The doctor's fiancée lived out of town. After talking with him several times, she decided that he was just trying to be friendly.

I thought how nice it would be to spend a platonic evening with a sympathetic ear. The first couple of hours were just that— good conversation, a wonderful meal, and a bottle of wine. He lived in a nice apartment with expensive furniture.

After we finished eating, I felt ready to go. He pleaded with me to stay a bit longer. He had some pot he wanted to share and told me that it would relax me and lift my spirits.

Paula had smoked marijuana before, but never anything as potent. Looking back now, she believes it was medical-strength marijuana, the kind that is sometimes given by prescription to chemotherapy patients to ease their pain.

I got real delusional. I felt like I was having hallucinations. I remember his face and it seemed disconnected from his body. It was distorted. I can remember losing muscular control.

Her date, however, was having no such problem. He took off her clothes and dragged her up some stairs to a bedroom.

I started to cry. It was the only coping mechanism I had. I remember saying, "No, no, no," and crying profusely.

I remember feeling like it was never going to stop. He was able to maintain an erection for a long time without coming. I remember thinking, "Oh, I can't stand this anymore. Either I have to die or he has to stop." It got to the point where the crying wasn't working; nothing was working. I was feeling like I was going to burst if he didn't stop doing these things to me because it was oral sex and he tried anal sex. He was forcing me to have oral sex and I said something like, "I'm going to throw up," and I think that's what spurred him to finish.

He finished and that's when I was really in shock. I was in denial and disbelief up to that point, but when it was over with, I was very much in shock and really quite unable to maneuver around much. I think he must have helped me get dressed and sort of dragged me to the door. His demeanor was real sheepish.

I remember somehow getting in my car, somehow driving home. I have no idea how I got home, none whatsoever. I'm lucky I didn't kill somebody on the road.

Paula went home and told her sister-in-law, who immediately wanted to go back and confront the man. Instead, Paula made her promise that she wouldn't tell anyone. Several days later, Paula saw the doctor at work; she glared ferociously at him, but said nothing.

Acquaintance rape was an unknown thing, at least in my world it was, so the anger at him was in the form of "You lied to me. You tricked me. You conned me." I was aware of that, but I was totally unaware that what he had done to me was a crime. I had no idea I could report it to the police. I had no idea I could charge him with anything.

A month later I moved more than a thousand miles away and lived with my folks for a while. I couldn't stand my father to touch me; I didn't even like to be real close to him. I just didn't want any bodily contact at all.

I cut off all my hair. I did not want to be attractive to men. I started wearing real androgynous clothes—nothing tight, nothing revealing—and reduced my makeup to almost nil. I just wanted to look neutered for a while because that felt safer.

It was several years before Paula started dating again, years filled with anger and distrust and

sexual problems. As for the man who assaulted her, she did not speak to him before she quit her job and left town. But she has thought about him since.

At the time, it never crossed my mind that he would do this again and again. Now I am acutely aware that he probably used the same plan of action to rape a lot of women.

Deborah: An Older Woman

Deborah had been married for 15 years when she and her husband separated. Among her friends at the time was a man named Alex.

Alex and I had been good friends for about five years. We were both involved in community activities for children, mainly softball.

During the first four months [of the separation], Alex and I became closer. He helped me tremendously mentally. One thing led to another and we became sexually intimate. That lasted approximately six weeks.

Deborah, who was 34 at the time, and her husband decided to try to make their marriage work again. Alex was not happy with her decision. After six months, she and her husband again separated. Alex was ready to begin their relationship again, but she told him she needed time alone. One night, drunk and angry, Alex confronted her outside a restaurant near their California hometown. He threw her against a wall and started to choke her. She kneed him in the crotch, broke free, and ran inside where a female friend was waiting. Alex jumped in his car and drove off.

My friend and I left. She wanted me to spend the night with her because she was afraid for me. I told her I'd be okay and went on home.

At 4:00 A.M., I woke up with a start. Alex was standing over me, just staring. I told him if he didn't leave, I would call the police. He made no response. I picked up the phone, he grabbed it, ripped it out of the wall, and came after me. He started hitting me, throwing me, and became verbally abusive.

At one point I grabbed a ceramic bowl and hit him on the head with it as hard as I could. He didn't even flinch. Blood was everywhere.

Finally he got me pinned down on the bed. There was no fight left in me.

Then, as sometimes happens in rapes, Alex lost his erection although he had partially penetrated Deborah. He screamed at her and began hitting her again. He told her to lie still on the bed. When she moved, he would hit her. Finally, he got dressed and left, without ejaculating. He had been there for two hours.

There was enough evidence that I didn't have to press charges—the D.A. did. Alex was arrested that morning . . . on charges of rape, burglary, assault, and destruction of telephone equipment. At the preliminary hearing he plea-bargained to assault with attempt to rape. He pleaded guilty and got four years. He's now in state prison.

My year anniversary [of the rape] is coming up, but I feel I'll do fine. I have a lot of family and friend support. The only exception is my ex-husband. He says I got what I deserved.

Pornography

In recent years a strong movement to censor pornography has arisen. Feminists and religious leaders, often for somewhat different reasons, have worked together to shut down pornographic movie houses and video rental stores and to eliminate the sale of certain sexually explicit magazines. The debate over whether sexually explicit material degrades women, causes sexual violence, and endangers public morality, or whether it simply is a form of harmless free expression with important social functions, is not likely to be resolved.

In *Roth* v *United States* (1957), the Supreme Court declared that "obscene" material is not constitutionally protected speech. Hence, such material can be censored without the need to "strictly scrutinize" the purposes of the law. Since no constitutional right is violated, legislators need only show a "rational relation to a legitimate state end" (as opposed to a "necessary means to a compelling state interest" when a constitutional right is violated). This did not mean, of course, that pornographic materials were then to be eliminated.

In 1970 the Commission on Obscenity and Pornography recommended to then-President Richard Nixon that all legislation prohibiting the sale of pornographic material to consenting adults be eliminated. Although the committee was careful to reaffirm the view that minors and nonconsenting adults must be protected from obscene materials, it concluded that there was no significant harm to the individual who watches pornography or any link between the distribution of pornography and criminal behavior. Needless to say, President Nixon, many members of Congress, and much of the public were less than pleased with this conclusion.

In 1985, President Ronald Reagan's Attorney General, Edwin Meese, formed another commission to study the effects of pornography. This commission strongly endorsed the procensorship position. In fact, the Meese Commission found that violent and nonviolent but degrading pornography relates significantly to sexual violence and antisocial attitudes and that child pornography relates directly to child abuse.

Like the Meese Commission, those who argue against pornography feel that there is a definite link between pornography and violent antisocial behavior. Men are more inclined to rape, assault, sexually harass, and generally be violent toward women after watching pornography, it is said. This connection, of course, is widely debated.

The claim is also made that pornography is harmful to those who watch it. The dehumanizing element in pornography and the lies it teaches about both male and female sexuality make it damaging to those who see it. Furthermore, it is argued that pornography challenges the moral and social framework of our society; decay in our shared moral values leads to a breakdown of the family structure.

Feminists argue that pornography is degrading to women and therefore must be eliminated, although they have no objection to sexually explicit material per se. Thus feminists draw the distinction between pornography (i.e., sexually explicit material that is degrading to women) and erotica (sexually explicit material that depicts sexuality in a mutually empowering manner).

Those who argue against censorship maintain that there is no connection between pornography and violent crime. Indeed, some even contend that it may reduce such crime by satisfying fantasies that would otherwise be acted out.

As for harm to self, the claim is made that no one has any business telling another what is for his or her own good. Censorship in an open society is wrong, regardless of the constitutional status of obscene material. Furthermore, Justice William Brennan, in his dissenting opinion in *Paris Adult Theatre I* v *Slaton* (1973), argues that the concept "obscene" is so vague that any widespread attempt to censor pornography will necessarily tread on constitutionally protected material.

It is important to note that not all pornography depicts women. Pornography depicting males is central to much of the gay community. Hence, when feminists wish to censor pornography and shut down pornographic shops because it causes violence to women, they often end up shutting down one of the few avenues for gay male sexuality.

It has also been suggested that pornography plays an important role in the lives of disabled men who are not able to have any substantial sex lives. Men who are confined to wheelchairs and in hospitals often find pornographic materials to be their only available means of sexuality.

Another argument is that pornography is no more degrading to women than are advertising and other media. Many daytime soaps are extremely sexually explicit and depict women in degrading and dehumanizing positions, as do commercials and other advertisements. Opponents, to be consistent, would have to advocate widespread censorship of material that is clearly constitutionally protected.

34. Pornography, Civil Rights, and Speech

Catharine MacKinnon

Catharine MacKinnon, along with Andrea Dworkin, has been arguing, often in court and before legislators, that pornography is a form of sex discrimination that is injurious to women. She asserts that, since pornography legitimizes violence against women and children, laws should be passed prohibiting the production, sale, and distribution of pornographic material.

. . . There is a belief that this is a society in which women and men are basically equals. Room for marginal corrections is conceded, flaws are known to exist, attempts are made to correct what are conceived as occasional lapses from the basic condition of sex equality. Sex discrimination law has concentrated most of its focus on these occasional lapses. It is difficult to overestimate the extent to which this belief in equality is an article of faith for most people, including most women, who wish to live in self-respect in an internal universe, even (perhaps especially) if not in the world. It is also partly an expression of natural law thinking: if we are inalienably equal, we can't "really" be degraded.

This is a world in which it is worth trying. In this world of presumptive equality, people make money based on their training or abilities or diligence or qualifications. They are

For permission to photocopy this selection, please contact Harvard University Press. Reprinted by permission of the publisher from *Feminism Unmodified,* by Catharine MacKinnon. Cambridge, MA: Harvard University Press. Copyright © 1987 by the President and Fellows of Harvard College.

employed and advanced on the basis of merit. In this world of just deserts, if someone is abused, it is thought to violate the basic rules of the community. If it doesn't, victims are seen to have done something they could have chosen to do differently, by exercise of will or better judgment. Maybe such people have placed themselves in a situation of vulnerability to physical abuse. Maybe they have done something provocative. Or maybe they were just unusually unlucky. In such a world, if such a person has an experience, there are words for it. When they speak and say it, they are listened to. If they write about it, they will be published. If certain experiences are never spoken about, if certain people or issues are seldom heard from, it is supposed that silence has been chosen. The law, including much of the law of sex discrimination and the First Amendment, operates largely within the realm of these beliefs.

Feminism is the discovery that women do not live in this world, that the person occupying this realm is a man, so much more a man if he is white and wealthy. This world of potential credibility, authority, security, and just rewards, recognition of one's identity and capacity, is a world that some people do inhabit as a condition of birth, with variations among them. It is not a basic condition accorded humanity in this society, but a prerogative of status, a privilege, among other things, of gender.

I call this a discovery because it has not been an assumption. Feminism is the first theory, the first practice, the first movement, to take seriously the situation of all women from the point of view of all women, both on our situation and on social life as a whole. The discovery has therefore been made that the implicit social content of humanism, as well as the standpoint from which legal method has been designed and injuries have been defined, has not been women's standpoint. Defining feminism in a way that connects epistemology with power as the politics of women's point of view, this discovery can be summed up by saying that women live in another world: specifically, a world of *not* equality, a world of inequality.

Looking at the world from this point of view, a whole shadow world of previously invisible silent abuse has been discerned. Rape, battery, sexual harassment, forced prostitution, and the sexual abuse of children emerge as common and systematic. We find that rape happens to women in all contexts, from the family, including rape of girls and babies, to students and women in the workplace, on the streets, at home, in their own bedrooms by men they do not know and by men they do know, by men they are married to, men they have had a social conversation with, and least often, men they have never seen before. Overwhelmingly, rape is something that men do or attempt to do to women (44 percent of American women according to a recent study) at some point in our lives. Sexual harassment of women by men is common in workplaces and educational institutions. Based on reports in one study of the federal workforce, up to 85 percent of women will experience it, many in physical forms. Between a quarter and a third of women are battered in their homes by men. Thirty-eight percent of little girls are sexually molested inside or outside the family. Until women listened to women, this world of sexual abuse was *not spoken* of. It was the unspeakable. What I am saying is, if you *are* the tree falling in the epistemological forest, your demise

doesn't make a sound if no one is listening. Women did not "report" these events, and overwhelmingly do not today, because no one is listening, because no one believes us. This silence does not mean nothing happened, and it does not mean consent. It is the silence of women of which Adrienne Rich has written, "Do not confuse it with any kind of absence."

Believing women who say we are sexually violated has been a radical departure, both methodologically and legally. The extent and nature of rape, marital rape, and sexual harassment itself, were discovered in this way. Domestic battery as a syndrome, almost a habit, was discovered through refusing to believe that when a woman is assaulted by a man to whom she is connected, that it is not an assault. The sexual abuse of children was uncovered, Freud notwithstanding, by believing that children were not making up all this sexual abuse. Now what is striking is that when each discovery is made, and somehow made real in the world, the response has been: it happens to men too. If women are hurt, men are hurt. If women are raped, men are raped. If women are sexually harassed, men are sexually harassed. If women are battered, men are battered. Symmetry must be reasserted. Neutrality must be reclaimed. Equality must be reestablished.

The only areas where the available evidence supports this, where anything like what happens to women also happens to men, involve children—little boys are sexually abused—and prison. The liberty of prisoners is restricted, their freedom restrained, their humanity systematically diminished, their bodies and emotions confined, defined, and regulated. If paid at all, they are paid starvation wages. They can be tortured at will, and it is passed off as discipline or as means to a just end. They become compliant. They can be raped at will, at any moment, and nothing will be done about it. When they scream, nobody hears. To be a prisoner means to be defined as a member of a group for whom the rules of what can be done to you, of what is seen as abuse of you, are reduced as part of the definition of your status. To be a woman is that kind of definition and has that kind of meaning.

Men *are* damaged by sexism. (By men I mean the status of masculinity that is accorded to males on the basis of their biology but is not itself biological.) But whatever the damage of sexism to men, the condition of being a man is not defined as subordinate to women by force. Looking at the facts of the abuses of women all at once, you see that a woman is socially defined as a person who, whether or not she is or has been, can be treated in these ways by men at any time, and little, if anything, will be done about it. This is what it means when feminists say that maleness is a form of power and femaleness is a form of powerlessness.

In this context, all of this "men too" stuff means that people don't really believe that the things I have just said are true, though there really is little question about their empirical accuracy. The data are extremely simple, like women's pay figure of fifty-nine cents on the dollar. People don't really seem to believe that either. Yet there is no question of its empirical validity. This is the workplace story: what women do is seen as not worth much, or what is not worth much is seen as something for women to do. *Women* are seen as not worth much, is the thing. Now why are these basic realities of the subordination of women to men, for example, that only 7.8 percent of women have never been sexually assaulted, not effectively believed, not perceived as real in the face of all this evidence? Why don't *women* believe our own experiences? In the face of all this evidence, especially of systematic sexual abuse—subjection to violence with impunity is one extreme expression, although not the only expression, of a degraded status—the view that basically the sexes are equal in this society remains unchallenged and unchanged. The day I got this was the day I understood its real message, its real coherence: *This is equality for us.*

I could describe this, but I couldn't explain it until I started studying a lot of pornography. In pornography, there it is, in one place, all of the abuses that women had to struggle so long even to begin to articulate, all the *unspeakable* abuse: the rape, the battery, the sexual harassment, the prostitution, and the sexual abuse of children. Only in the pornography it is called something else: sex, sex, sex, sex, and sex, respectively. Pornography sexualizes rape, battery, sexual harassment, prostitution, and child sexual abuse; it thereby celebrates, promotes, authorizes, and legitimizes them. More generally, it eroticizes the dominance and submission that is the dynamic common to them all. It makes hierarchy sexy and calls that "the truth about sex" or just a mirror of reality. Through this process pornography constructs what a woman is as what men want from sex. This is what the pornography means.

Pornography constructs what a woman is in terms of its view of what men want sexually, such that acts of rape, battery, sexual harassment, prostitution, and sexual abuse of children become acts of sexual equality. Pornography's world of equality is a harmonious and balanced place. Men and women are perfectly complementary and perfectly bipolar. Women's desire to be fucked by men is equal to men's desire to fuck women. All the ways men love to take and violate women, women love to be taken and violated. The women who most love this are most men's equals, the most liberated; the most participatory child is the most grown-up, the most equal to an adult. Their consent merely expresses or ratifies these preexisting facts.

The content of pornography is one thing. There, women substantively desire dispossession and cruelty. We desperately want to be bound, battered, tortured, humiliated, and killed. Or, to be fair to the soft core, merely taken and used. This is erotic to the male point of view. Subjection itself, with self-determination ecstatically relinquished, is the content of women's sexual desire and desirability. Women are there to be violated and possessed, men to violate and possess us, either on screen or by camera or pen on behalf of the consumer. On a simple descriptive level, the inequality of hierarchy, of which gender is the primary one, seems necessary for sexual arousal to work. Other added inequalities identify various pornographic genres or subthemes, although they are always added through gender: age, disability, homosexuality, animals, objects, race (including anti-Semitism), and so on. Gender is never irrelevant.

What pornography *does* goes beyond its content: it eroticizes hierarchy, it sexualizes inequality. It makes dominance and submission into sex. Inequality is its central dynamic; the illusion of freedom coming together with the reality of force is central to its working.

Perhaps because this is a bourgeois culture, the victim must look free, appear to be freely acting. Choice is how she got there. Willing is what she is when she is being equal. It seems equally important that then and there she actually be forced and that forcing be communicated on some level, even if only through still photos of her in postures of receptivity and access, available for penetration. Pornography in this view is a form of forced sex, a practice of sexual politics, an institution of gender inequality.

From this perspective, pornography is neither harmless fantasy nor a corrupt and confused misrepresentation of an otherwise natural and healthy sexual situation. It institutionalizes the sexuality of male supremacy, fusing the erotization of dominance and submission with the social construction of male and female. To the extent that gender is sexual, pornography is part of constituting the meaning of that sexuality. Men treat women as who they see women as being. Pornography constructs who that is. Men's power over women means that the way men see women defines who women can be. Pornography is that way. Pornography is not imagery in some relation to a reality elsewhere constructed. It is not a distortion, reflection, projection, expression, fantasy, representation, or symbol either. It is a sexual reality.

In Andrea Dworkin's definitive work, *Pornography: Men Possessing Women,* sexuality itself is a social construct gendered to the ground. Male dominance here is not an artificial overlay upon an underlying inalterable substratum of uncorrupted essential sexual being. Dworkin presents a sexual theory of gender inequality of which pornography is a constitutive practice. The way pornography produces its meaning constructs and defines men and women as such. Gender has no basis in anything other than the social reality its hegemony constructs. Gender is what gender means. The process that gives sexuality its male supremacist meaning is the same process through which gender inequality becomes socially real.

In this approach, the experience of the (overwhelmingly) male audiences who consume pornography is therefore not fantasy or simulation or catharsis but sexual reality, the

level of reality on which sex itself largely operates. Understanding this dimension of the problem does not require noticing that pornography models are real women to whom, in most cases, something real is being done; nor does it even require inquiring into the systematic infliction of pornography and its sexuality upon women, although it helps. What matters is the way in which the pornography itself provides what those who consume it want. Pornography *participates* in its audience's eroticism through creating an accessible sexual object, the possession and consumption of which *is* male sexuality, as socially constructed; to be consumed and possessed as which, *is* female sexuality, as socially constructed; pornography is a process that constructs it that way.

The object world is constructed according to how it looks with respect to its possible uses. Pornography defines women by how we look according to how we can be sexually used. Pornography codes how to look at women, so you know what you can do with one when you see one. Gender is an assignment made visually, both originally and in everyday life. A sex object is defined on the basis of its looks, in terms of its usability for sexual pleasure, such that both the looking—the quality of the gaze, including its point of view—and the definition according to use become eroticized as part of the sex itself. This is what the feminist concept "sex object" means. In this sense, sex in life is no less mediated than it is in art. Men have sex with their image of a woman. It is not that life and art imitate each other; in this sexuality, they *are* each other.

To give a set of rough epistemological translations, to defend pornography as consistent with the equality of the sexes is to defend the subordination of women to men as sexual equality. What in the pornographic view is love and romance looks a great deal like hatred and torture to the feminist. Pleasure and eroticism become violation. Desire appears as lust for dominance and submission. The vulnerability of women's projected sexual availability, that acting we are allowed (that is, asking to be acted upon), is victimization. Play conforms to scripted roles. Fantasy expresses ideology, is not exempt from it. Admiration of natural physical beauty becomes objectification. Harmlessness becomes harm. Pornography is a harm of male supremacy made difficult to see because of its pervasiveness, potency, and, principally, because of its success in making the world a pornographic place. Specifically, its harm cannot be discerned, and will not be addressed, if viewed and approached neutrally, because it *is* so much of "what is." In other words, to the extent pornography succeeds in constructing social reality, it becomes invisible as harm. If we live in a world that pornography creates through the power of men in a male-dominated situation, the issue is not what the harm of pornography is, but how that harm is to become visible.

Obscenity law provides a very different analysis and conception of the problem of pornography. In 1973 the legal definition of obscenity became that which the average person, applying contemporary community standards, would find that, taken as a whole, appeals to the prurient interest; that which depicts or describes in a patently offensive way—you feel like you're a cop reading someone's *Miranda* rights—sexual conduct specifically defined by the applicable state law; and that which, taken as a whole, lacks serious literary, artistic, political or scientific value. Feminism doubts whether the average person gender-neutral exists; has more questions about the content and process of defining what community standards are than it does about deviations from them; wonders why prurience counts but powerlessness does not and why sensibilities are better protected from offense than women are from exploitation; defines sexuality, and thus its violation and expropriation, more broadly than does state law; and questions why a body of law that has not in practice been able to tell rape from intercourse should, without further guidance, be entrusted with telling pornography from anything less. Taking the work "as a whole" ignores that which the victims of pornography have long known: legitimate settings diminish the perception of injury done to those whose trivialization and objectification they contextualize. Besides, and this is a heavy one, if a woman is subjected, why should it matter that the work has other value? Maybe what re-

deems the work's value is what enhances its injury to women, not to mention that existing standards of literature, art, science, and politics, examined in a feminist light, are remarkably consonant with pornography's mode, meaning, and message. And finally—first and foremost, actually—although the subject of these materials is overwhelmingly women, their contents almost entirely made up of women's bodies, our invisibility has been such, our equation as a sex *with* sex has been such, that the law of obscenity has never even considered pornography a women's issue.

Obscenity, in this light, is a moral idea, an idea about judgments of good and bad. Pornography, by contrast, is a political practice, a practice of power and powerlessness. Obscenity is ideational and abstract; pornography is concrete and substantive. The two concepts represent two entirely different things. Nudity, excess of candor, arousal or excitement, prurient appeal, illegality of the acts depicted, and unnaturalness or perversion are all qualities that bother obscenity law when sex is depicted or portrayed. Sex forced on real women so that it can be sold at a profit and forced on other real women: women's bodies trussed and maimed and raped and made into things to be hurt and obtained and accessed, and this presented as the nature of women in a way that is acted on and acted out, over and over; the coercion that is visible and the coercion that has become invisible—this and more bothers feminists about pornography. Obscenity as such probably does little harm. Pornography is integral to attitudes and behaviors of violence and discrimination that define the treatment and status of half the population.

At the request of the city of Minneapolis, Andrea Dworkin and I conceived and designed a local human rights ordinance in accordance with our approach to the pornography issue. We define pornography as a practice of sex discrimination, a violation of women's civil rights, the opposite of sexual equality. Its point is to hold those who profit from and benefit from that injury accountable to those who are injured. It means that women's injury—our damage, our pain, our enforced inferiority—should outweigh their pleasure and their profits, or sex equality is meaningless.

We define pornography as the graphic sexually explicit subordination of women through pictures or words that also includes women dehumanized as sexual objects, things, or commodities; enjoying pain or humiliation or rape; being tied up, cut up, mutilated, bruised, or physically hurt; in postures of sexual submission or servility or display; reduced to body parts, penetrated by objects or animals, or presented in scenarios of degradation, injury, torture; shown as filthy or inferior; bleeding, bruised, or hurt in a context that makes these conditions sexual. Erotica, defined by distinction as not this, might be sexually explicit materials premised on equality. We also provide that the use of men, children, or transsexuals in the place of women is pornography. The definition is substantive in that it is sex-specific, but it covers everyone in a sex-specific way, so is gender neutral in overall design. . . .

This law aspires to guarantee women's rights consistent with the First Amendment by making visible a conflict of rights between the equality guaranteed to all women and what, in some legal sense, is now the freedom of the pornographers to make and sell, and their consumers to have access to, the materials this ordinance defines. Judicial resolution of this conflict, if the judges do for women what they have done for others, is likely to entail a balancing of the rights of women arguing that our lives and opportunities, including our freedom of speech and action, are constrained by—and in many cases flatly precluded by, in, and through—pornography, against those who argue that the pornography is harmless, or harmful only in part but not in the whole of the definition; or that it is more important to preserve the pornography than it is to prevent or remedy whatever harm it does.

In predicting how a court would balance these interests, it is important to understand that this ordinance cannot now be said to be either conclusively legal or illegal under existing law or precedent, although I think the weight of authority is on our side. This ordinance enunciates a new form of the previously recognized governmental interest in sex equality. Many laws make sex equality a governmental interest. Our law is designed to

further the equality of the sexes, to help make sex equality real. Pornography is a practice of discrimination on the basis of sex, on one level because of its role in creating and maintaining sex as a basis for discrimination. It harms many women one at a time and helps keep all women in an inferior status by defining our subordination as our sexuality and equating that with our gender. It is also sex discrimination because its victims, including men, are selected for victimization on the basis of their gender. But for their sex, they would not be so treated.

The harm of pornography, broadly speaking, is the harm of the civil inequality of the sexes made invisible as harm because it has become accepted as the sex difference. Consider this analogy with race: if you see Black people as different, there is no harm to segregation; it is merely a recognition of that difference. To neutral principles, separate but equal was equal. The injury of racial separation to Blacks arises "solely because [they] choose to put that construction upon it." Epistemologically translated: how you see it is not the way it is. Similarly, if you see women as just different, even or especially if you don't know that you do, subordination will not look like subordination at all, much less like harm. It will merely look like an appropriate recognition of the sex difference.

Pornography does treat the sexes differently, so the case for sex differentiation can be made here. But men as a group do not tend to be (although some individuals may be) treated the way women are treated in pornography. As a social group, men are not hurt by pornography the way women as a social group are. Their social status is not defined as *less* by it. So the major argument does not turn on mistaken differentiation, particularly since the treatment of women according to pornography's dictates makes it all too often accurate. The salient quality of a distinction between the top and the bottom in a hierarchy is not difference, although top is certainly different from bottom; it is power. So the major argument is: subordinate but equal is not equal.

Particularly since this is a new legal theory, a new law, and "new" facts, perhaps the situation of women it newly exposes deserves to be considered on its own terms. Why do the problems of 53 percent of the population have to look like somebody else's problems before they can be recognized as existing? Then, too, they can't be addressed if they do look like other people's problems, about which something might have to be done if something is done about these. This construction of the situation truly deserves inquiry. Limiting the justification for this law to the situation of the sexes would serve to limit the precedential value of a favorable ruling.

Its particularity to one side, the *approach* to the injury is supported by a whole array of prior decisions that have justified exceptions to First Amendment guarantees when something that matters is seen to be directly at stake. What unites many cases in which speech interests are raised and implicated but not, on balance, protected, is harm, harm that counts. In some existing exceptions, the definitions are much more open-ended than ours. In some the sanctions are more severe, or potentially more so. For instance, ours is a civil law; most others, although not all, are criminal. Almost no other exceptions show as many people directly affected. Evidence of harm in other cases tends to be vastly less concrete and more conjectural, which is not to say that there is necessarily less of it. None of the previous cases addresses a problem of this scope or magnitude—for instance, an eight-billion-dollar-a-year industry. Nor do other cases address an abuse that has such widespread legitimacy. Courts have seen harm in other cases. The question is, will they see it here, especially given that the pornographers got there first. I will confine myself here to arguing from cases on harm to people, on the supposition that, the pornographers notwithstanding, women are not flags. . . .

To reach the magnitude of this problem on the scale it exists, our law makes trafficking in pornography—production, sale, exhibition, or distribution—actionable. Under the obscenity rubric, much legal and psychological scholarship has centered on a search for the elusive link between harm and pornography defined as obscenity. Although they were not very clear on what obscenity was, it was its harm they truly could not find. They looked

high and low—in the mind of the male consumer, in society or in its "moral fabric," in correlations between variations in levels of antisocial acts and liberalization of obscenity laws. The only harm they have found has been harm to "the social interest in order and morality." Until recently, no one looked very persistently for harm to women, particularly harm to women through men. The rather obvious fact that the sexes *relate* has been overlooked in the inquiry into the male consumer and his mind. The pornography doesn't just drop out of the sky, go into his head, and stop there. Specifically, men rape, batter, prostitute, molest, and sexually harass women. Under conditions of inequality, they also hire, fire, promote, and grade women, decide how much or whether we are worth paying and for what, define and approve and disapprove of women in ways that count, that determine our lives.

If women are not just born to be sexually used, the fact that we are seen and treated as though that is what we are born for becomes something in need of explanation. If we see that men relate to women in a pattern of who they see women as being, and that forms a pattern of inequality, it becomes important to ask where that view came from or, minimally, how it is perpetuated or escalated. Asking this requires asking different questions about pornography than the ones obscenity law made salient.

Now I'm going to talk about causality in its narrowest sense. Recent experimental research on pornography shows that the materials covered by our definition cause measurable harm to women through increasing men's attitudes and behaviors of discrimination in both violent and nonviolent forms. Exposure to some of the pornography in our definition increases the immediately subsequent willingness of normal men to aggress against women under laboratory conditions. It makes normal men more closely resemble convicted rapists attitudinally, although as a group they don't look all that different from them to start with. Exposure to pornography also significantly increases attitudinal measures known to correlate with rape and self-reports of aggressive acts, measures such as hostility toward women, propensity to rape, condoning rape, and predicting that one would rape or force sex on a woman if one knew one would not get caught. On this latter measure, by the way, about a third of all men predict that they would rape, and half would force sex on a woman.

As to that pornography covered by our definition in which normal research subjects seldom perceive violence, long-term exposure still makes them see women as more worthless, trivial, nonhuman, and objectlike, that is, the way those who are discriminated against are seen by those who discriminate against them. Crucially, all pornography by our definition acts dynamically over time to diminish the consumer's ability to distinguish sex from violence. The materials work behaviorally to diminish the capacity of men (but not women) to perceive that an account of a rape is an account of a rape. The so-called sex-only materials, those in which subjects perceive no force, also increase perceptions that a rape victim is worthless and decrease the perception that she was harmed. The overall direction of current research suggests that the more expressly violent materials accomplish with less exposure what the less overtly violent— that is, the so-called sex-only materials— accomplish over the longer term. Women are rendered fit for use and targeted for abuse. The only thing that the research cannot document is which individual women will be next on the list. (This cannot be documented experimentally because of ethics constraints on the researchers—constraints that do not operate in life.) Although the targeting is systematic on the basis of sex, for individuals it is random. They are selected on a roulette basis. Pornography can no longer be said to be just a mirror. It does not just reflect the world or some people's perceptions. It *moves* them. It increases attitudes that are lived out, circumscribing the status of half the population.

What the experimental data predict will happen actually does happen in women's real lives. You know, it's fairly frustrating that women have known for some time that these things do happen. As Ed Donnerstein, an experimental researcher in this area, often puts it, "We just quantify the obvious." It is women,

primarily, to whom the research results have been the obvious, because we live them. But not until a laboratory study predicts that these things *will* happen do people begin to believe you when you say they *did* happen to you. There is no—*not any*—inconsistency between the patterns the laboratory studies predict and the data on what actually happens to real women. Show me an abuse of women in society, I'll show it to you made sex in the pornography. If you want to know who is being hurt in this society, go see what is being done and to whom in pornography and then go look for them other places in the world. You will find them being hurt in just that way. We did in our hearings.

In our hearings women spoke, to my knowledge for the first time in history in public, about the damage pornography does to them. We learned that pornography is used to break women, to train women to sexual submission, to season women, to terrorize women, and to silence their dissent. It is this that has previously been termed "having no effect." The way men inflict on women the sex they experience through the pornography gives women no choice about seeing the pornography or doing the sex. Asked if anyone ever tried to inflict unwanted sex acts on them that they knew came from pornography, 10 percent of women in a recent random study said yes. Among married women, 24 percent said yes. That is a lot of women. A lot more don't know. Some of those who do testified in Minneapolis. One wife said of her ex-husband, "He would read from the pornography like a textbook, like a journal. In fact when he asked me to be bound, when he finally convinced me to do it, he read in the magazine how to tie the knots." Another woman said of her boyfriend. "[H]e went to this party, saw pornography, got an erection, got me . . . to inflict his erection on . . . There is a direct causal relationship there." One woman, who said her husband had rape and bondage magazines all over the house, discovered two suitcases full of Barbie dolls with rope tied on their arms and legs and with tape across their mouths. Now think about the silence of women. She said, "He used to tie me up and he tried those things on me." A therapist in private practice reported:

Presently or recently I have worked with clients who have been sodomized by broom handles, forced to have sex with over 20 dogs in the back seat of their car, tied up and then electrocuted on their genitals. These are children, [all] in the ages of 14 to 18, all of whom [have been directly affected by pornography,] [e]ither where the perpetrator has read the manuals and manuscripts at night and used these as recipe books by day or had the pornography present at the time of the sexual violence.

One woman, testifying that all the women in a group of ex-prostitutes were brought into prostitution as children through pornography, characterized their collective experience: "[I]n my experience there was not one situation where a client was not using pornography while he was using me or that he had not just watched pornography or that it was verbally referred to and directed me to pornography." "Men," she continued, "witness the abuse of women in pornography constantly and if they can't engage in that behavior with their wives, girl friends or children, they force a whore to do it."

Men also testified about how pornography hurts them. One young gay man who had seen *Playboy* and *Penthouse* as a child said of such heterosexual pornography: "It was one of the places I learned about sex and it showed me that sex was violence. What I saw there was a specific relationship between men and women. . . .[T]he woman was to be used, objectified, humiliated and hurt; the man was in a superior position, a position to be violent. In pornography I learned that what it meant to be sexual with a man or to be loved by a man was to accept his violence." For this reason, when he was battered by his first lover, which he described as "one of the most profoundly destructive experiences of my life," he accepted it.

Pornography also hurts men's capacity to relate to women. One young man spoke about this in a way that connects pornography—not the prohibition on pornography—with fascism. He spoke of his struggle to repudiate the thrill of dominance, of his difficulty finding connection with a woman to whom he is close.

He said: "My point is that if women in a society filled by pornography must be wary for their physical selves, a man, even a man of good intentions, must be wary for his mind. . . . I do not want to be a mechanical, goose-stepping follower of the Playboy bunny, because that is what I think it is. . . .[T]hese are the experiments a master race perpetuates on those slated for extinction." The woman he lives with is Jewish. There was a very brutal rape near their house. She was afraid; she tried to joke. It didn't work. "She was still afraid. And just as a well-meaning German was afraid in 1933, I am also very much afraid."

Pornography stimulates and reinforces, it does not cathect or mirror, the connection between one-sided freely available sexual access to women and masculine sexual excitement and sexual satisfaction. The catharsis hypothesis is fantasy. The fantasy theory is fantasy. Reality is: pornography conditions male orgasm to female subordination. It tells men what sex means, what a real woman is, and codes them together in a way that is behaviorally reinforcing. This is a real five-dollar sentence, but I'm going to say it anyway: pornography is a set of hermeneutical equivalences that work on the epistemological level. Substantively, pornography defines the meaning of what a woman is seen to be by connecting access to her sexuality with masculinity through orgasm. What pornography means *is* what it does.

So far, opposition to our ordinance centers on the trafficking provision. This means not only that it is difficult to comprehend a group injury in a liberal culture—that what it *means* to be a woman is defined by this and that it is an injury for all women, even if not for all women equally. It is not only that the pornography has got to be accessible, which is the bottom line of virtually every objection to this law. It is also that power, as I said, is when you say something, it is taken for reality. If you talk about rape, it will be agreed that rape is awful. But rape is a conclusion. If a victim describes the facts of a rape, maybe she was asking for it or enjoyed it or at least consented to it, or the man might have thought she did, or maybe she had had sex before. It is now agreed that

there is something wrong with sexual harassment. But describe what happened to you, and
it may be trivial or personal or paranoid, or
maybe you should have worn a bra that day.
People are against discrimination. But describe the situation of a real woman, and they
are not so sure she wasn't just unqualified. In
law, all these disjunctions between women's
perspective on our injuries and the standards
we have to meet go under dignified legal rubrics like burden of proof, credibility, defenses, elements of the crime, and so on.
These standards all contain a definition of
what a woman is in terms of what sex is and the
low value placed on us through it. They reduce injuries done to us to authentic expressions of who we are. Our silence is written
all over them. So is the pornography.

We have as yet encountered comparatively
little objection to the coercion, force, or assault
provisions of our ordinance. I think that's
partly because the people who make and
approve laws may not yet see what they do as
that. They *know* they use the pornography as
we have described it in this law, and our law
defines that, the reality of pornography, as a
harm to women. If they suspect that they
might on occasion engage in or benefit from
coercion or force or assault, they may think
that the victims won't be able to prove it—and
they're right. Women who charge men with
sexual abuse are not believed. The
pornographic view of them is: they want it;
they all want it. When women bring charges of
sexual assault, motives such as veniality or sexual repression must be invented, because we
cannot really have been hurt. Under the
trafficking provision, women's lack of credibility cannot be relied upon to negate the harm.
There's no woman's story to destroy, no credi-
bility-based decision on what happened. The
hearings establish the harm. The definition
sets the standard. The grounds of reality definition are authoritatively shifted. Pornography is bigotry, *period*. We are now—*in* the
world pornography has decisively defined—
having to meet the burden of proving, once
and for all, for all of the rape and torture and
battery, all of the sexual harassment, all of the
child sexual abuse, all of the forced prostitution, *all* of it that the pornography is part of
and that is part of the pornography, that the

harm *does happen* and that when it happens it
looks like this. Which may be why all this evidence never seems to be enough.

It is worth considering what evidence has
been enough when other harms involving
other purported speech interests have been
allowed to be legislated against. By comparison to our trafficking provision, analytically
similar restrictions have been allowed under
the First Amendment, with a legislative basis
far less massive, detailed, concrete, and conclusive. Our statutory language is more ordinary, objective, and precise and covers a harm
far narrower than the legislative record sub-
stantiates. Under *Miller*, obscenity was allowed
to be made criminal in the name of the "danger of offending the sensibilities of unwilling
recipients, or exposure to juveniles." Under
our law, we have direct evidence of harm, not
just a conjectural danger, that unwilling
women in considerable numbers are not simply offended in their sensibilities, but are violated in their persons and restricted in their
options. Obscenity law also suggests that the
applicable standard for legal adequacy in
measuring such connections may not be statistical certainty. The Supreme Court has said
that it is not their job to resolve empirical uncertainties that underlie state obscenity legislation. Rather, it is for them to determine
whether a legislature could reasonably have
determined that a connection might exist between the prohibited material and harm of a
kind in which the state has legitimate interest.
Equality should be such an area. The Supreme
Court recently recognized that prevention of
sexual exploitation and abuse of children is, in
their words, "a governmental objective of sur-
passing importance." This might also be the
case for sexual exploitation and abuse of
women, although I think a civil remedy is initially more appropriate to the goal of
empowering adult women than a criminal prohibition would be.

Other rubrics provide further support for
the argument that this law is narrowly tailored
to further a legitimate governmental interest
consistent with the goals underlying the First
Amendment. Exceptions to the First Amendment—you may have gathered from this—
exist. The reason they exist is that the harm

done by some speech outweighs its expressive value, if any. In our law a legislature recognizes that pornography, as defined and made actionable, undermines sex equality. One can say—and I have—that pornography is a causal factor in violations of women; one can also say that women will be violated so long as pornography exists; but one can also say simply that pornography violates women. Perhaps this is what the woman had in mind who testified at our hearings that for her the question is not just whether pornography causes violent acts to be perpetrated against some women. "Porn is already a violent act against women. It is our mothers, our daughters, our sisters, and our wives that are for sale for pocket change at the newsstands in this country." *Chaplinsky v. New Hampshire* recognized the ability to restrict as "fighting words" speech which, "by [its] very utterance inflicts injury." Perhaps the only reason that pornography has not been "fighting words"—in the sense of words that by their utterance tend to incite immediate breach of the peace—is that women have seldom fought back, yet.

Some concerns that are close to those of this ordinance underlie group libel laws, although the differences are equally important. In group libel law, as Justice Frankfurter's opinion in *Beauharnais* illustrates, it has been understood that an individual's treatment and alternatives in life may depend as much on the reputation of the group to which that person belongs as on their own merit. Not even a partial analogy can be made to group libel doctrine without examining the point made by Justice Brandeis and recently underlined by Larry Tribe: would more speech, rather than less, remedy the harm? In the end, the answer may be yes, but not under the abstract system of free speech, which only enhances the power of the pornographers while doing nothing substantively to guarantee the free speech of women, for which we need civil equality. The situation in which women presently find ourselves with respect to the pornography is one in which more *pornography* is inconsistent with rectifying or even counterbalancing its damage through speech, because so long as the pornography exists in the way it does there *will not be more speech by women*. Pornography strips and devastates women of credibility, from our

accounts of sexual assault to our everyday reality of sexual subordination. We are stripped of authority and reduced and devalidated and silenced. Silenced here means that the purposes of the First Amendment, premised upon conditions presumed and promoted by protecting free speech, do not pertain to women because they are not our conditions. Consider them: individual self-fulfillment—how does pornography promote our individual self-fulfillment? How does sexual inequality even permit it? Even if she can form words, who listens to a woman with a penis in her mouth? Facilitating consensus—to the extent pornography does so, it does so one-sidedly by silencing protest over the injustice of sexual subordination. Participation in civic life—central to Professor Meiklejohn's theory—how does pornography enhance women's participation in civic life? Anyone who cannot walk down the street or even lie down in her own bed without keeping her eyes cast down and her body clenched against assault is unlikely to have much to say about the issues of the day, still less will she become Tolstoy. Facilitating change—*this law* facilitates the change that existing First Amendment theory had been used to throttle. Any system of freedom of expression that does not address a problem where the free speech of men silences the free speech of women, a real conflict between speech interests as well as between people, is not serious about securing freedom of expression in this country.

For those of you who still think pornography is only an idea, consider the possibility that obscenity law got one thing right. Pornography is more actlike than thoughtlike. The fact that pornography, in a feminist view, furthers the idea of the sexual inferiority of women, which is a political idea, doesn't make the pornography itself into a political idea. One can express the idea a practice embodies. That does not make that practice into an idea. Segregation expresses the idea of the inferiority of one group to another on the basis of race. That does not make segregation an idea. A sign that says "Whites Only" is only words. Is it therefore protected by the First Amendment? Is it not an act, a practice, of segregation because what it means is inseparable from what it does? *Law* is only words.

The issue here is whether the fact that words and pictures are the central link in the cycle of abuse will immunize that entire cycle, about which we cannot do anything without doing something about the pornography. As Justice Stewart said in *Ginsburg,* "When expression occurs in a setting where the capacity to make a choice is absent, government regulation of that expression may coexist with and *even implement* First Amendment guarantees." I would even go so far as to say that the pattern of evidence we have closely approaches Justice Douglas' requirement that "freedom of expression can be suppressed if, and to the extent that, it is so closely brigaded with illegal action as to be an inseparable part of it." Those of you who have been trying to separate the acts from the speech—that's an act, that's an act, there's a law against that act, regulate that act, don't touch the speech—notice here that the illegality of the acts involved doesn't mean that the speech that is "brigaded with" it *cannot* be regulated. This is when it *can* be.

I take one of two penultimate points from Andrea Dworkin, who has often said that pornography is not speech for women, it is the silence of women. Remember the mouth taped, the woman gagged, "Smile, I can get a lot of money for that." The smile is not her expression, it is her silence. It is not her expression not because it didn't happen, but because it *did* happen. The screams of the women in pornography are silence, like the screams of Kitty Genovese, whose plight was misinterpreted by some onlookers as a lovers' quarrel. The flat expressionless voice of the woman in the New Bedford gang rape, testifying, is silence. She was raped as men cheered and watched, as they do in and with the pornography. When women resist and men say, "Like this, you stupid bitch, here is how to do it" and shove their faces into the pornography, this "truth of sex" is the silence of women. When they say, "If you love me, you'll try," the enjoyment we fake, the enjoyment we learn is silence. Women who submit because there is more dignity in it than in losing the fight over and over live in silence. Having to sleep with your publisher or director to get access to what men call speech is silence. Being humiliated on the basis of your appearance, whether by approval or disapproval, because you have to look a certain way for a certain job, whether you get the job or not, is silence. The absence of a woman's voice, everywhere that it cannot be heard, is silence. And anyone who thinks that what women say in pornography is women's speech—the "Fuck me, do it to me, harder," all of that—has never heard the sound of a woman's voice.

The most basic assumption underlying First Amendment adjudication is that, socially, speech is free. The First Amendment says Congress shall not abridge the freedom of speech. Free speech, get it, *exists.* Those who wrote the First Amendment *had* speech—they wrote the Constitution. *Their* problem was to keep it free from the only power that realistically threatened it: the federal government. They designed the First Amendment to prevent government from constraining that which, if unconstrained by government, was free, meaning *accessible to them.* At the same time, we can't tell much about the intent of the framers with regard to the question of women's speech, because I don't think we crossed their minds. It is consistent with this analysis that their posture toward freedom of speech tends to presuppose that whole segments of the population are not systematically silenced socially, prior to government action. If everyone's power were equal to theirs, if this were a nonhierarchical society, that might make sense. But the place of pornography in the inequality of the sexes makes the assumption of equal power untrue.

This is a hard question. It involves risks. Classically, opposition to censorship has involved keeping government off the backs of people. Our law is about getting some people off the backs of other people. The risks that it will be misused have to be measured against the risks of the status quo. Women will never have that dignity, security, compensation that is the promise of equality so long as the pornography exists as it does now. The situation of women suggests that the urgent issue of our freedom of speech is not primarily the avoidance of state intervention as such, but getting affirmative access to speech for those to whom it has been denied.

35.   False Promises:
Feminist Antipornography Legislation

Lisa Duggan, Nan D. Hunter, and Carole S. Vance

Duggan, Hunter, and Vance disagree with Catharine MacKinnon that pornography constitutes sex discrimination. These authors feel that, since the laws as conceived are overbroad, they could ban anything that is sexually explicit and could in fact be damaging to the feminist movement. Following up on this claim, Duggan, Hunter, and Vance argue that pornography is no more injurious to women than are other forms of sexist material not covered by the legislation.

On February 24, 1986, the U.S. Supreme Court ruled that the Indianapolis version of the antipornography ordinance was unconstitutional. Although this ruling settles the legal question of the ordinance's validity, the political debate on the wisdom of invoking state power to suppress sexual materials continues. That debate, which will be with us for many years to come, encompasses many of the same points of disagreement—over the social meanings of language and imagery and the political risks to women of protectionist strategy—which we analyze in this article.

In the United States, after two decades of increasing community tolerance for dissenting or disturbing sexual or political materials, there is now growing momentum for retrenchment. In an atmosphere of increased conservatism, evidenced by a wave of book banning and anti-gay harassment, support for new repressive legislation of various kinds—from an Oklahoma law forbidding schoolteachers from advocating homosexuality to new antipornography laws passed in Minneapolis and Indianapolis—is growing.

The antipornography laws have mixed roots of support, however. Though they are popular with the conservative constituencies that traditionally favor legal restrictions on sexual expression of all kinds, they were drafted and are endorsed by antipornography feminists who oppose traditional obscenity

From *Women Against Censorship*, Varda Burstyn, ed., Toronto: Douglas and McIntyre, pp. 130–151, 1985. Copyrighted by and reprinted with permission of the authors.

and censorship laws. The model law of this type, which is now being widely copied, was drawn up in the politically progressive city of Minneapolis by two radical feminists, author Andrea Dworkin and attorney Catharine MacKinnon. It was passed by the city council there, but vetoed by the mayor. A similar law was passed in Indianapolis, but later declared unconstitutional in federal court. The city is appealing that ruling to the Supreme Court. Other versions of the legislation have been considered, and either discarded or defeated, in several other cities including Suffolk County, New York, Madison, Wisconsin, Los Angeles County, California, and Cambridge, Massachusetts. Pennsylvania Senator Arlen Specter has introduced legislation modeled on parts of the Dworkin-MacKinnon bill in Congress, and the Reagan-initiated Attorney General's Commission on Pornography is weighing its merits as a censorship strategy.

Dworkin, MacKinnon and their feminist supporters believe that the new antipornography laws are not censorship laws. They also claim that the legislative effort behind them is based on feminist support. Both of these claims are dubious at best. Though the new laws are civil laws that allow individuals to sue the makers, sellers, distributors, or exhibitors of pornography, and not criminal laws leading to arrest and imprisonment, their censoring impact would be substantially as severe as criminal obscenity laws. Materials could be removed from public availability by court injunction, and publishers and booksellers could be subject to potentially endless legal harassment. Passage of the laws was therefore achieved with the support of right-wing elements who expect the new laws to accomplish what censorship efforts are meant to accomplish. Ironically, many antifeminist conservatives backed these laws, while many feminists opposed them. In Indianapolis, the law was supported by extreme right-wing religious fundamentalists, including members of the Moral Majority, while there was *no* local feminist support. In other cities, traditional procensorship forces have expressed interest in the new approach to banning sexually explicit materials. Meanwhile, anticensorship feminists have become alarmed at these new developments and are seeking to galvanize feminist opposition to the new antipornography legislative strategy pioneered in Minneapolis.

One is tempted to ask in astonishment, how can this be happening? How can feminists be entrusting the patriarchal state with the task of legally distinguishing between permissible and impermissible sexual images? But in fact this new development is not as surprising as it at first seems. For the reasons explored by Ann Snitow*, pornography has come to be seen as a central cause of women's oppression by a significant number of feminists. Some even argue that pornography is the root of virtually all forms of exploitation and discrimination against women. It is a short step from such a belief to the conviction that laws against pornography can end the inequality of the sexes. But this analysis takes feminists very close— indeed far too close—to measures that will ultimately support conservative, anti-sex, procensorship forces in American society, for it is with these forces that women have forged alliances in passing such legislation.

The first feminist-inspired antipornography law was passed in Minneapolis in 1983. Local legislators had been frustrated when their zoning restrictions on porn shops were struck down in the courts. Public hearings were held to discuss a new zoning ordinance. The Neighborhood Pornography Task Force of South and South Central Minneapolis invited Andrea Dworkin and Catharine MacKin-

*See *Caught Looking: Feminism, Pornography, and Censorship,* Feminist Anti-Censorship Task Force, East Haven, CT: Long River Books, 1992, page 10.

non, who were teaching a course on pornography at the University of Minnesota, to testify. They proposed an alternative that, they claimed, would completely eliminate, rather than merely regulate, pornography. They suggested that pornography be defined as a form of sex discrimination, and that an amendment to the city's civil rights law be passed to proscribe it. City officials hired Dworkin and MacKinnon to develop their new approach and to organize another series of public hearings.

The initial debate over the legislation in Minneapolis was intense, and opinion was divided within nearly every political grouping. In contrast, the public hearings held before the city council were tightly controlled and carefully orchestrated; speakers invited by Dworkin and MacKinnon—sexual abuse victims, counselors, educators and social scientists—testified about the harm pornography does women. (Dworkin and MacKinnon's agenda was the compilation of a legislative record that would help the law stand up to its inevitable court challenges.) The legislation passed, supported by antipornography feminists, neighborhood groups concerned about the effects of porn shops on residential areas, and conservatives opposed to the availability of sexually explicit materials for "moral" reasons.

In Indianapolis, the alignment of forces was different. For the previous two years, conservative antipornography groups had grown in strength and public visibility, but they had been frustrated in their efforts. The police department could not convert its obscenity arrests into convictions; the city's zoning law was also tied up in court challenges. Then Mayor William Hudnut III, a Republican and a Presbyterian minister, learned of the Minneapolis law. Mayor Hudnut thought Minneapolis's approach to restricting pornography might be the solution to the Indianapolis problems. Beulah Coughenour, a conservative Republican stop-ERA activist, was recruited to sponsor the legislation in the city-county council.

Coughenour engaged MacKinnon as consultant to the city—Dworkin was not hired, but then, Dworkin's passionate radical feminist rhetoric would not have gone over well in Indianapolis. MacKinnon worked with the Indianapolis city prosecutor (a well-known anti-vice zealot), the city's legal department and Coughenour on the legislation. The law received the support of neighborhood groups, the Citizens for Decency and the Coalition for a Clean Community. There were no crowds of feminist supporters—in fact, there were no feminist supporters at all. The only feminists to make public statements opposed the legislation, which was nevertheless passed in a council meeting packed with 300 religious fundamentalists. All 24 Republicans voted for its passage; all five Democrats opposed it to no avail.

A group of publishers and booksellers challenged the law in Federal District Court, where they won the first round. This initial decision was then upheld by the Federal Appeals Court. The city is appealing again to the Supreme Court, though it may take a year or two for a final decision to be reached.

In the meantime, other versions of the Dworkin-MacKinnon bill have appeared. A version of the law introduced in Suffolk County on Long Island in New York emphasized its conservative potential—pornography was said to cause "sodomy" and "disruption" of the family unit, in addition to rape, incest, exploitation and other acts "inimical to the public good." In Suffolk, the law was put forward by a conservative, anti-ERA male legislator who wishes to "restore ladies to what they used to be." The Suffolk County bill clearly illustrates the repressive antifeminist potential of the new antipornography legislation.

Versions of the bill, nearer to the original intent of the authors, have been considered in Madison, Los Angeles and Cambridge. In these cities, feminist opposition to antipornography ordinances was organized, and Feminist Anti-Censorship Taskforce groups helped to defeat the idea. In Madison, the measure was not introduced after a FACT press conference wiped out support for an ordinance on the Dane County Board of Supervisors. In Los Angeles, FACT efforts helped defeat a measure before the County Board of Supervisors, though the vote was close and individual supervisors responded little to feminist opinion on either side. In Cambridge, voters defeated the measure after a heated referendum campaign in which feminists dominated both sides of the debate.

At present, Edwin Meese's Commission on Pornography is preparing a report on new ways to control pornography. The Commission is controlled by moral conservatives, and it is expected to issue repressive recommendations designed to help legislators and courts suppress sexual images. The Commission is considering the "feminist" antipornography arguments and legislation. It is likely to try to use what it can, while discarding those aspects of the feminist approach which conflict with a conservative outlook. The Meese Commission's report may very well show how far the right-wing will go in coopting feminist language and laws in the service of its own repressive agenda.

Yet it is true that some of the laws have been proposed and supported by antipornography feminists. This is therefore a critical moment in the feminist debate over sexual politics. As anticensorship feminists work to develop alternatives to antipornography campaigns, we also need to examine carefully the new laws and expose their underlying assumptions. We need to know why these laws, for all their apparent feminist rhetoric, actually appeal to conservative antifeminist forces, and why feminists should be preparing to move in a different direction.

Definitions: The Central Flaw

The antipornography ordinances passed in Minneapolis and Indianapolis were framed as amendments to municipal civil rights laws. They provide for complaints to be filed against pornography in the same manner that complaints are filed against employment discrimination. If enforced, the laws would make illegal public or private availability (except in libraries) of any materials deemed pornographic.

Such material could be the object of a lawsuit on several grounds. The ordinance would penalize four kinds of behavior associated with pornography: its production, sale, exhibition or distribution ("trafficking"); coercion into pornographic performance; forcing pornography on a person; and assault or physical attack due to pornography.

Under this law, a woman "acting as a woman against the subordination of women" could file a complaint; men could also file complaints if they could "prove injury in the same way that a woman is injured." The procedural steps in the various versions differ, but they generally allow the complainant either to file an administrative complaint with the city's equal opportunity commission, or to file a lawsuit directly in court. If the local commission found the law had been violated, it would file a lawsuit. By either procedure, the court—not "women"—would have the final say on whether the materials fit the definition of pornography, and would have the authority to award monetary damages and issue an injunction (or court order) preventing further distribution of the material in question.

The Minneapolis ordinance defines pornography as "the sexually explicit subordination of women, graphically depicted, whether in pictures or words." To be actionable, materials would also have to fall within one of a number of categories: nine in the Minneapolis ordinance, six in the Indianapolis version.

Although proponents claim that these ordinances represent a new way to regulate pornography, the strategy is still laden with our culture's old, repressive approach to sexuality. The implementation of such laws hinges on the definition of pornography as interpreted by the court. The definition provided in the Minneapolis legislation is vague, leaving critical phrases such as "the explicit subordination of women," "postures of sexual submission" and "whores by nature" to the interpretation of the citizen who files a complaint and to the civil court judge who hears the case. The legislation does not prohibit just the images of gross sexual violence that most supporters claim to be its target, but instead drifts toward covering an increasingly wide range of sexually explicit material.

The most problematic feature of this approach, then, is a conceptual flaw embedded in the law itself. Supporters of this type of legislation say that the target of their efforts is misogynist, sexually explicit and violent representation, whether in pictures or words. Indeed, the feminist antipornography movement is fueled by women's anger at the most repugnant examples of pornography. But a close examination of the wording of the model legislative text, and examples of purportedly actionable material offered by proponents of the legislation in court briefs suggest that the law is actually aimed at a range of material considerably broader than what proponents claim is their target. The discrepancies between the law's explicit and implicit aims have been almost invisible to us, because these distortions are very similar to distortions about sexuality in the culture as a whole. The legislation and supporting texts deserve close reading. Hidden beneath illogical transformations, non-sequiturs, and highly permeable definitions are familiar sexual scripts drawn from mainstream, sexist culture that potentially could have very negative consequences for women.

The Venn diagram illustrates the three areas targeted by the law, and represents a scheme that classifies words or images that have any of three characteristics: violence, sexual explicitness or sexism.

Clearly, a text or an image might have only one characteristic. Material can be violent but not sexually explicit or sexist: for example, a war movie in which both men and women suffer injury or death without regard to or because of their gender. Material can be sexist but not sexually explicit and violent. A vast number of materials from mainstream media—television, popular novels, magazines, newspapers—come to mind, all of which depict either distraught housewives or the "happy sexism" of the idealized family, with mom self-sacrificing, other-directed and content. Finally, material can be sexually explicit but not violent or sexist: for example, the freely chosen sexual behavior depicted in sex education films or women's own explicit writing about sexuality.

As the diagram illustrates, areas can also intersect, reflecting a range of combinations of the three characteristics. Images can be violent and sexually explicit without being sexist—for example, a narrative about a rape in a men's prison, or a documentary about the effect of a rape on a woman. The latter example illustrates the importance of context in evaluating whether material that is sexually explicit and violent is also sexist. The intent of the maker, the context of the film and the perception of the viewer together render a depiction of a rape sympathetic, harrowing, even educational, rather than sensational, victim-blaming and laudatory.

Another possible overlap is between material that is violent and sexist but not sexually explicit. Films or books that describe violence directed against women by men in a way that clearly shows gender antagonism and inequality, and sometimes strong sexual tension, but no sexual explicitness fall into this category—for example, the popular genre of slasher films in which women are stalked, terrified and killed by men, or accounts of mass murder of women, fueled by male rage. Finally, a third point of overlap arises when material is sexually explicit and sexist without being violent—that is, when sex is consensual but still reflects themes of male superiority and female abjectness. Some sex education materials could be included in this category, as well as a great deal of regular pornography.

The remaining domain, the inner core, is one in which the material is simultaneously violent, sexually explicit and sexist—for example, an image of a naked woman being slashed by a knife-wielding rapist. The Minneapolis law, however, does not by any means confine itself to this material.

To be actionable under the law as pornography, material must be judged by the courts to be "the sexually explicit subordination of women, graphically depicted whether in pictures or in words that also includes at least one or more" of nine criteria. Of these, only four involve the intersection of violence, sexual explicitness and sexism, and then only arguably. Even in these cases, many questions remain about whether images with all three characteristics do in fact cause violence against women. And the task of evaluating material that is

ostensibly the target of these criteria becomes complicated—indeed, hopeless—because most of the clauses that contain these criteria mix actions or qualities of violence with those that are not particularly associated with violence.

The section that comes closest to the stated purpose of the legislation is clause (iii): "women are presented as sexual objects who experience sexual pleasure in being raped." This clause is intended to cover depictions of rape that are sexually explicit and sexist; the act of rape itself signifies the violence. But other clauses are not so clearcut, because the list of characteristics often mixes signs or by-products of violence with phenomena that are unrelated or irrelevant to judging violence.

For example, clause (iv) presents: "women are presented as sexual objects tied up or cut up or mutilated or bruised or physically hurt." All these except the first, "tied up," generally occur as a result of violence. "Tied up." if part of consensual sex, is not violent and, for some practitioners, not particularly sexist. Women who are tied up may be participants in nonviolent sex play involving bondage, a theme in both heterosexual and lesbian pornography. (See, for example, *The Joy of Sex* and *Coming to Power*.) Clause (ix) contains another mixed list, in which "injury," "torture," "bleeding," "bruised" and "hurt" are combined with words such as "degradation" and "shown as filthy and inferior," neither of which is violent. Depending on the presentation, "filthy" and "inferior" may constitute sexually explicit sexism, although not violence. "Degradation" is a sufficiently inclusive term to cover most acts of which a viewer disapproves.

Several other clauses have little to do with violence at all; they refer to material that is sexually explicit and sexist, thus falling outside the triad of characteristics at which the legislation is supposedly aimed. For example, movies in which "women are presented as dehumanized sexual objects, things, or commodities" may be infuriating and offensive to feminists, but they are not violent.

Finally, some clauses describe material that is neither violent nor necessarily sexist. Clause (v), "women . . . in postures of sexual submission or sexual servility, including by inviting penetration," and clause (viii), "women`. . . being penetrated by objects or animals," are sexually explicit, but not violent and not obviously sexist unless one believes that penetration—whether heterosexual, lesbian, or autoerotic masturbation—is indicative of gender inequality and female oppression. Similarly problematic are clauses that invoke representations of "women . . . as whores by nature" and "women's body parts . . . such that women are reduced to those parts."

Briefs filed in support of the Indianapolis law show how broadly it could be applied. In the amicus brief filed on behalf of Linda Marchiano ("Linda Lovelace," the female lead in *Deep Throat*) in Indianapolis, Catharine MacKinnon offered *Deep Throat* as an example of the kind of pornography covered by the law. *Deep Throat* served a complicated function in this brief, because the movie, supporters of the ordinance argue, would be actionable on two counts: coercion into pornographic performance, because Marchiano alleges that she was coerced into making the movie; and trafficking in pornography, because the content of the film falls within one of the categories in the Indianapolis ordinance's definition—that which prohibits presenting women as sexual objects "through postures or positions of servility or submission or display." Proponents of the law have counted on women's repugnance at allegations of coerced sexual acts to spill over and discredit the sexual acts themselves in this movie.

The aspects of *Deep Throat* that MacKinnon considered to be indicative of "sexual subordination" are of particular interest, since any movie that depicted similar acts could be banned under the law. MacKinnon explained in her brief that the film "subordinates women by using women . . . sexually, specifically as eager servicing receptacles for male genitalia and ejaculate. The majority of the film represents 'Linda Lovelace' in, minimally, postures of sexual submission and/or servility." In its brief, the City of Indianapolis concurred: "In the film *Deep Throat* a woman is being shown as being ever eager for oral penetration by a series of men's penises, often on her hands and knees. There are repeated scenes in which her genitalia are graphically displayed and she is shown as enjoying men ejaculating on her face."

These descriptions are very revealing, since they suggest that multiple partners, group sex and oral sex subordinate women and hence are sexist. The notion that the female character is "used" by men suggests that it is improbable that a woman would engage in fellatio of her own accord. *Deep Throat* does draw on several sexist conventions common in the entire visual culture—the woman as object of the male gaze, and the assumption of heterosexuality, for example. But it is hardly an unending paean to male dominance, since the movie contains many contrary themes. In it, the main female character is shown as both actively seeking her own pleasure and as trying to please men; a secondary female character is shown as actually directing encounters with multiple male partners. Both briefs described a movie quite different from the one viewers see.

As its heart, this analysis implies that heterosexual sex itself is sexist; that women do not engage in it of their own volition; and that behavior pleasurable to men is necessarily repugnant to women. In some contexts, for example, the representation of fellatio and multiple partners can be sexist, but are we willing to concede that they always are? If not, then what is proposed as actionable under the Indianapolis law includes merely sexually explicit representation (the traditional target of obscenity laws), which proponents of the legislation vociferously insist they are not interested in attacking.

Some other examples offered through exhibits submitted with the City of Indianapolis brief and also introduced in the public hearing further illustrate this point. Many of the exhibits are depictions of sadomasochism. The court briefs treat SM material as depicting violence and aggression, not consensual sex, in spite of avowals to the contrary by many SM practitioners. With this legislation, then, a major question for feminists that has only begun to develop would be closed for discussion. Instead, a simplistic reduction has been advanced as the definitive feminist position. The description of the material in the briefs focused on submissive women and implied male domination, highlighting the similarity proponents would like to find between all SM narratives and male/female inequality. The actual exhibits, however, illustrated plots and power relations far more diverse than the descriptions provided by MacKinnon and the City of Indianapolis would suggest, including SM between women and female dominant/male submissive SM. For example, the Indianapolis brief stated that in the magazine *The Bitch Goddesses,* "women are shown in torture chambers with their nude body parts being tortured by their 'master' for 'even the slightest offense'. . . . The magazine shows a woman in a scenario of torture." But the brief failed to mention that the dominants in this magazine are all female, with one exception. This kind of discrepancy characterized many examples offered in the briefs.

This is not to say that such representations do not raise questions for feminists. The current lively discussion about lesbian SM clearly demonstrates that the issue is still unresolved. But in the Indianapolis briefs all SM material was assumed to be male dominant/female submissive, thereby squeezing a nonconforming reality into prepackaged, inadequate—and therefore dangerous—categories. This legislation would virtually eliminate all SM pornography by recasting it as violent, thereby attacking a sexual minority while masquerading as an attempt to end violence against women.

Analysis of clauses in the Minneapolis ordinance and several examples offered in court briefs filed in connection with the Indianapolis ordinance show that the law targets material that is sexually explicit and sexist, but ignores material that is violent and sexist, violent and sexually explicit, only violent or only sexist.

Certain troubling questions arise here, for if one claims, as some antipornography activists do, that there is a direct relationship between images and behavior, why should images of violence against women or scenarios of sexism in general not be similarly proscribed? Why is sexual explicitness singled out as the cause of women's oppression? For proponents to exempt violent and sexist images, or even sexist images, from regulation is inconsistent, especially since they are so pervasive.

Even more difficulties arise from the vagueness of certain terms crucial in interpreting the ordinances. The term "subordination"

is especially important, since pornography is defined as the "sexually explicit subordination of women." The authors of this legislation intend it to modify each of the clauses, and they appear to believe that it provides a definition of sexism that each example must meet. The term is never defined in the legislation, yet the Indianapolis brief, for example, suggests that the average viewer, on the basis of "his or her common understanding of what it means for one person to subordinate another" should be able to decide what is pornographic. But what kind of sexually explicit acts place a woman in an inferior status? To some, *any* graphic sexual act violates women's dignity and therefore subordinates them. To others, consensual heterosexual lovemaking within the boundaries of procreation and marriage is acceptable, but heterosexual acts that do not have reproduction as their aim lower women's status and hence subordinate them. Still others accept a wide range of nonprocreative, perhaps even nonmarital, heterosexuality but draw the line at lesbian sex, which they view as degrading.

The term "sex object" is also problematic. The City of Indianapolis's brief maintains that "the term sexual object, often shortened to sex object, has enjoyed a wide popularity in mainstream American culture in the past fifteen years, and is used to denote the objectification of a person on the basis of their sex or sex appeal. . . . People know what it means to disregard all aspects of personhood but sex, to reduce a person to a thing used for sex." But, indeed, people do not agree on this point. The definition of "sex object" is far from clear or uniform. For example, some feminist and liberal cultural critics have used the term to mean sex that occurs without strong emotional ties and experience. More conservative critics maintain that any detachment of women's sexuality from procreation, marriage and family objectifies it, removing it from its "natural" web of associations and context. Unredeemed and unprotected by domesticity and family, women—and their sexuality—become things used by men. In both these views, women are never sexually autonomous agents who direct and enjoy their sexuality for their own purposes, but rather are victims. In the same vein, other problematic terms include "inviting penetration," "whores by nature" and "positions of display."

Through close analysis of the proposed legislation one sees how vague the boundaries of the definitions that contain the inner core of the Venn diagram really are. Their dissolution does not happen equally at all points, but only at some: the inner core begins to include sexually explicit and sexist material, and finally expands to include purely sexually explicit material. Thus "sexually explicit" becomes identified and equated with "violent" with no further definition or explanation.

It is also striking that so many feminists have failed to notice that the laws (as well as examples of actionable material) cover so much diverse work, not just that small and symbolic epicentre where many forms of opposition to women converge. It suggests that for us, as well as for others, sexuality remains a difficult area. We have no clearly developed framework in which to think about sex equivalent to the frameworks that are available for thinking about race, gender and class issues. Consequently, in sex, as in few other areas of human behavior, unexamined and unjustifiable prejudice passes itself off as considered opinion about what is desirable and normal. And finally, sex arouses considerable anxiety, stemming from both the meeting with individual difference and from the prospect—suggested by feminists themselves—that sexual behavior is constructed socially and is not simply natural.

The law takes advantage of everyone's relative ignorance and anxious ambivalence about sex, distorting and oversimplifying what confronts us in building a sexual politic. For example, antipornography feminists draw on several feminist theories about the role of violent, aggressive or sexist representations. The first is relatively straightforward: that these images trigger men into action. The second suggests that violent images act more subtly, to socialize men to act in sexist or violent ways by making this behavior seem commonplace and more acceptable, if not expected. The third assumption is that violent, sexually explicit or even sexist images are offensive to women, assaulting their sensibilities and sense of self. Although we have all used metaphor to exhort women to action or illustrate a point, antipornography proponents have frequently used these conventions of speech as if they were literal statements of fact. But these metaphors have gotten out of hand, as Julie Abraham has noted, for they fail to recognize that the assault committed by a wife beater is quite different from the visual "assault" of a sexist ad on TV. The nature of that difference is still being clarified in a complex debate within feminism that must continue; this law cuts off speculation, settling on a causal relationship between image and action that is starkly simple, if unpersuasive.

This metaphor also paves the way for reclassifying images that are merely sexist as also violent and aggressive. Thus, it is no accident that the briefs supporting the legislation first invoke violent images and rapidly move to include sexist and sexually explicit images without noting that they are different. The equation is made more easy by the constant shifts back to examples of depictions of real violence, almost to draw attention away from the sexually explicit or sexist material that in fact would be affected by the laws.

Most important, what underlies this legislation and the success of its analysis in blurring and exceeding boundaries is an appeal to a very traditional view of sex: sex is degrading to women. By this logic, any illustrations or descriptions of sexually explicit acts that involve women are in themselves affronts to women's dignity. In its brief, the City of Indianapolis was quite specific about this point: "The harms caused by pornography are by no means limited to acts of physical aggression. The mere existence of pornography in society degrades and demeans all women." Embedded in this view are several other familiar themes: that sex is degrading to women, but not to men; that men are raving beasts; that sex is dangerous for women; that sexuality is male, not female; that women are victims, not sexual actors; that men inflict "it" on women; that penetration is submission; that heterosexual sexuality, rather than the institution of heterosexuality, is sexist.

These assumptions, in part intended, in part unintended, lead us back to the traditional target of obscenity law: sexually explicit material. What initially appeared novel, then, is really the reappearance of a traditional theme. It's ironic that a feminist position on pornography incorporates most of the myths about sexuality that feminism has struggled to displace.

The Dangers of Application

The Minneapolis-style ordinances embody a political view that holds pornography to be a central force in "creating and maintaining" the oppression of women. This view appears in summary form in the legislative findings section at the beginning of the Minneapolis bill, which describes a chain reaction of misogynistic acts generated by pornography. The legislation is based on the interweaving of several themes: that pornography constructs the meaning of sexuality for women and, as well, leads to discrete acts of violence against women; that sexuality is the primary cause of women's oppression; that explicitly sexual images, even if not violent or coerced, have the power to subordinate women; and that women's own accounts of force have been silenced because, as a universal and timeless rule, society credits pornographic constructions rather than women's experiences. Taking the silencing contention a step further, advocates of the ordinance effectively assume that women have been so conditioned by the pornographic world view that if their own experiences of the sexual acts identified in the definition are not subordinating, then they must simply be victims of false consciousness.

The heart of the ordinace is the "trafficking" section, which would allow almost anyone to seek the removal of any materials falling within the law's definition of pornography. Ordinance defenders strenuously protest that the issue is not censorship because the state, as such, is not authorized to initiate criminal prosecutions. But the prospect of having to defend a potentially infinite number of privately filed complaints creates at least as much of a chilling effect against sexual speech as does a

criminal law. And as long as representatives of the state—in this case, judges—have ultimate say over the interpretation, the distinction between this ordinance and "real" censorship will not hold.

In addition, three major problems should dissuade feminists from supporting this kind of law: first, the sexual images in question do not cause more harm than other aspects of misogynist culture; second, sexually explicit speech, even in male-dominated society, serves positive social functions for women; and third, the passage and enforcement of antipornography laws such as those supported in Minneapolis and Indianapolis are more likely to impede, rather than advance, feminist goals.

Ordinance proponents contend that pornography does cause violence because it conditions male sexual response to images of violence and thus provokes violence against women. The strongest research they offer is based on psychology experiments that employ films depicting a rape scene, toward the end of which the woman is shown to be enjoying the attack. The ordinances, by contrast, cover a much broader range of materials than this one specific heterosexual rape scenario. Further, the studies ordinance supporters cite do not support the theory that pornography causes violence against women. Taken at their strongest, some studies indicate that exposure to some pornography promotes sexist attitudes and beliefs in some subjects. Interestingly, researchers have found that subjects exposed to "debriefing" sessions at the end of the experiments, in which rape myths are identified and dispelled, are found to have fewer sexist attitudes when tested months later than the "controls" who were not exposed to any pornography. This indicates that education efforts can indeed be effective in countering the sexist messages of pornography.

In addition, the argument that pornography itself plays a major role in the general oppression of women contradicts the evidence of history. It need hardly be said that pornography did not lead to the burning of witches or the English common law treatment of women as chattel property. If anything functioned then as the prime communication medium for woman-hating, it was probably religion. Nor can pornography be blamed for the enactment of laws from at least the eighteenth century that allowed a husband to rape or beat his wife with impunity. In any period, the causes of women's oppression have been many and complex, drawing on the fundamental social and economic structures of society. Ordinance proponents offer little evidence to explain how the mass production of pornography—a relatively recent phenomenon—could have become so potent a causative agent so quickly.

The silencing of women is another example of the harm attributed to pornography. Yet if this argument were correct, one would expect that as the social visibility of pornography has increased, the tendency to credit women's accounts of rape would have decreased. In fact, although the treatment of women complainants in rape cases is far from perfect, the last 15 years of work by the women's movement has resulted in marked improvements. In many places, the corroboration requirement has now been abolished; cross-examination of victims as to past sexual experiences has been prohibited; and a number of police forces have developed specially trained units and procedures to improve the handling of sexual assault cases. The presence of rape fantasies in pornography may in part reflect a backlash against these women's movement advances, but to argue that most people routinely disbelieve women who file charges of rape belittles the real improvements made in social consciousness and law.

The third type of harm suggested by the ordinance backers is a kind of libel: the maliciously false characterization of women as a group of sexual masochists. The City of Indianapolis brief argues that pornography, like libel, is "a lie [which] once loosed" cannot be effectively rebutted by debate and further speech.

To claim that all pornography as defined by the ordinance is a lie is a false analogy. If truth is a defence to charges of libel, then surely depictions of consensual sex cannot be thought of as equivalent to a falsehood. For example, some women (and men) do enjoy bondage or display. The declaration by fiat that sadomasochism is a "lie" about sexuality reflects an arrogance and moralism that feminists should combat, not engage in. When mutually desired sexual experiences are depicted, pornography is not "libelous."

Not only does pornography not cause the kind and degree of harm that can justify the restraint of speech, but its existence serves some social functions which benefit women. Pornographic speech has many, often anomalous, characteristics. One is certainly that it magnifies the misogyny present in the culture and exaggerates the fantasy of male power. Another, however, is that the existence of pornography has served to flout conventional sexual mores, to ridicule sexual hypocrisy and to underscore the importance of sexual needs. Pornography carries many messages other than woman-hating: it advocates sexual adventure, sex outside of marriage, sex for no reason other than pleasure, casual sex, anonymous sex, group sex, voyeuristic sex, illegal sex, public sex. Some of these ideas appeal to women reading or seeing pornography, who may interpret some images as legitimating their own sense of sexual urgency or desire to be sexually aggressive. Women's experience of pornography is not as universally victimizing as the ordinance would have it.

The new antipornography laws, as restrictions on sexual speech, in many ways echo and expand upon the traditional legal analysis of sexually explicit speech under the rubric of obscenity. The U.S. Supreme Court has consistently ruled that sexual speech defined as "obscenity" does not belong in the system of public discourse, and is therefore an exception to the First Amendment and hence not entitled to protection under the free speech guarantee. (The definition of obscenity has shifted over the years and remains imprecise.) In 1957 the Supreme Court ruled that obscenity could be suppressed regardless of whether it presented an imminent threat of illegal activity. In the opinion of the Supreme Court, graphic sexual images do not communicate "real" ideas. These, it would seem, are only found in the traditionally defined public arena. Sexual themes can qualify as ideas if they use sexuality for argument's sake, but not if they speak in the words and images of "private" life—that is, if they graphically depict sex itself. At least theoretically, and insofar as the law functions as a pronouncement of moral judgment, sex is consigned to remain un-expressed and in the private realm.

The fallacies in this distinction are obvious. Under the U.S. Constitution, for example, it is acceptable to write "I am a sadomasochist" or even "Everyone should experiment with sadomasochism in order to increase sexual pleasure." But to write a graphic fantasy about sadomasochism that arouses and excites read-ers is not protected unless a court finds it to have serious literary, artistic or political value, despite the expressive nature of the content. Indeed, the fantasy depiction may com-municate identity in a more compelling way than the "I am" statement. For sexual minori-ties, sexual acts can be self-identifying and affirming statements in a hostile world. Im-ages of those acts should be protected for that reason, for they do have political content. Just as the personal can be political, so can the specifically and graphically sexual.

Supporters of the antipornography ordi-nances both endorse the concept that pornographic speech contains no ideas or ex-pressive interest, and at the same time attri-bute to pornography the capacity to trigger violent acts by the power of its misogyny. The city's brief in defence of the Indianapolis ordi-nance expanded this point by arguing that all sexually explicit speech is entitled to less con-stitutional protection than other speech. The antipornography groups have cleverly capital-ized on this approach—a product of a totally nonfeminist legal system—and are now attempting, through the mechanism of the ordinances, to legitimate a new crusade for protectionism and sexual conservatism.

The consequences of enforcing such a law, however, are much more likely to obstruct than advance feminist political goals. On the level of ideas, further narrowing of the public realm of sexual speech coincides all too well with the privatization of sexual, reproductive and family issues sought by the far right—an agenda described very well, for example, by Rosalind Petchesky in "The Rise of the New Right," in *Abortion and Woman's Choice.* Prac-tically speaking, the ordinances could result in attempts to eliminate the images associated with homosexuality. Doubtless there are het-erosexual women who believe that lesbianism is a "degrading" form of "subordination."

Since the ordinances allow for suits against materials in which men appear "in place of women," far-right antipornography crusaders could use these laws to suppress gay male por-nography. Imagine a Jerry Falwell-style con-servative filing a complaint against a gay book-store for selling sexually explicit materials showing men with other men in "degrading" or "submissive" or "objectified" postures—all in the name of protecting women.

And most ironically, while the ordinances would do nothing to improve the material con-ditions of most women's lives, their high visibility might well divert energy from the drive to enact other, less popular laws that would genuinely empower women—compara-ble worth legislation, for example, or affirma-tive action requirements or fairer property and support principles in divorce laws.

Other provisions of the ordinances concern coercive behavior: physical assault which is im-itative of pornographic images, coercion into pornographic performance and forcing por-nography on others. On close examination, however, even most of these provisions are problematic.

Existing law already penalizes physical assault, including when it is associated with pornography. Defenders of the laws often cite the example of models who have been raped or otherwise harmed while in the process of making pornographic images. But victims of this type of attack can already sue or prosecute those responsible. (Linda Marchiano, the ac-tress who appeared in the film *Deep Throat*, has not recovered damages for the physical assaults she describes in her book *Ordeal* be-cause the events happened several years be-fore she decided to try to file a suit. A lawsuit was thus precluded by the statute of limita-tions.) Indeed, the ordinances do not cover assault or other harm incurred while produc-ing pornography, presumably because other laws already achieve that end.

The ordinances do penalize coercing, in-timidating or fraudulently inducing anyone into performing for pornography. Although existing U.S. law already provides remedies for fraud or contracts of duress, this section of the ordinance seeks to facilitate recovery of damages by, for example, pornography mod-els who might otherwise encounter substantial prejudice against their claims. Supporters of this section have suggested that it is comparable to the Supreme Court's ban on child pornography. The analogy has been stretched to the point where the City of Indianapolis brief argued that women, like children, need "special protection." "Children are incapable of consenting to engage in pornographic conduct, even absent physical coercion and therefore require special protection," the brief stated. "By the same token, the physical and psychological well-being of women ought to be afforded comparable protection, for the coercive environment in which most pornographic models work vitiates any notion that they consent or 'choose' to perform in pornography."

The reality of women's lives is far more complicated. Women do not become pornography models because society is egalitarian and they exercise a "free choice," but neither do they "choose" this work because they have lost all power for deliberate, volitional behavior. Modeling or acting for pornography, like prostitution, can be a means of survival for those with limited options. For some women, at some points in their lives, it is a rational economic decision. Not every woman regrets having made it, although no woman should have to settle for it. The fight should be to expand the options and to insure job safety for women who do become porn models. By contrast, the impact of the ordinance as a whole would be either to eliminate jobs or drive the pornography industry further underground.

One of the vaguest provisions in the ordinance prohibits "forcing" pornography on a person. "Forcing" is not defined in the law, and one is left to speculate whether it means forced to respond to pornography, forced to read it or forced to glance at it before turning away. Also unclear is whether the perpetrator must in fact have some superior power over the person being forced—that is, is there a meaningful threat that makes the concept of force real.

Again, widely varying situations are muddled and a consideration of context is absent. "Forcing" pornography on a person "in any public space" is treated identically to using it as a method of sexual harassment in the workplace. The scope of "forcing" could include

walking past a newstand or browsing in a bookstore that had pornography on display. The force involved in such a situation seems mild when compared, for example, to the incessant sexist advertising on television.

The concept behind the "forcing" provision is appropriate, however, in the case of workplace harassment. A worker should not have to endure, especially on pain of losing her job, harassment based on sex, race, religion, nationality or any other factor. But this general policy was established by the U.S. courts as part of the guarantees of Title VII of the 1964 Civil Rights Act. Pornography used as a means of harassing women workers is already legally actionable, just as harassment by racial slurs is actionable. Any literature endorsing the oppression of women—whether pornography or the Bible—could be employed as an harassment device to impede a woman's access to a job, or to education, public accommodations or other social benefits. It is the usage of pornography in this situation, not the image itself, that is discriminatory. Appropriately, this section of the ordinances provides that only perpetrators of the forcing, not makers and distributors of the images, could be held liable.

Forcing of pornography on a person is also specifically forbidden "in the home." In her testimony before the Indianapolis City Council, Catharine MacKinnon referred to the problem of pornography being "forced on wives in preparation for later sexual scenes." Since only the person who forces the pornography on another can be sued, this provision becomes a kind of protection against domestic harassment. It would allow wives to sue husbands for court orders or damages for some usages of pornography. Although a fascinating attempt to subvert male power in the domestic realm, it nonetheless has problems. "Forcing" is not an easy concept to define in this context. It is hard to know what degree of intrusion would amount to forcing images onto a person who shares the same private space.

More important, the focus on pornography seems a displacement of the more fundamental issues involved in the conflicts that occur between husbands and wives or lovers over sex. Some men may invoke images that reflect their greater power to pressure women into performing the supposedly traditional role of acceding to male desires. Pornography may facilitate or enhance this dynamic of male dominance, but it is hardly the causative agent. Nor would removing the pornography do much to solve the problem. If the man invokes instead his friends' stories about sexual encounters or his experiences with other women, is the resulting interaction with his wife substantially different? Focusing on the pornography rather than on the relationship and its social context may serve only to channel heterosexual women's recognition of their own intimate oppression toward a movement hailed by the far right as being antiperversion rather than toward a feminist analysis of sexual politics.

The last of the sections that deals with actual coercive conduct is one that attempts to deal with the assault, physical injury or attack of any person in a way that is directly caused by specific pornography. The ordinances would allow a lawsuit against the makers and distributors of pornographic materials that were imitated by an attacker—the only provision of the ordinance that requires proof of causation. Presenting such proof would be extremely difficult. If the viewer's wilful decision to imitate the image were found to be an intervening, superceding cause of the harm, the plaintiff would not recover damages.

The policy issues here are no different from those concerning violent media images that are nonsexual: Is showing an image sufficient to cause an act of violence? Even if an image could be found to cause a viewer's behavior, was that behavior reasonably foreseeable? So far, those who have produced violent films have not been found blameworthy when third persons acted out the violence depicted. If this were to change, it would mean, for example, that the producer of the TV movie *The Burning Bed,* which told the true story of a battered wife who set fire to her sleeping husband, could be sued if a woman who saw the film killed her husband in a similar way. The result, of course, would be the end of films depicting real violence in the lives of women.

The ordinances' supporters offer no justification for singling out sexual assault from other kinds of violence. Certainly the experience of sexual assault is not always worse than that of being shot or stabbed or suffering other kinds of nonsexual assault. Nor is sexual assault the only form of violence that is fueled by sexism. If there were evidence that sexual images are more likely to be imitated, there might be some justification for treating them differently. But there is no support for this contention.

These laws, which would increase the state's regulation of sexual images, present many dangers for women. Although the ordinances draw much of their feminist support from women's anger at the market for images of sexual violence, they are aimed not at violence, but at sexual explicitness. Far-right elements recognize the possibility of using the full potential of the ordinances to enforce their sexually conservative world view, and have supported them for that reason. Feminists should therefore look carefully at the text of these "model" laws in order to understand why many believe them to be a useful tool in *anti*feminist moral crusades.

The proposed ordinances are also dangerous because they seek to embody in law an analysis of the role of sexuality and sexual images in the oppression of women with which all feminists do not agree. Underlying virtually every section of the proposed laws there is an assumption that sexuality is a realm of unremitting, unequaled victimization for women. Pornography appears as the monster that made this so. The ordinances' authors seek to impose their analysis by putting state power behind it. But this analysis is not the only feminist perspective on sexuality. Feminist theorists have also argued that the sexual terrain, however power-laden, is actively contested. Women are agents, and not merely victims, who make decisions and act on them, and who desire, seek out and enjoy sexuality.

The key provisions of the original Minneapolis ordinance are reprinted below:

(1) *Special Findings on Pornography*: The council finds that pornography is central in creating and maintaining the civil inequality of the sexes. Pornography is a systematic practice of exploitation and subordination based on sex which differentially harms women. The bigotry and contempt it promotes, with the acts

of aggression it fosters, harm women's opportunities for equality of rights in employment, education, property rights, public accommodations and public services; create public harassment and private denigration; promote injury and degradation such as rape, battery and prostitution and inhibit just enforcement of laws against these acts; contribute significantly to restricting women from full exercise of citizenship and participation in public life, including in neighborhoods; damage relations between the sexes; and undermine women's equal exercise of rights to speech and action guaranteed to all citizens under the constitutions and laws of the United States and the State of Minnesota.

(gg)*Pornography.* Pornography is a form of discrimination on the basis of sex.

(1) Pornography is the sexually explicit subordination of women, graphically depicted, whether in pictures or in words, that also includes one or more of the following:

(i) women are presented as dehumanized sexual objects, things or commodities; or

(ii) women are presented as sexual objects who enjoy pain or humiliation; or

(iii) women are presented as sexual objects who experience sexual pleasure in being raped; or

(iv) women are presented as sexual objects tied up or cut up or mutilated or bruised or physically hurt; or

(v) women are presented in postures of sexual submission; [or sexual servility, including by inviting penetration;]* or

(vi) women's body parts—including but not limited to vaginas, breasts, and buttocks—are exhibited, such that women are reduced to those parts; or

(vii) women are presented as whores by nature; or

(viii) women are presented being penetrated by objects or animals; or

(ix) women are presented in scenarios of degradation, injury, abasement, torture, shown as filthy or inferior, bleeding, bruised, or hurt in a context that makes these conditions sexual.

(2) The use of men, children, or transsexuals in the place of women . . . is pornography for purposes of . . . this statute.

(1) *Discrimination by trafficking in pornography*: The production, sale, exhibition, or distribution of pornography is discrimination against women by means of trafficking in pornography:

(1) City, state, and federally funded public libraries or private and public university and college libraries in which pornography is available for study, including on open shelves shall not be construed to be trafficking in pornography but special display presentations of pornography in said places is sex discrimination.

(2) The formation of private clubs or associations for purposes of trafficking in pornography is illegal and shall be considered a conspiracy to violate the civil rights of women.

(3) Any woman has a cause of action hereunder as a woman acting against the subordination of women. Any man or transsexual who alleges injury by pornography in the way women are injured by it shall also have a cause of action.

(m) *Coercion into pornographic performances.* Any person, including a transsexual, who is coerced, intimidated, or fraudulently induced (hereafter, "coerced") into performing for pornography shall have a cause of action against the maker(s), seller(s), exhibitor(s) or distributor(s) of said pornography for damages and for the elimination of the products of the performance(s) from the public view.

(1) *Limitation of action.* This claim shall not expire before five years have elapsed from the date of the coerced performance(s) or from the last appearance

---

*The bracketed phrase appears in an early version of the Minneapolis ordinance but may have been removed before the bill was formally introduced in the city council. It has reappeared, however, in subsequent defences of the ordinance by its supporters. See J. Miller, "Civil Rights, Not Censorship," *Village Voice*, Nov. 6, 1984, p. 6.

or sale of any product of the performance(s); whichever date is later;

(2) Proof of one or more of the following facts or conditions shall not, without more, negate a finding of coercion:

(aa) that the person is a woman; or

(bb) that the person is or has been a prostitute; or

(cc) that the person has attained the age of majority; or

(dd) that the person is connected by blood or marriage to anyone involved in or related to the making of the pornography; or

(ee) that the person has previously had, or been thought to have had, sexual relations with anyone including anyone involved in or related to the making of the pornography; or

(ff) that the person has previously posed for sexually explicit pictures for or with anyone, including anyone involved in or related to the making of the pornography at issue; or

(gg) that anyone else, including a spouse or other relative, has given permission on the person's behalf; or

(hh) that the person actually consented to a use of the performance that is changed into pornography; or

(ii) that the person knew that the purpose of the acts or events in question was to make pornography; or

(jj) that the person showed no resistance or appeared to cooperate actively in the photographic sessions or in the sexual events that produced the pornography; or

(kk) that the person signed a contract, or made statements affirming a willingness to cooperate; or

(ll) that no physical force, threats, or weapons were used in the making of the pornography; or

(mm) that the person was paid or otherwise compensated.

(n) *Forcing pornography on a person.* Any woman, man, child, or transsexual who has pornography forced on them in any place of employment, in education, in a home, or in any public place has a cause of action against the perpetrator and/or institution.

(o) *Assault or physical attack due to pornography.* Any woman, man, child, or transsexual who is assaulted, physically attacked or injured in a way that is directly caused by specific pornography has a claim for damages against the perpetrator, the maker(s), distributor(s), seller(s), and/or exhibitor(s), and for an injunction against the specific pornography's further exhibition, distribution, or sale. No damages shall be assessed (A) against maker(s) for pornography made, (B) against distributor(s) for pornography distributed, (C) against seller(s) for pornography sold, or (D) against exhibitor(s) for pornography exhibited prior to the effective date of this act.

(p) *Defenses.* Where the materials which are the subject matter of a cause of action under subsections (l), (m), (n), or (o) of this section are pornography, it shall not be a defense that the defendant did not know or intend that the materials are pornography or sex discrimination.

36. Pornography and the Alienation of Male Sexuality

Harry Brod

Harry Brod discusses the role of pornography in the social construction of male sexuality. He feels that pornography misrepresents the "normal" sexual development of men—a point that is crucial to understanding the link among pornography, male sexuality, and violence against women.

This paper is intended as a contribution to an ongoing discussion. It aims to augment, not refute or replace, what numerous commentators have said about pornography's role in the social construction of sexuality. I have several principal aims in this paper. My primary focus is to examine pornography's model of male sexuality. Furthermore, in the discussion of pornography's role in the social construction of sexuality, I wish to place more emphasis than is common on the social construction of pornography. As I hope to show, these are related questions. One reason I focus on the image of male sexuality in pornography is that I believe this aspect of the topic has been relatively neglected. In making this my topic here, I do not mean to suggest that this is the most essential part of the picture. Indeed, I am clear it is not. It seems clear enough to me that the main focus of discussion about the effects of pornography is and should be the harmful effects of pornography on women, its principal victims. Yet, there is much of significance which needs to be said about pornography's representation, or perhaps I should more accurately say misrepresentation, of male sexuality. My focus shall be on what is usually conceived of as "normal" male sexuality, which for my purposes I take to be consensual, non-violent heterosexuality, as these terms are conventionally understood. I am aware of analyses which argue that this statement assumes distinctions which are at least highly problematic, if not outright false, which

Copyright 1988 by *Social Theory and Practice*, Vol. 14, No. 3 (Fall 1988), pp. 265–284. Reprinted by permission.

argue that this "normal" sexuality is itself coercive, both as compulsory heterosexuality and as containing implicit or explicit coercion and violence. My purpose is not to take issue with these analyses, but simply to present an analysis of neglected aspects of the links between mainstream male sexuality and pornography. I would argue that the aspect of the relation between male sexuality and pornography usually discussed, pornography's incitement to greater extremes of violence against women, presupposes such a connection with the more accepted mainstream. Without such a link, pornography's messages would be rejected by rather than assimilated into male culture. My intention is to supply this usually missing link.

My analysis proceeds from both feminist and Marxist theory. These are often taken to be theories which speak from the point of view of the oppressed, in advocacy for their interests. That they indeed are, but they are also more than that. For each claims not simply to speak for the oppressed in a partisan way, but also to speak a truth about the social whole, a truth perhaps spoken in the name of the oppressed, but a truth objectively valid for the whole. That is to say, Marxism is a theory which analyzes the ruling class as well as the proletariat, and feminism is a theory which analyzes men as well as women. It is not simply that Marxism is concerned with class, and feminism with gender, both being united by common concerns having to do with power. Just as Marxism understands class as power, rather than simply understanding class differences as differences of income, lifestyle, or opportunities, so the distinctive contribution of feminism is its understanding of gender as power, rather than simply as sex role differentiation. Neither class nor gender should be reified into being understood as fixed entities, which then differentially distribute power and its rewards. Rather, they are categories continually constituted in ongoing contestations over power. The violence endemic to both systems cannot be understood as externalized manifestations of some natural inner biological or psychological drives existing prior to the social order, but must be seen as emerging in and from the relations of power which constitute social structures. Just as capitalist exploitation is caused not by capitalists' excess greed but rather by the structural imperatives under which capitalism functions, so men's violence is not the manifestation of some inner male essence, but rather evidence of the bitterness and depth of the struggles through which genders are forged.[1]

For my purposes here, to identify this as a socialist feminist analysis is not, in the first instance, to proclaim allegiance to any particular set of doctrinal propositions, though I am confident that those I subscribe to would be included in any roundup of the usual suspects, but rather to articulate a methodological commitment to make questions of power central to questions of gender, and to understand gendered power in relation to economic power, and as historically, materially structured.[2] If one can understand the most intimate aspects of the lives of the dominant group in these terms, areas which would usually be taken to be the farthest afield from where one might expect these categories to be applicable, then I believe one has gone a long way toward validating claims of the power of socialist feminist theory to comprehend the totality of our social world. This is my intention here. I consider the analysis of male sexuality I shall be presenting part of a wider socialist feminist analysis of patriarchal capitalist masculinity, an analysis I have begun to develop elsewhere.[3]

As shall be abundantly clear, I do not take a "sexual liberationist" perspective on pornography. I am aware that many individuals, particularly various sexual minorities, make this claim on pornography's behalf. I do not minimize nor negate their personal experiences. In the context of our society's severe

sexual repressiveness, pornography may indeed have a liberating function for certain individuals. But I do not believe an attitude of approval for pornography follows from this. Numerous drugs and devices which have greatly helped individual women have also been medical and social catastrophes—the one does not negate the other.

I shall be claiming that pornography has a negative impact on men's own sexuality. This is a claim that an aspect of an oppressive system, patriarchy, operates, at least in part, to the disadvantage of the group it privileges, men. This claim does not deny that the overall effect of the system is to operate in men's advantage, nor does it deny that the same aspect of the system under consideration, that is, male sexuality and pornography under patriarchy, might not also contribute to the expansion and maintenance of male power even as it also works to men's disadvantage. Indeed, I shall be arguing precisely for such complementarity. I am simply highlighting one of the "contradictions" in the system. My reasons for doing so are in the first instance simply analytic: to, as I said, bring to the fore relatively neglected aspects of the issue. Further, I also have political motivations for emphasizing this perspective. I view raising consciousness of the prices of male power as part of a strategy through which one could at least potentially mobilize men against pornography's destructive effects on both women and men.

It will aid the following discussion if I ask readers to call to mind a classic text in which it is argued that, among other things, a system of domination also damages the dominant group, and prevents them from realizing their full humanity. The argument is that the dominant group is "alienated" in specific and identifiable ways. The text I have in mind is Marx's "Economic and Philosophic Manuscripts of 1844." Just as capitalists as well as workers are alienated under capitalism according to Marxist theory (in a certain restricted sense, even more so), so men, I shall argue, and in particular male modes of sexuality, are also alienated under patriarchy. In the interests of keeping this paper a manageable length, I shall here assume rather than articulate a working familiarity with Marx's concept of alienation, the process whereby one becomes a stranger to oneself and one's own powers come to be powers over and against one. Since later in the paper I make use of some of Marx's more economistic concepts, I should however simply note that I see more continuity than rupture between Marx's earlier, more philosophical writings and his later, more economic ones.[4] While much of this paper presents an analysis of men's consciousness, I should make clear that while alienation may register in one's consciousness (as I argue it does), I follow Marx in viewing alienation not primarily as a psychological state dependent on the individual's sensibilities or consciousness but as a condition inevitably caused by living within a system of alienation. I should also note that I consider what follows an appropriation, not a systematic interpretation, of some of Marx's concepts.

Alienated pornographic male sexuality can be understood as having two dimensions, what I call the objectification of the body and the loss of subjectivity. I shall consider each in greater detail, describing various aspects of pornographic male sexuality under each heading in a way which I hope brings out how they may be conceptualized in Marx's terms. Rather than then redoing the analysis in Marx's terms, I shall then simply cite Marx briefly to indicate the contours of such a translation.

1. Objectification of the Body

In terms of both its manifest image of and its effects on male sexuality, that is, in both intrinsic and consequentialist terms, pornography restricts male sensuality in favor of a genital, performance oriented male sexuality. Men become sexual acrobats endowed with oversized and overused organs which are, as the chapter title of a fine book on male sexuality describes what it calls "The Fantasy Model of Sex: Two Feet Long, Hard as Steel, and Can Go All Night."[5] To speak non-euphemistically, using penile performance as an index of male strength and potency directly contradicts biological facts. There is no muscle tissue in

the penis. Its erection when aroused results simply from increased blood flow to the area. All social mythology aside, the male erection is physiologically nothing more than localized high blood pressure. Yet this particular form of hypertension has attained mythic significance. Not only does this focusing of sexual attention on one organ increase male performance anxieties, but it also desensitizes other areas of the body from becoming what might otherwise be sources of pleasure. A colleague once told me that her favorite line in a lecture on male sexuality I used to give in a course I regularly taught was my declaration that the basic male sex organ is not the penis, but the skin.

The predominant image of women in pornography presents women as always sexually ready, willing, able, and eager. The necessary corollary to pornography's myth of female perpetual availability is its myth of the male perpetual readiness. Just as the former fuels male misogyny when real-life women fail to perform to pornographic standards, so do men's failures to similarly perform fuel male insecurities. Furthermore, I would argue that this diminishes pleasure. Relating to one's body as a performance machine produces a split consciousness wherein part of one's attention is watching the machine, looking for flaws in its performance, even while one is supposedly immersed in the midst of sensual pleasure. This produces a self-distancing self-consciousness which mechanizes sex and reduces pleasure. (This is a problem perpetuated by numerous sexual self-help manuals, which treat sex as a matter of individual technique for fine-tuning the machine rather than as human interaction. I would add that men's sexual partners are also affected by this, as they can often intuit when they are being subjected to rote manipulation.)

2. Loss of Subjectivity

In the terms of discourse of what it understands to be "free" sex, pornographic sex comes "free" of the demands of emotional intimacy or commitment. It is commonly said as a generalization that women tend to connect sex with emotional intimacy more than men do. Without romantically blurring female sexuality into soft focus, if what is meant is how each gender consciously thinks or speaks of sex, I think this view is fair enough. But I find it takes what men say about sex, that it doesn't mean as much or the same thing to them, too much at face value. I would argue that men do feel similar needs for intimacy, but are trained to deny them, and are encouraged further to see physical affection and intimacy primarily if not exclusively in sexual terms. This leads to the familiar syndrome wherein, as one man put it:

> Although what most men want is physical affection, what they end up thinking they want is to be laid by a Playboy bunny.[6]

This puts a strain on male sexuality. Looking to sex to fulfill what are really non-sexual needs, men end up disappointed and frustrated. Sometimes they feel an unfilled void, and blame it on their or their partner's inadequate sexual performance. At other times they feel a discomfitting urgency or neediness to their sexuality, leading in some cases to what are increasingly recognized as sexual addiction disorders (therapists are here not talking about the traditional "perversions," but behaviors such as what is coming to be called a "Don Juan Syndrome," an obsessive pursuit of sexual "conquests"). A confession that sex is vastly overrated often lies beneath male sexual bravado. I would argue that sex seems overrated because men look to sex for the fulfillment of non-sexual emotional needs, a quest doomed to failure. Part of the reason for this failure is the priority of quantity over quality of sex which comes with sexuality's commodification. As human needs become subservient to market desires, the ground is laid for an increasing multiplication of desires to be exploited and filled by marketable commodities.[7]

For the most part the female in pornography is not one the man has yet to "conquer," but one already presented to him for the "taking." The female is primarily there as sex object, not sexual subject. Or, if she is not completely objectified, since men do want to be desired themselves, hers is at least a subjugated subjectivity. But one needs another independent subject, not an object or a captured subjectivity, if one either wants one's own prowess validated, or if one simply desires human interaction. Men functioning in the pornographic mode of male sexuality, in which men dominate women, are denied satisfaction of these human desires.[8] Denied recognition in the sexual interaction itself, they look to gain this recognition in wider social recognition of their "conquest."

To the pornographic mind, then, women become trophies awarded to the victor. For women to serve this purpose of achieving male social validation, a woman "conquered" by one must be a woman deemed desirable by others. Hence pornography both produces and reproduces uniform standards of female beauty. Male desires and tastes must be channeled into a single mode, with allowance for minor variations which obscure the fundamentally monolithic nature of the mold. Men's own subjectivity becomes masked to them, as historically and culturally specific and varying standards of beauty are made to appear natural and given. The ease with which men reach quick agreement on what makes a woman "attractive," evidenced in such things as the "1-10" rating scale of male banter and the reports of a computer program's success in predicting which of the contestants would be crowned "Miss America," demonstrates how deeply such standards have been internalized, and consequently the extent to which men are dominated by desires not authentically their own.

Lest anyone think that the analysis above is simply a philosopher's ruminations, too far removed from the actual experiences of most men, let me just offer one recent instantiation, from among many known to me, and even more, I am sure, I do not know. The following is from the *New York Times Magazine*'s "About Men" weekly column. In an article titled "Couch Dancing," the author describes his reactions to being taken to a place, a sort of cocktail bar, where women "clad only in the skimpiest of bikini underpants" would "dance" for a small group of men for a few minutes for about 25 or 30 dollars, men who "sat immobile, drinks in hand, glassy-eyed, tapping their feet to the disco music that throbbed through the room."

Men are supposed to like this kind of thing, and there is a quite natural part of each of us that does. But there is another part of us—of me, at least—that is not grateful for the traditional male sexual programming, not proud of the results. By a certain age, most modern men have been so surfeited with images of unattainably beautiful women in preposterous contexts that we risk losing the capacity to respond to the ordinarily beautiful women we love in our bedrooms. There have been too many times when I have guiltily resorted to impersonal fantasy because the genuine love I felt for a woman wasn't enough to convert feeling into performance. As in those sorry, secret moments, I have resented deeply my lifelong indoctrination into the esthetic of the centerfold.[9]

3. Alienation and Crisis

I believe that all of the above can be translated without great difficulty into a conceptual framework paralleling Marx's analysis of the alienation experienced by capitalists. The essential points are captured in two sentences from Marx's manuscripts:

1. *All* the physical and intellectual senses have been replaced by the simple alienation of *all* these senses; the sense of *having*.[10]

2. The wealthy man is at the same time one who *needs* a complex of human manifestations of life, and whose own self-realization exists as an inner necessity, a need.[11]

Both sentences speak to a loss of human interaction and self-realization. The first articulates how desires for conquest and control prevent input from the world. The second presents an alternative conception wherein wealth is measured by abilities for self-expression, rather than possession. Here Marx expresses his conceptualization of the state of alienation as a loss of sensuous fulfillment, poorly replaced by a pride of possession, and a lack of self-consciousness and hence actualization of one's own real desires and abilities. One could recast the preceding analysis of pornographic male sexuality through these categories. In Marx's own analysis, these are more properly conceived of as the results of alienation, rather than the process of alienation itself. This process is at its basis a process of inversion, a reversal of the subject-object relationship, in which one's active powers become estranged from one, and return to dominate one as an external force. It is this aspect which I believe is most useful in understanding the alienation of male sexuality of which pornography is part and parcel. How is it that men's power turns against them, so that pornography, in and by which men dominate women, comes to dominate men themselves?

To answer this question I shall find it useful to have recourse to two other concepts central to Marxism, the concept of "crisis" in the system and the concept of "imperialism."[12] Marx's conception of the economic crisis of capitalism is often misunderstood as a prophecy of a cataclysmic doomsday scenario for the death of capitalism. Under this interpretation, some look for a single event, perhaps like a stock market crash, to precipitate capitalism's demise. But such events are for Marx at most triggering events, particular crises which can shake the system, if at all, only because of the far more important underlying structural general crisis of capitalism. This general crisis is increasingly capitalism's ordinary state, not an extraordinary occurrence. It is manifest in the ongoing fiscal crisis of the state as well as recurring crises of legitimacy, and results from basic contradictory tensions within capitalism. One way of expressing these tensions is to see them as a conflict between the classic laissez-faire capitalist market mode, wherein capitalists are free to run their own affairs as individuals, and the increasing inability of the capitalist class to run an increasingly complex system without centralized management. The result of this tension is that the state increasingly becomes a managerial committee for the capitalist class, and is increasingly called upon to perform functions previously left to individuals. As entrepreneurial and laissez-faire capitalism give way to corporate capitalism and the welfare state, the power of capitalism becomes increasingly depersonalized, increasingly reft from the hands of individual capitalists and collectivized, so that capitalists themselves come more and more under the domination of impersonal market forces no longer under their direct control.

To move now to the relevance of the above, there is currently a good deal of talk about a perceived crisis of masculinity, in which men are said to be confused by contradictory imperatives given them in the wake of the women's movement. Though the male ego feels uniquely beleaguered today, in fact such talk regularly surfaces in our culture—the 1890's in the United States, for example, was another period in which the air was full of a "crisis of masculinity" caused by the rise of the "New Woman" and other factors.[13] Now, I wish to put forward the hypothesis that these particular "crises" of masculinity are but surface manifestations of a much deeper and broader phenomenon which I call the "general crisis of patriarchy," paralleling Marx's general crisis of capitalism. Taking a very broad view, this crisis results from the increasing depersonalization of patriarchal power which occurs with the development of patriarchy from its pre-capitalist phase, where power really was often directly exercised by individual patriarchs, to its late capitalist phase where men collectively exercise power over women, but are themselves as individuals increasingly under the domination of those same patriarchal powers.[14] I would stress that the sense of there being a "crisis" of masculinity arises not from the decrease or increase in patriarchal power as such. Patriarchal imperatives for men to retain power over women remain in force throughout. But there is a shift in the mode of that power's exercise, and the sense of crisis results from the simultaneous promulgation throughout society of two conflicting modes of patriarchal power, the earlier more personal form and the later more institutional form. The crisis results from the incompatibility of the two conflicting ideals of masculinity embraced by the different forms of patriarchy, the increasing conflicts between behavioral and attitudinal norms of the political/economic and the personal/familial spheres.

4. From Patriarchy to Fratriarchy

To engage for a moment in even broader speculation than that which I have so far permitted myself, I believe that much of the culture, law, and philosophy of the nineteenth century in particular can be re-interpreted as marking a decisive turn in this transition. I believe the passing of personal patriarchal power and its transformation into institutional patriarchal power in this period of the interrelated consolidation of corporate capitalism is evidenced in such phenomena as the rise of what one scholar has termed "judicial patriarchy," the new social regulation of masculinity through the courts and social welfare agencies, which through new support laws, poor laws, desertion laws and other changes transformed what were previously personal obligations into legal duties, as well as in the "Death of God" phenomenon and its aftermath.[15] That is to say, I believe the loss of the personal exercise of patriarchal power and its diffusion through the institutions of society is strongly implicated in the death of God the Father and the secularization of culture in the nineteenth century, as well as the modern and postmodern problem of grounding authority and values.

I would like to tentatively and preliminarily propose a new concept to reflect this shift in the nature of patriarchy caused by the de-individualization and collectivization of male power. Rather than speak simply of advanced capitalist patriarchy, the rule of the *fathers,* I suggest we speak of fratriarchy, the rule of the *brothers.* For the moment, I propose this concept more as a metaphor than as a sharply defined analytical tool, much as the concept of patriarchy was used when first popularized. I believe this concept better captures what I could argue is one of the key issues in conceptualizing contemporary masculinities, the disjunction between the facts of public male power and the feelings of individual male powerlessness. As opposed to the patriarch, who embodied many levels and kinds of authority in his single person, the brothers stand in uneasy relationships with each other, engaged in sibling rivalry while trying to keep the power of the family of man as a whole intact. I note that one of the consequences of the shift from patriarchy to fratriarchy is that some people become nostalgic for the authority of the benevolent patriarch, who if he was doing his job right at least prevented one of the great dangers of fratriarchy, fratricide, the brothers' killing each other. Furthermore, fratriarchy is an intragenerational concept, whereas patriarchy is intergenerational. Patriarchy, as a father-to-son transmission of authority, more directly inculcates traditional historically grounded authority, whereas the dimension of temporal continuity is rendered more problematic in fratriarchy's brother-to-brother relationships. I believe this helps capture the problematic nature of modern historical consciousness as it emerged from the nineteenth century, what I would argue is the most significant single philosophical theme of that century. If taken in Freudian directions, the concept of fratriarchy also speaks to the brothers' collusion to repress awareness of the violence which lies at the foundations of society.

To return to the present discussion, the debate over whether pornography reflects men's power or powerlessness, as taken up, recently by Alan Soble in his book *Pornography: Marxism, Feminism, and the Future of Sexuality*, can be resolved if one makes a distinction such as I have proposed between personal and institutional male power. Soble cites men's use of pornographic fantasy as compensation for their powerlessness in the real world to argue that "pornography is therefore not so much an expression of male power as it is an expression of their lack of power."[16] In contrast, I would argue that by differentiating levels of power one should more accurately say that pornography is both an expression of men's public power and an expression of their lack of personal power. The argument of this paper is that pornography's image of male sexuality works to the detriment of men personally even

as its image of female sexuality enhances the powers of patriarchy. It expresses the power of alienated sexuality, or, as one could equally well say, the alienated power of sexuality.

With this understanding, one can reconcile the two dominant but otherwise irreconcilable images of the straight male consumer of pornography: on the one hand the powerful rapist, using pornography to consummate his sexual violence, and on the other hand the shy recluse, using it to consummate his masturbatory fantasies. Both images have their degree of validity, and I believe it is a distinctive virtue of the analysis presented here that one can understand not only the merits of each depiction, but their interconnection.

5. Embodiment and Erotica

In the more reductionist and determinist strains of Marxism, pornography as ideology would be relegated to the superstructure of capitalism. I would like to suggest another conceptualization: that pornography is not part of patriarchal capitalism's superstructure, but part of its infrastructure. Its commodification of the body and interpersonal relationships paves the way for the ever more penetrating ingression of capitalist market relations into the deepest reaches of the individual's psychological makeup. The feminist slogan that "The Personal is Political" emerges at a particular historical moment, and should be understood not simply as an imperative declaration that what has previously been seen solely as personal should now be viewed politically, but also as a response to the real increasing politicization of personal life.

This aspect can be illuminated through the Marxist concept of imperialism. The classical Marxist analysis of imperialism argues that it is primarily motivated by two factors: exploitation of natural resources and extension of the market. In this vein, pornography should be understood as imperialism of the body. The greater public proliferation of pornography, from the "soft-core" pornography of much commercial advertising to the greater availability of "hard-core" pornography, proclaims the greater colonization of the body by the market.[17] The increasing use of the male body as a sex symbol in contemporary culture is evidence of advanced capitalism's increasing use of new styles of masculinity to promote images of men as consumers as well as producers.[18] Today's debates over the "real" meaning of masculinity can be understood in large part as a struggle between those espousing the "new man" style of masculinity more suited to advanced corporate, consumerist patriarchal capitalism and those who wish to return to an idealized version of "traditional" masculinity suited to a more production-oriented, entrepreneurial patriarchal capitalism.[19]

In a more theoretical context, one can see that part of the reason the pornography debate has been so divisive, placing on different sides of the question people who usually find themselves allies, is that discussions between civil libertarians and feminists have often been at cross purposes. Here one can begin to relate political theory not to political practice, but to metaphysical theory. The classical civil liberties perspective on the issue remains deeply embedded in a male theoretical discourse on the meaning of sexuality. The connection between the domination of nature and the domination of women has been argued from many Marxist and feminist points of view.[20] The pivot of this connection is the masculine overlay of the mind-body dualism onto the male-female dichotomy. Within this framework, morality par excellence consists in the masculinized mind restraining the feminized body, with sexual desires seen as the crucial test for these powers of restraint. From this point of view, the question of the morality of pornography is primarily the quantitative question of how much sexual display is allowed, with full civil libertarians opting to uphold the extreme end of this continuum, arguing that no sexual expression should be repressed. But the crucial question, for at least the very important strain of feminist theory which rejects these dualisms which frame the debate for the malestream mainstream, is not *how much* sexuality is displayed but rather *how* sexuality is displayed. These theories speak not of mind-body dualism, but of mind/body wholism, where the body is seen not as the limitation or barrier for the expression of the free moral self, but rather as the most immediate and intimate vehicle for the expression of that self. The question of sexual morality here is not that of restraining or releasing sexual desires as they are forced on the spiritual self by the temptations of the body, but that of constructing spirited and liberating sexual relationships with and through one's own and others' bodies. Here sexual freedom is not the classical liberal freedom *from* external restraint, but the more radical freedom *to* construct authentically expressive sexualities.

I have argued throughout this paper that pornography is a vehicle for the imposition of socially constructed sexuality, not a means for the expression of autonomously self-determined sexuality. (I would add that in contrasting imposed and authentic sexualities I am not endorsing a sexual essentialism, but simply carving out a space for a more personal freedom.) Pornography is inherently about commercialized sex, about the eroticization of power and the power of eroticization. One can look to the term's etymology for confirmation of this point. It comes from the classical Greek "*pornographos,* meaning 'writing (sketching) of harlots,'" sometimes women captured in war.[21] Any distinction between pornography and erotica remains problematic, and cannot be drawn with absolute precision. Yet I believe some such distinction can and must be made. I would place the two terms not in absolute opposition, but at two ends of a continuum, with gray areas of necessity remaining between them. The gradations along the continuum are marked not by the explicitness of the portrayal of sexuality or the body, nor by the assertiveness vs. passivity of persons, nor by any categorization of sexual acts or activities, but by the extent to which autonomous personhood is attributed to the person or persons portrayed. Erotica portrays sexual subjects, manifesting their personhood in and through their bodies. Pornography depicts sex objects, persons reduced to their bodies. While the erotic nude presents the more pristine sexual body before the social persona is adopted through donning one's clothing, the pornographic nude portrays a body whose clothing has been more or less forcibly removed, where the absence of that clothing remains the most forceful presence in the image. Society's objectification remains present, indeed emphasized, in pornography, in a way in which it does not in erotica. Erotica, as sexual art, expresses a self, whereas pornography, as sexual commodity, markets one. The latter "works" because the operation it performs on women's bodies resonates with the "pornographizing" the male gaze does to women in other areas of society.[22] These distinctions remain problematic, to say the least, in their application, and disagreement in particular cases will no doubt remain. Much more work needs to be done before one could with any reasonable confidence distinguish authentic from imposed, personal from commercial, sexuality. Yet I believe this is the crucial question, and I believe these concepts correctly indicate the proper categories of analysis. Assuming a full definition of freedom as including autonomy and self-determination, pornography is therefore incompatible with real freedom.

6. Conclusions

It has often been noted that while socialist feminism is currently a major component of the array of feminisms one finds in academic feminism and women's studies, it is far less influential on the playing fields of practical politics.[23] While an analysis of male sexuality may seem an unlikely source to further socialist feminism's practical political agenda, I hope this paper's demonstration of the interconnections between intimate personal experiences and large scale historical and social structures, especially in what may have initially seemed unlikely places, may serve as a useful methodological model for other investigations.

In one sense, this paper hopes to further the development of socialist feminist theory via a return to Hegel, especially the Hegel of the *Phenomenology*. Not only is Hegel's master-servant dialectic the *sine qua non* for the use of the concept of alienation in this paper, but the inspiration for a mode of analysis which is true to the experiential consciousness of social actors while at the same time delimiting that consciousness by showing its partiality and placing it in a broader context is rooted in Hegel's *Phenomenology*. It is not a coincidence that the major wave of socialist feminist theory and practice in the late 60's and early 70's coincided with a wave of Marxist interest in Hegel, and that current signs of a new feminist interest in Hegel coincide with signs of the resurgence of radical politics in the United States.[24] Analogous to the conception of socialist feminism I articulated in the Introduction to this paper, my conception of Hegelianism defines Hegelianism as method rather than doctrine.[25] In some sense, contemporary Marxism and feminism can already be said to be rooted in Hegel, in the case of Marxism through Marx himself, and in the case of feminism through Beauvoir's *The Second Sex*. A more explicitly Hegelian influenced socialist feminism would embody a theory and practice emphasizing the following themes: the dialectic between individual consciousness and social structure, a thoroughly historical epistemology, a non-dualistic metaphysics, an understanding of gender, class, and other differences as being constituted through interaction rather than consisting of isolated "roles," the priority of political over moralistic or economistic theory, a probing of the relations between state power and cultural hegemony, a program for reaching unity through difference rather than through sameness, a tolerance of if not preference for ambiguity and contradiction, and an orientation toward process over end product.[26]

I would like to conclude with some remarks on the practical import of this analysis. First of all, if the analysis of the relationship between pornography and consumerism and the argument about pornography leading to violence are correct, then a different conceptualization of the debate over the ethics of the feminist anti-pornography movement emerges. If one accepts, as I do, the idea that this movement is not against sex, but against sexual abuse, then the campaign against pornography is essentially not a call for censorship but a consumer campaign for product safety. The proper context for the debate over its practices is then not issues of free speech or civil liberties, but issues of business ethics. Or rather, this is the conclusion I reach remaining focused on pornography and male sexuality. But we should remember the broader context I alluded to at the beginning of this paper, the question of pornography's effects on women. In that context, women are not the consumers of pornography, but the consumed. Rather than invoking the consumer movement, perhaps we should then look to environmental protection as a model.[27] Following this line of reasoning, one could in principle then perhaps develop under the tort law of product liability an argument to accomplish much of the regulation of sexually explicit material some are now trying to achieve through legislative means, perhaps developing a new definition of "safe" sexual material.

Finally, for most of us most of our daily practice as academics consists of teaching rather than writing or reading in our fields. If one accepts the analysis I have presented, a central if not primary concern for us should therefore be how to integrate this analysis into our classrooms. I close by suggesting that we use this analysis and others like it from the emerging field of men's studies to demonstrate to the men in our classes the direct relevance of feminist analysis to their own lives, at the most intimate and personal levels, and that we look for ways to demonstrate to men that feminism can be personally empowering and liberating for them without glossing over, and in fact emphasizing, the corresponding truth that this will also require the surrender of male privilege.[28]

Notes

1. I am indebted for this formulation to Tim Carrigan, Bob Connell, and John Lee, "Toward a New Sociology of Masculinity," in Harry Brod, ed., *The Making of Masculinities: The New Men's Studies* (Boston: Allen & Unwin, 1987).

2. For the *locus classicus* of the redefinition of Marxism as method rather than doctrine, see George Lukács, *History and Class Consciousness: Studies in Marxist Dialectics*, trans. Rodney Livingstone (Cambridge, MA: MIT Press, 1972).

3. See my Introduction to Brod, *The Making of*

Masculinities. For other recent books by men I consider to be engaged in essentially the same or a kindred project, see Jeff Hearn, *The Gender of Oppression: Men, Masculinity, and the Critique of Marxism* (New York: St. Martin's Press, 1987) and R. W. Connell, *Gender and Power* (Stanford, CA: Stanford University Press, 1987), particularly the concept of "hegemonic masculinity," also used in Carrigan, Connell, and Lee, "Toward a New Sociology of Masculinity." Needless to say, none of this work would be conceivable without the pioneering work of many women in women's studies.

4. For book length treatments of Marx's concept of alienation, see István Mészáros, *Marx's Theory of Alienation* (New York: Harper & Row, 1972), and Bertell Ollman, *Alienation: Marx's Conception of Man in Capitalist Society* (Cambridge: Cambridge University Press, 1971).

5. Bernie Zilbergeld, *Male Sexuality: A Guide to Sexual Fulfillment* (Boston: Little, Brown and Company, 1978).

6. Michael Betzold, "How Pornography Shackles Men and Oppresses Women," in *For Men Against Sexism: A Book of Readings,* ed. Jon Snodgrass (Albion, CA: Times Change Press, 1977), p. 46.

7. I am grateful to Lenore Langsdorf and Paula Rothenberg for independently suggesting to me how this point would fit into my analysis.

8. See Jessica Benjamin, "The Bonds of Love: Rational Violence and Erotic Domination," *Feminist Studies* 6 (1980): 144–74.

9. Keith McWalter, "Couch Dancing," *New York Times Magazine,* December 6, 1987, p. 138.

10. Karl Marx, "Economic and Philosophic Manuscripts: Third Manuscript," in *Early Writings,* ed. and trans. T. B. Bottomore (New York: McGraw-Hill, 1964), pp. 159–60.

11. Marx., pp. 164–65.

12. An earlier version of portions of the following argument appears in my article "Eros Thanatized: Pornography and Male Sexuality" with a "1988 Postscript," forthcoming in Michael Kimmel, ed., *Men Confronting Pornography* (New York: Crown, 1989). The article originally appeared (without the postscript) in *Humanities in Society* 7 (1984), pp. 47–63.

13. See the essays by myself and Michael Kimmel in Brod, *The Making of Masculinities.*

14. Compare Carol Brown on the shift from pri-

vate to public patriarchy: "Mothers, Fathers, and Children: From Private to Public Patriarchy" in Lydia Sargent, ed., *Women and Revolution* (Boston: South End Press, 1981).

15. According to Martha May in her paper 'An Obligation on Every Man': Masculine Breadwinning and the Law in Nineteenth Century New York," presented at the American Historical Association, Chicago, Illinois, 1987, from which I learned of these changes; the term "judicial patriarchy" is taken from historian Michael Grossberg's *Governing the Hearth: Law and the Family in Nineteenth Century America* (Chapel Hill: University of North Carolina Press, 1985) and "Crossing Boundaries: Nineteenth Century Domestic Relations Law and the Merger of Family and Legal History," *American Bar Foundation Research Journal* (1985): 799–847.

16. Alan Soble, *Pornography: Marxism, Feminism, and the Future of Sexuality* (New Haven: Yale University Press, 1986), p. 82. I agree with much of Soble's analysis of male sexuality in capitalism, and note the similarities between much of what he says about "dismemberment" and consumerism and my analysis here.

17. See John D'Emilio and Estelle B. Freedman, *Intimate Matters: A History of Sexuality in America* (New York: Harper & Row, 1988).

18. See Barbara Ehrenreich, *The Hearts of Men: American Dreams and the Flight from Commitment* (New York: Anchor-Doubleday, 1983); and Wolfgang Fritz Haug, *Critique of Commodity Aesthetics: Appearance, Sexuality, and Advertising in Capitalist Society,* trans. Robert Bock (Minneapolis: University of Minnesota Press, 1986).

19. See my "Work Clothes and Leisure Suits: The Class Basis and Bias of the Men's Movement," originally in *Changing Men* 11 (1983) 10–12 and 38–40, reprint forthcoming in *Men's Lives: Readings in the Sociology of Men and Masculinity,* ed. Michael Kimmel and Michael Messner (New York: MacMillan, 1989).

20. This features prominently in the work of the Frankfurt school as well as contemporary ecofeminist theorists.

21. Rosemarie Tong, "Feminism, Pornography and Censorship," *Social Theory and Practice* 8 (1982): 1–17.

22. I learned to use "pornographize" as a verb in this way from Timothy Beneke's "Introduction" to his *Men on Rape* (New York: St. Martin's Press, 1982).

23. See the series of ten articles on "Socialist-Feminism Today" in *Socialist Review* 73–79 (1984–1985).

24. For the most recent feminist re-examinations of Hegel, see Heidi M. Raven, "Has Hegel Anything to Say to Feminists?" *The Owl of Minerva* 19 (1988) 149–168. Patricia Jagentowicz Mills, *Women, Nature, and Psyche* (New Haven: Yale University Press, 1987); and Susan M. Easton, "Hegel and Feminism," in David Lamb, ed., *Hegel and Modern Philosophy* (London: Croom Helm, 1987). Hegel enters contemporary radical legal thought primarily through the Critical Legal Studies movement. Especially relevant here is the work of Drucilla Cornell, for example, "Taking Hegel Seriously: Reflections on Beyond Objectivism and Relativism," *Cardozo Law Review* 7 (1985): 139; "Convention and Critique," *Cardozo Law Review* 7 (1986): 679; "Two Lectures on the Normative Dimensions of Community in the Law," *Tennessee Law Review* 54 (1987): 327; "Toward a Modern/Postmodern Reconstruction of Ethics," *University of Pennsylvania Law Review* 133 (1985): 291. See also papers from the Conference on "Hegel and Legal Theory," March 1988 at the Cardozo Law School of Yeshiva University, New York City, forthcoming in a special issue of the *Cardozo Law Review.* For signs of radical resurgence in the United States, I would cite such phenomena as the Jackson candidacy and the 1988 National Student Convention. In a recent issue of *The Nation* (actually, the current issue as I write this) Jefferson Morley writes: "The most fundamental idea shared by popular movements East and West is the principle of 'civil society.' " Jefferson Morley, "On 'Civil Society,' " *The Nation,* May 7, 1988, p. 630.

25. I believe this is true to Hegel's own conception of Hegelianism, for Hegel put the Logic at the core of his system, and at the center of the Logic stands the transfiguration and transvaluation of form and content.

26. Much of the feminist critique of the philosophical mainstream echoes earlier critiques of the mainstream made in the name of "process thought." See *Feminism and Process Thought: The Harvard Divinity School/Claremont Center for Process Studies Symposium Papers,* ed. Sheila Greeve

Davaney (Lewiston, NY: Edwin Mellen Press, 1981).

27. I am indebted to John Stoltenberg for this point.

28. I attempt to articulate this perspective principally in the following: *The Making of Masculinities,* Introduction and "The Case for Men's Studies," *A Mensch Among Men: Explorations in Jewish Masculinity* (Freedom, CA: The Crossing Press, 1988), especially the Introduction; and "Why Is

This 'Men's Studies' Different From All Other Men's Studies?" *Journal of the National Association for Women Deans, Administrators, and Counselors* 49 (1986): pp. 44–49. See also generally the small men's movement magazines *Changing Men: Issues in Gender, Sex and Politics* (306 North Brooks St., Madison, WI 53715), *Brother: The Newsletter of the National Organization for Changing Men* (1402 Greenfield Ave., #1, Los Angeles, CA 90025), and *Men's Studies Review* (Box 32, Harriman, TN 37748).

Case 8.a　*American Booksellers* v. *Hudnutt*

U.S. District Court and Court of Appeals

In this case, the federal court struck down an Indianapolis ordinance that prohibited pornography on the grounds of sex discrimination. The court felt that the ordinance restricted constitutionally protected speech.

Indianapolis enacted an ordinance defining "pornography" as a practice that discriminates against women. "Pornography" is to be redressed through the administrative and judicial methods used for other discrimination.

"Pornography" under the ordinance is "the graphic sexually explicit subordination of women, whether in pictures or in words, that also includes one or more of the following:

1. Women are presented as sexual objects who enjoy pain or humiliation; or

2. Women are presented as sexual objects who experience sexual pleasure in being raped; or

3. Women are presented as sexual objects tied up or cut up or mutilated or bruised or physically hurt, or as dismembered or truncated or fragmented or severed into body parts; or

4. Women are presented as being penetrated by objects or animals; or

5. Women are presented in scenarios

of degradation, injury, abasement, torture, shown as filthy or inferior, bleeding, bruised, or hurt in a context that makes these conditions sexual; or

6. Women are presented as sexual objects for domination, conquest, violation, exploitation, possession, or use, or through postures or positions of servility or submission or display." . . .

First Amendment Requirements

This Ordinance cannot be analyzed adequately without first recognizing this: the drafters of the Ordinance have used what appears to be a legal term of art, "pornography," but have in fact given the term a specialized meaning which differs from the meanings ordinarily assigned to that word in both legal and common parlance. In Section 16-3(v) (page 6), the Ordinance states:

Pornography shall mean the sexually explicit subordination of women, graphically depicted, whether in pictures or in words, that includes one or more of the following: . . .

There follows at that point a listing of five specific presentations of women in various settings which serve as examples of "pornography" and as such further define and describe that term under the Ordinance.

As is generally recognized, the word "pornography" is usually associated, and sometimes synonymous, with the word, "obscenity." "Obscenity" not only has its own separate and specialized meaning in the law, but in laymen's use also, and it is a much broader meaning than the definition given the word "pornography" in the Ordinance which is at issue in this action. There is thus a considerable risk of confusion in analyzing this ordinance unless care and precision are used in that process.

The Constitutional analysis of this Ordinance requires a determination of several underlying issues: first, the Court must determine whether the Ordinance imposes restraints on speech or behavior (content versus conduct); if the Ordinance is found to regulate speech, the Court must next determine whether the subject speech is protected or not protected under the First Amendment; if the speech which is regulated by this Ordinance is protected speech under the Constitution, the Court must then decide whether the regulation is constitutionally permissible as being based on a compelling state interest justifying the removal of such speech from First Amendment protections.

Do the Ordinances Regulate Speech or Behavior (Content or Conduct)?

It appears to be central to the defense of the Ordinance by defendants that the Court accept their premise that the City-County Council has not attempted to regulate speech, let alone protected speech. Defendants repeat throughout their briefs the incantation that their Ordinance regulates conduct, not speech. They contend (one senses with a certain sleight of hand) that the production, dissemination, and use of sexually explicit words

and pictures is the actual subordination of women and not an expression of ideas deserving of First Amendment protection. . . .

Defendants claim support for their theory by analogy, arguing that it is an accepted and established legal distinction that has allowed other courts to find that advocacy of a racially "separate but equal" doctrine in a civil rights context is protected speech under the First Amendment though "segregation" is not constitutionally protected behavior. Accordingly, defendants characterize their Ordinance here as a civil rights measure, through which they seek to prevent the distribution, sale, and exhibition of "pornography," as defined in the Ordinance, in order to regulate and control the underlying unacceptable conduct.

The content-versus-conduct approach espoused by defendants is not persuasive, however, and is contrary to accepted First Amendment principles. Accepting as true the City-County Council's finding that pornography conditions society to subordinate women, the means by which the Ordinance attempts to combat this sex discrimination is nonetheless through the regulation of speech.

For instance, the definition of pornography, the control of which is the whole thrust of the Ordinance, states that it is "the sexually explicit subordination of women, graphically *depicted*, whether in *pictures* or in *words*, that includes one or more of the following:" (emphasis supplied) and the following five descriptive subparagraphs begin with the words, "Women are *presented*. . . ." . . .

The unlawful acts and discriminatory practices under the Ordinance are set out in Section 16-3(g):

4. Trafficking in pornography: the production, sale, exhibition, or distribution of pornography. . . .

5. Coercion into pornographic performance: coercing, intimidating or fradulently inducing any person . . . into performing for pornography. . . .

6. Forcing pornography on a person:. . . .

7. Assault or physical attack due to pornography: the assault, physical attack,

or injury of any woman, man, child or transsexual in a way that is directly caused by specific pornography. . . .

Section (7), *supra,* goes on to provide a cause of action in damages against the perpetrators, makers, distributors, sellers and exhibitors of pornography and injunctive relief against the further exhibition, distribution or sale of pornography.

In summary, therefore, the Ordinance establishes through the legislative findings that pornography causes a tendency to commit these various harmful acts, and outlaws the pornography (that is, the "depictions"), the activities involved in the production of pornography, and the behavior caused by or resulting from pornography.

Thus, though the purpose of the Ordinance is cast in civil rights terminology—"to prevent and prohibit all discriminatory practices of sexual subordination or inequality through pornography" . . . —it is clearly aimed at controlling the content of the speech and ideas which the City-County Council has found harmful and offensive. Those words and pictures which depict women in sexually subordinate roles are banned by the Ordinance. Despite defendants' attempt to redefine offensive speech as harmful action, the clear wording of the Ordinance discloses that they seek to control speech, and those restrictions must be analyzed in light of applicable constitutional requirements and standards.

Is the Speech Regulated by the Ordinance Protected or Unprotected Speech under the First Amendment?

The First Amendment provides that government shall make no law abridging the freedom of speech. However, "the First and Fourteenth Amendments have never been thought to give absolute protection to every individual to speak whenever or wherever he pleases or to use any form of address in any circumstances that he chooses." *Cohen v. California,* . . . (1971). Courts have recognized only a "relatively few categories of instances," . . . where the government may regulate certain forms of

individual expression. The traditional categories of speech subject to permissible government regulation include "the lewd and obscene, the profane, the libelous, and the insulting or 'fighting' words—those which by their very utterance inflict injury or tend to incite an immediate breach of the peace" *Chaplinsky v. State of New Hampshire,* . . . (1942). In addition, the Supreme Court has recently upheld legislation prohibiting the dissemination of material depicting children engaged in sexual conduct. *New York v. Ferber,* . . . (1982).

Having found that the Ordinance at issue here seeks to regulate speech (and not conduct), the next question before the Court is whether the Ordinance, which seeks to restrict the distribution, sale, and exhibition of "pornography" as a form of sex discrimination against women, falls within one of the established categories of speech subject to permissible government regulation, that is, speech deemed to be unprotected by the First Amendment.

It is clear that this case does not present issues relating to profanity, libel, or "fighting words." In searching for an analytical "peg," the plaintiffs argue that the Ordinance most closely resembles obscenity, and is, therefore, subject to the requirements set forth in *Miller v. California,* . . . (1973). . . . But the defendants admit that the scope of the Ordinance is not limited to the regulation of legally obscene material as defined in *Miller.* . . . In fact, defendants concede that the "pornography" they seek to control goes beyond obscenity, as defined by the Supreme Court and excepted from First Amendment protections. Accordingly, the parties agree that the materials encompassed in the restrictions set out in the Ordinance include to some extent what have traditionally been protected materials.

The test under *Miller* determining whether material is legal obscenity is:

(a) whether "the average person, applying contemporary community standards" would find that the work, taken as a whole, appeals to the prurient interest, . . .; (b) whether the work depicts or describes, in a patently offensive way, sexual conduct specifically defined by the applicable state law; and (c) whether the work, taken as a whole, lacks serious literary, artistic, political, or scientific value. . . .

It is obvious that this three-step test is not directly applicable to the present case, because, as has been noted, the Ordinance goes beyond legally obscene material in imposing its controls. The restrictions in the Indianapolis Ordinance reach what has otherwise traditionally been regarded as protected speech under the *Miller* test. Beyond that, the Ordinance does not speak in terms of a "community standard" or attempt to restrict the dissemination of material that appeals to the "prurient interest." Nor has the Ordinance been drafted in a way to limit only distributions of "patently offensive" materials. Neither does it provide for the dissemination of works which, though "pornographic," may have "serious literary, artistic, political or scientific value." Finally, the Ordinance does not limit its reach to "hard core sexual conduct," though conceivably "hard core" materials may be included in its proscriptions.

Because the Ordinance spans so much more broadly in its regulatory scope than merely "hard core" obscenity by limiting the distribution of "pornography," the proscriptions in the Ordinance intrude with defendants' explicit approval into areas of otherwise protected speech. Under ordinary constitutional analysis, that would be sufficient grounds to overturn the Ordinance, but defendants argue that this case is not governed by any direct precedent, that it raises a new issue for the Court and even though the Ordinance regulates protected speech, it does so in a constitutionally permissible fashion.

Does Established First Amendment Law Permit the Regulation Provided for in the Ordinance of Otherwise Protected Speech?

In conceding that the scope of this Ordinance extends beyond constitutional limits, it becomes clear that what defendants actually seek by enacting this legislation is a newly-defined class of constitutionally unprotected speech, labeled "pornography" and characterized as sexually discriminatory.

Defendants vigorously argue that *Miller* is not the " 'constitutional divide' separating protected from unprotected expression in this area." . . . Defendants point to three cases which allegedly support their proposition that *Miller* is not the exclusive guideline for disposing of pornography/obscenity cases, and that the traditional obscenity test should not be applied in the present case. . . .

Defendants first argue that the Court must use the same reasoning applied by the Supreme Court in *New York v. Ferber*, . . . which upheld a New York statute prohibiting persons from promoting child pornography by distributing material which depicted such activity, and carve out another similar exception to protected speech under the First Amendment.

Defendants can properly claim some support for their position in *Ferber*. There the Supreme Court allowed the states "greater leeway" in their regulation of pornographic depictions of children in light of the State's compelling interest in protecting children who, without such protections, are extraordinarily vulnerable to exploitation and harm. The Court stated in upholding the New York statute:

> "The prevention of sexual exploitation and abuse of children constitutes a government objective of surpassing importance. The legislative findings accompanying passage of the New York laws reflect this concern:. . . ."

. . . The Supreme Court continued in *Ferber* by noting that the *Miller* standard for legal obscenity does not satisfy the unique concerns and issues posed by child pornography where children are involved; it is irrelevant, for instance, that the materials sought to be regulated contain serious literary, artistic, political or scientific value. In finding that some speech, such as that represented in depictions of child pornography, is outside First Amendment protections, the *Ferber* court stated:

> When a definable class of material, . . . bears so heavily and pervasively on the welfare of children engaged in its production, we think the balance of compet-

ing interests is clearly struck and that it is permissible to consider these materials as without the protection of the First Amendment.

Defendants, in the case at bar, argue that the interests of protecting women from sex-based discrimination are analogous to and every bit as compelling and fundamental as those which the Supreme Court upheld in *Ferber* for the benefit of children. But *Ferber* appears clearly distinguishable from the instant case on both the facts and law.

As has already been shown, the rationale applied by the Supreme Court in *Ferber* appears intended to apply solely to child pornography cases. In *Ferber,* the court recognized "that a state's interest in 'safeguarding the physical and psychological well-being of a minor' is 'compelling.' " . . . Also, the obscenity standard in *Miller* is appropriately abandoned in child pornography cases because it "[does] not reflect the State's particular and more compelling interest in prosecuting those who promote the sexual exploitations of children." . . . Since a state's compelling interest in preventing child pornography outweighs an individual's First Amendment rights, the Supreme Court held that "the states are entitled to greater leeway in the regulation of pornographic depictions of children." . . .

In contrast, the case at bar presents issues more far reaching than those in *Ferber*. Here, the City-County Council found that the distribution, sale, and exhibition of words and pictures depicting the subordination of women is a form of sex discrimination and as such is appropriate for governmental regulation. The state has a well-recognized interest in preventing sex discrimination, and, defendants argue, it can regulate speech to accomplish that end.

But the First Amendment gives primacy to free speech and any other state interest (such as the interest of sex based equality under law) must be so compelling as to be fundamental: only then can it be deemed to outweigh the interest of free speech. This Court finds no legal authority or public policy argument which justifies so broad an incursion into First Amendment freedoms as to allow that which

defendants attempt to advance here. *Ferber* does not open the door to allow the regulation contained in the Ordinance for the reason that adult women as a group do not, as a matter of public policy or applicable law, stand in need of the same type of protection which has long been afforded children. This is true even of women who are subject to the sort of inhuman treatment defendants have described and documented to the Court in support of this Ordinance. The Supreme Court's finding in *Ferber* of the uncontroverted state interest in "safeguarding the physical and psychological well being of a minor" and its resultant characterization of that interest as "compelling," . . . is an interest which inheres to children and is not an interest which is readily transferrable to adult women as a class. Adult women generally have the capacity to protect themselves from participating in and being personally victimized by pornography, which makes the State's interest in safeguarding the physical and psychological well-being of women by prohibiting "the sexually explicit subordination of women, graphically depicted, whether in pictures or in words" not so compelling as to sacrifice the guarantees of the First Amendment. In any case, whether a state interest is so compelling as to be fundamental interest sufficient to warrant an exception from constitutional protections, therefore, surely must turn on something other than mere legislative dictate, which issue is discussed more fully further on in this Opinion. . . .

The second case relied upon by defendants to support their contention that *Miller* is not controlling in the present case is *FCC v. Pacifica Foundation*, . . . (1978). According to defendants, *Pacifica* exemplifies the Supreme Court's refusal to make obscenity the sole legal basis for regulating sexually explicit conduct.

In *Pacifica*, the Supreme Court was faced with the question of whether a broadcast of patently offensive words dealing with sex and excretion may be regulated on the basis of their content. . . . The Court held that this type of speech was not entitled to absolute constitutional protection in every context. . . . Since the context of the speech in *Pacifica* was broadcasting, it was determined only to be due "the most limited First Amendment protection." . . . The reason for such treatment was two-fold:

> First, the broadcast media have established a uniquely pervasive presence in all the lives of all Americans. Patently offensive, indecent material presented over the airwaves confronts the citizen, not only in public, but also in the privacy of the home, where the individual's right to be left alone plainly outweighs the First Amendment rights of an intruder.
>
> Second, broadcasting is uniquely accessible to children, even those too young to read. . . .

Although the defendants correctly point out that the Supreme Court did not use the traditional obscenity test in *Pacifica*, this Court is not persuaded that the rule enunciated there is applicable to the facts of the present case. The Ordinance does not attempt to regulate the airwaves; in terms of its restrictions, it is not even remotely concerned with the broadcast media. The reasons for the rule in *Pacifica,* that speech in certain contexts should be afforded minimal First Amendment protection, are not present here, since we are not dealing with a medium that "invades" the privacy of the home. In contrast, if an individual is offended by "pornography," as defined in the Ordinance, the logical thing to do is avoid it, an option frequently not available to the public with material disseminated through broadcasting.

In addition, the Ordinance is not written to protect children from the distribution of pornography, in contrast to the challenged FCC regulation in *Pacifica*. Therefore, the peculiar state interest in protecting the "well being of its youth," . . . does not underlie this Ordinance and cannot be called upon to justify a decision by this Court to uphold the Ordinance.

The third case cited by defendants in support of their proposition that the traditional obscenity standard in *Miller* should not be used to overrule the Ordinance is *Young v. American Mini Theatres, Inc.,* . . . (1976). In *Young* the Supreme Court upheld a city ordinance that restricted the location of movie theatres featuring erotic films. The Court, in a plurality opinion, stated that "[e]ven though the First Amendment protects communication in this area from total suppression, we hold that the State may legitimately use the content of these materials as the basis for placing them in a different classification from other motion pictures." . . . The Court concluded that the city's interest in preserving the character of its neighborhoods justified the ordinance which required that adult theatres be separated, rather than concentrated, in the same areas as it is permissible for other theatres to do without limitation. . . .

Young is distinguishable from the present case because we are not here dealing with an attempt by the City-County Council to restrict the time, place, and manner in which "pornography" may be distributed. Instead, the Ordinance prohibits completely the sale, distribution, or exhibition of material depicting women in a sexually subordinate role, at all times, in all places and in every manner.

The Ordinance's attempt to regulate speech beyond one of the well-defined exceptions to protected speech under the First Amendment is not supported by other Supreme Court precedents. The Court must, therefore, examine the underlying premise of the Ordinance: that the State has so compelling an interest in regulating the sort of sex discrimination imposed and perpetuated through "pornography" that it warrants an exception to free speech.

Is Sex Discrimination a Compelling State Interest Justifying an Exception to First Amendment Protections?

It is significant to note that the premise of the Ordinance is the sociological harm, *i.e.,* the discrimination, which results from "pornography" to degrade women as a class. The Ordinance does not presume or require specifically defined, identifiable victims for most of its proscriptions. The Ordinance seeks to protect adult women, as a group, from the diminution of their legal and sociological status as women, that is, from the discriminatory stigma which befalls women *as women* as a result of "pornography." On page one of the introduction to defendants' *Amicus Brief,* counsel explicitly argues that the harm which underlies this legislation is the "harm to the treatment and *status* of women . . . on the basis of sex." . . .

This is a novel theory advanced by the defendants, an issue of first impression in the courts. If this Court were to accept defendants' argument—that the State's interest in protecting women from the humiliation and degradation which comes from being depicted in a sexually subordinate context is so compelling as to warrant the regulation of otherwise free speech to accomplish that end—one wonders what would prevent the City-County Council (or any other legislative body) from enacting protections for other equally compelling claims against exploitation and discrimination as are presented here. Legislative bodies, finding support here, could also enact legislation prohibiting other unfair expression—the publication and distribution of racist material, for instance, on the grounds that it causes racial discrimination,* or legislation prohibiting ethnic or religious slurs on the grounds that they cause discrimination against particular ethnic or religious groups, or legislation barring literary depictions which are uncomplimentary or oppressive to handicapped persons on the grounds that they cause discrimination against that group of people, and so on. If this Court were to extend to this case the rationale in *Ferber* to uphold the Amendment, it would signal so great a potential encroachment upon First Amendment freedoms that the precious liberties reposed within those guarantees would not survive. The compelling state interest, which defendants claim gives constitutional life to their Ordinance, though important and valid as that interest may be in other contexts, is not so fundamental an interest as to warrant a broad intrusion into otherwise free expression.

Defendants contend that pornography is not deserving of constitutional protection because its harms victimize all women. It is argued that "pornography" not only negatively affects women who risk and suffer the direct abuse of its production, but also, those on whom violent pornography is forced through such acts as compelled performances of "dangerous acts such as being hoisted upside down by ropes, bound by ropes and chains, hung from trees and scaffolds or having sex with animals. . . ." It is also alleged that exposure to pornography produces a negative impact on its viewers, causing in them an increased willingness to aggress toward women, *ibid.* . . ., and experience self-generated rape fantasies, increases in sexual arousal and a rise in the self-reported possibility of raping. . . . In addition, it causes discriminatory attitudes and behavior toward all women. . . . The City-County Council, after considering testimony and social research studies, enacted the Ordinance in order to "combat" pornography's "concrete and tangible harms to women." . . .

Defendants rely on *Paris Adult Theatre I v. Slaton,* . . . (1973), to justify their regulation of "pornography." In that case the Supreme Court held "that there are legitimate state interests at stake in stemming the tide of commercialized obscenity . . . [which] include the interest of the public in the quality of life and the total community environment, the tone of commerce in the great city centers, and, possibly, the public safety itself." . . .

The Georgia Legislature had determined that in that case exposure to obscene material adversely affected men and women, that is to say, society as a whole. Although the petitioners argued in that case that there was no scientific data to conclusively prove that proposition, the Court said, "[i]t is not for us to resolve empirical uncertainties underlying state legislation, save in the exceptional case where that legislation plainly impinges upon rights protected by the constitution itself." . . .

*In *Beauharnais v. Illinois,* . . . (1952), the Supreme Court upheld an Illinois libel statute prohibiting the dissemination of materials promoting racial or religious hatred and which tended to produce a breach of the peace and riots. It has been recognized that "the rationale of that decision turns quite plainly on the strong tendency of the prohibited utterances to cause violence and disorder." *Collin v. Smith,* . . . (7th Cir. 1978). The Supreme Court has recognized breach of the peace as the traditional justification for upholding a criminal libel statute. *Beauharnais,* . . . Therefore, a law preventing the distribution of material that causes racial discrimination, an attitude, would be upheld under this analysis. Further, the underlying reasoning of the *Beauharnais* opinion, that the punishment of libel raises no constitutional problems, has been questioned in many recent cases. . . .

Based on this reasoning, defendants argue that there is more than enough "empirical" evidence in the case at bar to support the City-County Council's conclusion that "pornography" harms women in the same way obscenity harms people, and, therefore, this Court should not question the legislative finding. As has already been acknowledged, it is not the Court's function to question the City-County Council's legislative finding. The Court's solitary duty is to ensure that the Ordinance accomplishes its purpose without violating constitutional standards or impinging upon constitutionally protected rights. In applying those tests, the Court finds that the Ordinance cannot withstand constitutional scrutiny.

It has already been noted that the Ordinance does not purport to regulate legal obscenity, as defined in *Miller*. Thus, although the City-County Council determined that "pornography" harms women, this Court must and does declare the Ordinance invalid without being bound by the legislative findings because "pornography," as defined and regulated in the Ordinance, is constitutionally protected speech under the First Amendment and such an exception to the First Amendment protections is constitutionally unwarranted. This Court cannot legitimately embark on judicial policy-making, carving out a new exception to the First Amendment simply to uphold the Ordinance, even when there may be many good reasons to support legislative action. To permit every interest group, especially those who claim to be victimized by unfair expression, their own legislative exceptions to the First Amendment so long as they succeed in obtaining a majority of legislative votes in their favor demonstrates the potentially predatory nature of what defendants seek through this Ordinance and defend in this lawsuit.

It ought to be remembered by defendants and all others who would support such a legislative initiative that, in terms of altering sociological patterns, much as alteration may be necessary and desirable, free speech, rather than being the enemy, is a long-tested and worthy ally. To deny free speech in order to engineer social change in the name of accomplishing a greater good for one sector of our society erodes the freedoms of all and, as such, threatens tyranny and injustice for those subjected to the rule of such laws. The First Amendment protections presuppose the evil of such tyranny and prevent a finding by this Court upholding the Ordinance. . . .

Case 8.b   Mapplethorpe or 2 Live Crew: "As Nasty As They Wanna Be"?

Within a span of two days, a judge in Cincinnati, Ohio, ruled that Robert Mapplethorpe's photographs were not obscene but a judge in Ft. Lauderdale, Florida, ruled that the music of 2 Live Crew was. The former involved homoerotic art and nude depictions of children; the latter was a rap album that, among other things, described sexual violence against women. The confusion over what sort of art can legitimately be considered obscene has made serious waves in funding for the National Endowment of the Arts and for the museums and artists they sponsor.

Contrasting obscenity verdicts in Ohio and Florida last week signaled a clear victory for art museums and a setback for rap music. Cincinnati's Contemporary Arts Center and its director, Dennis Barrie, were acquitted of obscenity charges for displaying graphic photographs by the late Robert Mapplethorpe. But two days earlier, Charles Freeman, a Ft. Lauderdale record-store owner, was convicted for selling a copy of 2 Live Crew's "As Nasty As They Wanna Be" album to an undercover policeman. (Members of the group go on trial this week in Ft. Lauderdale for performing the same material, which a federal judge had previously deemed obscene.) With a tenuous compromise on the National Endowment for the Arts' obscenity policy about to be tested in Congress, the country continues to struggle with an issue that seems to defy objective standards.

To most observers, the Barrie verdict was a stunner. It was the first time an American arts gallery had faced obscenity charges, and the case seemed to be running in the prosecution's favor. The mostly working-class, churchgoing jury of four men and four women reflected Cincinnati's status as an XXX-less, politically conservative city. Only three had ever set foot in an arts museum. During the two-week trial, Judge David Albanese resolved issue after

From *Newsweek*, October 15, 1990, p. 74. © 1990, Newsweek, Inc. All rights reserved. Reprinted by permission.

issue in the prosecution's favor, allowing only seven photographs out of the exhibition's 175 to be admitted as evidence. Prosecutor Frank Prouty became so sure of a conviction that he began walking around with a Cheshire cat grin, even alluding to it in his closing statements. "We've presented our case and the smile is because it's almost over from our standpoint," he said.

But Prouty had relied entirely on the shock value of the seven photos to make his case. His only witnesses had been three police officers sent to videotape the exhibition, and an "expert" rebuttal witness whose main credentials were taking some junior-college art classes and writing music videos for "Captain Kangaroo." Prouty had to convince the jury that the photos met all three of the obscenity criteria laid down by the Supreme Court. The "average person" must find the work appeals to "prurient interests," that it "depicts or describes in a patently offensive way sexual conduct," and that it lacks serious artistic value.

Even the defense conceded that the pictures are disturbing: five depict homosexual and sadomasochistic activities; two feature children with exposed genitals. But an array of art experts testified that, content aside, the photos were the work of a serious, even brilliant artist. Prouty tried to turn the jurors against the experts: "Are they saying they're better than us?" And he slashed at Barrie's high-road, goodness-of-art defense. "Tell me the artistic value," he asked sarcastically, "in the photo with the man's finger inserted in the penis?" But it only took the jury two hours to reach a verdict. In the end they apparently weren't as queasy as the local woman who'd seen the show and found Mapplethorpe's *flower* photographs offensive: one man's pistil is another man's stamen.

That's the attitude store owner Freeman had been banking on in his trial. But after listening to a copy of 2 Live Crew's "As Nasty As They Wanna Be," the all-white jury decided the album was obscene, and Freeman was convicted for selling it. He faces a maximum sentence of a year in jail and a $1,000 fine. "They don't know nothing about the goddam ghetto," Freeman fumed after leaving court. "They don't know where my store is. The verdict does not reflect my community standards as a black man in Broward County." His lawyers plan to appeal.

Washington lawmakers, meanwhile, are backing off from imposing content restrictions on funded artists. While a battle over the NEA's pending reauthorization still seems likely, they're apparently willing to let the courts decide what art is too raunchy for government funding. The deal proposed by committee negotiators would simply require anyone convicted of making obscene art to return all grant money and refrain from reapplying for three years. Predictably, conservatives accuse their colleagues of wimping out on moral standards once more, while arts activists regard the sanctions as draconian and deliberately intimidating.

Many artists, however, aren't easing off. They're even thumbing their noses at would-be censors. In New York, the Brooklyn Museum has unveiled an exhibition of historical art works that have been deemed objectionable in the past—or could be in the future. And in Ann Arbor, Mich., artists have put together a show called "Fear No Art," which includes drawings of a man clubbing a 2-year-old with a mallet and a man performing a sex act on himself. The city attorney in the liberal college town says he doesn't foresee any prosecutions.

Economic Justice and Welfare Rights

Despite substantial state ownership of property and significant market regulation, ours is clearly a "capitalist" economy. For the most part, productive property is privately owned and is traded on a relatively free market. We distribute resources principally on an ability-to-pay basis. And yet many in our society, especially during these "recessionary" times, are not able to afford even the most basic necessities. To what extent, within our system of private ownership, do we have an obligation to support those who need it? Are such benefits entitlements, property, or charity? Or, perhaps, is the whole system that makes us ask these questions inherently immoral (perhaps we would be better off with some sort of socialized system)? In his article in this chapter, Native-American scholar Ward Churchill challenges the idea that any Euro-Americans have any claim to property in this country.

Concerning distributive justice, we can consider three different types: libertarian, liberal, and socialist. Libertarian conceptions of justice rest on the notion that individuals have a fundamental right to be left alone. This "classical liberal" position places ultimate emphasis on the freedom of the individual in a *negative* sense. *Negative rights* can be defined roughly as rights of *noninterference:* X's right to life, in the sense that others have a duty not to kill X, is negative—others have a duty not to interfere with X's living. *Positive rights,* on the other hand, are welfare rights—that is, rights to be provided with something. So, for example, X may have a right to life such that others have a duty to provide X with food. Libertarians reject any conception of positive rights, defining freedom strictly in negative terms. Each person has, on this view, only the right not to be harmed and the right not to have his or her property interfered with. Hence, a just society is one in which a "minimal state" (as philosopher Robert Nozick calls it) exists to protect against such things as rape, murder, assault, theft, and fraud and to enforce contracts. Any state that respects these basic rights is inherently just, no matter the outcome.

Libertarianism is inextricably bound up with capitalist forms of economy. The right to private property, and to the free trade of that property, is essential to both. The contemporary liberal perspective (as opposed to the libertarian or classical liberal) accepts this basic social formation. Liberals generally agree that we must protect basic rights to own productive property privately and that the state should protect against physical harm. The liberal today, however, also wishes to assure some form of basic assistance to the least advantaged, some form of social welfare.

Liberals integrate some sense of positive freedom (i.e., the right to be provided with some basic necessities) into the framework of capitalism. Hence there are limits to the level of social inequality that the liberal will tolerate. Whereas much of society can starve without the libertarian raising a cry (as long as each person has the opportunity to compete, survival is the responsibility of the individual), the liberal will accept only so much deprivation. John Rawls, in his famous book *A Theory of Justice* (Cambridge, MA: Harvard University Press, 1971), suggests that a given level of inequality is justified only when such inequality in provision of goods and services will be to the benefit of the representative *least advantaged* of that society.

The main difference between socialists and the libertarian/liberal perspective is the rejection of the right to hold productive property privately. All productive property, on this model, must be held collectively and distributed on the basis of "*From each according to his or her need to each according to his or her ability.*" The primary emphasis here is on positive forms of freedom. The socialist wishes to provide each person with the necessary means for subsistence and with the sorts of goods needed to flourish as an authentic human being. Negative freedom, the socialist argues, is of little value if one does not have enough to eat or if one is denied basic access to available social resources. Individual ownership of private property means that others do not own and, hence, have little say in their productive life.

It must be noted that socialism can admit of competition and differential reward systems. Different agencies can be in competition with each other; the difference lies in the fact that the "loser" of the competition gets reassigned rather than thrown out of work. Similarly, in socialism there is no reason why some cannot be paid more than others if they work harder. It is the basic needs that must be met.

It is also important to note that socialism is an economic concept that can be combined with different political systems. Forms of democratic socialism are concerned with social equality but can be just as committed to negative individual civil rights as either the libertarian or the liberal perspective is. There is no reason to believe that in a socialist state one cannot have the same political rights to free speech, religion, due process of law, and so on, that one would have in a nonsocialist society.

37. Radical Egalitarianism

Kai Nielsen

Kai Nielson argues in favor of radical egalitarianism, in which the basic needs of all persons must be met. He suggests that such an arrangement satisfies the most fundamental elements of justice by providing a fair distribution of benefits and liberty.

I

I have talked of equality as a right and of equality as a goal. And I have taken, as the principal thing, to be able to state what goal we are seeking when we say equality is a goal. When we are in a position actually to achieve that goal, then that same equality becomes a right. The goal we are seeking is an equality of basic condition for everyone. Let me say a bit what this is: everyone, as far as possible, should have equal life prospects, short of genetic engineering and the like and the rooting out any form of the family and the undermining of our basic freedoms. There should, where this is possible, be an equality of access to equal resources over each person's life as a whole, though this should be qualified by people's varying needs. Where psychiatrists are in short supply only people who are in need of psychiatric help should have equal access to such help. This equal access to resources should be such that it stands as a barrier to

Abridged from *Equality and Liberty* (1985), pp. 283–292, 302–306, 309. Reprinted by permission of Rowman & Allanheld, Publishers. Notes renumbered.

their being the sort of differences between people that allow some to be in a position to control and to exploit others; such equal access to resources should also stand as a barrier to one adult person having power over other adult persons that does not rest on the revokable consent on the part of the persons over whom he comes to have power. Where, because of some remaining scarcity in a society of considerable productive abundance, we cannot reasonably distribute resources equally, we should first, where considerations of desert are not at issue, distribute according to stringency of need, second according to the strength of unmanipulated preferences and third, and finally, by lottery. We should, in trying to attain equality of condition, aim at a condition of autonomy (the fuller and the more rational the better) for everyone and at a condition where everyone alike, to the fullest extent possible, has his or her needs and wants satisfied. The limitations on the satisfaction of people's wants should be only where that satisfaction is incompatible with everyone getting the same treatment. Where we have conflicting wants, such as where two persons want to marry the same person, the fair thing to do will vary with the circumstances. In the marriage case, freedom of choice is obviously the fair thing. But generally, what should be aimed at is having everyone have their wants satisfied as far as possible. To achieve equality of condition would be, as well, to achieve a condition where the necessary burdens of the society are equally shared, where to do so is reasonable, and where each person has an equal voice in deciding what these burdens shall be. Moreover, everyone, as much as possible, should be in a position—and should be equally in that position—to control his own life. The goals of egalitarianism are to achieve such equalities.

Minimally, classlessness is something we should all aim at if we are egalitarians. It is necessary for the stable achievement of equalities of the type discussed in the previous paragraph. Beyond that, we should also aim at a statusless society, though not at an undifferentiated society or a society which does not recognize merit. . . . It is only in such a classless, statusless society that the ideals of equality (the conception of equality as a very general goal to be achieved) can be realized. In aiming for a statusless society, we are aiming for a society which, while remaining a society of material abundance, is a society in which there are to be no extensive differences in life prospects between people because some have far greater income, power, authority or prestige than others. This is the *via negativia* of the egalitarian way. The *via positiva* is to produce social conditions, where there is generally material abundance, where well-being and satisfaction are not only maximized (the utilitarian thing) but, as well, a society where this condition, as far as it is achievable, is sought equally for all (the egalitarian thing). This is the underlying conception of the egalitarian commitment to equality of condition.

II

Robert Nozick asks "How do we decide how much equality is enough?"[1] In the preceding section we gestured in the direction of an answer. I should now like to be somewhat more explicit. Too much equality, as we have been at pains to point out, would be to treat everyone identically, completely ignoring their differing needs. Various forms of "barracks equality" approximating that would also be too much. Too little equality would be to limit equality of condition, as did the old egalitarianism, to achieving equal legal and political rights, equal civil liberties, to equality of opportunity and to a redistribution of gross disparities in wealth sufficient to keep social peace, the rationale for the latter being that such gross inequalities if allowed to stand would threaten social stability. This Hobbesist stance indicates that the old egalitarianism proceeds in a very pragmatic manner. Against the old egalitarianism I would argue that we must at least aim at an equality of whole life prospects, where that is not read simply as the right to compete for scarce positions of advantage, but where there is to be brought into being the kind of equality of condition that would provide everyone equally, as far as possible, with the resources and the social conditions to satisfy their needs as fully as possible compatible with everyone else doing likewise. (Note that between people these needs will be partly the same but will still often be importantly different as well.) Ideally, as a kind of ideal limit for a society of wondrous abundance, a radical egalitarianism would go beyond that to a similar thing for wants. We should, that is, provide all people equally, as far as possible, with the resources and social conditions to satisfy their wants, as fully as possible compatible with everyone else doing likewise. (I recognize that there is a slide between wants and needs. As the wealth of a society increases and its structure changes, things that started out as wants tend to become needs, e.g., someone in the Falkland Islands might merely reasonably want an auto while someone in Los Angeles might not only want it but need it as well. But this does not collapse the distinction between wants and needs. There are things in any society people need, if they are to survive at all in anything like a commodious condition, whether they want them or not, e.g., they need food, shelter, security, companionship and the like. An egalitarian starts with basic needs, or at least with what are taken in the cultural environment in which a given person lives to be basic needs, and moves out to other needs and finally to wants as the productive power of the society increases.)

I qualified my above formulations with "as far as possible" and with "as fully as possible compatible with everyone else doing likewise." These are essential qualifications. Where, as in societies that we know, there are scarcities, even rather minimal scarcities, not everyone can have the resources or at least all the resources necessary to have their needs satisfied. Here we must first ensure that, again as far as possible, their basic needs are all satisfied and then we move on to other needs and finally to wants. But sometimes, to understate it, even in very affluent societies, everyone's needs cannot be met, or at least they cannot be equally met. In such circumstances we have to make some hard choices. I am thinking of a situation where there are not enough dialysis machines to go around so that everyone who needs one can have one. What then should we do? The thing to aim at, to try as far as possible to approximate, if only as a heuristic ideal, is the full and equal meeting of needs and wants of everyone. It is when we have that much equality that we have enough equality. But, of course, "ought implies can," and where we can't achieve it we can't achieve it. But where we reasonably can, we ought to do it. It is something that fairness requires.

The "reasonably can" is also an essential modification: we need situations of sufficient abundance so that we do not, in going for such an equality of condition, simply spread the misery around or spread very Spartan conditions around. Before we can rightly aim for the equality of condition I mentioned, we must first have the productive capacity and resource conditions to support the institutional means that would make possible the equal satisfaction of basic needs and the equal satisfaction of other needs and wants as well.

Such achievements will often not be possible; perhaps they will never be fully possible, for, no doubt, the physically handicapped will always be with us. Consider, for example, situations where our scarcities are such that we cannot, without causing considerable misery, create the institutions and mechanisms that would work to satisfy all needs, even all basic needs. Suppose we have the technology in place to develop all sorts of complicated life-sustaining machines all of which would predictably provide people with a quality of life

that they, viewing the matter clearly, would rationally choose if they were simply choosing for themselves. But suppose, if we put such technologies in place, we will then not have the wherewithal to provide basic health care in outlying regions in the country or adequate educational services in such places. We should not, under those circumstances, put those technologies in place. But we should also recognize that where it becomes possible to put these technologies in place without sacrificing other more pressing needs, we should do so. The underlying egalitarian rationale is evident enough: produce the conditions for the most extensive satisfaction of needs for everyone. Where A's need and B's need are equally important (equally stringent) but cannot both be satisfied, satisfy A's need rather than B's if the satisfaction of A's need would be more fecund for the satisfaction of the needs of others than B's, or less undermining of the satisfaction of the needs of others than B's. (I do not mean to say that that is our only criterion of choice but it is the criterion most relevant for us here.) We should seek the satisfaction of the greatest compossible set of needs where the conditions for compossibility are (a) that everyone's needs be considered, (b) that everyone's needs be *equally* considered and where two sets of needs cannot both be satisfied, the more stringent set of needs shall first be satisfied. (Do not say we have no working criteria for what they are. If you need food to keep you from starvation or debilitating malnutrition and I need a vacation to relax after a spate of hard work, your need is plainly more stringent than mine. There would, of course, be all sorts of disputable cases, but there are also a host of perfectly determinate cases indicating that we have working criteria.) The underlying rationale is to seek compossible sets of needs so that we approach as far as possible as great a satisfaction of needs as possible for everyone.

This might, it could be said, produce a situation in which very few people got those things that they needed the most, or at least wanted the most. Remember Nozick with his need for the resources of Widner Library in an annex to his house. People, some might argue, with expensive tastes and extravagant needs, say a need for really good wine, would never, with a stress on such compossibilia, get things they are really keen about.[2] Is that the kind of world we would reflectively want? Well, *if* their not getting them is the price we have to pay for everyone having their basic needs met, then it is a price we ought to pay. I am very fond of very good wines as well as fresh ripe mangos, but if the price of my having them is that people starve or suffer malnutrition in the Sahel, or indeed anywhere else, then plainly fairness, if not just plain human decency, requires that I forego them.

In talking about how much equality is enough, I have so far talked of the benefits that equality is meant to provide. But egalitarians also speak of an equal sharing of the necessary burdens of the society as well. Fairness requires a sharing of the burdens, and for a radical egalitarian this comes to an equal sharing of the burdens where people are equally capable of sharing them. Translated into the concrete this does *not* mean that a child or an old man or a pregnant woman are to be required to work in the mines or that they be required to collect garbage, but it would involve something like requiring every able bodied person, say from nineteen to twenty, to take his or her turn at a fair portion of the necessary unpleasant jobs in the world. In that way we all, where we are able to do it, would share equally in these burdens—in doing the things that none of us want to do but that we, if we are at all reasonable, recognize the necessity of having done. (There are all kinds of variations and complications concerning this— what do we do with the youthful wonder at the violin? But, that notwithstanding, the general idea is clear enough.) And, where we think this is reasonably feasible, it squares with our considered judgments about fairness.

I have given you, in effect appealing to my considered judgments but considered judgments I do not think are at all eccentric, a picture of what I would take to be enough equality, too little equality and not enough equality. But how can we know that my proportions are right? I do not think we can avoid or should indeed try to avoid an appeal to considered judgments here. But working with them there are some arguments we can appeal, to get them in wide reflective equilibrium. Suppose we go back to the formal principle of justice, namely that we must treat like cases

alike. Because it does not tell us *what* are like cases, we cannot derive substantive criteria from it. But it may, indirectly, be of some help here. We all, if we are not utterly zany, want a life in which our needs are satisfied and in which we can live as we wish and do what we want to do. Though we differ in many ways, in our abilities, capacities for pleasure, determination to keep on with a job, we do not differ about wanting our needs satisfied or being able to live as we wish. Thus, *ceterus paribus*, where questions of desert, entitlement and the like do not enter, it is only fair that all of us should have our needs equally considered and that we should, again *ceterus paribus*, all be able to do as we wish in a way that is compatible with others doing likewise. From the formal principle of justice and a few key facts about us, we can get to the claim that *ceterus paribus* we should go for this much equality. But this is the core content of a radical egalitarianism.

However, how do we know that *ceterus* is *paribus* here? What about our entitlements and deserts? Suppose I have built my house with my own hands, from materials I have purchased and on land that I have purchased and that I have lived in it for years and have carefully cared for it. The house is mine and I am entitled to keep it even if by dividing the house into two apartments greater and more equal satisfaction of need would obtain for everyone. Justice requires that such an entitlement be respected here. (Again, there is an implicit *ceterus paribus* clause. In extreme situations, say after a war with housing in extremely short supply, that entitlement could be rightly overridden.)

There is a response on the egalitarian's part similar to a response utilitarianism made to criticisms of a similar logical type made of utilitarians by pluralistic deontologists. One of the things that people in fact need, or at least reflectively firmly want, is to have such entitlements respected. Where they are routinely overridden to satisfy other needs or wants, we would *not* in fact have a society in which the needs of everyone are being maximally met. To the reply, but what if more needs for everyone were met by ignoring or overriding such entitlements, the radical egalitarian should respond that that is, given the way we are, a thoroughly hypothetical situation and that theories of morality cannot be expected to give guidance for all logically possible worlds but only for worlds which are reasonably like what our actual world is or plausibly could come to be. Setting this argument aside for the moment, even if it did turn out that the need satisfaction linked with having other things—things that involved the overriding of those entitlements—was sufficient to make it the case that more need satisfaction all around for *everyone* would be achieved by overriding those entitlements, then, for reasonable people who clearly saw that, these entitlements would not have the weight presently given to them. They either would not have the importance presently attached to them or the need for the additional living space would be so great that their being overridden would seem, everything considered, the lesser of two evils (as in the example of the postwar housing situation).

There are without doubt genuine entitlements and a theory of justice must take them seriously, but they are not absolute. If the need is great enough we can see the merit in overriding them, just as in law as well as morality the right of eminent domain is recognized. Finally, while I have talked of entitlements here, parallel arguments will go through for desert.

III

I want now to relate this articulation of what equality comes to my radically egalitarian principles of justice. My articulation of justice is a certain spelling out of the slogan proclaimed by Marx "From each according to his ability, to each according to his needs." The egalitarian conception of society argues for the desirability of bringing into existence a world, once the springs of social wealth flow freely, in which everyone's needs are as fully satisfied as possible and in which everyone gives according to his ability. Which means, among other things, that everyone, according to his ability, shares the burdens of society. There is an equal giving and equal responsibility here according to ability. It is here, with respect to giving according to ability and with respect to receiving

according to need, that a complex equality of result, i.e., equality of condition, is being advocated by the radical egalitarian. What it comes to is this: each of us, where each is to count for one and none to count for more than one, is to give according to ability and receive according to need.

My radical egalitarian principles of justice read as follows:

1. Each person is to have an equal right to the most extensive total system of equal basic liberties and opportunities (including equal opportunities for meaningful work, for self-determination and political and economic participation) compatible with a similar treatment of all. (This principle gives expression to a commitment to attain and/or sustain equal moral autonomy and equal self-respect.)

2. After provisions are made for common social (community) values, for capital overhead to preserve the society's productive capacity, allowances made for differing unmanipulated needs and preferences, and due weight is given to the just entitlements of individuals, the income and wealth (the common stock of means) is to be so divided that each person will have a right to an equal share. The necessary burdens requisite to enhance human well-being are also to be equally shared, subject, of course, to limitations by differing abilities and differing situations. (Here I refer to different natural environments and the like and not to class position and the like.)

Here we are talking about equality as a right rather than about equality as a goal as has previously been the subject matter of equality in this chapter. These principles of egalitarianism spell out rights people have and duties they have under *conditions of very considerable productive abundance*. We have a right to certain basic liberties and opportunities and we have, subject to certain limitations spelled out in the second principle, a right to an equal share of the income and wealth in the world. We also have a duty, again subject to the qualifications mentioned in the principle, to do our equal share in shouldering the burdens necessary to protect us from ills and to enhance our well-being.

What is the relation between these rights and the ideal of equality of condition discussed earlier? That is a goal for which we can struggle now to bring about conditions which will some day make its achievement possible, while these rights only become rights when the goal is actually achievable. We have no such rights in slave, feudal or capitalist societies or such duties in those societies. In that important way they are not natural rights for they depend on certain social conditions and certain social structures (socialist ones) to be realizable. What we can say is that it is always desirable that socio-economic conditions come into being which would make it possible to achieve the goal of equality of condition so that these rights and duties I speak of could obtain. But that is a far cry from saying we have such rights and duties now.

It is a corollary of this, if these radical egalitarian principles of justice are correct, that capitalist societies (even capitalist welfare state societies such as Sweden) and statist societies such as the Soviet Union or the People's Republic of China cannot be just societies or at least they must be societies, structured as they are, which are defective in justice. (This is not to say that some of these societies are not juster than others. Sweden is juster than South Africa, Canada than the United States and Cuba and Nicaragua than Honduras and Guatemala.) But none of these statist or capitalist societies can satisfy these radical egalitarian principles of justice, for equal liberty, equal opportunity, equal wealth or equal sharing of burdens are not at all possible in societies having their social structure. So we do not have such rights now but we can take it as a goal that we bring such a society into being with a commitment to an equality of condition in which we would have these rights and duties. Here we require first the massive development of productive power.

The connection between equality as a goal and equality as a right spelled out in these principles of justice is this. The equality of condition appealed to in equality as a goal would, if it were actually to obtain, have to contain the rights and duties enunciated in those principles. There could be no equal life prospects between all people or anything approximating an equal satisfaction of needs if there were not in place something like the system of equal basic liberties referred to in the first principle. Furthermore, without the rough equality of wealth referred to in the second principle, there would be disparities in power and self-direction in society which would render impossible an equality of life prospects or the social conditions required for an equal satisfaction of needs. And plainly, without a roughly equal sharing of burdens, there cannot be a situation where everyone has equal life prospects or has the chance equally to satisfy his needs. The principles of radical egalitarian justice are implicated in its conception of an ideally adequate equality of condition.

IV

The principles of radical egalitarian justice I have articulated are meant to apply globally and not just to particular societies. But it is certainly fair to say that not a few would worry that such principles of radical egalitarian justice, if applied globally, would force the people in wealthier sections of the world to a kind of financial hari-kari. There are millions of desperately impoverished people. Indeed millions are starving or malnourished and things are not getting any better. People in the affluent societies cannot but worry about whether they face a bottomless pit. Many believe that meeting, even in the most minimal way, the needs of the impoverished is going to put an incredible burden on people—people of all classes—in the affluent societies. Indeed it will, if acted on non-evasively, bring about their impoverishment, and this is just too much to ask. Radical egalitarianism is forgetting Rawls' admonitions about "the strains of commitment"—the recognition that in any rational account of what is required of us, we must at least give a minimal healthy self-interest its due. We must construct our moral philosophy for human beings and not for saints. Human nature is less fixed than conservatives are wont to assume, but it is not so elastic that we can reasonably expect people to impoverish themselves to make the massive transfers between North and South—the industrialized world and the Third World—required to begin to approach a situation where even Rawls' principles would be in place on a global level, to say nothing of my radical egalitarian principles of justice.[3]

The first thing to say in response to this is that my radical egalitarian principles are meant actually to guide practice, to directly determine what we are to do, only in a world of extensive abundance where, as Marx put it, the springs of social wealth flow freely. If such a world cannot be attained with the undermining of capitalism and the full putting into place, stabilizing, and developing of socialist relations of production, then such radical egalitarian principles can only remain as heuristic ideals against which to measure the distance of our travel in the direction of what would be a perfectly just society.

Aside from a small capitalist class, along with those elites most directly and profitably beholden to it (together a group constituting not more than 5 percent of the world's population), there would, in taking my radical egalitarian principles as heuristic guides, be no impoverishment of people in the affluent societies, if we moved in a radically more egalitarian way to start to achieve a global fairness. There would be massive transfers of wealth between North and South, but this could be done in stages so that, for the people in the affluent societies (capitalist elites apart), there need be no undermining of the quality of their lives. Even what were once capitalist elites would not be impoverished or reduced to some kind of bleak life though they would, the incidental Spartan types aside, find their life styles altered. But their health and general well-being, including their opportunities to do significant and innovative work, would, if anything, be enhanced. And while some of the sources of their enjoyment would be a thing of the past, there would still be a considerable range of enjoyments available to them sufficient to afford anyone a rich life that could be lived with verve and zest.

A fraction of what the United States spends on defense spending would take care of immediate problems of starvation and malnutri-tion for most of the world. For longer range problems such as bringing conditions of life in the Third World more in line with conditions of life in Sweden and Switzerland, what is necessary is the dismantling of the capitalist system and the creation of a socio-economic system with an underlying rationale directing it toward producing for needs—everyone's needs. With this altered productive mode, the irrationalities and waste of capitalist production would be cut. There would be no more built-in obsolescence, no more merely cosmetic changes in consumer durables, no more fashion roulette, no more useless products and the like. Moreover, the enormous expenditures that go into the war industry would be a thing of the past. There would be great transfers from North to South, but it would be from the North's capitalist fat and not from things people in the North really need. (There would, in other words, be no self-pauperization of people in the capitalist world.) . . .

V

It has been repeatedly argued that equality undermines liberty. Some would say that a society in which principles like my radical egalitarian principles were adopted, or even the liberal egalitarian principles of Rawls or Dworkin were adopted, would not be a free society. My arguments have been just the reverse. I have argued that it is only in an egalitarian society that full and extensive liberty is possible.

Perhaps the egalitarian and the anti-egalitarian are arguing at cross purposes? What we need to recognize, it has been argued, is that we have two kinds of rights both of which are important to freedom but to rather different freedoms and which are freedoms which not infrequently conflict.[4] We have rights to *fair terms of cooperation* but we also have rights to *non-interference*. If a right of either kind is overridden our freedom is diminished. The reason why it might be thought that the egalitarian and the anti-egalitar-

402   Chapter 9   Economic Justice and Welfare Rights

ian may be arguing at cross purposes is that the egalitarian is pointing to the fact that rights to fair terms of cooperation and their associated liberties require equality while the anti-egalitarian is pointing to the fact that rights to non-interference and their associated liberties conflict with equality. They focus on different liberties.

What I have said above may not be crystal clear, so let me explain. People have a right to fair terms of cooperation. In political terms this comes to the equal right of all to effective participation in government and, in more broadly social terms, and for a society of economic wealth, it means people having a right to a roughly equal distribution of the benefits and burdens of the basic social arrangements that affect their lives and for them to stand in such relations to each other such that no one has the power to dominate the life of another. By contrast, rights to non-interference come to the equal right of all to be left alone by the government and more broadly to live in a society in which people have a right peacefully to pursue their interests without interference.

The conflict between equality and liberty comes down to, very essentially, the conflicts we get in modern societies between rights to fair terms of cooperation and rights to non-interference. As Joseph Schumpeter saw and J. S. Mill before him, one could have a thoroughly democratic society (at least in conventional terms) in which rights to non-interference might still be extensively violated. A central anti-egalitarian claim is that we cannot have an egalitarian society in which the very precious liberties that go with the rights to non-interference would not be violated.

Socialism and egalitarianism plainly protect rights to fair terms of cooperation. Without the social (collective) ownership and control of the means of production, involving with this, in the initial stages of socialism at least, a workers' state, economic power will be concentrated in the hands of a few who will in turn, as a result, dominate effective participation in government. Some right-wing libertarians blind themselves to that reality, but it is about as evident as can be. Only an utter turning away from the facts of social life could lead to any doubts about this at all. But then this means that in a workers' state, if some people have

capitalistic impulses, that they would have their rights peacefully to pursue their own interests interfered with. They might wish to invest, retain and bequeath in economic domains. In a workers' state these capitalist acts in many circumstances would have to be forbidden, but that would be a violation of an individual's right to non-interference and the fact, if it was a fact, that we by democratic vote, even with vast majorities, had made such capitalist acts illegal would still not make any difference because individuals' rights to non-interference would still be violated.

We are indeed driven, by egalitarian impulses, of a perfectly understandable sort, to accept interference with laissez-faire capitalism to protect non-subordination and non-domination of people by protecting the egalitarian right to fair terms of cooperation and the enhanced liberty that that brings. Still, as things stand, this leads inevitably to violations of the right to non-interference and this brings with it a diminution of liberty. There will be people with capitalist impulses and they will be interfered with. It is no good denying, it will be said, that egalitarianism and particularly socialism will not lead to interference with very precious individual liberties, namely with our right peacefully to pursue our interests without interference.[5]

The proper response to this, as should be apparent from what I have argued throughout, is that to live in any society at all, capitalist, socialist or whatever, is to live in a world in which there will be some restriction or other on our rights peacefully to pursue our interests without interference. I can't lecture in Albanian or even in French in a standard philosophy class at the University of Calgary, I can't jog naked on most beaches, borrow a book from your library without your permission, fish in your trout pond without your permission, take your dog for a walk without your say so and the like. At least some of these things have been thought to be things which I might peacefully pursue in my own interests. Stopping me from doing them is plainly interfering with my peaceful pursuit of my own interests. And indeed it is an infringement on liberty, an interference with my doing what I may want to do.

However, for at least many of these activities, and particularly the ones having to do with property, even right-wing libertarians think that such interference is perfectly justified. But, justified or not, they still plainly constitute a restriction on our individual freedom. However, what we must also recognize is that there will always be some such restrictions on freedom in any society whatsoever, just in virtue of the fact that a normless society, without the restrictions that having norms imply, is a contradiction in terms.[6] Many restrictions are hardly felt as restrictions, as in the attitudes of many people toward seat-belt legislation, but they are, all the same, plainly restrictions on our liberty. It is just that they are thought to be unproblematically justified.

To the question would a socialism with a radical egalitarianism restrict some liberties, including some liberties rooted in rights to noninterference, the answer is that it indeed would; but so would laissez-faire capitalism, aristocratic conceptions of justice, liberal conceptions or any social formations at all, with their associated conceptions of justice. The relevant question is which of these restrictions are justified.

The restrictions on liberty proferred by radical egalitarianism and socialism, I have argued, are justified for they, of the various alternatives, give us both the most extensive and the most abundant system of liberty possible in modern conditions with their thorough protection of the right to fair terms of cooperation. Radical egalitarianism will also, and this is central for us, protect our civil liberties and these liberties are, of course, our most basic liberties. These are the liberties which are the most vital for us to protect. What it will not do is to protect our unrestricted liberties to invest, retain and bequeath in the economic realm and it will not protect our unrestricted freedom to buy and sell. There is, however, no good reason to think that these restrictions are restrictions of anything like a basic liberty. Moreover, we are justified in restricting our freedom to buy and sell if such restrictions strengthen, rather than weaken, our total system of liberty. This is in this way justified, for only by such market restrictions can the rights of the vast majority of people to effective participation in government and an equal role in the control of their social lives be protected. I say this because if we let the market run free in this way, power will pass into the hands of a few who will control the lives of the many and determine the fundamental design of the society. The actual liberties that are curtailed in a radically egalitarian social order are inessential liberties whose restriction in contemporary circumstances enhances human well-being and indeed makes for a firmer entrenchment of basic liberties and for their greater extension globally. That is to say, we here restrict some liberty in order to attain more liberty and a more equally distributed pattern of liberty. More people will be able to do what they want and have a greater control over their own lives than in a capitalist world order with its at least implicit inegalitarian commitments.

However, some might say I still have not faced the most central objection to radical egalitarianism, namely its statism. (I would prefer to say its putative statism.) The picture is this. The egalitarian state must be in the redistribution business. It has to make, or make sure there is made, an equal relative contribution to the welfare of every citizen. But this in effect means that the socialist state or, for that matter, the welfare state, will be deeply interventionist in our personal lives. It will be in the business, as one right-winger emotively put it, of cutting one person down to size in order to bring about that person's equality with another person who was in a previously disadvantageous position.[7] That is said to be morally objectionable and it would indeed be deeply morally objectionable in many circumstances. But it isn't in the circumstances in which the radical egalitarian presses for redistribution. (I am not speaking of what might be mere equalizing upwards.) The circumstances are these: Capitalist A gets his productive property confiscated so that he could no longer dominate and control the lives of proletarians B, C, D, E, F, and G. But what is wrong with it where this "cutting down to size"—in reality the confiscation of productive property or the taxation of the capitalist—involves no violation of A's civil liberties or the harming of his actual well-being (health, ability to work, to cultivate the arts, to have fruitful personal relations, to live in comfort and the like) and where B, C, D, E, F, and G will have their freedom and their well-being thoroughly enhanced if such confiscation or taxation occurs? Far from being morally objectionable, it is precisely the sort of state of affairs that people ought to favor. It certainly protects more liberties and more significant liberties than it undermines.

There is another familiar anti-egalitarian argument designed to establish the liberty-undermining qualities of egalitarianism. It is an argument we have touched upon in discussing meritocracy. It turns on the fact that in any society there will be both talents and handicaps. Where they exist, what do we want to do about maintaining equal distribution? Egalitarians, radical or otherwise, certainly do not want to penalize people for talent. That being so, then surely people should be allowed to retain the benefits of superior talent. But this in some circumstances will lead to significant inequalities in resources and in the meeting of needs. To sustain equality there will have to be an ongoing redistribution in the direction of the less talented and less fortunate. But this redistribution from the more to the less talented does plainly penalize the talented for their talent. That, it will be said, is something which is both unfair and an undermining of liberty.

The following, it has been argued, makes the above evident enough.[8] If people have talents they will tend to want to use them. And if they use them they are very likely to come out ahead. Must not egalitarians say they ought not to be able to come out ahead no matter how well they use their talents and no matter how considerable these talents are? But that is intolerably restrictive and unfair.

The answer to the above anti-egalitarian argument is implicit in a number of things I have already said. But here let me confront this familiar argument directly. Part of the answer comes out in probing some of the ambiguities of "coming out ahead." Note, incidentally, that (1) not all reflective, morally sensitive people will be so concerned with that, and (2) that being very concerned with that is a mentality that capitalism inculcates. Be that as it may, to turn to the ambiguities, note that some take "coming out ahead" principally to mean "being paid well for the use of those talents" where "being paid well" is being paid

sufficiently well so that it creates inequalities sufficient to disturb the preferred egalitarian patterns. (Without that, being paid well would give one no relative advantage.) But, as we have seen, "coming out ahead" need not take that form at all. Talents can be recognized and acknowledged in many ways. First, in just the respect and admiration of a fine employment of talents that would naturally come from people seeing them so displayed where these people were not twisted by envy; second, by having, because of these talents, interesting and secure work that their talents fit them for and they merit in virtue of those talents. Moreover, having more money is not going to matter much—for familiar marginal utility reasons—where what in capitalist societies would be called the welfare floors are already very high, this being made feasible by the great productive wealth of the society. Recall that in such a society of abundance everyone will be well off and secure. In such a society people are not going to be very concerned about being a little better off than someone else. The talented are in no way, in such a situation, robbed to help the untalented and handicapped or penalized for their talents. They are only prevented from amassing wealth (most particularly productive wealth), which would enable them to dominate the untalented and the handicapped and to control the social life of the world of which they are both a part. . . .

I think that the moral authority for abstract egalitarianism, for the belief that the interests of everyone matters and matters equally, comes from its being the case that it is *required by the moral point of view*.[9] What I am predicting is that a person who has a good understanding of what morality is, has a good knowledge of the facts, is not ideologically mystified, takes an impartial point of view, and has an attitude of impartial caring, would, if not conceptually confused, come to accept the abstract egalitarian thesis. I see no way of arguing someone into such an egalitarianism who does not in this general way have a love of humankind.[10] A hard-hearted Hobbesist is not reachable here. But given that a person has that love of humankind—that impartial and impersonal caring—together with the other qualities mentioned above, then, I predict, that that person would be an egalitarian at least to the extent of accepting the abstract egalitarian thesis. What I am claiming is that if these conditions were to obtain (if they ceased to be just counterfactuals), then there would be a consensus among moral agents about accepting the abstract egalitarian thesis. . . .

Notes

---

1. See the debate between Robert Nozick, Daniel Bell and James Tobin, "If Inequality Is Inevitable What Can Be Done About It?" *The New York Times,* January 3, 1982, p. E5. The exchange between Bell and Nozick reveals the differences between the old egalitarianism and right-wing libertarianism. It is not only that the right and left clash but sometimes right clashes with right.

2. Amartya Sen, "Equality of What?" *The Tanner Lectures on Human Values,* vol. 1 (1980), ed. Sterling M. McMurrin (Cambridge, England: Cambridge University Press, 1980), pp. 198–220.

3. Henry Shue, "The Burdens of Justice," *The Journal of Philosophy* 80, no. 10 (October 1983): 600–601; 606–608.

4. Richard W. Miller, "Marx and Morality," in *Marxism,* eds. J. R. Pennock and J. W. Chapman.

Nomos 26 (New York: New York University Press, 1983), pp. 9–11.

5. Ibid., p. 10.

6. This has been argued from both the liberal center and the left. Ralf Dahrendorf, *Essays in the Theory of Society* (Stanford, Cal.: Stanford University Press, 1968), pp. 151–178; and G. A. Cohen, "Capitalism, Freedom and the Proletariat" in *The Idea of Freedom: Essays in Honour of Isaiah Berlin,* ed. Alan Ryan (Oxford: Oxford University Press, 1979).

7. The graphic language should be duly noted. Jan Narveson, "On Dworkinian Equality," *Social Philosophy and Policy* 1, no. 1 (autumn 1983): 4.

8. Ibid., p. 1–24.

9. Some will argue that there is no such thing as a moral point of view. My differences with him about the question of whether the amoralist can be argued into morality not withstanding, I think Kurt Baier, in a series of articles written subsequent to his *The Moral Point of View,* has clearly shown that there is something reasonably determinate that can, without ethnocentrism, be called "the moral point of view."

10. Richard Norman has impressively argued that this is an essential background assumption of the moral point of view. Richard Norman, "Critical Notice of Rodger Beehler's *Moral Life,*" *Canadian Journal of Philosophy* 11, no. 1 (March 1981): 157–183.

---

38.   From Liberty to Welfare

James P. Sterba

Traditional libertarian views of justice fundamentally reject the concept of state-coerced redistribution of property. Liberty is fundamentally negative (i.e., it involves the absence of constraints), and hence the state has no duty to provide for the needy on the basis of liberty. James P. Sterba disagrees. He argues that welfare can be given a libertarian justification.

Libertarians today are deeply divided over whether a night watchman state can be morally justified. Some, like Robert Nozick, hold

From *Social Theory and Practice,* vol. 11, no. 3 (Fall 1985), pp. 285–305. Reprinted by permission.

that a night watchman state would tend to arise by an invisible-hand process if people generally respected each other's Lockean rights.[1] Others, like Murray Rothbard, hold that even the free and informed consent of all the members of a society would not justify such a state.[2] Despite this disagreement, libertarians are strongly united in opposition to welfare rights and the welfare state. According to Nozick, "the state may not use its coercive apparatus for the purpose of getting some citizens to aid others."[3] For Rothbard, "the libertarian position calls for the complete abolition of governmental welfare and reliance on private charitable aid."[4] Here I argue that this libertarian opposition to welfare rights and a welfare state is ill-founded. Welfare rights can be given a libertarian justification, and once this is recognized, a libertarian argument for a welfare state, unlike libertarian arguments for the night watchman state, is both straightforward and compelling. . . .

Libertarians have defended their view in basically two different ways. Some libertarians, following Herbert Spencer, have (1) defined liberty as the absence of constraints, (2) taken a right to liberty to be the ultimate political ideal, and (3) derived all other rights from this right to liberty. Other libertarians, following John Locke, have (1) taken a set of rights, including, typically, a right to life or self-ownership and a right to property, to be the ultimate political ideal, (2) defined liberty as the absence of constraints in the exercise of these fundamental rights, and (3) derived all other rights, including a right to liberty, from these fundamental rights.

Each of these approaches has its difficulties. The principal difficulty with the first approach is that unless one arbitrarily restricts what is to count as an interference, conflicting liberties will abound, particularly in all areas of social life.[5] The principal difficulty with the second approach is that as long as a person's rights have not been violated, her liberty would not have been restricted either, even if she were kept in prison for the rest of her days.[6] I don't propose to try to decide between these two approaches. What I do want to show, however, is that on either approach welfare rights and a welfare state are morally required.

Spencerian Libertarianism

Thus suppose we were to adopt the view of those libertarians who take a right to liberty to be the ultimate political ideal. According to this view, liberty is usually defined as follows:

The Want Conception of Liberty: Liberty is being unconstrained by other persons from doing what one wants.

This conception limits the scope of liberty in two ways. First, not all constraints whatever their source count as a restriction of liberty; the constraints must come from other persons. For example, people who are constrained by natural forces from getting to the top of Mount Everest do not lack liberty in this regard. Second, constraints that have their source in other persons, but that do not run counter to an individual's wants, constrain without restricting that individual's liberty. Thus, for people who do not want to hear Beethoven's Fifth Symphony, the fact that others have effectively proscribed its performance does not restrict their liberty, even though it does constrain what they are able to do.

Of course, libertarians may wish to argue that even such constraints can be seen to restrict a person's liberty once we take into account the fact that people normally want, or have a general desire, to be unconstrained by others. But other philosophers have thought that the possibility of such constraints points to a serious defect in this conception of liberty,[7] which can only be remedied by adopting the following broader conception of liberty:

The Ability Conception of Liberty: Liberty is being unconstrained by other persons from doing what one is able to do.

Applying this conception to the above example, we find that people's liberty to hear Beethoven's Fifth Symphony would be restricted even if they did not want to hear it (and even if, perchance, they did not want to be unconstrained by others) since other people would still be constraining them from doing what they are able to do. . . .

Of course, there will be numerous liberties determined by the Ability Conception that are not liberties according to the Want Conception. For example, there will be highly talented students who do not want to pursue careers in philosophy, even though no one constrains them from doing so. Accordingly, the Ability Conception but not the Want Conception would view them as possessing a liberty. And even though such liberties are generally not as valuable as those liberties that are common to both conceptions, they still are of some value, even when the manipulation of people's wants is not at issue.

Yet even if we accept all the liberties specified by the Ability Conception, problems of interpretation still remain. The major problem in this regard concerns what is to count as a constraint. On the one hand, libertarians would like to limit constraints to positive acts (that is, acts of commission) that prevent people from doing what they are otherwise able to do. On the other hand, welfare liberals and socialists interpret constraints to include, in addition, negative acts (that is, of omission) that prevent people from doing what they are otherwise able to do. In fact, this is one way to understand the debate between defenders of "negative liberty" and defenders of "positive liberty." For defenders of negative liberty would seem to interpret constraints to include only positive acts of others that prevent people from doing what they otherwise are able to do, while defenders of positive liberty would seem to interpret constraints to include both positive and negative acts of others that prevent people from doing what they are otherwise able to do.[8]

Suppose we interpret constraints in the manner favored by libertarians to include only positive acts by others that prevent people from doing what they are otherwise able to do, and let us consider a typical conflict situation between the rich and the poor.

In this conflict situation, the rich, of course, have more than enough resources to satisfy their basic needs. By contrast, the poor lack the resources to meet their most basic nutritional needs even though they have tried all the means available to them that libertarians regard as legitimate for acquiring such resources. Under circumstances like these, libertarians usually maintain that the rich should have the liberty to use their resources to satisfy their luxury needs if they so wish. Libertarians recognize that this liberty might well be enjoyed at the expense of the satisfaction of the most basic nutritional needs of the poor. Libertarians just think that a right to

liberty always has priority over other political ideals, and since they assume that the liberty of the poor is not at stake in such conflict situations, it is easy for them to conclude that the rich should not be required to sacrifice their liberty so that the basic nutritional needs of the poor may be met.

From a consideration of the liberties involved, libertarians claim to derive a number of more specific requirements, in particular, a right to life, a right to freedom of speech, press and assembly, and a right to property.

Here it is important to observe that the libertarian's right to life is not a right to receive from others the goods and resources necessary for preserving one's life; it is simply a right not to be killed unjustly. Correspondingly, the libertarian's right to property is not a right to receive from others the goods and resources necessary for one's welfare, but rather a right to acquire goods and resources either by initial acquisition or by voluntary agreement.

Rights such as these, libertarians claim, can at best support only a limited role for government. That role is simply to prevent and punish initial acts of coercion—the only wrongful actions for libertarians. And, as we noted before, libertarians are deeply divided over whether a government with even such a limited role, that is, a night watchman state, can be morally justified.

Of course, libertarians would allow that it would be nice of the rich to share their surplus resources with the poor. Nevertheless, according to libertarians, such acts of charity should not be coercively required, because the liberty of the poor is not thought to be at stake in such conflict situations.

In fact, however, the liberty of the poor is at stake in such conflict situations. What is at stake is the liberty of the poor to take from the surplus possessions of the rich what is necessary to satisfy their basic nutritional needs. When libertarians are brought to see that this is the case, they are often genuinely surprised, for they had not previously seen the conflict between the rich and the poor as a conflict of liberties.[9]

When the conflict between the rich and the poor is viewed as a conflict of liberties, we can either say that the rich should have the liberty to use their surplus resources for luxury purposes, or we can say that the poor should have the liberty to take from the rich what they require to meet their basic nutritional needs. If we choose one liberty, we must reject the other. What needs to be determined, therefore, is which liberty is morally preferable: the liberty of the rich or the liberty of the poor.

I submit that the liberty of the poor, which is the liberty to take from the surplus resources of others what is required to meet one's basic nutritional needs, is morally preferable to the liberty of the rich, which is the liberty to use one's surplus resources for luxury purposes. To see that this is the case we need only appeal to one of the most fundamental principles of morality, one that is common to all political perspectives, namely, the "ought" implies "can" principle. According to this principle, people are not morally required to do what they lack the power to do or what would involve so great a sacrifice that it would be unreasonable to ask them to perform such an action.[10] For example, suppose I promised to attend a meeting on Friday, but on Thursday I am involved in a serious car accident which puts me into a coma. Surely it is no longer the case that I ought to attend the meeting now that I lack the power to do so. Or suppose instead that on Thursday I develop a severe case of pneumonia for which I am hospitalized. Surely I could legitimately claim that I no longer ought to attend the meeting on the grounds that the risk to my health involved in attending is a sacrifice that it would be unreasonable to ask me to bear.

Now applying the "ought" implies "can" principle to the case at hand, it seems clear that the poor have it within their power to willingly relinquish such an important liberty as the liberty to take from the rich what they require to meet their basic nutritional needs. Nevertheless, it would be unreasonable to require them to make so great a sacrifice. In the extreme case, it would involve requiring the poor to sit back and starve to death. Of course, the poor may have no real alternative to relinquishing this liberty. To do anything else may involve worse consequences for themselves and their loved ones and may invite a painful death. Accordingly, we may expect that the poor would acquiesce, albeit unwillingly, to a political system that denied them the welfare rights supported by such a liberty,

at the same time that we recognize that such a system imposed an unreasonable sacrifice upon the poor—a sacrifice that we could not morally blame the poor for trying to evade.[11] Analogously, we might expect that a woman whose life was threatened would submit to a rapist's demands, at the same time that we recognize the utter unreasonableness of those demands.

By contrast, it would not be unreasonable to require the rich to sacrifice the liberty to meet some of their luxury needs so that the poor can have the liberty to meet their basic nutritional needs. Naturally, we might expect that the rich for reasons of self-interest and past contribution might be disinclined to make such a sacrifice. We might even suppose that the past contribution of the rich provides a good reason for not sacrificing their liberty to use their surplus for luxury purposes. Yet, unlike the poor, the rich could not claim that relinquishing such a liberty involved so great a sacrifice that it would be unreasonable to require them to make it; unlike the poor, the rich could be morally blameworthy for failing to make such a sacrifice.

Consequently, if we assume that however else we specify the requirements of morality, they cannot violate the "ought" implies "can" principle, it follows that, despite what libertarians claim, the right to liberty endorsed by libertarians actually favors the liberty of the poor over the liberty of the rich.

Yet, couldn't libertarians object to this conclusion, claiming that it would be unreasonable to require the rich to sacrifice the liberty to meet some of their luxury needs so that the poor could have the liberty to meet their basic nutritional needs? As I have pointed out, libertarians don't usually see the situation as a conflict of liberties, but suppose they did. How plausible would such an objection be? Not very plausible at all, I think.

Consider this: what are libertarians going to say about the poor? Isn't it clearly unreasonable to require the poor to sacrifice the liberty to meet their basic nutritional needs so that the rich can have the liberty to meet their luxury needs? Isn't it clearly unreasonable to require the poor to sit back and starve to death? If it is, then there is no resolution of this conflict that would be reasonable to require both the rich and the poor to accept. But that would mean that the libertarian ideal of liberty cannot be a moral ideal that resolves conflicts of interest in ways that it would be reasonable to require everyone affected to accept. Therefore, as long as libertarians think of themselves as putting forth such a moral ideal, they cannot allow that it would be unreasonable both to require the rich to sacrifice the liberty to meet some of their luxury needs in order to benefit the poor and to require the poor to sacrifice the liberty to meet their basic nutritional needs in order to benefit the rich. But I submit that if one of these requests is to be judged reasonable, then, by any neutral assessment, it must be the requirement that the rich sacrifice the liberty to meet some of their luxury needs so that the poor can have the liberty to meet their basic nutritional needs; there is no other plausible resolution, if libertarians intend to be putting forth a moral ideal that reasonably resolves conflicts of interest.

But might not libertarians hold that putting forth a moral ideal means no more than being willing to universalize one's fundamental commitments? Surely we have no difficulty imagining the rich willing to universalize their commitments to relatively strong property rights. Yet, at the same time, we have no difficulty imagining the poor and their advocates willing to universalize their commitments to relatively weak property rights. Consequently, if the libertarian's moral ideal is interpreted in this fashion, it would not be able to provide a basis for reasonably resolving conflicts of interest between the rich and the poor. But without such a basis for conflict resolution, how could societies flourish, as libertarians claim they would, under a minimal state or with no state at all?[12] Surely, in order for societies to flourish in this fashion, the libertarian ideal must resolve conflicts of interest in ways that it would be reasonable to require everyone affected to accept. But, as we have seen, that requirement can only be satisfied if the rich sacrifice the liberty to meet some of their luxury needs so that the poor can have the liberty to meet their basic nutritional needs.

It should also be noted that this case for restricting the liberty of the rich depends upon the willingness of the poor to take advantage of whatever opportunities are available to them for satisfying their basic needs by engaging in mutually beneficial work, so that failure of the poor to take advantage of such opportunities would normally either cancel or at least significantly reduce the obligation of the rich to restrict their own liberty for the benefit of the poor.[13] In addition, the poor would be required to return the equivalent of any surplus possessions they have taken from the rich once they are able to do so and still satisfy their basic needs. Nor would the poor be required to keep the liberty to which they are entitled. They could give up part of it, or all of it, or risk losing it on the chance of gaining a greater share of liberties or other social goods.[14] Consequently, the case for restricting the liberty of the rich for the benefit of the poor is neither unconditional nor inalienable.

Even so, libertarians would have to be disconcerted about what turns out to be the practical upshot of taking a right to liberty to be the ultimate political ideal. For libertarians contend that their political ideal would support welfare rights only when constraints are "illegitimately" interpreted to induce both positive and negative acts by others that prevent people from doing what they are otherwise able to do. By contrast, when constraints are interpreted to include only positive acts, libertarians contend, no such welfare rights can be justified.

Nevertheless, what the foregoing argument demonstrates is that this view is mistaken. For even when the interpretation of constraints favored by libertarians is employed, a moral assessment of the competing liberties still requires an allocation of liberties to the poor that will be generally sufficient to provide them with the goods and resources necessary for satisfying their basic nutritional needs.

One might think that once the rich realize that the poor should have the liberty not to be interfered with when taking from the surplus possessions of the rich what they require to satisfy their basic needs, it would be in the interest of the rich to stop producing any surplus whatsoever. Yet that would only be the case if first, the recognition of the rightful claims of the poor would exhaust the surplus of the rich and second, the poor would never be in a position to be obligated to repay what they appropriated from the rich. Fortunately for the poor both of these conditions are unlikely to obtain.

Of course, there will be cases where the poor fail to satisfy their basic nutritional needs, not because of any direct restriction of liberty on the part of the rich, but because the poor are in such dire need that they are unable even to attempt to take from the rich what they require to meet their basic nutritional needs. Accordingly, in such cases, the rich would not be performing any act of commission that prevents the poor from taking what they require. Yet, even in such cases, the rich would normally be performing acts of commission that prevent other persons from aiding the poor by taking from the surplus possessions of the rich. And when assessed from a moral point of view, restricting the liberty of these other persons would not be morally justified for the very same reason that restricting the liberty of the poor to meet their own basic nutritional needs would not be morally justified: it would not be reasonable to ask all of those affected to accept such a restriction of liberty. . . .

In brief, what this shows is that if a right to liberty is taken to be the ultimate political ideal, then, contrary to what libertarians claim, not only would a system of welfare rights be morally required, but also such a system would clearly benefit the poor.

Lockean Libertarianism

Yet suppose we were to adopt the view of those libertarians who do not take a right to liberty to be the ultimate political ideal. According to this view, liberty is defined as follows:

The Rights Conception of Liberty. Liberty is being unconstrained by other persons from doing what one has a right to do.

The most important ultimate rights in terms of which liberty is specified are, according to this view, a right to life understood as a right not to be killed unjustly and a right to property understood as a right to acquire goods and resources either by initial acquisition or voluntary agreement. In order to evaluate this view, we must determine what are the practical implications of these rights.

Presumably, a right to life understood as a right not to be killed unjustly would not be violated by defensive measures designed to protect one's person from life-threatening attacks. Yet would this right be violated when the rich prevent the poor from taking what they require to satisfy their basic nutritional needs? Obviously, as a consequence of such preventive actions poor people sometimes do starve to death. Have the rich, then, in contributing to this result, killed the poor, or simply let them die; and, if they have killed the poor, have they done so unjustly?

Sometimes the rich, in preventing the poor from taking what they require to meet their basic nutritional needs, would not in fact be killing the poor, but only causing them to be physically or mentally debilitated. Yet since such preventive acts involve resisting the life-preserving activities of the poor, when the poor do die as a consequence of such acts, it seems clear that the rich would be killing the poor, whether intentionally or unintentionally.

Of course, libertarians would want to argue that such killing is simply a consequence of the legitimate exercise of property rights, and hence, not unjust. But to understand why libertarians are mistaken in this regard, let us appeal again to that fundamental principle of morality, the "ought" implies "can" principle. In this context, the principle can be used to assess two opposing accounts of property rights. According to the first account, a right to property is not conditional upon whether other persons have sufficient opportunities and resources to satisfy their basic needs. This view holds that the initial acquisition and voluntary agreement of some can leave others, through no fault of their own, dependent upon charity for the satisfaction of their most basic needs. By contrast, according to the second account, initial acquisition and voluntary agreement can confer title of property on all goods and resources except those surplus goods and resources of the rich that are required to satisfy the basic needs of those poor who through no fault of their own lack opportunities and resources to satisfy their own basic needs.

Clearly, only the first of these two accounts of property rights would generally justify the killing of the poor as a legitimate exercise of the property rights of the rich. Yet it would be unreasonable to require the poor to accept anything other than some version of the second account of property rights. Moreover, according to the second account, it does not matter whether the poor would actually die or are only physically or mentally debilitated as a result of such acts of prevention. Either result would preclude property rights from arising. Of course, the poor may have no real alternative to acquiescing to a political system modeled after the first account of property rights, even though such a system imposes an unreasonable sacrifice upon them—a sacrifice that we could not blame them for trying to evade. At the same time, although the rich would be disinclined to do so, it would not be unreasonable to require them to accept a political system modeled after the second account of property rights—the account favored by the poor.

Consequently, if we assume that however else we specify the requirements of morality, they cannot violate the "ought" implies "can" principle, it follows that, despite what libertarians claim, the right to life and the right to property endorsed by libertarians actually support a system of welfare rights. . . .

Nevertheless, it might be objected that the welfare rights that have been established against the libertarian are not the same as the welfare rights endorsed by welfare liberals. We could mark this difference by referring to the welfare rights that have been established against the libertarian as "action welfare rights" and referring to the welfare rights endorsed by welfare liberals as both "action and recipient welfare rights." The significance of this difference is that a person's action welfare right can be violated only when other people through acts of commission interfere with a person's exercise of that right, whereas a person's action and recipient welfare right can be violated by such acts of commission and by acts of omission as well. However, this difference will have little practical import. For once

libertarians come to recognize the legitimacy of action welfare rights, then in order not to be subject to the poor person's discretion in choosing when and how to exercise her action welfare right, libertarians will tend to favor two morally legitimate ways of preventing the exercise of such rights. First, libertarians can provide the poor with mutually beneficial job opportunities. Second, libertarians can institute adequate recipient welfare rights that would take precedence over the poor's action welfare rights. Accordingly, if libertarians adopt either or both of these ways of legimately preventing the poor from exercising their action welfare rights, libertarians will end up endorsing the same sort of welfare institutions favored by welfare liberals.

Finally, once a system of welfare rights is seen to follow irrespective of whether one takes a right to liberty or rights to life and property as the ultimate political ideal, the justification for a welfare state becomes straightforward and compelling. For while it is at least conceivable that rights other than welfare rights could be adequately secured in a society without the enforcement agencies of a state, it is inconceivable that welfare rights themselves could be adequately secured without such enforcement agencies. Only a welfare state would be able to effectively solve the large-scale coordination problem necessitated by the provision of welfare. Consequently, once a system of welfare rights can be seen to have a libertarian justification, the argument for a welfare state hardly seems to need stating.[15]

Notes

1. Robert Nozick, *Anarchy, State and Utopia* (New York: Basic Books, 1974), Part I.

2. Murray Rothbard, *The Ethics of Liberty* (Atlantic Highlands: Humanities Press, 1982), p. 230.

3. Nozick, *Anarchy, State and Utopia*, p. ix.

4. Murray Rothbard, *For a New Liberty* (New York: Collier Books, 1978), p. 148.

5. See, for example, James P. Sterba, "Neo-Libertarianism," *American Philosophical Quarterly* 15 (1978): 17–19; Ernest Loevinsohn, "Liberty

and the Redistribution of Property," *Philosophy and Public Affairs* 6 (1977): 226–39; David Zimmerman, "Coercive Wage Offers," *Philosophy and Public Affairs* 10 (1981): 121–45. To limit what is to count as coercive, Zimmerman claims that in order for P's offer to be coercive:

(I)t must be the case that P does more than merely prevent Q *from taking from* P resources necessary for securing Q's strongly preferred preproposal situation; P must prevent Q *from acting on his own* (or with the help of others) *to produce or procure* the strongly preferred preposal situation.

But this restriction seems arbitrary, and Zimmerman provides little justification for it. See David Zimmerman, "More on Coercive Wage Offers," *Philosophy and Public Affairs* 12 (1983): 67–68.

6. It might seem that this second approach could avoid this difficulty if a restriction of liberty is understood as the curtailment of one's prima facie rights. But in order to avoid the problem of a multitude of conflicting liberties, which plagues the first approach, the specification of prima facie rights must be such that they only can be overridden when one or more of them is violated. And this may involve too much precision for our notion of prima facie rights.

7. Isaiah Berlin, *Four Essays on Liberty* (New York: Oxford University Press, 1969), pp. XXXVIII-XL.

8. On this point, see Maurice Cranston, *Freedom* (New York: Basic Books, 1953), pp. 52–53; C. B. Macpherson, *Democratic Theory* (Oxford: Oxford University Press, 1973), p. 95; Joel Feinberg, *Rights, Justice and the Bounds of Liberty* (Princeton, N.J.: Princeton University Press, 1980), Chapter 1.

9. See John Hospers, *Libertarianism* (Los Angeles: Nash Publishing Co., 1971), Chapter 7.

10. Alvin Goldman, *A Theory of Human Action* (Englewood Cliffs, N.J.: Prentice-Hall, 1970), pp. 208–15; William Frankena, "Obligation and Ability," in *Philosophical Analysis*, edited by Max Black (Ithaca, N.Y.: Cornell University Press, 1950), pp. 157–75.

Judging from some recent discussions of moral dilemmas by Bernard Williams and Ruth Marcus, one might think that the "ought" implies "can" principle would only be useful for illustrating moral conflicts rather than resolving them.

See Bernard Williams, *Problems of the Self* (Cambridge: Cambridge University Press, 1977), Chapters 11 and 12; Ruth Marcus, "Moral Dilemmas and Consistency," *The Journal of Philosophy* 80 (1980): 121–36. See also Terrance C. McConnell, "Moral Dilemmas and Consistency in Ethics," *Canadian Journal of Philosophy* 18 (1978): 269–87. But this is only true if one interprets the "can" in the principle to exclude only "what a person lacks the power to do." If one interprets the "can" to exclude in addition "what would involve so great a sacrifice that it would be unreasonable to ask the person to do it" then the principle can be used to resolve moral conflicts as well as state them. Nor would libertarians object to this broader interpretation of the "ought" implies "can" principle since they do not ground their claim to liberty on the existence of irresolvable moral conflicts.

11. See James P. Sterba, "Is there a Rationale for Punishment?", *The American Journal of Jurisprudence* 29 (1984): 29–44.

12. As further evidence, notice that those libertarians who justify a minimal state do so on the grounds that such a state would arise from reasonable disagreements concerning the application of libertarian rights. They do not justify the minimal state on the grounds that it would be needed to keep in submission large numbers of people who could not come to see the reasonableness of libertarian rights.

13. Obviously, the employment opportunities offered to the poor must be honorable and supportive of self-respect. To do otherwise would be to offer the poor the opportunity to meet some of their basic needs at the cost of denying some of their other basic needs.

14. The poor cannot, however, give up the liberty to which their children are entitled.

15. Of course, someone might still want to object to welfare states on the grounds that they "force workers to sell their labor" (see G. A. Cohen, "The Structure of Proletarian Unfreedom," *Philosophy and Public Affairs* 12 (1982): 3–33) and subject workers to "coercive wage offers." (See Zimmerman, "Coercive Wage Offers.") But for a defense of at least one form of welfare state against such an objection, see James P. Sterba, "A Marxist Dilemma for Social Contract Theory," *American Philosophical Quarterly* 21 (1981): 51–59.

39.   The Nonexistence of Basic Welfare Rights

Tibor Machan

In opposition to James Sterba, Tibor Machan defends a traditional libertarian perspective. Machan argues that humans have a right not to be attacked, killed, or deprived of their property. However, we do not, he suggests, have a *right* to receive the resources necessary for survival.

James Sterba and others maintain that we all have the right to "receive the goods and resources necessary for preserving" ourselves. This is not what I have argued human beings have a right to. They have the right, rather, not to be killed, attacked, and deprived of their property—by persons in or outside of government. As Abraham Lincoln put it, "no man is good enough to govern another man, without that other's consent."[1]

Sterba claims that various political outlooks would have to endorse these "rights." He sets out to show, in particular, that welfare rights follow from libertarian theory itself.[2] Sterba wishes to show that *if* Lockean libertarianism is correct, then we all have rights to welfare and equal (economic) opportunity. What I wish to show is that since Lockean libertarianism—as developed in this work—is true, and since the rights to welfare and equal opportunity require their violation, no one has these latter rights. The reason some people, including Sterba, believe otherwise is that they have found some very rare instances in which some citizens could find themselves in circumstances that would require disregarding rights altogether. This would be in situations that cannot be characterized to be "where peace is possible."[3] And every major libertarian thinker from Locke to the present has treated these kinds of cases.[4]

Let us be clear about what Sterba sets out to show. It is that libertarians are philosophically unable to escape the welfare-statist implication of their commitment to negative liberty. This

Reprinted from *Individuals and Their Rights* by Tibor Machan by permission of Open Court Publishing Company, La Salle, Illinois.

means that despite their belief that they are only supporting the enforceable right of every person not to be coerced by other persons, libertarians must accept, by the logic of their own position, that individuals also possess basic enforceable rights to being provided with various services from others. He holds, then, that basic negative rights imply basic positive rights.

To Lockean libertarians the ideal of liberty means that we all, individually, have the right not to be constrained against our consent within our realm of authority—ourselves and our belongings. Sterba states that for such libertarians "Liberty is being unconstrained by persons from doing what one has a right to do."[5] Sterba adds, somewhat misleadingly, that for Lockean libertarians "a right to life [is] a right not to be killed unjustly and a right to property [is] a right to acquire goods and resources either by initial acquisition or voluntary agreement."[6] Sterba does realize that these rights do not entitle one to receive from others the goods and resources necessary for preserving one's life.

A problem with this foundation of the Lockean libertarian view is that political justice—not the justice of Plato, which is best designated in our time as "perfect virtue"—for natural-rights theorists presupposes individual rights. One cannot then explain rights in terms of justice but must explain justice in terms of rights.

For a Lockean libertarian, to possess any basic right to receive the goods and resources necessary for preserving one's life conflicts with possessing the right not to be killed, assaulted, or stolen from. The latter are rights Lockean libertarians consider to be held by all individual human beings. Regularly to protect and maintain—that is, enforce—the former right would often require the violation of the latter. A's right to the food she has is incompatible with B's right to take this same food. Both the rights could not be fundamental in an integrated legal system. The situation of one's having rights to welfare, and so forth, and another's having rights to life, liberty, and property is thus theoretically intolerable and practically unfeasible. The point of a system of rights is the securing of mutually peaceful and consistent moral conduct on the part of human beings. As Rand observes,

> "Rights" are . . . the link between the moral code of a man and the legal code of a society, between ethics and politics. *Individual rights are the means of subordinating society to moral law.*[7]

Sterba asks us—in another discussion of his views—to consider what he calls "a *typical* conflict situation between the rich and the poor." He says that in his situation "the rich, of course, have more than enough resources to satisfy their basic needs. By contrast, the poor lack the resources to meet their most basic needs even though *they have tried all the means available to them that libertarians regard as legitimate for acquiring such resources*"[8] (my emphasis).

The goal of a theory of rights would be defeated if rights were typically in conflict. Some bureaucratic group would have to keep applying its moral intuitions on numerous occasions when rights claims would *typically* conflict. A constitution is workable if it helps remove at least the largest proportion of such decisions from the realm of arbitrary (intuitive) choice and avail a society of men and women of objective guidelines that are reasonably integrated, not in relentless discord.

Most critics of libertarianism assume some doctrine of basic needs which they invoke to show that whenever basic needs are not satisfied for some people, while others have "resources" which are not basic needs for them, the former have just claims against the latter. (The language of resources of course loads the argument in the critic's favor since it suggests that these goods simply come into being and happen to be in the possession of some people,

quite without rhyme or reason, arbitrarily [as John Rawls claims].)[9]

This doctrine is full of difficulties. It lacks any foundation for why the needs of some persons must be claims upon the lives of others. And why are there such needs anyway—to what end are they needs, and whose ends are these and why are not the persons whose needs they are held responsible for supplying the needs? (Needs, as I have already observed, lack any force in moral argument without the prior justification of the purposes they serve or the goals they help to fulfill. A thief has a basic need of skills and powers that are clearly not justified if theft is morally unjustified. If, however, the justification of basic needs, such as food and other resources, presupposes the value of human life, and if the value of human life justifies, as I have argued earlier, the principle of the natural rights to life, liberty and property, then the attainment or fulfillment of the basic need for food may not involve the violation of these rights.)

Sterba claims that without guaranteeing welfare and equal-opportunity rights, Lockean libertarianism violates the most basic tenets of any morality, namely, that "ought" implies "can." The thrust of " 'ought' implies 'can' " is that one ought to do that which one is free to do, that one is morally responsible only for those acts that one had the power either to choose to engage in or to choose not to engage in. (There is debate on just how this point must be phrased—in terms of the will being free or the person being free to will something. For our purposes, however, all that counts is that the person must have [had] a genuine option to do X or not to do X before it can be true that he or she ought to do X or ought to have done X.) If an innocent person is forced by the actions of another to forgo significant moral choices, then that innocent person is not free to act morally and thus his or her human dignity is violated.

This is not so different from the commonsense legal precept that if one is not sound of mind one cannot be criminally culpable. Only free agents, capable of choosing between right and wrong, are open to moral evaluation. This indeed is the reason that many so-called moral theories fail to be anything more than value theories. They omit from consideration the issue of self-determination. If either hard or soft determinism is true, morality is impossible, although values need not disappear.[10]

If Sterba were correct about Lockean libertarianism typically contradicting " 'ought' implies 'can,' " his argument would be decisive. (There are few arguments against this principle that I know of and they have not convinced me. They trade on rare circumstances when persons feel guilt for taking actions that had bad consequences even though they could not have avoided them.)[11] It is because Karl Marx's and Herbert Spencer's systems typically, normally, indeed in every case, violate this principle that they are not bona fide moral systems. And quite a few others may be open to a similar charge.[12]

Sterba offers his strongest argument when he observes that " 'ought' implies 'can' " is violated "when the rich prevent the poor from taking what they require to satisfy their basic needs even though they have tried all the means available to them that libertarians regard as legitimate for acquiring such resources."[13]

Is Sterba right that such are—indeed, must be—typical conflict cases in a libertarian society? Are the rich and poor, even admitting that there is some simple division of people into such economic groups, in such hopeless conflict all the time? Even in the case of homeless people, many find help without having to resort to theft. The political factors contributing to the presence of helpless people in the United States and other Western liberal democracies are a hotly debated issue, even among utilitarians and welfare-state supporters. Sterba cannot make his argument for the typicality of such cases by reference to history alone. (Arguably, there are fewer helpless poor in near-libertarian, capitalist systems than anywhere else—why else would virtually everyone wish to live in these societies rather than those where welfare is guaranteed, indeed enforced? Not, at least originally, for their welfare-statist features. Arguably, too, the disturbing numbers of such people in these societies could be due, in part, to the lack of consistent protection of all the libertarian natural rights.)

Nonetheless, in a system that legally protects and preserves property rights there will be cases where a rich person prevents a poor person from taking what belongs to her (the rich person)—for example, a chicken that the poor person might use to feed herself. Since after such prevention the poor person might starve, Sterba asks the rhetorical question, "Have the rich, then, in contributing to this result, killed the poor, or simply let them die; and if they have killed the poor, have they done so unjustly?"[14] His answer is that they have. Sterba holds that a system that accords with the Lockean libertarian's idea that the rich person's preventive action is just "imposes an unreasonable sacrifice upon" the poor, one "that we could not blame them for trying to evade." Not permitting the poor to act to satisfy their basic needs is to undermine the precept that " 'ought' implies 'can' " since, as Sterba claims, that precept means, for the poor, that they ought to satisfy their basic needs. This they must have the option to do if they ought to do it. . . .

When people defend their property, what are they doing? They are protecting themselves against the intrusive acts of some other person, acts that would normally deprive them of something to which they have a right, and the other has no right. As such, these acts of protectiveness make it possible for men and women in society to retain their own sphere of jurisdiction intact, protect their own "moral space."[15] They refuse to have their human dignity violated. They want to be sovereigns and govern their own lives, including their own productive decisions and actions. Those who mount the attack, in turn, fail or refuse to refrain from encroaching upon the moral space of their victims. They are treating the victim's life and its productive results as though these were unowned resources for them to do with as they choose.

Now the argument that cuts against the above account is that on some occasions there can be people who, with no responsibility for their situation, are highly unlikely to survive without disregarding the rights of others and taking from them what they need. This is indeed possible. It is no less possible that there be cases in which someone is highly unlikely to survive without obtaining the services of a doctor who is at that moment spending time healing someone else, or in which there is a person who is highly unlikely to survive without obtaining one of the lungs of another person, who wants to keep both lungs so as to be able to run the New York City marathon effectively. And such cases could be multiplied indefinitely.

But are such cases typical? The argument that starts with this assumption about a society is already not comparable to the libertarianism that has emerged in the footsteps of Lockean natural-rights doctrine, including the version advanced in this book. That system is developed for a human community in which "peace is possible." Libertarian individual rights, which guide men and women in such an adequately hospitable environment to act without thwarting the flourishing of others, are thus suitable bases for the legal foundations for a human society. It is possible for people in the world to pursue their proper goals without thwarting a similar pursuit by others.

The underlying notion of society in such a theory rejects the description of human communities implicit in Sterba's picture. Sterba sees conflict as typically arising from some people producing and owning goods, while others having no alternative but to take these goods from the former in order to survive. But these are not the typical conflict situations even in what we today consider reasonably free human communities—most thieves and robbers are not destitute, nor are they incapable of doing something aside from taking other people's property in order to obtain their livelihood.

The typical conflict situation in society involves people who wish to take shortcuts to earning their living (and a lot more) by attacking others, not those who lack any other alternative to attacking others so as to reach that same goal. This may not be evident from all societies that team with human conflict—in the Middle East, or Central and South America, for example. But it must be remembered that these societies are far from being even near-libertarian. Even if the typical conflicts there involved the kind Sterba describes, that would not suffice to make his point. Only if it were true that in comparatively free countries the typical conflict involved the utterly destitute and helpless arrayed against the well-to-do, could his argument carry any conviction.

The Lockean libertarian has confidence in the willingness and capacity of *virtually all persons* to make headway in life in a free society. The very small minority of exceptional cases must be taken care of by voluntary social institutions, not by the government, which guards self-consistent individual rights.

The integrity of law would be seriously endangered if the government entered areas that required it to make very particular judgments and depart from serving the interest of the public as such. We have already noted that the idea of "satisfying basic needs" can involve the difficulty of distinguishing those whose actions are properly to be so characterized. Rich persons are indeed satisfying their basic needs as they protect and preserve their property rights. . . . Private property rights are necessary for a morally decent society.

The Lockean libertarian argues that private property rights are morally justified in part because they are the concrete requirement for delineating the sphere of jurisdiction of each person's moral authority, where her own judgment is decisive.[16] This is a crucial basis for the right to property. And so is the contention that we live in a metaphysically hospitable universe wherein people normally need not suffer innocent misery and deprivation—so that such a condition is usually the result of negligence or the violation of Lockean rights, a violation that has made self-development and commerce impossible. If exceptional emergencies set the agenda for the law, the law itself will disintegrate. (A just legal system makes provision for coping with emergencies that are brought to the attention of the authorities, for example, by way of judicial discretion, without allowing such cases to determine the direction of the system. If legislators and judges don't uphold the integrity of the system, disintegration ensues. This can itself encourage the emergence of strong leaders, demagogues, who promise to do what the law has not been permitted to do, namely, satisfy people's sense of justice. Experience with them bodes ill for such a prospect.)

Normally persons do not "lack the opportunities and resources to satisfy their own basic needs." Even if we grant that some helpless, crippled, retarded, or destitute persons could offer nothing to anyone that would merit wages enabling them to carry on with their lives and perhaps even flourish, there is still the other possibility for most actual, known hard cases, that is, seeking help. I am not speaking here of the cases we know: people who drop out of school, get an unskilled job, marry and have kids, only to find that their personal choice of inadequate preparation for life leaves them relatively poorly off. " 'Ought' implies 'can' " must not be treated ahistorically—some people's lack of current options results from their failure to exercise previous options prudently. I refer here to the "truly needy," to use a shop-worn but still useful phrase—those who have never been able to help themselves and are not now helpless from their own neglect. Are such people being treated *unjustly,* rather than at most uncharitably, ungenerously, indecently, pitilessly, or in some other respect immorally—by those who, knowing of the plight of such persons, resist forcible efforts to take from them enough to provide the ill-fated with what they truly need? Actually, if we tried to pry the needed goods or money from the well-to-do, we would not even learn if they would act generously. Charity, generosity, kindness, and acts of compassion presuppose that those well enough off are not coerced to provide help. These virtues cannot flourish, nor can the corresponding vices, of course, without a clearly identified and well-protected right to private property for all.

If we consider the situation as we are more likely to find it, namely, that desperate cases not caused by previous injustices (in the libertarian sense) are rare, then, contrary to what Sterba suggests, there is much that unfortunate persons can and should do in those plausible, non-emergency situations that can be considered typical. They need not resort to violating the private-property rights of those who are better off. The destitute can appeal for assistance both from the rich and from the many voluntary social service agencies which emerge from the widespread compassion of people who know about the mishaps that can at times strike perfectly decent people.

Consider, as a prototype of this situation on which we might model what concerns Sterba,

that if one's car breaks down on a remote road, it would be unreasonable to expect one not to seek a phone or some other way of escaping one's unfortunate situation. So one ought to at least try to obtain the use of a phone.

But should one break into the home of a perfect stranger living nearby? Or ought one instead to request the use of the phone as a favor? " 'Ought' implies 'can' " is surely fully satisfied here. Actual practice makes this quite evident. When someone is suffering from misfortune and there are plenty of others who are not, and the unfortunate person has no other avenue for obtaining help than to obtain it from others, it would not be unreasonable to expect, morally, that the poor seek such help as surely might be forthcoming. We have no justification for assuming that the rich are all callous, though this caricature is regularly painted by communists and by folklore. Supporting and gaining advantage from the institution of private property by no means implies that one lacks the virtue of generosity. The rich are no more immune to virtue than the poor are to vice. The contrary view is probably a legacy of the idea that only those concerned with spiritual or intellectual matters can be trusted to know virtue—those concerned with seeking material prosperity are too base.

The destitute typically have options other than to violate the rights of the well-off. " 'Ought' implies 'can' " is satisfiable by the moral imperative that the poor ought to seek help, not loot. There is then no injustice in the rich preventing the poor from seeking such loot by violating the right to private property. " 'Ought' implies 'can' " is fully satisfied if the poor can take the kind of action that could gain them the satisfaction of their basic needs, and this action could well be asking for help.

All along here I have been considering only the helplessly poor, who through no fault of their own, nor again through any rights violation by others, are destitute. I am taking the hard cases seriously, where violation of " 'ought' implies 'can' " would appear to be most probable. But such cases are by no means typical. They are extremely rare. And even rarer are those cases in which all avenues regarded as legitimate from the libertarian point of view have been exhausted, including appealing for help.

The bulk of poverty in the world is not the result of natural disaster or disease. Rather it is political oppression, whereby people throughout many of the world's countries are not legally permitted to look out for themselves in production and trade. The famines in Africa and India, the poverty in the same countries and in Central and Latin America, as well as in China, the Soviet Union, Poland, Rumania, and so forth, are not the result of lack of charity but of oppression. It is the kind that those who have the protection of even a seriously compromised document and system protecting individual negative human rights, such as the U.S. Constitution, do not experience. The first requirement for men and women to ameliorate their hardship is to be free of other people's oppression, not to be free to take other people's belongings.

Of course, it would be immoral if people failed to help out when this was clearly no sacrifice for them. But charity or generosity is not a categorical imperative, even for the rich. There are more basic moral principles that might require the rich to refuse to be charitable—for example, if they are using most of their wealth for the protection of freedom or a just society. Courage can be more important than charity or benevolence or compassion. But a discussion of the ranking of moral virtues would take us far afield. One reason that many critics of libertarianism find their own cases persuasive is that they think the libertarian can only subscribe to *political* principles or values. But this is mistaken.[17]

There can be emergency cases in which there is no alternative available to disregarding the rights of others. But these are extremely rare, and not at all the sort invoked by critics such as Sterba. I have in mind the desert-island case found in ethics books where instantaneous action, with only one violent alternative, faces persons—the sort we know from the law books in which the issue is one of immediate life and death. These are not cases, to repeat the phrase quoted from Locke by H. L. A. Hart, "where peace is possible." They are discussed in the libertarian literature and considerable progress has been made in integrating them with the concerns of law and politics.

Since we are here discussing law and politics, which are general systematic approaches to how we normally ought to live with one another in human communities, these emergency situations do not help us except as limiting cases. And not surprisingly many famous court cases illustrate just this point as they now and then confront these kinds of instances after they have come to light within the framework of civilized society. . . .

Notes

1. Quoted in Harry V. Jaffa, *How to Think About the American Revolution* (Durham, NC: Carolina Academic Press, 1978), p. 41 (from *The Collected Works of Abraham Lincoln* [R. Basler (ed.), 1953], pp. 108–115).

2. See, in particular, James Sterba, "A Libertarian Justification for a Welfare State," *Social Theory and Practice*, vol. 11 (Fall 1985), 285–306. I will be referring to this essay as well as a more developed version, titled "The U.S. Constitution: A Fundamentally Flawed Document" in *Philosophical Reflections on the United States Constitution*, edited by Christopher Gray (1989).

3. H. L. A. Hart, "Are There Any Natural Rights?" *Philosophical Review*, vol. 64 (1955), 175.

4. See, for my own discussions, Tibor R. Machan, *Human Rights and Human Liberties* (Chicago: Nelson-Hall, 1975), pp. 213–222; "Prima Facie versus Natural (Human) Rights," *Journal of Value Inquiry*, vol. 10 (1976), 119–131; "Human Rights: Some Points of Clarification," *Journal of Critical Analysis*, vol. 5 (1973), 30–39.

5. Sterba, op. cit., "A Libertarian Justification," p. 295.

6. Ibid.

7. Ayn Rand, "Value and Rights," in J. Hospers (ed.), *Readings in Introductory Philosophical Analysis* (Englewood Cliffs, NJ: Prentice-Hall, 1968), p. 382.

8. Sterba, "The U.S. Constitution: A Fundamentally Flawed Document."

9. John Rawls, *A Theory of Justice* (Cambridge, MA: Harvard University Press, 1971), pp. 101–02. For a discussion of the complexities in the differential attainments of members of various

ethnic groups—often invoked as evidence for the injustice of a capitalist system, see Thomas Sowell, *Ethnic America: A History* (New York: Basic Books, 1981). There is pervasive prejudice in welfare-state proponents' writings against crediting people with the ability to extricate themselves from poverty without special political assistance. The idea behind the right to negative liberty is to set people free from others so as to pursue their progressive goals. This is the ultimate teleological justification of Lockean libertarian natural rights. See Tibor R. Machan, *Human Rights and Human Liberties: A Radical Reconsideration of the American Political Tradition* (Chicago: Nelson-Hall, 1975). Consider also this thought from Herbert Spencer:

The feeling which vents itself in "poor fellow!" on seeing one in agony, excludes the thought of "bad fellow," which might at another time arise. Naturally, then, if the wretched are unknown or but vaguely known, all the demerits they may have are ignored: and thus it happens that when the miseries of the poor are dilated upon, they are thought of as the miseries of the deserving poor, instead of being thought of as the miseries of undeserving poor, which in large measure they should be. Those whose hardships are set forth in pamphlets and proclaimed in sermons and speeches which echo throughout society, are assumed to be all worthy souls, grievously wronged; and none of them are thought of as bearing the penalties of their own misdeeds. (*Man versus the State* [Caldwell, ID: Caxton Printers, 1940], p. 22)

10. Tibor R. Machan, "Ethics vs. Coercion: Morality of Just Values?" in L. H. Rockwell, Jr. et al., (ed.), *Man, Economy and Liberty: Essays in Honor of Murray N. Rothbard* (Auburn, AL: Ludwig von Mises Institute, 1988), pp. 236–246.

11. John Kekes, " 'Ought Implies Can' and Two Kinds of Morality," *The Philosophical Quarterly,* vol. 34 (1984), 459–467.

12. Tibor R. Machan, "Ethics vs. Coercion." In a vegetable garden or even in a forest, there can be good things and bad, but no morally good things and morally evil things (apart from people who might be there).

13. Sterba, "The U.S. Constitution: A Fundamentally Flawed Document."

14. Sterba, "A Libertarian Justification," pp. 295–296.

15. Robert Nozick, *Anarchy, State, and Utopia* (New York: Basic Books, 1974), p. 57. See, also, Tibor R. Machan, "Conditions for Rights, Sphere of Authority," *Journal of Human Relations,* vol. 19 (1971), 184–187, where I argue that "within the context of a legal system where the *sphere of authority* of individuals and groups of individuals cannot be delineated independently of the sphere of authority of the public as a whole, there is an inescapable conflict of rights specified by the same legal system." (186) See, also, Tibor R. Machan, "The Virtue of Freedom in Capitalism," *Journal of Applied Philosophy,* vol 3 (1986), 49–58, and Douglas J. Den Uyl, "Freedom and Virtue," in Tibor R. Machan (ed.), *The Main Debate: Communism versus Capitalism* (New York: Random House, 1987), pp. 200–216. This last essay is especially pertinent to the understanding of the ethical or moral merits of coercion and coerced conduct. Thus it is argued here that "coercive charity" amounts to an oxymoron.

16. See, Machan, op. cit., "The Virtue of Freedom in Capitalism" and "Private Property and the Decent Society," in J. K. Roth and R. C. Whittemore (eds.), *Ideology and American Experience* (Washington, DC: Washington Institute Press, 1986).

17. E.g., James Fishkin, *Tyranny and Legitimacy* (Baltimore, MD: Johns Hopkins University Press, 1979). Cf., Tibor R. Machan, "Fishkin on Nozick's Absolute Rights," *Journal of Libertarian Studies,* vol. 6 (1982), 317–320.

40.   Women, Welfare, and the Politics of Need Interpretation

Nancy Fraser

Nancy Fraser argues that social-welfare struggles are central to the feminist political agenda. This is so because of the underlying gender norms and presumptive definition of women's needs inherent in the administrative practices of the U.S. welfare system. Fraser addresses the importance of the interpretation of women's needs.

What some writers are calling "the coming welfare wars" will be largely wars about, even against, women. Because women comprise the overwhelming majority of social-welfare program recipients and employees, women and women's needs will be the principal stakes in the battles over social spending likely to dominate national politics in the coming period. Moreover, the welfare wars will not be limited to the tenure of Reagan or even of Reaganism. On the contrary, they will be protracted wars both in time and in space. What James O'Connor (1973) theorized nearly fifteen years ago as "the fiscal crisis of the state" is a long-term, structural phenomenon of international proportions. Not just the U.S., but every late-capitalist welfare state in Western Europe and North America is facing some version of it. And the fiscal crisis of the welfare state coincides everywhere with a second long-term, structural tendency: the feminization of poverty. This is Diana Pearce's (1979) term for the rapidly increasing proportion of women in the adult poverty population, an increase tied to, *inter alia,* the rise in "female-headed households." In the U.S., this trend is so pronounced and so steep that analysts project that, should it continue, the poverty population will consist entirely of women and their children before the year 2000 (Ehrenreich and Piven 1984).

This conjunction of the fiscal crisis of the state and the feminization of poverty suggests

From *Unruly Practices: Power, Discourse, and Gender in Contemporary Social Theory,* by Nancy Fraser. Reprinted by permission of the University of Minnesota Press.

that struggles around social-welfare will and should become increasingly focal for feminists. But such struggles raise a great many problems. Some of these, like the following, can be thought of as structural: On the one hand, increasing numbers of women depend directly for their livelihoods on social-welfare programs; and many others benefit indirectly, since the existence of even a minimal and inadequate "safety net" increases the leverage of women who are economically dependent on individual men. Thus, feminists have no choice but to oppose social-welfare cuts. On the other hand, economists like Pearce (1979), Nancy Barrett (1984) and Steven Erie, Martin Rein and Barbara Wiget (1983) have shown that programs like Aid to Families with Dependent Children actually institutionalize the feminization of poverty. The benefits they provide are system-conforming ones which reinforce rather than challenge basic structural inequalities. Thus, feminists cannot simply support existing social-welfare programs. To use the suggestive but ultimately too simple terms popularized by Carol Brown (1981): If to eliminate or to reduce welfare is to bolster "private patriarchy," then simply to defend it is to consolidate "public patriarchy."[1]

Feminists also face a second set of problems in the coming welfare wars. These problems, seemingly more ideological and less structural than the first set, arise from the typical way in which issues get framed as a result of the institutional dynamics of the political system.[2] Typically, social-welfare issues are posed as follows: Shall the state undertake to satisfy the social needs of a given constituency and to what degree? Now, this way of framing issues permits only a relatively small number of answers; and it tends to cast debates in quantitative terms. More importantly, it takes for granted the definition of the needs in question, as if that were self-evident and beyond dispute. It therefore occludes the fact that the interpretation of people's needs is itself a political stake, indeed sometimes *the* political stake. Clearly, this way of framing issues poses obstacles for feminist politics, since at the heart of such politics lie questions like, what do various groups of women really need, and whose interpretations of women's needs should be authoritative. Only in terms of a discourse oriented to the *politics of need interpretation*[3] can feminists meaningfully intervene in the coming welfare wars. But this requires a challenge to the dominant policy framework.

Both sets of problems, the structural and the ideological, are extremely important and difficult. In what follows, I shall not offer solutions to either of them. Rather, I want to attempt the much more modest and preliminary task of exploring how they might be thought about in relation to one another. Specifically, I want to propose a framework for inquiry which can shed light on both of them simultaneously.

Consider that, in order to address the structural problem, it will be necessary to clarify the phenomenon of "public patriarchy." One type of inquiry which is useful here is the familiar sort of economic analysis alluded to earlier, analysis which shows, for example, that "workfare" programs function to subsidize employers of low-wage, "women's work" in the service sector and thus to reproduce the sex-segmented, dual-labor market. Now, important as such inquiry is, it does not tell the whole story, since it leaves out of focus the discursive or ideological dimension of social-welfare programs. By the discursive or ideological dimension, I do not mean anything distinct from or epiphenomenal with respect to welfare practices; I mean, rather, the tacit norms and implicit assumptions which are constitutive of those practices. To get at this dimension requires a meaning-oriented sort of inquiry, one which considers welfare programs as, among other things, institutionalized patterns of interpretation.[4] Such

inquiry would make explicit the social meanings embedded within welfare programs, meanings which tend otherwise simply to go without saying.

In spelling out such meanings, the inquiry I am proposing could do two things simultaneously. First, it could tell us something important about the structure of the U.S. welfare system, since it might identify some underlying norms and assumptions which lend a measure of coherence to diverse programs and practices. Second, it could illuminate what I called "the politics of need interpretation," since it could expose the processes by which welfare practices construct women and women's needs according to certain specific and in principle contestable interpretations, even as they lend those interpretations an aura of facticity which discourages contestation. Thus, this inquiry could shed light on both the structural and ideological problems identified earlier.

The principal aim of this paper is to provide an account of this sort for the present U.S. social-welfare system. The account is intended to help clarify some key structural aspects of male dominance in welfare-capitalist societies. At the same time, it is meant to point the way to a broader, discourse-oriented focus which can address political conflicts over the interpretation of women's needs.

The paper proceeds from some relatively "hard," uncontroversial facts about the U.S. social-welfare system (section I) through a series of increasingly interpreted accounts of that system (sections II and III). These culminate (in section IV) in a highly theorized characterization of the welfare system as a "juridical-administrative-therapeutic state apparatus" (JAT). Finally (in section V), the paper situates that apparatus as one actor among others in a larger and highly contested political field of discourse about needs which also includes the feminist movement.

I

Long before the emergence of welfare states, governments have defined legally secured arenas of societal action. In so doing, they have at the same time codified corresponding patterns of agency or social roles. Thus, early modern states defined an economic arena and the corresponding role of an economic person capable of entering into contracts. More or less at the same time, they codified the "private sphere" of the household and the role of household head with dependents. Somewhat later, governments were led to secure a sphere of political participation and the corresponding role of citizen with (limited) political rights. In each of these cases, the original and paradigmatic subject of the newly codified social role was male. Only secondarily and much later was it conceded that women, too, could occupy these subject-positions, without however er entirely dispelling the association with masculinity.

Matters are different, however, with the contemporary welfare state. When this type of government defined a new arena of activity— call it "the social"—and a new societal role, the welfare client, it included women among its original and paradigmatic subjects. Today, in fact, women have become the principal subjects of the welfare state. On the one hand, they comprise the overwhelming majority both of program recipients and of paid social service workers. On the other hand, they are the wives, mothers and daughters whose unpaid activities and obligations are redefined as the welfare state increasingly oversees forms of caregiving. Since this beneficiary-social worker-caregiver nexus of roles is constitutive of the social-welfare arena, one might even call the latter as feminized terrain.

A brief statistical overview confirms women's greater involvement with and dependence on the U.S. social-welfare system. Consider first women's greater dependence as program clients and beneficiaries. In each of the major "means-tested" programs in the U.S., women and the children for whom they are responsible now comprise the overwhelming majority of clients. For example, more than 81% of households receiving Aid to Families with Dependent Children (AFDC) are headed by women; more than 60% of families receiving food stamps or Medicaid are headed by women; and 70% of all households in publicly owned or subsidized housing are headed by women (Erie, Rein, Wiget 1983;

Nelson 1984). High as they are, these figures actually underestimate the representation of women. As Barbara Nelson (1984) notes, in the androcentric reporting system, households counted as female-headed by definition contain no healthy adult men. But healthy adult women live in most households counted as male-headed. Such women may directly or indirectly receive benefits going to "male-headed" households, but they are invisible in the statistics, even though they usually do the work of securing and maintaining program eligibility.

Women also predominate in the major U.S. "age-tested" programs. For example, 61.6% of all adult beneficiaries of Social Security are women; and 64% of those covered by Medicare are women (Erie, Rein, Wiget 1983; Nelson 1984). In sum, because women as a group are significantly poorer than men—indeed they now comprise nearly two-thirds of all U.S. adults below the official poverty line— and because women tend to live longer than men, women depend more on the social-welfare system as clients and beneficiaries.

But this is not the whole story. Women also depend more on the social-welfare system as paid human service workers—a category of employment which includes education and health, as well as social work and services administration. In 1980, 70% of the 17.3 million paid jobs in this sector in the U.S. were held by women. This accounts for one-third of U.S. women's total paid employment and a full 80% of all professional jobs held by women. The figures for women of color are even higher than this average, since 37% of their total paid employment and 82.4% of their professional employment is in this sector (Erie, Rein, Wiget 1983). It is a distinctive feature of the U.S. social-welfare system, as opposed to, say, the British and Scandinavian systems, that only 3% of these jobs are in the form of direct federal government employment. The rest are in state and local government, in the "private non-profit" sector and in the "private" sector. But the more decentralized and privatized character of the U.S. system does not make paid welfare workers any less vulnerable in the face of federal program cuts. On the contrary, the level of federal social-welfare spending affects the level of human service employment in *all* sectors. State and local government jobs depend on federal and federally-financed state and local government contracts; and private profit and non-profit jobs depend on federally financed transfer payments to individuals and households for the purchase of services like health care in the market (Erie, Rein, Wiget 1983). Thus, reductions in social spending mean the loss of jobs for women. Moreover, as Barbara Ehrenreich and Frances Fox Piven (1984) note, this loss is not compensated when spending is shifted to the military, since only 0.5% of the entire female paid workforce is employed in work on military contracts. In fact, one study they cite estimates that with each one billion dollar increase in military spending, 9500 jobs are lost to women.

Finally, women are subjects of and to the social-welfare system in their traditional capacity as unpaid caregivers. It is well known that the sexual division of labor assigns women primary responsibility for the care of those who cannot care for themselves. (I leave aside women's traditional obligations to provide personal services to adult males—husbands, fathers, grown sons, lovers—who can very well care for themselves.) Such responsibility includes child care, of course, but also care for sick and/or elderly relatives, often parents. For example, a 1975 British study cited by Hilary Land (1978) found that three times as many elderly people live with married daughters as with married sons, and that those without a close female relative were more likely to be institutionalized, irrespective of degree of infirmity. As unpaid caregivers, then, women are more directly affected than men by the level and character of government social services for children, the sick and the elderly.

As clients, paid human service workers and unpaid caregivers, then, women are the principal subjects of the social-welfare system. It is as if this branch of the state were in effect a "Bureau of Women's Affairs."

II

Of course, the welfare system does not deal with women on women's terms. On the contrary, it has its own characteristic ways of interpreting women's needs and positioning women as subjects. In order to understand these, we need to examine how gender norms and meanings are reflected in the structure of the U.S. social-welfare system.

This issue is quite complicated. On the one hand, nearly all U.S. social-welfare programs are officially gender neutral. Yet the system as a whole is a dual or two-tiered one; and it has an unmistakable gender subtext.[5] There is one set of programs oriented to *individuals* and tied to participation in the paid workforce, for example, unemployment insurance and Social Security. These programs are designed to supplement and compensate for the primary market in paid labor power. There is a second set of programs oriented to *households* and tied to combined household income, for example, AFDC, food stamps and Medicaid. These programs are designed to compensate for what are considered to be family failures, generally the absence of a male breadwinner.

What integrates the two sets of programs is a common core of assumptions, underlying both, concerning the sexual division of labor, domestic and non-domestic. It is assumed that families do or should contain one primary breadwinner who is male and one unpaid domestic worker (homemaker and mother) who is female. It is further assumed that when a woman undertakes paid work outside the home this is or should be in order to supplement the male breadwinner's wage and so it neither does nor ought override her primary housewifely and maternal responsibilities. It is assumed, in other words, that society is divided into two separate spheres of home and outside work and that these are women's and men's spheres respectively.[6]

These assumptions are increasingly counterfactual. At present, fewer than 15% of U.S. families conform to the normative ideal of a domicile shared by a husband who is the sole breadwinner, a wife who is a full-time homemaker and their offspring.

Nonetheless, the separate spheres norms determine the structure of the social-welfare system. They determine that it contain a primary labor market-related subsystem and a family or household-related subsystem. Moreover, they determine that these subsystems be gender-linked, that the labor market-related system be implicitly "masculine" and the family-related system be implicitly "feminine."

Consequently, the normative, ideal-typical recipient of primary labor market-oriented programs is a (white) male, while the normative, ideal-typical client of household-based programs is a female.

This gender subtext of the U.S. welfare system is confirmed when we take a second look at participation figures. Consider again the figures just cited for the "feminine" or family-based programs, which I earlier referred to as "means-tested" programs: more than 81% of households receiving AFDC are female-headed, as are more than 70% of those receiving housing assistance and more than 60% of those receiving Medicaid and food stamps. Now recall that these figures do not compare female vs. male individuals, but rather female vs. male headed-*households*. They therefore confirm four things: 1) these programs have a distinctive administrative identity in that their recipients are not individualized but *familialized;* 2) they serve what are considered to be defective families, overwhelmingly families without a male breadwinner; 3) the ideal-typical (adult) client is female; and 4) she makes her claim for benefits on the basis of her status as an unpaid domestic worker, a homemaker and mother, not as a paid worker based in the labor market.

Now contrast this with the case of a typical labor market-based and thus "masculine" program, namely, unemployment insurance. Here the percentage of female claimants drops to 38%, a figure which contrasts female vs. male *individuals,* as opposed to households. As Diana Pearce (1979) notes, this drop reflects at least two different circumstances. First, and most straightforwardly, it reflects women's lower rate of participation in the paid workforce. Second, it reflects the fact that many women wage-workers are not eligible to participate in this program, for example, paid household service workers, part-time workers, pregnant workers and workers in the "irregular economy" such as prostitutes, baby-sitters and home typists. The exclusion of these predominantly female wage-workers testifies to the existence of a gender segmented labor market, divided into "primary" and "secondary" employment. It reflects the more general assumption that women's earnings are "merely supplementary," not on a par with those of the primary (male) breadwinner. Altogether, then, the figures tell us four things about programs like unemployment insurance: 1) they are administered in a way which *individualizes* rather than familializes recipients; 2) they are designed to compensate primary labor market effects, such as the temporary displacement of a primary breadwinner; 3) the ideal-typical recipient is male; and 4) he makes his claim on the basis of his identity as a paid worker, not as an unpaid domestic worker or parent.

One final example will round out the picture. The Social Security system of retirement insurance presents the interesting case of a hermaphrodite or androgyne. I shall soon show that this system has a number of characteristics of "masculine" programs in virtue of its link to participation in the paid workforce. However, it is also internally dualized and gendered, and thus stands as a microcosm of the entire dual-benefit welfare system. Consider that, while a majority—61.6%—of adult beneficiaries are female, only somewhat more than half of these—or 33.3% of all recipients—claim benefits on the basis of their own paid work records (Nelson 1984; Erie, Rein and Wiget 1983). The remaining female recipients claim benefits on the basis of their husbands' records, that is, as wives or unpaid domestic workers. By contrast, virtually no male recipients claim benefits as husbands. On the contrary, they claim benefits as paid workers, a labor market-located as opposed to family-located identity. So the Social Security system is hermaphroditic or androgynous; it is internally divided between family-based, "feminine" benefits, on the one hand, and labor market-based, "masculine" benefits, on the other hand. Thus, it too gets its structure from gender norms and assumptions.

III

So far, we have established the dualistic structure of the U.S. social-welfare system and the gender subtext of the dualism. Now, we can better tease out the system's implicit norms and tacit assumptions by examining its mode of operation. To see how welfare programs interpret women's needs, we should consider what benefits consist in. To see how programs position women as subjects, we should examine administrative practices. In general, we shall see that the "masculine" and "feminine" subsystems are not only separate but also unequal.

Consider that the "masculine" social-welfare programs are social insurance schemes. They include unemployment insurance, Social Security (retirement insurance), Medicare (age-tested health insurance) and Supplemental Social Security Insurance (disability insurance for those with paid work records). These programs are contributory; wage-workers and their employers pay into trust funds. They are administered on a national basis and benefit levels are uniform across the country. Though bureaucratically organized and administered, they require less, and less demeaning effort on the part of beneficiaries in qualifying and maintaining eligibility than do "feminine" programs. They are far less subject to intrusive controls and in most cases lack the dimension of surveillance. They also tend to require less of beneficiaries in the way of benefit-collection efforts, with the notable exception of unemployment insurance.

In sum, "masculine" social insurance schemes position recipients primarily as *rights-bearers*. The beneficiaries of these programs are in the main not stigmatized. Neither administrative practice nor popular discourse constitutes them as "on the dole." They are constituted rather as receiving what they deserve, what they, in "partnership" with their employers, have already paid in for, what they, therefore, have a *right* to. Moreover, these beneficiaries are also positioned as *purchasing consumers*. They receive cash as opposed to "in kind" benefits and so are positioned as having "the liberty to strike the best bargain they can in purchasing services of their choice on the open market." In sum, these beneficiaries are what C. B. MacPherson (1964) calls "possessive individuals." Proprietors of their own persons who have freely contracted to sell their labor-power, they become participants in social insurance schemes and, thence, paying consumers of human services. They therefore qualify as *social citizens* in

virtually the fullest sense that term can acquire within the framework of a male-dominated capitalist society.

All this stands in stark contrast to the "feminine" sector of the U.S. social-welfare system. This sector consists in relief programs, such as AFDC, food stamps, Medicaid and public housing assistance. These programs are not contributory, but are financed out of general tax revenues, usually with one-third of the funds coming from the federal government and two-thirds coming from the states. They are not administered nationally but rather by the states. As a result, benefit levels vary dramatically, though they are everywhere inadequate, deliberately pegged below the official poverty line. The relief programs are notorious for the varieties of administrative humiliation they inflict upon clients. They require considerable work in qualifying and maintaining eligibility; and they have a heavy component of surveillance.

These programs do not in any meaningful sense position their subjects as rights-bearers. Far from being considered as having a right to what they receive, recipients are defined as "beneficiaries of governmental largesse" or "clients of public charity."[7] In the androcentric-administrative framework, "welfare mothers" are considered not to work and so are sometimes required, that is to say coerced, to work off their benefits via "workfare." They thus become inmates of what Diana Pearce (1979) calls a "workhouse without walls." Indeed, the only sense in which the category of rights is relevant to these clients' situation is the somewhat dubious one according to which they are entitled to treatment governed by the standards of formal-bureaucratic procedural rationality. But if that right is construed as protection from administrative caprice, then even it is widely and routinely disregarded. Moreover, recipients of public relief are generally not positioned as purchasing consumers. A significant portion of their benefits is "in kind" and what cash they get comes already carved up and earmarked for specific, administratively designated purposes. These recipients are therefore essentially *clients,* a subject-position which carries far less power and dignity in capitalist societies than does the alternative position of purchaser. In these societies, to be a client in the sense relevant to relief recipients is to be an abject dependent. Indeed, this sense of the term carries connotations of a fall from autonomy, as when we speak, for example, of "the client-states of empires or superpowers." As clients, then, recipients of relief are *the negatives of possessive individuals.* Largely excluded from the market, both as workers and as consumers, claiming benefits not as individuals but as members of "failed" families, these recipients are effectively denied the trappings of social citizenship as the latter are defined within male-dominated capitalist societies.[8]

Clearly, this system creates a double-bind for women raising children without a male breadwinner. By failing to offer them day care, job training, a job that pays a "family wage" or some combination of these, it constructs them exclusively as mothers. As a consequence, it interprets their needs as maternal needs and their sphere of activity as that of "the family." Now, according to the ideology of separate spheres, this should be an honorific social identity. Yet the system does not honor these women. On the contrary, instead of providing them a guaranteed income equivalent to a family wage as a matter of right, it stigmatizes, humiliates and harasses them. In effect, it decrees that these women must be, yet cannot be, normative mothers.

Moreover, the way in which the U.S. social-welfare system interprets "maternity" and "the family" is race- and culture-specific. The bias is made plain in Carol Stack's (1974) study, *All Our Kin.* Stack analyzes domestic arrangements of very poor Black welfare recipients in a midwestern city. Where ideologues see "the disorganization of *the* [sic] black family," she finds complex, highly organized kinship structures. These include kin-based networks of resource pooling and exchange which enable those in direst poverty to survive economically and communally. The networks organize delayed exchanges or "gifts," in Mauss' (1967) sense, of prepared meals, food stamps, cooking, shopping, groceries, furniture, sleeping space, cash (including wages and AFDC allowances), transportation, clothing, child care, even children. They span several physically distinct households and so transcend the principal administrative category which organizes

relief programs. It is significant that Stack took great pains to conceal the identities of her subjects, even going so far as to disguise the identity of their city. The reason, though unstated, is obvious: these people would lose their benefits if program administrators learned that they did not utilize them within the confines and boundaries of a "household."

We can summarize the separate and unequal character of the two-tiered, gender-linked, race- and culture-biased U.S. social-welfare system in the following formulae: Participants in the "masculine" subsystem are positioned as *rights-bearing beneficiaries and purchasing consumers of services.* Participants in the "feminine" subsystem, on the other hand, are positioned as *dependent clients.*

IV

Clearly, the identities and needs which the social-welfare system fashions for its recipients are *interpreted* identities and needs. Moreover, they are highly political interpretations which are in principle subject to dispute. Yet these needs and identities are not always recognized as interpretations. Too often, they simply go without saying and are rendered immune from analysis and critique.

Doubtless one reason for this "reification effect" is the depth at which gender meanings and norms are embedded in our general culture. But there may also be another reason more specific to the welfare system.

Let me suggest yet another way of analyzing the U.S. social-welfare system, this time as a "juridical-administrative-therapeutic state apparatus" (JAT).[9] The point is to emphasize a distinctive style of operation. *Qua* JAT, the welfare system works by linking together a series of juridical, administrative and therapeutic procedures. As a consequence, it tends to translate political issues concerning the interpretation of people's needs into legal, administrative and/or therapeutic matters. Thus, the system executes political policy in a way which appears nonpolitical and tends to be depoliticizing.

Consider that, at an abstract level, the subject-positions constructed for beneficiaries of *both* the "masculine" and the "feminine" components of the system can be analyzed as combinations of three distinct elements. The first element is a *juridical* one which positions recipients vis-a-vis the legal system by according or denying them various *rights*. Thus, the subject of the "masculine" subsystem has a right to benefits and is protected from some legally sanctioned forms of administrative caprice, while the subject of the "feminine" subsystem largely lacks rights.

This juridical element is then linked with a second one, an *administrative* element. For in order to qualify to receive benefits, subjects must assume the stance of petitioners with respect to an administrative body; they must petition a bureaucratic institution empowered to decide their claims on the basis of administratively defined criteria. In the "masculine" subsystem, for example, claimants must prove their "cases" meet administratively defined criteria of entitlement; in the "feminine" subsystem, on the other hand, they must prove conformity to administratively defined criteria of need. The enormous qualitative differences between the two sets of procedures notwithstanding, both are variations on the same administrative moment. Both require claimants to translate their experienced situations and life-problems into administerable needs, to present the former as bonafide instances of specified generalized states of affairs which could in principle befall anyone (Habermas 1981).

If and when they qualify, social-welfare claimants get positioned either as purchasing consumers or dependent clients. In either case, their needs are redefined as correlates of bureaucratically administered satisfactions. This means they are quantified, rendered as equivalents of a sum of money (Habermas 1981). Thus, in the "feminine" subsystem, clients are positioned passively to receive monetarily measured, predefined and prepackaged services; in the "masculine" subsystem, on the other hand, they receive a specified, predetermined amount of cash.

In both subsystems, then, people's needs are subject to a sort of rewriting operation. Experienced situations and life-problems are translated into administerable needs. And since the latter are not necessarily isomorphic

to the former, the possibility of a gap between them arises. This possibility is especially likely in the "feminine" subsystem. For there, as we saw, clients are constructed as deviant and service provision has the character of normalization—albeit normalization designed more to stigmatize than to "reform."

Here, then, is the opening for the third, *therapeutic* moment of the JAT's *modus operandi*. Especially in the "feminine" subsystem, service provision often includes an implicit or explicit therapeutic or quasi-therapeutic dimension. In AFDC, for example, social workers concern themselves with the "mental health" aspects of their clients' lives, often construing these in terms of "character problems." More explicitly and less moralistically, municipal programs for poor, unmarried, pregnant teenage women include not only pre-natal care, mothering instruction and tutoring or schooling, but also counseling sessions with psychiatric social workers. As observed by Prudence Rains (1971), such sessions are intended to bring girls to acknowledge what are considered to be their true, deep, latent, emotional problems on the assumption that this will enable them to avoid future pregnancies. Ludicrous as this sounds, it is only an extreme example of a more pervasive phenomenon, namely, the tendency of especially "feminine" social-welfare programs to construct gender-political and political-economic issues as individual, psychological problems. In fact, some therapeutic or quasi-therapeutic welfare services can be regarded as second-order services. In any case, the therapeutic dimension of the U.S. social-welfare system encourages clients to close gaps between their culturally shaped lived experience and their administratively defined situation by bringing the former into line with the latter.

Clearly, this analysis of the U.S. welfare system as a "juridical-administrative-therapeutic state apparatus" lets us see both subsystems more critically. It suggests that the problem is not only that women are disempowered by the *denial* of social citizenship in the "feminine" subsystem, although they are. It is also that women and men are disempowered by the *realization* of an androcentric, possessive individualist form of social citizenship in the "masculine" subsystem. In *both* subsystems, including the "masculine" one, the JAT positions its subjects in ways which do not empower them. It individualizes them as "cases" and so militates against collective identification. It imposes monological, administrative definitions of situation and need and so preempts dialogically achieved self-definition and self-determination. It positions its subjects as passive client or consumer recipients and not as active co-participants involved in shaping their life-conditions. Lastly, it construes experienced discontent with these arrangements as material for adjustment-oriented, usually sexist therapy and not as material for empowering processes of consciousness-raising.

All told, then, the form of social citizenship constructed even in the *best* part of the U.S. social-welfare system is a degraded and depoliticized one. It is a form of passive citizenship in which the state preempts the power to define and satisfy people's needs.

This form of passive citizenship arises in part as a result of the JAT's distinctive style of operation. The JAT treats the interpretation of people's needs as pregiven and unproblematic, while itself redefining them as amenable to system-conforming satisfactions. Thus, the JAT shifts attention away from the question: Who interprets social needs and how? It tends to substitute the *juridical, administrative and therapeutic management of need satisfaction* for the *politics of need interpretation.* That is, it tends to substitute *monological, administrative processes of need definition* for *dialogical, participatory processes of need interpretation.*[10]

V

Usually, analyses of social complexes as "institutionalized patterns of interpretation" are implicitly or explicitly functionalist. They purport to show how culturally hegemonic systems of meaning are stabilized and reproduced over time. As a result, such analyses often screen out "dysfunctional" events like micro- and macro-political resistances and conflicts. More generally, they tend to obscure the active side of social processes, the ways in which even the most routinized practice of social agents involves the active construction, deconstruction and reconstruction of social meanings. It is no wonder, then, that many feminist scholars have become suspicious of functionalist methodologies; for, when applied to gender issues, these methods occult female agency and construe women as mere passive victims of male dominance.

In order to avoid any such suggestion here, I want to conclude by situating the foregoing analysis in a broader, nonfunctionalist perspective. I want to sketch a picture according to which the social-welfare apparatus is one agent among others in a larger and highly contested political arena.

Consider that the ideological (as opposed to economic) effects of the JAT's mode of need interpretation operate within a specific and relatively new societal arena. I call this arena "the social" in order to mark its noncoincidence with the familiar institutionalized spaces of family and official-economy. As I conceive it, the social is not exactly equivalent to the traditional public sphere of political discourse defined by Jürgen Habermas (1975, 1981); nor is it coextensive with the state. Rather, the social is a site of discourse about people's needs, specifically about those needs which have broken out of the domestic and/or official-economic spheres that earlier contained them as "private matters." Thus, the social is a site of discourse about problematical needs, needs which have come to exceed the apparently (but not really) self-regulating domestic and economic institutions of male-dominated, capitalist society.[11]

As the site of this excess, the social is by definition a terrain of contestation. It is a space in which conflicts among rival interpretations of people's needs are played out. "In" the social, then, one would expect to find a plurality of competing needs discourses. And in fact what we do find here are at least three major kinds: (1) "expert" needs discourses of, for example, social workers and therapists, on the one hand, and welfare administrators, planners and policy makers, on the other; (2) oppositional movement needs discourses of, for example, feminists, lesbians, and gays, people of color, workers and welfare clients; and (3) "reprivatization" discourses of constituencies seeking to repatriate newly problematized needs to their former domestic or official-economic enclaves. Such discourses, and others, compete with one another in addressing the fractured social identities of potential adherents.

Seen from this vantage point, the social has a two-fold character. It is simultaneously a new arena of state activity and, equally important, a new terrain of wider political contestation. It is both the home turf of the JAT and, also, a field of struggle which the JAT does not simply control, but on which it acts as one contestant among others.

It would be a mistake, then, to treat the JAT as the undisputed master of the terrain of the social. In fact, much of the growth and activity of the social branch of the state has come in response to the activities of social movements, especially the labor, Black, feminist and Progressive movements. Moreover, as Theda Skocpol (1980) has shown, the social state is not simply a unified, self-possessed political *agent*. It is rather in significant respects a *resultant,* a complex and polyvalent nexus of compromise-formations in which are sedimented the outcomes of past struggles as well as the conditions for present and future ones. In fact, even when the JAT does act as an agent, the results are often unintended. When it takes responsibility for matters previously left to the family and/or economy, it tends to denaturalize those matters and thus risks fostering their further politicization.

In any case, social movements, too, act on the terrain of the social (as do, on a smaller scale, clients who engage the JAT in micropolitical resistances and negotiations). In fact, the JAT's monological, administrative approach to need definition can also be seen as a strategy to contain social movements. Such movements tend, by their very nature, to be dialogic and participatory. They represent the emergent capacities of newly politicized groups to cast off the apparently natural and prepolitical interpretations which enveloped their needs in the official-economy and/or family. In social movements, people come to articulate alternative, politicized interpretations of their needs as they engage in processes of dialogue and collective struggle. Thus, the confrontation of

such movements with the JAT on the terrain of the social is a confrontation between *conflicting logics of need definition.*

Feminists, too, then, are actors on the terrain of the social. Indeed, from this perspective, we can distinguish several analytically distinct, but practically intermingled kinds of feminist struggles worth engaging in the coming welfare wars. First, there are struggles to secure the political status of women's needs, that is, to legitimate women's needs as genuine political issues as opposed to "private" domestic or market matters. Here, feminists would engage especially anti-welfarist defenders of privatization. Second, there are struggles over the interpreted content of women's needs, struggles to challenge the apparently natural, traditional interpretations still enveloping needs only recently sprung from domestic and official-economic enclaves of privacy. Here feminists would engage all those forces in the culture which perpetuate androcentric and sexist interpretations of women's needs, including but not only the social state. Third, there are struggles over the who and how of need interpretation, struggles to empower women to interpret their own needs and to challenge the anit-participatory, monological practices of the welfare system *qua* JAT. Fourth, there are struggles to elaborate and win support for policies based on feminist interpretations of women's needs, policies which avoid both the Scylla of private patriarchy and the Charybdis of public patriarchy.

In all these cases, the focus would be as much on need interpretation as on need satisfaction. This is as it should be, since any satisfactions we are able to win will be problematic to the degree we fail to fight and win the battle of interpretation.

Notes

1. I believe that Brown's terms are too simple on two counts. First, for reasons elaborated by Gayle Rubin (1975), I prefer not to use 'patriarchy' as a generic term for male dominance but rather as the destination of a specific historical social formation. Second, Brown's public/private contrast oversimplifies the structure of both laissez-

faire and welfare capitalism, since it posits two major societal zones where there are actually four (family, official-economy, state, and sphere of public political discourse) and conflates two distinct public-private divisions. (For a discussion of this second problem, see Fraser 1985b.) These problems notwithstanding, it remains the case that Brown's terms are immensely suggestive and that we currently have no better terminology. Thus, in what follows I occasionally use 'public patriarchy' for want of an alternative.

2. For an analysis of the dynamics whereby late-capitalist political systems tend to select certain types of interests while excluding others, see Claus Offe (1972, 1974, 1980). For a feminist application of Offe's approach, see Drude Dahlerup (1984).

3. This phrase owes its inspiration to Jürgen Habermas (1975).

4. I owe this phrase to Thomas McCarthy (personal communication).

5. I owe the phase 'gender subtext' to Dorothy Smith (1984). A number of writers have noticed the two-tiered character of the U.S. social-welfare system. Andrew Hacker (1985) correlates the dualism with class but not with gender. Diana Pearce (1979) and Erie, Rein and Wiget (1983) correlate the dualism with gender and with the dual labor market, itself gender-correlated. Barbara Nelson (1984) correlates the dualism with gender, the dual labor market and the sexual division of paid *and unpaid* labor. My account owes a great deal to all of these writers, especially Barbara Nelson.

6. Hilary Land (1978) identifies similar assumptions at work in the British social-welfare system. My formulation of them is much indebted to her.

7. I owe these formulations to Virginia Held (personal communication).

8. It should be noted that I am here taking issue with the view of some left theorists that "decommodification" in the form of in kind social-welfare benefits represents an emancipatory or progressive development. In the context of a two-tiered welfare system like the one described here, this assumption is clearly false, since in kind benefits are qualitatively and quantitatively inferior to the corresponding commodities and since they function to stigmatize those who receive them.

9. This term echoes Louis Althusser's (1984) term, "ideological state apparatus." Certainly, the U.S. social-welfare system as described in the present section of this paper counts as an "ISA" in Althusser's sense. However, I prefer the term "juridical-administrative-therapeutic state apparatus" as more concrete and descriptive of the specific ways in which welfare programs produce and reproduce ideology. In general, then, a JAT can be understood as a subclass of an ISA. On the other hand, Althusserian-like terminology aside, readers will find that the account in this section owes more to Michel Foucault (1979) and Jürgen Habermas (1981) than to Althusser. Of course, neither Habermas nor Foucault is sensitive to the gendered character of social-welfare programs. For a critique of Habermas in this respect, see Fraser (1985b). For my views about Foucault, see Fraser (1981, 1983 and 1985a).

10. These formulations owe much to Jürgen Habermas (1975, 1981).

11. I borrow the term "social" from Hannah Arendt (1958). However, my use of it differs from hers in several important ways. First, Arendt and I both understand the social as an historically emergent societal space specific to modernity. And we both understand the emergence of the social as tending to undercut or blur an earlier, more distinct separation of public and private spheres. But she treats the emergence of the social as a fall or lapse and she valorizes the earlier separation of public and private as a preferred state of affairs appropriate to "the human condition." I, on the other hand, make no assumptions about the human condition; nor do I regret the passing of the private/public separation; nor do I consider the emergence of the social a fall or lapse. Secondly, Arendt and I agree that one salient, defining feature of the social is the emergence of heretofore "private" needs into public view. But Arendt treats this as a violation of the proper order of things. She assumes that needs are wholly natural and are forever doomed to be things of brute compulsion. Thus, she supposes needs can have no genuinely political dimension and that their emergence from the private sphere into the social spells the death of authentic politics. I, on the other hand, assume that needs are irreducibly interpretive and that need interpretations are in principle contestable. It follows from my view

that the emergence of needs from the "private" into the social is a generally positive development since such needs thereby lose their illusory aura of naturalness, while their interpretations become subject to critique and contestation. I, therefore, suppose that this represents the (possible) flourishing of politics, rather than the (necessary) death of politics. Finally, Arendt assumes that the emergence of the social and of public concern with needs necessarily means the triumph of administration and instrumental reason. I, on the other hand, assume that instrumental reason represents only one possible way of defining and addressing social needs; and that administration represents only one possible way of institutionalizing the social. Thus, I would argue for the existence of another possibility: an alternative socialist-feminist "dialogic of need interpretation" and a participatory-democratic-institutionalization of the social.

References

Althusser, Louis. 1984. Ideology and ideological state apparatuses: Notes towards an investigation. In *Essays on ideology,* ed. Althusser. London: Verso.

Arendt, Hannah. 1958. *The human condition.* Chicago and London: The University of Chicago Press.

Barrett, Nancy S. 1984. Mothers, fathers, and children: From private to public patriarchy. In *Women and revolution,* ed. Lydia Sargent. Boston: South End Press.

Dahlerup, Drude. 1984. Overcoming the barriers: An approach to the study of how women's issues are kept from the political agenda. In *Women's views of the political world of men,* ed. Judith H. Stiehm. Dobbs Ferry, NY: Transnational Publishers.

Ehrenreich, Barbara and Frances Fox Piven. 1984. The feminization of poverty. *Dissent,* Spring: 162–170.

Erie, Steven P., Martin Rein, and Barbara Wiget. 1983. Women and the Reagan's revolution: Thermidor for the social welfare economy. In *Families, politics, and public policies: A feminist dialogue on women and the state,* ed. Irene Di-amond. New York and London: Longman.

Foucault, Michel. 1979. *Discipline and punish: The birth of the prison.* Trans. Alan Sheridan. New York: Vintage.

Fraser, Nancy. 1981. Foucault on modern power: Empirical insights and normative confusions. *Praxis International* 1:272–87.

———. 1983. Foucault's body-language: A posthumanist political rhetoric? *Salmagundi* 61:55–70.

———.1985a. Michel Foucault: A "Young Conservative"? The case of Habermas and Gender. *New German Critique* 35:97–131.

Habermas, Jürgen. 1975. *Legitimation crisis.* Boston: Beacon.

———. 1981. *Theorie des kommunikativen Handelns,* Band II, *Zur Kritik der funktionalistischen Vernunft.* Frankfurt am Main: Suhrkamp Verlag.

Hacker, Andrew. 1985. 'Welfare': The future of an illusion. *New York Review of Books* February 28:37–43.

Land, Hilary. 1978. Who cares for the family? *Journal of Social Policy* 7:257–284.

MacPherson, C. B. 1964. *The political theory of possessive individualism: Hobbes to Locke.* New York and London: Oxford University Press.

Mauss, Marcel. 1967. *The gift: Forms and functions of exchange in archaic societies.* Trans. Ian Cunnison. New York and London: W. W. Norton & Company.

Nelson, Barbara J. 1984. Women's poverty and women's citizenship: Some political consequences of economic marginality. *Signs: Journal of Women in Culture and Society* 10:209–231.

O'Connor, James. 1973. *The fiscal crisis of the state.* New York: St. Martin's Press.

Offe, Claus. 1972. Political authority and class structure: An analysis of late capitalist societies. *International Journal of Sociology* 2:73–108.

———. 1974. Structural problems of the capitalist state: Class rule and the political system. On the selectiveness of political institutions. In *German Political Studies,* ed. Klaus von Beyme. London: Sage Publications.

———. 1980. The separation of form and content in liberal democratic politics. *Studies in Political Economy* 3:5–16.

Pearce, Diana. 1979. Women, work, and welfare: The feminization of poverty. In *Working Women and Families*, ed. Karen Wolk Feinstein. Beverly Hills, CA: Sage Publications.

Rains, Prudence Mors. 1971. *Becoming an unwed mother: A sociological account.* Chicago: Aldine Atherton, Inc.

Rubin, Gayle. 1975. The traffic in women: Notes on the "Political Economy" of sex. In *Towards an Anthropology of Women*, ed. Rayna R. Reiter.

New York: Monthly Review Press.

Skocpol, Theda. 1980. Political response to capitalist crisis: Neo-Marxist theories of the state and the case of the new Deal. *Politics and Society* 10:155–201.

Smith, Dorothy. 1984. The gender subtext of power. Unpublished manuscript.

Stack, Carol B. 1974. *All our kin: Strategies for survival in a black community.* New York, Evanston, San Francisco, London: Harper & Row.

41. Perversions of Justice: A Native-American Examination of the Doctrine of U.S. Rights to Occupancy in North America

Ward Churchill

Traditionally, philosophers have debated the extent to which the wealthy are obligated, if at all, to share their property with the poor, with women, and with impoverished ethnic minorities. In a more radical vein, Native-American scholar Ward Churchill argues that Euro-Americans have little or no claim to property in what is now called the United States. Churchill rejects modern claims to sovereignty and extrapolates this analysis to the contemporary international political order.

For the nation, there is an unrequited account of sin and injustice that sooner or later will call for national retribution.
—George Catlin, 1844

Recognition of the legal and moral rights by which it occupies whatever land base it calls its own is perhaps the most fundamental issue confronting any nation. Typically, such claims to sovereign and proprietary interest in national territorialities devolve, at least in considerable part, upon supportable contentions that the citizenry is preponderantly composed of persons directly descended from peoples who have dwelt within the geographical area claimed since "time immemorial." The matter becomes infinitely more complex in situations

in which the dominant—or dominating—population comprises either the representatives of a foreign power or immigrants ("settlers") who can offer no such assertion of "aboriginal" lineage to justify their presence or ownership of property in the usual sense.

History is replete with instances in which various peoples have advanced philosophical, theological, and juridical arguments concerning their alleged entitlement to the homelands of others, only to have them rebuffed by the community of nations as lacking both moral force and sound legal principle. In such cases, the trend has been that international rejection of "imperial" pretensions has led to the inability of those nations extending such claims to sustain them. Modern illustrations of this tendency include the dissolution of the classic European empires—those of France, the Netherlands, Portugal, and Great Britain, in particular—during the post-World War II period, as well as the resounding defeat of the Axis powers' territorial ambitions during the war itself. Even more recent examples may be found in the breakup of the Soviet (Great Russian) and Yugoslavian (Serbian) states and in the extreme controversy attending maintenance of such settler states as Northern Ireland, Israel, and South Africa.

The purpose of this essay is to examine the basis upon which another contemporary settler state, the United States of America, contends that it possesses legitimate—indeed, inviolate—rights to approximately 2.25 billion acres of territory in North America. Through such scrutiny, the philosophical validity of U.S. legal claims to territorial integrity can be understood and tested against the standards of both logic and morality. This, in turn, is intended to provide a firm foundation from which readers may assess the substance of that image generated by the sweeping pronouncements so frequently offered by official America and its adherents over the years: that this is a country so essentially "peaceful," so uniquely enlightened in its commitments to the rule of law and concept of liberty, that it has inevitably emerged as the natural leader of a global drive to consolidate a "new world order" in which the conquest and occupation of the territory of any nation by another "cannot and will not stand."

Rights to Territorial Acquisition in International Law

From the outset of the "Age of Discovery" precipitated by the Columbian voyages, the European powers, eager to obtain uncontested title to at least some portions of the lands their emissaries were encountering, quickly recognized the need to establish a formal code of juridical standards to legitimate what they acquired. To some extent, this was meant to lend a patina of "civilized"—and therefore, it was imagined, inherently superior—legality to the actions of the European Crowns in their relations with the peoples indigenous to the desired geography. More importantly, however, the system was envisioned as a necessary means of resolving disputes among the Crowns themselves, each of which was vying with the others in a rapacious battle over the prerogative to benefit from wealth accruing through ownership of given regions in the "New World." In order for any such regulatory code to be considered effectively binding by all Old World parties, it was vital that it be sanctioned by the Church.

Hence, the mechanism deployed for this purpose was a theme embodied in a series of Papal bulls begun by Pope Innocent IV during the late-13th-century First Crusade. The bulls were designed to define the proper ("lawful") relationship between Christians and "Infidels" in all such worldly matters as property rights. Beginning in the early 16th century, Spanish jurists in particular did much to develop this theory into what have come to be known as the "Doctrine of Discovery" and an attendant dogma, the "Rights of Conquest." Through the efforts of legal scholars such as Franciscus de Vitoria and Matías de Paz, Spanish articulations of Discovery Doctrine, endorsed by the pope, rapidly evolved to hold the following as primary tenets of international law:

1. Outright ownership of land accrued to the Crown represented by a given Christian (European) discoverer only when the land discovered proved to be uninhabited (*territorium res nullius*).

2. Title to inhabited lands discovered by Crown representatives was recognized as belonging inherently to the indigenous people thereby encountered, but rights to acquire land from, and to trade with, the natives of the region accrued exclusively to the discovering Crown vis-à-vis other European powers. In exchange for this right, the discovering power committed itself to proselytizing the Christian gospel among the natives.

3. Acquisition of land title from indigenous peoples could occur only by their consent—by an agreement usually involving purchase—rather than through force of arms, so long as the natives did not arbitrarily

decline to trade with Crown representatives, refuse to admit missionaries among them, or inflict gratuitous violence upon citizens of the Crown.

4. In the absence of these last three conditions, utilization of armed force to acquire aboriginally held territory was considered to be unjust and claims to land title accruing therefrom to be correspondingly invalid.

5. Should one or more of the three conditions be present, then it was held that the Crown had a legal right to use whatever force was required to subdue native resistance and impound their property as compensation. Land title gained by prosecution of such "just wars" was considered valid.

Although this legal perspective was hotly debated at the time (it still is, in certain quarters), and saw considerable violation by European colonists, it was generally acknowledged as the standard against which international conduct would be weighed. By the early 17th century, the requirements of Discovery Doctrine had led the European states (England in particular) to adopt a policy of entering into formal treaties—full-fledged international instruments in which the sovereignty of the indigenous parties to such agreements were, by definition, officially recognized as equivalent to that of the respective Crowns—as an expedient to obtaining legally valid land titles from American Indian peoples, first in what is now the State of Virginia and then in areas further north. Treaties concerning trade, professions of peace and friendship, and military alliances were also quite common. Undeniably, there is a certain overweening arrogance embedded in the proposition that Europeans were somehow intrinsically imbued with an authority to unilaterally restrict the range of those to whom Native Americans might sell their property, assuming they wished to sell it at all. Nonetheless, in its recognition that indigenous peoples constituted bona fide nations holding essentially the same rights to land and sovereignty as any other, the legal posture of early European colonialism seems rather advanced and refined in retrospect. In these respects, the Doctrine of Discovery is widely viewed as one of the more important cornerstones of modern international law and diplomacy.

With its adoption of Protestantism, however, Britain had already begun to mark its independence from papal regulation by adding an element of its own to the doctrine. Usually termed the "Norman Yoke," this concept asserted that land rights devolve in large part upon the extent to which the owners demonstrate a willingness and ability to "develop" their territories in accordance with a scriptural obligation to exercise "dominium" over nature. In other words, a person or a people is ultimately entitled to only that quantity of real estate which he/she/they convert from "wilderness" to a "domesticated" state. By this criterion, English settlers were seen as possessing an inherent right to dispossess native people of all land other than that which the latter might be "reasonably expected" to put to such "proper" uses as cultivation. By the same token, this doctrinal innovation automatically placed the British Crown on a legal footing from which it could contest the discovery rights of any European power not adhering to the requirement of "overcoming the wilderness" per se.

This last allowed England to simultaneously "abide by the law" *and* directly confront Catholic France for ascendancy in the Atlantic regions of North America. After a series of "French and Indian Wars" beginning in the late 1600s and lasting nearly a century, the British were victorious, but at a cost more than negating the expected financial benefits to the Crown that had led it to launch its colonial venture in the first place. As one major consequence, King George II, in a move intended to preclude further warfare with indigenous nations, issued the Proclamation of 1763. This royal edict stipulated that all settlement or other forms of land acquisition by British subjects west of a line running along the Allegheny and Appalachian Mountains from Canada to the Spanish colony of Florida would be suspended indefinitely, and perhaps permanently. English expansion on the North American continent was thereby brought to an abrupt halt.

Enter the United States

The new British policy conflicted sharply with the desires for personal gain evident among a voracious elite that had been growing within England's seaboard colonial population. Most of the colonies held some pretense of title to "western" lands, much of it conveyed by earlier Crown grant, and had planned to use it as a means of bolstering their respective economic positions. Similarly, members of the landed gentry such as George Washington, Thomas Jefferson, John Adams, James Madison, and Anthony Wayne all possessed considerable speculative interests in land parcels on the far side of the 1763 demarcation line. The only way in which these could be converted into profit was for the parcels to be settled and developed. Vociferous contestation and frequent violation of the proclamation, eventually enforced by George III, became quite common. All in all, this dynamic became a powerful precipitating factor in the American Revolution, during which many rank-and-file rebels were convinced to fight against the Crown by promises of western land grants "for services rendered" in the event their revolt was successful.

There was, however, a catch. The United States emerged from its decolonization struggle against Britain—perhaps the most grievous offense that could be perpetrated by any subject people under then-prevailing law—as a pariah, an outlaw state that was shunned as an utterly illegitimate entity by most other countries. Desperate to establish itself as a legitimate nation, and lacking any other viable alternatives with which to demonstrate its aptitude for complying with international legality, the new government was virtually compelled to observe the strictest of protocols in its dealings with Indians. Indeed, what the Continental Congress needed more than anything at the time was for indigenous nations, already recognized as respectable sovereignties via their treaties with the European states, to bestow a comparable recognition upon the fledgling United States by entering into treaties with *it*. The urgency of the matter was compounded by the fact that the Indians maintained military parity with, and in some cases superiority to, the U.S. Army all along the frontier.

As a result, both the Articles of Confederation and the subsequent Constitution of the United States contained clauses explicitly and exclusively restricting relations with indigenous nations to the federal government, insofar as the former were recognized as enjoying the same politicolegal status as any other foreign power. The United States also officially renounced, in the 1789 Northwest Ordinance and elsewhere, any aggressive intent concerning indigenous nations, especially with regard to their respective land bases:

> The utmost good faith shall always be observed towards the Indians; their land and property shall never be taken from them without their consent; and in their property, rights, and liberty, they shall never be disturbed . . . but laws founded in justice and humanity shall from time to time be made, for wrongs done to them, and for peace and friendship with them.[1]

This rhetorical stance, reflecting an impeccable observance of international legality, was also incorporated into such instruments of agreement with European states as the United States was able to obtain during its formative years. For instance, in the 1803 Louisiana Purchase from France of much of North America west of the Mississippi, the federal government solemnly pledged itself to protect "the inhabitants of the ceded territory . . . in the free enjoyment of their liberty, property and the religion they profess."[2] Other phraseology in the purchase agreement makes it clear that federal authorities understood they were acquiring from the French, not the land itself, but France's monopolistic trade rights and prerogative to buy any acreage within the area its indigenous owners wished to sell.

The same understanding certainly pertained to all unceded Indian Country claimed by Britain under Discovery Doctrine east of the Mississippi, after it was quit-claimed by George III in the Treaty of Paris concluding the Revolution. Even if English discovery rights somehow "passed" to the new republic by virtue of this royal action (an extremely dubious premise in itself), there still remained the matter of obtaining native consent to literal U.S. ownership of any area beyond the 1763 proclamation line. Hence, the securing of indigenous agreement to land cessions must be added to the impressive list of diplomatic and military reasons why treaty-making with Indians constituted the main currency of American diplomacy throughout the immediate postrevolutionary period. Moreover, the need to secure valid land title from native people through treaties far outlasted the motivations of diplomatic and military necessity, these having been greatly diminished in importance after U.S. victories over Tecumseh's alliance in 1794 and 1811, over Britain in the War of 1812, and over the Red Stick Confederacy during 1813–1814. The treaties were and remain, in substance, the basic real-estate documents anchoring U.S. claims to land title—and thus to rights of occupancy—in North America.

What was most problematic in this situation for early federal policymakers was the fact that, in gaining diplomatic recognition and land cessions from indigenous nations through treaties, the United States was simultaneously admitting not only that Indians ultimately owned virtually all of the coveted territory but also that they were really under no obligation to part with it. As William Wirt, an early attorney general, put it in 1821: "[Legally speaking,] so long as a tribe exists and remains in possession of its lands, its title and possession are sovereign and exclusive. We treat with them as separate sovereignties, and while an Indian nation continues to exist within its acknowledged limits, we have no more right to enter upon their territory than we have to enter upon the territory of a foreign prince."[3] A few years later, Wirt amplified this point:

> The point, once conceded, that the Indians are independent to the purpose of treating, their independence is to that purpose as absolute as any other nation. Being competent to bind themselves by

treaty, they are equally competent to bind the party that treats with them. Such party cannot take benefit of [a] treaty with the Indians, and then deny them the reciprocal benefits of the treaty on the grounds that they are not independent nations to all intents and purposes. . . . Nor can it be conceded that their independence as a nation is a limited independence. Like all other independent nations, they have the absolute power of war and peace. Like all other independent nations, their territories are inviolate by any other sovereignty. . . . They are entirely self-governed, self-directed. They treat, or refuse to treat, at their pleasure; and there is no human power that can rightly control them in the exercise of their discretion in this respect.[4]

Such enjoyment of genuine sovereign rights and status by indigenous nations served, during the 20 years following the Revolution (roughly 1790–1810), to considerably retard the assumption of lawful possession of their land grants by revolutionary soldiers, as well as consummation of the plans of the elite caste of prerevolutionary land speculators. Over the next two decades (1810–1830), the issue assumed an ever-increasing policy importance as the matter of native sovereignty came to replace Crown policy in being construed as *the* preeminent barrier to U.S. territorial consolidation east of the Mississippi. Worse, as Chief Justice of the Supreme Court John Marshall pointed out in 1822, any real adherence to the rule of law in regard to native rights might not only block U.S. expansion but— since not all the territory therein had been secured through Crown treaties—cloud title to significant portions of the original 13 states as well. Perhaps predictably, it was perceived in juridical circles that the only means of circumventing this dilemma was through construction of a legal theory—a subterfuge, as it were—by which the more inconvenient implications of international law might be voided even while the republic maintained an appearance of holding to its doctrinal requirements.

Emergence of the Marshall Doctrine

Not unnaturally, the task of forging the required "interpretation" of existing law fell to Marshall, who was widely considered one of the great legal minds of his time. Whatever his scholarly qualifications, the chief justice can hardly be said to have been a disinterested party, given not only his vociferous ideological advocacy of the rebel cause before and during the Revolution but also the fact that both he and his father were consequent recipients of 10,000-acre grants west of the Appalachians, in what is now the State of West Virginia. His first serious foray into land-rights law thus centered in devising a conceptual basis to secure title for his own and similar grants. In the 1810 *Fletcher* v. *Peck* case, he invoked the Norman Yoke tradition in a manner that far exceeded previous British applications, advancing the patently absurd contention that the areas involved were effectively "vacant" even though very much occupied—and in many instances stoutly defended—by indigenous inhabitants. On this basis, he declared that individual Euro-American deeds within recognized Indian territories might be considered valid whether or not native consent was obtained.

Although *Peck* was obviously useful from the U.S. point of view, resolving as it did a number of short-term difficulties in meeting obligations already incurred by the government vis-à-vis individual citizens, it was in itself a tactical opinion, falling far short of accommodating the country's overall territorial goals and objectives. In the 1823 *Johnson* v. *McIntosh* case, however, Marshall followed up with a more clearly strategic enunciation, reaching for something much closer to the core of what he had in mind. Here he opined that, because discovery rights purportedly constricted native discretion in disposing of property, the sovereignty of discoverers was to that extent inherently superior to that of indigenous nations. From this point of departure, he then proceeded to invert all conventional understandings of Discovery Doctrine, ultimately asserting that native people occupied land within discovered regions at the sufferance of their discoverers rather than the other way around. A preliminary rationalization was thus contrived by which to explain the fact that the United States had already begun depicting its borders as encompassing rather vast portions of unceded Indian country.

Undoubtedly aware that neither *Peck* nor *McIntosh* was likely to withstand the gaze of even minimal international scrutiny, Marshall next moved to bolster the logic undergirding his position. In the two "Cherokee Cases" of the early 1830s, he hammered out the thesis that native nations within North America were "nations like any other" in the sense that they possessed both territories they were capable of ceding and recognizable governmental bodies empowered to cede these areas through treaties. On the other hand, he argued on the basis of the reasoning deployed in *McIntosh,* they were nations of a "peculiar type," both "domestic to" and "dependent upon" the United States, and therefore possessed of a degree of sovereignty intrinsically less than that enjoyed by the United States itself. The essential idea boils down to a presumption that, although native peoples are entitled to exercise some range of autonomy in managing their affairs within their own territories, both the limits of that autonomy and the extent of the territories involved can be "naturally" and unilaterally established by the federal government. At base, this is little more than a judicial description of the classic relationship between colonizer and colonized, but it was put forth in such a way as to seem at first glance to be the exact opposite.

Although it might be contended (and has been, routinely enough) that Marshall's framing of the circumstances pertaining to the Cherokee Nation, already completely surrounded by the territorality of the United States by 1830, bore some genuine relationship to then-prevailing reality, it must be reiterated that he did not confine his observations of the situation to Cherokees, or even to native nations east of the Mississippi. Rather, he purported to articulate the legal status of *all* indigenous nations, including those west of the Mississippi—the Lakota, Cheyenne, Arapaho, Comanche, Kiowa, Navajo, and Chiricahua Apache, to name but a few—that had not yet encountered the United States in any appreciable way. Self-evidently, these nations could not have been described with the faintest accuracy as domestic to or dependent upon the United States. The clear intent belied by Marshall's formulation was that they be made so in the future. The doctrine completed with elaboration of the Cherokee Cases was thus the pivotal official attempt to rationalize and legitimate a vast campaign of conquest and colonization—absolutely contrary to the customary law of the period—upon which the United States was planning to embark in the years ahead.

A final inversion of accepted international legal norms and definitions stems from this: an outright reversal of what was meant by "just" and "unjust" warfare.[5] Within Marshall's convoluted and falsely premised reasoning, it became arguable that indigenous nations acted unlawfully whenever and wherever they attempted to physically prevent exercise of the U.S. "right" to expropriate their property. Put another way, Indians could be construed as committing "aggression" against the United States at any point when they attempted to resist the invasion of their homelands by American citizens. In this sense the United States could declare itself to be waging a "just"—and therefore lawful—war against native people on virtually any occasion when force of arms was required to realize its territorial ambitions. *Ipso facto,* all efforts of native people to defend themselves against systematic dispossession and subordination could thereby be categorized as "unjust"—and thus unlawful—by the United States.[6]

In sum, the Marshall Doctrine shredded significant elements of the existing Laws of Nations. Given the understandings of these very same legal requirements placed on record by federal judicial officials such as Attorney General Wirt and Marshall himself, not to mention the embodiment of such understandings in the Constitution and formative federal statutes, this cannot be said to have been unintentional or inadvertent. Instead, the chief justice engaged in a calculated exercise in juridical cynicism, quite deliberately confusing and deforming accepted legal principles as an expedient to "justifying" his country's pursuit of a thoroughly illegitimate course of territorial acquisition. Insofar as federal courts and policymakers elected to adopt his doctrine as the predicate to all subsequent relations with American Indians, it may be said that he not only replicated the initial posture of the United States as an outlaw state but rendered it permanent.

Evolution of the Marshall Doctrine

The Cherokee Cases were followed by a half-century hiatus in important judicial determinations regarding American Indians. On the foundation provided by the Marshall Doctrine, the government felt confident in entering into the great bulk of the at least 371 treaties with indigenous nations by which it professed to have gained the consent of Indians in ceding huge portions of the native land base, assured all the while that, because of its self-anointed position of superior sovereignty, it would be under "no legal obligation" to live up to its end of the various bargains struck. Well before the end of the 19th century, the United States stood in default on virtually every treaty agreement it had made with native people, and there is considerable evidence in many instances that this was intended to be so from the outset. Aside from the fraudulent nature of U.S. participation in the treaty process, there is an ample record that many of the instruments of cession were militarily coerced while the government implemented Marshall's version of "just wars" against Indians. As the U.S. Census Bureau put it in 1894:

The Indian wars under the United States government have been about 40 in number [most of them occurring after 1835]. They have cost the lives of . . . about 30,000 Indians [at a minimum]. . . . The actual number of killed and wounded Indians must be very much greater than the number given, as they conceal, where possible, their actual loss in battle. . . .

Fifty percent additional would be a safe number to add to the numbers given.[7]

The same report noted that some number "very much more" than 8,500 Indians were known to have been killed by government-sanctioned private citizen action—dubbed "individual affairs"—during the course of U.S./Indian warfare.[8] In reality, such citizen action is known to have been primarily responsible for the reduction of the native population of Texas from about 100,000 in 1828 to under 10,000 in 1880.[9] Similarly, in California, an aggregate indigenous population that still numbers approximately 300,000 had been reduced to fewer than 35,000 by 1860, mainly because of "the cruelties and wholesale massacres perpetrated by [American] miners and early settlers."[10] Either of these illustrations offers a death toll several times that officially acknowledged as having accrued through individual affairs within the whole of the 48 contiguous states.

Even while this slaughter was occurring, the government was conducting what it itself frequently described as a "policy of extermination" in its conduct of wars against those indigenous nations that proved "recalcitrant" about giving up their land and liberty. This manifested itself in a lengthy series of massacres of native people—men, women, children, and old people alike—at the hands of U.S. troops. Among the worst were those at Blue River (Nebraska, 1854), Bear River (Idaho, 1863), Sand Creek (Colorado, 1864), Washita River (Oklahoma, 1868), Sappa Creek (Kansas, 1875), Camp Robinson (Nebraska, 1878), and Wounded Knee (South Dakota, 1890). Somewhat different, but comparable, methods of destroying indigenous peoples were evidenced in the forced march of the entire Cherokee Nation along the "Trail of Tears" to Oklahoma during the 1830s (55% attrition)[11] and in the internment of the bulk of the Navajo Nation under abysmal conditions at the Bosque Redondo from 1864 to 1868 (35–50% attrition).[12] Such atrocities against humans were coupled with an equally systematic extermination of an entire animal species, the buffalo or North American bison, as part of a military strategy to starve resistant Indians into submission by "destroying their commissary."

All told, it is probable that more than a quarter-million Indians perished as a direct result of U.S. extermination campaigns directed against them.[13] By the turn of the century, only 237,196 native people were recorded by census as still being alive within the United States,[14] perhaps 2% of the total indigenous population of the U.S. portion of North America at the point of first contact with Europeans.[15] Correlating rather precisely with this genocidal reduction in the number of native inhabitants was an erosion of Indian land holdings to approximately 2.5% of the "lower 48" states.[16] Small wonder that, barely 50 years later, Adolf Hitler would explicitly anchor his concept of *lebensraumpolitik* ("politics of living space") directly upon U.S. practice against American Indians. Meanwhile, even as the 1890 census figures were being tallied, the United States had already moved beyond the "Manifest Destiny" embodied in the conquest phase of its continental expansion and was emphasizing the development of colonial administration over residual indigenous land and lives through the Bureau of Indian Affairs (BIA), a subpart of the War Department that had been reassigned for this purpose to the Department of the Interior.

This was begun as early as 1871, when Congress—having determined that the military capacity of indigenous nations had finally been sufficiently reduced by incessant wars of attrition—elected to consecrate Marshall's description of their "domestic" status by suspending further treaty making with them. In 1885, the United States moved for the first time to directly extend its internal jurisdiction over reserved Indian territories through passage of the Major Crimes Act. When this was immediately challenged as a violation of international standards, Supreme Court Justice Samuel F. Miller rendered an opinion that consolidated and extended Marshall's earlier assertion of federal plenary power over native nations, contending that the government held an "incontrovertible right" to exercise authority over Indians as it saw fit and "for their own good." Miller also concluded that Indians lacked any legal recourse in matters of federal interest, their sovereignty being defined as whatever Congress did not remove through specific legislation. This decision opened the door to enactment of more than 5,000 statutes regulating affairs in Indian Country through the present day.

One of the first of these was the General Allotment Act of 1887, "which unilaterally negated Indian control over land tenure patterns within the reservations, forcibly replacing the traditional mode of collective use and occupancy with the Anglo-Saxon system of individual property ownership."[17] The act also imposed for the first time a formal eugenics code—dubbed "blood quantum"—by which American Indian identity would be federally defined on racial grounds rather than by native nations themselves on the basis of group membership/citizenship.[18]

The Allotment Act set forth that each American Indian recognized as such by the federal government would receive an allotment of land according to the following formula: 160 acres for family heads, eighty acres for single persons over eighteen years of age and orphans under eighteen, and forty acres for [non-orphan] children under eighteen. "Mixed blood" Indians received title by fee simple patent; "full bloods" were issued "trust patents," meaning they had no control over their property for a period of twenty-five years. Once each person recognized by the government as belonging to a given Indian nation had received his or her allotment, the "surplus" acreage was "opened" to non-Indian homesteading or conversion into the emerging system of national parks, forests, and grasslands.[19]

Needless to say, there proved to be far fewer Indians identifiable as such under federal eugenics criteria than there were individual parcels available within the reserved land areas of the 1890s. Hence, "not only was the cohesion of indigenous society dramatically disrupted by allotment, and traditional government prerogatives preempted, but it led to the loss of some two-thirds of all the acreage [about 100 million of 150 million acres] still held by native people at the time it was passed.[20] Moreover, the land assigned to individual Indians during the allotment process fell overwhelmingly within arid and semi-arid locales considered to be the least productive in North America; uniformly, the best-watered and otherwise useful portions of the reservations were declared surplus and quickly stripped away. This, of course, greatly reinforced the "dependency" aspect of the Marshall thesis and led U.S. Indian Commissioner Francis Leupp to conclude approvingly that allotment should be considered as "a mighty pulverizing engine for breaking up [the last vestiges of] the tribal mass" that stood as a final barrier to complete Euro-American hegemony on the continent.

As with the Major Crimes Act, native people attempted to utilize their treatied standing in federal courts to block the allotment process and corresponding erosion of the reservation land base. In the 1903 *Lonewolf* v. *Hitchcock* case, however, Justice Edward D. White extended the concept of federal plenary power to hold that the government possessed a right to unilaterally abrogate whatever portion of any treaty with Indians it found inconvenient while continuing to consider the remaining terms and provisions binding upon the Indians. In essence, this meant that the United States could point to the treaties as being the instruments that legally validated much of its North American land title while simultaneously avoiding whatever reciprocal obligations it had incurred by way of payment. White also opined that the government's plenary power over Indians lent it a "trust responsibility" over residual native property such that it might opt to "change the form" of this property—from land, say, to cash or "services"—whenever and however it chose to do so. This final consolidation of the Marshall Doctrine effectively left native people with *no* true national rights under U.S. law while voiding the remaining pittance of conformity to international standards the United States had exhibited with regard to its Indian treaties.

The Open Veins of Native America

A little-discussed aspect of the Allotment Act is that it required each Indian, as a condition of receiving the deed to his or her land parcel, to accept U.S. citizenship. By the early 1920s, when most of the allotment the United States wished to accomplish had been completed, there were still a significant number of native people who still not been "naturalized," either because they'd been left out of the process for one reason or another or because they'd refused to participate. Consequently, in 1924 the Congress passed a "clean-up bill" entitled the Indian Citizenship Act, which imposed citizenship upon all remaining indigenous people within U.S. borders whether they wished it or not.

> The Indian Citizenship Act greatly confused the circumstances even of many of the blooded and federally certified Indians insofar as it was held to bear legal force, and to carry legal obligations, whether or not any given Indian or group of Indians wished to be U.S. citizens. As for the host of non-certified, mixed-blood people residing in the U.S., their status was finally "clarified"; they had been definitionally absorbed into the American mainstream at the stroke of the congressional pen. And, despite the fact that the act technically left certified Indians occupying the status of citizenship within their own indigenous nation as well as the U.S. (a "dual form" of citizenship so awkward as to be sublime), the juridical door had been opened by which the weight of Indian obligations would begin to accrue more to the U.S. than to themselves.[21]

All of this—suspension of treaty making, extension of federal jurisdiction, plenary power and "trust" prerogatives, blood quantum and allotment, and imposition of citizenship—was bound up in a policy officially designated as the compulsory assimilation of American Indians into the dominant (Euro-American) society. Put another way, U.S. Indian policy was carefully (and openly) designed to bring about the disappearance of all recognizable Indian groups, as such. The methods used included the general proscription of native languages and spiritual practices, the systematic and massive transfer of Indian children into non-Indian settings via mandatory attendance at boarding schools remote from their communities, and the deliberate suppression of reservation economic structures. As Indian Commissioner Charles Burke put it at the time, "It is not consistent with the general welfare to promote [American Indian national] characteristics and organization."[22]

The assimilationist policy trajectory culminated during the 1950s with the passage of House Concurrent Resolution 108, otherwise known as the "Termination Act of 1953," a measure through which the United States moved to unilaterally dissolve 109 indigenous nations within its borders. Termination was coupled to the "Relocation Act," a statute passed in 1956 and designed to coerce reservation residents to disperse to various urban centers around the country. As a result of the ensuing programmatic emphasis on creating an American Indian diaspora, by 1990 over half of all U.S. Indians had been severed from their respective land bases and generally acculturated to non-Indian mores. Meanwhile, the enactment of Public Law 280, placing many reservations under the jurisdiction of individual states, thereby reduced the level of native sovereignty to that held by counties or municipalities. This voided one of the last federal pretenses that Indians retained "certain characteristics of sovereign nations."

The question arises, of course, as to why, given the contours of this aspect of federal policy, the final obliteration of the indigenous nations of North America has not long since occurred. The answer, apparently, resides within something of a supreme irony: unbeknownst to the policymakers who implemented allotment policy against Indians during the late 19th century, much of the ostensibly useless land to which native people were consigned has turned out to be some of the most mineral rich on earth. It is presently estimated that as much as two-thirds of all known U.S. "domestic" uranium reserves lie beneath reservation lands, as well as perhaps a quarter of the readily accessible low-sulphur coal and about a fifth of the oil and natural gas. In addition, the reservations are now known to hold substantial deposits of copper, zinc, iron, nickel, molybdenum, bauxite, zeolites, and gold.

These facts began to surface in the early 1920s. Federal economic planners quickly discerned a distinct advantage in retaining these abundant resources within the framework of governmental trust control, an expedient to awarding extractive leases, mining licenses, and the like to preferred corporate entities in ways that might have proven impossible had the reservations been liquidated altogether. Hence, beginning in 1921, it was determined that selected indigenous nations should be maintained in some semblance of being, and Washington began to experiment with the creation of "tribal governments" intended to administer what was left of Indian Country in behalf of an emerging complex of interlocking federal/corporate interests. In 1934, this resulted in the passage of the Indian Reorganization Act (IRA), a bill that served to supplant virtually every remaining traditional indigenous government in the country, replacing them with federally designed "tribal councils" structured along the lines of corporate boards and empowered primarily to sign off on mineral leases and similar instruments.

The arrangement led to a recapitulation of the Marshall Doctrine's principle of indigenous "quasi-sovereignty" in slightly revised form: now, native nations were cast as always being sovereign enough to legitimate Euro-American mineral exploitation on their reservations but never sovereign enough to prevent it. Predictably, under such circumstances the BIA negotiated mining leases, duly endorsed by the puppet governments it had installed, "in behalf of" its "Indian wards" that typically paid native people 15% or less of market royalty rates on minerals taken from their lands. The "superprofits" thus generated for major corporations have had a significant positive effect on U.S. economic growth since 1950, a matter amplified by the fact that the BIA also "neglected" to include land restoration and other environmental cleanup clauses into contracts pertaining to reservation land (currently, Indians are always construed as being sovereign enough to waive such things as environmental protection regulations but never sovereign enough to enforce them). One consequence of this trend is that, on reservations where uranium mining has occurred, Indian Country has become so contaminated by radioactive substances that the government has actively considered designating them as "National Sacrifice Areas" unfit for human habitation. At this juncture, planning is also afoot to utilize several reservations as dump sites for high-level nuclear wastes and toxic chemical substances that cannot be otherwise conveniently disposed of.

Further indications of the extent and virulence of the colonial system by which the United States has come to rule Native America are not difficult to find. For instance, dividing the 50-million-odd acres of land still nominally reserved for Indian use and occupancy in the United States by the approximately 1.6 million Indians the government recognized in its 1980 census reveals that native people—on paper, at least—remain the largest landholders on a per capita basis of any population sector on the continent.[23] Given this, in combination with the resources known to lie within their land and the increasingly intensive "development" of these resources over the past 40 years, simple arithmetic strongly suggests that they should also be the wealthiest of all aggregate groups. Instead, according to the federal government's own data, Indians are far and away the poorest in terms of both annual and lifetime per capita income. Correspondingly, we suffer all the standard indices of dire poverty: North America's highest rates of infant mortality and teen suicide and of death from malnutrition, exposure, and plague. Overall, we consistently experience the highest rate of unemployment, lowest level of educational attainment, and one of the highest rates of incarceration of any group. The average life expectancy of a reservation-based American Indian male is currently less than 45 years; that of a reservation-based female, barely over 47.

In Latin America, there is a core axiom that guides understanding of the interactive dynamics between the northern and southern continents of the Western Hemisphere. "Your wealth," Ladino analysts point out to their Yanqui counterparts, "is our poverty."[24] Plainly, the structure of the relationship forged by the United States vis-à-vis the indigenous nations of the northern continent itself follows exactly the same pattern of parasitic domination. The economic veins of the prostrate Native North American host have been carefully opened, their contents provided lifeblood to the predatory creature that applied the knife. Such are the fruits of John Marshall's doctrine after a century and a half of continuous application to the "real world" context.

International Sleight of Hand

It's not that the United States has ever attempted to mask the face of this reality. Indeed, in the wake of World War II, even as the United States was engaged in setting a "moral example" to all of humanity by assuming a lead role in prosecuting former Nazi leaders for having ventured down much the same road of continental conquest that the United States itself had pioneered, Congress passed what it called the Indian Claims Commission Act. The premise of the bill was that all nonconsensual—and therefore illegal—seizures of native property that had transpired during the course of American history had been "errors," sometimes "tragic" ones. As a means, at least figuratively, of separating U.S. historical performance and expansionist philosophy from the more immediate manifestations of the Nazis, the new law established a commission empowered to review the basis of U.S. land title in every quarter of the country and to award retroactive monetary compensation to indigenous nations shown to have been unlawfully deprived of their lands. Tellingly, the commission was authorized to set compensation amounts only on the basis of the estimated per-acre value of illegally taken land *at the time it was taken* (often a century or more before), and was specifically disempowered from restoring land to Indian control, no matter *how* the land was taken or *what* the desires of the impacted native people might be.

Although the life of the commission was originally envisioned as being only ten years, the magnitude of the issues it encountered, and the urgency with which its mission came to be viewed by the Euro-American status quo, caused it to be repeatedly extended. When it was ultimately suspended on September 30, 1978, it still had 68 cases docketed for review, despite having heard and ostensibly "disposed of" several hundred others over a period of three decades. In the end, although its intent

had been the exact opposite, it had accomplished nothing so much as to establish with graphic clarity how little of North America the United States could be said to legally own.

> The fact is that about half the land area of the country was purchased by treaty or agreement at an average price of less than a dollar an acre; another third of a [billion] acres, mainly in the West, were confiscated without confiscation; another two-thirds of a [billion] acres were claimed by the United States without pretense of a unilateral action extinguishing native title.[25]

This summary, of course, says nothing at all about the approximately 44 million acres of land presently being taken from the Indians, Aleuts, and Inuits of the Arctic North under provision of the 1971 Alaska Native Claims Settlement Act, or the several million acres of Hawaii stripped away from the natives of those islands. Similarly, it says nothing of the situation in such U.S. "possessions" as Guam, Puerto Rico, the "U.S." Virgin Islands, "American" Samoa, and the Marshall Islands.

Serious challenges to commission findings have been mounted in U.S. courts, based largely in the cumulative contradictions inherent to federal Indian law. As a consequence, the Supreme Court has been compelled to resort to ever more convoluted and logically untenable argumentation as a means of upholding certain governmental assertions of "legitimate" land title. In its 1980 opinion in the Black Hills Land Claim case, for example, the high court was forced to extend the Marshall Doctrine's indigenous domesticity thesis to a ludicrous extreme, holding that the United States had merely exercised its rightful internal power of "imminent domain" over the territory of the Lakota Nation when it expropriated 90% of the latter's land a century earlier, in direct violation of the 1868 Treaty of Fort Laramie. Similarly, in the Western Shoshone Land Claim case, where the government could show no documentation that it had ever even pretended to assume title to the native land at issue, the Supreme Court let stand the Claims Commission's assignment of an arbitrary date on which a transfer supposedly took place.

During the 1970s, the American Indian Movement (AIM), an organization militantly devoted to the national liberation of Native North America, emerged in the United States. In part, the group attempted the physical decolonization of the Pine Ridge Reservation in South Dakota (home of the Oglala Lakota people) but was met with a counterinsurgency war waged by federal agencies such as the FBI and U.S. Marshalls Service and by surrogates associated with the reservation's IRA Council. Although unsuccessful in achieving a resumption of indigenous self-determination at Pine Ridge, the tenacity of AIM's struggle (and the ferocity of the government's repression of it) attracted considerable international attention. This led, in 1980, to the establishment of a United Nations Working Group on Indigenous Populations, under auspices of the U.N. Economic and Social Council (UNESCO), an entity mandated to assess the situation of native peoples globally and produce a universal declaration of their rights as a binding element of international law.

Within this arena, the United States, joined by Canada, has consistently sought to defend its relations with indigenous nations by trotting out the Marshall Doctrine's rationalization that the United States has assumed a trust responsibility over rather than outright colonial domination of Native North America. Native delegates have countered, correctly, that trust prerogatives, in order to be valid under international law, must be tied to some clearly articulated time interval after which the trustee nations resume independent existence. This has been successfully contrasted to the federal (and Canadian) government's presumption that it enjoys a permanent trust authority over indigenous nations; assumption of permanent plenary authority over another nation's affairs and property is the essential definition of colonialism, it is argued, and is illegal under a number of international covenants.

The United States and Canada have responded with prevarication, contending that their relationship to Native North America cannot be one of colonialism insofar as United Nations Resolution 1541 (XV), the "Blue Water Thesis," specifies that in order to be defined as a colony a nation must be separated from its colonizer by at least 30 miles of open ocean. The representatives of both countries have also done everything in their power to delay or prevent completion of the Universal Declaration of the Rights of Indigenous Peoples, arguing, among other things, that the term "peoples," when applied to native populations, should not carry the force of law implied by its use in such international legal instruments as the Universal Declaration of Human Rights (1948), Covenant on Civil and Political Rights (1978), and the International Convention on Elimination of All Forms of Racial Discrimination (1978). The United States in particular has implied that it will not abide by any declaration of indigenous rights that runs counter to what it perceives as its own interests, a matter that would replicate its posture with regard to the authority of the International Court of Justice (the "World Court")[26] and elements of international law such as the 1948 Convention on Prevention and Punishment of the Crime of Genocide.[27]

Meanwhile, the United States has set out to "resolve things internally" through what may be intended as a capstone extrapolation of the Marshall Doctrine. This strategy has involved a drive to convince Indians to accept the premise that, rather than struggling to regain the self-determining rights to separate sovereign existence embodied in their national histories and treaty relationships, they should voluntarily merge themselves with the U.S. polity. In this scenario, the IRA administrative apparatus created during the 1930s would assume a position as a "third level of the federal government," finally making indigenous rights within the United States inseparable from those of the citizenry as a whole. This final assimilation of native people into the "American sociopolitical mainstream" would obviously void most (or perhaps all) potential utility for Indian rights that exist or might emerge from international law over the next few years. The option is therefore being seriously pursued at this juncture by a Senate Select Committee on Indian Affairs, chaired by Hawaii Senator Daniel Inouye (who has already done much to undermine the last vestiges of rights held by the native people of his own state).

United States out of North America

During the fall of 1990, President George Bush stepped onto the world stage beating the drums for what he termed a "just war" to roll back the "naked aggression" of Iraq's invasion and occupation of neighboring Kuwait. Claiming to articulate "universal principles of international relations and human decency," Bush stated that such aggression "cannot stand," that "occupied territory must be liberated, legitimate governments must be reinstated, the benefits of their aggression must be denied to aggressive powers."[28] Given the tone and tenor of this Bushian rhetoric—and the undeniable fact that Iraq had a far better claim to Kuwait (its 19th province, separated from the Iraqis by the British as an administrative measure following World War I) than the United States has to virtually any part of North America[29]—one could only wait with baited breath for the American president to call airstrikes in upon his own Capitol as a means of forcing his own government to withdraw from Indian Country. Insofar as he did not, the nature of the "New World Order" his war in the Persian Gulf harkened tends to speak for itself.

The United States does not now possess, nor has it ever possessed, a legitimate right to occupancy in at least half the territory it claims as its own on this continent. It began its existence as an outlaw state, and, given the nature of its expansion to its present size, it has adamantly remained so through the present moment. In order to make things appear otherwise, its legal scholars and its legislators have persistently and often grotesquely manipulated and deformed accepted and sound legal principles, both internationally and domestically. They have done so in precisely the same fashion, and on the same basis, as the Nazi leaders they stood at the forefront in condemning for Crimes against Humanity at Nuremberg.

In no small part because of its success in consolidating its position on other people's land in North America, the United States may well continue to succeed where the Nazis failed. With the collapse of the Soviet Union, it has emerged as *the* ascendant military power on the planet during the late 20th century. As the sheer margin of its victory over Iraq has revealed, it now possesses the capacity to extend essentially the same sort of relationships it has already imposed upon American Indians to the remainder of the world. And, given the experience it has acquired in Indian Affairs over the years, it is undoubtedly capable of garbing this process of planetary subordination in a legalistic attire symbolizing its deep-seated concern with international freedom and dignity, the sovereignty of other nations, and the human rights of all peoples. At a number of levels, the Marshall Doctrine reckons to become truly globalized in the years ahead.

This is likely to remain the case, unless and until significant numbers of people within the United States as well as without come to recognize the danger, and the philosophical system that underpins it, for what they are. More importantly, any genuine alternative to a consummation of the Bushian vision of world order is predicated upon these same people acting upon their insights, opposing the order implicit to the U.S. status quo both at home and abroad. Ultimately, the dynamic represented by the Marshall Doctrine must be reversed, and the structure it fostered dismantled, within the territorial corpus of the United States itself. In this, nothing can be more central than the restoration of indigenous land and indigenous national rights in the fullest sense of the term. The United States—at least as it has come to be known, and in the sense that it knows itself—must be driven from North America. In its stead resides the possibility, likely the *only* possibility, of a genuinely just and liberatory future for all humanity.

Notes

1. 1 *Stat.* 50, 1789.

2. Quoted in Lazarus, Edward, *Black Hills, White Justice: The Sioux Nation versus the United States,*

1775 to the Present, Harper-Collins, New York, 1991, p. 158.

3. Opinion rendered by the Attorney General (Op. Atty. Gen.), April 26, 1821, p. 345.

4. Op. Atty. Gen., 1828, pp. 623–4. For further background, see Berman, Howard, "The Concept of Aboriginal Rights in the Early Legal History of the United States," *Buffalo Law Review,* No. 28, 1978, pp. 637–67. Also see Cohen, Felix S., "Original Indian Land Title," *Minnesota Law Review,* No. 32, 1947, pp. 28–59.

5. For a comprehensive survey of the meanings of these terms in the international legal vernacular, see Walzer, Michael, *Just and Unjust Wars: A Moral Argument with Historical Illustrations,* Basic Books, New York, 1977.

6. One indicator of the pervasiveness with which this outlook has been implanted is that armed conflicts between the United States and indigenous nations are inevitably described as "Indian Wars" despite the fact that each one was demonstrably initiated by the invasion by American citizens of territory belonging to one or more native peoples. The so-called Indian Wars would thus be accurately depicted as "Settlers' Wars" (or, more appropriately yet, "Wars of Aggression by the United States").

7. U.S. Bureau of the Census, *Report on Indians Taxed and Indians Not Taxed in the United States (except Alaska) at the Eleventh U.S. Census: 1890,* U.S. Government Printing Office, Washington, D.C., 1894, pp. 637–38.

8. *Ibid.*

9. See Stiffarm and Lane, *op. cit.,* pp. 35–36. The government of first the Republic, and then the State of Texas maintained a bounty on Indian—*any* Indian—scalps until well into the 1870s; see Newcome, W. W., Jr., *The Indians of Texas,* University of Texas Press, Austin, 1961.

10. Mooney, James, "Population," in Frederick W. Dodge (ed.), *Handbook of the Indians North of Mexico, Vol. 2,* Bureau of American Ethnology Bulletin No. 30, Smithsonian Institution, U.S. Government Printing Office, Washington, D.C., 1910, pp. 286–87. Also see Cook, Sherburn F., *The Conflict between the California Indian and White Civilization,* University of California Press, Berkeley, 1976.

11. See Thornton, Russell, "Cherokee Population Losses during the Trail of Tears: A New Perspective and Estimate," *Ethnohistory,* No. 31, 1984, pp. 289–300.

12. See Johansson, S. Ryan, and S. H. Preston, "Tribal Demography: The Navajo and Hopi Populations as Seen through Manuscripts from the 1900 Census," *Social Science History,* No. 3, 1978, p. 26. Also see Salmon, Roberto Mario, "The Disease Complaint at Bosque Redondo (1864–1868)," *The Indian Historian,* No. 9, 1976.

13. Scholarly sources suggest the actual total may have been as high as a half-million. See Thornton, Russell, *American Indian Holocaust and Survival: A Population History since 1492,* University of Oklahoma Press, Norman, 1987, p. 49.

14. This nadir figure is reported in U.S. Bureau of the Census, *Fifteenth Census of the United States, 1930: The Indian Population of the United States and Alaska,* U.S. Government Printing Office, Washington, D.C., 1937. Barely 101,000 Canadian Indians were estimated as surviving in the same year.

15. Estimating native population figures at the point of first contact is, at best, a slippery business. Recent demographic work has, however, produced a broad consensus that the standard anthropological estimates of "about one million north of the Rio Grande" fashioned by James Mooney and Alfred Kroeber, as well as Harold Driver's subsequent upward revision of their calculations to "approximately two million," are *far* too low. The late Henry Dobyns, using more appropriate methodologies than his predecessors, computed a probable aggregate pre-contact North American Indian population of 18.5 million, about 15 million of them within present U.S. borders (*Their Numbers Become Thinned: Native American Population Dynamics in Eastern North America,* University of Tennessee Press, Knoxville, 1983). A somewhat more conservative successor, the Cherokee demographer Russell Thornton, counters that the figure was more likely about 12.5 million, perhaps 9.5 million of them within the United States (*American Indian Holocaust and Survival, op. cit.*). Splitting the difference between Dobyns and Thornton leaves one with an approximate 15 million North American population total, about 12.5 million in the United States. Interestingly, no matter which set of the newer estimates one uses, the overall attrition by 1900 is in the upper 90th percentile range.

16. The figure is arrived at by relying upon Royce, Charles C., *Indian Land Cessions in the United States* (2 Vols.), Bureau of American Ethnography, 18th Annual Report, 1896–97, Smithsonian Institution, Washington, D.C., 1899.

17. Ch. 119, 24 *Stat.* 388, now codified as amended at 25 U.S.C. 331 *et seq.*, better known as the "Dawes Act," after its sponsor, Massachusetts Senator Henry Dawes. The quote is from Robbins, Rebecca L., "Self-Determination and Subordination: The Past, Present, and Future of American Indian Governance," in Jaimes, *op. cit.*, p. 93.

18. See Jaimes, M. Annette, "Federal Indian Identification Policy: A Usurpation of Indigenous Sovereignty in North America," in Jaimes, *op. cit.*, pp. 123–38. It is noteworthy that official eugenics codes have been employed by very few states, mostly such unsavory examples as Nazi Germany (against the Jews), South Africa (against "Coloreds"), and Israel (against Palestinian Arabs).

19. Robbins, *op. cit.* Also see McDonnell, Janet A., *The Dispossession of the American Indian, 1887–1934*, Indiana University Press, Bloomington/Indianapolis, 1991.

20. Robbins, *op. cit.* Also see Kicking Bird, Kirk, and Karen Ducheneaux, *One Hundred Million Acres*, Macmillan, New York, 1973.

21. Jaimes, "Federal Indian Identification Policy," *op. cit.*, pp. 127–28.

22. Letter, Charles Burke to William Williamson, September 16, 1921; William Williamson Papers, Box 2, File—Indian Matters, Miscellaneous, I.D. Weeks Library, University of South Dakota, Vermillion. Such articulation of official sensibility was hardly isolated; see Kvasnicka, Robert M., and Herman J. Viola (eds.), *The Commissioners of Indian Affairs, 1824–1977*, University of Nebraska Press, Lincoln, 1979.

23. See U.S. Bureau of the Census, *1980 Census of the Population, Supplementary Reports, Race of the Population by States, 1980*, U.S. Government Printing Office, Washington, D.C., 1981. Also see U.S. Bureau of the Census, *Ancestry of the Population by State, 1980*, Supp. Rep. PC80-SI-10, U.S. Government Printing Office, Washington, D.C., 1983.

24. The quote is taken from Galeano, Eduardo, *The Open Veins of Latin America: Five Centuries of the Pillage of a Continent*, Monthly Review Press, New York, 1973.

25. Barsh, Russell, "Indian Land Claims Policy in the United States," *North Dakota Law Review*, No. 58, 1982, pp. 1–82.

26. In October 1985, President Ronald Reagan withdrew a 1946 U.S. declaration accepting ICJ jurisdiction in all matters of "international dispute." The withdrawal took effect in April 1986. This was in response to the ICJ determination in *Nicaragua* v. *United States*, the first substantive case ever brought before it to which the United States was a party. The ICJ ruled the U.S. action of mining Nicaraguan harbors in times of peace to be unlawful. The Reagan administration formally rejected the authority of the ICJ to decide the matter (but removed the mines). It is undoubtedly significant that the Reagan instrument contained a clause accepting continued ICJ jurisdiction over matters pertaining to "international commercial relationships," thus attempting to convert the world court into a mechanism for mere trade arbitration. See *U.S. Terminates Acceptance of ICJ Compulsory Jurisdiction*, Department of State Bulletin No. 86, Washington, D.C., January 1986.

27. The United States declined to ratify the Genocide Convention until 1988, 40 years after it became international law (and after more than 100 other nations had ratified it), and then only with an attached "Sovereignty Package" purporting to subordinate the convention to the U.S. Constitution (thereby seeking to protect certain aspects of genocidal conduct). The U.S. stipulation in this regard is, of course, invalid under Article 27 of the 1969 Vienna Convention on the Law of Treaties and has been protested as such by such countries as Britain, Denmark, and the Netherlands. Further, the Genocide Convention is now customary international law, meaning—according to the United States' own Nuremberg Doctrine—that it is binding upon the United States, whether Congress ratifies its terms or not. For further analysis, see LeBlanc, Lawrence J., *The United States and the Genocide Convention*, Duke University Press, Durham (N.C.)/London, 1991.

28. For the context of this rhetoric, see Chomsky, Noam, " 'What We Say Goes': The Middle East in the New World Order," in Cynthia Peters (ed.), *Collateral Damage: The "New World Order" at Home*

and Abroad, South End Press, Boston, 1992, pp. 49–92.

29. For further information, see Chomsky, Noam, and Eqbal Ahmed, "The Gulf Crisis: How

We Got There," in Greg Bates (ed.), *Mobilizing Democracy: Changing the U.S. Role in the Middle East,* Common Courage Press, Monroe, ME, 1991, pp. 3–24.

42.   Justice for Farm Workers

Thomas Auxter

Through informal interviews, meetings, and published statements by migrant farm workers, Thomas Auxter attempts to generate an understanding of justice for farm workers. Auxter analyzes the arguments presented by growers, as well as the statements of farm workers, in order to understand social justice in this context.

This paper is in part a chronicle and in part a theory of social justice. The chronicle will recount what farm workers have said about their situation in published statements, in meetings, and in personal interviews at farm labor camps. Letting farm workers speak in their own words is essential if we truly want to hear about their lives.

As it happens, there are some who would prefer that farm workers did not tell their story. Growers often fall into this category, as do certain professors of economics. But growers cannot conceal the facts about the condition of farm workers. Well-publicized reports, beginning with Edward R. Murrow's *Harvest of Shame,* have taken away that option. So the growers face a dilemma: how do they explain to the public that they are not responsible for the conditions that exist on their property, or within their domain, into which they seek to bring farm workers? After we hear the farm workers, we will consider the growers' response, before asking what conditions must be met to ensure justice for farm workers and what issues the answer to this question raises for understanding social justice.

From George Lucas, Jr., ed., *Poverty, Justice, and the Law: New Essays on Needs, Rights, and Obligations.* University Press of America, 1986, pp. 149–163. Reprinted by permission.

I

Cesar Chavez cites the following cases at the Bruce Church Company:[1]

1. Manuel Amaya was an employee of Bruce Church for twelve years—before his right arm became infected from the powerful herbicide he was required to use in his job as a farm worker. Because Mr. Amaya did not have the money to pay a physician, he asked Bruce Church for help. Bruce Church refused. Cesar Chavez tells the outcome: "By the time he saved the money for a doctor, his hand had to be amputated. The company fired Manuel Amaya. It had little use for a one-handed worker."

2. Aurelia Pena, another farm worker at Bruce Church, was exposed to toxic fumes from the heated plastic used for wrapping lettuce. Three times she asked permission to leave the job when she became ill and three times the foreman refused. When Mrs. Pena fainted, she was placed in a company bus parked in the field for several hours. Then, after her lips turned blue, the company finally drove her home but delivered her to the wrong house. By the time her relatives found her and took her to the hospital, she

was dead. Fifteen days later Mr. Pena received what was to be the only communication ever sent by Bruce Church after his wife's death: Mrs. Pena, Bruce Church, Inc., said, was fired.

3. Martina Zuniga turned down the sexual propositions of company foremen in her area. They threatened retaliation if she continued to refuse their advances. When Ms. Zuniga stood her ground, she was demoted. Ms. Zuniga went with other women farm workers and with union officials to complain to Bruce Church, Inc., about these abuses of power and about the problem of sexual harassment on the job. They asked whether the company approved of these practices by its representatives. They wanted to know whether the company was allowing its managers to use company power in this way. Most of all, they wanted to know whether Bruce Church, Inc., would put a stop to a situation in which women farm workers were forced to submit to the sexual demands of Bruce Church managers or else lose financial support for families that badly needed the money. They were angry that they had to choose between their dignity and their livelihood. Bruce Church refused to put an end to the practice or to do anything to reduce the amount of sexual coercion by its managers. The answer from the Bruce Church lawyer typified the company attitude: he expressed surprise over such concern and then added, "I didn't know the union is opposed to love."

When we talk about justice for farm workers, we are talking about justice for people like Manuel Amaya, Aurelia Pena, and Martina Zuniga. Justice for farm workers means, among other things, that we restore conditions of life, insofar as that is possible, to people like these three farm workers. But when there is extreme injustice, as in these cases, it is not possible to change the world enough to compensate victims for what they have lost, for what they can no longer do, for what they must face, for life itself. Our commitment to justice must take other forms as well. We must ask what conditions are responsible for generating these kinds of abuses, what structural changes are required to eliminate them, and what we can do to make these changes so that others will not suffer these fates.

Understanding what has happened to these three farm workers involves more than examining individual circumstances. It involves noticing in a general way what the condition of farm workers is like. Although these are extreme examples, they are not rare examples. These examples illustrate a more general problem. A theme runs through all of these cases. It is a theme that runs through the lives of most farm workers. Cesar Chavez states it:

> For most of the men, women, and children who produce the food we eat, earning a living is a daily battle with toxic poisons, sexual harassment, unsafe conditions . . . and multi-million dollar corporations that treat them like agricultural implements instead of human beings.

II

How do growers respond when presented with the evidence that farm workers are suffering subhuman conditions within the growers' sphere of influence? We have already heard the kinds of responses given by representatives of Bruce Church, Inc. Another set of responses comes from growers interviewed in documentaries such as Edward R. Murrow's *Harvest of Shame* and Chet Huntley's *Migrant*. Here the responses have generally been (1) to condemn farm workers as "lazy" or "irresponsible" and as deserving their condition, or (2) to insist that critics of current farm labor practices are not facing up to "economic realities." Because the first sort of reply involves a stereotyping of farm workers, along with racial and ethnic slurs, it is obvious why we do not have to consider these answers when we are asking what it would take to achieve justice—except insofar as the answers betray an attitude that is itself an obstacle with which we must reckon. Of course, there is a long history, dating to times of slavery, in which some growers (including plantation owners) attempted to justify subhuman conditions for farm labor by claiming that whatever population was involved was a subhuman group and therefore "deserved" subhuman treatment. But this would be a classic example of an immoral argument, not a moral argument.

Nevertheless, the economic argument does need to be considered because it is the argument offered by the official representatives of the growers, namely, the farm bureaus. If the farm bureau of a particular state discusses farm labor, it is likely to emphasize that these are economic issues, not moral issues. The question is how much growers can afford to pay farm workers and still stay in business, not how much the grower can improve life for farm workers. Answering the question involves knowing how much the consumer will pay for produce. Improvements for farm workers, the growers say, can only come at the expense of the consumer. When the consumer indicates a greater willingness to pay for these expenses, the growers will respond to the new market conditions.

The growers' argument has also been advanced by certain professors of economics who are quick to dismiss moral questions about treatment of farm workers. In a recent paper, "Ethical Issues and Farm Labor: The Contribution of Economic Analysis," Professor Daniel Sumner claims that "much moral self-righteousness and indignation have been spent because of misunderstanding of facts and of economic cause and consequence with respect to farm labor."[2] He believes, however, that if we simply consider "what common economic reasoning can contribute," we will discover that the most good is generated by allowing growers and workers to set the rates of exchange in a free market. Appealing to Milton Friedman's conception of "the ethics of exchange," Sumner argues that the only real moral issue is whether we allow "the exercise of human rights" in the free exchange of goods and services. He concludes that we will generate the greatest well-being by unleashing "the power of exchange" and "encouraging trading rather than stealing." He notes that people who feel bad about the plight of farm workers are free to contribute to charity.

III

How do we compare the moral appeals of the farm workers with the economic analysis of the growers? Does justice for farm workers mean securing decent treatment for farm workers? Or does it mean protecting the right of growers to offer jobs at whatever rates, and under whatever conditions, they can get farm workers to accept them? Is our most basic ethical consciousness connected with regarding human beings in certain special ways so that we do not treat them as instruments? Or is our ethical awareness a concern to protect "the power of exchange," regardless of how degrading work becomes, as long as there are still people left who will accept the work?

The debate over this question has been going on for a long time and in many forms. At stake in the debate are sharply opposed ideas of the value of human beings and of the value of money. The debate is as old as Socrates' comparison of conceptions of the nature of justice in Book I of the *Republic*. Socrates was searching for a concept of justice that would recognize the importance of the full development of the soul. In contrast to those who believe justice is nothing more than honoring the conditions for the fulfillment of business contracts, namely, telling the truth and repaying debts, Socrates believed that human life is more than the acquisition of wealth and that justice will have something to do with honoring this "something more."

In the *Republic,* justice turns out to be recognizing *all* that is excellent in human beings and creating a unity among these characteristics—both in the individual and in society. Within the individual, justice is the harmony of the basic sides of human personality—recognizing more than just the concupiscent side of human nature (the side that says 'I want this' and 'I want that') and insisting on an acknowledgment of the rational and spiritual sides of human nature to such an extent that every option in the realm of acquisition and the satisfaction of bodily desire is assessed, and accepted or rejected, based on whether it can be harmonized with the elements of a more complete and well-rounded life. In contrast to those who want justice to consist of the conditions for unimpeded acquisition, Socrates insists that the other sides of us are so important that acquisitive impulses must fit into a harmony in which the other sides set the terms of the unity. This does not abolish desire for material and bodily gratification; it means that acting on this desire depends on whether or not such action is compatible with the overall moral identity, the unity of the soul, that a person should be trying to create. The moral ideal is *not* to extinguish all material desires but to bring them into alignment with the other, more important sides of personality. Accordingly, justice cannot be devotion to the acquisitive side of personality—either in the individual or in society. At the individual level, Socrates notes that an emphasis on making fortunes produces people who are "very bad company for they can talk about nothing but the praises of wealth." He also observes that with such an emphasis the ideal society would consist of the most clever thieves, those who could acquire the most without anyone objecting. To the end (*Republic* X) Socrates urges us "to be undazzled by the desire of wealth or the other allurements of evil" and to attend to the soul.

Justice is a central theme in Aristotle's ethics, as well. He goes to great lengths to define the terms of the discussion so that we will know what we are talking about. The "unjust person," he tells us in the *Nicomachean Ethics,* is "an unfair self-aggrandizer"—one who is always "taking more than one's share of the good and less than one's share of the bad." The "unjust" are distinguished from "profiteers" only in the magnitude of scale of their operations: the unjust are "those who take the wrong things from the wrong source on a large scale," while profiteers (such as gamblers and highway robbers) must be willing to "endure notoriety for the sake of profit" inasmuch as their imaginations and abilities limit them to "ways of taking" that are "stingy and mean." It is the limited scale of operation that marks them as profiteers; they share with the unjust the "wish to gain profit from the wrong sources" (1122a).

So much for the motivation and orientation of the unjust person. How do we identify an unjust act? "Acting unjustly" means "harming a person knowing the person affected, the instrument, the manner of action, and that it is against that person's wish." Acting unjustly involves knowing that what you propose will bring harm to someone or some group and, in full knowledge of the harm that will be done, going through with it for the sake of self-aggrandizement.

Aristotle, too, believes that justice is the unity of the virtues. In fact, his discussion of justice follows a detailed examination of these basic types of human excellence and of the sense of proportion necessary to cultivate each type of excellence. Each virtue is a sense of proportion concerning a sphere of activity, and justice is a sense of proportion with regard to the coordination of the spheres. The just person will give the just or due response in each type of situation. Within the individual this means choosing a course that harmonizes with all of the virtues.

But individuals do not live in self-enclosed worlds. The human world is inescapably social. Within society, justice is a condition in which each person "acts well" and "fares well" in encounters with others, a condition in which no one acts the part of the "self-aggrandizer" who is "taking more than one's share of the good and less than one's share of the bad." Here it is important to notice that justice goes beyond the domain called "public legal justice." It is not merely a legal matter. Indeed, Aristotle highlights this point in his discussion of equity. Recognizing the need for equity is tantamount to admitting that "law falls short by reason of its universality" and often requires rectification—possibly including "a special decree" (1137b). Because justice involves having a sense of proportion, no set of general laws can be anything more than a crude estimation of justice—*calling* for rectification. This point will become important later on when we consider the growers' claim that a legal framework establishing the free exchange of goods and services is a sufficient condition for justice.

In more modern times, philosophers who have written about questions in ethics have, for the most part, adopted this ancient orientation and have sought to develop and refine certain aspects of it. Kant, for example, emphasizes the importance of moral choice to such an extent that it would be impossible to justify ever letting an economic reason override a moral one. For him, respecting what is human in us supersedes every other value that could possibly compete with it for attention. Like Socrates, Kant believes that personal integrity and concern for the development of the soul generally are far more important than material gain. Knowing the importance of these values means knowing the difference between treating people as ends in themselves and merely using them as a means toward other ends. It means knowing the difference between a human being and some object that can be used as a mere instrument. It means knowing the difference between a person and a thing.

Of course, of those who know this difference, not all act as if they do. Indeed, it is of the very essence of evil to know the difference and to behave as if one did not. This also means that one is never justified in treating people in the present merely as means in order to generate some imagined future good—even if that imagined good is supposedly for human beings. Thus it is wrong when Hitler orders genocide for the sake of the future "purity" of the human race, and it is wrong when Stalin orders the killing of peasants to put into effect his agricultural policies. It is also wrong when someone lies to another human being about a product in order to make a profit or when someone takes advantage of another's powerlessness in order to achieve some personal gain. The question this raises for us is whether it is acceptable to treat farm workers as less than fully human even if the purpose is to provide either an extra margin of surplus for the growers or less expensive agricultural products for consumers.

Kant also discusses the "morally dead," whom he sometimes calls "the pathological." They are the ones who disregard all moral considerations in the pursuit of their self-interest, however they may define it, and treat people as objects to be used and disposed of at will. Slaveholders would be the most obvious example of the morally dead. They use others to generate profits for themselves—coercing others to work on projects in which they have no stake and using up their lives for the promotion of ends they do not share. In other words, the morally dead disregard the human-

ity of people in order to be more effective in using them as instruments.

It is significant that the founders of another great current of modern ethical thought, namely, utilitarianism, also acknowledge roots in Greek ethics. But the continuity of utilitarianism with Greek ethics runs much deeper than these acknowledgments of forebears. The classical sensitivity to variations in circumstances that have a bearing on character formation, the recognition of the need for ongoing deliberation in evaluating choices, and the sense of proportion in making judgments are all reflected in the utilitarian's careful assessment of the greatest balance of good consequences over bad consequences. Now that the long and divisive controversy over the nature and status of pleasure has been pushed to the back burner of utilitarian theory, it is much easier to notice these continuities and to appreciate a tradition utilitarians share with others in the approach to morality and justice. Like the major Greek philosophers, the utilitarians reject the notion that ethical awareness is solely a matter of noninterference with those who manage to accumulate wealth without fraud. Creating the greatest happiness, which is the goal of moral reasoning and effort, is a project sufficiently expansive and encompassing that no amount of individual, privately interested activity can approach it. Not only are those who devote themselves to acquisition "bad company," as Socrates observes; they have thrown away the opportunity for a larger, more complete happiness and joy in life "by caring for nobody but themselves," as Mill would say. Those who cultivate "a fellow-feeling with the collective interests of mankind will retain as lively an interest in life on the eve of death as in the vigor of youth and health."[3] Human existence is naturally, necessarily, and habitually a "social state."

The greatest happiness cannot be consistently pursued unless this larger domain of human life—including the social arrangements that can maximize happiness—is covered by the assessment of the consequences of various courses of action. The path to the greatest happiness lies in cultivating "social feelings" for a "strengthening of social ties" and a "healthy growth of society." This will increase the personal interest of each individual in considering the welfare of others and will lead each to identify personal feelings with a practical regard for others. Each person "comes, as though instinctively, to be conscious of himself as a being who *of course* pays regard to others."[4] The "others" are not merely those with wealth and power, who are difficult to disregard in any case, but also those who are poor and powerless. In contrast to a society of masters and slaves, whether this is understood literally or in some extended sense, a "society between equals can only exist on the understanding that the interests of all are to be regarded equally."[5] As Bentham says, "Everybody to count for one, nobody for more than one." Mill pointedly sums up this attitude:

> Few but those whose mind is a moral blank could bear to lay out their course of life on the plan of paying no regard to others except so far as their own private interest compels.[6]

Justice cannot be merely a legal insurance policy for the orderly pursuit of private interests largely for the sake of those who are best at it. Justice is, among other things, a set of social accommodations for the sake of a progressively viable and fulfilling set of social relations—those engendering the greatest happiness. "Justice remains the appropriate name for certain social utilities which are vastly more important, and therefore more absolute and imperative, than any others are as a class."[7]

IV

In *Adventures of Ideas* Whitehead discusses the emergence in Greek society of "the ideal of the intellectual and moral grandeur of the human soul."[8] This general idea, especially as it was formulated by Plato in the dialogues, "haunted" the ancient world—both in the sense that people found it to be inspiring and in the sense that a slaveowning society would have to find this emphasis on the dignity of human nature a great danger. While there are always those who rush forward to explain that such an idea is not really a threat to the existing social order, provided that certain small adjustments are made, the very generality

of the idea means that it remains a danger to the social structure promoting injustice.

> The whole bundle of [the idea's] conceivable special embodiments in various usages of society constitutes a program of reform. At any moment the smoldering unhappiness of mankind may seize on some such program and initiate a period of rapid change guided by the light of its doctrines.[9]

However, we should not believe that a great idea is merely lurking in the background until there are enough good people to implement it. On the contrary, we could not account for the eventual success of the idea unless its duration in the background had involved "promoting the gradual growth of the requisite communal customs, adequate to sustain the load of its exemplification."[10]

We can estimate moral progress in the Western tradition by the extent to which the generality of the humanitarian ideal, which is traceable to "the speculations of the philosophical Greeks upon functions of the human soul," has found exemplification in society.[11] While the history of ideas can be construed as "a history of mistakes," it can also be understood as "the history of the gradual purification of conduct."[12] Throughout this process, the major philosophers in the West who have given a detailed, positive account of the relationship between ethical awareness and justice have appealed to and built on this tradition stemming from the Greeks. But the very fact that it would take centuries before this ideal would prevail in the West, finally leading to the general abolition of the most overt forms of slavery, means that the forces opposing the ideal are both powerful and potentially able to reverse this moral progress. Under these circumstances it would be wise to remember how far we have come and how we got here. It would also be wise to be on the alert for reversals.

Nothing said so far has been meant to suggest that a succession of intellectuals is responsible for the abolition of slavery. Ideas can be powerful, but they are not that powerful. The most vigorous opposition to slavery comes from slaves themselves. They know from their own experience what others often discover in their hearts only after consulting a general ideal for the treatment of human beings.

Moral principles do not topple oppressive institutions. People do. Yet we need to reconstruct this history of ideas so that we can give ourselves some basic orientation on what the struggle over justice has been all about. The end of injustice comes sooner when we realize what the debate has been, where it has taken us, and what these lessons show about what still needs to be done.

V

What is at stake in the debate between farm workers and growers comes into sharper focus against the background of the Western moral tradition. This is not the only tradition or context that is relevant to the issue. However, the lessons on freedom and slavery, hard-won through a long process of cultural evolution, should not be ignored. Considering what it has cost to learn these lessons, we should not fail to draw out the implications for basic issues of justice.

This history is relevant for another reason as well. Slavery is a live issue for farm workers and is often a topic of discussion in their meetings. It is no accident that recent cases of slavery discovered in the United States (in Florida and North Carolina) were cases in which migrant farm laborers were held as slaves. Such practices trade upon a more general attitude among growers of contempt for farm workers and point up the laborers' condition of relative powerlessness. But the problem goes beyond merely dealing with these overt forms of slavery. After slavery was officially abolished in the United States, virtually identical conditions could still be found for decades under a "new" arrangement called "sharecropping." For many former slaves, sharecropping was little different from slavery. The terms of the arrangement were dictated to impoverished agricultural laborers who were already heavily in debt to the owner of the land. The owner could count on support from the law enforcement system, which could easily distinguish between law-abiding citizens who "amounted to something" and impoverished farm workers who might try to escape to avoid legal obligations to repay debts. If the sharecropper was different from the slave, it was only because the owner decided to recognize a difference and not because there was any major change in either the poverty or the powerlessness of the agricultural laborer.

The connection between their condition and that of the sharecropper has not escaped the notice of the farm workers. Baldemar Velasquez, President of the Farm Labor Organizing Committee which represents two thousand farm workers in Ohio and Michigan who are on strike against Campbell's Soup, states the point:

> We keep scratching away at the symptoms and don't really look at the underlying situation that causes these things to persist. We now believe that the basic problem is the whole system of sharecropping.[13]

The basic idea of sharecropping is that those who tend to and harvest crops receive a portion of what they have produced while the owner of the land takes the rest. Sharecropping is a crop contracting system: workers make a contract with growers to harvest a crop for a portion of its worth. The advantage to growers of such a system is that they need take no responsibility for the conditions into which they bring farm workers. Because growers can claim that farm workers are "independent contractors," they can refuse responsibility for complying with the Fair Labor Standards Act, minimum wage, child labor laws, and deductions for Social Security. In short, they can employ farm workers and subject them to adverse conditions while taking no responsibility for the effect of this employment on the workers. Although we are accustomed to thinking that a sharecropping system has been superseded by a more enlightened attitude toward labor relations, Baldemar Velasquez alerts us to the fact that current crop contracting arrangements are not substantially different from an older form of sharecropping which was itself merely a subterfuge for continuing the social relations involved in slavery.[14]

The problem is compounded, as it was in the past, by the influence growers are able to exercise on the legal system. Working in tandem with a conservative federal administration, growers have recently convinced the courts (in cases in Ohio and Michigan) to absolve them of any responsibility for working conditions—including both child labor and the spraying of pesticide on farm workers (a common occurrence). The federal government joined growers in promoting this idea of farm workers as independent contractors; it has even unleashed agents on farm workers who have migrated to the south—pursuing them for payment of the payroll deductions that had in the past been paid by the growers they had worked for in the north.

The "free exercise of human rights" advocated by Friedman and Sumner has another consequence for the condition of farm workers—the labor contractor system. If justice is simply a matter of protecting the right of everyone to be an "independent contractor," then there is no reason why growers should not be free to make a contract with a "crew leader," stipulating that all of the agricultural labor necessary for tending and harvesting a crop will be provided by the crew leader for a certain price. The growers need take no responsibility for conditions of farm labor since the labor contractor has assumed it for them. The labor contractor in turn insists that each farm worker is an independent contractor—selling his or her labor by contract—and thereby "voluntarily" assuming responsibility for labor conditions.

This is a system that lends itself to abuses—abuses well known to all the parties to these contracts. The labor contractor receives a lump sum for all of the labor to be performed; therefore, there is an incentive to cut corners on labor expenses since the labor contractor keeps all money left over. Farm workers often find themselves with less than they bargained for, as little as that was in the first place, because there were "misunderstandings" due to language problems, or a "bonus system" in which a portion of the money cannot be collected until a date when farm workers will have migrated to a new harvest, or "coincidental" raids by the immigration service on the morning of pay day so that illegal aliens will not have to be paid, etc. While labor contractors typically make incomes of $20,000–$40,000 per year, the farm workers trapped in this system make less than $2.00 per hour.

Friedman's "free exercise of human rights" in forming independent contracts with farm workers results in a system that is a sublimated form, adapted to new conditions, of the original sharecropping system, itself a sublimated form of slavery. What is common to each of these systems is the powerlessness of agricultural laborers to deal with continual assaults on their dignity and well-being—the requirement that they subject themselves to subhuman conditions in order to survive.

Some growers create much worse conditions than others. Not all should be blamed for what the worst do. Still, if growers are silent about these problems, and even join organizations that seek to quiet these concerns, then we may wonder whether they do not all share responsibility for the conditions. Or, if growers know of practices by their own labor contractors that they would rather not have disclosed, even as they defend the labor contractor system itself, then we may also wonder what real difference there is between them and the worst growers.

The long struggle to abolish slavery is not over. Slavery has not died out; it has become more subtle—a matter of "independent contracts." The emphasis that growers and their academic allies have placed on these contracts is significant. As Aristotle said, it is difficult to claim there has been an injustice if the supposed victim willingly accepts it. No doubt this accounts for the great interest growers have shown in "protecting" the right of the individual farm worker to make such an agreement. Not only have growers divested themselves of legal responsibility for the long list of abuses; they can ease their consciences with the thought that all of this is actually desired by the "individual" farm worker who makes the contract. Emphasis on the "individual" farm worker has the further advantage for growers that the testimony of *groups* of farm workers, denying that such contracts express their will, becomes irrelevant. But let us not forget that during the early stages of the civil rights movement, whites who were against civil rights for blacks would say that they had talked this over with their servants and reported having been assured that blacks didn't really want these rights.

The principal feature of slavery is powerlessness to resist what the slave master desires. I believe that Baldemar Velasquez is right when he says there is a continual history of exploitation of agricultural labor from times of slavery to sharecropping to crop contracting. The powerlessness of farm workers is no doubt related to the fact that most are migrant laborers and therefore have difficulty in voting and exercising political power. But there is a more general problem: the rest of society is still willing to tolerate a situation in which farm workers are exempted from most of the workplace protections normally afforded other workers. This in itself should cause us to wonder whether Baldemar Velasquez does not have a point. When we also consider the ways in which immigration policies have been used to flood the labor market, with the consequence of creating an urgent, even desperate, need to accept work under even the most miserable conditions, his thesis becomes even more plausible.

Is justice for farm workers the decent treatment they demand? Or is it restricted to protecting their right to make independent contracts, as the growers claim? If we examine the details of the farm workers' situation and consider their argument against the background of an evolving moral tradition, the answer will be obvious. If we agree with Socrates that the full development of the soul is more important than unbridled acquisition; if we agree with Aristotle that we must guard against self-aggrandizers and profiteers who would restrict and corrupt our sense of proportion and justice, the better to pursue their own narrow ends; if we believe a more amplified conception of justice will include equity and consequent "special decrees"; if we agree with Kant that it is wrong to treat people merely as instruments and that consistently engaging in such practices is the hallmark of the morally dead; if we agree with Mill that the human condition is at its best when it involves a mutually supportive set of social relations; and if we agree with Whitehead that an awareness

of the evolution of this general idea means that we will promote the growth of "the requisite communal customs," then we will not be puzzled about how to react to the growers' claim that justice is merely the legal support system for the successful entrepreneur.

But suppose we do understand these things about justice and therefore understand that we must help change the condition of farm workers, in spite of the growers' protest. What are we to do? Any correction of what is wrong with the condition of farm workers must address the issue of powerlessness. The scales of power are so heavily tipped in favor of the growers that incremental or piecemeal attempts at reform will fail until this issue is squarely faced. Strict enforcement of child labor laws simply makes the economic viability of farm worker families even more precarious until there is compensation adequate to replace what children have contributed previously—especially during harvest time when whole families must take whatever opportunities they can find in order to produce a subsistence income. Enforcing codes in deplorable farm labor camps simply means workers and their families will sleep in their cars or under bridges. The only way to ensure that each incremental victory is not turned into defeat is to empower farm workers to correct the overall condition through unionization, which means strengthening the legal support system for such activity in agriculture. The changes after unionization are dramatic—abolition of child labor, prohibitions against spraying pesticides while farm workers are in the fields, sanitary farm labor camps, etc. The evidence is there. We simply have to look at it—and make the changes. The direction is clear.

Notes

1. Cesar Chavez, letter to farm worker support groups, August 1983.

2. Daniel Sumner, "Ethical Issues and Farm Labor: The Contribution of Economic Analysis," in *Agriculture, Change and Human Values*, ed. Richard Hayes (Gainesville: University of Florida, 1983), Vol. 1, pp. 337–47.

3. John Stuart Mill, *Utilitarianism,* in *The Utilitarians* (Garden City: Dolphin Books, 1961), p. 414.

4. Mill, *Utilitarianism,* p. 435.

5. Mill, *Utilitarianism,* p. 435.

6. Mill, *Utilitarianism,* p. 437.

7. Mill, *Utilitarianism,* p. 470.

8. Alfred North Whitehead, *Adventures of Ideas* (New York: The Free Press, 1967), p. 15.

9. Whitehead, *Adventures of Ideas,* p. 15.

10. Whitehead, *Adventures of Ideas,* p. 10.

11. Whitehead, *Adventures of Ideas,* p. 24.

12. Whitehead, *Adventures of Ideas,* p. 12.

13. Baldemar Velasquez, "Sharecropping Is the Root of Our Problem," *Newsletter of the National Migrant Farm Worker Ministry,* 1984.

14. Velasquez, "Sharecropping."

Case 9.a *Plyler* v. *Doe:*
Educating the Children of Illegal Aliens

U.S. Supreme Court

Justice Brennan, writing for the majority of the Supreme Court, struck down the Texas statute that denied state funds for schools that admitted or educated children who were illegally admitted to the United States. Although public education is not a right guaranteed by the Constitution, Brennan argued that, because of the crucial importance of education to our society, and because of the economic benefits derived by the State of Texas from illegal workers, the state does not have a legitimate interest in denying the educational benefits. In dissent, Chief Justice Burger argued that illegal aliens are not protected by the equal protection clause and that the state law bears a reasonable relation to a legitimate state interest.

Justice *Brennan,* writing for the majority:

. . . In May 1975, the Texas Legislature revised its education laws to withhold from local school districts any state funds for the education of children who were not "legally admitted" into the United States. The 1975 revision also authorized local school districts to deny enrollment in their public schools to children not "legally admitted" to the country. . . . These cases involve constitutional challenges to those provisions.

[*Plyler v. Doe*] is a class action, filed in the United States District Court for the Eastern District of Texas in September 1977, on behalf of certain school-age children of Mexican origin residing in Smith County, Tex., who could not establish that they had been legally admitted into the United States. The action complained of the exclusion of plaintiff children from the public schools of the Tyler Independent School District. The Superintendent and members of the Board of Trustees of the School District were named as defendants; the State of Texas intervened as a party-defendant. After certifying a class consisting of all undocumented school-age children of Mexican origin residing within the School District, the District Court preliminarily enjoined defendants from denying a free education to members of the plaintiff class. In December 1977, the court conducted an extensive hearing on plaintiffs' motion for permanent injunctive relief. . . .

The District Court held that illegal aliens were entitled to the protection of the Equal Protection Clause of the Fourteenth Amendment, and that [this section] violated that Clause . . .

The Court of Appeals for the Fifth Circuit

upheld the District Court's injunction. . . .

The Fourteenth Amendment provides that "[n]o State shall . . . deprive any person of life, liberty, or property, without due process of law; nor deny to *any person within its jurisdiction* the equal protection of the laws." . . . (Emphasis added.) Appellants argue at the outset that undocumented aliens, because of their immigration status, are not "persons within the jurisdiction" of the State of Texas, and that they therefore have no right to the equal protection of Texas law. We reject this argument. . . .

. . . The Equal Protection Clause was intended to work nothing less than the abolition of all caste-based and invidious class-based legislation. That objective is fundamentally at odds with the power the State asserts here to classify persons subject to its laws as nonetheless excepted from its protection.

Although the congressional debate concerning . . . the Fourteenth Amendment was limited, that debate clearly confirms the understanding that the phrase "within its jurisdiction" was intended in a broad sense to offer the guarantee of equal protection to all within a State's boundaries, and to all upon whom the State would impose the obligations of its laws. Indeed, it appears from those debates that Congress, by using the phrase "person within its jurisdiction," sought expressly to ensure that the equal protection of the laws was provided to the alien population. Representative Bingham reported to the House of the draft resolution of the Joint Committee of Fifteen on Reconstruction (H.R. 63) that was to become the Fourteenth Amendment. . . . Two days later, Bingham posed the following question in support of the resolution:

Is it not essential to the unity of the people that the citizens of each State shall be entitled to all the privileges and immunities of citizens in the several States? Is it not essential to the unity of the Government and the unity of the people that all persons, *whether citizens or strangers, within this land,* shall have equal protection in every State in this Union in the rights of life and liberty and property?"

. . . Our conclusion that the illegal aliens who are plaintiffs in these cases may claim the benefit of the Fourteenth Amendment's guarantee of equal protection only begins the inquiry. The more difficult question is whether the Equal Protection Clause has been violated by the refusal of the State of Texas to reimburse local school boards for the education of children who cannot demonstrate that their presence within the United States is lawful, or by the imposition by those school boards of the burden of tuition on those children. It is to this question that we now turn. . . .

. . . In applying the Equal Protection Clause to most forms of state action, we thus seek only the assurance that the classification at issue bears some fair relationship to a legitimate public purpose.

Of course, undocumented status is not irrelevant to any proper legislative goal. Nor is undocumented status an absolutely immutable characteristic since it is the product of conscious, indeed unlawful, action. But [this statute] is directed against children, and imposes its discriminatory burden on the basis of a legal characteristic over which children can have little control. It is thus difficult to conceive of a rational justification for penalizing these children for their presence within the United States. Yet that appears to be precisely the effect of [this statute].

Public education is not a "right" granted to individuals by the Constitution. *San Antonio Independent School Dist. v. Rodriguez* . . . (1973). But neither is it merely some governmental "benefit" indistinguishable from other forms of social welfare legislation. Both the importance of education in maintaining our basic institutions, and the lasting impact of its deprivation on the life of the child, mark the distinction. The "American people have always regarded education and [the] acquisition of knowledge as matters of supreme importance." *Meyer v. Nebraska* . . . (1923). We have recognized "the public schools as a most vital civic institution for the preservation of a democratic system of government," *Abington School District v. Schempp* . . . (1963) . . . and as the primary vehicle for transmitting "the values on which our society rests." *Ambach v. Norwick* . . . (1979). "[A]s . . . pointed out early in our history, . . . some degree of education is necessary to prepare citizens to participate effectively and intelligently in our open political system if we are to preserve freedom and independence." *Wisconsin v. Yoder* . . . (1972). And these historic "perceptions of the public schools as inculcating fundamental values necessary to the maintenance of a democratic political system have been confirmed by the observations of social scientists." *Ambach v. Norwick.* . . . In addition, education provides the basic tools by which individuals might lead economically productive lives to the benefit of us all. In sum, education has a fundamental role in maintaining the fabric of our society. We cannot ignore the significant social costs borne by our Nation when select groups are denied the means to absorb the values and skills upon which our social order rests.

In addition to the pivotal role of education in sustaining our political and cultural heritage, denial of education to some isolated group of children poses an affront to one of the goals of the Equal Protection Clause: the abolition of governmental barriers presenting unreasonable obstacles to advancement on the basis of individual merit. Paradoxically, by depriving the children of any disfavored group of an education, we foreclose the means by which that group might raise the level of esteem in which it is held by the majority. But more directly, "education prepares individuals to be self-reliant and self-sufficient participants in society." *Wisconsin v. Yoder.* . . . Illiteracy is an enduring disability. The inability to read and write will handicap the individual deprived of a basic education each and every day of his life. The inestimable toll of that deprivation on the social, economic, intellectual, and psychological well-being of the individual, and the obstacle it poses to individual achievement, make it most difficult to reconcile the cost or the principle of a status-based denial of basic education with the framework of equality embodied in the Equal Protection Clause. What we said 28 years ago in *Brown v. Board of Education,* . . . (1954), still holds true:

Today, education is perhaps the most important function of state and local governments. Compulsory school attendance laws and the great expenditures for education both demonstrate our recognition of the importance of education to our democratic society. It is required in the performance of our most basic public

responsibilities, even service in the armed forces. It is the very foundation of good citizenship. Today it is a principal instrument in awakening the child to cultural values, in preparing him for later professional training, and in helping him to adjust normally to his environment. In these days, it is doubtful that any child may reasonably be expected to succeed in life if he is denied the opportunity of an education. Such an opportunity, where the state has undertaken to provide it, is a right which must be made available to all on equal terms.". . .

. . . [A]ppellants appear to suggest that the State may seek to protect itself from an influx of illegal immigrants. While a State might have an interest in mitigating the potentially harsh economic effects of sudden shifts in population, [this statute] hardly offers an effective method of dealing with an urgent demographic or economic problem. There is no evidence in the record suggesting that illegal entrants impose any significant burden on the State's economy. To the contrary, the available evidence suggests that illegal aliens underutilize public services, while contributing their labor to the local economy and tax money to the state fisc. . . . The dominant incentive for illegal entry into the State of Texas is the availability of employment; few if any illegal immigrants come to this country, or presumably to the State of Texas, in order to avail themselves of a free education. Thus, even making the doubtful assumption that the net impact of illegal aliens on the economy of the State is negative, we think it clear that "[c]harging tuition to undocumented children constitutes a ludicrously ineffectual attempt to stem the tide of illegal immigration," at least when compared with the alternative of prohibiting the employment of illegal aliens. . . .

Accordingly, the judgment of the Court of Appeals in each of these cases is *Affirmed.*

Justice *Marshall,* concurring.

While I join the Court's opinion, I do so without in any way retreating from my opinion in *San Antonio Independent School District v. Rodriguez.* . . . I continue to believe that an individual's interest in education is fundamental, and that this view is amply supported "by the unique status accorded public education by our society, and by the close relationship between education and some of our most basic constitutional values.". . . Furthermore, I believe that the facts of these cases demonstrate the wisdom of rejecting a rigidified approach to equal protection analysis, and of employing an approach that allows for varying levels of scrutiny depending upon "the constitutional and societal importance of the interest adversely affected and the recognized invidiousness of the basis upon which the particular classification is drawn.". . . It continues to be my view that a class-based denial of public education is utterly incompatible with the Equal Protection Clause of the Fourteenth Amendment.

Justice *Blackmun,* concurring.

I join the opinion and judgment of the Court.

Like Justice Powell, I believe that the children involved in this litigation "should not be left on the streets uneducated.". . . I write separately, however, because in my view the nature of the interest at stake is crucial to the proper resolution of these cases.

The "fundamental rights" aspect of the Court's equal protection analysis—the now-familiar concept that governmental classifications bearing on certain interests must be closely scrutinized—has been the subject of some controversy. . . .

[This controversy], combined with doubts about the judiciary's ability to make fine distinctions in assessing the effects of complex social policies, led the Court in *Rodriguez* to articulate a firm rule: fundamental rights are those that "explicitly or implicitly [are] guaranteed by the Constitution.". . . It therefore squarely rejected the notion that "an ad hoc determination as to the social or economic importance" of a given interest is relevant to the level of scrutiny accorded classifications involving that interest, . . . and made clear that "[i]t is not the province of this Court to create substantive constitutional rights in the name of guaranteeing equal protection of the laws.". . .

I joined Justice Powell's opinion for the Court in *Rodriguez,* and I continue to believe that it provides the appropriate model for

resolving most equal protection disputes. Classifications infringing substantive constitutional rights necessarily will be invalid, if not by force of the Equal Protection Clause, then through operation of other provisions of the Constitution. Conversely, classifications bearing on non-constitutional interests—even those involving "the most basic economic needs of impoverished human beings.". . .—generally are not subject to special treatment under the Equal Protection Clause, because they are not distinguishable in any relevant way from other regulations in "the area of economics and social welfare."

With all this said, however, I believe the Court's experience has demonstrated that the *Rodriguez* formulation does not settle every issue of "fundamental rights" arising under the Equal Protection Clause. Only a pedant would insist that there are *no* meaningful distinctions among the multitude of social and political interests regulated by the States, and *Rodriguez* does not stand for quite so absolute a proposition. To the contrary, *Rodriguez* implicitly acknowledged that certain interests, though not constitutionally guaranteed, must be accorded a special place in equal protection analysis. Thus, the Court's decisions long have accorded strict scrutiny to classifications bearing on the right to vote in state elections, and *Rodriguez* confirmed the "constitutional underpinnings of the right to equal treatment in the voting process." . . . Yet "the right to vote, *per se,* is not a constitutionally protected right." . . . Instead, regulation of the electoral process receives unusual scrutiny because "the right to exercise the franchise in a free and unimpaired manner is preservative of other basic civil and political rights." . . . In other words, the right to vote is accorded extraordinary treatment because it is, in equal protection terms, an extraordinary right: a citizen cannot hope to achieve any meaningful degree of individual political equality if granted an inferior right of participation in the political process. Those denied the vote are relegated, by state fiat, in a most basic way to second-class status. . . .

In my view, when the State provides an education to some and denies it to others, it immediately and inevitably creates class distinctions of a type fundamentally inconsistent with those purposes, mentioned above, of the Equal Protection Clause. Children denied an education are placed at a permanent and insurmountable competitive disadvantage, for an uneducated child is denied even the opportunity to achieve. And when those children are members of an identifiable group, that group—through the State's action—will have been converted into a discrete underclass. Other benefits provided by the State, such as housing and public assistance, are of course important; to an individual in immediate need, they may be more desirable than the right to be educated. But classifications involving the complete denial of education are in a sense unique, for they strike at the heart of equal protection values by involving the State in the creation of permanent class distinctions. . . . In a sense, then, denial of an education is the analogue of denial of the right to vote: the former relegates the individual to second-class social status; the latter places him at a permanent political disadvantage.

This conclusion is fully consistent with *Rodriguez.* The Court there reserved judgment on the constitutionality of a state system that "occasioned an absolute denial of educational opportunities to any of its children," noting that "no charge fairly could be made that the system . . . fails to provide each child with an opportunity to acquire . . . basic minimal skills." . . . And it cautioned that in a case "involv[ing] the most persistent and difficult questions of educational policy, . . . [the] Court's lack of specialized knowledge and experience counsels against premature interference with the informed judgments made at the state and local levels." . . . Thus *Rodriguez* held, and the Court now reaffirms, that "a State need not justify by compelling necessity every variation in the manner in which education is provided to its population." . . . Similarly, it is undeniable that education is not a "fundamental right" in the sense that it is constitutionally guaranteed. Here, however, the State has undertaken to provide an education to most of the children residing within its borders. And, in contrast to the situation in *Rodriguez*, it does not take an advanced degree to predict the effects of a complete denial of education upon those children targeted by the State's classification. In such circumstances,

the voting decisions suggest that the State must offer something more than a rational basis for its classification. . . .

Chief Justice *Burger*, with whom Justice *White*, Justice *Rehnquist*, and Justice *O'Connor* join, dissenting.

Were it our business to set the Nation's social policy, I would agree without hesitation that it is senseless for an enlightened society to deprive any children—including illegal aliens—of an elementary education. I fully agree that it would be folly—and wrong—to tolerate creation of a segment of society made up of illiterate persons, many having a limited or no command of our language. However, the Constitution does not constitute us as "Platonic Guardians" nor does it vest in this Court the authority to strike down laws because they do not meet our standards of desirable social policy, "wisdom," or "common sense." . . . We trespass on the assigned function of the political branches under our structure of limited and separated powers when we assume a policymaking role as the Court does today.

The Court makes no attempt to disguise that it is acting to make up for Congress' lack of "effective leadership" in dealing with the serious national problems caused by the influx of uncountable millions of illegal aliens across our borders. . . . The failure of enforcement of the immigration laws over more than a decade and the inherent difficulty and expense of sealing our vast borders have combined to create a grave socioeconomic dilemma. It is a dilemma that has not yet even been fully assessed, let alone addressed. However, it is not the function of the Judiciary to provide "effective leadership" simply because the political branches of government fail to do so.

The Court's holding today manifests the justly criticized judicial tendency to attempt speedy and wholesale formulation of "remedies" for the failures—or simply the laggard pace—of the political processes of our system of government. The Court employs, and in my view abuses, the Fourteenth Amendment in an effort to become an omnipotent and omniscient problem solver. That the motives for doing so are noble and compassionate does not alter the fact that the Court distorts our constitutional function to make amends for the defaults of others. . . .

The Court acknowledges that, except in those cases when state classifications disadvantage a "suspect class" or impinge upon a "fundamental right," the Equal Protection Clause permits a state "substantial latitude" in distinguishing between different groups of persons. . . . Moreover, the Court expressly—and correctly—rejects any suggestion that illegal aliens are a suspect class, . . . or that education is a fundamental right. . . . Yet by patching together bits and pieces of what might be termed quasi-suspect-class and quasi-fundamental-rights analysis, the Court spins out a theory custom-tailored to the facts of these cases.

In the end, we are told little more than that the level of scrutiny employed to strike down the Texas law applies only when illegal alien children are deprived of a public education. . . . If ever a court was guilty of an unabashedly result-oriented approach, this case is a prime example. . . .

Once it is conceded—as the Court does—that illegal aliens are not a suspect class, and that education is not a fundamental right, our inquiry should focus on and be limited to whether the legislative classification at issue bears a rational relationship to a legitimate state purpose. . . .

It is significant that the Federal Government has seen fit to exclude illegal aliens from numerous social welfare programs, such as the food stamp program, . . . the old-age assistance, aid to families with dependent children, aid to the blind, aid to the permanently and totally disabled, and supplemental security income programs, . . . the Medicare hospital insurance benefits program, . . . and the Medicaid hospital insurance benefits for the aged and disabled program. . . . Although these exclusions do not conclusively demonstrate the constitutionality of the State's use of the same classification for comparable purposes, at the very least they tend to support the rationality of excluding illegal alien residents of a state from such programs so as to preserve the state's finite revenues for the benefit of lawful residents. . . .

Denying a free education to illegal alien children is not a choice I would make were I a legislator. Apart from compassionate considerations, the long-range costs of excluding any children from the public schools may well outweigh the costs of educating them. But that is not the issue; the fact that there are sound *policy* arguments against the Texas Legislature's choice does not render that choice an unconstitutional one. . . .

The Constitution does not provide a cure for every social ill, nor does it vest judges with a mandate to try to remedy every social problem. . . . Moreover, when this Court rushes in to remedy what it perceives to be the failings of the political processes, it deprives those processes of an opportunity to function. When the political institutions are not forced to exercise constitutionally allocated powers and responsibilities, those powers, like muscles not used, tend to atrophy. Today's cases, I regret to say, present yet another example of unwarranted judicial action which in the long run tends to contribute to the weakening of our political processes.

Congress, "vested by the Constitution with the responsibility of protecting our borders and legislating with respect to aliens," . . . bears primary responsibility for addressing the problems occasioned by the millions of illegal aliens flooding across our southern border. Similarly, it is for Congress, and not this Court, to assesss the "social costs borne by our Nation when select groups are denied the means to absorb the values and skills upon which our social order rests." . . . While the "specter of a permanent caste" of illegal Mexican residents of the United States is indeed a disturbing one, . . . it is but one segment of a larger problem, which is for the political branches to solve. I find it difficult to believe that Congress would long tolerate such a self-destructive result—that it would fail to deport these illegal alien families or to provide for the education of their children. Yet instead of allowing the political processes to run their course—albeit with some delay—the Court seeks to do Congress' job for it, compensating for congressional inaction. It is not unreasonable to think that this encourages the political branches to pass their problems to the Judiciary.

The solution to this seemingly intractable problem is to defer to the political processes, unpalatable as that may be to some.

Case 9.b *Goldberg* v. *Kelly:* Welfare, Prior Notice, and Property

U.S. Supreme Court

The City of New York wished to terminate federally assisted programs, such as Aid to Families with Dependent Children, without prior notice or a hearing. Justice Brennan argued in 1970 that a hearing is necessary for due process of law to be met. He further opined that welfare payments are not "gratuities" to be taken away at will but fundamental entitlements, more like "property."

Justice *Brennan,* writing for the majority:

The constitutional issue to be decided . . . is the narrow one whether the Due Process Clause requires that the recipient be afforded an evidentiary hearing before the termination of benefits. The District Court held that only a pre-termination evidentiary hearing would satisfy the constitutional command, and rejected the argument of the state and city officials that the combination of the post-termination "fair hearing" with the informal pre-termination review disposed of all due process claims. The court said: "While post-termination review is relevant, there is one overpowering fact which controls here. By hypothesis, a welfare recipient is destitute, without funds or assets. . . . Suffice it to say that to cut off a welfare recipient in the face of . . . 'brutal need' without a prior hearing of some sort is unconscionable, unless overwhelming considerations justify it." . . . The court rejected the argument that the need to protect the public's tax revenues supplied the requisite "overwhelming consideration." "Against the justified desire to protect public funds must be weighed the individual's overpowering need in this unique situation not to be wrongfully deprived of assistance. . . . While the problem of additional expense must be kept in mind, it does not justify denying a hearing meeting the ordinary standards of due process. Under all the circumstances, we hold that due process requires an adequate hearing before termination of welfare benefits, and the fact that there is a later constitutionally fair proceeding does not alter the result." . . .

Appellant does not contend that procedural due process is not applicable to the termination of welfare benefits. Such benefits are a matter of statutory entitlement for persons qualified to receive them.[1] Their termination involves state action that adjudicates important rights. The constitutional challenge cannot be answered by an argument that public assistance benefits are "a 'privilege' and not a 'right'." . . . Relevant constitutional restraints apply as much to the withdrawal of public assistance benefits as to disqualification for unemployment compensation; . . . or to denial of a tax exemption; . . . or to discharge from public employment. The extent to which procedural due process must be afforded the recipient is influenced by the extent to which he may be "condemned to suffer grievous loss," . . . and depends upon whether the recipient's interest in avoiding that loss outweighs the governmental interest in summary adjudication. Accordingly, as we said in *Cafeteria & Restaurant Workers Union, etc. v. McElroy* (1961), . . . "consideration of what procedures due process may require under any given set of circumstances must begin with a determination of the precise nature of the government function involved as well as of the private interest that has been affected by governmental action." . . .

It is true of course, that some governmental benefits may be administratively terminated without affording the recipient a pre-termination evidentiary hearing.[2] But we agree with the District Court that when welfare is discontinued, only a pre-termination evidentiary hearing provides the recipient with procedural due process. . . . Thus the crucial factor in this context—a factor not present in the case of the blacklisted government contractor, the discharged government employee, the taxpayer denied a tax exemption, or virtually anyone else whose governmental entitlements are ended—is that termination of aid pending resolution of a controversy over eligibility may deprive an eligible recipient of the very means by which to live while he waits. Since he lacks independent resources, his situation becomes immediately desperate. His need to concentrate upon finding the means for daily subsistence, in turn, adversely affects his ability to seek redress from the welfare bureaucracy.

Moreover, important governmental interests are promoted by affording recipients a pre-termination evidentiary hearing. From its founding the Nation's basic commitment has been to foster the dignity and well-being of all persons within its borders. We have come to recognize that forces not within the control of the poor contribute to their poverty. This perception, against the background of our traditions, has significantly influenced the development of the contemporary public assistance system. Welfare, by meeting the basic demands of subsistence, can help bring within the reach of the poor the same opportunities that are available to others to participate meaningfully in the life of the community. At the same time, welfare guards against the societal malaise that may flow from a widespread sense of unjustified frustration and insecurity. Public assistance, then, is not mere charity, but a means to "promote the general Welfare, and secure the Blessings of Liberty to ourselves and our Posterity." The same governmental interests that counsel the provision of welfare, counsel as well its uninterrupted provision to those eligible to receive it; pre-termination evidentiary hearings are indispensable to that end.

Appellant does not challenge the force of these considerations but argues that they are outweighed by countervailing governmental interests in conserving fiscal and administrative resources. These interests, the argument goes, justify the delay of any evidentiary hearing until after discontinuance of the grants. Summary adjudication protects the public fisc by stopping payments promptly upon discovery of reason to believe that a recipient is no longer eligible. Since most terminations are accepted without challenge, summary adjudication also conserves both the fisc and administrative time and energy by reducing the number of evidentiary hearings actually held.

We agree with the District Court, however, that these governmental interests are not overriding in the welfare context. The requirement of a prior hearing doubtless involves some greater expense, and the benefits paid to ineligible recipients pending decision at the hearing probably cannot be recouped, since these recipients are likely to be judgment-proof. But the State is not without weapons to minimize these increased costs. Much of the drain on fiscal and administrative resources can be reduced by developing procedures for prompt pre-termination hearings and by skillful use of personnel and facilities. Indeed, the very provision for a post-termination evidentiary hearing in New York's Home Relief program is itself cogent evidence that the State recognizes the primacy of the public interest in correct eligibility determinations and therefore in the provision of procedural safeguards. Thus, the interest of the eligible recipient in uninterrupted receipt of public assistance, coupled with the State's interest that his payments not be erroneously terminated, clearly outweighs the State's competing concern to prevent any increase in its fiscal and administrative burdens. As the District Court correctly concluded, "the stakes are simply too high for the welfare recipient, and the possibility for honest error or irritable misjudgment too great, to allow termination of aid without giving the recipient a chance, if he so desires, to be fully informed of the case against him so that he may contest its basis and produce evidence in rebuttal."

Notes

1. It may be realistic today to regard welfare entitlements as more like "property" than a "gratuity". Much of the existing wealth in this country takes the form of rights that do not fall

within traditional common-law concepts of property. It has been aptly noted that:

"Society today is built around entitlement. The automobile dealer has his franchise, the doctor and lawyer their professional licenses, the worker his union membership, contract, and pension rights, the executive his contract and stock options; all are devices to aid security and independence. Many of the most important of these entitlements now flow from government: subsidies to farmers and businessmen, routes for airlines and channels for television stations; long term contracts for defense, space, and education; social security pensions for individuals. Such sources of security, whether private or public, are no longer regarded as luxuries or gratuities; to the recipients they are essentials, fully deserved, and in no sense a form of charity. It is only the poor whose entitlements, although recognized by public policy, have not been effectively enforced."

Reich, *Individual Rights and Social Welfare: The Emerging Legal Issues,* 74 Yale L. J. 1245, 1255 (1965). See also Reich, *The New Property,* 73 Yale L. J. 733 (1964).

2. One Court of Appeals has stated: "In a wide variety of situations, it has long been recognized that where harm to the public is threatened, and the private interest infringed is reasonably deemed to be of less importance, an official body can take summary action pending a later hearing."

Case 9.c   *Wyman* v. *James:* Welfare Visits as Search and Seizure

U. S. Supreme Court

Barbara James, a recipient of Aid to Families with Dependent Children, refused a home visit by a caseworker. On that basis, Commissioner Wyman of the New York Department of Social Services terminated her benefits. James, however, argued that such a visit amounted to an unwarranted search of her home in violation of the Fourth and Fifth Amendments. In 1971 Justice Blackmun overruled the District Court of New York. In his decision against James, he asserted that home visitation constitutes a reasonable administration tool. By considering welfare payments a form of charity, rather than a "right" or entitlement, Blackmun needed to be concerned only with reasonableness, rather than with the more difficult strict scrutiny test.

Justice *Blackmun,* arguing for the majority:

I

Plaintiff Barbara James is the mother of a son, Maurice, who was born in May 1967. They reside in New York City. Mrs. James first applied for AFDC assistance shortly before Maurice's birth. A caseworker made a visit to her apartment at that time without objection. The assistance was authorized.

Two years later, on May 8, 1969, a caseworker wrote Mrs. James that she would visit her home on May 14. Upon receipt of this advice, Mrs. James telephoned the worker that, although she was willing to supply information "reasonable and relevant" to her need for public assistance, any discussion was not to take place at her home. The worker told Mrs. James that she was required by law to visit in her home and that refusal to permit the visit would result in the termination of assistance. Permission was still denied.

On May 13 the City Department of Social Services sent Mrs. James a notice of intent to discontinue assistance because of the visitation refusal. The notice advised the beneficiary of her right to a hearing before a review officer. The hearing was requested and was held on May 27. Mrs. James appeared with an attorney at that hearing. They continued to refuse permission for a worker to visit the James home, but again expressed willingness to cooperate and to permit visits elsewhere. The review officer ruled that the refusal was a proper ground for the termination of assistance. His written decision stated:

> "The home visit which Mrs. James refuses to permit is for the purpose of determining if there are any changes in her situation that might affect her eligibility to continue to receive Public Assistance, or that might affect the amount of such assistance, and to see if there are any social services which the Department of Social Services can provide to the family."

A notice of termination was issued on June 2.

Thereupon, without seeking a hearing at the state level, Mrs. James, individually and on behalf of Maurice, and purporting to act on behalf of all other persons similarly situated, instituted the present civil rights suit. She alleged the denial of rights guaranteed to her under the First, Third, Fourth, Fifth, Sixth, Ninth, Tenth, and Fourteenth Amendments, and under Subchapters IV and XVI of the Social Security Act and regulations issued thereunder. She further alleged that she and her son have no income, resources, or support other than the benefits received under the AFDC program. . . .

II

When a case involves a home and some type of official intrusion into that home, as this case appears to do, an immediate and natural reaction is one of concern about Fourth Amend-

ment rights and the protection which that Amendment is intended to afford. Its emphasis indeed is upon one of the most precious aspects of personal security in the home: "The right of the people to be secure in their persons, houses, papers, and effects. . . ." This Court has characterized that right as "basic to a free society." And over the years the Court consistently has been most protective of the privacy of the dwelling. . . .

III

This natural and quite proper protective attitude, however, is not a factor in this case, for the seemingly obvious and simple reason that we are not concerned here with any search by the New York social service agency in the Fourth Amendment meaning of that term. It is true that the governing statute and regulations appear to make mandatory the initial home visit and the subsequent periodic "contacts" (which may include home visits) for the inception and continuance of aid. It is also true that the caseworker's posture in the home visit is perhaps, in a sense, both rehabilitative and investigative. But this latter aspect, we think, is given too broad a character and far more emphasis than it deserves if it is equated with a search in the traditional criminal law context. We note, too, that the visitation in itself is not forced or compelled, and that the beneficiary's denial of permission is not a criminal act. If consent to the visitation is withheld, no visitation takes place. The aid then never begins or merely ceases, as the case may be. There is no entry of the home and there is no search.

IV

If however, we were to assume that a caseworker's home visit, before or subsequent to the beneficiary's initial qualification for benefits, somehow (perhaps because the average beneficiary might feel she is in no position to refuse consent to the visit), and despite its interview nature, does possess some of the characteristics of a search in the traditional sense, we nevertheless conclude that the visit does not fall within the Fourth Amendment's proscription. This is because it does not descend to the level of unreasonableness. It is unreasonableness which is the Fourth Amendment's standard. . . .

There are a number of factors that compel us to conclude that the home visit proposed for Mrs. James is not unreasonable:

1. The public's interest in this particular segment of the area of assistance to the unfortunate is protection and aid for the dependent child whose family requires such aid for that child. The focus is on the *child* and, further, it is on the child who is *dependent.* There is no more worthy object of the public's concern. The dependent child's needs are paramount, and only with hesitancy would we relegate those needs, in the scale of comparative values, to a position secondary to what the mother claims as her rights.

2. The agency, with tax funds provided from federal as well as from state sources, is fulfilling a public trust. The State, working through its qualified welfare agency, has appropriate and paramount interest and concern in seeing and assuring that the intended and proper objects of that tax-produced assistance are the ones who benefit from the aid it dispenses. Surely it is not unreasonable, in the Fourth Amendment sense or in any other sense of that term, that the State have at its command a gentle means, of limited extent and of practical and considerate application, of achieving that assurance.

3. One who dispenses purely private charity naturally has an interest in and expects to know how his charitable funds are utilized and put to work. The public, when it is the provider, rightly expects the same. It might well expect more, because of the trust aspect of public funds, and the recipient, as well as the caseworker, has not only an interest but an obligation.

4. The emphasis of the New York statutes and regulations is upon the home, upon "close contact" with the beneficiary, upon restoring the aid recipient "to a condition of self-support," and upon the relief of his distress.

The federal emphasis is no different. It is upon "assistance and rehabilitation," upon maintaining and strengthening family life, and upon "maximum self-support and personal independence consistent with the maintenance of continuing parental care and protection. . . ." It requires cooperation from the state agency upon specified standards and in specified ways. . . .

5. The means employed by the New York agency are significant. Mrs. James received written notice several days in advance of the intended home visit.[1] . . .

6. Mrs. James, in fact, on this record presents no specific complaint of any unreasonable intrusion of her home. . . . She alleges only, in general and nonspecific terms, that on previous visits and, on information and belief, on visitation at the home of other aid recipients, "questions concerning personal relationships, beliefs and behavior are raised and pressed which are unnecessary for a determination of continuing eligibility." . . . What Mrs. James appears to want from the agency that provides her and her infant son with the necessities for life is the right to receive those necessities upon her own informational terms, to utilize the Fourth Amendment as a wedge for imposing those terms, and to avoid questions of any kind. . . .

V

Our holding today does not mean, of course, that a termination of benefits upon refusal of a home visit is to be upheld against constitutional challenge under all conceivable circumstances. The early morning mass raid upon homes of welfare recipients is not unknown. But that is not this case. Facts of that kind present another case for another day.

We therefore conclude that the home visitation as structured by the New York statutes and regulations is a reasonable administrative tool; that it serves a valid and proper administrative purpose for the dispensation of the AFDC program; that it is not an unwarranted invasion of personal privacy; and that it violates no right guaranteed by the Fourth Amendment. . . .

Justice *Douglas,* dissenting:

We are living in a society where one of the most important forms of property is government largesse which some call the "new property." The payrolls of government are but one aspect of that "new property." Defense contracts, highway contracts, and the other multifarious forms of contracts are another part. So are subsidies to air, rail, and other carriers. So are disbursements by government for scientific research. So are TV and radio licenses to use the air space which of course is part of the public domain. Our concern here is not with those subsidies but with grants that directly or indirectly implicate the *home life* of the recipients.

In 1969 roughly 127 billion dollars were spent by the federal, state, and local governments on "social welfare." To farmers alone almost four billion dollars were paid, in part for not growing certain crops. Almost 129,000 farmers received $5,000 or more, their total benefits exceeding $1,450,000,000. Those payments were in some instances very large, a few running a million or more a year. But the majority were payments under $5,000 each.

Yet almost every beneficiary whether rich or poor, rural or urban, has a "house"—one of the places protected by the Fourth Amendment against "unreasonable searches and seizures." The question in this case is whether receipt of largesse from the government makes the *home* of the beneficiary subject to access by an inspector of the agency of oversight, even though the beneficiary objects to the intrusion and even though the Fourth Amendment's procedure for access to one's *house* or *home* is not followed. The penalty here is not, of course, invasion of the privacy of Barbara James, only her loss of federal or state largesse. That, however, is merely rephrasing the problem. Whatever the semantics, the central question is whether the government by force of its largesse has the power to "buy up" rights guaranteed by the Constitution. But for the assertion of her constitutional right, Barbara James in this case would have received the welfare benefit. . . .

. . . In *See v. City of Seattle* (1967) we [decided] that the "businessman, like the occupant of a residence, has a constitutional right to go about his business free from unreasonable official entries upon his private commercial property." There is not the slightest hint in *See* that the Government could condition a business license on the "consent" of the licensee to the administrative searches we held violated the Fourth Amendment. It is a strange jurisprudence indeed which safeguards the businessman at his place of work from warrantless searches but will not do the same for a mother in her *home*.

Is a search of her home without a warrant made "reasonable" merely because she is dependent on government largesse?

Judge Skelly Wright has stated the problem succinctly:

"Welfare has long been considered the equivalent of charity and its recipients have been subjected to all kinds of dehumanizing experiences in the government's effort to police its welfare payments. In fact, over half a billion dollars are expended annually for administration and policing in connection with the Aid to Families with Dependent Children program. Why such large sums are necessary for administration and policing has never been adequately explained. No such sums are spent policing the government subsidies granted to farmers, airlines, steamship companies, and junk mail dealers, to name but a few. The truth is that in this subsidy area society has simply adopted a double standard, one for aid to business and the farmer and a different one for welfare." Poverty, Minorities, and Respect For Law, 1970 Duke L. J. 425, 437–438.

If the welfare recipient was not Barbara James but a prominent, affluent cotton or wheat farmer receiving benefit payments for not growing crops, would not the approach be different? Welfare in aid of dependent children, like social security and unemployment benefits, has an aura of suspicion. There doubtless are frauds in every sector of public welfare whether the recipient be a Barbara James or someone who is prominent or influential. But constitutional rights—here the privacy of the *home*—are obviously not dependent on the poverty or on the affluence of the beneficiary. It is the precincts of the *home* that the Fourth Amendment protects; and their privacy is as important to the lowly as to the mighty. . . .

I would place the same restrictions on inspectors entering the *homes* of welfare beneficiaries as are on inspectors entering the *homes* of those on the payroll of government, or the *homes* of those who contract with the government, or the *homes* of those who work for those having government contracts. The values of the *home* protected by the Fourth Amendment are not peculiar to capitalism as we have known it; they are equally relevant to the new form of socialism which we are entering. Moreover, as the numbers of functionaries and inspectors multiply, the need for protec-

tion of the individual becomes indeed more essential if the values of a free society are to remain. . . .

Note

1. It is true that the record contains 12 affidavits, all essentially identical, of aid recipients (other than Mrs. James) which recite that a caseworker "most often" comes without notice; that when he does, the plans the recipient had for that time cannot be carried out; that the visit is "very embarrassing to me if the caseworker comes when I have company"; and that the caseworker "sometimes asks very personal questions" in front of children.

Affirmative Action, Comparable Worth, and Sexual Harassment

Discrimination

In its most general sense, to discriminate simply means to pick and choose, to distinguish, to differentiate. There is nothing wrong with that per se. However, there are certain categories—what the courts call "constitutionally suspect classes"—for which it is typically considered immoral to pick and choose, such as on the basis of race, gender, religion, sexual orientation, etc. But even this is not necesssarily the case. Where these categories constitute a *Bona Fide Occupational Qualification* (or BFOQ), selection on that ground in employment is acceptable. Would anyone feel it wrong to hire for the job of priest or rabbi and not discriminate on the basis of the applicant's religion?

We seem to be left, then, with the claim that discrimination is morally wrong when the category is not relevant to, for example, a job or to school admission. But even then there are questions. Is "relevancy" to the job the only issue? Slavery was immoral independent of the fact that the criterion for being a slave (i.e., being black) was not relevant. Had we chosen slaves on some relevant criteria, would the institution of slavery then be morally acceptable? (See the article in this chapter by Wasserstrom.) To find out what is really wrong with discrimination, we must look at its purposes. Discrimination against women and people of color is wrong because its intent is to exclude them from positions of money and power.

There are two basic ways to look at the issue of discrimination. From a traditional liberal perspective, discrimination is wrong because it violates the *principle of equality:* like things should be treated alike and different things in accordance with their differences. Hence, discrimination is wrong because it makes irrelevant distinctions. Marxist theory, on the other hand, starts from the notion that all societies are class divided: one class dominates, exploits, and obtains the surplus wealth produced by a dependent class. Here discrimination is wrong because it functions to maintain that system of exploitation. In other words, discrimination against women and people of color exists, and is morally unacceptable, because it helps to maintain an unfair distribution of power and property.

Affirmative Action

One strategy put forward to deal with discrimination in business and educational settings is *affirmative action.* Rather than simply sitting back and ensuring *equal opportunity* by passive nondiscrimination (i.e., by making sure no one in the company actually discriminates), affirmative action attempts to deal with the unfair race/gender distribution of power and wealth in our society by actively seeking to hire or include women and people of color.

Affirmative action can be employed on either a *case by case* or *quota* basis. With the case-by-case approach, an institution attempts to achieve greater race/gender balance by hiring as many qualified applicants as they can find, proportionate to their needs. There are no hard and fast numbers, and no pressure or goals to hire a specific number of people. This method gives the institution a great degree of flexibility to deal with the problem, while making sure to get only the best qualified candidates. Unfortunately, a case-by-case approach is of little use with recalcitrant institutions. If an institution does not wish to integrate, a case-by-case plan will provide little incentive for change. The value of numerical goals or hard quotas is found in the ability to force integration and change in uncooperative institutions. Change is more rapid and apparent when little room for discretion is allowed. Unfortunately, with hard quotas, the pressure entails a greater chance that less qualified people will be hired to fill the slots.

One of the first important legal decisions on affirmative action was *DeFunis* v. *Overgaard* (1973). The Supreme Court of Washington ruled that racial and ethnic classifications were not unconstitutional if a compelling state interest was involved. Since the need for more minority attorneys, judges, prosecutors, public officials, etc., constitutes such an interest, the classifications at the University of Washington Law School were held constitutional. The major Supreme Court decision, *Bakke* v. *Davis*

(1978), ruled, to the contrary, that quotas were not constitutionally acceptable. However, case-by-case methods, which treat each applicant as an individual and use race as only one factor, are constitutionally sound. The Court did grant, though, that quotas are acceptable when there is evidence that the institution has illegally discriminated in the past.

Those who favor affirmative action typically do so on grounds of compensation and social change. As a group, women and people of color have been, and still are, discriminated against. Hence affirmative action is justified as fair compensation. In response, it is often argued that compensation is not just if the person paying the compensation (e.g., the white man who does not get the job) never harmed anyone or if the person being compensated never actually suffered any discrimination.

As for social change, it is typically argued that affirmative action rapidly increases the number of women and people of color in positions of power. Racism, sexism, and discrimination will be ended only by a fundamental shift in power, with women and people of color receiving fair opportunities. In response, many people argue that affirmative action engenders anger and resentment and hence actually brings out racism and sexism.

Those who disagree with affirmative action usually maintain that it violates the rights of white men. In response, it is argued that discrimination is wrong because of its purposes. Discriminating on the basis of race or gender is wrong when it perpetuates a system of racist/sexist domination, acceptable when it breaks down that system. Others argue against affirmative action based on merit: only the best and brightest should be considered. Of course, the concepts of "best" and "merit" are defined largely by white men. Furthermore, white men have the opportunity, given social and economic benefits, to "merit" or do better.

Comparable Worth

Another way to deal with gender discrimination is a *comparable worth* program. Since women are often channeled into lower-paying, less responsible careers—into "pink-collar" jobs, or what is often called "women's work"—it has been argued that they should be paid for those jobs salaries equal to those enjoyed by men in "comparable" occupations. In 1986 the State of Washington began such a program to adjust what it saw as a manifest inequality in pay between occupations that were male dominated and jobs requiring similar skills and training that were occupied predominantly by women.

Advocates of comparable worth consider it a matter of justice. Women have traditionally been pushed into lower-paying jobs with a biased wage system. Jobs, it is argued, should be evaluated objectively in terms of skills, responsibilities, training, risk, and other relevant criteria so that pay scales between traditionally male and traditionally female jobs can be fairly adjusted. Opponents to comparable worth argue either that women freely choose to enter these occupations or that the programs are impractical because such comparisons are vague and imprecise. It is responded, of course, that social pressures compel women into certain occupations and that the kinds of comparisons being made are not as contentious as some may think.

Sexual Harassment

Another form of discrimination, which until recently has been given only scant attention, is sexual harassment. Sexual harassment is not merely a matter of little jokes or inevitable flirtations at the office. Rather, sexual harassment has been a long-standing feature of our institutional structures and has served as a discriminatory practice to keep women out of positions of power. Title VII of the Civil Rights Act allows women to sue for damages for, among other things, sexual harassment. The courts have acknowledged that sexual harassment is part of a wider system that reinforces sexist attitudes about women and maintains inequality in employment.

Sexual harassment may involve unwelcome

sexual advances or unwanted verbal or be-havioral sexual conduct. In the most extreme situations, threats may be issued or job bene-fits offered in return for sexual favors. But harassment need not always be so dramatic. Leering, repeated lewd remarks, and offen-sive gestures can often seriously interfere with a woman's ability to perform her job. In gener-al, the less disturbing the activity is to the re-cipient, the more it has to be a repeated pat-tern of behavior in order to count as sexual harassment.

Sexual harassment may come from co-workers and peers, as well as from supervisors. It may even come about from a substantially sexist atmosphere. It is often claimed that pornographic pictures and calendars, and even persistent and pervasive sexist attitudes in the workplace, can constitute sexual harass-ment.

Men can also be sexually harassed. And when a man is denied a job, or otherwise in-hibited in his career, due to sexual harass-ment, whether from a woman or from another man, it is morally wrong. However, because harassment against men is quite rare and is not part of an institutional practice of discrimina-tion, it is given significantly less attention.

Overall, our society reflects pervasive dis-crimination—discrimination based on race, gender, religion, sexual orientation, and more. Unfortunately, no matter what policies we may adopt, it is not likely to go away in the near future.

43.   A Defense of Programs of Preferential Treatment

Richard Wasserstrom

Richard Wasserstrom presents a limited defense of preferential treatment pro-grams by showing how some of the major arguments against them—arguments based on justice—do not work. Wasserstrom responds to charges that preferen-tial treatment programs involve intellectual inconsistency and emphasize race and gender over the only important criterion: qualifications.

Many justifications of programs of preferen-tial treatment depend upon the claim that in one respect or another such programs have good consequences or that they are effective means by which to bring about some desirable end, e.g., an integrated, equalitarian society. I mean by "programs of preferential treatment" to refer to programs such as those at issue in the *Bakke* case—programs which set aside a certain number of places (for example, in a

From *National Forum (The Phi Kappa Phi Journal)*, vol. LVIII, no. 1 (Winter 1978), pp. 15–18. Reprinted by permission.

law school) as to which members of minority groups (for example, persons who are non-white or female) who possess certain minimum qualifications (in terms of grades and test scores) may be preferred for admission to those places over some members of the major-ity group who possess higher qualifications (in terms of grades and test scores).

Many criticisms of programs of preferential treatment claim that such programs, even if effective, are unjustifiable because they are in some important sense unfair or unjust. In this paper I present a limited defense of such pro-grams by showing that two of the chief argu-ments offered for the unfairness or injustice of these programs do not work in the way or to the degree supposed by critics of these programs.

The first argument is this. Opponents of preferential treatment programs sometimes assert that proponents of these programs are guilty of intellectual inconsistency, if not racism or sexism. For, as is now readily acknowledged, at times past employers, universities, and many other social institutions did have racial or sexual quotas (when they did not practice overt racial or sexual exclusion), and many of those who were most concerned to bring about the eradication of those racial quotas are now untroubled by the new programs which reinstitute them. And this, it is claimed, is inconsistent. If it was wrong to take race or sex into account when blacks and women were the objects of racial and sexual policies and practices of exclusion, then it is wrong to take race or sex into account when the objects of the policies have their race or sex reversed. Simple considerations of intellectual consistency—of what it means to give racism or sexism as a reason for condemning these social policies and practices—require that what was a good reason then is still a good reason now.

The problem with this argument is that despite appearances, there is no inconsistency involved in holding both views. Even if contemporary preferential treatment programs which contain quotas are wrong, they are not wrong for the reasons that made quotas against blacks and women pernicious. The reason why is that the social realities do make an enormous difference. The fundamental evil of programs that discriminated against blacks or women was that these programs were a part of a larger social universe which systematically maintained a network of institutions which unjustifiably concentrated power, authority, and goods in the hands of white male individuals, and which systematically consigned blacks and women to subordinate positions in the society.

Whatever may be wrong with today's affirmative action programs and quota systems, it should be clear that the evil, if any, is just not the same. Racial and sexual minorities do not constitute the dominant social group. Nor is the conception of who is a fully developed member of the moral and social community one of an individual who is either female or black. Quotas which prefer women or blacks do not add to an already relatively overabundant supply of resources and opportunities at the disposal of members of these groups in the way in which the quotas of the past did maintain and augment the overabundant supply of resources and opportunities already available to white males.

The same point can be made in a somewhat different way. Sometimes people say that what was wrong, for example, with the system of racial discrimination in the South was that it took an irrelevant characteristic, namely race, and used it systematically to allocate social benefits and burdens of various sorts. The defect was the irrelevance of the characteristic used—race—for that meant that individuals ended up being treated in a manner that was arbitrary and capricious.

I do not think that was the central flaw at all. Take, for instance, the most hideous of the practices, human slavery. The primary thing that was wrong with the institution was not that the particular individuals who were assigned the place of slaves were assigned there arbitrarily because the assignment was made in virtue of an irrelevant characteristic, their race. Rather, it seems to me that the primary thing that was and is wrong with slavery is the practice itself—the fact of some individuals being able to own other individuals and all that goes with that practice. It would not matter by what criterion individuals were assigned; human slavery would still be wrong. And the same can be said for most if not all of the other discrete practices and institutions which comprised the system of racial discrimination even after human slavery was abolished. The practices were unjustifiable—they were oppressive—and they would have been so no matter how the assignment of victims had been made. What made it worse, still, was that the institutions and the supporting ideology all interlocked to create a system of human oppression whose effects on those living under it were as devastating as they were unjustifiable.

Again, if there is anything wrong with the programs of preferential treatment that have begun to flourish within the past ten years, it should be evident that the social realities in respect to the distribution of resources and opportunities make the difference. Apart from everything else, there is simply no way in which all of these programs taken together could plausibly be viewed as capable of relegating white males to the kind of genuinely oppressive status characteristically bestowed upon women and blacks by the dominant social institutions and ideology.

The second objection is that preferential treatment programs are wrong because they take race or sex into account rather than the only thing that does matter—that is, an individual's qualifications. What all such programs have in common and what makes them all objectionable, so this argument goes, is that they ignore the persons who are more qualified by bestowing a preference on those who are less qualified in virtue of their being either black or female.

There are, I think, a number of things wrong with this objection based on qualifications, and not the least of them is that we do not live in a society in which there is even the serious pretense of a qualification requirement for many jobs of substantial power and authority. Would anyone claim, for example, that the persons who comprise the judiciary are there because they are the most qualified lawyers or the most qualified persons to be judges? Would anyone claim that Henry Ford II is the head of the Ford Motor Company because he is the most qualified person for the job? Part of what is wrong with even talking about qualifications and merit is that the argument derives some of its force from the erroneous notion that we would have a meritocracy were it not for programs of preferential treatment. In fact, the higher one goes in terms of prestige, power and the like, the less qualifications seem ever to be decisive. It is only for certain jobs and certain places that qualifications are used to do more than establish the possession of certain minimum competencies.

But difficulties such as these to one side, there are theoretical difficulties as well which cut much more deeply into the argument about qualifications. To begin with, it is important to see that there is a serious inconsistency present if the person who favors "pure qualifications" does so on the ground that the most qualified ought to be selected because this promotes maximum efficiency. Let us suppose that the argument is that if we have the most qualified performing the relevant tasks we will get those tasks done in the most economical and efficient manner. There is nothing wrong in principle with arguments based upon the good consequences that will flow from maintaining a social practice in a certain way. But it is inconsistent for the opponent of preferential treatment to attach much weight to qualifications on this ground, because it was an analogous appeal to the good consequences that the opponent of preferential treatment thought was wrong in the first place. That is to say, if the chief thing to be said in favor of strict qualifications and preferring the most qualified is that it is the most efficient way of getting things done, then we are right back to an assessment of the different consequences that will flow from different programs, and we are far removed from the considerations of justice or fairness that were thought to weigh so heavily against these programs.

It is important to note, too, that qualifications—at least in the educational context—are often not connected at all closely with any plausible conception of social effectiveness. To admit the most qualified students to law school, for example—given the way qualifications are now determined—is primarily to admit those who have the greatest chance of scoring the highest grades at law school. This says little about efficiency except perhaps that these students are the easiest for the faculty to teach. However, since we know so little about what constitutes being a good, or even successful lawyer, and even less about the correlation between being a very good law student and being a very good lawyer, we can hardly claim very confidently that the legal system will operate most effectively if we admit only the most qualified students to law school.

To be at all decisive, the argument for qualifications must be that those who are the most qualified deserve to receive the benefits (the job, the place in law school, etc.) because they are the most qualified. The introduction of the concept of desert now makes it an objection as to justice or fairness of the sort promised by the original criticism of the programs. But now the problem is that there is no reason to think that there is any strong sense of "desert" in which it is correct that the most qualified deserve anything.

Let us consider more closely one case, that of preferential treatment in respect to admission to college or graduate school. There is a logical gap in the inference from the claim that a person is most qualified to perform a task, e.g., to be a good student, to the conclusion that he or she deserves to be admitted as a student. Of course, those who deserve to be admitted should be admitted. But why do the most qualified deserve anything? There is simply no necessary connection between academic merit (in the sense of being the most qualified) and deserving to be a member of a student body. Suppose, for instance, that there is only one tennis court in the community. Is it clear that the two best tennis players ought to be the ones permitted to use it? Why not those who were there first? Or those who will enjoy playing the most? Or those who are the worst and, therefore, need the greatest opportunity to practice? Or those who have the chance to play least frequently?

We might, of course, have a rule that says that the best tennis players get to use the court before the others. Under such a rule the best players would deserve the court more than the poorer ones. But that is just to push the inquiry back one stage. Is there any reason to think that we ought to have a rule giving good tennis players such a preference? Indeed, the arguments that might be given for or against such a rule are many and varied. And few if any of the arguments that might support the rule would depend upon a connection between ability and desert.

Someone might reply, however, that the most able students deserve to be admitted to the university because all of their earlier schooling was a kind of competition, with university admission being the prize awarded to the winners. They deserve to be admitted because that is what the rule of the competition provides. In addition, it might be argued, it would be unfair now to exclude them in favor of others, given the reasonable expectations they developed about the way in which their industry and performance would be re-

warded. Minority-admission programs, which inevitably prefer some who are less qualified over some who are more qualified, all possess this flaw.

There are several problems with this argument. The most substantial of them is that it is an empirically implausible picture of our social world. Most of what are regarded as the decisive characteristics for higher education have a great deal to do with things over which the individual has neither control nor responsibility: such things as home environment, socioeconomic class of parents, and, of course, the quality of the primary and secondary schools attended. Since individuals do not deserve having had any of these things vis-à-vis other individuals, they do not, for the most part, deserve their qualifications. And since they do not deserve their abilities they do not in any strong sense deserve to be admitted because of their abilities.

To be sure, if there has been a rule which connects, say, performance at high school with admission to college, then there is a weak sense in which those who do well at high school deserve, for that reason alone, to be admitted to college. In addition, if persons have built up or relied upon their reasonable expectations concerning performance and admission, they have a claim to be admitted on this ground as well. But it is certainly not obvious that these claims of desert are any stronger or more compelling than the competing claims based upon the needs or advantages to women or blacks from programs of preferential treatment. And as I have indicated, all rule-based claims of desert are very weak unless and until the rule which creates the claim is itself shown to be a justified one. Unless one has a strong preference for the status quo, and unless one can defend that preference, the practice within a system of allocating places in a certain way does not go very far at all in showing that that is the right or the just way to allocate those places in the future.

A proponent of programs of preferential treatment is not at all committed to the view that qualifications ought to be wholly irrelevant. He or she can agree that, given the existing structure of any institution, there is probably some minimal set of qualifications without which one cannot participate meaningfully within the institution. In addition, it can be granted that the qualifications of those involved will affect the way the institution works and the way it affects others in the society. And the consequences will vary depending upon the particular institution. But all of this only establishes that qualifications, in this sense, are relevant, not that they are decisive. This is wholly consistent with the claim that race or sex should today also be relevant when it comes to matters such as admission to college or law school. And that is all that any preferential treatment program—even one with the kind of quota used in the *Bakke* case—has ever tried to do.

I have not attempted to establish that programs of preferential treatment are right and desirable. There are empirical issues concerning the consequences of these programs that I have not discussed, and certainly not settled. Nor, for that matter, have I considered the argument that justice may permit, if not require, these programs as a way to provide compensation or reparation for injuries suffered in the recent as well as distant past, or as a way to remove benefits that are unde-

servedly enjoyed by those of the dominant group. What I have tried to do is show that it is wrong to think that programs of preferential treatment are objectionable in the centrally important sense in which many past and present discriminatory features of our society have been and are racist and sexist. The social realities as to power and opportunity do make a fundamental difference. It is also wrong to think that programs of preferential treatment are in any strong sense either unjust or unprincipled. The case for programs of preferential treatment could, therefore, plausibly rest both on the view that such programs are not unfair to white males (except in the weak, rule-dependent sense described above) and on the view that it is unfair to continue the present set of unjust—often racist and sexist—institutions that comprise the social reality. And the case for these programs could rest as well on the proposition that, given the distribution of power and influence in the United States today, such programs may reasonably be viewed as potentially valuable, effective means by which to achieve admirable and significant social ideals of equality and integration.

---

44.   Reverse Discrimination as Unjustified

Lisa Newton

Lisa Newton argues against programs of preferential treatment on the grounds that they constitute reverse discrimination. Relying on the writings of Aristotle, Newton suggests that discrimination of any type violates basic principles of justice.

I have heard it argued that "simple justice" requires that we favor women and blacks in employment and educational opportunities, since women and blacks were "unjustly" excluded from such opportunities for so many years in the not so distant past. It is a strange

From *Ethics*, 83:4 (July 1973), pp. 308–312. © 1973 The University of Chicago Press. Reprinted by permission.

argument, an example of a possible implication of a true proposition advanced to dispute the proposition itself, like an octopus absent-mindedly slicing off his head with a stray tentacle. A fatal confusion underlies this argument, a confusion fundamentally relevant to our understanding of the notion of the rule of law.

Two senses of justice and equality are involved in this confusion. The root notion of justice, progenitor of the other, is the one that Aristotle (*Nichomachean Ethics* 5.6; *Politics* 1.2; 3.1) assumes to be the foundation and proper virtue of the political association. It is the condition which free men establish among themselves when they "share a common life in order that their association bring them self-sufficiency"—the regulation of their relationship by law, and the establishment, by law, of equality before the law. Rule of law is the name and pattern of this justice; its equality stands against the inequalities—of wealth, talent, etc.—otherwise obtaining among its participants, who by virtue of that equality are called "citizens." It is an achievement—complete, or, more frequently, partial—of certain people in certain concrete situations. It is fragile and easily disrupted by powerful individuals who discover that the blind equality of rule of law is inconvenient for their interests. Despite its obvious instability, Aristotle assumed that the establishment of justice in this sense, the creation of citizenship, was a permanent possibility for men and that the resultant association of citizens was the natural home of the species. At levels below the political association, this rule-governed equality is easily found; it is exemplified by any group of children agreeing together to play a game. At the level of the political association, the attainment of this justice is more difficult, simply because the stakes are so much higher for each participant. The equality of citizenship is not something that happens of its own accord, and without the expenditure of a fair amount of effort it will collapse into the rule of a powerful few over an apathetic many. But at least it has been achieved, at some times in some places; it is always worth trying to achieve, and eminently worth trying to maintain, wherever and to whatever degree it has been brought into being.

Aristotle's parochialism is notorious; he really did not imagine that persons other than Greeks could associate freely in justice, and the only form of association he had in mind was the Greek *polis*. With the decline of the *polis* and the shift in the center of political thought, his notion of justice underwent a sea change. To be exact, it ceased to represent a political type and became a moral ideal: the ideal of equality as we know it. This ideal demands that all men be included in citizenship—that one Law govern all equally, that all men regard all other men as fellow citizens, with the same guarantees, rights, and protections. Briefly, it demands that the circle of citizenship achieved by any group be extended to include the entire human race. Properly understood, its effect on our associations can be excellent: it congratulates us on our achievement of rule of law as a process of government but refuses to let us remain complacent until we have expanded the associations to include others within the ambit of the rules, as often and as far as possible. While one man is a slave, none of us may feel truly free. We are constantly prodded by this ideal to look for possible unjustifiable discrimination, for inequalities not absolutely required for the functioning of the society and advantageous to all. And after twenty centuries of pressure, not at all constant, from this idea, it might be said that some progress has been made. To take the cases in point for this problem, we are now prepared to assert, as Aristotle would never have been, the equality of sexes and of persons of different colors. The ambit of American citizenship, once restricted to white males of property, has been extended to include all adult free men, then all adult males including ex-slaves, then all women. The process of acquisition of full citizenship was for these groups a sporadic trail of half-measures, even now not complete; the steps on the road to full equality are marked by legislation and judicial decisions which are only recently concluded and still often not enforced. But the fact that we can now discuss the possibility of favoring such groups in hiring shows that over the area that concerns us, at least, full equality is presupposed as a basis for discussion. To that extent, they are full citizens, fully protected by the law of the land.

It is important for my argument that the moral ideal of equality be recognized as logically distinct from the condition (or virtue) of justice in the political sense. Justice in this sense exists *among* a citizenry, irrespective of the number of the populace included in that citizenry. Further, the moral ideal is parasitic upon the political virtue, for "equality" is unspecified—it means nothing until we are told in what respect that equality is to be realized.

In a political context, "equality" is specified as "equal rights"—equal access to the public realm, public goods and offices, equal treatment under the law—in brief, the equality of citizenship. If citizenship is not a possibility, political equality is unintelligible. The ideal emerges as a generalization of the real condition and refers back to that condition for its content.

Now, if justice (Aristotle's justice in the political sense) is equal treatment under law for all citizens, what is injustice? Clearly, injustice is the violation of that equality, discriminating for or against a group of citizens, favoring them with special immunities and privileges or depriving them of those guaranteed to the others. When the southern employer refuses to hire blacks in white-collar jobs, when Wall Street will only hire women as secretaries with new titles, when Mississippi high schools routinely flunk all black boys above ninth grade, we have examples of injustice, and we work to restore the equality of the public realm by ensuring that equal opportunity will be provided in such cases in the future. But of course, when the employers and the schools *favor* women and blacks, the same injustice is done. Just as the previous discrimination did, this reverse discrimination violates the public equality which defines citizenship and destroys the rule of law for the areas in which these favors are granted. To the extent that we adopt a program of discrimination, reverse or otherwise, justice in the political sense is destroyed, and none of us, specifically affected or not, is a citizen, a bearer of rights—we are all petitioners for favors. And to the same extent, the ideal of equality is undermined, for it has content only where justice obtains, and by destroying justice we render the ideal meaningless. It is, then, an ironic paradox, if not a contradiction in terms, to assert that the ideal of equality justifies the violation of justice; it is as if one should argue, with William Buckley, that an ideal of humanity can justify the destruction of the human race.

Logically, the conclusion is simple enough: all discrimination is wrong prima facie because it violates justice, and that goes for reverse discrimination too. No violation of justice among the citizens may be justified (may over-come the prima facie objection) by appeal to the ideal of equality, for that ideal is logically dependent upon the notion of justice. Reverse discrimination, then, which attempts no other justification than an appeal to equality, is wrong. But let us try to make the conclusion more plausible by suggesting some of the implications of the suggested practice of reverse discrimination in employment and education. My argument will be that the problems raised there are insoluble, not only in practice but in principle.

We may argue, if we like, about what "discrimination" consists of. Do I discriminate against blacks if I admit none to my school when none of the black applicants are qualified by the tests I always give? How far must I go to root out cultural bias from my application forms and tests before I can say that I have not discriminated against those of different cultures? Can I assume that women are not strong enough to be roughnecks on my oil rigs, or must I test them individually? But this controversy, the most popular and well-argued aspect of the issue, is not as fatal as two others which cannot be avoided: if we are regarding the blacks as a "minority" victimized by discrimination, what is a "minority"? And for any group—blacks, women, whatever—that has been discriminated against, what amount of reverse discrimination wipes out the initial discrimination? Let us grant as true that women and blacks were discriminated against, even where laws forbade such discrimination, and grant for the sake of argument that a history of discrimination must be wiped out by reverse discrimination. What follows?

First, are there other groups which have been discriminated against? For they should have the same right of restitution. What about American Indians, Chicanos, Appalachian Mountain whites, Puerto Ricans, Jews, Cajuns, and Orientals? And if these are to be included, the principle according to which we specify a "minority" is simply the criterion of "ethnic (sub) group," and we're stuck with every hyphenated American in the lower-middle class clamoring for special privileges for *his* group—and with equal justification. For be it noted, when we run down the Harvard roster, we find not only a scarcity of blacks (in comparison with the proportion in the population) but an even more striking scarcity of those second-, third-, and fourth-generation ethnics who make up the loudest voice of Middle America. Shouldn't they demand *their* share? And eventually, the WASPs will have to form their own lobby, for they too are a minority. The point is simply this: there is no "majority" in America who will not mind giving up just a bit of their rights to make room for a favored minority. There are only other minorities, each of which is discriminated against by the favoring. The initial injustice is then repeated dozens of times, and if each minority is granted the same right of restitution as the others, an entire area of rule governance is dissolved into a pushing and shoving match between self-interested groups. Each works to catch the public eye and political popularity by whatever means of advertising and power politics lend themselves to the effort, to capitalize as much as possible on temporary popularity until the restless mob picks another group to feel sorry for. Hardly an edifying spectacle, and in the long run no one can benefit: the pie is no larger—it's just that instead of setting up and enforcing rules for getting a piece, we've turned the contest into a free-for-all, requiring much more effort for no larger a reward. It would be in the interests of all the participants to reestablish an objective rule to govern the process, carefully enforced and the same for all.

Second, supposing that we do manage to agree in general that women and blacks (and all the others) have some right of restitution, some right to a privileged place in the structure of opportunities for a while, how will we know when that while is up? How much privilege is enough? When will the guilt be gone, the price paid, the balance restored? What recompense is right for centuries of exclusion? What criterion tells us when we are done? Our experience with the Civil Rights movement shows us that agreement on these terms cannot be presupposed: a process that appears to some to be going at a mad gallop into a black takeover appears to the rest of us to be at a standstill. Should a practice of reverse discrimination be adopted, we may safely predict

that just as some of us begin to see "a satisfactory start toward righting the balance," others of us will see that we "have already gone too far in the other direction" and will suggest that the discrimination ought to be reversed again. And such disagreement is inevitable, for the point is that we could not *possibly* have any criteria for evaluating the kind of recompense we have in mind. The context presumed by any discussion of restitution is the context of rule of law: law sets the rights of men and simultaneously sets the method for remedying the violation of those rights. You may exact suffering from others and/or damage payments for yourself if and only if the others have violated your rights; the suffering you have endured is not sufficient reason for them to suffer. And remedial rights exist only where there is law: primary human rights are useful guides to legislation but cannot stand as reasons for awarding remedies for injuries sustained. But then, the context presupposed by any discussion of restitution is the context of preexistent full citizenship. No remedial rights could exist for the excluded; neither in law nor in logic does there exist a right to *sue* for a standing to sue.

From these two considerations, then, the difficulties with reverse discrimination become evident. Restitution for a disadvantaged group whose rights under the law have been violated is possible by legal means, but restitution for a disadvantaged group whose grievance is that there was no law to protect them simply is not. First, outside of the area of justice defined by the law, no sense can be made of "the group's rights," for no law recognizes that group or the individuals in it, qua members, as bearers of rights (hence *any* group can constitute itself as a disadvantaged minority in some sense and demand similar restitution). Second, outside of the area of protection of law, no sense can be made of the violation of rights (hence the amount of the recompense cannot be decided by any objective criterion). For both reasons, the practice of reverse discrimination undermines the foundation of the very ideal in whose name it is advocated; it destroys justice, law, equality, and citizenship itself, and replaces them with power struggles and popularity contests.

45. Debate over Comparable Worth: Facts and Rhetoric

Judith Olans Brown, Phyllis Tropper Baumann, and Elaine Millar Melnick

Brown, Baumann, and Melnick defend the principle of "equal pay for comparable work" against the major criticisms of comparable worth: namely, that the situation is not due to discrimination, that comparable worth comparisons are impossible, and that such policies would seriously damage the free-market system.

A. Definitions: The Heart of the Debate

"Comparable worth" means that workers, regardless of their sex, should earn equal pay for work of comparable value to their common employer. Imprecise use of the phrase hinders meaningful discussion. Comparable worth is equated indiscriminately with comparable work, work of equal worth, work of equal value, or pay equity; however, these terms are not synonymous. Comparable worth theory addresses wage inequities that are associated with job segregation. The basic premise of comparable worth theory is that women should be able to substantiate a claim for equal wages by showing that their jobs and those of male workers are of equal value to their common employer. The doctrine allows comparison of jobs which are different but which require comparable skills, effort and responsibility.[1] In other words, this doctrine permits comparison of jobs which do not come within the ambit of the Equal Pay Act requirement of equal pay for jobs which are "substantially equal."

Opponents of comparable worth, however,

Reprinted by permission from "Equal Pay for Jobs of Comparable Worth: An Analysis of the Rhetoric," *Harvard Civil Rights Civil Liberties Law Review* 21 (Winter 1986). Copyright © 1986 by the Harvard Civil Rights Civil Liberties Law Review.

focus on jobs that are not demonstrably equivalent and where a comparable worth claim is thus not present. Their rhetoric too often sacrifices accuracy to ideology.[2] In a popular but mistaken example, comparable worth opponents ask why such unrelated workers as nurses (not generally unionized) and truck drivers (highly unionized) should receive the same wages.[3] Opponents also ask why nurses and teamsters, who do not even work for the same employer, should receive the same pay. The response must emphasize that comparable worth cases always involve the same employer. The cases also always involve occupations which, according to a rational standard, are of comparable value to that employer.

The nurse/truck driver example implies that comparable worth requires equal pay for randomly selected job categories simply because the jobs being compared are ordinarily performed by members of one sex. What is really at issue, however, is equal pay for demonstrably equivalent jobs, as measured by either job content or a standard of experience, skill, or responsibility. An appropriate index against which to measure nurses' salaries might be the salaries of hospital sanitarians. Similarly, the appropriate comparable job for a truck driver is one which, although perhaps different in job content, is rated as equivalent in a job evaluation study, or which is capable of being so rated.[4]

Comparable worth doctrine differs from the Equal Pay Act formula in that it permits comparison of jobs which are not substantially similar in content. The Equal Pay Act of 1963 requires equal pay for work of equal skill, effort and responsibility performed under similar working conditions. But the statute requires pay equality only for jobs which are *substantially equal*. If the jobs are relatively equivalent yet not sufficiently similar to meet that standard, no Equal Pay Act violation exists.

[In 1981 the Supreme Court] eliminated the requirement that Title VII plaintiffs prove the substantial equality of the jobs being compared.[5] . . . All Title VII plaintiffs alleging gender-based discrimination are comparing jobs which may have dissimilar functions but are of comparable value to the common employer.

The question for Title VII plaintiffs invoking comparable worth theory then becomes how to demonstrate that their jobs and those of male workers are of equal value to their common employer. [After the Court's 1981 decision] plaintiffs need not demonstrate job equivalency. Nor does a successful comparable worth claim require proof of underevaluation due to historical discrimination.[6] Instead, comparable worth requires proof that the employer's male and female workers perform work of comparable value and that the female workers are paid less. Such a demonstration necessarily depends upon the evaluation of jobs which are different in content.

B. Job Evaluation: The Red Herring of the Comparable Worth Debate

Job evaluation techniques provide a method for comparing jobs which are dissimilar in content. Job evaluation is a formal procedure which classifies a set of jobs on the basis of their relative value to the employer. Although the courts are uncomfortable with the concept of comparable worth, the technique of job evaluation has been familiar to American industry for decades.[7] Contrary to the claims of comparable worth critics, job evaluation does not require governmental participation.

Evaluation merely eliminates resort to guess-work or unsubstantiated assertions of comparability. It provides a way of identifying situations in which wages remain artificially low because of sex, but where men and women are not performing identical or nearly identical operations.

Formal job evaluation originated in the late nineteenth century as part of a generalized expansion of organizational techniques and a restructuring of workplace control systems. Indeed, job evaluation was such a familiar method for comparing jobs that it provided the theoretical underpinning for the Equal Pay Act of 1963.[8] The various evaluation techniques all use similar methods to inject objectivity and equity into pay structures. The first stage requires a formal description of the duties, requirements and working conditions of each job within the unit being evaluated. Next, jobs are evaluated in terms of "worth" to the organization. The outcome of these two processes is a ranking of all jobs in the evaluation unit. The third stage involves setting wage rates for each job in accordance with the evaluation—the higher the ranking, the higher the wages. The job itself, not the worker performing it, is the subject of evaluation.

Any attempt to raise wages on the basis of comparable worth turns on effective use of wage rate, job classification, promotion policy and contractual data. Job evaluations assemble the relevant information in a form useful to employers, employees, and courts. Firmly grounded in existing industrial relations practice, job evaluation itself is hardly controversial. What is new is the use of this practice to address sex discrimination in wages.

Women in diverse occupations have begun to use job evaluation to demonstrate the discriminatory nature of their employers' male/female pay discrepancies.[9] The public rhetoric that characterizes job evaluation as an impossible task of comparing "apples and oranges" merely ignores the factual basis of the technique. The employer has already fashioned a wholly rational hierarchy of "apples and oranges" on the basis of relative worth to the employer. Unfortunately, the mistaken but popular notion of job evaluation has nonetheless prejudiced the courts against evaluation techniques that are essential to plaintiffs' cases.

C. Arguments against Comparable Worth: The Crux of the Rhetoric

Intense hostility has surrounded the idea of comparable worth. In order to understand this hostility, it is necessary to examine the arguments used by opponents of comparable worth. These arguments involve three related contentions: the male/female earnings gap results, at least in large part, from factors unrelated to discrimination by particular employers; comparable worth analysis is logistically impossible since there is no objective basis for establishing comparisons between different jobs; and, third, pay equity based on comparable worth would cripple the so-called free market.

1. The Non-Discriminatory Nature of the Wage Gap

The argument that the wage gap between men and women results from non-discriminatory factors is clearly expressed in a report by the U.S. Civil Rights Commission. In its findings, the Civil Rights Commission states that:

> The wage gap between female and male earnings in America results, at least in significant part from a variety of things having nothing to do with discrimination by employers, including job expectations resulting from socialization beginning in the home; educational choices of women who anticipate performing child-bearing and child-rearing functions in the family and who wish to prepare for participation in the labor force in a manner which accommodates the performance of those functions, like the desire of women to work in the kinds of jobs which accommodate their family roles and the intermittency of women's labor force participation.

Essentially, one can reduce the Commission's argument to three basic propositions: women choose low-paying jobs because of their sociological predisposition; women make educational choices which lead to low-paying jobs; and the interrupted participation of women in the labor force leads to lower pay.

The first contention is misguided; comparable worth does not raise job *access* issues. Instead, it addresses situations where women who are already employed are paid less for jobs demonstrably similar to those of male co-workers. In comparable worth cases, women are not socialized to hold "easier" jobs: they are paid less for work of equivalent value. While the effect of socialization on job expectations is relevant to a woman's choice to become a nurse rather than a doctor, it does not address why female nurses are paid less than male orderlies or sanitarians at the same hospital. Comparable worth theory addresses inequities subsequent to access. The Commission simply misses the point in arguing that disadvantage results from the victim's choice, based on her own lower expectations.

The second and third contentions reflect the analytical framework used by human capital theorists to account for employment discrimination.[10] The touchstone of human capital theory as an explanation of wage differentials is productivity. Wages are viewed as a return on investments in human capital. The argument proceeds from the premise that individuals make investments in their productive capacity through education and training. These investments have costs, but they also produce returns in the form of higher wages. The male/female wage differential, therefore, merely reflects the different investments that men and women make.

Mincer and Polachek provide the classic formulation of the theory that women's lower wages merely reflect lower investments in human capital.[11] Productivity of men and women arguably differs . . . [due to] differences in education, training, or length of experience. [However] comparable worth theory does not rely on generalized statistical assertions; it requires a demonstration that in a particular case no other factor appears capable of explaining a proven disparity.

2. Comparing "Apples and Oranges"

The second major argument espoused by opponents of comparable worth is that no objective technique exists for comparing jobs that are not identical in content. The Civil Rights Commission contends that in comparable worth litigation job evaluations are inherently subjective and cannot establish jobs' intrinsic worth. Instead, the Commission claims that such studies function only "to establish rational pay-setting policies within an organization, satisfactory to the organization's employees and management."

This objection, though partially valid, goes too far. Although job evaluation is not absolutely objective, it is a well-established technique in American industry for determining relative wage levels. Representatives of business interests successfully sought to incorporate the concepts of job evaluation into the definition of equality in the Equal Pay Act of 1963. They argued that such a course was necessary because the use of job evaluation techniques was so widespread in industry. For example, E. G. Hester, the director of industrial relations research for Corning Glass, told the Senate Committee on Labor and Public Welfare of his company's concern over the proposed equality criteria. According to Mr. Hester, the proposed criteria would require equal pay "for equal work on jobs the performance of which requires equal skills." He asserted that this approach:

. . . could give a great deal of difficulty to that large part of American industry and business which has relied upon systematic methods of job evaluation for establishment of equitable rate relationships. Such job evaluation plans depend for their reliability upon other factors than skill alone.

Mr. Hester's statement to the Committee included evidence of the extent to which job evaluation was used. He argued that:

With this general acceptance of job evaluation throughout industry on the part of both management and labor, we feel it most desirable that legislation related to the equal-pay principle incorporate in its language, recognition of job evaluation (or job classification) principles that have been developed, accepted, and are in general use.

In arguing for the incorporation of job evaluation principles, Mr. Hester conceded that job evaluation was "not a precise science governed by natural laws" but still lauded it as "a systematic approach to establish relative job order . . ." He pointed out the industries using job evaluation principles had customarily constructed the hierarchy on the basis of "effort, skill, responsibility, and working conditions." The Equal Pay Act incorporates these same four factors.

Even a cursory examination of industrial relations practices demonstrates that business and industry have long used specific techniques to determine the relative wage rates of jobs which are dissimilar in content. While evaluation techniques are not absolutely objective, they are a logical starting point in any meaningful wage determination process. Comparable worth cases do not require an abstract showing of intrinsic value. Instead, plaintiffs' cases turn on proof that the employer's job worth determinations are gender-based. Since comparable worth cases always address alleged discrimination of a particular employer, they compare "pay-setting policies within an organization." The Commission itself admits that this use of job evaluation is "rational."

3. Laissez-Faire Economics and Antidiscrimination Law

The third argument commonly raised against comparable worth is that it requires an unwarranted intrusion into the market. Again, the Civil Rights Commission report provides an example. The Commission notes that: "The setting of wages is not and cannot be divorced from the forces of labor supply and demand. These factors heavily influence the setting of pay in many jobs and play an important role in setting wages for virtually all other jobs." The Commission then argues that there is nothing in the language or legislative history of Title VII to indicate that Congress intended to prevent employers from relying on the operation of the market in setting wages.

Courts have also made this assertion. However, any statute governing the employment relationship must by its very nature interfere with an employer's absolute freedom to determine wages by reference to the market. The enactment of Title VII indicates congressional intent to intervene in the market to further significant policy interests.

Those who argue that comparable worth is an unwarranted interference insist that supply and demand curves create the wage disparity at issue. Thus, comparable worth theory is not a legitimate response to discrimination but rather a specious definition of discrimination. If there is no impermissible discrimination, they argue, there is no social justification for judicial interference with market forces. A recent article called equal pay for work of comparable worth "a fallacious notion that apples are equal to oranges and that prices for both should be the same, even if that means overriding the law of supply and demand."[12] Market forces are the only relevant measure of value.

The argument's proponents would cloak impermissible sex-based discrimination in the putative legality of "market operation." Yet the argument sidesteps the contention of comparable worth proponents that, despite a pay differential, the jobs are equivalent according to a rational standard. Extolling the overriding authority of supply and demand is to ignore the possibility that that "law" conflicts with Title VII, which like other regulatory legislation necessarily interferes with a laissez-faire economy. The market-based argument against comparable worth is nonetheless instructive since it links criticisms of the allegedly spurious nature of comparable worth with antipathy to the remedy—interference with the market—that comparable worth purportedly implies. It is this connection which is critical to an understanding of judicial opinions in the comparable worth area, since judges often defer to the operation of the market.

Notes

1. See, e.g., Newman and Wilson, "Comparable Worth: A Job Inequity By Any Other Name," *Manual On Pay Equity: Raising Wages for Women's Work* 54 (J. Grune ed. undated) (on file with Harv. C.R.-C.L. L. Rev.)

2. President Reagan even dismissed comparable worth as a "cockamamie idea." Connant & Paine, "A Loss for Comparable Worth," *Newsweek,* Sept. 16, 1985, 36.

3. See, e.g., Krucoff, "Money: The Question of Men, Women, and 'Comparable Worth,'" *Wash. Post,* Nov. 13, 1979, B5, col. 1.

4. The point is not to assert that equal pay *must* be based on similarity of job content, although it may be so based. Jobs which are quite different in content may properly be the basis for an equal pay claim if it can be demonstrated that they are of equal worth. A case brought under the British Equal Pay Act of 1970 provides an illustration. In *Hayward v. Cammell Laird Shipbuilders Ltd.,* IRLR 463 (1984), ICR 71 (1985), a female cook employed in the works cafeteria at the employer's shipyard sought equal pay with men employed as painters, thermal insulation engineers and joiners. An independent expert appointed by the industrial tribunal hearing the claim assessed the various jobs under five factors: physical demands, environmental demands, planning and decisionmaking, skill and knowledge required, and responsibility involved. On the basis of this evaluation he found the jobs to be of equal value.

5. "Respondent's claims of discriminatory undercompensation are not barred by § 703(h) of Title VII merely because respondents do not perform work equal to that of male jail guards." *Gunther,* 452 U.S. at 181.

6. For a discussion of the historic undervaluation of women's jobs, see Blumrosen, "Wage Discrimination, Job Segregation, and Title VII of the Civil Rights Act of 1964," 12 *U. Mich. J. L. Ref.* 397 (1979).

7. See, e.g., *Laffey v. Northwest Airlines,* 567 F.2d 429 (D.C. Cir. 1976), vacating and remanding in part, aff'g in pertinent part, 366 F. Supp. 763 (D.D.C. 1973), cert. denied, 434 U.S. 1080 (1978) (Court of Appeals agreeing with District Court judge who found, after testimony from expert

witnesses on job evaluation presented by both plaintiff and defendant, that "pursers" and "stewardesses" performed substantially equal work even though jobs had different titles, descriptions and responsibilities).

8. The "effort, skill, responsibility and working conditions" criteria which the Equal Pay Act uses to determine whether jobs are equal were derived from then-current job evaluation systems.

9. See American Federation of State, County, and Municipal Employees, AFL-CIO (AFSCME), *Guide to Comparable Worth, in Pay Equity: A Union Issue for the 1980's* 11–12 (1980). Unions representing women workers have begun to use evaluation techniques to demonstrate the extent to which women's work is undervalued and underpaid. AFSCME bargained for job evaluation studies in San Jose, California, Lane County, Oregon, and statewide in Minnesota, Wisconsin, and Michigan. *Manual on Pay Equity: Raising Wages for Women's Work* 152–53 (J. Grune ed. undated) (on file with Harv. C.R.-C.L. L. Rev.). The trend has been especially pronounced in the public sector where 100 municipalities are now re-evaluating their job classification systems. See Noble, "Comparable Worth: How It's Figured," *New York Times*, Feb. 27, 1985, p. C7, col. 1.

10. See Amsden, "Introduction," in *The Economics of Women and Work* 13–18 (A. Amsden ed. 1980).

11. See Mincer & Polachek, "Family Investments in Human Capital: Earnings of Women," 82 *J. Pol. Econ.* 76 (1974) (supp.).

12. Smith, "The EEOC's Bold Foray into Job Evaluation," *Fortune*, Sept. 11, 1978, 58. The author goes on to talk of the "enormous inflationary effect" of comparable worth, which "at the extreme [would] raise the aggregate pay of the country's 27.3 million full-time working women high enough . . . [to] add a staggering $150 billion a year to civilian payrolls." *Id.* at 59. The statement is typical of the hyperbole on which comparable worth arguments often are based. The author fails to acknowledge that no comparable worth advocate has suggested that all American working women will benefit from the implementation of the doctrine—only those doing work of demonstrably comparable value to that of a male worker of the same employer.

---

46. An Argument against Comparable Worth

June O'Neill

June O'Neill argues against programs of equal pay for comparable work on the grounds that they violate important elements of the market economy. This, she suggests, goes against the traditional goals feminists have of providing equal opportunity to women within a market economy. In her analysis, she examines the roles that prices and wages play in an economy, as well as the topics of discrimination and its unintended effects and other options for feminists.

The traditional goal of feminists has been equal opportunity for women—the opportunity for women to gain access to the schools, training, and jobs they choose to enter, on the same basis as men. This goal, however, basically accepts the rules of the game as they operate in a market economy. In fact the thrust has

From *Comparable Worth: An Issue for the 80's*, vol. 1. (U.S. Commission on Civil Rights, 1984).

been to improve the way the market functions by removing discriminatory barriers that restrict the free supply of workers to jobs. By contrast, the more recent policy of "comparable worth" would dispense with the rules of the game. In place of the goal of equality of opportunity it would substitute a demand for equality of results, and it would do this essentially through regulation and legislation. It proposes, therefore, a radical departure from the economic system we now have, and so should be scrutinized with the greatest care.

The topics I will cover in this paper and the main points I will make are as follows:

1. The concept of comparable worth rests on a misunderstanding of the role of wages and prices in the economy.
2. The premises on which a comparable worth policy is based reflect a misconception about the reasons why women and men are in different occupations and have different earnings. Both the occupational differences and the pay gap to a large extent are the result of differences in the roles of women and men in the family and the effects these role differences have on the accumulation of skills and other job choices that affect pay. Discrimination by employers may account for some of the occupational differences, but it does not, as comparable worth advocates claim, lower wages directly in women's occupations.
3. Comparable worth, if implemented, would lead to capricious wage differentials, resulting in unintended shortages and surpluses of workers in different occupations with accompanying unemployment. Moreover, it would encourage women to remain in traditional occupations.
4. Policies are available that can be better targeted than comparable worth on any existing discriminatory or other barriers. These policies include the equal employment and pay legislation now on the books.

The Concept of Comparable Worth

By comparable worth I mean the view that employers should base compensation on the inherent value of a job rather than on strictly market considerations. It is not a new idea—since the time of St. Thomas Aquinas, the concept of the "just price," or payment for value, has had considerable appeal. Practical considerations, however, have won out over metaphysics. In a free market, wages and prices are not taken as judgments of the inherent value of the worker or the good itself, but reflect a balancing of what people are willing to pay for the services fo these goods with how much it costs to supply them. Market prices are the efficient signals that balance supply and demand. Thus, in product markets we do not require that a pound of soybeans be more expensive than a pound of Belgian chocolates because it is more nutritious, or that the price of water be higher than that of diamonds because it is so much more important to our survival. If asked what the proper scale of prices should be for these products, most people—at least those who have taken Economics I—would give the sensible answer that there is no proper scale—it all depends on the tastes and needs of millions of consumers and the various conditions that determine the costs of production and the supplies of these products.

What is true of the product market is equally true of the labor market. There is simply no independent scientific way to determine what pay should be in a particular occupation without recourse to the market. Job skills have "costs of production" such as formal schooling and on-the-job training. Different jobs also have different amenities that may be more or less costly for the employer to provide—for example, part-time work, safe work, flexible hours, or a pleasant ambience. And individuals vary in their talents and tastes for acquiring skills and performing different tasks. The skills required change over time as the demand for products changes and as different techniques of production are introduced. And these changes may vary by geographic region. In a market system, these changing conditions are reflected in changing wage rates, which in turn provide workers with the incentive to acquire new skills or to migrate to different regions.

The wage pattern that is the net outcome of these forces need not conform to anyone's independent judgment based on preconceived notions of comparability or of relative desirability. The clergy, for example, earn about 30 percent less than brickmasons.[1] Yet the clergy are largely college graduates; the brickmasons are not. Both occupations are more than 95 percent male—so one cannot point to sex discrimination. Possibly the reason for the wage disparity lies in unusual union power of construction workers and is an example of market imperfections. But other explanations are possible too. The real compensation to the clergy, for example, may include housing and spiritual satisfaction as fringe benefits. On the other hand, the high risk of unemployment and exposure to hazards of brickmasons may be reflected in additional monetary payments. If enough people require premiums to become brickmasons and are willing to settle for nonmonetary rewards to work as clergy, and if the buyers of homes are willing to pay the higher costs of brickmasons, while churchgoers are satisfied with the number and quality of clergy who apply, the market solution may well be satisfactory.[2]

One can also think of examples of jobs that initially may seem quite comparable but that would not command the same wage, even in nondiscriminatory and competitive markets. The following example is based on a case that has been used before, but it illustrates the point so well it bears repeating.[3] Consider two jobs—one a Spanish-English translator and the other a French-English translator. Most job evaluators would probably conclude that these jobs are highly comparable and should be paid the same. After all, the skills required, the mental demands, the working conditions, and responsibility would seem to be nearly identical. But "nearly" is not equal, and the difference in language may in fact give rise to a legitimate pay differential. The demand for the two languages may differ—for example, if trade with Spanish-speaking countries is greater. But the supply of Spanish-English translators may also be greater. And this would vary by geographic area. It would be difficult to predict which job will require the higher wage and by how much in order to balance supply and demand.

What the market does is to process the scarcity of talents, the talents of heterogeneous individuals and the demands of business and consumers in arriving at a wage. The net outcome would only coincidentally be the same as a comparable worth determination. There are simply too many factors interacting in highly complex ways for a study to find the market clearing wage.

Why Abandon the Market?

The argument for abandoning market determination of wages and substituting "comparable worth," where wage decisions would be based on an independent assessment of the "value" of occupations, is based on the following premises: (1) the pay gap between women and men is due to discrimination and has failed to narrow over time; (2) this discrimination takes the form of occupational segregation, where women are relegated to low-paying jobs; and (3) pay in these female-dominated occupations is low simply because women hold them.

The Pay Gap

In 1983 the pay gap, viewed as the ratio of women's to men's hourly pay, was about 72 percent overall (Table 1).[4] Among younger groups the ratio is higher (and the pay gap smaller)—a ratio of 89 percent for 20–24-year-olds and 80 percent for the age 25–34 years old. Among groups age 35 and over the ratio is about 65 percent.

What accounts for the pay gap? Clearly, not all differentials reflect discrimination. Several minorities (Japanese and Jewish Americans, for example) have higher than average wages, and I do not believe anyone would ascribe these differences to favoritism towards these groups and discrimination against others.

A growing body of research has attempted to account for the pay gap, and the researchers have come to different conclusions. These studies, however, use different data sources, refer to different populations and control for many, but not always the same set of variables. Even the gross wage gap—the hourly earnings differential before adjusting for diverse characteristics—varies from study to study, ranging from 45 to 7 percent depending on the type of population considered. Studies based on national samples covering the full age range tend to show a gross wage gap of 35 to 40 percent. Studies based on more homogeneous groups, such as holders of advanced degrees or those in specific professions, have

TABLE 1. Female–Male Ratios of Median Usual Weekly Earnings of Full-Time Wage and Salary Workers, by Age, 1971–1983

I. UNADJUSTED RATIOS

Age	May 1971	May 1973	May 1974	May 1975	May 1976	May 1977	May 1978	2nd Quarter 1979	Annual Average 1979	1982	1983
16–19	.89	.82	.82	.86	.86	.88	.86	.85	.87	.88	.94
20–24	.78	.77	.76	.76	.80	.78	.75	.75	.76	.83	.84
25–34	.65	.64	.65	.66	.67	.65	.66	.67	.66	.72	.73
35–44	.59	.54	.55	.57	.55	.56	.53	.58	.58	.60	.60
45–54	.57	.57	.57	.59	.57	.56	.54	.57	.56	.59	.58
55–64	.62	.63	.60	.63	.61	.59	.60	.60	.58	.60	.62
Total, 16 years and over	.62	.62	.61	.62	.61	.61	.61	.62	.62	.65	.66

II. ADJUSTED FOR MALE-FEMALE DIFFERENCES IN FULL-TIME HOURS[1]

Age	May 1971	May 1973	May 1974	May 1975	May 1976	May 1977	May 1978	2nd Quarter 1979	Annual Average 1979	1982	1983
16–19	.94	.86	.87	.90	.90	.92	.91	.90	.92	.91	.96
20–24	.85	.83	.82	.82	.86	.84	.80	.81	.82	.88	.89
25–34	.73	.72	.72	.73	.74	.72	.73	.74	.73	.79	.80
35–44	.66	.61	.61	.63	.61	.62	.59	.64	.64	.66	.66
45–54	.62	.62	.62	.63	.62	.61	.59	.63	.61	.64	.63
55–64	.67	.69	.65	.67	.67	.65	.65	.66	.64	.65	.67
Total, 16 years and over	.68	.68	.67	.68	.68	.67	.67	.68	.68	.71	.72

[1]Female–male earnings ratios were adjusted for differences in hours worked by multiplying by age-specific male–female ratios of average hours worked per week (for nonagricultural workers on full-time schedules).

SOURCE: [Data from] Earnings by age and sex are from unpublished tabulations from the Current Population Survey provided by the Bureau of Labor Statistics, U.S. Department of Labor. Hours data are from U.S. Bureau of Labor Statistics, Employment and Earnings series, January issues, annual averages.

found considerably smaller gross wage gaps.

After adjusting for various characteristics, the wage gap narrows. Generally, the most important variables contributing to the adjustment are those that measure the total number of years of work experience, the years of tenure on current job, and the pattern or continuity of previous work experience.

Traditional home responsibilities of married women have been an obstacle to their full commitment to a career. Although women are now combining work and marriage to a much greater extent than in the past, older women in the labor force today have typically spent many years out of the labor force raising their families. Data from the National Longitudinal Survey (NLS) indicate that in 1977 employed white women in their forties had worked only 61 percent of the years after leaving school, and employed black women had worked 68 percent of the years.[5] By contrast, men are usually in the labor force or the military on a continuing basis after leaving school.

In a recent study I examined the contribution of lifetime work experience and other variables using the NLS data for men and women aged 25 to 34. White women's hourly wage rate was found to be 66 percent of white men's—a wage gap of 34 percent. This wage gap narrowed to 12 percent after accounting for the effects of male-female differences in work experience, job tenure, and schooling, as well as differences in plant size and certain job characteristics, such as the years of training required to learn a skill, whether the occupation was hazardous, and whether the occupation had a high concentration of women.

The gross wage gap between black men and black women was 18 percent. The gross wage gap was smaller for blacks than for whites because job-related characteristics of black women and black men are closer than those of white women and white men. Black women have somewhat fewer years of work experience in their teens and early twenties than white women, which may be related to earlier childbearing. They are more likely to work continuously and full time later on, however, and thus accumulate more total work experience and longer tenure on their current jobs than white women. The adjustment for differences in the measured characteristics cited above narrowed the wage gap of black men and women to 9 percent.

Are the remaining, unaccounted-for differences a measure of discrimination in the labor market?

If all the productivity differences between women and men are not accurately identified and measured, labor market discrimination would be overestimated by the unexplained residual. Many variables were omitted from this analysis and from other studies because relevant data are not available. These include details on the quality and vocational orientation of education; on the extent of other work-related investments, such as job search; and on less tangible factors, such as motivation and effort. Differences in these factors could arise from the priority placed on earning an income versus fulfilling home responsibilities. If women, by tradition, assume the primary responsibility for homemaking and raising children, they may be reluctant to take jobs that demand an intense work commitment.

On the other hand, the unexplained residual may underestimate discrimination if some of the included variables, such as years of training to learn a job, or the sex typicality of occupations, partially reflect labor market discrimination. Some employers may deny women entry into lengthy training programs or be reluctant to hire them in traditionally male jobs. It is difficult with available data to distinguish this situation from one where women choose not to engage in training because of uncertainty about their long-run career plans or choose female occupations because they are more compatible with competing responsibilities at home.

Occupational Segregation

Although occupational segregation clearly exists, it is in large part the result of many of the same factors that determine earnings: years of schooling, on-the-job training, and other human capital investments, as well as tastes for particular job characteristics. In a recently completed study, I found that women's early expectations about their future life's work— that is, whether they planned to be a homemaker or planned to work outside the home— are strongly related to the occupations they ultimately pursue.[6] Many women who initially planned to be homemakers, in fact, become labor force participants, but they were much more likely to pursue stereotyped female occupations than women who had formed their plans to work at younger ages. Early orientation influences early training and schooling decisions, and as a result women may be locked into or out of certain careers. Some women, however, by choice, maintain an ongoing dual career—combining work in the home with an outside job—and this leads to an accommodation in terms of the number of hours that women work and other conditions that influence occupational choice.

Women and men were also found to differ sharply in the environmental characteristics of their occupations. Women were less likely to be in jobs with a high incidence of outdoor work, noisy or hazardous work, or jobs requiring heavy lifting. These differences may reflect employer prejudice or the hostile attitudes of male coworkers, but they may also reflect cultural and physical differences.

In sum, a substantial amount of the differences in wages and in occupations by sex has been statistically linked to investments in work skills acquired in school or on the job. Varied interpretations of these results are possible, however. Thus, the precise amount that can be labeled as the result of choices made by women and their families rather than the result of discrimination by employers is not known.

The Trend in the Pay Gap

A major source of frustration to feminists and a puzzle to researchers has been the failure of the gap to narrow over the post-World War II period, despite large increases in women's labor force participation. In fact, the gap in 1982 is somewhat larger than it was in 1955.

The wage gap would not, however, narrow significantly over time unless the productivity or skill of women in the labor force increased relative to men's, or discrimination in the workplace diminished. Because the gross wage gap widened somewhat after 1955, either discrimination increased or women's skills decreased relative to men's. Findings from a recent study suggest that changes in skill, as measured by the changes in the education and work experience of men and women in the labor force, strongly contributed to an increase in the wage gap.[7]

In 1952 women in the labor force had completed 1.6 more years of schooling than men. This difference narrowed sharply so that by 1979 it had disappeared. One reason for this is that the educational level of men advanced more rapidly than that of women during the 1950s. Aided by the GI bill educational benefits, more men attended college. Another reason is that the labor force participation of less educated women increased more rapidly than the participation of highly educated women. Thus, the female labor force became increasingly less selective over time in terms of schooling attainment.

The rise in the number of women in the labor force may also have had an effect on the lifetime work experience of the average working women. A large number of less experienced women entering the labor force may have diluted the experience level of the working women. Although the total number of years of work experience of women is not available for periods of time before the late 1960s, data on job tenure—years with current employer—show that in 1951 men's job tenure exceeded women's job tenure by 1.7 years. This difference widened to 2.7 years in 1962 and then slowly declined, reaching 1.9 years in 1978 and 1.5 years in 1981.

The decline in working women's educational level relative to men's alone would have caused the pay gap to widen by 7 percentage points. The initial widening in the job tenure differential contributed another 2 percentage points to the gap. Together the change in education and job tenure would have increased the wage gap by more than it actually increased. Possibly then, discrimination declined during this period even though the wage gap widened. Since the mid-1960s, educational and work experience differences have moved in different directions. Male educational attainment rose slightly more than that of working women, which alone would have widened the pay gap slightly. Difference in work experience declined overall. Recently (between 1979 and 1983), a narrowing has occurred in the wage gap, from 68 percent to 72 percent overall.

Evidence from the NLS and other sources suggests that the pay gap is likely to narrow perceptibly in the next decade. Not only are young women working more continuously, but they are also getting higher pay for each year of work experience than they were in the late 1960s. This could reflect a reduction in sex discrimination by employers or a greater willingness of women to invest in market skills, or both. Women's career expectations also seem to be rising. In response to an NLS question asked in 1973, 57 percent of women between 25 and 29 indicated their intention to hold jobs rather than be homemakers when they reach age 35. Among women reaching ages 25 to 29 in 1978, 77 percent expressed their intention to work.

Young women have also greatly increased their educational level relative to men. Female college enrollment increased significantly during the 1970s, while male enrollment fell between 1975 and 1980. Moreover, women have made impressive gains in professional degrees during the 1970s. Work roles and work expectations of women and men may well be merging. As these younger women become a larger component of the female labor force, it is anticipated that the overall wage gap will be reduced.

Are Women's Occupations Underpaid?

A major contention of comparable worth supporters is that pay in women's occupations is lower because employers systematically downgrade them. The argument differs from the idea that pay in women's occupations is depressed because of an oversupply of these occupations. An oversupply could arise either because large numbers of women entering the labor force choose these occupations (which is compatible with no discrimination) or because women are barred from some causing an oversupply in others (a discriminatory situation). Although comparable worth advocates have taken the view that overcrowding is caused by restrictive measures, they have lately come to believe that this explanation is not the whole cause of "low payment" in women's jobs.[8] The argument is made that employers can pay less to women's jobs regardless of supply considerations, simply reflecting prejudice against such jobs because they are held by women.

The ability of firms to wield such power is highly questionable. If a firm underpaid workers in women's occupations, in the sense that their wages were held below their real contributions to the firm's receipts, other firms would have a strong incentive to hire workers in these occupations away, bidding up the wages in these occupations. Thus, competition would appear to be a force curtailing employer power. This process could only be thwarted by collusion, an unrealistic prospect considering the hundreds of thousands of firms.

Killingsworth (1984) has suggested that the market for nurses may be an example of collusion by a centralized hospital industry that has conspired to hold wages down. Without more careful analysis of the hospital industry, it is difficult to verify whether this is a valid hypothesis. Basic facts about wages and supply in nursing, however, suggest that collusion either does not exist or is ineffective. Despite a perennial "shortage" of nurses that seems to have existed as far back as one can go, the number of nurses has increased dramatically, both absolutely and as a percentage of the population. In 1960 there were 282 registered nurses per 100,000 population. In 1980 there were 506 nurses per 100,000. This rate of increase is even more rapid than the increase in doctors over the past decade, and the supply of doctors has been rapidly increasing. Why did the increase occur? Were women forced into nursing because they were barred from other occupations? That does not seem to be the case in recent times. What has happened is that nursing, along with other medical professions, has experienced a large increase in demand since the middle 1960s when medicare and medicaid were introduced, and private health insurance increased. As a result, the pay of nurses increased more rapidly than in other fields. Between 1960 and 1978 the salary of registered nurses increased by 250 percent, while the pay of all men rose by 206 percent and the pay of all women rose by 193 percent. During the 1970s the rate of pay increase for nurses slowed, which is not surprising considering the increase in supply. And entry of women into nursing school has recently slowed, suggesting a self-correcting mechanism is at work.

Another way to attempt to evaluate the contention that lower pay in female-dominated occupations reflects discrimination is through statistical analysis of the determinants of earnings in occupations. In a recent study, I asked the question—after accounting for measurable differences in skill, do these predominantly female occupations still pay less? In an analysis of data on more than 300 occupations, I found that after adjusting for schooling, training, part-time work, and environmental conditions (but not actual years of work experience or job tenure, which were not available), the proportion female in an occupation was associated with lower pay in that occupation for both women and for men. But the effect was not large. For each 10 percentage point increase in the percent female in an occupation, the wage in the occupation went down by 1.5 percent. Again, however, one is left with a question mark. Are there other characteristics of occupations that women, on the average, may value more highly than men because of home responsibilities or differences in tastes and for which women, more so than men, are willing to accept a lower wage in exchange? Characteristics that come to mind might be a long summer vacation, such as teaching provides, or a steady 9 to 5 job close to home that certain office or shop jobs may provide. The true effect of sex on occupational differences or wage rates is, therefore, another unresolved issue. There are many good reasons why women would be in lower paying occupations than men, even in the absence of sex discrimination on the part of employers. That does not rule out the existence of discrimination, but it weakens the case for seeking an alternative to the market determination of occupational wage rates.

Comparable Worth in Practice—The Washington State Example

What would happen if wages were set in accordance with comparable worth standards and independently of market forces? Any large-scale implementation of comparable worth would necessarily be based on job evaluations that assign points for various factors believed to be common to disparate jobs. For example, in the State of Washington, where a comparable worth study was commissioned, a job evaluation firm assisted a committee of 13 politically chosen individuals in rating the jobs used as benchmarks in setting pay in State employment. The committee's task was to assign points on the basis of knowledge and skills, mental demands, accountability, and working conditions. In the 1976 evaluation a registered nurse at level IV was assigned 573 points, the highest number of points of any job—280 points for knowledge and skills, 122 for mental demands, 160 for accountability, and 11 for working conditions. A computer systems analyst at the IV level received a total of only 426 points—212 points for knowledge and skills, 92 points for mental demands, 122 points for accountability, and no points for working conditions. In the market, however, computer systems analysts are among the

highest paid workers. National data for 1981 show that they earn 56 percent more than registered nurses. The Washington job evaluation similarly differs radically from the market in its assessment of the value of occupations throughout the job schedule. A clerical supervisor is rated equal to a chemist in knowledge and skills and mental demands, but higher than the chemist in accountability, thereby receiving more total points. Yet the market rewards chemists 41 percent higher pay. The evaluation assigns an electrician the same points for knowledge and skills and mental demands as a level I secretary and 5 points less for accountability. Auto mechanics are assigned lower points than the lowest level homemaker or practical nurse for accountability as well as for working conditions. Truckdrivers are ranked at the bottom, assigned lower points on knowledge and skills, mental demands, and accountability than the lowest ranked telephone operator or retail clerk. The market, however, pays truckdrivers 30 percent more than telephone operators, and the differential is wider for retail clerks.

Should the market pay according to the comparable worth scale? Or is the comparable worth scale faulty? In Washington State, AFSCME, the American Federation of State, County, and Municipal Employees, brought suit against the State on the grounds that failure to pay women according to the comparable worth scale constituted discrimination. Judge Jack E. Tanner agreed and ruled in favor of the union. The decision was based largely on the fact that the State had conducted the study. Whether or not the study was a reasonable standard for nondiscriminatory wage patterns was never an issue. The State, in fact, was disallowed from presenting a witness who would have critically evaluated the study.

What would happen if comparable worth were to be adopted as a pay-setting mechanism? Take the example of registered nurses and computer systems analysts. Nurses are 95 percent female. If a private firm employing both occupations were required to adopt the rankings from the Washington State comparable worth study, it would likely have to make a significant pay adjustment. It could either lower the salary of systems analysts below that of nurses or raise the pay of nurses above systems analysts. If it lowered the pay of systems analysts, it would likely find it impossible to retain or recruit them. The more popular remedy would be to raise the pay of nurses. If the firm did so, it would also be compelled to raise its prices. Most likely, demand for the firm's product would fall, and the firm would of necessity be required to cut back production. It would seek ways of lowering costs—for example, by reducing the number of registered nurses it employed, trying to substitute less skilled practical nurses and orderlies where possible. Some women would benefit—those who keep their jobs at the higher pay. But other women would lose—those nurses who become unemployed, as well as other workers who are affected by the cutback.

Of course, if the employer is a State government, the scenario may be somewhat different. The public sector does not face the rigors of competition to the same extent as a private firm. I suspect this is one reason why public sector employees seem to be in the forefront of the comparable worth movement. The public sector could not force workers to work for them if the remedy was to lower the wage in high-paying male jobs. But that is not usually what employee groups request. It can, however, pay the bill for the higher pay required to upgrade wages in female-dominated occupations by raising taxes. But in the long run, the State may have financing problems, since taxpayers may not be willing to foot the bill, and the result would be similar to that in the private firm—unemployment of government workers, particularly women in predominantly female occupations, as government services are curtailed.

Concluding Remarks

Advocates of comparable worth see it as a way of raising women's economic status and, quite expectedly, tend to minimize costs. A typical comment is as follows (Center for Philosophy and Public Policy):

Certainly, the costs incurred would vary widely depending on the scope of the approach chosen. But the economic costs of remedying overt discrimination should not prove staggering. Employers and business interests have a long history of protesting that fair treatment of workers will result in massive economic disruption. Similar claims were made preceding the abolishment of child labor and the establishment of the minimum wage, and none of the dire predictions came to pass.

Evidently the author is unaware of the numerous economic studies showing the disemployment effects of the minimum wage. However, what this statement fails to see is that comparable worth is in a bigger league than the child labor law or the minimum wage laws that have actually been implemented. It is far more radical. Instituting comparable worth by means of studies such as the one conducted in Washington State could be more like instituting a $15 an hour minimum wage or passing sweeping legislation like Prohibition. Moreover, the costs in terms of economic distortion would be much more profound than the dollars required to pay the bills. Curiously, this is recognized by one comparable worth proponent,[9] who then suggests "that we give very serious consideration to the idea that firms that do raise pay for 'disadvantaged occupations' get special tax incentives for capital equipment that will raise the productivity of these workers. We can't expect firms to swallow these losses; that's crazy." Barrett is willing to go to these lengths because she thinks it might be a way to raise the incomes of poor women heading families on welfare. Long-term welfare recipients, however, are not the women holding the jobs covered by comparable worth schemes. The work participation of women in this situation is very low. Moreover, the lesson of studies of minimum wage effects has been that those who are most vulnerable to disemployment as a result of wage hikes that exceed national market rates are the disadvantaged—those with little education, poor training, and little work experience. Comparable worth would hurt, not help, these women.

Subsidies to try to prevent these effects from occurring would be impractical to implement and prohibitively costly.

With all the difficulties that would ensue from implementing comparable worth, it is striking that it would not achieve many of the original goals of the women's movement such as the representation of women as electricians, physicists, managers, or plumbers. In fact, it would likely retard the substantial progress that has been made in the past decade. Younger women have dramatically shifted their school training and occupational choices. They have been undertaking additional training and schooling because the higher pay they can obtain from the investment makes it worthwhile. Raising the pay of clerical jobs, teaching, and nursing above the market rates would make it less rewarding to prepare for other occupations and simply lead to an oversupply to women's fields, making it still harder to find a stable solution to the problem of occupational segregation.

Another byproduct of comparable worth is that it diverts attention away from the real problems of discrimination that may arise. Such problems need not be confined to women in traditional jobs. Pay differences between men and women performing the same job in the same firm at the same level of seniority may no longer be an important source of discrimination. The form discrimination more likely takes is through behavior that denies women entry into on-the-job training or promotions on the same basis as men. The obvious solution is the direct one—namely, allowing or encouraging women whose rights are being denied to bring suit. Existing laws were intended to cover this very type of problem.

The pay-setting procedure in all levels of government employment is another area where remedies other than comparable worth would be more direct and effective. Governments usually do not have the flexibility to meet market demands. The need to adhere to rigid rules under considerable political pressure may result in paying wages that are too high in some occupations and too low in others. (By "too high" I mean that an ample supply of workers could be obtained at a lower wage.) This could occur if the private plants covered in a pay survey for a particular occupation are themselves paying above market—for example, as the result of a powerful union. Such a situation could lead to unnecessary pay differentials between certain occupations that are male dominated (which are more likely to be represented by such strong unions) and other male, mixed, and female occupations whose private sector wages are more competitive. Comparable worth is not the solution, however, since it does not address the problem. Pay-setting procedures can be improved by changing the nature of the pay surveys and by introducing market criteria—for example, by considering the length of the queue to enter different government jobs and the length of time vacancies stay open. Such changes may help women and also improve the efficiency of government.

Dramatic changes have occurred in women's college enrollment, in labor force participation, and in entrance into formerly male occupations, particularly in the professions. These changes are taking place because of fundamental changes in women's role in the economy and in the family—changes that themselves reflect a response to rising wage rates as well as changing social attitudes. Pay set according to comparable worth would distort wage signals, inducing inappropriate supply response and unemployment. If women have been discouraged by society or barred by employers from entering certain occupations, the appropriate response is to remove the barriers, not try to repeal supply and demand. Comparable worth is no shortcut to equality.

Notes

1. These statistics are based on the median hourly earnings of workers in these occupations in 1981. Rytina, 1982.

2. If brickmasons' wages are artificially high because of union power, the market would be unstable. More workers would desire to be brickma-

sons than would be hired at the artificially high wage. Would comparable worth policy help the situation? Not likely. A comparable worth solution would likely require higher pay for clergy than for brickmasons because of the heavy weight placed on readily measured items like education. A wage for clergy that is too high would also be unstable. Only the removal of the union power or restrictions on unions would satisfactorily resolve the issue.

3. This example was originated by Sharon Smith and described in Killingsworth (1984), who notes it is cited in Gold (1983).

4. The commonly cited pay gap—where women are said to earn 59 cents out of every dollar earned by men—is based on a comparison of the annual earnings of women and men who work year round and are primarily full time. In 1982 this ratio was 62 percent. This figure is lower than the figure of 72 percent cited above because the annual earnings measure is not adjusted for differences in hours worked during the year, and men are more likely than women to work overtime or on second jobs.

5. O'Neill, 1984.

6. O'Neill, 1983.

7. O'Neill, 1984.

8. Hartmann, 1984.

9. Barrett, 1984.

References

Barrett, Nancy. 1984. "Poverty, Welfare and Comparable Worth," in Phyllis Schlafly, ed., *Equal Pay for Unequal Work, A Conference on Comparable Work.*

Hartmann, Heidi I. 1984. "The Case for Comparable Worth," in Phyllis Schlafly, ed., *Equal Pay for Unequal Work, A Conference on Comparable Work.*

Killingsworth, Mark. 1984. *Statement on Comparable Worth.* Testimony before the Joint Economic Committee, U.S. Congress, Apr. 10, 1984.

O'Neill, June. 1983. "The Determinants and Wage Effects of Occupational Segregation." Working Paper, The Urban Institute.

O'Neill, June, 1984. "Earnings Differentials: Empirical Evidence and Causes" in G. Schmid, ed., *Discrimination and Equalization in the Labor Market: Employment Policies for Women in Selected Countries.*

O'Neill, June. 1984. "The Trend in the Male–Female Wage Gap in the United States." *Journal of Labor Economics,* October.

Rytina, Nancy F. 1982. "Earnings of Men and Women: A Look at Specific Occupations." *Monthly Labor Review,* April 1982.

47. Sexual Harassment

Susan M. Dodds, Lucy Frost, Robert Pargetter, and Elizabeth W. Prior

Dodds et al. discuss the need for a clear, just, and enforceable policy on sexual harassment. They try to understand sexual harassment in terms of how it is connected to harassment in general, how it can be distinguished from legitimate sexual interaction, and how it can be useful for policy purposes.

Mary has a problem. Her boss, Bill, gives her a bad time. He is constantly making sexual innuendoes and seems always to be blocking her way and brushing against her. He leers at her, and on occasions has made it explicitly clear that it would be in her own best interests to go to bed with him. She is the one woman in the office now singled out for this sort of treatment, although she hears that virtually all other attractive women who have in the past worked for Bill have had similar experiences. On no occasion has Mary encouraged Bill. His attentions have all been unwanted. She has found them threatening, unpleasant and objectionable. When on some occasions she has made these reactions too explicit, she has been subjected to unambiguously detrimental treatment. Bill has no genuinely personal feelings for Mary, is neither truly affectionate nor loving: his motivation is purely sexual.

Surely this is a paradigmatic case of sexual harassment. Bill discriminates against Mary, and it seems that he would also discriminate against any other attractive woman who worked for him. He misuses his power as an employer when he threatens Mary with sex she does not want. His actions are clearly against her interests. He victimizes her at present and will probably force her to leave the office, whatever the consequences to her future employment.

Not all cases of sexual harassment are so clear. Indeed, each salient characteristic of the paradigmatic case may be missing and yet sexual harassment still occur. Even if all the features are missing, it could still be a case of sexual harassment.

We aim to explicate the notion of sexual

harassment. We note that our aim is not to provide an analysis of the ordinary language concept of sexual harassment. Rather we aim to provide a theoretical rationale for a more behavioral stipulative definition of sexual harassment. For it is an account of this kind which proves to be clearly superior for policy purposes. It provides the basis for a clear, just and enforceable policy, suitable for the workplace and for society at large. Of course ordinary language intuitions provide important touchstones. What else could we use to broadly determine the relevant kind of behavior? But this does not mean that all ordinary language considerations are to be treated as sacrosanct. Sexual harassment is a concept with roots in ordinary language, but we seek to develop the concept as one suitable for more theoretical purposes, particularly those associated with the purposes of adequate policy development.

In brief we aim to provide an account which satisfies three desiderata. The account should:

a. show the connection between harassment in general and sexual harassment
b. distinguish between sexual harassment and legimate sexual interaction
c. be useful for policy purposes.

1. Sexual Harassment and Sexual Discrimination

It seems plausible that minimally harassment involves discrimination, and more particularly, sexual harassment involves sexism. Sexual discrimination was clearly part of the harassment in the case of Mary and Bill.

The pull towards viewing sexual harassment as tied to sexual discrimination is strengthened by consideration of the status of most harassers and most harassees. In general, harassers are men in a position of power over female harassees. The roles of these men and women are reinforced by historical and cultural features of systematic sexual discrimination against women. Generally men have control of greater wealth and power in our society, while women are economically dependent on men. Men are viewed as having the (positive) quality of aggression in sexual and social relations, while women are viewed as (appropriately) passive. These entrenched attitudes reflect an even deeper view of women as fundamentally unequal, that is in some sense, less fully persons than men. Sexual harassment, then, seems to be just one more ugly manifestation of the sexism and sexual inequality which is rampant in public life.

MacKinnon sees this connection as sufficient to justify treating cases of sexual harassment as cases of sexual discrimination.[1] Sexual discrimination, for MacKinnon, can be understood through two approaches. The first is the "difference approach," under which a "differentiation is based on sex when it can be shown that a person of the opposite sex in the same position is not treated the same." The other is the "inequality approach," which "requires no comparability of situation, only that a rule or practice disproportionately burden one sex because of sex."[2] Thus, even when no comparison can be made between the situation of male and female employees (for example, if the typing pool is composed entirely of women, then the treatment a woman in the pool receives cannot be compared with the treatment of a man in the same situation), if a rule or practice disproportionately burdens women, because they are women, that rule or practice is sexually discriminatory. For MacKinnon all cases of sexual harassment will be cases of sexual discrimination on one or other of these approaches.

Closer consideration reveals, however, that while discrimination may be present in cases of harassment, it need not be. More specifically, while sexual discrimination may be (and often is) present in cases of sexual harassment, it is not a necessary feature of sexual harassment.

The fact that in most cases women are (statistically, though not necessarily) the objects of

sexual harassment, is an important feature of the issue of sexual harassment, and it means that in many cases where women are harassed, the harassment will involve sexual discrimination. However, sexual harassment need not entail sexual discrimination.

Consider the case of Mary A and Bill A, a case very similar to that of Mary and Bill. The only relevant difference is that Bill A is bisexual and is sexually attracted to virtually everyone regardless of sex, appearance, age or attitude. Perhaps all that matters is that he feels that he has power over them (which is the case no matter who occupies the position now occupied by Mary A). Mary A or anyone who filled her place would be subjected to sexual harassment.

The point of this variant case is that there appears to be no discrimination, even though there clearly is harassment. Even if it is argued that there is discrimination against the class of those over whom Bill A has power, we can still describe a case where no one is safe. Bill A could sexually harass anyone. This particular case clearly defeats both of MacKinnon's conceptual approaches to sexual discrimination; it is neither the case that Bill A treats a man in Mary A's position differently from the way in which he treats Mary A, nor is it the case that (in Bill A's office) the burden of Bill A's advances is placed disproportionately on one sex, because of that person's sex (for the purpose of sex, perhaps, but not on account of chromosomes).[3]

A different point, but one worth making here, is that there is a difference between sexual harassment and sexist harassment. A female academic whose male colleagues continually ridicule her ideas and opinions may be the object of sexist harassment, and this sexist harassment will necessarily involve sexual discrimination. But she is not, on this basis, the object of sexual harassment.

2. Negative Consequences and Interests

Perhaps sexual harassment always involves action by the harasser which is against the interests of the harassee, or has overall negative consequences for the harassee.

However, consider Mary B who is sexually harassed by Bill B. Mary B gives in, but as luck would have it, things turn out extremely well; Mary B is promoted by Bill B to another department. The long term consequences are excellent, so clearly it has been in Mary B's best interests to be the object of Bill B's attentions. One could also imagine a case where Mary B rejects Bill B, with the (perhaps unintentional) affect that the overall consequences for Mary B are very good.

Crosthwaite and Swanton argue for a modification of this view. They urge that, in addition to being an action of a sexual nature, an act of sexual harassment is an action where there is no adequate consideration of the interests of the harassee. They in fact suggest that this is both a necessary and sufficient condition for sexual harassment.[4]

We think is is not sufficient. Consenting to sex with an AIDS carrier is not in an antibody-negative individual's best interests. If the carrier has not informed the other party, the antibody-positive individual has not given adequate consideration to those interests. But this case need not be one of sexual harassment.

Nor is this condition necessary for sexual harassment. Of course Bill B may believe that it is in Mary B's interests to come across. (A sexual harasser can be deceitful or just intensely egotistical.) Bill B may believe that it would conform with Mary B's conception of her interests. And, as we noted earlier, it may even be objectively in her own best interests. Yet still we think this would not prevent the action of Bill B against Mary B—which is in other ways similar to Bill's actions against Mary—being a case of sexual harassment.

In general, harassment need not be against the interests of the harassee. You can be harassed to stop smoking, and harassed to give up drugs. In these cases the consequences may well be good, and the interests of the harassee adequately considered and served, yet it is still harassment. This general feature seems equally applicable to sexual harassment.

3. Misuse of Power

Bill has power over Mary and it is the misuse of this power which plays an important role in making his treatment of Mary particularly immoral. For, on almost any normative theory, to misuse power is immoral. But is this misuse of power what makes this action one of sexual harassment?

If it is, then it must not be restricted to the formal power of the kind which Bill has over Mary—the power to dismiss her, demote her, withhold benefits from her, and so on. We also usually think of this sort of formal power in cases of police harassment. But consider the harassment of women at an abortion clinic by Right-To-Lifers. They cannot prevent the women having abortions and indeed lack any formal power over them. Nonetheless, they do possess important powers—to dissuade the faint-hearted (or even the over-sensitive), and to increase the unpleasantness of the experience of women attending the clinic.

Now consider the case of Mary C. Bill C and Mary C are co-workers in the office, and Bill C lacks formal power over Mary C. He sexually harasses her—with sexual innuendoes, touches, leers, jokes, suggestions, and unwanted invitations. To many women Bill C's actions would be unpleasant. But Mary C is a veteran—this has happened to her so many times before that she no longer responds. It is not that she desires or wants the treatment, but it no longer produces the unpleasant mental attitudes it used to produce—it just rolls off her. She gives the negative responses automatically, and goes on as though nothing had happened.

It would still seem to us that Mary C has been sexually harassed. But what power has Bill C misused against Mary C? He has not used even some informal power which has caused her some significantly unpleasant experience.

Crosthwaite and Swanton also argue against the necessary connection between misuse of power and sexual harassment. They note that one case where there is a lack of power and yet harassment takes place (like the Mary C and Bill C case), is the case where there is a use of pornographic pictures and sexist language by work colleagues. They also note that there are cases in which a sexually-motivated misuse of power leads to events advantaging the woman in the long run. Misuse of power cannot in itself therefore constitute sexual harassment.[5]

4. Attitudes, Intentions and Experiences

In our discussions so far, it seems that we have not taken into account, to any significant extent, how Mary and Bill feel about things. It may be argued that what defines or characterizes sexual harassment is the mental state of the harasser, or harassee, or both.

Bill wanted to have sex with Mary. He perceived her as a sex object. He failed to have regard for her as a person. He failed to have regard for how she might feel about things. And his actions gave him egotistical pleasure. These attitudes, intentions and experiences may help constitute Bill's action as a case of sexual harassment.

Mary also had very specific kinds of mental states. She found Bill's actions unpleasant, and unwanted. She wished Bill would not act in that way towards her, and she disliked him for it. She was angry that someone would treat her that way, and she resented being forced to cope with the situation. So again we have attributed attitudes and mental experiences to Mary in describing this case as one of sexual harassment.

We do not want to have to label as sexual harassment all sexual actions or approaches beween people in formally structured relationships. Cases of sexual harassment and non-harassing sexual interaction may appear very similar (at least over short time intervals). It seems that in the two kinds of cases only the mental features differ. That is, we refer to attitudes, intentions or experiences in explaining the difference between the two cases. But attention to this feature of sexual harassment is not enough in itself to identify sexual harassment.

We will now consider one of the more salient features of the mental attitudes of Bill and Mary, and show that sexual harassment is not dependent on these or similar features. Then we shall describe a case where the mental experiences are very different, but where sexual harassment does, in fact, still occur.

Consider the claim that Bill uses (or tries to use) Mary as a sex object. The notion of sex object is somewhat vague and ill-defined, but we accept that it is to view her as merely an entity for sexual activity or satisfaction, with no interest in her attributes as a person and without any intention of developing any personal relationship with her.

This will not do as a sufficient condition for sexual harassment. We normally do not think of a client sexually harassing a prostitute. And surely there can be a relationship between two people where each sees the other merely as a sex object without there being harassment. Nor is viewing her merely as a sex object a necessary condition.[6] For surely Bill could love Mary deeply, and yet by pursuing her against her wishes, still harass her.

Now consider the claim that what is essential is that Mary not want the attentions of Bill. This is not a sufficient condition—often the most acceptable of sexual approaches is not wanted. Also a woman may not want certain attentions, and even feel sexually harassed, in situations which we would not want to accept as ones of sexual harassment.

Imagine that Mary D is an abnormally sensitive person. She feels harassed when Bill D comments that the color she is wearing suits her very well, or even that it is a cold day. Bill D is not in the habit of making such comments, nor is he in the habit of harassing anyone. He is just making conversation and noting something (seemingly innocuous) that has caught his attention. Mary D feels harassed even though she is not being harassed.

Perhaps this condition is a necessary one. But this too seems implausible. Remember Mary C, the veteran. She is now so immune to Bill C that she has no reaction at all to his approaches. He does not cause unpleasantness for her for she does not care what he does. Yet nonetheless Bill C is harassing Mary C.

Mary E and Bill E interact in a way which shows that sexual harassment is not simply a matter of actual attitudes, intentions or experiences. Bill E is infatuated with Mary E and wants to have sex with her. In addition to this, he genuinely loves her and generally takes an interest in her as a person. But he is hopeless on technique. He simply copies the brash actions of those around him and emulates to perfection the actions of the sexual harasser. Most women who were the object of his infatuation (for instance, someone like our original Mary) would feel harassed and have all the usual emotions and opinions concerning the harasser. But Mary E is different. Outwardly, to all who observe the public interactions between them, she seems the typical harassee—doing her best to politely put off Bill E, seeming not to want his attentions, looking as though she is far from enjoying it. That is how Bill E sees it too, but he thinks that that is the way women are.

Inwardly Mary E's mental state is quite different. Mary E is indifferent about Bill E personally, and is a veteran like Mary C in that she is not distressed by his actions. But she decides to take advantage of the situation and make use of Bill E's attentions. By manipulating the harassing pressures and invitations, she believes she can obtain certain benefits that she wants and can gain certain advantages over others. The attention from Bill E is thus not unwanted, nor is the experience for her unpleasant. In this case neither the harasser nor the harassee have mental states in any way typical of harassers and harassees, yet it is a case of sexual harassment.

Such a case, as hypothetical and unlikely as it is, demonstrates that the actual mental states of the people involved cannot be what is definitive of sexual harassment. They are not even necessary for sexual harassment.

5. A Behavioral Account of Sexual Harassment

The case of Mary E and Bill E persuades us that we require a behavioral account of sexual harassment. For a harasser to sexually harass a harassee is for the harasser to behave in a certain way towards the harassee. The causes of that behavior are not important, and what that behavior in turn causes is not important. The behavior itself constitutes the harassment.

But how then are we to specify the behavior that is to count as sexual harassment? We shall borrow a technique from the functionalist theory of the mind.

Functionalists usually identify mental states in terms of the functional roles they play. However, some functionalist theories allow a variation on this. If we talk instead of the kind

of mental state which *typically* fills a functional role or the functional role *typically* associated with a mental state, we maintain the functionalist flavor, but allow unusual combinations of kinds of inner states and kinds of functional roles to be accommodated. We shall follow a similar technique when describing the kinds of behavior associated with sexual harassment.

Consider the behavior which is typically associated with a mental state representing an attitude which seeks sexual ends without any concern for the person from whom those ends are sought, and which typically produces an unwanted and unpleasant response in the person who is the object of the behavior. Such behavior we suggest is what constitutes sexual harassment. Instances of the behavior are instances of sexual harassment even if the mental states of the harasser or harassee (or both) are different from those typically associated with such behavior. The behavior constitutes a necessary and sufficient condition for sexual harassment.

According to this view, the earlier suggestion that attitudes, intentions and experience are essential to an adequate characterization of sexual harassment is correct. It is correct to the extent that we need to look at the mental states typical of the harasser, rather than those present in each actual harasser, and at those typical of the harassee. The empirical claim is that connecting these typical mental states is a kind of behavior—behavior not incredibly different from instance to instance, but with a certain sameness to it. Thus it is a behavior of a definite characteristic *type*. This type of behavior is sexual harassment.

This preferred account may at first appear surprising. But let us look at some of its features to alleviate the surprise, and at the same time increase the plausibility of the account.

Most importantly, the account satisfies our three desiderata: to show the connection between harassment in general and sexual harassment, to distinguish between sexual harassment and legitimate sexual interaction, and to assist in guiding policy on sexual harassment.

The relationship between harassment and sexual harassment is to be accounted for in terms of a behavioral similarity. This at first may seem to be a sweeping suggestion, since *prima facie,* there need be no descriptive similarity between sexual harassment, harassment by police, harassment of homosexuals, harassment of Jews, and so on. But the behavioral elements on which each kind of harassment supervenes will have enough in common to explain our linking them all as harassment, while at the same time being sufficiently different to allow for their differentiation into various kinds of harassment. The most plausible similarity, as we shall argue later, will be in the presence of certain behavioral dispositions, though the bases for these dispositions may differ.

Our approach allows for an adequate distinction between sexual harassment and legitimate sexual approaches and interactions. The approach requires that this be a behavioral difference. There is something intrinsically different about the two kinds of activity. Given that the typical causal origin of each of the kinds of behavior is different and so too is the typical reaction it in turn produces, it is to be expected that there would be a difference in the behavior itself. It is important to note that the constitutive behavior will be within a particular context, in particular circumstances. (The importance of this is well illustrated in cases such as a student and her lecturer at a university.[7]) Further it will include both overt and covert behavior (subtle differences count). In many cases it will also be behavior over a time interval, not just behavior at a time.

From the policy guiding perspective the account is very attractive. It is far easier to stipulate a workable, practical, defensible, and legally viable policy on harassment if it is totally definable in behavioral terms. Definition in terms of mental experiences, intentions and attitudes spells nothing but trouble for a viable social policy on sexual harassment.

The analysis we have offered entails that if there were no such characteristic kind of behavior there would be no sexual harassment. This seems to be right. In this case no legislation to ground a social policy would be possible. We would instead condemn individual actions on other moral grounds—causing pain and distress, acting against someone's best interests, misusing power, and so on.

In addition to satisfying these three de-

siderata, our account has numerous other positive features. First our account is culturally relative. It is highly likely that the kind of behavior constitutive of sexual harassment will vary from culture to culture, society to society. That is, it will be a culture-relative kind of behavior that determines sexual harassment. In any culture our reference to the typical mental states of the harasser and harassee will identify a kind of behavior that is constitutive of sexual harassment in that culture. This kind of behavior matches well with the empirical observations. There is so much variation in human behavior across cultures that behavior which may be sexual harassment in one need not be in another. The same is true of other kinds of human behavior. In the middle east, belching indicates appreciation of a meal. In western society, it is considered bad manners. The practice of haggling over the price of a purchase is acceptable (indeed expected) in some societies, and unacceptable in others. But in almost any culture, some kind of behavior may reasonably be judged to be sexual harassment.

Second, while we have cast our examples in terms of a male harasser and female harassee, there is nothing in the account which necessitates any gender restriction on sexual harassment. All that is required is that the behavior is sexual in nature and has other behavioral features which make it an instance of sexual harassment. The participants could be of either sex in either role, or of the same sex.

We acknowledge that we use the notion of an action being sexual in nature without attempting any explication of that notion. Such an explication is a separate task, but we believe that for our purposes there is no problem in taking it as primitive.

Third, the account allows for the possibility of sexual harassment without the presence of the mental states typical of the harasser or the harassee. There is an important connection between these typical mental states and sexual harassment, but it does not restrict instances of sexual harassment to instances where we have these typical mental states.

Further as the account focuses on behavior, rather than mental states, it explains why we feel so skeptical about someone who behaves as Bill behaves, yet pleads innocence and claims he had no bad intentions. The intentions are not essential for the harassment, and such a person has an obligation to monitor the responses of the other person so that he has an accurate picture of what is going on. Moreover, he has an obligation to be aware of the character of his own behavior. He also has an obligation to give due consideration to the strength and the weight of the beliefs upon which he is operating before he makes a decision to act in a manner that may have unpleasant consequences for others. Strength of belief concerns the degree of confidence it is rational to have in the belief, given the evidence available. Weight of belief concerns the quality of the evidential basis of the belief, and the reasonableness of acting on the evidence available.[8] If a person is acting in a way which has a risk of bad consequences for others, that person has an obligation to be aware of the risks and to refrain from acting unless he has gained evidence of sufficient strength and weight to be confident that the bad consequences will not arise. In the case of someone who wishes to engage in legitimate sexual interaction and to avoid sexual harassment, he must display a disposition to be alive to the risks and to seek appropriate evidence from the other person's behavior, as to whether that person welcomes his attentions. He must also display a disposition to refrain from acting if such evidence is lacking.

In the case of Mary E and Bill E, Bill E relies on the harassing behavior of other men as a guide to his actions regarding Mary E. Mary E has displayed standard forms of avoidance behavior (although she has ulterior motives). Bill E does not pay sufficient heed to the strength and weight of the beliefs which guide his actions, and it is just fortunate that Mary E is not harmed by what he does. Given Bill E's total disregard of Mary E's interests and reactions, it seems that his behavior could have caused, just as easily, significant distress to any other Mary who might have filled that role. A policy intended to identify sexual harassment should not rely on such luck, although the actual mental states (where they are as atypical as Mary E's) may mitigate blameworthiness. Bill E's harassing behavior should be checked and evaluated, regardless of any of Mary's actual mental states.[9]

Consider an example taken from an actual case[10] which highlights this obligation. Suppose Tom is married to Jane. He invites Dick (an old friend who has never met Jane) home to have sex with Jane. He tells Dick that Jane will protest, but that this is just part of the game (a game she very much enjoys). Dick forces Jane, who all the time protests violently, to have sex with him. Jane later claims to have been raped. Dick has acted culpably because he has acted without giving due consideration to the weight of the belief which guided his action, that is, to how rational it was to act on the belief given such a minimal evidential base. The only evidence he had that Jane did consent was Tom's say-so, and the consequences of acting on the belief were very serious. All of Jane's actions indicated that she did not consent.

In the case of Bill E and Mary E, Bill has an obligation to consider the strength and weight of the beliefs which guide his action before he acts. He is not justified in claiming that he is innocent, when he has been provided with signals that indicate that Mary does not welcome his attentions.

We acknowledge that it will be difficult in many situations to obtain sufficient evidence that a proposed act will not be one of sexual harassment. This will be true especially in cases where the potential harassee may believe that any outward indication of her displeasure would have bad consequences for her. The awareness of this difficulty is probably what has led others to promote the policy of a total ban on sexual relationships at the office or work place. While we acknowledge the problem, we feel that such a policy is both unrealistic and overrestrictive.

Fourth, the account allows an interesting stance on the connection between sexual harassment and morality. For consequentialist theories of morality, it is possible (though unlikely) that an act of sexual harassment may be, objectively, morally right. This would be the case if the long term good consequences outweighed the bad effects (including those on the harassee at the time of the harassment). For other moral theories it is not clear that this is a possibility, except where there are sufficiently strong overriding considerations present, such as to make the sexual harassment morally permissible. From the agent's point of view, it would seem that the probable consequences of sexual harassment (given the typical attitude of the typical harasser and the typical effects on the typical harassee) will be bad. Hence it is very likely, on any moral theory, that the agent evaluation for a harasser will be negative. The possible exceptions are where the harasser's actual mental state is not typical of a harasser, or the harassee's is not typical of a harassee.

Further, on this account many of the salient features of the case of Mary and Bill—such as misuse of power, discrimination, unfair distribution of favors, and so on—are not essential features of sexual harassment. They are usually immoral in their own right, and their immorality is not explained by their being part of harassment. But the behavior characteristic of sexual harassment will be constituted by features which we commonly find in particular instances of sexual harassment. For sexual harassment must supervene on the behavioral features which constitute its instances, but there is a range of such behavior, no one element of which need be present on any particular occasion. Similarly the morality of an instance of sexual harassment (at least for the consequentialist) will supervene on the morality of those same features of behavior.

6. Objections to the Behavioral Account

It may be objected that we have made no significant progress. We acknowledged at the beginning of the paper that many different kinds of behavior were instances of sexual harassment, even though there seemed to be no specific kind of behavior commonly present in all these instances.

Our reply is to concede the point that there is no first order property commonly possessed by all the behaviors. However, other important similarities do exist.

The property of being an instance of sexual harassment is a second order property of a particular complex piece of behavior. It is a property of the relevant specific behavioral features, and these features may be from a list of disjunctive alternatives (which may be altered as norms of behavior change). Also, the behavior of a typical harassee will possess the property of being an instance of avoidance behavior. Avoidance behavior is a disposition. Hence, even if two lots of behavior are descriptively similar they may differ in their dispositional properties. Finally the behavior of the typical harasser will possess the property of being sexually motivated, which again is dispositional in nature.

A second objection goes as follows: couldn't we have the very same piece of behavior and yet have no sexual harassment? To take the kind of example well tried as an objection to behaviorism, what would we say about the case of two actors, acting out a sexual harassment sequence?

There are a variety of replies we may make here. We could "bite the bullet" and admit the case to be one of sexual harassment. On the model proposed, we may do this while still maintaining that the behavior in this case is not morally wrong. Or, instead, we could insist that certain kinds of behavior only become harassment when they are carried on over a sufficiently lengthy time interval, the circumstances surrounding the behavior also being relevant. The case of the actors would not count as an instance of harassment because the behavior has not been recurrent over a sufficiently long period of time, especially as the behavior before and after the acting period are significantly different. Also the circumstances surrounding an acting exercise would be typically different from those of an instance of sexual harassment.

Still another response to the acting example is to argue that if the actual mental states of "harasser" and "harassee" are sufficiently different from those of the prototypical harasser and harassee, there can be no sexual harassment as there will be behavioral differences. This is not a logical necessity, but a physical one given the causal relations which hold between the mental states and the behavior. We should also keep in mind that many of the features of sexual harassment are dispositional. Thus, even if such features of sexual harassment are not manifested in particular circumstances, they would in other circumstances, and it is in these other circumstances that the observable behavior would be significantly different if it is the manifestation of harassment from that which would be associated with non-harassment.[11]

A third objection to our behavioral account focuses on our use of the mental state *typical* of harassers and harassees. We have noted that it is possible that some instances of harassment will involve a harasser or harassee with mental states significantly different from those of the typical harasser or harassee. So it is possible that the harassee is not even offended or made to feel uncomfortable, and it is possible that the harasser did not have intentions involving misuse of power against, and disregard for the interests of, the harassee. It is even possible that one or both of the harasser and harassee could know about the atypical mental states of the other. Why, at least in this last case, insist that the behavior is sufficient for sexual harassment?

From our concern to provide an account of sexual harassment adequate for policy purposes, we would be inclined to resist this kind of objection, given the clear advantage in policy matters of a behavioral account. But there is more to say in reply to this objection. Policy is directed at the action of agents, and in all cases except where at least one of the agents involved has justified beliefs about the atypical actual mental states of the agents involved, it is clearly appropriate to stipulate behavior associated with the states of mind typical of harassers and harassees as sexual harassment. For agents ought to be guided by what it is reasonable to predict, and rational prediction as to the mental states of those involved in some kind of behavior will be determined by the mental states typically associated with that behavior. So only in cases where we have reliable and justified knowledge of atypical mental states does the objection have any substance at all.

But even in these cases it seems the behavior should not be regarded as innocuous. Instances of behavior all form parts of behavioral patterns. People are disposed to behave similarly in similar circumstances. Hence we ought not to overlook instances of behavior which would typically be instances of sexual

harassment. Agents ought not be involved in such patterns of behavior. It is for similar reasons that while we allow for cultural relativity in the behavior constitutive of sexual harassment, this relativity should not be taken to legitimate patterns of behavior which do constitute sexual harassment but which are taken as the standard mode of behavior by a culture.[12]

There are three final notes about our account of sexual harassment. Provided that the kind of behavior so specified is characteristically different from behavior having other typical causes and effects, the desired distinction between sexual harassment and other kinds of sexual activity is assured.

The required connection between sexual harassment and other forms of harassment seems assured by a kind of behavioral similarity. Other forms of harassment are not sexual and vary in many ways from the pattern of behavior characteristic of sexual harassment. But there will be corresponding accounts for each kind of harassment in terms of typical causes and typical effects. The connection between all the different kinds of harassment may well be revealed by looking at these typical causes and typical effects. But despite the noted differences, the contention is that there will be an empirically verifiable behavioral similarity, and this will justify the claim that they are all forms of harassment. It may be that the relevant features of the behavior characteristic of the various forms of harassment are dispositional.

We have made two claims about behavior constitutive of sexual harassment, and we should now see how they relate. The behavior is identified in terms of its typical causes and typical effects, that is, in terms of the typical mental states of harassers and harassees. But harassment is recognized by reference to features of the behavior itself, and any legislation to ground social policy will also refer to such features. The philosophical claim is that there will be a range of such behavior features some combination of which will be present in each case of sexual harassment. The empirical job is to tell us more about the nature of such behavior and help determine the practical social policy and legislation.[13]

Notes

1. Catherine MacKinnon, *Sexual Harassment of Working Women* (London: Yale University Press, 1979), Ch. 6.

2. MacKinnon, p. 225.

3. Given that sexual harassment is possible between men, by a woman harassing a man, among co-workers, and so on, MacKinnon's view of sexual harassment as nothing but one form of sexual discrimination is even less persuasive. It is also interesting that the problems which MacKinnon recognizes in trying to characterize "offence" of sexual harassment (p. 162 ff.), indicate a need for a behavioral analysis of sexual harassment, like the one we offer.

4. Jan Crosthwaite and Christine Swanton, "On the Nature of Sexual Harassment," *Women and Philosophy: Australasian Journal of Philosophy,* supplement to 64 (1986): 91–106; pp. 100–101.

5. Crosthwaite and Swanton, p. 99.

6. If it is, it needs to be connected to a general view that women are sex objects, for pornographic pin-ups and sexist jokes and language may harass a woman without anyone viewing *that* woman as a sex object. (See Nathalie Hadjifotiou, *Women and Harassment at Work* (London: Pluto Press, 1983), p. 14.) Note that we have urged that sexual harassment should be a special case of harassment. But what is the general form of the sex object account? It seems implausible that for each form of harassment there is something corresponding to the notion of sex object.

7. See, for example, Billie Wright Dzeich and Linda Weiner, *The Lecherous Professor: Sexual Harassment on Campus* (Boston: Beacon Press, 1984).

8. For a discussion of this concept of weight see Barbara Davidson and Robert Pargetter, "Weight" *Philosophical Studies* 49 (1986): 219–30.

9. Some might say that this behavioristic account of sexual harassment is similar to having strict liability for murder, that is to say, that mental states do need to be taken into account when judging and penalizing someone's actions. What we are arguing for is a way of *identifying* sexual harassment, not how (or even if) it should be

penalized. The appropriate response to a case of sexual harassment may very well take mental states into account, along with the harm caused, or likely to be caused, and so forth. One advantage of our account is that it demands that potential harassers become aware of their behavior and to be alert to the responses of those around them. The response of Bill E (that he thought women liked to be treated that way) ought not be considered adequate especially in public life where a person's livelihood could hang in the balance.

10. This example is based on the British case, D.P.P. v. Morgan (1975), 2 All E.R. 347 (House of Lords): Morgan (1975), 1 All E.R. 8 (Court of Appeal); see also Frank Jackson, "A Probabilistic Approach to Moral Responsibility," in Ruth Barcan Marcus, *et al.* (eds.), *Logic, Methodology and Philosophy of Science VII* (North Holland, 1986), pp. 351–66.

11. For a useful account of dispositional properties, their manifestations, and their categorical bases, see Elizabeth Prior, Robert Pargetter and Frank Jackson, "Three Theses about Dispositions," *American Philosophical Quarterly* 19 (1982): 251–58.

The case of pressing solicitation by a prostitute towards a reluctant john can be viewed in the same manner as that of the actors. It is quite likely that there would be sufficient difference in the mental states of the pressing prostitute and the typical harasser to yield behavioral differences (for instance the prostitute is more interested in making money than having sex, so her behavior will reflect this insofar as, say, she would not keep on pressing if the john proved to have no money). The pressing behavior of the prostitute may be seen as a nuisance by the reluctant john, but it is not sexual harassment.

12. What will be culturally relative are types of behavior incidental to their being viewed as constituting sexual harassment in a particular culture. Acceptable standards concerning modes of address, physical proximity, touching, and so forth will vary among cultures, so the behavior patterns which will constitute sexual harassment will also vary. Of course, we must be careful not to confuse socially accepted behavior with behavior which is not sexually harassing, especially in cultures where men have much greater power to determine what is to count as socially acceptable behavior. However, so long as there are

typical mental states of harassers and harassees, the behavior which constitutes sexual harassment will be identifiable in each culture.

13. We acknowledge useful comments from Robert Young and various readers for this journal.

48.   Sex, Lies, and the Public Sphere: Some Reflections on the Confirmation of Clarence Thomas

Nancy Fraser

Nancy Fraser examines the gender, race, and class struggles highlighted in the confirmation hearings of Supreme Court Justice Clarence Thomas. In this essay, Fraser exposes the weaknesses inherent in the liberal theory of the public sphere vis à vis the impact race and gender have on how individuals stand in relation to the domains of public and private.

1. Introduction

The recent struggle over the confirmation of Clarence Thomas and the credibility of Anita Hill raises in a dramatic and pointed way many of the issues at stake in theorizing the public sphere in contemporary society. At one level, the Senate Judiciary Committee hearings on Hill's claim that Thomas sexually harassed her constituted an exercise in democratic publicity as it has been understood in the classical liberal theory of the public sphere. The hearings opened to public scrutiny a function of government, namely, the nomination and confirmation of a Supreme Court justice. They thus subjected a decision of state officials to the force of public opinion. Through the hearings, in fact, public opinion was constituted and brought to bear directly on the decision itself, affecting the process by which the decision was made as well as its substantive outcome. As a result, state officials were held accountable to the public by means of a discursive process of opinion and will formation.

Yet that classical liberal view of the public sphere does not tell the whole story of these events.[1] If we examine the Thomas confirmation struggle more closely, we see that the very meaning and boundaries of the concept of publicity was at stake. The way the struggle unfolded, moreover, depended at every point on who had the power to successfully and authoritatively define where the line between the public and the private would be drawn. It depended as well on who had the power to police and defend that boundary.

Consider how those issues underlay many of the questions that were explicitly debated: Was the public disclosure on 6 October 1991 of Anita Hill's accusations against Clarence Thomas a leak that represented a breach of proper procedure and confidentiality, or was it an act of whistle-blowing that exposed a cover-up? Was Anita Hill's failure to go public with her accusations prior to 6 October grounds for doubting her account, or was it consistent with her story? Should the behavior Hill ascribed to Thomas be considered innocent comraderie or abuse of power? Is such behavior "normal" or "pathological"?

Moreover, do men and women have different views of these issues, and are they positioned differently with respect to privacy and publicity? Did the efforts of Thomas's supporters to undermine the credibility of Anita Hill constitute an invasion of her privacy or a proper exercise of public scrutiny? Were there significant differences in the ability of Thomas

From *Critical Inquiry* 18 (Spring 1992). ©1992 by The University of Chicago. All rights reserved. Reprinted by permission.

and Hill respectively to define and defend their privacy?

Was the injection of the issue of race by Clarence Thomas a mere smoke screen, or did the convening of an all-white public tribunal to adjudicate on television a dispute between two blacks signal the existence of real racial-ethnic differences in relation to privacy and publicity? Is "sexual harassment" a figment of the fevered imagination of puritanical, sexually repressed, elite white feminists or an instrument of gender, race, and class power? Does the vindication in this case of a black man's ability to defend his privacy against a white-dominated public represent an advance for his race or a setback for black women?

Did the hearings themselves constitute an unseemly circus that degraded the democratic process, or were they a rare exercise in democratic publicity, a national teach-in on sexual harassment? Was the airing in public hearings of the charge of sexual harassment another case of the American obsession with the private lives of public figures, an obsession that displaces real politics onto questions of character? Or was it instead a historic breakthrough in an ongoing struggle to achieve a more equitable balance in the social relations of privacy and publicity?

Finally, is democratic publicity best understood as a check on the public power of the state, or should it be understood more broadly as a check against illegitimate "private" power as well? And what is the relationship between various publics that emerged here: for example, the official public sphere within the state (the hearings); the extragovernmental public sphere constituted by the mass media; various counterpublics associated with oppositional social movements like feminism and with ethnic enclaves like the black community (the feminist press, the black press); various secondary associations active in forming public opinion (interest groups, lobbies); the ephemeral but intense constitution of informal public spheres at various sites in everyday life—at workplaces, restaurants, campuses, street corners, shopping centers, private homes, wherever people gathered to discuss the events? In each of those public arenas, whose words counted in the conflict of interpretations that determines the official public story of what "really" happened? And why?

Underlying all these questions are two more general problems that are centered on power and inequality: Who has the power to decide where to draw the line between public and private? What structures of inequality underlie the hegemonic understandings of these categories as well as the struggles that contest them?

2. Gender Struggle

The first phase of the struggle was played out as a gender struggle, and it laid bare important gender asymmetries concerning privacy and publicity. These were not the familiar orthodoxies of an earlier stage of feminist theory, which protested women's alleged confinement to the private sphere. Rather, the asymmetries here concerned women's greater vulnerability to unwanted, intrusive publicity and lesser ability to define and defend their privacy.

These issues first emerged when the public at large learned of a struggle that had been waged behind closed doors for several weeks between Anita Hill and members of the Senate Judiciary Committee over the handling of her accusations against Clarence Thomas. In her first public news conference after her charges had been publicly reported, Hill focused on what she called her lack of "control" over the routing, timing, and dissemination of her information. She was already having to defend herself against two apparently contradictory charges: first, that she had failed to make public her allegations in a timely fashion, as any bona fide victim of sexual harassment supposedly would have; but second, that in making these charges she was seeking publicity and self-aggrandizement. Hill sought to explain her actions, first, by insisting that "control" over these disclosures "had never been with me," and second, by acknowledging her difficulty in balancing her need for privacy against her duty to disclose information in response to the committee's inquiry.[2] As it turned out, she never succeeded in fully dispelling many Americans' doubts on these points.

For its part, the committee's initial decision not to publicize her sexual harassment charges against Thomas represented an effort to de-limit the scope of the first round of public hearings in September and to contain public debate about the nomination. Once Hill's charges were made public, however, the committee lost control of the process. Instead, its members became embroiled in a public struggle with feminists who objected to the privatization of an important gender issue and accused the senators of "sexism" and "insensitivity."

This gender struggle was widely reported in the media in counterpoint with a counter-discourse of outrage over "the leak." These two themes of "The Senate and Sexism" and leaks were for a time the two principal con-tenders in the battle for preeminence in in-terpreting the events, as the struggle over whether or not to delay the Senate vote on the nomination was being waged.[3] The vote *was* of course delayed, and the feminists succeeded in broadening the space of the official national political public sphere to encompass, for the first time, the subject of sexual harassment.

Getting an issue on the public agenda, however, does not guarantee success in con-trolling the discussion of it. Even as it was being decided that the vote on Thomas's nom-ination would be delayed and that public hear-ings on the sexual harassment charges would be held, there began a fierce backstage contest to shape the public debate over the issues. While public debate focused on the question of the Senate's "insensitivity," White House strategists worked behind the scenes to shape the focus of the hearings and the interpreta-tion of events.

As it turned out, the administration's plan to shape public debate and limit the scope of the hearings had three crucial features. First, the White House sought to prevent or marginalize any new allegations of sexual ha-rassment by other victims in order to shape the hearings as a he-said-she-said affair. Second, they sought to rule off-limits any interrogation of what was defined as Thomas's "private life," including what the *New York Times* called his "well-documented taste for watching and dis-cussing pornographic movies while he was at Yale Law School."[4] Third, and last, they sought to exclude expert testimony about the nature of sexual harassment and the characteristic responses of victims, so that, in the words of one administration spin doctor, they could "prevent this from turning into a referendum on 2000 years of male dominance and sexual harassment."[5]

Together these three moves cast Clarence Thomas and Anita Hill in very different rela-tions to privacy and publicity. Thomas was enabled to declare key areas of his life "pri-vate" and therefore off-limits. Hill, in contrast, was cast as someone whose motives and char-acter would be subjects of intense scrutiny and intrusive speculation, since her "credibility" was to be evaluated in a conceptual vacuum. When the Senate Judiciary Committee adopt-ed these ground rules for the hearings, they sealed in place a structural differential in rela-tion to publicity and privacy that worked over-whelmingly to Thomas's advantage and to Hill's disadvantage.

Once these ground rules were in place, the administration could concentrate on its hard-ball attempt to undermine Hill. They sought to insure, as Senator Alan K. Simpson pre-sciently predicted, that "Anita Hill will be sucked right into the maw, the very thing she wanted to avoid most. She will be injured and destroyed and belittled and hounded and harassed, real harassment, different from the sexual kind."[6]

While open season was being declared on Hill, Clarence Thomas was attempting to de-fine and defend his privacy. His attempts had a certain ironic flavor, to be sure, given his insistence in the first round of hearings on substituting his personal life story—or at least his version thereof—for discussion of his polit-ical, legal, and constitutional views. Having first tried to make his private character the public issue, he was nearly undone by the focus on his character when Hill's accusation was made public.

In the second round of hearings, Thomas responded to Hill's charges by trying to define what he thought was or should be his private life. He refused to accept questions that breached his privacy as he defined it. And he objected to "reporters and interest groups . . . looking for dirt" as un-American and Kaf-kaesque.

> I am not here . . . to put my private life on display for prurient interests or other

reasons. I will not allow this committee or anyone else to probe into my private life. . . . I will not provide the rope for my own lynching or for further humiliation. I am not going to engage in discussions nor will I submit to roving questions of what goes on in the most intimate parts of my private life, or the sanctity of my bedroom. These are the most intimate parts of my privacy, and they will remain just that, private.[7]

Certainly, Thomas was not entirely successful in enforcing his definitions of privacy and publicity, as the mere airing of Hill's charges attested. Yet within the limits imposed by the fact of the hearings, he was more successful than not. His questioners on the committee generally accepted his definition of privacy, and their questions did not trespass on that space as he had defined it. They didn't inquire into his sexual history or his fantasy life, and he was not in fact questioned about his practice of viewing and discussing pornographic films. The one time when this subject was broached, at the session of 12 October 1991, Thomas successfully repulsed the inquiry:

[Senator Leahy]: Did you ever have a discussion of pornographic films with . . . any other women [than Professor Hill]?

[Thomas]: Senator, I will not get into any discussions that I might have about my personal life or my sex life with any person outside of the workplace.[8]

The question was not pursued. Later, after the Senate confirmed the nomination, Democratic members of the Judiciary Committee defended their failure to cross-examine Thomas vigorously by saying that he had put up a "wall" and refused to answer questions about his private life.[9]

The relative success of Thomas's efforts to define and defend his privacy can be seen in the fact that while the country was awash in speculation concerning the character, motives, and psychology of Anita Hill, there was no comparable speculation about him. No one wondered, it seemed, what sort of anxieties and hurts could lead a powerful and successful self-made black man from a very poor background to sexually harass a black female subordinate from a similar background.

Anita Hill also sought to define and defend her privacy, but she was far less successful than Thomas. Events constantly eluded her efforts to keep the focus on her complaint and on the evidence that corroborated it. Instead, the principal focus soon became *her* character. During the course of the struggle, it was variously suggested that Hill was a lesbian, a heterosexual erotomaniac, a delusional schizophrenic, a fantasist, a vengeful spurned woman, a perjurer, and a malleable tool of liberal interest groups. Not only the Republican hit men, Arlen Specter, Orrin Hatch, and Alan Simpson, but even her female coworkers from the Equal Employment Opportunity Commission tarred her with many of the classical sexist stereotypes: "stridently aggressive," "arrogant," "ambitious," "hard," "tough," "scorned," "opinionated." Nor did any of the Democratic committee members succeed, or for that matter even try, to limit the scope of inquiry into her "privacy."[10]

Hill's lesser success in drawing the line between public and private testifies to the gendered character of these categories and to the way their constitution reflects the asymmetry or hierarchy of power along gender lines. That asymmetry is reflected in the phenomenon of sexual harassment as well. Consider the following account by Hill in response to the questioning of Howell Heflin, who first read to her portions of her own opening statement:

"I sense[d] that my discomfort with [Thomas's] discussions [of pornography] only urged him on as though my reaction of feeling ill at ease and vulnerable was what he wanted."

Then, in response to Heflin's request for elaboration, Hill replied: "It was almost as though he wanted me at a disadvantage . . . so that I would have to concede to whatever his wishes were. . . . I would be under his control. I think it was the fact that I had said no to him that caused him to want to do this."[11] As Hill saw it, then, Thomas's behavior had been an assertion (or reassertion) of power, aimed simultaneously at compensating himself and punishing her for rejection. She herself had lacked the power to define the nature of their interaction; he, in contrast, had had the power to inject what liberals consider private sexual elements into the public sphere of the workplace against her wishes and over her objections.

Given the gender differential in ability to define and protect one's privacy, we can understand some of the deeper issues at stake in Thomas's insistence on avoiding the "humiliation" of a "public probe" into his "privacy." This insistence can be understood in part as a defense of his masculinity; to be subject to having one's privacy publicly probed is to risk being feminized.

Women's difficulty in defining and defending their privacy is also attested by an extremely important absence from the hearings: the non-appearance of Angela Wright, a second black woman who claimed to have been sexually harassed by Thomas and whose testimony to that effect was to have been corroborated by another witness, Rose Jordain, in whom Wright had confided at the time. Given that disbelief of Hill was often rationalized by the claim that there were no other complainants, the non-appearance of Wright was significant. We can speculate that had she testified and proved a credible witness, the momentum of the struggle might have shifted decisively. Why then did Angela Wright not appear? Both sides had reasons to privatize her story. Thomas's supporters feared a second accusation would be extremely damaging and threatened to discredit her by introducing information concerning her personal history. Thomas's opponents may have feared that a woman described in the press as presenting "a more complex picture than Professor Hill"[12] would appear to lack credibility and undermine Hill's as well. Thus, the silencing of a complainant who was thought to lack Hill's respectability was a crucial and possibly even decisive factor in the dynamics and outcome of the struggle.

3. The Struggle over Race

During the first, gender-dominated phase of the struggle, the issue of race was barely discussed, despite repeated, but unelaborated references to the Senate as an all-white body.[13] The relative silence about race was soon shattered, however, when Thomas himself broached the issue. Moving quickly to occupy an otherwise vacant discursive terrain, he and his supporters managed to establish a near-monopoly on "race" talk, and the result proved disastrous for Hill.

Thomas claimed that the hearings were a "high-tech lynching" designed to stop "uppity Blacks who in any way deign to think for themselves."[14] He also spoke repeatedly about his defenselessness before charges that played into racial stereotypes of black men as having large penises and unusual sexual prowess.[15]

Here it is important to note that by combining references to lynching with references to stereotypes about black men's sexual prowess, Thomas artfully conflated two stereotypes, which, although related, are far from identical. The first is the stereotype of the black man as sexual stud, highly desired by women and capable of providing them great sexual pleasure. This was the figure that emerged from Hill's testimony, according to which Thomas bragged to her about his heterosexual virtuosity. The second stereotype is that of the black man as rapist, a lust-driven animal, whose sexuality is criminal and out of control. There was no hint of that stereotype in Hill's testimony.

It is possible that at an unconscious level there are affinities between these two stereotypes. But they differ importantly in at least one crucial respect. While both have been embraced by white racists, the first, but not the second, has also been embraced by some black men.[16] Thus, while it may be inconceivable that Thomas would have elected to affect the persona of black man as rapist, it is not inconceivable that he would have affected the persona of the black male sexual stud. Yet by conflating these two stereotypes, Thomas was able to suggest that Hill's reports of his behavior as a would-be stud were equivalent to southern white racist fabrications of criminal sexuality and rape. This turned out to be a rhetorical master stroke. The Democrats on the committee were too cowed by the charge of racism to question the nominee's logic. Many leading black liberals seemed caught off guard and unable to respond effectively; most simply denied that race had any relevance in the case at all.

The mainstream press contributed to the confusion. For example, the *New York Times* printed solemn quotations from Harvard psychiatrist Alvin Poussaint about the effects of Hill's charges on black men:

> "Black men will feel [her allegations] reinforce negative stereotypes about them as sexual animals out of control. . . . It will increase their level of tension and vulnerability around charges of this type. . . . There's a high level of anger among black men . . . that black women will betray them; that black women are given preference over them; that white men will like to put black women in between them to use them. Black men feel that white men are using this black woman to get another black man."[17]

I have no way of knowing whether or to what extent Poussaint is accurately reporting the views and feelings of black men. What is clear however is the lack of any comparable discussion of the effects of the case on black women. In the absence of such discussion, moreover, the fears ascribed to black men seem to acquire legitimacy. They are not contextualized or counterpointed by any other perspective. The press coverage of the racial dimensions of the struggle generally slighted black women. It focused chiefly on questions such as whether or not all black men would be tarred in the eyes of white America, and whether or not another black man would get a shot at a seat on the Supreme Court.

One of the most important features of the entire struggle was the absence from the hearings and from the mainstream public sphere debate of a black feminist analysis. No one who was in a position to be heard in the hearings or in the mainstream mass media spoke about the historic vulnerability of black women to sexual harassment in the United States and about the use of racist-misogynist stereotypes to justify such abuse and to malign black women who protest.[18] As a result, black women were yet again "asked to choose . . . whether to stand against the indignities done them as women, sometimes by men of their own race, or to remember that black men take enough of a beating from the white world and to hold their peace."[19] In other words, there was no widely disseminated perspective that persuasively integrated a critique of sexual harassment with a critique of racism. At this stage the struggle was cast as either a gender struggle or a race struggle. It could not, apparently, be both at once.

The result was that it became difficult to see Anita Hill as a black woman. She became, in effect, functionally white. Certainly, Thomas's references to lynching had the effect of calling into question her blackness. The lynching story requires a white woman as "victim" and pretext. To my knowledge, no black man has ever been lynched for the sexual exploitation of a black woman. Thomas's charge thus implied that Hill might not really be black. Perhaps because she was a tool of white interest groups. Or perhaps because she had internalized the uptight, puritanical sexual morality of elite white feminists and had mistaken his lower class, black courting style for abuse, a view propounded by Orlando Patterson.[20] Or perhaps most ingeniously of all, because, like Adela Quested, the white female protagonist of E. M. Forster's *A Passage to India,* Hill was an erotomaniacal spinster who fantasized abuse at the hands of a dark-skinned man out of the depths of her experiences of rejection and sexual frustration, a view apparently originated by John Doggett, but more effectively—because less self-servingly—presented by Hatch and other Thomas supporters.

Whichever of these scenarios one chose to believe, the net effect was the same: Anita Hill became functionally white. She was treated, consequently, very differently from the way that Angela Wright would probably have been treated had *she* testified. Wright might very well have been cast as Jezebel, opposite Hill's Adela Quested, in a bizarre melodramatic pastiche of traditional and nontraditional casting.

The "whitening" of Anita Hill had much broader implications, however, since it cast black women who seek to defend themselves against abuse at the hands of black men as traitors or enemies of the race. Consequently, when the struggle was cast exclusively as a racial struggle, the sole black protagonist became the black man. He was made to stand synecdochically for the entire race, and the black woman was erased from view.

A recent development holds out some hope for redressing this erasure and for overcoming the definition of the struggle as either a gender or a race struggle. This is the founding of a group called African American Women in Defense of Ourselves, whose inaugural statement is worth quoting at some length:

Many have erroneously portrayed the allegations against Clarence Thomas as an issue of either gender or race. As women of African descent, we understand sexual harassment as both. We further understand that Clarence Thomas outrageously manipulated the legacy of lynching in order to shelter himself from Anita Hill's allegations. To deflect attention away from the reality of sexual abuse in African American women's lives, he trivialized and misrepresented this painful part of African American people's history. This country, which has a long legacy of racism and sexism, has never taken the sexual abuse of Black women seriously. Throughout U.S. history Black women have been sexually stereotyped as immoral, insatiable, perverse; the initiators in all sexual contacts—abusive or otherwise. The common assumption in legal proceedings as well as in the larger society has been that Black women cannot be raped or otherwise sexually abused. As Anita Hill's experience demonstrates, Black women who speak of these matters are not likely to be believed.

In 1991, we cannot tolerate this type of dismissal of any one Black woman's experience or this attack upon our collective character without protest, outrage, and resistance. . . . No one will speak for us but ourselves.[21]

What is so important about this statement is its rejection of the view, held by many supporters of Anita Hill, that race was simply irrelevant to this struggle, apart from Thomas's manipulation of it. Instead, the statement implies that the categories of privacy and publicity are not simply gendered categories; they are racialized categories as well. Historically blacks have been denied privacy in the sense of domesticity. As a result, black women have been highly vulnerable to sexual harassment at the hands of masters, overseers, bosses, and supervisors. At the same time, they have lacked the public standing to claim state protection against abuse, whether suffered at work or at home. Black men, meanwhile, have lacked the rights and prerogatives enjoyed by white men, including the right to exclude white men from "their" women and the right to exclude the state from their "private" sphere.

Perhaps, then, it is worth exploring the hypothesis that in making his case before the white tribunal, Clarence Thomas was trying to claim the same rights and immunities of masculinity that white men have historically enjoyed, especially the right to maintain open season on black women. Or perhaps he was not claiming *exactly* the same rights and immunities as white men. Perhaps he was not seeking these privileges vis-à-vis all women. After all, no white woman claimed to have been sexually harassed by him. Is that because in fact he never sexually harassed a white woman, although he married one? And if so, is *that* because he felt less of a sense of entitlement in his interactions with his white female subordinates at work? If so, then perhaps his references to lynching were not *merely* a smoke screen, as many people assumed. Perhaps they were also traces of the racialization of his masculinity. In any event, we need more work that theorizes the racial subtext of the categories of privacy and publicity and its intersection with the gender subtext.[22]

4. Class Struggle?

Sexual harassment is not only a matter of gender and racial domination but one of status and class domination as well. The scene of harassment is the workplace or educational institution; the protagonists are bosses, supervisors, or teachers, on the one hand, and employees or students, on the other; the effect of the practice is to maintain the power of the former over the latter.[23] Sexual harassment, therefore, implicates the classic issues of workers' power in the workplace and student power in the school. It should be high on the agenda of every trade union, labor organization, and student association.

Yet the class and status dimensions of the struggle over Thomas's confrontation were not aired in the public sphere debates. No trade unionist or workers' or students' representative testified in the hearings. Nor did any publish an op-ed piece in the *New York Times*. In general, no one in a position to be widely heard articulated support for Anita Hill grounded in class or status solidarity. No one foregrounded the accents of class to rally workers and students to her side.

The absence of a discourse of class conflict in the United States is no surprise. What is surprising perhaps was the deployment in the final phase of the struggle of a counterdiscourse of class resentment to mobilize support for Thomas.

On the day before the Senate confirmation vote, the *New York Times* printed an op-ed piece by that longtime friend of labor, former speech-writer for presidents Reagan and Bush, Peggy Noonan. Noonan predicted victory for Thomas based on a "class division" between the "chattering classes" supporting Hill and the "normal humans," who believed Thomas. She also glossed this as a division between the "clever people who talk loudly in restaurants and those who seat them":

You could see it in the witnesses. For Anita Hill, the professional, movement-y and intellectualish Susan Hoerchner, who spoke with a sincere, unmakeupped face

of inherent power imbalances in the workplace. For Clarence Thomas, the straight-shooting Maybellined J. C. Alvarez, who once broke up a mugging because she hates bullies and paid $900 she doesn't have to get there because she still hates 'em. . . . Ms. Alvarez was the voice of the real, as opposed to the abstract, America: she was like a person who if a boss ever sexually abused her would kick him in the gajoobies and haul him straight to court.[24]

Here Noonan appealed in familiar terms to the "real American" workers (tough and macho, even if wearing eyeliner) to resist the effeminate (albeit make-up-free) intellectuals who impersonate them and feign concern for their interests, but whose Americanness is suspect (shades of Communism). The scenario thus appeared to oppose "the real worker," J. C. Alvarez, to "the intellectual," Susan Hoerchner. Yet Alvarez here actually represented Thomas, the boss, while the actual aggrieved subordinate, Anita Hill, disappeared altogether behind the representation of Hoerchner. Moreover, by painting "the worker" as a Maybellined tough guy, Noonan simultaneously updated and perpetuated masculinist stereotypes. It became hard to see most women, who do not repay sexual harassment with a kick to the groin, as "workers."

Noonan's rhetoric mobilized class resentment in support of Thomas by disappearing Anita Hill as a worker. A similar tack was taken by Orlando Patterson, whose own *New York Times* op-piece appeared the following week in the guise of a more analytical postmortem. Although Patterson acknowledged Hill's lower class origins, he nonetheless treated her as an instrument of "elitist" (read: "bourgeois") forces. In his scenario she was a tool, not simply of whites or of feminists, but of *elite, upper-class* white feminists bent on using the law to impose a class-specific sexual morality on poor and working-class populations with different, less repressive norms. Workers were in effect called to defend their class culture—by siding with the boss against his assistant.[25]

Both Noonan and Patterson in effect bourgeoisified Anita Hill, just as Thomas had earlier whitened her. Her actual social origins in rural poverty, which she had stressed in her opening statement to the committee, had by the end of the affair become so clouded by the rhetoric of class resentment that to many she was just another yuppie. The way, once again, was paved by Thomas. Very early on, even before the sexual harassment story broke, he staked out a strong claim to the discourse of impoverished origins. And as in the case of race, here too he retained a near-monopoly.

The "class struggle" in this affair, then, was largely a matter of manipulating the signifiers of class to mobilize resentment in the interests of management. But was class not relevant in any other sense? Were there no class differences in the way Americans viewed these events and in the way they chose sides?

Some news reports following closely on Thomas's confirmation portrayed white working-class women and women of color of all classes as unsympathetic to Hill. For example, in a story titled "Women See Hearing from a Perspective of Their Own Jobs," the *New York Times* reported that blue-collar women were put off by her soft-spokenness and what they construed as her inability to take care of herself. The story contrasted this "blue-collar" view with the views of female "lawyers, human service professionals, and politicians," who strongly sympathized with and believed Hill.[26] Despite the title of the article, the *Times* did not consider the possibility that these putative class differences could be rooted in different class work cultures. It could be the case, for example, that working-class people who felt that Hill should simply have told Thomas off and quit and found another job were not attuned to professional career structures, which require cultivation of one's reputation in the profession via networking and long-term maintenance of relationships.

There was another sense in which class affected this struggle, but it remained largely unspoken and implicit. Polls taken on the last night of the hearings showed that party affiliation was the most statistically significant factor distinguishing Thomas's supporters from Hill's.[27] This suggests that a large part of what was at stake in the confirmation of this and other recent Supreme Court nominees was the continuation—or not—of the Reagan-Bush

agenda, broadly conceived. For a moment, the question of sexual harassment became the condensation point for a host of anxieties, resentments, and hopes about who gets what and who deserves what in America. In our current political culture, those anxieties, resentments, and hopes are often articulated in terms of gender and race, but they are also necessarily about status and class. Noonan and Patterson notwithstanding, class remains the great unarticulated American secret. As such, it remains highly susceptible to manipulation and abuse.

5. Conclusion: Some Morals of the Story

This extraordinary series of struggles proves the continuing importance of the public sphere in relation to state power. However, it also shows the need to revise the standard liberal view of the public sphere, since the categories of publicity and privacy are multivalent and contested, and not all understandings of them promote democracy.

For example, male-supremacist constructions enshrine gender hierarchy by privatizing practices of domination like sexual harassment. They enforce men's privacy rights to harass women with impunity in part by smearing in public any woman who protests. As a result, women are in effect asked to choose between quiet abuse in private and noisy discursive abuse in public.

However, the gendered character of the categories publicity and privacy cannot today be understood in terms of the Victorian separate-spheres ideology, as some feminists have assumed. It is not the case now, and never was, that women are simply excluded from public life; nor that men are public and women are private; nor that the private sphere is women's sphere and the public sphere is men's; nor that the feminist project is to collapse the boundaries between public and private. Rather, feminist analysis shows the political, ideological nature of these categories. And the feminist project aims in part to overcome the gender hierarchy that gives men more power than women to draw the line between public and private.

Yet even that more complicated view is still too simple because the categories of public and private also have a racial-ethnic dimension. The legacy of American slavery and racism has denied black women even the minimal protections from abuse that white women have occasionally managed to claim, even as their disadvantaged economic position has rendered them more vulnerable to sexual harassment. That same legacy has left black men without white men's privacy rights; they have sometimes tried to claim them in ways that endanger black women. That suggests the need to develop an antiracist project that does not succeed at black women's expense, one that simultaneously attacks the racial and gender hierarchy embedded in hegemonic understandings of privacy and publicity.

Recognizing how these categories become defined by gender and race points up several inadequacies of the liberal theory of the public sphere. For one thing, it is not correct to view publicity as always and unambiguously an instrument of empowerment and emancipation. For members of subordinate groups, it will always be a matter of balancing the potential political uses of publicity against the dangers of loss of privacy. Likewise, it is not adequate to analyze these categories as supports for and challenges to state power exclusively. Rather, we need also to understand the ways in which discursive privatization supports the "private" power of bosses over workers, husbands over wives, and whites over blacks. Publicity, then, is not only a weapon against state tyranny, as its bourgeois originators and current Eastern European devotees assume. It is also potentially a weapon against the extrastate power of capital, employers, supervisors, husbands, fathers, among others. There was no more dramatic proof of the emancipatory potential of publicity in relation to "private" power than the way in which these events momentarily empowered many women to speak openly for the first time of heretofore privately suffered humiliations of sexual harassment.

Yet these events also show that publicity as a political weapon cannot be understood simply in terms of making public what was previously private. They demonstrate that merely publicizing some action or practice is not always sufficient to discredit it; that is only the case where the view that the practice is wrong is already widely held and uncontroversial. Where, in contrast, the practice is widely approved or contested, publicity means staging a discursive struggle over its interpretation. Certainly, a key feature of the Thomas-Hill confrontation was the wider struggle it sparked over the meaning and moral status of sexual harassment.

The way that struggle played out, moreover, reflected the current state of American political culture. The drama unfolded at a point at which a feminist vocabulary for naming and interpreting the behavior ascribed to Thomas had already been created in the feminist counter-public sphere and disseminated to a broader public. Not only was that vocabulary thus available and ready to hand, but it was also even encoded in law. However, the feminist interpretation of sexual harassment was neither deeply rooted nor widely accepted in the culture at large. Consequently, it was contested and resisted throughout these events despite its official legal standing. In fact, it was precisely the disjuncture between its official legal acceptance, on the one hand, and the widespread popular resistance it met, on the other, that helped determine the shape of the struggle. Much of the disbelief of Anita Hill may well have been a disguised rejection of the feminist view of sexual harassment as a wrong, a rejection that could not easily be openly expressed and that was displaced onto doubts about Hill. Moreover, because the feminist understanding had legal legitimacy before it had widespread popular legitimacy, it could become a target for the expression of class, ethnic, and racial resentments. While it is not the case, in other words, that the feminist perspective is elitist, white, upper class, and so forth, it was vulnerable to being coded as such. Consequently, people with any number of a range of class, ethnic, or racial resentments, as well as those with gender resentments, could express them by disbelieving Hill.[28] Yet the result was a sharpening and broadening of the battle of interpretation.

If one result of this struggle was some increased consciousness-raising about sexual harassment, another was the fracturing of the myth of homogeneous "communities." "The black community," for example, is now fractured into black feminists versus black conservatives versus black liberals versus various other strands of opinion that are less easy to fix with ideological labels. The same fracturing holds for "the women's community." This struggle showed that women don't necessarily side with women just because they are women. Rather, the polls, for what they are worth (and it may not be much), showed that a plurality of women in every age, income, and education group said they believed Clarence Thomas more than Anita Hill.[29] Perhaps these events should lead us to consider replacing the homogenizing, ideological category of "community" with the potentially more critical category of "public" in the sense of a discursive arena for staging conflicts.

This last point suggests that if these events expose some weaknesses in the liberal theory of the public sphere, they also point in the direction of a better theory. Such a theory would need to take as its starting point the multivalent, contested character of the categories of privacy and publicity with their gendered and racialized subtexts. It would have to acknowledge that in highly stratified late capitalist societies, not everyone stands in the same relation to privacy and publicity; some have more power than others to draw and defend the line. Further, an adequate theory of the public sphere would need to theorize both the multiplicity of public spheres in contemporary late capitalist societies and also the power differentials among them. It would need to distinguish, for example, official governmental public spheres, mass-mediated mainstream public spheres, counterpublic spheres, and informal public spheres in everyday life; and it would have to show how some of these publics marginalize others. Such a theory would certainly help us better understand discursive struggles like the Clarence Thomas-Anita Hill confrontation. Perhaps it could also help inspire us to imagine, and to fight for, a more egalitarian and democratic society.[30]

Notes

1. See Jürgen Habermas, *The Structural Transformation of the Public Sphere: An Inquiry into a Category of Bourgeois Society,* trans. Thomas Burger (Cambridge, Mass., 1989).

2. "Excerpts of News Conference on Harassment Accusations against Thomas," *New York Times,* 8 Oct. 1991, p. A20.

3. Maureen Dowd, "The Senate and Sexism," *New York Times,* 8 Oct. 1991, p. A1.

4. Dowd, "Image More Than Reality Became Issue, Losers Say," *New York Times,* 16 Oct. 1991, p. A14. The mainstream press frequently referred to Thomas's alleged porn habit. See Michael Wines, "Stark Conflict Marks Accounts Given by Thomas and Professor," *New York Times,* 10 Oct. 1991, p. A18, for an account by one of his fellow Yale law school students.

5. "Bush Emphasizes He Backs Thomas in Spite of Uproar," *New York Times,* 10 Oct. 1991, p. B14.

6. Alan K. Simpson, *Congressional Record–Senate,* 102d Cong. 1st sess., 1991, 137, pt. 143:14546.

7. Clarence Thomas, "Hearing of the Senate Judiciary Committee," 11 Oct. 1991, morning sess., in Nexis Library, FEDNWS file, Federal News Service.

8. "Excerpts from Senate's Hearings on the Thomas Nomination," *New York Times,* 13 Oct. 1991, p. A30.

9. Quoted in Dowd, "Image More Than Reality Became Issue, Losers Say," p. A14.

10. Dowd, "Republicans Gain in Battle by Getting Nasty Quickly," *New York Times,* 15 Oct. 1991, p. A18.

11. "Excerpts from Senate's Hearings on the Thomas Nomination," *New York Times,* 12 Oct. 1991, p. A14.

12. Peter Applebone, "Common Threads between the 2 Accusing Thomas of Sexual Improprieties," *New York Times,* 12 Oct. 1991, p. A11.

13. See Anna Quindlen, "Listen to Us," *New York Times,* 9 Oct. 1991, p. A25. These references rendered invisible the Asian-Americans and Hispanic-Americans in the Senate, thereby attesting

to the American cultural tendency to turn race into the stark opposition of white versus black.

14. "Thomas Rebuts Accuser: 'I Deny Each and Every Allegation,' " *New York Times,* 12 Oct. 1991, p. A1.

15. See Richard L. Berke, "Thomas Backers Attack Hill; Judge, Vowing He Won't Quit, Says He Is Victim of Race Stigma," *New York Times,* 13 Oct. 1991, p. A1.

16. In a roundtable discussion on a local Chicago television talk show, three black male journalists, Salim Muwakkil *(In These Times),* Ty Wansley (WVON radio), and Don Wycliff *(Chicago Tribune)* agreed with the suggestion of black political satirist Aaron Freeman (author of the play "Do the White Thing") that many black men embrace the stereotype of the sexual stud.

17. Alvin Poussaint, quoted in Lena Williams, "Blacks Say the Blood Spilled in the Thomas Case Stains All," *New York Times,* 14 Oct. 1991, p. A16.

18. The one exception was Ellen Wells, a witness who corroborated Hill's version of events by testifying that Hill had told her that Thomas was harassing her at the time. In the course of her testimony, Wells explained why Hill might have nonetheless maintained contact with Thomas:

> My mother told me, and I'm sure Anita's mother told her. When you leave, make sure you leave friends behind, because who don't know who you may need later on. And so you do at least want to be cordial. I know I get Christmas cards from people that I . . . quite frankly do not wish to [see]. And I also return their cards and will return their calls. And these are people who have insulted me and done things which perhaps have degraded me at times. But these are things that you have to put up with. And being a black woman you know you have to put up with a lot. And so you grit your teeth and you do it. ["Questions to Those Who Corroborated Hill Account," *New York Times,* 14 Oct. 1991, p. A13]

19. Quindlen, "The Perfect Victim," *New York Times,* 16 Oct. 1991, p. A25.

20. See Orlando Patterson, "Race, Gender, and Liberal Fallacies," *New York Times,* 20 Oct. 1991, p. E15.

21. "African American Women in Defense of Ourselves," advertisement, *New York Times,* 17 Nov. 1991, p. A19.

22. A good beginning has been made in two important articles that appeared shortly after the end of the struggle. See Nell Irvin Painter, "Who Was Lynched?" *The Nation,* 11 Nov. 1991, p. 577, and Rosemary L. Bray, "Taking Sides against Ourselves," *New York Times Magazine,* 17 Nov. 1991, pp. 56, 94–95, 101.

23. There is in addition another variety of sexual harassment, in which male workers harass female coworkers who are not formally under their supervisory authority. This sort of harassment is frequent when very small numbers of women enter heavily male-dominated and masculinized occupations such as construction, fire fighting, and military service. Women in these fields are often subject to harassment from coworkers who are technically their peers in the occupational hierarchy—in the form, for example, of the display of pornography in the workplace, sexual taunts, noncooperation or sabotage, and even having male coworkers urinate in front of them. This sort of "horizontal" harassment differs significantly from the "vertical" variety discussed in the present essay, which involves harassment of an occupational subordinate by a superordinate. "Horizontal" harassment merits a different sort of analysis.

24. Peggy Noona, "A Bum Ride," *New York Times,* 15 Oct. 1991, p. A15.

25. Patterson, "Race, Gender, and Liberal Fallacies," p. E15.

26. Felicity Barringer, "Women See Hearing from a Perspective of Their Own Jobs," *New York Times,* Midwest ed., 18 Oct. 1991, p. A1.

27. See Elizabeth Kolbert, "Most in National Survey Say Judge Is the More Believable," *New York Times,* 15 Oct. 1991, pp. A1, A20.

28. Perhaps this helps explain the otherwise surprising fact, disclosed in polls, that large numbers of people who claimed to believe Hill nonetheless supported Thomas's confirmation, either minimizing the seriousness of her accusations, or judging her to be too prudish, or insisting that she should have handled the situation herself by simply telling him where to get off.

29. See *New York Times,* 15 Oct. 1991, pp. A1, A10.

30. For an attempt to develop such a theory, see Nancy Fraser, "Rethinking the Public Sphere: A Contribution to the Critique of Actually Existing Democracy," *Social Text,* no. 25/26 (Fall 1990): 56–80.

Case 10.a *Memphis Firefighters* v. *Stotts*

U.S. Supreme Court

The Supreme Court overrode lower court decisions upholding the city of Memphis's attempts to ignore seniority in layoffs of firefighters. At issue was the city's desire to preserve affirmative action gains made in recent years by African-American firefighters. Layoffs on the basis of seniority, during the time of fiscal crisis, would have disproportionately affected the African Americans recently hired through an affirmative action program. The Supreme Court upheld the seniority system.

Justice *White* delivered the opinion of the Court.

Petitioners challenge the Court of Appeals' approval of an order enjoining the City of Memphis from following its seniority system in determining who must be laid off as a result of a budgetary shortfall. Respondents contend that the injunction was necessary to effectuate the terms of a Title VII consent decree in which the City agreed to undertake certain obligations in order to remedy past hiring and promotional practices. Because we conclude that the order cannot be justified, either as an effort to enforce the consent decree or as a valid modification, we reverse. . . .

In early May, 1981, the City announced that projected budget deficits required a reduction of non-essential personnel throughout the City Government. Layoffs were to be based on the "last hired, first fired" rule under which city-wide seniority, determined by each employee's length of continuous service from the latest date of permanent employment, was the basis for deciding who would be laid off. . . .

On May 4, at respondents' request, the District Court entered a temporary restraining order forbidding the layoff of any black employee. . . . [C]oncluding that the layoffs would have a racially discriminatory effect and that the seniority system was not a bona fide one, the District Court ordered that the City "not apply the seniority policy insofar as it will decrease the percentage of black lieutenants,

drivers, inspectors and privates that are presently employed. . . ."

[The] Court of Appeals concluded that the District Court had acted properly. . . .

The issue at the heart of this case is whether the District Court exceeded its powers in entering an injunction requiring white employees to be laid off, when the otherwise applicable seniority system would have called for the layoff of black employees with less seniority. We are convinced that the Court of Appeals erred in resolving the issue and in affirming the District Court. . . .

The Court of Appeals held that even if the injunction is not viewed as compelling compliance with the terms of the decree, it was still properly entered because the District Court had inherent authority to modify the decree when an economic crisis unexpectedly required layoffs which, if carried out as the City proposed, would undermine the affirmative action outlined in the decree and impose an undue hardship on respondents. This was true, the court held, even though the modification conflicted with a bona fide seniority system adopted by the City. The Court of Appeals erred in reaching this conclusion.

Section 703(h) of Title VII provides that it is not an unlawful employment practice to apply different standards of compensation, or different terms, conditions, or privileges of employment pursuant to a bona fide seniority system, provided that such differences are not the result of an intention to discriminate because of race. It is clear that the City had a seniority system, that its proposed layoff plan conformed to that system, and that in making the settlement the City had not agreed to award competitive seniority to any minority employee whom the City proposed to lay off. The District Court held that the City could not follow its seniority system in making its proposed layoffs because its proposal was discriminatory in effect and hence not a bona fide plan. Section 703(h), however, permits the routine application of a seniority system absent proof of an intention to discriminate. Here, the District Court itself found that the layoff proposal was not adopted with the purpose or intent to discriminate on the basis of race. Nor had the City in agreeing to the decree admitted in any way that it had engaged in intentional discrimination. The Court of Appeals was therefore correct in disagreeing with the District Court's holding that the layoff plan was not a bona fide application of the seniority system, and it would appear that the City could not be faulted for following the seniority plan expressed in its agreement with the Union. The Court of Appeals nevertheless held that the injunction was proper even though it conflicted with the seniority system. This was error. . . .

The difficulty with this approach is that it overstates the authority of the trial court to disregard a seniority system in fashioning a remedy after a plaintiff has successfully proved that an employer has followed a pattern or practice having a discriminatory effect on black applicants or employees. If individual members of a plaintiff class demonstrate that they have been actual victims of the discriminatory practice, they may be awarded competitive seniority and given their rightful place on the seniority roster. . . . *Teamsters,* however, also made clear that mere membership in the disadvantaged class is insufficient to warrant a seniority award; each individual must prove that the discriminatory practice had an impact on him. Even when an individual shows that the discriminatory practice has had an impact on him, he is not automatically entitled to have a non-minority employee laid off to make room for him. He may have to wait until a vacancy occurs, and if there are non-minority employees on layoff, the Court must balance the equities in determining who is entitled to the job. . . .

Our ruling in *Teamsters* that a court can award competitive seniority only when the beneficiary of the award has actually been a victim of illegal discrimination is consistent with the policy behind § 706(g) of Title VII, which affects the remedies available in Title VII litigation. That policy, which is to provide make-whole relief only to those who have been actual victims of illegal discrimination, was repeatedly expressed by the sponsors of the Act during the congressional debates. . . .

Accordingly the judgment of the Court of Appeals is reversed.

Case 10.b   *City of Richmond* v. *Croson*

U.S. Supreme Court

This case involved the issue of minority set-aside programs, whereby a certain percentage of government contracts must be awarded to minorities. In this case, the city of Richmond adopted a "Minority Business Utilization Plan," subcontracting at least 30% of all business to minority enterprises. Justice O'Connor argued that such programs violate the Equal Protection Clause of the Fourteenth Amendment. Justice Scalia agreed with O'Connor and further rejected minority set-asides on the ground that programs should be race-blind. On the other hand, Justice Marshall argued that, because minorities had previously been wrongly excluded by the city of Richmond, such programs amounted to fair remedy.

Justice *O'Connor* announced the judgment of the Court. . . .

In this case, we confront once again the tension between the Fourteenth Amendment's guarantee of equal treatment to all citizens, and the use of race-based measures to ameliorate the effects of past discrimination on the opportunities enjoyed by members of minority groups in our society. . . .

On April 11, 1983, the Richmond City Council adopted the Minority Business Utilization Plan (the Plan). The Plan required prime contractors to whom the city awarded construction contracts to subcontract at least 30% of the dollar amount of the contract to one or more Minority Business Enterprises (MBEs). . . .

. . . The 30% set-side did not apply to city contracts awarded to minority-owned prime contractors. . . .

The Plan defined an MBE as "[a] business at least fifty-one (51) percent of which is owned and controlled . . . by minority group members." . . . "Minority group members" were defined as "[c]itizens of the United States who are Blacks, Spanish-speaking, Orientals, Indians, Eskimos, or Aleuts.". . . There was no geographic limit to the Plan; an otherwise qualified MBE from anywhere in the United States could avail itself of the 30% set-aside. The Plan declared that it was "remedial" in nature, and enacted "for the purpose of promoting wider participation by minority business enterprises in the construction of public projects."

There was no direct evidence of race discrimination on the part of the city in letting contracts or any evidence that the city's prime contractors had discriminated against minority-owned subcontractors.

On September 6, 1983, the city of Richmond issued an invitation to bid on a project for the provision and installation of certain plumbing fixtures at the city jail. On September 30, 1983, Eugene Bonn, the regional manager of J. A. Croson Company (Croson), a mechanical plumbing and heating contractor, received the bid forms. The project involved the installation of stainless steel urinals and water closets in the city jail. Products of either of two manufacturers were specified, Acorn Engineering Company (Acorn) or Bradley Manufacturing Company (Bradley). Bonn determined that to meet the 30% set-aside requirement, a minority contractor would have to supply the fixtures. The provision of the fixtures amounted to 75% of the total contract price.

[Though Croson turned out to be the low bidder, it encountered difficulties in meeting the MBE requirement, and eventually asked that it be waived. The City refused; Croson sued, challenging the constitutionality of the Plan—*Ed.*]

The Equal Protection Clause of the Fourteenth Amendment provides that "[N]o State shall . . . deny to *any person* within its jurisdiction the equal protection of the laws" (emphasis added). As this Court has noted in the past, the "rights created by the first section of the Fourteenth Amendment are, by its terms, guaranteed to the individual. The rights established are personal rights." *Shelly* v. *Kraemer,* 334 U.S. 1, 22 (1948). The Richmond Plan denies certain citizens the opportunity to compete for a fixed percentage of public contracts based solely upon their race. To whatever racial group these citizens belong, their "personal rights" to be treated with equal dignity and respect are implicated by a rigid rule erecting race as the sole criterion in an aspect of public decisionmaking.

Absent searching judicial inquiry into the justification for such race-based measures, there is simply no way of determining what classifications are "benign" or "remedial" and what classifications are in fact motivated by illegitimate notions of racial inferiority or simple racial politics. Indeed, the purpose of strict scrutiny is to "smoke out" illegitimate uses of race by assuring that the legislative body is pursuing a goal important enough to warrant use of a highly suspect tool. The test also ensures that the means chosen "fit" this compelling goal so closely that there is little or no possibility that the motive for the classification was illegitimate racial prejudice or stereotype.

Classifications based on race carry a danger of stigmatic harm. Unless they are strictly reserved for remedial settings, they may in fact promote notions of racial inferiority and lead to a politics of racial hostility. . . .

. . . We thus reaffirm the view . . . that the standard of review under the Equal Protection Clause is not dependent on the race of those burdened or benefited by a particular classification.

Even were we to accept a reading of the guarantee of equal protection under which the level of scrutiny varies according to the ability of different groups to defend their interests in the representative process, heightened scrutiny would still be appropriate in the circumstances of this case. One of the central arguments for applying a less exacting standard to "benign" racial classifications is that such measures essentially involve a choice made by dominant racial groups to disadvantage themselves. If one aspect of the judiciary's role un-

der the Equal Protection Clause is to protect "discrete and insular minorities" from majoritarian prejudice or indifference . . ., some maintain that these concerns are not implicated when the "white majority" places burdens upon itself. See J. Ely, Democracy and Distrust 170 (1980).

In this case, blacks comprise approximately 50% of the population of the city of Richmond. Five of the nine seats on the City Council are held by blacks. The concern that a political majority will more easily act to the disadvantage of a minority based on unwarranted assumptions or incomplete facts would seem to militate for, not against, the application of heightened judicial scrutiny in this case. See Ely, The Constitutionality of Reverse Racial Discrimination, 41 U. Chi. L. Rev. 723, 739, n. 58 (1974) ("Of course it works both ways: a law that favors Blacks over Whites would be suspect if it were enacted by a predominantly Black legislature").

. . . The District Court found the city council's "findings sufficient to ensure that, in adopting the Plan, it was remedying the present effects of past discrimination in the *construction industry*." . . . Like the "role model" theory . . ., a generalized assertion that there has been past discrimination in an entire industry provides no guidance for a legislative body to determine the precise scope of the injury it seeks to remedy. It "has no logical stopping point." . . . "Relief" for such an ill-defined wrong could extend until the percentage of public contracts awarded to MBEs in Richmond mirrored the percentage of minorities in the population as a whole.

Appellant argues that it is attempting to remedy various forms of past discrimination that are alleged to be responsible for the small number of minority businesses in the local contracting industry. Among these the city cites the exclusion of blacks from skilled construction trade unions and training programs. This past discrimination has prevented them "from following the traditional path from laborer to entrepreneur." . . .

While there is no doubt that the sorry history of both private and public discrimination in this country has contributed to a lack of opportunities for black entrepreneurs, this observation, standing alone, cannot justify a rigid racial quota in the awarding of public contracts in Richmond, Virginia. Like the claim that discrimination in primary and secondary schooling justifies a rigid racial preference in medical school admissions, an amorphous claim that there has been past discrimination in a particular industry cannot justify the use of an unyielding racial quota.

It is sheer speculation how many minority firms there would be in Richmond absent past societal discrimination, just as it was sheer speculation how many minority medical students would have been admitted to the medical school at Davis absent past discrimination in educational opportunities. Defining these sorts of injuries as "identified discrimination" would give local governments license to create a patchwork of racial preferences based on statistical generalizations about any particular field of endeavor.

These defects are readily apparent in this case. The 30% quota cannot in any realistic sense be tied to any injury suffered by anyone.

In sum, none of the evidence presented by the city points to any identified discrimination in the Richmond construction industry. We, therefore, hold that the city has failed to demonstrate a compelling interest in apportioning public contracting opportunities on the basis of race. To accept Richmond's claim that past societal discrimination alone can serve as the basis for rigid racial preferences would be to open the door to competing claims for "remedial relief" for every disadvantaged group. The dream of a Nation of equal citizens in a society where race is irrelevant to personal opportunity and achievement would be lost in a mosaic of shifting preferences based on inherently unmeasurable claims of past wrongs. . . .

. . . We think such a result would be contrary to both the letter and spirit of a constitutional provision whose central command is equality.

Justice *Scalia*, concurring in the judgment.

I agree with much of the Court's opinion, and, in particular, with its conclusion that strict scrutiny must be applied to all governmental classification by race, whether or not its asserted purpose is "remedial" or "be-

nign." . . . I do not agree, however, with the Court's dicta suggesting that, despite the Fourteenth Amendment, state and local governments may in some circumstances discriminate on the basis of race in order (in a broad sense) "to ameliorate the effects of past discrimination." . . . The benign purpose of compensating for social disadvantages, whether they have been acquired by reason of prior discrimination or otherwise, can no more be pursued by the illegitimate means of racial discrimination than can other assertedly benign purposes we have repeatedly rejected. . . .

. . . The difficulty of overcoming the effects of past discrimination is as nothing compared with the difficulty of eradicating from our society the source of those effects, which is the tendency—fatal to a nation such as ours—to classify and judge men and women on the basis of their country of origin or the color of their skin. A solution to the first problem that aggravates the second is no solution at all.

. . . At least where state or local action is at issue, only a social emergency rising to the level of imminent danger to life and limb—for example, a prison race riot, requiring temporary segregation of inmates . . . can justify an exception to the principle embodied in the Fourteenth Amendment that "[o]ur Constitution is color-blind, and neither knows nor tolerates classes among citizens," *Plessy* v. *Ferguson*, 163 U.S. 537, 559 (1896) (Harlan, J., dissenting).

It is plainly true that in our society blacks have suffered discrimination immeasurably greater than any directed at other racial groups. But those who believe that racial preferences can help to "even the score" display, and reinforce, a manner of thinking by race that was the source of the injustice and that will, if it endures within our society, be the source of more injustice still. The relevant proposition is not that it was blacks, or Jews, or Irish who were discriminated against, but that it was individual men and women, "created equal," who were discriminated against. And the relevant resolve is that that should never happen again. Racial preferences appear to "even the score" (in some small degree) only if one embraces the proposition that our society is appropriately viewed as divided into races, making it right that an injustice rendered in the past to a black man should be compensated for by discriminating against a white. Nothing is worth that embrace. Since blacks have been disproportionately disadvantaged by racial discrimination, any race-neutral remedial program aimed at the disadvantaged *as such* will have a disproportionately beneficial impact on blacks. Only such a program, and not one that operates on the basis of race, is in accord with the letter and the spirit of our Constitution. . . .

Justice *Marshall*, with whom Justice *Brennan* and Justice *Blackmun* join, dissenting.

It is a welcome symbol of racial progress when the former capital of the Confederacy acts forthrightly to confront the effects of racial discrimination in its midst. In my view, nothing in the Constitution can be construed to prevent Richmond, Virginia, from allocating a portion of its contracting dollars for businesses owned or controlled by members of minority groups. . . .

A majority of this Court holds today, however, that the Equal Protection Clause of the Fourteenth Amendment blocks Richmond's initiative. The essence of the majority's position is that Richmond has failed to catalogue adequate findings to prove that past discrimination has impeded minorities from joining or participating fully in Richmond's construction contracting industry. I find deep irony in second-guessing Richmond's judgment on this point. As much as any municipality in the United States, Richmond knows what racial discrimination is; a century of decisions by this and other federal courts has richly documented the city's disgraceful history of public and private racial discrimination. In any event, the Richmond City Council *has* supported its determination that minorities have been wrongly excluded from local construction contracting. Its proof includes statistics showing that minority-owned businesses have received virtually no city contracting dollars and rarely if ever belonged to area trade associations; testimony by municipal officials that discrimination has been widespread in the local construction industry; and . . . exhaustive

and widely publicized federal studies . . ., which showed that pervasive discrimination in the Nation's tight-knit construction industry had operated to exclude minorities from public contracting. These are precisely the types of statistical and testimonial evidence which, until today, this Court had credited in cases approving of race-conscious measures designed to remedy past discrimination.

Today, for the first time, a majority of this Court has adopted strict scrutiny as its standard of Equal Protection Clause review of race-conscious remedial measures. . . . This is an unwelcome development. A profound difference separates governmental actions that themselves are racist, and governmental actions that seek to remedy the effects of prior racism or to prevent neutral governmental activity from perpetuating the effects of such racism.

I am also troubled by the majority's assertion that, even if it did not believe generally in strict scrutiny of race-based remedial measures, "the circumstances of this case" require this Court to look upon the Richmond City Council's measure with the strictest scrutiny. . . . The sole such circumstance which the majority cites, however, is the fact that blacks in Richmond are a "dominant racial grou[p]" in the city.

It cannot seriously be suggested that nonminorities in Richmond have any "history of purposeful unequal treatment." . . . Nor is there any indication that they have any of the disabilities that have characteristically afflicted those groups this Court has deemed suspect.

The majority today sounds a full-scale retreat from the Court's longstanding solicitude to race-conscious remedial efforts "directed toward deliverance of the century-old promise of equality of economic opportunity." . . . The new and restrictive tests it applies scuttle one city's effort to surmount its discriminatory past, and imperil those of dozens more localities. I, however, profoundly disagree with the cramped vision of the Equal Protection Clause which the majority offers today and with its application of that vision to Richmond, Virginia's, laudable set-aside plan. The battle against pernicious racial discrimination or its effects is nowhere near won. I must dissent.

Case 10.c   A Quota on Excellence?
The Asian American Admissions Debate

Don Toshiaki Nakanishi

Unlike many ethnic minorities, Asian Americans have, in recent years, found a great measure of success in higher education—so much so, in fact, that many prestigious colleges and universities have been accused of finding ways to limit the number of Asian Americans. In this article, Don Toshiaki Nakanishi examines the points of contention surrounding bias in admissions and the social/political context of the current controversy.

Allegations of possible quotas or limitations in the admission and enrollment of Asian American applicants to some of the country's most selective public and private colleges are fueling one of the hottest educational policy controversies in recent years. From the White House to the California State House, from Berkeley to Cambridge, and from New York's Chinatown to Los Angeles's Koreatown, the so-called "Asian American admissions issue" has been the focus of extensive media scrutiny, unprecedented bipartisan political intervention, and prolonged protests by Asian American students, professors, and civil rights groups. And although some colleges have responded by formally apologizing to the Asian American community, by launching fact-finding studies, and by revising admissions procedures, it is highly likely that this issue will be with us for some time. The major competing social forces as well as perspectives of change and tradition that gave rise to this controversy still remain in an uneasy tug-of-war.

For over five years—beginning in 1983 at Brown and other private Ivy League colleges in the Northeast, and shortly after at the Berkeley and Los Angeles campuses of the public, taxpayer-supported University of California system—this admissions controversy has placed Asian Americans on an unexpected collision course with their most prized vehicle for social mobility. Indeed, despite the growth and heterogeneity of the Asian American population during the past two decades—with respect to national origin, religion, social class, and generation—there is unmistakeable unanimity in the belief that higher education is the *sine qua non* for individual and group survival and advancement in American society.

Consequently, it is not surprising that the admissions debate has elicited powerful emotional responses from Asian American students and parents alike, and has been an ongoing front-page news story in the Asian American ethnic press for several years. It also now occupies the top rung of the leadership agenda of Asian American civil rights and educational groups across the country.

However, probably not so obvious is why this admissions issue has escalated far beyond a simple tête-à-tête between Asian Americans and college administrators. Why, for example, have Presidents Reagan and Bush joined an unusually diverse group of liberals and conservatives from both political parties in Congress and in state legislatures—like Democratic U.S. Senators Paul Simon and Thomas Daschle, Republican U.S. Representatives Patricia Saiki and Dana Rohrabacher, and top Democratic California state legislators Tom Hayden, Willie Brown, David Roberti, and Art Torres—in embracing this admissions issue, denouncing "exclusionary racial quotas," and

From *Change*, November/December 1989, pp. 39–47. Reprinted with permission of the Helen Dwight Reid Educational Foundation. Published by Heldref Publications, 1319 18th St. NW, Washington, DC 20036–1802. Copyright © 1989.

spearheading numerous hearings in Washington and across the country?

Why is the Office of Civil Rights of the Department of Education conducting full-scale Title VI anti-bias compliance investigations of potentially discriminatory admissions practices and policies toward Asian American applicants at UCLA and Harvard? And why is it highly likely that other colleges will be targeted in the future? Why has almost every major newspaper and magazine in the nation, many television news programs, as well as just about every syndicated columnist from left to right on the political spectrum—including Doonesbury—found this controversy to be so newsworthy and symptomatic of much of what is wrong with American education?

Above all, why does the Asian American admissions debate represent a serious challenge to a number of long-standing institutional goals and practices of American higher education, whether the goal is socially engineering a "diverse" or "balanced" undergraduate student body or seeking the meritocratic ideal of choosing the best of the brightest? And what, if anything, can be done to resolve this issue?

The answers to these questions, I believe, require an understanding of not only the specific points of contention regarding possible bias and unfairness in evaluating Asian American applicants, but also the social and political context within which this controversy has emerged.

The Emergence of the Debate

The Asian American admissions debate probably could not have been foreseen. Unitl recently, the Asian American college-going population received little media, policy, or scholarly attention, because of their relatively small numbers nationally and their seemingly strong academic performance levels. In two of the more highly regarded comparative studies of minority students—Alexander Astin's *Minorities in Higher Education* (1982) and John Ogbu's *Minority Education and Caste* (1978)—Asian Americans were not included in the data collection and analysis because they were not considered to be "educationally disadvantaged" like other non-white minority groups. Indeed, there is much to suggest that the admissions debate might not have become so explosive if there had been a body of empirical knowledge that all parties to the dispute could have used to test or verify their largely unfounded assumptions and assertions about Asian American students. (One major point of contention has focused on the predictive value of admissions criteria—high school GPA, SAT verbal and math, and achievement tests—in explaining future college performance of Asian American and other groups of students. Contrary to conventional wisdom, a comparative study of University of California students found that the SAT math score was a better predictor of first-year grades than the SAT verbal for Asian Americans. For whites, the SAT verbal score remained the stronger predictor. Similarly, math achievement was a better predictor than English composition for Asian Americans, while the opposite was true for whites. The study served to challenge the common admissions practice of placing greater weight on verbal rather than math scores. See Stanley Sue and Jennifer Abe, "Predictors of Academic Achievement Among Asian American and White Students," *College Board Report,* No. 88-11, 1988.) Instead, much of this controversy has evolved in a virtual scholarly vacuum.

Beginning in the early 1980s, the national press became increasingly interested in the Asian American college-going population. They initially wrote stories touting the individual academic achievements of some of the most gifted Asian American students—such as the winners of the Westinghouse Talent Search—and what appeared to be their dramatic rise in enrollment at many of the country's most selective institutions. *U.S. News and World Report* wrote that "Asians are, in fact, flocking to top colleges. They make up about 10 percent of Harvard's freshman class and 20 percent of all students at the Juilliard School. In California, where Asians are 5.5 percent of the population, they total 23.5 percent of all Berkeley undergraduates." And

Newsweek asked rhetorically: "Is it true what they say about Asian American students, or is it mythology? They say that Asian Americans are brilliant. They say that Asian Americans behave as a model minority, that they dominate mathematics, engineering, and science courses—that they are grinds who are so dedicated to getting ahead that they never have any fun."

Beginning in 1985, however, journalists and syndicated columnists began portraying Asian American undergraduates not only as "Whiz Kids," as *Time* magazine boldly proclaimed in a major cover story, but also as possible victims of racially discriminatory admissions practices. In a highly influential 1986 *Chronicle of Higher Education* article, Lawrence Biemiller wrote, "Charges that some elite colleges and universities may be purposefully limiting the admission of persons of Asian descent continue to worry students and parents. . . . The allegations come at a time when reports of racially motivated violence against Asians are increasing and talk of 'trade wars' with Asian countries continues, prompting concern about a possible resurgence of anti-Asian sentiment."

Historical analogies often were drawn to the situation facing American Jewish students before World War II when invidious, discriminatory policies and procedures officially were adopted to limit their access to many of the same selective institutions now concerning Asian Pacific Americans. As *Los Angeles Times* reporter Linda Mathews wrote, "There may be a parallel between what is happening to Asian Americans now and what happened to Jews in the 1920s and 1930s at some Ivy League schools. . . . To keep a lid on the number of Jewish students—denounced as 'damned curve raisers' by less talented classmates—the universities imposed quotas, sometimes overt, sometimes covert. . . . Today's 'damned curve raisers' are Asian Americans, who are winning academic prizes and qualifying for prestigious universities in numbers out of proportion to their percentage of the population. And, like Jews before them, the members of the new model minority contend that they have begun to bump up against artificial barriers to their advancement."

Conservative and liberal commentators alike also joined the fray, linking the Asian American admissions issue to their ongoing ideological donneybrooks on a range of such unsettled policy topics as affirmative action programs, the nation's competitiveness with foreign economic powers, or recent educational reform measures. George F. Will, writing in April 1989, shortly after Berkeley Chancellor Ira Michael Heyman apologized to the Asian American community for his administration's past admissions policies that "indisputably had a disproportionate impact on Asian Americans," declared that liberalism was to blame for the admissions controversy. In echoing the highly controversial views expressed a few months earlier by former Assistant Attorney General William Bradford Reynolds, columnist Will argued that the discrimination that Asian American students encountered was due to affirmative action policies, one of the major cornerstones of the liberal social agenda. He wrote, "Affirmative action discriminated against Asian Americans by restricting the social rewards open to competition on the basis of merit. We may want a modified meritocracy, but it should not be modified by racism and the resentment of excellence. . . . At a time of high anxiety about declining educational standards and rising competition from abroad, and especially from the Pacific Rim, it is lunacy to punish Asian Americans—the nation's model minority—for their passion to excel."

Clarence Page was one of many liberal commentators, along with major Asian American community leaders, who denounced the conservatives' attack on affirmative action and their attempt to connect it with the situation facing Asian American students at Berkeley. As Page wrote, "Since this announcement offers ammunition in their relentless fight against affirmative action programs, some political conservatives applaud it. Conservatives often offer the success of Asian Americans as evidence that the American system is so fair to all that blacks and other minorities jolly well better look to themselves, not to the government or 'reverse discrimination,' for solutions to their problems. But the Berkeley problem was not 'reverse discrimination.' It was plain, old-fashioned discrimination of a sort affirmative action programs were intended to remedy, not create. The big difference this time is that it penalizes a people who have a reputation for overachievement."

During the past decade, the media's changing portrayal of Asian American college students may have appeared to reflect a zealous search for not only good, but provocative, news stories rather than focusing on policy. However, beyond the catchy headlines and one-line history lessons, a new and potentially far-reaching controversy about undergraduate admissions was gradually, and unexpectedly, unfolding. In many respects, the points of contention appeared quite familiar, and somehow *seemed* to be settled, especially in the aftermath of *Bakke*. Like other recent conflicts dealing with access and representation of women or historically underrepresented racial minorities in America's institutions of higher education, the Asian American admissions debate eventually focused on the potential bias and arbitrariness of selection criteria procedures, and policies that might limit equal educational opportunities. Broad philosophical concepts (like meritocracy) and seemingly widely shared, long-standing institutional goals (like the deliberate social engineering of a "diverse" or "balanced" undergraduate student body) were again debated, and their procedural role in the admissions process was both questioned and justified.

And yet not anticipated was that this new admissions controversy would involve Asian Americans, a group that had not figured prominently in the earlier policy and legal disputes over admissions, and a group that did not have a reputation for being particularly assertive, visible, or efficacious in the political or other decision-making arenas. However, during the 1980s, a new and different Asian American population emerged as a result of unprecedented demographic, economic, and political trends. Higher education officials, like others who were not population specialists, probably could not have foreseen the dramatic changes that were occurring among Asian Americans, nor could they have fully realized how these trends would seriously challenge their seemingly well-established institutional practices and policies.

Contrary to the media's interpretation, the extraordinary rise in Asian American enrollment in many of the country's most competitive institutions starting in the early 1980s probably had far less to do with Asian American students' suddenly becoming more academically motivated and qualified than it did with their phenomenal demographic growth. According to the 1980 U.S. Census, Asian Americans were America's fastest-growing group. Between 1970 and 1980, they increased nationally by 128 percent from 1.5 million to 3.5 million. Recent projections estimate that Asian Americans will again double in size to 7 million by 1990 because of the continued large influx of refugees and immigrants from East and Southeast Asia, along with the Pacific Islands.

By extension, Asian Americans also are the fastest-growing group in the American college-going population, and the large increases in enrollment that the media reported with such surprise and awe for the most competitive private colleges were simultaneously occurring at other, less selective institutions as well. In the fall of 1976, there were 150,000 Asian American undergraduates in American higher education nationwide. A decade later, in fall of 1986, there were almost three times as many—448,000 Asian Americans in colleges and universities across the country, with almost half enrolled in two-year institutions. All demographic projections of the Asian American college-age sector indicate that this exceptionally fast growth pattern will continue well into the next century.

Coinciding with this demographic upsurge during the '80s was the Asian American population's growing political maturity and influence at both the national and local levels. Perhaps at no other period in the over 150-year history of Asians in the United States have so many individuals and organizations participated in such a wide array of political and civil rights activities, not only in relation to the American political system, but also to the affairs of their ancestral homelands in Asia. In traditional electoral politics, what had come to be taken as a common occurrence in Hawaii—namely the election of Asian Americans to public office—suddenly became a less than surprising novelty in the so-called mainland states with the election and appointment of

Asian Americans to federal, state, and local positions in California, Washington, New York, and elsewhere. And perhaps most significantly, the Asian American population came to demonstrate that it, too, had resources and talents—organizational, financial, or otherwise—to advance its specific concerns in a variety of political arenas, and to confront political issues that potentially are damaging to its group interests. Two widely reported grass-roots campaigns illustrate this new collective determination: the successful drive by Japanese Americans to gain redress and reparations for their World War II incarceration, and the effective national movement to appeal and overturn the light sentences given to two unemployed Detroit auto workers who, in 1982, used a baseball bat to kill Chinese American Vincent Chin. (The two men mistook Chin for a Japanese and, therefore, someone who was viewed as having taken away their jobs.)

The Asian American population's enhanced political participation during the '80s had several idiosyncratic features, with peculiar consequences for the Asian American admissions controversy. For example, other ethnic groups register and vote in overwhelming proportions for one or the other of the two major political parties—for example, blacks and American Jews for the Democratic party—which makes them largely beholden to the electoral success of that one party. Asian Americans, however, began during the '80s to exhibit a very different pattern of political affiliations at both the mass and elite levels. In numerous studies I conducted for the UCLA Asian Pacific American Voter Registration Project, Asian Americans were almost evenly divided between Democrats and Republicans in their registration and voting behavior. Both political parties, especially the Republicans, have attempted to register the hundreds of thousands of recent Asian immigrants and refugees who annually become naturalized citizens—most notably in key electoral states like California. At the same time, Asian Americans have been cultivating a strong reputation as major financial contributors to Republican and Democratic candidates alike. Their estimated $10 million in contributions to the 1988 presidential election were divided almost equally between George Bush and Michael Dukakis. This 1980s pattern of supporting both parties at the voting and campaign fund-raising levels will likely continue. In turn, Democratic and Republican leaders, attempting to appeal to their growing and valued Asian American constituents, are addressing issues of special concern to them.

This unusual pattern of bipartisan affiliations among Asian Americans might well explain why the Asian American admissions issue is gaining the support of top leaders from both political parties. In California, for example, the state legislature's foremost liberal Democratic leaders—like Tom Hayden, Art Torres, David Roberti, and Willie Brown—have actively monitored the admissions controversy at the public University of California campuses for close to five years. They held numerous fact-finding hearings, intervened by bringing together university officials and Asian American community leaders, passed special resolutions on admissions, and had the state Auditor General undertake an unprecedented audit of admissions procedures at Berkeley. When addressing local Asian American communities, these politicians—along with other key municipal leaders like Mayor Tom Bradley of Los Angeles—have frequently spoken out against potentially discriminatory admissions practices. At the national level, in Washington, where politics often do make for very strange bedfellows, the issue has been championed by liberals like Senator Paul Simon and conservatives like Congressman Dana Rohrabacher. Simon and Rohrabacher, on separate occasions, both expressed a keen interest in the current Title VI compliance investigations by the Office of Civil Rights at UCLA and Harvard, and indicated they may request that other institutions be formally reviewed in the future.

Rohrabacher, whose Southern California congressional district has a large number of Asian American voters, and Hawaiian representative Patricia Saiki, a Japanese American, introduced a bill in Congress last June dealing with bias against Asian American applicants. Hearings were scheduled this fall in cities across the nation. And although many Asian American liberals fear that conservative Republicans like Rohrabacher will attempt to use the Asian American issue to dismantle or discredit affirmative action programs and policies in higher education, it also is evident that Republican leaders are attempting to address one of the foremost concerns raised by their own constituents and the increasingly influential group of Asian American leaders in the Republican party.

For Asian Americans, then, the admissions controversy has gone beyond party or ideological differences, and has come to rest at the top of the leadership agenda for Asian Americans of all political persuasions. It is highly likely, therefore, that Republican and Democratic Asian American leaders, working together or independently, will continue pushing officials from both parties to resolve this issue.

The Asian American admissions controversy evolved out of the largely unexpected convergence of dramatic demographic and political changes among the Asian American population during the 1980s. Although higher education officials probably could not have anticipated these extraordinary social trends, it was their general reluctance and inability to fully and expeditiously address the complaints raised initially by Asian American students and professors on their own campuses that dramatically escalated this controversy.

Some commentators speculate that university administrators were fully convinced their customary policies and procedures were sound and fair and did not believe there were compelling reasons to change them. Writing in *The New Republic*, David Bell said, "The universities, however, consider their idea of the academic community to be liberal and sound. They are understandably hesitant to change it because of a demographic shift in the admissions pool."

Still others suggest that university administrators simply did not believe the admissions debate involving Asian Americans would get out of control or receive such prominent national media and political attention. These observers speculate that higher education officials were blinded by stereotypic images of Asian Americans as being politically passive and ineffectual, and did not anticipate how a new and more assertive Asian American population would use its many resources and

alliances to confront a potentially discriminatory situation.

Whatever the case, the Asian American admissions controversy emerged and continues to be played out in this broader social context. Specific points of contention of the ongoing debate must be considered in terms of the interplay of these larger social forces and perspectives.

The Pros and Cons

All parties to the controversy—the critics as well as the admissions officers—agree that Asian American applicants to many of the nation's most selective undergraduate Ivy League institutions, as well as Stanford and the flagship Berkeley and Los Angeles campuses of the UC system, now have lower rates of admission than other groups of applicants, including whites (see Tables 1 and 2 for Harvard and Berkeley).

Although disparities have existed and been acknowledged officially for several years, data for the fall 1985 entering class are illustrative. At Princeton, 17 percent of all applicants and 14 percent of the Asian American applicants were admitted. At Harvard, 15.9 percent of all applicants and 12.5 percent of the Asian Americans were accepted. And at Yale, 18 percent of all applicants and 16.7 percent of Asian Americans were admitted. Put another way, Asian American applicants to Princeton were admitted at a rate that was only 82.4 percent of that for other applicants; to Harvard at 78.6 percent; and to Yale at 92.6 percent. Likewise, a study undertaken by a Standard University Academic Senate committee found that, between 1982 and 1985, "Asian American applicants to Stanford had admission rates ranging between 66 percent and 70 percent of admission rates for whites."

Similarly, in perhaps the most exhaustive external investigation of the admissions controversy performed to date (at the time this article was being written, the Office of Civil Rights of the U.S. Department of Education had not completed its Title VI compliance investigations of potentially biased admissions

Table 1. 1978–87 Admissions Rates at Harvard for Asian Americans and Whites

	1978	1979	1980	1981	1982	1983	1984	1985	1986	1987
Asian Americans	12%	15%	15%	14%	13%	14%	13%	12%	11%	12%
Whites	17%	16%	15%	16%	18%	19%	18%	17%	18%	16%

Harvard University, Office of Admissions

practices toward Asian American applicants at Harvard and UCLA), the California State Auditor General, at the State Senate's request, conducted a full-scale audit of white and Asian Pacific American freshman applicants to the UC-Berkeley campus. Academic records for applicants to Berkeley's seven different undergraduate colleges and programs from 1981 through 1987 were examined, producing a total of 49 different categories of comparison between Asian Pacifics and whites. In 37 of the 49 cases, whites had higher admission rates than Asian Pacifics, even though Asian Pacific applicants were found to have higher academic qualifications in practically all comparison groups.

Indeed, the academic qualifications of Asian American applicants have never been an issue, nor have they been used in rebuttal to explain lower admission rates. Every campus that launched its own *ad hoc* inquiry to examine and resolve this debate—Brown, Princeton, Harvard, Berkeley, and Stanford, among others—has found that Asian Pacific applicants have stronger group-level academic profiles as measured by high school grades and standardized tests, and that those who are ul-

timately admitted usually have far stronger academic qualifications than other groups of admits.

Bunzel and An wrote in *Public Interest* that, of the students who were admitted to Harvard in 1982, "Asian Americans had average verbal and math scores of 742 and 725, respectively, for an average combined score of 1467, while the scores for Caucasians were 666 and 689, for a total of 1355, or 112 points lower." An official letter sent by Harvard's admissions office to its alumni recruiters nationwide challenged these figures while acknowledging that Asian/Pacific admits usually had higher test scores than whites: "The actual difference for the year cited in the article was 50 points, and the typical difference in a given year is 40 points for the verbal and mathematics SATs combined."

The findings by these individual campuses are consistent with other formal studies. The California Postsecondary Education Commission's periodic investigations of eligibility rates for the UC system consistently show that Asian/Pacific Americans have the largest proportion of "academically eligible" students of any group and, thus, should have the highest

Table 2. 1981–87 Admission Rates at U.C. Berkeley for Asian Americans and Whites

	1981	1982	1983	1984	1985	1986	1987
Asian Americans	50.4%	60.3%	66.8%	45.0%	44.4%	28.4%	27.7%
Whites	54.3%	64.5%	70.5%	56.4%	52.3%	32.7%	31.4%

University of California, Berkeley, Chancellor's Report.

admission rate if grades and test scores were the *only* selection criteria. In the most recent study, based on the state's 1986 high school graduating class, 32.8 percent of the Asian American graduates were found to be eligible for the University of California, in contrast to 15.8 percent for whites, 5 percent for Latinos, and 4.5 percent for blacks. Similar patterns of university eligibility by ethnic group have been found in previous years.

Several major explanations have been offered to account for these disparities in admission rates. Critics contend that admissions officers at both highly selective public and private institutions are engaging in intentionally discriminatory practices to limit the representation of Asian/Pacific students—who tend to be the fastest-growing group of applicants at these campuses. For example, over 20 percent of the fall 1987 entering class at Berkeley was Asian American. Given that Asian Americans make up approximately 2 percent of the nation's population and 6 percent of California's population, at first glance this figure might provide credence to the claim that Asian Americans were "overrepresented." However, what is not apparent is that Asian/Pacific Americans now represent an increasingly sizeable proportion of the total applicant pools at these colleges. Of the 16,318 applicants who competed for regular admissions slots at Berkeley for the fall 1987 class, 5,032—or 30.8 percent—were Asian Americans.

Critics also contend that public institutions like the UC campuses have secretly, without adequate public and legislative discussion, deviated from their long-standing academic, merit-based admissions policies by giving weight to a variety of subjective criteria in the selection process. They also argue that Asian/Pacific American faculty and administrators at the institutions are systematically excluded from participating in decision-making committees and activities dealing with undergraduate selection policies and procedures.

Admissions officers, on the other hand, deny that quotas, informal or formal, exist for Asian/Pacific Americans or any other group, especially in the post-*Bakke* era. They contend that admission rates are simplistic indicators of discrimination and do not fully describe the highly professional, multilevel process of admissions review that all applicants receive. They further argue that privacy laws, like the so-called Buckley Amendment of 1974, prevent access to all the relevant materials that are reviewed in an applicant's file, especially personal essays and letters of recommendation that can play a far more decisive role in highly competitive admissions situations than is generally recognized.

Finally, admissions officers at private institutions, and increasingly at public colleges as well, have argued that their admissions policies are not entirely meritocratic, but encompass other significant institutional goals and traditions. A common explanation offered to account for lower admission rates among Asian/Pacific American applicants is that they are less likely to be proportionately represented among a range of criteria that underlie a broad and flexible interpretation of the goal of seeking undergraduate diversity. Ironically, current officials at many of the nation's most prestigious research universities, like their predecessors who dealt with the upsurge in American Jewish applicants, have found themselves defending their institutional need to enroll good football players and the siblings of loyal and wealthy alumni rather than a meritocratic ideal of choosing the best of the brightest.

Geographic diversity, for example, is a well-established and widely accepted goal of private elite institutions, which is explicitly routinized in the admissions process. Recruiting in certain cities and states, specific admissions officers not only identify, but are advocates for, the top students in admissions committee deliberations, which systematically reflect geographic considerations rather than a random review of the entire applicant pool. As a result, only a few of the many applicants from any particular geographic area can be admitted. Thus, the various talents and characteristics of student diversity, or other institutional priorities, must be encompassed within this formal geographic quota.

Admissions officers argue that Asian Americans are at a disadvantage because the vast majority of their applicants are from New York, California, or the western states, and, as a result, their representation in the entering class is a function of the size and strength of their local applicant pools. Ironically, this goal of geographic diversity was first instituted by many of these same undergraduate institutions to limit indirectly the enrollment of American Jews before World War II, who were concentrated mainly in New York and other parts of the Northeast.

However, the geographic skewing of the Asian Americans and American Jewish applicant pools may not be unique. Indeed, New York probably provides more applicants and matriculants overall to the Ivy colleges than any other state. California, the site of intensive recruiting campaigns by institutions from across the nation, usually ranks second or third in its overall representation of these student bodies. For example, during the 1985–86 academic year, there were 1,094 students from New York, 747 from Yale's home state of Connecticut, and 455 Californians among Yale's total undergraduate enrollment of 5,190. Together, these three top feeder states accounted for 44.2 percent of Yale's undergraduate student body. Similarly, Harvard's entering class of 1985 had 290 students from New York, 279 from its home state of Massachusetts, and 168 from California. Although all 50 states were represented among the 1,525 domestic freshman students, Harvard's top three feeder states of New York, Massachusetts, and California accounted for 48.3 percent of its entering class.

Admissions officers at the nation's selective institutions, public and private, also argue that Asian American applicants show a disproportionate interest in specific future college programs, especially pre-med studies, engineering, and the natural and physical sciences. For example, an official faculty and student committee investigating Asian American admissions at Princeton in 1985 argued that "Asian American applicants have not been strongly represented in those subgroups tending to have higher than average rates of admission (e.g., alumni children, athletes); on the other hand, Asian Americans are strongly represented in the one applicant group with a somewhat lower rate of admission (engineering school candidates)." Similarly, L. Fred Jewitt, former dean of admissions at Harvard, made an analogous assessment: "A terribly high proportion of Asian students are heading toward the sciences. In the interests of diversity, then, more of them must be left out."

Admissions to these majors, of course, tends to be extremely competitive because of the oversupply of highly qualified applicants and the formal and informal restrictions placed on the number of potential admits by specific departments. Thus, university administrators argue that the lower admission rate for Asian American applicants is due to their overconcentration in particular majors of choice that are designated when filing applications. Put another way, they believe that if Asian Americans were less homogeneous and were equally distributed among a range of majors, then there would be no disparities in admission rates.

A comparative analysis of data on the characteristics of California SAT test-takers in 1977 and 1985 tends to support the notion of "lack of diversity of major." Approximately 70 percent of the state's Asian/Pacific American males and over 50 percent of the females who took the test in 1985 indicated at the time that they intended to major in engineering, the sciences, or mathematics. For the males, interest in majoring specifically in engineering or computer science jumped from 26.1 percent to 46.1 percent from 1977 to 1985, while for females there was an increase from 5.3 percent to 15.8 percent. Interest in being a premed major declined slightly for Asian American males from 8.6 percent to 7.8 percent, and rose slightly for females from 6.2 percent to 8.6 percent (Table 3).

However, admissions data from UC's Los Angeles and Berkeley campuses, as well as Stanford, empirically support the more important hypothesis that there are disparities in admit rates across fields. As Table 4 illustrates, Asian American applicants to UCLA from 1983–85 had lower overall admission rates than other applicants, including white applicants, that cannot be explained by analyzing separate admissions statistics for the institution's three undergraduate colleges. Aside from the College of Fine Arts, which accounts for a small proportion of applicants and admits for all groups, Asian Americans consistently had lower rates than whites and other applicants in engineering, as well as letters and science at UCLA. Similarly, as noted earlier, the situation at the Berkeley campus for applicants to the seven different undergraduate colleges and programs from 1981–87 demon-

Table 3. Changes in Intended Undergraduate Majors for Asian Pacific American Students*

Intended Major	Males		Females	
	1977 *N = 3699*	1985 *N = 6730*	1977 *N = 3738*	1985 *N = 7008*
All sciences and engineering combined**	2325 (62.9%)	4672 (69.4%)	1876 (50.2%)	3590 (51.2%)
Engineering and computer science only	966 (26.1%)	3104 (46.1%)	200 (5.3%)	1106 (15.8%)

*Based on SAT data tapes for California test-takers, 1977 and 1985.
**Includes all test-takers who indicated a preference for majoring in the biological sciences, computer science, engineering, health and medicine, mathematics, physical sciences, and psychology.
Source: UCLA Project on Asian Pacific Americans in Higher Education

strated comparable differences in admission rates for Asian and white applicants in engineering, the sciences, and the liberal arts. A Stanford University Academic Senate report found that for *every* category of intended majors, Asian Americans had a lower admission rate than whites.

Finally, another common argument for explaining away admission rate disparities is that Asian Americans are less likely than whites to be among specific categories of applicants who receive, by tradition or official decree, special consideration in the admission process—alumni children and athletes. Applicants from these "special" groups usually are admitted at twice or more the rate of other applicants and tend to be largely white at Ivy League and other private elite institutions. For example, the overall admission rate for Brown's entering class in fall of 1987 was an extremely competitive 18.5 percent for all who applied. The admission rates, on the other hand, for alumni legacies and athletes, were 46.1 percent and 56 percent, respectively. The rationale for giving such added preference to special groups of applicants is usually embedded in long-standing institutional policies and practices.

Admissions officers argue that differences in admit rates would not be apparent if Asian Americans were proportionately represented among applicants with alumni and athletic preferences. They also believe that such disparities will vanish in the future as those who are currently enrolled become alumni and urge their own siblings to apply to their alma maters. For example, as Harvard's admissions office wrote, "Today, relatively few Asian Americans are the children of alumni/ae, although the recent dramatic increases in the percentages of Asian Americans in the college will obviously change this significantly in the coming years."

What Should Be Done?

Since the Asian American admissions issue evolved out of an extraordinary historical convergence of social, political, and demographic changes among the Asian American population—a pattern projected to continue for many more years—positive steps must be taken to resolve the major points of the dispute. If they are not resolved, it is highly likely we will witness further intervention by legislative bodies and governmental compliance agencies; more protests by Asian American students, professors, and civil rights leaders; and continued attention by the news media. There might also be an individual or class-

Table 4. 1983–85 Applicants and Admits to the UCLA School of Engineering, College of Letters and Science, and College of Fine Arts

	1983			1984			1985		
	Appli-cants	Admits	Admit Rate	Appli-cants	Admits	Admit Rate	Appli-cants	Admits	Admit Rate
School of Engineering									
All Applicants	655	368	56.2%	1665	596	35.8%	1780	712	40.0%
Asian									
Americans	174	94	54.0%	617	145	23.5%	719	241	33.5%
Whites	350	161	46.0%	807	281	34.8%	860	319	37.0%
College of Letters and Science									
All Applicants	7184	4826	67.2%	8271	4787	57.9%	8426	4620	54.8%
Asian									
Americans	1296	804	62.0%	1356	647	47.7%	1325	595	44.9%
Whites	3903	2480	63.5%	4479	2362	52.7%	4496	2137	47.5%
College of Fine Arts									
All Applicants	514	231	45.0%	614	319	51.9%	680	299	44.0%
Asian									
Americans	63	25	40.0%	72	42	58.3%	97	46	47.4%
Whites	374	165	44.1%	437	220	50.3%	478	211	44.1%
Combined Total									
All Applicants	8852	5508	63.2%	10550	5782	53.9%	10889	5631	51.7%
Asian									
Americans	1533	923	60.2%	2047	834	40.7%	2141	882	41.2%
Whites	4627	2806	60.6%	5727	2863	50.0%	5834	2667	45.7%

Source: UCLA Planning Office

action lawsuit. (In the January 1989 issue of the *Yale Law Journal,* attorney Grace Tsuang provided the necessary legal foundation for a possible future lawsuit, which might be filed by an Asian American who is denied admission to either a public or private college because of an upper-limit quota on Asian Americans.)

The Asian American admissions controversy represents only the most recent dispute focusing on issues of equal and fair access and representation in higher education. If the Asian American applicant pool continues to increase in the future, two complex policy issues will become increasingly significant and controversial. First, how large a difference in admission rates between Asian Americans and other groups of applicants will be tolerated by university administrators before they take, or are compelled by others to take, corrective measures? As indicated earlier, the present disparities in admission rates are not closely guarded secrets, but rather are openly and publicly acknowledged facts. Although several campuses have initiated fact-finding studies, most admissions officers have only speculated on the causes of what they perceive to be less than compelling differences. What would be compelling? If Asian American applicants to a college were 75 percent, 50 percent, or 25 percent as likely as other applicants to gain admission, would this constitute sufficient cause for university administrators to address the issue more rigorously? Would such disparities lead to further external intervention or perhaps legal challenges?

The second issue relates directly to the first, and it deals with the broader issue of how much of an Asian American presence will be accepted and tolerated by institutions of higher learning. University officials usually do not maintain an inflexible and predetermined score card on how much varied representation they seek from different groups. However, they do not seem to have given sufficient thought and attention to relating institutional goals of academic-based meritocracy and valued diversity to the Asian American representation on their campuses. Indeed, it seems that Asian American applicants are evaluated exclusively with the non-minority, regular admission pool and tend to be strong candidates. Their presence in the pool, and ultimately in the college, strengthens the academic profile of the university's entering class. However, because Asian American applicants are counted as minorities, university officials also can boast about the racial diversity of their entering class. There is something at least peculiar, and perhaps insidious, about this relationship that demands closer and more serious attention.

The continuation of an adversarial relationship is not in the best interests of any of the parties involved in the Asian American admissions debate. There is definitely more to be gained by seeking a mutually advantageous partnership between the new and growing Asian American population and institutions of higher education. Berkeley Professor Ling-Chi Wang, a major national spokesperson for fair and equal admissions practices toward Asian Americans, best summarized what should be done. "Universities, public or private, should allow full access to their admissions policies and data to avoid suspicion and abuse of power. Asian Americans are not asking for numerical increases in their enrollments, nor are they challenging the merit of existing affirmative action programs. Not unlike whites, they are asking only for fair and equal treatment and demanding equal participation in decision-making processes. In other words, Asian Americans want only equality and justice, no more and no less."

Case 10.d   Raising the Ante

This article raises the issue of equal pay for comparable work. The practical, social, and even personal problems that arise in cases of comparable worth are illustrated.

Having spearheaded the women's cause on behalf of equal pay for jobs of equal value, Phyllis Warren was elated when the board decided to readjust salaries. Its decision meant Phyllis and the other women employed by the crafts firm would receive pay equivalent to men do-

From William H. Shaw and Vincent Barry, *Moral Issues in Business,* 5th ed., pp. 449–450. Belmont, CA: Wadsworth, 1992. Reprinted by permission.

ing comparable jobs. But in a larger sense it constituted an admission of guilt on the part of the board, acknowledgment of a history blemished with sexual discrimination.

In the euphoria that followed the board's decision, neither Phyllis nor any of the other activists thought much about the implied admission of female exploitation. But some weeks later, Herm Leggett, a sales dispatcher, half-jokingly suggested to Phyllis over lunch that she shouldn't stop with equal pay now. Phyllis asked Herm what he meant.

"Back pay," Herm said without hesitation. "If they're readjusting salaries for women," he explained, "they obviously know that salaries are out of line and have been for some time." Then he asked her pointedly, "How long you been here, Phyl?" Eleven years, she told him. "If those statistics you folks were passing around last month are accurate," Herm said, "then I'd say you've been losing about $500 a year, or $5,500 over eleven years." Then he added with a laugh, "Not counting interest, of course."

"Why not?" Phyllis thought. Why shouldn't she and other women who'd suffered past inequities be reimbursed?

That night Phyllis called a few of the other women and suggested that they press the board for back pay. Some said they were satisfied and didn't think they should force the issue. Others thought the firm had been fair in readjusting the salary schedule, and they were willing to let bygones be bygones. Still others thought that any further efforts might, in fact, roll back the board's favorable decision. Yet a nucleus agreed that workers who had been unfairly treated in the past ought to receive compensation. They decided, however, that since their ranks were divided, they shouldn't wage as intense an in-house campaign as previously but instead take the issue directly to the board, while it might still be inhaling deeply the fresh air of social responsibility.

The following Wednesday, Phyllis and four other women presented their case to the board, intentionally giving the impression that they enjoyed as much support from other workers as they had the last time they appeared before it. Although this wasn't true, Phyllis suggested it as an effective strategic ploy.

Phyllis's presentation had hardly ended when board members began making their feelings known. One called her proposal "industrial blackmail." "No sooner do we try to right an injustice," he said testily, "than you take our good faith and threaten to beat us over the head with it unless we comply with your request."

Another member just as vigorously argued that the current board couldn't be held accountable for the actions, policies, and decisions of previous boards. "Sure," he said, "we're empowered to alter policies as we see fit, as new conditions chart new directions. And we've done that. But to expect us to bear the full financial liability of decisions we never made is totally unrealistic—and unfair."

Still another member wondered where it would all end. "If we agree," he asked, "will you then suggest we should track down all those women who ever worked for us and provide them compensation?" Phyllis said no, but the board should readjust retirement benefits for those affected.

At this point the board asked Phyllis if she had any idea what her proposal would cost the firm. "Whatever it is, it's a small price to pay for righting wrong," she said firmly.

"But is it a small price to pay for severely damaging our profit picture?" one of the members asked. Then he added, "I needn't remind you that our profit outlook directly affects what we can offer our current employees in terms of salary and fringe benefits. It directly affects our ability to revise our salary schedule." Finally, he asked Phyllis whether she'd accept the board reducing everyone's current compensation to meet what Phyllis termed the board's "obligation to the past."

Despite its decided opposition to Phyllis's proposal, the board agreed to consider it and render a decision at its next meeting. As a final broadside, Phyllis hinted that, if the board didn't comply with the committee's request, the committee was prepared to submit its demand to litigation.

Case 10.e   *Vinson* v. *Taylor*: Sexual Harassment

In the case of *Vinson* v. *Taylor,* Vinson sued Taylor and the bank at which they worked, Capital City Savings, for compensation for sexual harassment. At issue is whether Vinson voluntarily entered into a relationship with Taylor, or whether his constant pressure, and later violent behavior, amounted to sexual harassment.

In the recent case of *Vinson* v. *Taylor,* heard before the federal District Court for the District of Columbia, Vinson alleged that Taylor, her supervisor at Capital City Savings and Loan, sexually harassed her, but the facts of the case are contested. In court, Vinson testified that about a year after she began working at the bank Taylor asked her to have sexual relations with him. She claimed that Taylor said that she "owed" him because he had obtained the job for her.

Although she turned down Taylor at first, she eventually became involved with him. She and Taylor engaged in sexual relations, both during and after business hours, during the remaining three years that she worked at the bank. The encounters included intercourse in a bank vault and in a storage area in the bank basement. Vinson also testified that Taylor often actually "assaulted or raped" her. She contended that she was forced to submit to Taylor or jeopardize her employment.

Taylor, for his part, denied the allegations. He testified that he had never had sex with Vinson. On the contrary, he alleged that Vinson had made advances toward him and that he declined them. He contended that Vinson had brought the charges against him in order to "get even" with him because of a work-related dispute.

In its ruling on the case, the court held that if Vinson and Taylor engaged in a sexual relationship, that relationship was voluntary on the part of Vinson and was not employment related. The court also held that Capital City Federal Savings and Loan did not have

From William H. Shaw and Vincent Barry, *Moral Issues in Business,* 5th ed., pp. 452–453. Belmont, CA: Wadsworth, 1992. Reprinted by permission.

"notice" of the alleged harassment and was, therefore, not liable. Although Taylor was Vinson's supervisor, the court reasoned that notice to him was not notice to the bank.

Vinson appealed the case, and the court of appeals held that the district court had erred in three ways. First, the district court had overlooked the fact that there are two possible kinds of sexual harassment. Writing for the majority, Chief Judge Robinson distinguished cases where the victim's continued employment or promotion is conditioned on giving into sexual demands and those cases in which the victim must tolerate a "substantially discriminatory work environment." The lower court had failed to consider Vinson's case as possible harassment of the second kind.

Second, the higher court also overruled the district court's finding that because Vinson voluntarily engaged in a sexual relationship with Taylor, she was not a victim of sexual harassment. Voluntariness on Vinson's part had "no bearing," the judge wrote, on "whether Taylor made Vinson's toleration of sexual harassment a condition of her employment." Third, the court of appeals held that *any* discriminatory activity by a supervisor is attributable to the employer, regardless of whether the employer had specific notice.

In his dissent to the court of appeals's decision, Judge Bork rejected the majority's claim that "voluntariness" did not automatically rule out harassment. He argued that this would have the result of depriving the accused person of any defense since he could no longer establish that the supposed victim was really "a willing participant." Judge Bork contended further that an employer should not be held vicariously liable for a supervisor's acts that it didn't know about.

Case 10.f   Sexual Harassment in the Locker Room: The Case of Lisa Olson

In this recent case, sports reporter Lisa Olson sued the New England Patriots for sexual harassment after several players allegedly exposed themselves and made rude comments to her in the locker room. This case illustrates how sexual harassment becomes a barrier for women in many male-dominated occupations.

The early morning, at five or six o'clock, is when sportswriter Lisa Olson can leave her apartment with the least worry. She can walk the empty streets of her Boston neighborhood and buy her newspapers and her groceries. No one will gawk or point or shout at her. No one will notice her. This is her small window of freedom.

She usually has been awake for most of the night. She has worried and thought and worried some more. The phone? Who can that be? For a while she used a system of rings for friends and co-workers, just to know if a stranger was calling, but she has changed her number often and the latest number seems to be safe. For now. Who knows when that new number will land in strange hands?

"I have your number," a voice might say again. "I know where you live. I have battery acid that I will throw on your face. I know the way you go to work."

The whole thing is crazy. What did she do to anyone? The letters. The hate. A man wrote recently that she should jump off the Mystic River bridge, just as Chuck Stuart, the alleged murderer, had done.

She does not answer the doorbell. She mostly does not go out to dinner or to the movies. She does not do anything, really, except work and go home. She is covering the Bruins now for the *Boston Herald,* and the Bruins are in the Stanley Cup playoffs and this should be a wonderful time. But she covers only the games that are played on the road. There has been

too much trouble at the Boston Garden, where she has been spit upon and otherwise demeaned and where the two mailboxes on Causeway Street have graffiti addressed to her written on them: LISA IS A CLASSIC BITCH . . . LISA IS A SLUT.

She stays in her apartment during the Bruins' home games, watches them on television, thinks of the stories that she would have written about them. The games end and the news ends and the scoreboard shows end, and she is left to fret through the night. At five or six, she can buy her papers and her groceries and come back to the apartment and close her eyes. Just for a little bit.

How did all this happen?

"She appeared one day in my office," *Herald* executive sports editor Bob Sales says. "She said she was taking some grad school classes at Harvard, but what she always wanted to do was become a sportswriter. She asked if I had any jobs. I did have one. It wasn't much. I needed someone to do the horse racing agate part time at night. She took it."

She was from Phoenix, 22 years old then, in 1986, and as convinced as anyone could be about what she wanted from life. She had been writing sports since she was seven, when she made up her own little newsletter that reported on neighborhood sports events. She almost learned to read with SPORTS ILLUSTRATED and her brothers' *Boy's Life.* This would be the greatest job, writing sports.

She continued with school and worked at the *Herald* and sometimes did some stringing for United Press International. Her big chance to write came from doing the anonymous roundups of sports news that the *Herald* ran daily. She wrote them, Sales noticed, with a nice touch.

In August 1987, when he decided to expand coverage of scholastic sports, Sales hired Olson full time. It wasn't an affirmative-action hire, bringing in another female name for public display; it was a talent hire. "She did nice stories portraying athletes as human beings," Sales says. "These were stories about high school volleyball players and swimmers, and she made you want to read them. I liked what she did a lot."

Olson wrote scholastic and collegiate sports for a year and a half. Sales thought she wrote the best scholastic stories in the city. When a Bruin beat writer became ill in the middle of the 1988–89 season, Sales turned the job over to Olson. He liked her hockey stories and began to expand her range. He told her to continue what she had been doing, to write about athletes in human terms. He sent her to a prizefight and included her on the team of reporters that covered the 1990 Super Bowl. Human stories. Last summer, Sales promoted Michael Gee, who was covering the Patriots, to columnist and that opened up a spot on the Pats' beat. The choice to fill it was Olson.

She started covering the Pats in training camp. For two months, there were no problems. On Sept. 17, she was working on a story on cornerback Maurice Hurst, who had intercepted two passes in a game the day before. Olson said later that she had asked twice to get Hurst to meet her in the media room at Foxboro Stadium. Hurst said he would do the interview after practice, in the locker room, where Olson had been only twice before. This was the beginning of her ordeal. The human stories, alas, became stories about the woman who wrote human stories.

The events of Sept. 17 are old news now, but their effects do not seem to end. Especially for Olson. The story—studied, debated, played across the pages of virtually every newspaper and magazine in the country—was that at least three Patriots players, Zeke Mowatt, Robert Perryman and Michael Timpson, gathered around her and made lewd suggestions while she interviewed Hurst. This was a locker room. The players were naked. The reporter was a woman. The story took off in that cheesy, wink-wink style that some newspapers like to print and readers like to read. Jim Bakker meets Donna Rice at Au Pair Bar in Palm Beach. Or something like that. Sports-page version.

There was a three-day stutter at the beginning, the time frame in which the Pats could have closed the gates. Olson had reported the incident to Sales, who had contacted the Patriots, but nothing happened. "The sad thing is how easily all of this could have been avoided," Sales says. "All she wanted was a chance to sit down with the players involved and explain herself, to explain that she was doing a job and she should be treated that way. That's all the Patriots would have had to do. Get the players together and meet with her."

The Boston Globe printed an account of the lockerroom incident first, on Sept. 21, and the *Herald* followed suit, and then two sportswriters overheard Pats owner Victor Kiam calling Olson "a classic bitch," and there was no stopping this story. The Boston chapter of the National Organization for Women urged a boycott of products by Remington Products, Kiam's company. Kiam apologized for the remark through paid newspaper ads. The issue of "a woman in the locker room," supposedly decided a decade earlier, was rehashed.

Oprah wanted Olson. Phil wanted Olson. Geraldo wanted Olson. She went on none of the shows. She did NBC's *NFL Live* and *CBS This Morning,* appearing uneasy and timid, and then stopped doing TV. She did not have to defend herself. What did she do? She was a reporter who was doing her job and had been insulted, if not actually threatened.

This did not seem to matter. *Playboy* called asking if she was interested in doing a "pictorial layout." Representatives for producers Aaron Spelling and Steven Bochco called asking about the chances of filming her story. She did not return the calls. Andrew Dice Clay did a routine about her. *Saturday Night Live* did a routine. The local disc jockeys did routines. The White House sent a telegram urging her to hang tough on the same day she received her first death threat. The sickos of the land moved to their desks and began to type with two fingers.

"I do a lot of civil-rights cases, so I've seen a lot of things that have gone through the mails, but this was the worst stuff I've ever read," says Michael Avery, one of Olson's lawyers. "The sexual references, the obscene drawings. Things that make you sick."

For a few weeks, Olson continued covering the Pats. It was ridiculous. At a Sept. 30 game against the New York Jets at Foxboro, fans chanted her name and bounced one of those inflated rubber women around the stands. She walked a gauntlet of abuse as she went to the locker room for interviews. She has electric red hair and is easily recognizable. How could she hide? Following the game, Sales moved her off the beat, told her to take a vacation and get away from the noise.

The NFL was strangely quiet for the longest time, and when commissioner Paul Tagliabue finally took action on Oct. 1 by appointing Philip Heymann as special counsel to investigate the locker room incident and its aftermath, the story stayed alive as a lengthy study was conducted. The investigation culminated in the Heymann Report, a 60-page indictment of the Pats players' behavior and their team's handling of the situation, which was released on Nov. 27. The three players and Pats management were fined. Olson supposedly was vindicated. Vindicated? When she had returned to work in mid-October, she covered the Celtics and Bruins, but reporting on NBA games brought her to courtside at Boston Garden, where she still was jostled and touched and hooted at. The words were graphic. At an exhibition game in Worcester, a man poured a beer on her.

In early December, Sales moved Olson exclusively to the Bruin beat, partly because the hockey press box is located almost at the top of the Garden. On Feb. 4, Kiam, continuing in his buffoon's role, told a joke at a dinner in Stamford, Conn., saying that what Olson and the Iraqi army had in common was that they both had seen Patriot missiles up close. Kiam apologized again. Nothing changed. People spit on her head from the luxury boxes, the only seats in the Garden located above the hockey press box. She started to wear a hat for protection. Someone spray-painted *classic bitch* on the front of her apartment house.

Her tires were slashed. The letters continued. She changed her phone number again and again. In Hartford, a group of male fans seated in front of the press box chanted all night at her, asking her to show them her breasts.

"Isn't the thing in America supposed to be that you can be whatever you want to be?" asks Bruin public relations director Heidi Holland. "What do these people tell their daughters? That you can't do it because of idiots like me who are missing a chromosome somewhere?"

On April 25, Olson filed suit in Suffolk (County) Superior Court against the Patriots, Kiam, former general manager Pat Sullivan, former media relations director Jimmy Oldham, Mowatt, Perryman and Timpson. She asked for unspecified monetary damages for sexual harassment, civil-rights violations, intentional infliction of emotional distress and intentional damage to her professional reputation. The Patriots have declined to comment on the situation.

The news now is that Olson is leaving Boston. She will finish covering the NHL playoffs and then she will leave the city, leave the country, go work in a foreign country for another paper owned by Rupert Murdoch, proprietor of the *Herald*. She probably will not cover sports, but she will be able to walk the streets and answer the phone and sleep. She has to wonder if she ever will cover sports again.

The suit probably will not be heard for two years, maybe three. It is not one of her great worries. She never wanted to sue anybody in the first place. The continual harassment, sparked anew by Kiam's tasteless dinner joke, forced her hand. She never wanted to be especially famous or rich. She wanted only to do a job that she always wanted to hold. Is that a crime? The rage around her is a puzzle. The buzz wherever she goes is a puzzle. What did she do?

"I'm working on a story about you for SPORTS ILLUSTRATED," a reporter says to her.

"Do you have to?" Lisa Olson says, politely refusing to be quoted in the magazine she read as a child.

The whole thing does not end.

Animals and the Environment

The Environment

It seems like a long time in coming, but the environment is beginning to be a major issue in the contemporary political and social scene. From the decimation of the rain forests to the depletion of the ozone, governments, businesses, and the media are finally waking up and focusing on these issues.

Probably the most discussed environmental problem today is ozone depletion. Ozone is an element in the earth's stratosphere that screens out harmful ultraviolet rays. Even small depletions of this precious element can cause significant increases in skin cancers, damage to crops, and serious ecological change. We may already be experiencing global warming and environmental shifts caused by ozone depletion. The release into the atmosphere of chlorofluorocarbons (CFCs), which are used in refrigeration equipment, styrofoam, and aerosol sprays, is largely responsible for ozone depletion. Until recently, the United States was willing to do little about CFCs. However, when an ozone hole was discovered over North America, President Bush decided to act. Using the Clean Air Act, he called for the elimination of CFCs within the decade. Unfortunately, our government has repeatedly rejected the rest of the world's insistence that limits be set on carbon dioxide emissions.

Our environment is also threatened by acid rain, or pollutants caused by the burning of fossil fuels. The resulting pollutants fall in rainwater, causing damage to fish, plants, ground water, and even buildings.

Today our environment is threatened by countless tons of trash, toxic and nuclear waste, and other pollutants. Plant and animal species are becoming extinct at an alarming rate, and the long-term environmental change caused by global warming is not fully understood.

The moral issues involved in environmental concerns are typically presented in an *anthropocentric* manner. Damage to the environment is immoral because it infringes on the needs and interests of human beings. Whether it threatens our lives directly, or simply damages the quality of our lives, the destruction of our environment is morally unacceptable. Anthropocentric interests invariably come into conflict with economic and social interests. However it is the long-term good of our species that, according to this way of thinking, is ultimately of primary importance.

The *biocentric* approach, like that of environmentalist Aldo Leopold, holds that we must see ourselves as part of an environmental whole. All life, on this view, is inherently valuable, and the environment is not our "property" to be used solely in our own best interests. Rather, we have a responsibility to preserve the environment because we are a part of a biotic community.

The women's movement also has brought out a new way of understanding environmentalism, a view called *ecofeminism*. Ecofeminism owes as much to concrete political struggles for the environment as it does to feminist social theory. Fundamentally, ecofeminism attempts to underscore the relationship between the domination of women and the exploitation of the environment, both of which can be attributed to patriarchal conceptions of reason and nature.

Animal Rights and Animal Experimentation

Throughout history human beings have consumed nonhuman animals as food, kept them as pets, killed them for sport, and, in recent times, used them for scientific projects. Humans today still subordinate the fundamental interests of other animals to their own desires, reflecting what Peter Singer has called *speciesism*. Discriminating against other animals, Singer says, is just as morally reprehensible as racial, gender, or other forms of discrimination. According to Singer and others, animals have moral standing because they have "interests." Nonhuman animals, at least those that are sentient (i.e., have conscious experience), can feel pain, pleasure, fear, and happiness and have an interest in these things just as we do. On a utilitarian basis, Singer argues that we must maximize the happiness of all animals capable of such feelings, not just the human ones. Other philosophers take a deontological approach, attributing rights and moral standing to nonhuman animals based on their inherent value.

Many people disagree with the attribution of rights and moral standing to nonhuman animals, arguing that humans are the only animals with rights and that the interests of nonhuman animals are important only insofar as mistreatment of them offends human sensibilities. Moral standing is rejected because nonhuman animals, lacking the capacity for moral judgment and the ability to identify and live by moral rules, hence cannot be members of a moral community.

For years nonhuman animals have been used in often painful scientific experiments. Often these experiments have constituted medical research; just as frequently, however, they have been conducted by private industry for the purpose of testing and marketing new products such as cosmetics or household cleansers. In both types of experimentation, animals have been subjected to the most hid-eous forms of torture in the name of science.

Recently, animal rights groups have begun campaigns to stop animal experimentation. Such groups have resorted to demonstrations, boycotts, and even terrorist-style break-ins to "liberate" animals that are being used in painful experiments. Corporations like U.S. Surgical have launched a counteroffensive by using the media to picture the use of animals in medical experiments as the source of "medical miracles."

From a moral perspective, many object to animal experimentation on the grounds that, since animals have inherent value, they have rights that protect them from being used for the needs of others. Of course, many feel that animals have no inherent value and that whatever suffering may be caused is justified in terms of the benefits it provides to humans. This, to be sure, does not mean that every experiment is justified. Not all experiments lead to advances in human knowledge. Hence, those that inflict needless suffering may still be unacceptable, even to those who feel that animals do not have the same moral standing as humans.

49. Ecology and Morality

Peter S. Wenz

Peter S. Wenz argues for a deep ecology, namely the position that we have moral obligations towards the ecosystem itself. He describes a healthy ecosystem, and creates two cases that are intended to show that we have prima facie obligations to the ecosystem independent of any claims about human or non-human animals.

In the first section of this article I characterize good or healthy ecosystems. In the second I argue that we have a *prima facie* obligation to protect such ecosystems irrespective of all possible advantage to human beings.

Reprinted with permission of Humana Press from *Ethics and Animals* (1983), edited by Harlan B. Miller and William H. Williams, pp. 185–191.

Good Ecosystems

An ecosystem is what Aldo Leopold referred to as a "biotic pyramid." He describes it this way (1970, p. 252):

> Plants absorb energy from the sun. This energy flows through a circuit called

the biota, which may be represented by a pyramid consisting of layers. The bottom layer is the soil. A plant layer rests on the soil, an insect layer on the plants, a bird and rodent layer on the insects, and so on up through various animal groups to the apex layer, which consists of the large carnivores.

Proceeding upward, each successive layer decreases in numerical abundance. Thus, for every carnivore there are hundreds of his prey, thousands of their prey, millions of insects, uncountable plants.

The lines of dependency for food and other services are called food chains. Thus soil-oak-deer-Indian is a chain that has now largely converted to soil-corn-cow-farmer. Each species, including ourselves, is a link in many chains. The deer eats a hundred plants other than oak, and the cow a hundred plants other than corn. Both, then, are links in a hundred chains. The pyramid is a tangle of chains so complex as to seem disorderly, yet the stability of the system proves it to be a highly organized structure.[1]

It is so highly organized that Leopold and others write of it, at times, as if it were a single organism which could be in various stages of health or disease (p. 274):

Paleontology offers abundant evidence that wilderness maintained itself for immensely long periods; that its component species were rarely lost, neither did they get out of hand: that weather and water built soil as fast or faster than it was carried away. Wilderness, then, assumes unexpected importance as a laboratory for the study of land-health.

By contrast,

When soil loses fertility, or washes away faster than it forms, and when water systems exhibit abnormal floods and shortages, the land is sick (p. 272).

The disappearance of plant and animal species without visible cause, despite efforts to protect them, and the irruption of others as pests despite efforts to control them, must, in the absence of simpler explanations, be regarded as symptoms of sickness in the land organism (pp. 272–273).

In general, a healthy ecosystem consists of a great diversity of flora and fauna, as "the trend of evolution is to elaborate and diversify the biota" (p. 253). This flora and fauna is in a relatively stable balance, evolving slowly rather than changing rapidly, because its diversity enables it to respond to change in a flexible manner that retains the system's integrity. In all of these respects a healthy ecosystem is very much like a healthy plant or animal.

A description of one small part of one ecosystem will conclude this account of the nature of ecosystems. It is Leopold's description of a river's sand bar in August (1970, p. 55):

The work begins with a broad ribbon of silt brushed thinly on the sand of a reddening shore. As this dries slowly in the sun, goldfinches bathe in its pools, and deer, herons, killdeers, raccoons, and turtles cover it with a lacework of tracks. There is no telling, at this stage, whether anything further will happen.

But when I see the silt ribbon turning green with Eleocharis,* I watch closely thereafter, for this is the sign that the river is in a painting mood. Almost overnight the Eleocharis becomes a thick turf, so lush and so dense that the meadow mice from the adjoining upland cannot resist the temptation. They move *en masse* to the green pasture, and apparently spend the nights rubbing their ribs in its velvety depths. A maze of neatly tended mouse-trails bespeaks their enthusiasm. The deer walk up and down in it, apparently just for the pleasure of feeling it underfoot. Even a stay-at-home mole has tunneled his way across the dry bar

---

Editor's note: Eleocharis is a type of sedge.

to the Eleocharis ribbon, where he can heave and hump the sod to his heart's content.

At this stage the seedlings of plants too numerous to count and too young to recognize spring to life from the damp warm sand under the green ribbon.

Three weeks later (pp. 55–56):

The Eleocharis sod, greener than ever is now spangled with blue mimulus, pink dragonhead, and the milk-white blooms of Sagittaria. Here and there a cardinal flower thrusts a red spear skyward. At the head of the bar, purple ironweeds and pale pink joepyes stand tall against the wall of willows. And if you have come quietly and humbly, as you should to any spot that can be beautiful only once, you may surprise a fox-red deer, standing knee-high in the garden of his delight (pp. 55–56).

Human Obligations to Ecosystems

Let us now consider whether or not we, you and I, have *prima facie* obligations towards ecosystems, in particular, the obligation to avoid destroying them, apart from any human advantage that might be gained by their continued existence. My argument consists in the elaboration of two examples, followed by appeals to the reader's intuition. The second, Case II, is designed to function as a counterexample to the claim that human beings have no obligations to preserve ecosystems except when doing so serves human interests or prevents the unnecessary suffering of other sentient beings.

Some clarifications are needed at the start. By "*prima facie* obligation" I mean an obligation that would exist in the absence of other, countervailing moral considerations. So I will construct cases in which such other considerations are designedly absent. A common

consideration of this sort is the effect our actions have on intelligent beings, whether they be humans, extraterrestrials, or (should they be considered intelligent enough) apes and aquatic mammals. Accordingly, I will construct my cases so that the destruction of the environment affects none of these. Finally, the obligation in question is not to preserve ecosystems from any and every threat to their health and existence. Rather, the obligation for which I am contending is to protect ecosystems from oneself. The differences here may be important. A duty to protect the environment from any and every threat would have to rest on some principle concerning the duty to bring aid. Such principles concern positive duties, which are generally considered less stringent than negative duties. The duty to protect the environment from oneself, on the other hand, rests on a principle concerning the duty to do no harm, which is a negative duty. Those not convinced that we have a duty to bring aid may nevertheless find a *prima facie* duty not to harm the environment easy to accept.

Case I

Consider the following situation. Suppose that you are a pilot flying a bomber that is low on fuel. You must release your bombs over the ocean to reduce the weight of the plane. If the bombs land in the water they will not explode, but will, instead, deactivate harmlessly. If, on the other hand, any lands on the islands that dot this part of the ocean, it will explode. The islands contain no mineral or other resources of use to human beings, and are sufficiently isolated from one another and other parts of the world that an explosion on one will not affect the others, or any other part of the world. The bomb's explosion will not add to air pollution because it is exceedingly "clean." However, each island contains an ecosystem, a biotic pyramid of the sort described by Aldo Leopold, within which there are rivers, sandbars, Eleocharis, meadow mice, cardinal flowers, blue mimulus, deer, and so forth, but no intelligent life. (Those who consider mice, deer, and other such animals so intelligent as to fall under some ban against killing intelligent life are free to suppose that in their wisdom, all such creatures have emigrated.) The bomb's explosion will ruin the ecosystem of the island on which it explodes, though it will not cause any animals to suffer. We may suppose that the islands are small enough and the bombs powerful enough that all animals, as well as plants, will be killed instantly, and therefore painlessly. The island will instantly be transformed from a wilderness garden to a bleakness like that on the surface of the moon.

Suppose that with some care and attention, but with no risk to yourself, anyone else or the plane, you could release your bombs so as to avoid hitting any of the islands. With equal care and attention you could be sure to hit at least one of the islands. Finally, without any care or attention to the matter, you might hit one of the islands and you might not. Assuming that you are in no need of target practice, and are aware of the situation as described, would you consider it a matter of moral indifference which of the three possible courses of action you took? Wouldn't you feel that you ought to take some care and pay some attention to insure that you avoid hitting any of the islands? Those who can honestly say that in the situation at hand they feel no more obligation to avoid hitting the islands than to hit them, who think that destroying the balanced pyramidal structure of a healthy ecosystem is morally indifferent, who care nothing for the islands' floral displays and interactions between flora, fauna, soil, water, and sun need read no further. Such people do not share the intuition on which the argument in this paper rests.

I assume that few, if any readers of the last paragraph accepted my invitation to stop reading. I would have phrased things differently if I thought they would. Many readers may nevertheless be skeptical of my intuitive demonstration that we feel a *prima facie* obligation to avoid destroying ecosystems. Even though no pain to sentient creatures is involved, nor the destruction of intelligent life nor pollution or other impairment of areas inhabited by human beings or other intelligent creatures, some readers may nevertheless explain their reluctance to destroy such an ecosystem by reference, ultimately, to human purposes. They can thereby avoid the inference I am promoting. They might point out

that the islands' ecosystems may be useful to scientists who might someday want to study them. No matter that there are a great many such islands. The ecosystem of each is at least slightly different from the others, and therefore might provide some information of benefit to human beings that could not be gleaned elsewhere. Alternatively, though scientists are studying some, it might be to the benefit of humanity to establish Holiday Inns and Hilton Hotels on the others. Scientists have to relax too, and if the accommodations are suitable they will be more likely to enjoy the companionship of their families.

I believe that such explanations of our intuitive revulsion at the idea of needlessly destroying a healthy ecosystem are unhelpful evasions. They represent the squirming of one who intellectually believes ethics to concern only humans and other intelligent creatures, perhaps with a rider that one ought not to cause sentient creatures unnecessary suffering, with the reality of his or her own moral intuitions. The next case will make this clearer.

Case II

Suppose that human beings and all other intelligent creatures inhabiting the earth are becoming extinct. Imagine that this is the effect of some cosmic ray that causes extinction by preventing procreation. There is no possibility of survival through emigration to another plant, solar system or galaxy because the ray's presence is so widespread that no humans would survive the lengthy journey necessary to escape from its influence. There are many other species of extraterrestrial, intelligent creatures in the universe whom the cosmic ray does not affect. Nor does it affect any of the non-intelligent members of the earth's biotic community. So the earth's varied multitude of ecosystems could continue after the extinction of human beings. But their continuation would be of no use to any of the many species of intelligent extraterrestrials because the earth is for many reasons inhospitable to their forms of life, and contains no mineral or other resources of which they could make use.

Suppose that you are the last surviving human being. All other intelligent animals, if there were any, have already become extinct.

Before they died, other humans had set hydrogen explosives all around the earth such that, were they to explode, all remaining plant and animal life on the earth would be instantly vaporized. No sentient creature would suffer, but the earth's varied multitude of ecosystems would be completely destroyed. The hydrogen explosives are all attached to a single timing mechanism, set to explode next year. Not wishing to die prematurely, you have located this timing device. You can set it ahead fifty or one hundred years, insuring that the explosion will not foreshorten your life, or you can, with only slightly greater effort, deactivate it so that it will never explode at all. Who would think it a matter of moral indifference which you did? It seems obvious that you ought to deactivate the explosives rather than postpone the time of the explosions.

How can one account for this "ought"? One suggestion is that our obligations are to intelligent life, and that the chances are improved and the time lessened for the evolution of intelligent life on earth by leaving the earth's remaining ecosystems intact. But this explanation is not convincing. First, it rests on assumptions about evolutionary developments under different earthly conditions that seem very plausible, but are by no means certain. More important, as the case was drawn, there are many species of intelligent extraterrestrials who are in no danger of either extinction or diminished numbers, and you know of their existence. It is therefore not at all certain that the obligations to intelligent life contained in our current ethical theories and moral intuitions would suggest, much less require, that we so act as to increase the probability of and decrease the time for the development of another species of intelligent life on earth. We do not now think it morally incumbent upon us to develop a form of intelligent life suited to live in those parts of the globe that, like Antarctica, are underpopulated by human beings. This is so because we do not adhere to a principle that we ought to so act as to insure the presence of intelligent life in as many earthly locations as possible. It is therefore doubtful that we adhere to the more extended principle that we ought to promote the development of as many different species of intelligent life as possible in as many different locations in the universe

as possible. Such a problematic moral principle surely cannot account for our clear intuition that one obviously and certainly ought not to reset the explosives rather than deactivate them. It is more plausible to suppose that our current morality includes a *prima facie* obligation to refrain from destroying good ecosystems irrespective of both the interests of intelligent beings and the obligation not to cause sentient beings unnecessary suffering.

It is not necessary to say that ecosystems have rights. It is a commonplace in contemporary moral philosophy that not all obligations result from corresponding rights, for example, the obligation to be charitable. Instead, the obligation might follow from our concept of virtuous people as ones who do not destroy any existing things needlessly. Or perhaps we feel that one has a *prima facie* obligation not to destroy anything of esthetic value, and ecosystems are of esthetic value. Alternatively, the underlying obligation could be to avoid destroying anything that is good of its kind—so long as the kind in question does not make it something bad in itself—and many of the earth's ecosystems are good.

Our intuition might, on the other hand, be related more specifically to those characteristics that make good ecosystems good. Generally speaking, one ecosystem is better than another if it incorporates a greater diversity of life forms into a more integrated unity that is relatively stable, but not static. Its homeostasis allows for gradual evolution. The leading concepts, then, are diversity, unity, and a slightly less than complete homeostatic stability. These are, as a matter of empirical fact, positively related to one another in ecosystems. They may strike a sympathetic chord in human beings because they correspond symbolically to our personal, psychological need for a combination in our lives of both security and novelty. The stability and unity of a good ecosystem represents security. That the stability is cyclically homeostatic, rather than static, involves life forms rather than merely inorganic matter, and includes great diversity, corresponds to our desires for novelty and change. Of course, this is only speculation. It must be admitted that some human beings seem to so value security and stability as to prefer a purely static unity. Parmenides and the eastern religious thinkers who promote nothingness as a goal might consider the surface of the moon superior to that of the earth, and advocate allowing the earth's ecosystems to be vaporized under the conditions described in Case II.

My intuitions, however, and I assume those of most readers, favor ecosystems over static lifelessness and, perhaps for the same reason, good ecosystems over poorer ones. In any case, the above speculations concerning the psychological and logical derivations of these intuitions serve at most to help clarify their nature. Even the correct account of their origin would not necessarily constitute a justification. Rather than try to justify them, I will take

them as a starting point for further discussion. So I take the cases elaborated above to establish that our current morality includes a *prima facie* obligation to avoid destroying good ecosystems, absent considerations of both animal torture and the well-being of intelligent creatures. . . .

Note

1. Leopold, A. 1970. *A Sand County Almanac, with essays on conservation from Round River*. New York: Ballantine Books.

---

50.   People or Penguins

William F. Baxter

Unlike the deep ecological view expressed in the previous section, William F. Baxter argues for an anthropocentric perspective. Rights, and the respect associated with them, should not, Baxter says, be extended to nonhuman animals. He prefers a cost/benefit, economically oriented form of reasoning to decide the case for what he calls "optimal pollution" relative to human interests.

I start with the modest proposition that, in dealing with pollution, or indeed with any problem, it is helpful to know what one is attempting to accomplish. Agreement on how and whether to pursue a particular objective, such as pollution control, is not possible unless some more general objective has been identified and stated with reasonable precision. We talk loosely of having clean air and clean water, of preserving our wilderness areas, and so forth. But none of these is a sufficiently general objective: each is more accurately viewed as a means rather than as an end.

With regard to clean air, for example, one may ask, "how clean?" and "what does clean

mean?" It is even reasonable to ask, "why have clean air?" Each of these questions is an implicit demand that a more general community goal be stated—a goal sufficiently general in its scope and enjoying sufficiently general assent among the community of actors that such "why" questions no longer seem admissible with respect to that goal.

If, for example, one states as a goal the proposition that "every person should be free to do whatever he wishes in contexts where his actions do not interfere with the interests of other human beings," the speaker is unlikely to be met with a response of "why." The goal may be criticized as uncertain in its implications or difficult to implement, but it is so basic a tenet of our civilization—it reflects a cultural value so broadly shared, at least in the abstract—that the question "why" is seen as impertinent or imponderable or both.

I do not mean to suggest that everyone would agree with the "spheres of freedom" objective just stated. Still less do I mean to suggest that a society could subscribe to four or five such general objectives that would be adequate in their coverage to serve as testing criteria by which all other disagreements might be measured. One difficulty in the attempt to construct such a list is that each new goal added will conflict, in certain applications, with each prior goal listed; and thus each goal serves as a limited qualification on prior goals.

Without any expectation of obtaining unanimous consent to them, let me set forth four goals that I generally use as ultimate testing criteria in attempting to frame solutions to problems of human organization. My position regarding pollution stems from these four criteria. If the criteria appeal to you and any part of what appears hereafter does not, our disagreement will have a helpful focus: which of us is correct, analytically, in supposing that his position on pollution would better serve these general goals. If the criteria do not seem acceptable to you, then it is to be expected that our more particular judgments will differ, and the task will then be yours to identify the basic set of criteria upon which your particular judgments rest.

My criteria are as follows:

1. The spheres of freedom criterion stated above.
2. Waste is a bad thing. The dominant feature of human existence is scarcity—our available resources, our aggregate labors, and our skill in employing both have always been, and will continue for some time to be, inadequate to yield to every man all the tangible and intangible satisfactions he would like to have. Hence, none of those resources, or labors, or skills, should be wasted—that is, employed so as to yield less than they might yield in human satisfactions.
3. Every human being should be regarded as an end rather than as a means to be used for the betterment of another. Each should be afforded dignity and regarded as having an absolute claim to an evenhanded applica-

tion of such rules as the community may adopt for its governance.
4. Both the incentive and the opportunity to improve his share of satisfactions should be preserved to every individual. Preservation of incentive is dictated by the "no-waste" criterion and enjoins against the continuous, totally egalitarian redistribution of satisfactions, or wealth; but subject to that constraint, everyone should receive, by continuous redistribution if necessary, some minimal share of aggregate wealth so as to avoid a level of privation from which the opportunity to improve his situation becomes illusory.

The relationship of these highly general goals to the more specific environmental issues at hand may not be readily apparent, and I am not yet ready to demonstrate their pervasive implications. But let me give one indication of their implications. Recently scientists have informed us that use of DDT in food production is causing damage to the penguin population. For the present purposes let us accept that assertion as an indisputable scientific fact. The scientific fact is often asserted as if the correct implication—that we must stop agricultural use of DDT—followed from the mere statement of the fact of penguin damage. But plainly it does not follow if my criteria are employed.

My criteria are oriented to people, not penguins. Damage to penguins, or sugar pines, or geological marvels is, without more, simply irrelevant. One must go further, by my criteria, and say: Penguins are important because people enjoy seeing them walk about rocks; and furthermore, the well-being of people would be less impaired by halting use of DDT than by giving up penguins. In short, my observations about environmental problems will be people-oriented, as are my criteria. I have no interest in preserving penguins for their own sake.

It may be said by way of objection to this position, that it is very selfish of people to act as if each person represented one unit of importance and nothing else was of any importance. It is undeniably selfish. Nevertheless I think it is the only tenable starting place for analysis for several reasons. First, no other position corresponds to the way most people really think and act—i.e., corresponds to reality.

Second, this attitude does not portend any massive destruction of nonhuman flora and fauna, for people depend on them in many obvious ways, and they will be preserved because and to the degree that humans do depend on them.

Third, what is good for humans is, in many respects, good for penguins and pine trees—clean air for example. So that humans are, in these respects, surrogates for plant and animal life.

Fourth, I do not know how we could administer any other system. Our decisions are either private or collective. Insofar as Mr. Jones is free to act privately, he may give such preferences as he wishes to other forms of life: he may feed birds in winter and do with less himself, and he may even decline to resist an advancing polar bear on the ground that the bear's appetite is more important than those portions of himself that the bear may choose to eat. In short my basic premise does not rule out private altruism to competing life-forms. It does rule out, however, Mr. Jones' inclination to feed Mr. Smith to the bear, however hungry the bear, however despicable Mr. Smith.

Insofar as we act collectively on the other hand, only humans can be afforded an opportunity to participate in the collective decisions. Penguins cannot vote now and are unlikely subjects for the franchise—pine trees more unlikely still. Again each individual is free to cast his vote so as to benefit sugar pines if that is his inclination. But many of the more extreme assertions that one hears from some conservationists amount to tacit assertions that they are specially appointed representatives of sugar pines, and hence that their preferences should be weighted more heavily than the preferences of other humans who do not enjoy equal rapport with "nature." The simplistic assertion that agricultural use of DDT must stop at once because it is harmful to penguins is of that type.

Fifth, if polar bears or pine trees or penguins, like men, are to be regarded as ends rather than means, if they are to count in our calculus of social organization, someone must tell me how much each one counts, and someone must tell me how these life-forms are to be permitted to express their preferences, for I do not know either answer. If the answer is that certain people are to hold their proxies, then I want to know how those proxy-holders are to be selected: self-appointment does not seem workable to me.

Sixth, and by way of summary of all the foregoing, let me point out that the set of environmental issues under discussion—although they raise very complex technical questions of how to achieve any objective—ultimately raise a normative question: what *ought* we to do. Questions of *ought* are unique to the human mind and world—they are meaningless as applied to a nonhuman situation.

I reject the proposition that we *ought* to respect the "balance of nature" or to "preserve the environment" unless the reason for doing so, express or implied, is the benefit of man.

I reject the idea that there is a "right" or "morally correct" state of nature to which we should return. The word "nature" has no normative connotation. Was it "right" or "wrong" for the earth's crust to heave in contortion and create mountains and seas? Was it "right" for the first amphibian to crawl up out of the primordial ooze? Was it "wrong" for plants to reproduce themselves and alter the atmospheric composition in favor of oxygen? For animals to alter the atmosphere in favor of carbon dioxide both by breathing oxygen and eating plants? No answers can be given to these questions because they are meaningless questions.

All this may seem obvious to the point of being tedious, but much of the present controversy over environment and pollution rests on tacit normative assumptions about just such nonnormative phenomena: that it is "wrong" to impair penguins with DDT, but not to slaughter cattle for prime rib roasts. That it is wrong to kill stands of sugar pines with industrial fumes, but not to cut sugar pines and build housing for the poor. Every man is entitled to his own preferred definition of Walden Pond, but there is no definition that has any moral superiority over another, except by reference to the selfish needs of the human race.

From the fact that there is no normative definition of the natural state, it follows that there is no normative definition of clean air or pure water—hence no definition of polluted air—or of pollution—except by reference to the needs of man. The "right" composition of the atmosphere is one which has some dust in it and some lead in it and some hydrogen sulfide in it—just those amounts that attend a sensibly organized society thoughtfully and knowledgeably pursuing the greatest possible satisfaction for its human members.

The first and most fundamental step toward solution of our environmental problems is a clear recognition that our objective is not pure air or water but rather some optimal state of pollution. That step immediately suggests the question: How do we define and attain the level of pollution that will yield the maximum possible amount of human satisfaction?

Low levels of pollution contribute to human satisfaction but so do food and shelter and education and music. To attain ever lower levels of pollution, we must pay the cost of having less of these other things. I contrast that view of the cost of pollution control with the more popular statement that pollution control will "cost" very large numbers of dollars. The popular statement is true in some senses, false in others; sorting out the true and false senses is of some importance. The first step in that sorting process is to achieve a clear understanding of the difference between dollars and resources. Resources are the wealth of our nation; dollars are merely claim checks upon those resources. Resources are of vital importance; dollars are comparatively trivial.

Four categories of resources are sufficient for our purposes: At any given time a nation, or a planet if you prefer, has a stock of labor, of technological skill, of capital goods, and of natural resources (such as mineral deposits, timber, water, land, etc.). These resources can be used in various combinations to yield goods and services of all kinds—in some limited quantity. The quantity will be larger if they are combined efficiently, smaller if combined inefficiently. But in either event the resource stock is limited, the goods and services that they can be made to yield are limited; even the most efficient use of them will yield less than our population, in the aggregate, would like to have.

If one considers building a new dam, it is appropriate to say that it will be costly in the sense that it will require x hours of labor, y tons of steel and concrete, and z amount of capital goods. If these resources are devoted to the dam, then they cannot be used to build hospitals, fishing rods, schools, or electric can openers. That is the meaningful sense in which the dam is costly.

Quite apart from the very important question of how wisely we can combine our resources to produce goods and services, is the very different question of how they get distributed—who gets how many goods? Dollars constitute the claim checks which are distributed among people and which control their share of national output. Dollars are nearly valueless pieces of paper except to the extent that they do represent claim checks to some fraction of the output of goods and services. Viewed as claim checks, all the dollars outstanding during any period of time are worth, in the aggregate, the goods and services that are available to be claimed with them during that period—neither more nor less.

It is far easier to increase the supply of dollars than to increase the production of goods and services—printing dollars is easy. But printing more dollars doesn't help because each dollar then simply becomes a claim to fewer goods, i.e., becomes worth less.

The point is this: many people fall into error upon hearing the statement that the decision to build a dam, or to clean up a river, will cost $X million. It is regrettably easy to say: "It's only money. This is a wealthy country, and we have lots of money." But you cannot build a dam or clean a river with $X million—unless you also have a match, you can't even make a fire. One builds a dam or cleans a river by diverting labor and steel and trucks and factories from making one kind of goods to making another. The cost in dollars is merely a shorthand way of describing the extent of the diversion necessary. If we build a dam for $X million, then we must recognize that we will have $X million less housing and food and medical care and electric can openers as a result.

Similarly, the costs of controlling pollution

are best expressed in terms of the other goods we will have to give up to do the job. This is not to say the job should not be done. Badly as we need more housing, more medical care, and more can openers, and more symphony orchestras, we could do with somewhat less of them, in my judgment at least, in exchange for somewhat cleaner air and rivers. But that is the nature of the trade-off, and analysis of the problem is advanced if that unpleasant reality is kept in mind. Once the trade-off relationship is clearly perceived, it is possible to state in a very general way what the optimal level of pollution is. I would state it as follows:

People enjoy watching penguins. They enjoy relatively clean air and smog-free vistas. Their health is improved by relatively clean water and air. Each of these benefits is a type of good or service. As a society we would be well advised to give up one washing machine if the resources that would have gone into that washing machine can yield greater human satisfaction when diverted into pollution control. We should give up one hospital if the resources thereby freed would yield more human satisfaction when devoted to elimination of noise in our cities. And so on, trade-off by trade-off, we should divert our productive capacities from the production of existing goods and services to the production of a cleaner, quieter, more pastoral nation up to—and no further than—the point at which we value more highly the next washing machine or hospital that we would have to do without than we value the next unit of environmental improvement that the diverted resources would create.

Now this proposition seems to me unassailable but so general and abstract as to be unhelpful—at least unadministerable in the form stated. It assumes we can measure in some way the incremental units of human satisfaction yielded by very different types of goods. The proposition must remain a pious abstraction until I can explain how this measurement process can occur. In subsequent chapters I will attempt to show that we can do this—in some contexts with great precision and in other contexts only by rough approximation. But I insist that the proposition stated describes the result for which we should be striving—and again, that it is always useful to know what your target is even if your weapons are too crude to score a bull's eye.

51.   Feminism and Ecology: Making Connections

Karen J. Warren

Karen J. Warren assesses the importance of the ecology movement to feminist theory and to the different schools of feminism—namely, liberal feminism, traditional Marxist feminism, radical feminism, and socialist feminism. According to Warren, eco-feminism shows that each form of feminism is incomplete; hence she argues for a transformative feminism that moves beyond traditional approaches.

The current feminist debate over ecology raises important and timely issues about the theoretical adequacy of the four leading versions of feminism—liberal feminism, traditional Marxist feminism, radical feminism,

From *Environmental Ethics*, Vol. 9, No. 1, pp. 3–20 (Spring 1987). Reprinted by permission.

and socialist feminism. In this paper I present a minimal condition account of ecological feminism, or *eco-feminism*. I argue that if eco-feminism is true or at least plausible, then each of the four leading versions of feminism is inadequate, incomplete, or problematic as a theoretical grounding for eco-feminism. I conclude that, if eco-feminism is to be taken seriously, then a transformative feminism is needed that will move us beyond the four familiar feminist frameworks and make an eco-feminist perspective central to feminist theory and practice.

Introduction

In *New Woman/New Earth,* Rosemary Ruether writes:

> Women must see that there can be no liberation for them and no solution to the ecological crisis within a society whose fundamental model of relationship continues to be one of domination. They must unite the demands of the women's movement with those of the ecological movement to envision a radical reshaping of the basic socioeconomic relations and the underlying values of this society.[1]

According to Ruether, the women's movement and the ecology movement are intimately connected. The demands of both require "transforming that world-view which underlies domination and replacing it with an alternative value system."[2] Recent writings by feminists Elizabeth Dodson Gray, Susan Griffin, Mary Daly, Carolyn Merchant, Joan Griscom, Ynestra King, and Ariel Kay Salleh, underscore Ruether's basic point: ecology is a feminist issue.[3]

Why is this so? Feminists who debate the ecology issue agree that there are important connections between the oppression of women and the oppression of nature,[4] but they disagree about both the nature of those connections and whether those connections are "potentially liberating or simply a rationale for the continued subordination of women."[5] Stated slightly differently, while many feminists agree that ecology is a feminist issue, they disagree about the nature and desirability of "ecological feminism," or *eco-feminism.*

This disagreement is to be expected. Just as there is not one version of feminism, there is not one version of eco-feminism. The varieties of eco-feminism reflect not only differences in the analysis of the woman/nature connection, but also differences on such fundamental issues as the nature of and solutions to women's oppression, the theory of human nature, and the conceptions of freedom, equality, and epistemology on which the various feminist theories depend.

In order to accomodate the varieties of eco-feminist perspectives, it is important to provide a minimal condition account of eco-feminism which captures the basic claims to which all eco-feminists are committed. As I use the term, *eco-feminism* is a position based on the following claims: (i) there are important connections between the oppression of women and the oppression of nature; (ii) understanding the nature of these connections is necessary to any adequate understanding of the oppression of women and the oppression of nature; (iii) feminist theory and practice must include an ecological perspective; and (iv) solutions to ecological problems must include a feminist perspective.[6]

Suppose that eco-feminism is true or at least plausible. To what extent do the four leading versions of feminism—liberal feminism, traditional Marxist feminism, radical feminism, and socialist feminism—capture or make a place for eco-feminism? To answer this question is to determine the extent to which the leading versions of feminism constitute an adequate theoretical grounding for eco-feminism.

My primary aim in this paper is to assess the adequacy of the four leading versions of feminism from the perspective of eco-feminism. I argue that while each may provide important insights into the oppression of women and nature, nonetheless, in its present form and taken by itself, each is inadequate, incomplete, or at least sufficiently problematic as a theoretical grounding for eco-feminism. I conclude by suggesting that if eco-feminism is to be taken seriously, then what is needed is a new "transformative" feminism, one which moves us beyond the current debate over the four leading versions of feminism and makes an eco-feminist perspective central to feminist theory and practice.

Two qualifications on the scope of the paper are in order. First, eco-feminism is a relatively new movement. In some cases, the leading versions of feminism have not, in fact, articulated a position on ecology or on the nature of the connection between the oppression of women and the oppression of nature. As such, in some cases, the ecological implications attributed in this paper to a given feminist theory are only hypothetical: they are suppositions about what such feminist accounts *might* be like, given what is known of the more general tenets of those feminist positions, rather than accounts of viewpoints actually stated.

Second, I provide neither a defense of eco-feminism nor a defense of a "transformative feminism." Rather, on the assumption that eco-feminism is true or plausible, I attempt to clarify the extent to which the four leading versions of feminism are problematic as a theoretical basis for eco-feminism. The concluding discussion of a transformative feminism is intended mainly to be suggestive of possible directions to pursue which will both expand upon the insights of current feminisms and include eco-feminism as an integral aspect of feminist theory and practice.

Eco-Feminism and Patriarchal Conceptual Frameworks

Eco-feminists take as their central project the unpacking of the connections between the twin oppressions of women and nature. Central to this project is a critique of the sort of thinking which sanctions that oppression. One way to understand this critique is to talk about conceptual frameworks.

Underlying eco-feminism is the view that, whether we know it or not, each of us operates out of a socially constructed mind set or *conceptual framework,* i.e., a set of beliefs, values, attitudes, and assumptions which shape, reflect, and explain our view of ourselves and our world. A conceptual framework is influenced by such factors as sex-gender, race, class, age, sexual preference, religion, and nationality. A *patriarchal conceptual framework* is one which takes traditionally male-identified beliefs, values, attitudes, and assumptions as

the only, or the standard, or the superior ones; it gives higher status or prestige to what has been traditionally identified as "male" than to what has been traditionally identified as "female."

A patriarchal conceptual framework is characterized by *value-hierarchical thinking.* In the words of eco-feminist Elizabeth Dodson Gray, such thinking "is a perception of diversity which is so organized by a spatial metaphor (Up-and-Down) that greater value is always attributed to that which is higher."[7] It puts men "up" and women "down," culture "up" and nature "down," minds "up" and bodies "down."

Such patriarchal value-hierarchical thinking gives rise to *a logic of domination,* i.e., a value-hierarchical way of thinking which explains, justifies, and maintains the subordination of an "inferior" group by a "superior" group on the grounds of the (alleged) inferiority or superiority of the respective group. By attributing greater value to that which is higher, the up-down organization of perceptions, mediated by a logic of domination, serves to legitimate inequality "when, in fact, prior to the metaphor of Up-Down one would have said only that there existed diversity."[8]

Eco-feminists assume that patriarchal value-hierarchical thinking supports the sort of "either-or" thinking which generates *normative dualisms,* i.e., thinking in which the disjunctive terms (or sides of the dualism) are seen as exclusive (rather than inclusive) and oppositional (rather than complementary), and where higher value or superiority is attributed to one disjunct (or, side of the dualism) than the other. It, thereby, conceptually separates as opposites aspects of reality that in fact are inseparable or complementary; e.g., it opposes human to nonhuman, mind to body, self to other, reason to emotion.[9]

According to eco-feminism, then, the connections between the oppression of women and the oppression of nature ultimately are *conceptual:* they are embedded in a patriarchal conceptual framework and reflect a logic of domination which functions to explain, justify, and maintain the subordination of both women and nature. Eco-feminism, therefore, encourages us to think ourselves out of "patriarchal conceptual traps,"[10] by *reconceptualiz-*

ing ourselves and our relation to the nonhuman natural world in nonpatriarchal ways.

What makes a critique of patriarchal conceptual frameworks distinctively "eco-feminist" has to do with the interconnections among the four minimal condition claims of eco-feminism. First, and most obviously, the critique is used to show that there are important connections between the oppression of women and the oppression of nature (condition [i]). Second, by understanding how a patriarchal conceptual framework sanctions the oppression of both women and nature (condition [ii]), eco-feminists are in a position to show why "naturism" (i.e., the domination of nature) ought to be included among the systems of oppression maintained by patriarchy. This opens the door for showing how, in Sheila Collins' words,

> Racism, sexism, class exploitation, and ecological destruction are four interlocking pillars upon which the structure of patriarchy rests.[11]

Third, the critique of patriarchal conceptual frameworks is grounded in familiar ecological principles: everything is interconnected with everything else; all parts of an ecosystem have equal value; there is no free lunch; "nature knows best"; healthy, balanced ecosystems must maintain diversity; there is unity in diversity.[12] This grounding is the basis for the uniquely eco-feminist position that an adequate feminist theory and practice embrace an ecological perspective (condition [iii]). Fourth, the critique goes two ways: not only must a proper feminist theory and practice reflect an ecological perspective (condition [iii]); the ecological movement must embrace a feminist perspective (condition [iv]). Otherwise, the ecological movement will fail to make the conceptual connections between the oppression of women and the oppression of nature (and to link these to other systems of oppression), and will risk utilizing strategies and implementing solutions which contribute to the continued subordination of women.

The stakes are high. If eco-feminism is correct, then a feminist debate over ecology is much deeper and more basic to both the feminist and ecology movements than traditional construals of feminism or ecology might have us believe. What is at stake is not only the success of the feminist and ecology movements, but the theoretical adequacy of feminism itself.

An Eco-Feminist Critique of the Four Leading Versions of Feminism

Feminism traditionally has been construed as the movement to end the oppression of women. All feminists agree that the oppression of women (i.e., the unequal and unjust status of women) exists, is wrong, and ought to be changed. But feminists disagree markedly about how to understand that oppression and how to bring about the necessary changes.

In her book *Feminist Politics and Human Nature*, Alison Jaggar offers an extensive analysis of the four leading versions of feminism and the key respects in which these theories differ. In what follows, I use Jaggar's analysis as the basis for my account of the eco-feminist critique of the leading versions of feminism.

Liberal Feminism

Liberal feminism emanates from the classical liberal tradition that idealizes a society in which autonomous individuals are provided maximal freedom to pursue their own interests. Liberal feminists trace the oppression of women to the lack of equal legal rights and unfair disadvantages in the public domain. Hence, the liberation of women requires the elimination of those legal and social constraints that prevent women from exercising their right of self-determination.

Liberal feminism endorses a highly individualistic conception of human nature. Humans are essentially separate, rational agents engaged in competition to maximize their own interests. The "mental" capacity to reason, i.e., the capacity to act in accordance with objective principles and to be consistent in the pursuit of ends, is what grounds the basic, essential, and equal dignity of all individuals. Basic human properties (e.g., rationality, autonomy, dignity) are ascribed to individuals independent of any historical or social context, and moral consideration is due humans on the basis of these distinctive human properties.

Because humans are conceived as essentially separate rational agents, a liberal feminist epistemology construes the attainment of knowledge as an individual project. The liberal feminist epistemological goal is to formulate value-neutral, intersubjectively verifiable, and universalizable rules that enable any rational agent to attain knowledge "under a veil of ignorance." Both genuine knowledge and "the moral point of view" express the impartial point of view of the rational, detached observer.

There are two sorts of ecological implications of liberal feminism. Both are generated within a liberal framework that applies traditional moral and legal categories to nonhumans. They are liberal feminist insofar as the ecological perspective is based on the same sorts of considerations that liberal feminists have appealed to traditionally in arguments for equal rights, equal opportunities, or fair consideration for women.

The first ecological implication draws the line of moral considerability at humans, separating humans from nonhumans and basing any claims to moral consideration for nonhumans either on the alleged rights or interests of humans, or on the consequences of such consideration for human well-being. Liberal feminists who do (or might) take this stance justify such practices as legal protection of endangered species, restrictions on the use of animals in laboratory research, or support for the appropriate technology, anti-nuclear, and peace movements on the grounds that they are mandated by consideration of the rights, interests, or well-being of present or future generations of humans (including women, mothers, and children).

The second extends the line of moral considerability to qualified nonhumans on the grounds that they, like women (or humans), are deserving of moral consideration in their own right: they are rational, sentient, interest carriers, or right holders.[13] According to this second sort of ecological stance, responsible environmental practices toward nonhumans are justified on the grounds that individual

nonhumans share certain morally relevant characteristics with humans in virtue of which they are deserving of protection or moral consideration.

From an eco-feminist perspective, both sorts of ecological implications are inadequate or at least seriously problematic. First, both basically keep intact a patriarchal conceptual framework characterized by value-hierarchical thinking and oppositional normative dualisms: humans over and against nature, the "mind" (or "rational") over and against the "body" (or the "nonrational"). As such, although liberal feminist ecological concerns may expand the traditional ethical framework to include moral and legal consideration of qualified nonhumans, or even to include the instrumental value of ecosystemic well-being for human welfare, they will be unacceptable to eco-feminists.

Second, the extreme individualism of a liberal feminist ecological perspective conflicts with the eco-feminist emphasis on the independent value of the integrity, diversity, and stability of ecosystems, and on the ecological themes of interconnectedness, unity in diversity, and equal value to all parts of the human-nature system. It also conflicts with "ecological ethics" per se. Ecological ethics are holistic, not individualistic; they take the value and well-being of a species, community, or ecosystem, and not merely of particular individuals, let alone human individuals, as basic. For eco-feminists, an ecological ethics based on a "web-like" view of relationships among all life forms conflicts with the hierarchical rules- and individual rights-based ethics of the liberal ethical tradition.

The eco-feminist critique of hierarchical rights- and rules-based ethical models reflects current feminist scholarship on ethics and moral reasoning. For example, in her recent book *In A Different Voice,* psychologist Carol Gilligan compares highly individualized and hierarchical rules- and rights-oriented ethics (embedded in the liberal tradition) with web-like and contextual ethics of care and reciprocal responsibility.[14] She argues that the two ethical orientations reflect important differences in moral reasoning between men and women, and on such basic issues as the conception of the self, morality, and conflict resolution. In her article "Moral Revolution," philosopher Kathryn Pyne Addelson argues that there is a bias in "our world view" by the near exclusion of women from the domain of intellectual pursuits, "a bias that requires a revolutionary change in ethics to remedy."[15] According to Addelson:

> It is a bias that allows moral problems to be defined from the top of various hierarchies of authority in such a way that the existence of the authority is concealed, and so the existence of alternative definitions that might challenge that authority and radically change our social organization is also concealed.[16]

Addelson's criticism of traditional ethics is at the same time a criticism of liberal feminism: the liberal feminist ethical tradition (what Addelson calls "the Judith Thomson tradition") assumes that defining moral problems from the top of the hierarchy is the "official" or "correct" or "legitimate" point of view;[17] it does not notice that "dominant-subordinate social structures are *creators* of inequality."[18] By contrast, what Addelson calls "the Jane tradition" uses the perceptions and power of a subordinate group—women—"to eliminate dominant-subordinate structures through the creation of new social forms which do not have that structure."[19] The women of the Jane tradition, unlike those of the Thomson tradition, challenge the patriarchal conceptual framework which defines "our" world view, how things "really are," and how things "ought to be," and which assumes the superiority of the hierarchical rules- and rights-approach to ethics.

Whatever else the strengths and weaknesses of the Gilligan and Addelson accounts of alternative ethical frameworks, their contributions to a discussion of eco-feminism are noteworthy. Each provides important reasons for being suspicious of approaches to feminism, ethics, or ecological concerns based on a patriarchal conceptual framework. To the extent that the ecological implications of liberal feminism do so, they perpetuate the sort of thinking and bias which, according to Gilligan and Addelson, fails to pay adequate attention to other values (e.g., care, friendship, rec-

iprocity in relationships) and to the epistemological and moral point of view of a subordinate group in our society: women. The Gilligan and Addelson accounts thereby provide the sorts of reasons eco-feminists offer for rejecting a liberal feminist ecology.

Traditional Marxist Feminism

Traditional Marxist feminism views the oppression of women, like the oppression of workers, as a direct result of the institution of class society and, under capitalism, of private property. The specific oppression of women is due to the sexual division of labor whereby women are excluded from the public realm of production and occupy dependent economic positions in the traditional monogamous family. Thus, the liberation of women requires that the traditional family be dissolved as an economic (though not necessarily as a social) unit. As Engels states in a much quoted sentence, "The first condition of the liberation of the wife is to bring the whole female sex into public industry."[20] Since women's oppression is a class oppression, women's liberation will be a class movement accomplished together with male workers by overthrowing capitalism.

For traditional Marxist feminists (like traditional Marxists generally), the essential human activity is not pure thought or reason (as liberals assume) but conscious and productive activity—*praxis*. Praxis is conscious physical labor directed at transforming the material world to meet human needs. Humans are distinguished from nonhumans by their ability to consciously and purposefully transpose their environment to meet their material needs through the activity of praxis.[21]

Since human nature is developed historically and socially through praxis, human nature is not a fixed or immutable condition. Furthermore, since human nature is understood in terms of praxis, humans are only truly free when they engage in productive activity which extends beyond the satisfaction of basic survival needs. For traditional Marxist feminists, women will be free when they are economically independent and when their work expresses the full development of human productive activity (or praxis), rather than the coercion of economic necessity.

A Marxist feminist epistemology is a radical departure from that of liberal feminism. Since humans are viewed as necessarily existing in dialectical relationship with each other, knowledge is viewed as a social construction; it is part of the basic shared human activity of praxis. The development of knowledge is not an individual undertaking, and there is no value-neutral knowledge accessible to some impartial, detached observer. For traditional Marxist feminists, "all forms of knowledge are historically determined by the prevailing mode of production."[22]

In *Marx and Engels on Ecology*, Howard L. Parsons discusses four general sorts of ecological criticisms which have been raised against traditional Marxism:

> Marx, Engels, and Marxism, generally have been criticized for certain alleged positions on ecological matters: (1) they have pitted man against nature; (2) they have anthropocentrically denied the values of external nature; (3) they have overstressed the conflicts in nature and have understressed its harmony; and (4) they have denied basic human values.[23]

These criticisms rest on such Marxist claims as "nature is man's inorganic body," man is "the real conscious master of Nature," and "the purely natural material in which *no* human labor is objectified . . . has no value."[24] The alleged criticisms are that since such claims emphasize the use value of the natural world in the production of economic goods (e.g., food, clothing, shelter), the transformation of nature to meet human material needs in the essential human activity of praxis, and the domination, mastery, or control of nature "by man," Marxism is not a suitable basis for an ecological ethic.[25]

Whether traditional Marxism can overcome these objections is being rigorously debated; it is beyond the scope of this paper to discuss that issue here. Nonetheless, it is important to indicate what the particular challenges are for traditional Marxist feminism from an eco-feminist perspective.

First, given the primacy of class in the traditional Marxist feminist account of oppression and liberation, a Marxist feminist must recon-cile traditional Marxist claims about nature with a political vision that does not pit men and women, as one class, over and against nature. Otherwise, the sort of patriarchal conceptual framework which traditionally has sanctioned the exploitation of nature will survive relatively unscathed, even if women get elevated to equal status with men (but against nature).

Second, traditional Marxists argue that environmental problems under capitalism will continue as long as the means of production (i.e., the raw materials, land, energy resources) and forces of production (i.e., the factories, machinery, skills) are used to support environmental research and development in the interest of expanding capital. Marxist feminists must show that a liberating or appropriate technology and science, based on ecological principles, could help protect and preserve, rather than exploit, nature.

Perhaps the most significant challenge to a plausible Marxist eco-feminism, however, lies in a third area of difficulty, viz., its general failure to take seriously gender as a constitutive category of social reality. This "gender blindness" in traditional Marxist analyses of women's oppression serves to distort, rather than clarify, the nature of women's oppression. Since eco-feminism assumes that the connections between the oppression of women and the oppression of nature have to do with sex-gender systems, a "gender blind" traditional Marxist feminism will be hard pressed to make visible those connections.

Radical Feminism

Radical feminism departs from both liberal feminism and traditional Marxist feminism by rooting women's oppression in reproductive biology and a sex-gender system. According to radical feminists, patriarchy (i.e., the systematic domination by men) oppresses women in sex-specific ways by defining women as beings whose primary functions are either to bear and raise children (i.e., to be mothers) or to satisfy male sexual desires (i.e., to be sex objects). Since the oppression of women is based on "male control of women's fertility and women's sexuality," the liberation of women is to "end male control of women's bodies" by dismantling patriarchy.[26] Women will be free when no longer bound by the constraints of compulsory heterosexuality and compulsory child-bearing and child-rearing roles.

Insofar as there is one radical feminist conception of human nature,[27] it is that humans are essentially embodied. We are not (as the Cartesian philosophical tradition might have us suppose) bodiless minds, i.e., "mental" or thinking beings whose essential nature exists independently from our own or others' physical, emotional, or sexual existence. By taking women's bodies, and, in particular, women's reproductive biology, as indispensable to women's nature, radical feminism brings child-bearing and child-rearing functions into the political arena. It makes women's sex politically significant. It is in this way that for the radical feminist, "the personal is (profoundly) political."

A radical feminist epistemology self-consciously explores strategies (e.g., consciousness-raising processes) to correct the distortions of patriarchal ideology. It emphasizes a variety of sources of reliable knowledge (e.g., intuition, feelings, spiritual or mystical experiences) and the integration of women's felt mystical/intuitive/spiritual experiences into feminist theory and epistemology. Challenging the traditional "political versus spiritual" dichotomy, many radical feminists support a "politics of women's spirituality" which makes a spiritual ingredient necessary to any adequate feminist political theory.[28]

Radical feminists have had the most to say about eco-feminism. Taking up the question "Are women closer to nature than men?" some radical feminists (e.g., so-called "nature feminists," Mary Daly, Susan Griffin, Starhawk) have answered "yes." They applaud the close connections between women and nature, and urge women to celebrate their bodies, rejoice in our place in the community of inanimate and animate beings, and seek symbols that can transform our spiritual consciousness so as to be more in tune with nature. Other radical feminists answer "no"; they criticize nature feminists for regressing to harmful patriarchal sex-role stereotyping which feeds the prejudice that women have specifically female or womanly interests in preventing pollution, nurturing animals, or saving the planet.[29]

Even though to date eco-feminism has tended to be associated with radical feminism, there are noteworthy worries about radical feminism from an eco-feminist perspective. First, since radical feminism generally pays little attention to the historical and material features of women's oppression (including the relevance of race, class, ethnic, and national background), it insufficiently articulates the extent to which women's oppression is grounded in concrete and diverse social structures. In this respect, it lacks the sort of theoretical leverage needed to reveal the interconnections between the oppression of nature and women, on the one hand, and other forms of oppression (e.g., racism, classism).

Second, it mystifies women's experiences to locate women closer to nature than men, just as it underplays important aspects of the oppression of women to deny the connection of women with nature, for the truth is that women, like men, are both connected to nature and separate from it, natural and cultural beings. Insofar as radical feminism comes down in favor of one side or the other of the nature-culture dualism—by locating women either on the nature or on the culture side—it mistakenly perpetuates the sort of oppositional, dualistic thinking for which patriarchal conceptual frameworks are criticized.

This last point raises a conceptual and methodological worry about radical feminism as a grounding of eco-feminist concerns; the worry has to do with framing the feminist debate over ecology in terms of the question, "Are women closer to nature than men?"[30] In order for the question to be meaningfully raised, one must presuppose the legitimacy of the nature-culture dualism. The idea that one group of persons is, or is not, closer to nature than another group assumes the very nature-culture split that eco-feminism denies. As Joan Griscom puts it, "the question itself is flawed."[31] She argues:

> Since we are all part of nature, and since all of us, biology and culture alike, is part of nature, the question ultimately makes no sense.[32]

It is "unwitting complicity"[33] in the patriarchal mind set that accounts for the question being raised at all. Insofar as radical feminism engages in such complicity, its approach to the feminist debate over ecology is methodologically suspect and conceptually flawed.

Socialist Feminism

Socialist feminism attempts to integrate the insights of traditional Marxist feminism with those of radical feminism by making domination by class and by sex gender fundamental to women's oppression. The socialist feminist program applies the historical materialist method of traditional Marxism to issues of sex and gender made visible by radical feminists.[34] By widening the Marxist notions of praxis and production to include procreation and child rearing, socialist feminists argue that the economic system and sex-gender system are dialectically reinforced in historically specific ways.[35] Thus, for socialist feminists, the liberation of women requires the end of both capitalism and patriarchy.

The socialist feminist view of human nature is that humans are created historically and culturally through the dialectical interrelation of human biology, physical environment, and society.[36] Since contemporary society consists of groups of individuals defined by age, sex, class, race, nationality, and ethnic background, each of these is included in the conception of human nature. Differences between men and women are viewed as social constructions, not pre-social or biological givens. For the socialist feminist, even if human biology is in some sense determined, it is nonetheless also socially conditioned. As Jaggar puts it, "Biology is 'gendered' as well as sexed."[37] In this respect, according to Jaggar,

> The goal of socialist feminism is to abolish the social relations that constitute humans not only as workers and capitalists but also as women and men. . . . the ideal of socialist feminism is that women (and men) will disappear as socially constructed categories.[38]

Like traditional Marxist feminists, socialist feminists view knowledge as a social construction; like radical feminists, they claim that women, as a subordinate group, have a "special epistemological standpoint that makes possible a view of the world that is unavailable to capitalist or to working class men."[39] This "standpoint of women," as Jaggar calls it, is historical materialist as well as sex-gendered; it is constructed from and accounts for the felt experiences of women of different ages, classes, races, and ethnic and national backgrounds.[40]

Since socialist feminism is an attempt to wed the insights of traditional Marxist feminism and radical feminism, it might seem that it would provide the most promising theoretical framework for eco-feminist concerns. In fact, however, many socialist feminists have been quite guarded in their enthusiasm for ecological matters.[41] This is understandable. The Marxist side of their politics makes them suspicious of a radical feminist grounding of ecological concerns in women's spiritual or sex-gender-based connection with nature.

Some socialist feminists have attempted to make a place for eco-feminist concerns by interpreting the Marxist attitude of domination over nature as "the psychological result of a certain mode of organizing production."[42] They argue that what is needed are new modes of conceptualizing and organizing production which allow for both reproductive freedom for women and recognition of the independent value of nonhuman nature. From an eco-feminist perspective, such a reconceptualization of traditional Marxist views is necessary if women are not to be brought into public production with men over and against nature.

The attractiveness of socialist feminism from an eco-feminist perspective lies in its emphasis on the importance of factors in addition to sex gender and class for an understanding of the social construction of reality and the interconnections among various systems of oppression. But, as is, it is incomplete. From an eco-feminist perspective, insofar as socialist feminism does not explicitly address the systematic oppression of nature, it fails to give an account of one of the "four interlocking pillars upon which the structure of patriarchy rests"—sexism, racism, classism, *and* naturism.

Transformative Feminism

So far I have argued that, from an eco-feminist perspective, there are good reasons to worry about the adequacy of each of the four leading versions of feminism as a theoretical grounding for eco-feminism. If this view is correct, what, then, is needed?

If one takes seriously eco-feminist claims about the nature and importance of the connections between the oppression of women and the oppression of nature, then I think what is needed is an integrative and transformative feminism, one that moves us beyond the current debate over the four leading versions of feminism and makes a responsible ecological perspective central to feminist theory and practice. In what follows, I offer a few suggestions about how such a transformative feminism might be developed.

First, a transformative feminism would expand upon the traditional conception of feminism as "the movement to end women's oppression" by recognizing and making explicit the interconnections between all systems of oppression. In this regard, a transformative feminism would be informed by the conception of feminism which has been advanced by many black feminists and Third World feminists articulating the needs and concerns of black women and women in development. These feminists have argued that because of the basic connections between sexist oppression and other forms of systematized oppression, feminism, properly understood, is a movement to end *all* forms of oppression.[43]

Socialist feminism has opened the door for such a transformative feminism by acknowledging the structural interconnections between sexism, racism, and classicism; eco-feminism contributes insights about the important connections between the oppression of women and the oppression of nature. A transformative feminism would build on these insights to develop a more expansive and complete feminism, one which ties the liberation of women to the elimination of all systems of oppression.

Second, a transformative feminism must provide a central theoretical place for the diversity of women's experiences, even if this means abandoning the project of attempting to formulate one overarching feminist theory or one woman's voice.[44] This is in accordance with the basic goal of any theory. As Evelyn Fox Keller puts it:

> The essential goal of theory in general I take to be to represent our experience of the world in as comprehensive and inclusive a way as possible; in that effort we seek a maximal intersubjectivity.[45]

A transformative feminism would acknowledge the social construction of knowledge and conception of epistemology that takes seriously the felt experiences of women as a subordinate group—however different those experiences may be. As a related point, it would be a call to oppressed groups to collectively assert *for themselves* their felt experiences, needs, and distinctiveness. In this respect, it would reflect a commitment to what Iris Young calls "a politics of difference," viz., one that asserts the value and specificity of group difference in political theory and practice.[46]

Third, a transformative feminism would involve a rejection of a logic of domination and the patriarchal conceptual framework which gives rise to it. By showing how systems of oppression are rooted in this common conceptual framework, it would address the conceptual and structural interconnections among all forms of domination. In this way, it would encourage feminists concerned with ecology to join allegiance with those seeking to end oppression by race and class. Otherwise, feminist concerns over ecology would degenerate into a largely white middle-class movement. As Rosemary Ruether warns:

> The ethic of reconciliation with the earth has yet to break out of its snug corners of affluence and find meaningful cohesion with the revolution of insurgent people.[47]

The promise of a transformative feminism requires making connections with "the revolution of insurgent people."

Fourth, a transformative feminism would involve a rethinking of what it is to be human, especially as the conception of human nature becomes informed by a nonpatriarchal conception of the interconnections between human and nonhuman nature. This would involve a psychological restructuring of our attitudes and beliefs about ourselves and "our world" (including the nonhuman world), and a philosophical rethinking of the notion of the self such that we see ourselves as both co-members of an ecological community and yet different from other members of it.

Fifth, a transformative feminism would involve recasting traditional ethical concerns to make a central place for values (e.g., care, friendship, reciprocity in relationships, appropriate trust, diversity) underplayed or lost in traditional, particularly modern and contemporary, philosophical construals of ethics. It would include nonhierarchical models of morality and conflict resolution (e.g., consensual decision making and mediation) and involve a rethinking of the "moral point of view" in light of the social and historical context of human nature.

Sixth, a transformative feminism would involve challenging patriarchal bias in technology research and analysis and the use of appropriate science and technologies, i.e., those brought into the service of preserving, rather than destroying, the Earth.[48] Only then would the eco-feminist reconceptualization of the relationship between human and nonhuman nature come around full circle.

Conclusion

In this paper I have argued that from the perspective of eco-feminism, the four leading versions of feminism are inadequate, incomplete, or seriously problematic as a theoretical grounding of eco-feminist concerns. I have suggested that if eco-feminism is correct, then what is needed is a "transformative feminism." The adequacy of such a transformative feminism would depend on how accurately it captures and systematizes the points of view of women as oppressed persons, the insights of eco-feminism, and the interconnections between all systems of oppression.

When one describes a lake by looking down at it from above, or by only skimming across its surface, one gets a limited and partial view of the nature of the lake. It is only when one dives deep and looks at the lake from the bottom up that one sees the diversity and richness of the various life forms and processes that constitute the lake.

So, too, it is with feminist theorizing. It is only when we dive deep and conceptualize reality from the various points of view of women of different ages, races, ethnic and national backgrounds, however different those experiences may be, that our feminist theories will see the diversity and richness of those points of view. It is only when we dive deep and see the interconnections between various systems of oppression that our feminist theories will hold much water. A transformative feminism has the potential to make these connections. It has the potential for making the connections between feminism and ecology from the bottom up.

Notes

1. Rosemary Radford Ruether, *New Woman/New Earth: Sexist Ideologies and Human Liberation* (New York: The Seabury Press, 1975), p. 204.

2. Ibid.

3. Elizabeth Dodson Gray, *Green Paradise Lost* (Wellesley, Mass.: Roundtable Press, 1981), and *Patriarchy As A Conceptual Trap* (Wellesley, Mass.: Roundtable Press, 1982); Susan Griffin, *Women and Nature* (New York: Harper and Row, 1978); Mary Daly, *Gyn/Ecology: The Meta-Ethics of Radical Feminism* (Boston: Beacon Press, 1978); Carolyn Merchant, *The Death of Nature: Women, Ecology, and the Scientific Revolution* (New York: Harper and Row, 1983), and "Earthcare: Women and the Environmental Movement," *Environment* 23 (1981): 2–13, 38–40; Joan L. Griscom, "On Healing the Nature/History Split in Feminist

Thought," *Heresies #13: Feminism and Ecology* 4 (1981): 4–9; Ynestra King, "Feminism and the Revolt of Nature," *Heresies #13: Feminism and Ecology* 4 (1981): 12–16, and "The Eco-feminist Imperative," in Leonie Caldecott and Stephanie Leland, eds, *Reclaim the Earth: Women Speak Out for Life on Earth* (London: The Women's Press, 1983), pp. 12–16, and "Toward an Ecological Feminism and a Feminist Ecology," in Joan Rothschild, ed., *Machina Ex Dea: Feminist Perspectives on Technology* (New York: Pergamon Press, 1983), pp. 118–29; Ariel Kay Salleh, "Deeper than Deep Ecology: The Eco-Feminist Connection." *Environmental Ethics* 3 (1984): 339–45.

4. Although more traditional uses of the term *oppression* refer to domination or subordination of humans by humans, eco-feminists use the expression "oppression of nature" to refer to the domination or subordination of nonhuman nature by humans.

5. Ynestra King, "Feminism and a Revolt of Nature," p. 12.

6. The minimal condition account given here does not, by itself, specify what counts as a "feminist perspective," an "ecological perspective," "feminist theory and practice," or "solutions to ecological problems." Nor does it specify whether a "science of ecology" must reflect a commitment to gender ideologies or in some sense be a "feminist science." Questions about the meaning, scope, and application of conditions (i) to (iv) are deliberately left open.

7. Elizabeth Dodson Gray, *Green Paradise Lost,* p. 20.

8. Ibid.

9. Alison M. Jaggar, *Feminist Politics and Human Nature* (Totowa, N.J.: Rowman and Allanheld, 1983), p. 96. Joyce Trebilcot argues that "In feminism, there is a movement toward the elimination of all dualisms" because dualisms not only function evaluatively (to justify the "superior's" power over the "inferior") and epistemologically (they determine perceptions); they also function to determine in part the conception or meaning of the things related. Joyce Trebilcot, "Conceiving Women: Notes on the Logic of Feminism," in Marilyn Pearsall, ed., *Women and Values: Readings in Recent Feminist Philosophy* (Belmont, Calif.: Wadsworth Publishing Co., 1986), pp.. 358–63.

10. Elizabeth Dodson Gray describes a "conceptual trap" as "a set of outmoded beliefs" and "a way of thinking that is like a room which—once inside—you cannot imagine a world outside." Gray, *Patriarchy as a Conceptual Trap,* pp. 16, 17.

11. Sheila D. Collins, *A Different Heaven and Earth* (Valley Forge: Judson Press, 1974), p. 161. I take it that this account is compatible with there being other "pillars" on which patriarchal structures rest (e.g., "imperialism" in capitalist patriarchal structures).

12. See the discussions of eco-feminism given by King, "Toward an Ecological Feminism and a Feminist Ecology;" Don E. Marietta, Jr., "Environmentalism, Feminism, and the Future of American Society," *The Humanist* 44 (1984): 15–18, 30; Merchant, "Earthcare: Women and the Environmental Movement."

13. For example, consider animal liberationism. According to Tom Regan's rights-based version of animal liberationism, individual nonhuman animals have moral rights against humans which impose on us obligations to treat them in certain ways. Tom Regan, *All That Dwell Therein: Essays on Animal Rights and Environmental Ethics* (Berkeley: University of California Press, 1982). According to Peter Singer's utilitarian-based version, our obligations to nonhuman animals are grounded in their capacity to feel pain and pleasure; failure to acknowledge that animals and other sentient nonhumans deserve moral consideration is just "speciesism," akin to racism, sexism, and classism, i.e., the view that humans are morally superior to animals. Peter Singer, *Animal Liberation* (New York: New York Review/Random House, 1975). Both Regan and Singer's versions of animal liberation extend traditional liberal ethical concerns to individual nonhumans on the basis of certain morally relevant characteristics they allegedly share with humans.

14. Carol Gilligan, *In a Different Voice* (Cambridge, Mass.: Harvard University Press, 1982).

15. Kathryn Pyne Addelson, "Moral Revolution," in *Women and Values,* p. 306.

16. Ibid., p. 307.

17. Ibid.

18. Ibid., p. 306.

19. Ibid.

20. Frederick Engels, *The Origin of the Family,*

Private Property and the State (New York: International Publishers, 1972), pp. 137–38.

21. For example, Marx writes "Men can be distinguished from animals by consciousness, by religion or by anything else you like. They themselves begin to distinguish themselves from animals as soon as they begin to *produce* their means of subsistence, a step which is conditioned by their physical organization." Karl Marx and Frederick Engels, *The German Ideology,* ed. with an introduction by C. J. Arthur (New York: International Publishers, 1970), p. 42.

22. Jaggar, *Feminist Politics and Human Nature,* p. 358.

23. *Marx and Engels on Ecology,* ed. Howard L. Parsons (Westport, Conn.: Greenwood Press, 1977), p. 35. Parsons defends Marx, Engels, and Marxism against each of these criticisms.

24. Ibid., pp. 133, 141, and 122.

25. For recent discussions of problems for an environmentally attractive interpretation of traditional Marxist doctrine, see Val Routley, "On Karl Marx as an Environmental Hero," *Environmental Ethics,* 3 (1981): 237–44; Hwa Yol Jung, "Marxism, Ecology, and Technology," *Environmental Ethics* 5 (1983): 169–71; Charles Tolman, "Karl Marx, Alienation, and the Mastery of Nature," *Environmental Ethics* 3 (1981): 63–74. For a defense of a Marxian ecological ethic, see Donald C. Lee, "On the Marxian View of the Relationship between Man and Nature," *Environmental Ethics* 2 (1980): 3–16, and "Toward a Marxian Ecological Ethic: A Response to Two Critics," *Environmental Ethics* 4 (1982): 339–43; Howard L. Parsons, *Marx and Engels on Ecology.*

26. Jaggar, *Feminist Politics and Human Nature,* p. 266.

27. Jaggar identifies four radical feminist conceptions of human nature. Ibid., pp. 11–12, 85–105.

28. See Charlene Spretnak, "Introduction," in Charlene Spretnak, ed., *The Politics of Women's Spirituality* (New York: Doubleday, 1982), p. xxx, n. 20.

29. For a discussion of these two radical feminist positions, see Ynestra King, "Feminism and the Revolt of Nature."

30. Sherry B. Ortner was one of the first to address this question in her article, "Is Female to Male As Nature Is to Culture?" in Michelle Rosaldo and Louise Lamphere, eds., *Woman, Culture, and Society* (Stanford: Stanford University Press, 1974), pp. 67–87.

31. Griscom, "On Healing the Nature/Culture Split in Feminist Thought," p. 9.

32. Ibid.

33. The phrase "unwitting complicity" is from Ynestra King, "Feminism and the Revolt Against Nature," p. 15.

34. Jaggar, *Feminist Politics and Human Nature,* p. 124.

35. Ibid., p. 129.

36. Ibid., p. 125.

37. Ibid., p. 126.

38. Ibid., p. 132.

39. Ibid., p. 126.

40. According to Jaggar, a "standpoint" is "a position in society from which certain features of reality come into prominence and from which others are obscured" (ibid., p. 382). The "standpoint of women" is "that perspective which reveals women's true interests and this standpoint is reached only through scientific and political struggle. Those who construct the standpoint of women must begin from women's experience as women describe it, but they must go beyond that experience theoretically and ultimately may require that women's experiences be redescribed" (ibid., p. 384).

41. For example, in her otherwise thorough treatment of socialist feminism in *Feminist Politics and Human Nature,* Alison Jaggar explicitly addresses the issue of the connection between socialist feminism and ecology in less than one full page (pp. 306–07). From an eco-feminist perspective, such a limited treatment of the feminism-ecology connection leaves the incorrect impression that ecology is not, or is not a very important, feminist issue. Furthermore, this (what might be called "ecology blindness") reinforces oppositional thinking which separates discussions of political philosophy from the life sciences (e.g., ecology) and discussions of human nature from non-human nature. From an eco-feminist perspective, it thereby reinforces the mistaken view that an adequate feminist political theory can be articulated without incorporation of an ecological perspective, and that an adequate theory of human nature can be articulated without essential reference to nonhuman nature.

42. Ibid., p. 306.

43. See, e.g., Bell Hooks, *Feminist Theory: From Margin to Center* (Boston: South End Press, 1984), pp. 17–31; "The Combahee River Collective Statement," in Barbara Smith, ed., *Home Girls: A Black Feminist Anthology* (New York: Kitchen Table Women of Color Press, 1983), p. 272; Gita Sen and Caren Gowen, *Development, Crisis and Alternative Visions: Third World Women's Perspectives* (New Delhi: DAWN, 1985), p. 13.

44. For an account of reasons to be wary of attempts to articulate "the women's voice," see Maria Lugones and Elizabeth V. Spelman "Have We Got a Theory for You! Feminist Theory, Cultural Imperialism and the Woman's Voice," *Women's Studies International Forum* 6 (1983): 573–81.

45. Evelyn Fox Keller, "Women, Science, and Popular Mythology," in Joan Rothschild, ed., *Machina Ex Dea: Feminist Perspectives on Technology* (New York: Pergamon Press, 1983), p. 134.

46. Iris Marion Young, "Elements of a Politics of Difference," read at the Second Annual North American Society for Social Philosophy, Colorado Springs, August 1985.

47. Rosemary Radford Ruether, "Mother Earth and the Megamachine," in Carol Christ and Judith Plaskow, eds., *Woman-Spirit Rising: A Feminist Reader in Religion* (San Francisco: Harper and Row, 1979), p. 51.

48. For a discussion of a variety of feminist perspectives on science and technology, see Rothschild, ed., *Machina Ex Dea;* see also Judy Smith, *Something Old, Something New, Something Borrowed, Something Due* (Missoula, Mont.: Women and Technology Network, 1980).

52. All Animals Are Equal

Peter Singer

Peter Singer rejects what he calls "speciesism," or prejudice against another species. As with racism and sexism, we have an obligation to oppose speciesism, because animals have the capacity to suffer and have an interest in not suffering. Singer applies his ideas to animal experimentation.

"Animal Liberation" may sound more like a parody of other liberation movements than a serious objective. The idea of "The Rights of Animals" actually was once used to parody the case for women's rights. When Mary Wollstonecraft, a forerunner of today's feminists, published her *Vindication of the Rights of Woman* in 1792, her views were widely regarded as absurd, and before long an anonymous publication appeared entitled *A Vindication of the Rights of Brutes*. The author of this satirical work (now known to have been Thomas Taylor, a distinguished Cambridge philosopher) tried to refute Mary Wollstonecraft's arguments by showing that they could be car-

Reprinted with permission of the author from *Animal Liberation*, New York Review, second edition (1990), pp. 1–9, 36–37, 40, 81–83, 85–86.

ried one stage further. If the argument for equality was sound when applied to women, why should it not be applied to dogs, cats, and horses? The reasoning seemed to hold for these "brutes" too; yet to hold that brutes had rights was manifestly absurd. Therefore the reasoning by which this conclusion had been reached must be unsound, and if unsound when applied to brutes, it must also be unsound when applied to women, since the very same arguments had been used in each case.

In order to explain the basis of the case for the equality of animals, it will be helpful to start with an examination of the case for the equality of women. Let us assume that we wish to defend the case for women's rights against the attack by Thomas Taylor. How should we reply?

One way in which we might reply is by

saying that the case for equality between men and women cannot validly be extended to nonhuman animals. Women have a right to vote, for instance, because they are just as capable of making rational decisions about the future as men are; dogs, on the other hand, are incapable of understanding the significance of voting, so they cannot have the right to vote. There are many other obvious ways in which men and women resemble each other closely, while humans and animals differ greatly. So, it might be said, men and women are similar beings and should have similar rights, while humans and nonhumans are different and should not have equal rights.

The reasoning behind this reply to Taylor's analogy is correct up to a point, but it does not go far enough. There are obviously important differences between humans and other animals, and these differences must give rise to some differences in the rights that each have. Recognizing this evident fact, however, is no barrier to the case for extending the basic principle of equality to nonhuman animals. The differences that exist between men and women are equally undeniable, and the supporters of Women's Liberation are aware that these differences may give rise to different rights. Many feminists hold that women have the right to an abortion on request. It does not follow that since these same feminists are campaigning for equality between men and women they must support the right of men to have abortions too. Since a man cannot have an abortion, it is meaningless to talk of his right to have one. Since dogs can't vote, it is meaningless to talk of their right to vote. There is no reason why either Women's Liberation or Animal Liberation should get involved in such nonsense. The extension of the basic principle of equality from one group to another does not imply that we must treat both groups in exactly the same way, or grant exactly the same rights to both groups. Whether we should do so will depend on the nature of the members of the two groups. The basic principle of equality does not require equal or identical *treatment;* it requires equal consideration. Equal consideration for different beings may lead to different treatment and different rights.

So there is a different way of replying to Taylor's attempt to parody the case for women's rights, a way that does not deny the obvious differences between human beings and nonhumans but goes more deeply into the question of equality and concludes by finding nothing absurd in the idea that the basic principle of equality applies to so-called brutes. At this point such a conclusion may appear odd; but if we examine more deeply the basis on which our opposition to discrimination on grounds of race or sex ultimately rests, we will see that we would be on shaky ground if we were to demand equality for blacks, women, and other groups of oppressed humans while denying equal consideration to nonhumans. To make this clear we need to see, first, exactly why racism and sexism are wrong. When we say that all human beings, whatever their race, creed, or sex, are equal, what is it that we are asserting? Those who wish to defend hierarchical, inegalitarian societies have often pointed out that by whatever test we choose it simply is not true that all humans are equal. Like it or not we must face the fact that humans come in different shapes and sizes; they come with different moral capacities, different intellectual abilities, different amounts of benevolent feeling and sensitivity to the needs of others, different abilities to communicate effectively, and different capacities to experience pleasure and pain. In short, if the demand for equality were based on the actual equality of all human beings, we would have to stop demanding equality.

Still, one might cling to the view that the demand for equality among human beings is based on the actual equality of the different races and sexes. Although, it may be said, humans differ as individuals, there are no differences between the races and sexes as such. From the mere fact that a person is black or a woman we cannot infer anything about that person's intellectual or moral capacities. This, it may be said, is why racism and sexism are wrong. The white racist claims that whites are superior to blacks, but this is false; although there are differences among individuals, some blacks are superior to some whites in all of the capacities and abilities that could conceivably be relevant. The opponent of sexism would say the same: a person's sex is no guide to his or her abilities, and this is why it is unjustifiable to discriminate on the basis of sex.

The existence of individual variations that cut across the lines of race or sex, however, provides us with no defense at all against a more sophisticated opponent of equality, one who proposes that, say, the interests of all those with IQ scores below 100 be given less consideration than the interests of those with ratings over 100. Perhaps those scoring below the mark would, in this society, be made the slaves of those scoring higher. Would a hierarchical society of this sort really be so much better than one based on race or sex? I think not. But if we tie the moral principle of equality to the factual equality of the different races or sexes, taken as a whole, our opposition to racism and sexism does not provide us with any basis for objecting to this kind of inegalitarianism.

There is a second important reason why we ought not to base our opposition to racism and sexism on any kind of factual equality, even the limited kind that asserts that variations in capacities and abilities are spread evenly among the different races and between the sexes: we can have no absolute guarantee that these capacities and abilities really are distributed evenly, without regard to race or sex, among human beings. So far as actual abilities are concerned there do seem to be certain measurable differences both among races and between sexes. These differences do not, of course, appear in every case, but only when averages are taken. More important still, we do not yet know how many of these differences are really due to the different genetic endowments of the different races and sexes, and how many are due to poor schools, poor housing, and other factors that are the result of past and continuing discrimination. Perhaps all of the important differences will eventually prove to be environmental rather than genetic. Anyone opposed to racism and sexism will certainly hope that this will be so, for it will make the task of ending discrimination a lot easier; nevertheless, it would be dangerous to rest the case against racism and sexism on the belief that all significant differences are environmental in origin. The op-

ponent of, say, racism who takes this line will be unable to avoid conceding that if differences in ability did after all prove to have some genetic connection with race, racism would in some way be defensible.

Fortunately there is no need to pin the case for equality to one particular outcome of a scientific investigation. The appropriate response to those who claim to have found evidence of genetically based differences in ability among the races or between the sexes is not to stick to the belief that the genetic explanation must be wrong, whatever evidence to the contrary may turn up; instead we should make it quite clear that the claim to equality does not depend on intelligence, moral capacity, physical strength, or similar matters of fact. Equality is a moral idea, not an assertion of fact. There is no logically compelling reason for assuming that a factual difference in ability between two people justifies any difference in the amount of consideration we give to their needs and interests. *The principle of the equality of human beings is not a description of an alleged actual equality among humans: it is a prescription of how we should treat human beings.*

Jeremy Bentham, the founder of the reforming utilitarian school of moral philosophy, incorporated the essential basis of moral equality into his system of ethics by means of the formula: "Each to count for one and none for more than one." In other words, the interests of every being affected by an action are to be taken into account and given the same weight as the like interests of any other being. A later utilitarian, Henry Sidgwick, put the point in this way: "The good of any one individual is of no more importance, from the point of view (if I may say so) of the Universe, than the good of any other." More recently the leading figures in contemporary moral philosophy have shown a great deal of agreement in specifying as a fundamental presupposition of their moral theories some similar requirement that works to give everyone's interests equal consideration—although these writers generally cannot agree on how this requirement is best formulated.[1]

It is an implication of this principle of equality that our concern for others and our readiness to consider their interests ought not to depend on what they are like or on what abilities they may possess. Precisely what our concern or consideration requires us to do may vary according to the characteristics of those affected by what we do: concern for the well-being of children growing up in America would require that we teach them to read; concern for the well-being of pigs may require no more than that we leave them with other pigs in a place where there is adequate food and room to run freely. But the basic element—the taking into account of the interests of the being, whatever those interests may be —must, according to the principle of equality, be extended to all beings, black or white, masculine or feminine, human or nonhuman.

Thomas Jefferson, who was responsible for writing the principle of the equality of men into the American Declaration of Independence, saw this point. It led him to oppose slavery even though he was unable to free himself fully from his slaveholding background. He wrote in a letter to the author of a book that emphasized the notable intellectual achievements of Negroes in order to refute the then common view that they had limited intellectual capacities:

> Be assured that no person living wishes more sincerely than I do, to see a complete refutation of the doubts I myself have entertained and expressed on the grade of understanding allotted to them by nature, and to find that they are on a par with ourselves . . . but whatever be their degree of talent it is no measure of their rights. Because Sir Isaac Newton was superior to others in understanding, he was not therefore lord of the property or persons of others.[2]

Similarly, when in the 1850s the call for women's rights was raised in the United States, a remarkable black feminist named Sojourner Truth made the same point in more robust terms at a feminist convention:

> They talk about this thing in the head; what do they call it? ["Intellect," whispered someone nearby.] That's it. What's that got to do with women's rights or Negroes' rights? If my cup won't hold but a pint and yours holds a quart, wouldn't you be mean not to let me have my little half-measure full?[3]

It is on this basis that the case against racism and the case against sexism must both ultimately rest; and it is in accordance with this principle that the attitude that we may call "speciesism," by analogy with racism, must also be condemned. Speciesism—the word is not an attractive one, but I can think of no better term—is prejudice or attitude of bias in favor of the interests of members of one's own species and against those of members of other species. It should be obvious that the fundamental objections to racism and sexism made by Thomas Jefferson and Sojourner Truth apply equally to speciesism. If possessing a higher degree of intelligence does not entitle one human to use another for his or her own ends, how can it entitle humans to exploit nonhumans for the same purpose?[4]

Many philosophers and other writers have proposed the principle of equal consideration of interests, in some form or other, as a basic moral principle; but not many of them have recognized that this principle applies to members of other species as well as to our own. Jeremy Bentham was one of the few who did realize this. In a forward-looking passage written at a time when black slaves had been freed by the French but in the British dominions were still being treated in the way we now treat animals, Bentham wrote:

> The day *may* come when the rest of the animal creation may acquire those rights which never could have been withholden from them but by the hand of tyranny. The French have already discovered that the blackness of the skin is no reason why a human being should be abandoned without redress to the caprice of a tormentor. It may one day come to be recognized that the number of the legs, the villosity of the skin, or the termination of the *os sacrum* are reasons equally insufficient for abandoning a sensitive being to the same fate. What else is it that should trace the insuperable line? Is it

the faculty of reason, or perhaps the faculty of discourse? But a full-grown horse or dog is beyond comparison a more rational, as well as a more conversable animal, than an infant of a day or a week or even a month, old. But suppose they were otherwise, what would it avail? The question is not, Can they *reason?* nor Can they *talk?* but, Can they *suffer?*[5]

In this passage Bentham points to the capacity for suffering as the vital characteristic that gives a being the right to equal consideration. The capacity for suffering—or more strictly, for suffering and/or enjoyment or happiness—is not just another characteristic like the capacity for language or higher mathematics. Bentham is not saying that those who try to mark "the insuperable line" that determines whether the interests of a being should be considered happen to have chosen the wrong characteristic. By saying that we must consider the interests of all beings with the capacity for suffering or enjoyment Bentham does not arbitrarily exclude from consideration any interests at all—as those who draw the line with reference to the possession of reason or language do. The capacity for suffering and enjoyment is *a prerequisite for having interests at all,* a condition that must be satisfied before we can speak of interests in a meaningful way. It would be nonsense to say that it was not in the interests of a stone to be kicked along the road by a schoolboy. A stone does not have interests because it cannot suffer. Nothing that we can do to it could possibly make any difference to its welfare. The capacity for suffering and enjoyment is, however, not only necessary, but also sufficient for us to say that a being has interests—at an absolute minimum, an interest in not suffering. A mouse, for example, does have an interest in not being kicked along the road, because it will suffer if it is.

Although Bentham speaks of "rights" in the passage I have quoted, the argument is really about equality rather than about rights. Indeed, in a different passage, Bentham famously described "natural rights" as "nonsense" and "natural and imprescriptable rights" as "nonsense upon stilts." He talked of moral rights as a shorthand way of referring to protections that people and animals morally ought to have; but the real weight of the moral argument does not rest on the assertion of the existence of the right, for this in turn has to be justified on the basis of the possibilities for suffering and happiness. In this way we can argue for equality for animals without getting embroiled in philosophical controversies about the ultimate nature of rights.

In misguided attempts to refute the arguments of this book, some philosophers have gone to much trouble developing arguments to show that animals do not have rights.[6] They have claimed that to have rights a being must be autonomous, or must be a member of a community, or must have the ability to respect the rights of others, or must possess a sense of justice. These claims are irrelevant to the case for Animal Liberation. The language of rights is a convenient political shorthand. It is even more valuable in the era of thirty-second TV news clips than it was in Bentham's day; but in the argument for a radical change in our attitude to animals, it is in no way necessary.

If a being suffers there can be no moral justification for refusing to take that suffering into consideration. No matter what the nature of the being, the principle of equality requires that its suffering be counted equally with the like suffering—insofar as rough comparisons can be made—of any other being. If a being is not capable of suffering, or of experiencing enjoyment or happiness, there is nothing to be taken into account. So the limit of sentience (using the term as a convenient if not strictly accurate shorthand for the capacity to suffer and/or experience enjoyment) is the only defensible boundary of concern for the interests of others. To mark this boundary by some other characteristic like intelligence or rationality would be to mark it in an arbitrary manner. Why not choose some other characteristic, like skin color?

Racists violate the principle of equality by giving greater weight to the interests of members of their own race when there is a clash between their interests and the interests of those of another race. Sexists violate the principle of equality by favoring the interests of their own sex. Similarly, speciesists allow the interests of their own species to override the greater interests of members of other species. The pattern is identical in each case.

Animals and Research

Most human beings are speciesists. . . . Ordinary human beings—not a few exceptionally cruel or heartless humans, but the overwhelming majority of humans—take an active part in, acquiesce in, and allow their taxes to pay for practices that require the sacrifice of the most important interests of members of other species in order to promote the most trivial interests of our own species. . . .

The practice of experimenting on nonhuman animals as it exists today throughout the world reveals the consequences of speciesism. Many experiments inflict severe pain without the remotest prospect of significant benefits for human beings or any other animals. Such experiments are not isolated instances, but part of a major industry. In Britain, where experimenters are required to report the number of "scientific procedures" performed on animals, official government figures show that 3.5 million scientific procedures were performed on animals in 1988.[7] In the United States there are no figures of comparable accuracy. Under the Animal Welfare Act, the U.S. secretary of agriculture publishes a report listing the number of animals used by facilities registered with it, but this is incomplete in many ways. It does not include rats, mice, birds, reptiles, frogs, or domestic farm animals used for experimental purposes; it does not include animals used in secondary schools; and it does not include experiments performed by facilities that do not transport animals interstate or receive grants or contracts from the federal government.

In 1986 the U.S. Congress Office of Technology Assessment (OTA) published a report entitled "Alternatives to Animal Use in Research, Testing and Education." The OTA researchers attempted to determine the number of animals used in experimentation in the U.S. and reported that "estimates of the animals used in the United States each year range from 10 million to upwards of 100 million."

They concluded that the estimates were unreliable but their best guess was "at least 17 million to 22 million."[8]

This is an extremely conservative estimate. In testimony before Congress in 1966, the Laboratory Animal Breeders Association estimated that the number of mice, rats, guinea pigs, hamsters, and rabbits used for experimental purposes in 1965 was around 60 million.[9] In 1984 Dr. Andrew Rowan of Tufts University School of Veterinary Medicine estimated that approximately 71 million animals are used each year. In 1985 Rowan revised his estimates to distinguish between the number of animals produced, acquired, and actually used. This yielded an estimate of between 25 and 35 million animals used in experiments each year.[10] (This figure omits animals who die in shipping or are killed before the experiment begins.) A stock market analysis of just one major supplier of animals to laboratories, the Charles River Breeding Laboratory, stated that this company alone produced 22 million laboratory animals annually.[11]

The 1988 report issued by the Department of Agriculture listed 140,471 dogs, 42,271 cats, 51,641 primates, 431,457 guinea pigs, 331,945 hamsters, 459,254 rabbits, and 178,249 "wild animals": a total of 1,635,288 used in experimentation. Remember that this report does not bother to count rats and mice, and covers at most an estimated 10 percent of the total number of animals used. Of the nearly 1.6 million animals reported by the Department of Agriculture to have been used for experimental purposes, over 90,000 are reported to have experienced "unrelieved pain or distress." Again, this is probably at most 10 percent of the total number of animals suffering unrelieved pain and distress—and if experimenters are less concerned about causing unrelieved pain to rats and mice than they are to dogs, cats, and primates, it could be an even smaller proportion.

Other developed nations all use large numbers of animals. In Japan, for example, a very incomplete survey published in 1988 produced a total in excess of eight million.[12] . . .

Among the tens of millions of experiments performed, only a few can possibly be regarded as contributing to important medical research. Huge numbers of animals are used in university departments such as forestry and psychology; many more are used for commercial purposes, to test new cosmetics, shampoos, food coloring agents, and other inessential items. All this can happen only because of our prejudice against taking seriously the suffering of a being who is not a member of our own species. Typically, defenders of experiments on animals do not deny that animals suffer. They cannot deny the animals' suffering, because they need to stress the similarities between humans and other animals in order to claim that their experiments may have some relevance for human purposes. The experimenter who forces rats to choose between starvation and electric shock to see if they develop ulcers (which they do) does so because the rat has a nervous system very similar to a human being's, and presumably feels an electric shock in a similar way.

There has been opposition to experimenting on animals for a long time. This opposition has made little headway because experimenters, backed by commercial firms that profit by supplying laboratory animals and equipment, have been able to convince legislators and the public that opposition comes from uninformed fanatics who consider the interests of animals more important than the interests of human beings. But to be opposed to what is going on now it is not necessary to insist that all animal experiments stop immediately. All we need to say is that experiments serving no direct and urgent purpose should stop immediately, and in the remaining fields of research, we should whenever possible, seek to replace experiments that involve animals with alternative methods that do not. . . .

When are experiments on animals justifiable? Upon learning of the nature of many of the experiments carried out, some people react by saying that all experiments on animals should be prohibited immediately. But if we make our demands as absolute as this, the experimenters have a ready reply: Would we be prepared to let thousands of humans die if they could be saved by a single experiment on a single animal?

This question is, of course, purely hypothetical. There has never been and never could be a single experiment that saved thousands of lives. The way to reply to this hypothetical question is to pose another: Would the experimenters be prepared to carry out their experiment on a human orphan under six months old if that were the only way to save thousands of lives?

If the experimenters would not be prepared to use a human infant then their readiness to use nonhuman animals reveals an unjustifiable form of discrimination on the basis of species, since adult apes, monkeys, dogs, cats, rats, and other animals are more aware of what is happening to them, more self-directing, and, so far as we can tell, at least as sensitive to pain as a human infant. (I have specified that the human infant be an orphan, to avoid the complications of the feelings of parents. Specifying the case in this way is, if anything, overgenerous to those defending the use of nonhuman animals in experiments, since mammals intended for experimental use are usually separated from their mothers at an early age, when the separation causes distress for both mother and young.)

So far as we know, human infants possess no morally relevant characteristic to a higher degree than adult nonhuman animals, unless we are to count the infants' potential as a characteristic that makes it wrong to experiment on them. Whether this characteristic should count is controversial—if we count it, we shall have to condemn abortion along with experiments on infants, since the potential of the infant and the fetus is the same. To avoid the complexities of this issue, however, we can alter our original question a little and assume that the infant is one with irreversible brain damage so severe as to rule out any mental development beyond the level of a six-month-old infant. There are, unfortunately, many such human beings, locked away in special wards throughout the country, some of them long since abandoned by their parents and other relatives, and, sadly, sometimes unloved by anyone else. Despite their mental deficiencies, the anatomy and physiology of these infants are in nearly all respects identical with those of normal humans. If, therefore, we were to force-feed them with large quantities of floor polish or drip concentrated solutions of cosmetics into their eyes [as has been done in experiments using animals], we would have a much more reliable indication of the safety of these products for humans than we now get by attempting to extrapolate the results of tests on a variety of other species. . . .

So whenever experimenters claim that their experiments are important enough to justify the use of animals, we should ask them whether they would be prepared to use a brain-damaged human being at a similar mental level to the animals they are planning to use. I cannot imagine that anyone would seriously propose carrying out the experiments described in this chapter on brain-damaged human beings. Occasionally it has become known that medical experiments have been performed on human beings without their consent; one case did concern institutionalized intellectually disabled children, who were given hepatitis. When such harmful experiments on human beings become known, they usually lead to an outcry against the experimenters, and rightly so. They are, very often, a further example of the arrogance of the research worker who justifies everything on the grounds of increasing knowledge. But if the experimenter claims that the experiment is important enough to justify inflicting suffering on animals, why is it not important enough to justify inflicting suffering on humans at the same mental level? What difference is there between the two? Only that one is a member of our species and the other is not? But to appeal to that difference is to reveal a bias no more defensible than racism or any other form of arbitrary discrimination. . . .

We have still not answered the question of when an experiment might be justifiable. It will not do to say "Never!" Putting morality in such black-and-white terms is appealing, because it eliminates the need to think about particular cases; but in extreme circumstances, such absolutist answers always break down. Torturing a human being is almost always wrong, but it is not absolutely wrong. If torture were the only way in which we could discover the location of a nuclear bomb hidden in a New York City basement and timed to go off within the hour, then torture would be justifiable. Similarly, if a single experiment could cure a disease like leukemia, that experiment would be justifiable. But in actual life the benefits are always more remote, and more often than not they are nonexistent. So how do

we decide when an experiment is justifiable?

We have seen that experimenters reveal a bias in favor of their own species whenever they carry out experiments on nonhumans for purposes that they would not think justified them in using human beings, even brain-damaged ones. This principle gives us a guide toward an answer to our question. Since a speciesist bias, like a racist bias, is unjustifiable, an experiment cannot be justifiable unless the experiment is so important that the use of a brain-damaged human would also be justifiable.

This is not an absolutist principle. I do not believe that it could never be justifiable to experiment on a brain-damaged human. If it really were possible to save several lives by an experiment that would take just one life, and there were no other way those lives could be saved, it would be right to do the experiment. But this would be an extremely rare case. Admittedly, as with any dividing line, there would be a gray area where it was difficult to decide if an experiment could be justified. But we need not get distracted by such considerations now. . . . We are in the midst of an emergency in which appalling suffering is being inflicted on millions of animals for purposes that on any impartial view are obviously inadequate to justify the suffering. When we have ceased to carry out all those experiments, then there will be time enough to discuss what to do about the remaining ones which are claimed to be essential to save lives or prevent greater suffering. . . .

Notes

1. For Bentham's moral philosophy, see his *Introduction to the Principles of Morals and Legislation*, and for Sidgwick's see *The Methods of Ethics*, 1907 (the passage is quoted from the seventh edition; reprint, London: Macmillan, 1963), p. 382. As examples of leading contemporary moral philosophers who incorporate a requirement of equal consideration of interests, see R. M. Hare, *Freedom and Reason* (New York: Oxford University Press, 1963), and John Rawls, *A Theory of Justice* (Cambridge: Harvard University Press,

Belknap Press, 1972). For a brief account of the essential agreement on this issue between these and other positions, see R. M. Hare, "Rules of War and Moral Reasoning," *Philosophy and Public Affairs* 1 (2) (1972).

2. Letter to Henry Gregoire, February 25, 1809.

3. Reminiscences by Francis D. Gage, from Susan B. Anthony, *The History of Woman Suffrage*, vol. 1; the passage is to be found in the extract in Leslie Tanner, ed., *Voices From Women's Liberation* (New York: Signet, 1970).

4. I owe the term "speciesism" to Richard Ryder. It has become accepted in general use since the first edition of this book, and now appears in *The Oxford English Dictionary*, second edition (Oxford: Clarendon Press, 1989).

5. *Introduction to the Principles of Morals and Legislation*, chapter 17.

6. See M. Levin, "Animal Rights Evaluated," *Humanist* 37:14–15 (July/August 1977); M. A. Fox, "Animal Liberation: A Critique," *Ethics* 88:134–138 (1978); C. Perry and G. E. Jones,

"On Animal Rights," *International Journal of Applied Philosophy* 1:39–57 (1982).

7. *Statistics of Scientific Procedures on Living Animals, Great Britain, 1988*, Command Paper 743 (London: Her Majesty's Stationery Office, 1989).

8. U.S. Congress Office of Technology Assessment, *Alternatives to Animal Use in Research, Testing and Education* (Washington, D.C.: Government Printing Office, 1986), p. 64.

9. Hearings before the Subcommittee on Livestock and Feed Grains of the Committee on Agriculture, U.S. House of Representatives, 1966, p. 63.

10. See A. Rowan, *Of Mice, Models and Men* (Albany: State University of New York Press, 1984), p. 71; his later revision is in a personal communication to the Office of Technology Assessment; see *Alternatives to Animal Use in Research, Testing and Education*, p. 56.

11. OTA, *Alternatives to Animal Use in Research, Testing and Education*, p. 56.

12. *Experimental Animals* 37:105 (1988).

53. The Case for the Use of Animals in Biomedical Research

Carl Cohen

Carl Cohen defends speciesism and the use of animals in experimentation. He asserts that animals have no rights because they lack the capacity for autonomous moral judgments and moral reasoning. Speciesism, Cohen argues, is not like racism or sexism. Moreover, we have an obligation to expand medical research.

Using animals as research subjects in medical investigations is widely condemned on two grounds: first, because it wrongly violates the *rights* of animals,[1] and second, because it wrongly imposes on sentient creatures much avoidable *suffering*.[2] Neither of these arguments is sound. The first relies on a mistaken understanding of rights; the second relies on a mistaken calculation of consequences. Both deserve definitive dismissal.

Why Animals Have No Rights

A right, properly understood, is a claim, or potential claim, that one party may exercise against another. The target against whom

Reprinted with permission from *The New England Journal of Medicine*, vol. 315 (October 2, 1986), pp. 865–870.

such a claim may be registered can be a single person, a group, a community, or (perhaps) all humankind. The content of rights claims also varies greatly: repayment of loans, non-discrimination by employers, noninterference by the state, and so on. To comprehend any genuine right fully, therefore, we must know *who* holds the right, *against whom* it is held, and *to what* it is a right.

Alternative sources of rights add complexity. Some rights are grounded in constitution and law (e.g., the right of an accused to trial by jury); some rights are moral but give no legal claims (e.g., my right to your keeping the promise you gave me); and some rights (e.g., against theft or assault) are rooted both in morals and in law.

The differing targets, contents, and sources of rights, and their inevitable conflict, together weave a tangled web. Notwithstanding all such complications, this much is clear about rights in general: they are in every case claims, or potential claims, within a community of moral agents. Rights arise, and can be intelligibly defended, only among beings who actually do, or can, make moral claims against one another. Whatever else rights may be, therefore, they are necessarily human; their possessors are persons, human beings.

The attributes of human beings from which this moral capability arises have been described variously by philosophers, both ancient and modern: the inner consciousness of a free will (Saint Augustine[3]); the grasp, by human reason, of the binding character of moral law (Saint Thomas[4]); the self-conscious participation of human beings in an objective ethical order (Hegel[5]); human membership in an organic moral community (Bradley[6]); the development of the human self through the consciousness of other moral selves (Mead[7]); and the underivative, intuitive cognition of the rightness of an action (Prichard[8]). Most influential has been Immanuel Kant's emphasis on the universal human possession of a uniquely moral will and the autonomy its use entails.[9] Humans confront choices that are purely moral; humans—but certainly not dogs or mice—lay down moral laws, for others and for themselves. Human beings are self-legislative, morally *auto-nomous.*

Animals (that is, nonhuman animals, the ordinary sense of that word) lack this capacity for free moral judgment. They are not beings of a kind capable of exercising or responding to moral claims. Animals therefore have no rights, and they can have none. This is the core of the argument about the alleged rights of animals. The holders of rights must have the capacity to comprehend rules of duty, governing all including themselves. In applying such rules, the holders of rights must recognize possible conflicts between what is in their own interest and what is just. Only in a community of beings capable of self-restricting moral judgments can the concept of a right be correctly invoked.

Humans have such moral capacities. They are in this sense self-legislative, are members of communities governed by moral rules, and do possess rights. Animals do not have such moral capacities. They are not morally self-legislative, cannot possibly be members of a truly moral community, and therefore cannot possess rights. In conducting research on animal subjects, therefore, we do not violate their rights, because they have none to violate.

To animate life, even in its simplest forms, we give a certain natural reverence. But the possession of rights presupposes a moral status not attained by the vast majority of living things. We must not infer, therefore, that a live being has, simply in being alive, a "right" to its life. The assertion that all animals, only because they are alive and have interests, also possess the "right to life"[10] is an abuse of that phrase, and wholly without warrant.

It does not follow from this, however, that we are morally free to do anything we please to animals. Certainly not. In our dealings with animals, as in our dealings with other human beings, we have obligations that do not arise from claims against us based on rights. Rights entail obligations, but many of the things one ought to do are in no way tied to another's entitlement. Rights and obligations are not reciprocals of one another, and it is a serious mistake to suppose that they are.

Illustrations are helpful. Obligations may arise from internal commitments made: physicians have obligations to their patients not grounded merely in their patients' rights.

Teachers have such obligations to their students, shepherds to their dogs, and cowboys to their horses. Obligations may arise from differences of status: adults owe special care when playing with young children, and children owe special care when playing with young pets. Obligations may arise from special relationships: the payment of my son's college tuition is something to which he may have no right, although it may be my obligation to bear the burden if I reasonably can; my dog has no right to daily exercise and veterinary care, but I do have the obligation to provide these things for her. Obligations may arise from particular acts or circumstances: one may be obliged to another for a special kindness done, or obliged to put an animal out of its misery in view of its condition—although neither the human benefactor nor the dying animal may have had a claim of right.

Plainly, the grounds of our obligations to humans and to animals are manifold and cannot be formulated simply. Some hold that there is a general obligation to do no gratuitous harm to sentient creatures (the principle of nonmaleficence); some hold that there is a general obligation to do good to sentient creatures when that is reasonably within one's power (the principle of beneficence). In our dealings with animals, few will deny that we are at least obliged to act humanely—that is, to treat them with the decency and concern that we owe, as sensitive human beings, to other sentient creatures. To treat animals humanely, however, is not to treat them as humans or as the holders of rights.

A common objection, which deserves a response, may be paraphrased as follows:

If having rights requires being able to make moral claims, to grasp and apply moral laws, then many humans—the brain-damaged, the comatose, the senile—who plainly lack those capacities must be without rights. But that is absurd. This proves [the critic concludes] that rights do not depend on the presence of moral capacities.[1,10]

This objection fails; it mistakenly treats an essential feature of humanity as though it were a screen for sorting humans. The capacity for moral judgment that distinguishes humans from animals is not a test to be administered to human beings one by one. Persons who are unable, because of some disability, to perform the full moral functions natural to human beings are certainly not for that reason ejected from the moral community. The issue is one of kind. Humans are of such a kind that they may be the subject of experiments only with their voluntary consent. The choices they make freely must be respected. Animals are of such a kind that it is impossible for them, in principle, to give or withhold voluntary consent or to make a moral choice. What humans retain when disabled, animals have never had.

A second objection, also often made, may be paraphrased as follows:

Capacities will not succeed in distinguishing humans from the other animals. Animals also reason; animals also communicate with one another; animals also care passionately for their young; animals also exhibit desires and preferences.[11,12] Features of moral relevance—rationality, interdependence, and love—are not exhibited uniquely by human beings. Therefore [this critic concludes], there can be no solid moral distinction between humans and other animals.[10]

This criticism misses the central point. It is not the ability to communicate or to reason, or dependence on one another, or care for the young, or the exhibition of preference, or any such behavior that marks the critical divide. Analogies between human families and those of monkeys, or between human communities and those of wolves, and the like, are entirely beside the point. Patterns of conduct are not at issue. Animals do indeed exhibit remarkable behavior at times. Conditioning, fear, instinct, and intelligence all contribute to species survival. Membership in a community of moral agents nevertheless remains impossible for them. Actors subject to moral judgment must be capable of grasping the generality of an ethical premise in a practical syllogism. Humans act immorally often enough, but only they—never wolves or monkeys—can discern, by applying some moral rule to the facts of a case, that a given act ought or ought not to be performed. The moral restraints imposed by humans on themselves are thus highly abstract and are often in conflict with the self-interest of the agent. Communal behavior among animals, even when most intelligent and most endearing, does not approach autonomous morality in this fundamental sense.

Genuinely moral acts have an internal as well as an external dimension. Thus, in law, an act can be criminal only when the guilty deed, the actus reus, is done with a guilty mind, mens rea. No animal can ever commit a crime; bringing animals to criminal trial is the mark of primitive ignorance. The claims of moral right are similarly inapplicable to them. Does a lion have a right to eat a baby zebra? Does a baby zebra have a right not to be eaten? Such questions, mistakenly invoking the concept of right where it does not belong, do not make good sense. Those who condemn biomedical research because it violates "animal rights" commit the same blunder.

In Defense of "Speciesism"

Abandoning reliance on animal rights, some critics resort instead to animal sentience—their feelings of pain and distress. We ought to desist from the imposition of pain insofar as we can. Since all or nearly all experimentation on animals does impose pain and could be readily forgone, say these critics, it should be stopped. The ends sought may be worthy, but those ends do not justify imposing agonies on humans, and by animals the agonies are felt no less. The laboratory use of animals (these critics conclude) must therefore be ended—or at least very sharply curtailed.

Argument of this variety is essentially utilitarian, often expressly so[13]; it is based on the calculation of the net product, in pains and pleasures, resulting from experiments on animals. Jeremy Bentham, comparing horses and dogs with other sentient creatures, is thus commonly quoted: "The question is not, Can they reason? nor Can they talk? but, Can they suffer?"[14]

Animals certainly can suffer and surely ought not to be made to suffer needlessly. But in inferring, from these uncontroversial premises, that biomedical research causing animal distress is largely (or wholly) wrong, the critic commits two serious errors.

The first error is the assumption, often explicitly defended, that all sentient animals have equal moral standing. Between a dog and a human being, according to this view, there is no moral difference; hence the pains suffered by dogs must be weighed no differently from the pains suffered by humans. To deny such equality, according to this critic, is to give unjust preference to one species over another; it is "speciesism." The most influential statement of this moral equality of species was made by Peter Singer:

> The racist violates the principle of equality by giving greater weight to the interests of members of his own race when there is a clash between their interests and the interests of those of another race. The sexist violates the principle of equality by favoring the interests of his own sex. Similarly the speciesist allows the interests of his own species to override the greater interests of members of other species. The pattern is identical in each case.[2]

This argument is worse than unsound; it is atrocious. It draws an offensive moral conclusion from a deliberately devised verbal parallelism that is utterly specious. Racism has no rational ground whatever. Differing degrees of respect or concern for humans for no other reason than that they are members of different races is an injustice totally without foundation in the nature of the races themselves. Racists, even if acting on the basis of mistaken factual beliefs, do grave moral wrong precisely because there is no morally relevant distinction among the races. The supposition of such differences has led to outright horror. The same is true of the sexes, neither sex being entitled by right to greater respect or concern than the other. No dispute here.

Between species of animate life, however—between (for example) humans on the one hand and cats or rats on the other—the morally relevant differences are enormous, and almost universally appreciated. Humans engage in moral reflection; humans are morally autonomous; humans are members of moral communities, recognizing just claims against their own interest. Human beings do have rights; theirs is a moral status very different from that of cats or rats.

I am a speciesist. Speciesism is not merely plausible; it is essential for right conduct, because those who will not make the morally relevant distinctions among species are almost certain, in consequence, to misapprehend their true obligations. The analogy between speciesism and racism is insidious. Every sensitive moral judgment requires that the differing natures of the beings to whom obligations are owed be considered. If all forms of animate life—or vertebrate animal life?—must be treated equally, and if therefore in evaluating a research program the pains of a rodent count equally with the pains of a human, we are forced to conclude (1) that neither humans nor rodents possess rights, or (2) that rodents possess all the rights that humans possess. Both alternatives are absurd. Yet one or the other must be swallowed if the moral equality of all species is to be defended.

Humans owe to other humans a degree of moral regard that cannot be owed to animals. Some humans take on the obligation to support and heal others, both humans and animals, as a principal duty in their lives; the fulfillment of that duty may require the sacrifice of many animals. If biomedical investigators abandon the effective pursuit of their professional objectives because they are convinced that they may not do to animals what the service of humans requires, they will fail, objectively, to do their duty. Refusing to recognize the moral differences among species is a sure path to calamity. (The largest animal rights group in the country is People for the Ethical Treatment of Animals; its codirector, Ingrid Newkirk, calls research using animal subjects "fascism" and "supremacism." "Animal liberationists do not separate out the *human* animal," she says, "so there is no rational basis for saying that a human being has special rights. A rat is a pig is a dog is a boy. They're all mammals."[15])

Those who claim to base their objection to the use of animals in biomedical research on their reckoning of the net pleasures and pains produced make a second error, equally grave. Even if it were true—as it is surely not—that the pains of all animate beings must be counted equally, a cogent utilitarian calculation requires that we weigh all the consequences of the use, and of the nonuse, of animals in laboratory research. Critics relying (however mistakenly) on animal rights may claim to ignore the beneficial results of such research, rights being trump cards to which interest and advantage must give way. But an argument that is explicitly framed in terms of interest and benefit for all over the long run must attend also to the disadvantageous consequences of not using animals in research, and to all the achievements attained and attainable only through their use. The sum of the benefits of their use is utterly beyond quantification. The elimination of horrible disease, the increase of longevity, the avoidance of great pain, the saving of lives, and the improvement of the quality of lives (for humans and for animals) achieved through research using animals is so incalculably great that the argument of these critics, systematically pursued, establishes not their conclusion but its reverse: to refrain from using animals in biomedical research is, on utilitarian grounds, morally wrong.

When balancing the pleasures and pains resulting from the use of animals in research, we must not fail to place on the scales the terrible pains that would have resulted, would be suffered now, and would long continue had animals not been used. Every disease eliminated, every vaccine developed, every method of pain relief devised, every surgical procedure invented, every prosthetic device implanted—indeed, virtually every modern medical therapy is due, in part or in whole, to experimentation using animals. Nor may we ignore, in the balancing process, the predictable gains in human (and animal) well-being that are probably achievable in the future but that will not be achieved if the decision is made now to desist from such research or to curtail it.

Medical investigators are seldom insensitive to the distress their work may cause animal subjects. Opponents of research using animals are frequently insensitive to the cruelty of the results of the restrictions they would impose.[2] Untold numbers of human beings—real persons, although not now identifiable—would suffer grievously as the consequence of this well-meaning but shortsighted tenderness. If the morally relevant differences between humans and animals are borne in mind, and if all relevant considerations are weighed, the calculation of long-term consequences must give overwhelming support for biomedical research using animals.

Concluding Remarks

Substitution

The humane treatment of animals requires that we desist from experimenting on them if we can accomplish the same result using alternative methods—in vitro experimentation, computer simulation, or others. Critics of some experiments using animals rightly make this point.

It would be a serious error to suppose, however, that alternative techniques could soon be used in most research now using live animal subjects. No other methods now on the horizon—or perhaps ever to be available—can fully replace the testing of a drug, a procedure, or a vaccine, in live organisms. The flood of new medical possibilities being opened by the successes of recombinant DNA technology will turn to a trickle if testing on live animals is forbidden. When initial trials entail great risks, there may be no forward movement whatever without the use of live animal subjects. In seeking knowledge that may prove critical in later clinical applications, the unavailability of animals for inquiry may spell complete stymie. In the United States, federal regulations require the testing of new drugs and other products on animals, for efficacy and safety, before human beings are exposed to them.[16,17] We would not want it otherwise.

Every advance in medicine—every new drug, new operation, new therapy of any kind—must sooner or later be tried on a living being for the first time. That trial, controlled or uncontrolled, will be an experiment. The subject of that experiment, if it is not an animal, will be a human being. Prohibiting the use of live animals in biomedical research, therefore, or sharply restricting it, must result either in the blockage of much valuable research or in the replacement of animal subjects with human subjects. These are the consequences—unacceptable to most reasonable persons—of not using animals in research.

Reduction

Should we not at least reduce the use of animals in biomedical research? No, we should increase it, to avoid when feasible the use of humans as experimental subjects. Medical investigations putting human subjects at some risk are numerous and greatly varied. The risks run in such experiments are usually unavoidable, and (thanks to earlier experiments on animals) most such risks are minimal or moderate. But some experimental risks are substantial.

When an experimental protocol that entails substantial risk to humans comes before an institutional review board, what response is appropriate? The investigation, we may suppose, is promising and deserves support, so long as its human subjects are protected against unnecessary dangers. May not the investigators be fairly asked, Have you done all that you can to eliminate risk to humans by the extensive testing of that drug, that procedure, or that device on animals? To achieve maximal safety for humans we are right to require thorough experimentation on animal subjects before humans are involved.

Opportunities to increase human safety in this way are commonly missed; trials in which risks may be shifted from humans to animals are often not devised, sometimes not even considered. Why? For the investigator, the use of animals as subjects is often more expensive, in money and time, than the use of human subjects. Access to suitable human subjects is often quick and convenient, whereas access to appropriate animal subjects may be awkward, costly, and burdened with red tape. Physician-investigators have often had more experience working with human beings and know precisely where the needed pool of subjects is to be found and how they may be enlisted. Animals, and the procedures for their use, are often less familiar to these investigators. Moreover, the use of animals in place of humans is now more likely to be the target of zealous protests from without. The upshot is that humans are sometimes subjected to risks that animals could have borne, and should have borne, in their place. To maximize the protection of human subjects, I conclude, the wide and imaginative use of live animal subjects should be encouraged rather than discouraged. This enlargement in the use of animals is our obligation.

Consistency

Finally, inconsistency between the profession and the practice of many who oppose research using animals deserves comment. This frankly ad hominem observation aims chiefly to show that a coherent position rejecting the use of animals in medical research imposes costs so high as to be intolerable even to the critics themselves.

One cannot coherently object to the killing of animals in biomedical investigations while continuing to eat them. Anesthetics and thoughtful animal husbandry render the level of actual animal distress in the laboratory generally lower than that in the abattoir. So long as death and discomfort do not substantially differ in the two contexts, the consistent objector must not only refrain from all eating of animals but also protest as vehemently against others eating them as against others experimenting on them. No less vigorously must the critic object to the wearing of animal hides in coats and shoes, to employment in any industrial enterprise that uses animal parts, and to any commercial development that will cause death or distress to animals.

Killing animals to meet human needs for food, clothing, and shelter is judged entirely reasonable by most persons. The ubiquity of these uses and the virtual universality of moral support for them confront the opponent of research using animals with an inescapable difficulty. How can the many common uses of animals be judged morally worthy, while their use in scientific investigation is judged unworthy?

The number of animals used in research is but the tiniest fraction of the total used to satisfy assorted human appetites. That these appetites, often base and satisfiable in other ways, morally justify the far larger consumption of animals, whereas the quest for improved human health and understanding cannot justify the far smaller, is wholly implausible. Aside from the numbers of animals involved, the distinction in terms of worthiness of use, drawn with regard to any single animal, is not defensible. A given sheep is surely not more justifiably used to put lamb chops on the supermarket counter than to serve in testing a new contraceptive or a new prosthetic device. The needless killing of animals is wrong; if the common killing of them for our food or convenience is right, the less common but more humane uses of animals in the service of medical science are certainly not less right.

Scrupulous vegetarianism, in matters of food, clothing, shelter, commerce, and recreation, and in all other spheres, is the only fully coherent position the critic may adopt. At great human cost, the lives of fish and crustaceans must also be protected, with equal vigor, if speciesism has been forsworn. A very few consistent critics adopt this position. It is the reductio ad absurdum of the rejection of moral distinctions between animals and human beings.

Opposition to the use of animals in research is based on arguments of two different kinds—those relying on the alleged rights of animals and those relying on the consequences for animals. I have argued that arguments of both kinds must fail. We surely do have obligations to animals, but they have, and can have, no rights against us on which research can infringe. In calculating the consequences of animal research, we must weigh all the long-term benefits of the results achieved—to animals and to humans—and in that calculation we must not assume the moral equality of all animate species.

Notes

1. Regan T. The case for animal rights. Berkeley, Calif.: University of California Press, 1983.

2. Singer P. Animal liberation. New York: Avon Books, 1977.

3. St. Augustine. Confessions. Book Seven. 397 A.D. New York: Pocketbooks, 1957:104–26.

4. St. Thomas Aquinas. Summa theologica. 1273 A.D. Philosophic texts. New York: Oxford University Press, 1960:353–66.

5. Hegel GWF. Philosophy of right. 1821. London: Oxford University Press, 1952:105–10.

6. Bradley FH. Why should I be moral? 1876. In: Melden AI, ed. Ethical theories. New York: Prentice-Hall, 1950:345–59.

7. Mead GH. The genesis of the self and social control. 1925. In: Reck AJ, ed. Selected writings. Indianapolis: Bobbs-Merrill, 1964:264–93.

8. Prichard HA. Does moral philosophy rest on a mistake? 1912. In: Cellars W, Hospers J, eds.

Readings in ethical theory. New York: Appleton-Century-Crofts, 1952:149–63.

9. Kant I. Fundamental principles of the metaphysics of morals. 1785. New York: Liberal Arts Press, 1949.

10. Rollin BE. Animal rights and human morality. New York: Prometheus Books, 1981.

11. Hoff C. Immoral and moral uses of animals. N Engl J Med 1980; 302:115–8.

12. Jamieson D. Killing persons and other beings. In: Miller HB, Williams WH, eds. Ethics and animals. Clifton, N.J.: Humana Press, 1983:135–46.

13. Singer P. Ten years of animal liberation. New York Review of Books. 1985; 31:46–52.

14. Bentham J. Introduction to the principles of morals and legislation. London: Athlone Press, 1970.

15. McCabe K. Who will live, who will die? Washingtonian Magazine. August 1986:115.

16. U.S. Code of Federal Regulations, Title 21, Sect. 505(i). Food, drug, and cosmetic regulations.

17. U.S. Code of Federal Regulations, Title 16, Sect. 1500.40-2. Consumer product regulations.

54.   Immoral and Moral Uses of Animals

Christina Hoff

With respect to the use of animals in experimentation, Christina Hoff takes an intermediate position. She does not feel that animals have rights. And, although they are capable of suffering, there are significant moral differences between human and nonhuman animals. She concludes that painful experiments may be acceptable if they substantially help human and other nonhuman animals.

One can do something wrong to a tree, but it makes no sense to speak of wronging it. Can one wrong an animal? Many philosophers think not, and many research scientists adopt

From *The New England Journal of Medicine*, Vol. 302, No. 2, pp. 115–118, January 10, 1980. Reprinted with permission of the publisher.

the attitude that the use of laboratory animals raises no serious moral questions. It is understandable that they should do so. Moral neutrality toward the objects of one's research is conducive to scientific practice. Scientists naturally wish to concentrate on their research and thus tend not to confront the problems that may arise in the choice of techniques. In support of this attitude of indifference, they could cite philosophers who point to features peculiar to human life, by virtue of which painful experimentation on unwilling human beings is rightly to be judged morally reprehensible and that on animals not. What are these features?

Rationality and the ability to communicate meaningfully with others are the most commonly mentioned differentiating characteristics. Philosophers as diverse as Aristotle, Aquinas, Descartes, and Kant point to man's deliberative capacities as the source of his moral preeminence. Animals, because they are irrational, have been denied standing. The trouble is that not all human beings are rational. Mentally retarded or severely brain-damaged human beings are sometimes much less intelligent than lower primates that have been successfully taught to employ primitive languages and make simple, logical inferences beyond the capacity of the normal three-year-old child. The view that rationality is the qualifying condition for moral status has the awkward consequence of leaving unexplained our perceived obligations to nonrational humanity.

Some philosophers have therefore argued that man's privileged moral status is owed to his capacity for suffering. To be plausible, this way of explaining man's position as the only being who can be wronged must discount the apparent suffering of mammals and other highly organized creatures. It is sometimes assumed that the subjective experience of pain is quite different for animals and human beings. Descartes, for example, maintains that animals are machines: he speaks of tropisms of avoidance and desire rather than pleasure and pain.[1] Although it is true that human beings can suffer in ways that animals cannot, the idea that animals and human beings experience physical pain differently is physiologically incoherent. We know that animals feel pain because of their behavioral reactions (including writhing, screaming, facial contortions, and desperate efforts to escape the source of pain), the evidence of their nervous systems, and the evolutionary value of pain. (By "animals" I mean mammals, birds, and other organisms of comparable evolutionary complexity.)

There are other sources of human suffering besides pain, but they too are not peculiarly human. One has only to consult the reports of naturalists or go to the zoo or own a pet to learn that the higher animals, at least, can suffer from loneliness, jealousy, boredom, frustration, rage, and terror. If, indeed, the capacity to suffer is the morally relevant characteristic, then the facts determine that animals, along with all human beings, are the proper subjects of moral consideration.

There is, however, another common way of defending human privilege. It is sometimes asserted that "just being human" is a sufficient basis for a protected moral status, that sheer membership in the species confers exclusive moral rights. Each human life, no matter how impoverished, has a depth and meaning that transcends that of even the most gifted dolphin or chimpanzee. One may speak of this as the humanistic principle. Cicero was one of its earliest exponents: "Honor every human being because he is a human being."[2] Kant called it the Principle of Personality and placed it at the foundation of his moral theory.[3] The principle appears evident to us because it is embodied in the attitudes and institutions of most civilized communities. Although this accounts for its intuitive appeal, it is hardly an adequate reason to accept it. Without further argument the humanistic principle is arbitrary. What must be adduced is an acceptable criterion for awarding special rights. But when we proffer a criterion based, say, on the capacity to reason or to suffer, it is clearly inadequate either because it is satisfied by some but not all members of the species Homo sapiens, or because it is satisfied by them all—and many other animals as well.

Another type of argument for denying equal consideration to animals goes back at least to Aristotle. I refer to the view that man's tyranny over animals is natural because his superiority as an animal determines for him the dominant position in the natural scale of things. To suggest that man give up his dominance over animals is to suggest that he deny his nature. The argument assumes that "denial of nature" is ethically incoherent. But conformity with nature is not an adequate condition for ethical standards. Being moral does not appear to be a question of abiding by the so-called laws of nature; just as often it seems to require us to disregard what is "natural" in favor of what is compassionate. We avoid slavery and child labor, not because we have discovered that they are unnatural, but because we have discovered that slaves and children have their own desires and interests and they engage our sympathy. Social Darwinism was an ethical theory that sought to deduce moral rules from the "facts" of nature. Wealthy 19th-century industrialists welcomed a theory that seemed to justify inhumane labor practices by reference to the "natural order of things." It has become clear that these so-called "laws" of nature cannot provide an adequate basis for a moral theory, if only because they may be cited to support almost any conceivable theory.

It is fair to say that no one has yet given good reasons to accept a moral perspective that grants a privileged moral status to all and only human beings. A crucial moral judgment is made when one decides that a given course of action with respect to a certain class of beings does not fall within the range of moral consideration. Historically, mistakes at this level have proved dangerous: they leave the agent free to perpetrate heinous acts that are not regarded as either moral or immoral and are therefore unchecked by normal inhibition. The exclusion of animals from the moral domain may well be a similar and equally benighted error. It is, in any case, arbitrary and unfounded in good moral argument.

Whatever belongs to the moral domain can be wronged. But if one rejects the doctrine that membership in the moral domain necessarily coincides with membership in the human species, then one must state a satisfactory condition for moral recognition. Bentham offers an intuitively acceptable starting point. "The question is not, Can they *reason?*, nor, Can they *talk?* but Can they *suffer?*"[4] The capacity to suffer confers a minimal prima facie moral status on any creature, for it seems reasonable that one who is wantonly cruel to a sentient creature wrongs that creature. Animals too can be wronged; the practical consequences of such a moral position are, however, not as clear as they may seem. We must consider what we may and may not do to them.

I begin with a word about the comparative worthiness of human and animal life. Although animals are entitled to moral consideration, it does not follow that animals and human beings are always equal before the moral law. Distinctions must still be made. One may acknowledge that animals have rights without committing oneself to a radical egalitarianism that awards to animals complete parity with human beings. If hunting animals for sport is wrong, hunting human beings for the same purpose is worse, and such a distinction is not inconsistent with recognizing that animals have moral status. Although some proponents of animal rights would deny it, there are morally critical differences between animals and human beings. Animals share with human beings a common interest in avoiding pain, but the complexities of normal human life clearly provide a relevant basis for assigning to human beings a far more serious right to life itself. When we kill a human being, we take away his physical existence (eating, sleeping, and feeling pleasure and pain), but we deprive him of other things as well. His projects, his friendships, and his sense of himself as a human being are also terminated. To kill a human being is not only to take away his life, but to impugn the special meaning of his life. In contrast, an animal's needs and desires are restricted to his place in time and space. He lives "the life of the moment." Human lives develop and unfold; they have a direction. Animal lives do not. Accordingly, I suggest the following differential principle of life worthiness: Human lives are generally worthier than animal lives, and the right to life of a human being generally supersedes the right to life of an animal.

This differential principle rejects the Cartesian thesis, which totally dismisses animals from moral consideration, and it is consistent with two other principles that I have been tacitly defending: animals are moral subjects with claims to considerations that should not be ignored; and an animal's experience of pain is similar to a human being's experience of pain.

In the light of these principles I shall try to determine what general policies we ought to adopt in regulating the use of animals in experimental science. I am limiting myself to the moral questions arising in the specific area of painful or fatal animal experimentation, but some of the discussion will apply to other areas of human interaction with animals. Space does not allow discussion of killing animals for educational purposes.

Scientists who perform experiments on animals rarely see the need to justify them, but when they do they almost always stress the seriousness of the research. Although it may be regrettable that animals are harmed, their suffering is seen as an unavoidable casualty of scientific progress. The moral philosopher must still ask: is the price in animal misery worth it?

That the ends do not always justify the means is a truism, and when the means involve the painful treatment of unwilling innocents, serious questions arise. Although it is notoriously difficult to formulate the conditions that justify the consequences, it is plausible that desired ends are not likely to justify onerous means in the following situations: when those who suffer the means are not identical with those who are expected to enjoy the ends; when there is grave doubt that the justifying ends will be brought about by the onerous means; and when the ends can be achieved by less onerous means.

When a competent surgeon causes pain he does not run afoul of these conditions. On the other hand, social policies that entail mass misery on the basis of tenuous sociopolitical assumptions of great future benefits do run afoul of the last two conditions and often of the first as well. The use of laboratory animals often fails to satisfy these conditions of consequential justification; the first is ignored most frequently (I shall argue that this can often be justified), but scientists often violate the others as well when they carry out painful or fatal experiments with animals that are poorly designed or could have been just as well executed without intact living animals.

We can be somewhat more specific in formulating guidelines for animal experimentation if we consider the equality of animals and human beings with respect to pain. Because there are no sound biologic reasons for the idea that human pain is intrinsically more intense than animal pain, animals and men may be said to be equals with respect to pain. Equality in this case is a measure of their shared interest in avoiding harm and discomfort. The evil of pain, unlike the value of life, is unaffected by the identity of the individual sufferer.

Animals and human beings, however, do differ in their experience of the aftereffects of pain. When an injury leaves the subject cosmetically disfigured, for example, a human being may suffer from a continuing sense of shame and bitterness, but for the animal the trauma is confined to the momentary pain. Even the permanent impairment of faculties has more serious and lasting aftereffects on human beings than on animals. It can be argued that a person who is stricken by blindness suffers his loss more keenly than an animal similarly stricken.

More important than the subjective experience of privation is the objective diminishment of a valuable being whose scope of activity and future experience have been severely curtailed. In terms of physical privation animals and human beings do not differ, but the measure of loss must be counted far greater in human beings. To sum up: human beings and animals have a parity with respect to the trauma of a painful episode but not with respect to the consequences of the trauma. Yet when an experiment involves permanent impairment or death for the subject and thus considerations of differential life worthiness make it wrong to use most human beings, the pain imposed on the animals should still be counted as intrinsically bad, as if human beings had been made to suffer it, regardless of the aftereffects.

Although I believe that the general inferiority of animal lives to human life is relevant to the formation of public policy, I cannot accept the view that their relative inferiority licenses harming animals except for very serious purposes in rather special circumstances. However, the special circumstances are not necessarily extraordinary. Many experiments, although not as many as is generally supposed, are medically important and needed. The researcher who is working to control cancer and other fatal and crippling diseases may be able to satisfy the conditions that justify the use of laboratory animals. Because I believe that normal human lives are of far greater worth than animal lives, I accept a policy in which those who suffer the means are not those who may enjoy the ends, which violates the first of the conditions of consequential justification mentioned above, by permitting the infliction of pain on animals to save human lives or to contribute substantially to their welfare. However, when researchers intend to harm an animal, they need more than a quick appeal to the worthiness of human life. They ought to be able to show that the resulting benefits are outstandingly compensatory; if the scientist cannot make a good case for the experiment, it should be proscribed. (On the other hand, if suffering is the main consideration in judging the admissibility of experiments with animals, then nonpainful experiments, even fatal ones, may be under fewer constraints than painful, nonfatal experiments. Although this idea may seem paradoxical, it is in accord with the common moral intuition that condones those who put a kitten "to sleep" while condemning those who torment one.) The implementation of this policy raises questions that cannot be dealt with here. Yet one might expect that research proposals involving painful animal experimentation should be reviewed by a panel of experts, perhaps composed of two scientists in the field of the experiment and a scientifically knowledgeable philosopher versed in medical ethics.

In closing, I wish to indicate how I would deal with a possible objection. It may appear that my criteria of life worthiness place human idiots on a par with animals. On what grounds could I prohibit the painful or fatal experimental use of human subjects whose capacity does not differ from that of many animals? I would be prepared to rethink or even abandon a position that could not distinguish between animal and human experimentation. Fortunately, this distinction can be made.

I oppose painful or fatal experimentation on defective, nonconsenting human beings not because I believe that any person, just because he is human, has a privileged moral status, but because I do not believe that we can safely permit anyone to decide which human beings fall short of worthiness. Judgments of this kind and the creation of institutions for making them are fraught with danger and

open to grave abuse. It is never necessary to show that an animal's life is not as valuable as that of a normal human being, but just such an initial judgment of exclusion would have to be made for idiots. Because there is no way to circumvent this problem, experiments on human beings are precluded and practically wrong. There are other arguments against experimenting on mentally feeble human beings, but this one seems to me to be the strongest and to be sufficient to support the view that whereas animal experimentation is justifiable, no dangerous or harmful experiments involving unwilling human subjects could be.

Accordingly, I have reached the following conclusions concerning the painful exploitation of animals for human rewards. Animals should not be used in painful experiments when substantial benefits are not expected to result. Even when the objective is important, there is a presumption against the use of animals in painful and dangerous experiments that are expected to yield tenuous results of doubtful value. Animals but not human beings may be used in painful and dangerous experiments that are to yield vital benefits for human beings (or other animals).

Vast numbers of animals are currently being used in all kinds of scientific experiments, many of which entail animal misery. Some of these studies, unfortunately, do not contribute to medical science, and some do not even require the use of intact animals. Even the most conservative corrective measures in the implementation of a reasonable and morally responsible policy would have dramatic practical consequences.

Notes

1. Descartes, R. Letter to the Marquess of Newcastle. In: Kenny A., ed. *Philosophical letters.* Oxford: Oxford University Press, 1970.

2. Cicero. *De Finibus.*

3. Kant, I. In: Paton H. J., ed. *Groundwork for a metaphysic of morals.*

4. Bentham, J. *The principles of morals and legislation.* New York: Hafner Publishing, 1948:311n.

Case 11.a Acid Rain and the Uses of Coal

Nancy Blanpied and Tom L. Beauchamp

In this case study, the frightening results of acid rain are described. This case raises questions about our obligations to the environment, to nonhuman animals, and, of course, to other people.

Acid rain is created by burning coal and other fossil fuels. It has been cited in numerous scientific studies as the leading cause of lake acidification and fish kills in the northeastern United States and southeastern Canada. It may also adversely affect forest ecosystems, farmlands, and groundwater. Environmental activists have targeted the coal industry and its power-generating and industrial consumers as primary causes of acid rain.

Scientists do not fully understand the chemical process creating acid rain and its environmental impact. However, experts believe that gaseous sulfur dioxide is released into the air when coal with a high sulfur content is burned (primarily in utility power plants and some industrial plants). The sulfur dioxide and nitrogen oxides from transportation vehicles and unregulated oil burner emissions combine with water vapor to produce sulfuric and nitric acids. Carried by prevailing winds perhaps far from the emission source, these acids infiltrate precipitation and lower the pH levels. Pure rain is naturally somewhat acidic, with a pH level of 5.6. The degree of acidity increases exponentially as the pH level decreases. Rainfall with pH levels of 3 or 4 is common in the eastern United States and Canada, and thus is anywhere from ten to over a hundred times more acidic than a normal 5.6. Levels as low as 1.5, roughly the acidity of battery acid, have been reported in Wheeling, West Virginia.[1]

This article was revised by Sarah Westrick, Cathleen Kaveny, Joanne L. Jurmu, and John Cuddihy. Copyright © 1992 by Tom L. Beauchamp. From Tom L. Beauchamp, ed., *Case Studies in Business, Society, and Ethics*, 3rd ed. (Englewood Cliffs, NJ: Prentice-Hall, 1992). Reprinted by permission.

Ecological systems have natural alkaline properties that can neutralize moderately acidic rain, but continued precipitation of low pH levels endangers the environment. Large fish kills often occur in the early spring because, as environmentalist Anne LaBastille has graphically depicted:

All winter, the pollutant load from storms accumulates in the snowpack as if in a great white sponge. When mild weather gives the sponge a "squeeze," acids concentrated on the surface of the snow are released with the first melt. . . . This acid shock . . . produces drastic changes in water chemistry that destroy fish life.[2]

Those highly acidified areas in the northeastern United States and southeastern Canada are naturally low in alkaline buffers, which neutralize the acids. As an acidification by-product, toxic metals such as aluminum are leached from the earth's surface. The aluminum proves lethal to fish and other life forms, and fish that survive may become poisonous to predators who eat them, including, in some cases, humans.[3]

In the Adirondack region, which receives some acid rain, residents have noticed a steady decrease in the number of fish and other forms of wildlife. A forest ranger and lifelong area resident has noted that

the snowshoe rabbit is down, the fox is way down, deer are down, way down, the bobcat is down, the raccoon is down. Even the porcupine is disappearing. . . . Frogs and crayfish are way down. The loon has disappeared. . . . You don't see fish jump anymore. There are no fish to jump, and even if there were, there'd be no insects to make them jump.[4]

Some lakes have also become crystal clear and devoid of life.

Another example of the concern over acid rain is found in Scandinavia, where regional scientists have studied the effects of acid precipitation in response to alarming changes in their rivers and lakes. Folke Andersson, coordinator of the Swedish acid rain research on soils, forests, and waters found that "75 percent of nitrogen needed by forests comes from the work of soil organisms. Laboratory studies show that increased acidity kills these microorganisms. Over the long term we ought to see a decrease in forest productivity due to the decrease in organisms releasing nitrogen to the soil. We can't see this yet."[5] Swedish researchers have found that soils retain liquid pollution. Even if all sulfur emissions stopped today, the sulfur would not stop flowing from the soil for decades. It has been estimated that 80 percent of acid rain's sulfur is retained in the soil and slowly bleeds out.[6] This effect is compounded by the fact that normal fertilizer use contributes to soil acidity.[7]

In the United States, many of those who wish to prevent acid rain and its possibly devastating consequences focus their attention on the midwestern coal mines. Coal mining is a major industry in southern Ohio and the West Virginia panhandle, employing 15,000 miners. Ohio coal, which has a particularly high sulfur content, is used throughout the region and is thought by environmentalists to be one of the primary sources of the acid rain falling in the United States and Canada. However, existing environmental regulations (see below) controlling the use of high-sulfur coal have already decimated the region's economy. The state of Michigan has slashed orders for Ohio coal, and some area power plants have switched to a low-sulfur coal. Miners fear for their jobs, and unemployment in these regions is increasing.

However, the National Coal Association reports that because of greater use of low-sulfur coal and scrubbers in power plants, there is little more sulfur dioxide in the air than there was in the late 1940s. The Environmental Protection Agency (EPA) found a 28 percent decrease in sulfate levels from 1973, when the Clean Air Act was passed, to 1983. From 1980 to 1985 sulfur dioxide emissions decreased by 2.7 percent, while coal usage increased by 23 percent. Furthermore, ambient levels of sulfur dioxide dropped by 36 percent from 1975 to 1984.[8] As of 1986, 98 percent of all U.S. counties had complied with the national standard for sulfur dioxide and nitrogen oxide.[9] Because of the many unknowns about acid rain, the *Wall Street Journal* cautioned as follows in mid-1980:

At least five more years of study is required to identify correctly the causes and effects of acidic rainfall. Precipitous regulatory action by EPA could cost utilities and other industries billions of dollars. Until more is genuinely known about acid rain, these expenditures may end up only going down the drain.[10]

Despite such warnings, EPA proceeded with regulatory efforts (by targeting coal- and oil-fired power plants) until the Reagan administration ordered the *Wall Street Journal's* advice to become official policy. However, a 1981 National Research Council report thwarted this strategy. It reported that nitrogen oxide levels have tripled in the last 25 years, and the panel placed the burden of responsibility for environmental deterioration on coal-burning industries. The "circumstantial evidence" of a causal connection between coal-burning and environmental damage, it argued, is overwhelming. It recommended stringent control measures.[11]

Scrubbers, which remove sulfur dioxide from coal, are generally regarded as the most effective control technology, although decreased reliance on fossil fuel may be the most promising policy. To install scrubbers is costly, but it has proven effective. A cheaper though less efficient alternative is to wash coal prior to combustion. Many small industrial Ohio coal users have found it difficult to survive in today's regulatory environment.

It is also difficult to determine with precision who is responsible for the deteriorating situation. Tracking the atmosphere routes of acid rain from sources to destinations is a complex problem that some believe must be solved if emissions are to be controlled effectively. Sulfur dioxide over the Adirondacks may vary only 10 percent through a given period while rainfall acid concentration may change 100 percent.[12] A DOE report has cast doubt altogether on the major role of acid rain that once was assigned to imported coal-produced pollutants, focusing instead on local automobile and oil-burner emissions as the source.[13] (This report was filed approximately nine months before the National Research Council panel report mentioned earlier. The studies ran concurrently.)

The issue of acid precipitation across the U.S.–Canadian border has received extensive attention. In March 1985 the U.S. and Canada appointed special envoys to study the issue and make recommendations for its resolution. One major recommendation in their January 1986 report was a 5-year, $5-billion program to develop innovative technology for new and existing discharge sources. (This is not to imply that the United States has not been actively funding acid rain research. Between 1982 and 1989 the National Acid Precipitation Assessment Program appropriated over $500 million for such research.[14])

Coal industry representatives generally contend that there are too few definite answers to warrant further emission regulations, and should they be instituted too quickly, needless expenditures would result. The Electric Power Research Institute has developed an extensive international research plan to examine acid rain's causes and effects. The Tennessee Valley Authority, the U.S. Geological Survey, and the other government agencies mentioned above are also pursuing further research.[15] Industry spokespersons believe that further research is all that can and should be done until we better understand the acid rain phenomenon. For example, Al Courtney, the designated spokesperson for the nation's investor-owned electric utilities, offers the following as that industry's preferred policy:

A careful examination of the available facts leads to four conclusions: first, the only adverse effect which has been documented is the acidification of certain local water bodies; second, the causes of the acidification are not clear; third, the contribution of power plant emissions to this problem is not known, and as a result, it is not known whether emission reductions would retard or reverse this acidification; and further, requiring substantial additional emission reductions by the electric utility industry would impose great economic burdens on the financially troubled nation and on the already weak economy without assurance of commensurate benefits to the public. . . . It is clear that many of the critical chemical, meteorological, ecological, and economic questions related to acid rain remain unanswered. . . . Pending the completion of the research program established by the Acid Precipitation Act of 1980, claims regarding irreversible ecological impact should be investigated, and mitigating measures, such as liming, should be instituted where appropriate. . . . In enacting the Acid Precipitation Act of 1980, Congress recognized this essential prerequisite and in response, instituted a program designated to explore the acid deposition phenomenon in a deliberate, methodical manner. We should permit this rational, problem-solving approach to produce the information which we so badly need.[16]

The acid rain receivers, on the other hand, have asked for international cooperation and quick responses to what they consider to be a worsening environmental situation. In 1984 and again in 1986, Representative Henry Waxman (D–CA) introduced legislation to respond to the acid rain problem. His 1986 bill (HR 4567) involved a two-phase plan to decrease sulfur dioxide and nitrogen oxide emissions by 1997. It allowed the states to develop new methods for reduction. In addition, HR 4567 levied a nationwide fee on electricity to create a trust fund. The fund would be used to limit consumer utility fee increases to 10 percent or less. Many observers agree that the legislation would cause Midwest consumers to pay increases of over 10 percent unless the fund existed. Costs to utilities for decreased sulfur and nitrogen emissions would have been in the range of $4.3 to $5.6 billion annually.[17] The bill did not survive.

Cost estimates vary, but whatever the method of calculation, the cost of effectively controlling sulfur dioxide emissions has long been agreed to be substantial. According to Sheldon Meyers of the EPA, to install one scrubber on an existing 300 megawatt utility boiler would cost between $60 and $90 million in 1985 dollars.[18] Because the scrubber creates a sludge, scientists need to develop new sludge disposal methods. Also, levels of reduction vary in costs:

There are annual dollar values usually assigned to the phased reductions: $2 billion would buy a reduction of four million tons annually in the thirty-one states east of the Mississippi; $4 billion would buy a reduction of eight million tons per year; and $8 to $10 billion would buy reductions of 12 million tons per year below the 1980 level.[19]

Even the basic facts about acid rain remain disputed, and the legislative and regulatory situation is uncertain. A report by Milton J. Socolar, Acting Comptroller General of the United States on the debate over acid precipitation summed up the situation as of 1981 as follows.[20]

Summing up the evidence on the acid precipitation debate, even the most conciliatory representatives of the opposite sides arrive at different conclusions.

Those most concerned with the additional costs and problems expected for further emissions controls argue for the point that there is no firm proof that reductions of emissions would result in lessening acid deposition. Therefore, they conclude, it is inappropriate to take any additional control actions at this time, because the controls would be certain to involve costs but would stand the risk of producing no benefits.

On the other side, those most concerned with the present and anticipated damage due to acid precipitation start from the point that the oxide precursors of deposited acids, particularly SO_2, come predominantly from man-made emissions. From this they conclude that reducing oxide emissions upwind from threatened areas is most likely to prevent or reduce damage, so they urge that at least moderate steps in the direction should be started promptly. They view as inequitable the present situation, in which they see all costs and risks being borne by the regions suffering damage, contending that the emitting regions should also take some share of risks and costs.

A decade after this statement, in November 1990, President George Bush signed amendments to the Clean Air Act into law. Among the amendments' major provisions are a nationwide utility emissions cap on sulfur dioxide emissions of 8.9 million tons a year by the year 2000. After 2000, emissions must be kept at this level. The Bush administration argued that this cap represents a 10-million-ton reduction from the levels of a decade ago. The largest sulfur dioxide cuts for the first five years are scheduled to come from the dirtiest plants, roughly 100 plants located mainly in Appalachia and the Midwest. Cleaner plants will be required to cut emissions only after the five-year period, but before 2001.

Title IV of these amendments details acid rain controls. A major part of the projected reduction in sulfur dioxide is to come by substituting low-sulfur coals for the now popular high-sulfur coal. Industry watchers call the acid rain provisions "a boon for low-sulfur coal producers, since a large part of this reduction will be obtained through substituting low-sulfur coals for the higher-sulfur fuels now used" and also a boon for rail carriers, which now must truck the coal farther and in larger quantities.[21]

By contrast, the costs for public utilities will be substantially higher. They already operate in a regulatory environment that has placed many utilities at increased risk by reducing or disallowing rate increases, sometimes reducing or eliminating common-stock dividends. Some coal-burning utilities already operate on the margin of profitability, and the new amendments increase their risk. Many utilities have already begun to look into nontraditional forms of financing.

The amendments also establish a pollution credits system that provides an incentive to plants to restrict sulfur dioxide emissions beyond federally required levels. The legislation provides credits for cleaner plants, to allow them greater production flexibility beyond the mandated cap, and calls for annual reductions of nitrogen oxides, which contribute to acid rain, through 1996.

The Clean Air Act and some joint ventures between the U.S. and Canada have strengthened the anti-pollution activity in North America. Environmentalists have been quick to praise these initiatives. However, the new legislation is inadequate from the perspective of many environmentalists, in part because of the go-slow provisions of the legislation. There also are no specific provisions to regulate the emissions of midwestern utilities' tall stacks, which disperse emissions that are generally believed to be primary causes of the damage to the ecology of the northeastern U.S. and southeastern Canada.

Environmentalists have long viewed acid rain as a dire emergency. Yet the 1990 amendments are not likely to produce ecological improvements for at least a decade. Environmentalists believe that in the long struggle between environmental protection and increased costs, fear of costs has once again dominated ecological interests. Opponents of the new legislation take a diametrically opposed view. Senator Steve Symms (R–Idaho), for example, maintained that the bill was "so costly that it probably will do more damage to the economy than the good it may do for the air."[22] (Costs of compliance with the new amendments are projected to be $4 billion to $6 billion per year.)

The continuing effects of acid rain and the economic and environmental impact of the new legislation are still today being debated in much the same terms they were debated ten years ago. Moreover, government studies of costs and projected damage often reach sharply conflicting conclusions. For example, at the present writing it is not clear whether the acidity in streams and lakes has been increasing or decreasing since the Clean Air Act of 1973. The American public also seems confused and

ambivalent. Although public opinion polls have consistently shown that Americans say they are willing to pay higher rates for cleaner air, the polls also indicate that Americans favor the reduction or denial of proposed rate increases for public utilities.[23]

Notes

1. Lois R. Ember, "Acid Pollutants: Hitchhikers Ride the Wind," *Chemical and Engineering News* (September 14, 1981), p. 29.

2. Anne LaBastille, "Acid Rain: How Great a Menace?" *National Geographic* 160 (November 1981), p. 672.

3. Robert H. Boyle, "An American Tragedy," *Sports Illustrated* (September 21, 1981), p. 75.

4. *Ibid.,* p. 74.

5. Ember, "Acid Pollutants," p. 24.

6. Fred Pierce, "Unravelling a Century of Acid Pollution," *New Scientist* 111 (September 25, 1986), p. 24.

7. "Acid Rain Briefing Reviews Recent Research," *Journal of the Air Pollution Control Association* 33 (August 1983), p. 782.

8. Carl E. Bagge, "A Tale of UFO's and Other Random Anxieties," *Vital Speeches of the Day* 52 (September 1, 1986), p. 702.

9. Richard E. Benedick, "U.S. Policy on Acid Rain," *Department of State Bulletin* 86 (September 1986), p. 56.

10. "Review and Outlook: Acid Rain," *Wall Street Journal,* June 20, 1980.

11. Committee on the Atmosphere and the Biosphere, *Atmosphere-Biosphere Interactions* (Washington, D.C.: National Academy Press, 1981).

12. "Review and Outlook," *Wall Street Journal.*

13. Michael Woods, "Theory Blamed Midwest Utilities: Study Disputes Cause of Acid Rain," *Toledo Blade,* January 28, 1981.

14. Alan Skrainka and Daniel Burkhardt, "Acid Rain: What's an Investor to Do?" *Public Utilities Fortnightly,* August 31, 1989, p. 33.

15. "Acid Rain," *Energy Researcher,* Electric Power Research Institute (June 1981).

16. Edison Electric Institute Information Service, Release of October 21, 1981, pp. 1–2.

17. "Waxman Unveils Acid Rain Bill: Support Is Strong," *Wall Street Journal*, April 11, 1986, p. 2.

18. Sheldon Meyers, "Acid Deposition: A Search for Solutions," in Diane Suitt Gilland and James H. Swisher, eds., *Acid Rain Control: The Cost of Compliance* (Carbondale: Southern Illinois University Press, 1985), p. 7.

19. *Ibid.*, p. 8.

20. *The Debate over Acid Precipitation: Opposing Views; Status of Research,* Report by the Comptroller General of the United States (Wash-

ington, D.C.: General Accounting Office, September 11, 1981), pp. 7–8.

21. Richard G. Sharp, "The Clean Air Act Amendments: Impacts on Rail Coal Transportation," *Public Utilities Fortnightly*, March 1, 1991, p. 26.

22. "Congress, Breaking 10-Year Deadlock, Passes Landmark Clean Air Measure," *Washington Post*, October 28, 1990, p. A16.

23. See Alan Skrainka and Daniel A. Burkhardt, "Acid Rain: What's an Investor to Do?" *Public Utilities Fortnightly*, August 31, 1989, pp. 33–34.

Case 11.b   Native American Grave Sites at Risk

Brenda K. Marshall

Archeology, research, resource exploration, and, in this case, even the need for fill dirt for a landfill often jeopardize Native American grave sites. Issues related to land ownership and the effects on the culture and customs of Native Americans, as well as a simple respect for the dead, have to be addressed.

One by one they kneel in the cool autumn dark of the Tennessee night and crawl through the small opening into a deeper dark. "All my relations," each says in passage, in English, in Cherokee, in Apache.

Inside the sweat lodge, a voice begins: "We are here to pray. When we pray to the Great Father, we pray for all our relations, for all our brothers and sisters, for all those who lived before us, for the land and the trees, for the animals, for Mother Earth. We are all related."

"Do not pray for yourself," comes the admonition. "Someone else will do that for you. And remember why we are here."

The "here" is Bells Bend, just outside Nashville. The "why" is the threatened desecration of what Native Americans consider to be sacred burial ground. At issue is an 808-acre site intended to provide fill dirt for a proposed sanitary landfill across the road.

From *The Progressive*, January 1991, p. 14. Reprinted by permission.

Members of the Alliance for Native American Indian Rights, a Nashville-based nonprofit lobbying group formed in October 1989 to fight grave desecration and seek reburial of Native American remains, pointed to archaeological reports showing there are hundreds of known ancient Indian grave sites on that parcel of land, and possibly thousands more. Metropolitan Nashville and Spicewood Services, the developer involved in the project, assured Alliance members that any digging would be done "sensitively."

"The 808 acres the Native Americans are concerned about is to be used only for borrow material," says Rick Runyeon, press secretary to the mayor. "Yes, there are known burial sites on the entire 808 acres, so we selected a 124-acre piece [within the larger site] with no known burial sites. On this piece there are three archaeological sites, remains of Indian habitats, and one of the three may have potential for human burial. We want to survey the entire area, and then do about twenty drill core samples. If we find graves we'll fence them off."

But that's Catch-22, points out Archie Mouse, a Cherokee who is president of the Alliance. "In essence," he says, "they're going down with the intent to find grave sites. In order to do that they have to desecrate the graves."

Modern Native Americans are not a homogeneous group, but most share a belief in the "sacred hoop," the idea that the spirit of the Native American cannot complete his or her trip back to Mother Earth until the bones turn to dust. To disrupt this spiritual journey is desecration.

Distrust is also a factor. Why, ask the Native Americans, do the developers plan to buy 808 acres if they only intend to use 124? Why are they paying Eastman-Kodak, the seller, $10,500 per acre—purportedly more than three times the highest price ever paid for such land in Bells Bend? What is to keep them from using the area as a landfill after they have taken the available cover dirt? "How do you suppose Americans would react if we were to suggest taking fill dirt from the Arlington National Cemetery?" asks Jeff Carnahan, of Cherokee descent.

Thus, when the developers arrived with core-drilling equipment for preliminary testing on the land, Native Americans and Bells Bend residents, who had been maintaining a prayer vigil across the road, were there to block access.

In response, Metro and Spicewood filed a suit seeking a temporary injunction to keep Native Americans off the land and prevent them from blocking access. Attorneys for the Alliance filed a countersuit seeking an injunction to prevent Metro from digging landfill cover dirt on the site.

In late October, a judge ruled in favor of Metro and Spicewood Services, saying, "The site has not been identified as a place any person or group uses for religious practice. Nor has it been identified as a place which has been considered over time sacred to person or group."

A week later, when protesters gathered at the site entrance to block access by the drilling rig, thirty people were arrested for obstructing

traffic. That same day, a state appeals court denied the Native Americans' request to stop the work.

Nick Mejia, a Comanche member of the Alliance, says he and other members were "absolutely astounded" by the original ruling. But, he says, "We have every intention of abiding by the law. Our civil disobedience was a way to make a statement, not a blatant disregard of the law."

For a short while, it looked as if a medicine man, a Lakota Sioux from South Dakota, would be allowed on site to watch the core drilling and perform a pipe ceremony, "to say to the Ancient Ones, 'something is being done. We have not forgotten about you,'" explains Mejia. But these plans fell through when Spicewood denied the Native Americans' request that at least one more Indian accompany the medicine man.

Core drilling was completed within a week and no Indian remains or archaeological sites were encountered, according to Spicewood. "No comment," was the Native American response.

Nick Fielder, director of Tennessee's Division of Archaeology, disagrees with the Native Americans' religious concerns. "We have no idea," he says, "what the spiritual beliefs were of the people who did the burying, which happened 3,000 to 110,000 years ago."

Native Americans, however, point out that for them, community is something that transcends time. Responsibility is directed backward as well as forward.

Even if we don't understand the religious bond the Native Americans feel they share with their ancestors, we still should respect it, says Susan Garner, attorney for the Alliance. "There is an obvious analogy," she says, "to what happened with black people in this country. They weren't seen as human. There weren't rights and laws protecting black people. We see that in our laws here and now with Indians. These laws are evolving. This is a human-rights as well as a religious issue.

"There is a lot more litigation to come," Garner adds. "The first ruling was on a preliminary motion. Ahead now is a trial with witnesses." Garner and Dan Norwood, another Alliance attorney, will be arguing the case as cooperating counsel from the Trial Lawyers for Public Justice, a public-interest group based in Washington, D.C., that includes approximately 700 lawyers who work pro-bono on such cases.

"This is a very winnable situation," says Garner. Regardless of what happens in court,

she says, "People in the county will be outraged when they look at the exorbitant amount of money being spent here that could be used in other ways. People think this is a case of corruption and greed." She pauses, and adds, "This is a case of good versus evil if there ever was one."

Case 11.c   Environmental Racism: Hispanics Fight a Toxic Waste Incinerator

Is it an accident that toxic waste incinerators, pollution, and other environmental hazards are disproportionately located in areas whose residents are predominantly poor people of color? Is this a form of environmental racism? This article describes how, for the first time, a Hispanic group fought a toxic waste incinerator on the grounds of discrimination.

No wonder the folks at Chemical Waste Management Inc. were pumped up after winning approval in January to build California's first commercial toxic-waste incinerator. Since 1987, they had been haggling with state and county officials to get permission to burn hazardous waste at their Kettleman Hills dump site in the rural San Joaquin Valley.

But weeks after winning the nod, the nation's largest hazardous-waste company, the state, and the county were slapped with a novel suit alleging they had discriminated by placing the incinerator near mostly Hispanic Kettleman City. Filed by People for Clean Air & Water, the suit claims the Oak Brook (Ill.) company's decision was part of a national pattern of siting hazardous-waste facilities near minority areas.

Profit Plunge

Lawsuits are routine in the $10 billion hazardous-waste business. But this one is unusually worrisome. The suit marks one of the first uses of the civil rights laws to fight a waste facility. If successful, it would give activists another weapon to attack "Lulus"—locally unpopular land uses. "We are taking this lawsuit very seriously," says Chem Waste Senior Counsel Philip L. Comella.

Chem Waste hardly needs more woes. On Apr. 16, it reported a 31% plunge in first-quarter earnings, to $24 million. Last year, it agreed to pay the Environmental Protection Agency a record civil penalty—$3.75 million—for polluting at its Chicago South Side facility. And the EPA just disclosed its intent to fine Chem Waste $7.1 million for improprieties at its landfill in Model City, N.Y.

At a minimum, the Kettleman suit could delay construction of the facility. Kay Hahn, a Chicago Corp. analyst, estimates that the incinerator would burn 100,000 tons of toxic waste annually and add $25 million to Chem Waste's $1.1 billion in yearly revenues. She says the incinerator is key to the company's long-term strategy because federal rules last year began barring untreated land disposal of hazardous wastes. Now, it must ship its untreated waste in California to another state to be processed.

While the Kettleman suit tests the theory of "environmental racism," the issue isn't just local. The EPA is studying whether minorities bear the brunt of the nation's toxic pollution. And studies by the General Accounting Office, the United Church of Christ, and others show that waste sites are mostly in black or Hispanic communities.

Sometimes poor areas welcome the sites—they bring jobs and more taxes. But mostly, "it's a pattern of picking the path of least resistance," argues Robert D. Bullard, a University of California at Riverside professor. "Minority communities are the least likely to fight."

Chem Waste doesn't dispute that its incinerator sites are in largely minority areas (table). But it says it didn't engage in discriminatory siting, because the sites had incinerators or landfills when it bought them.

Protracted Battle

Chances are Chem Waste will defeat the civil rights claims. In the only prior case alleging civil rights violations over a dump siting, the plaintiffs failed in 1979 to prove the company intentionally discriminated. But even if the industry avoids such awards, it can expect more battles. "We're just not ready to accept them at their word that these incinerators are a safe method of disposal," says plaintiff Joe Maya.

In one sense, the Kettleman suit is just a variation of the "not in my backyard" syndrome. The poor and minorities, like everyone else, don't want to live next to toxic dumps. And that's a key reason few incinerators have been built lately—despite federal laws designating incineration as the preferred destruction method for most toxic waste. Building the sites near nobody's backyard would seem to be the optimal solution. But even that's no guarantee: A few years ago, Chem Waste abandoned plans to burn toxic waste at sea because of environmentalists' protests. A more practical fix? Set national policies for deciding where to put the Lulus.

Case 11.d   The Cosmetics Industry and the Draize Test

Andrew N. Rowan

This article discusses the use of animals by the cosmetics industry for the purpose of testing the safety of certain cosmetics. The Draize eye test is a standard test for determining the possibility of eye damage from the use of shampoos, toiletries, and certain occupational compounds. The question remains as to whether the painful use of animals is justified for these purposes.

In a survey conducted in the United Kingdom, the vast majority of respondents objected to cosmetic testing on animals.[1] More recently, *Glamour* magazine asked its readers whether

we should do cosmetic tests on animals and 84 percent said no.[2] However, in a 1977 BBC television program on animal experimentation, the following question was put to a number of shoppers: Would you use a shampoo if it had not been safety-tested on animals? All answered that they would not. The difference in the responses to the two surveys illustrates the complex nature of the problem.

Some argue that society does not need cosmetics but offer few constructive suggestions as to how a $10 billion industry should be prevented from innovation in Western "free" market economies. Others argue that the products should not be tested on animals since humanity has no right to subject animals to pain and suffering for the sake of frivolous vanity products. However, many consumer organizations consider that cosmetics should be even more closely regulated and subjected to more intensive animal tests.[3]

Faced with the continuing threat of litigation as a result of adverse reactions, the cosmetics industry is unlikely to retreat from animal testing. It is known that tests do not necessarily protect consumers from all risk, but they reduce the extent of risk and also provide some protection for a company in the event of a large claim for damages.

Nevertheless, in a case against Beacon Castile, in which a woman accidentally splashed concentrated shampoo in her eye, the verdict went against the FDA and in favor of the company.[4] The judge's ruling was based primarily on the contention that the concentrated shampoo would be unlikely to enter the eye under normal conditions. However, he also noted that "the rabbit studies, standing alone, do not warrant condemnation of this product." This indicated that this court, at least, was not impressed by the applicability of the rabbit data.

Historical Background On Eye Testing

The Draize eye test is a standard testing procedure for eye irritation. It is named after the principal author of a paper that outlined the main element of the test, together with a numerical scoring system to provide an idea of the irritancy of the tested substance.[5] Such irritancy testing primarily involves cosmetics, toiletries, agricultural chemicals, occupational and environmental hazards, and certain therapeutics, especially ophthalmological formula-

tions. The development of the test followed the passage of the Federal Food, Drug, and Cosmetic Act of 1938 that required, *inter alia*, that cosmetics be free of poisonous or deleterious substances to the user.

In 1933, a woman suffered ulceration of both corneas as a result of having her eyelashes dyed with a coal-tar product called "Lash-lure." She was left blind and disfigured and the American Medical Association (AMA) documented seventeen similar cases, some resulting in death. "Lash-lure" remained on the market for five more years because the federal government did not have the authority to seize the product under the 1906 Food and Drug Act because the "Lash-lure" manufacturer made no medical claims.[6] However, the 1938 act did not prevent accidents resulting in eye damage. In a 1952 hearing in Congress, a case was presented of an anti-dandruff shampoo containing a new polyoxyethylene compound that caused semi-permanent injuries.[7] A recent study of 35,490 people, covering a three-month period, turned up 589 adverse reactions that were confirmed by dermatologists as most likely to have been caused by cosmetics. Of the 589 reactions, 3 percent were classified as severe, 11 percent as moderate, and 86 percent as mild.[8] It is thus clear that there is a need to determine whether or not a new cosmetic product is likely to cause eye irritancy before it is released on the market. The question, therefore, concerns the method of determining a product's potential hazard, rather than whether or not testing is required.

Eye irritation usually has one or more of the following characteristics—ulceration or opacity of the cornea, iris inflammation, and conjunctival inflammation. The Draize test utilizes this fact and scores the extent of the injury to each part of the eye. The various scores are then combined to give a total, which is used to indicate the irritancy potential of the test substance.

The Draize test has undergone several modifications since 1944 and was adapted for use in enforcing the Hazardous Substances Labeling Act. In the modified version, 0.1 ml is instilled into the conjunctival sac of one eye of each of six rabbits, the other eye serving as a control. The lids are held together for one second and the animal is then released. The eyes are examined at 24, 48, and 72 hours.[9] The scoring system is heavily weighted towards corneal damage (80 out of 110) because corneal damage leads quickly to impairment of vision.

The Interagency Regulatory Liaison Group issued draft guidelines for acute eye irritation tests a few years ago.[10] They selected the albino rabbit as the preferred test animal and recommended the use of a single, large-volume dose (0.1 ml) despite the advantages (obtaining a dose-response effect) of using a range of volumes.[11] They also recommended that, in most cases, anesthetics should not be used. However, if the test substance were likely to cause extreme pain, the use of a local anesthetic (0.5 percent proparacaine or 2 percent butacaine) was recommended for humane reasons.[12] The eyes should not be washed. Observations should be made 1, 24, 72, and 168 hours after treatment. The cut-off point for a nonirritant is set very low (*i.e.*, minimal reaction) in order to provide a large margin of safety in extrapolating the human response.

Comparative Studies

The parts of the eye that are most affected by topically applied substances are the cornea, the bulbar and palpebral conjunctivae, and the iris. The corneas of laboratory mammals are very similar in construction[13] and variations are, for the most part, minor. (The mean thickness of the cornea does vary: In man it is 0.51 mm; in the rabbit, 0.37 mm; and in the cat, 0.62 mm. The composition of the corneas of man and other species differs in the quantity and kind of enzymes.)[14]

The rabbit has historically been the animal of choice for the Draize eye test, but this seems to have occurred more by accident than by design. The use of the rabbit eye for predicting human ophthalmic response has been challenged from time to time. It has been suggested that the greater thickness of the human cornea and other anatomical differences may contribute to the rabbit's greater susceptibility to alkali burns of the cornea.[15] However, the rabbit is less sensitive than man to some other substances.[16] Tears are produced in smaller quantities in the rabbit than in man, but the rabbit nictitating membrane may supplement the cleansing effect of tears.

Procter & Gamble produced an extensive critique of the Draize test in their comments on the draft IRLG Guidelines for Acute Toxicity Tests.[17] They expressed disappointment at the fact that federal agencies have been singularly unresponsive to widespread criticism of the Draize test and have made little or no effort to encourage innovation. They commented on the differences between the human and rabbit eye[18] and the fact that the rabbit's response to the test material is greatly exaggerated when compared to human responses.[19] Procter & Gamble suggest that, when the rabbit result is equivocal, organizations should have the option of using monkeys.

The monkey has been proposed as a more suitable model because it is phylogenetically closer to man,[20] but there are still species differences.[21] In addition, use of monkeys for eye irritancy testing is inappropriate, in part because of their diminishing availability. Also, the expense does not warrant the purported fine-tuning involved in the use of monkeys. The rat has also been suggested as an alternative model but has not been investigated in any depth. Studies at Avon indicate that it may be less sensitive than the rabbit.[22] If one must use an animal for eye irritancy testing, then the rabbit would appear to be as appropriate as any other species.

Technical

It has already been stressed that the Draize eye irritancy test cannot be *routinely* used to grade substances according to their potential irritancy for human beings but only as a "pass-fail" test. In 1971, Weil and Scala[23] reported the results of a survey of intra- and interlaboratory variability of the Draize eye and skin test. Twenty-four laboratories cooperated on the eye irritancy testing, including the Food and Drug Directorate (Canada), Hazleton

Laboratories (USA), Huntingdom Research Centre (UK), Avon Products (USA), Colgate-Palmolive (USA), General Foods (USA), and American Cyanamid (USA). Twelve chemicals were selected for ophthalmic irritancy testing and distributed as unknowns to the various companies for testing according to a standard reference procedure employing the original grading scale.[24] Three of the substances were recorded as nonirritants by all the laboratories but there was considerable variation in the results for the other nine. For example, cream peroxide was recorded as a nonirritant by certain laboratories but as an irritant by others.

As a result of this study. Weil and Scala[25] concluded that "the rabbit eye and skin procedures currently recommended by the federal agencies for use in the delineation of irritancy of materials should not be recommended as standard procedures in any new regulations. Without careful re-education these tests result in unreliable results." It is pertinent to note that Scala considers that the Draize test can be used to grade irritants, but only by experienced and careful researchers.[26]

Recent Proposals and Political Activity

Development of the Coalition to Abolish the Draize Test. During the last decade, the humane movement has increasingly called into question the testing of cosmetics on laboratory animals. With one or two minor exceptions, the campaigns that have been launched against such cosmetic testing have been poorly planned and their effectiveness has been undercut by inadequately researched position papers and a dissipation of energy in different directions. All this changed with the development of a coalition of over 400 humane societies aimed specifically at the use of the Draize eye irritancy test by cosmetic companies. This coalition was the brainchild of a New York English teacher, Henry Spira, and the Draize test was selected as the target for the following reasons. First, the test has been criticized in scientific literature as being inappropriate and, in routine use, the data produced are

unreliable for regulatory purposes.[27] Second, the Draize test can cause trauma to rabbit eyes that is readily visible and that produces a strong reaction among the general public as well as scientists. As Henry Spira states, "it is the type of test that people can identify with—people know what it feels like to get a little bit of soap in their eyes."[28] Third, the test has remained essentially unchanged for over thirty years despite the fact that the prospects for humane modifications are good. Also, relatively little research has been undertaken in a search for an *in vitro* alternative and even fewer results have been made available in the scientific literature.

The cosmetics industry was selected as the target because it is vulnerable to the image problem raised by the use of the Draize eye test. The picture of the sultry model advertising a new beauty product does not juxtapose readily with an inflamed and swollen rabbit eye. It has been argued that the selection of the cosmetics industry is unfair since their products are, by and large, the least irritant. However, the coalition took the view that the cosmetics industry is not a discrete group, totally separate from other manufacturing companies. In many instances, a single company will make a range of products including household cleaners, toiletries, cosmetics, and drugs. From the coalition's point of view, it is important that the activities of all the members be narrowly focused in order to create the maximum impact and ultimately persuade policy makers that it is worth their while to change their priorities on the Draize test. The campaign's success may be measured by the following actions taken after it started in March 1980.

Government Responses   The Consumer Product Safety Commission started, on May 8, 1980, a temporary (6-month) moratorium on all in-house Draize testing until the effects of using local anesthetics to reduce pain could be elucidated. They have now identified tetracaine (a double dose) as an effective local anesthetic. The Office of Pesticides and Toxic Substances of the Environmental Protection Agency established a similar moratorium on October 1, 1980. Furthermore, they proposed to "establish the search for alternative test methods to the Draize as a research priority for the coming year." The FDA committed funds in 1981 to study a new *in vitro* technique.[29] In Congress, Senator D. Durenberger (R-Minn) and Congressman A. Jacobs (D-Ind) introduced resolutions that it was the sense of Congress that funds should be allocated to the development of a non-animal alternative to the Draize. The National Toxicology Program has yet to make a serious commitment to look for an alternative.

Public pressure on government agencies regarding the Draize test in particular has abated since 1981. Until a feasible alternative (a battery of non-animal tests) becomes available, little more will be expected of the regulatory bodies than that they exhibit sensitivity to the issue. Recently, however, there has been some suggestion that the agencies could be more responsive. Scientists at Procter and Gamble have produced evidence indicating that use of a smaller test volume (0.01 ml instead of 0.1 ml) improves the predictive accuracy of the Draize test.[30] Nevertheless, the Environmental Protection Agency has not yet shown any inclination to change its testing requirements.

Industry Actions The Cosmetics, Toiletries and Fragrances Association (CTFA) established a special task force to review alternative test systems. They sponsored a closed workshop of scientists to investigate the potential for modifying the Draize test and to develop an alternative.

A major breakthrough in the controversy occurred on December 23, 1980, when Revlon announced that it was giving Rockefeller University a grant of $750,000 to fund a three-year research effort aimed at finding an alternative to the Draize test. Revlon executives commented that while it would be naive to deny that the campaign, including an effort focused specifically on Revlon, did not have any effect, the grant was part of an ongoing program to research and develop possible alternatives. According to Donald Davis, editor of *Drug and Cosmetic Industry*, Revlon's plight engendered a great deal of sympathy from other leaders in the industry but there was a distinct lack of volunteers to help take the heat off Revlon. Revlon also called upon

other cosmetic companies, including Avon, Bristol-Myers, Gillette, Johnson and Johnson, Max Factor, and Procter and Gamble, to join them as full partners in supporting this research effort.

The other cosmetic companies were taken by surprise by Revlon's action, but they moved rapidly. Early in 1981, the CTFA announced the formation of a special research fund or trust to support research into alternatives. Avon committed $750,000, Estee-Lauder $350,000, and Bristol-Myers $200,000. Chanel, Mary Kay, and Max Factor also contributed undisclosed amounts. These funds have now been passed on to the Johns Hopkins School of Hygiene and Public Health to establish a Center for Alternatives Research. In the meantime, a number of proposed modifications were suggested that would answer some of the humane concerns.

Possible Modifications to the Draize Test Since there is no satisfactory non-animal alternative currently available for eye irritancy testing, any modifications that can be incorporated now to make the test more "humane" would be welcomed by humane groups. Such modifications range from not doing the test at all to the use of smaller volumes or local anesthetics. These proposals include the following:

i. *Do not test substances with physical properties known to produce severe irritation* such as alkalis (above pH 12) and acids (below pH 3).[31] (Adopted by the IRLG, 1981)

ii. Screen out irritants using *in vitro* or less stressful tests. The *in vitro* eye preparations described above could be used to screen unknown substances and irritant substances either labeled as such or discarded. One could also utilize results from skin irritancy studies and human patch testing to avoid testing substances that produce trauma since the skin is likely to be less sensitive than the delicate tissues of the eye.[32]

iii. When the test is conducted in the living animal, smaller volumes should be used. It has been argued that the use of 10 μl, rather than the standard 100 μl, would be a far more realistic test in terms of assessing possible human hazard. The use of smaller volumes would produce less trauma and one could also do some superficial dose-response studies to ensure that a nonirritant has a sufficient margin of safety.

iv. Where it is necessary to test substances that cause pain and irritation in the rabbit, then local anesthetics should be used. This is recommended by the IRLG.[33]

Recent Developments

Since 1981, over $5 million has been provided by industry to support research in America into alternatives to the Draize test. Additional funds have been provided to scientists in Europe, not to mention the costs of intramural industry programs. A number of meetings have been organized to explore the issue. In 1986, as a result of an initiative by Henry Spira, Bausch and Lomb contracted with the Johns Hopkins Center for Alternatives to Animal Testing to produce a critical evaluation of the research to date and to identify the most promising tests. The resulting monograph reviewed thirty-five different test methods that have been developed but stopped short of naming the five or six with the most promise on the grounds of insufficient data.[34] However, the volume does provide ample evidence of the thought and effort that have gone into the search for an alternative to the Draize since 1980.

Industry has also re-evaluated its safety testing program. Procter and Gamble took the opportunity to review and revamp its toxicology group and has made a serious commitment to reduce animal use. Avon has opened its own cell culture laboratory to validate *in vitro* assays and has reduced its use of rodents and rabbits from 14,500 in 1981 to 4,715 in 1986. Avon has asserted that it intends to be a leader in the industry in switching to *in vitro* assays. Bristol Myers, Noxell, Colgate, and others have also pursued aggressive programs to promote alternatives and the Soap and Detergent Association organized a validation study for eight *in vitro* tests. Ironically, the study was not made public because there was so much difficulty in obtaining sound, quantified animal data to compare with the *in vitro* results.

Conclusion

The results of the campaign indicate that before 1980, the companies and government agencies affected could have made more effort to seek an alternative to the Draize test or to modify the procedure to make it more humane. However, until the public raised the stakes on the issue, there was little motivation for action. Revlon ended up spending $1.25 million instead of the $17,000 suggested at the beginning by the coalition, and all the companies had to deal with large numbers of consumer complaints. Seven years later, some companies have made considerable strides in addressing the concerns raised by the animal movement but others have been less progressive. Nonetheless, it is clear that there is a trend to reduce animal use in testing.

Notes

1. National Opinion Polls, *Report to Annual General Meeting of Royal Society for the Prevention of Cruelty to Animals* (June 28, 1974).

2. *Glamour* (December 1981).

3. R. Nader, on the regulation of the safety of cosmetics, in S. S. Epstein and R. D. Grundy, eds., *The Legislation of Product Safety: Consumer Health and Product Hazards—Cosmetics and Drugs, Pesticides, Food Additives*, vol. 2 (Boston, Mass.: MIT Press, 1974), pp. 73–141.

4. U.S. District Court of the Northern District of Ohio, Eastern Division, No. C71–53. January 7, 1974, pp. 164–166.

5. J. H. Draize, G. Woodard, and H. O. Calvery, on methods for the study of irritation and toxicity of substances applied topically to the skin and mucous membranes, in *Journal of Pharmacology and Experimental Therapy* 82 (1944), pp. 377–390.

6. R. D. Lamb, *American Chamber of Horrors* (New York: Farrar & Reinhart, 1936).

7. T. Stabile, *Cosmetics: Trick or Treat* (New York: Houston Books, 1966).

8. M. Morrison, "Cosmetics: Some Statistics on Safety," *FDA Consumer* (March 1976), pp. 15–17.

9. F. N. Marzulli and M. E. Simon, on eye irritation from topically applied drugs and cosmetics: preclinical studies, in *American Journal of Optometry, Archives of the American Academy of Optometry* 48 (1971), pp. 61–78.

10. Interagency Regulatory Liaison Group, Testing Standards and Guidelines Workgroup, *Draft IRLG Guidelines for Selected Acute Toxicity Test* (Washington, D.C.: IRLG, 1979).

11. J. F. Griffith, G. A. Nixon, R. D. Bruce, P. J. Reer, and E. A. Bannan, on dose-response studies with chemical irritants in the albino rabbit eye as a basis for selecting optimum testing conditions for predicting hazard to the human eye, in *Toxicology and Applied Pharmacology* 55 (1980), pp. 501–513.

12. A. G. Ulsamer, P. L. Wright, and R. E. Osterbert, "A Comparison of the Effects of Model Irritants on Anesthetized and Nonanesthetized Rabbit Eyes," *Toxicology and Applied Pharmacology* 41 (1977), pp. 191–192 (abstract).

13. S. Duke-Elder, *System of Ophthalmology, Volume 1: The Eye in Evolution* (St. Louis, Mo.: C. V. Mosby Co., 1958), p. 452.

14. R. Kuhlman, on species variation in the enzyme content of the corneal epithelium, in *Journal of Cell Composition Physiology* 53 (1959), pp. 313–326.

15. C. P. Carpenter and H. F. Smyth, on chemical burns of the rabbit cornea, in *American Journal of Ophthalmology* 29 (1946), pp. 1363–1372.

16. Marzulli and Simon, on eye irritation.

17. Procter and Gamble Company, Comments on Draft IRLG Guidelines for Acute Toxicity Tests (Washington, D.C.: IRLG, 1979).

18. J. H. Beckley, "Comparative Eye Testing: Man versus Animal," *Toxicology and Applied Pharmacology* 7 (1965), pp. 93–101, and E. V. Buehler, "Testing to Predict Potential Ocular Hazards of Household Chemicals," *Toxicology Annual*, ed. C. L. Winek (New York: Marcel Dekker, 1974).

19. R. O. Carter and J. F. Griffith, on experimental bases for the realistic assessment of safety of topical agents, in *Toxicology and Applied Pharmacology* 7 (1965), pp. 60–73.

20. J. H. Beckley, T. J. Russell, and L. F. Rubin, on the use of rhesus monkey for predicting human responses to eye irritants, in *Toxicology and Applied Pharmacology* 15 (1969), pp. 1–9.

21. W. R. Green, J. B. Sullivan, R. M. Hehir, L. G. Scharpf, and A. W. Dickinson, *A Systematic Comparison of Chemically Induced Eye Injury in the Albino Rabbit and Rhesus Monkey* (New York: Soap and Detergent Association, 1978).

22. G. Foster, 1980, personal communication.

23. C. S. Weil and R. A. Scala, on the study of intra- and inter-laboratory variability in the results of rabbit eye and skin irritation test, in *Toxicology and Applied Pharmacology* 19 (1971), pp. 276–360.

24. Draize, et al., on methods for the study of irritation and toxicity.

25. Weil and Scala, on the study of intra- and inter-laboratory variability.

26. R. A. Scala, 1980, personal communication.

27. Weil and Scala, on the study of intra- and inter-laboratory variability.

28. L. Harriton, "Conversation with Henry Spira: Draize Test Activist," *Lab Animal* 10 (1) (1981), pp. 16–22.

29. *Congressional Record* E2953, June 15, 1981.

30. F. E. Freebert, J. F. Griffith, R. D. Bruce, and F. H. S. Bay, "Correlation of Animal Test Methods with Human Experience of Household Products," *Journal of Toxicology—Cut. Ocular. Toxicology* 1 (1984), pp. 53–64.

31. Interagency Regulatory Liaison Group, *Recommended Guidelines for Acute Eye Irritation Testing* (Washington, D.C.: IRLG, 1981).

32. *Ibid.*

33. *Ibid.*

34. J. M. Frazier, S. C. Gad, A. M. Goldberg, and J. P. McCulley, *A Critical Evaluation of Alternatives to Acute Ocular Irritation Testing* (New York: Mary Ann Liebert Inc., 1987).

Amendments to the Constitution

Amendment I [1791]

Congress shall make no law respecting an establishment of religion, or prohibiting the free exercise thereof; or abridging the freedom of speech, or of the press; or the right of the people peaceably to assemble, and to petition the Government for a redress of grievances.

Amendment II [1791]

A well regulated Militia, being necessary to the security of a free State, the right of the people to keep and bear Arms, shall not be infringed.

Amendment III [1791]

No Soldier shall, in time of peace be quartered in any house, without the consent of the Owner, nor in time of war, but in a manner to be prescribed by law.

Amendment IV [1791]

The right of the people to be secure in their persons, houses, papers, and effects, against unreasonable searches and seizures, shall not be violated, and no Warrants shall issue, but upon probable cause, supported by Oath or affirmation, and particularly describing the place to be searched, and the persons or things to be seized.

Amendment V [1791]

No person shall be held to answer for a capital, or otherwise infamous crime, unless on a presentment or indictment of a Grand Jury, except in cases arising in the land or naval forces, or in the Militia, when in actual service in time of War or public danger; nor shall any person be subject for the same offence to be twice put in jeopardy of life or limb; nor shall be compelled in any criminal case to be a witness against himself, nor be deprived of life, liberty, or property, without due process of law; nor shall private property be taken for public use, without just compensation.

Amendment VI [1791]

In all criminal prosecutions, the accused shall enjoy the right to a speedy and public trial, by an impartial jury of the State and district wherein the crime shall have been committed, which district shall have been previously ascertained by law, and to be informed of the nature and cause of the accusation; to be confronted with the witnesses against him; to have compulsory process for obtaining witnesses in his favor, and to have the Assistance of Counsel for his defence.

Amendment VII [1791]

In Suits at common law, where the value in controversy shall exceed twenty dollars, the right of trial by jury shall be preserved, and no fact tried by jury, shall be otherwise reexamined in any Court of the United States, than according to the rules of the common law.

Amendment VIII [1791]

Excessive bail shall not be required, nor excessive fines imposed, nor cruel and unusual punishments inflicted.

Amendment IX [1791]

The enumeration in the Constitution, of certain rights, shall not be construed to deny or disparage others retained by the people.

Amendment X [1791]

The powers not delegated to the United States by the Constitution, nor prohibited by it to the States, are reserved to the States respectively, or to the people.

Amendment XI [1798]

The Judicial power of the United States shall not be construed to extend to any suit in law or equity, commenced or prosecuted against one of the United States by Citizens of another State, or by Citizens or Subjects of any Foreign State.

Amendment XII [1804]

The Electors shall meet in their respective states and vote by ballot for President and Vice-President, one of whom, at least, shall not be an inhabitant of the same state with themselves; they shall name in their ballots the person voted for as President, and in distinct ballots the person voted for as Vice-President, and they shall make distinct lists of all persons voted for as President, and of all persons voted for as Vice-President, and of the number of votes for each, which lists they shall sign and certify, and transmit sealed to the seat of the government of the United States, directed to the President of the Senate;—The President of the Senate shall, in the presence of the Senate and House of Representatives, open all the certificates and the votes shall then be counted;—The person having the greatest number of votes for President, shall be the President, if such number be a majority of the whole number of Electors appointed; and if no person have such majority, then from the persons having the highest numbers not exceeding three on the list of those voted for as President, the House of Representatives shall choose immediately, by ballot, the President.

But in choosing the President, the votes shall be taken by states, the representation from each state having one vote; a quorum for this purpose shall consist of a member or members from two-thirds of the states, and a majority of all the states shall be necessary to a choice. And if the House of Representatives shall not choose a President whenever the right of choice shall devolve upon them before the fourth day of March next following, then the Vice-President shall act as President, as in the case of the death or other constitutional disability of the President.—The person having the greatest number of votes as Vice-President, shall be the Vice-President, if such number be a majority of the whole number of Electors appointed, and if no person have a majority, then from the two highest numbers on the list, the Senate shall choose the Vice-President; a quorum for the purpose shall consist of two-thirds of the whole number of Senators, and a majority of the whole number shall be necessary to a choice. But no person constitutionally ineligible to the office of President shall be eligible to that of Vice-President of the United States.

Amendment XIII [1865]

Section 1. Neither slavery nor involuntary servitude, except as a punishment for crime whereof the party shall have been duly convicted, shall exist within the United States, or any place subject to their jurisdiction.

Section 2. Congress shall have power to enforce this article by appropriate legislation.

Amendment XIV [1868]

Section 1. All persons born or naturalized in the United States, and subject to the jurisdiction thereof, are citizens of the United States and of the State wherein they reside. No State shall make or enforce any law which shall abridge the privileges or immunities of citizens of the United States; nor shall any State deprive any person of life, liberty, or property, without due process of law; nor deny to any person within its jurisdiction the equal protection of the laws.

Section 2. Representatives shall be apportioned among the several States according to their respective numbers, counting the whole number of persons in each State, excluding Indians not taxed. But when the right to vote at any election for the choice of electors for President and Vice President of the United States, Representatives in Congress, the Executive and Judicial officers of a State, or the members of the Legislature thereof, is denied to any of the male inhabitants of such State, being twenty-one years of age, and citizens of the United States, or in any way abridged, except for participation in rebellion, or other crime, the basis of representation therein shall be reduced in the proportion which the number of such male citizens shall bear to the whole number of male citizens twenty-one years of age in such State.

Section 3. No person shall be a Senator or Representative in Congress, or elector of President and Vice President, or hold any office, civil or military, under the United States, or under any State, who having previously taken an oath, as a member of Congress, or as an officer of the United States, or as a member of any State legislature, or as an executive or judicial officer of any State, to support the Constitution of the United States, shall have engaged in insurrection or rebellion against the same, or given aid or comfort to the enemies thereof. But Congress may by a vote of two-thirds of each House, remove such disability.

Section 4. The validity of the public debt of the United States, authorized by law, including debts incurred for payment of pensions and bounties for services in suppressing insurrection or rebellion, shall not be questioned. But neither the United States nor any State shall assume or pay any debt or obligation incurred in aid of insurrection or rebellion against the United States, or any claim for the loss or emancipation of any slave; but all such debts, obligations and claims shall be held illegal and void.

Section 5. The Congress shall have power to enforce, by appropriate legislation, the provisions of this article.

Amendment XV [1870]

Section 1. The right of citizens of the United States to vote shall not be denied or abridged by the United States or by any State on account of race, color, or previous condition of servitude.

Section 2. The Congress shall have power to enforce this article by appropriate legislation.

Amendment XVI [1913]

The Congress shall have power to lay and collect taxes on incomes, from whatever source derived, without apportionment among the several States, and without regard to any census or enumeration.

Amendment XVII [1913]

[1] The Senate of the United States shall be composed of two Senators from each State, elected by the people thereof, for six years; and each Senator shall have one vote. The electors in each State shall have the qualifications requisite for electors of the most numerous branch of the State legislatures.

[2] When vacancies happen in the representation of any State in the Senate, the executive authority of such State shall issue writs of election to fill such vacancies: *Provided,* That the legislature of any State may empower the executive thereof to make temporary appointments until the people fill the vacancies by election as the legislature may direct.

[3] This amendment shall not be so construed as to affect the election or term of any Senator chosen before it becomes valid as part of the Constitution.

Amendment XVIII [1919]

Section 1. After one year from the ratification of this article the manufacture, sale, or transportation of intoxicating liquors within, the importation thereof into, or the exportation thereof from the United States and all territory subject to the jurisdiction thereof for beverage purposes is hereby prohibited.

Section 2. The Congress and the several States shall have concurrent power to enforce this article by appropriate legislation.

Section 3. This article shall be inoperative unless it shall have been ratified as an amendment to the Constitution by the legislatures of the several States, as provided in the Constitution, within seven years from the date of the submission hereof to the States by the Congress.

Amendment XIX [1920]

[1] The right of citizens of the United States to vote shall not be denied or abridged by the United States or by any State on account of sex.

[2] Congress shall have power to enforce this article by appropriate legislation.

Amendment XX [1933]

Section 1. The terms of the President and Vice President shall end at noon on the 20th day of January, and the terms of Senators and Representatives at noon on the 3d day of January, of the years in which such terms would have ended if this article had not been ratified; and the terms of their successors shall then begin.

Section 2. The Congress shall assemble at least once in every year, and such meeting shall begin at noon on the 3d day of January, unless they shall by law appoint a different day.

Section 3. If, at the time fixed for the beginning of the term of the President, the President elect shall have died, the Vice President elect shall become President. If the President shall not have been chosen before the time fixed for the beginning of his term, or if the President elect shall have failed to qualify, then the Vice President elect shall act as President until a President shall have qualified; and the Congress may by law provide for the case wherein neither a President elect nor a Vice President elect shall have qualified, declaring who shall then act as President, or the manner in which one who is to act shall be selected, and such person shall act accordingly until a President or Vice President shall have qualified.

Section 4. The Congress may by law provide for the case of the death of any of the persons from whom the House of Representatives may choose a President whenever the right of choice shall have devolved upon them, and for the case of the death of any of the persons from whom the Senate may choose a Vice President whenever the right of choice shall have devolved upon them.

Section 5. Sections 1 and 2 shall take effect on the 15th day of October following the ratification of this article.

Section 6. This article shall be inoperative unless it shall have been ratified as an amendment to the Constitution by the legislatures of three-fourths of the several States within seven years from the date of its submission.

Amendment XXI [1933]

Section 1. The eighteenth article of amendment to the Constitution of the United States is hereby repealed.

Section 2. The transportation or importation into any State, Territory, or possession of the United States for delivery or use therein of intoxicating liquors, in violation of the laws thereof, is hereby prohibited.

Section 3. This article shall be inoperative unless it shall have been ratified as an amendment to the Constitution by conventions in the several States, as provided in the Constitution, within seven years from the date of the submission hereof to the States by the Congress.

Amendment XXII [1951]

Section 1. No person shall be elected to the office of the President more than twice, and no person who has held the office of President, or acted as President, for more than two years of a term to which some other person was elected President shall be elected to the office of President more than once. But this Article shall not apply to any person holding the office of President when this Article was proposed by the Congress, and shall not prevent any person who may be holding the office of President, or acting as President, during the term within which this Article becomes operative from holding the office of President or acting as President during the remainder of such term.

Section 2. This article shall be inoperative unless it shall have been ratified as an amendment to the Constitution by the legislatures of three-fourths of the several States within seven years from the date of its submission to the States by the Congress.

Amendment XXIII [1961]

Section 1. The District constituting the seat of Government of the United States shall appoint in such manner as the Congress may direct:

A number of electors of President and Vice President equal to the whole number of Senators and Representatives in Congress to which the District would be entitled if it were a State, but in no event more than the least populous state; they shall be in addition to those appointed by the states, but they shall be considered, for the purposes of the election of President and Vice President, to be electors appointed by a state; and they shall meet in the District and perform such duties as provided by the twelfth article of amendment.

Section 2. The Congress shall have power to enforce this article by appropriate legislation.

Amendment XXIV [1964]

Section 1. The right of citizens of the United States to vote in any primary or other election for President or Vice President, for electors for President or Vice President, or for Senator or Representative in Congress, shall not be denied or abridged by the United States, or any State by reason of failure to pay any poll tax or other tax.

Section 2. The Congress shall have power to enforce this article by appropriate legislation.

Amendment XXV [1967]

Section 1. In case of the removal of the President from office or of his death or resignation, the Vice President shall become President.

Section 2. Whenever there is a vacancy in the office of the Vice President, the President shall nominate a Vice President who shall take office upon confirmation by a majority vote of both Houses of Congress.

Section 3. Whenever the President transmits to the President pro tempore of the Senate and the Speaker of the House of Representatives his written declaration that he is unable to discharge the powers and duties of his office, and until he transmits to them a written declaration to the contrary, such powers and duties shall be discharged by the Vice President as Acting President.

Section 4. Whenever the Vice President and a majority of either the principal officers of the executive departments or of such other body as Congress may by law provide, transmit to the President pro tempore of the Senate and the Speaker of the House of Representatives their written declaration that the President is unable to discharge the powers and duties of his office, the Vice President shall immediately assume the powers and duties of the office as Acting President.

Thereafter, when the President transmits to the President pro tempore of the Senate and the Speaker of the House of Representatives his written declaration that no inability exists, he shall resume the powers and duties of his office unless the Vice President and a majority of either the principal officers of the executive department or of such other body as Congress may by law provide, transmit within four days to the President pro tempore of the Senate and the Speaker of the House of Representatives their written declaration and the President is unable to discharge the powers and duties of his office. Thereupon Congress shall decide the issue, assembling within forty-eight hours for that purpose if not in session. If the Congress, within twenty-one days after receipt of the latter written declaration, or, if Congress is not in session, within twenty-one days after Congress is required to assemble, determines by two-thirds vote of both Houses that the President is unable to discharge the powers and duties of his office, the Vice President shall continue to discharge the same as Acting President; otherwise, the President shall resume the powers and duties of his office.

Amendment XXVI [1971]

Section 1. The right of citizens of the United States, who are eighteen years of age or older, to vote shall not be denied or abridged by the United States or by any State on account of age.

Section 2. The Congress shall have power to enforce this article by appropriate legislation.